SMITH AND BAILEY
ON
THE MODERN ENGLISH LEGAL
SYSTEM

SMITH AND BAILEY
ON
THE MODERN ENGLISH LEGAL SYSTEM

by

S. H. BAILEY, M.A., LL.B.,

Professor of Public Law at the
University of Nottingham

and

M. J. GUNN, LL.B.,

Senior Lecturer in Law at the
University of Nottingham

LONDON
SWEET & MAXWELL
1991

Published in 1991 by
Sweet & Maxwell Limited of
South Quay Plaza, 183 Marsh Wall, London E14 9FT
Computerset by
M.F.K. Typesetting Ltd., Hitchin, Herts.
Printed and bound in Great Britain by
BPCC Hazell Books
Aylesbury, Bucks, England
Member of BPCC Ltd.

A CIP Catalogue Record
for this book is available
from the British Library

PREFACE

The production of this second edition has turned out to be a more protracted exercise than originally anticipated. In the event, Peter Smith, who is now managing director of the Norton Rose M5 group, was unfortunately unable to take any part in the preparation of this edition, and bears no responsibility for it. Michael Gunn has joined Stephen Bailey as co-author of the present edition, for which we bear joint responsibility.

Since the first edition was published in 1984 there have been significant changes affecting many aspects of the legal system. Much of the book has required substantial revision both to take account of these changes and to respond to some, at least, of the comments directed to the first edition. For example, the chapter on lawyers has had to be extended to deal with the radical changes to the legal profession effected both by and in anticipation of the Courts and Legal Services Act 1990. The chapter on pre-trial criminal procedure now commences with a treatment of the role of the police in the investigation of crime. The chapters concerned with civil justice have been affected by both the Civil Justice Review and the 1990 Act. We have, regretfully, had to drop the separate chapters on remedies and sentencing, although some aspects of these are now dealt with in the chapters on the civil and criminal trial.

The pace of change shows little sign of slackening. As we write, a Royal Commission has been established to consider the criminal justice process. We await with interest to see how the new institutions established by the Courts and Legal Services Act 1990 settle down to their work. The proposals for the training of solicitors continue to progress. At the same time there are serious concerns over the public provision of legal services. On the one hand, record sums are being spent on the statutory legal aid and advice schemes; on the other, the schemes are declining in scope and the number of people who are eligible for assistance under them is steadily diminishing.

In the course of producing this edition, we have received assistance from many people, but we wish to record our particular thanks to Diane Birch, Maeve Doggett, Edward Griew, Ian Hooker, Nottinghamshire Law Society, Peter Seago, Vivien Shrubsall, Rabinder Singh and Mark Smith. They of course bear no responsibility for any errors that remain in the text.

We are also greatly indebted to our publishers, and in particular to the editorial department, who have been very supportive of us through the various difficulties that have arisen.

We have endeavoured to state the law as at January 1, 1991, but have managed to incorporate some later developments at the proof stage.

S.H.B.
M.J.G.

April 19, 1991
Nottingham

v

ACKNOWLEDGMENTS

The authors and publishers would like to thank the following for permission to reproduce material from publications in which they have copyright.

Crown copyright material reproduced with permission of the Controller of Her Majesty's Stationery Office.

Extracts from various law reports reproduced by kind permission of The Incorporated Council for Law Reporting for England and Wales.

Various forms reproduced by kind permission of the Lord Chancellor's Department.

The Green Form Key Card and accompanying notes reproduced by kind permission of the Legal Aid Board.

Various forms reproduced by kind permission of the Solicitor's Law Stationery Society Ltd.

CONTENTS

PART I: COURTS, PERSONNEL AND SOURCES OF LAW

PART IV: THE HEARING

TABLE OF CASES

xiii

TABLE OF STATUTES

TABLE OF STATUTORY INSTRUMENTS

RULES OF THE SUPREME COURT

EUROPEAN COMMISSION CASES

PART I

COURTS, PERSONNEL AND
SOURCES OF LAW

Chapter 1

INTRODUCTION

A. THE ENGLISH LEGAL SYSTEM

THE study of the English legal system is a vital part of any law student's course. Not only are the legal institutions and processes integral to every other legal course he or she will study, they are also the subject of necessary scrutiny for assessing how well the law provides solutions to the problems it is intended to meet.

Law students are not always aware of the social context in which the rules of law they learn about will actually operate. Some of their teachers are more enthusiastic than others about ensuring that their study is not directed solely to the rules of law contained in statutes or gleaned from the decisions of the superior courts. In respect of the institutions, processes and people of the English legal system in particular, some students affect impatience at the study of matters which they think are better left to social scientists. Some even have the misguided belief that the study of the institutions and processes of our law does not carry the intellectual challenge of other legal subjects. Yet a failure to understand the English legal system will make much of what the student learns of those other subjects either incomprehensible or misleading.

For example, those studying the law of negligence need to know the basic elements of the tort and their respective functions. They will discover that until comparatively recently its scope has been confined to cases of physical damage to person or property and that the great majority of cases actually brought arise out of accidents on the road or at work. Liability in tort will be compared with other sources of accident compensation, such as social security, and related to the insurance position. As regards a tort claim, however, the student should not only be aware of the rules which prescribe who has a right to bring a claim for damages, but also of the processes whereby legal rights are actually vindicated, and indeed the enormous practical difficulties that face potential claimants. These processes form an important part of the subject matter of this book.

Almost every aspect of life in the modern state is regulated or affected in some way by law. There are laws which provide for the remedying of defined grievances (*e.g.* by the payment of damages in respect of accidentally inflicted injuries), laws which prohibit anti-social activities and provide for the imposition of penal sanctions for breach (*e.g.* the criminal law of murder or theft), laws which regulate potentially harmful activities by, for example, systems for licensing, registration or inspection, usually in conjunction with the prescription of standards (*e.g.* liquor licensing, the protection of health and safety at work), laws which confer state benefits upon individuals (*e.g.*

3

education, highways, social security, national health service) and laws which facilitate private arrangements (*e.g.* marriages, contracts, wills).[1] In a sense, the whole body of English law could be said to constitute the English legal system. However, we use the term in a narrower sense to cover the distinctive legal institutions and processes that come into operation when for some reason there is doubt or disagreement as to how the law applies in a given situation: there may be recourse to a lawyer or some other agency for legal advice, or, usually as a last resort, involvement in litigation before a court or tribunal.

The label "English legal system" is convenient, but has to be treated with a little care. For one thing, it extends to both England and Wales (Scotland, Northern Ireland, the Isle of Man and the Channel Islands have separate systems). For another, it is not as systematically organised as a "system" perhaps should be.

B. SOME BASIC CONCEPTS

There is not room here for an introduction to the theoretical background of the role of law in society.[2] There are, however, certain concepts that will appear at various points in this book and require some explanation here.

1. "COMMON LAW" AND "CIVIL LAW"

The "common law" was the term that came to be used for the laws and customs applied by the royal courts which emerged after the Norman Conquest, and which progressively replaced local laws and customs applied in sundry local courts.[3] As the decisions of these courts came to be recorded and published, so the practice developed whereby past decisions would be cited in argument before the courts, and would be regarded as being of persuasive or even binding authority.[4] The point that decisions of the superior courts are a source of law in their own right is a distinctive feature of "common law systems," the term here being used to distinguish such systems from continental, "civil law,"[4a] systems based in origin upon Roman law but now upon a series of codes established in the nineteenth and twentieth centuries. The basic elements of English law have become established in a number of Commonwealth countries (most notably Australia, New Zealand and Canada, excluding Quebec) and the United States (except Louisiana).

---

[1] These five legal techniques were distinguished by R. Summers, "The Technique Element in Law," 59 Calif. L.R. 733 (1971). See also J. Farrar and A. M. Dugdale, *Introduction to Legal Method* (3rd ed., 1990), Chap. 2, who distinguish two further techniques: the "constitutive" technique whereby the law recognises a group of people as constituting a legal person (*e.g.* a company), and the "fiscal" technique whereby the government raises money by taxation.

[2] See B. Roshier and H. Teff, *Law and Society in England* (1980); P. S. Atiyah, *Law and Modern Society* (1983); R. Cotterell, *The Sociology of Law: An Introduction* (1984).

[3] See below, pp. 31–34 on the growth of the royal courts.

[4] See Chap. 7.

[4a] This usage of the term "civil" should be distinguished from its uses "as opposed to (i) ecclesiastical; (ii) criminal; (iii) military": *Osborn's Concise Law Dictionary* (7th ed., 1983).

2. "Common Law" and Statute

Apart from its use as a convenient label for one kind of legal system, the term "common law" is used, in a narrower sense, for one of a number of distinct sources of law that exist within such a system. Laws enacted by the Queen in Parliament ("Acts of Parliament" or "statutes"), or made under delegated powers conferred by statute, have come to be of arguably greater significance than the decisions of the courts.[5] The common law has always been particularly associated with the protection of such matters as personal freedom, rights of property and contract, and individual interests in reputation and bodily security. However, the nineteenth and twentieth centuries have seen a substantial expansion of the accepted role of government to include the pursuit of such collective purposes as the protection of public health and welfare and the direction of the economy. The National Health Service, state education and social security are all examples of services established and regulated by legislation. It has also come to be felt that important changes in areas still dominated by the common law are more legitimately made by statute than by judges, although the vein of judicial creativity is by no means exhausted.[6]

The term "common law" is thus used to denote rules derived from decisions of the superior courts in contrast to those derived from statute. There is, however, one usage that is narrower still. Only some judge-made rules are rules of the common law in this narrower sense—the others are rules of "equity" which are of distinct historical origin.

3. "Common Law" and "Equity"

By the thirteenth century, the Crown had, in effect, delegated its inherent power to dispense justice to the judges of three royal courts: the Exchequer, the Common Bench—or as it came to be known in Tudor times, the Common Pleas—and the King's (or Queen's) Bench.[7] At this time, the Common Bench was by far the busiest court as regards civil cases, with jurisdiction over matters between subject and subject such as disputes over rights to land and actions for debt.[8] Proceedings were commenced by the plaintiff's purchase of a writ from the Chancery.[9] The Chancery was originally the royal secretariat, the place where all kinds of royal documents were prepared and authenticated by the Great Seal. Its head was the Chancellor,[10] whose office came to be one of the great offices of state. In medieval

---

[5] See Chaps. 5 and 6.
[6] See pp. 232–239.
[7] See further below, pp. 31–32 on the development of these courts.
[8] The King's Bench shared with the Common Bench cases of "trespass" (the term then simply meaning "wrong" as in the Lord's Prayer) and heard proceedings to correct errors in the Common Bench and local courts. Its main function was to deal with what are now called criminal cases—pleas of the Crown. By the end of the sixteenth century it had by a series of procedural devices obtained a civil jurisdiction comparable with the Common Pleas.
[9] Proceedings in the King's Bench were commenced by a petition known as a "bill" addressed directly to the court by the plaintiff, a simpler and cheaper procedure.
[10] Where a Chancellor was not appointed, the Great Seal could be entrusted to temporary "Keepers of the Seal." Occasionally, a permanent appointment was made to the office of "Lord Keeper of the Great Seal" where it was wished not to make an appointment to the more dignified office of Lord Chancellor; the powers of the two offices were the same.

times, most Chancellors were bishops and graduates in civil or canon law. Some holders of the office were in effect the King's chief minister.

The plaintiff was obliged to obtain a writ in a form appropriate to the claim. At first, if there was no precedent the Chancery would be prepared to draft a new one, but by the end of the thirteenth century this could no longer be done. Once the writ was obtained it governed the detailed form the action would take: if the wrong one had been chosen, the plaintiff was required to recommence proceedings.

Among the duties of the Chancellor were those of determining questions relating to Crown property, hearing common law actions concerning his clerks, servants and officials, and entertaining "petitions of right" (*i.e.* claims against the Crown). In addition, the Chancellor came to deal exclusively with petitions addressed to the King or the Council in respect of grievances which for some reason were not redressed or redressible by proceedings in the common law courts. This might be because of corruption or undue influence affecting proceedings (*e.g.* the bribery of jurors), or because in a particular case strict common law requirements for proof appeared to lead to injustice, or because the matter did not fall within the scope of writs recognised by the common law. The Chancellor would give relief in particular cases by an order directed to the parties, his intervention being based on the dictates of their consciences judged in accordance with his own view of what was just. Proceedings before the Chancellor were simpler, and were in other respects advantageous when compared with the procedures of the common law courts. Moreover, the Chancellor developed several remedies which were not available in other courts, most notably specific performance and the injunction—an order requiring the person to whom it is addressed to perform or to refrain from performing a stated act. When performing these judicial functions, the Chancellor came to be regarded as constituting a court: the Court of Chancery.

The standard illustration of how the Chancellor operated was provided by the person who borrowed money, acknowledged the debt by entering into a bond under seal, subsequently paid the debt, but failed to have the bond cancelled. For a common law court, the sealed bond provided incontrovertible proof of the existence of the debt: the court would enforce a second payment if proceedings were instituted by the creditor. However, the Chancellor could restrain such unconscionable action on the part of the creditor by an injunction directed to him, and order that the bond be cancelled.

At first it was not thought that there were separate systems of "law" and "equity." The Chancellor was frequently advised by the common law judges, and there were suggestions that the common law courts could take account of matters of conscience. However, tensions developed. The arguments on each side indeed reflected what is an inevitable dilemma in any system of law, the problem of reconciling the competing demands of justice and certainty. The more general a rule, the less likely it is to do justice in all the particular cases to which it applies; moreover, an attempt to construct in advance the qualifications to the rule necessary to do justice in all cases would lead to a system of rules of enormous complexity, even if all the problems could be foreseen. Hence, the need for some means whereby particular cases could be dealt with justly. Ad hoc decision-making can however be unjust if like cases are treated differently and, in any event, tends to be unpredictable.[11] The Chancellors reacted to criticisms from common lawyers and to the need to introduce regularity into the processing of an increasing caseload by developing principles of "equity" or justice from their ad hoc interventions. At times, however, the tensions also reflected personal difficulties between the Chancellor and common lawyers. In the sixteenth century Cardinal Wolsey caused much discontent among common lawyers by his preference for his own robust "common sense" over legal learning, and in the early seventeenth century a dispute between Lord Chancellor Ellesmere and Sir Edward Coke, the Chief Justice of the King's Bench, was settled by King James I in favour of the former. The Chancellor's power to issue injunctions preventing a litigant from suing at common law or enforcing a judgment obtained at law was confirmed.[12] By the end of the century the common lawyers had given up the struggle. By this time it was also the established practice for lawyers rather than ecclesiastics to be appointed to the office of Lord Chancellor,[13] and, indeed, men trained in English common law and equity rather than civil law.

The principles of equity were progressively refined and developed, most notably during the course of the seventeenth and eighteenth centuries. Of fundamental significance was the development of the concept of the "trust," whereby property could be legally owned by one person, but held by that person for the benefit of another, the latter's rights being recognised and enforced by the Court of Chancery. By the nineteenth century the organisation of the Court of Chancery was totally incapable of dealing with the business, and a series of reforms increased the number of judges sharing the work of the court with the Lord Chancellor. It was also obvious that the presence of two systems with separate courts was highly inconvenient for litigants. Further reforms in the middle of the century made some of the procedural devices of the Court of Chancery (discovery of documents, injunctions) available in the common law courts, allowed those courts to consider equitable defences, and empowered the Chancery to decide questions of common law, receive oral evidence, determine issues of fact by jury trial and award damages. One aspect of the general reorganisation of the superior courts by the Supreme Court of Judicature Acts 1873 and 1875[14] was the *procedural* fusion of law and equity. Matters of both law and equity can now be determined in the course of one set of proceedings: if there is any conflict between rules of law and rules of equity, the latter are to prevail.[15] In most instances there are differences between the operation of law and equity rather than conflict. For example, different remedies may be available in respect of what both systems acknowledge to be a wrong (*e.g.* damages (common law) and an injunction (equity) in respect of a nuisance). Equity

---

[11] This point was made in the 17th century by John Selden (*Table Talk*, edited by F. Pollock, 1927)—"Equity is a roguish thing, for law we have a measure, knowing what to trust to. Equity is according to the conscience of him that is Chancellor, and as it is larger or narrower so is equity. It is all one as if they should make the standard for the measure we call a foot to be the Chancellor's foot; what an uncertain measure would this be; one Chancellor has a long foot, another a short foot, a third an indifferent foot; it is the same thing in the Chancellor's conscience." These matters are considered further, below, at pp. 12–15.

[12] See J. H. Baker, "The Common Lawyers and the Chancery: 1616" (1969) 4 Ir. Jur. (N.S.) 368.

[13] It became customary for the Chancellor to be ennobled.

[14] See below p. 32.

[15] 1873 Act, s.25(11). See now the Supreme Court Act 1981, s.49.

may impose additional obligations on a person while recognising his or her rights at common law (*e.g.* by accepting that a trustee is the legal owner of property while requiring him or her to hold it for the benefit of another).

4. "LAW" AND "FACT"

(i) *Historical background*

Today, English law is expounded to law students as a system of substantive rules, derived from the common law and statute, which confer rights, impose obligations, create immunities, confer legal powers and so on. This is, however, a comparatively modern way of looking at the law.[16]

The earliest methods of conducting a law suit, adopted by royal courts from the practice of local courts, involved the intervention of the Almighty. The plaintiff was required to state his claim in the appropriate form. The defendant would make a formal denial of the claim. One of them, usually the defendant, would then be required to swear on oath that his cause was just, and the oath would be tested, or put to proof. This might be done by "compurgation," whereby a fixed number of persons (eventually 12) swore oaths in his support; by "battle" where a party or a person swearing an oath in his support could be compelled to prove his veracity by successfully defending himself in a fight, it being presumed that God would aid the righteous, or by "ordeal"—

"we find that the person who can carry red-hot iron, who can plunge his hand or his arm into boiling water, who will sink when thrown into the water, is deemed to have right on his side."[17]

By the thirteenth century all these methods were regarded with disfavour although compurgation lingered on as the method of proof in actions of debt, and detinue (*i.e.* actions to recover money owed or property) for several centuries beyond. In such systems there was comparatively little scope for legal learning outside the forms of writs and the correct formulation of claim and defence.

These modes of proof were replaced in both civil and criminal cases by trial by jury, whereby the sheriff (a local officer appointed by the Crown) was required to bring 12 men before the court to enquire into the disputed matter and state the truth of it. At first the "jurors" might be aware of this themselves or might be informed before they came to court, but it came to be the rule that they should only act upon evidence given in open court, and that their verdict should be unanimous. The development of the jury caused an elaboration of legal technique in disputes as to what was the material question to be put to the jury.

In civil cases, the material question would be an issue of fact, alleged in pleadings on behalf of the plaintiff and denied by the defendant, which would decide the case one way or another. The lawyers appearing on behalf

[16] On the historical background see J. H. Baker, *An Introduction to English Legal History* (3rd ed., 1990), Chaps. 4, 5; S. F. C. Milsom, *Historical Foundations of the Common Law* (2nd ed., 1981), Chaps. 2, 3.

[17] Sir William Holdsworth, *A History of English Law* (7th ed., 1956), Vol. 1, p. 310. The person who sunk in water was of course rescued—this was not a medieval "Catch-22" situation. See also R. Bartlett, *Trial by Fire and Water* (1986).

of each party could debate with the judges in court the appropriate wording of their pleas before they were formally enrolled in the court records. Furthermore, a party was entitled to admit all the facts alleged by his or her opponent but claim that they did not give rise to a good claim: this process of "demurrer" raised an issue of law for the judges to decide. Again, it was possible for tentative demurrers to be debated in court. These debates provided the opportunity for an increasing level of sophistication in legal argument. The judges were, however, reluctant to commit themselves to formal legal exceptions to general rules. Where possible, parties were encouraged to "plead the general issue," *i.e.* simply to deny all the allegations put forward by the opponent. This form of plea remains the standard form of plea in a criminal trial ("not guilty") but originally it was the norm in civil trials as well. This meant that many matters that today would be reflected in detailed rules of law were left to the jury for it to do justice on the facts of the particular case. The best example was the issue of whether a defendant was liable in trespass if he or she was not at fault. For a long time it was thought that the absence of any legal rule on the point meant that liability was strict—the better view held today is that the jury was entitled to acquit the defendant if he or she was not at fault, but that that was never recorded as it was not then a matter for the lawyers. By contrast "special" pleas were only permitted where there was a serious chance that the jury was likely to go wrong if the "general issue" was left to it. Much of the lawyers' debate in court would, in practice, turn on whether a special plea was permitted in the given situation rather than on the substantive question of which of the parties in that situation ought to "win."

In the sixteenth century, the judges evinced a much greater willingness to refine and determine questions of law. Pleadings became written rather than oral, and were entered before the appearance in court rather than at it. Informal, tentative discussions of pleas before formal enrolment were replaced by procedures that enabled matters of law to be raised at Westminster after the jury trial.[18] These procedures[19] enabled the lawyers to argue and the judges to determine the legal implications of facts that had already been found: there could be, for example, an objection to the opponent's plea or to the direction on the law given by the judge for the guidance of the jury. The court at Westminster could order that the plaintiff or defendant should succeed notwithstanding the jury verdict against him or her. A later development was the power to order a new trial.[20] In the same period demurrers became much more common and the judges permitted greater use to be made of the "special verdict" whereby the jury would answer specific questions of fact put to them rather than return a general verdict for one or other of the parties, and the court would enter judgment in the light of these findings. Formal errors could be corrected by a "writ of error."[21]

The development of procedures such as these enabled attention to be switched from matters of form to matters of the substance of the law. The distinction between matters for the judge and matters for the jury now

---

[18] The jury trial would normally be conducted away from Westminster: see below, p. 32.

[19] The defendant could enter a "motion in arrest of judgment" and the plaintiff a motion *non obstante verdicto*.

[20] This was of wider significance in that the court could quash a verdict that was against the weight of evidence or where there was a misdirection on a point of law.

[21] See below, pp. 33, 823–824.

corresponded much more closely to the present day distinction between matters of "law" and matters of "fact."

In the nineteenth century the various procedures whereby decisions could be challenged on procedural or substantive legal grounds were replaced by appeals on points of law (and in some circumstances points of fact) to the High Court, the Court of Appeal and the House of Lords,[22] and as the decisions of these courts constitute precedents for the future,[23] it is in the course of such appeals that common law and equity can be developed.

In criminal cases, special pleading was virtually never permitted, and the general plea of "not guilty" has remained the standard form of pleading for the defendant. Questions of law concerning the indictment or the evidence could be raised informally at the trial, an indictment could be removed on a writ of certiorari into the Queen's Bench where the defendant could challenge it for insufficiency in form, and the trial judge could adjourn a difficult case for discussion in Serjeants' Inn or the Exchequer Chamber. This last procedure was only regularised in the nineteenth century. In 1908 it was replaced by a proper appeal to a Court of Criminal Appeal.[24] The scope for the systematic development of criminal law has thus, until comparatively recent times, been limited.

(ii) *The distinction today*

A distinction between matters of "law" and matters of "fact" is drawn for a number of different purposes: one of the consequent difficulties is that it is possible for the line between "law" and "fact" to be drawn in slightly different places for each of these purposes. Three areas[25] where the distinction is of importance for the operation of the English legal system are (1) the division of function between judge and jury; (2) the rule that only a decision on a point of law can constitute a precedent that can be cited in future cases; and (3) the question whether a particular point may be raised on an appeal limited to matters of law.

The first of these situations has declined in significance with the dramatic reduction over the last hundred years in the use of the jury in civil cases.[26] In all but a tiny proportion of cases the judge determines the facts in issue, states and applies the law and decides what remedy or remedies should be given. The discursive statement of reasons delivered by the judge may well contain a mixture of factual and legal determinations, and will be arranged for convenience of exposition rather than in clearly separated sections. The components of the mixture will normally, however, be appropriately "labelled," and the precedent status and the scope of any further appeal will of course vary according to the true nature of the particular determination. The judge/jury distinction remains of significance in criminal cases where the mode of trial for the numerically small proportion of contested serious cases is still trial by jury.[27]

---

[22] See below, pp. 33, 90–94.

[23] See Chap. 7.

[24] See further below, pp. 88–89.

[25] There are others, *e.g.* the effect of a misrepresentation in contract, estoppel and judicial review of administrative action under the *ultra vires* doctrine.

[26] See below p. 703.

[27] See below, p. 797. A few factual matters are determined by the judge, *e.g.* those relating to admissibility of evidence and those relating to mitigation.

Rights of appeal can only be created by statute, and the grounds on which an appeal may be taken are almost invariably expressed in the statute. The commonest pattern is for a person aggrieved by the decision of a court, or, in numerous but certainly not all situations, a public authority, to be given one chance to appeal on a matter of fact but several chances to raise a matter of law.[28] Appeals from tribunals are normally limited to points of law.[29]

Some aspects of the law/fact distinction are fairly clear. An issue is one of fact where its resolution depends on the reliability or credibility of direct evidence such as a witness's testimony.[30] An issue whose resolution depends on probabilities, for example by way of inference from circumstantial evidence, is also one of fact.[31] These issues normally constitute answers to the question "what happened?" By contrast, if there is a dispute as to the existence or exact scope of a rule of the common law or a dispute over the meaning of the words of a statute, it is a dispute concerning a matter of law. This leaves one kind of issue that is difficult to classify: whether facts found fall within a common law rule or statutory description. This kind of question, one of "application,"[32] has been variously characterised as "law," "fact," "mixed law and fact," "fact and degree," "degree" or *sui generis*. As a matter of theory it is difficult to resist the conclusion that this is really a question of law.[33] However, there have been many cases in which it has not been so categorised.

A number of arguments have been advanced to support the classification of a question of application as one of fact.

(1) The matter can as well be determined by a layman as by a trained lawyer.[34]

(2) The words to be applied are "ordinary words of the English language." This argument was used by the House of Lords in *Cozens* v. *Brutus*.[35] Here, the application of "insulting" in section 5 of the Public Order Act 1936, which made it an offence to use threatening, abusive or insulting words or behaviour where that was conducive to a breach of the peace, was held to be a matter of fact for the magistrates. Lord Reid stressed the undesirability of courts providing definitions of "ordinary" statutory words, whether from dictionaries or otherwise:

> "we have been warned time and again not to substitute other words for the words of a statute. And there is very good reason for that. Few words have exact synonyms. The overtones are almost always different."[36]

---

[28] See generally Chap. 17.

[29] See below, p. 869.

[30] These are sometimes termed "primary facts." Such facts may be admitted, or "judicial" notice of them may be taken (*i.e.* the facts are of general knowledge or can easily be ascertained from standard reference works).

[31] These are sometimes termed "secondary facts." An example would be inferring the speed of a vehicle from tyre marks left on the road.

[32] The term used by E. Mureinik, "The Application of Rules: Law or Fact?" (1982) 98 L.Q.R. 587.

[33] *Ibid. Cf.* G. J. Pitt, "Law, Fact and Casual Workers" (1985) 101 L.Q.R. 217.

[34] Denning L.J. in *British Launderers' Association* v. *Borough of Hendon* [1949] 1 K.B. 462.

[35] [1973] A.C. 854.

[36] *Ibid.* p. 861.

Similarly, it has been held that whether an appropriation is "dishonest" for the purpose of the law of theft is, within certain limits, a question of fact for the jury.[37]

(3) The rule in question sets a standard, such as one of "reasonableness."[38] The best example here is whether a defendant's conduct has been "unreasonable" and accordingly in breach of a duty to take care imposed by the law of negligence. This is clearly regarded as a question of fact.[39]

(4) The question is one of "degree." In *Edwards* v. *Bairstow*[40] the question was whether a particular transaction was an "adventure in the nature of trade." If it was, the profit was subject to tax. Lord Radcliffe stated that this matter was one "in which the facts warrant a determination either way" and "in which it could not be said to be wrong to arrive at a conclusion either way."[41] It was a question of degree and therefore a question of fact.

Running through all these points is the wish to avoid the multiplication of decisions that can be cited as a precedent, and an increase in the number of decisions that can be taken further on appeal.[42]

The view that some questions of application are to be classified as ones of fact is a classic illustration of the competing requirements of principle and pragmatism. On the one hand it is, for example, difficult to see that there is any clear distinction between matters requiring the attention of a "trained lawyer" and those that do not, or between English words that are "ordinary" and those that are not. The "ordinary English word" argument in particular has occasioned much academic criticism[43] and in practice has been ignored much more often than applied.[44] On the other hand it is equally possible to appreciate the dangers of excessive complexity. It would, for example, cause chaos, even in an age of computerised legal data bases, if every decision on whether a defendant had behaved "unreasonably" for the purposes of the law of negligence could potentially be cited as an authority.

Finally, there are two factors which further blur the distinction between law and fact. First, there may sometimes be a tendency for an appellate court, if it is satisfied that the decision on a point is wrong, to classify the point as one of law precisely to enable it to intervene. Secondly, if a decision on an undoubted question of fact is unsupported by any evidence, or is a decision which no reasonable person could have reached, it is regarded as erroneous in point of law.[45] This convenient fiction enables an appellate court to retain control over factual determinations that are palpably wrong.

5. "Rules" and "Discretion"

As has already been touched upon, it is inherent in any decision-making

---

[37] *R.* v. *Feely* [1973] Q.B. 530; *R.* v. *Ghosh* [1982] Q.B. 1053. See below, pp. 791–792.
[38] This is described by Glanville Williams as raising a question of "evaluative fact": [1976] Crim.L.R. 472.
[39] See *Qualcast (Wolverhampton) Ltd.* v. *Haynes* [1959] A.C. 743, below, p. 371.
[40] [1956] A.C. 14.
[41] *Ibid.* p. 33.
[42] See, *e.g.* the statements in *Qualcast (Wolverhampton) Ltd.* v. *Haynes*, below, p. 371, n.11.
[43] See Glanville Williams, *Textbook of Criminal Law* (2nd ed., 1983), pp. 59–67 and [1976] Crim.L.R. 472, 532; J. C. Smith and B. Hogan, *Criminal Law* (6th ed., 1988) pp. 120, 490, 525–532). These authors point out that many apparently ordinary words have been the subject of judicial definition for the guidance of juries.
[44] See D. W. Elliott, "Brutus v. Cozens: Decline and Fall" [1989] Crim.L.R. 323.
[45] See below, p. 862.

process that is required to handle more than a small number of cases (1) that consistency and certainty are likely to be regarded as important objectives (albeit not the only ones) but (2) that their achievement is likely to be at the expense of an individualised consideration of and reaction to the merits of each case. This is as true of the handling of cases by courts and tribunals as it is of programmes established by government for the administration of, for example, state welfare benefits. In each of these situations it can loosely be said that the basic rules are made by Parliament (statute) or under the authority of Parliament (delegated legislation) or by certain senior judges (common law), and then put into effect by others (judges, magistrates, tribunal members, administrators in government offices and so on).[46]

It will be difficult, and usually impossible, for the "rulemaker" to draft a set of rules that covers all the possible cases that may arise and indicate with precision the outcome desired in each of them. The consequence will be that a measure of "discretion" will be conferred on the "implementer": the word "discretion" being used here to mean an ability to choose among alternative courses of action or inaction. The inevitable imprecisions of language will be such that the persons charged with the task of implementation will have to interpret some of the words used and decide whether the words apply to the circumstances before them. Indeed, a measure of flexibility or uncertainty may be created deliberately to enable the rules to be applied to situations not anticipated by the rulemaker. This can be done by the use of words of general rather than particular meaning, or by the incorporation in the rules of a standard such as "reasonable," "fair" or "just." The element of choice that may be present here is limited.[47] The rulemaker may go further and *expressly* confer a discretion upon the implementer. This express discretion may to a greater or lesser extent be hedged around by restrictions or limits set by the rulemaker. It must be emphasised that it is not possible to draw a clear line between rule-based and discretion-based decision-making processes: the implementation of rules tends to involve the exercise of a measure of discretion, and discretions tend to be hedged around by rules. All that can be said is that the element of discretion may be weaker or stronger as the case may be.

These points may be illustrated by some examples, both real and hypothetical. Parliament, at the instigation of the government, has enacted that a person who is injured in an "accident arising out of and in the course of his employment" is entitled to certain welfare benefits.[48] This phrase, which first appeared in the Workmen's Compensation Act 1897, has to be applied by the DSS officer who decides in the first instance whether a particular claim for benefit is made out. The issue then may be taken on appeal to a Social Security Appeal Tribunal, then to a Social Security Commissioner and then to the courts.[49] The application of the phrase has indeed given rise to a vast number of cases.[50] It would clearly be absurd to expect any person

[46] The two groups overlap in the person of a High Court judge who can propound a rule of the common law and apply it in successive breaths.

[47] It is also less usual, although not incorrect, to use the term "discretion" here than in the situations about to be described.

[48] See Social Security Act 1975, s.50. The range of benefits specially linked to this concept was reduced by the Social Security and Housing Benefits Act 1982.

[49] See below, pp. 60–63.

[50] See A. I. Ogus and E. M. Barendt, *The Law of Social Security* (3rd ed., 1988), pp. 261–278.

to construct a set of rules which would cover in advance all the possible circumstances that might arise where there could be doubts as to the applicability of the phrase: even assuming a perfect set of rules *could* be constructed, it would be equally absurd to expect mere mortals to find their way around them, as the rules would be of great complexity. Moreover, an attempt to spell out in detail what would count as an "accident" and the "course of employment" might prevent the extension of the right to benefit to persons injured in novel ways or when employed in novel kinds of employment, where the extension would have been desired by the rule-maker. Accordingly, a certain measure of judgment has to be exercised by those determining the applicability of the statutory phrase, and in the sense that their task is not simple and mechanical they can be said to exercise a discretion.

It would, however, have been possible for an Act of Parliament to have provided that a sum of money should be allocated to a board, and that the board could "pay such sum as it thinks fit to any person who in the opinion of the board has suffered an accident at work." This would have entailed the delegation of a considerably greater measure of discretion than is inherent in the present statutory scheme. Moreover, the wording of the board's powers could have been varied so as to increase or decrease the area of choice open to it. The area of choice could be increased by, for example, deleting the words "at work." Conversely, it could be decreased by, for example, replacing "may" by "shall," by setting a limit to the sum payable in any one case, by deleting the words "in the opinion of the board" or by listing a number of factors that the board would be required to take into account. The wider the area of choice, the better able the board would be to reach the "right" or "most appropriate" decision in each individual case (according to its own concept of "rightness" or "propriety"). On the other hand, its greater freedom of action would enable it more easily to diverge from the rule-maker's conception of justice. Even if the board were comparatively free of fetters imposed by the rulemaker it might still have wished to develop policies for its own guidance to ensure a reasonable measure of flexibility.

A good example of a discretion-based decision making process concerned the "exceptional circumstances additions" and the "exceptional needs payments" which were formerly part of the supplementary benefits scheme. These provided, respectively, for an increase in the weekly payment, or a lump sum, in "exceptional cases" at the discretion of the Supplementary Benefits Commission. In practice, the Commission produced detailed codes for the guidance of the local officials who determined the claims on a day-to-day basis, although the codes were not published.[51] These arrangements contrasted with the rule-based system of national insurance including those for industrial injuries. Following what was the classic "rules" v. "discretion" debate, these discretions were replaced by a rule-based structure,[52] although, more recently, the introduction of the Social Fund has seen in part a return to a discretion-based approach.[53]

---

[51] See generally, J. A. Farmer, *Tribunals and Government* (1974), pp. 89–99; M. Adler and A. Bradley, *Justice, Discretion and Poverty* (1975).

[52] See Ogus and Barendt (1988), pp. 414–415. For a spirited defence of discretion see R. Titmuss, "Welfare 'Rights,' Law and Discretion" (1971) 42 *The Political Quarterly*, p. 113; answered by R. White in P. Morris *et al*, *Social Needs and Legal Action* (1973), pp. 23–32; *cf.* M. Adler and S. Asquith (eds.), *Discretion and Welfare* (1981), especially Chaps. 1, 7, 11.

[53] See below, pp. 62–63.

Accordingly, among the advantages[54] of predetermined rules over discretions are that like cases will be treated alike (consistency), that persons will not in effect be punished by rules applied *ex post facto* (predictability), that the rulemaker is more likely than a person exercising a discretion to be accountable to an electorate, that the implementer will have a more limited scope to deviate from the rulemaker's objective by arbitrary decision-making, that such divergent decisions can more easily be challenged, that the rules will normally be open to public criticism and that decision-making processes can more easily be planned and routinised. Conversely, rules can be inflexible, and can "permit unreasoned official behaviour."[55]

The "rules" v. "discretion" issue crops up at a number of points in the English legal system. The original development of equity was a discretionary case-by-case response to the generality or inadequacy of common law rules or procedures.[56] The subsequent development of rules of equity was a response to the arbitrariness of a system which could vary as the length of the Chancellor's foot.[57] The issue also arises in debates as to the extent to which courts and tribunals should be bound by precedent,[58] the comparative merits of different styles of statutory drafting,[59] whether it is proper for a jury to acquit a defendant who would by a strict application of the rules of criminal law be liable to be convicted, and the extent to which the discretion of a criminal court as to sentence should be limited or "structured" by the provision of guidelines.[60] As the widest discretionary powers are allocated to administrative bodies such as ministers, officials and local authorities, the extent to which the courts should control or review exercises or non-exercises of power is an important feature of administrative law[61]; however, analogous principles apply to the control by appellate courts of exercises of discretion by judges.[62] The "rules" v. "discretion" issue does not admit of easy or general solutions: the appropriate balance has to be sought depending upon the precise context in which the issue arises.

C. THE BASIC INSTITUTIONS OF THE ENGLISH LEGAL SYSTEM

A number of institutions are of central importance to the creation of law. Statute law is enacted by Parliament; a vast quantity of delegated legislation is made under powers conferred by Act of Parliament.[63] Both processes are heavily dominated by the government of the day; indeed, most of the delegated powers are exerciseable by government departments.[64] Legislative authority has also been accorded to the institutions of the European

[54] See generally J. Jowell, "The Legal Control of Administrative Discretion" [1973] P.L. 178, 184–194; the pioneering work in the field is K. C. Davis, *Discretionary Justice, A Preliminary Inquiry* (1969) (see P. P. Craig, *Administrative Law* (2nd ed., 1989), pp. 315–319).
[55] [1973] P.L. 178 at p. 193.
[56] See above pp. 6–7.
[57] See above pp. 7–8.
[58] See below, pp. 232–239.
[59] See below, pp. 252–253.
[60] See below, pp. 796–797.
[61] See below, p. 873.
[62] See below, pp. 859–861.
[63] See Chaps. 5 and 6.
[64] A detailed consideration of Parliament and government may be found in such works as S. A. de Smith and R. Brazier, *Constitutional and Administrative Law* (6th ed., 1989).

Communities: the Council of Ministers and the Commission.[65] Decisions of the superior courts may also constitute sources of law.[66]

The administration of the legal system, in the sense of the mechanisms for the provision of legal services, the courts and tribunals established for the resolution of legal disputes and the processes for effecting law reform, is almost entirely a matter for central government. In many countries, responsibility for legal affairs is exercised by a "Minister of Justice." However, in the United Kingdom, responsibility for different aspects of the legal system is divided among separate ministries or departments of state, the main ones being the Lord Chancellor's Department, the Home Office, the Law Officers' Departments and the Treasury.[67]

1. THE LORD CHANCELLOR'S DEPARTMENT[68]

As is mentioned elsewhere,[69] the Lord Chancellor exercises a wide range of disparate functions, including those of judge, Speaker of the House of Lords, cabinet minister and government legal adviser. He also has extensive responsibilities concerning the administration of justice, including making or advising on judicial appointments,[70] arranging judicial business in the House of Lords and Privy Council and acting as chairman of the committees that make procedural rules for the Supreme Court and Crown Court.[71] He controls the unified court service, which provides administrative support for the Court of Appeal, High Court, Crown Court and county courts,[72] and supervises the legal aid and advice schemes.[73] Under the Courts and Legal Services Act 1990, he is responsible for the appointment of an Advisory Committee on Legal Education and Conduct, a Legal Services Ombudsman, an Authorised Conveyancing Practitioners Board and a Conveyancing Ombudsman.[74] He is also generally responsible for law reform in civil matters, although other government departments have their own specialised areas of concern. For example, company law is within the province of the Department of Trade and Industry and employment law within that of the Department of Employment. Finally, he has a number of miscellaneous

---

[65] See below, pp. 282–284.

[66] See Chaps. 2, 7.

[67] For a general survey, see R. Brazier, "Government and the Law: Ministerial Responsibility for Legal Affairs" [1989] P.L. 64. See also G. Zellick (ed.), *Law Reform and the Law Commission* (1988), Appendix 7.

[68] See P. Polden, *Guide to the Records of the Lord Chancellor's Department* (H.M.S.O., 1988), which covers the development of the department from about 1870 (systematic record keeping started in 1889) to November 1951. See also R. B. Stevens, "A View from the Lord Chancellor's Office," (1987) 40 C.L.P. 181 and "The Independence of the Judiciary: The View from the Lord Chancellor's Office" (1988) 8 O.J.L.S. 222; Sir D. Oulton, *Counsel,* Michaelmas 1986, p. 3.

[69] See below, p. 209.

[70] See below, p. 214.

[71] See below, p. 85.

[72] See below, pp. 84–85.

[73] See below pp. 443–458, 506–517, 672–680. The Lord Chancellor has been responsible for civil legal aid since its introduction and responsibility for criminal legal aid was transferred from the Home Secretary in July 1980.

[74] See below, pp. 114–115, 128–129, 132–133, 161–162, 174.

responsibilities, for example for the Land Registry,[75] the Public Record Office and the Official Receiver.

Since the Second World War the Lord Chancellor's Department has grown from a small office of personal assistants and advisers to the Lord Chancellor into a medium-sized government department employing a staff of about 10,000. It has its headquarters in the House of Lords and at Trevelyan House, Great Peter Street, London. The most senior official holds the offices of Permanent Secretary to the Lord Chancellor and Clerk of the Crown in Chancery. There are several Divisions dealing, respectively, with Judicial Appointments and Legislation, Court Service Management, Policy and Legal Services, and Establishment and Finance. For the purposes of courts administration the country is divided into six areas or "Circuits," each controlled by a Circuit Administrator.[76]

There is no departmental minister in the House of Commons[77]: instead, the Attorney-General acts as spokesman for the Lord Chancellor. This seems unsatisfactory, given the many other calls on the Attorney-General's time and the fact that he is not actually responsible for any aspect of the work of the Lord Chancellor's Department. A further anomaly was that the Department resisted attempts by the Parliamentary Commissioner for Administration to investigate allegations of maladministration by the Department's staff in the course of administering the courts, maintaining that the administrative functions of the courts were not to be regarded as part of the administrative functions of the Department, even though they were performed by the Department's staff.[78] The case for amendment was overwhelming, and the necessary change was effected by the Courts and Legal Services Act 1990.[79]

2. THE HOME OFFICE

The Home Secretary is responsible for the maintenance of law and order, and as a result performs various functions that might be regarded as those of a Minister of Justice. These include[80] overall responsibility for prisons and

---

[75] Responsible for the compulsory registration of titles to land under the Land Registration Acts 1925–1986 and the maintenance of land charges registered under the Land Charges Act 1972. See National Audit Office, *Review of the Operations of H.M. Land Registry* (1986–87 H.C. 39).

[76] See below, p. 75.

[77] The nearest has been Sir Eric Fletcher, a solicitor, who was Minister without Portfolio between 1964 and 1966. His main responsibility was the passage of the Law Commission Bill through the Commons, and he otherwise assisted the law officers and government departments: see J. H. Farrar, *Law Reform and the Law Commission* (1974), pp. 23–24.

[78] See the Annual Reports of the P.C.A. for 1986 (1986–87 H.C. 248), pp. 15–16; 1987 (1987–88 H.C. 363), pp. 18–19; 1988 (1988–89 H.C. 301), pp. 21–22; Minutes of Evidence of the Select Committee on the P.C.A. (1986–87 H.C. 284–ii): evidence of Lord Hailsham on March 31, 1983 and (1988–89 H.C. 159): evidence of Lord Mackay on January 26, 1989.

[79] s.110, providing that the administrative functions in respect of courts and tribunals are to be taken as the Department's functions, although there is an exception where action is taken at the direction or on the authority of a judicial officer.

[80] For a full list see R. Brazier, [1989] P.L. 64, 93.

other aspects of the penal system, the working of magistrates' courts[81] and the reform of the criminal law, on which he may be advised by the Criminal Law Revision Committee. The Home Secretary advises the Queen on the exercise of the royal prerogative of mercy to grant a free pardon in respect of a conviction or to remit all or part of a penalty.

3. THE LAW OFFICERS[82]

The Attorney-General and the Solicitor-General are the Law Officers of the Crown for England and Wales.[83] They are members of and the chief legal advisers to the government,[84] and are normally members of the House of Commons. Occasionally the Attorney-General has been appointed to the cabinet. The Law Officers may appear on behalf of the Crown at the International Court in the Hague and the European Court of Human Rights in Strasbourg. In this country they may appear in civil litigation or conduct prosecutions. They may not, however, undertake private work.

In civil matters the Attorney may institute proceedings in the High Court for the enforcement of public rights[85] or on behalf of the interests of charity. His consent is required for the institution of criminal proceedings for a large number of criminal offences,[86] and he may stop trials on indictment by entering a *nolle prosequi*.[87] He superintends the work of the Queen's Proctor, who has certain duties in matrimonial cases. He exercises ministerial responsibility for the Director of Public Prosecutions, the Crown Prosecution Service and the Serious Fraud Office[88] and, from 1989, the Treasury Solicitor's Department.[89] The Law Officers are assisted by a small staff of civil servants, the Legal Secretariat to the Law Officers, based in the Attorney-General's chambers in the Royal Courts of Justice, and generally

---

[81] The Lord Chancellor appoints magistrates and makes procedural rules for magistrates' courts; certain administrative functions are performed by magistrates' courts committees: see below pp. 54–55. The division of responsibility between Lord Chancellor and Home Secretary can cause problems: see Sir Thomas Skyrme, *The Changing Image of the Magistracy* (2nd ed., 1983), pp. 32–35.

[82] See J. Ll. J. Edwards, *The Law Officers of the Crown* (1964) and *The Attorney-General, Politics and the Public Interest* (1984); Sir Elwyn Jones, [1969] C.L.J. 43; S. C. Silkin, (1980) 4 Trent L.J. 21; Sir Michael Havers, (1984) 52 Medico-Legal Jo. 98. For a list of the Law Officers' functions see Vol. 67, H.C.Deb., November 12, 1984, col. 63, written answer by the Attorney-General; R. Brazier, [1989] P.L. 64, 94.

[83] Since 1972, the Attorney has been Attorney-General for Northern Ireland (see Northern Ireland Constitution Act 1973, s.10). The Solicitor-General is authorised to act as his deputy (*ibid.*). See Edwards (1984), Chap. 9. There are separate Law Officers for Scotland: the Lord Advocate and the Solicitor-General for Scotland see Edwards (1984), Chap. 10.

[84] The settled constitutional practice that Law Officers' advice to government remains confidential was breached in the Westland affair: see R. Austin, (1986) 39 C.L.P. 269, 277–278; M. Linklater and D. Leigh, *Not With Honour* (1986).

[85] *e.g.* to seek an injunction to restrain a public nuisance or to restrain repeated or threatened breaches of the criminal law.

[86] See below, p. 619.

[87] See below, pp. 618–619.

[88] See below.

[89] Following the recommendations of the *Review of Government Legal Services* by Sir Robert Andrew (H.M.S.O., 1989). See Vol. 145 H.C.Deb., January 19, 1989 cols. 262–263, written answer by the Prime Minister. These departments, together with the Legal Secretariat to the Law Officers, are now collectively known as the Law Officers Departments.

divide the duties between them according to their own preferences.[90] The Attorney is also the head of the Bar.[91]

When taking decisions in respect of criminal matters, the Attorney-General is expected to act independently of the government. While in an appropriate case he may seek the views of ministers as to the consequences of a prosecution, there should be no pressure from them in favour of or against a prosecution: the ultimate decision is his.[92] However, it has recently been asserted that the position is different where the government is acting as government in civil proceedings and the Attorney is the nominal plaintiff: here a decision whether to proceed is the government's collectively.[93]

4. THE DIRECTOR OF PUBLIC PROSECUTIONS

In 1879 pressure for the introduction of a system of public prosecution led to the establishment of the office of Director of Public Prosecutions.[94] It was originally contemplated that he would be provided with a number of locally-based assistants, but this development never took place. The Director and his staff have thus always been based in London. The first Director took a narrow view of the scope of his functions, and between 1884 and 1908 the office was combined with that of Treasury Solicitor.

The Director's responsibilities are now set out in the Prosecution of Offences Act 1985. He is appointed by the Attorney-General and must be a barrister or solicitor of not less than 10 years' standing.[95] Prior to the establishment of the Crown Prosecution Service his main functions were to conduct prosecutions in serious cases and to give advice and assistance to chief officers of police respecting the conduct of other prosecutions. He was assisted by a Deputy Director and Assistant Directors, and had a head-quarters staff of about 60.[96] He is now head of the Crown Prosecution Service,[97] which is responsible for the conduct of most proceedings instituted by the police. The Director heads a management team comprising the Deputy Director and Chief Executive, responsible for C.P.S. operations; the Director of Headquarters Casework, responsible for developing C.P.S. casework policies and supervising cases referred to headquarters; the Field

[90] Technically, the Solicitor-General is the Attorney-General's deputy. He may act in the Attorney's place if that office is vacant, if the Attorney is away ill, or if the Attorney authorises him to act: Law Officers Act 1944.

[91] This caused some difficulty in 1989 when the Bar was severely critical of the Lord Chancellor's proposals for reform of the legal profession: see below, p. 133.

[92] The classic statement of principle was made by Sir Hartley Shawcross in 1951: Vol. 483, H.C.Deb., January 29, 1951, cols. 683–684: see Edwards (1964), pp. 220–225 and (1984), pp. 318–324.

[93] Sir Michael Havers (Vol. 106, H.C.Deb., December 1, 1986, cols. 619–620), referring to the decision not to seek an injunction to restrain publication of Chapman Pincher's book, *Their Trade is Treachery*, a decision to which he was not a party. Analogous decisions in the *Gouriet* (*Gouriet* v. *Union of Post Office Workers* [1978] A.C. 435) and *Crossman Diaries* (*Att. Gen.* v. *Jonathan Cape Ltd.* [1976] Q.B. 752) cases had, by contrast, been taken independently by the Attorney: see J. Michael "The Wright Case—The Attorney-General's Role" (1986) 136 N.L.J. 1199.

[94] Prosecution of Offences Act 1879, J. Ll. J. Edwards, *The Law Officers of the Crown* (1964), Chaps. 16, 17 and *The Attorney-General, Politics and the Public Interest* (1984), Chaps. 1–5; G. Mansfield and J. Peay, *The Director of Public Prosecutions* (1987).

[95] 1985 Act, s.2.

[96] See below, pp. 618–619.

[97] Below, pp. 623–628, 633–636, 689–692.

Director (Resources), concerned with Area plans, targets and resources; the Field Director (Operations), responsible for operational practice; managerial performance and the implementation of legal operational policies and procedures in the field, the Director, Policy and Communications Group; and the Principal Establishment and Finance Officer.[98] The Service is organised into 31 Areas, each headed by a Chief Crown Prosecutor.

The Serious Fraud Office was established by the Criminal Justice Act 1987 with powers to investigate any suspected offence involving serious or complex fraud and to institute and have the conduct of any criminal proceedings appearing to relate to such fraud.[99] Its operations extend to Northern Ireland, and are wider than that of the C.P.S., which is only responsible for the conduct of proceedings investigated and instituted by the police. It comprises lawyers and accountants, and works in close co-operation with police officers, seconded from a number of forces, who occupy the same building. It aims to carry a caseload of about 60, selecting cases by reference to criteria of complexity, the amount of money at risk (sums in excess of £1m) or the public interest.[1] There continues to be a Fraud Investigation Group attached to the headquarters of the C.P.S. to deal with fraud cases not taken over by the S.F.O.

The D.P.P. may be directed by the Divisional Court to appear for the prosecution on any criminal appeal to the House of Lords, and by the Court of Appeal (Criminal Division) to appear in appeals to that court from the Crown Court or from it to the House of Lords.[2] He also has the power to intervene in prosecutions.[3] This power is used rarely, for example where private prosecutions are instituted maliciously. It includes the right to discontinue proceedings.[4] Finally, the Director's consent to prosecution is required by statute in certain classes of case.[5]

5. THE TREASURY AND OTHER GOVERNMENT DEPARTMENTS

The Treasury is involved in the administration of justice at a number of points. It has overall responsibilities for government expenditure and the organisation of the civil service. The Parliamentary draftsmen are technically Parliamentary Counsel to the Treasury. The Treasury Solicitor heads a large legal department which does legal work for the Treasury and for other government departments which do not have their own legal sections. He also presides over inter-departmental management machinery for civil service lawyers and was for many years and for most purposes the *de facto* head of the civil service Civil Legal Group in England and Wales.[6] In 1989 the government legal service was reorganised following a report by Sir

---

[98] Annual Report of the Crown Prosecution Service 1989–90 (1989–90 H.C. 305), p. 5 and Annex B.
[99] s.1. See further below, pp. 628–629.
[1] Serious Fraud Office: First Annual Report, 1988–89 (1988–89 H.C. 485); J. Wood, [1989] Crim.L.R. 175.
[2] Prosecution of Offences Act 1985, s.3(*f*). See below, p. 624.
[3] *Ibid.*, s.6. Below, pp. 618, 626.
[4] *Raymond* v. *Att.-Gen.* [1982] Q.B. 839, decided under the equivalent provision (s.4) of the Prosecution of Offences Act 1979.
[5] See below, pp. 618, 628.
[6] See G. Drewry, "The Office of Treasury Solicitor" (1980) 130 N.L.J. 753 and "Lawyers in the U.K. Civil Service" (1981) 59 *Public Administration* 15.

Robert Andrew.[7] The Treasury Solicitor was recognised as head of the service, with the responsibility of advising on the personnel management of lawyers across departments and supported by a lawyers management unit.[8]

6. THE OFFICIAL SOLICITOR

While the Treasury Solicitor is concerned with the government's legal business, the official solicitor to the Supreme Court heads an office in that court. He is appointed by the Lord Chancellor and must be a solicitor of 10 years' standing.[9] His functions broadly fall into five categories[10]: the liberty of the subject (making bail applications for remand prisoners, reviewing the cases of persons committed to prison for contempt of court,[11] investigating applications for leave to issue a writ of habeas corpus); the paternalistic jurisdiction (representing wards of court in wardship proceedings, acting as guardian of a minor's estate, dealing with the affairs of mental patients); the conduct of litigation for children and mental patients; the administration of the estates of deceased persons when there is no-one else willing or able to do so; and assisting the court (investigating the conduct of litigation, briefing counsel to appear as *amicus curiae*).

D. LAW REFORM

It is inevitable that any legal system cannot be static: there will always be aspects both of the substantive law and the institutional and procedural features of the system that require change. Many aspects of the common law are developed by the decisions of the superior courts. However, the judges seem generally to hold the view that this power should be exercised with caution, although this caution is from time to time thrown to the winds.[12] Commonly, a distinction is drawn between the application of an existing principle to new circumstances, which is regarded as a legitimate exercise for the judges, and the creation of a new principle, which is regarded as a matter for government and Parliament.[13]

Reform by the judges is further handicapped by the fact that the accidents of litigation may not throw up the right cases, that the precise issues in dispute are formulated by the parties (the opinions of the judges on other

---

[7] *Review of Government Legal Services* (H.M.S.O., 1989). On the appointment of the enquiry see G. Drewry, "Government Lawyers under Scrutiny" (1988) 138 N.L.J. 219.

[8] Vol. 145, H.C.Deb., January 19, 1989, cols. 262–263, written answer by the Prime Minister. See M. Mair, (1989) L.S.Gaz. March 22, 1989, pp. 12, 37: interview with the Treasury Solicitor, James Nurshaw.

[9] Supreme Court Act 1981, s.90. See N. Lowe and R. White, *Wards of Court* (2nd ed., 1986), Chap. 9; J. M. L. Evans, (1966) 63 L.S.G. 270, 335; C. Dyer, *The Law Magazine*, June 12, 1987, p. 27; D. Venables, (1990) 20 Fam. Law 53.

[10] M. Hinchliffe, (1989) J. of Child Law, pp. 64–67.

[11] It was in this capacity that the Official Solicitor came into prominence in 1972 in obtaining the release of trade unionists committed to prison for disobedience to orders of the National Industrial Relations Court in the course of a national dock strike: *Churchman* v. *Joint Shop Stewards Committee* [1972] I.C.R. 222; *Midland Cold Storage Ltd.* v. *Turner*, The Times, July 27, 1972. See N. Lowe, *Borrie and Lowe's Law of Contempt* (2nd ed., 1983), pp. 446–448; B. A. Hepple, (1972) 1 I.L.J. 198; Lord Denning, *The Due Process of Law* (1980), pp. 36–39.

[12] See below, pp. 232–239.

[13] See, *e.g.* Lord Pearson and Lord Salmon in *Launchbury* v. *Morgans* [1973] A.C. 127, 142, 151.

matters amounting to *obiter dicta* which are not binding in future cases),[14] and that the judges must normally confine themselves to the arguments and information presented by the parties. The judges cannot in any event commission empirical research and even the information derived from existing research is not admissible in evidence. Judicial reforms tend also to be retrospective in nature and hence potentially unfair.[15] Accordingly, most significant law reforms must be achieved by statute.

There are several mechanisms which exist to further the cause of law reform by statute, including one permanent body, the Law Commission, several part-time bodies such as the Law Reform Committee and the Criminal Law Revision Committee, and any number of ad hoc Royal Commissions and departmental committees.

1. THE LAW COMMISSION[16]

Calls for a permanent law reform institution were answered in 1965 by the establishment of two Law Commissions, one for England and Wales and one for Scotland.[17] This move was associated particularly with Lord Gardiner L.C.[18] The Law Commission for England and Wales comprises five "persons appearing . . . to be suitably qualified by the holding of judicial office or by experience as a barrister or solicitor or as a teacher of law in a university."[19] In practice, the chairman has been a High Court judge, who works full-time for the Commission and normally subsequently receives promotion to the Court of Appeal. The pattern for the other appointments has become settled with one common law Q.C. experienced in criminal law, a solicitor with experience of land law and equity and two academics. There is a legal secretary, a staff of barristers and solicitors from the legal Civil Service and several parliamentary draftsmen.[20]

The Commission's task is:

"to take and keep under review all the law with which [it is] concerned with a view to its systematic development and reform, including in particular the codification of such law, the elimination of anomalies, the

[14] See below, pp. 372–377.
[15] *Cf.* below, p. 397.
[16] See generally on the work of the Law Commission, J. H. Farrar, *Law Reform and the Law Commission* (1974); G. J. Zellick (ed.), *Law Reform and the Law Commission* (1988); N. Marsh, (1971) 13 William and Mary L.R. 263; L. C. B. Gower, (1973) 23 Univ. of Toronto L.J. 257; A. L. Diamond, (1976) 10 L.T. 11, and (1977) 51 A.L.J. 396; Sir Michael Kerr, (1980) 96 L.Q.R. 515; P. M. North, (1985) 101 L.Q.R. 338; S. Cretney, (1985) 48 M.L.R. 493; Sir Ralph Gibson, (1986) 39 C.L.P. 57; Sir Roy Beldam, (1987) 16 Kingston L.R. 21. The Commission reviewed the first 20 years of its operations in its 20th Annual Report, 1984–85 (Law Com. No. 155), Part I: see Editorial, (1986) 136 N.L.J. 201. For a critical account of its operations by a former member of its staff, see R. T. Oerton, *Lament for the Law Commission* (1987). For a proposal for its abolition, see A. Samuels, (1986) 136 N.L.J. 747; response by Oerton, *ibid.*, p. 1071.
[17] Law Commissions Act 1965; Lord Chorley and G. Dworkin, (1965) 28 M.L.R. 675.
[18] He had argued the case for such a body in Chap. 1 of G. Gardiner and A. Martin (eds.), *Law Reform NOW* (1963) and *cf.* (1953) 69 L.Q.R. 46.
[19] 1965 Act, s.1(2). Under the Courts and Legal Services Act 1990, Sched. 10, para. 25, the reference to a barrister or solicitor is to be replaced by possession of a general qualification under s.71 of the Act.
[20] Sir Michael Kerr, (1980) 96 L.Q.R. 515, 523. Four of the five senior Civil Service legal posts have, however, been abolished ((1984) 134 N.L.J. 467), the Law Commission relying instead on commissioning work from academic lawyers, some of whom join it on secondment (see 21st Annual Report, 1985–86 (Law Com. No. 159), pp. 1–2, 17).

repeal of obsolete and unnecessary enactments, the reduction of the number of separate enactments and generally the simplification and modernisation of the law."[21]

The topics investigated are either referred to it by the Lord Chancellor or are aspects of one of the programmes for examination of different branches of the law with a view to reform that have been approved by the Lord Chancellor and laid before Parliament.[22] The Commission is also required to provide advice and information to government and other bodies concerned with law reform.[23]

In the course of its existence the Law Commission has dealt with a large number of substantive legal topics and projects for the consolidation of statutes and the repeal of obsolete provisions ("Statute Law Reform").[24] It has also worked on the codification of the law of contract and of the law of landlord and tenant, although these tasks have proved too onerous and the work has been suspended indefinitely.[25] The prospects for codification of the criminal law are brighter,[26] a draft code having been produced.

A notable feature of the Law Commission's working methods in connection with the reform of a substantive legal topic is the circulation of a "working paper." This consists of a detailed statement of the present law on the topic, an account of the criticisms and supposed defects of the law and a statement of the options for change. The Commission normally states a provisional view as to the option that should be preferred. The paper, in both full and summarised forms, is circulated widely and the views of interested parties sought.[27] Following consultation a final report is produced, which includes a draft bill prepared by the parliamentary draftsmen seconded to the Commission. The chances of implementation are reasonably high, although they are less where the matter falls within the purview of a government department other than the Lord Chancellor's Department (most notably the Home Office and the Department of the Environment), and have generally become lower with the passage of time.[28] Problems

---

[21] 1965 Act s.3(1).

[22] Ibid. ss.3(1)(a)(b), (2). There have been four general programmes (approved in 1965, 1968, 1973 and 1989) with major items on criminal law, family law and private international law. The programme arrangements are considered by S. Cretney in Zellick (1988), pp. 3–20. The Commission may also consider reform proposals from other quarters.

[23] The Commission publishes a quarterly bulletin *Law Under Review*, giving details of the progress of government law reform projects.

[24] See below, pp. 246–248.

[25] See A. L. Diamond, (1968) 31 M.L.R. 361; Sir Michael Kerr, (1980) 96 L.Q.R. 515, 527–530.

[26] See J. C. Smith, (1984) Stat.L.R. 17 and [1987] Denning L.J. 137; I. Dennis, (1986) 50 J. of Crim.Law 161; *Codification of the Criminal Law: A Report to the Law Commission* (Law Com. No. 143, 1985); Symposium, [1986] Crim.L.R. 285–323; *Criminal Code for England and Wales* (Law Com. No. 177, 1989); R. Buxton, (1989) 139 N.L.J. 639.

[27] See P. M. North, "Law Reform: the Consultation Process" (1982) 66 Trent L.J. 19 and (1985) 101 L.Q.R. 338–346 (expressing some scepticism as to the effectiveness of consultation). The Commission has not followed the example of the Australian Law Reform Commission and organised public meetings or hearings: see the paper by the A.L.R.C. Chairman, Mr. Justice M. D. Kirby, "Reforming Law Reform: New Methods of Law Reform in Australia," to the 1979 Colloquium of the U.K. National Committee on Comparative Law, summarised in M. Zander, *The Law-Making Process* (3rd ed., 1989), pp. 441–445.

[28] See Lord Hailsham, "Obstacles to Law Reform" (1981) 34 C.L.P. 279; P. M. North, (1981) III (I) *Liverpool Law Review* 5 and (1985) 101 L.Q.R. 338, 346–357; Lord Hooson Q.C., "Reform of the Legislative Process in the Light of the Law Commission's Work" (1983) 17 L.T. 67; S. Cretney, (1985) 48 M.L.R. 493; G. Drewry in Zellick (1988), pp. 28–43.

identified include the pressures on Parliamentary time and the lack of political support. It has also been argued that the "problem" of non-implementation has been exaggerated, in that some reports simply prove unacceptable to the government on policy grounds, with even apparently technical areas of law concealing significant policy elements.[29]

2. THE LAW REFORM COMMITTEE[30]

A part-time Law Revision Committee was appointed by Lord Sankey in 1934 and produced eight reports between then and 1939, most of which were implemented. It was reconstituted by Lord Simonds in 1952 under the present title of Law Reform Committee, and comprises judges, practising lawyers and academics. Its permanent secretariat is provided by the Lord Chancellor's Department, but it lacks research facilities and suffers from the inevitable problems of any part-time body. By 1982 it had produced 23 reports.

3. THE CRIMINAL LAW REVISION COMMITTEE

This committee, the counterpart to the Law Reform Committee, but responsible to the Home Secretary rather than the Lord Chancellor, was established in 1959, and includes judges, academics and the D.P.P.[31] Its reports have led to important reforming legislation, most notably the Theft Acts 1968 and 1978. Perhaps the best known report was its 11th Report on Evidence, which aroused a storm of opposition, in part at least, according to its defenders, based on the misrepresentation of some of its recommendations.[32] For the purposes of its review of sexual offences, the Committee was advised by a Policy Advisory Committee comprising five members of the C.L.R.C. and ten members from other disciplines, including probation officers, a consultant psychiatrist, a social worker and a sociologist. There was here a greater potentional for fundamental disagreement about what it is that the law should be attempting to achieve than there had been on earlier references to the C.L.R.C.[33] The Committee has not been convened since 1985.

4. OTHER BODIES

Other bodies which require mention include the rule committees which make procedural rules for the courts[34] and the newly established committee to consider reforms in the Supreme Court.[35]

---

[29] S. Cretney, *op. cit.*; P. M. North, *op. cit.* pp. 351–355 distinguishes between the rejection of proposals, which should not be regarded as a problem, and failure to decide on the fate of proposals, which should. The Law Commission expressed its concern in its 25th Annual Report (Law Com. No. 195, 1990), pp. 1–2.

[30] See E. C. S. Wade, (1961) 24 M.L.R. 3; J. H. Farrar, *Law Reform and the Law Commission* (1974), pp. 9–14, 133–137; M. C. Blair, (1982) 1 C.J.Q. 64.

[31] See generally, Glanville Williams, "The Work of Criminal Law Reform" (1975) 13 J.S.P.T.L. 183; J. C. Smith, "An academic lawyer and law reform" (1981) 1 L.S. 119.

[32] See the articles cited in the previous footnote and M. Zander in P. Glazebrook (ed.), *Reshaping the Criminal Law* (1978).

[33] Criminal Law Revision Committee, 15th Report on Sexual Offences (Cmnd. 9213, 1984), pp. 1, 100.

[34] See below, pp. 54, 71, 85.

[35] See below, p. 85.

5. AD HOC COMMITTEES[36]

Investigations by Royal Commissions and departmental committees have long been a familiar feature of the law reform scene. They have the advantage over part-time advisory committees of a much greater commitment of resources, both of the time of their members and in money for research. They have the disadvantage when compared with permanent bodies that, having accumulated a large amount of information and expertise, their members disperse once the body has done its work. Other points of contrast with the law reform bodies discussed above are that ad hoc committees usually have a majority, or at least a large contingent of non-lawyers, and are more likely than those others to be employed in connection with institutional reforms. Since 1960, there have been four Royal Commissions of particular importance for the English legal system. The Royal Commission on Assizes and Quarter Sessions,[37] chaired by Lord Beeching, made proposals for the reorganisation of the criminal courts (other than magistrates courts) which were speedily implemented.[38] The Royal Commission on Civil Liability and Compensation for Personal Injury reported in 1978.[39] It found the private law system for claiming damages in tort to be too dependent on chance, unduly slow and expensive to operate, but felt unable because of its terms of reference to recommend a comprehensive state scheme for the compensation of all accident victims. Such a scheme would have had serious implications for the large number of lawyers, particularly barristers, who specialise in tort work. In the event, the Commission made a large number of piecemeal proposals for reform, only some of which have been implemented.

The Royal Commission on Legal Services, chaired by an accountant, Sir Henry Benson, reported in 1979.[40] Its terms of reference were:

"to inquire into the law and practice relating to the provision of legal services in England, Wales and Northern Ireland, and to consider whether any, and if so what, changes are desirable in the public interest in the structure, organisation, training, regulation of and entry to the legal profession, including the arrangements for determining its remuneration, whether from private sources or public funds, and in the rules which prevent persons who are neither barristers nor solicitors from undertaking conveyancing and other legal business on behalf of other persons."

The report was widely regarded as a disappointment.[41] It was criticised for its pedestrian style, its paucity of reasoning, the fact that only a limited amount of research[42] was commissioned and its apparent over-dependence

---

[36] A list of major reports of official committees and commissions on law reform is given in G. Zellick (ed.), *Law Reform and the Law Commission* (1988), Appendix 6.

[37] Cmnd. 4153, 1969.

[38] See below, pp. 71–72, 75.

[39] Cmnd. 7054, Chairman: Lord Pearson.

[40] Cmnd. 7648.

[41] See C. Glasser, *L.A.G. Bull*, September 1979, p. 201; (1979) 129 N.L.J. 1116–1122, 1131–1135, 1140–1146, 1223–1224; M. Elliott, (1980) J.S.W.L. 1; O. Hanson and J. Levin, (1979) *Yearbook of Social Policy*, Chap. 12; (1980) 43 M.L.R. 543–566; (1981) *Windsor Yearbook of Access to Justice* 121 (T. A. Downes, P. R. Hopkins and W. M. Rees) and 179 (P. A. Thomas); P. A. Thomas (ed.), *Law in the Balance* (1982).

[42] See C. Glasser, *op. cit.*

on the information and arguments presented by the legal profession. The *Legal Action Group Bulletin* was tempted to ignore the report: it would certainly be kinder so shaky were its foundations.[43] Professor Zander, who had played a significant role in securing the establishment of the Commission and who had submitted a considerable body of evidence, was more welcoming: he counted well over a hundred recommendations that he thought would amount to valuable changes.[44] The only real enthusiasts were the two branches of the legal profession, which was unsurprising given that on many issues their position was endorsed by the Commission. Aspects of the report will be considered at various points in the book. Many of the recommendations directed at the profession were the subject of action; those directed at the government had little impact, except that responsibility for criminal legal aid was transferred from Home Secretary to Lord Chancellor.[45] Indeed, the government subsequently decided, contrary to the recommendation of a majority of members of the Royal Commission, to end the solicitors' conveyancing "monopoly," and fundamental changes have followed the Lord Chancellor's White Paper, *Legal Services: A Framework for the Future*,[46] many comprised in the Courts and Legal Services Act 1990.

The Royal Commission on Criminal Procedure[47] provided an interesting contrast. It was established in 1978 to consider the powers and duties of the police in respect of the investigation of criminal offences and the rights and duties of suspects and accused persons, the process of and responsibility for the prosecution of criminal offences and related matters. Three features of the report were especially noteworthy. First, the Commission was much more active than the Royal Commission on Legal Services in sponsoring research. Second, there was a clear intention to identify basic points of principle to which the specific recommendations were to be related.[48] Third, the report indicated the lines that reform should take leaving the details to be worked out. In consequence, the Police and Criminal Evidence Bill was presented to Parliament in 1983, together with proposals for the establishment of a national prosecution service.

In more recent times, Royal Commissions and departmental committees have been conspicuous by their absence. Questions of policy have tended to be determined by government, with the use of teams of civil servants, perhaps with an independent chairman or advisers, to work out the details of implementation. Examples in the context of the law include the Civil Justice Review,[49] the Magistrates' Courts Scrutiny[50] and the Working Group on the Right of Silence.[51] The Green Papers on Reform of the Legal Profession

---

[43] November 1979, p. 246.

[44] (1980) 33 C.L.P. 33, 50.

[45] See *The Government Response to the Report of the Royal Commission on Legal Services* (Cmnd. 9077, 1983). The Law Society and the Bar also published their responses: see *L.A.G. Bulletin*, December 1983, pp. 3, 6.

[46] Cm. 740, 1989. See below, p. 119.

[47] Cmnd. 8092, 1981.

[48] The Commission applied three standards for judging both the existing system and its own recommendations: are the arrangements, actual or proposed, fair and clear?; are they open, that is, not secret, and is there accountability?; are they workable and efficient?

[49] *Report of the Review Body on Civil Justice* (Cm. 394, 1988). See I. Ramsey, (1988) 15 J.L.S. 416.

[50] *Magistrates' Courts: Report of a scrutiny* (H.M.S.O., 1989).

[51] *Report of the Working Group on the Right of Silence* (Home Office, 1989).

were simply published as such. This kind of approach is certainly more convenient for government. It leads to a speedier conclusion, and also avoids the risk of an independent body producing unwelcome recommendations. There are, however, corresponding doubts as to the quality of the reports produced. In early 1991, there was a departure from recent practice with the appointment of a Royal Commission to consider the criminal justice system.

E. POSSIBLE INSTITUTIONAL REFORMS

Proposals have regularly been made for the establishment of a Ministry of Justice, performing all the functions concerning justice at present divided among separate ministries.[52] The calls have commonly been associated with demands for a more systematic approach to law reform,[53] and have equally commonly been resisted on the highly dubious ground that the establishment of such a ministry might pose a threat to the administration of justice. In 1918, the Machinery of Government Committee chaired by Lord Haldane[54] proposed a redistribution of functions between Lord Chancellor and Home Secretary. The former would cease to be Speaker of the House of Lords and to sit judicially, but would be responsible for all judicial appointments, would continue as chief constitutional adviser to the Crown and would "watch and master all questions relating to legislation." Other matters concerning the administration of justice would pass to the Home Secretary, who would be redesignated as Minister of Justice, and would probably sit in the Commons. These proposals were supported by the Law Society but opposed by the Bar. Four years later, the case against a Ministry of Justice (albeit a ministry on the continental pattern including responsibility for the judiciary) was powerfully made by Lord Birkenhead.[55] Some of the steam was taken out of the case for a Ministry by the establishment of the Law Commissions in 1965. However, the large increases in the amount of money spent on courts' administration and the provision of legal services, and the general argument in favour of greater political accountability have led both the Labour and Liberal parties, and in turn the S.D.P./Liberal Alliance and the Liberal Democrats, to favour the appointment of a minister answerable to the House of Commons to take charge of these matters.[56] It would also seem desirable for the Home Affairs Committee of the House of Commons to extend its remit to include matters concerning the administration of

---

[52] See JUSTICE Conference, *Do we Need a Ministry of Justice?* (1970); G. Drewry, "Ministry of Justice—a Matter of Meaning" (1982) 132 N.L.J. 602–603; G. Drewry, "Lord Haldane's Ministry of Justice—Stillborn or Strangled at Birth?" (1983) 61 *Public Administration*, 396.

[53] See, *e.g.* Glanville Williams (ed.) *The Reform of the Law* (1951); *cf.* G. Gardiner and A. Martin (eds.), *Law Reform NOW* (1963); P. Archer and A. Martin (eds.), *More Law Reform NOW* (1983), pp. 15–20.

[54] Cd. 9230.

[55] *Points of View* (1922), Vol. I, p. 112. This was apparently prepared by Sir Claud Schuster, Permanent Secretary to the Lord Chancellor 1915–1944: Drewry (1983) *op. cit.*

[56] See A. Davidson Q.C., M.P., and T. Clement-Jones, *L.A.G. Bulletin*, May 1983, pp. 12, 13; A. Lester, (1984) 134 N.L.J. 138; S.C. Silkin, [1984] P.L. 179; R. Smith, "Ministry of Justice" *Legal Action*, November 1988, pp. 6–7, and "Labour and legal services" *Legal Action*, July 1989, p. 7; R. Brazier, "Government and the Law: Ministerial Responsibility" [1989] P.L. 64.

justice other than judicial appointments.[57] At present, it is limited to conducting inquiries into matters concerning the administration of the criminal
law falling within the remit of the Home Office.[58]

Another proposed development has been the creation of a Legal Services
Council of laymen and lawyers to review and carry out research on the
provision of legal services, to advise the Lord Chancellor and possibly to
carry out some executive functions. This was recommended by the Royal
Commission on Legal Services,[59] but rejected by the government. More
generally, there is a good case for a permanent body analogous to the Law
Commission to concern itself with the reform of civil and criminal procedure
and the operation of the legal system.[60]

F. INFORMATION ABOUT THE LEGAL SYSTEM

Statistical and factual information about the operation of the English legal
system can be gleaned from various official sources. Official publications are
grouped into a number of classes.[61] "Command papers" are "Presented to
Parliament by Command of Her Majesty"[62] and include reports of Royal
Commissions, departmental committees and the Law Commission. "House
of Commons" and "House of Lords Papers" are published on behalf of the
respective Houses of Parliament.[63] Other documents are published as "Non-
Parliamentary Publications" by Her Majesty's Stationery Office[64] or by the
department concerned.[65]

[57] See G. Drewry "The Administration of Justice and Parliamentary Scrutiny" (1983) 133
N.L.J. 959–960. The Select Committee on Procedure, 1977–78 H.C. 588, recommended that
the L.C.D. and Law Officers' Department should be subject to scrutiny by the H.A.C., but
this was not accepted by the government: N. St. John Stevas: "the new Committees should
not be allowed to threaten either the independence of the judiciary or the judicial process."
"Civil Law administration" was regarded as a "minor part of the work of those departments."
H.C. Deb., Vol. 969, col. 38, June 25, 1979). In 1983 the Liaison Committee proposed that
the original recommendation should be implemented: 1982–83 H.C. 92, para. 24, and it did
so again in 1990: 1989–90 H.C. 19–I, paras. 287–290.
[58] See, *e.g.*, First Report from the Home Affairs Committee (1983–84 H.C. 252), *Remands in
Custody*; Government Reply (Cmnd. 9322, 1984). The government now publishes fuller
information on its expenditure plans (see, *e.g. The Government's Expenditure Plans 1991–92
to 1993–94* (Cm. 1509, Home Office; Cm. 1510, Lord Chancellor's and Law Officers'
Department, 1991)) and these are subject to comments by the Committee: see Fourth Report
from the Home Affairs Committee (1988–89) H.C. 314), *Home Office Expenditure*. The
Lord Chancellor's Department submits memoranda to the committee.
[59] R.C.C.P. Report, pp. 125–170; R.C.L.S., Vol. 1, pp. 62–65. See below, pp. 461–462;
Government Response (above, p. 26, n. 45) p. 6.
[60] See M. Zander, "Promoting Change in the Legal System" (1979) 42 L.Q.R. 489, 502–505.
The suggested model is the Vera Institute of Justice of New York, which has assisted in
various reform projects in the U.K. A "complete and systematic review of civil procedure"
was instituted by the Lord Chancellor see the *Government Response* (above, p. 26, n. 45) pp.
31–32), but took the form of the *ad hoc Civil Justice Review*.
[61] See generally J. E. Pemberton, *British Official Publications* (2nd ed., 1973).
[62] These papers are numbered in series and since 1870 have been prefixed by an abbreviation
for "Command": 1st series [1]–[4222] 1833–1869; 2nd series [C.1]–[C.9550] 1870–1899; 3rd
series [Cd.1]–[Cd.9239] 1900–1918; 4th series [Cmd.1]–Cmd.9889, 1919–1956; 5th series
Cmnd.1–9927, 1956–1986; 6th series Cm.1– , 1986– .
[63] These are numbered in the session of publication (*e.g.* 1983–84 H.C. or H.L. 1).
[64] H.M.S.O. also publish Command Papers and Parliamentary Papers: see the daily, monthly
and annual H.M.S.O. lists.
[65] See the *Catalogue of British Official Publications Not Published by H.M.S.O.* (1980–).

Statistical information may be found in the series of *Judicial Statistics* (1856–1922) published by the Home Office and covering both civil and criminal matters; and *Criminal Statistics* (1922 to date) also published by the Home Office. There are also Home Office Statistical Bulletins, which provide regular statistical information on some topics, such as the use of the Prevention of Terrorism Acts, and occasional information on others, such as comparative figures on remands in custody by magistrates' courts in different areas. The Lord Chancellor's Department has published various series: *Civil Judicial Statistics* (1922–1974); *Statistics on Judicial Administration* (1972–1974) and *Judicial Statistics: England and Wales* (1975 to date). Information on legal services has given in the Annual Report of the Law Society and the Lord Chancellor's Advisory Committee, first issued in 1951 and from 1974–75 termed the *Legal Aid Annual Reports*, and now in the Annual Reports of the Legal Aid Board. The Lord Chancellor is required to publish annual reports on the business of the Supreme Court and county courts,[66] and the Master of the Rolls issues annual Reviews of the work of the Court of Appeal (Civil Division).[67]

---

[66] Courts and Legal Services Act 1990, s.1(12).
[67] See below, p. 91, fn. 46.

CHAPTER 2

COURTS AND TRIBUNALS

A. INTRODUCTION

THERE are several ways in which a legal dispute (which the parties also characterise as "legal") may be resolved. It may be settled by force or by agreement. The dispute may be referred informally or formally to a third party for him or her to arbitrate. Exceptionally, the dispute may be referred to one of the institutions established by the state expressly for the purpose of resolving such matters. Some of these institutions are termed "courts," others "tribunals." These terms cannot be defined with precision, and, for the most part, little turns on whether a particular institution is labelled a court or a tribunal, or whether an institution, however labelled, falls within the legal definition of a "court."

The term "tribunal" can be used very generally to mean any "judicial assembly,"[1] including a court; in the present context it is commonly used for "judicial assemblies" other than courts. If established by the state they are generally described as "administrative tribunals" to distinguish them from "domestic tribunals" established by non-state institutions such as professional and sporting associations and trade unions as part of their disciplinary procedures. The label "administrative" reflects the fact that most such tribunals are established to perform judicial functions as part of the administration of some government scheme or programme.

Finally, it should be remembered that while the settlement of disputes is the main function of almost all courts and most tribunals, it is not the only one: a number of administrative functions have also been allocated to them.[2]

B. COURTS

1. SIGNIFICANCE

Apart from the police, the courts of law are perhaps the most visible feature of the English legal system. Only the courts have power to impose punishment in criminal cases; reports of these, and important civil cases decided by the superior courts, commonly appear in the national and local press, and they may be covered by radio and television. Lawyers, and to an even greater extent, law students and lecturers place great emphasis on the

---

[1] O.E.D.

[2] *e.g.* the licensing functions of magistrates and the discretionary powers of the High Court in relation to the administration of estates or the supervision of the affairs of infants and mental patients; *cf.* below, pp. 78–79.

decisions of the superior courts. It is, however, difficult to estimate the significance of the courts in the legal system as a whole. The number of cases determined by the courts is small, and by the superior courts[3] minute, in comparison with the number of disputes settled by other means. Moreover, in a high proportion of the cases dealt with by the magistrates' courts and county courts the proceedings are merely mechanical processes for, respectively, the fining of minor traffic offenders and the collection of debts, with no live issue to be determined.

On the other hand, the courts do have a much wider indirect impact, given, first, that the chances of success in legal proceedings will influence the settlement of disputes,[4] and, secondly, that the decisions of superior courts are a source of law.[5]

2. HISTORICAL BACKGROUND[6]

(a) Courts of common law and equity

As we have said, the main function of almost all courts today is the adjudication of disputes. They can, however, trace their origins to local and central institutions in which no distinctions were drawn between the functions of administration, legislation and adjudication. At the local level in the Dark Ages there were community assemblies or "moots" which, *inter alia*, dealt with disputes according to local custom. These assemblies, apart from the smallest, village, assemblies, came to be based on administrative units established by the Crown, the shires, and their subdivisions, the hundreds and the boroughs. At the centre was the *Curia Regis* (King's Court).

Three related themes in early legal development can be discerned. First, the administration of justice came to be regarded as an adjunct of feudal lordship rather than a matter for the community as a whole. Then there was a further shift whereby it came in particular to be one of the prerogatives of the Crown. Thirdly, the administration of justice came to be differentiated from other functions of government. The strengthening of royal justice at the expense of local, communal, justice was a gradual process, and was neither intended nor planned, but it took place at all levels. This process involved the establishment of distinct royal courts, the placing of royal officials in the localities, whether temporarily or permanently, and the development of the supervisory jurisdiction of the royal courts over local courts.

At the centre, three common law courts evolved at different times out of the *Curia Regis*: the Exchequer,[7] the Common Pleas and the King's (or Queen's) Bench. They sat at Westminster Hall. The jurisdictional lines between these courts were complex. In theory, the Exchequer dealt with matters concerning the revenues of the Crown, the Common Pleas suits between subject and subject in which the Crown had no interest, and the King's Bench "pleas of the Crown" (*i.e.* criminal matters and civil cases involving a breach of the King's peace or some other royal interest). By the

[3] See below, p. 43.
[4] See below, pp. 493–502.
[5] See below, Chap. 7.
[6] See generally J. H. Baker, *An Introduction to Legal History* (3rd ed., 1990), Chaps. 1–7.
[7] As well as a common law jurisdiction, this court had an established equity jurisdiction, which was transferred to the Court of Chancery as late as 1842.

eighteenth century a variety of fictions had enabled each court to exercise a jurisdiction that was similar in substance although different in form to the others.

Parallel to the development of the common law courts at the centre was that of the Court of Chancery, and in particular its function of dealing with petitions.[8] For a time in the sixteenth and seventeenth centuries a number of "conciliar courts" also assumed importance, being courts established under the prerogative to handle judicial matters that came before the Privy Council but were not dealt with by the Chancellor. These included the Court of Star Chamber, which became notorious towards the end of its life for its handling of political crimes, the Court of Requests and several regional offshoots. They were looked on with suspicion by the common law courts and were abolished in the 1640s. The pattern of superior courts otherwise remained substantially unchanged until the nineteenth century, when some new courts were created, and there was subsequently a general reorganisation under the Supreme Court of Judicature Acts 1873–75.[9] In this reorganisation the various superior courts[10] were replaced by one Supreme Court of Judicature comprising the High Court (in five divisions) and the Court of Appeal. The intention initially was for the appellate jurisdiction of the House of Lords to be abolished, but a successful rearguard action was fought for its retention.[11]

Royal justices from the common law courts were also sent out to travel the country. Originally, they conducted all manner of governmental affairs, but they came to concentrate on judicial proceedings. There were two bases for their jurisdiction. In criminal and some civil cases they were given ad hoc commissions from the Crown. In other civil cases they sat with a jury to try issues that arose in litigation in the superior courts at Westminster: the juries technically were summoned to Westminster "unless before then (*nisi prius*) the King's justices have come" into the country. It was obviously more convenient to try the issues locally and transmit the result to London. The system came to be known as the "assize system" and continued until the 1970s,[12] and even the present arrangements have maintained the concept of High Court judges hearing cases in the provinces, albeit now reinforced by local judges.

The significant development in the handling of criminal cases less serious than those dealt with at the assizes was the appointment by the Crown of justices of the peace and the progressive widening of their criminal jurisdiction from the thirteenth century onwards.[13] Civil cases were heard by the successors of the old community assemblies, a variegated pattern of county, hundred, manorial and borough courts. These courts were subject to the supervisory jurisdiction of the superior royal courts and came to apply the common law. They declined for different reasons and at different times,

---

[8] See above, pp. 6–7.

[9] This followed the recommendations of the First Report of the Judicature Commission (H.M.S.O., 1869).

[10] *i.e.* the Courts of Chancery, Queen's Bench, Common Pleas, Exchequer, Admiralty (see below, p. 33), Probate (below, p. 34), and Divorce and Matrimonial Causes (*ibid.*). The London Court of Bankruptcy, originally established by an Act of 1831 to relieve the Court of Chancery of some of its business, was incorporated in 1884.

[11] See below, pp. 92–93.

[12] See below, pp. 71–72.

[13] See below, pp. 181–182. The justices also had many administrative responsibilities.

although many were only formally abolished in the 1970s.[14] The important step in the establishment of a regular system of local civil courts was the creation of new, statutory, county courts in 1846.[15]

(b) Appeals[16]

Provision for appeals was complex. The record of a court's proceedings could be reviewed for error[17] by another common law court[18] or a special court, a number of which were established by statute at various times to sit in a room at Westminster Hall known as the Exchequer Chamber.[19] Error lay from the Courts of Exchequer Chamber to Parliament, this jurisdiction being exercised by the House of Lords. Another, informal, method of review was the practice of judges to reserve cases for the opinion of their brethren, expressed at meetings held in Serjeants' Inn or the Exchequer Chamber.[20] In Chancery proceedings, a case argued before the Master of the Rolls or a Vice-Chancellor[20a] could be re-argued before the Chancellor, and the Chancellor could review his own previous decisions and those of his predecessors. In the seventeenth century it was established that proceedings in error lay from the Court of Chancery to the House of Lords. A Court of Appeal in Chancery with appellate judges (Lords Justices) specially appointed to it was created in 1851 to hear appeals from the Master of the Rolls and the Vice-Chancellors. This became the model for the Court of Appeal established by the Judicature Acts 1873–75. The nineteenth century also saw the replacement of proceedings in error by statutory appeals in the modern form.

(c) Other courts

Apart from the courts of common law and equity there were courts that followed civil law procedure: the High Court of Admiralty,[21] which dealt with maritime matters and the High Court of Chivalry,[22] a court of honour.

---

[14] Courts Act 1971, ss.42, 43; Administration of Justice Act 1977, s.23, Sched. 4.

[15] See below, p. 63. These must not be confused with the old shire or county courts presided over by the sheriff.

[16] See Baker (1990), Chap. 9.

[17] This process was more akin to the modern application for judicial review than statutory appeal: see Chap. 17.

[18] Proceedings in error lay from the Common Pleas to the King's Bench until 1830.

[19] (1) One was established in 1357 to hear error from the Exchequer. This comprised the Chancellor and the Treasurer with judges as assistants. (2) A second was established in 1585 to hear error from the Queen's Bench, this court comprising the justices of the Common Pleas and the barons of the Exchequer. (3) In 1830 a new Court of Exchequer Chamber was established to hear error from each of the common law courts. This comprised all the judges of the superior courts, error from one court being heard by the judges of the other two.

[20] In criminal cases such meetings became formalised with the creation of the Court for Crown Cases Reserved in 1848.

[20a] See below pp. 210, 211.

[21] This court became part of the Supreme Court of Judicature in the 1873–75 reorganisation. See F. Wiswall, *The Development of Admiralty Jurisdiction and Practice since 1800* (1971).

[22] This court has sat once since 1737: *Manchester Corporation* v. *Manchester Palace of Varieties Ltd.* [1955] P. 133. See G. D. Squibb, *The High Court of Chivalry* (1959). It has jurisdiction over such questions as the right to arms, precedence and descent. In the 1955 case the corporation claimed successfully that the company should be prevented from using the former's arms in their seal and displayed above the main curtain at the Palace Theatre, Manchester.

Canon law was administered by archdeacons' courts, the bishops' consistory courts, each presided over by the chancellor of the diocese, and the archbishops' provincial courts, the Chancery Court of York and the Court of Arches.[23] Further appeals lay to the Pope or to Papal Delegates. Following the Reformation this jurisdiction passed to the Court of High Commission, which lapsed in the 1640s, and the Court of Delegates. The latter court was replaced by the Privy Council in 1832. The relationship between the ecclesiastical courts and the royal courts was stormy and complicated.[24] The jurisdiction of ecclesiastical courts over marriage, divorce and probate ended in 1857 with the creation of the Court of Divorce and Matrimonial Causes and the Court of Probate.[25] Since then, their jurisdiction has been confined to church matters. The present court structure was introduced by the Ecclesiastical Jurisdiction Measure 1963, which retained the consistory courts, but created an appellate system of gothic complexity, largely replacing the appellate jurisdiction of the Privy Council.[26] Appeals in matters of doctrine, ritual or ceremonial lie from the consistory courts to the Court of Ecclesiastical Causes Reserved, which comprises three bishops and two judges, appointed by the Queen.[26a]

C. TRIBUNALS

1. INTRODUCTION

The significant role played by administrative tribunals in the adjudication of legal disputes is a development of the present century, although it is possible to find examples of similar institutions in earlier centuries.[27] For example, the General and Special Commissioners of Income Tax were established in 1799 and 1805 respectively, with both assessment and appellate functions. The Railway and Canal Commission was established in 1873, *inter alia*, to settle disputes between railway companies and between companies and their customers, and subsequently evolved into the Transport Tribunal.

The most important factors behind the expansion of the number of tribunals and the range of their work have been the advent of the welfare state and the development of state economic controls. The National Insurance Act 1911 set up the unemployment benefit scheme. All questions concerning claims to benefit were to be determined initially by an insurance officer. A workman dissatisfied with a determination could have it referred to a "court of referees" consisting of a chairman appointed by the Board of Trade, one member from an "employers' panel" and one from a "workmens' panel." A further right of appeal lay to an "umpire"—a national appellate authority appointed by the Crown. This arrangement proved superior to alternative methods of adjudication used in legislation of the

[23] So called because it usually sat in the arched crypt of the church of St. Mary le Bow in London. Its judge became known as the Dean of Arches.
[24] See Baker (1990), Chap. 8.
[25] These courts became part of the Supreme Court of Judicature in the 1873–75 reorganisation.
[26] See E. Garth Moore, *An Introduction to Canon Law* (1967), Chap. XIV.
[26a] The first two cases before this court were *In re St. Michael and All Angels, Great Torrington* [1985] Fam. 81 and *In re St. Stephen's, Walbrook* [1987] Fam. 146: see J. D. C. Harte, (1988) 2 Ecc.L.J. 22.
[27] See R. E. Wraith and P. G. Hutchesson, *Administrative Tribunals* (1973), Chap. 1.

period,[28] and was adopted as the general model for many of the new tribunals established in the following decades:

"The extension of governmental responsibility for welfare provision, regulation of the economy, employment policy and resource development has created new statutory rights, obligations and restraints. Consequently, new areas of potential dispute have opened up, the boundaries of which have been progressively extended, and which require legislative provision for adjudication. The tendency, for a variety of reasons, has been to use tribunals rather than ordinary courts for settling disputes of this kind."[29]

This is not to say that there have been clear principles governing either the decision to allocate a particular decision to a tribunal or the details of the machinery established:

"Parliament's selection of subjects to be referred to tribunals and inquiries does not form a regular pattern. Certain basic guidelines can be detected, but the choice is influenced by the interplay of various factors—the nature of the decisions, accidents of history, departmental preferences and political considerations—rather than by the application of a set of coherent principles."[29a]

These tribunals commonly determine disputes between the citizen and the state arising out of the administration of a statutory scheme.[30] In addition, some determine disputes between citizens, normally arising out of protective legislation enacted for the benefit of one of the parties.[31]

2. THE FRANKS REPORT

A significant landmark in the development of tribunals was the 1957 report of the Committee on Administrative Tribunals and Enquiries chaired by Sir Oliver Franks.[32] Part of the terms of reference required the Committee to review the constitution and working of tribunals other than the ordinary courts of law, constituted by a minister or for the purposes of a minister's functions.[33] Among the general points made by the Committee were, first, that the special procedures within their terms of reference should be marked by the characteristics of "openness, fairness and impartiality"[34]:

"In the field of tribunals openness appears to us to require the publicity of proceedings and knowledge of the essential reasoning

---

[28] i.e. Workmen's Compensation Act 1897: disputes concerning compensation for industrial injuries were supposed to be settled by arbitration but in practice went to county court judges and beyond on appeal; Old Age Pensions Act 1908: pensions were administered by pensions committees of local authorities, which also adjudicated disputes, with an appeal to the Local Government Board; National Insurance Act 1911, Part I: national health insurance was administered by friendly societies with an appeal to one of four Insurance Commissioners.

[29] The Functions of the Council on Tribunals: Special Report by the Council (Cmnd. 7805, 1980), p. 1.

[29a] Ibid., pp. 1–2.

[30] e.g. disputes concerning claims to welfare benefits.

[31] e.g. disputes between landlord and tenant arising out of rent controls, and between employer and employee concerning allegedly unfair dismissals.

[32] Cmnd. 218.

[33] The other part of the terms of reference concerned public inquiry procedures.

[34] Cmnd. 218, p. 5.

underlying the decisions; fairness to require the adoption of a clear procedure which enables parties to know their rights, to present their case fully and to know the case which they have to meet; and impartiality to require the freedom of tribunals from the influence, real or apparent, of Departments concerned with the subject matter of their decisions."[35]

Secondly, the Committee noted that tribunals as a system for adjudication had come to stay, and indeed that the tendency to refer issues arising from legislative schemes to special tribunals was likely to grow rather than to diminish.[36]

Thirdly, the Committee recommended the establishment of two permanent Councils on Tribunals, one for England and Wales and one for Scotland, to supervise tribunal and inquiry procedures.

In addition, the report made a whole series of detailed recommendations concerning both the constitution and procedures of tribunals generally and icular tribunals. Most of the proposals were implemented in the Tribuand Inquiries Act 1958, subsequently consolidated in the Tribunals and iries Act 1971, and in changes of regulation and departmental practice.

3. THE COUNCIL ON TRIBUNALS[37]

)58 Act established one Council on Tribunals, with a Scottish Committee. Its functions in respect of tribunals are:

"(a) to keep under review the construction and working of the tribunals specified in Schedule 1 to the [1971] Act;

(b) to consider and report on particular matters referred to the Council by the Lord Chancellor and the Lord Advocate with respect to any tribunal other than a court of law whether or not specified in Schedule 1; ...."[38]

Thus, its powers are consultative and advisory. It was not given the executive powers recommended by the Franks Report as to the appointment of tribunal members, the review of remuneration and the formulation of procedural codes.[39] Certainly it has no power to reverse or require reconsideration of specific tribunal decisions. The Council has 15 members appointed by the Lord Chancellor and the Lord Advocate, and the Parliamentary Commissioner for Administration is a member *ex officio*. The membership comprises a mixture of lawyers, both practising and academic, and non-lawyers, with the latter predominating. The Council's requests for additional powers, put forward in its Special Report of 1980, were generally not accepted, although a code for consultation with government depart-

---

[35] *Ibid.* p. 10.

[36] *Ibid.* p. 8.

[37] See *The Functions of the Council on Tribunals*: Special Report by the Council (Cmnd. 7805, 1980); the Council's Annual Reports; H. W. R. Wade, [1960] P.L. 351; J. F. Garner, [1965] P.L. 321; D. G. T. Williams, [1984] P.L. 73 and (1990) 9 C.J.Q. 27; O. Lomas, (1985) 48 M.L.R. 694; C. Harlow and R. Rawlings, *Law and Administration* (1984), Chap. 6.

[38] Special Report, p. 3. It has similar, although not identical functions in respect of procedures involving inquiries held on behalf of a minister.

[39] It must be consulted before procedural rules are made for Schedule 1 tribunals, but does not make the rules itself: 1971 Act, s.10.

ments has been introduced.[40] The Council has done much useful work in minor matters, securing, for example, many amendments to draft bills, rules and regulations, and some changes in tribunal practice. However, its political position is weak, its resources are inadequate[41] and it "remains an inconspicuous advisory committee."[42]

4. ADJUDICATION OR ADMINISTRATION

There has been some debate on whether tribunals are to be regarded as part of the machinery of justice or part of the machinery of administration. The Franks Committee stated[43]:

"Tribunals are not ordinary courts, but neither are they appendages of Government Departments. Much of the official evidence, including that of the Joint Permanent Secretary to the Treasury, appeared to reflect the view that tribunals should properly be regarded as part of the machinery of administration, for which the Government must retain a close and continuing responsibility. Thus, for example, tribunals in the social service field would be regarded as adjuncts to the administration of the services themselves. We do not accept this view. We consider that tribunals should properly be regarded as machinery provided by Parliament for adjudication rather than as part of the machinery of administration. The essential point is that in all these cases Parliament has deliberately provided for a decision outside and independent of the Department concerned, either at first instance (for example in the case of Rent Tribunals and the Licensing Authorities for Public Service and Goods Vehicles) or on appeal from a decision of a Minister or of an official in a special statutory position (for example a valuation officer or an insurance officer). Although the relevant statutes do not in all cases expressly enact that tribunals are to consist entirely of persons outside the Government service, the use of the term 'tribunal' in legislation undoubtedly bears this connotation, and the intention of Parliament to provide for the independence of tribunals is clear and unmistakable."

The supposed characteristic of independence cannot, however, be taken too far. Clearly it is desirable that the expression of the "departmental view" in an individual case should be confined to the representations made at the hearing itself. However, in many respects the departments retain a general influence over tribunal decision-making. They are responsible for the formulation of the relevant primary legislation and procedural rules, albeit in consultation with the Council on Tribunals, and indeed for the "detailed

[40] See the Council's Annual Reports for 1980–81 (1981–82 H.C. 89), pp. 6–7 and 1981–82 (1982–83 H.C. 64), p. 8 and Appendix C. The Code was recirculated in 1986: Annual Report for 1986–87 (1987–88 H.C. 234), pp. 2, 7–8.

[41] The Lord Chancellor's Department took over two years to consider and reject a request for additional staff: Annual Report for 1985–86 (1986–87 H.C. 42), pp. 28–30. In 1989–90 the Council's expenditure was £410,530, and it had a staff of 13, including a part-time research officer appointed to co-ordinate research on tribunals conducted in universities and elsewhere: see Annual Reports for 1986–87 (1987–88 H.C. 234), pp. 11, 16; for 1989–90 (1990–91 H.C. 64), pp. 49, 57.

[42] Sir William Wade, *Administrative Law* (6th ed., 1988), p. 920.

[43] Cmnd. 218, p. 9.

arrangements" for the working of tribunals.[44] There has, however, been a trend in recent years for the Lord Chancellor's Department to take over responsibility for the operation of a growing list of tribunals. This has occurred in the case of the Special Commissioners of Income Tax,[45] V.A.T. Tribunals,[46] the Social Security Commissioners,[47] the Transport Tribunal,[48] and the Immigration Adjudicators and administrative responsibility for the immigration appellate authorities.[49] The Council on Tribunals has set out some broad guidelines as to the allocation of administrative responsibility for tribunals, suggesting that the main consideration should be the independence of the tribunal and the public perception of that independence. It was necessary to show that there was real independence, especially where the outcome of a tribunal's hearings would affect the public purse on a policy seen by the government or a department as vitally important. There could be a long term aim for the Lord Chancellor's Department to take over responsibility for all such tribunals, but this would not be realistic for the present. Other relevant factors were the tribunal's size and geographical spread, level and involvement with the law. The Council noted that most of the tribunals currently administered by the Department were relatively senior, relatively closely involved with specifically legal issues, and comparatively small, and only sat in a small number of places.[50]

A further aspect of the role of the Lord Chancellor's Department is that it is involved in the consideration of proposals to create new tribunals and provides advice and guidance to other departments on tribunal matters when so requested.[51]

The Franks view on this point has been criticised in two respects. First, it has been pointed out that some tribunals are "policy-oriented" rather than "court substitute":

> "For instance, where there is a dispute about social security entitlement, tribunals are basically used in place of the ordinary courts because the latter have become too expensive, formal and technical in their procedure. On the other hand, many matters of planning, whether in transport, land use, or industrial expertise, are given to tribunals because of the lack of expertise and doctrinal flexibility, or policy consciousness, on the part of the courts. Thus different weaknesses in the courts give rise to different types of tribunals."[52]

---

[44] Annual Report of the Council on Tribunals for 1975–76 (1976–77 H.C. 236), p. 3. The Council recognises that it is not always practicable for a tribunal to use non-departmental staff and premises: Annual Report for 1981–82 (1982–83 H.C. 64), pp. 26–27.

[45] Finance Act 1984, Sched. 22 (amending the Taxes Management Act 1970).

[46] Finance Act 1985, ss.27(3), 30, Sched. 8 (amending the Value Added Tax Act 1983).

[47] Transfer of Functions (Social Security) (Commissioners) Order 1984 (S.I. 1984, No. 1818).

[48] Transfer of Functions (Transport Tribunal) Order 1989 (S.I. 1989 No. 495).

[49] Transfer of Functions (Immigration Appeals) Order 1987 (S.I. 1987, No. 465).

[50] Annual Report for 1984–85 (1985–86 H.C. 54), pp. 13–14.

[51] Annual Report for 1986–87 (1987–88 H.C. 42), p. 13.

[52] B. Abel-Smith and R. Stevens, *In Search of Justice* (1968), p. 220; see J. A. Farmer, *Tribunals and Government* (1974), Chap. 8, for an argument in favour of the establishment of more policy-oriented tribunals as an alternative to ministerial decision-making.

Examples of policy-oriented tribunals include the Transport Tribunal[53] and the Civil Aviation Authority.[54]

Secondly, it has been argued that even court-substitute tribunals should be seen as hybrid in nature; not only machinery for adjudication but, as well, "vital components of administration."[55]

5. SUPPOSED ADVANTAGES OF TRIBUNALS AS COURT-SUBSTITUTES

The Franks Committee noted that tribunals have certain characteristics which often give them advantages over the courts: "cheapness, accessibility, freedom from technicality, expedition and expert knowledge of their particular subject."[56] Generally, tribunal proceedings are cheaper, speedier,[57] and more expert than courts of law. However, accessibility is hindered by the great complexity of the system of tribunals and the lack of publicity given to their work. Moreover, the Council on Tribunals has stated that:

"Significant changes have ... taken place in the general constitutional and administrative climate. There is, for example, a movement towards greater formalism in procedures for settling disputes. The process started with reforms following the Franks Report which, in general, made tribunals more like courts.... Since then the trend towards judicialisation has gathered momentum with the result that tribunals are becoming more formal, expensive and procedurally complex. Consequently they tend to become more difficult for an ordinary citizen to comprehend and cope with on his own."[58]

Associated with this movement are the Council's arguments in favour of the extension of legal aid to tribunals, the appointment of lawyer chairmen and the extension of rights of appeal to the courts. It has also been pointed out that, despite declarations by tribunals that they are not bound by precedent, the requirements of consistency and predictability of decision lead to the development of general principles and an informal *de facto* system of precedent,[59] especially as the decisions of certain tribunals are systematically reported.

Accordingly, it is perhaps more true today than ever that "such differences as there are between [courts and tribunals] are not in any sense fundamental but at most differences in degree...."[60] In particular, it is not

---

[53] Goods vehicle licensing appeals: Transport Act 1968, s.70.

[54] Air transport licensing: Civil Aviation Acts 1971, 1980, 1982: see R. Baldwin, *Regulating the Airlines* (1985). Other possible candidates were the Patents Appeal Tribunal (now the Patents Court), the Lands Tribunal and the Industrial Court (renamed the Industrial Arbitration Board in 1971 and the Central Arbitration Committee in 1976): Abel-Smith and Stevens (1968), p. 225.

[55] K. Hendry, "The Tasks of Tribunals: Some Thoughts" (1982) 1 C.J.Q. 253, 259; *cf.* J. A. G. Griffith, "Tribunals and Inquiries" (1959) 22 M.L.R. 125, 129.

[56] Cmnd. 218, p. 9.

[57] The problem of delays is, however, a frequently recurring theme of Annual Reports of the Council on Tribunals.

[58] *The Functions of the Council on Tribunals*: Special Report by the Council (Cmnd. 7805, 1980), p. 21.

[59] J. A. Farmer, *Tribunals and Government* (1974), pp. 174–180 and Chap. 3; below, p. 398.

[60] B. Abel-Smith and R. Stevens, *In Search of Justice* (1968), pp. 224, 228. This is perhaps not true of the policy-oriented tribunals: see Farmer (1974), p. 189.

possible to argue that courts administer rules of law while tribunals administer both law and policy:

"[N]o such clear line can or should be drawn. Indeed it was the evolution of this myth which helped establish the tribunal system by convincing the judges of the ordinary courts that they were concerned with legal but not with policy questions. . . . Properly understood, tribunals are a more modern form of court. In some cases they may have more discretion than the courts, and this is particularly true of the policy oriented tribunals. But certainly they have no more discretion than the Chancery Division has in handling trusts, wards or companies."[61]

Other, more pragmatic, reasons for establishing tribunals rather than entrusting matters to courts include the need not to overburden the judiciary,[62] the avoidance of Ministerial responsibility for sensitive decisions and the easing of the workload of government departments.[63]

6. THE TRIBUNALS AND INQUIRIES ACT 1971

Apart from establishing the Council on Tribunals, the 1971 Act makes provision for the selection of chairmen of certain tribunals,[64] requires reasons to be given by Schedule 1 tribunals,[65] provides in many cases for an appeal on a point of law to the High Court[66] and renders inoperative most clauses in statutes passed before August 1, 1958 purporting to exclude judicial review.[67]

D. THE SYSTEM IN OUTLINE

1. COURTS

The courts structure is shown on pp. 41–42 in diagrammatic form, with a table below showing the current workload. The main courts are considered in detail in section E.

---

[61] Abel-Smith and Stevens (1968), pp. 227–228.

[62] Franks Report, Cmnd. 218, p. 9. In evidence the Permanent Secretary to the Lord Chancellor had stated that the wholesale transfer of tribunal work to the courts would necessitate the creation of a large number of additional judges, particularly in the county courts. Much of the work did not need the services of a highly remunerated judge. Moreover, a dilution of the bench was undesirable. Since then, there has been a large increase in the number of such judges, but they have been directed towards criminal and not tribunal work: see below, pp. 73, 206–208.

[63] See K. Hendry, (1982) 1 C.J.Q. 253, 257–58, giving the immigration appeals system as an example. See also J.A.G. Griffith, (1959) 22 M.L.R. 125, 129 in relation to national insurance and rent tribunals: "the truth was that the Department did not wish to be bothered with these decisions. And this for the most obvious of reasons: that the Department did not mind what the decisions were, for no questions of policy were involved."

[64] s.7. See below, pp. 201–203.

[65] s.12.

[66] s.13.

[67] s.14. Such clauses are not to prevent applications for certiorari or mandamus: see below, pp. 876–877.

THE COURTS EXERCISING CRIMINAL JURISDICTION

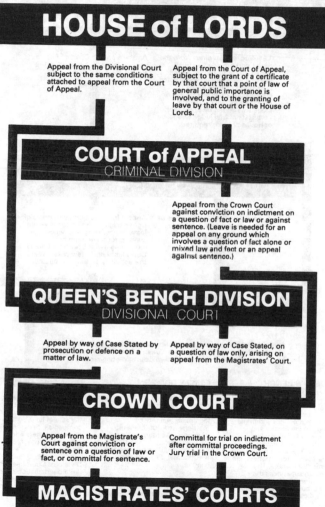

HOUSE of LORDS

Appeal from the Divisional Court subject to the same conditions attached to appeal from the Court of Appeal.

Appeal from the Court of Appeal, subject to the grant of a certificate by that court that a point of law of general public importance is involved, and to the granting of leave by that court or the House of Lords.

COURT of APPEAL
CRIMINAL DIVISION

Appeal from the Crown Court against conviction on indictment on a question of fact or law or against sentence. (Leave is needed for an appeal on any ground which involves a question of fact alone or mixed law and fact or an appeal against sentence.)

QUEEN'S BENCH DIVISION
DIVISIONAL COURT

Appeal by way of Case Stated by prosecution or defence on a matter of law.

Appeal by way of Case Stated, on a question of law only, arising on appeal from the Magistrates' Court.

CROWN COURT

Appeal from the Magistrate's Court against conviction or sentence on a question of law or fact, or committal for sentence.

Committal for trial on indictment after committal proceedings. Jury trial in the Crown Court.

MAGISTRATES' COURTS

SUMMARY JURISDICTION

Trial of summary offences and other offences triable summarily with the consent of the accused.

EXAMINING JUSTICES

The conduct of committal proceedings to establish the existence of prima facie case against an accused on a charge on indictment.

THE PRINCIPAL COURTS
EXERCISING CIVIL JURISDICTION

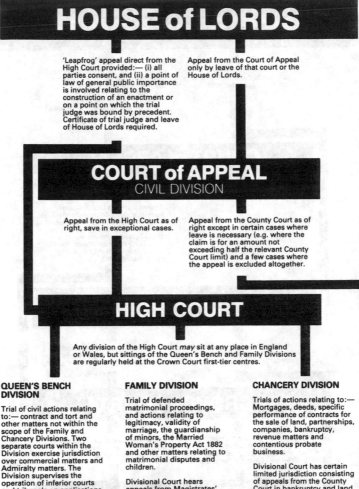

HOUSE of LORDS

'Leapfrog' appeal direct from the High Court provided:— (i) all parties consent, and (ii) a point of law of general public importance is involved relating to the construction of an enactment or on a point on which the trial judge was bound by precedent. Certificate of trial judge and leave of House of Lords required.

Appeal from the Court of Appeal only by leave of that court or the House of Lords.

COURT of APPEAL
CIVIL DIVISION

Appeal from the High Court as of right, save in exceptional cases.

Appeal from the County Court as of right except in certain cases where leave is necessary (e.g. where the claim is for an amount not exceeding half the relevant County Court limit) and a few cases where the appeal is excluded altogether.

HIGH COURT

Any division of the High Court *may* sit at any place in England or Wales, but sittings of the Queen's Bench and Family Divisions are regularly held at the Crown Court first-tier centres.

QUEEN'S BENCH DIVISION

Trial of civil actions relating to:— contract and tort and other matters not within the scope of the Family and Chancery Divisions. Two separate courts within the Division exercise jurisdiction over commercial matters and Admiralty matters. The Division supervises the operation of inferior courts and tribunals on applications for judicial review.

FAMILY DIVISION

Trial of defended matrimonial proceedings, and actions relating to legitimacy, validity of marriage, the guardianship of minors, the Married Woman's Property Act 1882 and other matters relating to matrimonial disputes and children.

Divisional Court hears appeals from Magistrates' and County Courts on family matters (e.g. affiliation, guardianship, adoption).

CHANCERY DIVISION

Trials of actions relating to:— Mortgages, deeds, specific performance of contracts for the sale of land, partnerships, companies, bankruptcy, revenue matters and contentious probate business.

Divisional Court has certain limited jurisdiction consisting of appeals from the County Court in bankruptcy and land registration matters.

COUNTY COURT

JURISDICTION INCLUDES

(i) Actions in contract or tort where the claim does not exceed £5,000 (except defamation);

(ii) Equity matters (trusts, mortgages, partnership etc.) where the value of the fund does not exceed £30,000;

(iii) Actions for recovering land where the rateable value does not exceed £1,000;

(iv) Undefended and some defended matrimonial cases;

(v) Bankruptcy.

Workload of the courts: Proceedings commenced
Comparative Tables[68]

	1938	1963	1977	1982	1989
1. Appellate Courts					
Judicial Committee of the Privy Council	107	46	48	62	55
House of Lords:					
From courts in England & Wales	32	21	58	65	51
From elsewhere	11	18	6	6	12
Court of Appeal					
Civil Division	574	711	1,359	1,627	1,622
Criminal Division	—	2,065	6,399	6,674	7,076
High Court	263	484	1,029	1,482	2,535
2. Crown Court (disposals)					
Committals for trial	—	—	53,118	66,184	101,232
Committals for sentence	—	—	12,846	14,544	8,267
Appeals	—	—	15,497	20,775	16,860
3. High Court					
Chancery Division	9,826	16,137	14,651	17,119	30,813
Queen's Bench	83,641	123,998	176,128	164,396	288,287
4. Family matters (High Court and County Court)					
Probate (grants issued)	149,752	—	251,703	279,127	231,883
Wardship	—	—	1,491	2,301	4,327
Adoption	—	—	10,724	9,102	7,516
Guardianship	—	—	628	1,540	3,351
Custodianship	—	—	—	—	961
Dissolution of marriage	9,970	36,385	170,149	173,452	184,610
Nullity	263	919	1,095	921	478
Judicial separation	71	206	1,980	7,480	2,741
5. County Courts					
Plaints entered	1,262,402	1,543,324	1,673,966	2,048,568	2,615,508
Judgments on hearing	30,821	34,746	141,950	168,682	179,006
6. Magistrates' Courts					
Indictable offences	—	—	470,000	539,000	449,000
Summary offences (excluding motoring)	—	—	458,000	469,000	568,000
Motoring offences	—	—	1,165,000	1,214,000	847,000
7. Other courts and tribunals					
Restrictive Practices Court	—	33	4	0	10
Employment Appeal Tribunal	—	—	748	829	615

[68] Based on *Judicial Statistics 1989* (Cm. 1154) and earlier volumes, and (for magistrates' courts) *Criminal Statistics: England and Wales 1989* (Cm. 1322, 1990).

2. TRIBUNALS

There are now approximately 60 types of tribunal within the jurisdiction of the Council on Tribunals,[69] and several others outside it. They may be roughly grouped according to subject matter.[70] The table on pp. 45–49 does not, however, purport to be a comprehensive list. Some tribunals are considered in detail in the next section.

Other tribunals of note that have not been included within the jurisdiction of the Council on Tribunals include the Criminal Injuries Compensation Board, set up under the royal prerogative to consider claims for *ex gratia* compensation from the victims of crimes of violence,[71] the Attendance Allowance Board, which determines whether the medical conditions are satisfied for the payment of attendance allowance, and the Housing Benefit Review Boards set up[72] to hear appeals by claimants for rent or rates rebate or rent allowance (housing benefit) who remain dissatisfied with their local authority's determination of their claims.[73] The Foreign Compensation Commission, which considers claims by British subjects as a result of nationalisation or sequestration in foreign countries, was placed under the Council's supervision, as regards its adjudicatory functions, in 1984.[74]

E. PARTICULAR COURTS AND TRIBUNALS

In this section we consider the courts and tribunals that feature most prominently in the English legal system, by virtue either of their status in the hierarchy or their caseload. For reasons of space it is not possible to cover all tribunals in detail. We have not divided this section into "courts" and "tribunals" but have incorporated coverage of certain tribunals approximately in accordance with their position in the overall hierarchy.

1. MAGISTRATES' COURTS

(a) Introduction

Magistrates' courts are the inferior criminal courts. In addition they exercise certain family law, administrative law and minor civil functions. England and Wales is divided into "commission areas": each county, the City of London, and five London commission areas (inner London, north-

[69] An alphabetical list is published as an appendix to each Annual Report.
[70] See R. E. Wraith and P. G. Hutchesson, *Administrative Tribunals* (1973), Chap. 2. See also the table in Sir William Wade, *Administrative Law* (6th ed., 1988), pp. 948; B. L. Jones, *Garner's Administrative Law* (6th ed., 1989), Chap. VIII; and D. Price, *Appeals* (1982).
[71] See the White Paper on Compensation for Victims of Crimes of Violence (Cmnd. 2323, 1964); Annual Reports of the Board; Review of the Criminal Injuries Compensation Scheme: Report of an Interdepartmental Working Party (H.M.S.O., 1978). The Board is to be reconstituted as a statutory tribunal under Part VII of the Criminal Justice Act 1988, and placed under the Council's jurisdiction, although implementation has been delayed.
[72] Housing Benefits Regulations 1982 (S.I. 1982, No. 1124): see now the Housing Benefits (General) Regulations 1987 (S.I. 1987, No. 1971), regs. 81–87 and Sched. 7.
[73] These Boards comprise members of the authority whose officers' decisions are in question. The claim of such Boards to be independent does not seem to be supportable.
[74] Tribunals and Inquiries (Foreign Compensation Commission) Order 1984 (S.I. 1984, No. 1247).

Table of Tribunals

General Subject Matter	Tribunal	Jurisdiction	Cases in 1989—England and Wales[75]	Number of Tribunals as at 31.12.89 England and Wales[75]
(a) *Social Administration* (1) Personal Welfare	Social Security Appeal Tribunals	National insurance; industrial injuries; others Income support; family credit; others	32,063[76] 51,460[76]	180[76]
	Social Security Commissioners	See p.62	4,113	1 Chief Commissioner 16 full-time Commissioners
	Medical Appeal Tribunals	Appeals concerning disablement questions arising in claims for disablement benefit	10,979	22
	Mental Health Review Tribunals	Review of the compulsory admission to hospital of mental patients	3,908	15
	Vaccine Damage Payment Tribunals	Medical Appeal Tribunals specially constituted to review refusals of vaccine damage payments	10	6
(2) Pensions	Pensions Appeal Tribunals	Appeals from decisions of the Secretary of State for Social Security concerning war pensions	2,196	Ad hoc
(3) Education	Education Appeal Committees	Appeals against allocation of school places	15,427	Not available

[75] Figures from Annual Report of the Council on Tribunals for 1989–90 (1990–91 H.C. 64), Appendix C.
[76] These figures include Scotland.

Table of Tribunals

General Subject Matter	Tribunal	Jurisdiction	Cases in 1989—England and Wales[78a]	Number of Tribunals as at 31.12.89 England and Wales[78a]
(4) Employment	Independent Schools Tribunals	Complaints concerning regulation of independent schools	1	1
	Industrial Tribunals	See pp.57–59	8,918[77]	11 Regional offices with sittings in other centres as necessary
(5) National Health Service	Family Practitioner Committees and Service Committees	Complaints by patients of practitioner's failure to comply with terms of service	2,128	90 (FPC) 360 (SC)
	National Health Service Tribunal	Appeals against a decision that a practitioner should be removed from the N.H.S.	4	2
(6) Immigration	Immigration Adjudicators	Appeals against decisions of Immigration Officers	13,777	1 Chief 11 full-time 71 part-time
	Immigration Appeal Tribunal	Appeals from Immigration Officers and Adjudicators	686	1 sitting in 4 divs.
(7) Residential Care Homes	Registered Homes Tribunals	Appeals concerning the registration of residential, nursing and children's homes	26	Ad hoc, drawn from a panel of 6 chairmen and 9 expert members
(b) *Economic matters* (8) Agriculture	Agricultural Land Tribunals	Disputes between landlord and tenant in respect of notice to quit, bad husbandry and drainage	52	7

[77] 19,015 cases were withdrawn or settled before a hearing.

				Ad hoc[78]
	Arbitrators under the Agricultural Holdings Act 1988	Certain disputes over agricultural tenancies	46	Ad hoc[78]
	Dairy Produce Quota Tribunal	Appeals against milk quota decisions	1	1
	Milk and Dairies Tribunals	Objections against decisions concerning registration of dairy farms and farmers	1	5
	Commons Commissioners	Determination of claims in respect of common land	340	1 Chief Commissioner, 1 full-time and 1 part-time Commissioners
	Plant Varieties and Seeds Tribunal	Disputes between citizens concerning plant variety rights	Nil	1
(9) Commerce	Comptroller of Patents	Adjudication in respect of patents, registered designs and trade marks	5,681	3
	Director-General of Fair Trading	Licensing decisions concerning consumer credit and estate agent activities	233	5
	Copyright Tribunal	Disputes between citizens concerning licences for copyright material	1	1
	Financial Services Tribunal[79]	References concerning authorisations to act as a practitioner concerning investment businesses	2	1

[78] Arbitrators are appointed *ad hoc* by the President of the Royal Institute of Chartered Surveyors (formerly by the Minister of Agriculture) from a panel of 223 members nominated by the Lord Chancellor.

[78a] Figures from Annual Report of the Council on Tribunals for 1989–90 (1990–91 H.C. 64), Appendix C.

[79] There is also an Insolvency Practitioners Tribunal under the Insolvency Act 1986, a Banking Appeal Tribunal under the Banking Act 1987 and a Building Societies Appeal Tribunal under the Building Societies Act 1986. None were convened in 1989.

Table of Tribunals

General Subject Matter	Tribunal	Jurisdiction	Cases in 1989—England and Wales[83a]	Number of Tribunals as at 31.12.89 England and Wales[83a]
	Data Protection Registrar	Registration of data users and computer bureaux	99,010	2
	Data Protection Tribunal	Appeals from the Registrar	0	1
(10) Transport	Traffic Commissioners	Licensing of public service passenger vehicles / Licensing of goods vehicles	1,893 / 1,007[80]	8 serving 9 regional traffic areas
	Transport Tribunal	Appeals from Traffic Commissioners	24	1
	Civil Aviation Authority	Air transport and travel organisers' licensing	1,370	1
(11) Housing	Rent assessment committees	Appeals concerning rents	15,931	Appointed ad hoc from 14 panels
	Rent Tribunals[81]	Disputes between landlord and tenant relating to the rent or security of tenure of certain dwellings	1,703	Appointed ad hoc from 14 panels

[80] Heard at public inquiry. 37,559 applications were dealt with in total.
[81] Under the Housing Act 1980, s.72, the functions of rent tribunals are to be performed by rent assessment committees, although when so acting the committees are to be known as "rent tribunals."

(12) Foreign Compensation			
Leasehold Valuation Tribunals[82]	Valuation of leaseholds for purposes of the Leasehold Reform Act 1967	Not available[83]	Appointed ad hoc from 14 panels
Foreign Compensation Commission	Distribution of compensation from foreign governments	1,206	1
(c) Revenue			
(13) Taxation			
Special and General Commissioners of Income Tax	Tax appeals	Special: 149 General: 1,156,704 (delay) 12,313 (contentious)[84]	Special: 1 presiding, 3 full-time, 2 part-time General: 4,081[85]
Value Added Tax Tribunals	V.A.T. appeals	1,227	2
Tribunal for Part XVII of the Income and Corporation Taxes Act 1988	Nullification of tax advantages from certain transactions in securities, e.g. dividend-stripping	2	1
(14) Statutory Levies			
Levy Exemption Referees	Disputes concerning refusal of industrial training boards to grant certificates of exemption from industrial training levy	2	1
Betting Levy Appeal Tribunal	Appeals in respect of levy on bookmakers by the Horserace Betting Levy Board	16	2
(15) Property, Valuation and Rating			
Valuation and Community Charge Tribunals[85a]	Rating and community charge appeals	40,870[86]	Tribunals drawn from 64 panels
Lands Tribunal	See p. 86	369	1
London Building Act Tribunal of Appeal	Appeals under the Acts	Nil	Ad hoc

82 Under the Housing Act 1980, s.142, rent assessment committees are established as leasehold valuation tribunals.
83 Figures are to be collected for 1990.
83a Figures from Annual Report of the Council on Tribunals for 1989–90 (1990–91 H.C. 64), Appendix C.
84 Figures are estimates of cases listed for the U.K.
85 Vol. 151, H.C.Deb., April 29, 1989, col. 552, Sir Nicholas Lyell, Solicitor-General.
85a Formerly, Local Valuation Courts.
86 A further 129,053 cases were settled or withdrawn.

east London, south-east London, south-west London and Middlesex).[87]
Each non-metropolitan county and metropolitan district, the City of
London, the inner London area and each outer London borough constitutes
a "petty sessions area" unless it is divided into "petty sessional divisions" in
which case each division constitutes a petty sessions area.[88] Each petty
sessions area has its own "bench" of justices with an elected chairman and
one or more deputy chairmen.[89] Each justice is a justice of the peace for the
commission area and not merely for the petty session area in which he or she
normally sits.[90]

(b) Criminal jurisdiction

Magistrates' courts are involved in some way in virtually all criminal
prosecutions. Proceedings may be commenced by a summons or an arrest
warrant issued by a justice of the peace.[91] Magistrates' courts try those
offences triable only summarily, and act as examining justices to determine
whether persons charged with offences triable only on indictment should be
committed for trial in the Crown Court. Where proceedings are brought in
respect of the intermediate category of offences "triable either way," the
court must decide whether the offence appears more suitable for summary
trial or for trial on indictment. Once this is decided, and subject to the right
of the accused to insist on trial by a jury, the court proceeds either to
summary trial or committal proceedings.[92]

A magistrates' court must be composed of at least two justices of the
peace[93] unless there is express provision for a single justice to act,[94] as there
is, for example, in the case of committal proceedings. Stipendiary magistrates[95] normally sit alone.

---

[87] Justices of the Peace Act 1979, ss.1, 2.
[88] *Ibid.* s.4, as amended by the Local Government Act 1985, s.12. See the Local Government
(Petty Sessional Divisions etc.) Order 1973 (S.I. 1973 No. 1593), as amended, and, for
London, the Petty Sessional Divisions (Inner London) Order 1964 (S.I. 1964, No. 853), as
amended, which divides the Inner London area into 9 divisions and the Local Government
(Magistrates' Courts etc.) Order 1986 (S.I. 1986 No. 399), which made provision for Outer
London following the constitution of the Outer London boroughs as petty sessions areas by
the Local Government Act 1985.
[89] See the Justices of the Peace (Size and Chairmanship of Bench) Rules 1990 (S.I. 1990 No.
1554); see (1990) 154 J.P.N. 683. The Home Office and the Lord Chancellor's Department
have produced a joint paper on "The Size of Benches" (1986) 42 *The Magistrate* 118 (benches
should normally have more than 12 Justices, and have at least 134 planned sittings a year if
they are not to be candidates for amalgamation; where a bench has more than 150 justices or
1,750 planning sittings, a stipendiary appointment (below, p. 199) should be considered).
[90] 1979 Act, s.6. This facilitates the cross-remanding of cases from one petty sessions area to
another within the same commission area: see *R.* v. *Avon Magistrates' Courts Committee, ex
p. Bath Law Society* [1988] Q.B. 409.
[91] Magistrates' Courts Act 1980, s.1. The other methods of commencing proceedings are by an
arrest without warrant and by a voluntary bill of indictment: see below, pp. 664–665. Only
this last method by-passes the magistrates' court. As to the geographical limits of the
jurisdiction of magistrates' courts, see the 1980 Act, s.2.
[92] These proceedings are explained more fully in the chapters on criminal procedure.
[93] The office of justice of the peace is considered below, pp. 180–194.
[94] Magistrates' Courts Act 1980, s.121(1). Normally, three justices sit.
[95] See below, pp. 199–201.

(c) Proceedings concerning juveniles[96]

(i) Juvenile courts

A juvenile court must be composed of not more than three justices, and must normally include a man and a woman.[97] The justices must be drawn from the juvenile court panel appointed by the justices for each petty sessions area at their annual meeting.[98] They must be under 65 and should be "specially qualified for dealing with juvenile cases."[99] Each panel elects a chairman and deputy chairman, one of whom must normally preside over each juvenile court. Stipendiary magistrates are members of the panel *ex officio* although one may only sit alone if he or she thinks it inexpedient in the interests of justice for there to be an adjournment.[1] A court may be held in buildings set apart for the purpose, or, as is more usually the case, in a courtroom normally used for an adult magistrates' court.[2] However, a juvenile court may not sit in a room that has been or will be used within an hour by another court.[3]

(ii) Jurisdiction

Criminal proceedings may not be instituted against children who are under 10: it is conclusively presumed that they cannot be guilty of any offence.[4] Where children between 10 and 14 are prosecuted it must be proved that they were children of a "mischievous discretion," *i.e.* that they

---

[96] See H. K. Bevan, *Child Law* (1989); G. Walters, *Criminal Proceedings against Juveniles* (1984); K. W. Pain, *Minors: The Law and the Practice* (1987). For research into the "consumer's" view of the juvenile justice system see H. Parker *et al., Receiving Juvenile Justice* (1981).

[97] The Juvenile Courts (Constitution) Rules 1954 (S.I. 1954 No. 1711), r. 12.

[98] Children and Young Persons Act 1933, Sched. 2. In London, the panels are appointed by the Lord Chancellor. Outside London there has been little progress towards the amalgamation of panels in areas where juvenile courts do not sit often enough for the justices to gain adequate experience of the work: see C. Ball, (1983) 147 J.P.N. 148. In 1986, the Lord Chancellor, having accepted a recommendation from the Judicial Studies Board (see pp. 224–225), required a minimum of 12 sittings per annum for each panel member, with a suggested target of 15 sittings per annum.

[99] 1954 Rules, r. 1. The rules do not specify any qualifications. The Home Secretary has suggested that they "should include some direct practical experience of dealing with young persons (*e.g.* through working with youth organisations, teaching or similar work) and a real appreciation of the surroundings and way of life of the children who are likely to come before courts." The most suitable age for first appointment would be between 30 and 40 and no one should normally be first appointed when over 50: Home Office Circular No. 138/1979, printed in *Clarke Hall and Morrison on Children* (10th ed., 1985), pp. E.390–399. See also Circulars 67/1982 (pp. E.514–523) and 61/1983 (pp. E.699–718).

[1] 1954 Rules, rr. 2, 12(2).

[2] Guidance on the design of juvenile courts was given in Home Office Circular No. 39/1971 (*Clarke Hall and Morrison* (9th ed., 1979), pp. 1154–6). For a description of some courtrooms see L. Hilgendorf, *Social Workers and Solicitors in Child Care Cases* (H.M.S.O., 1981), pp. 89–98, criticising the poor conditions provided in many courts for waiting areas, the scheduling of care and criminal proceedings for the same day, and the continued use of old-fashioned magistrates' courts for care cases.

[3] Children and Young Persons Act 1933, s.47, as amended by the 1963 Act, s.17.

[4] Children and Young Persons Act 1933, s.50, as amended by the 1963 Act, s.16(1). At common law the relevant age was seven. Section 4 of the Children and Young Persons Act 1969 provides for the age to be raised to 14, but this has not been, and is unlikely to be, implemented.

knew that what they were doing was legally or morally wrong. Young persons of 14 and over are regarded as fully responsible for their acts.

There are two main branches to the juvenile court's jurisdiction. First, all criminal proceedings against juveniles[5] must normally take place in a juvenile court. The main exceptions are that an adult magistrates' court *must* deal with juveniles where they are charged jointly with an adult and *may* do so where different charges are made against an adult arising out of the same or connected circumstances or where either an adult or a juvenile is charged with aiding, abetting, causing, procuring, allowing or permitting the other's alleged offence.[6] The juvenile court will try the case summarily except (1) where the charge is murder or manslaughter in which case the juvenile *must* be committed for trial in the Crown Court and (2) where the offence is one which carries a penalty for an adult of 14 years' imprisonment or more and the defendant is over 14, in which event the court *may* commit for trial.[7]

Any person may institute criminal proceedings against a juvenile,[8] but they must notify the appropriate local authority.[9]

Secondly, a juvenile court may entertain civil "care proceedings" in relation to juveniles.[10] The structure of the law relating to children is, however, to be substantially altered by the Children Act 1989.[11] Care proceedings are to be re-modelled, and transferred to the family proceedings courts (see below).

(iii) *Procedure*

The procedure of juvenile courts is less formal than for adult magistrates' courts.[12] Only members and officers of the court, the parties, their lawyers, witnesses and other persons directly concerned, press, representatives, and other persons specially authorised may be present.[13] There are strict limits as to what may be reported.[14] In the case of juveniles dealt with summarily the

---

[5] This term applies to children and young persons under 17. For most purposes under the 1933 Act "child" is defined as a person under 14 and "young person" as a person of 14 or over but under 17: s.107(1). The term "child" is differently defined for other purposes: see *Halsbury's Laws of England* (4th ed.) Vol. 24, para. 403.

[6] Children and Young Persons Act 1933, s.46 as extended by the 1963 Act, s.18. Applications for bail or for a remand may be heard by any justice or justices (1933 Act, s.46(2)). The adult magistrates' court will normally try the juvenile summarily but may commit him or her for trial in the Crown Court (Magistrates' Courts Act 1980, s.24) or remit for trial (*ibid*. s.29) or sentence (Children and Young Persons Act 1969, s.7(8)) in the juvenile court.

[7] Magistrates' Courts Act 1980, s.24. This enables the Crown Court to invoke the power under section 53(2) of the Children and Young Persons Act 1933 to impose a long sentence of detention.

[8] The provisions of section 5 of the Children and Young Persons Act 1969 which restrict private prosecutions have not been implemented.

[9] 1969 Act, s.5(8), (9).

[10] See P. M. Bromley and N. V. Lowe, *Bromley's Family Law* (7th ed., 1987), pp. 448–465; Children and Young Persons Act 1969, ss.1–3, as amended.

[11] The Act follows the D.H.S.S. *Review of Child Care Law* (1985) and the White Paper, *The Law on Child Care and Family Services* (Cm. 62. 1987). See J. Masson, Annotations in *Current Law Statutes Annotated 1989*; S. Cretney and J. Masson, *Principles of Family Law* (5th ed., 1990), Part VI.

[12] See the Magistrates' Courts (Children and Young Persons) Rules 1988 (S.I. 1988 No. 913).

[13] Children and Young Persons Act 1933, s.47, as amended by the Children and Young Persons Act 1963, s.17(2).

[14] 1933 Act, s.49, as amended by the Children and Young Persons Acts 1963, s.57 and 1969, s.10.

expression "finding of guilt" must be used instead of "conviction" and the expression "order made upon a finding of guilt" instead of "sentence."[15]

(d) Family proceedings

Magistrates have an extensive jurisdiction in family law matters.[16] The list includes powers to make orders for financial provision for, or the protection of, parties to a marriage and children of the family, for the custody or supervision of children and committing children to the care of a local authority, guardianship orders and adoption orders. Proceedings concerning these matters are termed "domestic proceedings" and the courts when hearing them "domestic courts."[17] The justices must be appointed from a domestic court panel constituted on a similar basis to the juvenile court panel.[18] Under the Children Act 1989[19] these are to become "family proceedings" "family proceedings courts" and "family panel" respectively.[20]

The law relating to child care is to be substantially altered by the 1989 Act, which re-states the respective powers and responsibilities of parents, courts and local authorities. The courts will have power to grant, *inter alia*, "contact orders" (replacing access orders) and "residence orders" (replacing custody orders) and a variety of emergency orders; the grounds on which care or supervision orders may be granted are simplified and narrowed.[21] The magistrates' courts, county courts and High Courts will have concurrent jurisdiction under the 1989 Act and the Adoption Act 1976; the Lord Chancellor has power to make orders specifying the level of court and the description of court at which different classes of proceedings should be commenced, and makes provision for the transfer of proceedings.[22] His intention is to require care cases to start in the magistrates' court.[23] Most orders will, however, continue to be made in divorce or matrimonial proceedings which are commenced in the county court.[24]

The courts will have power to make care or supervision orders in respect of children under 17 (16 if married), if they are satisfied that (a) the child is suffering or likely to suffer significant harm; and (b) this is attributable to (i) the care given to the child, or likely to be given to him or her if the order were not made, not being what it would be reasonable to expect a parent to give; or (ii) the child's being beyond parental control.[25] The welfare of the child is the paramount consideration, and the court must take other specified matters into account.[26] Under a care order, the child is taken into the care of the local authority; a supervision order places the child under the supervision of a designated local authority or a probation officer.[27]

---

[15] *Ibid.* s.59.
[16] Magistrates' Courts Act 1980, s.65.
[17] *Ibid.* s.67(1).
[18] *Ibid.* s.66(1); Domestic Courts (Constitution) Rules 1979 (S.I. 1979 No. 757), as amended by S.I. 1983 No. 676 and S.I. 1988 No. 868.
[19] s.92(1).
[20] Existing members of domestic panels will not automatically be appointed to family panels. A substantial training programme has been put into effect.
[21] See below.
[22] Children Act 1989, s.92 and Sched. 11; Courts and Legal Services Act 1990, s.9.
[23] (1989) 139 N.L.J. at p. 506.
[24] See below, pp. 66, 82–83.
[25] Children Act 1989, Part IV.
[26] *Ibid.* s.1.
[27] *Ibid.* s.31.

(e) Civil jurisdiction

Apart from domestic (family) proceedings, magistrates' courts have powers in relation to certain other civil matters, including enforcement of the payment of rates, the community charge, income tax and charges for supplies of gas, electricity and water. They also have an important jurisdiction in respect of the granting of liquor licences to public houses and clubs, and licences for bookmakers, betting offices, and premises for gaming and bingo. Finally, there is a vast number[28] of statutory provisions enabling appeals to be brought against administrative decisions of various kinds.

(f) Appeals[29]

Appeals lie from a magistrates' court either as of right to the Crown Court,[30] where proceedings take the form of a complete rehearing, or to the High Court by a procedure whereby the magistrates state a case for the opinion of the High Court on a point of law. In family matters the appeal is heard by the Family Division, otherwise the appeal will lie to the Queen's Bench Division. Any further appeal from the High Court lies to the House of Lords in criminal cases and to the Court of Appeal and House of Lords in civil cases.

(g) Administration

Procedural rules are made by the Lord Chancellor after consultation with a Rule Committee, comprising the Lord Chief Justice, the President of the Family Division, the chief metropolitan stipendiary magistrate, and other persons appointed by the Lord Chancellor, who must include a justices' clerk, and specified lawyers.[31] There is a "magistrates' courts committee" for each non-metropolitan county, metropolitan district and outer London borough and for the City of London.[32] The committee consists of magistrates appointed by the magistrates for each petty sessions area at their annual meeting.[33] Each committee may co-opt a High Court judge, Circuit judge or recorder,[34] and must appoint a chairman and a clerk. The clerk is usually

---

[28] D. Price, *Appeals* (1982) pp. 53–96, including appeals against refusal of a petshop licence, of a driving licence or a knacker's yard licence, a notice requiring a fire certificate and a notice requiring that an earth closet be replaced by a water closet. For discussion of the jurisdiction of magistrates to entertain appeals concerned with the licensing of pilots see G. Browne, "The Admiralty Jurisdiction of Inner London Magistrates" (1987) 151 J.P.N. 23.

[29] See generally, Chap. 17, below.

[30] See below, pp. 71–77, 825–827.

[31] Magistrates' Courts Act 1980, s.144, and see also ss.145–146. S.144, as amended by the Courts and Legal Services Act 1990, Sched. 18, para. 25(7), requires the appointment of one person with a Supreme Court qualification under s.71 of the Courts and Legal Services Act, and one with the right to conduct litigation in the Supreme Court.

[32] Justices of the Peace Act 1979, ss.19–22, as amended by the Local Government Act 1985, s.12. In Inner London there is a "committee of magistrates" under ss.35–38.

[33] See the Magistrates' Courts Committees (Constitution) Regulations 1973 (S.I. 1973 No. 1522), as amended by S.I.s 1980 No. 1258 and 1985 No. 1393, which determine the number appointed for each division where an area is so divided.

[34] 1979 Act, s.20(2).

either the local clerk to the justices or the clerk to the local authority.[35] The functions of the committee include making proposals as to the division of their area into petty sessional divisions,[36] the appointment or removal of justices' clerks and other staff,[37] the indemnification of justices and clerks[38] and the provision of courses of instruction.[39] It is also responsible for determining what accommodation, books and equipment should be provided, although the actual provision is made by the local non-metropolitan county, metropolitan district, or outer London borough council or the City of London.[40] The council also pays the committee's expenses, including staff salaries. A council may appeal to the Secretary of State against a determination by the committee. This division of function can cause problems, although there seems to be a general desire to avoid confrontation.[41]

In recent years, the Home Office, which provides a grant covering 80 per cent. of the cost of running the service, has taken a greater interest in its management. It has taken a number of steps designed to secure greater efficiency and economy,[42] including the commissioning of studies,[43] the development of a Management Information System to help assess performance at a local level and (from 1992) the introduction of cash limits.[44] There has been some debate as to whether magistrates' courts committees would be able to respond to the challenge of improving the management of the service.[45] Indeed, a Home Office scrutiny[46] has concluded that they will not, and has recommended that they be replaced by a Magistrates' Courts

[35] If the area of the committee coincides with a petty sessions area it must be the clerk to the justices: *ibid.* s.22(2). In 1988, in 22 out of the 47 non-metropolitan counties the post was filled by a justices' clerk, in 20 by a senior council officer (usually the chief executive or county secretary/solicitor) and in 5 by an independent, full-time clerk: J. Bowden and J. W. Raine, (1988) 152 J.P.N. at p. 501.

[36] *Ibid.* ss.23, 24.

[37] *Ibid.* ss.25–27.

[38] *Ibid.* s.53.

[39] *Ibid.* s.63. See below, pp. 190–191.

[40] *Ibid.* ss.55, 56. In 1971–72 the Justices' Clerks' Society and the Magistrates' Association pressed unsuccessfully for the link with local authorities to be broken and the administration of magistrates' courts to be merged with the new unified court service: see (1971) *The Magistrate*, pp. 52–56, 93, 109, 124–125, 142–43; (1972) *The Magistrate*, p. 49.

[41] See generally the *Report of the Working Group on Magistrates' Courts* (Home Office, 1982) Chap. 2; comments by C. Moiser (1983) 133 N.L.J. 149–150, 517–519.

[42] See J. W. Raine and L. G. Henshaw, *Resource Requirements and Value for Money in the Magistrates' Courts Service* (Home Office, 1985); J. W. Raine, (1986) 150 J.P.N. 761, 777, noting significant variations from area to area in patterns of expenditure and, generally, J. W. Raine, *Local Justice* (1989), Chap. 5.

[43] *e.g.* D. Moxon and R. Tarling, *Waiting Time on the day in magistrates' courts: a review of case listing practices* (Home Office Research and Planning Unit Paper 45, 1988), summarised at (1988) 152 J.P.N. 534.

[44] Home Office Consultation Document on "Distribution of Specific Grant" for the Magistrates' Courts Service, discussed by J. W. Raine, (1988) 152 J.P.N. 358; I. S. Lomax, (1990) 154 J.P.N. 672. The Scrutiny Report (below, fn. 46, recommended against cash limits: Vol. 1, paras. 10.6–10.7.

[45] J. W. Raine, (1986) 150 J.P.N. 260, 280: J. Bowden and J. W. Raine, (1988) 152 J.P.N. 489, 501, 521.

[46] *Magistrates' Courts: Report of A Scrutiny 1989* (H.M.S.O., 1989 (the Le Vay Scrutiny)). For reactions, see (1989) 153 J.P.N. 489, 553, 627–8, 660–1; T. Kavanagh, *ibid.* p. 589; R. Burriss, *ibid.*, p. 655; W. M. S. Tildesley, *ibid.*, p. 670; J. W. Raine, *ibid.*, p. 684; R. L. Jones, (1990) 154 J.P.N. 538. Coopers & Lybrand Deloitte were commissioned to cost the options for change: *ibid.* p. 666. *Cf.* the less radical proposals of the Justices' Clerks Society: *Administering Magistrates' Courts: The Role of the Justices' Clerk* (1989).

Agency, an executive agency accountable to, but operationally independent of, the Home Office. The Scrutiny found the present arrangements had led to a service which was highly fragmented, lacked a coherent management structure and failed to deliver value for money. Instead, there should be a national service, funded entirely by the government, but with maximum delegation of managerial responsibility and control of resources to the local level. Overall policy responsibility should rest with government, but the service should not be administered directly by a government department, so as to minimise the risk of government interference in judicial decision-making.

The organisation of magistrates' courts varies according to the workload:

"In the dignified Victorian courthouse of one Midlands city 15 adult and two juvenile courts are held each morning, and up to 10 adult courts in the afternoon. Over 300 magistrates are on the rota, the staff numbers 150, fines collected annually amount to £1½ million, and the turnover in the maintenance department is £3 million.

At the opposite end of the scale you find a country district with eight different courts, each several miles from the next, but all served by one Justices' Clerk. . . .

The majority of courts, however, lie between these two extremes, with perhaps two to five courts a day."[47]

In a small court the list may be a mixture of all kinds of case; in a large court there may be specialised courts to hear traffic offences or applications, or to deal with debtors.

The administration is headed by the justices' clerk.[48] In a large court there may be separate sections for documentation concerning court proceedings, fines and fees, maintenance and licensing. In smaller courts the functional divisions are more blurred.[49]

Justices comprise at least two-thirds of the membership of the 56 "probation and after care committees" that are responsible, under the overall supervision of the Home Office, for the Probation and After-Care Service.[50] Probation officers have responsibilities in connection with probation orders, supervision orders for young offenders, suspended sentence supervision orders, community service orders, the after-care of persons released from custody and the preparation of social inquiry reports and reports concerning the custody of children and the selection of prisoners for parole. They also provide a welfare service in domestic and matrimonial cases, and work in prison establishments. The government has published a Green Paper, *Supervision, Punishment and the Community*, setting out options for restructuring the Probation Service.[51] One possibility for it to become a national service.

[47] *A Career in the Magistrates Courts* (H.M.S.O., 1979), p. 7.
[48] See below, pp. 194–198.
[49] Procedures for the scheduling of cases and fine enforcement were examined in the Report, *op. cit.* n. 41 above, and the Le Vay Scrutiny.
[50] See *The Probation and After-Care Service in England and Wales* (H.M.S.O., 5th ed., 1973); F. V. Jarvis, *Probation Officers' Manual* (4th ed., 1987); M. Vizard, (1986) 150 J.P.N. 299; A. Rich and J. Waters, (1989) 45 *The Magistrate* 77; D. E. R. Faulkner, (1989) 153 J.P.N. 606.
[51] Cm. 966, 1990.

2. INDUSTRIAL TRIBUNALS[52]

Industrial tribunals were first established by the Industrial Training Act 1964 to hear appeals by employers assessed for levy payable to an industrial training board. They were then given jurisdiction over disputes about redundancy pay. The Royal Commission on Trade Unions and Employers' Associations[53] recommended that the tribunal's jurisdiction should be enlarged to comprise, subject to certain limitations, all disputes between the individual worker and employer, the primary aim being to make available "a procedure which is easily accessible, informal, speedy and inexpensive, and which gives them the best possible opportunities of arriving at an amicable settlement of their differences."[54] To a large extent this recommendation has been fulfilled. In addition to the points already mentioned industrial tribunals have jurisdiction in respect of complaints of unfair dismissal,[55] questions as to terms required to be included in a contract of employment,[56] claims to equal pay,[57] appeals against improvement notices or prohibition notices served by a health and safety inspector[58] and certain complaints relating to sex[59] and race[60] discrimination. Apart from matters arising between employer and employee, they also handle claims by individuals against trade unions for unreasonable exclusion or expulsion in closed shop situations and claims for compensation in respect of pressure on the employer to take action against an individual by reason of membership or non-membership of a union.[61] This list is not exhaustive.

The tribunals sit at over 50 centres, grouped under 13 Regional Offices of Industrial Tribunals and the Central Office of Industrial Tribunals in London. There is a President of Industrial Tribunals (England and Wales) who both sits as a chairman and has important administrative responsibilities in relation to the system.[62] Each tribunal has a legally qualified chairman and two "wingmen."[63]

A common criticism of industrial tribunals has been that they have become increasingly "legalistic":

> "First, it is observed that the immense quantity of case law reported and cited in the courts is complicating the work of tribunals. Secondly,

---

[52] See K. Whitesides and G. Hawker, *Industrial Tribunals* (1975); M. J. Goodman, *Industrial Tribunals: Practice and Procedure* (4th ed., 1987); B. A. Hepple and P. O'Higgins, *Encyclopedia of Labour Relations Law*, Part 4A; JUSTICE Report, *Industrial Tribunals* (1987); L. Dickens, *et al.*, *Dismissed: A Study of Unfair Dismissal and the Industrial Tribunal System* (1987); A. M. Leonard, *Judging Inequality* (Cobden Trust., 1987).
[53] Cmnd. 3623, 1968: Chairman: Lord Donovan.
[54] *Ibid.*, para. 572.
[55] Employment Protection (Consolidation) Act 1978, s.67.
[56] *Ibid.* s.11.
[57] Equal Pay Act 1970, as amended.
[58] Health and Safety at Work etc. Act 1974, ss.21–24.
[59] Sex Discrimination Act 1975, ss.63, 72, 73.
[60] Race Relations Act 1976, s.54.
[61] Employment Act 1980, ss.4, 5; Employment Act 1982.
[62] See the Industrial Tribunals (England and Wales) Regulations 1965 (S.I. 1965 No. 1101), as amended.
[63] See below, pp. 201–205.

statutes, which were intended to be straightforward enactments, are increasingly being subjected to subtle lawyers' reasoning."[64]

Lord Denning M.R. suggested that some limit be placed on the reporting of cases:

"If we are not careful, we shall find the Industrial Tribunals bent down under the weight of the law books or, what is worse, asleep under them. Let principles be reported, but not particular instances."[65]

On the other hand, it has been suggested that growing "legalism" is inevitable given that the legislation is in fact complex and interpretative difficulties unavoidable, that there is a legally qualified chairman, that legal representation is increasingly common, that in practice litigants require consistency in decision-making, and that there must be a reliable yardstick for the conciliatory procedures incorporated in the legislation to work:

"Naturally, tribunals will continue to dispense with the flummery and much of the procedural and evidential paraphernalia of the law courts—in this sense they are informal and comparatively free. But in most important respects, tribunals do closely resemble courts. Thus, if charges of legalism mean that they interpret the law in legal fashion, one would expect to find these charges fully proven for it is quite impossible to see how else tribunals could be expected to behave."[66]

Industrial tribunals do not have jurisdiction over common law claims arising out of breaches of contracts of employment.[67] In accordance with the recommendation of the Donovan Commission they have not been given jurisdiction over tort actions arising out of accidents at work.

A JUSTICE Report on Industrial Tribunals[68] has made a number of proposals for change. For the vast majority of cases the investigative approach should be improved, so as to reduce the need for representation, while, for a minority of cases, the adversarial system should be improved by providing legal aid for representation and establishing an upper tier Industrial Court, with senior chairmen and members, to hear them. The Industrial Court would also assume the appellate functions of the Employment Appeal Tribunal. The Committee confirmed that industrial tribunals did have a number of advantages over ordinary courts, being more accessible, less formal, more expeditious, less expensive and possessed of special expertise.[69] However, complaints of excessive "legalism" were to an extent justified. One cause was the present state of substantive employment law, which was in need of clarification and consolidation in a comprehensible form. The other main cause was the adversarial system which was a major obstacle to

---

[64] R. Munday, "Tribunal Lore: Legalism and the Industrial Tribunals" (1981) 10 I.L.J. 146, 147.

[65] *Walls Meat Co. Ltd.* v. *Khan* [1979] I.C.R. 52, 57, *cf.* Lawton L.J. in *Clay Cross (Quarry Services) Ltd.* v. *Fletcher* [1979] 1 All E.R. 474, 479.

[66] Munday, *op. cit.* p. 159. On the procedure of industrial tribunals see below, pp. 585 ff, 721–722.

[67] Where there is a termination of employment these are termed claims for wrongful dismissal, to distinguish them from the statutory claims in respect of unfair dismissal arising out of the Employment Protection (Consolidation) Act 1978. There is a power, as yet unused, for industrial tribunals to be given jurisdiction over certain wrongful dismissal claims: 1978 Act, s.131.

[68] Chairman: Bob Hepple (1987).

[69] pp. 7–9.

informality in the conduct of hearings.[70] The Committee also noted that research indicated that industrial tribunals were particularly weak in understanding and applying the legislation concerning complaints of sex or race discrimination.[71] Special training was necessary for chairmen and members who dealt with such cases.[72]

Appeals lie on a point of law[73] in most cases to the Employment Appeal Tribunal,[74] and in the others[75] to the Queen's Bench Division.

3. THE EMPLOYMENT APPEAL TRIBUNAL

The Employment Appeal Tribunal[76] was established by the Employment Protection Act 1975[77] as the successor of the politically controversial National Industrial Relations Court, inheriting the latter's appellate functions. Its membership comprises judges of the High Court or Court of Appeal[78] nominated by the Lord Chancellor, at least one judge of the Court of Session nominated by the Lord President of that court, and lay members appointed by the Queen on the recommendation of the Lord Chancellor and the Secretary of State, being persons who "appear . . . to have special knowledge or experience of industrial relations, either as representatives of employers or as representatives of workers."[79] One of the judges is appointed President. Each appeal is normally heard by a judge sitting with two or four lay members. Decisions can be by a majority, and the judge can be outvoted, even on a point of law, by the lay members. The E.A.T. hears appeals from industrial tribunals and from the Certification Officer, who performs various functions in respect of trade unions, mostly on points of law. The Court of Appeal has expressed the view that the E.A.T. has taken too wide a view of what constitutes an error of law and has thus interfered too readily with the decisions of industrial tribunals.[80] It suggested that the E.A.T. should be less ready to lay down "guidelines" for industrial tribunals. For example, whether a dismissal is "fair" should essentially be

---

[70] Chap. 2.
[71] V. C. Kumar, *Industrial Tribunal Applicants under the Race Relations Act 1976* (Commission for Racial Equality 1986); A. Leonard, *Judging Inequality* (1987).
[72] pp. 35–38.
[73] Fact or law where the question is whether a person has been unreasonably excluded or expelled from membership of a trade union in a closed shop situation.
[74] See below.
[75] *e.g.* industrial training levy assessments, appeals against an improvement or prohibition notice.
[76] A superior court of record. See Phillips J., "Some notes on the Employment Appeal Tribunal" (1978) 7 I.L.J. 137; Browne-Wilkinson J., "The role of the EAT in the 1980s" (1982) 11 I.L.J. 69; Sir John Waite, "Lawyers and Laymen as Judges in Industry" (1986) 15 I.L.J. 32; Sir John Wood, (1990) 19 I.L.J. 133.
[77] See now the Employment Protection (Consolidation) Act 1978, ss.135, 136, Sched. 11.
[78] Only the former have so far been nominated. In 1990 there were four High Court judges (including the President) and one judge of the Court of Session nominated to the E.A.T.
[79] The lay members do not in practice act in a partisan manner.
[80] See *Retarded Children's Aid Society* v. *Day* [1978] I.C.R 437; *Methven* v. *Cow Industrial Polymers Ltd.* [1980] I.C.R. 463; *Pedersen* v. *Camden London B.C.* [1981] I.C.R. 674; *Woods* v. *W. M. Car Services (Peterborough) Ltd.* [1982] I.C.R. 693; and the articles cited in n. 76 above. See also *O'Kelly* v. *Trusthouse Forte plc* [1983] I.C.R. 728.

regarded as a question of fact. The consequent advantage of greater flexibility for industrial tribunals has to be balanced against the consequent inconsistency amongst them.[81]

Appeals lie on a point of law from the E.A.T. to the Court of Appeal,[82] with the leave of either court.

4. SOCIAL SECURITY TRIBUNALS[83]

A variety of cash benefits are available under the Social Security Act 1975 (*e.g.* unemployment benefit, invalidity and sickness benefit, retirement pension, widow's benefit, child's special allowance, maternity allowance, and non-contributory attendance, invalid care and mobility allowances), the Child Benefit Act 1975 and the Social Security Act 1986 (*e.g.* income support, family credit and housing benefit). Several tribunals have been established to determine questions arising in the administration of these benefits.

Two discernible trends in the development of the structure of social security tribunals have been, first, the amalgamation of different tribunal jurisdictions and, secondly, the integration of tribunals within the court system. However most recently there has also been a tendency for the government to restrict rights of appeal to an independent tribunal against decisions concerning benefits.

(a) The position to 1984

Prior to 1984, a distinction was drawn between the schemes based on the insurance principle, where entitlement to benefit depended on the claimant having made appropriate contributions and otherwise falling within the rules of the scheme, and the provision of means-tested benefits involving the exercise of discretion. As regards the former, claims and questions arising under the Social Security Act 1975 and the Child Benefit Act 1975 were determined initially by an insurance officer appointed by the Secretary of State for Social Services or, for unemployment benefit, by the Secretary of State for Employment. An appeal lay to a National Insurance Local Tribunal,[84] comprising a legally qualified chairman,[85] the member from a panel representing employers and self-employed earners and one from a panel representing employed earners.[86] As regards the latter, tribunals were first set up in the 1930s and subsequently evolved into Supplementary Benefit Appeal Tribunals. These comprised a chairman appointed by the Secretary of State from a panel drawn up by the Lord Chancellor, one "ordinary member" from a panel appointed by the Secretary of State from people "appearing to have knowledge or experience of conditions in the area to

---

[81] See Browne-Wilkinson J., *op. cit.* n. 71, p. 72: "... there are signs that ... Industrial Tribunals are beginning to demonstrate a lack of uniformity in their approach to what constitutes fair industrial practice." His Lordship suggested that it would be desirable to aim for a middle way between the early practice of the E.A.T. and the restrictive approach of the Court of Appeal.

[82] In Scotland, appeals lie to the Court of Session.

[83] See generally A. I. Ogus and E. M. Barendt, *The Law of Social Security* (3rd ed., 1988), Chap. 15.

[84] This term did not appear in the legislation, but was the title commonly used. Another label sometimes found was "Social Security Local Tribunal."

[85] This was not a legal requirement but was the almost invariable practice: see below, p. 202.

[86] Social Security Act 1975, s.97(2): see below, p. 203.

which the panel relates and of the problems of people living on low incomes" and one from a panel "appearing ... to represent work people."[87] The procedures and decision-making of S.B.A.T.s were contrasted unfavourably with those of N.I.L.T.s.[88]

(b) Social Security Appeal Tribunals

In 1980 the supplementary benefit scheme was reformed, with detailed rules of entitlement replacing discretions, thereby bringing it closer in form to the national insurance scheme.[89] The Health and Social Services and Social Security Adjudications Act 1983[90] provided for the merger of the two adjudication systems. Most claims are now submitted to an "adjudication officer" appointed by the Secretary of State for Social Security (including some officers of the Department of Employment to deal with unemployment benefit).[91] There is a Chief Adjudication Officer, who is required to advise adjudication officers and keep their work under review, and to report annually to the Secretary of State on standards of adjudication.[92]

Appeals lie to a Social Security Appeal Tribunal,[93] which now exercises the jurisdictions formerly exercised by N.I.L.T.s and S.B.A.T.s. S.S.A.T.s are organised in seven regions, each headed by a Regional Chairman, and the whole system is headed by the President of Social Security Appeal Tribunals and Medical Appeal Tribunals.[94] The President must be a lawyer of not less than 10 years' standing, and the regional and other full-time chairmen of not less than five years' standing. All are appointed by the Lord Chancellor. There is also a panel of part-time chairmen appointed by the Lord Chancellor or the Lord President of the Court of Session under the Tribunals and Inquiries Act 1971.[95] These must be a lawyer of not less than five years' standing.[96] There is a single panel of members constituted by the President for the whole of Great Britain. Each tribunal comprises a chairman, nominated by the President, and two members. The President is also responsible for assigning clerks to tribunals, and it is the duty of the clerk to summon members from the panel. In practice, arrangements are made by staff at the Regional Chairman's office.

(c) Other adjudicating bodies

Certain questions, including whether a person is an "earner," whether he

---

[87] Supplementary Benefits Act 1976, Sched. 4.
[88] See the first edition of this book, pp. 55–57.
[89] Social Security Act 1980, Sched. 2.
[90] Sched. 8: in force from April 23, 1984. See J. Mesher, (1983) 10 J.L.S. 135; M. Partington, "The Restructuring of SSATs: a Personal View" in C. Harlow (ed.), *Public Law and Politics* (1986), Chap. 9.
[91] Social Security Act 1975, ss.97–99, substituted by the HSSSSA Act 1983.
[92] *Ibid.* s.97 (1B)–(1E). See R. Sainsbury, "The Social Security Chief Adjudication Officer: The First Four Years" [1989] P.L. 323.
[93] *Ibid.* s.97(2)–(2E), (4), 100, Sched. 10.
[94] The first President was Judge Byrt, who held the office from 1984 to 1989: see J. Fulbrook, (1989) 18 I.L.J. 177; Interview, *Legal Action*, September 1989, p. 7.
[95] s.7.
[96] By virtue of the Courts and Legal Services Act 1990, Sched. 10, para. 37, the qualifications in England became, respectively, a 10 year (President) and 5 year (Chairmen) general qualification under s.71 of the Act, *i.e.* a right of audience in any part of the Supreme Court or in all proceedings in county courts or magistrates' courts.

or she is "employed" or "self-employed" and whether he or she complies with "contribution conditions" necessary for receipt of contributory benefits, are still determined by the Secretary of State: in practice by a member of the DSS Solicitors' Office.[97] The Secretary of State may refer a point of law, and a dissatisfied claimant may appeal on such a point, to the High Court.

Certain questions concerning disablement benefit are determined by "Medical Boards" of two medical practitioners, which also hear certain appeals on medical questions from the decisions of a medical practitioner, or adjudication officers. There is a right of appeal to a Medical Appeal Tribunal, comprising a legally qualified chairman and two doctors of consultant status.[98]

The Attendance Allowance Board,[99] most members of which are medical practitioners, determine whether the medical conditions for attendance allowance are satisfied. In practice the Board delegates the decision to a medical practitioner.

(d) Social Security Commissioners[1]

The National Insurance Commissioners heard appeals from N.I.L.T.s, and appeals on a point of law from Medical Appeal Tribunals and the Attendance Allowance Board. In 1980, a right of appeal on a point of law was created from S.B.A.T.s to the Commissioners,[2] who were renamed Social Security Commissioners.[3] From April 23, 1984, they have heard appeals from S.S.A.T.s and from 1987 these have been restricted to points of law in all cases.[4] At present there is a Chief Social Security Commissioner and 16 Commissioners.[5] In practice two sit in Edinburgh, one in Cardiff and the others in London. The Chief Commissioner may convene a Tribunal of three Commissioners to hear an appeal involving a point of law of special difficulty. He is also responsible for selecting the decisions that are to be reported. Until 1980, the only further possibility of review was an application for judicial review. There is now a right of appeal on a point of law to the Court of Appeal, with the leave of the Commissioner or the court. From 1985, they have been administered by the Lord Chancellor's Department.

(e) Limitation of rights of appeal

Reforms to the social security system under Part III of the Social Security

---

[97] Social Security Act 1975, ss.93–95.
[98] *Ibid*. s.108.
[99] *Ibid*. Sched. 11.
[1] See R. Micklethwait, *The National Insurance Commissioners* (1976): below, p. 201. Under the 1946 legislation there was a National Insurance Commissioner and an Industrial Injuries Commissioner, each with several deputies. The same man commonly held appointments under both schemes. In 1966, these posts were merged, the National Insurance Commissioner was retitled the Chief National Insurance Commissioner, and the deputies became full Commissioners.
[2] Supplementary Benefits Act 1976, s.15A, inserted by the Social Security Act 1979, s.6. This replaced an appeal from S.B.A.T.s to the High Court that had been created in 1978.
[3] Social Security Act 1980, s.14.
[4] Social Security Act 1975, s.101, amended by the HSSSSA Act, Sched. 8 and the Social Security Act 1986, Sched. 5.
[5] The same qualifications are specified as for appointment as President of SSATs and MATs: *supra*.

Act 1986 included the replacement of lump sum "single payments" and "urgent need payments" under the supplementary benefit legislation by payments from the, cash-limited, Social Fund. In one sense this involved a return to a system of discretionary payments. The payments, most in the form of loans, are made by social fund officers appointed by the Secretary of State. In practice, however, the detailed directions given to the officers by the Secretary of State operate very much in the manner of regulations.[6] Controversially, the government decided that there should be no rights of appeal within the tribunals system.[7] The legislation provides instead for internal review by social fund inspectors, who are DSS officials appointed as inspectors by the Social Fund Commissioner. The Commissioner is in turn appointed by the Secretary of State. The inspectors are subject to the guidance and directions issued to the social fund officers.[8]

5. COUNTY COURTS

(a) Establishment

The present county courts were originally established by the County Courts Act 1846. This Act followed a lengthy campaign, which aroused hostility in several quarters, including the Bar and certain large London solicitors' firms.[9] The hostility was based essentially on fears of loss of business to provincial attornies and solicitors. In the case of the Bar there was also resistance to the development of provincial Bars, which were seen to be the only effective way of competing for county court business.[10] The aim of the Act was to set up an effective local court for minor cases, and, in particular, the recovery of small debts: proceedings in the superior courts were prohibitively expensive and civil proceedings at the assizes were prone to delay. It is ironic that similar criticisms of ordinary county court proceedings in recent times have led to the development of new, more informal, procedures for small claims, and arguments that a further tier of small claims courts should be established.[11] Indeed, right from the outset the new courts were much more heavily used by shopkeepers, traders, and other creditors than by ordinary people, their establishment leading to "an infinite expansion of credit."[12]

(b) Organisation

England and Wales is divided into districts and at least one court is held in

---

[6] See R. v. Secretary of State for Social Services, ex p. Stitt, The Times, July 5, 1990.

[7] See H. Bolderson, (1988) 15 J.L.S. 279. The Council on Tribunals registered their objections in a Special Report, Social Security—Abolition of independent appeals under the proposed Social Fund (Cmnd. 9722, 1986). See generally R. Drabble and T. Lynes, [1989] P.L. 297.

[8] Social Security Act 1986, ss.34, 35; Social Fund (Application for Review) Regulations 1988 (S.I. 1988 No. 34).

[9] See B. Abel-Smith and R. Stevens, Lawyers and the Courts (1967), pp. 32–37.

[10] See R. Cocks, Foundations of the Modern Bar (1983), pp. 25–26, 56–57.

[11] See below, pp. 531–535.

[12] Lord Westbury L.C., quoted by Abel-Smith and Stevens (1967), p. 35.

each district.[13] The districts and locations are specified by the Lord Chancellor.[14] In 1989 there were about 270 county courts; 47 courts had Admiralty jurisdiction, 174 divorce jurisdiction, and 135 bankruptcy jurisdiction.[15] About 30 offered trial facilities under which one or more judges were available on a continuous basis to hear trials.[16]

(c) Judges

Under the original arrangements the districts were grouped into 60 county court circuits, each with its own judge appointed by the Lord Chancellor from barristers of at least seven years' standing. On the re-organisation of the criminal courts under the Courts Act 1971[17] the existing county court judges became Circuit judges.[18] Every Circuit judge is by virtue of his or her office capable of sitting as a judge for any county court district and at least one is assigned to each district by the Lord Chancellor.[19] The regular sittings are normally taken by the assigned judges. In addition, a district judge is appointed for each county court district by the Lord Chancellor, and assistant and deputy district judges may also be appointed.[20] A full-time district judge is barred from legal practice.[21] District judges were formerly called registrars; the change of title reflected the fact that their functions are now judicial. They are responsible for procedural steps in court proceedings, this responsibility being analogous to those of Masters and Registrars of the High Court, and they try or arbitrate most small claims. Their administrative functions have now been transferred to the chief clerk or some other administrative officer, in accordance with the Lord Chancellor's directions.[22] County courts are administered by the unified court service.[23] There are substantial staffs of clerks and bailiffs.

(d) Jurisdiction

A county court has jurisdiction in almost the whole range of civil proceedings. In some matters the jurisdiction is exclusive, in others it is exercised concurrently with the High Court. In the latter event there is normally a

---

[13] County Courts Act 1984, s.1; Civil Courts Order 1983 (S.I. 1983 No. 713), as amended. The county court for the City of London is known as the Mayor's and City of London Court: the name is that of a court of similar jurisdiction abolished by the Courts Act 1971. The court is maintained by the City of London rather than the Department of the Environment.
[14] County Courts Act 1984, s.2.
[15] *Judicial Statistics 1989* (Cm. 1154), p. 37.
[16] *Civil Justice Review* (Cm. 394, 1988), para. 176.
[17] See below, pp. 71–72.
[18] See below, pp. 206–208.
[19] County Courts Act 1984, s.5. A judge of the Court of Appeal or the High Court or a recorder may also sit as a county court judge: *ibid.*
[20] County Courts Act 1984, ss.6–9; Courts and Legal Services Act 1990, s.74 and Sched. 10 para. 57. A deputy district judge is appointed as a temporary measure. The eligibility requirement is now possession of a 7 year general qualification (*i.e.* right of audience in any part of the Supreme Court or in all proceedings in county courts or magistrates courts); it was formerly being a solicitor of at least 7 years' standing.
[21] Courts and Legal Services Act 1990, s.75 and Sched. 11.
[22] County Court Rules 1981, Ord. 1, r. 3.
[23] See below, p. 75.

monetary limit to the county court's jurisdiction, the "county court limit," specified by Order in Council.[24]

A county court may hear and determine the following matters—

(i) Contract and tort

An action founded on contract or tort where the amount claimed is not more than £5,000, whether the full original claim or the balance left after an arrangement or set off between the parties.[25] A plaintiff may abandon the excess of a claim over the limit to give the county court jurisdiction.[26] This head of jurisdiction covers the bulk of cases brought in the county court.

(ii) Actions in respect of land

An action for the recovery of land or in respect of title to any hereditament, or for an injunction or declaration relating to any land, where the net rateable value does not exceed £1,000.[27]

(iii) Equity proceedings

A variety of equity proceedings where the amount involved is not more than £30,000[28]: these include proceedings for the administration of the estate of a deceased person, for foreclosure or redemption of a mortgage, for the specific performance of an agreement for the sale of property, for the maintenance or advancement of an infant and for the dissolution of a partnership. These correspond to matters that would be dealt with in the Chancery Division of the High Court.

(iv) Admiralty proceedings

A variety of Admiralty matters,[29] such as claims for damage done by or to a ship, for loss or damage to goods carried in a ship, or for salvage, towage or pilotage. The jurisdictional limit is £5,000, except for salvage claims, where it is £15,000. Only some county courts are appointed by the Lord Chancellor to take Admiralty proceedings, most of which are on or near the coast.[30]

(v) Probate proceedings

Contentious matters arising in respect of the grant or revocation of probate or administration of estates where the value of the estate is less than £30,000.[31]

---

[24] Made under section 145 of the County Courts Act 1984. The current limits are set by the County Court Jurisdiction Order 1981 (S.I. 1981 No. 1123) and s.147 of the 1984 Act.
[25] County Courts Act 1984, s.15. This head does not apply to actions for the recovery of land, any action where title to any hereditament is in question or any action for libel or slander: *ibid*. There is a similar jurisdiction in respect of money recoverable under a statute: *ibid*. s.16.
[26] *Ibid*. s.17.
[27] *Ibid*. ss.21, 22. In London, the figure is £1,500.
[28] *Ibid*. s.23. In addition, many specific powers under the Trustee Act 1925 and the Law of Property Act 1925 are conferred by the 1984 Act, Sched. 2.
[29] County Courts Act 1984, ss.26, 27.
[30] Civil Courts Order 1983 (S.I. 1983 No. 713).
[31] County Courts Act 1984, s.32, substituted by the Administration of Justice Act 1985, s.51(1).

(vi) *Jurisdiction by agreement*

Matters outside the monetary limits where the parties confer jurisdiction on a county court by agreement.[32]

(vii) *Family matters*

Any county court which has been designated by the Lord Chancellor as a "divorce county court" has jurisdiction to hear and determine any matrimonial cause,[33] although it only has jurisdiction to try the cause if it is also designated as a court of trial.[34] A divorce county court also has jurisdiction to make orders in relation to financial relief and custody of children ancillary to proceedings for divorce, nullity or separation,[35] and, if designated by the Lord Chancellor, to make orders for financial relief where a marriage has been terminated abroad.[36] The jurisdiction of divorce county courts, so far as is exercisable by judges of such courts, is to be exercised by such Circuit judges as the Lord Chancellor may direct.[37]

Every matrimonial cause must be commenced in a divorce county court,[38] and will be heard there unless it is transferred to the High Court.[39] There is also provision for the transfer of family proceedings from the High Court to the county court.[40] Principles governing the distribution and transfer of business between the High Court and county courts are set out in Directions given by the President of the Family Division.[41] Other family matters may be dealt with by divorce county courts, or, in some cases, any county court. There is a concurrent jurisdiction with magistrates' courts and the High Court in adoption and guardianship matters, and there will be a concurrent jurisdiction under the Children Act 1989.[42]

(viii) *Other proceedings*

Jurisdiction in a large number of other matters is conferred by specific statutory provisions, including hire-purchase, consumer credit, the Rent

---

[32] *Ibid.* ss.18 (Queen's Bench Division matters), 24 (many equity proceedings), 27(6) (most Admiralty proceedings).

[33] *i.e.* an action for divorce, nullity of marriage or judicial separation: Matrimonial and Family Proceedings Act 1984, s.32, as amended by the Family Law Act 1986, Sched. 1, para. 27.

[34] 1984 Act, s.33(1); Civil Courts Order 1983 (S.I. 1983 No. 713), as amended. In London, the Divorce Registry of the Family Division is deemed to be a county court for this purpose; see the 1984 Act, s.42.

[35] Under Parts II and III of the Matrimonial Causes Act 1973: 1984 Act, s.34(1)(*a*).

[36] Under Part III of the 1984 Act: *ibid*, ss.33(4), 34(1)(*b*).

[37] 1984 Act, s.36.

[38] *Ibid.* s.33(3).

[39] Under *ibid.* s.39 (which applies to any family proceedings), or section 41 of the County Courts Act 1984. Prior to April 26, 1986, *all* defended causes had to be transferred to the High Court.

[40] Matrimonial and Family Proceedings Act 1984, s.38.

[41] *Ibid.* s.37. See *Practice Direction* (*Family Division: Business: Distribution*) [1988] 1 W.L.R. 558, replacing earlier directions. The new provisions set out in Part V of the 1984 Act were preceded by a Consultation Paper issued by the Lord Chancellor's Department, *Family Jurisdiction of the High Court and County Courts* (1983). A defect in the transitional arrangements led to thousands of divorces being technically invalid: see *Nissim* v. *Nissim* (1987) 137 N.L.J. Rep. 1207; N. Wikeley, (1988) 7 C.J.Q. 97. They were retrospectively validated by the Matrimonial Proceedings (Transfers) Act 1988.

[42] See above, p. 53.

Acts, landlord and tenant, housing and sex discrimination.[43] Designated county courts have jurisdiction in bankruptcy matters[44] and race relations.[45] Appeals also lie to the county court in a number of administrative matters.[46]

(ix) *Jurisdiction of the district judge*

District judges have jurisdiction:
(1) to determine interlocutory applications;
(2) to conduct pre-trial reviews;
(3) to hear any action or matter
—where the defendant fails to appear at the hearing or admits the claim;
—where the amount involved does not exceed £1,000[47];
—where jurisdiction is expressly conferred; or
—with the leave of the judge and the consent of the parties.[48]

Their determinations may be reviewed by the judge. The role of the district judge is particularly significant in family matters,[49] where, *inter alia*, they determine interlocutory applications and applications for ancillary relief,[50] and, in undefended divorces under the special procedure, where they examine the evidence and issue a certificate which enables the judge to pronounce the decree.

Where the amount involved is £500 or less, defended claims are referred for arbitration by the district judge unless he or she otherwise orders.[51]

(e) The boundary between High Court and County Court

As regards those matters where there is concurrent jurisdiction with the High Court the usual arrangement is for there to be a maximum monetary limit for the county court, but no minimum limit for the High Court. There is, however, provision for the transfer of cases from High Court to county court, and vice versa, and for costs sanctions for those who use the High Court where there is no reason not to use the county court.

(i) *Transfer*[52]

(1) *High Court to county court.* Any proceedings in the High Court which a county court would have jurisdiction to hear,[53] apart from any monetary limit, may be transferred by the High Court to a county court either on its own motion or on the application of a party. One of four conditions must be established—

[43] See the annual *County Court Practice* (the "Green Book").
[44] Civil Courts Order 1983 (S.I. 1983 No. 713), as amended.
[45] *Ibid.*
[46] D. Price, *Appeals* (1982), pp. 46–49 lists 29 situations.
[47] Raised from £500 by the County Court (Amendment) Rules 1986, r. 25. This is to be raised to £5,000.
[48] County Court Rules 1981, Ord. 21, r. 5.
[49] See W. Barrington-Baker *et al.*, *The Matrimonial Jurisdiction of Registrars* (S.S.R.C., 1977).
[50] *e.g.* financial provision and adjustment of property rights on divorce.
[51] See below, pp. 531–535, on small claims in the county court. The limit is to be raised to £1,000.
[52] County Courts Act 1984, ss.40–45. By comparison with the provisions replaced, the powers to transfer proceedings to or retain them in the county court were strengthened.
[53] Excluding certain family law matters.

1. the parties consent to the transfer; or

2. the High Court is satisfied that the subject matter in dispute is or is likely to be within the relevant county court jurisdictional limit; or

3. where only a counterclaim remains in dispute, the High Court considers that the amount recoverable is likely to be within the relevant limit; or

4. the High Court considers that the proceedings are not likely to raise any important question of law or fact and are suitable for determination by a county court.

The proceedings are transferred to such county court as the High Court considers convenient to the parties, and the county court may award any relief, including any amount of damages, which could have been awarded by the High Court.

The High Court has begun to make more active use of its power to initiate transfer of its own motion. A High Court judge has been placed in charge of the lists in the Queen's Bench Division and he scrutinises cases, other than personal injury cases, in London, to consider whether they should be transferred.[54] Personal injury cases in London are scrutinised by a master.[55] Outside London, cases commenced in a district registry are to be scrutinised by the district judge, with an appeal lying against a transfer decision to the presiding judge or to a High Court judge invited to act on his behalf.[56]

(2) *County court to High Court by order of the High Court.* The High Court may order the transfer of the whole or any part of proceedings in a county court if it "thinks it desirable."

(3) *County court to High Court by order of the county court.* The whole or any part of the proceedings in a county court which the High Court would have jurisdiction to hear and determine may be transferred by the county court to the High Court either on its own motion or on the application of any party. The same family law matters are excluded as in respect of transfers the other way. One of three conditions must be established:

1. the court considers that some important question of law or fact is likely to arise; or

2. the court considers that one or other of the parties is likely to be entitled to an amount exceeding the amount recoverable in the county court; or

3. any counterclaim or set off and counterclaim of a defendant involves matters beyond the county court's jurisdiction.

These provisions are to be substantially modified by sections 1 and 2 of the Courts and Legal Services Act 1990. Section 1 gives the Lord Chancellor wide powers to make orders allocating business between the High Court and county courts. Such orders may reallocate jurisdiction between these courts, specify that certain proceedings can only be taken or must be commenced in one or other court. No order can, however, confer jurisdiction on any county court to hear an application for judicial review. Section 2 amends sections 40 to 42 of the County Courts Act 1984. Thus, the High Court will have a general power to transfer any proceedings (other than family proceedings) to a county court, either on its own motion, or on the application

---

[54] *Practice Statement (Listings), The Times,* January 13, 1988; J. Jacob, (1988) 7 C.J.Q. 91; *Practice Note* [1989] 2 All E.R. 128 (jury cases).

[55] *Practice Direction (County Court: Transfer of Action)* [1984] 1 W.L.R. 1023.

[56] *Practice Direction (County Court: Transfers outside London)* [1988] 3 All E.R. 95.

of any party. If it is satisfied that any proceedings are required by any enactment to be in a county court, it must order transfer or, if satisfied that the person bringing the proceedings knew or ought to have known of that requirement, order that they be struck out. Similar provisions apply to transfer from the county court to the High Court. The power for the High Court to require proceedings to be transferred to the High Court remains, subject to any order under section 1 or any other enactment.

(ii) *The costs sanction*

Given that there is no minimum limit for High Court jurisdiction it has been thought necessary to encourage litigants to use the county court by the imposition of a "costs sanction."[57] Thus, if an action in contract or tort is commenced in the High Court which could have been commenced in the county court,
—a plaintiff who recovers less than £3,000 may only be awarded costs on the county court scale.
—a plaintiff who recovers less than £600 is not entitled to any costs.

This is so unless it appears either that there was reasonable ground for supposing the amount recoverable to be in excess of the county court limit or that there was sufficient reason for bringing the action in the High Court or that the defendant objected to transfer to the county court.

(f) Reform

(i) *Integration with the High Court*

From time to time it has been proposed that the county court should be integrated with the High Court.[58] The main advantage would be the ending of the existing differences in practice and procedure between two courts which to a significant extent exercise jurisdiction in respect of the same subject-matter. On the other hand, improvements can be and have been achieved by procedural reforms, without raising problems that integration would create such as the extension of rights of audience for solicitors. This last consideration has impelled the Bar to oppose increases in the monetary limits of county court jurisdiction,[59] although not always with success. Proposals for integration were considered and rejected by the Gorell Committee on County Court Procedure,[60] mainly on the ground that the county courts should not take larger cases which would affect prejudicially the handling of small claims, and by the Beeching Commission on Assizes and Quarter Sessions,[61] more on the ground that full consideration of the question would have seriously delayed their report. The current trend seems to be for the greater assimilation of the standard county court and High Court procedures, with a greater contrast between both of these and the small claims procedures.

[57] County Courts Act 1984, ss.19, 20.
[58] See, *e.g.* Sir Jack Jacob, *The Reform of Civil Procedural Law* (1982), pp. 7–13.
[59] See B. Abel-Smith and R. Stevens, *Lawyers and the Courts* (1967), pp. 92–93, 249–250.
[60] 1908–09 H.C. 71.
[61] Cmnd. 4153, 1969, p. 73.

(ii) *Monetary limits*

The limits are raised periodically. Other possible arrangements would include making the jurisdiction of the county court exclusive within its limit, unless leave is obtained for a hearing in the High Court.[62]

(iii) *The Civil Justice Review*

The relationship between the High Court and the county court was one of the main matters considered by the Civil Justice Review Body.[63] They rejected proposals for amalgamation on the grounds that major changes could be made within the present system, there was not general support for a unified court,[64] the financial implications were uncertain, a unified court would require major legislation and a lengthy implementation period, and would possibly have adverse effects on the standing of the High Court judiciary. Their more selective proposals were as follows:

— the High Court should try public law cases, other specialist cases and general list cases of importance, complexity and substance (cases of substance being those where the amount in issue exceeds £25,000);
— there should be a flexible band between £25,000 and £50,000 within which cases could be tried in the county court or the High Court:
— there should be no upper limit of county court jurisdiction;
— there should be a single point of entry in the county court for personal injury cases;
— the costs sanction system should be reviewed in due course;
— the general trial jurisdiction of county court registrars should be increased to £5,000;
— the upper limit of the automatic small claims jurisdiction should be £1,000;
— county court trials should be concentrated at centres at which continuous trial facilities are made available;
— there should be an upper tier of Circuit judges who take responsibility for heavier civil work, with appropriate remuneration;
— barristers as well as solicitors should be eligible for appointment as county court and district registrars and registrars should be given the title of judge;
— the same remedies should be available in the county court as in the High Court, including remedies by way of injunction and summary judgment, except that the power to grant *Mareva* and *Anton Piller* orders should be reserved to High Court judges.[65]

Effect is being given to many of the Review's recommendations by Part I of the Courts and Legal Services Act 1990 and regulations.

[62] This was recommended by the Payne Committee on the *Enforcement of Judgment Debts* in respect of debt recovery (Cmnd. 3909, 1969), paras. 119–120, but was not accepted.
[63] Cm. 394, Chap. 3.
[64] Supported by the Law Society, the County Court Registrars, Chancery Masters, Family Division Registrars and National Association of Citizens' Advice Bureaux; opposed by the judges of the High Court and Court of Appeal, the Queen's Bench Masters and the Bar.
[65] For responses, see *Legal Action*, July 1988, pp. 3, 4.

(g) Procedural Rules

The County Court Rules are made by a rule committee consisting of eleven persons appointed by the Lord Chancellor (five judges of county courts, two district judges, two lawyers with a Supreme Court qualification, and two lawyers with the right to conduct litigation in the Supreme Court). They are subject to the approval of the Lord Chancellor, either as submitted or after amendment by him.[66] The rules were substantially revised in 1981 and are to be found in the current edition of the *County Court Practice* (the "Green Book").[67]

(h) Register of judgments

A register recording all county court judgments for £10 or more (subject to some exceptions) is maintained by a private company, Registry Trust Ltd. by agreement with the Lord Chancellor.[68] It was formerly maintained by the County Courts Branch of the Lord Chancellor's Department.

(i) Appeals[69]

Appeals lie to the Court of Appeal (Civil Division)[70] on questions of fact, law or evidence. The leave of either court is in general necessary if the claim is for an amount not exceeding half the relevant county court limit, or the matter came to the county court on appeal. In a few cases appeals lie to the High Court.[71]

6. THE CROWN COURT[72]

(a) The Beeching Royal Commission

In 1966 the Royal Commission on Assizes and Quarter Sessions was appointed, under the chairmanship of Lord Beeching, to inquire into the arrangements for the administration of justice at assizes and quarter sessions outside London, and to report what reforms should be made for the more convenient, economic and efficient disposal of the civil and criminal business dealt with by those courts. The *assize courts* were presided over by High Court judges sent out "on circuit," a system that could be traced back to the twelfth century and which had changed comparatively little since medieval times.[73] There were seven circuits of assize towns. Assizes had jurisdiction

---

[66] County Courts Act 1984, s.75, as amended by the Courts and Legal Services Act 1990, s.16, Sched. 18, para. 47.

[67] County Court Rules 1981, (S.I. 1981 No. 1687). See R.C.L. Gregory Q.C. "The Genesis of the County Court Rules" (1983) 2 C.J.Q. 1.

[68] County Courts Act 1984 ss.73, as amended, and 73A, inserted by the Administration of Justice Act 1985, s.54; Register of County Court Judgments Regulations 1985 (S.I. 1985 No. 1807), as amended by S.I. 1986 No. 2001. See also the Courts and Legal Services Act 1990, Sched. 17, para. 14.

[69] See generally, Chap. 17.

[70] See below, pp. 90–91, 848–849.

[71] *e.g.* bankruptcy matters are heard by the Divisional Court of the Chancery Division.

[72] See I.R. Scott, *The Crown Court* (1971); *The Crown Court. A guide to good practice* (four separate guides published under this or a similar title by the LCD, the CPS, the Bar Council and the Law Society.

[73] See above, p. 32. Additional "Commissioners of Assize," usually senior Q.C.s, could be appointed ad hoc.

over all indictable criminal offences and exclusive jurisdiction over some, including homicide, serious crimes of violence and rape. In addition, assize courts had the same civil jurisdiction as the High Court sitting in London, although priority was given to criminal cases. There were *courts of quarter sessions* for each of the 58 counties and for 93 boroughs; there were five such courts in Greater London and one for the City of London. The borough quarter sessions were presided over by a part-time Recorder, sitting alone. The county quarter sessions comprised a bench of magistrates normally with a legally qualified Chairman or Deputy Chairman, some of whom were whole-time appointments. These courts had jurisdiction to try many indictable offences with a jury, and to hear appeals from magistrates' courts and from a variety of administrative orders. In London, the *Central Criminal Court* at the Old Bailey was in effect the Assize court for criminal cases. It had a number of full time judges, including the Recorder of London and the Common Serjeant; in addition some cases would be taken by High Court judges. In 1956, new courts known as *Crown Courts* were established for Liverpool and Manchester to deal with both quarter sessions and assize work. A full time Recorder was appointed for each court. Responsibility for providing judges, court staff and court buildings was "as fragmented as the system itself."[74]

The Beeching Report identified many defects of assizes and quarter sessions and recommended a fundamental reorganisation. A number of features which a good court system should provide were identified[75]:

Convenience	(a)	Ease of physical access.
	(b)	An early hearing.
	(c)	The assurance of trial on a date of which reasonable notice has been given.
Quality	(d)	Suitable accommodation.
	(e)	Judicial expertise.
	(f)	Adequate and dependable legal representation.
Economy	(g)	Efficient use of all manpower.
	(h)	Optimum use of buildings.

The restricting factors were cost and the capacity of the Bar. The report's proposals were designed to[76]:

"(a) simplify the structure of the courts;
 (b) deploy judge power as flexibly as possible;
 (c) relate court locations to travelling facilities for the public;
 (d) secure the efficient administration of all court services;
 (e) ensure that courts are built and maintained as economically and efficiently as possible."

The proposals, which involved the creation of a new superior court of criminal jurisdiction, to be called the Crown Court, were largely accepted. They were enacted in the Courts Act 1971, substantial parts of which were re-enacted in the Supreme Court Act 1981.

---

[74] Beeching Report, p. 31.
[75] *Ibid.*, p. 48.
[76] *Ibid.*, p. 64.

(b) The constitution of the Crown Court

The Crown Court is part of the Supreme Court of England and Wales.[77] It is a single court, but sittings may be conducted at any place in England and Wales, in accordance with directions given by the Lord Chancellor.[78] There are at present over 90 centres and over 130 separate court houses.[79] The name "Central Criminal Court" has been retained for the Crown Court sitting in the City of London at the Old Bailey. There are three kinds of Crown Court centre: "first-tier" centres are visited by High Court judges, Circuit judges and recorders for the complete range of Crown Court business, and by High Court judges for High Court civil work; "second-tier" centres are the same as first-tier except that no civil business is done; "third-tier" centres are visited only by Circuit judges and recorders. The centres are grouped into six circuits: Midland and Oxford, North Eastern, Northern, South Eastern, Wales and Chester, and Western.[80]

The jurisdiction of the Crown Court is exerciseable by any judge of the High Court, Circuit judge or recorder.[81] In some cases one of these may sit with not more than four justices of the peace[82]: a court must normally be so comprised when hearing an appeal or proceedings on committal for sentence,[83] and may be so comprised for other proceedings, but not cases listed for pleas of not guilty.[84]

(c) Jurisdiction

The Crown Court has exclusive jurisdiction with respect to criminal trials on indictment.[85] It also has an extensive appellate jurisdiction inherited from quarter sessions, including appeals from magistrates' courts in criminal cases and appeals in a wide variety of administrative matters, such as betting, gaming and liquor licensing. Magistrates' courts may also commit convicted persons to the Crown Court for sentence.

(d) Distribution of business

The classes of cases in the Crown Court suitable for allocation respectively to a High Court judge, Circuit judge or recorder, and to a court including justices, are prescribed in directions given by the Lord Chief Justice, with the concurrence of the Lord Chancellor.[86] For the purposes of trial in the Crown Court, offences are grouped in four classes.

---

[77] Supreme Court Act 1981, s.1. Procedural rules can be prescribed by the Crown Court Rule Committee: *ibid.* s.86, as amended by the Courts and Legal Services Act 1990, Sched. 18, para. 36(2).
[78] *Ibid.* s.78.
[79] See *Shaw's Directory of Courts in the United Kingdom*.
[80] See H.L. Deb. Vol. 314, col. 948, January 26, 1971; H.L. Deb. Vol. 321, col. 572, July 1, 1971; H.L. Deb. Vol. 343, col. 968, June 14, 1973.
[81] Supreme Court Act 1981, s.8. See below pp. 206–208.
[82] *Ibid.* and see below, pp. 198–199.
[83] Supreme Court Act 1981, s.74; Crown Court Rules 1982 (S.I. 1982 No. 1109).
[84] See below, p. 199.
[85] Supreme Court Act 1981, s.46.
[86] Supreme Court Act 1981, s.75; *Practice Direction* (*Crown Court Business: Classification*) [1987] 1 W.L.R. 1671; see Home Office Circular 3/1988, ((1988) 152 J.P.N. 58).

Class 1

These offences are to be tried by a High Court judge and include any offence carrying the death penalty, murder, genocide and offences under section 1 of the Official Secrets Act 1911. A case of murder may be released by the authority of a presiding judge, for trial by a Circuit judge approved for the purpose by the Lord Chief Justice.

Class 2

These offences are to be tried by a High Court judge unless a particular case is released by or on the authority of a presiding judge, and include manslaughter, infanticide, abortion, rape, sexual intercourse or incest with a girl under 13 and sedition. A case of rape, or a serious sexual offence against a child, may be released by a presiding judge for trial only by a Circuit judge approved for that purpose by the Lord Chief Justice.

Class 3

These offences may be listed for trial by a High Court judge, or, in accordance with general or particular directions given by a presiding judge, by a Circuit judge, or a recorder. They comprise all offences triable only on indictment other than those in classes, 1, 2 and 4.

Class 4

These may be tried by a High Court judge, Circuit judge, recorder, or assistant recorder. They are normally listed for trial by a Circuit judge or recorder, and include all offences triable either way and a number of specific offences including wounding, causing grievous bodily harm and robbery.

Presiding judges, with the approval of the senior presiding judge, must issue directions as to the need where appropriate to reserve a case for trial by a High Court judge, the allocation of work between Circuit judges, recorders and assistant recorders, and, where necessary, the devolved responsibility of resident or designated judges for such allocation.[87] Specific provision must be made in these directions for cases in 15 specified categories, including, for example, cases involving death or serious risk to life or the use of loaded firearms, arson or criminal damage with intent to endanger life, a number of offences involving serious violence, cases where the trial may last more than 10 days or involve more than five defendants and cases involving difficult issues of law.

Most other Crown Court proceedings are normally listed for hearing by a court presided over by a Circuit judge or a recorder. Any proceedings listed for hearing by a Circuit judge or recorder, except pleas of not guilty, are stated to be suitable for allocation to a court including justices of the peace.

---

[87] These are Circuit judges appointed by the presiding judges to have responsibility, at one or more centres, for seeing to the efficient and orderly running of the lists: *Civil Justice Review* (Cm. 394, 1988), para. 307.

Appeals and committals for sentence are to be heard by (i) a resident or designated judge; (ii) a Circuit judge, nominated by the resident or designated judge, who regularly sits at the Crown Court centre; (iii) an experienced recorder specifically approved by the presiding judges for the purpose; or, otherwise, (iv) a Circuit judge or recorder selected by the resident or designated judge for a specific case or cases.

The same Practice Direction prescribes the general principles for the distribution of business among the different court centres geographically. Generally, the magistrates committing for trial should select the "most convenient location" of the appropriate tier of Crown Court centre, having regard to the convenience of defence, prosecution and witnesses and the expediting of the trial,[88] and to the location or locations designated by the presiding judge as the normal ones for committals from their petty sessions area. It is possible for the location to be changed.[89] In addition, the "catchment areas" are varied if the work-load at a particular Crown Court centre requires cases to be directed to a less busy centre. Arrangements can be made for a case to be transferred from one circuit to another.[90] 31 centres have been designated for the trial of serious and complex fraud trials.[91]

(e) Administration

Another important feature of the Beeching Report and the Courts Act 1971 was the establishment of a "unified court service" under the direction of the Lord Chancellor, providing administrative support to the Supreme Court, including the Crown Court and county courts.[92] The service is organised on a circuit basis. The administration in each circuit is headed by a Circuit Administrator, a civil servant of Under Secretary rank responsible to the Lord Chancellor. Each of these has a small headquarters staff and three or four Courts Administrators working under him or her, each responsible for a particular area.[93] Each court has a chief clerk responsible to one of the Courts Administrators. The Circuit Administrators work closely with the presiding judges and deal with such matters as personnel management, finance and accommodation. The Courts Administrator has responsibility for planning the courts' sittings and ensuring the smooth disposal of business between courts, and is a point of contact for the various parties concerned with the running of the courts.

Two High Court judges are assigned to each circuit by the Lord Chief Justice to act as presiding judges: at least one should be present in the circuit at any given time. Presiding judges have certain functions in relation to the allocation of cases.[94]

Their position has been summarised as follows[95]:

---

[88] Magistrates' Courts Act 1980, s.7.
[89] Supreme Court Act 1981, s.76.
[90] *Practice Direction* (*Crown Court Business: Classification*) [1987] 1 W.L.R. 1671: Allocation of Business, para. 9.
[91] *Practice Direction* (*Crown Court: Fraud Trials (No. 2)*) [1990] 1 W.L.R. 1310.
[92] Courts Act 1971, s.27. See I. R. Scott, *The Crown Court* (1971), Chap. IV; E. C. Friesen and I. R. Scott, *English Criminal Justice* (1977), pp. 121–5 and I. R. Scott, *Court Administration: The Case for a Judicial Council* (1979).
[93] There is a Courts Administrator responsible for the Central Criminal Court.
[94] See above, p. 74.
[95] Friesen and Scott (1977), p. 124.

"The presiding judges are the judicial authority for the circuit paralleling the administrative authority of the Circuit Administrators. . . . Where they perform properly (and there is some unevenness) the presiding judges make a substantial effort to control judicial performance on their circuits. They know the capabilities of the Circuit judges and in consultation with the Circuit Administrators they see that these judges are properly assigned and utilised according to skill and expertise."

However, it has also been noted that the presiding judges frequently lack confidence when dealing with their more senior colleagues, that some do not capture the respect of Circuit judges in their circuit, that there is too much doubt as to their proper role, that uncertainty is created by the fact that so much depends on the respective personalities of presiding judge and Circuit Administrator and that the judge's position is weakened by the fact that appointments are only for short periods.[96]

A Lord Justice of Appeal has been appointed as a senior presiding judge who is available for consultation by the presiding judges and relieves the Lord Chief Justice of certain administrative responsibilities.[97] The offices of presiding judge and senior presiding judge now have statutory recognition.[98]

(f) Workload

The workload of the Crown Court has increased significantly since it was established:

"It is undoubtedly true to say that in the light of the inexorable increase in caseloads chaos would have ensued but for the implementation of the Beeching Reforms. The number of persons working in the court service is now about 10,000 and the range of quasi-judicial and administrative tasks undertaken by this bureaucracy is far greater and much more sophisticated than those attempted under the pre-1971 arrangements."[99]

Between 1979 and 1989 committals for trial received by the Crown Court have more than doubled, with an average annual growth rate of over 7 per cent.[1]

Other important factors have been the establishment of the circuit bench and the increase in the number of High Court judges, and the court-building

---

[96] Scott (1979), p. 16. An account of Judge James Pickles' relations with presiding judges on his circuit and the Lord Chief Justice is given in his book, *Straight from the Bench* (1987), Chap. 1.

[97] (1983) 133 N.L.J. 732.

[98] Courts and Legal Services Act 1990, s.72.

[99] Scott (1979), p. 5.

[1] *Judicial Statistics 1989* (Cm. 1154), p. 67.

programme. Nevertheless, the increase in workload meant that waiting times increased dramatically.[2]

(g) Appeals[3]

Appeals in relation to trials on indictment and in cases where a defendant has been committed for sentence to the Crown Court lie to the Court of Appeal (Criminal Division).[4] Appeals from an exercise of the Crown Court's appellate jurisdiction lie to the High Court on the same basis as appeals there from the magistrates' court.

7. THE HIGH COURT

(a) Constitution

The High Court of Justice is a court of unlimited civil jurisdiction and also has an important appellate jurisdiction in both civil and criminal matters. It is part of the Supreme Court of England and Wales,[5] and was created as part of the reorganisation of the superior courts under the Supreme Court of Judicature Acts 1873–75. It sits at the Royal Courts of Justice in the Strand[6] and at 26 first-tier Crown Court centres outside London.[7] There are three divisions: the Chancery Division, Queen's Bench Division and Family Division,[8] headed, respectively, by the Vice-Chancellor,[9] the Lord Chief Justice and the President of the Family Division.[10] Each High Court judge[11] is attached to one of the divisions, but they may be transferred to one of the others with their consent, and they may act as an additional judge of one of them at the request of the Lord Chancellor.[12] Different classes of business are allocated for administrative convenience to each division by rules of court,[13] although technically all the jurisdiction of the High Court belongs to

---

[2] In 1973, of the 13,925 defendants disposed of on indictment and who had awaited trial in custody, 74 per cent. were dealt with within eight weeks of committal and 96 per cent. within 20 weeks. In 1980 the figures were 16,088, 54 per cent. and 87 per cent. respectively. See generally, I. R. Scott, "Crown Court Productivity" [1980] Crim.L.R. 193, noting the growing proportion of not guilty pleas and the lengthening of hearing times in contested cases. By 1987 of 31,443 defendants in custody, 58 per cent. waited less than eight weeks and 85 per cent. less than 16 weeks. Between 1980 and 1983 the average waiting time for all defendants committed for trial fell from 17.3 weeks to 14.2 weeks. It stayed at roughly that figure until 1987 (12.3 weeks), 1988 (12.2 weeks)), the lowest annual average level since 1976, and 1989 (12.4 weeks): *Judicial Statistics 1989*, Tables 6.14 to 6.19. See pp. 492–493.

[3] See generally, Chap. 17, below.

[4] See below, pp. 88–89, 830–845.

[5] The Supreme Court was thus re-titled by the Supreme Court Act 1981.

[6] The Supreme Court moved here from Westminster Hall in 1883. See F. W. Maitland, (1942) 8 C.L.J. 2; J. Kinnard in P. Ferriday (ed.), *Victorian Architecture* (1963); M. H. Port, "The New Law Courts Competition, 1866–67" (1968) *Architectural History* 75–93.

[7] See above, p. 73.

[8] Supreme Court Act 1981, s.5(1). The number of divisions can be altered by Order in Council: *ibid.* s.7.

[9] Technically, the Lord Chancellor is the president and the Vice-Chancellor the vice-president of the Chancery Division, but the latter is the effective head.

[10] See below, pp. 82, 210–211.

[11] See below, p. 208.

[12] Supreme Court Act 1981, s.5(2) (3).

[13] Supreme Court Act 1981, s.61.

all the divisions alike.[14] There have been two major reorganisations. In 1881 the Exchequer and Common Pleas Divisions were merged into the Queen's Bench Division,[15] and in 1971 the Probate, Divorce and Admiralty Division was re-named the Family Division, with Admiralty business assigned to the Queen's Bench Division, probate business other than non-contentious or common form matters assigned to the Chancery Division, and wardship, guardianship and adoption jurisdiction transferred from Chancery Division to Family Division.[16] A joint committee of High Court judges and civil servants has recommended abolition of the three separate divisions of the High Court,[17] but this recommendation has not been implemented.

Most High Court work is taken by a single judge sitting alone.[18] This should be in open court, except where under rules of court or in accordance with the practice of the court it is dealt with in chambers.[19] A proportion of the appellate and supervisory work of the High Court is dealt with by "divisional courts," which comprise two or more judges.[20]

The business is mainly conducted by the heads of division and the puisne[21] judges of the High Court. In addition, High Court work may be taken by a deputy High Court judge, a Circuit judge, a recorder, a judge of the Court of Appeal or a former judge of the High Court or the Court of Appeal.[22]

(b) The Chancery Division

The division deals with property, trusts, the administration of estates, bankruptcy, partnership, companies, revenue cases, probate business other than non-contentious common form business, and other matters specifically assigned.[23] The Patents Court established in 1977[24] is part of this division. In addition the judges of the division have been assigned to deal with the management of the property and affairs of mental patients under the Mental

[14] *Ibid.* s.5(5). Any Division to which a cause or matter is assigned has jurisdiction to grant any remedy or relief sought notwithstanding that proceedings for such remedy or relief are assigned to another Division: *Practice Direction (High Court: Divisions)* [1973] 1 W.L.R. 627. Cases may be transferred between Divisions: see J. Jacob, (1988) 7 C.J.Q. 94; *Barclays Bank* v. *Bemister* and *Pryke* v. *Gibbs Hartley Cooper Ltd.* [1989] 1 All E.R. 10, C.A.

[15] This was done by an Order in Council which was made on December 16, 1880 and which came into force on February 26, 1881.

[16] Administration of Justice Act 1970, with effect from August 2, 1971.

[17] Committee on the Deployment of the High Court: *Legal Action*, June 1988, p. 5; (1988) L.S.Gaz. May 25, p. 3.

[18] There is provision for a judge to sit with assessors who are specially qualified in relation to the proceedings in question: 1981 Act, s.70. They are mainly used in Admiralty proceedings. See below, p. 80.

[19] Supreme Court Act 1981, s.67.

[20] *Ibid.* s.66.

[21] See below, p. 208.

[22] *Ibid.* s.9. There have been complaints that too many High Court cases have been heard by Circuit judges and recorders sitting as deputy High Court judges. The Civil Justice Review Body thought it excessive that 30 per cent. of High Court sittings were by persons who were not High Court judges: their proposals for the transfer of business to the county court (see p. 70) should mean that deputy judges would only be appointed to give them experience or to cover peaks of work or temporary shortages of judge power: (Cm. 394, para. 192).

[23] *Ibid.* Sched. 1. The judges who deal with bankruptcy are referred to as the "High Court of Justice in Bankruptcy" and those who deal with company matters as the "Companies Court," but these are not formally constituted as courts under the 1981 Act.

[24] Patents Act 1977. The judge may sit with scientific advisers: Supreme Court Act 1981, s.70.

Health Act 1983. This work is the responsibility of the "Court of Protection" which is in fact an office of the Supreme Court rather than a court.

The business is at present handled by the Vice-Chancellor and 13 puisne judges, two of whom are nominated to the Patents Court although they are available to help with the other work of the Division. One judge (Scott J.) has been appointed Vice-Chancellor of the Duchy of Lancaster.[25] The judges are assisted by five Chancery masters and four registrars in bankruptcy.[26] The work is done in London and at eight centres in the provinces.[27] In the latter the work is done by the Vice-Chancellor of the Duchy of Lancaster, by High Court judges sitting at Bristol and Cardiff and by Circuit judges who specialise in Chancery work and who sit for this purpose as judges of the High Court.[28] The Vice-Chancellor of the Duchy of Lancaster has arranged to sit at Manchester or Liverpool in the north and at Leeds to the north east for approximately one half of each term.[29] Steps have also been taken to transfer less onerous cases to the county court,[30] Chancery expertise for this purpose being concentrated at the Mayor's and City of London County Court.[31]

The administrative arrangements for the Chancery Division were substantially revised in 1982[32] following the Report of the Review Body on the Chancery Division of the High Court.[33] Amongst other matters the changes were designed to produce greater flexibility in the deployment of judges and a new approach to the drafting of orders "which should eliminate their present sesquipedalian pedantry."[34] As from October 1, 1982, orders have been simpler in form and drawn by clerks (known as associates) rather than professionally qualified officers, thus bringing practice more into line with the other divisions.

(c) The Queen's Bench Division

This Division deals mainly with claims in contract and tort, and also exercises supervisory and appellate jurisdiction over inferior courts and tribunals. The supervisory jurisdiction includes most applications for habeas corpus and all applications for judicial review.[35] The appellate jurisdiction includes appeals by case stated on a point of law from magistrates' courts and the Crown Court. Also part of this division are the Admiralty Court and the

---

[25] This Office, to which the appointment is made by the Chancellor of the Duchy, was formerly held by a Circuit judge: see p. 206.

[26] See R. E. Ball, "The Chancery Master" (1961) 77 L.Q.R. 331. See generally, E. Heward, *Chancery Practice* (2nd ed., 1990).

[27] Leeds, Liverpool, Manchester, Newcastle-upon-Tyne, Preston, and, as from October 10, 1982, Birmingham, Bristol and Cardiff. See *Practice Direction* (*Proceedings outside London*) [1972] 1 W.L.R. 1 and (*No. 2*) [1973] 1 W.L.R. 657; *Practice Direction* (*Chancery Chambers*) [1982] 1 W.L.R. 1189; *Practice Directions* (*Chancery: Proceedings Outside London*) [1984] 1 W.L.R. 417 and [1988] 1 W.L.R. 630; *Practice Notes* [1989] 1 W.L.R. 134, 135.

[28] See below, p. 212. They may also take equity work in county courts.

[29] *Practice Direction* (*Chancery: Hearings in North*) [1988] 1 W.L.R. 739.

[30] Under s.40 of the County Courts Act 1984.

[31] *Practice Direction* (*Chancery: Transfer of Business*) [1988] 1 W.L.R. 741.

[32] See R.S.C. (Amendment No. 2) 1982 (S.I. 1982 No. 1111); *Practice Direction* (*Chancery Chambers*), n. 27 above.

[33] Cmnd. 8205, 1981: report by Oliver L.J. and J. M. Woolf Esq.: see R. Blackford, (1981) 78 L.S.Gaz. 590.

[34] Blackford (1981), p. 590.

[35] Supreme Court Act 1981, s.61 and Sched. 1. See below, pp. 871–878.

Commercial Court.[36] The work is at present handled by the Lord Chief Justice[37] and 53 puisne judges. The business is done in London and at the 26 first-tier Crown Court centres in the provinces.

In London, the judges are assisted by 12[38] masters of the Queen's Bench Division. A master can perform all the functions of the High Court or a judge in chambers, with certain exceptions, and, with the parties' consent, may try actions.[39] Much of the work involves the determination of interlocutory applications.[40] One master sits each day as the Practice Master, to deal with procedural and practice problems arising in the Central Office and generally to supervise the work of the office. The right of audience before a master is not limited to barristers; solicitors and their clerks may appear, including unadmitted clerks. The work is normally done in chambers, which lead off from an ante-chamber generally known as "the Bear Garden."

(i) The Admiralty Court

This court has jurisdiction in a wide variety of matters concerning ships and aircraft, including claims arising out of collisions, claims for damage to cargo, for goods supplied and for repairs.[41] When necessary, it also exercises the jurisdiction of the High Court as a prize court.[42]

(ii) The Commercial Court[43]

There were a number of attempts in the nineteenth century to establish some form of specialised commercial court.[44] A Commercial List was established in the Queen's Bench Division in 1895, partly as the result of dissatisfaction with the handling of a commercial case by Lawrance J.[45] This did not, however, end the drift to arbitration.[46] The list was transformed into a court in 1970.[47] The interlocutory stages are handled by the judge rather than a master and pleadings must be "as brief as possible."[48] A judge of the Commercial Court may be appointed as an arbitrator, provided the Lord

---

[36] Supreme Court Act 1981, s.6.

[37] The Lord Chief Justice's time is mainly spent on appellate criminal work in the Divisional Court of the Queen's Bench Division or the Court of Appeal (Criminal Division). He no longer takes applications for judicial review at first instance.

[38] This figure includes the Master of the Crown Office, who is also Registrar of the Criminal Appeal Office. These offices were combined by the Courts and Legal Services Act 1990, s.78.

[39] See A. S. Diamond, "The Queen's Bench Master" (1960) 76 L.Q.R. 504; Sir Jack Jacob, "The Masters of the Queen's Bench Division" (1971) reprinted in The Reform of Civil Procedural Law (1982); R.S.C. Ords. 36, 63.

[40] e.g. in relation to the extension of time, pleadings, striking out, discovery, summons for directions, summary judgment under R.S.C., Ord. 14: see pp. 535–566.

[41] Supreme Court Act 1981, ss.20–24.

[42] Ibid. s.62.

[43] A. D. Colman, The Practice and Procedure of the Commercial Court (2nd ed., 1986); Civil Justice Review (Cm. 394, 1988), Chap. 11.

[44] Colman (1986), Chap. 1.

[45] See below, p. 216; (1895–96) 1 Com.Cas. pp. i–x; MacKinnon L.J., (1944) 60 L.Q.R., 324–325; Lord Parker C.J., History and Development of Commercial Arbitration (1959).

[46] See G. Wilson, Cases and Materials on the English Legal System (1973), pp. 31–43; R. B. Ferguson, "The Adjudication of commercial disputes and the legal system in modern England" (1980) 7 B.J.L.S. 141.

[47] Administration of Justice Act 1970, s.3(1).

[48] R.S.C., Ord. 72, rr. 2, 7.

Chief Justice agrees that he or she can be made available.[49] Separate lists have been established in the district registries in Liverpool and Manchester, and cases set down in them are tried by designated circuit commercial judges sitting as High Court judges.[50]

A Commercial Court Committee was established in 1977 to consider and keep under review the working of the Court and the appeal procedures in arbitration proceedings, and to report to the Lord Chancellor.[51] A report of this committee[52] led to the enactment of the Arbitration Act 1979, which was designed to limit rights of appeal to the courts from the decisions of arbitrators, and thereby to halt a decline in the standing of London as a leading centre of international commercial arbitration.[53]

In recent years the caseload of the Commercial Court has increased significantly,[54] although it is still small in relation to the number of arbitrations. Waiting times for trial have increased dramatically.[55] Three features of its work are that in many cases either one or both litigants are foreigners, that a significant part of the court's work comes from London arbitrations, and that it is commonplace for cases to involve millions of pounds.[56]

Concern over waiting times led to the establishment of a working party of practitioner members of the Commercial Court Committee to examine possible reforms.[57] Its report was adopted by the Committee and its recommendations as to improved practice, particularly as to documentation and the conduct of the hearing, commended to court users in a *Guide to Commercial Court Practice*.[58] A new combined Admiralty and Commercial Court Registry was established.[59] The operation of the court was also scrutinised by the Civil Justice Review Body,[60] which made a number of recommendations, including the introduction of a minimum jurisdictional

---

[49] Administration of Justice Act 1970, s.4; Colman (1986), pp. 160–165. Such appointments are rare.

[50] *Practice Direction (Commercial Lists: Manchester and Liverpool)* [1990] 1 W.L.R. 331; G. Wingate-Saul, (1990) 140 N.L.J. 539.

[51] See its Annual Report for 1980 (1981) 78 L.S.Gaz. 100; Colman (1986), Chap. 2.

[52] Commercial Court Committee, *Report on Arbitration* (Cmnd. 7284, 1978).

[53] See Ferguson (1980), pp. 151–154; Kerr J., "The Arbitration Act 1979" (1980) 43 M.L.R. 45.

[54] The number of cases heard and disposed of increased from an average of 20 a year between 1946 and 1959 (*Report of the Commercial Court Users' Conference* (Cmnd. 1616, 1962) Appendix G) to a high point of 157 in 1981, declining to 108 in 1986 (*Civil Justice Review*, para. 789).

[55] From eight months in 1980 to 24 months in 1984 for a trial due to last longer than three days. In January 1987, trials estimated to last between two and four weeks were being given fixed dates for hearing in October 1990; those estimated at over four weeks were listed for February 1991; *Civil Justice Review*, paras. 791, 792. A number of applications for transfer to another division were rejected if the sole ground was to obtain an earlier trial: see J. Jacob, (1988) 7 C.J.Q. 5.

[56] Goff. J., "The Commercial Court—How it Works" (1980) 77 L.S.Gaz. 1035. See generally on the working of the court, Colman, *op. cit.*

[57] See F. Meisel, "Commercial Court Reform" (1986) 5 C.J.Q. 196.

[58] The *Guide* was revised in 1990. *Supreme Court Practice 1991* Vol. 1, paras. 72/A1—72/A25. See (1990) 9 C.J.Q. 225; *Practice Direction (Commercial Court: Revised Practice)* [1990] 1 W.L.R. 481.

[59] R.S.C. (Amendment) 1987 (S.I. 1987 No. 1423); *Practice Direction (Q.B.D.)* (*New Admiralty and Commercial Court Registry*) [1987] 1 W.L.R. 1459.

[60] Report, Cm. 394, 1988, Chap. 11. The Review Body commissioned a Factual Study by Coopers & Lybrand, which did not endorse all the assumptions that had been made by the earlier working party: see F. Meisel, "Commercial Court Reform—The Lord Chancellor's Consultation Paper" (1987) 6 C.J.Q. 95.

limit of £50,000 (with special exceptions for complex or difficult cases), the provision of extra judge power on a temporary basis, and dealing with formal or uncontested business by consent or by applications on paper.

(d) The Family Division

This division exercises the matrimonial and domestic jurisdiction of the High Court, which includes defended divorce cases[61] and matters relating to the wardship, guardianship, custody, maintenance or adoption of children, and deals with non-contentious or common form probate business. It also hears appeals from magistrates' courts in domestic (family) proceedings.[62] The work is at present handled by the President, 16 puisne judges, and 13 district judges of the principal registry of the Family Division. It is done in London and at first-tier Crown Court centres.[63]

Many important aspects of High Court family work are dealt with by the registrars of the Family Division and district judges of the High Court, including decisions on ancillary matters (*e.g.* maintenance, adjustment of property rights and the arrangements for access to children).

A number of proposals have been made for the establishment of "family courts."[64] Under the present system, there has been jurisdictional confusion as between magistrates' courts, county courts and the High Court,[65] and there are also discrepancies in the substantive law applied and doubts as to whether a system of accusatorial hearings is appropriate for family matters. The Finer Committee on One Parent Families[66] recommended the establishment of family courts to take over all family matters dealt with in magistrates' courts, county courts and the High Court. The family courts would be organised in tiers, on the analogy of the Crown Court. The lowest tier would comprise Circuit judges and magistrates and sit in county courts: magistrates' court buildings would not be used. There would be facilities for conciliation and support by a professional welfare service. The government was, however, unwilling to provide extra court buildings or add to the workload of the circuit bench. Many of the significant differences between the law applicable by the High Court and county court on the one hand and by magistrates' courts on the other were removed,[67] moves were made to keep the domestic jurisdiction of magistrates' courts separate from criminal

---

[61] See above, p. 66.

[62] Supreme Court Act 1981, Sched. 1. See above, p. 54.

[63] Most of these have been designated as "divorce towns" for the purpose of hearing defended matrimonial causes and ancillary applications: see *Practice Direction* (*Divorce Towns*: *Defended Causes*) [1971] 1 W.L.R. 1762; Matrimonial Causes Rules 1977 (S.I. 1977 No. 344) rr. 2, 43, 44. The cases here may be dealt with by High Court judges or Circuit judges sitting as High Court judges.

[64] See B. M. Hoggett and D. S. Pearl, *The Family, Law and Society* (2nd ed., 1987), pp. 628–636; Lord McGregor, (1987) 6 C.J.Q. 44; B. M. Hoggett, (1986) 6 L.S.1; D. Allen (ed.), *Family justice—a structure for the family court* (1986).

[65] See *The Overlapping Family Jurisdiction of Magistrates' Courts and County Courts*, Research Report of the Socio-Legal Centre for Family Studies, University of Bristol, June 1987, summarised by J. Graham Hall and D. F. Martin, (1987) 151 J.P.N. 659.

[66] Cmnd. 5629, 1974.

[67] Domestic Proceedings and Magistrates' Courts Act 1978.

proceedings,[68] and steps were taken to widen the jurisdiction of the county court and improve the distribution of business between the High Court and county courts.[69]

The Lord Chancellor's Department began to take a greater interest in the question, issuing consultation documents in 1983[70] and 1986.[71] The Family Courts Campaign, a consortium of major organisations and individuals, began action in 1984. They showed, *inter alia*, that the net costs of reform were not as great as have been thought.[72] Lord Havers and Lord Mackay, who in turn succeeded Lord Hailsham as Lord Chancellor in 1987, showed markedly more enthusiasm for change than their predecessor. The 1986 Review identified three options; (a) to retain the existing structure but with a revised distribution of jurisdiction to eliminate duplication and overlap; (b) to create a unified court within the existing High Court and county court structure; (c) to create a wholly new court with its own structure and judiciary. In the event, however, it is Option (a) in some form which is reflected in arrangements under the Children Act 1989.[73]

The number of cases dealt with by magistrates although falling, has not declined to the extent at one time thought.[74]

(e) Official Referees' business

There are six Circuit judges nominated by the Lord Chancellor to deal with "Official Referees' business."[75] This is a business appropriate to be dealt with by an official referee (as these judges are still commonly known) because (a) it involves a prolonged examination of documents or accounts or a technical, scientific or local investigation, or (b) because that is in the interests of one or more of the parties on grounds of expedition, economy or

---

[68] See the Justices' Clerks' Society, *Resolving Family Conflict in the 1980s* (1982); "Making the Domestic Proceedings Act Work: A joint declaration by the Magistrates' Association and the Justices' Clerks' Society" (1982) 146 J.P.N. 756–758; C. Latham, "Magistrates' courts and the family jurisdiction: A re-assessment of the Finer Concept of Family Court" (1983) 147 J.P.N. 233–236, 246–247.

[69] See p. 66.

[70] Lord Chancellor's Department, *Family Jurisdiction of the High Court and County Courts, A Consultative Paper* (1983). See J. Levin, *L. A. G. Bull*, March 1983, pp. 5–6.

[71] Lord Chancellor's Department, *Interdepartmental Review of Family and Domestic Jurisdiction*. For responses, see, *e.g.* (1987) 17 *Family Law* 33–34, 64–66 (Family Courts Campaign), 75–76 (Magistrates' Association); J. S. W. Black, (1986) 150 J.P.N. 422; J. Graham Hall and D. F. Martin, *ibid.* p. 436; N. Wikely, (1986) 5 C.J.Q. 288; C. Yates, (1987) J.S.W.L. 300.

[72] J. Stringer and P. M. Smith, *Family Courts—The Price is Right*, summarised by J. Graham Hall and D. F. Martin, "Family Courts—Analysing the Cost" (1988) 152 J.P.N. 517. See also Graham Hall and Martin, "Towards a Unified Family Court—the Cost Factor" (1983) 4 C.J.Q. 223.

[73] See above, p. 53.

[74] "The Domestic Court: A declining jurisdiction" (1982) 146 J.P.N. 754–755; (1984) 148 J.P.N. 179–180; but *cf.* J. Graham Hall and D. F. Martin, *ibid.* p. 355; (1987) 151 J.P.N. 482.

[75] Supreme Court Act 1981, s.68. See E. Fay, *Official Referees' Business* (2nd ed., 1988); F. Meisel, (1984) 3 C.J.Q. 97; (1986) 83 L.S.Gaz. 1294; S. Knafler, *Legal Action*, November 1989, p. 12. The office of Official Referee, first established by the Supreme Court of Judicature Act 1873, was abolished by the Courts Act 1971. Existing holders became Circuit judges: 1971 Act, Sched. 2. On each circuit other than the South Eastern two Circuit judges are appointed to conduct this business, although most is taken in London: see T. Heald, "Official referee's business in the provinces" (1983) Constr.L.J. 91.

convenience or otherwise.[76] A matter for trial may either be commenced as official referees' business or transferred to a referee.[77] A matter may also be referred for inquiry and report concerning any issue of fact.[78]

In practice, official referees' business;

> "covers a surprisingly wide range of subject matter, but much of it involves very substantial building and civil engineering claims with allied disputes about the provision of materials and services, often including a technical or design element, together with the associated liabilities of architects, engineers, surveyors and other professional men."[79]

An Official Referees' Users Committee and an Official Referees' Bar Association have been established.[80]

(f) Administration

Administrative support for the High Court is provided by officials who are technically part of the unified court service.[81] Apart from the masters and registrars appointed under the Supreme Court Act 1981, the officials are civil servants who are members of the Lord Chancellor's Department.[82] In London, the principal offices are the Central Office of the Supreme Court, Chancery Chambers, the Principal Registry of the Family Division,[83] the Admiralty and Commercial Court Registry and the Accounting Department.

Outside London there are district registries of the High Court in about 130 locations.[84] A district judge[85] is appointed by the Lord Chancellor as district judge of the High Court for each registry,[86] and there is provision for the appointment of deputy and assistant district judges.[87] Writs and originating summonses in the Queen's Bench Division may be issued in any district registry; writs and originating summonses in most Chancery actions may be issued out of eight Chancery district registries[88] and in certain specified cases out of any district registry.[89] The other interlocutory steps are also taken here. Matrimonial causes and most other proceedings in the Family Division may be dealt with at those district registries that have a divorce county court

---

[76] R.S.C., Ord. 36, rr., 1, as substituted by S.I. 1982 No. 1111, para. 100.

[77] *Ibid.* rr. 2, 3.

[78] *Ibid.* r. 8.

[79] "Referens," "Official Referee's Business—A New Dawn?" (1983) 80 L.S.Gaz. 478, 479. The author noted a trend away from arbitration to official referees in professional negligence cases.

[80] *Ibid.*

[81] The Review Body on the Chancery Division found that the establishment of the service had had little impact on the Division, and were highly critical of the Division's administrative arrangements.

[82] Appointed under the Courts Act 1971, s.27.

[83] Referred to as Principal Probate Registry or the Divorce Registry depending on which branch of the Division's work is concerned.

[84] Supreme Court Act 1981, s.99; Civil Courts Order 1983 (S.I. 1983 No. 713), as amended.

[85] See above, p. 64.

[86] Supreme Court Act 1981, s.100.

[87] *Ibid.* ss.102, 103. Formerly they were entitled district registrars.

[88] *i.e.* the district registries for the eight centres mentioned above, p. 79, n. 27.

[89] See R. Blackford and C. Jacque, *Chancery Practice Handbook* (1983), pp. 78–80, 100–101.

within its district,[90] although they can only be tried at the Royal Courts or one of the divorce towns.[91] There are district probate registries in 11 places and sub-registries in 18 others.[92] District probate registrars are appointed by the Lord Chancellor.[93]

(g) Procedural rules

Rules for the purpose of regulating and prescribing the practice and procedure to be followed in the High Court and Court of Appeal may be made by the Supreme Court Rule Committee.[94] Most cases[95] are regulated by the Rules of the Supreme Court.[96] These first appeared in 1885 and the most recent major revision was in 1965. They are regularly amended, and are printed, with extensive annotations, in the current edition of *The Supreme Court Practice* (known as the "White Book"). The rules may not alter any matter of substantive law.[97] In 1982, a Supreme Court Procedure Committee was established by the Lord Chief Justice and the other heads of the divisions, in conjunction with the Presidents of the Senate and the Law Society, to consider and recommend reforms in practice and procedure for saving time and costs. Their recommendations are placed before the Rule Committee.[98]

(h) Appeals[99]

Appeals lie either to the Court of Appeal (Civil Division)[1] or direct to the House of Lords.[2] The appeal lies direct to the House of Lords where the case has reached the High Court on appeal from a magistrates' court or the Crown Court in a criminal matter, or, otherwise, under the "leap frog" procedure.

---

[90] See the Matrimonial Causes Rules 1977 (S.I. 1977 No. 344), r. 2 (definition of "district registry" for the purpose of the rules), r. 43; R.S.C., Ord. 9, rr. 3, 5, 17.

[91] Above, p. 82, n. 63.

[92] Supreme Court Act 1981, s.104; District Probate Registries Order 1982 (S.I. 1982 No. 379).

[93] Supreme Court Act 1981, s.89, Sched. 2.

[94] Supreme Court Act 1981, ss.84, 85, as amended by the Courts and Legal Services Act 1990, Sched. 18, para. 36(1). The Committee comprises the heads of division, three High Court judges, two lawyers with a Supreme Court qualification and two lawyers with the right to conduct litigation in the Supreme Court. See Sir Jack Jacob, "The Machinery of the Rule Committee of the Supreme Court" (1971) reprinted in *The Reform of Civil Procedural Law* (1982).

[95] There are separate sets of rules for bankruptcy, the winding up of companies, non-contentious or common form probate proceedings, prize matters, certain proceedings under the Mental Health Act 1983 and matrimonial proceedings.

[96] The Rules are divided into Orders, rules and paragraphs, and are referred to in abbreviated form as (*e.g.*) R.S.C., Ord 1, r. 1.

[97] *e.g.* doubts as to whether certain aspects of the "New Order 53," which introduced the "application for judicial review," were *ultra vires* were settled by the enactment of section 31 of the Supreme Court Act 1981 (see below, p. 875).

[98] (1982) 79 L.S.Gaz. 711. The membership includes judges, masters, barristers, and solicitors. There is a sub-committee for each division of the High Court.

[99] See generally Chap. 17.

[1] See below, pp. 90–91.

[2] See below, pp. 91–94.

8. THE LANDS TRIBUNAL

The Lands Tribunal was set up in 1949[3] to take over the jurisdiction of official arbitrators to determine disputes concerning the assessment of compensation for the compulsory acquisition of land. It consists of a President, who must be a person who has held judicial office or a lawyer of at least seven years' standing, a number of members who are lawyers of seven years' standing, and a number who are persons with experience in land valuation (*i.e.* qualified surveyors).[4] All are appointed by the Lord Chancellor, the valuation experts after consultation with the president of the Royal Institute of Chartered Surveyors. The Tribunal's jurisdiction may be exercised by any one or more of its members, as selected by the President, and the selection depends on the nature of the matters at issue. The Tribunal's permanent office and secretariat are in London, although it may sit in the provinces if appropriate, for example to facilitate the inspection of the relevant land and buildings. In addition to the jurisdiction in respect of compensation, it has the power to determine disputes as to the valuation of land for taxation, it hears appeals from valuation and community charge tribunals, in matters concerning disputed assessments of land and buildings for rating and disputes concerning the community charge, and from leasehold valuation tribunals, and it has a discretionary power to vary, modify or discharge restrictive covenants under section 84 of the Law of Property Act 1925. An appeal lies to the Court of Appeal by case stated on a point of law. The Lands Tribunal is regarded as having a high status in the court structure, notwithstanding that, unlike the Transport Tribunal and the Employment Appeal Tribunal, it is not constituted under the 1949 Act as a court of record.[5] Its proceedings are conducted fairly formally.

9. THE RESTRICTIVE PRACTICES COURT

An institution of some analytical interest is the Restrictive Practices Court, which started its operations in 1958 and is now constituted under the Restrictive Practices Court Act 1976. It consists of three puisne judges of the High Court nominated by the Lord Chancellor, one judge of the Court of Session nominated by the Lord President of that Court, one judge of the Supreme Court of Northern Ireland nominated by the Lord Chief Justice of Northern Ireland and up to 10 non-judicial members appointed by the Crown on the recommendation of the Lord Chancellor. One of the High Court judges is selected by the Lord Chancellor to be the president. The "appointed members" must be persons appearing to the Lord Chancellor to be qualified by their knowledge of or experience in industry, commerce or public affairs, and the appointments are for periods of at least three years. The Court, which is a superior court of record, has its central office in

---

[3] Lands Tribunal Act 1949. For its rules of procedure see the Lands Tribunal Rules 1975 (S.I. 1975 No. 299), as amended.

[4] 1949 Act, s.2(2), as amended by the Courts and Legal Services Act, 1990, Sched. 10, para. 7. To be eligible, a lawyer must possess a 7 year general qualification under s.71 of the 1990 Act, *i.e.* a right of audience in any part of the Supreme Court or all proceedings in county courts or magistrates' courts.

[5] See *Att.-Gen.* v. *British Broadcasting Corporation* [1981] A.C. 303, 338, (Viscount Dilhorne). *Cf.* the Annual Report of the Council on Tribunals, 1980–81 (1981–82 H.C. 89), p. 8: "The Lands Tribunal is generally regarded as of High Court standing. . . ."

London, and although it may sit anywhere in the United Kingdom it normally sits in the Royal Courts of Justice. For the hearing of a case the court consists of a judge and at least two other members, although the opinion of the judge or judges must prevail on any question of law. The rights of audience before the court when sitting in England and Wales are limited to those who would have such a right before the High Court.

The main functions of the court are derived from the Restrictive Trade Practices Act 1976.[6] It must determine whether restrictive agreements[7] as to goods or services are contrary to the public interest. The agreements have to be registered with the Director-General of Fair Trading, and it is for him to refer an agreement to the court. A number of professional services, including legal services, were expressly exempted from the scope of the legislation.[8] There is a presumption that a restriction is contrary to the public interest unless the court is satisfied that one (or more) of eight specified conditions (known as "gateways") both exists and outweighs the detriment caused by the restriction.[9] Much of the debate concerning the justiciability of the issues before the court centred on whether these conditions were sufficiently precisely drawn to enable the court to operate in a judicial manner. Stevens and Yamey[10] concluded that they were not. The early decision-making of the courts showed that it would be difficult for firms to justify restrictive agreements, and a large number were ended without recourse to proceedings under the Act:

"The cases require considerable preparation and the hearing of some of the more recent ones has lasted over 40 days. The trade witnesses, often pillars of the establishment, frequently find that being cross-examined for several consecutive days is a considerable strain and the costs, both in lawyers' fees and in time that might otherwise be spent managing the business, are high. Consequently, apart from three lengthy hearings under the Resale Prices Act 1964, there have been only two contested hearings since 1965 as to whether an agreement is contrary to the public interest."[11]

---

[6] This consolidated the original powers included in the Restrictive Trade Practices Act 1956, and the extra powers granted by the Restrictive Trade Practices Act 1968. See generally, R. B. Stevens and B. S. Yamey, *The Restrictive Practices Court* (1965); D. Swann *et al.*, *Competition in British Industry* (1974); V. Korah, *Competition Law of Britain and the Common Market* (3rd ed., 1982); R. Whish, *Competition Law* (2nd ed., 1989), Chap. 5; T. Frazer, *Monopoly, Competition and the Law* (1988).

[7] *e.g.* price-fixing agreements, quota agreements, market sharing agreements and collective boycotts. The controls may be extended to agreements to exchange information about prices, quantities produced, etc.

[8] See the Restrictive Trade Practices Act 1976, s.13, Sched. 1.

[9] *Ibid.* ss.10(1), 19(1). For example, the restriction is reasonably necessary to protect the public against injury (gateway (a)); or provides "specific and substantial benefits" to the public (gateway (b)); removal of the restriction "would be likely to have a serious and persistent adverse effect on the general level of unemployment" (gateway (e)); or to cause a substantial reduction in export earnings (gateway (f)).

[10] *Op. cit.* n. 6, above, Chap. 6. Particularly problematic has been the necessity for the court "to decide which of two or more economic hypotheses is the appropriate one on which to base specific economic predictions." *Ibid.* p. 49.

[11] Korah (1982), p. 95.

Moreover:

"Most of the judgments that have upheld agreements have been subjected to devastating criticism showing logical inconsistencies or complex and unlikely assumptions that are not expressly mentioned in the judgments."[12]

The Court also has jurisdiction in respect of the exemption of resale price maintenance agreements from prohibition[13] and applications by the Director-General of Fair Trading for an order directing the respondent to refrain from conduct detrimental to the interests of consumers.[14]

The Department of Trade and Industry published a Green Paper, *Review of Restrictive Trade Practices Policy*,[15] which listed the major weaknesses of the present arrangements[16] and proposed its complete replacement by a system based on European Community competition law. The coverage of U.K. law should be defined in terms of the effects of agreements and concerted practices on competition, rather than in terms of their legal form; agreements with anti-competitive effects would be prohibited, the registration system being scrapped; exemptions would be determined on a case-by-case basis by reference to a broad test rather than specific grounds for exemption, and with a reduced scope for block exemptions; and the existing exemptions for many sectors, including the provision of professional legal services would be reappraised. Enforcement would be initially in the hands of a new administrative agency, based on the Office of Fair Trading, and with rights of appeal to the Restrictive Practices Court,[17] which was rather doubtfully characterised[18] as "a court especially equipped for the task of economic analysis." However, the government's revised proposals for enforcement, as set out in the White Paper, *OpeningMarkets: New Policy on Restrictive Trade Practices*[19] envisage the court's abolition.

10. THE COURT OF APPEAL (CRIMINAL DIVISION)

The Court of Appeal (Criminal Division) hears appeals from trials on indictment or sentences passed by the Crown Court,[20] and references by the Attorney-General under the Criminal Justice Acts 1972 and 1988.[21] It replaced the Court of Criminal Appeal[22] with effect from October 1, 1966.[23] The Lord Chief Justice is the president of the division, and the Lord

---

[12] *Ibid.*, p. 179.
[13] Resale Prices Act 1976, ss.14–21.
[14] Fair Trading Act 1973, ss.35–39.
[15] Cm. 331, 1988. For comments, see T. Frazer, (1988) 51 M.L.R. 493; C. S. Newell, (1988) 138 N.L.J. 312; M. Burke-Gaffney, (1988) 85 L.S.Gaz. June 22, 1988, pp. 23, 25–26.
[16] Neatly summarised in the headings in Chap. 2: "lack of bite against damaging agreements," "catching trivia," "scope for avoidance," "too many exemptions," "complexity," "burdensome and costly."
[17] "recalled from retirement": T. Frazer, (1988) 51 M.L.R. 493, 500.
[18] Green Paper, para. 6, 14.
[19] Cm. 727, 1989. See Whish (1989), pp. 755–765.
[20] Criminal Appeal Act 1968, Parts I and II. See below, pp. 830–845.
[21] See below, pp. 839–841 and 843–844.
[22] Established by the Criminal Appeal Act 1907. This Act for the first time established a right of appeal for the *accused*, as distinct from the discretion of the *judge* to refer a point to his fellow judges (see above, p. 33).
[23] Criminal Appeal Act 1966. This followed the Report of the Committee on the Court of Criminal Appeal (Chairman: Lord Donovan; Cmnd. 2755, 1965).

Chancellor may appoint a vice-president.[24] The work is done by the Lord Chief Justice, Lords Justices and High Court judges.[25] For the following purposes, a court of the division must comprise an uneven number of judges not less than three[26]:

(i) determining appeals against conviction;
(ii) determining appeals against a verdict of not guilty by reason of insanity;
(iii) determining appeals against a finding of unfitness to be tried because of a disability;
(iv) determining applications for leave to appeal to the House of Lords;
(v) refusing leave to appeal in situations (i), (ii), (iii) above except where the application has already been refused by a single judge;
(vi) determining reviews of sentencing.

Otherwise, matters may be determined by a court comprising two judges.[27] A single judge may grant leave to appeal, grant bail and perform certain other functions.[28] Any number of courts may sit at the same time. The court gives a single judgment unless the judge presiding states that in his or her opinion the question is one of law on which it is convenient that separate judgments should be pronounced by the members of the court.[29] Procedural rules may be made by the Crown Court Rule Committee.[30] The administration of criminal appeals is handled by the Criminal Appeal Office, headed by the Registrar of Criminal Appeals.[31]

Appeals lie to the House of Lords, with the leave of the House or the Court of Appeal, where the Court of Appeal has certified that a point of law of general public importance is involved.[32]

---

[24] Supreme Court Act 1981, s.3.
[25] On occasion, one or more of the Law Lords (see below, p. 208) may sit: *e.g. R.* v. *Husseyn* (Note) (1977) 67 Cr.App.R. 131, "explained" in *Attorney-General's References (Nos. 1 and 2 of 1979)* [1980] Q.B. 180, see below p. 844.
[26] Supreme Court Act 1981, s.55, as amended by the Criminal Justice Act 1988, Sched. 15, para. 80.
[27] *Ibid., e.g.* appeals against sentence. If the court is equally divided the case must be re-argued before an uneven number of judges not less than three: *ibid.* s.55(5).
[28] Criminal Appeal Act 1968, s.31.
[29] Supreme Court Act 1981, s.59. See *R.* v. *Head* [1958] 1 Q.B. 132, 137; *R.* v. *Harz* [1967] 1 A.C. 760, 765.
[30] *Ibid.* s.86, as amended by the Courts and Legal Services Act 1990, Sched. 18, para. 36(2). This comprises the Lord Chancellor and any four of: the Lord Chief Justice, two other judges of the Supreme Court, two Circuit judges, the Registrar of Criminal Appeals, a J.P., two lawyers with a Supreme Court qualification under s.71 of the 1990 Act and two lawyers with the right to conduct litigation in the High Court. See the Criminal Appeal Rules 1968 (S.I. 1968 No. 1262), as amended; *A Guide to Proceedings in the Court of Appeal Criminal Division* [1983] Crim.L.R. 415; D. Thompson and H. W. Wollaston, *Court of Appeal—Criminal Division* (1969); M. Knight, *Criminal Appeals* (1970) and I. McLean, *Criminal Appeals* (2nd ed., 1986).
[31] This office is held in combination with that of Master of the Crown Office. See above, p. 80, fn. 38.
[32] See below, pp. 91–94 and 845–847.

11. THE COURT OF APPEAL (CIVIL DIVISION)[33]

The Court of Appeal was established as part of the Supreme Court by the Supreme Court of Judicature Acts 1873 and 1875. It was reconstituted with Civil and Criminal Divisions in 1966.[34] The jurisdiction of the Civil Division includes appeals from the High Court and county courts in civil matters, and from certain other courts and tribunals.[35] The Master of the Rolls[36] is president of the division, and the Lord Chancellor may appoint a vice-president.[37] The work is mainly done by the Master of the Rolls and the Lords Justices,[38] with occasional assistance from Law Lords, heads of division in the High Court, High Court judges and former judges of the Court of Appeal or High Court.

A court of two judges may hear appeals in interlocutory matters, any other appeal with the consent of the parties, and, as a recent development, certain other appeals, including appeals from county courts.[39] Otherwise the court must comprise an uneven number of judges of three or more.[40] A single judge may determine an application for leave to appeal and deal with other matters arising incidentally.[41]

The work of the division is administered by the Registrar of Civil Appeals. This office was created by the Supreme Court Act 1981,[42] following the report of a Working Party headed by Lord Scarman.[43] The Scarman Committee had identified four main sources of wasted time in the Court of Appeal: (1) failure of parties to an appeal to provide the necessary documentation in a suitable form; (2) the requirement that at least two Lords Justices hear procedural applications; (3) the absence of a flexible and co-ordinated listing system; (4) the length of oral hearings. The Registrar's functions include ensuring that the proper documentation is prepared, advising those unfamiliar with the procedure and practice of the court and the establishment of a co-ordinated listing system. The Scarman Committee

[33] For accounts of the working of the Court of Appeal see Lord Asquith, (1947–51) 1 J.S.P.T.L. (N.S.) 350, reproduced in L.Blom-Cooper, *The Language of the Law* (1965); Sir R. Evershed, *The Court of Appeal in England* (1950); D. Karlen, *Appellate Courts in the United States and England* (1963) Chap. 6; Sir John Donaldson M.R., *The Problems of a Master of the Rolls* (Holdsworth Club Presidential Address, 1985) and "The Court of Appeal" (1985) 53 Medico-Legal Jo. 148.

[34] Criminal Appeal Act 1966.

[35] See below, pp. 848–863.

[36] See below, p. 210.

[37] Supreme Court Act 1981, s.3.

[38] See below, p. 208.

[39] Supreme Court Act 1981, s.54; Court of Appeal (Civil Division) Order 1982 (S.I. 1982 No. 543). If a court is evenly divided the case is re-argued before an uneven number of judges not less than three: s.54(5). There were about 12 such rehearings between 1982 and 1986: *Court of Appeal (Civil Division): Review of the Legal Year 1985–86* (1986) 130 S.J. 767, 770. In cases of real difficulty counsel should consider whether an application for a three-judge court should be made: *Coldunell Ltd.* v. *Gallon* [1986] Q.B. 1184, 1202.

[40] Lord Denning M.R. used occasionally to convene courts of five judges "because it was believed in his day that a five-judge court would get out of a precedent set by a three-judge court. That has now been exploded, so there is no point in sitting in a five-judge Court. I do not see any point in it. I have never done it and I have no present intention of doing it": Sir John Donaldson M.R., (1985) 53 Medico-Legal Jo. 148, 161.

[41] *Ibid.* ss.54(6), 58.

[42] s.89 and Sched. 2.

[43] *Practice Note (Court of Appeal: New Procedure)* [1982] 1 W.L.R. 1312 (Sir John Donaldson M.R.).

considered and rejected a change to the system of written briefs and limitations on the time allowed for oral argument which is the practice, for example, in the Supreme Court of the United States. This system was regarded as alien to the British tradition of oral presentation and argument, and not necessarily less expensive because of the time devoted to preparing highly complex briefs. Instead, arrangements have been made for the pre-reading of documents before the oral hearing begins, and for the submission of "skeleton arguments" (*i.e.* an abbreviated note of arguments and other matters which would otherwise be dictated to the court at the oral hearing).[44]

Decisions as to the composition of the courts and the allocation of the cases are made by the Registrar acting in consultation with the Master of the Rolls. In general, the constitution of the civil courts is changed about every six weeks and that of the criminal court every three weeks. Civil courts are "multi-disciplinary" rather than "specialised" (*e.g.* all former Chancery judges sitting on a Chancery appeal) although, where possible, no appeal on a specialist topic is listed before a court none of whose members are familiar with that speciality.[45] The aim is to have between 6 and 8 courts sitting simultaneously. Overall, the introduction of greater efficiency in the administration of the Court of Appeal has enabled the court to handle an increasing workload, while not being able significantly to reduce the burden of outstanding appeals.[46] A small team of "in-house" lawyers has been appointed, each taking charge of the case management of a group of applications and appeals, defined by reference to subject matter. They will also give procedural advice to litigants in person and, where necessary, provide summaries of the issues raised for the use of judges.[47]

Appeals lie to the House of Lords, with the leave of the court or the House, on questions of law or fact.[48]

12. THE HOUSE OF LORDS[49]

The House of Lords hears appeals (1) from the Court of Appeal; (2) in certain circumstances, direct from the High Court; (3) from the Court of Session (the highest civil court in Scotland)[50]; (4) from the Court of Appeal in Northern Ireland; (5) in certain circumstances, direct from the High

---

[44] *Practice Note (Court of Appeal: skeleton arguments)* [1983] 2 All E.R. 34; *Practice Direction (Court of Appeal: Presentation of Argument)* [1989] 1 W.L.R. 281; *Practice Direction (Court of Appeal: Skeleton Argument Time Limits)* [1990] 1 W.L.R. 794. The Master of the Rolls has stated that there is no scope for a further shift to prereading: *Court of Appeal (Civil Division)*, *Review of the Legal Year 1985–86* (1986) 130 S.J. 767, 768.

[45] Sir John Donaldson M.R., *The Problems of A Master of the Rolls* (Holdsworth Club Presidential Address, 1985), pp. 9–10.

[46] See the Annual Reviews by the Master of the Rolls: 1982–83 (*The Times*, October 5, 1983); 1983–84 ((1984) 134 N.L.J. 883); 1984–85 ((1985) 129 S.J. 701); 1985–86 ((1986) 130 S.J. 767); 1986–87 (1987) 131 S.J. 1393; 1987–88 (*The Times*, November 1, 1988); 1988–89 (*The Times*, October 13, 1989); 1989–90 (*The Times*, October 25, 1990; (1990) 140 N.L.J. 1569).

[47] Annual Review 1988–89, *supra*. See *Practice Statement (Civil Appeals: Setting Down)* [1990] 1 W.L.R. 1436.

[48] See below, and pp. 864–866.

[49] See L. Blom-Cooper and Gavin Drewry, *Final Appeal* (1972); R. Stevens, *Law and Politics* (1978); A. Paterson, *The Law Lords* (1982); Lord Fraser of Tullybelton, 1986 S.L.T. 33.

[50] There is no right of appeal from the highest Scottish criminal court, the High Court of Justiciary: *Mackintosh* v. *Lord Advocate* (1876) 3 R. (H.L.) 34; Criminal Procedure (Scotland) Act 1887, s.72. See A. J. Maclean, "The House of Lords and Appeals from the High Court of Justiciary 1707–1887" 1985 J.R. 192.

Court of Justice in Northern Ireland and (6) from the Courts-Martial Appeal Court.[51]

An appeal may not be heard or determined unless at least three from the following list are present: (1) the Lord Chancellor[52]; (2) the Lords of Appeal in Ordinary[53]; (3) any peer who has held one of the high judicial offices of Lord Chancellor, member of the Judicial Committee of the Privy Council, Lord of Appeal in Ordinary, judge of the Supreme Court of England and Wales or Northern Ireland or judge of the Court of Session.[54] Technically, it seems that all members of the House of Lords have the right to vote on appeals, but the practice has fallen into disuse. In the early nineteenth century lay peers were used to make up the necessary quorum but by the 1830s there were sufficient Law Lords[55] for a "professional" court to be possible.[56] In 1844 the convention that lay peers did not vote was established in *O'Connell* v. *R.*[57] Daniel O'Connell appealed against a conviction for conspiracy. Three Law Lords were in favour of allowing the appeal, two were against it. Several lay peers purported to vote with the minority, but were persuaded to withdraw on the ground that in reality the "Court of Law" in the House was constituted by the Law Lords and interference by lay peers would greatly lessen the authority of the House. The last occasion when a lay peer attempted to vote was in *Bradlaugh* v. *Clarke*[58] when Lord Denman[59] attended throughout the proceedings and purported to vote with Lord Blackburn against the majority of the Law Lords. His attempt was ignored by the Lord Chancellor and the Law Reports, but was noted by *The Times.*[60] In response to a question in the House of Commons, the Home Secretary stated that as the Appellate Jurisdiction Act 1876 had not excluded lay peers, it had been competent for Lord Denman to sit: had his opinion affected the result, he would have been asked to withdraw his vote on the precedent of *O'Connell's* case.[61]

Under the original arrangements for reorganisation incorporated in the Supreme Court of Judicature Act 1873 the appellate role of the House of Lords was to be abolished. The Court of Appeal was to be the final appeal court for England, and ultimately for Scotland, Ireland and the colonies. However, before the arrangements came into effect opposition developed in

---

[51] Appeals in English cases are considered in detail below, pp. 845–847, 863–866.
[52] Above, pp. 16–17; below, p. 209.
[53] Below, p. 208.
[54] Appellate Jurisdiction Act 1876, ss.5, 25; Appellate Jurisdiction Act 1887, s.5. The current list includes 10 retired Lords of Appeal, two former Lord Chancellors (Hailsham and Havers) and several Scottish judges: see *Waterlow's Solicitors and Barristers Diary 1991*.
[55] The term then covered the Lord Chancellor, the Lord Chancellor of Ireland, former Lord Chancellors, ennobled judges, and occasionally a peer who had held a minor judicial office.
[56] Stevens (1978), p. 29.
[57] (1844) 11 Cl. & F. 155, 421–426.
[58] (1883) 8 App.Cas 354. See R. E. Megarry, (1949) 65 L.Q.R. 22–24.
[59] This was the second Lord Denman, son of the Lord Chief Justice and brother of Denman J., a High Court judge, 1872–1892. "Lord Denman was aged seventy-eight at the time of his fling, and he had been a peer for nearly thirty years and a barrister for fifty, so that his was no mere indiscretion of youth and inexperience" (Megarry (1949), p. 24). He "won notoriety rather from his eccentricities than any eminent qualifications" (D.N.B.).
[60] April 10, 1883, p. 4.
[61] Sir William Harcourt, H.C. Deb. Vol. 278, col. 68, April 12, 1883.

several quarters, the appeal to the House was retained and provision was made for the appointment of salaried Law Lords.[62]

Up to 1948, appeals to the House of Lords were heard in the chamber of the House. In that year, the process of repairing the Palace of Westminister caused the House to commit the hearing of appeals to an Appellate Committee meeting in a committee room and this practice has been maintained ever since. The committee hears appeals and reports its conclusions to the House, where judgment is delivered at a judicial sitting.[63] The House, or the Appellate Committee, as the case may be, is presided over by the Lord Chancellor or, as is more usually the case, the senior Lord of Appeal in Ordinary present.[64] The Appellate Committee must be distinguished from the "Appeal Committee" which sits to consider and report on petitions for leave to appeal and other incidental matters and which normally comprises three Law Lords.

Selection of Law Lords to sit on Appeal Committees is done by the Principal Clerk to the Judicial Office: selection of Appellate Committees, although theoretically in the hands of the Lord Chancellor, is delegated to his Permanent Secretary, who consults the Lord Chancellor in cases of difficulty.[65] Normally, the most convenient panel available is chosen; occasionally, special considerations may apply, such as the exclusion of judges with a political background from adjudicating in a case with party-political implications,[66] the strong desirability of one or both of the Scottish Law Lords sitting on an appeal from Scotland and the desirability of the presence of a Chancery judge in a Chancery appeal. The room for manoeuvre is in practice limited.

Procedure on appeals to the House of Lords is regulated by Directions and Standing Orders of the House.[67] Each side must submit a "printed Case," drawn up by counsel, which is a "succinct statement of their argument in the Appeal,"[68] although in practice the oral submissions of counsel and the interchange between them and the Law Lords are of greater significance.[69] The Law Lords are generally expected to confine their propositions of law to matters covered by the argument of counsel, although this view is

---

[62] See Stevens (1979), Chap. 2 and R. Stevens, "The Final Appeal: Reform of the House of Lords and Privy Council, 1867–1876" (1964) 80 L.Q.R. 343.

[63] A morning sitting in the Chamber of the House. Some appeals may be heard in the Chamber, e.g. during Parliamentary recesses.

[64] Seniority formerly depended on the date of first appointment to the office: Blom-Cooper and Drewry (1972), p. 179. From 1984, the first and second senior Law Lords have been specifically appointed as such by the Queen: H.L. Deb. Vol. 453, cols. 914–919, June 27, 1984: see L. Blom-Cooper, [1984] P.L. 376; A. A. Paterson, 1988 J.R. 235, 251, n. 59. The presiding judge may exert significant influence over the course of proceedings: Paterson (1982), pp. 66–72. The most recent senior Lords of Appeal have been Lord Simonds (1954–1962); Lord Reid (1962–1975); Lord Wilberforce (1975–1982); Lord Diplock (1982–1984); Lord Fraser of Tullybelton (1984–1985); Lord Scarman (1985–1986); Lord Keith of Kinkel (1986–).

[65] See Paterson (1982), pp. 87–89. The selections have to be co-ordinated with those for the Judicial Committee of the Privy Council.

[66] This was done for Heaton's Transport Co. v. T.G.W.U. [1973] A.C. 15. See A. Paterson, (1979) 1 B.J.L.S. 118, 126.

[67] See Supreme Court Practice 1991, Vol. 2, Part 16, Directions as to Procedure, July 1988.

[68] Ibid.

[69] See A. Paterson, The Law Lords (1982), Chaps. 3 and 4.

held today less strongly than formerly.[70] Moreover, they will not normally consider a point not raised in the courts below,[71]

> "But if [the Law Lords] think it is something that really goes to the root of the thing, if they think the whole thing would be rather a mess if they did not allow it to be argued, then they would probably allow it on terms as to costs."[72]

Informal discussions among the Law Lords take place during the hearing of an appeal.[73] Judgment is invariably reserved. At the conclusion of the hearing there is a conference at which provisional opinions are expressed, and a general discussion follows. If there appears to be general agreement, it may also be agreed that a particular Law Lord should write the major opinion. Occasionally, a second conference may be convened.

Each Law Lord is entitled to write his own opinion,[74] although they attempt to avoid the unnecessary multiplication of opinions. Views differ on the desirability of multiple opinions.[75] Paterson found that of those studied:

> "although in non-criminal common law cases only two active Law Lords generally favoured a single judgment in criminal appeals on a point of statutory construction, probably a majority of the active Law Lords favoured that approach."[76]

The main problem with multiple assenting judgments is that the differences in language may make it difficult to discern the *ratio decidendi*[77]; conversely, the same feature may leave subsequent judges greater scope for developing the law. The main problem with single opinions is that they may reflect an uneasy compromise. Recently, the proportion of cases with a single opinion has increased.[78]

The House of Lords has a limited original, as distinct from appellate, jurisdiction, which includes the power to determine peerage claims and the power to conduct impeachment proceedings.[79] The right of a peer to be tried by his peers in cases of treason, felony or misprision of felony was abolished in 1948.[80]

---

[70] *Ibid.* pp. 38–45.

[71] *Ibid.* pp. 45–49.

[72] Lord Cross, cited by Paterson (1982), p. 47.

[73] The interaction among the Law Lords is discussed by Paterson (1982), Chap. 5.

[74] Occasionally the presiding judge may press for a single opinion: see *D.P.P.* v. *Smith* [1961] A.C. 290 and *Heaton's Transport Ltd.* v. *T.G.W.U.* [1973] A.C. 15: *cf.* the position in the Judicial Committee of the Privy Council, below, p. 96.

[75] See Blom-Cooper and Drewry (1972), Chap. V; R. Cross, (1977) 93 L.Q.R. 378; Paterson (1982), pp. 96–109 and 183–187.

[76] *Op. cit.*, p. 185.

[77] See, *e.g. Boys* v. *Chaplin* [1971] A.C. 356; *British Railways Board* v. *Herrington* [1972] A.C. 877: below, pp. 376–377.

[78] See P. V. Baker, (1983) 99 L.Q.R. 371; Lord Diplock *In re Prestige Group plc* [1984] 1 W.L.R. 335, 338, referring to this as "a frequent practice in this House when dealing with questions of statutory construction"; A. Bradney, "The changing face of the House of Lords" 1985 J.R. 178 (statistical analysis of judgments between January 30, 1974 and March 1, 1984).

[79] The last such cases were those of Warren Hastings (1788–1795: see P. J. Marshall, *The Impeachment of Warren Hastings* (1965)) and Viscount Melville (1806); *cf.* below, p. 221.

[80] Criminal Justice Act 1948, s.30. The last trial was that of Lord de Clifford 1935. See, W. T. West, *The Trial of Lord de Clifford 1935* (1984), and, generally P. Marsden, *In Peril Before Parliament* (1965).

13. THE JUDICIAL COMMITTEE OF THE PRIVY COUNCIL

The Judicial Committee of the Privy Council was established in 1833,[81] largely as the result of the efforts of Lord Brougham.[82] Previously, appeals to the Crown from the colonies, which arose out of the prerogative right of the Sovereign as the fountainhead of all justice, were dealt with by a committee of the Privy Council which did not have a regular judicial composition. The 1833 Act limited the membership almost exclusively to senior judges. The present position is that the Committee comprises the Lord President of the Council, the Lord Chancellor, the Lords of Appeal in Ordinary and other members of the Privy Council who hold "high judicial office,"[83] and former holders of these offices.[84] In addition, privy councillors who hold or have held one of a number of judicial offices in New Zealand and other Commonwealth countries may also be members.[85]

The Judicial Committee hears appeals from certain Commonwealth countries, from the Channel Islands, in certain admiralty and ecclesiastical matters and from the General Medical Council[86] and other professional bodies.[87] The Commonwealth appellate jurisdiction was formerly regarded as an important unifying influence: it has now dwindled significantly as an increasing number of Commonwealth countries have abandoned the appeal.[88] For example, Canada and India abolished appeals in 1949, Sri Lanka in 1971, and Australia in 1986.[89] At present appeals lie from over 25 Commonwealth countries. The Committee's decision takes the form of advice to the Queen, to which effect is given by an Order in Council.[90] It is binding on the relevant Commonwealth courts.[91] A proportion of the cases heard by the Privy Council raise questions of constitutional interpretation.

---

[81] Judicial Committee Act 1833.

[82] See P. A. Howell, *The Judicial Committee of the Privy Council 1833–1876* (1979), Chap. 12, D. B. Swinfen, "Henry Brougham and the Judicial Committee of the Privy Council" (1975) 90 L.Q.R. 396; L. P. Beth, [1975] P.L. 219. See generally D. B. Swinfen, *Imperial Appeal* (1987).

[83] As defined by the Appellate Jurisdiction Acts 1876, ss.5, 25 and 1877, s.5. This extends the membership of the Committee to the Lords Justices of Appeal, although they rarely sit in practice.

[84] Judicial Committee Act 1833, s.1; Appellate Jurisdiction Act 1876, s.6; Appellate Jurisdiction Act 1887, s.3.

[85] Judicial Committee Amendment Act 1895, s.1, Sched.; Appellate Jurisdiction Act 1908, s.3. The list in 1991 included six from New Zealand and one from The Bahamas: *Waterlow's Solicitors and Barristers' Diary 1991*, p. 1–2.

[86] Medical Act 1983, s.40.

[87] *e.g.* dentists, vets, chiropodists and remedial gymnasts: Dentists Act 1984, s.29; Veterinary Surgeons Act 1966, s.17; Professions Supplementary to Medicine Act 1960, ss.1, 9. See, *e.g.* *Libman* v. *General Medical Council* [1972] A.C. 217; *McEniff* v. *General Dental Council* [1980] 1 W.L.R. 328 (Dentist struck off for allowing an assistant and a receptionist to fill teeth after he had completed the drilling); *Le Scroog* v. *General Optical Council* [1982] 1 W.L.R. 1238 (optician struck off for advertising).

[88] Dominions were given the power to do this by the Statute of Westminster 1931, ss.2, 3.

[89] Australia Act 1986, s.11. For arguments for and against appeals to the Privy Council from New Zealand, see C. Cato, [1988] N.Z.L.J. 110 and E. Garnett, [1989] N.Z.L.J. 105.

[90] For Malaysia, an independent monarchy, the advice is tendered to the Head of Malaysia (Yang di-pertuan Agong); for the republics (The Gambia, Singapore, Trinidad and Tobago) the Committee itself is the decision-making authority.

[91] At least while that country retains the appeal to the Privy Council. For example, in *Viro* v. *R.* (1978) 18 A.L.R. 257, the High Court of Australia held that it was no longer bound by decisions of the Privy Council: see R. S. Geddis, (1978) 9 Fed.L.R. 427.

The handling of these cases has been analysed for guidance as to how the House of Lords might deal with matters arising under a written constitution with a Bill of Rights for the United Kingdom. The consensus appears to be that the judges seem not particularly well suited to handling such issues.[92] The Committee sits in London. The recording of dissenting opinions has only been permitted since 1966.[93] There is either one unanimous opinion, or one for the majority and one for the minority. Lord Reid thought that the single opinion rule had led to Privy Council judgments being much inferior to speeches in the House of Lords:

> "They are perfectly adequate to decide the particular case but not often of wider importance. Yet the same Law Lords have sat and they have taken just as much trouble. The reason is that a single judgment must get the agreement of at least all in the majority so it tends to be no more than the highest common factor of all the views."[94]

Apart from the appellate jurisdiction, the Judicial Committee may entertain an application for a declaration that a person purporting to be a member of the House of Commons is disqualified by the House of Commons Disqualification Act 1975.[95] Finally, Her Majesty may refer any matter to the Judicial Committee for hearing or consideration.[96]

14. The Court of Justice of the European Communities[97]

(a) Establishment

This Court is one of the four major institutions created by the Treaties establishing the European Communities. There was originally a Court of Justice for the European Coal and Steel Community, but when the treaties establishing the European Economic Community and Euratom were concluded it was agreed that there should be one court for the three communities. The Single European Act of 1986 made provision for the establishment of a Court of First Instance to ease the Court's work load.[98]

---

[92] P. Wallington and J. McBride, *Civil Liberties and a Bill of Rights* (1976), pp. 32–33 "We come away with a rather neutral impression of the talents available"; G. J. Zellick "Fundamental Rights in the Privy Council" [1982] P.L. 344 (criticising the decision in a case concerning the death penalty, *Riley* v. *Attorney General of Jamaica* [1983] 1 A.C. 719); B. de Smith, "The Judicial Committee as a Constitutional Court" [1984] P.L. 557; N. S. Price, "Constitutional Adjudication in the Privy Council and Reflections on the Bill of Rights debate" (1986) 35 I.C.L.Q. 946, criticising *Robinson* v. *R.* [1985] A.C. 956; *cf.* M. Zander, *A Bill of Rights?* (3rd ed., 1985), pp. 62–64, who takes a more favourable view. On the rôle of the Privy Council in developing the common law, see J. W. Harris, (1990) 106 L.Q.R. 574.

[93] Judicial Committee (Dissenting Opinion) Order 1966. See D. B. Swinfen, "Single Judgment in the Privy Council 1833–1966" 1975 20 J.R. 153.

[94] "The Judge as Law Maker" (1972) XII J.S.P.T.L. (N.S.) 22, 29.

[95] See s.7.

[96] Judicial Committee Act 1833, s.4. See D. B. Swinfen, "Politics and the Privy Council: Special Reference to the Judicial Committee" 1978 23 J.R. 126.

[97] T. C. Hartley, *The Foundations of European Community Law* (2nd ed., 1988); L. Neville Brown and F. G. Jacobs, *The Court of Justice of the European Communities* (3rd ed., 1989); J. Usher, *European Court Practice* (1983); K. P. E. Lasok, *The European Court of Justice: Practice and Procedure* (1984); Office for Official Publications of the European Communities, *The Court of Justice of the European Community* (4th ed., 1986); H. Rasmussen, *On Law and Policy in the European Court of Justice* (1986) (reviewed by M. Cappelletti, (1987) 12 E.L.Rev. 3, J. H. H. Weiler, (1987) 24 C.M.L. Rev. 555); C. O. Leng, (1989) 14 E.L.Rev. 127.

[98] See section (f), below.

(b) Composition

The Court consists of thirteen judges,[99] assisted by six advocates general.[1] It may sit either in "plenary session" (*i.e.* with all the judges entitled to be present) or, where permitted by the Rules of Procedure, in "chambers" of three or five judges. It must sit in plenary session—

(1) to hear cases brought by a member State or Community institution, or

(2) to give preliminary rulings under Article 177/EEC, unless the case may be dealt with by a chamber under the Rules of Procedure.

Otherwise, matters may be dealt with by a chamber, as, for example, may cases brought by an official against an institution, matters concerning costs and legal aid, and references for a preliminary ruling or direct actions where the difficulty or importance of the case or the circumstances are not such as to require a decision of the court in plenary session. Only one judgment is delivered by the Chamber or Court and it is not revealed whether the decision was unanimous or reached by a majority.

The function of the advocate general is:

"acting with complete impartiality, and independence, to make, in open court, reasoned submissions on cases brought before the Court of Justice, in order to assist the Court. . . ."[2]

This office has no exact equivalent in any national legal system although it is loosely based on that of *commissaire du gouvernement* in proceedings before French administrative courts, especially the Conseil d'Etat. One advocate general is assigned to each case. He or she sits on the bench, next to the judges, and may put questions to the parties. His or her opinion on the case is normally expressed about three weeks after the submissions of counsel have been heard, and, unlike such submissions on behalf of a client, "the Advocate General speaks for no-one but himself."[3] The opinion sets out the facts and relevant legal provisions, analyses the issues in the light of the case law of the court and suggests the appropriate decision for the court to adopt. It tends to be longer, more informative and less bland in style than the judgments of the court. The advocate general does not attend the deliberations of the judges. It is thought that his or her opinion is followed in about 70 per cent. of cases, but this may be an overestimate.[4]

The judges and advocates general are chosen by agreement among the governments of the Member States. They have to be:

"chosen from persons whose independence is beyond doubt and who possess the qualifications required for appointment to the highest judicial offices in their respective countries or who are jurisconsults of recognised competence,"[5]

and are appointed for a term of six years. A proportion[6] of the judges and advocates general are replaced every three years. The incumbents are

---

[99] Art. 165/EEC (*i.e.* Article 165 of the EEC Treaty), as amended.

[1] Art. 166/EEC, as amended.

[2] Art. 166/EEC. See A. A. Dashwood, "The Advocate General in the Court of Justice of the European Communities" (1982) 2 L.S. 202; K. Borgsmidt, "The Advocate General at the European Court of Justice: A Comparative Study" (1988) 13 E.L.Rev. 106.

[3] Dashwood, *op. cit.*, p. 207.

[4] *Ibid.* p. 212.

[5] Art. 167/EEC. See also the Protocols on the Statute of the Court of Justice.

[6] Six or seven judges; three advocates general.

eligible for re-appointment. The judges elect one of their number to be President for a (renewable) three year term. The President's functions are to direct the judicial business and the administration of the court and to preside at hearings. One of the advocates general is designated as first advocate general, and performs certain administrative functions, including the distribution of cases among his or her colleagues.

There is one judge of each of the 12 nationalities: the thirteenth judge will serve a single term and will be drawn in rotation from France, Germany, Italy and the United Kingdom.[7] There is one advocate general from each of the four large states[8] and one each from two of the smaller states.

(c) Jurisdiction

The jurisdiction of the Court of Justice under the EEC Treaty[9] can be classified under four main heads: (i) Applications for preliminary rulings under Article 177/EEC in the course of proceedings in a national court or tribunal; (ii) Direct actions against Member States or Community institutions; (iii) Staff cases; (iv) Opinions.

(i) *Applications for Preliminary rulings*

These are considered in Chapter 17.

(ii) *Direct actions*

(1) *Actions against Member States.*[10] Under Article 169/EEC, if the Commission considers that a Member State has failed to fulfil an obligation imposed by the Treaty or secondary Community legislation, it must deliver a reasoned opinion on the matter, after giving the State concerned the opportunity to submit its observations.[11] If the State does not comply with the opinion within the period laid down by the Commission, the Commission may bring the matter before the Court of Justice.[12] Under Article 170/EEC a Member State may bring similar proceedings against another Member State, after bringing the matter to the Commission's attention. If a breach is established the Court will make a declaratory order to that effect.[13] The

---

[7] These are not legal requirements but are the consequence in practice of the need for the agreement of all the member states. The U.K. judges have been Lord Mackenzie Stuart, formerly a judge of the Court of Session, (1973–1988, President 1984–1988); Sir Gordon Slynn; formerly a High Court judge and then an Advocate General (1988–).

[8] France, Germany, Italy, the United Kingdom. Those from the U.K. have been J.-P. Warner (1973–1981); Sir Gordon Slynn (1981–1988); Prof. F. Jacobs Q.C. (1988–).

[9] There are analogous procedures under the other Treaties, with some differences in point of detail between the E.C.S.C. and the others.

[10] Hartley (1988), Chap. 10; H. A. H. Audretsch, *Supervision in European Community Law* (2nd ed., 1986); A. Dashwood and R. White, (1989) 14 E.L.Rev. 388.

[11] A reasonable time must be allowed: Case 293/85, *Commission* v. *Belgium* [1989] 2 C.M.L.R. 527. See A. Arnull, (1988) 13 E.L.Rev. 260.

[12] See, *e.g.* Case 232/78 *Commission* v. *France* [1979] E.C.R. 2729: French ban on the import of mutton and lamb from the U.K. held to be an infringement of the Treaty; the dispute was eventually compromised.

[13] Only one case under Art. 170 has proceeded to judgment: Case 141/78 *France* v. *United Kingdom* [1979] E.C.R. 2923. *Cf.* the procedure under Art. 93/EEC. whereby the Commission may require a state to abolish or alter a state aid that distorts or threatens to distort competition: if the state does not comply the matter may be referred to the court.

Member State is required by Article 171/EEC to take the necessary measures to comply, but the sanctions are political rather than legal.[14] A majority of cases are settled before they reach the Court.

(2) *Actions against community institutions*. These include (1) actions under Article 173/EEC for the annulment of acts of the Council and Commission[15]; (2) actions under Article 175/EEC against the Council or the Commission where either has, contrary to the requirements of the Treaty, failed to act[16]; (3) actions under Article 172/EEC to review penalties or fines imposed by the Commission; (4) actions under Article 178/EEC for damages based on the non-contractual (including tortious) liability of the Communities.[17]

(iii) *Staff cases*

The court has jurisdiction under Article 179/EEC in any dispute between the Community and its servants within the limits and under the conditions laid down in the Staff Regulations or the Conditions of Employment.

(iv) *Opinions*

The court may under Article 228/EEC give an opinion as to whether an international agreement that the Community proposes to enter is compatible with the Treaty.

(d) Some aspects of procedure

Proceedings before the court are governed by the Rules of Procedure[18] drawn up by the court with the approval of the Council. There are four stages—
(1) Written proceedings. Proceedings are commenced by filing an application specifying the subject matter of the dispute, the grounds, the form of order sought and certain other matters. A defence must be filed within one month, and a reply and rejoinder may follow.
(2) Investigation or preliminary inquiry. The case will have been assigned by the President to one of the six chambers. He will also nominate one of the judges in that chamber to act as rapporteur. After the close of pleadings the judge-rapporteur makes a preliminary report which enables the court to decide whether the submission of any evidence is required, such as the oral

---

[14] Although Art. 171 does not specify a time limit within which a judgment must be complied with, implementation must start immediately and be completed as soon as possible: Case 131/84, *Commission* v. *Italian Republic* [1985] E.C.R. 3531 (unreasonable delay in implementing judgment in Case 91/81, [1982] E.C.R. 2133). Implementation must be by national provisions of a binding nature, not merely by administrative circulars or practices: Case 168/85, *Commission* v. *Italy* [1986] E.C.R. 2945.

[15] See below, pp. 310–312. Community legislation is considered below at pp. 281–297, and its interpretation at pp. 361–368.

[16] See below, pp. 313–314.

[17] Art. 215/EEC provides that "the Community shall, in accordance with the general provisions common to the laws of the Member States, make good any damage caused by its institutions or by its servants in the performance of their duties."

[18] A codified version of the 1974 rules as amended was published in the Official Journal 1982, C.39/1. See *Encyclopedia of European Community Law*, B8–142 *et seq.*

testimony of witnesses, an expert's report or the personal appearance of the parties. These matters are dealt with at this stage. The judge-rapporteur then prepares a report summarising facts and arguments.

(3) Oral proceedings. At this stage the parties' lawyers address the court.[19] Interchange between court and advocate is a comparatively recent development. The final step of this stage is the delivery of the advocate general's opinion, which takes place in open court, normally a few weeks later.

(4) Judgment. Proceedings may be conducted in Danish, Dutch, English, French, German, Greek, Irish, Italian, Portuguese or Spanish. The language is chosen by the applicant except where an application is made against a Member State, where the state's language is used, and in applications for preliminary rulings, which are conducted in the language of the referring court or tribunal. In practice, the working language is normally French.

There are no court fees. Costs are normally awarded to the successful party against his or her opponent. The court may grant legal aid: aid for an application for a preliminary ruling is, however, regarded as an aspect of the national proceedings, and aid will only be granted by the court if it is not available in those proceedings.

(e) Administration

This is the responsibility of the Registrar and his staff. There is a Registry, translation, library and documentation and interpretation services and an information office. In addition, two legal secretaries are attached to each judge and advocate general.

(f) The Court of First Instance[20]

The European Court has pressed since 1974 for the establishment of a separate administrative tribunal to deal with staff cases and thereby relieve the pressure on the Court. For over twenty years, nothing came of this, although changes were made in the Court's procedures, including the greater use of Chambers, and the number of Judges and Advocates General were periodically increased. Eventually, the Single European Act amended the main Treaties[21] to enable the Council, by a Decision, to establish a Court of First Instance of the European Communities, and amend the Rules of Procedure accordingly. The necessary Decision was made in 1988,[22] and provides for a court of twelve members "attached to the Court of Justice of the European Communities"[23] and with its seat at the Court. It will normally sit in chambers of three or five judges, but may exceptionally sit in plenary

---

[19] Any lawyer entitled to practice before a court of a Member State may appear. Thus, either a barrister or solicitor from the U.K. may appear. A litigant may not normally appear in person. *Cf.* below, pp. 176–177.

[20] The background is fully considered by T. Kennedy, "The Essential Minimum: The Establishment of the Court of First Instance" (1989) 14 E.L.Rev. 7. See also H. G. Schermers, (1988) 25 C.M.L.Rev. 541; Select Committee on the European Communities, Fifth Report 1987–88 (1987–88 H.L. 20); A. Barav, (1989) 139 N.L.J. 1299; O. Due, (1988) 4 Y.E.L. 1; T. Kennedy, (1990) 15 E.L.Rev. 54; A. G. Toth in R. White and B. Smythe (eds.), *Current Issues in European and International Law* (1990), Chap. 2.

[21] Art. 168A/EEC; Art. 32D/ECSC; Art. 140A/Euratom.

[22] Dec. 88/591/ECSC, EEC, Euratom, October 24, 1988, [1988] O.J.L. 319/1 (November 25, 1988), [1989] 1 C.M.L.R. 323.

[23] *Ibid.*, Art. 1.

session, in accordance with its Rules of Procedure. The members are appointed by common accord of the governments of the Member States for (renewable) six year terms, and with the membership partly renewed every three years.[24] They must be "chosen from persons whose independence is beyond doubt and who possess the ability required for appointment to judicial office."[25] No separate advocates general are appointed, but the judges "may be called upon to perform the task of an advocate general,"[26] again in accordance with the Rules of Procedure. A President is elected by the judges for a (renewable) three year term.[27] The Court also is to appoint a Registrar.

The Court will exercise the jurisdiction of the European Court in (1) staff cases[28]; (2) competition cases[29]; and (3) coal and steel cases arising from the application of the ECSC Treaty.[30] After two years, the Council will consider whether to extend the Court's jurisdiction to include anti-dumping and subsidies cases: these raise complex questions of fact and would seem suitable for it.[31]

The Court of First Instance is to establish its own Rules of Procedure, in agreement with the European Court and with the unanimous approval of the Council.[32] Until then, the European Court's Rules are to apply *mutatis mutandis*.[33]

An appeal lies to the European Court[34] against final decisions of the Court of First Instance, and decisions disposing of the substantive issues in part only or disposing of a procedural issue concerning a plea of lack of competence or inadmissibility. An appeal may be brought by (1) any unsuccessful party (except that interveners other than Member States or Community institutions may only appeal where the Court's decision directly affects them); and (2) (except in staff cases) any non-intervening Member State or Community institution. The appeal is limited to points of law, including lack of competence of the Court of First Instance, and a breach of procedure which adversely affects the appellant's interests. If the appeal is well founded, the European Court is to quash the decision and either itself give final judgment or remit the case to the Court of First Instance. In the latter event, the European Court's decision on points of law is binding.

---

[24] Art. 168/A(3)/EEC. The first judge from the U.K. is Prof. D. Edward.
[25] *Ibid.*
[26] *Ibid.*, Art. 2(3).
[27] *Ibid.*, Art. 2(2). The first President may be appointed as such by the Member States: Art. 11.
[28] Disputes between the Communities and their servants under Art. 179/EEC and Art. 152/Euratom.
[29] Actions against Community institutions under Arts. 173(2) and 175(3)/EEC relating to the implementation of the competition rules applicable to undertakings.
[30] Actions against the Commission under Arts. 33(2) and 35/ECSC by undertakings or associations of undertakings concerning individual acts relating to the application of Arts. 50, 57–66/ECSC.
[31] The Commission had opposed this transfer as the procedure was already cumbersome.
[32] Art. 168A(4)/EEC. For Draft Rules see [1990] 2 C.M.L.R. 420.
[33] Dec. 88/591/ECSC, EEC, Euratom, Art. 11.
[34] Articles 50–55 of the Protocol on the Statute of the Court of Justice, as amended by Dec. 88/591/ECSC/EEC/Euratom.

15. THE EUROPEAN COURT OF HUMAN RIGHTS[35]

Decisions of the European Court of Human Rights have become of increasing significance for the English legal system in recent years. The Convention for the Protection of Human Rights and Fundamental Freedoms of November 4, 1950, generally known as the European Convention on Human Rights, was one of the first achievements of the Council of Europe, an association of 21 states. It came into force in 1953 and by 1982 all these states were parties to the Convention.[36] Article 1 provides that these parties "shall secure to everyone within their jurisdiction" the rights and freedoms defined in Articles 2 to 18. These are mostly civil and political rights,[37] including the right to life (Art. 2), the right not to be subjected to torture or to inhuman or degrading treatment or punishment (Art. 3), the right to liberty and security of person (Art. 5), the right to a fair trial in both civil and criminal cases (Art. 6), the right to respect for private and family life, home and correspondence (Art. 8), the right to freedom of thought, conscience and religion (Art. 9), the right to freedom of expression (Art. 10) and the right to freedom of peaceful assembly and to freedom of association with others (Art. 11). Further rights are specified in the First Protocol to the Convention.[38] Article 13 requires that persons whose guaranteed rights are violated "have an effective remedy before a national authority."

For the purposes of enforcement the Convention established the European Commission of Human Rights and the European Court of Human Rights, each with one member in respect of each party. Each member is elected by the Consultative Assembly of the Council of Europe and sits in an individual capacity and not as a representative of his or her country.

Alleged breaches of the Convention may be raised either by a state party[39] or, if the state against which the complaint is made has accepted the right of individual petition, by an individual.[40] All applications are made first to the Commission. They must normally be made after all effective domestic remedies have been exhausted and within six months from the date when the final decision was taken.[41] They are investigated by the Commission, which may seek to secure a friendly settlement.[42] If a solution is not reached the

---

[35] See F. G. Jacobs, *The European Convention on Human Rights* (1975); R. Beddard, *Human Rights in Europe* (2nd ed., 1980); J. E. S. Fawcett, *The Application of the European Convention on Human Rights* (2nd ed., 1987).

[36] The United Kingdom was the first state to ratify the Convention in 1951. In addition, in 1989 the Convention was ratified by San Marino and signed by Finland.

[37] Economic, social and cultural rights are protected under the European Social Charter 1961: see D. J. Harris, *The European Social Charter* (1984); A. Ph. C. M. Jaspers and L. Betten (eds.), *25 years: European Social Charter* (1988).

[38] In force 1954; all member states except Spain, Switzerland, Finland and Liechtenstein are parties to the protocol. Fifteen states, not including the U.K., are parties to the Fourth Protocol.

[39] Art. 24. Few such applications have been made. One example is *Ireland* v. *United Kingdom*. Eur. Court H.R. No. 25 Series A, Judgment of January 18, 1978.

[40] Art. 25. On May 5, 1989, 22 states had made the necessary declarations: Council of Europe, Human Rights Information Sheet Nos. 24 and 25. The U.K. first made a declaration on January 14, 1966, and this was renewed for five years from January 14, 1981, and from January 14, 1986.

[41] Art. 26. There are other grounds on which an application may be considered inadmissible: Art. 27.

[42] Art. 28.

Commission draws up a Report on the facts, and also states in the Report its opinion[43] as to whether a breach of the Convention has been established. The Report is sent to the Committee of Ministers of the Council of Europe and the states concerned. If the question is not referred to the Court within three months, the matter is dealt with by the Committee.

A matter may only be referred to the Court if the state against which the complaint is made has accepted the compulsory jurisdiction of the Court,[44] or otherwise consents and may only be referred by (1) the Commission; (2) a state party to the Convention whose national is alleged to be a victim; (3) a state party which referred the case to the Commission; and (4) a state party against which the complaint has been lodged.[45] The individual concerned has no right to insist on a reference to the Court.[46]

Each case is heard either by a Chamber of the Court composed of seven judges,[47] or by the full or "plenary" Court.[48]

As from January 1, 1983, an individual applicant may be represented by an advocate authorised to practise in any of the party states or any other person approved by the President of the Court, or may be given leave to present his or her own case.[49]

Legal aid may be awarded in respect of proceedings before the Commission and the Court. The official languages are English and French.[50] There is provision for the submission of written documents and an oral hearing.[51] The Court deliberates and votes on its decision in private. A judgment of the Court is prepared: each judge is entitled to annex a separate opinion, whether concurring or dissenting, or a bare statement of dissent.[52] In most cases a declaratory judgment is given. If the Court finds that a decision or measure taken by an authority of a state party is in conflict with the obligations imposed by the Convention, it must "if necessary afford just satisfaction to the injured party."[53] In a number of cases monetary compensation has been awarded as "just satisfaction" covering costs and expenses, pecuniary losses and non-pecuniary loss.

As of April 1988, the Court has determined 27 cases[54] involving the United Kingdom. In 20 the Court found there to be violations of one or more

---

[43] This may be reached by a majority: Art. 34.

[44] Art. 46. On October 31, 1987 all Members except Turkey had done so.

[45] Art. 48.

[46] By January 1, 1989, 590 applications had been declared admissible, 160 cases had been referred to the Court and 78 had been decided by the Council of Ministers: Stocktaking on the European Convention on Human Rights, Supplement 1988. See generally, V. Berger, *Case Law of the European Court of Human Rights, Vol. 1 1960–1987* (1989).

[47] Art. 43. The seven must include the President or Vice-President, and the judge who is a national of any state party concerned. If the national judge is unable to sit or withdraws, the relevant state may appoint another member of the court or an ad hoc judge.

[48] See the Revised Rules of Court (adopted on November 24, 1982): Cour. (82) 107 of December 2, 1982, r. 50.

[49] *Ibid.* r. 30: see P. J. Duffy, [1983] P.L. 32–33. Previously, the applicant technically had no independent right to appear although in practice his or her lawyer was permitted to address the Court as part of the Commission's case.

[50] Revised Rules of Court, r. 27. Another language may be used at the oral stage, with the leave of the President.

[51] Revised Rules of Court, rr. 37, 39, 41–46.

[52] *Ibid.* r. 52.

[53] Art. 50.

[54] Excluding separate applications under Art. 50 where the merits have already been determined.

articles. Either as a consequence, or in anticipation of these findings,[55] English law has been changed in a number of significant respects.[56] For example, the law of contempt of court was amended following the *Sunday Times* case[57]; the law relating to the correspondence of persons in prisons has been radically altered[58]; the law in Northern Ireland concerning homosexual acts has been brought into line with the rest of the United Kingdom[59]; Isle of Man courts have been advised that birching is contrary to the European Convention[60]; and phonetapping has been regulated by statute.[61] The Convention has also had some influence in statutory interpretation,[62] although judges have emphasised on a number of occasions that it is not part of English law.[63]

---

[55] There are also some changes that can be traced to friendly settlements or Commission decisions.

[56] See P. J. Duffy, (1980) 29 I.C.L.Q. 585–618; A. Drzemczewski, *European Human Rights Convention in Domestic Law* (1983), pp. 314–322; M. P. Furmston, *et al.*, (eds.), *The Effect on English Domestic Law of Membership of the European Communities and of Ratifications of the European Convention on Human Rights* (1983); F. J. Hampson, "The United Kingdom Before the European Court of Human Rights" (1989) 9 Y.E.L. 121.

[57] See *Sunday Times Case*, Series A No. 30, Judgment of April 26, 1979: violation of Art. 10; Contempt of Court Act 1981; S.H. Bailey, (1982) 45 M.L.R. 301. It is not certain that the Act went far enough.

[58] See the *Golder Case*, Series A No. 18, Judgment of February 21, 1975; *Case of Silver and Others*: Series A No. 61, Judgment of March 25, 1983: violations of Arts. 6 §1 and 3; *Case of Campbell and Fell*, Series A No. 80, Judgment of June 28, 1984; *Case of Boyle and Rice*, Series A No. 131, Judgment of April 27, 1988; S. H. Bailey, D. J. Harris and B. Jones, *Civil Liberties: Cases and Materials* (2nd ed., 1985), pp. 535–551; G. J. Zellick, [1981] P.L. 435–438, [1983] P.L. 167–169.

[59] *Dudgeon Case*, Series A No. 45 Judgment of October 22, 1981: violation of Art. 8; Homosexual Offences (Northern Ireland) Order 1982.

[60] *Tyrer Case*, Series A No. 26, Judgment of April 25, 1978; G. J. Zellick, [1982] P.L. 4–5. The United Kingdom does not now accept the rights of individual petition in respect of the Isle of Man.

[61] *Malone Case*, Series A No. 82, Judgment of August 2, 1984; Bailey, Harris and Jones (1985), pp. 381–392; Interception of Communications Act 1985 (see annotations in *Current Law Statutes 1985* by D. Foulkes). The Convention has also influenced the law affecting mental patients, children in secure accommodation, immigration, and the right of parents to forbid the imposition by a school of corporal punishment on their children.

[62] See below, p. 349; A. Drzemczewski, *European Human Rights Convention in Domestic Law* (1983), pp. 166–187.

[63] *Ibid.* pp. 314–322. See, *e.g. Malone* v. *Metropolitan Police Commissioner* [1979] Ch. 344; *Att.-Gen.* v. *B.B.C.* [1981] A.C. 303 (Lord Scarman); *R.* v. *Secretary of State for the Home Department, ex p. Brind* [1991] 2 W.L.R. 702.

CHAPTER 3

LAWYERS

A. INTRODUCTION: THE "LEGAL PROFESSION"

THE title "lawyer" is reserved for those who have achieved the special status of membership of the "legal profession."[1] It is not a straightforward job description: many non-lawyers perform legal tasks, some of them full-time. For example, accountants may specialise in revenue law, trade union officials may appear regularly before industrial tribunals on behalf of their members,[2] and solicitors may delegate work to legal executives.[3] Conversely, many of the tasks performed by lawyers are not strictly "legal."[4] Membership of the legal profession in England and Wales involves qualification as either a solicitor or a barrister; it is usual to speak of two branches of the profession although historically it would be more accurate to refer to two professions.[5]

It is significant that lawyers are accepted to be members of a "profession." Much has been written about the supposedly distinctive attributes of professions, and how and why occupational groups seek professional status.[6] Medicine and law have been regarded as classic models, although important differences between them have been perceived.[7] The self-conception of the legal profession was articulated by the Law Society in evidence to the Monopolies Commission in 1968[8]:

> "When a profession is fully developed it may be described as a body of men and women (a) identifiable by reference to some register or

---

[1] "Barrack-room" lawyers don't count. Law lecturers commonly refer to themselves as "academic lawyers" even if they are not qualified. See M. Partington, Academic lawyers and "legal practice" in Britain: a preliminary reappraisal (1988) 15 J.L.S. 374.

[2] See below, p. 737.

[3] See below, p. 175.

[4] See below, p. 115.

[5] M. Birks, *Gentlemen of the Law* (1960), p. 3. See further, below pp. 107–113.

[6] See T. J. Johnson, *Professions and Power* (1972), pp. 21–38. For an argument that the concept of "profession . . . obscures more than it reveals about the work people do" see M. Cain, (1979) 7 *International Journal of the Sociology of Law* 331. See generally R. Dingwall and P. Lewis (eds.), *The Sociology of the Professions* (1983), in which Cain's paper is reprinted. See also R. Dingwall and P. Fenn, "A respectable profession?" (1987) 7 Int. Rev. Law and Econ. 51; R. L. Abel, *The Legal Profession in England and Wales* (1988), Chap. 1 "Theories of the professions," and note the extensive bibliography.

[7] D. Rueschemeyer, "Lawyers and Doctors: a Comparison of Two Professions" in V. Aubert (ed.) *Sociology of Law* (1969), pp. 267–277, abridged from (1964) 1 *Canadian Review of Sociology and Anthropology*, 17–30.

[8] Quoted in the Report of the Royal Commission on Legal Services (Cmnd. 7648, 1969) Vol. 1, p. 30.

record; (b) recognised as having a special skill and learning in some field of activity in which the public needs protection against incompetence, the standards of skill and learning being prescribed by the profession itself; (c) hold themselves out as being willing to serve the public; (d) voluntarily submitting themselves to standards of ethical conduct beyond those required of the ordinary citizen by law; (e) undertaking to accept personal responsibility to those whom they serve for their actions and to their profession for maintaining public confidence."

This approach was accepted uncritically by the Royal Commission on Legal Services.[9] They emphasised five main features of a profession: (a) central organisation: a governing body with powers of control and discipline; (b) the primary function of giving advice or service in a specialised field of knowledge; (c) the restriction of admission to those with the required standard of education and training; (d) a measure of self-regulation by the profession; and (e) the paramountcy of the duty owed to the client, subject only to responsibility to the court. A rule of conduct or restriction on practice should "stand or fall on its capacity to protect the interests of, or to enhance the level of service to the public." Thus, in theory at least, "altruistic service" is offered subject to self-regulation, in return for considerable autonomy from external control.[10] The Royal Commission, having noted that these features existed, found that they promoted the public interest, subject to points of detail, and proposed no fundamental changes. There was no exploration of other features that have been associated with the "rise of professionalism." For example, Larson has described professionalisation as:

> "the process by which producers of special services sought to constitute *and control* a market for their expertise . . . a collective assertion of special social status (and) a collective process of upward social mobility."[11]

Arguments for maintaining standards tend to coincide with arguments for monopolies, restrictions on practice and high rewards.[12] There was also no proper analysis of the ways in which professionalism may impede the expansion of legal services.[13] Thus, problems may be defined in the professional's terms and alternative definitions regarded as irrelevant; outsiders, whether lay people or members of other disciplines, may be ignored on the grounds that they are not competent either to assist or to criticise; "specialised knowledge" may be guarded by such means as "the creation of special forms of jargonised discourse and the fostering of an air of impenetrable mystery"[14]; the emphasis on the individual lawyer-client relationship may inhibit

---

[9] R.C.L.S., Vol. 1, pp. 28, 30. Johnson has mentioned the error made by many sociologists in accepting the professions' own definitions of themselves: Johnson (1972), p. 25. The Commission did not discuss the literature on the sociology of the professions.

[10] Johnson sees professionalism as a form of occupational control rather than an expression of the inherent nature of particular occupations: Johnson (1972), p. 45.

[11] M. S. Larson, *The Rise of Professionalism* (1977), p. xvi.

[12] See below, pp. 125–140.

[13] R. Cotterell, "Legal Services and Professional Ideology" (1980) (Paper presented at the Conference on Legal Services in the Eighties, University College, Cardiff). P. Fennell, "Solicitors, their markets and their 'ignorant public': the crisis of the professional ideal" in Z. Bankowski and G. Mungham (eds.), *Essays in Law and Society* (1980), p. 1.

[14] Cotterell, *op. cit.*, p. 10.

the development of group representation and test-case strategies[15]; the proper advertisement of legal services may be prevented.

Many of these problematic features of professionalism have come under attack in recent years. The general preference of the Royal Commission to endorse the *status quo* has not prevailed. What he terms "the decline of professionalism" has been charted by Prof. R. L. Abel, who has written extensively on the English legal profession, applying in particular Weberian theories developed by writers such as Larson.[16] We return to his work at the end of the chapter.[17]

In the following sections, we deal briefly with the historical development of the legal profession, showing how it progressively acquired the indicia of professionalism and control over the market for legal services, and then with the main features of the profession today.

B. FROM "OCCUPATION" TO "PROFESSION"

1. MEDIEVAL LAWYERS

In medieval times, legal life in London outside the courts was centred on the four inns of court (Lincoln's Inn, Gray's Inn, the Inner Temple and the Middle Temple) and the nine or so inns of chancery. Together they constituted a "great legal university situated in the western suburbs of London."[18] Membership of an inn was the clearest indicator of professional status, but not a sufficient one as most of the members attended only for general social and educational purposes and took no part in the legal learning exercises. Each inn had a chapel and a library, and a hall which was used both for meals and for moots, readings and debates. A moot was a form of mock trial consisting of the submission of legal argument relating to a given set of facts. The hypothetical pleadings were recited by "inner barristers" and the arguments conducted by "utter barristers," so called because they spoke from outside the bar of the inn. The moots were judged by senior members of the inn: the "benchers." The inns of chancery were lower in status than the inns of court; a man might spend a couple of years in an inn of chancery before moving to an inn of court, or he might remain a member of an inn of chancery all his life.

Baker[19] has distinguished six classes of common lawyer in late medieval times. Of the legal practitioners other than judges and court clerks, the most senior were the *serjeants-at-law*. The serjeants were appointed by the judges of the Court of Common Pleas, the main common-law court in London. They had the exclusive right of audience in that court, and the exclusive right to be appointed judges of the Common Pleas and King's Bench. On appointment, a serjeant would move from his inn of court to one of the two

[15] See below, pp. 422–423.
[16] R. L. Abel, "The decline of professionalism?" (1986) 49 M.L.R.1, *The Legal Profession in England and Wales* (1988), and "Between market and state: the legal profession in turmoil" (1989) 52 M.L.R. 285; R. L. Abel and P. S. C. Lewis (eds.), *Lawyers in Society: The Common Law World* (1988).
[17] Below, pp. 177–179.
[18] J. H. Baker, "The English Legal Profession, 1450–1550" in W. Prest, *Lawyers in Early Modern Europe and America* (1981), p. 17.
[19] *Ibid.* See also J. H. Baker, *Introduction to Legal History* (3rd ed., 1990), Chap. 10; Birks (1960); H. Kirk, *Portrait of a Profession* (1976), Chap. 1.

serjeant's inns, joining his fellow serjeants and the judges. *Apprentices-at-law* were, notwithstanding the name, "fully-fledged advocates below the degree of serjeant,"[20] who appeared in the King's Bench and other courts. They were senior members of the inns of court. The *utter barristers* did not at this stage appear as advocates in the superior courts. The largest group were the *attorneys*. Litigants were originally required to act personally in the course of litigation, meeting their adversaries face to face. This rule was progressively relaxed.[21] A litigant could then appoint an attorney to act in his name for specific or general purposes. He could appoint a friend, a relation or a stranger as he wished; court clerks and sheriff's officers were often selected. The appointments were supervised by the judges, and the names of the attorneys entitled to practise in a particular court would be endorsed in that court's records. By the fifteenth century a number of people earned a living as "common attorneys" prepared to act for any client wishing to employ them. Most were members of inns of chancery; the more affluent and those intending to become barristers joined one of the inns of court. Attorneys also came to be permitted in local courts, although they would not necessarily be members of an inn.[22] They took formal steps in litigation, which bound their clients, and "also acted as general practitioners, retaining counsel and giving it."[23] *Solicitors* performed a variety of miscellaneous clerical tasks for employers such as land owners and attorneys. Their name was derived from their function of "soliciting" or prosecuting actions in courts of which they were not officers or attorneys. Thus the nomenclature of early common lawyers was confusing. Some titles indicated a public position or status (*e.g.* serjeants); others a position within one of the inns, which might not be of significance outside (*e.g.* utter barrister, bencher); yet others were descriptive of a type of legal work (*e.g.* attorney, solicitor). Strict lines of demarcation were few. For example, serjeants, apprentices and attorneys might all give legal advice and an apprentice or utter barrister might act as an attorney.

A separate set of lawyers practised in the ecclesiastical courts, the Admiralty and the Court of Chivalry. The *doctors of law* acted as advocates; the *proctors* as attorneys.[24] Other quasi-legal functionaries included *scriveners*, who drew up legal and other documents and enjoyed a monopoly over the drawing of deeds in London and York, and *notaries*, who authenticated documents to be used abroad.[25]

2. SPECIALISATION AND DEMARCATION

A dramatic increase of legal business in the late sixteenth and early seventeenth centuries was accompanied by a rise in the number of barristers and attorneys in the common law courts and a reduction in the number of attorneys attached to local courts.[26] Much more work came to be available in

[20] Baker (1981), p. 27.
[21] Birks (1960), Chap. 1; Kirk (1976), pp. 1–4.
[22] C. W. Brooks, "The Common Lawyers in England, c.1558–1642" in Prest (1981), pp. 46–50.
[23] Baker (1981), p. 24.
[24] Baker (1990), pp. 193–194; G. D. Squibb, *Doctors' Commons* (1977); B. P. Levack, "The English Civilians, 1500–1750" in Prest (1981), p. 108.
[25] Birks (1960), Chap. 4; Baker (1981), p. 27.
[26] Brooks (1981), pp. 51–54 and *Pettyfoggers and Vipers of the Commonwealth: The 'Lower Branch' of the Legal Profession in Early Modern England* (1986); W. R. Prest, *The Rise of the Barristers: A Social History of the English Bar 1590–1640* (1986).

the King's Bench and this came to be done by utter barristers as well as apprentices. The slow decline of the order of serjeants which set in was closely related to the decline in the importance of the Common Pleas compared to the other superior courts, and to the fact that holders of the new office of "King's Counsel" which became established in the seventeenth century took precedence. By 1600, practice at the Bar was limited by royal proclamation and judicial decision to utter barristers of the inns of court and their seniors.[27] Barristers concentrated more on advocacy and less on counselling. At the same time, the judges began to object to men acting as "solicitors." Intermeddling in another person's law suit constituted "maintenance," which was both a crime and a tort.[28] Serjeants and barristers obviously had a good defence, as did an attorney acting in his own court. A servant could act as solicitor for his master. However, "common solicitors" prepared to act for any client were regarded by many judges as "maintainers." They were described by Lord Keeper Egerton as "caterpillars of the common weal" and by one Hudson as:

"a new sort of people . . . who, like grasshoppers of Egypt, devour the whole land . . . ; these are the retainers of causes, and devourers of men's estates by contention, and prolonging suits to make them without end."[29]

Some judges thought that solicitors' work should be done by young barristers rather than "ignorant and vagrant" solicitors. Nevertheless, the attempt to abolish solicitors failed. A statute of 1605[30] instead subjected both attorneys and solicitors to a measure of control to prevent overcharging and to cut their numbers; only "skilful" and "honest" men were to be allowed to practise. Solicitors became particularly associated with the Court of Chancery where there was a rule that only court clerks could be appointed as attorneys; there was, however, too much work for the clerks to handle.

At the same time, the judges and benchers began the process of excluding attorneys from the inns of court and prohibiting such persons from being called to the bar while in practice, thereby asserting the bar's intellectual and social superiority.[31] The Judges' Order of 1614 described attorneys and solicitors as "but ministerial persons *and* of an inferior nature. . . ." In the seventeenth century, the superior status of barristers was further consolidated by their growing unwillingness to accept instructions directly from a lay client without the intervention of an attorney or solicitor,[32] by rules which prohibited social contact between barristers and solicitors, and by the development of the presumption that fees paid to barristers were *honoraria* which if unpaid could not be recovered by an action.[33] In the long term, attorneys and solicitors benefited financially from the Bar's pursuit of a separate elite status and continued reluctance to perform "mechanic" legal

[27] See J.H. Baker, "Solicitors and the Law of Maintenance 1590–1640" [1973] C.L.J. 56, 59–66.
[28] *Ibid.* pp. 66–80.
[29] *Ibid.* pp. 72, 73–4.
[30] 3 Jac. 1, c.7.
[31] J. H. Baker, "Counsellors and Barristers" [1969] C.L.J. 205, 222–224; H.H.L. Bellot, "The Exclusion of Attorneys from the Inns of Court" (1910) 26 L.Q.R. 137.
[32] This was a clear rule of etiquette by the second half of the eighteenth century: it was not, however, a rule of law: *Doe d. Bennett* v. *Hale* (1850) 15 Q.B. 171.
[33] Baker [1969] C.L.J. at pp. 222–229. Fees were then usually paid in advance and so the *honorarium* concept reinforced the barrister's status without seriously affecting his pocket.

work even when it fell on harder times. Moreover, barristers came to be dependent upon the patronage of attorneys and solicitors.

By the eighteenth century[34] the judges and the government had ceased to attempt to exercise any control over the Bar. The government of the inns of court had long since passed from the membership as a whole into the hands of the benchers.[35] The inns' educational functions disappeared; the only requirements for call to the Bar were enrolment as a student for a number of years and the eating of dinners for twelve terms in one of the inns. The lines of demarcation between barristers and solicitors were strengthened during the century. Common practice became firm rules of etiquette. The expulsion of attorneys from the inns was completed.[36]

3. THE RISE OF THE SOLICITORS' PROFESSION

The eighteenth century saw the establishment of a professional organisation for attorneys and solicitors,[37] the development of statutory controls and subsequently the expansion of work associated with the Industrial Revolution. The inns of chancery were dominated by the attorneys and their links with the bar were severed. However, the inns did not develop as a professional organisation as they had no control over admission to practice or discipline. Attorneys were still admitted to the rolls by the judges,[38] and, albeit only in serious cases of a misbehaviour, struck off by them.[39] Solicitors were not subject to any formal control until the 1728 Act "for the better regulation of Attornies and Solicitors."[40] A roll of solicitors was then established in the Court of Chancery.[41] An applicant for admission as an attorney or solicitor had to have been articled to a practitioner and the judges had to be satisfied of his fitness. This Act established the mechanisms of control but the judges did not examine applicants for admission and some of its provisions were easily evaded.

In the early 1730s some London lawyers formed the Society of Gentlemen Practisers in the Courts of Law and Equity, for the purpose of "supporting the honour and independence of the profession, promoting fair and liberal practice, and preventing unnecessary expense and delay to suitors.[42] It did not claim to be representative of the profession, or even of London practitioners, but it did attempt, with limited success, to ensure compliance with the legislation and to promote the profession's interests. In 1831[43] a new society received its Royal Charter: "The Society of Attorneys Solicitors Proctors and others not being barristers practising in the Courts of Law and Equity in the United Kingdom." Its original object had been the estab-

---

[34] See D. Duman, "The English Bar in the Georgian Era" in Prest (1981), pp. 86–107.
[35] A. W. B. Simpson, "The Early Constitution of the Inns of Court" [1970] C.L.J. 241; "The Early Constitution of Gray's Inn" [1975] C.L.J. 131.
[36] Duman (1981), pp. 100–104.
[37] Kirk (1976), Chap. 2.
[38] By the late eighteenth century this was a formality: Birks (1960), pp. 171–172.
[39] An attorney struck off was physically pitched over the bar, presumably not by the judges personally.
[40] 2 Geo. 2, c.23. The Act was renewed in 1739 and 1749, made perpetual in 1757, and amended on these and other occasions.
[41] "Accordingly they became entitled to call themselves 'gentlemen'. This is the origin of the jibe that solicitors are gentlemen by Act of Parliament": Birks (1960), p. 136.
[42] Kirk (1976), Chap. 2.
[43] Its inaugural meeting was in 1825.

lishment of a central "Law Institution" where lawyers could meet. The idea was popular, and a Hall was erected in Chancery Lane. The society's objects widened. It never actually amalgamated with the Society of Gentlemen Practisers but began to undertake disciplinary proceedings in the courts against attorneys and solicitors and to lobby on behalf of the profession's interests. In 1833 it decided to use the name "The Incorporated Law Society of the United Kingdom."[44] The Solicitors Act 1843 provided that it was to be the Registrar of Attorneys and Solicitors.

Another nineteenth century preoccupation of attorneys and solicitors[45] was the improvement of their status in society. Improvements in the general educational standards of entrants and in their subsequent legal education were regarded as prerequisites.[46] In 1836 the common law judges were persuaded to revive a rule of 1654 enabling them to appoint persons to examine those wishing to be admitted as attorneys. The examiners nominated included 12 members of the Council of The Incorporated Law Society. Similar steps were taken by the Court of Chancery and examinations were duly held.[47] Nevertheless, a Select Committee of the House of Commons reported in 1846 that the state of legal education was still extremely unsatisfactory.[48] For solicitors and attorneys they recommended the introduction of a preliminary examination to ensure a sound general education, the provision of lectures for articled clerks, higher standards in the final examination, and, eventually, a college of law. These recommendations were progressively adopted. In 1860, a preliminary and an intermediate examination were introduced, the latter intended to be taken midway through articles. In 1877 The Incorporated Law Society acquired control of the education and qualifying arrangements for admission. Tuition by private coaches such as Messrs. Gibson and Weldon proved more attractive than Law Society lectures, although the Society did establish a law school in 1903.[49] Failure rates in the final examination increased, particularly at times when there was concern that there were too many solicitors.[50]

University legal education also developed from slender origins in the second half of the century.[51] Graduates were exempted from the preliminary examination in 1877 and law graduates from the intermediate as late as 1922. It has indeed been a notable feature of legal education in this country that the universities and polytechnics have played a much more minor role in the education of intending practitioners than in other systems, including, for example, those in Scotland and the United States. The profession has fought hard to retain ultimate control.[52]

---

[44] By a charter of 1903 it became "The Law Society."
[45] By now solicitors were regarded as more respectable than attorneys. Most practitioners were qualified as both. The offices of attorney and proctor were abolished in 1875 as one of the consequences of the reorganisation of the superior courts. See above, p. 32.
[46] See Kirk (1976), Chap. 3.
[47] Birks (1960), pp. 176–180. All the entrants passed the first attorneys' examination.
[48] *Report from the Select Committee on Legal Education*, August 25, 1846, H.C. 686.
[49] The Society's school and Gibson and Weldon's were amalgamated to form the College of Law in 1961, perhaps on the "if you can't beat 'em join 'em" principle.
[50] *Cf.* S. Hughes, *Legal Action*, July 1984, p. 10.
[51] *Report of the Committee on Legal Education* (1971, Cmnd. 4595), pp. 5–9; J. H. Baker, "University College and Legal Education 1826–1976" (1977) 30 C.L.P.1. Until the eighteenth century the universities taught only Roman-based Civil law.
[52] See further, pp. 171–175 below.

Parliament confirmed the authority of the Law Society in 1888 and 1919 when disciplinary functions in respect of all solicitors, including those not members of the Society, were transferred from the courts to a disciplinary committee appointed by the Master of the Rolls from past and present members of the Council of the Law Society.[53] According to Abel-Smith and Stevens:

> "it is almost certain that it was in the fifty years after 1860 that the solicitors' branch of the profession built its financial prosperity and social respectability."[54]

The nineteenth century development of an active professional organisation with educational and disciplinary responsibilities was no doubt associated with this transformation. Two factors of particular significance were the right of solicitors to appear as advocates in the new county courts created in 1846 and an increase in income from conveyancing following the introduction of scale fees in 1883.[55]

In the twentieth century, further steps were taken to deal with dishonest solicitors, and those who indulged in the supposedly objectionable practices of touting and of undercutting on conveyancing. The Solicitors Act 1933 enabled the Council of the Law Society to make rules about the keeping of clients' accounts and for regulating any other matter of professional practice. Solicitors' Account Rules came into effect in 1935, and Practice Rules in 1936. The Solicitors Act 1941 established a compensation fund to which all practising solicitors had to contribute, and required that solicitors' accounts be audited each year. Solicitors also lost their struggle to resist the entry of women to the profession.[56]

4. THE BAR IN THE NINETEENTH AND TWENTIETH CENTURIES

The main concerns of the Bar in the mid-nineteenth century were the problems created by a lack of work[57] and the improvement of legal education in response to sustained public criticism.[58] The 1846 Select Committee reported that the inns of court provided no legal education worthy of the name, and recommended the introduction of lectures and examinations and the establishment of a college of law. A Council of Legal Education was set up by the inns in 1852. Lectures were organised, but not compulsory examinations. A Royal Commission recommended in 1855 that there should be an entrance examination for non-graduates, compulsory lectures and pupillage and a final examination before call to the bar.[59] These proposals were

---

[53] Solicitors Acts 1888 and 1919. Between these dates the committee could investigate and dismiss complaints but only the High Court could punish offenders.

[54] *Lawyers and the Courts* (1967), p. 187.

[55] A. Offer, *Property and Politics 1870–1914* (1981), pp. 39–40. Part I of this work considers the relationship of solicitors to the land market and to land law reform.

[56] Sex Disqualification (Removal) Act 1919. In *Bebb* v. *Law Society* [1914] 1 Ch. 286 the Court of Appeal had held that women were not "persons" within the meaning of the Solicitors Act 1843, one of many similar cases in various fields: A. Sachs and J. H. Wilson, *Sexism and the Law* (1978), Chap. 1.

[57] Abel-Smith and Stevens (1967), pp. 53–57.

[58] *Ibid.* pp. 63–74; A. H. Manchester, *Modern Legal History* (1980), pp. 54–63. See generally, on the bar in the nineteenth century, D. Duman, *The English and Colonial Bars in the Nineteenth Century* (1983) and R. Cocks, *Foundations of the Modern Bar* (1983).

[59] *Report of the Commissioners appointed to inquire into arrangements in the Inns of Court and Inns of Chancery for promoting the study of Law and Jurisprudence*, 1855.

vetoed by Lincoln's Inn and Gray's Inn. Attempts in the second half of the nineteenth century to establish a "Law University" based on the inns were also successfully resisted, at the "cost" of the introduction of compulsory examinations in 1872.

Further problems were caused by the need of the Bar to adjust to the reforms introduced by the Supreme Court of Judicature Acts 1873–75. A Bar Committee was formed in 1883 to protest against new Rules of the Supreme Court which were thought likely to deprive younger barristers of work. It was felt that the benchers, who were mostly judges[60] and Q.C.s, could not adequately protect the interests of barristers. The Committee, and its replacement, the Bar Council, began to make representations on other matters and to make rulings on matters of etiquette.[61] Disciplinary powers remained with the inns, subject to an appeal to the judges.[62]

Significant improvements in the education and training of barristers did not take place until the 1960s when the Inns of Court School of Law was established with a full-time Dean, new premises, remodelled syllabuses and improved teaching. Pupillage became compulsory. Further structural changes did not take place until 1966 when a "Senate of the Four Inns of Court" was established. In 1974 this was replaced by the "Senate of the Inns of Court and the Bar." This was in theory the governing body of the barristers' branch of the profession although the inns retained significant financial autonomy, and the Bar Council also retained its separate identity.[63]

Much more momentous was the decision by the Bar in 1986 to take control into its own hands. A committee chaired by Lord Rawlinson recommended the replacement of the (unrepresentative) Senate by the General Council of the Bar of England and Wales, which would be strengthened and made more representative of the Bar, and on which the judges would not be represented.[64] This received overwhelming support and the new constitution took effect on January 1, 1987.

C. THE LEGAL PROFESSION TODAY

1. ORGANISATION

The governing body of the Bar is now the General Council of the Bar of England and Wales.[65]

---

[60] After the abolition of the order of serjeants in 1875 and the closure of Serjeants' Inn, the judges remained as benchers of the inns of court and began to take part in their management.

[61] The Judicature Act reforms, in conjunction with the development of the railways, significantly weakened the role of circuit messes (clubs formed by barristers travelling on circuit) as mechanisms for influencing or controlling the conduct of barristers: see Cocks (1983) and Duman (1983), Chap. 2.

[62] Abel-Smith and Stevens (1967), pp. 214–220.

[63] The Royal Commission recommended that the Senate should assume the central responsibility for all matters affecting barristers: R.C.L.S., Vol. 1, pp. 425–443.

[64] See P. Walker, Counsel, Easter Term 1986, pp. 36–37.

[65] It has 97 members: 3 officers; 13 ex-officio (the Attorney-General, the Solicitor-General, leaders of the 6 circuits, chairmen of 5 specialist associations); 12 representatives of the Inns; 12 circuit representatives; 5 association representatives; 39 practising barristers; 12 employed and non-practising barristers; 4 co-opted: (1986) 83 L.S.Gaz. 3828.

"It fulfils the function of what might be called a 'trade union,' pursuing the interests of the Bar and expanding the market for the Bar's services and is also a watchdog regulating its practices and activities."[66]

It co-operates with the Inns of Court through the Council of the Inns of Court, which comprises representatives of the four Inns, the Bar Council and the Council of Legal Education. The independence of the Inns has been reduced under the new arrangements; where the Council of the Inns and the Bar Council disagree, the latter's policy is to be implemented provided that it has the support of two-thirds of the profession.

The powers and duties of the Law Society are derived from the Solicitors Act 1974. Membership of the Society is not compulsory, although it is the governing body for the profession as a whole. Thus the Master of the Rolls may only admit as a solicitor a person certified by the Society to have complied with its training regulations and to be suitable for admission.[67] The Society also issues the "practising certificate" which each solicitor wishing to practise must obtain.[68] Many of its statutory functions relate to the maintenance of standards for the protection of the public. However, it is also the main professional association for solicitors. The inconsistency in these roles has led to concern that neither is performed satisfactorily. The Society was able to point to its success in defending solicitors' interests during the deliberations of the Royal Commission. There have, however, been a number of matters on which the Society has fallen out with sections of the rank-and-file[69] and its success in defending the solicitors' "conveyancing monopoly" proved short lived. The composition of the Council of the Law Society has long been criticised as unrepresentative, with very few members under 35, very few women, few from outside private practice and a disproportionate number from large firms.[70]

The Courts and Legal Services Act 1990 introduced a new statutory committee with responsibilities in the regulation of lawyers. This is the Lord Chancellor's Advisory Committee on Legal Education and Conduct and comprises a chairman and 16 other members appointed by the Lord Chancellor.[71] The chairman is to be a Lord of Appeal or judge of the Supreme Court[72]; of the members, one must be a judge who is or has been a Circuit judge; 2 practising barristers appointed after consultation with the General Council of the Bar; 2 practising solicitors appointed after consultation with the Law Society; 2 law teachers appointed after consultation with such institutions concerned with the teaching of law and such persons representing law teachers as the Lord Chancellor considers appropriate; and 9 lay

[66] General Council of the Bar, *A Career at the Bar* (1988), p. 7.
[67] Solicitors Act 1974, s.3.
[68] *Ibid.* ss.1, 9–18.
[69] *e.g.* education and training, the problems of sole practitioners, advertising, compulsory insurance: D. Podmore, "Bucher and Strauss Revisited—the Case of the Solicitors' Profession" (1980) 7 B.J.L.S. 1, 4–11.
[70] R. L. Abel, *The Legal Profession in England and Wales* (1988), pp. 242–245; see also below, p. 178.
[71] Courts and Legal Services Act 1990, s.19 and Sched. 1. It replaced the previous non-statutory Lord Chancellor's Advisory Committee on Legal Education.
[72] The first is Lord Griffiths.

members. The government was determined to ensure a lay majority.[73] The Committee is under a "general duty of assisting in the maintenance and development of standards in the education, training and conduct of those offering legal services,"[74] and has specific functions in relation to these matters, including giving advice to the General Council of the Bar, the Law Society and other authorised bodies on all aspects of their qualification regulations and rules of conduct, and on specialisation schemes.[75] It has a particular role in advising on the extension of rights of audience and rights to ·conduct litigation.[76] It is intended to be "operationally fully independent of Government," funded by a grant-in-aid from the Lord Chancellor's Department, and able to appoint its own staff, who will not be civil servants.[77] Given that members are appointed by the Lord Chancellor, and that the Committee is funded by his department, it is doubtful how far it will be truly independent.

2. LAWYERS AND THEIR WORK

(a) Introduction

In their study of the legal profession in the United States and England, Johnstone and Hopson identified nineteen different "work tasks" performed by lawyers in the United States: giving advice, both legal and non legal; negotiations; drafting letters and legal documents; litigation, including the preparation of cases and advocacy; investigation of facts; legal research and analysis; lobbying legislators and administrators; acting as broker; public relations; filing submissions to government and other organisations; adjudication; financing; property management; referral of clients to other sources of assistance; supervision of others; emotional support to clients; immoral and unpleasant tasks (taking care of disagreeable matters for clients which the clients could do themselves but prefer to have someone else do); acting as scapegoat; and getting business.[78] Any one lawyer might never perform all these tasks, and some, such as advising and negotiation, were generally more significant than others. The variety of combinations in which these tasks were performed by individual lawyers was "almost endless"[79] Laymen could be found performing any of them. English lawyers may be less likely than their American counterparts to act in some of these areas, but it is difficult to think of any of them that no English lawyer would touch. It has been noted that the expertise of many lawyers may be founded not so much on their mastery of legal technique as on their possession of "worldly knowledge" in "giving economic advice or providing organisational 'know-how' and in their interpersonal skills."[80]

---

[73] White Paper (Cm. 740, 1989), Chap. 7: "That balance aims to ensure that the Committee primarily represents the views and interests of the user of legal services, but contains wide representation from those who have experience of providing them" (*ibid.* p. 27). This has been described as a "needless affront to the legal profession": M. Zander (1989) 139 N.L.J. 300, 303.

[74] Court and Legal Services Act 1990, s.20.

[75] *Ibid.* Sched. 2.

[76] Below, pp. 132–133.

[77] White Paper, p. 27.

[78] Q. Johnstone and D. Hopson, *Lawyers and their Work* (1967), Chap. 3.

[79] *Ibid.* p. 77.

[80] Rueschemeyer, *op cit.*, p. 105, n. 7, at p. 271.

(b) Fusion[81]

The English pattern of work is complicated by the division of the legal profession into barristers and solicitors. It is not possible for anyone to be qualified in both branches at the same time. Traditionally, barristers have had an exclusive right of audience in the superior courts, and have not normally been instructed by a lay client direct without the intervention of a solicitor. There is not, however, any *kind* of work done by barristers which is not also done by solicitors. In the lower courts the advocacy work has been shared between the two branches; in tribunals it also has been shared with non-lawyers. Both barristers and solicitors do drafting work. Both may give legal advice, the solicitor direct to the client, the barrister only if he or she is approached for his oral or written opinion by a solicitor. This would be done where the solicitor lacks the time or resources to do the work personally, to satisfy a "difficult" client or simply because "counsel's opinion" is often regarded as especially authoritative.

The different emphases in the functions of solicitors and barristers have led to marked differences in their geographical distribution: solicitors' offices may be found throughout the country[82]; over 70 per cent. of barristers work from chambers in central London, where the superior courts sit, the rest being spread through over 30 provincial centres.[83] A further difference which affects the way that practices are organised is that each barrister must act on his or her own account, whereas solicitors may form partnerships.[84] Many solicitors' firms have several partners and a large employed staff, including fee-earners. Barristers are generally grouped in chambers, which provide administrative support, but a barrister may not share fees or employ fee-earners.

Over the years, there have been many advocates of fusion of the two branches. The profession was not always divided as it is today.[85] The legal professions of other countries are not normally divided. It was argued in submissions to the Royal Commission that the necessity of employing a solicitor as well as a barrister, where the latter's services are required, causes inefficiency (failures in communication, delay and the return of briefs by barristers who are doubled-booked), harms the confidence of clients (barristers being regarded by some clients as too remote or insufficiently prepared) and is more expensive for clients obliged to pay for two lawyers rather than one. Most of the professional bodies who gave evidence, including the Senate and the Law Society, opposed fusion. It was feared that fusion would lead to a serious fall in the quality of advocacy. The leading barristers might join the larger firms of solicitors and so be less accessible. Smaller practices might generate insufficient business to justify partnership with a barrister and find it increasingly difficult to brief a barrister of equal standing to the one retained by an opponent. The drift from smaller to larger firms might

---

[81] R.C.L.S., Vol. 1, pp. 187–202; G. Gardiner, "Two Lawyers or One" (1970) 23 C.L.P.1; M. Zander, *Lawyers and the Public Interest* (1968), pp. 271–332, (1976) 73 L.S.Gaz. 882, *Legal Services for the Community* (1978), pp. 170–174; F. A. Mann, "Fusion of the Legal Professions?" (1977) 93 L.Q.R. 367; P. Reeves, *Are Two Legal Professions Necessary?* (1986).

[82] See below, p. 122.

[83] See below, p. 140.

[84] See below, pp. 121–122.

[85] See above, pp. 146–147.

increase, with a corresponding reduction in the number of offices in smaller towns and rural areas. Smaller firms might be reluctant to refer a client to a large firm for fear of losing him permanently. A reduction in the number of specialist advocates might also contribute to the lowering of standards, and make it more difficult for the Lord Chancellor to make "suitable" appointments to the bench: the numbers for consideration would be increased but the candidates would not be as well known to the Lord Chancellor and his senior advisers.

Other arguments against fusion have centred on the English form of court procedure.[86] First, there is heavy reliance on the oral rather than written presentation of evidence and argument. Secondly, hearings are single and continuous, this being designed to make best use of judicial time at the cost of inconvenience to practitioners and clients. Barristers are more easily and more economically organised to meet such inconvenience than solicitors could be. Thirdly, there is the "principle of judicial unpreparedness." The judge relies upon the parties to present the case; he or she has no research or investigative staff, and limited time to do his or her own research. The requirement that the judges have confidence in the advocates appearing before them is particularly acute under such a system.[87]

It was not surprising that the Royal Commission unanimously recommended against fusion, notwithstanding the speculative nature of some of the arguments. They saw that the existing system had its advantages; fusion might lead to some saving, but only in small cases and in larger cases the expense might be greater. Employing two lawyers did not necessarily mean that work was duplicated. Some of the adverse criticisms of the present system could be met by other changes.

(c) The 1990 Reforms

As we shall see later in this chapter, as well as opposing fusion, the Royal Commission did not favour substantial changes to the various monopolies and restrictive practices enshrined in part in law and in part in professional rules. This position has not been maintained. In 1989, the government turned its attention to the legal profession, and indicated its determination to introduce significant reforms designed to open up the market for legal services. It was not its stated aim to secure fusion; the main theme was that of dismantling the various monopolies and restrictive practices operated by the two branches of the profession. The main targets were the restrictions preventing unqualified persons undertaking conveyancing, probate or litigation work for reward (especially the so-called "conveyancing monopoly" enjoyed by solicitors); the prohibition on solicitors entering multi-disciplinary partnerships; and the Bar's exclusive rights of audience in higher courts. How did this radical change come about?

In December 1983, a second reading was given to a Private Member's Bill, the House Buyer's Bill, sponsored by Austin Mitchell M.P., which proposed the introduction of a system whereby licensed conveyancers would be permitted to undertake the conveyancing of "houses" with registered title. In response, the government indicated its intention to promote legislation to

[86] See Mann, *op. cit.* n. 66.
[87] The advocate's "duty to the court" rests on rules of professional conduct: see below, pp. 150–161.

establish a system of licensed conveyancers and, moreover, to enable solicitors employed by building societies, banks and other organisations to undertake conveyancing for their employers' clients, whether or not the land was registered. This decision was reached by the cabinet over the objections of the then Lord Chancellor, Lord Hailsham, and was apparently motivated by a desire to see increased competition and lower charges.[88] In the event, a system of licensed conveyancers was established by Part II of the Administration of Justice Act 1985, but the government ultimately decided that banks and building societies should only be permitted to offer conveyancing services where they were not the lending institution. On the latter point it accepted the Law Society's argument that the provision of conveyancing services in conjunction with a mortgage loan would lead to an undesirable conflict of interest.[89]

Concern at the threat to conveyancing incomes led to the wholesale relaxation of the professional rules restricting advertising by solicitors, and the revival of arguments by the Law Society that the Bar's monopoly of rights of advocacy in the higher courts should be removed. The latter led to an acrimonious dispute between the two branches of the profession,[90] which was temporarily put into abeyance by the appointment by them of a Committee under the chairmanship of Lady Marre. The Marre Committee comprised (apart from the chairman), six barristers, six solicitors and six independent members, and was asked to report to the Bar Council and the Law Society on the extent to which the services offered by the legal profession met the needs and demands of the public for legal services; how the services of the profession could be made readily available to meet such needs and demands; and those areas where changes in the present education of the legal profession, and in the structure and practices of the profession, might be in the public interest. It reported in July 1988,[91] and, like the Royal Commission, tended to endorse the *status quo*. Its main recommendation affecting the structure of the profession was that solicitors recommended by a Rights of Audience Board and licensed by the Law Society should have extended rights of audience for all purposes in the Crown Court, and that professions other than solicitors should be permitted direct access to barristers.

Although there were moves to relax certain specific professional rules in each branch of the profession, the likelihood of fundamental changes seemed remote. The Marre Committee had not proposed anything that could be said to be radical. Lord Hailsham in particular was opposed to changes that might weaken the independent Bar. His immediate successor, Lord Havers, took a similar line during his brief period in office. However, the advent of Lord Mackay of Clashfern as Lord Chancellor, the first whose professional life had been at the Scottish and not the English Bar, made it easier for what may be termed a Thatcherite approach to reform to prevail.

---

[88] M. Zander, *A Matter of Justice* (Revised edn., 1989), pp. 9–10.
[89] *Ibid.* pp. 15–16. The Building Societies Act 1986, s.21 and Sched. 21 established a structure whereby banks, building societies and other financial institutions would be authorised to undertake conveyancing, subject to restrictions in regulations. These provisions were never brought into force and have been superseded by broader arrangements in the Courts and Legal Services Act 1990, below pp. 127–129.
[90] *Ibid.* pp. 24–31.
[91] *A Time for Change: Report of the Committee on the Future of the Legal Profession* (*Chairman: Lady Marre C.B.E.*) (General Council of the Bar, The Law Society, 1988).

On January 25, 1989, the Lord Chancellor published three Green Papers: *The Work and Organisation of the Legal Profession; Contingency Fees;* and *Conveyancing by Authorised Practitioners.*[92] The Papers were not founded on any form of research exercise, and took a line sharply different from those taken by the Royal Commission and the Marre Committee which, to an extent at least, had been based on research. Four months only were to be allowed for consultation. After consultation, the Lord Chancellor produced a White Paper, *Legal Services: A Framework for the Future,*[93] which took up proposals arising from the Civil Justice Review[93a], as well as the Green Papers. The tone of the White Paper differed from that in the Green Papers. The main Green Paper, on *The Work and Organisation of the Legal Profession,*[94] was prefaced by the statement that it was the government's overall objective "to see that the public has the best possible access to legal services and that those services are of the right quality for the particular needs of the client"; and that the government believed that this would be "best achieved by ensuring that:—

(a) a market providing legal services operates freely and efficiently so as to give clients the widest possible choice of cost effective services; and
(b) the public can be certain that those services are being supplied by people who have the necessary expertise to provide a service in the area in question."[95]

The resolve of the responsible section of the Lord Chancellor's Department had apparently been stiffened by the transfer of officials of the Department of Trade and Industry, and the result was a Green Paper "whose style and content paid little concession to the sensitivities of lawyers used to articulating, rightly or wrongly, their restrictive practices in terms of 'the interests of justice.' "[96] The White Paper was more moderate in tone, with more frequent reference to the need to secure the proper and efficient administration of justice.[97] There were some modifications in the content of the proposals to meet objections from professional bodies, but the fundamentals were for the most part little changed.[98]

The White Paper formed the basis of the Courts and Legal Services Act 1990, which was introduced in November 1989 and received Royal Assent a year later. The main features of Parts II to IV of the Act are

[92] Cm. 570, 571 and 572, 1989. See (1989) 139 N.L.J. 140–149; F. Cowper, *ibid.* p. 382; Responses, *ibid.* pp. 601–604; R. Smith, *ibid.* p. 897; (1989) 86 L.S.Gaz., February 1, pp. 2–7; M. Zander, *ibid.* March 1, pp. 14–15, 21; R. Abel, *ibid.* March 22, pp. 14, 18; I. R. Scott (1989) 8 C.J.Q. 202; B. Walsh (1989) P.N. 59.
[93] Cm. 740, 1989. See N. Stewart, (1989) 139 N.L.J. 1035; W. Merricks, *ibid.* p. 1036; I. R. Scott, (1990) 9 C.J.Q. 6; J. P. O'Brien, (1989) 133 S.J. 1046.
[93a] See above, p. 70.
[94] Cm. 570, 1989.
[95] *Ibid.* para. 1.1.
[96] R. Smith, "The Courts and Legal Services Bill: A View at Half-Time" (1990) 17 J.L.S. 242, 243.
[97] *e.g.* Cm. 740, para. 2.3, in respect of the need to maintain "the standards in the conduct of advocacy and ... litigation which are required in the interests of the proper and efficient administration of justice," and the intention to remove restrictions on practice "which are not necessary in the interests of justice."
[98] See generally R. Smith, *op. cit.*, and F. Cownie, "The reform of the legal profession or the end of civilization as we know it" in F. Patfield and R. White (eds.), *The Changing Law* (1990).

— the establishment, on a statutory basis, of the Lord Chancellor's Advisory Committee on Education and Conduct;
— the establishment of a Legal Services Ombudsman;
— the extension of rights of audience in all courts and rights to conduct litigation and undertake probate work to suitably qualified persons, whether or not barristers or solicitors;
— the removal of the restriction preventing banks and building societies offering conveyancing services to borrowers, subject to safeguards, including a Conveyancing Ombudsman Scheme.
— provision for new regulations and codes setting qualification standards and practice requirements for advocacy and the conduct of litigation, subject to the approval of the Lord Chancellor, assisted by his Advisory Committee;
— the ending of legal restrictions on multi-disciplinary and multi-national partnerships;
— changes to rule of eligibility for judicial appointments to reflect enjoyment of advocacy rights rather than status as a barrister or solicitor;
— the strengthening of the powers of the Law Society to deal with poor service by solicitors.

In addition, the professional bodies' rules and practices will be subject to review under the proposed restrictive practices legislation and, unless approved by the Lord Chancellor, open to prohibition.[99]

We consider these matters at the appropriate stages in the following sections.

(c) Solicitors' practices and their work

(i) *Numbers*

As at July 31, 1990, there were 54,736 solicitors with practising certificates; 46,652 were in private practice, on their own account (3,528) or as a partner (23,450), consultant (2,098) or assistant solicitor (13,365). The main categories outside private practice were local government (2,234), commerce or industry (2,177) and the Crown Prosecution Service (1,100).[1] The numbers have consistently increased, apart from periods of decline in the 1840s and between the wars, and have risen dramatically in the last twenty years.[2] The number per head of the population declined to the point that there was a period of acute shortage after the second world war; this trend was reversed in the late 1960s and 1970s. Thus in 1967 there were 22,233 solicitors (1 : 2164 of the population) and in 1977 32,812 (1 : 1497).[3] At one stage, fears were expressed that there were too many in and seeking entry to the solicitors' branch.[4] The number of law graduates doubled between 1967

[99] See the White Paper, *Opening Markets—New Policy on Restrictive Trade Practices* (Cm. 727, 1989).
[1] *Law Society Annual Statistical Report 1990*, pp. 8, 9.
[2] Podmore (1980), pp. 13–19; R. L. Abel, *The Legal Profession in England and Wales* (1988), 164–168, 406–413, Table 2.14: Changes in the size of the profession 1730–1985.
[3] *Ibid.*
[4] *e.g.* P. A. Leach, (1980) 77 L.S.Gaz. 29; J. Clarke (President of the Law Society), (1980) 77 L.S.Gaz. 981–982.

and 1977.[5] More recently, however, there has been a considerable increase in demand for recruits to the solicitors' profession, and by 1988, what has been seen as a recruitment crisis.[6] The position was easier by 1990, as the economy moved nearer recession.[7] Other trends in recent years have been a steady increase in the proportion of employed assistant solicitors in private practice, a decline in the proportion of sole practitioners,[8] and a slight increase in the proportion of solicitors outside private practice.

(ii) Solicitors firms: private practice

There are many kinds of solicitors' practice, ranging from large, highly specialised firms in the City of London to small provincial practices specialising in legal aid work.[9] At July 31, 1990, there were 10,272 private practice firms located in 15,551 separate offices.[10] According to the Law Society in 1978 the "typical firm" had three principals, five other fee earners (one assistant solicitor, two legal executives, one articled clerk, one junior clerk) ten other full time and three part-time staff (accounts clerks, an outdoor clerk, secretaries, a telephonist and a receptionist).[11] In 1989, 95 per cent. of firms had no more than ten principals[12] and 81 per cent. no more than four. 395 firms had eleven or more principals.[13] The overall ratio of partners to assistant solicitors was about 2 : 1; in the smallest firms it was 3 : 1 and in firms of 11 or more principals, about 1 : 1.[14] Large London firms employ a disproportionately large number of assistant solicitors.[15] There has been a distinct trend for the number and size of practices to increase.[16] Expansion has been particularly notable in the City, with lawyers taking an increasing proportion of office space.[17] A particular feature in recent years has been the number of firms growing through merger,[18] and the establishment, short of

---

[5] R.C.L.S., Vol. 2, p. 47.

[6] *The Recruitment Crisis: A Report by the Training Committee of the Law Society* (May 1988).

[7] J. Adams, "Evidence mounts of jobs crisis" (1990) 87 L.S.Gaz., October 10, pp. 8–9; M. Yuille, "Lay-offs hit City property lawyers," *The Lawyer*, September 18, 1990, p. 1.

[8] D. Podmore, (1979) 129 N.L.J. 356–357; Podmore (1980), pp. 21–22. This trend was reversed in 1984–86.

[9] Podmore suggests a classification of 14 groups, based on Abel-Smith and Stevens (1967), pp. 144–148: Podmore (1980), pp. 22–24.

[10] *Law Society Annual Statistical Report 1990*, pp. 11, 12.

[11] Memorandum No. 5 to the Royal Commission; (1978) 75 L.S.Gaz. 422, 426. 66 per cent. of all firms were of this size or smaller.

[12] *i.e.* solicitors entitled to a share of profits and not remunerated by salary only.

[13] *Law Society Annual Statistical Report 1990*, p. 15, Table 3.9. The figures excluded firms earning less than £15,000 p.a.

[14] *Ibid.* p. 16, Table 4.3.

[15] *Law Society Annual Statistical Report 1987*, pp. 19–20; and *1990*, p. 17.

[16] See R. L. Abel, *The Legal Profession in England and Wales* (1988), pp. 199–207, 419–423 (Tables 2.20–2.24); *Law Society Annual Statistical Reports*.

[17] (1990) 87 L.S.Gaz., March 7, p. 5; *The Lawyer*, July 10, 1990, pp. 12–13. Statistics of the growth of the top 20 City firms are given in P. Stewart, (1990) I.F.L. Rev., June, Law Firms Supplement.

[18] Particularly spectacular was the merger in 1987 of Clifford Turner and Coward Chance to form Clifford Chance, which by 1990 had over 200 partners: see P. Brown, (1987) 137 N.L.J. 377.

merger, of groups of firms with common central services covering such matters as recruitment, training and marketing.[19]

Geographically, the spread is uneven.[20] Foster's survey based on the 1971 Law List showed an irregular dispersal within towns, between urban and rural areas, and nationally. A majority of solicitors practised in the centre of urban areas, near each other, the courts and commercial and financial institutions. Solicitors' offices were, however, more widely dispersed than solicitors. For example, in Greater London 77 per cent. of solicitors were found to work in central London, but only 44 per cent. of solicitors' offices were found there. Nearly two-thirds of all solicitors practised in towns with over 100,000 people. The proportion of offices to population varied between 1 : 1896 (Guildford) and 1 : 66,629 (Huyton). A further survey was published in 1986, prepared as part of Exeter University's *Access to justice in rural Britain* project.[21] This found that, at the regional level, the southeast dominated, with almost half the total and the lowest regional value for the number of persons per solicitor; there was a broad band of relatively well-provided counties from the southwest to East Anglia and a core of poorly-provided counties covering the north and east Midlands. At the district level, there was an overwhelming concentration of solicitors in Central London, solicitors were disproportionately well represented in rural areas, and the districts where provision was worst were generally those with rapidly expanding suburban populations on the fringes of the major centres of population. Possible explanations for the relatively good provision in rural areas included high status within a small town community, easier or earlier acquisition of equity partnership and the quality of life in the countryside.

The Royal Commission on Legal Services thought the most likely reason for the lack of solicitors in areas of social deprivation to be the low level of remuneration for legally-aided contentious work rather than simply the "preference" of solicitors to practise elsewhere. Unless "mass production" methods were employed, legal aid work had to be subsidised by other more profitable work of a kind not generally available in the areas in question. They recommended that legal aid should be adequately remunerated, that law centres should be supported and that private solicitors should be encouraged to open in areas of need by the provision of interest-free loans.[22] These recommendations were not acted upon.

(iii) *Solicitors' work*

A remuneration survey commissioned by the Law Society showed that in

---

[19] *e.g.* the Norton Rose M5 Group, comprising firms in Manchester, Plymouth, Leeds, Bristol, Norwich and Birmingham, and, from 1990 the London firm Norton Rose: see C. Christian, (1987) S.J. 1056; J. Carr, (1990) I.F.L. Rev., May, pp. 11–13. Other examples include the Eversheds group, the Legal Resource Group and Law Net: (1990) 87 L.S.Gaz., October 18, pp. 26, 30.

[20] Podmore (1980), pp. 27–29; K. Foster, "The Location of Solicitors" (1973) 36 M.L.R. 153; L. Bridges *et al.*, *Legal Services in Birmingham* (1975), C. Watkins, *et al.*, The distribution of solicitors in England and Wales, AJRBP Working Paper 8, 1986, and (1988) 13 *Transactions of the Institute of British Geographers* 39–56.

[21] *Supra*; summarised by K. Economides and M. Blacksell, "Access to Justice in Rural Britain: Final Report" (1987) 16 Anglo-Am. L.R. 353, 356–359.

[22] R.C.L.S., Vol. 1, pp. 46–48, 181–182.

1985, 68 per cent. of the gross fees of solicitors in private practice came from non-contentious, and 32 per cent. from contentious work. The breakdown according to the category of work was: domestic conveyancing 29 per cent., company and commercial 25 per cent., probate and wills 9 per cent., other non contentious 5 per cent., matrimonial 7 per cent., crime 5 per cent. and other contentious 20 per cent.[23] The Survey found that there had overall been a serious decline in profitability between 1976–77 and 1984–85.[24]

Solicitors are generally much less dependent than barristers on legal aid.[25] There has been increasing pressure on firms with significant legal aid practices, given the declining profitability of legal aid work.[26] The trend seems to be more and more for such work to become the preserve of specialised firms able to handle high volumes of work efficiently, but even firms in this category have expressed concern at low increases in remuneration.[27] Solicitors have been forced to become less dependent on domestic conveyancing.[28]

Overall, the Royal Commission concluded that the earnings of private practice solicitors were not out of line with comparable occupations: middle management in industry and the legal and administrative class of the civil service.[29] However, no useful information was obtained for accountants, engineers, surveyors and members of other professions, and the general quality of the research was adversely criticised.[30] The Peat Marwick Survey in 1985 concluded that the average earnings of both principals and employed

[23] Peat Marwick Survey of the Structure and Finances of the Profession in Private Practice, January 6, 1986, cited in N.C.C., *Ordinary Justice* (H.M.S.O., 1989), p. 60. For earlier surveys see R.C.L.S., Vol. 2, pp. 486–489 (1975–76) and the Report of the Prices and Income Board, *Remuneration of Solicitors* (Cmnd. 3529, 1968). For a comprehensive survey of casework time devoted to different categories of work see G. Chambers and S. Harwood, *Solicitors in England and Wales: Practice, Organisation and Perceptions; First Report: Practice, Organisation and Perceptions* (1990), Chap. 6; Figure 6.1 (p. 26) shows the categories to be business affairs 20.6 per cent.; commercial property 18 per cent.; residential conveyancing 18.5 per cent.; family 10.6 per cent.; probate, wills etc. 7.2 per cent.; personal injury 7.1 per cent.; crime 6.7 per cent.; and other 11.3 per cent. The survey also contains much useful information on, *e.g.* work patterns over a career, the different work done by men and women. See further, below, p. 169.

[24] The Royal Commission had the "overall impression" that conveyancing was more profitable than the other classes of work apart from company and commercial (Vol. 2, p. 496); in 1968, the Prices and Incomes Board estimated that conveyancing accounted for 55.6 per cent. of solicitors' income, 40.8 per cent. of expenses and 41.4 per cent. of productive time (Cmnd. 3529, Tables 14 and 15).

[25] R.C.L.S., Vol. 2, p. 491. 65.7 per cent. of firms earned less than 10 per cent. from this source, and a further 20.9 per cent. less than 20 per cent.

[26] A survey conducted by the Law Society in 1988 showed that 40 per cent. of offices had since 1983 either given up or were seriously considering giving up criminal legal aid work, and 27 per cent. matrimonial legal aid work; of these over 80 per cent. gave inadequate remuneration as the reason: Law Society, *Survey of Legal Aid Provision* (April 1988). A survey by Touche Ross in 1989 found that only a small minority of firms in the provinces were making a profit on legal aid work: (1989) 86 L.S.Gaz., March 15, p. 21.

[27] See *The Lawyer*, October 9, 1990, pp. 13 (profiling four firms who have made legal aid pay); (1990) 87 L.S.Gaz., March 21, p. 2: a partner in one of these four spoke despondently about the future of legal aid practice; H. Hodge, "A legal aid practice—ten years on," *Legal Action*, September 1987, pp. 6–7, 24.

[28] See R. Bowles, (1987) 137 N.L.J. 401 and (1990) 140 N.L.J. 1340; M. Moffatt, (1990) 87 L.S.Gaz., May 23, pp. 16–17.

[29] See generally R.C.L.S., Vol. 1, pp. 507–542; Vol. 2, pp. 447–578 (earnings surveys) and 627–698 (comparisons).

[30] C. Glasser, *L.A.G. Bull.*, September 1979, p. 201.

solicitors were lower than those of most comparable professions and occupations.[31]

(iv) *Specialisation*

There has been an increasing tendency for solicitors to specialise. Larger firms will normally have, for example, separate litigation, company and property departments and further more specialised sections. Each solicitor will develop his or her career in a particular area. It has become common for league tables to be published comparing the reputation and workload of the leading firms in different areas of practice.[32] Until 1990, however, it was only in limited circumstances that firms could advertise their specialisms.[33] The Law Society established panels covering Mental Health Review Tribunals, child care and insolvency in 1984 and 1985. It also vets solicitors wishing to join duty solicitor schemes. The first two were set up to help clients identify solicitors with a particular competence in the relevant area. Those wishing to join must attend a course and an interview panel. The insolvency panel was established in consequence of sections 388 to 398 of the Insolvency Act 1986, which limited insolvency practice to practitioners licensed by the Law Society. The Council of the Law Society has also approved the establishment of a scheme for planning law. In 1989 it set up a Specialisation Committee to consider the whole question. In April 1990, the Committee proposed[34] the setting up of panels in seven areas: advocacy in the higher courts, personal injuries, medical negligence, employment law, pensions, revenue law and criminal law. Selection criteria would cover knowledge of relevant law and procedures, understanding of relevant ethical issues, and possession of relevant professional skills and experience. While the profession was being consulted on these proposals, however, the Council decided that in future the only restriction on a claim that a solicitor is a specialist or an expert should be that "such a claim can be justified."[35] As a result, it was predicted that the development of panels would be "stillborn": there would be little point in spending money and taking an examination to join a panel if the solicitor could anyway claim to be a specialist in the relevant area.[36] The decision was attacked by the National Consumer Council and the Legal Action Group, who favoured the introduction of formal specialisation schemes.[37] The N.C.C.'s position was that, in the light of American experience, well run schemes are in the interest of consumers because they

---

[31] The Law Society Special Committee on Remuneration, *Survey of the Structure and Finances of the Solicitors' Branch of the Legal Profession in Private Practice*, January 16, 1986, 3 vols.: see (1986) 83 L.S.Gaz. 316. Average salaries increased by 22 per cent. in 1988: (1989) 86 L.S.Gaz., May 31, p. 6. In 1990, estimated average earnings of solicitors 4–5 years qualified ranged from £42,000 in the City to £23,000 in the South West: *Chambers & Partners' Directory of the Legal Profession 1990*, p. 18; the earnings of equity partners were "kept a close secret": *ibid.*

[32] See, *e.g.* Chambers & Partners', *The Legal Profession 1990*; J. Pritchard, *The Legal Five Hundred* (1989).

[33] See below, p. 139.

[34] *Specialisation: The Way Forward. A Consultation Document* (April 1990). See (1990) 87 L.S.Gaz., March 7, p. 7; May 2, pp. 36, 39, 40.

[35] Solicitors' Publicity Code 1990, para. 2(*b*).

[36] See (1990) 87 L.S.Gaz., July 18, pp. 4–5. Personal injury and medical negligence panels may still be set up: M. McKeone, (1991) 88 L.S. Gaz., March 6, p. 4.

[37] (1990) 87 L.S.Gaz., August 22, p. 5; R. Smith, *ibid.*, October 3, p. 2; but *cf.* J. James, *ibid.*, October 10, p. 2. It has also been criticised by Lord Mackay: (1991) 88 L.S.Gaz., January 30, p. 7.

improve access and raise standards.[38] The need for such a development is, indeed, illustrated by research which demonstrates how accident victims may be at a serious disadvantage in pursuing claims for damages if they are advised by non-specialists.[39]

(v) *Employed solicitors*

A substantial number of solicitors are employed outside private practice, mainly in central[40] and local government, industry and commerce.[41] Their work is obviously geared to the needs of their employers, lawyers in industry being particularly concerned with employment law, property and commercial work,[42] lawyers in local government with prosecutions, property, rating and so on.[43] The rules on the kind of work that may be undertaken by employed solicitors were relaxed by the 1990 Solicitors' Practice Rules. Rule 4 now provides that solicitors who are employees of non-solicitors shall not as part of their employment do solicitors' work for any person other than their employers except as permitted by the Employed Solicitors Code, promulgated by the Law Society with the concurrence of the Master of the Rolls. Under the Code, employed solicitors may act for their fellow employees in any matter relating to their employment, excluding personal injuries; formerly, they were restricted to acting in conveyancing transactions where the employee was compulsorily moved. Solicitors employed by associations (now defined more widely[44]) may act for a member in both contentious and non-contentious matters; formerly, in non-contentious matters they could only advise. An employed solicitor may now act for a trade association of which the employer is a member. In each case, the employed solicitor must be satisfied that the person in question does not wish to instruct some other solicitor, and there must be no charge.

(vi) *"Monopolies"*

Solicitors have long enjoyed certain statutory monopolies.[45] Section 20 of the Solicitors Act 1974 makes it an offence for an unqualified person to act as a solicitor and as such commence or conduct litigation on behalf of another. An unqualified person may not pretend to be a solicitor.[46]

It is also an offence for an unqualified person[47] to prepare (directly or indirectly) any instrument "relating to real or personal estate, or any legal

---

[38] *Ordinary Justice* (H.M.S.O., 1989), pp. 144–153. See also A. A. Paterson, "Specialisation and the Legal Profession" (1986) 136 N.L.J. 697, 721.

[39] H. Genn, *Hard Bargaining* (1987).

[40] G. Drewry, "Lawyers in the UK Civil Service" (1981) 59 *Public Administration* 15; Sir Robert Andrew, *Review of Government Legal Services* (H.M.S.O., 1989): above, pp. 20–21.

[41] See above p. 120.

[42] See K. Mackie, *Lawyers in Business* (1989); *The Lawyer*, August 7, 1990, pp. 6–7.

[43] See *The Lawyer*, August 14, 1990, pp. 4–5, noting a variety of arrangements for the conduct of legal work for local councils.

[44] Membership of the associations must be limited to persons concerned in a particular trade, occupation or activity *or otherwise having a community of interest*. The words in italics were added in the 1990 Code to include, for example, groups based on sex, ethnic origin, nationality, religion or political affiliation: see (1990) 87 L.S.Gaz., August 22, p. 25.

[45] A non-lawyer may always act in person in matters affecting him- or herself. Some of the "monopolies" were shared with other relatively small groups.

[46] Solicitors Act 1974, s.21. See, *e.g. Carter* v. *Butcher* [1966] 1 Q.B. 526.

[47] Here the term covers a person who is not a solicitor, barrister or notary public, and there are some other exclusions: *ibid.* ss.22(2), 23(2).

proceedings,[48] to take instructions for a grant of probate or letters of administration, or to prepare papers on which to found or oppose such a grant,[49] unless he or she proves that this was not done for or in expectation of any fee, gain or reward. An offence is committed even where the unqualified person does not personally receive the fee.[50] No person may bring proceedings to recover costs in respect of anything done by an unqualified person acting as a solicitor.[51] The Royal Commission on Legal Services found these restrictions to be in the public interest.[52] In litigation heavy reliance was placed on the knowledge and integrity of solicitors, acting as they did as officers of the court. Solicitors had the responsibility of disclosing documents even where it would be contrary to the client's interests. A person "not subject to the same direct duty to the court and to professional disciplines"[53] could not be expected to exercise such responsibility. The Commission proposed a relaxation of the probate restrictions in non-contentious cases in favour of trust corporations, and resisted Law Society suggestions for new restrictions on unqualified persons preparing for reward wills or powers of attorney.

Conveyancing

The economic dependence of many solicitors upon conveyancing, when put alongside criticisms of the low quality of service provided[54] and the level of charges, naturally made the "conveyancing monopoly" one of the most controversial areas before the Royal Commission.[55] This monopoly had been sought by the Society of Gentlemen Practisers in the eighteenth century, and was finally granted by William Pitt in 1804 as a *quid pro quo* for an increase in the tax on practising certificates and articles.[56] The restriction was possibly designed to facilitate the collection of revenue rather than to protect the public interest. A majority[57] of the Commission accepted the Law Society's case that the restrictions were in the public interest in view of the complexity of the law relating to the ownership of land, the complexity of the conveyancing process and the need to protect clients from dishonesty, incompetence and overcharging. The Commission were unanimous that a "free-for-all" would not be in the public interest. By a majority they rejected proposals for a system of licensed conveyancers. Indeed they suggested that the restrictions should be extended to cover the preparation of the contract of sale as well as the final document and that the maximum penalty should be raised for the first time since 1894 from £50 to £500. They did not find that charges were excessive. In order to reintroduce more certainty to charging,

---

[48] *Ibid.* s.22. "Instrument" does not include a will, an agreement not under seal, a letter of power of attorney, or a "transfer of stock containing no trust or limitation thereof:" s.22(3). Thus a contract for the sale of land is not within the restriction whereas the deed which effects the conveyance is.

[49] *Ibid.* s.23(1).

[50] *Reynolds* v. *Hoyle* [1976] 1 W.L.R. 207; *cf. Green* v. *Hoyle* [1976] 1 W.L.R. 575.

[51] 1974 Act, s.25.

[52] R.C.L.S., Vol. 1, pp. 225–231.

[53] *Ibid.* p. 227.

[54] M. Joseph, *The Conveyancing Fraud* (2nd edn., 1989): a book by a practising solicitor.

[55] R.C.L.S., Vol. 1, pp. 243–282. The Commission preferred the expression "closed shop."

[56] Stamp Act 1804. See Abel-Smith and Stevens (1967), pp. 22–23, Kirk (1976), Chap. 7. It was moved from fiscal legislation to a Solicitors Act in 1932.

[57] A third of the members were unconvinced: R.C.L.S., Vol. 1, pp. 808, 809–812, 813–816.

they suggested there would be a scale of "standard" charges covering the general run of domestic conveyancing.

As we have seen, however, matters have not rested there. Part II of the Administration of Justice Act 1985,[58] founded on the First Report of the Conveyancing Committee, introduced a system of licensed conveyancers. The Act created a new body, The Council for Licensed Conveyancers,[59] with the responsibility of controlling the discipline, admission, training and professional standards of the new profession of "licensed conveyancer." The Council was required, *inter alia*, to make training rules, rules for regulating professional practice conduct and discipline, rules requiring compulsory indemnity insurance against civil liability and for setting up a compensation fund for the benefit of the victims of negligence, fraud or other dishonesty on the part of licensed conveyancers and rules for keeping accounts. The structure is similar to that applicable to the solicitors' profession as regulated by the Law Society, with some differences of detail.[60] The first licences were granted on May 1, 1987, and solicitors have been directed to proceed in their dealings with licensed conveyancers on the same basis as with solicitors, in recognition of their status as members of a regulated profession.[61]

The numbers of licensed conveyancers are as yet too small to have had much direct impact on the work of solicitors.[62] Their existence, coupled with the threat of institutional conveyancing, has, however, played a part in encouraging greater competitiveness among solicitors, with substantial reductions in charges for domestic conveyancing; the widespread use of advertising once the rules restricting it had been relaxed; decisions by solicitors' firms to undertake estate agency as well as conveyancing work, commonly establishing "solicitors' property centres"[63]; the introduction of TransAction, a new National Conveyancing Protocol designed to make the procedure for house transfer speedier and more efficient[64]; and the establishment by the Law Society of the Solicitors' Financial and Property Services Company, as a source of information and market support for firms wishing to offer clients a fully integrated package of financial services.[65]

By 1989, the government had reverted to the view that competition in the provision of conveyancing services could properly be extended, subject to safeguards. The White Paper,[66] which differed only on points of detail from

[58] See annotations by P. Kenny in *Current Law Statutes Annotated 1985*; A. Kenny, (1986) 277 E.G. 262, 394.
[59] (Chairman: Prof. J. T. Farrand) *Non-Solicitor Conveyancers—Competence and Consumer Protection* (H.M.S.O., 1984). See [1984] Conv. 393; R. C. A. White, (1985) P.N. 80.
[60] For commentaries on the Rules promulgated by Council of Licensed Conveyancers, see [1987] Conv. 396; P. Kenny, (1987) 131 S.J. 958.
[61] (1987) 84 L.S.Gaz., 1202.
[62] By 1990, there were more than 250 licensed conveyancers actively practising in the market and a further 500 or so in employment, accounting for only a small fraction of the conveyancing market: R. Bowles, (1990) 140 N.L.J. 1340, 1343.
[63] See (1989) 86 L.S.Gaz., February 22, pp. 4–5, noting the establishment by two firms of a chain of "property shops" in the London area, and the development of Crawley Solicitors Property Centre, set up by six firms.
[64] See (1990) 87 L.S.Gaz., March 21, p. 3 and March 28, p. 4 on TransAction's launch: the Law Society predicted a 90 per cent. take up; adoption of the Protocol is voluntary but preferred practice; see also L. A. Palmer, (1990) 87 L.S.Gaz., April 4, pp. 24–25.
[65] See K. Aldred, (1989) 86 L.S.Gaz., October 25, p. 26 and November 22, pp. 4–5; J. Ames, (1990) 87 L.S.Gaz., August 29, p. 8.
[66] Cm. 740, Chap. 5.

the Green Paper, proposed that the provision of conveyancing services should be open to any "authorised practitioner." The relevant provisions are to be found in the Courts and Legal Services Act 1990, ss.34–52, and Scheds. 5–7. The Act establishes the Authorised Conveyancing Practitioners Board,[67] comprising a chairman and between 4 and 8 other members appointed by the Lord Chancellor, who must have regard to the desirability of appointing people who have experience in or knowledge of the provision of conveyancing services, associated financial arrangements and consumer or commercial affairs, and securing a balance between the interests of authorised practitioners and those who use their services. The Board must, *inter alia*, seek to develop competition in the provision of conveyancing services, supervise the activities of authorised practitioners, and consider and report on matters referred by the Lord Chancellor. It has power to obtain information from authorised practitioners and those who act on their behalf, and to investigate and intervene in the affairs of an authorised practitioner.[68]

The restrictions in section 22 of the Solicitors Act 1974 will not apply where conveyancing services are provided by an authorised practitioner *i.e.* an individual or corporate body authorised by the Board.[69] The Board must grant authorisation if it is satisfied that the applicant is "fit and proper," and is of the opinion that the applicant will comply with applicable rules and regulations, will be able to meet claims made in connection with the provision of conveyancing services, will maintain satisfactory complaints procedures and satisfactory arrangements to protect clients in the event of ceasing to operate, and will be a member of the Conveyancing Ombudsman Scheme set up by the Act.[70] An authorisation may be refused, or may be granted subject to conditions, and may be revoked or suspended in accordance with rules to be made by the Board. Appeals lie to a Conveyancing Appeals Tribunal, and from the Tribunal, on a point of law, to the High Court.[71]

The Lord Chancellor may make regulations to secure that authorised practitioners maintain satisfactory standards of competence and conduct, that in providing conveyancing services (and in particular in fixing their charges) they act in a manner which is consistent with the maintenance of fair competition between authorised practitioners and others providing conveyancing services, and that the interests of clients are satisfactorily protected. The regulations may include provisions designed to promote efficiency and to avoid unnecessary delay and conflicts of interest, a requirement that, so far as is reasonably practicable, each transaction is under the overall control of one individual, and provisions as to the supervision of specified classes of work by qualified staff, terms and conditions of service, the information to be given to potential clients, the handling of clients' money and the disclosure of an accounting for commissions.[72] The Act also

---

[67] Courts and Legal Services Act 1990, ss.34, 35 and Sched. 5. These provisions and s.40 were the only sections in force at the time of writing.

[68] *Ibid.* ss.47–52.

[69] *Ibid.* s.36.

[70] *Ibid.* s.37. For the Conveyancing Ombudsman scheme see s.43, and the rules made thereunder and Sched. 7.

[71] *Ibid.* ss.38, 39, 41, 42.

[72] *Ibid.* s.40. Further details were set out in the *White Paper*, Cm. 740, paras. 5.12–5.14, including a requirement for a personal interview, safeguards against conflict of interest and the prevention of conveyancing services being offered at less than their true cost.

prohibits "tying-in arrangements": a loan for the purchase of residential property may not be made subject to a condition requiring the borrower to use other services (*e.g.* conveyancing services) provided or specified by the lender, and vice versa.[73] These provisions take account of the concern expressed by the Law Society that competition in the conveyancing market be placed on an equal footing.[74]

The obvious intended beneficiaries of the new arrangements are banks and building societies, but other professions may also become involved. The actual work will have to be carried out or supervised by qualified staff (*i.e.* solicitors, licensed conveyancers, and (subject to appropriate qualification) barristers and notaries.[75]

Rights of audience

An analogous area is that of rights of audience.[76] Prior to the Courts and Legal Services Act 1990, these were limited by the practice of the courts and tribunals concerned rather than by rules of law. Litigants in person had a right of audience throughout the legal system.[77] Barristers enjoyed a virtual monopoly of advocacy before the House of Lords, Court of Appeal and High Court.[78] They also had exclusive rights of audience in all Crown Court cases, except that a solicitor might appear (a) in appeals to the Crown Court from a magistrates' court in civil or criminal proceedings or on committal for sentence, if the solicitor or anyone in his or her firm appeared in the court below[79]; and (b) in a wider class of cases in certain remote areas.[80] Barristers and solicitors had rights of audience in the county courts and magistrates' courts; lay persons might be permitted to appear. For example, by custom magistrates allowed police officers, local government officials and civil servants employed by the D.P.P. to appear. In most tribunals there were no restrictions. Any person might attend a trial as a friend of a party to take notes and give advice but he or she would not be accorded a right of audience.[81]

The Royal Commission considered the question of rights of audience and came down resoundingly in favour of the *status quo*. They rejected suggestions that the rights of audience of lay persons should be extended, stressing, particularly for the higher courts, the importance of proceedings for the

---

[73] *Ibid.* ss.104–107.
[74] *e.g.* the Law Society, *Striking the Balance* (1989), pp. 5–8 and Annex A; *White Paper*, para. 5.14.
[75] Cm. 740, para. 5.9.
[76] R.C.L.S., Vol. 1, pp. 203–221. For a summary, see *ibid.* p. 221.
[77] Prosecutions in the Crown Court must be conducted by a barrister.
[78] Solicitors could appear before the single judge of the Court of Appeal (Criminal Division) sitting in chambers, in certain High Court bankruptcy applications and in any High Court proceedings heard in chambers (before a judge, official referee, master or registrar). Rights of audience before the Judicial Committee of the Privy Council were limited to English and Northern Ireland barristers, Scottish advocates and all advocates duly qualified in countries from which appeals lie to the Privy Council.
[79] *Practice Direction* [1972] 1 W.L.R. 307.
[80] *Practice Direction* [1972] 1 W.L.R. 5. The areas are Caernarvon, Barnstaple, Bodmin, Doncaster and Lincoln.
[81] *McKenzie* v. *McKenzie* [1971] P. 33; *Merry* v. *Persons Unknown* [1974] C.L.Y. 3003. There is, however, no right to a McKenzie Adviser: see below, p. 444. A superior court may exceptionally hear persons who technically have no right of audience: *Engineers' and Managers' Association* v. *A.C.A.S.* [1979] 1 W.L.R. 113 (trade union official).

individual concerned, the "special skill and expertise" called for, and their other proposals for the extension of financial support for legal services. The existing position of litigants in person and lay persons should not, however, be restricted. In the case of the former this was not because the Commission thought they were any good at advocacy, but because their right of audience was "long-established" and no-one had actually proposed its removal. In evidence, there had been some jockeying for position among lawyers. The Bar and the judges resisted solicitors' claims[82] for wider rights of audience, particularly in the Crown Court; the Law Society resisted the claims of legal executives.[83] By and large, the resisters won, apart from proposed minor changes to enable a solicitor to appear in any court to deal with formal or unopposed matters.[84] The Commission thought that any significant changes would lead to a lowering of standards. Crown Court advocacy required different skills (*e.g.* addressing a jury) or greater expertise (*e.g.* knowledge of the laws of evidence and experience in cross-examination) than advocacy in the magistrates' courts. The Commission's enthusiasm for solicitor-advocates was markedly lukewarm:

> "Many solicitors make competent advocates in magistrates' courts and some are very good. Some could achieve the same standard in the Crown Court if they could so arrange their professional lives as to enable them to concentrate on the work there."[85]

They thought it unlikely that many solicitors, except in large firms, would be able to have the constant practice in Crown Court advocacy which competence and progressive improvement required. However, they feared that enough solicitors would move into this area to have a "serious and disproportionate impact on the income and capacity of barristers to continue in practice."[86] The fear of fusion was thus in the background.

Again, as we have seen, matters have not stood still. The Law Society again raised the question of rights of audience in 1984,[87] and in 1985, widespread publicity surrounded the attempt by Cyril Smith M.P. to have the terms of the settlement of a libel action brought against him and Radio Trent by 25 other M.P.s read to the High Court by his solicitor. This act did not require the skills of an advocate, and Mr. Smith's solicitor took the view that it would be unnecessarily expensive to brief counsel for the task. Leonard J. held that he had no authority to allow a solicitor to appear before him, save in an emergency, and this was affirmed by the Court of Appeal,[88] on the ground that the public interest required that the High Court's general practices and procedures be known and not changed or departed from in

---

[82] The solicitors were refighting a battle lost when the criminal courts were reorganised in 1971: see the *Royal Commission on Assizes and Quarter Sessions* 1966–69, Cmnd. 4153, Written Evidence Nos. 32 and 47.

[83] See R.C.L.S., Vol. 1, pp. 413–415.

[84] Seven members of the Commission favoured some extension of the right of audience of solicitors in the Crown Court, particularly to make pleas in mitigation: Vol. 1, pp. 807, 816–823, 828–829.

[85] R.C.L.S., Vol. 1, p. 212. The competence of barristers was not discussed in the chapter on rights of audience. Their increasing prolixity was discussed in Vol. 1, pp. 307–308.

[86] R.C.L.S., Vol. 1, p. 216.

[87] Annual Statement, 1983–84, pp. 48–49; (1984) 81 L.S.Gaz. 1507.

[88] *Abse* v. *Smith* [1986] Q.B. 536.

piecemeal fashion by individual judges. However, it was acknowledged that the rule might be changed by the judges of the Supreme Court acting as a collegiate body. Accordingly, on May 9, a Practice Direction was issued on behalf of the judges of the High Court and Court of Appeal permitting solicitors to appear in the Supreme Court in formal or unopposed proceedings, and when judgment is delivered in open court following a hearing in Chambers at which that solicitor conducts the case for his or her client.[89] The Marre Committee subsequently supported, by a majority, the extension of rights of audience in the Crown Court to solicitors approved by a Rights of Audience Advisory Board.[90]

The government's proposals were more radical still.[91] The Courts and Legal Services Act 1990,[92] puts rights of audience in courts and in certain tribunals and inquiries[93] on a statutory footing. A person has a right of audience before a court

(a) where he or she has a right of audience granted by the appropriate authorised body,[94] and that body's qualification regulations and rules of conduct have been approved;

(b) where (a) does not apply but he or she has a statutory right of audience;

(c) where (a) does not apply but he or she has a right of audience granted by the court in question;

(d) where he or she is a party to the proceedings and would have had a right of audience as a party if the Act had not been passed;

(e) where he or she is a solicitor's clerk, or corresponding employee of a recognised body, and the proceedings are being heard in chambers in the High Court.

A right of audience can, however, be denied to a person for reasons which apply to him or her as an individual. Sections 20 and 25 of the Solicitors Act 1974 do not apply in relation to any act done in exercise of a right of audience duly granted under the Act.

Similar rules are to apply to rights to conduct litigation, except that the General Council of the Bar is not specified as an "authorised body."[95]

On the coming into force of section 27 of the 1990 Act,[95a] the rights of audience enjoyed by barristers and solicitors, and the right to conduct litigation enjoyed by solicitors, immediately before December 7, 1989, were deemed to have been granted, respectively, by the General Council of the Bar and the Law Society, and the relevant qualification regulations and rules

[89] *Practice Direction (Solicitors: Rights of Audience)* [1986] 1 W.L.R. 545. The Royal Commission's recommendation in favour of such a change (Vol. 1, p. 219) had previously been accepted in principle by the government (Government Response, Cmnd. 9077, 1983, p. 19) and the Senate of the Inns of Court and the Bar.

[90] Report of the Marre Committee, pp. 149–157. See J. Hodgson, (1988) 138 N.L.J. 615.

[91] *Green Paper*, Chap. 5, *White Paper*, Chap. 3.

[92] s.27.

[93] The term "court" includes (a) any tribunal under the jurisdiction of the Council on Tribunals (b) any court-martial and (c) a statutory inquiry within the meaning of the Tribunals and Inquiries Act 1971, s.19(1): 1990 Act, s.119.

[94] *i.e.* the General Council of the Bar, the Law Society, and a professional body designated by Order in Council (which may include the Council for Licensed Conveyancers: s.53). The procedures for securing and revoking designation are set out in ss.29 and 30 and Sched. 4.

[95] Courts and Legal Services Act 1990, s.28.

[95a] On January 1, 1991: see S.I. 1990 No. 2484.

of conduct relating to these rights were deemed to have been approved under section 27.[96]

The procedure whereby other professional bodies may become "authorised bodies," and their qualification regulations and rules of conduct approved for the purposes of section 27, is set out in Schedule 4, Part I. An application must be sent first to the Lord Chancellor's Advisory Committee for comment, and then to the Lord Chancellor, who is to consider the advice of the Committee, and that of the Director General of Fair Trading (who is to consider whether the regulations and rules would restrict, distort or prevent competition to any significant extent). The application needs the approval of the Lord Chancellor and each of four "designated judges" (the Lord Chief Justice, the Master of the Rolls, the President of the Family Division and the Vice-Chancellor.) The designated judges too must consider the advice of the Committee and the Director General. The applicant is entitled to written reasons for the decision. A similar procedure applies for obtaining approval for the alteration of the qualification regulations and rules of conduct of any authorised body (including the General Council of the Bar and the Law Society) (Schedule 4, Part II) or for revoking the designation of an authorised body (Schedule 4, Part III).

The grant or refusal of approval under Schedule 4 by the Lord Chancellor and the designated judges is not a matter of discretion: any one of them must refuse approval if satisfied that the application is incompatible with the "statutory objective" or the "general principle" laid down in section 17 of the Act. The former is the general objective of

"the development of legal services in England and Wales (and in particular the development of advocacy, litigation, conveyancing and probate services) by making provision for new or better ways of providing such services and a wider choice of persons providing them, while maintaining the proper and efficient administration of justice."

The latter is the general principle that the question whether a person should be granted a right of audience or to conduct litigation is to be determined only by reference to:

(a) whether he or she is qualified in accordance with the educational and training requirements appropriate to the court or proceedings;
(b) whether he or she is a member of a professional or other body which has rules of conduct which are the subject of an effective enforcement mechanism and are likely to be enforced;
(c) whether, in the case of a body whose members provide advocacy services, the body observes a form of the "cab-rank" principle: *i.e.* a satisfactory provision requiring its members not to withhold those services
   (i) on the ground that the nature of the case is objectionable to him or her or to any section of the public;
   (ii) on the ground that the conduct, opinions or beliefs of the prospective client are unacceptable to him or her or to any section of the public;
   (iii) on any ground relating to the prospective client's source of financial support (*e.g.* legal aid); and
(d) whether that body's rules of conduct are "appropriate in the interests of the proper and efficient administration of justice."

[96] *Ibid.* ss.31–33. Fully in force from April 1, 1991: see S.I. 1991 No. 608.

However, rules of conduct which allow advocacy services to be withheld on the ground that a proper fee has not been offered are not to be taken as incompatible with the general principle.[97]

These arrangements are a modification of those which were proposed in the Green Paper,[98] where it was suggested that it would be for the Lord Chancellor to decide on the education, qualifications and training of advocates appropriate for each of the various courts, and to specify principles on which Codes of Conduct regulating advocacy should be based. His decisions on rights of audience would be put into effect by subordinate legislation, following the receipt of advice from the Advisory Committee and after consultation with the judiciary. These proposals were attacked, with varying degrees of vehemence, by the judiciary, the Bar and the Law Society as constituting a serious threat to the independence of the legal profession from government.[99] Such new powers "in less wise hands, could be exercised so as to damage the legal profession and the judiciary in the interests of political dogma."[1] "There are warning lessons from other countries in the Commonwealth which have ceased to have Judges and legal professions independent of the diktat of Government."[2]

The revised arrangements, proposed in the White Paper and now enshrined in the Act, leave a lesser degree of control in the hands of the Lord Chancellor, and have given the designated judges a formal role in the procedure. In particular, these judges will have to approve changes to permit solicitors to appear as advocates in the superior courts. It is a matter of conjecture how far the designated judges will be able to resist this move. While that is likely to be their inclination,[3] any refusal must be reasoned, and may be subject to challenge on an application for judicial review, an unedifying prospect unless refusal can clearly be justified. It is true that exercise of the power of veto is made easier by incorporation into the legislation of a version of the "cab-rank" principle.[4] Nevertheless, it is likely that there will be at least some extension of rights of audience.

It has been predicted that solicitors' firms will be more likely to wish to take up advocacy in the High Court than in the Crown Court, given the organisation of work in the Crown Court and the low levels of remuneration for publicly funded legal work.[5]

---

[97] The practitioner must have reasonable ground to consider that it is not a proper fee having regard to the circumstances of the case, the nature of his or her practice or his or her experience and standing: s.17(5).

[98] *Green Paper: The Work and Organisation of the Legal Profession* (Cm. 570), Chaps. 4 and 5.

[99] F. Cownie, *op. cit.* p. 119, n. 98 *supra*, pp. 220–227; *Quality of Justice, The Bar's Response* (1989), Chap. 14; Council of the Law Society, *Striking the Balance* (1989), pp. 14–15; Lord Ackner, (1990) Bracton L.J. 4.

[1] *Quality of Justice*, para. 14.10.

[2] *Ibid.* para. 14.9.

[3] See F. Cownie, *op. cit.* p. 119, n. 98 *supra*, pp. 230–233, and M. Zander, (1989) 86 L.S.Gaz., October 25, pp. 17–18, citing a speech by Lord Donaldson to the Bar Council stating that the interests of justice might require that certain types of case, (*e.g.* concerning crime, judicial review, children) were conducted by full-time advocates; R. Smith, (1990) 17 J.L.S. 242, 248–249, citing the *Judges' Response* to the Green Papers.

[4] A House of Lords amendment directed at solicitors (the only government defeat in the House) was replaced by a government amendment applying it as a general principle to all rights of audience: (1990) 87 L.S.Gaz. April 25, p. 8, May 9, p. 3. This removed the main fears of solicitors and consumer groups aroused by the original version.

[5] See J. Hodgson, (1988) 138 N.L.J. 615, commenting on the proposals of the Marre Committee.

Probate

Section 54 of the 1990 Act will extend the right to perform probate work for reward to banks, building societies, insurance companies and their subsidiaries, provided that they operate a complaints scheme which complies with requirements prescribed by regulations, and to other bodies approved under section 55 and Schedule 9.[6] Possible candidates for inclusion include legal executives, licensed conveyancers,[7] authorised conveyancing practitioners and accountants.

(v) *Restrictions on practice*

Multi-disciplinary practices

A solicitor may employ, but may not form a partnership with a member of another profession.[8] This has prevented the development of "group practices" of lawyers and members of other professions. The Royal Commission was not in favour of any change. Some of the candidates for partnership, such as doctors, engineers, architects, patent agents and actuaries would most often be needed to give expert evidence in litigation; it would be inappropriate for them to be in partnership with the lawyers who were preparing the case for trial. If partnerships with estate agents were allowed, there was a danger that sole practitioners and small firms would be absorbed into large estate agents' firms, to the detriment of general practice in small towns and rural areas. The Commission thought that in general it was in the client's interest to be able to choose his or her adviser without restriction; with multi-disciplinary partnerships there would be a tendency to keep a client within the firm. There would also be difficulties in drawing up common codes of conduct. The Commission did, however, accept that solicitors' firms should be allowed to incorporate, with unlimited liability only, under the Companies Acts.[9] Provision for incorporated practices was made by section 9 of the Administration of Justice Act 1985, although this is not in force at the time of writing. The Law Society has made special rules for such practices.[10] They will have to be owned, managed and controlled by solicitors, and recognised by the Council of the Law Society as being a suitable body to undertake the provision of solicitors' services. Incorporation with limited liability will be permitted provided there is additional insurance cover.[11]

The debate over the issue of multi-disciplinary partnerships has nevertheless continued. Pressure for change has come from the Director General of

---

[6] See, the *Green Paper: The Work and Organisation of the Legal Profession* (Cm. 570), Chap. 14, and the *White Paper* (Cm. 740), Chap. 6.

[7] 1990 Act, s.53.

[8] Solicitors' Practice Rules 1990, r. 7(6).

[9] R.C.L.S., Vol. 1, pp. 401–404.

[10] Solicitors' Incorporated Practice Rules 1988, as amended.

[11] See (1988) 85 L.S.Gaz., February 3, p. 13: report of the January meeting of the Council of the Law Society, on the justification for permitting limited liability. See also (1985) 82 L.S.Gaz. 2253, discussing the pros and cons of incorporation.

Fair Trading, Sir Gordon Borrie. A report by him in 1986[12] supported the view that mixed practices should be encouraged, with suitable safeguards for the maintenance of professional standards and adequate consumer protection; the statutory impediments against their development[13] should be removed, paving the way for suitable alterations to the practice rules.

Support for the development of multi-disciplinary practices also came from the National Consumer Council.[14] They considered that there were a number of ways in which consumers could benefit, including the convenience of "one-stop" house transfer (covering a mortgage, a survey, help with selling and conveyancing services), the reduction in duplication, delay and extra cost in fields such as tax planning that could come with mixed practices of solicitors and accountants and the greater facility for bringing management expertise into the organisation of solicitors' practices. It has also been argued that such practices would have advantages for commercial clients.[15]

The Law Society has been more cautious. It issued a consultation paper in 1987 setting out both sides of the debate.[16] It emphasised the need to preserve "the solicitor's traditional role as an independent and impartial adviser of integrity enjoying a unique position as an officer of the court who is readily available to the public." Independence would be weakened if a solicitor were employed by a non-solicitor, or the practice was owned wholly or partly by a non-solicitor. Mixed practices might lead to confusion as members of the same firm would be subject to different sets of professional practice rules. The development of large practices might be at the expense of smaller ones and so reduce the number of solicitors' firms available to the public. On the other hand, mixed practices could enable solicitors to respond to a more competitive environment, by offering a broader range of services; overheads could be shared; it would be easier to run intensive training programmes; there could be economies of scale. Since then the Law Society has been engaged in discussions with other professions. The Marre Committee took the view that any action should await the outcome of these discussions.[17]

The Green Paper[18] proposed, in line with Sir Gordon Borrie's recommendation in 1986, that the statutory inhibitions on multi-disciplinary practices should be removed. In response, the Law Society's attitude hardened.[19] It

---

[12] *Restrictions on the kind of organisation through which members of professions may offer their services*: *A Report by the Director General of Fair Trading* (O.F.T., August 1986): see (1986) 136 N.L.J. 833. He repeated this call in an address to the Macfarlanes Seminar held at the University of Nottingham on November 18, 1987: see (1987) 34 L.S.Gaz. 3385 and (1988) 85 L.S.Gaz., February 3, p. 8.

[13] Solicitors Act 1974, ss.39 (preventing a solicitor from acting as an agent for an unqualified person in contentious matters) and 22 (preventing a solicitor sharing conveyancing fees with an unqualified person).

[14] *Ordinary Justice* (H.M.S.O., 1989), pp. 237–245.

[15] P. Couse (President of the Institute of Chartered Accountants in England and Wales), (1990) 87 L.S.Gaz. April 11, p. 2.

[16] *Multi-disciplinary partnerships and allied topics* (April 1987). For responses, see (1987) 84 L.S.Gaz., 2495, J. Harris, (1987) 131 S.J. 644.

[17] *A Time for Change* (1988), pp. 173–177.

[18] *The Work and Organisation of the Legal Profession* (Cm. 570), pp. 43–47.

[19] *Striking the Balance*: *The Final Response of the Council of the Law Society on the Green Papers* (1989), pp. 23–28.

argued that to allow such practices would undermine the network of solicitors' firms, threaten client confidentiality, create potential conflicts of interest, make it more difficult to pursue a complaint and handicap British firms in Europe. As these problems could not satisfactorily be overcome, the statutory prohibition should be maintained. Its view, however, did not prevail.

Section 66 of the Courts and Legal Services Act 1990 repeals section 39 of the Solicitors Act 1974, while providing that this is not to prevent the Law Society from making rules restricting multi-disciplinary partnerships. The matter will thus be left to professional rules. The *White Paper*[20] states that it is the government's intention that rules of practice approved by, among others, the Lord Chancellor under the procedure described above,[21] should be excluded from prohibition under the proposed new legislation on restrictive trade practices.[22]

One point stressed by the Law Society, the Marre Committee and the National Consumer Council is that if a practice is called "solicitors" it should have a majority of solicitor partners, should be controlled by solicitors and should be regulated by solicitors' rules as to accounts, insurance and compensation arrangements.[23]

Multi-national practices

The statutory inhibitions on multi-disciplinary practices have also, hitherto, prevented participation in multi-national practices in conjunction with lawyers in other jurisdictions. The pressure for such a development has grown as commercial operations have become more national, a trend reinforced in the European Communities with completion of the single market in 1992, and steps towards the mutual recognition of professional qualifications.[24] The Law Society saw far fewer difficulties of identity and regulation here, and agreed with the proposal in the Green Paper that the statutory inhibitions should be removed.[25] This is also achieved by section 66 of the Courts and Legal Services Act 1990.

There has been an increasing trend for larger solicitors' firms to open offices abroad, for foreign lawyers to establish offices in the U.K.,[26] and for U.K. firms to become associated with foreign firms.[27] The first steps towards the establishment of multi-national practices have already been taken, in anticipation of the legislation.[28] It is anticipated that such developments will accelerate.

[20] Cm. 740, para. 12.3.
[21] At pp. 132–133.
[22] See the White Paper, *Opening Markets—New Policy on Restrictive Trade Practices* (Cm. 727, 1989).
[23] *Striking the Balance*, p. 27; *A Time for Change*, p. 176; *Ordinary Justice*, p. 243.
[24] See below, pp. 176–177.
[25] *Green Paper: The Work and Organisation of the Legal Profession* (Cm. 570), pp. 47–48; *Striking the Balance*, p. 28; *White Paper* (Cm. 740), Chap. 13. The Council of the Law Society issued a consultation paper on multi-national partnerships in March 1988: see (1988) 85 L.S.Gaz., March 23, pp. 36–38, and on the regulation of such partnerships, in August 1989.
[26] See J. Carr and R. Morrissey, (1988) I.F.L. Rev. 5, noting the advantages for London of non-jury commercial courts, and being in a time zone between Tokyo and New York; *The Lawyer*, October 2, 1990, pp. 12–13.
[27] J. Carr, (1990) I.F.L. Rev. 13.
[28] (1990) 87 L.S.Gaz., February 14, p. 6.

Other developments

In the course of the on-going debate as to appropriate structures for solicitors' practices, the Law Society has relaxed some of its other rules. Thus solicitors may now share fees with non-solicitor employees and with an estate agent instructed as a sub-agent for the sale of a property[29]; the rules about introductions and referrals have been relaxed[30] and non-legal services may be "hived off" to a separate business.[31] On the other hand, new controls on persons (including solicitors) carrying on investment business were introduced by the Financial Services Act 1986. The concept of "investment business" is wide, and includes dealing in investments, arranging deals in investments, (e.g. arranging for a client to take out a life policy in connection with house purchase), managing investments, (e.g. as a trustee), and giving investment advice. The Law Society has obtained the status of a Recognised Professional Body under the Act, and so may authorise solicitors' firms to conduct investment business. The conduct of such business is regulated by the Solicitors' Investment Business Rules 1990.[32]

Advertising

Another important area of restriction has until recently concerned advertising by individual solicitors or firms.[33] "Touting" was regarded as unprofessional and associated with "trade."[34] Collective advertising by the profession and detailed referral lists[35] were, by contrast, officially acceptable. The Law Society was responsible for various national advertising campaigns,[36] financed by levies on practising certificates. They proved controversial.[37] The introduction of individual advertising, subject to restrictions preventing claims of superiority, inaccurate or misleading statements and publicity likely to bring the profession into disrepute, was recommended by both the

---

[29] Solicitors' Practice Rules 1990, Rule 7(1)(c), (2), first introduced in the 1988 Rules: (1988) 85 L.S.Gaz., February 3, p. 13.

[30] See below, p. 140.

[31] 1990 Rules, Rule 5; first modified in the 1988 Rules: (1988) 85 L.S.Gaz., February 3, p. 14.

[32] *The Guide to the Professional Conduct of Solicitors* (1990), Chap. 3 and pp. 318–365, 395–397. See P. Camp, (1988) 85 L.S.Gaz., October 20, pp. 35–36, November 16, pp. 17–18.

[33] It used to be prohibited: Solicitors' Practice Rules, 1936–72, r. 1. See below, p. 138; Zander (1978), pp. 46–54; P. Fennell in P. A. Thomas (ed.) *Law in the Balance* (1982), Chap. 6.

[34] Fennell notes that in fact "professional ideology is not exclusively anti-entrepreneurial, but . . . incorporates elements of the value systems of both the 'pre-industrial gentleman' and the tradesman." (*Law in the Balance* (1982), p. 144).

[35] See below, p. 138.

[36] The "Mr. Whatsisname" campaign in 1977 (see R. Neill, (1977) 74 L.S.Gaz. 883; G. Sanctuary (1978) 75 L.S.Gaz. 267), a second in 1979 and a third in 1980, the latter two produced by Saatchi and Saatchi. The 1980 theme was that people should "consult a solicitor before problems got out of hand;" one of the advertisements illustrated an action for damages in respect of an injured thumb: (1980) 77 L.S.Gaz. 501.

[37] D. Podmore, (1980) 7 B.J.L.S. 1, 8.

Monopolies Commission[38] and the Royal Commission.[39] Providing information to the public would thus be permitted; drumming up business would still
be prohibited.

The relaxation of the restrictions on advertising was regarded by the
Royal Commission not simply as helping to improve access to legal services
but also as the "necessary concomitant" to their conclusion that the solicitors' conveyancing monopoly should be retained. Individual advertising
should help the public to "shop around."[40] Ironically it was more the threat
of the loss of the conveyancing monopoly following the favourable reception
of Austin Mitchell's Bill that finally spurred the Law Society into action. It
responded by introducing a new national Solicitors' Directory, including
information as to the categories of work undertaken (published as part of the
Solicitors' and Barristers' Directory and Diary) and 28 regional directories
(replacing the *Legal Aid Solicitors' List*). It also agreed that individual
advertising on radio (but not television) and in the national and local press
should be permitted, subject to recommended restrictions, and that charges
might be advertised.[41] The new rules narrowly survived a ballot of the
profession in 1985,[42] but there was a further significant relaxation in 1987,[43]
prompted in part by the establishment of licensed conveyancers and the
(albeit limited) proposals to allow building societies to undertake conveyancing contained in the Building Societies Act 1986. The old rule 1 of the
Solicitors' Practice Rules 1936–72, which had prohibited (with exceptions)
inviting instructions for business, advertising and touting, was replaced by
new rules. They were modified in 1988,[44] and are now found in Rules 1 to 3 of
the Solicitors' Practice Rules 1990.

Rule 1 states that a solicitor must not do anything in the course of practice,
or permit another to do anything on his or her behalf, to compromise or
impair

(a) the solicitor's independence or integrity;
(b) a person's freedom to instruct a solicitor of his or her choice;
(c) the solicitor's duty to act in the best interest of the client;
(d) the good repute of the solicitor or of the solicitor's profession;
(e) the solicitor's proper standard of work;
(f) the solicitor's duty to the court.

Rule 2 states that solicitors may at their discretion publicise their practices,
or permit others to do so, or publicise the business or activities of other
persons, provided there is no breach of the Practice Rules, and compliance

---

[38] *Report on the supply of services of Solicitors in England and Wales in relation to restrictions on
advertising*, 1976 (1975–76 H.C. 557).
[39] Vol. 1, pp. 367–373. Similar guidelines were promulgated by the Consultative Committee of
the Bars and Law Societies of the European Community (C.C.B.E.) governing advertising of
lawyers' services in the Community: (1980) 77 L.S.Gaz. 662. In *Bates* v. *State Bar of Arizona*,
53 L.Ed. 2d 810 (1977) the United States Supreme Court held that it was unconstitutional to
prevent lawyers advertising the availability and cost of routine legal services.
[40] Sir Henry Benson, (1979) 76 L.S.Gaz. 1029, 1030.
[41] (1983) 80 L.S.Gaz. 1797, 3222 and 3223; (1984) 81 L.S.Gaz. 1802–3, 2583; (1985) 82
L.S.Gaz. 3057.
[42] (1985) 82 L.S.Gaz. 2137.
[43] (1987) 84 L.S.Gaz. 155, 234.
[44] See (1988) 85 L.S.Gaz. June 15, p. 11.

with the Solicitors' Publicity Code. Rule 3 states that solicitors may accept introductions and referrals of business from other persons and may make introductions and refer business to other persons, provided there is no breach of the Practice Rules, and compliance with the Solicitors' Introduction and Referral Code. The Codes mentioned in Rules 2 and 3 are promulgated by the Council of the Law Society with the concurrence of the Master of the Rolls.

The 1987 Publicity Code permitted, *inter alia*, advertising on television, direct mailing, advertising by a third party and references to the quality of the solicitor's service. Further changes followed in the 1990 version[45] permitting, *inter alia*, claims that a solicitor is a specialist or an expert, provided that such a claim can be justified, and relaxing the rules on naming clients and unsolicited visits and telephone calls.

The 1990 Code permits advertising provided that it complies with the Practice Rules, cannot reasonably be regarded as being in bad taste, is not misleading or inaccurate, and complies with any statutory requirements, (*e.g.* in regulations under the Consumer Credit Act 1974) and the British Code of Advertising Practice or I.B.A. Code of Advertising Standards and Practice. The publicity may be in any medium, may name clients (with their consent) and may include statements as to charges. It may not refer to a solicitor's success rate, make direct comparison or criticism in relation to the charges or quality of service of any other identifiable solicitor. Unsolicited telephone calls or visits are not permitted except for calls or visits to another professional, or to publicise a specific commercial property the solicitor has to sell or let, and calls to current or former clients.

A survey of 796 firms in 1986–87 showed that 45.5 per cent. had advertised in the media or in Yellow Pages in the previous six months. This figure concealed wide geographical variations, and a high level of "one-off" as opposed to repeat advertising. A wide variety of methods was employed.[46] Particular examples of advertising methods include local radio, the sponsorship of a football team, advertising on buses and the use of advertising hoardings.[47] A survey of advertisements in the local press and Yellow Pages led the National Consumer Council to conclude that solicitors advertising was a small step in the right direction, telling consumers the type of work a firm is willing to handle and helping to make conveyancing more price competitive. However, it rarely drew attention to legal remedies which people did not know about.[48] It has been suggested that firms are in fact wasting money on poor marketing.[49]

Rule 3, first introduced in the 1988 version of the Practice Rules, permits "arrangements" for the introduction of business. This enables solicitors to

[45] Solicitors' Publicity Code 1990: Law Society Professional Standards Bulletin No. 3, August 1990; (1990) 87 L.S.Gaz. August 22, 1990, p. 25.
[46] L. Farmer *et al.* "Advertising by Solicitors" (1988) 85 L.S.Gaz., October 20, p. 25. See also a survey of 350 firms in 1987: (1987) 131 S.J. 760. In 1989–90, over 1200 firms advertised in Yellow Pages through programmes organised by the Law Society: (1990) 87 L.S.Gaz., May 23, p. 13.
[47] M. Zander, *A Matter of Justice* (Revised edn., 1989), pp. 12–14.
[48] N.C.C., *Ordinary Justice* (H.M.S.O., 1989), pp. 138–141.
[49] Study by N. Morgan of 74 firms: (1989) 86 L.S.Gaz., April 26, p. 5. He found that marketing activity tended to be restricted to the responsible person or department operating within a narrow brief; market research was used infrequently; and there was little feedback from customers.

prepare or participate in a package of services together with other businesses or professional practices.[50] The Solicitors' Introduction and Referral Code 1990[51] applies to introductions and referrals other than between solicitors, between solicitors and barristers or between solicitors and lawyers of other jurisdictions. It states that solicitors should not allow themselves to become so reliant on a limited number of sources of referrals that the interests of the introducers affect the advice given by the solicitor to clients; each firm should conduct six-monthly reviews; where more than 20 per cent. of the firm's income arises from a single source of introduction, the firm should consider whether steps should be taken to reduce the proportion.

(d) Barristers and their work

(i) *Numbers*

In October 1990 there were 6,645 barristers (including 682 Q.C.s) practising in 374 sets of chambers. 4,638 were in 232 sets in central London, and the rest were spread through 30 provincial centres.[52] As was the case with solicitors, the numbers of practising barristers increased significantly in the late 1960s and 1970s following a period of shortage. They more than doubled between 1963 and 1979, and increased by almost a half between 1979 and 1989.[53] The net annual increase declined between 1975 and 1979, with increasing numbers ceasing practice.[54] The proportion of the profession of 10 years' call and under has also shown a marked increase: in 1966 there were 769 (34 per cent. of the practising Bar) and in 1983, 2,367 (47 per cent.).[55] The average size of sets of chambers has steadily increased.[56]

(ii) *Work*

A barrister may have a general or specialist common law practice (contract, crime, tort—especially personal injury cases, landlord and tenant, family matters), or may specialise in Chancery work (trusts, land law, conveyancing, wills, company law, revenue matters) or in one of a number of narrower fields (tax, patents, commercial matters, planning, admiralty,

---

[50] *e.g.* a solicitor may give an estate agent a price list to hand to the client or may work as part of an inclusive deal in which the agent charges the seller a fixed price and pays a fixed or hourly rate for the conveyancing service: *Ordinary Justice*, pp. 134–136. The N.C.C. thought the Code was difficult to interpret and enforce and suggested that the development of advertising was likely to reduce the importance of introductions by local businesses.

[51] See, "Arrangements: estate agents and solicitors" (1988) 85 L.S.Gaz., August 31, p. 11.

[52] Annual Report of the Bar Council 1990, pp. 20–21. Barristers in London may also join their provincial colleagues on one of the six Circuits: Northern, North Eastern, Midland and Oxford, Western, South Eastern and Wales and Chester. The circuits now are important as the units of regional court administration. Each Circuit elects a Leader and Committee. See *Counsel*, March 1990.

[53] R.C.L.S., Vol. 2, p. 54; Annual Report of the Bar Council 1990, pp. 20–21. The growth of the Bar is documented in R. L. Abel, *The Legal Profession in England and Wales* (1988), pp. 65–72, and see pp. 342–343, Table 1.16 (general figures for 1947–85) and pp. 358–359, Table 1.26 (growth of the provincial Bar).

[54] Annual Statement, 1983–84, p. 68. The figure since then has fluctuated, settling down between 1981 and 1985 to about 170, but becoming more variable thereafter.

[55] *Ibid.* p. 19. In 1988, about half of barristers in independent practice were 12 years or less since call: *Quality of Justice* (1989), p. 53.

[56] Abel (1988), pp. 360–361, Table 1.27.

libel, public law). Most of the recent increase in the size of this branch of the profession has been in the generalist common law area. In London, common law chambers are concentrated in the Temple; Chancery barristers are concentrated in Lincoln's Inn. There is no rule requiring chambers to be in one of the inns of court. Concentration there has been preferred because the inns until recently have charged barristers only a proportion of the market rent, for the convenience of access to the courts and because of long tradition.[57]

A "rough guide" to the specialist work done by barristers was given in the Bar's Response to the Green Papers[58]:

Analysis of Barristers' Practices

	0% — 10%	10% — 20%	20% — 30%	30% — 40%	40% — 50%	50% — 60%	60% — 70%	70% — 80%	80% — 90%	90% — 100%	Total
Admiralty	71	3	1	18	6	2	15	0	0	0	116
Commercial	544	204	124	72	89	38	45	45	42	62	1265
Criminal	512	275	268	324	344	268	310	408	431	1026	4166
Defamation	144	15	3	5	4	2	3	5	4	9	194
Employment	880	121	30	16	13	8	4	2	3	2	1079
European	73	9	6	5	2	1	0	3	6	10	115
Family	1131	524	367	212	152	79	58	66	47	65	2701
Immigration	188	24	15	5	5	3	1	7	2	2	252
Insolvency	429	63	22	10	11	4	1	2	2	2	546
International	85	19	13	8	8	2	0	0	1	12	148
Official Referees	541	97	50	31	42	16	10	9	1	2	799
Parliamentary	274	53	19	21	12	12	10	14	17	59	491
Patents	192	15	11	3	3	2	3	6	10	31	276
Restrictive Practices and Monopolies	28	4	7	3	1	3	0	1	1	0	48
Revenue	127	21	13	5	10	1	4	4	7	45	237
Chancery	649	136	73	48	43	43	36	67	57	86	1238
Common Law	1349	810	554	435	288	138	122	102	75	84	3957
Other	258	54	40	26	29	12	13	10	13	109	564

[57] R.C.L.S., Vol. 1, pp. 449–450. There is a set in Wellington St., Covent Garden, and other sets have opened outside the Inns.

[58] *Quality of Justice: The Bar's Response* (1989), pp. 43 and 44, Fig. 5.2.

The percentages of gross earnings by area of law for barristers were crime 30 per cent., general civil (common law) 17 per cent., commercial general 13 per cent., family 7 per cent., chancery 8 per cent., commercial specialist 9 per cent., tax 3 per cent., and 12 per cent., other specialisations.[59]

In the 1970s there were concerns that the recommendations of the Royal Commission on Civil Liability and Compensation and Legal Services might prove a threat to the work of barristers. In the event even the modest, piecemeal, proposals of the former were not implemented, apart from some changes to the law of damages.[60] As we have seen, the Bar's rights of audience were upheld by the latter,[61] and members of the Crown Prosecution Service established by the Prosecution of Offences Act 1985 were not given rights of audience in the Crown Court and above.[62] It seemed that prospects were not as bleak as had been feared. However, the Royal Commission on Legal Services confirmed that barristers were increasingly dependent on public funds,[63] and, since then, the low rates of increase in fees for legal aid work has caused increasing dissatisfaction. The renewed challenge of the Law Society on rights of audience and then the government's proposals for radical reform once again put the Bar on the defensive.[64] As we have seen, its case for preserving its monopoly of rights of audience in the higher courts has not prevailed. It remains to be seen how far the designated judges will be able to fight a rearguard action, and what use will in practice be made by solicitors and other professions of extended rights of audience.

As to remuneration, the Royal Commission concluded that the earnings of barristers were not out of line with those in comparable occupations, except that the earnings of barristers in the early years of practice were low.[65] A report by Coopers & Lybrand in 1985 of the remuneration levels of junior council carrying out publicly funded criminal defence work claimed that fees fell well below what was required to meet the principle of "fair and reasonable reward for work reasonably done," and that an increase of 30–40 per cent. was necessary to improve the position.[66] The Lord Chancellor rejected a claim for such an increase, casting doubt on some of the assumptions relied on in the Coopers & Lybrand report, and raised fees by 5 per cent. The Bar challenged the decision in court, proceedings being settled on the agreement

[59] *Ibid.* p. 45, Fig. 5.3.
[60] Royal Commission on Civil Liability and Compensation (Cmnd. 7054, 1979); Administration of Justice Act 1982. The Royal Commission did not even recommend the introduction of a comprehensive state scheme for compensating accident victims.
[61] Above, pp. 129–130.
[62] Below, pp. 623–624.
[63] In 1976–77, £23m out of £48m total gross fees were from public funds: R.C.L.S., Vol. 2, pp. 595–597.
[64] Illustrated by the substantial report, *Quality of Justice*, produced quickly in response to the Green Paper in 1989.
[65] See R.C.L.S., Vol. 1, pp. 507–542 and Vol. 2, pp. 579–626 (surveys of barristers' earnings). Figures for senior barristers are given in the Reports of the Top Salaries Review Board. Income Data Services Ltd. prepared estimates of barristers' earnings as at April 1988 for the Andrew Review of Government Legal Services (H.M.S.O., 1989), Annex to Chap. VIII (pp. 66–69). The median figure for those with between 15 and 35 years experience was £105,954 (Q.C.s) and £39,415 (juniors). The figures were substantially lower for those concentrating on criminal cases. In 1990 Chambers & Partners estimated that likely gross earnings for reasonably successful barristers ranged from £18,000 (early years) to £100,000+ (Q.C.s) in criminal work and £20–£40,000 (earlier years) to £300–600,000+ (Q.C.s) in commercial work: *Chambers & Partners' Directory of The Legal Profession 1990*, p. 19.
[66] Annual Statement of the Senate 1985–86, p. 76; (1985) 82 L.S.Gaz. 2636.

of the Lord Chancellor to a binding time-table for negotiations for an increase in fees.[67] The Lord Chancellor eventually awarded an additional 3 per cent., plus another 2 per cent. if the Bar would change its working practices.[68] The complaints have not gone away. The result has been an increasing polarisation of the Bar between specialists who can command enormous fees[69] and the large number of barristers who rely on public funds.

The late payment of fees by solicitors has been a serious cause for complaint among barristers. The Law Society and the Senate responded by tightening up the procedures for enforcing payments, and the Bar clarified the terms of work on which barristers are prepared to act. These developments did not satisfy all the critics.[70] In 1987, the Bar Council announced that, as from March 2, the Bar would withdraw credit facilities from solicitors who had failed to pay barristers' fees for over a year after reminders.[71] A revised code for barristers' terms of work was published in 1988.[72] The Law Society unsuccessfully sought changes, and advised solicitors to make it clear that, unless they thought it appropriate, they would not comply with the Bar's requirement that fees be paid within 3 months of delivery of the fee note, whether or not the solicitor had been placed in funds by the client and whether or not the case was still continuing.[73]

There are at least as many barristers employed in commerce, industry and central and local government as there are in private practice.[74] Their work compares much more closely with that done by employed solicitors in the same fields than with that done by barristers in private practice. Indeed, in 1976 the Chairman of the Solicitors' Commerce and Industry Group said that:

"Fusion is a word that we in commerce and industry never use in practice, because it is an accomplished fact with us. Barristers and solicitors are almost completely interchangeable. . . ."[75]

The Law Society has expressed the view that people who wish to practise as a solicitor should become a solicitor. It has also been suggested that one reason why such barristers do not change is snobbery.[76] However, the Bar Association for Commerce, Finance and Industry persuaded the Royal Commission that the rules preventing employed barristers from undertaking conveyancing and briefing other barristers in non-contentious matters

---

[67] R. v. Lord Chancellor, ex p. Alexander, The Times, March 21, 22, 24 and 27, 1986; Counsel, Easter Term 1986, pp. 24–25. For the background correspondence see the Annual Statement 1985–86, pp. 27–31, and for the proceedings of an angry extraordinary general meeting of the Bar, which authorised the proceedings, see ibid. pp. 32–41.

[68] (1986) 83 L.S.Gaz. 2282–7.

[69] M. Zander, A Matter of Justice (Revised edn., 1989), pp. 34–35.

[70] Annual Statement, 1982–83, pp. 23–41; J. Ferris, (1982) 132 N.L.J. 745; S. Best, (1982) 132 N.L.J. 803.

[71] (1987) 84 L.S.Gaz., 573; Counsel, Spring 1987, pp. 27, 28.

[72] (1988) 85 L.S.Gaz., September 28, pp. 40–41.

[73] Ibid.

[74] R. L. Abel, The Legal Profession in England and Wales (1988), pp. 111–113.

[75] (1976) 73 L.S.Gaz. 369.

[76] R.C.L.S., Vol. 1, p. 237; "Enobarbus" (1980) 77 L.S.Gaz. 766.

should be relaxed.[77] The Bar Council acted on this recommendation,[78] much to the displeasure of the Law Society.[79]

Further substantial changes took place in 1989 and 1990. In 1989, employed barristers became practising barristers in the same way as those in independent practice.[80] Employed barristers who have done pupillage and those who became employed barristers before January 1, 1989, and are of five years' standing, are now entitled to appear on behalf of their employers (or a fellow employee) as counsel in any courts, other than those in which barristers in independent practice have an exclusive right of audience. They need not be instructed by a solicitor. Any barrister employed by a public authority can now give instructions to a barrister in independent practice, as can employed barristers in the private sector (except in respect of criminal proceedings in the Crown Court or higher courts or where rules of court require the intervention of a solicitor). Employed barristers registered with the Bar Council can undertake conveyancing work for their employer (but not a fellow employee). Employed barristers are subject to many provisions of the Code of Conduct. An important restriction is that employed barristers may not offer legal services to the public.[81]

This last rule was flouted in a public way by a few barristers entering employment, particularly with firms of accountants, but also with surveyors or foreign lawyers. For example, Reginald Nock, a leading expert on stamp duty, joined the accountants, Coopers & Lybrand Deloitte. In response, a Bar Working Party, chaired by Mummery J., recommended that the Code of Conduct be amended to recognise a class of "non-practising barristers," free to advise members of the public, but unable to appear as counsel in any court. This recommendation was accepted.[82]

(iii) *Restrictions on practice*

One of the main restrictions has long been the general rule that they may only take instructions from a solicitor.[83] There are several long established exceptions,[84] covering such matters as foreign work, the examination of material to be published to check for libel and contempt, and briefing by a patent agent or parliamentary agent. There are also special rules covering barristers employed in law centres.[85] The general rule is of comparatively recent origin, being settled as regards contentious work in 1888 and non-contentious work in 1955. Significant exceptions were made to enable barristers to compete more effectively for foreign work. The Overseas

---

[77] R.C.L.S., Vol. 1, pp. 237–241.
[78] Annual Statement, 1979–80, pp. 52–55.
[79] Anon., "A Road to Fusion?" (1980) 77 L.S.Gaz. 637–8. This issue had previously been a bone of contention between the two branches: Abel-Smith and Stevens (1967) pp. 439–443.
[80] *Code of Conduct* (1990 edn.), paras. 401–405; P. Stivadoros, (1989) 139 N.L.J. 20.
[81] See *Code of Conduct*, Annex G.
[82] Report of the Employed Bar Working Party (1990); E. Gilvarry, (1990) 87 L.S.Gaz., September 26, p. 6.
[83] R.C.L.S., Vol. 1, pp. 222–5; In *Re T. (A Barrister)* [1982] Q.B. 430 the visitors to Lincoln's Inn upheld an order that a barrister be suspended for four months for breach of this rule and another act of professional misconduct.
[84] See now *Code of Conduct* (1990 edn.), paras. 305, 306 and Annexes E and F.
[85] See below, pp. 435–440.

Practice Rules were introduced in 1973[86] and relaxed many of the basic rules of conduct for barristers: apart from being able to receive instructions direct, barristers may negotiate fees direct, accept an annual retainer, a fixed fee or a contingent fee, and enter into partnership with any lawyer other than a solicitor for the purpose of sharing an office or services abroad.

From time to time there were rumblings from the Bar that their "self-denying ordinance" might be withdrawn,[87] but the Senate suggested to the Royal Commission that barristers were not equipped to deal with the office work necessary if they were to deal directly with clients. Having decided that fusion would not be in the public interest[88] it was inevitable that the Royal Commission would not favour the wholesale removal of restrictions on direct access.

Since then, access has been accorded to licensed conveyancers (in conveyancing matters), the Government Legal Service, the legal department of a local or public authority (if headed by a barrister or solicitor), employed barristers, arbitrators, and ombudsmen recognised by the Bar Council.[89] Indeed the governing provision in the Code of Conduct now requires that barristers in independent practice provide legal services only if instructed by a "professional client."[90] A major relaxation to allow direct access by members of recognised professional bodies took effect from April 1, 1989.[91] The principle had been approved in 1986 but implementation was delayed, *inter alia*, by the appointment of the Marre Committee. The criteria for recognition are that the body is regulated by a written constitution controlling admission and incorporating a disciplinary code, and that its members provide skilled and specialist services and are likely to have a significant requirement to retain barristers. Early recognised bodies covered accountants and surveyors.[92] Direct access here does not extend to appearances in the higher courts, the county court and the Employment Appeal Tribunal, in view of the objections of the judiciary. The Bar continues to oppose direct lay access on arguments similar to those put to the Royal Commission.[93] Both the Green Paper and the White Paper stated that questions of access should be left to the profession.[94] In the context of these various changes

---

[86] Annual Statement of the Bar Council, 1973–74, pp. 33–34. They were subsequently relaxed even further: see *Code of Conduct* (1990 edn.), para. 306 and Annex F (Overseas Practice Rules).

[87] R. Hazell, *The Bar on Trial* (1978) pp. 172–173.

[88] See above, pp. 116–117.

[89] See *Code of Conduct* (1990 edn.), paras. 204, 305 and 901 (definitions of "Direct Professional Access work" and "professional client") and Annex E (The Direct Professional Access Rules).

[90] *Ibid.*

[91] See A. Thornton Q.C., "Direct Professional Access" *Counsel*, March/April 1989, pp. 17–19.

[92] *Quality of Justice: Response of the Bar* (1989), p. 142. Others include the Royal Town Planning Institute, the Association of Average Adjusters, the Institution of Mechanical Engineers, the Institution of Chemical Engineers, the Institute of Taxation, the Institute of Chartered Secretaries & Administrators, and the Incorporated Society of Valuers and Auctioneers: *Counsel*, July/August 1989, p. 27.

[93] *Quality of Justice*, pp. 140–142.

[94] Cm. 570, Chap. 8; Cm. 740, p. 38.

widening direct access to the Bar, it was inevitable that the Bar's rules restricting advertising would be relaxed.[95]

A practising barrister may not enter a partnership with another practising barrister.[96] The Bar "is an intensely *individual* profession."[97] The Royal Commission recognised that partnerships might often be advantageous for barristers. An income could more easily be provided for a beginner, work could be distributed more evenly and provision for sickness and retirement would be easier. They concluded, however, that a change would not be in the public interest as it would restrict choice, on the assumption that partners would not be permitted to appear on opposite sides. Problems might be acute at the specialist and provincial bars.[98]

Individualism was tempered by requirements that practising barristers join a set of chambers[99] and have the services of the clerk to the chambers. It is possible for a set of chambers to contain only one member, but in 1984 the average number of barristers per set in London was 16.7 and only 3 per cent. of 222 sets had four or fewer members.[1] In evidence to the Royal Commission the Senate saw dangers in barristers practising alone, particularly in the criminal courts. They would be exposed to pressure to ignore the rules against touting and improper association with clients and witnesses; the younger the barrister, the greater the risk. Practice in chambers provided the "mutual support in respect of expenses and the allocation of work, professional association, informal advice and guidance, devilling and assistance to newcomers."[2] The Senate preferred to see "balanced" sets with barristers of all grades of seniority.[3] In addition to the provision of mutual aid and comfort, the chambers rule was seen by the Royal Commission as aiding the Senate in its task of "controlling backsliders" and maintaining standards.[4] In many respects chambers operate as *de facto* partnerships, with the sharing of expenses, the common fund of goodwill and the fact that briefs may be sent to a set of chambers rather than an individual barrister. Furthermore, a barrister may obtain the assistance of a fellow barrister in the preparation of his paperwork, and, with the consent of the instructing solicitor, at a hearing. Such arrangements are known as "devilling." The

---

[95] The rules were relaxed in 1987 to permit advertising in professional directories and chambers' brochures: see D. Farrer and A. Speight, *Counsel*, Spring 1987, p. 4 and January 1988, pp. 30–33; M. Findlay, *Law Magazine*, January 8, 1988, pp. 28–29; *Counsel*, March 1990, pp. 18–20 (brochures competition). They were relaxed further in 1989: see now *Code of Conduct* (1990 edn.), para. 307, permitting any advertising complying with the British Code of Advertising Practice. Barristers may now advertise their rates and methods of charging and make claims about the nature and extent of the services offered (but not quality, size of practice, or success rate).

[96] *Code of Conduct* (1990 edn.), para. 211.

[97] General Council of the Bar, *A Career at the Bar* (1988), p. 2.

[98] R.C.L.S., Vol. 1, pp. 462–465, Vol. 2, pp. 375–392. The case for allowing partnerships is argued in M. Zander, *Lawyers and the Public Interest* (1968), pp. 252–269 and Hazell (1978), pp. 123–129.

[99] New sets could only be opened with the consent of the Circuit or (in London) the Bar Council.

[1] R. L. Abel, *The Legal Profession in England and Wales* (1988), pp. 360–363. The average in the provinces was 12.6 and 8 per cent. of 119 sets had four or fewer members.

[2] R.C.L.S., Vol. 1, p. 455. The internal management of chambers has been made the subject of "Chambers Guidelines" issued by the Senate in 1977 (R.C.L.S., Vol. 1, pp. 475–478). See now *Action Pack: Counsel's Guide to Chambers Administration* (2nd edn., 1988).

[3] R.C.L.S., Vol. 1, p. 452.

[4] R.C.L.S., Vol. 1, pp. 454, 455.

barrister briefed retains his or her personal responsibility but must pay the "devil" adequate and reasonable remuneration, normally half the fee. So, while barristers are supposed to "stand on their own two feet," there are many ways in which their colleagues can help them remain upright. Purse-sharing arrangements have been permitted but have not been widely used.[5]

The Courts and Legal Services Act 1990 declares that no rule of common law prevents barristers from entering into any unincorporated association with persons who are not barristers, but that this is not to prevent the General Council of the Bar from making rules which prohibit or restrict such partnerships.[6] Such rules will be subject to review under the proposed restrictive practices legislation. The *Green Paper: The Work and Organisation of the Legal Profession*[7] stated the view that barristers should be permitted to operate in partnership if they chose to do so. The risk of diminishing clients' choice was outweighed by the advantages of greater efficiency and easing the entry of new barristers into the profession. Moreover, barristers should be permitted to enter multi-disciplinary partnerships.[8] These suggestions were strenuously resisted by the Bar: choice of advocate and access and competition would be reduced, standards would fall and costs would increase. The idea had been opposed by the Royal Commission, the Director General of Fair Trading and Lord Mackay himself when leader of the Scottish Bar. MDPs involving barristers would be in effect fusion with other professions, removing the benefits of independence and the cab-rank rule.[9] The White Paper merely stated that "the regulation of how the members of professional bodies organise themselves to meet their clients' needs is best left to the professions themselves, subject to a proper scrutiny to avoid unnecessary or undesirable anti-competitive effects."[10] This was reflected in the 1990 Act.

As a result of the recent growth in numbers, coupled with the lack of space, young barristers have found it increasingly difficult to obtain a permanent place ("seat" or "tenancy") in chambers, although a number have been allowed to remain after pupillage as "squatters" or "floaters." Insofar as the problem was caused by shortage of work, the Royal Commission felt there were no real remedies, although potential entrants should be informed of the difficulties.[11] However, the Senate "should adopt a vigorous policy to secure the provision of more accommodation."[12] The Senate's Accommodation Committee subsequently expressed the opinion that it was doing just that.[13] Since then, the demand for space has continued.[14] In

[5] See Annual Statement of the Senate 1985–86, p. 54; (1987) 84 L.S.Gaz. 566; *Quality of Justice* (1989), pp. 177–178. They were adopted in the Wellington Street Chambers: see Lord Gifford, *Counsel*, November/December 1988, p. 223, but *cf.* J. Hall, *Counsel*, March/April 1989, p. 28. In the view of the Bar Council, the experiment with purse-sharing "proved not to be beneficial": *Quality of Justice*, p. 178.
[6] s.66(5), (6).
[7] Cm. 570, p. 40.
[8] *Ibid.* pp. 46–47.
[9] *Quality of Justice* (1989), Chap. 15.
[10] Cm. 740, p. 39.
[11] R.C.L.S., Vol. 1, pp. 459–460.
[12] *Ibid.* pp. 460–462. Specific rules of conduct might also have to be waived.
[13] Annual Statement, 1979–80, p. 27.
[14] *Counsel*, Michaelmas 1985, pp. 17–18; a survey in 1986 showed that 10 per cent. of London barristers were sharing a desk and that in all there was a demand for over 400 more rooms: *Counsel*, Hilary 1986, p. 38.

response, the Inns have adopted a policy of charging full market rents and accommodation has been secured outside but in the vicinity of the Inns.[15]

Notwithstanding the arguments set out above, the Bar has now removed the requirement that barristers have the services of a clerk and practise from chambers established with the approval of the Bar Council.[16] The only requirement is that barristers of less than three years' post-pupillage call will be required to practise either from a Library, or from chambers containing at least one member of five years' post-pupillage call. The Bar has established a central Library in London, provided with office facilities, which can provide an alternative base to chambers. Such a system has long been adopted by the Bars of Northern Ireland, Scotland and the Republic of Ireland.[17] Apart from those in their early years, barristers will be able to practise from home. This may, for example, facilitate the continuation in practice of women with young children (assuming they can get work). In place of the requirement to have a clerk, a barrister in independent practice must take reasonable steps to ensure that his or her practice is efficiently and properly administered and that proper records are kept.[18]

Another distinctive feature of practice at the bar is the division into two ranks: Queen's Counsel[19] and "junior" barristers.[20] Appointment as a Q.C. is made by the Queen on the advice of the Lord Chancellor, and is today a mark of eminence in the profession rather than a retainer for Crown work. It is for the juniors who wish to "take silk" (Q.C.s wear silk gowns) to apply; between 20 per cent. and 30 per cent. of the applications are successful,[21] and re-applications are permissible. The main difference as regards work done is that Q.C.s do not normally do paperwork, except in those cases where they are briefed to appear alone: their role is that of the skilled and experienced advocate or specialist adviser, and they are in a position to concentrate on heavy cases. After his or her elevation a Q.C. would expect, or at least hope, to take work that is more remunerative, and to reduce his or her work load. The change can be something of a gamble,[22] but it may be that the risks are not as great as they used to be.[23] Most High Court judges are appointed from among the Q.C.s and there are many other judicial appointments available.

Formerly, there were rules of etiquette which prevented a Q.C. from appearing in court without a junior (the two-counsel rule) and which entitled the junior to a fee of two-thirds that of his or her leader. In 1966 the two-thirds rule was abolished[24]; the junior is now simply entitled to a

---

[15] Hirst J. (Chairman of the Accommodation Committee), *Counsel*, Summer 1986, pp. 15–16; P. Naughton, "Moving Out" *Counsel*, Summer/September 1987, pp. 12–13; Accommodation Committee, *ibid.* p. 36.

[16] *Code of Conduct* (1990 edn.), para. 301: a barrister must notify the Bar Council of the address and telephone number of his or her "chambers" but this is merely "the principal place at or from which one or more barristers in independent practice carry on their practice:" para. 901.

[17] *Quality of Justice* (1989), pp. 214–215.

[18] *Code of Conduct* (1990 edn.), para. 303.

[19] "One of Our Counsel learned in the Law." Q.C.s become K.C.s when there are Kings.

[20] R.C.L.S., Vol. 1, pp. 465–471. All barristers who are not Q.C.s are "juniors." There can be very senior "juniors."

[21] R.C.L.S., Vol. 1, p. 479. There were 52 appointments in 1981, 56 in 1982, 40 in 1983 and 42 in 1984.

[22] R. E. Megarry, *Lawyer and Litigant in England* (1962), pp. 90–92: "a great adventure with much to gain and much to lose."

[23] Hazell (1978), pp. 23–34. Q.C.s reliant on public funds may be at risk when there are pressures on public expenditure.

[24] See Zander (1968), pp. 146–152.

"proper fee."[25] Ten years later the Monopolies Commission reported that the two-counsel rule was contrary to the public interest.[26] The rule was accordingly abrogated as from October 1, 1977 and the Bar Council issued revised rules.[27] A Q.C. may appear alone but must decline to do so if he or she considers that the interest of the client require that a junior should also be instructed. The change seemed to make little practical difference.[28] In 1988, provision was made enabling solicitors to instruct Q.C.s to appear alone in certain criminal cases (guilty pleas, certain appeals and simple cases "with some sensitive overlay, whether political local or other").[29] This too has been little used.[30] A majority of the Royal Commission favoured continuance of the two-tier system, with minor changes.[31] The Green Paper and White Paper proposed that the two-tier system should be retained, with eligibility extended to all who have rights of audience in the High Court or the Crown Court.[32]

3. QUALITY OF SERVICE AND COMPLAINTS AGAINST LAWYERS

(a) Introduction

Most legal work is transacted well and efficiently and most clients are satisfied with the work of their lawyers.[33] A recent survey showed that 62 per cent. of the people who had used solicitors for personal business during the previous three years were completely satisfied. A further 22 per cent. were fairly satisfied, whereas only 7 per cent. were fairly dissatisfied and 7 per cent. very dissatisfied.[34] The main causes of complaint were delay, inefficiency, cost, incompetence and failure of communication. As regards barristers, the Royal Commission on Legal Services reported that the general opinion among judges and practising lawyers appeared to be that standards

---

[25] Annual Statement of the Bar Council, 1971–72, p. 20.

[26] *Barristers Services: A report on the supply by Her Majesty's Counsel alone of their services*, 1976 (1975–76 H.C. 512).

[27] Annual Statement, 1977–78, pp. 42–45; R.C.L.S., Vol. 1, pp. 480–481; *Code of Conduct*, (1990 edn.), para. 503.

[28] R.C.L.S., Vol. 1, pp. 468–470.

[29] (1988) 85 L.S.Gaz., November 2, p. 6.

[30] (1990) 87 L.S.Gaz., August 22, p. 5 (8 out of 1,700 eligible cases). The scheme also allowed for barristers to appear without a solicitor in Crown Court cases involving guilty pleas, appeals against sentence, and committals for sentence; the figures here were only slightly higher: *ibid*. See "Attendance at the Crown court with counsel" (1989) 86 L.S.Gaz., January 25, pp. 24–25, 38.

[31] *Ibid*. Four members thought that the title should be conferred as a mark of honour only: R.C.L.S., Vol. 1, pp. 823, 829. See A. Samuels, (1984) 134 N.L.J. 503.

[32] Cm. 570, Chap. 9; Cm. 740, p. 15. See *Quality of Justice* (1989), Chap. 17; the Bar suggested that there had been indications of a lack of knowledge in the L.C.D. resulting in the refusal of the title to those of distinction and the grant of the title to those not deserving it; appointment by the Judges rather than a government minister should be considered.

[33] J. Jenkins, E. Skordaki and C. F. Willis, *Public Use and Perception of Solicitors' Services* (1989), pp. 12–13; see also M. Zander, *A Matter of Justice* (Revised edn., 1989), pp. 78–80; R.C.L.S., Vol. 1, p. 292. This question is of course separate from the question whether there is work which lawyers should be doing but are not: see Chap. 8.

[34] Jenkins, Skordaki and Willis (1990), pp. 12–13, which confirms the results of other surveys, see R.C.L.S., Vol. 2, pp. 223–233 and M. Zander, *The State of Knowledge about the English Legal Profession* (1980), pp. 55–57. Convicted prisoners seem generally less enthusiastic about lawyers: M. Zander, [1972] Crim.L.R. 155. *Cf.* J. Bottoms and J. McLean, *Defendants in the Criminal Process* (1976), pp. 154–160. The role of solicitors in divorce proceedings is discussed in M. Murch, *Justice and Welfare in Divorce* (1980), Chap. 1.

fell in the 1960s and 1970s but were rising again.[35] However, dissatisfaction has been expressed, in particular, by Berlins in relation to advocacy at the Bar[36] and by Joseph in relation to conveyancing by solicitors and the handling of personal injury litigation by lawyers.[37] This cannot be ignored and, while many improvements have been made since the criticisms voiced by the Royal Commission,[38] further improvements are still needed in several areas, affecting aspects both of the way in which lawyers go about their work and of the legal system in which they operate.

A broad distinction may be drawn between factors which are designed to maintain standards by preventing problems arising and the procedures available whereby a client may obtain redress when things go wrong. The features of "professions" mentioned earlier,[39] such as education and training and rules of conduct, and other points such as supervision by the courts and fellow practitioners, control of fees by certification and taxation and control by the legal aid authorities, should assist in the maintenance of standards.[40] Following the recommendations of the Royal Commission on Legal Services, the Law Society and the General Council of the Bar have begun to introduce Written Professional Standards indicating what is good practice.[41]

When things go wrong, there are a number of avenues open to the client affected although there may be considerable practical difficulties in following them. The client may, for example, raise the matter with the firm to which the lawyer belongs. Solicitors' firms are required to have a complaints handling procedure which must, amongst other things, ensure that clients are informed whom to approach in the event of any problem with the service provided[42] and who is responsible for the day to day conduct of the matter and its overall supervision.[43] The client may complain to the Solicitors' Complaints Bureau, and this may lead to disciplinary action. The client may bring legal proceedings. The client may refuse to pay the lawyer's bill, and defend any proceedings for payment brought by the lawyer. A criminal offence such as theft may have been committed.

(b) Professional misconduct: solicitors[44]

Prior to the Courts and Legal Services Act 1990, the Law Society could make rules for regulating the professional practice, conduct and discipline of solicitors, subject to the concurrence of the Master of the Rolls.[45] Under the

[35] R.C.L.S., Vol. 1, p. 292.
[36] Reported in Zander (1989), pp. 75–76.
[37] M. Joseph, *The Conveyancing Fraud* (2nd ed. 1989) and *Lawyers Can Seriously Damage Your Health* (1984). For a valuable summary, see Zander (1989), pp. 76–79.
[38] R.C.L.S., Vol. 1, pp. 293–308. The problems discussed included delay, returned briefs, relations with clients and the listing of cases.
[39] Above, pp. 105–107.
[40] For an expression of this approach, see R.C.L.S., Vol. 1, pp. 288–290.
[41] The Law Society, *A Guide to the Professional Practice of Solicitors* (1990), Chap. 8, dealing with communication with the client, and *Code of Conduct* (1990), Annex H, dealing with general professional standards and standards in criminal proceedings.
[42] Solicitors' Practice Rules 1990, r. 15(1). In force from March 1, 1991.
[43] *Ibid.* r. 15(2). In force from March 1, 1991.
[44] See the Law Society, *A Guide to the Professional Practice of Solicitors* (1990) and F. Silverman, *Handbook of Professional Conduct for Solicitors* (1989).
[45] Solicitors Act 1974, s.31(1). In general, the principles and rules governing professional conduct are the responsibility of the Society's Standards and Guidance Committee and Professional Standards Directorate.

1990 Act such rules are also, to an extent, subject to review by the Lord Chancellor's Advisory Committee on Legal Education and Conduct. The Advisory Committee may give advice on all aspects of rules of conduct, and the Law Society is expressly required to have regard to that advice when it relates to rights of audience or rights to conduct litigation.[46] Further, when the Law Society seeks to be designated as an authorised body under the 1990 Act for the purposes of rights of audience or rights to conduct litigation,[47] any proposed rules of conduct in relation to those rights must be approved by the Advisory Committee.[48]

The rules are set out and amplified in *The Guide to the Professional Conduct of Solicitors*.[49] The *Guide* aims to provide "a clear and helpful source of reference for solicitors during the day to day conduct of their practice."

We have already set out the basic practice rules[50] governing the solicitor's general duties, publicity, introductions and referrals, employed solicitors, and multi-disciplinary partnerships.[51] The rules also prevent solicitors being involved in a business, other than a solicitor's practice, which offers what may be called solicitor's business,[52] and otherwise limit the extent to which solicitors may work with other professionals unless certain safeguards for the public are observed[53] and apart from the rules relating to multi-disciplinary practices. The rules also prevent solicitors accepting instructions from two or more clients in conflict.[54] Solicitors must ensure that every office where they or their firms practise is and can reasonably be seen to be properly supervised in accordance with certain minimum standards.[55]

[46] Courts and Legal Services Act 1990, Sched. 2, paras. 5(3), (4).

[47] See above, pp. 129–133.

[48] Courts and Legal Services Act 1990, ss.27, 28, 29 and Sched. 4, Part II and see above, pp. 131–133. The Committee was designed specifically to maintain quality of service in the public interest, see *Legal Services: A Framework for the Future* (Cm. 740, 1989), Part II, esp. para. 7.4.

[49] The latest edition is dated 1990, but must be read in conjunction with the Solicitors' Practice Rules 1990 and other amendments dealt with in the *Professional Standards Bulletin No. 3*.

[50] The Council of the Law Society may waive these rules in any particular case: Solicitors Practice Rules 1990, r. 17. The Council in its statement of January 17, 1990 confirmed that there are no general waivers, but that all existing individual waivers are continued, see *Professional Standards Bulletin No. 3*, pp. 28–29.

[51] See above, pp. 125, 134–136, 137–140.

[52] Solicitor's Practice Rules, 1990, r. 5. The business referred to in r. 5(2) involves the following services: the conduct of any matter which could proceed before any court, tribunal or inquiry, whether or not proceedings are commenced; advocacy before any court, tribunal or inquiry; instructing counsel; acting as executor or trustee; drafting any will; giving legal advice; property selling; investment business as defined by the Financial Services Act 1986; any activity reserved to solicitors by the Solicitors Act 1974, or other statute; drafting any other legal documents. If the only service ancillary to the business' main purpose is the latter, a solicitor may be involved in a management consultancy or company secretarial service: r. 5(4).

[53] Solicitors' Practice Rules 1990, r. 5(3). The safeguards for the public are that: the name of the business has no substantial element in common with the name of any solicitors' practice; the words "solicitor," "barrister" and "lawyer" are not used in connection with the solicitor's involvement with the business; clients referred by the solicitor to the business and, where business and practice premises are shared, all customers of the business are informed in writing that they do not enjoy the statutory protection attaching to a solicitor's clients.

[54] Solicitors' Practice Rules, 1990, r. 6. In addition this rule prevents a solicitor acting for both the seller and buyer of land, the lessor and lessee on the grant of a lease for value at arm's length or the lender and borrower in a private mortgage at arm's length, subject to a series of exceptions.

[55] *Ibid.* r. 13. The minimum standards are to be found in r. 13(1).

Further, in addition to the obligation to have a system for handling complaints,[56] solicitors must ensure that their clients know whom to approach when they have a problem with the service provided and receive any appropriate information as to the issues raised and the progress of the matter.[57] The prohibition on arrangements for contingency fees will be changed to comply with the Courts and Legal Services Act 1990.[58]

The practice rules require solicitors to account to their clients where they receive more than £10 as commission, unless the client agrees that the solicitor may retain it.[59] In addition, solicitors must comply with detailed rules made by the Law Society as to the holding of clients' money, in particular the requirement to maintain a separate clients' account and keep records.[60] An accountants' report must be made annually.[61] The Law Society may inspect a solicitor's books to ascertain whether the rules have been observed.[62] Clients are further protected by the Compensation Fund first set up in 1942.[63] The Council of the Law Society has a discretion to make a grant where it is satisfied that a person has suffered *loss* through the dishonesty of a solicitor or a solicitor's employee, or *hardship* through a solicitor's failure to account for money. A grant may also be made to a solicitor who has suffered loss or hardship following liability to a client on misappropriation by a partner or employee. This scheme is complementary to the requirement that solicitors be insured in respect of their civil liability as insurance is not available to cover deliberate misconduct.[64]

The Law Society has the power to deal with both professional misconduct and inadequate professional services. The Society has always had the power to deal with professional misconduct, which may involve moral turpitude or a criminal conviction for a serious offence or theft, but is now based mainly upon breaches of the practice rules.[65] The Society has only had the power to deal with inadequate professional services since the Administration of Justice Act 1985.[66] Inadequate professional services are defined as "the provi-

---

[56] Solicitors' Practice Rules 1990, r. 15(1). In force from March 1, 1991.
[57] *Ibid.* r. 15(2). In force from March 1, 1991.
[58] The existing rule is r. 8. As to the changes regarding contingency fees, see pp. 481–483 below.
[59] Solicitors Practice Rules 1990, r. 10.
[60] The Solicitors' Account Rules 1986 and the Solicitors' Trust Accounts Rules 1986, made under the Solicitors' Act 1974, s.32, see *The Guide to the Professional Conduct of Solicitors*, Chap. 19. Such rules were first made in 1935 following a period when the number of frauds by solicitors was causing public concern: Abel-Smith and Stevens (1967), pp. 190–192. Despite the Rules and the emphasis placed upon accounts in the solicitors' training, errors, both deliberate and accidental, still come to light. The Solicitor's Accounts (Deposit) Rules 1988 made under the Solicitors' Act 1974, s.33, deal with the accrual of interest arising on client's funds held by a solicitor, see *The Guide to the Professional Conduct of Solicitors*, pp. 155–158.
[61] Solicitors' Act 1974, s.34 and the Accountant's Report Rules 1986 (as amended). See *The Guide to the Professional Conduct of Solicitors*, Chap. 19.
[62] Solicitors' Account Rules 1988, r. 12, see *The Guide to the Professional Conduct of Solicitors*, pp. 151–152.
[63] It is now regulated by the Solicitors' Act 1974, s.36 and Schedule 2 and the Solicitors' Compensation Fund Rules 1975, see *The Guide to the Professional Conduct of Solicitors*, Chap. 20 and R.C.L.S., Vol. 1, pp. 321–324.
[64] See below, p. 163.
[65] The right of complaint in relation to a breach of the practice rules, etc., is granted by the Solicitors Act 1974, s.31(2).
[66] The provisions introduced by the 1985 Act have since been replaced by the Courts and Legal Services Act 1990, s.93 and now appear as section 37A and Sched. 1A in the Solicitors Act 1974.

sion by solicitors of services which are not of the quality which it is reasonable to expect of them."[67]

For the purposes of a complaint, the distinction between the two does not matter. All complaints are initially regarded as complaints of inadequate professional services.[68] The following are the sort of matters with which the Solicitors Complaints Bureau, exercising the disciplinary functions of the Law Society, may deal:

(a) delay in answering clients' letters or enquiries or failure to answer at all;
(b) delay in dealing with a client's case;
(c) failure to deal with clients' money properly;
(d) acting in the same case for a client and others where the client's interests are in conflict with those of the other clients;
(e) dishonesty or deception;
(f) failure to hand over a client's papers if the client has asked for them when the client does not owe the solicitor any money;
(g) incompetent or "shoddy" work;
(h) overcharging, although the Bureau cannot fix what is a fair charge.[69]

What the Solicitors Complaints Bureau cannot investigate are allegations of negligence. The dividing line between incompetent or "shoddy" work and negligence may be very difficult to draw. Negligence is conduct of a solicitor falling below that which may reasonably be expected and entitling the complainant to damages for any loss caused.[70]

Complaints about a solicitor[71] should first be made to the solicitor in question. If not satisfied, the complainant should refer the matter, where appropriate, to the senior partner of the firm for which the solicitor works. If still unsatisfied, the complainant may lodge a complaint with the Solicitors Complaints Bureau. The Bureau cannot investigate a complaint of alleged negligence, although it may refer the complainant to a solicitor on the "Negligence Panel" for advice about instituting an action for negligence in the courts. Should a complainant have difficulty formulating a complaint, he or she may be referred to a solicitor on the "Interview Panel" who will assist.

The Bureau will attempt to resolve complaints by local conciliation if at all possible. This is achieved by the Bureau referring the matter to a "local conciliation officer," who is a solicitor. That officer sees all the papers with regard to the complaint, discusses the problem with the complainant and the solicitor and assesses whether there is a way of resolving the complaint by putting forward the options to both the complainant and the solicitor. Any settlement which is achieved in consequence must be acceptable to both parties and if there is no settlement the matter will be referred back to the Bureau.

[67] Solicitors Act 1974, s.37A.
[68] Solicitors Complaints Bureau, *Annual Report 1989*, p. 12.
[69] This list is taken from the Solicitors Complaints Bureau own leaflet entitled, "The Solicitors Complaints Bureau: How and When." Fair charges are fixed by either obtaining a remuneration certificate from the Law Society or having the bill made subject to taxation, see pp. 475–476 below.
[70] Legal proceedings against lawyers are considered below at pp. 162–166.
[71] Complaints may be made not only by the solicitor's client, but also other lay complainants, see *The Guide to the Professional Conduct of Solicitors*, paras. 21.08 and 21.09.

If a case is referred back to the Bureau or is not a complaint for which local conciliation is appropriate, the Bureau will investigate through an "investigation officer."[72] If that officer is of the opinion that the solicitor is guilty of professional misconduct or has provided inadequate professional services, the matter is referred to the Adjudication Committee. If that Committee is satisfied that professional misconduct or inadequate professional services have been proved against the solicitor, it may exercise one or more of a number of powers.

If the allegation proved is that of inadequate professional services, the Committee has the power to take certain "steps." It may impose a reduction of costs,[73] or order the solicitor to refund or remit fees, waive the right to recover fees, rectify a mistake at his or her own expense, pay compensation to the client,[74] or take any other action in the interests of the client which the Committee may specify.[75]

If the allegation proved is that of professional misconduct, the Committee has the power to order an inspection of accounts, intervene in a solicitor's practice to protect the interests of clients, intervene to recover a particular file for the client or his or her new solicitor, refuse a practising certificate, impose conditions on the grant of a practising certificate,[76] prohibit a solicitor from taking an articled clerk, deprive a firm of its Investment Business Certificate under the Financial Services Act 1986,[77] invite a solicitor to take certain action such as to obtain a remuneration certificate to assess the fairness of charges made or to face disciplinary proceedings, and impose sanctions for misconduct which range from deprecation of a solicitor's conduct to calling a solicitor to be rebuked personally by the chair of the Committee.[78] Further, the Committee has the power to order payment out of the Solicitors Compensation Fund where a person has suffered as a consequence of a solicitor's dishonesty.[79] Finally, the Committee has the power to take disciplinary proceedings against a solicitor before the Solicitors' Disciplinary Tribunal.

It may not be possible or appropriate for the Bureau to deal with the matter. In that case it will be dealt with by the Solicitors' Disciplinary

---

[72] Before the greater use of local conciliation which now appertains, the majority of complaints were disposed of at this level: Zander (1989), p. 97.

[73] This is the most frequently used power: Solicitors Complaints Bureau, *Annual Report 1989*, p. 12.

[74] The amount of compensation cannot exceed £1,000, which limit can be increased by statutory instrument made by the Lord Chancellor after consultation with the Law Society: Solicitors Act 1974, Sched. 1A, para. 3 (as inserted by the Courts and Legal Services Act 1990, Sched. 15).

[75] Solicitors Act 1974, s.37A and Sched. 1A (as inserted by the 1990 Act, s.93 and Sched. 15).

[76] The power to impose this sanction under Solicitors Act 1974, s.13A has been extended to circumstances where a solicitor has been charged with or convicted of fraud or serious crime by the Courts and Legal Services Act 1990, s.94.

[77] See, further, F. T. Horne, *Cordery on Solicitors* (8th ed., 1988), pp. 288–290.

[78] Solicitors Act 1974, ss.12, 13, 31, 32, 35, Sched. 1. See further, *Cordery on Solicitors* (1988), pp. 292, 306–310. Appeals against the exercise of these powers must be made to the Master of the Rolls or the High Court depending upon which power is exercised. These powers may have an enormous effect upon the practice of a solicitor, and yet, unlike proceedings before the Solicitors' Disciplinary Tribunal, there are inadequate protections within the system to protect innocent solicitors, see, *e.g.* O. Hansen, "Solicitors' discipline" (1990) 140 N.L.J. 1345.

[79] Solicitors Act 1974, s.36 (as amended).

Tribunal.[80] Cases are referred to the Tribunal by the Adjudication Committee or directly by complainants. The Tribunal sits in divisions of three, comprising two solicitors and one lay member.[81] Applications are heard in private, but the findings are made public.[82] If a complaint is proved the Tribunal may impose any one or more of a number of sanctions dependent upon the nature of the case.[83] The solicitor concerned may be struck off the roll,[84] suspended from practice (indefinitely or for a specified period),[85] fined (not more than £5,000), excluded from legal aid work, or reprimanded. The Tribunal may inform the Council of the Law Society that it is of the view that "steps" in respect of inadequate professional services should be taken.[86] An appeal lies to the High Court[87] and then on a point of law to the Court of Appeal and the House of Lords. The High Court, the Crown Court and the Court of Appeal may also exercise disciplinary jurisdiction over solicitors as officers of the court.[88]

Thus the Solicitors Complaints Bureau exercises the power of the Law Society to deal with complaints and disciplinary issues. The day to day work of the Bureau in handling complaints against solicitors is undertaken by the Bureau staff comprising a director assisted by seven deputies. One of the deputies is the investigation accountant and the others deal with the administration and management of the Bureau; professional services; conduct and investigation; policy and development; the litigation compensation fund and professional and public relations. The Bureau staff work under the auspices of two Committees: the Adjudication Committee and the Investigation Committee. The powers of the Adjudication Committee, to which is delegated the functions of the Council of the Law Society in relation to determining matters concerning the conduct of solicitors and the quality of their work, have already been considered. Its membership comprises: nine members of the Council, from which group the Chair is appointed; three

---

[80] The Tribunal was established by the Solicitors Act 1974, s.46.

[81] Solicitors Act 1974, s.46(2)–(8).

[82] Solicitors Act 1974, s.48.

[83] Solicitors Act 1974, ss.37A, 47 and Sched. 1A, as amended by the Courts and Legal Services Act 1990, ss.92, 93. Reports of proceedings of the Solicitors Disciplinary Tribunal appear in the Law Society's Gazette, see, e.g. the Gazette for December 5, 1990, p. 43.

[84] This is obligatory in some cases, e.g. where a solicitor acts as agent for an unqualified person: Solicitors Act 1974, s.39; cf. s.41(4).

[85] The usual sentence is to suspend for up to five years.

[86] Solicitors Act 1974, Sched. 1A, para. 8.

[87] Solicitors Act 1974, s.49. In some cases the appeal lies to the Master of the Rolls (ss.43(4), 47(1)(b)) who makes a final decision. Examples of appeals include Re a Solicitor [1956] 1 W.L.R. 1312; Re a Solicitor [1960] 2 Q.B. 212 and Re a Solicitor [1975] Q.B. 475.

[88] Solicitors Act 1974, ss.50–53 and Supreme Court Practice 1991, Vol. 2, Part 11, Section D.1. The jurisdiction to strike off is rarely exercised. One instance involving striking off, the "Glanville Davies affair," was a major factor in moving the Law Society to amending its complaints procedures along the lines discussed in the text: see generally (1984) 134 N.L.J. 42, 48–49, 189–190; L.A.G. Bull. December 1983, pp. 11–14; Legal Action, Jan. 1984, pp. 3–4, Feb. 1984, pp. 406, Mar. 1984, pp. 4–5; R. Abel, The Legal Profession in England and Wales (1988), p. 255. More frequently exercised is the jurisdiction to order the solicitor to compensate others for neglect or misconduct in proceedings before the court: see Supreme Court Practice 1991, Vol. 2, Part 11, Section D.1, pp. 1295–1296. The jurisdiction is not readily exercised, see, e.g. Manor Electrics Ltd. v. Dickson; Re Knight, The Times, February 8, 1990, see also R. v. Smith (Martin) [1975] Q.B. 531 and R & T Thew Ltd. v. Reeves (No. 2) [1982] Q.B. 1283.

non-Council solicitors; and six lay members.[89] The Investigation Committee oversees the investigatory work of the Bureau. If a complainant is not happy with the work of the Bureau, the Investigation Committee's function is to look into the matter and see whether the complaint has been fully and fairly investigated or whether further investigation should be carried out. Consequently, no complaint file can be closed if a complainant is dissatisfied unless the Investigation Committee decides that there is nothing further to be done. The Committee membership comprises: ten lay members, from which group the Chair is appointed; four non-Council solicitors and only two Council solicitors.[90]

It will be noted that there is a marked distinction between the composition of the two Committees. This is deliberate. The Law Society on rethinking its complaints procedure perhaps surprisingly rejected the option of a wholly independent procedure whereby complaints would have been dealt with by an organisation completely outside the Law Society, an arrangement which would have demanded legislative change. Instead, a quasi-independent arrangement was adopted. Consequently, the composition of the Investigation Committee is dominated neither by solicitors nor by Council members. In addition, the Bureau stands separate from the Law Society, although technically its powers are given to it by the delegation from the Society.

The failure to opt for a completely independent complaints procedure, contrary to the recommendations of the management consultants, has been described as follows:

"In the final analysis, it is difficult to escape from the conclusion that the public interest has suffered and will continue to suffer while the conflict of interest within the Law Society endures. . . . [T]hey have only met the 'minimum requirements for independent complaints-handling and discipline.' . . . [Other debates about the profession] have clearly benefited the Law Society, for they have eclipsed complaints against solicitors and diverted critical attention to other issues. It may be doubted, however, whether the Society is wise to have, taken advantage of this situation. The complaints system will surely come into the foreground again before long and the Society's failure to have adequately tackles that issue will damage its reputation and weaken its voice on other subjects. It may thus come to regret, as so many others already do, that it came so close to an adequate reform of the system but drew back and substituted a manifestly inferior system."[91]

These criticisms lose some of their force when it is remembered that the complaints procedure has been subject to the overview of the Lay Observer since 1974 and is now subject to the overview of the Legal Services Ombudsman,[92] a development which the Council of the Law Society welcomed on the basis that it would strengthen "the independent element in the

---

[89] As to the current membership, see Solicitors' Complaints Bureau, *Annual Report 1989*, p. 18. The Adjudication Committee must have a majority of Council members otherwise it fails to satisfy the demands of the Solicitors Act 1974 when disciplinary powers are exercised. There are also a number of additional members of casework committees.

[90] See Solicitors' Complaints Bureau, *Annual Report 1989*, p. 25.

[91] A. L. Newbold and G. Zellick, "Reform of the Solicitors' Complaints Procedures: Fact or Fiction" (1987) 6 C.J.Q. 25, 42–43. See also Zander (1989), pp. 95–98.

[92] See below, pp. 161–162.

complaints procedure ... [and] might well help to secure greater public confidence in the complaints procedures."[93]

(c) Professional misconduct: barristers

The professional conduct of barristers is regulated, in the main, by the profession itself. It is the duty of every barrister to comply with the *Code of Conduct of the Bar of England and Wales*. The current *Code*, having been adopted by the Bar Council, came into force on March 31, 1990.[94] Prior to the Courts and Legal Services Act 1990, the Bar Council had sole responsibility for the creation and amendment of the *Code*. Judicial approval was not formally required, but it was provided through direct consultation with the judges, the judicial role in the disciplinary system and through the possibility that a particular rule could be held by a court to be contrary to public policy or liable to undermine the proper administration of justice, in which case the rule would be ineffective.[95] Under the 1990 Act the Lord Chancellor's Advisory Committee on Legal Education and Conduct may give the Bar Council advice in relation to all aspects of rules of conduct, and the Bar Council is expressly required to have regard to that advice when it relates to rights of audience.[96] Further, the 1990 Act requires the Bar Council, when seeking to be designated as an authorised body in relation to rights of audience, to obtain the approval of the Advisory Committee in relation to any alterations to rules of conduct in so far as they relate to rights of audience.[97]

The general purpose of the Code is "to provide the standards of conduct on the part of barristers which are appropriate in the interests of justice," and, in particular, to require barristers in independent practice to be completely independent in conduct and professional standing, to act only as consultants properly instructed and to "acknowledge a public obligation based on the paramount need for access to justice to act for any client (whether legally aided or not) in cases within his [or her] field of practice."[98]

To those ends, a barrister must comply with the *Code* generally, and in particular, must satisfy the "fundamental principles." The principles are grouped according to the nature of a barrister's work. There are four groups: all barristers; all barristers in independent practice; all practising barristers; and all non-practising barristers.

All barristers must not engage in conduct which is "dishonest or otherwise discreditable to a barrister" or "prejudicial to the administration of justice" or "likely to diminish public confidence in the legal profession or the

---

[93] The Law Society, *Striking the Balance* (1989), para. 8.13.
[94] The *Code* is subject to amendment, the first amendments being effective as from October 22, 1990.
[95] *Re T (a barrister)* [1982] Q.B. 430, and see General Council of the Bar, *Quality of Justice: The Bar's Response* (1989), pp. 193–194.
[96] Courts and Legal Service Act 1990, Sched. 2, para. 5(3), (4).
[97] s.29(3) and Sched. 4, Part II of the Courts and Legal Services Act 1990. The Bar was particularly concerned about the need to seek approval for any aspect of its Code of Conduct, see General Council of the Bar, *Quality of Justice: The Bar's Response* (1989), p. 194.
[98] *Code of Conduct*, para. 102.

administration of justice or otherwise bring the legal profession into disrepute."[99]

Barristers in independent practice must make that practice their primary occupation and be willing to render legal services for an appropriate fee.[1] In particular, such a barrister must comply with the "Cab-rank rule."[2]

All practising barristers must exercise personal and professional judgment in all matters, must "promote and protect fearlessly and by all proper and lawful means [a] client's best interests . . . without regard to [their] own interests or to any consequences to [themselves]," have "an overriding duty to the Court to ensure in the public interest that the proper and efficient administration of justice is achieved: [they] must assist the Court in the administration of justice and must not deceive or knowingly or recklessly mislead the Court," must act independently and must not discriminate on grounds of race, ethnic origin, sex, religion or political persuasion.[3]

Non-practising barristers must not appear as counsel in a court or, without indicating that he or she is not practising, supply legal services to any person.[4]

A wide range of matters is covered in the detailed provisions of the *Code*, including the acceptance or return of briefs and instructions, the administration of a barrister's practice, advertising and publicity, duties to client and court[5] and the obligations of employed barristers in so far as they are different from those of a barrister in independent practice.

One distinctive rule affecting barristers which requires emphasis is the so-called "cab-rank rule":

> "A barrister in independent practice must comply with the 'Cab-rank rule' and accordingly except only as otherwise provided . . . he [or she] must in any field in which he [or she] professes to practise in relation to work appropriate to his [or her] experience and seniority and irrespective or whether his [or her] client is paying privately or is legally aided or otherwise publicly funded:
> (a) accept any brief to appear before a court in which he [or she] professes to practice;
> (b) accept any instructions;
> (c) act for any person on whose behalf he [or she] is briefed or instructed;
> and do so irrespective of (i) the party on whose behalf he [or she] is briefed or instructed (ii) the nature of the case and (iii) any belief or opinion which he [or she] may have formed as to the character reputation cause conduct guilty or innocence of that person"[6]

The exceptions to its operation are concerned to ensure that a barrister will not accept any brief or instructions which would cause him or her to be

---

[99] *Code of Conduct*, para. 201(*a*). In addition, a barrister must not engage directly or indirectly in any occupation which may adversely affect the reputation of the Bar or prejudice a barristers' ability to attend properly to a client's interests: *ibid.* para. 201(*b*).
[1] *Code of Conduct*, paras. 202–205.
[2] See below.
[3] *Code of Conduct*, paras. 206–211.
[4] *Ibid.*, para. 212.
[5] For an argument that the advocate's duty to justice ought to be enshrined in law and not just rules of professional conduct, see D. L. Carey Miller, (1981) 97 L.Q.R. 127.
[6] *Code of Conduct*, para. 203.

"professionally embarrassed," which might arise as a result, *e.g.* of lack of sufficient experience or competence or lack of sufficient time to prepare because of other professional commitments[7]; or if, *e.g.* the fee is not appropriate[8]; or if the barrister is a Queen's Counsel and is being asked to do work generally only undertaken by a junior or to work without a junior where he or she believes that is inappropriate.[9]

It has been said that the rule "secures for the public a right of representation in the court which is a pillar of British liberty."[10] Its real significance lies in criminal cases, where it would obviously be undesirable for barristers to avoid unpopular causes, but barristers have also been looked on with disfavour[11] when they accept instructions in civil cases only from a "selected section of the community," by which was meant working class and ethnic minorities communities. This view was challenged on the basis that such an approach was taken in order to ensure that people receive representation which might not otherwise be available.[12] Lord Diplock doubted whether in civil litigation counsel often has to accept work which he or she would not otherwise be willing to undertake.[13]

Any failure of a barrister to comply with the provisions of the *Code of Conduct*[14] constitutes professional misconduct and renders that barrister liable to disciplinary proceedings in accordance with the Professional Conduct Committee Rules, the Disciplinary Tribunals Regulations and the Hearings before the Visitors Rules.[15] Complaints[16] against barristers are first dealt with by the Professional Conduct Committee.[17] The Secretary of the Committee makes such investigations and inquiries (if any) as appear to be necessary at that stage for the purpose of enabling the Committee to deal with the complaint.[18] The Secretary may then place the complaint before the Committee for summary dismissal if it is thought to be trivial or obviously lacking in validity or it is otherwise expedient to adopt this course of action.[19]

---

[7] *Ibid.* para. 501.

[8] *Ibid.* para. 502.

[9] *Ibid.* para. 503.

[10] R.C.L.S., Vol. 1, p. 31, based on the submission of the Senate of the Inns of Court.

[11] By the Senate in its submission to the R.C.L.S.

[12] See, *e.g.* the critical response of the members of chambers at 35, Wellington Street, London: "Barristers and the Cab Rank Rule: Some people can't afford taxis ..." *L.A.G. Bull.*, December 1978, pp. 279–281.

[13] *Saif Ali* v. *Sydney Mitchell & Co.* [1980] A.C. 198, 221.

[14] Including also the Consolidated Regulation contained in Annex A to the Code and the Code of Conduct for Lawyers in the European Community in Annex L to the Code: *Code of Conduct*, para. 802.1.

[15] *Code of Conduct*, para. 802.1. As to the relevant rules, see the *Code of Conduct*, Annexes M, N & O (as amended).

[16] If a barrister is convicted of a criminal offence, other than a minor road traffic offence, he or she must report it to the Bar Council (*Code*, para. 801(*b*)) and it is then treated as a complaint. "Complaint" also includes legal aid complaints, in which case the sentences available include the cancellation or reduction of fees or fixed period or temporary exclusion from legal aid work, and the Legal Aid Board must be informed of the finding and sentence: see Administration of Justice Act 1985, s.40(1) (as amended by the Legal Aid Act 1988) and the Disciplinary Tribunals Regulations 1990, rr. 18(3) and 21(3).

[17] The powers and functions of the Committee are spelt out at rule 2 of the Professional Conduct Committee Rules, see *Code*, Annex M. For a brief report of its work see The General Council of The Bar, *Annual Report 1990*, p. 13.

[18] The Professional Conduct Committee Rules, rule 3b.

[19] *Ibid.* r. 3c.

Otherwise the Secretary writes to the barrister asking for comments in writing or in person. Thereafter the Committee considers the complaint in the light of all the available material. It may dismiss the complaint (but only if all the lay representatives on the Committee agree); determine that no action should be taken; postpone further consideration of the complaint for further investigation or inquiry; where the matter is "domestic," refer it to the Treasurer of the Inn or the Leader of the Circuit of the barrister concerned; where informal treatment is required, draw the matter to the barrister's attention in writing and, if appropriate, require attendance before the Chair of the Committee; where there is a prima facie case of professional misconduct, but the matter is not sufficiently serious for it to be referred to the Disciplinary or Summary Tribunal, direct that the barrister attend on the Chair of the Committee to provide an explanation of conduct and, if necessary, to be given advice as to his or her future conduct or be admonished; where there is a prima facie case of professional misconduct, but there is no major dispute as to fact and no possibility of a sentence of disbarment or suspension, direct that the complaint should form the subject matter of a charge before the Summary Tribunal; where there is a prima facie case of professional misconduct, and the previously stated conditions do not apply, direct that the complaint should form the subject matter of a charge before the Disciplinary Tribunal; require the barrister to take a test in Oral English.[20] The Secretary is to take such steps as are reasonably practicable to inform the complainant of the progress and result of a complaint.[21]

If the matter is referred to either the Summary or Disciplinary Tribunal, a member of the Professional Conduct Committee takes charge of the proceedings on behalf of the Committee in preferring the charge at the Tribunal.[22] The Tribunals are established under the Disciplinary Tribunals Regulations.[23] A Disciplinary Tribunal must consist of a Judge (or a Judge or Queen's Counsel if a Summary Tribunal) as Chair, a lay representative and three barristers.[24] If a Disciplinary Tribunal is satisfied that a charge is proved a barrister may be sentenced[25] to be disbarred; suspended for a prescribed period (either unconditionally or subject to conditions); ordered to pay a fine up to £5,000 to his or her Inn; ordered to repay or forego fees; reprimanded by the Treasurer of his or her Inn; given advice by the Tribunal as to future conduct; or ordered by the Tribunal to attend on a nominated person to be admonished or given advice as to future conduct.[26] In a case

[20] *Ibid.* r. 3e.

[21] *Ibid.* r. 5.

[22] *Ibid.* r. 6.

[23] The Disciplinary Tribunals Regulations, see the *Code*, Annex N. As to further details relating to the procedure, designed to satisfy the rules of natural justice, see, *ibid.* rr. 5–16.

[24] *Ibid.* r. 2. Where the barrister is not working independently, one of the three barristers must normally be employed or non-practising as the case may be: *ibid.* r. 2(1)(*c*). In order to avoid the rule against bias, no barrister or lay representative may sit who has been at a P.C.C. meeting at which the matter was considered: *ibid.* r. 2(1), proviso (*ii*).

[25] The sentence is reported to the Lord Chancellor, Lord Chief Justice, Attorney-General, President, Chair of the Bar Council, Chair of the Professional Conduct Committee, barrister charged, Treasurer of the barrister's Inn of Call and the Treasurer of any other Inn of which the barrister is a member: *ibid.* r. 21(1), (2). The finding and sentence may also be publicised: *ibid.* r. 25.

[26] *Ibid.* r. 18(2)(*a*).

where a charge of professional misconduct is established, the Tribunal may decide that no action be taken against the barrister.[27]

If a Summary Tribunal is satisfied that a charge is proved it may impose any of the sentences above, except that it may not either disbar or suspend a barrister and cannot impose a fine greater than £500.[28]

As with solicitors complaints procedures, the Bar's complaints procedures are subject to the overview of the Legal Services Ombudsman through the complaints investigation procedure[29] and through the Bar Council's duty to have regard to any recommendation made by the L.S.O. about the arrangements in force for the investigation of complaints.[30] The creation of the L.S.O. may presage joint and local arrangements for handling complaints against solicitors and barristers.[31]

(d) The Legal Services Ombudsman

The office of the Legal Services Ombudsman (L.S.O.) has been created by section 21 of the Courts and Legal Services Act 1990 "to reinforce the existing system with more effective measures for dealing with complaints."[32] Section 22(1) provides the L.S.O. with the power to "investigate any allegation[33] which is properly made to him and which relates to the manner in which a complaint made to a professional body with respect to (a) an authorised advocate, authorised litigator, licensed conveyancer, recognised body or notary who is a member of that professional body; or (b) any employee of such a person, has been dealt with by that professional body." Excluded from this function are (1) the investigation of any allegation while it is being investigated by the professional body concerned unless the allegation is that that body has acted unreasonably in not starting an investigation or has failed to complete an investigation within a reasonable time or the L.S.O. believes that an investigation is justified despite the investigation by the professional body,[34] (2) the investigation of any complaint which has been dealt with by a court, the Solicitors Disciplinary Tribunal or the Disciplinary Tribunal of the Council of the Inns of Court, since the procedures in such tribunals satisfy the need for public accountability.[35]

It is of considerable importance to note that where the L.S.O. investigates an allegation he or she may also "investigate the matters to which the complaint relates."[36]

---

[27] *Ibid.* r. 18(2)(*b*).

[28] *Ibid.* r. 18(2)(*a*) proviso.

[29] See pp. 161–163, below.

[30] Courts and Legal Services Act 1990, s.24(1) and (2).

[31] *Legal Service: A Framework for the Future* (Cm. 740, 1989), para. 10.9.

[32] *Ibid.*, para. 10.13. The first L.S.O. is Mr. Michael Barnes, who took up his appointment on January 2, 1991.

[33] The L.S.O. may at any time discontinue an investigation: s.22(3). In conducting an investigation, the L.S.O. may require any person to furnish relevant information and produce relevant documents (s.25(1)). The L.S.O. has the same powers as the High Court with regard to the attendance and examination of witnesses and in respect of the production of documents (s.25(2)). Any person in contempt of the L.S.O. may be referred to the High Court (s. 25(4)–(7)).

[34] *Ibid.* s.22(5) and (6).

[35] *Ibid.* s.22(7), see General Council of the Bar, *Quality of Justice: The Bar's Response* (1989), p. 196.

[36] Courts and Legal Services Act 1990, s.22(2).

Upon completion of an investigation, the L.S.O. is required to send a written report of the conclusions to the person making the allegation, any person in respect of whom the complaint was made, and the professional body concerned.[37] In the report, which must be reasoned, the L.S.O. may make one of the following recommendations:

(1) that the complaint be reconsidered by the professional body;
(2) that the professional body (or any other relevant disciplinary body) should consider its powers in relation to the person about whom the complaint was made and any person who at the time was connected[38] with him or her;
(3) that the person about whom the complaint was made or any person who at the time was connected with him or her should pay compensation, as specified by the L.S.O., to the complainant for loss suffered or inconvenience or distress caused as a result of the matter about which there was a complaint;
(4) that the professional body concerned should pay such compensation;
(5) that a separate payment be made to the complainant in respect of costs related to the making of the allegation.[39]

These recommendations are backed by the requirement that a person to whom a report is sent must "have regard to the conclusions and recommendations set out in the report, so far as they concern that person."[40] Further, the person or body to whom a recommendation is made must, within three months of the date on which the report was sent, notify the L.S.O. of the action taken or proposed to be taken to comply with the recommendation.[41] Finally, any person or body failing to comply with a recommendation must publicise that failure and the reasons for it in such manner as the L.S.O. specifies.[42] If a person or body fails so to publicise, the L.S.O. may take such steps as are considered reasonable to publicise the failure.[43]

(e) Legal proceedings against lawyers

A lawyer's misconduct or incompetence may give rise to a cause of action against him or her. For example, a client may be able to sue for breach of

---

[37] *Ibid.*, s.23(1). The same people must be informed if the L.S.O. does not investigate: *ibid.* s.22(4).

[38] The person with respect to whom a complaint is made ("the first person") and another person ("the second person") are connected if (a) the second person employs the first and is an authorised advocate, authorised litigator, duly certificated notary public, licensed conveyancer or partnership, (b) they are both partners in the same partnership, (c) the second person is a recognised body which employs the first or of which the first is an officer: *Ibid.*, s.23(11).

[39] *Ibid.*, s.23(2). The L.S.O. also has the power to refer to the Lord Chancellor's Advisory Committee on Legal Education and Conduct any matters which come to his or her notice and are relevant to that committee's functions: *ibid.*, s.24(3).

[40] *Ibid.*, s.23(6).

[41] *Ibid.*, s.23(7).

[42] *Ibid.*, s.23(8).

[43] *Ibid.*, s.23(9). Any reasonable expenses incurred by the L.S.O. may be recovered as a civil debt from the person whose failure has been publicised: *ibid.*, s.23(10).

contract,[44] breach of trust[45] or the tort of negligence.[46] The scope of negligence liability has been wider since the decision of the House of Lords in 1963 in *Hedley, Byrne & Co. Ltd.* v. *Heller & Partners Ltd.*[47] where it was established that a special relationship could give rise to a duty of care in the giving of information or advice, and that there would be liability in damages in such cases in respect of losses that were purely economic. In *Midland Bank Trust Co. Ltd.* v. *Hett, Stubbs & Kemp*[48] Oliver J. stated that the case of a layman consulting a solicitor seemed:

"to be as typical a case as one could find of the sort of relationship in which the duty of care described in the *Hedley Byrne* case exists."[49]

His Lordship held that the authorities which indicated that the existence of a contract between a solicitor and client precluded any action in tort[50] were inconsistent with *Hedley Byrne* and should not be followed.[51] In *Ross* v. *Caunters*[52] Sir Robert Megarry V.-C. took matters a step further. Solicitors failed to warn a client that his will should not be witnessed by a spouse of a beneficiary and failed to notice that this had happened. They were held liable to the disappointed beneficiary whose bequest failed.

The position of the victims of incompetence is further secured by the requirement that solicitors carry indemnity insurance under the terms of a Master Policy taken out by the Law Society,[53] and the fact that all barristers must carry such insurance.[54] The Law Society's scheme has been unpopular with many solicitors, not because of any objection to the principle of

[44] Until the commencement of the Courts and Legal Services Act 1990, barristers could not have been sued in contract. However, s.61(1) now provides that "Any rule of law which prevents a barrister from entering into a contract for the provision of his services as a barrister is hereby abolished." But s.61(2) goes on to provide that "Nothing in subsection (1) prevents the General Council of the Bar from making rules (however described) restricting a barrister's right to enter into contracts." We wait to see what, if any, rules the Bar Council makes.

[45] *e.g. Re Bell's Indenture* [1980] 1 W.L.R. 1217.

[46] See R. M. Jackson and J. L. Powell, *Professional Negligence* (2nd ed., 1987), Chaps. 4 and 5 and A. M. Dugdale and K. M. Stanton, *Professional Negligence* (2nd ed., 1989), pp. 138–143.

[47] [1964] A.C. 465 and see Jackson and Powell (1987), *passim;* Dugdale and Stanton (1989), *passim;* W. V. H. Rogers (ed.) *Winfield and Jolowicz on Tort* (13th ed., 1989), pp. 272–288; M. A. Jones, *Textbook on Torts* (2nd ed., 1989), pp. 54–66.

[48] [1979] Ch. 384. Solicitors acting for both grantor and grantee of an option (to purchase the freehold reversion of a farm) carelessly failed to register the option. The grantor subsequently sold the reversion to a third party and thereby achieved the desired result of defeating the option. The executors of the grantee recovered damages from the solicitors.

[49] [1979] Ch. 384 at 417.

[50] *Groom* v. *Crocker* [1939] 1 K.B. 194, C.A.; *Clark* v. *Kirby-Smith* [1964] Ch. 506 (Plowman J.).

[51] Oliver J. held that the claim in contract succeeded as well as the claim in tort. The duty to register was a continuing one which lasted to the same date. The six year limitation period in tort ran from the time when the damage occurred, *i.e.* the date of the sale which defeated the option.

[52] [1980] Ch. 297.

[53] Solicitors Act 1974, s.37, the Solicitor's Indemnity Rules 1990. The precursor of the present rules were held to be *intra vires* the Law Society: *Swain* v. *The Law Society* [1982] 1 W.L.R. 52, C.A.

[54] Every barrister supplying legal services in independent practice must be a member of Bar Mutual Indemnity Fund Limited (BMIF) and have paid the appropriate insurance premium to and be insured with BMIF against claims for professional negligence: *Code of Conduct*, paras. 301, 302.

compulsory insurance, but because of the Society's insistence on a single centrally controlled scheme[55] and the high premiums charged.[56]

Even assuming the client has perceived that the lawyer has done his or her work incompetently, which is itself problematic, there are a number of problems facing those who wish to sue lawyers. First, legal assistance is advisable, but someone whose dealings with a lawyer have been unsatisfactory and probably protracted and a source of frustration and annoyance, is unlikely to relish the prospect of involvement with yet more lawyers. Moreover there may be difficulties in finding solicitors prepared to bring negligence proceedings against fellow practitioners. In order to alleviate this problem, the Law Society, with the co-operation of local law societies, established a panel of solicitors prepared to act in such cases (the "Negligence Panel").[57]

Secondly, there is a special immunity from an action for negligence which attaches in respect of acts or omissions in the conduct of litigation. The authorities have concerned barristers, but the immunity was regarded as extending to a solicitor acting as advocate.[58] The matter is put beyond doubt by section 62 of the Courts and Legal Services Act 1990, which states that anyone who is not a barrister but lawfully provides any legal services in relation to any proceedings has the same immunity as a barrister.[59]

The House of Lords in *Rondel* v. *Worsley*[60] held that a barrister was immune from action in respect of his or her conduct at trial. The immunity was justified by public policy:

"mainly upon the ground that a barrister owes a duty to the court as well as to his client and should not be inhibited through fear of an action by his client, from performing it; partly on the undesirability of relitigation as between barrister and client of what was litigated between the client and his opponent."[61]

In *Saif Ali* v. *Sydney Mitchell & Co.*[62] the House of Lords held that the immunity extended only to pre-trial work which was:

"so intimately connected with the conduct of the cause in Court that it can fairly be said to be a preliminary decision affecting the way that cause is to be conducted when it comes to a hearing."[63]

---

[55] D. Podmore, (1980) 7 B.J.L.S. 1 at 5–6. The Law Society is not liable to account to solicitors for the commission received from the insurance brokers: *Swain* v. *The Law Society* [1983] A.C. 598, H.L.

[56] The premium is assessed by reference to the average gross fee income per principal, with reduced rates, *e.g.* for small practices, practices in small areas, practices undertaking low risk work: Solicitors Indemnity Rules 1990, rr. 16, 17, Table 1.

[57] See above, p. 153.

[58] *Saif Ali* v. *Sydney Mitchell & Co.* [1980] A.C. 198, 215, 224, 227.

[59] If the advocate is immune from an action in negligence, there can be no liability for breach of any contract: Courts and Legal Services Act 1990, s.62(2).

[60] [1969] 1 A.C. 191. Until *Hedley Byrne* and *Rondel* v. *Worsley* were decided it was thought that a barrister could not be sued as he or she could not enter a contractual relationship with either the instructing solicitor or the lay client. This old rule of law has now been abolished, although it may be replaced by rules of conduct, see n. 44 above.

[61] *per* Lord Wilberforce in *Saif Ali* v. *Sydney Mitchell & Co.* [1980] A.C. 198 at 212.

[62] [1980] A.C. 198.

[63] *per* McCarthy P. in *Rees* v. *Sinclair* [1974] 1 N.Z.L.R. 180 at 187, endorsed by Lords Wilberforce, Diplock and Salmon. Lord Russell and Lord Keith favoured a wider test under which immunity would be extended to all work in connection with litigation.

It was alleged that a barrister negligently gave advice which led to the wrong person being joined as defendant. The House of Lords held that he was not immune as the alleged negligence had prevented the plaintiff's cause coming to court. The exact extent of the immunity is difficult to define, but it does appear to extend, *e.g.* to advice as to plea in a criminal case.[64]

The arguments in favour of the immunity are (1) that the barrister owes a duty to the court which transcends the duty to the client and that the necessary confidence between Bar and Bench would be undetermined by barristers' fear of suits, (2) that there should be a general immunity from suit for all participants in a trial again because of the adverse effects upon the administration of justice if the situation were otherwise, (3) that the "cab-rank rule" would be difficult to enforce if barristers had to take on clients who could then pursue actions against them, (4) that relitigation of cases is undesirable and the correct method of challenge is via an appeal.[65] These arguments can be challenged on two bases: the first that they are inherently unsound and the second that they are based on "dubious, empirical assertions about the legal process."[66] Zander has indicated that the first basis of challenge includes the arguments that it is not probable that barristers would be influenced to do their work much differently by the thought that they might be sued for negligence, that re-opening a case is not necessarily bad if, *e.g.* someone has gone to prison because of the negligence of the barrister, that there is little prospect of considerable litigation in view of the many barriers facing a potential litigant, and that no barrister is likely to know enough about a client for the prospect of litigation to have any effect upon accepting a brief or instruction.[67] Veljanowski and Whelan deal with the second basis of challenge, pointing out the lack of an empirical basis for the immunity, since there is no evidence to support the suggestion that a rash of suits would follow if there was no immunity, there is no evidence that "defensive" practices by barristers would abound, rather there is evidence that good practice might be encouraged, and, while the prospect of re-litigation appears to be the strongest argument, it may be that it has outlived its validity since "the very existence of an appellate framework suggests that the value of finality in judicial decisions is not absolute" and "it is hard to accept the proposition that an instrument capable of reducing negligence will bring the administration of justice into disrepute." Further, a barrister can only be liable for negligence and not for mere errors of judgment.[68] It is hard to avoid Miller's conclusion that the "immunity is an anachronism maintained by lawyers for lawyers."[69] Nevertheless, in 1979, the Royal Commission on Legal Services did not favour any change in this area[70] and the Government was convinced of the arguments in favour of the immunity

[64] *Somasundaram* v. *M. Julius Melchior & Co.* [1989] 1 All E.R. 129, C.A. See, further, Jackson and Powell (1987), pp. 273–280; Dugdale and Stanton (1989), pp. 158–162; Winfield (1989), pp. 103–104; Jones (1989), pp. 45–46.

[65] See C. G. Veljanowski and C. J. Whelan, "Professional Negligence and the Quality of Legal Services—An Economic Perspective" (1983) 46 M.L.R. 700, 711–712.

[66] Veljanowski and Whelan (1983), p. 712.

[67] M. Zander, *Legal Services for the Community* (1978), pp. 134–136.

[68] Veljanowski and Whelan (1983), pp. 712–717.

[69] D. L. Carey Miller, "The Advocate's Duty to Justice: Where Does It Belong" (1981) 97 L.Q.R. 127, 138. The Court of Appeal's support for the immunity in *Rondel* v. *Worsley* was met with scorn by the press, see Zander (1978), p. 136.

[70] R.C.L.S., Vol. 1, pp. 332–333.

not only to preserve it for barristers but to make it clear in the Courts and Legal Services Act 1990 that it extended to all advocates.[71]

Thirdly, it must be remembered that liability in negligence does not attach simply because a lawyer turns out to be wrong or makes an error of judgment. A lawyer is only liable if the error is "such as no reasonable well informed and competent member of that profession could have made."[72]

Fourthly, a solicitor who has done work for a client and remains unpaid has the right to retain the papers concerning the client's affairs and other personal property, that is a "retaining or general lien," and also a "lien on property recovered or preserved," that is a right to seek the court to direct that property, except real property, obtained under a court's judgment should be available to the solicitor to cover the client's costs in relation to that work.[73] This may cause both difficulty and resentment. If the solicitor declines to act further, the client or the new solicitor may obtain a court order for delivery of the papers on an undertaking to hold them without prejudice to the lien and to return them on completion of the matter.[74] If the client justifiably discharges the solicitor, the Law Society may gain possession of the documents.[75]

4. Social Background, Entry and Training

(a) Social Background

Lawyers predominantly come from middle class homes.[76] The same is true of law students. The College of Law reported to the Royal Commission on Legal Services that the parental occupation of 60.9 per cent. of its solicitor students and 67.3 per cent. of its bar students were professional or managerial, compared with 8 per cent. that were manual (whether skilled, semi-skilled or unskilled).[77] The system of admissions to law degrees appears to perpetuate the class structure of the legal profession.[78] Most

---

[71] S.62. See, *Legal Services: Framework for the Future* (Cm. 740, 1989), para. 10.10.

[72] *per* Lord Diplock in *Saif Ali* v. *Sydney Mitchell & Co.* [1980] A.C. 198, 220. For an example of a "reasonable mistake" see *Jones* v. *Jones* [1970] Q.B. 576.

[73] *Cordery on Solicitors* (1988), Chap. 8 and *Supreme Court Practice 1991*, Vol. 2, Part 11, section D.3.

[74] The Royal Commission recommended that this should be normal practice without a court order where a solicitor is replaced for any reason. No such reform has been introduced, see *Cordery on Solicitors* (1988), pp. 245–247.

[75] Solicitors Act 1974, s.35, Sched. 1. This power is rarely exercised. The Royal Commission recommendation that it should be exercised whether the client would otherwise suffer has not been implemented.

[76] See R. L. Abel, *The Legal Profession in England and Wales* (1988), pp. 74–76 and 170–172 and Table 1.21; R.C.L.S., Vol. 2, pp. 57–61; D. Podmore, (1977) 74 L.S.Gaz. 611; Podmore (1980), pp. 30–32, 90–93.

[77] M. Zander, *The State of Knowledge about the English Legal Profession* (1980), pp. 22–23. The accuracy of this information is emphasised by two further studies: P. McDonald, "The Class of '81: A Glance at the Social Class Composition of Recruits to the Legal Profession" (1982) 9 J.L.S. 267 and M. King, M. Israel and S. Goulbourne, *Ethnic Minorities and Recruitment to the Solicitor's Profession* (1990), pp. 32–34.

[78] See R. L. Abel, *The Legal Profession in England and Wales* (1988), Chap. 18, esp. pp. 271–275 and King, Israel and Goulbourne (1990), pp. 32–34 and 37–52. See also P. McDonald (1982); R. G. Lee, "Survey of law school admissions" (1984) 18 L.T. 165.

lawyers are graduates[79] and so the social imbalance seen at the academic stage of qualification maintains the social imbalance at the professional stage. The burden is upon the educational institutions to redress the social imbalance in the numbers of those reaching the required standard of admission to a university or profession.[80] Educational institutions have recognised this problem and are aiming to widen the backgrounds of people who come forward for tertiary education.[81] It remains to be seen whether any change occurs in student admission. Further, it remains to be seen whether the structure of the profession will be affected, since there are financial and other hurdles to be overcome.

The passage of the Sex Disqualification (Removal) Act 1919 meant that it was possible for women to be solicitors and that the theoretical possibility of women being barristers became a reality. However, women have not come into the professions in significant numbers until the last twenty years. Women are poorly represented in the legal profession as a whole,[82] and are particularly poorly represented at the upper echelons of both branches.[83]

---

[79] See R. L. Abel, *The Legal Profession in England and Wales* (1988), pp. 46–49 and 143–145. In 1989–90, 3,729 solicitors were admitted, of whom 67.3 per cent. were law graduates and 14.7 per cent. were non-law graduates; the remaining 18 per cent. consists not only of non-graduates, but also members of ILEX and of other legal professions, many of whom are graduates: *Law Society Annual Statistical Report 1990*, Table 9.1. Although effectively both branches of the profession are graduate entry, it is not formally required that all entrants be graduates, see below, p. 171–173.

[80] The Royal Commission on Legal Services made this clear in Vol. 1 at p. 629. The same point is made by the authors of the recent report on ethnic minorities and recruitment to the solicitors' profession: King, Israel and Goulbourne (1990) and see below, p. 170.

[81] *e.g.* through the "Access" scheme designed to enable people without the traditional "A" level qualifications to gain admission, see, *e.g.* N. Duncan, "Testing the Third Route: testing the effectiveness of Access courses in law" (1990) 24 L.T. 29. See also King, Israel and Goulbourne (1990), pp. 44–52; R. G. Lee (1984); R. Stone, "Prediction, Prize or Profile: Three Models of Admissions Policy" (1988) 22 L.T. 28.

[82] See *Women in the Professions*, a report compiled by the United Kingdom Inter-Professional Group Working Party on Women's Issues (1990). In 1989–90, 23 per cent. of the 54,734 solicitors with practising certificates were women: *Law Society Annual Statistical Report 1990*, pp. 6–7. See also the Law Society, *Equal in the Law* (1988), p. 10. At October 1, 1990, 18 per cent. of the 6,645 practising barristers in England and Wales were women: The General Council of The Bar, *Annual Report 1990*, p. 20.

[83] *Women in the Professions* shows that 11 of the 97 members of the ruling Bar Council were women and 3 of the 70 members of the ruling Council of the Law Society were women. In a survey of solicitors' careers (with 293 respondents) it was shown in relation to people working full-time or part-time in private practice that 91 per cent. of the men admitted to the Roll in 1977 and 61 per cent. of the men admitted in 1982 were sole practitioners or partners (13 per cent. and 23 per cent. respectively being salaried partners). The comparable figures for women were 60 per cent. (8 per cent. salaried) in 1977 and 36 per cent. (14 per cent. salaried) in 1982: P. Marks, *Solicitors' Career Structure Survey* (1988), see also the Law Society, *Equal in the Law* (1988), p. 11. Of the solicitors holding practising certificates at July 31, 1990, 41.5 per cent. of those who had been admitted within 9 years were women, 34.0 per cent. of those admitted within 10–19 years and a steadily reducing percentage to 1.2 per cent. of those who had been admitted for more than 50 years: *Law Society Annual Statistical Report 1990*, Table 2.3. At October 1, 1990, 4 per cent. of the 682 Queen's Counsel were women: The General Council of The Bar, *Annual Report 1990*, p. 21. The picture is replicated in the judiciary, where there is only one woman Court of Appeal judge, and in academic law, where women are noticeably under-represented at any of the promoted stages, but particularly as professors. See also G. Chambers and S. Harwood, *Solicitors in England and Wales: Practice, Organisation and Perceptions* (1990).

Women seem to be over-represented at certain lower levels of the profession, *e.g.* there appear to be proportionately more women working as assistant solicitors for longer before obtaining a partnership than men.[84] Needless to say this picture is changing. The proportion of women who hold practising certificates as solicitors is consistently increasing[85] and women have increasingly formed a large part of the entry to the profession.[86] No doubt the picture will continue to change.

It is not only in terms of recruitment and promotion that women have faced significant problems. Work practices and ethics adopted by the professions have added to the problems. It is now the case that in the solicitors' profession considerable attention is being paid to the need to change work practices so as to encourage women to stay in it[87] and to avoid the problem of requiring women to choose between family and career. Consequently, a Working Party of the Law Society has encouraged part-time work for men and women.[88] It also encouraged career-breaks for women so as to enable time to be taken out of a career, for example to have a family, and then to

[84] Of the 293 solicitors who responded in the Solicitors' Careers Survey, 40 per cent. of the women admitted to the Roll in 1977 and 64 per cent. of the women admitted in 1982 were Assistant Solicitors, whereas the figures for men were, respectively, 8 per cent. and 39 per cent. Marks (1988), p. 9. *Law Society Annual Statistical Report 1990*, Table 2.8 reports a similar marked difference.

[85] *e.g.* the proportion of solicitor practising certificate holders who are women is increasing consistently: in 1985–86 it was 15 per cent., 1986–87 18 per cent., 1987–88 20 per cent., 1988–89 21 per cent., and 1989–90 23 per cent.: *Law Society Annual Statistical Report 1990*, Table 2.2.

[86] The number of new members admitted to the Solicitors' Roll:

	Men	Women	
1900	593	0	0%
1920	606	0	0%
1940	309	14	4%
1960	671	40	6%
1965	947	62	6%
1970	1,712	165	16%
1975	1,871	332	15%
1980	2,515	1,023	29%
1985	1,563	1,123	43%
1988	1,746	1,499	46%

Source: *Women in the Professions*, p. 57. The proportion of women admitted to the Roll had increased to 47 per cent. in 1989: M. Chambers (ed.), *The Legal Profession 1990*, p. 20. In 1989 38 per cent. of those called to the Bar were women and 42 per cent. of those obtaining tenancies were women: C. Newman, "Women and the Bar" (1990) 87 L.S.Gaz., June 27, p. 39. In 1989–90, 40 per cent. of the 846 people called to the Bar were women: The General Council of the Bar, *Annual Report 1990*, p. 20.

[87] Significantly more women than men have left the professions, *e.g.* of the men solicitors admitted to the Roll in 1977 and 1982, 99 per cent. were working full-time and 1 per cent. part-time. On the other hand, of the women solicitors admitted in 1977, 56 per cent. were working full-time and 26 per cent. part-time and, of those admitted in 1982, 74 per cent. were working full-time and 11 per cent. part-time. Thus, the only people not working at the time of the survey (1987) were women. 18 per cent. of the women admitted in 1977 were not working at all and 15 per cent. of the women admitted in 1982 were not working at all: Marks (1988), p. 1. The Law Society views this picture with alarm: document reproduced in *Women in the Professions*, p. 65.

[88] *Equal in the Law* (1988), pp. 20–21.

make return relatively easy.[89] Consequently, it encouraged a retainer system and emphasised the importance of courses, at present organised by the Association of Women Solicitors, to provide up-dates on the law and skills and, in particular, to overcome any possible loss of confidence.[90] Since barristers are self-employed, the problems that arise are different. For example, attempts to be supportive of women with children by establishing child-care facilities have foundered for poor reasons.[91]

It is also the case, at least with regard to the solicitors' profession, that women earn less and that the work they do is different. For example, on average male assistant solicitors earn 9 per cent. more than their female counterparts, although there are significant regional variations.[92] Women are more likely to specialise in matrimonial law, probate, wills and trusts, and domestic conveyancing than men, who are more likely to specialise in company and commercial work.[93]

Although there have been few complaints about sex discrimination,[94] there has been an acceptance by some that it is a problem. Consequently, the Law Society has established a Code of Practice[95] to avoid sexual discrimination and the Code of Conduct for the Bar of England and Wales contains provisions designed to prevent sex discrimination by a practising barrister both generally and in particular in relation to pupillage.[96] Further, the Sex Discrimination Act 1975 now applies not only to the solicitors' profession but also to the offer of pupillage and tenancies at the Bar.[97] A Working Party of the Law Society has recommended that sex discrimination be a disciplinary offence, that interviewing styles should be amended to take account of the requirements of the legislation and that the implications of the legislation should be publicised generally throughout the profession.[98]

As regards racial discrimination, the Royal Commission on Legal Services concluded that the situation was not satisfactory and that the trends were unfavourable.[99] Historically speaking there has always been a significant number of people from ethnic minorities at the Bar, but they have usually been overseas residents. In a survey report of 1989 it was shown that 5 per

[89] Ibid., pp. 22–23.
[90] Ibid., p. 15.
[91] C. Newman (1990) 87 L.S.Gaz. June 27, p. 39.
[92] See M. Chambers (ed.), The Legal Profession 1990, p. 21.
[93] See, Marks (1988), p. 18 and Chambers (1990), pp. 20–21.
[94] It may be the case that women are afraid of making a complaint: C. Newman, op. cit.
[95] See, e.g. the Law Society's document entitled "The Treatment of Sexual Discrimination" reproduced in Women in the Professions at p. 18; see also R. L. Abel, The Legal Profession in England and Wales (1988), pp. 81–85 and 175–176, which also reports denial by some members of the professions of the existence of discrimination.
[96] See, The Guide to the Professional Conduct of Solicitors (1990), pp. 10–11 and The Code of Conduct of the Bar of England and Wales (1990), Annex C and para. 210.
[97] See the amendments to both the Sex Discrimination Act 1975 and the Race Relations Act 1976 introduced by s.64 of the Courts and Legal Services Act 1990. These provisions are also extended to advocates: ibid. s.65.
[98] Equal in the Law (1988), pp. 8–9, 17 and 23. The other recommendations made by the Working Party are that the Law Society should press for legislation enabling it to set different levels of practising certificate fees to enable women to retain a certificate whilst looking after children; change its procedures on the granting of practising certificates after a lapse of time, so as to make it easier for women to return after having had children; and adopt a policy to request tax relief for child care expenses for women solicitors who return to work: ibid. pp. 8, 14–15, 16.
[99] R.C.L.S., Vol. 1, pp. 501–504, see the Senate's Annual Statement, 1983–84, pp. 32–36.

cent. of all lawyers were ethnic minorities barristers, which the Bar believes to be a better proportion than in most other professions.[1] The problem of racial discrimination has been acknowledged. The Code of Conduct prohibits racial discrimination and the Bar Council and its Race Relations Committee have taken steps to combat racial discrimination and disadvantage at the Bar. However, the option of dealing with discrimination by affirmative action for the benefit of people from ethnic minorities was rejected.[2] Nevertheless, it is recognised that greater efforts need to be made, since ethnic minorities students appear to have greater difficulty obtaining pupillage and tenancies and many ethnic minorities barristers work in what have been called "ghetto" chambers, which are relatively isolated from the rest of the Bar.[3] Further, ethnic minorities barristers are clearly underrepresented in the upper echelons of the profession since the 1989 survey showed that they numbered only 1 per cent. of Q.C.s.[4] It may be the case that the extension of the statutory provisions relating to racial discrimination to the barristers' profession will have an effect, but it is doubted whether discrimination will be eliminated.[5]

There are few ethnic minorities solicitors.[6] Part of the problem has been that of racial discrimination, which the Law Society's Race Relations Committee constantly has under review.[7] Further, the Law Society has adopted a code of practice for the avoidance of racial discrimination.[8] Although steps have been taken to combat racial discrimination, there are still many problems. A recent report concerned with ethnic minorities and recruitment to the solicitors' profession[9] did not make the usual assumption that there is equality of opportunity, but examined the validity of that assumption. It examined the tests set at each stage of professional qualification and considered their effects upon people from disadvantaged backgrounds so as to determine what the barriers are and how they might be overcome both by

[1] General Council of the Bar, *Quality of Justice: The Bar's Response* (1989), pp. 267–268.
[2] R. L. Abel, *The Legal Profession in England and Wales* (1988), p. 78, and see *Quality of Justice* (1989), p. 267.
[3] Abel (1988), pp. 78–79; J. Morton, "Racial discrimination in the legal profession" (1990) 140 N.L.J. 1104–1107 (The Bar), 1146–1148 (the solicitors' profession), 1184–1185 (conclusion).
[4] *Quality of Justice* (1989), p. 267.
[5] J. Morton (1990), p. 1185.
[6] Abel (1988), p. 172. The *Law Society Annual Statistical Report 1990* reveals the following figures in Table 2.11:

Ethnic origin	Number	Per cent
White/European	37,403	68.3%
Afro-Caribbean	74	0.1%
Asian	477	0.9%
Chinese	98	0.2%
African	20	0.0%
Other ethnic origin	40	0.1%
Unanswered/refused	4,969	9.1%
Unknown	11,653	21.3%
Total	54,734	100.0%

81.2 per cent. of the students enrolling with the Law Society 1989–90 were white European: *ibid.*, Table 10.5.
[7] See, *e.g.* its publication entitled, *The Race Report* 1989.
[8] See, *The Guide to the Professional Conduct of Solicitors* (1990), pp. 10–11.
[9] King, Israel and Goulbourne, (1990).

the individual and the "gatekeepers."[10] There are barriers which are particularly difficult for ethnic minorities to overcome at all stages of qualification: the academic stage, the professional stage and seeking employment. One barrier is that created by class and race prejudice, *e.g.* prejudice in favour of Oxbridge applicants for articles. Further barriers are created by the tests used at various stages, *e.g.* for admission to Universities and Polytechnics, which are of such a nature that people who have experienced educational disadvantages, but who are talented, have significant problems in satisfying them; or for passing the L.S.F. course, which is wholly reliant upon assessment by examination and thus produces similar problems to those of admission to tertiary educational institutions. Finally, the candidate faces the barrier created by the method of informal, unstructured interviews for articles, which are not the best way to assess a candidate's ability. Numerous recommendations are made, including less reliance on A-level scores and greater reliance on a "Profile Model" for University and Polytechnic admission, less reliance on unseen written examinations in the L.S.F. examination and greater concentration on skills acquisition, and the introduction of a Code of Practice or a Model Interview Guide to minimise the influence of racial prejudice upon employment selection decisions.[11]

Further, one way to deal with discrimination may be highly disadvantageous to the legal system as a whole. Goulbourne pointed to this issue when she said, "the segregation of the profession which the Royal Commission warned against in 1979 continues not only because of historical forces but because many black solicitors and barristers believe that all black firms and chambers are the only way in which black lawyers can make progress within the profession."[12]

(b) Entry and training

Entry to the Bar has since 1975 been restricted to graduates and mature students.[13] An entrant must join one of the inns of court and complete two educational stages. The "academic stage" is satisfied by obtaining either a "qualifying law degree" recognised by the Council of Legal Education[14] or

---

[10] *Ibid.*, pp. 23–24. The method of assessing the barriers is to use the model established by Twining which requires the asking of four questions: (1) What are the barriers to progress beyond a particular stage? Do the barriers operate against members of disadvantaged groups? (2) Who controls entry and exit at this stage? (3) From the point of view of the individual, by what means might each barrier be surmounted? (4) From the point of view of the gatekeepers and of those concerned with general strategy, what are acceptable and feasible means of eliminating or circumnavigating the barriers or easing the passage of individual members of disadvantaged groups in the interests of improved access?: *ibid.* p. 24, adopting the Twining model: W. Twining, "Access to Legal Education and the Legal Profession: A Commonwealth Perspective" (1987) 7 *Windsor Yearbook of Access of Justice* 157.

[11] King, Israel and Goulbourne (1990), pp. 1–7 and 23–109.

[12] S. Goulbourne, "The Recent History of Black Ethnic Minorities in the Solicitors' Profession" in King, Israel and Goulbourne (1990). See also Abel (1988), p. 79.

[13] See the Consolidated Regulations of the Inns of Court published by the Council of Legal Education; R.C.L.S., Vol. 1, pp. 619–621; B. Hogan, *A Career in Law* (1981); E. Usher, *Careers in the Law in England and Wales* (1982).

[14] A law degree must include the six "core" subjects Contract, Tort, Criminal Law, Land Law, Constitutional and Administrative Law, Equity and Trusts, passed to a satisfactory standard. Partial exemption may be given on a subject by subject basis. From October 1981, at least 2(2) Honours standard has been required.

the Diploma in Law taught and examined by the City University and the Polytechnic of Central London.[15] The "vocational stage" comprises courses at the Inns of Court School of Law.[16] The new course is skills based in addition to providing and assessing basic information. In consequence the timetable for the course has been split into three parts:

(1) the knowledge which the students must acquire,[17]
(2) the skills the students must learn,[18]
(3) the practical exercises in which the students can deploy both knowledge and skills.[19]

Students wishing to practise must attend all elements as well as passing the examinations. Students who complete the two stages, and who have dined in the hall of their inn three times a term for eight terms,[20] are then "called to the Bar." They are not, however, entitled to practise unless they complete twelve months pupillage in the chambers of a barrister of at least five years' standing, and may not accept instructions until the second six months of pupillage.[21] There are special provisions for barristers from Ireland, Scottish advocates, Commonwealth lawyers and former solicitors.[22] The costs of entry are high, including not only tuition fees and maintenance, but also dining fees and special clothes and barristers may not earn enough to live on for some years. Discretionary grants may be available from local education authorities. In addition, the Council of Legal Education and the Inns of Court award a number of studentships, the Inns of Court make a variety of additional awards each year and the Bar Council has a Trusts Funds Committee which makes grants to assist students and pupils. Further, it is the policy of the Bar Council to encourage chambers to move towards a scheme of funded pupillages so that pupils receive a minimum of £3,000 per six months.

Entry to the solicitor's branch of the profession consists also of an academic stage followed by a vocational stage. The academic stage for about

[15] This is the method by which the person who is not a law graduate obtains the necessary "Certificate of Eligibility." The course for non-law graduates lasts one year; for mature students, two years. Students may be permitted to prepare by private study or by attendance at certain provincial polytechnics.

[16] The change towards a vocational course has meant a limitation on places available at the Inns of Court School of Law to only those people intending to practise in any member state of the E.C. In particular this excludes most overseas students. Courses not involving the skills training and simply leading to entry to the Bar examination are provided at a number of institutions, primarily the private Holborn Law Tutors.

[17] The knowledge is almost all confined to evidence, procedure and professional conduct. There is a multiple choice examination in civil and criminal procedure just before Christmas: Hoffmann J., "Change of Course at the CLE" (1989) *Counsel*, November, pp. 13–14.

[18] The skills concentrated on are legal research, information management and problem solving, opinion writing, interviewing, negotiating, drafting and advocacy: Hoffmann (1989), p. 14.

[19] Students are required to act as counsel in simulated cases, bringing together the various skills which they have been taught: Hoffmann (1989), p. 14.

[20] See the Consolidated Regulations, regs. 10–13. There are four "dining terms" of 23 days duration in each year. A pupil may keep up to four terms by dining in a Circuit Mess at least three times per term. The dining requirements have long been a matter of contention. The Royal Commission recommended their abolition unless improvement to ensure that benchers and barristers mix with the students are made and found to work satisfactorily: R.C.L.S., Vol. 1, pp. 641–642.

[21] Consolidated Regulations, regs. 39, 40.

[22] *Ibid.*, 34–48.

three-quarters of new solicitors is satisfied by them having obtained a law degree. A significant number take the "Common Professional Examination" after having obtained a non-law degree. Whilst 82 per cent. of people take a degree, some qualify by other routes. These other routes are available to people who, whilst they may be graduates, rely upon their qualifications as fellows of the Institute of Legal Executives[23] or as members of another legal profession.[24]

After the academic stage, all candidates must attend the first part of the professional stage, which is a vocational course leading to the taking of the Law Society's Final (L.S.F.) Examination. The L.S.F. course may be taken at one of the branches of the College of Law in London, Guildford, Chester or York, or one of the nine polytechnics offering the course, that is Birmingham, Bristol, Leeds, Leicester, City of London, Manchester, Newcastle, Nottingham and Wolverhampton.[25] The course is expressly designed not only to provide students with the requisite legal and procedural knowledge, but also with the vital skills necessary to fit someone to undertake practice as a solicitor. The courses taken are an attempt to reflect this essential mix and to reflect the basic areas of work that are the main work of a solicitor.[26] As with qualifying as a barrister, one of the main hurdles at the vocational stage is the financial one, since grants from an L.E.A. are discretionary and policy varies from area to area and from year to year. In consequence, the cost of tuition fees and maintenance must be either met from the student's own resources via, e.g. a loan, or by financial support from a future employer. Many solicitors' firms, in particular large London firms, offer assistance with funding the L.S.F. course. After the academic and vocational stages have been passed, a person enters articles for two years.[27] The formal educational requirements of a solicitor do not end with the successful completion of articles, since continuing education is a requirement for new solicitors, which it is expected will eventually extend to all solicitors admitted on or after August 1, 1965.

[23] It is still possible for school leavers and mature students (people over 25 with no degree) to qualify. School leavers must take and pass the "Solicitors' First Examination" as well as the Final Examination and then undertake five year articles. Mature students must pass an eight subject C.P.E. which takes two years, pass the Final Examination and do two years articles. The number of people entering the profession by this route is insignificant (one by each method in 1989–90). The Solicitors' First Examination is to be abolished: *Law Society Annual Statistical Report 1990*, para. 8.3. It is also possible for a justices' clerk to qualify through their Diploma.

[24] People transfer from being overseas solicitors, barristers and Scots and N. Ireland solicitors. Although relatively few take this route, there was a significant increase from 1988 to 1990: *Law Society Annual Statistical Report 1990*, para. 8.4. The manner in which transfer is facilitated is to be simplified.

[25] Fees at the College of Law are usually the most expensive, and fees at the polytechnics vary. Admissions are now undertaken through a centralised system, although the criteria for the College and polytechnics vary, e.g. the latter desire a reference in relation to the applicant. More information is available through the Association of Graduate Careers Advisory Services.

[26] The courses taken are: accounts; business organisations and insolvency; consumer protection and individual employment law; conveyancing; wills, probate and administration; family law; and litigation. In addition, professional conduct and revenue law can be tested in any of these papers.

[27] A Fellow of the Institute of Legal Executives may serve two years' articles instead of attending the L.S.F. course, but must pass the examination; if they attend the course, in certain circumstances they need not serve in articles.

The issue of legal education is a matter of public importance in view of the nature of the work performed by barristers and solicitors. In consequence, a publicly accountable committee, the Lord Chancellor's Advisory Committee on Legal Education and Conduct, is charged, amongst other things, with the general duty to assist "in the maintenance and development of standards in education [and] training ... of those offering legal services."[28] More specifically, the Advisory Committee is required to "keep under review the education and training of those who provide legal services," to "consider the need for continuing education and training for such persons and the form it should take," and to "consider the steps which professional and other bodies should take to ensure that their members benefit from such continuing education and training."[29]

The objectives of legal education in general have been considered on a number of occasions in the recent past. In particular, two reports have been published, one in 1971, by a committee chaired by Ormrod J.,[30] and one in 1988, by the Marre Committee.[31] Both committees were concerned with the financial burden of qualification. It may well be a significant additional factor in the skewed social background of the profession. The problem is slowly being tackled, at a time of great demand for lawyers, but only by the two branches of the profession. Government does not appear to recognise the obstacle which financial difficulties present to many potential lawyers.

Much of the recent discussion about legal education is concerned with the provision of essential legal skills.[32] This is already the avowed aim of the current vocational courses. Indeed, since the major changes to the vocational course at the Bar, the Law Society has undertaken a thoroughgoing examination of the L.S.F. course which is aimed to ensure that the education and training should "provide a supply of well trained solicitors sufficient to meet the needs of the profession and the consumer (both individual and corporate)."[33] In part this aim is to be achieved by more skills-based training. A further aspect of the future of legal education may be to encourage specialisation at the training stage, as well as the qualified stage.[34]

The Marre Committee commented not only on the need for the vocational stages to provide skills, but also the academic stage. It was pointed out, in particular, that many students arrive at the vocational stage exhibiting certain characteristics: "(1) insufficient ability to present clear and concise written arguments; (2) insufficient comprehensive knowledge of the core subjects; (3) inability to undertake independent legal research; (4) lack of ability in oral expression."[35] Many institutions already aim in their courses to provide students with the necessary skills, and the comments of the Marre

---

[28] Courts and Legal Services Act 1990, s.18(1). The precursor of this committee was established after the report of the Ormrod committee and the new committee partly responds to the recommendations for change made in *A Time for Change*, paras. 17.3–17.11.

[29] Courts and Legal Services Act 1990, Sched. 2, para. 1(1).

[30] Report of the Committee on Legal Education (Cmnd. 4595, 1971), see P. A. Thomas and G. Mungham (1972) 7 *Valparaiso Law Review* 87 and discussion reported at (1972) 12 J.S.P.T.L. (N.S.) 39.

[31] See above, p. 118.

[32] *A Time for Change*, at para. 12.21, provides a summary of the necessary legal skills, whilst recognising that at a time of rapid technological and social change it is not possible to provide a definitive list.

[33] The Law Society Training Committee, *Training Tomorrow's Solicitors* (1990), p. 9.

[34] *Legal Services: A Framework for the Future* (Cm. 740, 1989), paras. 9.7–9.11.

[35] *A Time for Change*, para. 13.5.

Committee inform debate about possible future developments. However, an inherent tension has to be recognised in considering what is the objective of a law degree. It has been suggested that it is a matter of concern that nearly one-half of law graduates do not go on to become lawyers.[36] However, a law degree is not simply one part of the process of qualifying as a lawyer. Law at a tertiary institution is an academic subject in its own right, taught for its own sake. It provides an insight into legal reasoning skills. Such reasoning skills are useful in many careers, not just the law. In consequence, there is often a tension between the perceived professional needs, *e.g.* reflected in the content and number of core subjects, as against the academic needs, *e.g.* to teach that which is of academic, intellectual and pedagogic significance.[37]

5. Unadmitted Personnel

Most solicitors' firms employ "legal executives," formerly known as "managing clerks," who are not admitted as solicitors but who do undertake professional work under their employers' supervision. The Institute of Legal Executives in evidence to the Royal Commission estimated their numbers at over 20,000, although the numbers of solicitors, particularly assistant solicitors, have been expanding more rapidly.[38] There are no requirements as to their qualification and training, although they may voluntarily take examinations in order to qualify as Associates or Fellows of the Institute of Legal Executives (ILEX). They tend to specialise in a particular class of work, and the amount of supervision exercised over an experienced executive may in practice be minimal. The Institute made various proposals to the Royal Commission for improving the professional status of legal executives. Having resisted suggestions that the two branches of the legal profession be fused, the Commission was unwilling to contemplate a third branch. The Institute's proposals for profit-sharing, enhanced pay for executives with ILEX qualifications or compulsory qualifications, compulsory arrangements for day release and payment for courses and extended right of audience all fell on stony ground, if not an impenetrable slab of concrete.[39] Legal executives have been among those who have qualified as licensed conveyancers.

Barristers' clerks have the rather different role in chambers of acting as office administrator and accountant for chambers as a whole, and as business manager and agent for each individual member. The employment of a clerk has until recently been a requirement of practice.[40] The Royal Commission recommended that this rule should be relaxed, provided a practice is administered efficiently, but recognised that a clerk would almost invariably be employed.[41] This was only finally implemented in 1990.[42]

[36] Reportedly the view of one member of the Marre Committee: *A Time for Change*, para. 13.3.
[37] See *e.g.* M. Zander, *A Matter of Justice* (1989), pp. 82–83.
[38] R.C.L.S., Vol. 1, p. 408.
[39] R.C.L.S., Vol. 1, pp. 406–417. See also R. L. Abel, *The Legal Profession in England and Wales* (1988), pp. 207–210.
[40] See above, p. 148. On barristers' clerks generally see R. Hazell, *The Bar on Trial* (1978) Chap. 5; J. Flood, "Barristers' Clerks," Warwick Law Working Paper No. 2, July 1977, and *Barristers' Clerks* (1983); M. Oldham, *Legal Executive Journal*, October 1990, pp. 2–3.
[41] R.C.L.S., Vol. 1, p. 484.
[42] See the General Council of the Bar, *Quality of Justice* (1989), p. 217; above, p. 148.

The clerk manipulates the flow of work in chambers by virtue of the functions of negotiating fees and arranging each barrister's timetable, and his or her relationships, built up over many years, with solicitors' firms. A minority are employed under a formal contract, although the Senate suggested that this should become the normal practice.[43] Many senior clerks are paid a percentage of gross fees, and their earnings are significantly higher than those of junior barristers.[44] The Royal Commission did not regard this disparity as justified by any difference in the nature and intensity of the work done. They suggested that clerks should be paid a fair remuneration for the work done, with a bonus of not more than one per cent. of gross fees to reward a high pressure of work (the present arrangements provide for a minimum of 5 per cent.[45]). The present system has the advantage for the barrister that the clerk has a "direct incentive to promote [his or her] practice,"[46] although the distinction between promoting the practice and simply "promoting" the level of fees is a fine one.[47] The Commission "deplored" cases where the clerk exercised too much authority, although all they could suggest was that barristers should not allow it to happen and that the head of chambers should exercise control in cases where a clerk restricted the flow of work to a particular barrister on grounds of supposed incompetence or inexperience, or simply personal dislike. The possibility of barristers arranging their own timetable and negotiating fees, leaving other administrative tasks to clerks, which system is operated by advocates in Ireland, Australia and South Africa,[48] was not seriously explored.

In recent years there have been some changes, with increasing number of senior clerk's appointments being advertised, and going to outsiders, the move away from remuneration based on a percentage of fees, the recruitment of graduates as junior clerks and the organisation of further education courses for junior clerks.[49] Overall, however, the cumulative effect of these changes seems limited.[50]

6. LAWYERS AND THE EUROPEAN COMMUNITY

A lawyer from another Community country may provide any service in connection with legal proceedings in the United Kingdom, provided that he or she acts in conjunction with a British lawyer entitled to provide that

---

[43] Chambers guidelines (1977); R.C.L.S., Vol. 1, p. 477. Forms of contracts have been recommended: Annual Statement, 1982–83, pp. 69–74; Counsels Guide to Chamber Administration (1988), pp. 11–15.

[44] R.C.L.S., Vol. 1, p. 487; see also Vol. 2, pp. 395–433.

[45] Annual Statement, 1969–70, pp. 33–36. The Bar responded to the effect that payment by commission is not wrong in principle, although steps should be taken to stop excessive earnings: Comments of the Senate on R.C.L.S. (November 1983), pp. 9–13.

[46] "Lincoln," (1980) 77 L.S.Gaz. 1275.

[47] "Lincoln" argues that it is the responsibility of the solicitor to protect his or her client when negotiating the fee.

[48] Hazell (1978), pp. 122–123.

[49] M. Findlay, "The discreet fixers behind the briefs" The Law Magazine, October 16, 1987; P. Shrubsall, Counsel, July/August 1988, pp. 9–10; J. Loyd Q.C., ibid. p. 11.

[50] Findlay, op. cit. noting that the success rate of outsiders was estimated by the Barristers Clerks Association at 50 per cent.

service.[51] The restrictions on conveyancing and probate work are not affected. In 1988, the Council adopted a Directive which established a system for the mutual recognition of higher education diplomas within the E.C.[52] This Recognition Directive was published on January 4, 1989, and is due to come into force on January 4, 1991 (as part of the Commission's 1992 programme). It applies generally to persons who have obtained a diploma as a necessary prerequisite for taking up a regulated profession in a member state, and who wish to have the diploma recognised in another member state where they wish to establish and take up the profession in question. The host member state may, however, require the applicant to complete an adaptation period not exceeding three years, or take an aptitude test, where the matters covered by the education and training in the original member state differ substantially from those covered by the diploma required in the host member state. The step of requiring an aptitude test has been taken, *inter alia*, by the U.K. and Germany.[53]

In October 1988, the Council of Bars and Law Societies of Europe agreed a Code of Professional Conduct to be applied to all cross-border activities by and between lawyers.[54] It has also been seeking agreement on the terms of a draft Directive to regulate the establishment of legal practices in other member states: some have argued that foreign lawyers should become full members of the local legal profession; others that they should have the option of relying on their original qualification and remaining subject to the exclusive disciplinary control of the home profession; yet others favour a compromise between those positions.[55]

It has been suggested, however, that the arrangements permitted by these developments will prove less efficient than the establishment of multi-national partnerships of lawyers from different jurisdictions.[56]

7. CONCLUSION

The various threads in the developments outlined in this chapter have been drawn together by Abel in his writings on the legal profession in England and Wales.[57] He notes that both branches have lost much of their control over the production *of* producers to academic legal education; financial barriers to entry to the profession have largely disappeared and all barristers

[51] Council Directive 77/249/EEC of March 22, 1977 (the Legal Services Directive); D. B. Walters (1978) 3 Eur.L.R. 265; European Communities (Services of Lawyers) Order 1978. (S.I. 1978, No. 1901). See also above, p. 136. The 1977 Directive did not provide for any right of establishment or mutual recognition of diplomas. In Case 427/85, *Re Lawyers' Services*: *E.C. Commission* v. *Germany* [1989] 2 C.M.L.R. 677, the Court of Justice held that the German Act implementing this directive was too restrictive in so far as it required a visiting lawyer to work in conjunction with a host lawyer even in cases where representation by a lawyer was not mandatory under German law: see H. Eidenmüller, (1990) 53 M.L.R. 604. See also D. Lasok and J. W. Bridge, *An Introduction to the Law and Institutions of the European Communities* (4th ed., 1987), pp. 79–83 and D. Edward, "The Legal Profession in the Community" in St. J. Bates, *et al.*, (eds.) *In Memoriam J.D.B. Mitchell* (1983).
[52] Council Directive 89/48/EEC of December 21, 1988.
[53] J. Toulmin Q.C., (1989) I.F.L. Rev. August, pp. 19–21 and (1990) 140 N.L.J. 1309; (1990) 87 L.S.Gaz., August 29, p. 41 and October 10, p. 7; H. Eidenmüller, (1990) 53 M.L.R. 604.
[54] J. Toulmin Q.C., *Counsel*, July/August 1989, p. 8.
[55] (1989) 86 L.S.Gaz., April 19, pp. 6–7; J. Toulmin Q.C., (1990) 140 N.L.J. 1309; P. Stewart, (1990) I.F.L. Rev., May, pp. 13–14.
[56] H. Eidenmüller, (1990) 53 M.L.R. 604, 607–608.
[57] Above, p. 107, fn. 16.

and most solicitors are now graduates. This development has facilitated a dramatic increase in the proportion of women entrants to the profession, although not of entrants from ethnic minorities and without a significant effect on the class composition of the profession. The monopolies and restrictive practices that enable profession to control production *by* producers have also come under serious scrutiny and challenge. Given the increasing difficulties in controlling their market by limiting supply, lawyers "have turned to the alternative strategy of creating demand" but "have done so slowly, reluctantly and ineffectively."[58] The expansion of demand for legal services fuelled by legal aid and the country's growing economic prosperity did not itself result from the activities of the profession (and is obviously vulnerable to, respectively, the government's wishes to curb legal aid expenditure, and economic recession).

These developments have led to heightened competition, and, in turn, an increase in the proportion of lawyers who are employed (in private practice[59] or by government, commerce or industry), the growth in the size of sets of chambers and solicitors' firms, and a decline in the authority of the profession's governing bodies, which "have lost significant power over their members, to both the state and the ever-larger and more bureaucratic units of production, such as public and private employers, barristers' chambers, and solicitors' firms."

Writing in 1986, Abel predicted the continuing growth in overall numbers and in the numbers employed by government, commerce and industry; the intensification of competition in private practice; the loss of solicitors' business to lay competitors; that the Bar would find it difficult to resist solicitors' claims to enhanced rights of audience given the similarity of academic education and professional training in the two branches; and the supplanting of collective self regulation "by both direct State control and bureaucratic controls within the units of production."[60] His conclusion is worth quoting in full:

> "Professionalism, in the sense in which both champions and critics have used that concept during the last two centuries, will not disappear. It will persist as both a nostalgic ideal and a source of legitimation for increasingly anachronistic practices, although it will lose much of its power to convince. And it still will reflect the experience of a dwindling elite—some profit-sharing partners in solicitors' firms and the handful of more successful barristers—who will remain largely impervious to State control and continue to dominate their markets and govern their professional associations. But for the mass of lawyers, occupational life will mean either employment by a large bureaucracy, dependence on a public paymaster, or competition within an increasingly free market. Whichever they choose, these lawyers no longer will enjoy the distinctive privileges of professionals: control over the market for their services and high social status. The age of professionalism is ending."[61]

---

[58] (1986) 49 M.L.R. 1, 21.
[59] The "more intensive and extensive exploitation of subordinated labour undoubtedly is part of the reason for the higher incomes enjoyed by principals in the larger firms:" *ibid.* p. 28.
[60] *Ibid.* p. 41.
[61] *Ibid.* See also R. L. Abel, *The Legal Profession in England and Wales* (1988), Chap. 19.

Recent developments have reinforced these predictions,[62] although the extent of government regulation in the Green Papers[63] was somewhat reduced in the White Paper and Courts and Legal Services Act 1990.[64]

There is every likelihood that the future will see growing divisions in legal practice. Private practice, with ever-larger firms increasingly devoted to delivering legal services to commercial clients, will move further away from the public sector, which will increasingly turn to the use of employed lawyers to deliver legal services to the poor. Public sector lawyers will enjoy inferior working conditions, lower salaries and higher caseloads than their counterparts in private practice. There is an obvious risk that only the less able or the altruistic will be attracted.[65]

---

[62] R. L. Abel, "Between Market and State: the Legal Profession in Turmoil" (1989) 52 M.L.R. 285; A. Sherr, (1990) 53 M.L.R. 406 (review of Abel (1988)).
[63] Criticised, *e.g.* by Abel in "Contradictions in the green papers" (1989) 86 L.S.Gaz., March 22, p. 14.
[64] See F. Cownie, in F. Patfield and R. White (eds.), *The Changing Law* (1990), Chap. 12.
[65] See A. Sherr, (1990) 53 M.L.R. 406.

CHAPTER 4

JUDGES

IN this chapter we consider the men and women who are appointed to adjudicate upon such disputes as are referred to a court or tribunal for determination. The term "judge" is used in the title of this chapter in its wide sense to cover all such persons. More commonly, however, the term is used in a narrower sense to cover those who are appointed to adjudicate in the House of Lords, the Supreme Court of England and Wales (*i.e.* the Court of Appeal, the High Court and the Crown Court) and county courts. In addition, some judicial functions are performed by officers below the rank of judge known as "masters" and "registrars." "Magistrates" or "justices of the peace" sit in the magistrates' courts (and in some cases in the Crown Court).[1] Those persons who sit on tribunals are normally simply referred to as tribunal "chairmen" or "members," although there are some with special designations, such as the Social Security Commissioners,[2] the Special and General Commissioners of Income Tax, Immigration Adjudicators and the Commons Commissioners.

A. MAGISTRATES[3]

1. NUMBERS AND FUNCTIONS

In January 1990 there were 28,667 active part-time lay magistrates or "justices of the peace."[4] There was provision for the appointment of up to 60 full-time, paid, "stipendiary magistrates" in London and up to 40 in the provinces.[5] In the City of London, the Lord Mayor and Aldermen are justices *ex officio*.[6] Magistrates sit in the magistrates' courts[7] and in the Crown Court,[8] perform certain administrative tasks such as the granting of liquor licences, issue arrest and search warrants and sign various forms for members of the public.

---

[1] When they are known as "judges of the Crown Court": Supreme Court Act 1981, s.8(1).
[2] Social Security Act 1975, s.97(3), as amended by the Social Security Act 1980, s.12. They were formerly known as National Insurance Commissioners. See above, p. 62.
[3] The major studies are Sir Thomas Skyrme, *The Changing Image of the Magistracy* (2nd ed., 1983); E. Burney, *J.P: Magistrate, Court and Community* (1979); M. King and C. May, *Black Magistrates* (1985).
[4] (1990) 154 J.P.N. 726.
[5] Justice of the Peace Act 1979, ss.13, 31. See below, pp. 199–201.
[6] 1979 Act, s.39.
[7] Above, pp. 44, 50–56.
[8] Above, pp. 71–77; below, pp. 198–199.

2. HISTORICAL ORIGINS OF JUSTICES OF THE PEACE[9]

The history of the justice of the peace as a judicial officer can be traced to the Justices of the Peace Act 1361, which provided:

"First, That in every County of *England* shall be assigned for the keeping of the Peace, one Lord, and with him three of four of the most worthy in the County, with some learned in the Law, and they shall have Power to restrain the Offenders, Rioters, and all other Barators, and to pursue, arrest, take, and chastise them according to their Trespass or Offence; and to cause them to be imprisoned and duly punished according to the Law and Customs of the Realm, and according to that which to them shall seem best to do by their Discretions and good Advisement; and also to inform them, and to enquire of all those that have been Pillors and Robbers in the Parts beyond the Sea, and be now come again, and go wandering, and will not labour as they were wont in Times past, and to take and arrest all those that they may find by Indictment, or by Suspicion, and to put them in Prison; and to take of all them that be not of good Fame, where they shall be found, sufficient Surety and Mainprise of their good behaviour towards the King and his People, and the other duly to punish, to the Intent that the People be not by such Rioters or Rebels troubled nor endamaged, nor the Peace blemished, nor Merchants nor other passing by the Highways of the Realm disturbed, nor put in the Peril which may happen of such Offenders. . . ."[10]

The Crown had previously appointed keepers or conservators of the peace (*Custodes Pacis*) with powers to arrest suspects and initiate criminal proceedings: the Act of 1361 gave in addition the power to determine proceedings. In 1362 the justices were required to hold formal meetings four times a year: these became known as quarter sessions. Over the ensuing centuries, more and more administrative duties were imposed by statute on the justices, including such matters as the construction and maintenance of fortifications, highways, bridges and gaols, the fixing of prices and the recruitment of soldiers. The list of provisions to be implemented or enforced became lengthy and burdensome.[11] Indeed, until the nineteenth century, the business of local government was largely entrusted to the justices. Different functions were committed to one, two or three justices or to quarter sessions. The informal meetings of two or more justices out of quarter sessions came to be known as "petty sessions," the forerunner of magistrates' courts.

The persons appointed in the counties were generally from the "gentry." In the eighteenth century, the justices came into growing disrepute. The

---

[9] On the historical development of the office see E. Moir, *The Justice of the Peace* (1969); J. H. Gleason, *The Justices of the Peace in England* (1969); L. J. K. Glassey, *Politics and the appointment of Justices of the Peace* (1979); N. Landau, *The Justices of the Peace 1679–1760* (1984).

[10] This is still in force, apart from the words "and also to inform . . . in Times past."

[11] In 1485 Lambard asked, "How many Justices, think you, may now suffice, without breaking their backs, to bear so many, not loads, but stacks of statutes?": 1 *Eirenarchia* (1581), Chap. 7. F. Milton (*The English Magistracy* (1967)) gives many examples of statutory provisions, including one forbidding a man who was not a Lord to wear a cloak that did not "cover his privy member and Buttocks (he being upright)" (p. 9).

corruption of the Middlesex Justices, described by Edmund Burke as "generally the scum of the earth," was such that they were replaced for most purposes by metropolitan stipendiary magistrates. Elsewhere, their administration of the Poor Law and the Game Laws attracted much criticism. In the nineteenth century they lost most of their administrative functions to central government departments and the new, elected, local authorities, the process of transfer culminating in the Local Government Act 1888. At the same time, their judicial functions were extended, with more offences becoming triable at petty sessions, and with the establishment and development of their matrimonial jurisdiction.[12]

3. APPOINTMENT

The Commission of the Peace is a document issued by the Crown setting out in very general terms the functions of the justices.[13] There is one Commission for each county, each of five London commission areas and the City of London.[14] Justices of the peace for any commission area are appointed in the name of the Queen by the Lord Chancellor,[15] or, in Greater Manchester, Merseyside and Lancashire, by the Chancellor of the Duchy of Lancaster.[16]

The only qualification for appointment laid down by statute is that the person resides in or within 15 miles of the commission area for which he or she is appointed.[17] However, the booklet *Justices of the Peace in England and Wales: Their Appointment and Duties Explained*, published on behalf of the Lord Chancellor, makes it clear that the following will not be appointed:

"(a) a person over 60 years of age;
 (b) a person convicted of certain offences, or subject to certain court orders[18];
 (c) an undischarged bankrupt[19];
 (d) a person whose sight or hearing is impaired, or who by reason of infirmity cannot carry out all the duties of a Justice;
 (e) a serving member of Her Majesty's Forces; a member of the Police; a traffic warden;
 (f) a close relative of a person who is already a Justice on the same Bench."

The notes on the application/recommendation form state that certain other classes of person will not be appointed:

[12] From the Matrimonial Causes Act 1878 onwards.
[13] Justices of the Peace Act 1979, s.5; The Crown Office (Commissions of the Peace) Rules 1973 (S.I. 1973 No. 2099).
[14] 1979 Act, s.1.
[15] *Ibid*. s.6. The work of the Lord Chancellor's Office concerning magistrates is dealt with by the Secretary of Commissions and his staff: see Skyrme (1983), Chap. 3; B. Cooke, (1984) 40 *The Magistrate* 69; J. Boothroyd, *The Law Magazine*, February 19, 1988, pp. 16–17.
[16] *Ibid*. s.68. The policy of the two offices is almost invariably identical: Skyrme (1983), p. 240. The Chancellor of the Duchy has concurrent powers with the Lord Chancellor on the appointment, removal and residence of justices, entry on or removal from the Supplemental List and records. On other matters the Lord Chancellor has exclusive powers.
[17] *Ibid*. s.7. The Lord Chancellor can direct that this restriction shall not apply: s.7(2).
[18] The notes on the application/recommendation form say "a serious offence or a series of minor offences."
[19] Justices of the Peace Act 1979, s.63A, inserted by the Statute Law (Repeals) Act 1989, Sched. 2.

"(g) a close relative of a member of the Crown Prosecution Service who appears before the Divison for which the candidate is proposed;

(h) a close relative of a member of the local police force;

(i) an officer or servant of a magistrates' court in his own Petty Sessional Division;

(j) an M.P., adopted candidate or full-time political agent for the local constituency;

(k) a person, the nature of whose work is such that it would conflict, or clearly be incompatible with, the duties of a magistrate."

The person must also be a British subject.[20] There is no property qualification[21] and women became eligible in 1919.[22]

The Lord Chancellor's booklet states that justices:

"should be personally suitable in character, integrity and understanding . . . and . . . should be generally recognised as such by those among whom they live and work."

They are appointed on the advice of Advisory Committees. These were first established following recommendations of the Royal Commission on the Selection of Justices of the Peace of 1910[23] in response to complaints that the Benches were dominated by Conservatives.

There are about 112 committees,[24] generally one for each non-metropolitan county and metropolitan district, the City of London, some of the larger urban areas and each London commission area. Most of the county committees have sub-committees or area panels. County committees are normally chaired by the Lord Lieutenant, the London Committees by Circuit judges. Most committees have eight to ten members, and sub-committees about six to eight. The term of office is normally six years. Appointments to a committee are made by the Lord Chancellor, usually after consulting the chairman.[25] Members are almost invariably existing magistrates.[26] Each committee has at least one Conservative and one Labour member; most have a Liberal, and some in Wales a member of Plaid Cymru. It is the practice to check with the party headquarters that they are known supporters. Until 1988, the names of the committee members were normally kept secret in order to keep them free from pressure and lobbying,[27] although the name and address of the secretary was published. In that year, the Lord Chancellor, Lord Mackay, announced that he had asked the committees to take steps to make themselves known. About half would have done so by the end of 1988, and it would be a requirement for all by 1992: the delay in the

[20] This is a policy not a rule of law: Skyrme (1983), p. 50.

[21] This was abolished by the Liberal government in 1906: Justices of the Peace Act, 1906, s.1.

[22] Sex Disqualification (Removal) Act 1919. Appointments do not, however, appear to fall within the scope of the Sex Discrimination Act 1975: see Skyrme (1983), p. 51. The proportion of women to men has increased steadily—from 1:3·5 in 1947 to 1:1·3 in 1990.

[23] Cd. 5250.

[24] 95 advising the Lord Chancellor, and 17 the Chancellor of the Duchy of Lancaster: Vol. 144 H.C.Deb., December 22, 1988, col. 418, written answer.

[25] Skyrme (1983), pp. 44–46. See also B. Cooke, (1984) 40 The Magistrate 69.

[26] In 1982, only 163 (8.6 per cent.) of the 1,900 or so members serving the Lord Chancellor, and only six of the members in the Duchy of Lancaster were neither serving nor retired magistrates: King and May (1985), p. 26.

[27] The Inner London Advisory Committee was an exception; membership of the Nottingham Committee was revealed in 1966.

imposition of the requirement of publicity would enable committee members, who had taken office on the understanding that their identity would not be revealed, and who wished to avoid publicity, to retire.[28] A candidate can be recommended to a committee by any person or organisation, or can put himself or herself forward. In turn, the recommendations of the committee can be rejected by the Lord Chancellor.[29]

The main areas of difficulty have been those of politics and social and ethnic background.[29a] The problems here are linked. The official position as to politics is stated in the Lord Chancellor's booklet:

> "Political views are neither a qualification nor a disqualification for appointment as a Justice of the Peace. When making appointments the Lord Chancellor has regard to political affiliations only in order that he may ensure that no Bench becomes unduly overweighted in favour of any one political party."

As regards politics, there have been a number of separate strands of thought. Firstly, some people have been recommended for appointment as a reward for political services rather than because of their fitness for the office. This was condemned by the Royal Commissions of both 1910 and 1946–48.[30] The latter noted that there were still "political appointments" in this sense, although their extent could not be stated with precision.[31]

Secondly, the 1910 Royal Commission stated unequivocally that "it is not in the public interest that there should be an undue preponderance of Justices drawn from one political party."[32] It is not clear whether this was intended to refer to the position nationally or the composition of particular benches, but the latter view seems to be emphasised today. It was certainly the contemporary preponderance of Conservatives on the bench that led to the appointment of both the Royal Commissions of 1910 and 1946–48, by, respectively, a Liberal and a Labour government. However, overall statistics kept of political affiliation are largely based on the declared position of each justice at the time of appointment and are thus of limited reliability. There is no policy to maintain "proportional representation" on the benches.[33] Conversely, it is not at all unusual for the Lord Chancellor to refuse to accept recommendations because a certain party is under-represented.[34]

[28] Vol. 499, H.L.Deb., July 20, 1988, cols. 1311–1313.

[29] In recent years he has rarely rejected a recommendation on the grounds of personal unsuitability, it being unlikely that he would have information about candidates other than that gathered by the Advisory Committee; recommendations have, however, been rejected on grounds of occupational and political balance: King and May (1985), pp. 29–30.

[29a] See R. Vogler, "Magistrates' Courts and the struggle for local democracy" in C. Sumner (ed.), *Censure, Politics and Criminal Justice* (1990), Chap. 4.

[30] Note 23, above; *Royal Commission on Justices of the Peace* (Cmd. 7463, 1948).

[31] *Ibid.*, para. 20.

[32] Cd. 5250, Summary of Conclusions: quoted in the 1946–48 Report (Cmd. 7463, p. 4).

[33] Skyrme (1983), p. 58. In 1983 the percentages, based on statements at the time of appointment, were Conservative 41, Labour 28, Liberal 11, S.D.P. 1, Plaid Cymru 0.3 and "Independent and not known" 18.7: Skyrme (1983), p. 58.

[34] *Ibid.* p. 59. It can prove difficult to find suitable candidates with a Labour background. A survey by the Labour Campaign for Criminal Justice showed that in one in three of 140 constituencies studied, people were unwilling to put their names forward because two in three Labour party nominees were not appointed. Of 1,500 J.P.s appointed a year there were 100 Labour party nominees, although that did not take account of Labour voters who were not members: *The Observer*, February 2, 1983.

Thirdly, the attention may be focused on the political affiliation of *new appointees*. This was emphasised by the 1946–48 Royal Commission, which stated that if after preliminary selection on merit:

"it is found that a considerable majority of the proposed new justices are of one political faith, the list should be revised with a view to seeing whether equally good, or better, nominations can be made from among members of political parties. If the answer is that they cannot, then the original list should stand."[35]

Fourthly, some have argued that political opinions should be ignored entirely.[36] This has, however, been regarded as impractical by successive Lord Chancellors.

Both Royal Commissions recommended that justices be drawn from different social backgrounds. The 1946–48 Report stated that:

"Care must be taken to see that there are persons in the commission representative of various sections of the community. It is an advantage that a justice should have knowledge of the way of life of other classes than the class to which he belongs, and it is essential that there should be many among the justices who know enough of the lives of the poorest people to understand their outlook and their difficulties."[37]

The Royal Commission's survey distinguished six classes[38]:

		% Male		% Female	
Class O	Persons without gainful occupation	3.5		16.7	
Class P	Professional	21.3	} 51.3	29.6	} 43.00
Class E	Employers of 10 or more, directors, higher managerial posts in business or industry	30.0		13.4	
Class OA	Persons in business on their own account or employing less than 10	16.5		11.2	
Class S	Persons paid salaries	13.7	} 28.7	10.5	} 18.2
Class W	Persons paid wages	15.0		7.7	
Not classifiable				10.9	

Subsequent studies have shown that there has been little change.[39]

---

[35] Cmd. 7463, para. 84.

[36] See the dissent by Lord Merthyr and two other members of the 1946–48 Royal Commission: Cmd. 7463, pp. 92–95.

[37] Para. 84.

[38] Minutes of Evidence, Appendix 4. Postal survey of all justices; 87% response rate.

[39] R. Hood, *Sentencing the Motoring Offender* (1972), Chap. 3. Sample of 650 justices from 32 benches in 1966–67 with an 83 per cent. response rate. Chairmen and deputy chairmen and small benches were overrepresented.

J. Baldwin, (1976) 16 B.J. Criminology 171. Sample of 339 (one in five of all magistrates newly appointed between July 1971 and June 1972, from 128 benches) with a 75.2 per cent. response rate.

In 1977, 8.2 per cent. of magistrates were manual workers: Skyrme (1983), p. 64, based on the Lord Chancellor's records. A survey of 129 magistrates produced similar results to earlier surveys: R.J. Henham, *Sentencing Principles and Magistrates' Behaviour* (1990), Chap. 5.

	Hood % Male		Baldwin % Male		% Female	
O	0.8		0.6		3.5	
P	30.8 ⎫	[52.6][40]	34.5 ⎫	53.0	44.8 ⎫	55.1
E	21.8 ⎭		18.5 ⎭		10.3 ⎭	
OA	14.6		12.5		13.8	
S	11.4 ⎫		17.2 ⎫		19.5	
	⎬ 27.3		⎬ 30.3			
W	15.9 ⎭		13.1 ⎭		3.5	
Not Classifiable	4.3		3.6		4.6	

Arranged according to the Registrar-General's Classification, the surveys of both Hood and Baldwin show the predominance of the professional and intermediate occupations, with figures of 76·9 per cent. and 83·9 per cent. respectively.[41]

Efforts have been made to increase the proportion of wage earners. In 1968, loss-of-earnings allowances were introduced.[42] The Employment Protection (Consolidation) Act 1978[43] provides that an employer must give an employee magistrate reasonable time off.[44] However, as Lord Hailsham pointed out,[45] the 1978 Act does not oblige an employer to give a magistrate a job, or to promote him or her if he or she has one. It provides no immunity from redundancy. Lord Mackay has indicated that he is prepared to appoint people who are over 60 in order to complement the categories of people on the bench:

> "For example, these days it is very difficult to find people who are in levels of manufacturing industry to go on the bench during their working lives. It is important however that people with that kind of background should be on the bench."[46]

These have been proper developments, but they seem to have had relatively little effect.

It is only comparatively recently that the ethnic background of magistrates has begun to be properly investigated. King and May's Cobden Trust report,[47] based on research conducted with the co-operation of the Lord Chancellor's Department, was in many respects critical. They found evidence of racial prejudice among some members of advisory committees and sub-committees, in the form of negative racial stereotyping. There was some evidence of direct racial discrimination, and considerable evidence of indirect discrimination in the procedure adopted and the criteria applied by

[40] Hood (1972), p. 51 gives this figure as 51·8 and attaches the wrong label to the column.
[41] Baldwin (1976) p. 172: the classes are I: Professional; II: Intermediate; III: Skilled; IV: Partly skilled; and V: Unskilled.
[42] Justices of the Peace Act 1968. See now the 1979 Act, s.12.
[43] s.29. See A. Samuels, (1986) 42 *The Magistrate* 58. A refusal to pay the person for the time off may constitute a failure to comply with the duty: see *Corner* v. *Buckinghamshire County Council* [1978] I.C.R. 836.
[44] Magistrates who are public employees and employees of nationalised industries are customarily given 18 days' extra paid leave to enable them to sit. Many large private firms have made similar arrangements.
[45] (1981) 37 *The Magistrate* 166.
[46] Vol. 503, H.L.Deb., January 19, 1989, col. 330.
[47] *Black Magistrates: A Study of Selection and Appointment* (1985), reviewed by R. Pearson, (1986) 13 J.L.S. 152.

selectors. There were no Afro-Caribbean and few Asians among the members of advisory committees. The procedures were inefficient and amateurish, with too much emphasis placed on interview performance, and the selection criteria of "suitability" and "balance" unacceptably vague. While in some areas there had been a significant increase in the number of black magistrates appointed, the proportion on the bench in many areas still fell far short of the proportion of black people in the local community. The number of black people coming forward as candidates was small. In the event, there was no discernible official reaction to the report.

The Lord Chancellor's Department has conducted a national survey of the ethnic composition of the magistracy, based on the figures on January 1, 1987.[48] At that date there were 455 (1.92%) black magistrates out of 23,730 active magistrates; 2.49% (338[49]) of male magistrates and 1.15% (117[50]) of female magistrates were black. The estimated proportions of black people in the general population and in the 35–54 age range (within which magistrates are normally appointed) were, respectively, 4.69% and 3.92%. The proportional rate of appointment of blacks had increased steadily from 1.77% in 1980 to 4.57% in 1986. The report also argued that

"the available pool in the black population from which magistrates can be drawn has been, and almost certainly still is, much smaller than the pool in the general population."

This was based on the points that in 1986 less than half of the black population were born in this country; that the first priority of many immigrants would have been "to establish themselves and their families before being ready to take part in public life"; and that "cultural differences, such as those affecting the position of women in some groups, will have prevented many blacks from seeing themselves as candidates for the magistracy." The report "illustrated the progress being made in the appointment of black magistrates." In an accompanying statement of "The qualities looked for in a justice of the peace," the Lord Chancellor emphasised that the magistracy

"is open to all eligible persons regardless of race, religion, colour, social class, sex or political opinion. These factors have no part to play in determining personal suitability for appointment. But second only to the requirement that candidates must be personally suitable is the desirability that each bench should include men and women from all backgrounds and walks of life throughout the petty sessions area and thereby broadly reflect the local community."

In view of this, the absence in the survey of any local breakdown of the statistics is a significant omission.[51]

---

[48] Published in (1988) 44 *The Magistrate* 77–78.
[49] 128 West Indian, Guyanese, African; 204 Indian, Pakistani, Bangladeshi; 6 others.
[50] 59 West Indian, Guyanese, African; 57 Indian, Pakistani, Bangladeshi; 1 other.
[51] See N. Dholakia, (1988) 44 *The Magistrate* 119, arguing in favour of regular ethnic monitoring, a proposal which had previously been rejected by Lord Hailsham. The author also proposed that selection panels be clearly informed of selection criteria, given guidance or training on the effects which generalised assumptions and prejudices about race can have, and made aware of possible misunderstandings that can occur in interviews between persons of different cultural backgrounds. The author argued that it was vital that advisory committees should have black people in their membership. The response in letters to the editor was generally critical: see (1988) 44 *The Magistrate* 123, 172, and see pp. 209–210 (A. Allott).

That a political and social balance is desirable has generally been assumed or asserted rather than explained. It is possible to detect three considerations: the interests of potential appointees; the need to maintain general public confidence in magistrates' courts; and the interests of defendants. The first factor lay behind the appointment of the Royal Commissions of 1910 and 1946–48, although the Reports played down what was clearly not a respectable consideration and placed more emphasis on the second factor. For example, Lord Loreburn L.C. said in evidence to the 1910 Royal Commission:

> "I regard it as an indignity and an injustice that any section of opinion should be, in practice, excluded from a legitimate ambition, and I think that it is contrary to the public interest that the authority of the bench of justices should be weakened by any widespread suspicion that the members of it are not fairly selected."[52]

The subsequent Report[53] simply took up the second strand of this reasoning. The interests of actual defendants came a poor third. It will of course be a matter of "pot luck" whether a working class defendant enjoys the supposed benefit of a court with one or more justices thought to be better able than the others to understand his or her outlook and difficulties. The respective social backgrounds of juries and justices do not seem to figure significantly among the considerations that affect the defendant's choice between summary trial and trial on indictment.[54] Lord Mackay has welcomed the increasing proportion of black magistrates on the basis that

> "In addition to the special knowledge and understanding of sections of the community which black magistrates can bring to the bench, their presence in a judicial capacity can be an important factor in reassuring black defendants, witnesses and others connected with legal proceedings that they will be treated impartially by the courts."[55]

A study[56] of 160 newly appointed magistrates in three English counties suggested that there were no significant differences according to social class in attitudes concerning penal philosophy, sentencing practice, the causes of crime, court procedure, and the role of the magistrate. It was noted, however, that there may have been a tendency to appoint magistrates with particular views, whatever the social class. There were differences in attitude related to different political background, with Conservatives tending particularly to be more punitive in their penal philosophy. The authors concluded that "although the relationship between attitudes and behaviour

---

[52] Minutes of Evidence. Lord Loreburn was caught between the pressure imposed by Liberal politicians and his own feelings that appointments should be made on merit without reference to politics: R. F. V. Heuston, *Lives of the Lord Chancellors* (1964), pp. 153–158.

[53] Report, p. 8.

[54] A. E. Bottoms and J. D. McClean, *Defendants in the Criminal Process* (1976), Chap. 4. The research did show that defendants in general had a higher opinion of the Crown Court than the magistrates, for a variety of reasons.

[55] (1988) 44 *The Magistrate* 218, 219.

[56] R. A. Bond and N. F. Lemon, "Changes in Magistrates' Attitudes During the First Year on the Bench" in D. P. Farrington *et al.* (eds.), *Psychology, Law and Legal Processes* (1979), Chap. 8.

is a problematic one, there is nevertheless a good prima facie case for arguing that differences in viewpoint expressed here are also likely to be expressed in some way in procedural and sentencing policies."[57] An earlier English study had not, however, found there to be such a correlation.[58] Indeed, the most significant factor seemed to be the general attitudes of the bench to which a particular magistrate belonged. Accordingly, it may well be that social and political background may neither be perceived to be of significance by defendants, nor actually of significance in affecting the way they are dealt with, although the evidence on the latter point is not entirely clear.

The authorities seem to take strong exception to charges that the processes of selection are shrouded in secrecy.[59] It is certainly true that the *formal* procedure is clearly stated in the booklet published by the Lord Chancellor's Department. It is also true that the detailed deliberations of the committees are kept confidential: rightly so, given that the debate will concern the personal qualities of individuals. What is noticeable, however, is the lack of general research on how the advisory committees operate in practice. Two exceptions have been the work of Elizabeth Burney,[60] and King and May.[61] In her study of six advisory committees or sub-committees Burney found that only 16 per cent. of the committee members were "non-aligned" politically, almost all of them were members of the Benches concerned and few were under 40. The selection of members of the committees was in practice normally left to the committee chairman. The local chairman of the bench commonly played a lead role. Some, but not all committees used interviews, which might be conducted by several magistrates, or by the chairman either alone or with the clerk. The two dominant routes to the bench seemed to be through personal recommendation from an existing magistrate or through some form of "voluntary work" background (churches, chambers of commerce, youth organisations, sports associations, political parties, etc.). The selectors would seek to weed out people of "extreme" views by pointed questions about the "Shrewsbury pickets." People who would be likely to "fit in" would be favoured. Burney's overall description was that selection "remains a largely personal and intimate

---

[57] *Ibid.* p. 141. *Cf.* J. Hogarth, *Sentencing as a Human Process* (1971) (survey of magistrates in Ontario); A. K. Bottomley, *Decisions in the Penal Process* (1973), Chap. 4. By contrast, a study based upon simulated sentencing exercises found that differences of sentence could not be explained by the group composition of "benches" in terms of age, political affiliation, education, sex or length of experience: A. Kapardis, (1981) 145 J.P.N. 289–291.

[58] R. Hood, *Sentencing the Motoring Offender* (1972); *Cf.* Hood, *Sentencing in Magistrates' Courts* (1962), where the author's findings suggested that the social composition of a bench, in combination with particular community conditions, might affect the prison rate (pp. 76–78, 119–120).

[59] Sir Thomas Skyrme, a former Secretary of Commissions, refers to the "myth of secrecy" and the "old chestnut of the clandestine routes to the magistracy" (Skyrme (1983), pp. 48, 49).

[60] Burney (1979), Chaps. 4 and 5. See also R. Pearson in Z. Bankowski and G. Mungham (eds.) *Essays in Law and Society* (1980), Chap. 5.

[61] King and May (1985). They examined the selection and appointment system from the particular perspective of the appointment of black magistrates, conducting postal surveys and detailed local studies in five areas.

affair, almost entirely dominated by existing magistrates who can too easily turn into self-perpetuating oligarchies."[62]

4. UNDERTAKINGS ON APPOINTMENT

A person selected to be a justice must give certain undertakings before being appointed. These are to complete the required training, to carry out a fair share of magisterial duties (normally to sit for at least 26 times a year[63]) and to resign if he or she fails to honour these undertakings or becomes unable to perform the duties of a justice through changes of residence, infirmity or any other cause, to inform the justices' clerk if he or she is summoned for or charged with a criminal offence or becomes a party to civil proceedings, and to inform the Secretary of Commissions of any conviction or court order against him or her.

5. TRAINING

Since 1953 it has been the duty of every magistrates' courts committee to provide courses of instruction for justices in their area, in accordance with arrangements approved by the Lord Chancellor.[64] All justices appointed since January 1, 1966[65] have been required to attend a course of basic training. The current arrangements[66] require newly appointed magistrates to attend an Induction Course, normally within three months of the date of appointment, before sitting to adjudicate in court. They will be given instruction on the obligations imposed by the judicial oath, human awareness, including awareness of the different ethnic, cultural and religious backgrounds of defendants and witnesses, the structure of the magistrates' courts system, the adversarial nature of the criminal trial, and an introduction to the operation of the criminal process. They will attend court as observers and participate in a series of practical exercises covering a bail application, mode of trial determination, a determination of guilt or innocence, and sentencing. Year 1 of Basic Training comprises sitting in court, visits to institutions (the probation service, an adult prison, a young offen-

---

[62] Burney (1979), p. 73. Similar views were expressed by King and May (1985), Chap. 4, emphasising the key roles of committee chairmen and secretaries. They proposed that the advisory committees and sub-committees should be completely independent of the local magistracy, and include people who know about magistrates' courts, the local community and selection techniques; the secretary should be a local court clerk, trained in selection procedures; and those procedures should incorporate a comprehension test (see Chap. 16).

[63] In practice, J.P.s are expected to sit more frequently: of 57 Petty Sessional Divisions surveyed by King and May, a majority (39) expected an average of between 35 and 50 court sessions: King and May (1985), pp. 72–73.

[64] See now the Justice of the Peace Act 1979, s.63.

[65] See *The Training of Justices of the Peace in England and Wales* (Cmnd. 2856, 1967) (White Paper). The Lord Chancellor was assisted from 1974 by an Advisory Committee on Training, chaired by Boreham J. This replaced a National Advisory Council which had been set up to consider the introduction of compulsory training. The Committee was absorbed into the Judicial Studies Board (see below, pp. 224–225) with effect from 1985. The Board's functions with respect to magisterial training are discharged by its Magisterial Committee (see the *Judicial Studies Board Report for 1983–1987* (H.M.S.O., 1988), Chap. 12: its function in this context is to supervise the training, not to perform it).

[66] See the looseleaf *Handbook for the Training of Magistrates* published by the Judicial Studies Board. The syllabus has been completely revised by the Board's Magisterial Committee.

ders institution) (6 hours) and further training courses (12 hours). Years 2 and 3 each require 4 hours' training.

Justices appointed after January 1, 1980 have also been required to undertake Refresher Training.[67] The commitment is for 12 hours training every three years. There is no complete prescribed syllabus, but there must be training in chairmanship and there is likely to be training for the Crown Court. There is a list of approved topics. In addition there are courses for justices appointed to juvenile court or domestic or family court panels.[68] From 1986, further training (12 hours every three years) has been compulsory for magistrates on each of these panels.[69]

The organisation of the courses is in the hands of Training Officers who are responsible to the Training Committee of the magistrates' courts committees. Most are justices' clerks, although the net is spread more widely for tutors.[70]

Within the limits laid down by the Lord Chancellor there is in fact considerable scope for local variation.[71] In the past, it has been claimed[72] that in spite of the Lord Chancellor's power to act in default if the required courses are not provided[73] the system "still falls short of what is needed to ensure that justices are trained in the most efficaceous and economic manner." Expenditure on training was "negligible." One problem seemed to be that training has been organised by magistrates' courts committees but paid for by local councils. Improvements can be expected as a result of the steps taken by the Judicial Studies Board's Magisterial Committee to monitor the effectiveness of training leading to the production of a revised *Handbook for the Training of Magistrates*. The *Handbook* provides a practical guide to Training Officers as well as a syllabus. The Committee has also produced a series of guidance notes for the use of magistrates on structured decision-making.[74]

The training programmes are not designed to turn magistrates into "experts": the best form of training is regarded as experience on the bench. The work of Bond and Lemon[75] suggests that experience is more likely than training to modify the attitudes of newly-appointed magistrates, although neither has much effect in changing previous attitudes on penal policy.

6. CONDUCT AND REMOVAL

A justice of the peace may be removed by the Lord Chancellor.[76] No

---

[67] *Ibid.* The requirement is operative to the age of 65, or, for those appointed after 1.1.90, the retiring age of 70.

[68] For example, there has been a substantial programme of training in respect of the Children Act 1989.

[69] LCD Circular MCC (86) 3 ((1986) 42 *The Magistrate* 124).

[70] J.W. Raine, *Local Justice* (1989), pp. 78–79.

[71] See Burney (1979), Chap. 12.

[72] Skyrme (1983), p. 80.

[73] Administration of Justice Act 1973, s.3; now the Justices of the Peace Act 1979, s.63(4).

[74] *Judicial Studies Board Report for 1983–1987* (H.M.S.O., 1988), paras. 12.8–12.15. See also the annual reports of the Lord Chancellor's Department Training Officer (on the 1986–87 report, see (1987) 43 *The Magistrate* 199, on the 1987–88 report, see (1988) 44 *The Magistrate* 179 and N. McKittrick, (1988) 152 J.P.N. 549, and on the 1988–89 report, see (1989) 45 *The Magistrate* 156 (outlining new Training Syllabuses)).

[75] *Op. cit.* n. 56 above.

[76] Justices of the Peace Act 1979, s.6.

grounds are specified in the Act. The Lord Chancellor also has power to direct that a justice be transferred to the "supplemental list" if he is satisfied either:

"(a) that by reason of the justice's age or infirmity or other like cause it is expedient that he should cease to exercise judicial functions as a justice for that area, or

(b) that the justice declines or neglects to take a proper part in the exercise of those functions."[77]

Justices are also automatically transferred to the supplemental list on reaching the age of 70, or, in the case of a justice who holds or who has held high judicial office, 75.[78] A justice who is on the list may not act as a justice except to authenticate a signature or written declaration, or to give a certificate of facts within his or her knowledge or of his or her opinion as to any matter.[79] He or she may, however, be authorised by the Lord Chancellor to sit in the Crown Court up to the age of 72.

In practice, a justice would only be removed for good cause. Most who leave office have to do so because they are unable to fulfil their share of the work or because they move outside the area.[80] In relation to misbehaviour, the "overriding consideration" is that "public confidence in the administration of justice may be preserved."[81] Justices have been removed if they or a spouse have been convicted of an offence, although a conviction for a minor motoring offence will lead to a reprimand rather than suspension or removal. Convictions for drunken driving have in recent years led to suspension during the period of disqualification rather than removal. Justices have also been removed for refusing to apply a law he or she has found distasteful,[82] and for demonstrating outside her own courthouse in support of a defendant on trial inside.[83] Allegations of incapacity or misbehaviour are normally referred to the Local Advisory Committee for investigation: if they conclude that the justice should be removed, that is reported to the Lord Chancellor. If the justice does not accept the committee's finding there is then a further inquiry by the Secretary of Commissions. The justice may be interviewed. A recent case shows, however, that the Committee may not permit the justice to appear before them in person and may act on allega-

---

[77] *Ibid*. s.8(4).

[78] *Ibid*. s.8(2).

[79] *Ibid*. s.10.

[80] Each year, about 1 per cent. of all justices on the active list are required to resign for the first reason, and 1 per cent. for the second: Skyrme (1983), p. 153.

[81] *Ibid*. p. 154.

[82] Colonel Delmer Davies-Evans, who disapproved of certain regulations governing the use of petrol, was removed in 1947 (see Skyrme (1983), pp. 156–7). A Welsh justice who stated that she was not prepared to impose penalties on people who, non-violently, broke laws which she considered unjust to the Welsh language, resigned in 1972: R. Pearson (*op. cit.* n. 60) pp. 89–90; see also Lord Hailsham, (1972) 28 *The Magistrate* 132–134: in a similar case, Lord Gardiner required a Welsh magistrate to resign. A number of magistrates have resigned rather than enforce the community charge.

[83] Her application for judicial review of the decision was rejected: *The Times*, September 25, 1985; (1985) 135 N.L.J. 976; Lord Hailsham, (1985) 41 *The Magistrate* 149.

tions of which he or she is not fully informed.[84] On three occasions in the 1940s the improper conduct of particular court proceedings led to an inquiry, and on one occasion Lord Dilhorne conducted a private inquiry into a lenient sentence imposed by three magistrates.[85]

7. DISQUALIFICATION

Justices are subject to the same common law rules as to disqualification for interest or bias as other judicial officers.[86] In addition, they are expressly disqualified from acting in a case involving a local authority if they are a member of that authority.[87] A celebrated case where a magistrate was sufficiently incautious as to admit actual bias was *R.* v. *Bingham JJ., ex p. Jowitt*.[88] The chairman of a bench hearing a speeding case, where the only evidence was that of the motorist and a police constable, said:

> "Quite the most unpleasant cases that we have to decide are those where the evidence is a direct conflict between a police officer and a member of the public. My principle in such cases has always been to believe the evidence of the police officer, and therefore we find the case proved."

The conviction was quashed.

8. LEGAL LIABILITY

A justice of the peace (or a justices' clerk exercising the functions of a single justice) enjoys a statutory immunity from any action for damages where he or she has acted in the execution of his or her duty and within jurisdiction. Where a justice (or clerk) has acted outside jurisdiction, but in the purported execution of his or her duty, an action will only lie if he or she has acted in bad faith.[89] The position is now similar to that of judges of superior

---

[84] *L.A.G. Bull.*, April 1983, pp. 9–12 (two magistrates removed on account of an "adulterous association," "conducted indiscreetly in a manner likely to give rise to scandal").

[85] Skyrme (1983), pp. 168–169.

[86] Below, p. 231. For cases concerning justices see *R.* v. *Altrincham JJ., ex p. Pennington* [1975] Q.B. 549; *R.* v. *Smethwick JJ., ex p. Hands, The Times*, December 4, 1980 (decision on allegation of statutory nuisance against local authority quashed because one of the justices was the wife of the former chairman of the housing committee); *R.* v. *Liverpool City JJ, ex. p. Topping* [1983] 1 W.L.R. 119; *R.* v. *Weston-super-Mare JJ., ex p. Shaw* [1987] Q.B. 640 (magistrates' knowledge of other outstanding charges against the defendant: see R. Stevens, (1986) 150 J.P.N. 788; (1986) 150 J.P.N. 805); *R.* v. *Metropolitan Stipendiary Magistrate, ex p. Gallagher* (1972) 136 J.P. 80; *R.* v. *Birmingham Magistrates' Court, ex p. Robinson* (1986) 150 J.P. 1 (see J. N. Spencer, (1986) 150 J.P.N. 307); *R.* v. *Blyth Valley Juvenile Court, ex p. S.* (1987) 151 J.P. 805; *R.* v. *Downham Market Magistrates' Court, ex p. Nudd* (1988) 152 J.P. 511 (see N. A. McKittrick, (1988) 152 J.P.N. 643) (magistrates' knowledge of defendant's previous record).

[87] Justices of the Peace Act 1979, s.64, as amended. For the rules relating to disqualification of licensing justices see the Licensing Act 1964, s.193 and *R.* v. *Barnsley Justices* [1960] 2 Q.B. 167.

[88] *The Times*, July 3, 1974.

[89] Justices of the Peace Act 1979, ss.44, 45, substituted by the Courts and Legal Services Act 1990, s.108. On the previous provisions see L. A. Sheridan, (1951) 14 M.L.R. 267; D. Thompson, (1958) 21 M.L.R. 517; "Suing the Beaks" (1990) 154 J.P.N. 212.

courts.[90] A justice or justices' clerk may be indemnified out of local funds for the expenses of defending proceedings, including any damages awarded against him or her. A justice or justices' clerk who has acted reasonably and in good faith is entitled to an indemnity.[91]

9. JUSTICES' CLERKS[92]

The justice's clerk is in charge of the administration of the magistrates' court and is also its chief legal advisor. Originally the clerks were the personal clerks to individual justices or benches. They are now appointed by the magistrates' courts committees subject to the approval of the Lord Chancellor.[93] They hold office "during the pleasure of the committee" although the approval of the Lord Chancellor is necessary for their removal where the magistrates for their division do not consent.[94] A candidate for appointment has to be a lawyer of five years' standing, an existing justices' clerk, a barrister or solicitor who has served as a justices' clerk's assistant[95] and, in special circumstances, a justices' clerk's assistant with 10 years' experience prior to 1960.[96] Remuneration is fixed by national negotiating machinery, and varies according to the size of the area served. In 1989 there were 285 clerkships in England and Wales. Of the 277 members of the Justices' Clerks' Society, 150 were solicitors, 119 barristers and eight qualified by experience.[97] The trend has been for the number of clerkships to be reduced by amalgamation of areas served by one clerk.[98]

The justices' clerk is the head of what may be a large staff. There will be a deputy[99] and a number of assistants. There are normally four categories of staff: court clerks, general administrative and clerical staff, staff employed on accounts and financial matters and ushers. There is also a trainee grade. Those who act as court clerks are senior assistants. As from October 1, 1980, a person may not act as a court clerk unless he or she possesses one of a series of prescribed qualifications.[1] These include being qualified for appointment

---

[90] See below, pp. 230–231. The Court of Appeal had stated the law of justices' immunity in similar broad terms in *Sirros* v. *Moore* [1975] Q.B. 118, but that was disapproved by the House of Lords in *In re McC (A Minor)* [1985] A.C. 528, holding that malice and lack of cause did not have to be established where an act was done outside jurisdiction. Following the award of damages against justices in a series of cases where they had acted outside jurisdiction (*In re McC (A Minor)*; *R.* v. *Waltham Forest JJ.*, *ex p. Solanke* [1986] Q.B. 983; *R.* v. *Manchester City Magistrates' Court*, *ex p. Davies (No. 2)* [1989] Q.B. 631), the Lord Chancellor acceded to pressure from the Magistrates' Association in favour of broadening the immunity.

[91] 1979 Act, s.53.

[92] K. C. Clarke, [1964] Crim.L.R. 620, 697; P. Darbyshire, (1980) 144 J.P.N., 186, 201, 219, 233; P. Darbyshire, *The Magistrates' Clerk* (1984); Justices' Clerks' Society, *Administering Magistrates' Courts: The Role of the Justices Clerk* (1989); H. McLaughlin, (1990) 30 Brit.J.Criminol. 358.

[93] Justices of the Peace Act 1979, s.25.

[94] *Ibid.*

[95] Or service in certain other clerkships before February 1, 1969.

[96] Justices of the Peace Act 1979, s.26. The reference to five years' standing as a lawyer means possession of a five year magistrates' court qualification (*i.e.* a right of audience in relation to all proceedings in magistrates' courts): Courts and Legal Services Act 1990, s.71 and Sched. 10, para. 45.

[97] (1989) 45 *The Magistrate* 34.

[98] (1980) 36 *The Magistrate* 44.

[99] See Justices of the Peace Act 1979, s.28(1A), inserted by the Courts and Legal Services Act 1990, s.117, which enables rules to be made authorising delegation to a deputy or assistant.

[1] The Justices' Clerks (Qualifications of Assistants) Rules 1979, S.I. 1979 No. 570, as amended by S.I. 1980 No. 1897.

as a justices' clerk, being a barrister or solicitor, possessing a certificate of competence or a training certificate granted by a magistrates' courts committee, or holding a "Diploma in Magisterial Law."[2]

In large offices the justices' clerk will rarely have time to act as a court clerk personally[3] although his or her advice on the law or procedure may be sought by a court clerk or bench of justices. He or she may act as clerk to the magistrates' courts committee,[4] to licensing committees, to the juvenile court panel and the Lord Chancellor's Advisory Committee. He or she may grant but not refuse legal aid, will supervise the listing of cases and organise the sittings of magistrates and will also normally arrange and participate in the training of magistrates. Under the Justices Clerks Rules 1970[5] a justices' clerk may perform a number of functions otherwise exercisable by a single justice, such as the issuing of a summons and adjourning a hearing with the consent of prosecutor and accused. Similarly, an information may be laid before either a justice or a justice's clerk. Judicial functions such as issuing a summons may not be delegated by the justices' clerk to an assistant[6]; the ministerial functions of receiving an information may, however, be performed by the court staff.[7]

One of the issues that has caused problems since the 1940s has been the role of the court clerk in magistrates' court proceedings.[8] The clerk's function is to advise on law and procedure, but not to participate in the decision on the facts. In *R. v. East Kerrier JJ., ex p. Mundy*[9] Lord Goddard C.J. stated that the clerk should not retire with the justices as a matter of course but should wait to be sent for should advice on a point of law be needed. Otherwise, observers might conclude that the clerk was influencing the justices on questions of fact, and this would constitute a breach of the principle that justice must be seen to be done. This apparently caused "alarm and despondency" in some quarters,[10] somewhat to Lord Goddard's surprise, and this led to some further "clarification,"[11] or back-pedalling (depending on one's point of view). At the same time Lord Goddard C.J.

---

[2] Courses for such a diploma are run by three polytechnics. The Government has rejected, apparently on financial grounds, a proposal that only those with a professional qualification be permitted to advise in court: (1985) 149 J.P.N. 721; (1987) 151 J.P.N. 1; J.C.S., *Administering Magistrates' Courts* (1989), Chap. 12. Low salaries, particularly in comparison with the Crown Prosecution Service, have led to great difficulties in recruiting and retaining qualified clerks: (1988) 152 J.P.N. 402; C. Clegg, (1988) 44 *The Magistrate* 211.

[3] "In 1947 the justices' clerk himself was present in about 9 courts in 10; by 1977 the average was not more than 1 in 10": Skyrme (1983), p. 179.

[4] Until the reorganisation of the areas of magistrates' courts committees as part of local government reorganisation in 1974 this clerkship was commonly held by the clerk to the local authority.

[5] S.I. 1970 No. 231, as amended.

[6] *R. v. Gateshead JJ., ex p. Tesco Stores Ltd.* [1981] Q.B. 470. This case caused consternation in magistrates' courts as it had been common practice to delegate such matters in line with the recommendations of the Justices' Clerks' Society.

[7] *R. v. Manchester Stipendiary Magistrate, ex p. Hill* [1983] 1 A.C. 328.

[8] The court clerk has been described as the "key worker in setting the tone of the courtroom atmosphere": H. Parker, M. Casburn and D. Turnbull, *Receiving Juvenile Justice* (1981), p. 48.

[9] [1952] 2 Q.B. 719.

[10] (1953) 10 *The Magistrate* 65.

[11] *R. v. Welshpool JJ., ex p. Holley* [1953] 2 Q.B. 403 (justices can invite the clerk to join them as they retire to advise on a point of law; the fact that he remains while the facts are discussed not sufficient to invalidate their decision); *Practice Note (Justices' Clerks)* [1953] 1 W.L.R. 1416.

threatened that justices who knowingly disobeyed the Divisional Court's directions would be reported to the Lord Chancellor.[12] Since then the trend has been for emphasis to be placed increasingly on the point that lay justices must be given proper professional advice, and less on the need to avoid the appearance that the clerk might have given an opinion on the facts.[13] A Practice Direction was issued in 1981 by Lord Lane C.J., with the concurrence of the President of the Family Division[14]:

"1. A justices' clerk is responsible to the justices for the performance of any of the functions set out below by any member of his staff acting as court clerk[15] and may be called in to advise the justices even when he is not personally sitting with the justices as clerk to the court.
    2. It shall be the responsibility of the justices' clerk to advise the justices, as follows: (a) on questions of law or of mixed law and fact[16]; (b) as to matters of practice and procedure.
    3. If it appears to him necessary to do so, or he is so requested by the justices, the justices' clerk has the responsibility to (a) refresh the justices' memory as to any matter of evidence and to draw attention to any issues[17] involved in the matters before the court, (b) advise the justices generally on the range of penalties which the law allows them to impose and on any guidance relevant to the choice of penalty provided by the law, the decisions of the superior courts or other authorities.[18] If no request for advice has been made by the justices, the justices' clerk shall discharge his responsibility in court in the presence of the parties.
    4. The way in which the justices' clerk should perform his functions should be stated as follows. (a) The justices are entitled to the advice of their clerk when they retire in order that the clerk may fulfil his responsibility outlined above. (b) Some justices may prefer to take their own notes of evidence. There is, however, no obligation on them to do so. Whether they do so or not, there is nothing to prevent them from enlisting the aid of their clerk and his notes if they are in any doubt as to the evidence which has been given.[19] (c) If the justices wish to consult their clerk solely about the evidence or his notes of it, this should ordinarily, and certainly in simple cases, be done in open court. The

[12] R. v. Barry JJ., ex p. Nagi Kasim [1953] 1 W.L.R. 1320, 1322.
[13] N. Crampton, (1979) 129 N.L.J. 208; R. v. Uxbridge Magistrates' Court, ex p. Smith (1985) 149 J.P. 620 (no objection where the clerk left court to advise the justices, who had retired, that certain legal submissions had been erroneous: criticised by A. Heaton-Armstrong, (1986) 150 J.P.N. 340, 357); cf. R. v. Bingham JJ., ex p. Bell, Unreported, discussed by Heaton-Armstrong, op. cit.; and R v. Eccles JJ., ex p. Fitzpatrick (1989) 89 Cr.App.R. 324 (certiorari granted where there was a reasonable suspicion of improper influence by the clerk). See also the joint statement by the Magistrates' Association and the Justices' Clerks' Society: (1975) 31 The Magistrate 4.
[14] Practice Direction (Justices: Clerk to Court) [1981] 1 W.L.R. 1163. See B. Harris, (1981) 145 J.P.N. 403. Some of these points as to the functions of a justices' clerk are also made in the Justices of the Peace Act 1979, s.28(3); it is stated that this subsection is not exhaustive (subs. (4)).
[15] The implication is that these rules apply to all court clerks.
[16] See, e.g. R. v. Consett JJ., ex p. Postal Bingo Ltd. [1967] 2 Q.B. 9.
[17] This is regarded as referring to issues of fact and evidence, and not isues of law or mixed law and fact: R. v. Uxbridge Magistrates' Court, ex p. Smith (1985) 149 J.P. 620.
[18] See (1976) 140 J.P.N. 496.
[19] This impliedly overrules the statements of Donaldson L.J. in R. v. Guildford JJ., ex p. Harding (1981) 145 J.P. 174.

object is to avoid any suspicion that the clerk has been involved in deciding issues of fact.

5. For the reasons stated in the practice direction of January 15, 1954, *Practice Note (Justices' Clerks)* [1954] 1 W.L.R. 213, which remains in full force and effect, in domestic proceedings it is more likely than not that the justices will wish to consult their clerk. In particular, where rules of court require the reasons for their decision to be drawn up in consultation with the clerk, they will need to receive his advice for this purpose."

If justices summon the clerk when only issues of fact are involved and the clerk has made no note of evidence, a conviction may well be quashed.[20]

It has been argued that the appearance of justice could only realistically be maintained if advice on points of law were always given in open court.[21] The right to give such advice in private seems, however, to be strongly supported by justices' clerks,[22] and the Home Offce and the courts are not inclined to interfere with it.[23]

It has been held that the clerk may ask questions in court in order to clear up ambiguities, so long as it is at the express or implied request of the bench,[24] and that it is proper for the clerk, in the absence of the justices and in conjunction with the prosecutor, to explain to an unrepresented defendant that if he or she attacks a prosecution witness his or her previous convictions can be revealed to the court.[25]

In some areas, clerks rule on questions of the admissibility of evidence in the absence of the justices. This is generally accepted to be irregular as the clerk has no legal authority to rule on such matters. On the other hand it is also accepted that it is undesirable for the justices who are to determine guilt to determine disputed questions of admissibility, which may well involve hearing evidence which subsequently has to be disregarded as inadmissible. There is in fact no reason why the parties should not by agreement submit the issue to the clerk and, once a ruling is made, voluntarily abide by it: the real limitation is that the ruling will not technically be binding. It is likely to be in the defendant's interests for this to be done in the absence of the justices: it is unlikely that the justices could be persuaded to differ from the clerk's view on such a question.

It is also a well established practice for lawyers to refer doubtful points of law to the clerk in advance of the hearing in order to obtain what in practice, although again not in theory, amounts to a ruling.[26]

---

[20] *R.* v. *Worley JJ.*, *ex p. Nash* [1982] C.L. 1932: see the comment at (1983) 147 J.P.N. 209. *Cf. R.* v. *Eccles JJ.*, *ex p. Fitzpatrick* (1989) 89 Cr.App.R. 324 (appearance of improper influence of decision to commit for trial).

[21] A. Heaton-Armstrong, (1986) 150 J.P.N. 340, 357.

[22] (1986) 42 *The Magistrate* 40–41: "the practice would have a disastrous effect upon the relationship between magistrates and their clerk. . . . The relationship . . . is the confidential relationship of the lay client and the professional adviser. . . ."

[23] See Heaton-Armstrong, *op. cit.*

[24] *R.* v. *Consett JJ.*, *ex p. Postal Bingo Ltd.* [1967] 2 Q.B. 9. In general, clerks should not otherwise take an active part in proceedings, except where an unrepresented party is not competent to examine witnesses properly: Lord Parker C.J. in *Simms* v. *Moore* [1970] 2 Q.B. 327, 332–333.

[25] *R.* v. *Weston-super-Mare JJ.*, *ex p. Townsend* [1968] 3 All E.R. 225. Magistrates may delegate to the clerk the function of telling a defendant his or her rights at a committal: *R.* v. *Horseferry Road JJ.*, *ex p. Farooki, The Times*, October 29, 1982.

[26] See P. Darbyshire, (1980) 144 J.P.N. 201.

From time to time, suggestions are made for changing the status of justices' clerks.[27] One possibility would be to appoint them to the bench, so that they would become, in those courts where they presided, a legally qualified chairman. Another possibility would be to give them the formal power to rule on points of law, while leaving the determination of the facts, as at present, to the lay justices. This is virtually the present position. There is a persistent minority of cases in which lay justices exert their power to determine a point of law contrary to the clerk's advice. Lord Widgery C.J., however, warned that if justices fly in the face of their clerk's advice and are subsequently reversed on appeal, costs may be awarded against them.[28]

10. MAGISTRATES IN THE CROWN COURT

The Beeching Committee[29] recommended that magistrates should sit as assessors with Circuit judges in the Crown Court. Before reorganization, justices had participated in quarter sessions in the counties, but not in the assizes or borough quarter sessions. The Courts Act 1971[30] provided that justices may sit with a Circuit judge or recorder when conducting a trial on indictment and must do so when the Crown Court is hearing an appeal or dealing with a person committed there for sentence. Moreover, it provided that the justices would act as judges of the Crown Court and not merely as assessors. Lord Gardiner L.C. and Lord Hailsham L.C. were advised to adopt this course by Sir Thomas Skyrme,[31] who argued, *inter alia*, that the experience would be of benefit to the justices; that justices could play a valuable part in sentencing, especially where the judge had no local knowledge; and that they could exercise a useful restriction on any idiosyncrasy of a judge or recorder. However, Skyrme subsequently acknowledged that the differences between the Crown Court and quarter sessions turned out to be greater than expected. Long trials that formerly would have been dealt with at assizes were now conducted by a court including justices at the Crown Court. The Crown Court was in continuous session. Trials might be conducted by judges with no experience of sitting with lay justices. Cases commonly ran over a day and this would cause problems for many lay justices. In some areas only those who could sit for several days were summoned: courts were accordingly composed disproportionately of women and the elderly. On the other hand, Circuit judges have been appointed as "liaison judges," and in some areas they have been able to improve relationships.[32]

---

[27] Here the suggestions are usually confined to the justices' clerk personally and do not extend to his or her assistants.

[28] *Jones* v. *Nicks* [1977] R.T.R. 72, 76. The advice concerned what might constitute a "special reason" for not imposing an endorsement following a speeding conviction.

[29] *Royal Commission on Assizes and Quarter Sessions* (Cmnd. 4153, 1969).

[30] See now the Supreme Court Act 1981, ss.8, 74, 75; the Crown Court Rules 1982, rr. 3–5.

[31] Skyrme (1983), pp. 125–130.

[32] Suggestions that liaison judges hold annual conferences of bench chairmen, sentencing conferences and meetings with justices' clerks have, however, been criticised as going beyond their proper role: see Judge Dyer, (1987) 43 *The Magistrate* 223, and for responses: D. H. Kidner, (1988) 44 *The Magistrate* 51, and (1988) 152 J.P.N. 97.

Dissatisfaction with the role of justices in the Crown Court continued in many places.[33] Eventually, the Lord Chancellor directed that justices no longer sit in contested Crown Court trials.[34]

The Lord Chancellor has asked that no justice should sit in the Crown Court unless he or she had completed basic training and had two years' experience. The justices may outvote the judge, although in the case of a tie the latter has a second and casting vote.[35] This is most likely to happen on a question of sentence, but may occur on other matters, such as the discretion to exclude evidence.[36]

11. STIPENDIARY MAGISTRATES

The Queen may appoint up to 60 "metropolitan stipendiary magistrates" for the inner London area,[37] and up to 40 "stipendiary magistrates" elsewhere.[38] The former can trace their existence back to 1792, when they took over criminal jurisdiction from the largely corrupt lay justices.[39] The Metropolitan Police Courts Act 1839 provided that only barristers were to be eligible for appointment. From 1964, they have shared their duties with lay justices, who, with the passage of time, have been restored to respectability.

In the provinces, stipendiaries were appointed in places where there were not enough justices to cope with the work, and where, at the same time, there was a resistance to the appointment of men who had acquired wealth through industry or trade. Boroughs might petition the Home Secretary to appoint a stipendiary; alternatively, a local Act of Parliament might provide for an appointment. The role of provincial stipendiaries was to supplement rather than to replace the lay justices. The 1948 Royal Commission noted that the determining factor behind whether a particular area had a stipendiary was "not a rational assessment of the present need but the course of past history."[40] The rationalisation of commission areas, which was a by-product of local government reorganisation, provided the opportunity for the right to take the initiative in the making of new appointments to be transferred from local authorities to the Lord Chancellor.[41] The requirements of each area were assessed by the Lord Chancellor's office.[42] The area of jurisdiction of some stipendiaries was increased to enable the post to be retained. One additional stipendiary was appointed in Sheffield.

[33] Skyrme (1983), pp. 125–130. See also G. Hawker, *Magistrates in the Crown Court* (1974): Survey by the Institute of Judicial Administration, University of Birmingham.

[34] *Practice Direction* (*Crime: Crown Court Business*) (*No. 2*) [1986] 1 W.L.R. 1041 (see now above pp. 73–75). The change was made with the agreement of the Magistrates' Association: (1987) 43 *The Magistrate* 81, 119 (the suggestion had previously been resisted: see Skyrme (1983), pp. 129–130).

[35] Supreme Court Act 1981, s.73.

[36] *R.* v. *Smith* (*Benjamin Walker*) [1978] Crim.L.R. 296.

[37] Justices of the Peace Act 1979, s.31. In 1990 there were 48.

[38] 1979 Act, s.13. In 1990 there were 26 posts.

[39] See generally F. Milton, *The English Magistracy* (1967), Chap. 2. Some of the existing justices managed to secure stipendiary appointments, but ministers in the early nineteenth century took greater care over appointments. See also, R. Bartle, (1986) 54 Medico-Legal Jo. 236.

[40] Cmd. 7463, p. 57.

[41] Administration of Justice Act 1973, s.2.

[42] Skyrme (1983), Chap. 13.

The question was further reviewed following the paper produced by the Home Office and the Lord Chancellor's Department on The Size of Benches,[43] which set out criteria for the appointment of stipendiaries. The paper stated that one stipendiary was the equivalent of 36 lay magistrates in terms of judicial resources, but that experience suggested that the average stipendiary works much faster than the average lay bench.[44] The aim of an appointment was to support the lay magistracy, not to supersede it. The work, both interesting and routine, would be fairly shared, although the stipendiary should normally hear cases likely to last several days or involving difficult points of law. Relevant criteria that would trigger consideration of an appointment were (a) excessive delays not remediable by other measures; (b) overloading the lay magistracy; and (c) keeping a lay bench down to a conveniently manageable size. In 1988 the Lord Chancellor announced five additional provincial appointments.[45] Where a bench is temporarily over-burdened, an acting stipendiary magistrate[46] may be assigned to assist.[47]

Appointments are made on the recommendation of the Lord Chancellor.[48] An appointee must be a lawyer[49] of seven years' standing.[50] Metropolitan stipendiaries may be removed by the Lord Chancellor for inability or misbehaviour[51]; provincial stipendiaries hold office "during pleasure" but may only be removed on the Lord Chancellor's recommendation.[52] The retiring age is 70, although the Lord Chancellor may authorise a stipendiary to continue in office up to the age of 72.[53] The Lord Chancellor may appoint acting stipendiary magistrates,[54] and a person will not normally be given a full-time appointment without prior experience as an acting stipendiary.[55] The current salary is £47,600,[56] stipendiaries being grouped with, *inter alia*, masters and registrars of the Supreme Court and chairmen of Industrial Tribunals.

---

[43] (1986) 42 *The Magistrate* 118 (see above, p. 50); for comments by the Magistrates' Association, see 67th Annual Report, 1986–87, Appendix II.
[44] Claims that a stipendiary can get through the work three times faster than a lay bench have been doubted: see P. Softley, (1985) 149 J.P.N. 710.
[45] For Portsmouth and Southampton, Brent, Nottingham, Rotherham and Birmingham: (1988) 44 *The Magistrate* at 219.
[46] See below.
[47] Popularly (or unpopularly) known as "flying stipes": they were, for example, employed in some areas during the miners' strike ((1984) 148 J.P.N. 578). There are lists of acting stipendiaries who sit regularly at certain provincial centres: L.C.D., *Judicial Appointments* (2nd ed., 1990), p. 14.
[48] This requirement is express as regards provincial stipendiaries: 1979 Act, s.14(3).
[49] The appointment of solicitors became possible under the Justices of the Peace Act 1949. The first was appointed in 1957. By 1983 20 solicitors had been appointed, 15 in London and five elsewhere: Skyrme (1983), p. 187.
[50] 1979 Act, ss.13(1), 31(2). The requirement is possession of a seven year general qualification (*i.e.* rights of audience in any part of the Supreme Court or in all proceedings in county courts or magistrates' courts) under amendments effected by the Courts and Legal Services Act 1990, s.71, Sched. 10, para. 44.
[51] 1979 Act, s.31(4)(c).
[52] 1979 Act, s.13(1).
[53] 1979 Act, s.14. The ages for persons appointed before October 25, 1968 are 72 and 75 respectively.
[54] 1979 Act, ss.15, 34.
[55] *Judicial Appointments* (2nd ed., 1990), pp. 18, 19. Candidates must normally be aged between 38 and 55: *ibid.* pp. 13, 14.
[56] As from April 1, 1991, subject to staging.

Traditionally, appointment to judicial office has been on the understanding that the appointee will remain in that office. Today there is a growing trend for judicial officers to be "promoted," although it is still very much the exception rather than the rule. Stipendiaries may be invited to sit as recorders. Some have been appointed to the Circuit Bench.

Proposals have been made on a number of occasions for extending the role of stipendiaries outside Inner London. One possibility would be to replace all lay justices by stipendiaries. Another would be to require that each bench of magistrates should comprise one stipendiary sitting with lay justices. A third would be to increase the numbers so that there is at least one in each area, operating on a peripatetic basis. The 1948 Royal Commission reported against any radical change in the system.[57] There would not be sufficient candidates for appointment. The cost of the salaries would be large. Legal training was not in fact necessary provided legal advice was available. The present system gave the citizen a part to play in the administration of the law. The third proposal was advanced by the Bar to the 1948 Royal Commission. The stipendiary would visit the various benches and sit as chairman and would be available to take difficult cases. However, the Royal Commission noted that it was difficult to predict those cases where guidance from a professional magistrate would be useful, and that it would be undesirable to dilute the responsibility and authority of lay justices.

B. TRIBUNAL CHAIRMEN AND MEMBERS

There are several patterns on which the composition of a tribunal may be organised.[58] The variations reflect partly the differences in the kind of work undertaken by different tribunals and partly their diverse historical origins. Full-time appointments are commonly of similar status to one or other of the ranks of the judiciary. The Presidents of the Lands Tribunal, of the Social Security Appeal Tribunals and Medical Appeal Tribunals and of Industrial Tribunals and the Chief Social Security Commissioner receive a higher salary than a Circuit judge[59]; members of the Lands Tribunal and Social Security Commissioners receive the same as a Circuit judge; chairmen of Industrial Tribunals receive the same as a stipendiary magistrate.[60] Most appointments are part-time.

It is not possible to consider here the details of appointment and tenure for all tribunals.[61] Some general observations can, however, be made.

1. WHO APPOINTS?

The Franks Committee on Administrative Tribunals and Enquiries[62] reported that appointments to tribunals were usually made by the minister responsible for the legislation under which they operated. They had

[57] Cmd. 7463, Chap. VIII.
[58] See above, pp. 34–40, 57–63, 86.
[59] £64,500, as from April 1, 1991, subject to staging. The first two may in practice carry out other judicial work in addition to their tribunal duties.
[60] Regional chairmen receive the same as Circuit judges.
[61] See B. L. Jones, *Garner's Administrative Law* (7th ed., 1989), Chap. 8; R. E. Wraith and P. G. Hutchesson, *Administrative Tribunals* (1973), Chap. 4.
[62] Cmnd. 218, 1957.

received no significant evidence that any influence was in fact exerted on tribunal members by government departments, but recommended, nevertheless, that chairmen, whether legally qualified or not, should be appointed by the Lord Chancellor and members by the Council on Tribunals.[63] The position today is that the Lord Chancellor is involved in the appointment of a majority of chairmen. He either appoints the chairman directly[64] or appoints a panel from which a selection is made by the relevant department or President of tribunals.[65] The appointment of members has, however, not been transferred to the Council on Tribunals, and it is not seriously argued that it should be. Most tribunal members are appointed by the relevant government department: some are appointed by the Crown or the Lord Chancellor, and some by the relevant President of tribunals.

2. QUALIFICATIONS FOR APPOINTMENT

The Franks Committee recommended that *chairmen* of tribunals:

> "should ordinarily have legal qualifications but that the appointment of persons without legal qualifications should not be ruled out when they are particularly suitable."[66]

There should be no such requirement for members. The possession of a legal qualification is thought to be desirable not so much for the expertise in handling legal rules as for the qualities necessary for good chairmanship. "Objectivity in the treatment of cases and the proper sifting of facts are most often best secured by having a legally qualified chairman...."[67] Many criticisms of Supplementary Benefit Appeal Tribunals were related to the general lack of legally qualified chairmen. They were regularly contrasted unfavourably with National Insurance Local Tribunals where a legal qualification was in practice required.[68] Not all commentators favoured a change to lawyer-chairmen, but the government indicated in 1977 that there would be a "gradual, but significant move to appoint more legally-qualified chairmen of S.B.A.T.s."[69] Between 1977 and 1980 the overall proportion of lawyer chairmen increased from 12 per cent. to 26·4 per cent.[70]

[63] Cmnd. 218 pp. 11–12.
[64] *e.g.* the President (and members) of the Lands Tribunal: Lands Tribunal Act 1949, s.2; chairman (and members) of Mental Health Review Tribunals: Mental Health Act 1983, s.65(2), Sched. 2. Some are Crown appointments: for example, the provisions governing the appointment and tenure of Social Security Commissioners (Social Security Act 1975, s.97(3), as amended; Social Security Act 1980, ss.12, 13) are very similar to those governing Circuit judges (see below, pp. 206–208), except that a solicitor is eligible for direct appointment as a Commissioner but only via a recordership or other office as a Circuit judge. See generally, L.C.D., *Judicial Appointments* (2nd ed., 1990), pp. 20–23.
[65] See the Tribunals and Inquiries Act 1971, s.7: examples include the chairmen of industrial tribunals and S.S.A.T.s (see above, pp. 57, 61).
[66] Cmnd. 218, p. 12.
[67] *Ibid.*
[68] See, *e.g.* Kathleen Bell *et al*, "National Insurance Local Tribunals: A Research Study" (1974) 3 *Journal of Social Policy* 289 and (1975) 4 *Journal of Social Policy* 1; Kathleen Bell, *Research Study on Supplementary Benefit Appeal Tribunals—Review of Main Findings: Conclusions: Recommendations* (1975); J. Fulbrook, *Administrative Justice and the Unemployed* (1978), pp. 209–220.
[69] Annual Report of the Council on Tribunals, 1976–77 (1977–78 H.C. 108), p. 26.
[70] N. Harris, "The Appointment of Legally Qualified Chairmen for S.B.A.T.s" (1982) 132 N.L.J. 495. There were some reports of consequential improvements in the conduct of proceedings.

In an increasing number of cases, a legal qualification or legal experience is required by statute[71]: in others it is normally required as a matter of practice.[72] Even here, however, there may be criticism that appointees may not have sufficient (or any) experience in the relevant area.[73] It has also been noted that it has become more common for people to hold part-time appointments to more than one tribunal,[74] or for a full-time chairman to sit in addition as a recorder or assistant recorder in the Crown Court.[75]

The background of *members* will obviously be related to the nature of the tribunal's work. For example, doctors sit on Medical Appeal Tribunals. A pattern that has been commonly adopted is that of the "representative panel." For example, in Industrial Tribunals, one "wingman" is taken from a panel representing employers and the other from a panel representing employed persons.[76] Similar arrangements were made for National Insurance Local Tribunals and Supplementary Benefit Appeal Tribunals.[77] However, there is a single members' panel for Social Security Appeal Tribunals, appointed by the President of Social Security Appeal Tribunals and Medical Appeal Tribunals, and composed of persons appearing to him "to have knowledge or experience of conditions in the area and to be representative of persons living or working in the area."[78] The change to a single panel was coupled with the intention that the range of organisations consulted about membership should be widened out from Trade Councils, Chambers of Commerce and the like to include, for example, groups representing ethnic minorities, the disabled and one-parent families.[79]

---

[71] *e.g.* Social Security Commissioners, (lawyer of 10 years' standing), chairmen of Social Security Appeal Tribunals (from April 23, 1989: lawyer of five years' standing), Lands Tribunal members (either lawyer or qualified surveyor), chairmen of Industrial Tribunals and of Medical Appeal Tribunals (lawyers of seven years' standing), chairmen of Mental Health Review Tribunals (persons of suitable legal experience). References to standing here mean the possession of a general qualification (*i.e.* right of audience in any part of the Supreme Court or in all proceedings in county courts or magistrates' courts) for the appropriate number of years: Courts and Legal Services Act 1990, s.71 and Sched. 10, paras. 7, 27, 36, 37, 46.

[72] *e.g.* Immigration Appeal Adjudicators.

[73] The JUSTICE Report on *Industrial Tribunals* (1987) notes (p. 47) that most appointees as chairman have little or no previous knowledge and experience of employment law and almost invariably lack industrial experience: it recommends that preference be given to candidates with previous experience in employment law, industrial relations and tribunal work; and that there should be closer links with the Circuit bench. The L.C.D. booklet (*supra*), p. 22, states in relation to S.S.A.T.s, I.T.s and M.A.T.s that "Candidates are not required to have extensive knowledge of the law applied by the tribunal, but experience in the field is helpful.

[74] Wraith and Hutchesson (1973), pp. 114–115; Fulbrook (1978), p. 212.

[75] JUSTICE, *Industrial Tribunals* (1987), p. 45.

[76] Industrial Tribunals (England and Wales) Regulations 1965 (S.I. 1965 No. 1101), reg. 5. One panel is appointed by the Secretary of State after consultation with *e.g.* the T.U.C., the other after consultation with *e.g.* the C.B.I: see JUSTICE, *Industrial Tribunals*, p. 49.

[77] See the previous edition of this book, pp. 151–152.

[78] Social Security Act 1975, Sched. 10, para. 1, as substituted by the Health and Social Service and Social Security Adjudications Act 1983, Sched. 8, paras. 7 and 8, and the Health and Social Security Act 1984, s.16(*b*).

[79] J. Mesher, *C.P.A.G.'s Income Support, The Social Fund and Family Credit: the Legislation* (1988), p. 292; *Social Security Appeal Tribunals: A guide to procedure* (H.M.S.O., 1985), pp. 13–14 (nominations are initially submitted to the appropriate regional chairman: *ibid.*).

Comparatively little has been written about the social and political background of tribunal chairmen and members,[80] although, as with the judiciary, women and members of ethnic minorities are seriously under-represented.[81] Part-time appointments are commonly for three years with the possibility of renewal, but there are variations.[82]

3. DISMISSAL

No power of a minister to terminate a person's membership of a tribunal is exercisable except with the consent of the Lord Chancellor.[83]

4. TRAINING

The Council on Tribunals has noted the benefits derived from regular meetings of tribunal chairmen, at which difficulties can be discussed and opinions ventilated,[84] and has stressed the importance of training for both chairmen and members.[85] In various contexts, shortcomings in the quality of decision-making have been related to the absence of adequate training.[86] There have also been developments in the training of tribunal chairmen, although these have lagged behind developments in the training of magistrates.[87] There has been little provision of training for tribunal members. The President of Social Security Appeals Tribunals and Medical Appeals Tribunals is under an express duty to arrange for such meetings of and training for chairmen and members of tribunals as he thinks appropriate.[88]

The Lord Chancellor has established a Tribunals Committee[89] as part of the enlarged Judicial Studies Board.[90] Its role is seen as complementary to

---

[80] See W. E. Cavanagh and G. N. Hawker, "Laymen on Administrative Tribunals" (1974) 52 *Public Administration* 215 (Rent Assessment Panels and S.B.A.T.s) and the study of N.I.L.T.s by Kathleen Bell and others: *op. cit.* n. 66 pp. 310–315; L. Dickens *et al.*, *Dismissed* (1985), pp. 52–59 (Industrial Tribunals) and JUSTICE, *Industrial Tribunals* (1987), pp. 45–50; J. Baldwin and S. Hill, (1987) 6 C.J.Q. 130 (Local Valuation Panels).

[81] See JUSTICE, *Industrial Tribunals* (1987), pp. 46, 47–48, 49–50. JUSTICE proposed positive action to promote their recruitment, involving a more open, accessible and democractic appointments process for members.

[82] Wraith and Hutchesson (1973), p. 109.

[83] Tribunals and Inquiries Act 1971, s.8. The tribunals to which this applies are specified in Sched. 1.

[84] Annual Report for 1976–77, pp. 19–20. In 1987, the Council organised the first conference of Presidents and Chairmen of major tribunals falling under its jurisdiction: Annual Report for 1986–87 (1987–88 H.C. 234), pp. 6–7.

[85] *e.g.* Annual Report for 1984–85 (1985–86 H.C. 54), p. 11; for 1986–87 (1987–88 H.C. 234), p. 18; for 1987–88 (1988–89 H.C. 102), pp. 31–32; for 1988–89 (1989–90 H.C. 114), pp. 26–27.

[86] *e.g.* in respect of General Commissioners of Income Tax (Annual Report for 1987–88, p. 6); education appeal committees (*ibid.*, p. 13); industrial tribunals, especially in sex discrimination and equal pay cases (A. Leonard, *Judging Inequality* (1987), pp. 71–72; JUSTICE, *Industrial Tribunals* (1987), pp. 35–38, 48, 50).

[87] For example, there was a system for training S.B.A.T. chairmen (see Annual Report of the Council on Tribunals for 1977–78 (1978–79 H.C. 74), pp. 16–17), and some training courses have been held for chairmen of Local Valuation Courts (Report for 1978–79 (1979–80 H.C. 359), p. 18).

[88] Social Security Act 1975, Sched. 10, para. 1D, inserted by the Health and Social Services and Social Security Adjudications Act 1983, Sched. 8, para. 8. The Regional chairmen assist in this task.

[89] Its first chairman, the President of Industrial Tribunals, was appointed with effect from April 1, 1987.

[90] See below, pp. 224–225.

the Council on Tribunals, and initially to be that of co-ordinating and advising, with perhaps some greater involvement in the case of tribunals for which the Lord Chancellor has administrative responsibility.[91] However, the Council has noted with disappointment the Board's indication that only modest resources will be available for this aspect of its work.[92]

5. CLERKS TO TRIBUNALS[93]

The Franks Committee noted that the practice

"whereby the majority of clerks of tribunals are provided by the Government Departments concerned from their local and regional staffs seems partly to be responsible for the feeling in the minds of some people that tribunals are dependent upon and influenced by those Departments."[94]

They considered the possibility of establishing under the Lord Chancellor's Department a central corps of clerks for all tribunals, but rejected it on the grounds that it was difficult to see how reasonable career prospects could be held out, that it would be difficult to arrange sittings to ensure that the clerks were fully occupied and that it was in any event desirable for the civil servants in social service departments to spend a period as tribunal clerk.[95] To ensure that clerks did not exert a departmental influence, the Committee stated that their duties and conduct should be regulated on the advice of the Council on Tribunals. The duties of a clerk should generally be confined to secretarial work, taking notes of evidence and tendering advice, when requested, on points connected with the tribunal's functions. He or she should not retire with the tribunal unless sent for to advise on a specific point.

The role of the clerk has proved problematic most notably in relation to hearings of Supplementary Benefit Appeal Tribunals.[96] In 1971, the D.H.S.S., following consultation with the Council on Tribunals, issued revised official instructions which curtailed the clerk's previous role. They were subsequently made a little less restrictive,[97] and are similar to those applicable to justices' clerks.[98] Kathleen Bell's study found that for the most part the clerk played a minor role in the hearing.[99]

Clerks to Social Security Appeal Tribunals and Medical Appeals Tribunals have from April 1984 been appointed by the President, and work from the regional offices of his organisation,[1] thus marking their independence from the Department of Social Security.

---

[91] Annual Report of the Council on Tribunals for 1986–87 (1987–88 H.C. 234), p. 18.
[92] Annual Report for 1987–88 (1988–89 H.C. 102), pp. 31–32, commenting on the Judicial Studies Board Report for 1983–87, pp. 10–11.
[93] See Wraith and Hutchesson (1973), Chap. 5, and pp. 300–306.
[94] Cmnd. 218, p. 13.
[95] Ibid., pp. 13–14.
[96] See Fulbrook (1978), pp. 229–236.
[97] Supplementary Benefit Appeal Tribunals: A guide to procedure (1977), Appendix 1; Annual Report of the Council on Tribunals, 1973–74 (1974–75 H.C. 289), pp. 22–23.
[98] See above, pp. 195–197.
[99] Op. cit. n. 68 above, p. 9.
[1] Social Security Act 1975, Sched. 10, para. 1B. The organisation is known as "OPSSAT" for short: see Judge Byrt (the first President), "Administering Appeals," Adviser, Oct.-Nov. 1987, p. 6.

C. THE CIRCUIT BENCH

The Circuit Bench was created by the Courts Act 1971 as part of the reorganisation of the criminal courts following the Beeching Commission.[2] The Queen may appoint Circuit judges and recorders on the recommendation of the Lord Chancellor.[3] Circuit judges are appointed to serve full-time in the Crown Court and county courts, recorders to serve as part-time judges in the Crown Court.[4] Under the 1971 Act, only a barrister or solicitor of 10 years' standing could be appointed as a recorder. A barrister of 10 years' standing or a recorder who had held office for at least three years could be appointed as a Circuit judge. A solicitor might accordingly reach the position of Circuit judge after time as a recorder.

On reorganisation, a number of middle-rank judges automatically became Circuit judges, including the Vice-Chancellor of the County Palatine of Lancaster, the Recorder of London, the Common Serjeant, the Recorders of Liverpool and Manchester, Official Referees, the Additional Judges of the Central Criminal Court, county court judges and the whole-time chairmen or deputy chairmen of quarter sessions.[5] Most of these offices were abolished, but some were retained. The Vice-Chancellor of the County Palatine of Lancaster conducts High Court Chancery business in the North.[6] The Common Serjeant and the Recorder of London[7] sit at the Central Criminal Court. Those appointed to these offices become Circuit judges *ex officio*. In addition, the senior Circuit judges at certain large court complexes (the Recorders of Liverpool and Manchester[8] and the Senior Circuit judge at Newington Causeway) and the Circuit judges who conduct Official Referees' business in London are regarded as holding appointments more burdensome than that of the ordinary Circuit judge, and are paid higher salaries.[9]

[2] Royal Commission on Assizes and Quarter Sessions (Cmnd. 4153, 1969).

[3] Courts Act 1971, s.16. In January 1991 there were 420 Circuit judges (including 19 women) and 747 recorders (including 42 women): (1991) 88 L.S.Gaz., February 20, p. 6.

[4] And to carry out such other judicial functions as may be conferred on them by statute. A Circuit judge or recorder may be requested to act as a judge of the High Court: Supreme Court Act 1981, s.9 as amended by the Administration of Justice Act 1982, s.58. They are addressed as "Your Honour," unless sitting as a judge of the High Court or at the Central Criminal Court when they are addressed as "My Lord" or "My Lady." Circuit judges are referred to as His (or Her) Honour Judge X and recorders as Mr. (or Mrs. but not Miss) recorder B: *Practice Direction (Judges: Mode of Address)* [1982] 1 W.L.R. 101.

[5] Courts Act 1971, Sched. 2, Part I.

[6] He is appointed by the Chancellor of the Duchy of Lancaster. From 1987, the post has been held by a High Court judge, Scott J., rather than a Circuit judge.

[7] The Recorder is elected by the City, but appointed by the Crown to exercise judicial functions. The Common Serjeant is appointed by the Crown. They are paid by the City of London authorities.

[8] These are honorary recorderships under the Courts Act 1971, s.54. The holders are addressed as "My Lord."

[9] £64,500 (£73,250 for official referees) as compared with £58,100, as from April 1, 1991, subject to staging. Six judges are assigned to Official Referees' business: see the Supreme Court Act 1981, s.68 above, pp. 83–84. There have for a number of years been difficulties in recruiting Circuit judges, with in 1987–88 three refusals for every one acceptance: salary was said to be a very important factor, especially for Q.C.s, and other factors included a perceived relative lack of status: *Review Body on Top Salaries*, Report No. 28 (Cm. 581, 1989), pp. 4–5. An additional 10% increase was recommended by the Board in 1990 (Cm. 938, 1990), chap. 5.

The Lord Chancellor may, if he thinks fit, remove a Circuit judge from office on the ground of incapacity or misbehaviour.[10] In 1983, Judge Bruce Campbell was removed from office following his conviction for smuggling whisky and cigarettes.[11] The retiring age is 72, although the Lord Chancellor may authorise a judge to continue in office up to the age of 75.

The appointment of a person as a recorder specifies the term for which he or she is appointed and the frequency and duration of the occasions when he or she will be required to sit. The term may not last beyond the year in which he or she attains 72. The Lord Chancellor may terminate the appointment on the grounds of incapacity, misbehaviour or a failure to comply with the conditions of the appointment.[12] The general terms and conditions for appointment were set out in a statement by the Lord Chancellor's office.[13] Those seeking appointment are invited to write to the Lord Chancellor's Department.[14] Appointments are normally for three years at a time. Appointments of recorders are not renewed where the Lord Chancellor is not satisfied as to their continuing fitness or suitability.[15] Recorders are expected to sit for not less than four working weeks (20 days) a year. A daily fee, travelling expenses and subsistence allowances are payable.

The Lord Chancellor may also appoint deputy Circuit judges and assistant recorders.[16] Any barrister or solicitor of 10 years' standing could be appointed an assistant recorder; only a former judge of the Court of Appeal or the High Court or former Circuit judge could be appointed as a deputy Circuit judge.

Under the present arrangements candidates for appointment as Circuit judges are normally expected to have proved themselves first by sitting as assistant recorders and recorders (or as holders of one of the other specified judicial offices[17]), and recorders are not appointed unless they have proved themselves as assistant recorders.[18] If an assistant recorder has not progressed to a full recordership after about three to five years, the appointment will be terminated.[19]

---

[10] Courts Act 1971, s.17(4).

[11] *The Times*, December 6, 1983.

[12] Courts Act 1971, s.21.

[13] (1971) 68 L.S.Gaz. 303.

[14] There is a Judicial Appointments Group within the L.C.D., headed by a Deputy Secretary, which assembles and records information about potential candidates: see L.C.D., *Judicial Appointments, The Lord Chancellor's Policies and Procedures* (2nd ed., 1990), pp. 26–28. The booklet also covers the appointment of Q.C.s. It is more informative about appointment to the lower ranks of the judiciary than to the High Court.

[15] "Where possible, the recorder is warned in advance of any cause for concern, so as to give him a chance to improve. However, this cannot always be done": L.C.D., *Judicial Appointments* (1986), p. 13. It was not effectively done in the case of Manus Nunan, whose appointment was not renewed in 1985: see *The Guardian*, 13, 14 and 16 June, and December 2, 1986; R. Brazier, *Constitutional Practice* (1988), pp. 249–250; Judge James Pickles, *Straight from the Bench* (1987), pp. 29–41, including notes of the interview between Nunan and Lord Hailsham L.C. The words in question were omitted from the 2nd ed. of the booklet.

[16] Courts Act 1971, s.24, as substituted by the Supreme Court Act 1981, s.146. Under section 24 as originally enacted there was no separate appointment of assistant recorder and the qualifications for a deputy Circuit judge were wider.

[17] See fn. 22, *infra*.

[18] L.C.D., *Judicial Appointments* (2nd ed., 1990), p. 9.

[19] Minimum age limits normally applied in practice are 35 (assistant recorders), 38 (recorders) and 45 (Circuit judges), and a person over 62 will not normally be appointed to a Circuit judgeship: *ibid.*, pp. 9, 10, 15.

The Courts and Legal Services Act 1990[20] introduced changes in the qualifications for judicial appointments, mostly reflecting the proposed changes in rights of audience.[21] Thus the qualification for the appointment of a practitioner as a Circuit judge, recorder or assistant recorder is now the enjoyment of general rights of audience in the Crown Court or the county courts for 10 years. Any person who has been a district judge, or equivalent judicial officer,[22] for at least three years is eligible for appointment as a Circuit judge. The requirement that a solicitor serve three years as a recorder before becoming eligible for appointment as a Circuit judge has been removed.

D. JUDGES OF THE SUPERIOR COURTS[23]

1. THE CLASSES OF JUDICIAL OFFICE

Appointments to the High Court Bench are to the office of *puisne*[24] *judge* or *Justice of the High Court*.[25] A High Court judge is almost invariably knighted (or made a Dame Commander of the British Empire) upon appointment, but is referred to as, for example, "Mr.[26] Justice Swallow."[27] Promotion to the Court of Appeal involves elevation to the position of *Lord Justice of Appeal*, which is normally associated with an appointment to membership of the Privy Council. "Swallow J." becomes "Lord Justice Swallow."[28] The next step is membership of the House of Lords as a *Lord of Appeal in Ordinary*,[29] one of the "Law Lords." Although he will have been addressed in court as "My Lord" from the time of his appointment as a High Court judge, it is only at this stage (in the normal course of events) that he actually acquires a life peerage, as, say, "Lord Swallow of Somerset."[30]

---

[20] Courts and Legal Services Act 1990, s.71 and Sched. 10, paras. 31, 32.

[21] See above, pp. 131–133.

[22] *e.g.* Social Security Commissioner, President of Tribunals, High Court Masters, stipendiary magistrates: see Part IA of Sched. 2 to the Courts Act 1971, inserted by the Courts and Legal Services Act 1990, Sched. 10, para. 31(2).

[23] See generally, J. A. G. Griffith, *The Politics of the Judiciary* (3rd ed., 1985); D. Pannick, *Judges* (1987); M. Zander (1987), Chap. 4; R. Brazier, "The appointment and removal of the lower judiciary" (1986) 15 Anglo-Am. L.R. 173 and *Constitutional Practice* (1988), Chap. 11. On the appointment, control and extra-judicial activities of the judges between 1945 and the mid–1950s, see R. B. Stevens, "The Independence of the judicary: the view from the Lord Chancellor's Office" (1988) 8 O.J.L.S. 222.

[24] Pronounced as if it were "puny." The two words are related, a puisne judge being a "junior" judge in the superior courts of common law.

[25] See the Supreme Court Act 1981, s.4(2).

[26] Or Mrs. There has not yet been a Miss and may never be a Ms. It has been suggested that an unmarried lady would be referred to as "Mrs. Justice": A. Samuels, (1982) 79 L.S.Gaz. 509.

[27] Written as Swallow J. If there are two Swallows on the bench, Christian names are also used.

[28] Written as Swallow L.J. The first woman appointed to this office was Dame Elizabeth Butler-Sloss in 1988: she is referred to as "Lord Justice," this being the designation in the Supreme Court Act 1981, s.2(3).

[29] "The word 'Ordinary' is a technical term used in law to describe a judge who has jurisdiction to hear cases by virtue of his office. In contrast to other persons who have jurisdiction only by being peers": Lord Denning, *The Family Story* (1981), p. 184.

[30] Lord Jenkins of Ashley Gardens apparently had wished to be styled Lord Jenkins of 24 Ashley Gardens, but was thwarted by the College of Arms.

In addition, there are several specific judicial offices. The *Lord Chancellor*[31] has long been regarded as the head of the judiciary, and has now received formal recognition as "president of the Supreme Court."[32] He is an *ex officio* member of the Court of Appeal,[33] and is the president of the Chancery Division[34] although the effective head of that Division is the Vice-Chancellor. If he sits as a judge at all it is in the House of Lords or the Privy Council, and only Lord Hailsham of St. Marylebone and Lord Mackay of Clashfern (previously a Lord of Appeal) of the recent Lord Chancellors have sat at all regularly.[35] The Lord Chancellor has many administrative functions to perform as head of the judiciary. For example, he has the effective say in most judicial appointments and assignments, and various powers to give directions affecting the business of the courts. He also has general responsibility for the unified court service,[36] the Law Commissions, the legal advice and assistance and legal aid schemes,[37] the Land Registry and the Public Records Office. He is normally a Cabinet minister, and is the Speaker of the House of Lords.[38] Lord Gardiner stated that his paperwork was about half political and half judicial administration.[39] He is appointed by the Queen on the advice of the Prime Minister, and, as a political appointment, holds office "during pleasure." He goes out of office with the government of which he is a member, and is, indeed, as subject to dismissal by the Prime Minister as any other minister.[40] There are no formal qualifications for appointment, but all have been barristers. Lord Mackay is the first who has not been a member of the English Bar.[41]

---

[31] *i.e.* the Lord High Chancellor of Great Britain. Written as Lord Mackay of Clashfern L.C. Incumbents since 1945 have been Lord Jowitt (1945–1951); Lord Simonds (1951–1954); Lord Kilmuir (1954–1962); Lord Dilhorne (1962–1964); Lord Gardiner (1964–1970); Lord Hailsham (1970–1974, 1979–1987); Lord Elwyn-Jones (1974–1979); Lord Havers (1987); Lord Mackay (1987–). See generally R. F. V. Heuston, *Lives of the Lord Chancellors, 1885–1940* (1964) and *1940–1970* (1987); I. S. Dickinson, "Aspects of appointments to the office of Lord Chancellor" 1988 S.L.T. 41 (which lists those appointed between 1830 and 1987).

[32] Supreme Court Act 1981, s.1. He is paid £2,000 more than the Lord Chief Justice: Ministerial and other Pensions and Salaries Act 1991, s.3.

[33] *Ibid.* s.2.

[34] *Ibid.* s.5(1)(*a*).

[35] See G. Drewry, "Lord Chancellor as Judge" (1972) 122 N.L.J. 855. Until the Second World War the legislative sittings of the House of Lords commenced at 4.15 p.m., enabling the Lord Chancellor to sit regularly on appeals during the standard hours of 10.30 a.m. to 4.00 p.m. However, wartime difficulties caused the start of legislative sittings to be advanced to 2.30 p.m. and the Lord Chancellor was compelled to choose between the two kinds of work: R.F.V. Heuston, *Lives of the Lord Chancellors, 1885–1940* (1964), p. xviii. See also A. Bradney, "The Judicial Activity of the Lord Chancellor 1946–1987" (1989) 16 J.L.S. 360: this sets out statistics of the judicial activity of Lord Chancellors and former Lord Chancellors in this period.

[36] Courts Act 1971, s.27(1).

[37] See below, pp. 443–468, 506–517, 672–680.

[38] See generally on the functions of the Lord Chancellor: *Halsbury's Laws of England* (4th ed.) Vol. 8, paras. 1171–1191; the accounts cited in Heuston (1964), p. xv, n. 1 and (1987), p. 1, n. 1; the addresses by Lord Gardiner (1968) and Lord Hailsham (1972) to the Holdsworth Club (published in B. W. Harvey (ed.) *The Lawyer and Justice* (1978)); and Lord Hailsham, *The Door Wherein I Went* (1975), pp. 244–258 and (1989) 8 C.J.Q. 308.

[39] Harvey (ed.) (1978), p. 216.

[40] Viscount Kilmuir was dismissed by Harold Macmillan on the "night of the long knives" in July 1962.

[41] He had previously been Lord Advocate, a judge of the Court of Session and a Lord of Appeal.

The *Lord Chief Justice of England*[42] takes precedence over all judges other than the Lord Chancellor. He is the president of the Court of Appeal (Criminal Division) and the Queen's Bench Division of the High Court. The office was created as part of the reorganisation of the superior courts under the Supreme Court of Judicature Acts 1873–75. Before then each of the superior common law courts had its own chief: the Chief Justices of the Queen's Bench and the Common Pleas, and the Chief Baron of the Exchequer. The first Lord Chief Justice of England appointed as such was, accordingly, Lord Coleridge,[43] Chief Justice of the Common Pleas from 1873, who took the office in 1880 following the deaths of Sir Alexander Cockburn C.J. of the Queen's Bench Division and Chief Baron Kelly.[44] From that date new incumbents have been ennobled if not already peers. The holder is referred to as Lord Lane, Chief Justice or Lord Lane, Lord Chief Justice.[45]

The office of *Master of the Rolls*[46] dates from at least the thirteenth century. He was originally the keeper of the rolls or records of the Chancery, but with the passage of time he became recognised as a judge in the Court of Chancery: until 1813 he was the only judge in that court other than the Chancellor. After the reorganisation of the courts under the Judicature Acts 1873–75 he continued as a judge of first instance, but the man appointed in 1873, Sir George Jessel, was such an able lawyer that it was thought appropriate for the Master of the Rolls to become a judge of the Court of Appeal.[47] He is now the president of the Court of Appeal (Civil Division).[48] In view of the large number of important civil cases determined in that court and the power of the Master of the Rolls over the allocation of cases, the holder of that office may exert considerable influence over the development of the civil law. It was for this reason that Lord Denning, then a Lord of Appeal in Ordinary, welcomed the appointment as Master of the Rolls.[49] The holder is referred to as Lord Donaldson, Master of the Rolls.[50]

The *President of the Family Division* and the *Vice-Chancellor* head, respectively, the Family and Chancery Divisions of the High Court, and are

---

[42] See F. Bresler, *Lord Goddard* (1977), Chap. 9.

[43] Lord Parker, (1961) 35 A.L.J. 97. Some Chief Justices of the King's Bench had styled themselves, or had been referred to informally as Lord Chief Justice of England, although this was technically incorrect. A notable example of the former was Sir Edward Coke, whose action was said to have displeased the King and to have been one of the causes of his dismissal.

[44] The opportunity was also taken to amalgamate the three common law divisions. The following have held the office: Lord Coleridge 1880–94; Lord Russell of Killowen 1894–1900; Lord Alverstone 1900–1914; Lord Reading 1914–1921; Lord Trevethin 1921–1922; Lord Hewart 1922–1940; Viscount Caldecote 1940–1946; Lord Goddard 1946–1958; Lord Parker 1958–1971; Lord Widgery 1971–1980; Lord Lane 1980– .

[45] Written as Lord Lane C.J. or Lord Lane L.C.J.

[46] See Lord Denning, *The Family Story* (1981), pp. 201–204; Sir John Donaldson, M.R., (1984) 17 Bracton L.J. 19 and *The Problems of A Master of the Rolls* (Holdsworth Club, 1985).

[47] Sir Robert Megarry, (1982) 98 L.Q.R. 370, 395.

[48] Supreme Court Act 1981, s.3(2).

[49] Lord Denning, *The Family Story* (1981), pp. 172, 197; "the Master of the Rolls is still one of the most coveted posts in the land": *ibid.* p. 204. Lord Denning also found himself "too often in a minority" in the House of Lords: *The Discipline of Law* (1979), p. 287.

[50] Written as Lord Donaldson M.R. It is common for the holder of the office to be ennobled, although not necessarily on appointment. Recent holders have been Lord Wright 1935–1949; Lord Evershed 1949–1962; Lord Denning 1962–1982; Sir John Donaldson (Lord Donaldson from 1988) 1982– .

ex officio members of the Court of Appeal. The former office was created in 1970, with the transition from the Probate, Divorce and Admiralty Division.[51] The holder is referred to as Sir Stephen Brown, President.[52] The latter office was created in 1970, the holder to be nominated by the Lord Chancellor.[53] It was made a royal appointment analogous to the other heads of division in 1982.[54] The holder is technically the vice-president of the Chancery Division,[55] but is effectively the head. He is referred to as Sir Nicolas Browne-Wilkinson, Vice-Chancellor.[56] The title "Vice Chancellor of England" was used in the nineteenth century for the judges appointed to assist the Lord Chancellor in the Court of Chancery.[57]

One of the Lords Justices of Appeal is to be appointed as Senior Presiding Judge by the Lord Chief Justice, with the agreement of the Lord Chancellor.[58]

2. MASTERS AND REGISTRARS

There are a number of officers of the Supreme Court below the ranks of the judges, who perform both administrative and judicial tasks, the latter in particular in interlocutory matters arising in the course of litigation. There are, for example,[59] a number of Masters of the Queen's Bench and Chancery Divisions, District Judges of the principal registry of the Family Division, Taxing Masters and Registrars in Bankruptcy. One of each of these groups is appointed as a "senior" or "chief."[60] Particularly important offices held by individuals are those of Master of the Crown Office and Registrar of Criminal Appeals,[61] and the Registrar of Civil Appeals.[62]

---

[51] See above, p. 78. The old division was also headed by a President. The incumbents have been Sir Jocelyn Simon 1962–1971; Sir George Baker 1971–1979; Sir John Arnold 1979–1988 and Sir Stephen Brown 1988– .

[52] Written as Sir Stephen Brown P. Sir Stephen is the first who was previously a Lord Justice of Appeal.

[53] Administration of Justice Act 1970, s.5.

[54] Supreme Court Act 1981, s.10(1). See generally Sir Robert Megarry, (1982) 98 L.Q.R. 370.

[55] 1981 Act, s.5(1)(*a*).

[56] Written as Sir Nicolas Browne-Wilkinson V.-C. Sir Nicolas is the fourth of the modern Vice-Chancellors and the first who was previously a Lord Justice of Appeal. The others were Sir John Pennycuick 1970–1974, Sir John Plowman 1974–1976 and Sir Robert Megarry, 1974–1985.

[57] 53 Geo III c. 24, 1813. In 1841 two additional Vice-Chancellors were appointed. With the death of the last Vice Chancellor of England (Sir Lancelot Shadwell) in 1850 the words "of England" were dropped. The Vice-Chancellors were transferred to the Chancery Division under the Judicature Act 1873. On their death or retirement their successors were styled as High Court justices. See A. B. Schofield, (1966) L.S.Gaz. 298; Megarry, *op. cit.*

[58] Courts and Legal Services Act 1990, s.72.

[59] Schedule 2 to the Supreme Court Act 1981, as substituted by the Courts and Legal Services Act 1990, Sched. 10, para. 49, lists 12 offices. See also s.89, as amended by the 1990 Act, Sched. 18, paras. 37, 38. On the work of the Queen's Bench Masters see A. S. Diamond, (1960) 76 L.Q.R. 504 and Sir Jack Jacob, *The Reform of Civil Procedural Law* (1982), p. 349; on Chancery Masters see R. E. Ball, (1961) 77 L.Q.R. 331.

[60] Supreme Court Act 1981, s.89(3).

[61] These were formerly separate posts, the first carrying responsibility for civil work and appeals in the Queen's Bench Division, the second for appeals to the Court of Appeal (Criminal Division). They were amalgamated by the 1990 Act, s.78.

[62] Supreme Court Act 1981, Sched. 2. This post carries responsibility for appeals to the Court of Appeal (Civil Division).

3. Eligibility for Appointment and Numbers

Prior to the Courts and Legal Services Act 1990, appointments as a judge of the Supreme Court were confined to members of the Bar[63]:

Position	Max. Number	Qualification
Puisne judges	85[64]	Barrister of at least 10 years' standing[65]
Lord Justices of Appeal	28[66]	Barrister of at least 15 years' standing or High Court judge.
Lord Chief Justice		
Master of the Rolls		Barrister of at least 15 years' standing or High Court judge or judge of
President of the Family Division		the Court of Appeal
Vice-Chancellor		

In order to be qualified for appointment as a Lord of Appeal in Ordinary a person had to have (1) practised for 15 years as a barrister in England or Northern Ireland or as an advocate in Scotland; or (2) have held for two years one or more of the "high judicial offices" of Lord Chancellor, or judge of the High Court, Court of Appeal, Court of Session or Supreme Court of Judicature of Northern Ireland.[67] There is a maximum number of 11.[68] By convention, two of the Lords of Appeal are Scots lawyers.[69] Most of the offices below the rank of judge could be held by barristers or solicitors, usually with a minimum of 10 years' standing.[70] These were very much in the way of minimum requirements: for example, a barrister would expect to wait much longer than 10 years before becoming a serious candidate for appointment to the High Court.

The most controversial issue relating to the list of qualifications for appointment was whether it was right that a solicitor could not become a judge of the Supreme Court or a Lord of Appeal in Ordinary.[71] Solicitors have become eligible for appointment as stipendiary magistrates, recorders and Circuit judges. The next logical step would seem to be to allow service as a Circuit judge to render the holder eligible for appointment to the Supreme Court irrespective of whether his or her career as a lawyer was as a solicitor

---

[63] Supreme Court Act 1981, s.10(3).

[64] *Ibid.* s.4(1)(*e*).

[65] A barrister of this standing was eligible for appointment as a deputy High Court judge: *ibid.* s.9(4).

[66] *Ibid.* s.2(1). The number of puisne judges and Lords Justices may be increased by Order in Council: ss.4(4) and 2(4). The maximum number of puisne judges was increased from 80 to 85, and Lords Justices from 23 to 28 by the Maximum Number of Judges Order 1987 (S.I. 1987 No. 2059): see Vol. 489, H.L.Deb., November 10 1987, cols. 1334–1344.

[67] Appellate Jurisdiction Act 1876, ss.6, 25.

[68] Administration of Justice Act 1968, s.1. This number may be increased by Order in Council: *ibid.*

[69] This has been observed notwithstanding the appointment of a Scots lawyer as Lord Chancellor: Lord Mackay was succeeded as Lord of Appeal by Lord Jauncey of Tullichettle.

[70] Supreme Court Act 1981, Sched. 2.

[71] A solicitor, or indeed a bus driver could theoretically be appointed Lord Chancellor, but neither is even a remote possibility.

or barrister. This was supported by the JUSTICE Sub-Committee in its Report on the Judiciary,[72] and strongly urged in Parliament during the passage of the Supreme Court Act 1981. However, it was successfully resisted by the government, mainly on the basis that experience as an advocate in the Supreme Court was necessary for appointment to the bench there.[73] The JUSTICE Sub-Committee argued that the Bar had become numerically inadequate to provide the exclusive source for appointment, unless the quality of possibly both the Bench and the Bar was to be jeopardised; it could not be said that *no* solicitor would make a competent judge; the larger the pool of candidates, the better the chance of a good appointment; and eligibility would enhance the dignity, self-respect and pride of the solicitors' branch of the legal profession. The committee doubted whether any particular experience or qualification was indispensible, but noted that many solicitors had experience of advocacy in the lower courts. As few solicitors would probably seek or receive appointment the attractions of the Bar as a profession would not significantly be reduced. A successful period as a Circuit judge would seem, as a matter of common sense, to be a rather better demonstration of one's qualities for *judicial* appointment than experience as an advocate.

The government's proposals for the substantial restructuring of the legal profession included consequential changes in the qualifications for judicial appointments.[74] The qualification for a practitioner in England and Wales to be appointed as a Lord of Appeal in Ordinary is now the enjoyment of general rights of audience in the Supreme Court for 15 years; as a Lord Justice of Appeal, High Court judge or deputy High Court judge, general rights of audience in the High Court for 10 years; and as a Master or Registrar of the Supreme Court, district judge (formerly High Court district or county court registrar) or stipendiary magistrate, a right of audience in any part of the Supreme Court or a general right of audience in the county courts or magistrates' courts for seven years. The existing qualifications of judges in the United Kingdom as a whole (and practitioners outside England and Wales) to be appointed as a Lord of Appeal remained unchanged. Any person who has been a Circuit judge for at least two years is eligible for appointment as a judge of the Supreme Court. These changes will enable the Lord Chancellor "to be free to consider the best practitioners of all kinds for appointment."

The expansion of eligibility for the highest judicial offices was widely welcomed during consultation on the Green Papers. One concern expressed in the course of it was that if members of the Crown Prosecution Service were to be given extended rights of audience they would thereby become eligible for a judicial appointment: it was, it was argued, wrong in principle for a person to be appointed as a judge whose experience was exclusively as a prosecutor. The White Paper pointed out that it was the Lord Chancellor's current practice not to appoint serving civil servants to any paid judicial office which would involve hearing criminal cases. As appointment to a full-time judicial office had in practice to be preceded by part-time judicial

[72] (1972), pp. 9–20. See also S. Shetreet, *Judges on Trial* (1976), pp. 55–58.
[73] See (1981) 131 N.L.J. 273; (1981) 79 L.S.Gaz. 193.
[74] *Legal Services: A Framework for the Future* (Cm. 740, 1989), pp. 42–43; Courts and Legal Services Act 1990, s.71 and Sched. 10.

experience, a member of any part of the government legal service could not become a judge without first returning to private practice for a substantial period. In the mean time, steps have been taken to encourage solicitor candidates for appointment to the Circuit bench.[75]

Academic lawyers are not appointed to the Bench in the United Kingdom, even if they are barristers of the requisite standing.[76] Moreover, it seems to have become progressively less common for academic lawyers to be a member of either branch of the profession. It is generally agreed that it would not be appropriate to appoint academic lawyers as trial judges, in view of their lack of experience with the process of ascertaining the facts of cases. It is, however, arguable that academics should be eligible for appointment to the Court of Appeal or the House of Lords.[77] The salary and prestige would be particularly attractive to professors of law, who are commonly required to retire at 65, and may currently be encouraged to retire earlier. It could not be disputed that there would be candidates with the appropriate qualities of intellect and scholarship; it would also be one method of widening the background, political and otherwise, of members of the judiciary, should that be thought to be desirable.

4. METHOD OF APPOINTMENT[78]

Appointment to the positions of Lord Chief Justice, Master of the Rolls, President of the Family Division, Vice-Chancellor, Lord of Appeal in Ordinary and Lord Justice of Appeal are made by the Queen,[79] acting by convention on the advice of the Prime Minister, who, in turn, will have consulted the Lord Chancellor. The effective voice in all appointments is normally that of the Lord Chancellor,[80] following consultations with members of the judiciary[81] and leading members of the Bar. Occasionally, the Prime Minister may override the Lord Chancellor's view in relation to senior appointments.[82] Records on potential candidates are maintained by the staff of the Lord Chancellor's Office, and candidates are interviewed.

[75] H.C.Deb. Vol. 157, col. 1022, July 28, 1989, written answer by the Solicitor-General.

[76] The only reference to "practising" barristers related to eligibility for appointment as a Law Lord, above p. 212: The word "practising" does not appear in the qualification substituted by the 1990 Act.

[77] The JUSTICE Sub-Committee on The Judiciary favoured this proposal: Report (1972) pp. 21–24.

[78] See L.C.D., *Judicial Appointments* (2nd ed., 1990); Shetreet (1976), pp. 46–84; Lord Hailsham, *The Door Wherein I Went* (1975), pp. 254–258; A. Paterson, "Becoming a Judge" in R. Dingwall and P.Lewis (eds.) *The Sociology of the Professions* (1983), Chap. 12; A. Samuels, "Appointing the Judges" (1984) 134 N.L.J. 85, 107; Sir Robert Megarry, "The anatomy of judicial appointment: change but not decay" (1985) 19 U.B.C. Law Rev. 113. *Cf.* G. Winterton, "Appointment of Federal Judges in Australia" (1987) 16 Melb. U.L.R. 185.

[79] Supreme Court Act 1981, s.10(1)(2).

[80] The Lord Advocate's influence in the appointment of Scots Law Lords has increased in the post-war period: see A.A. Paterson, "Scottish Lords of Appeal, 1876–1988" 1988 J.R. 235. "In the last 20 years, however, it is generally felt that, with promotion from the Bar being out of fashion and neither Lord President evincing any desire to move south, in the case of most appointments the candidates have almost selected themselves": *ibid.*, p. 241.

[81] There is a meeting between the Lord Chancellor and the Heads of Division at which "a consensus is usually arrived at": Lord Hailsham (1975), p. 254; *Cf.* Sir Robert Megarry, (1982) 98 L.Q.R. 370, 397. Lord Halsbury was exceptional in not consulting the Lord Chief Justice: R. F. V. Heuston, *Lives of the Lord Chancellors, 1885–1940* (1964), pp. 47–48.

[82] *e.g.* the appointment of Sir Ernest Pollock rather than Bankes L.J. as Master of the Rolls in 1923: Heuston, *Lives*, p. 428. *Cf.* Samuels (1984) 134 N.L.J. 85, 86.

Appointments to the High Court Bench are normally made from the ranks of Queen's Counsel. Junior barristers may be appointed direct but the only persons normally so appointed are the Junior Counsel to the Treasury, who, indeed, are normally elevated to the bench after their period in that position. From time to time there have been promotions from the positions of Official Referee,[83] county court judge,[84] Recorder of Liverpool or Manchester, Circuit judge[85] and Registrar of the Family Division,[86] but these constitute a fairly small minority.[87] One person has been appointed to the High Court Bench after being an advocate general of the Court of Justice of the European Communities.[88]

Put shortly, the qualities looked for would seem to be good character, success as an advocate and, if appropriate, in a lower judicial office, the rather mystical quality known as "common sense," and good health. Those appointed are normally in their fifties, although some are appointed in their forties.[89] Brilliance as a technical lawyer is not regarded as a necessary precondition, although greater weight is placed on legal ability when appointments to the Chancery Division or to the appellate courts are considered. It is normal for those appointed to have served previously as a recorder and, perhaps, a deputy High Court judge. Unlike the position in relation to appointments as recorder or Circuit judge, it is not the normal practice for barristers to apply for appointment to the High Court Bench: it is expected that they wait to be invited.

Several observers have noted an improvement in the quality of judges.[90] "On the whole, I have no doubt that judges are much better educated, more polite and more patient than they used to be."[91]

Political service was formerly a significant factor in many judicial appointments.[92] Of the 139 judges appointed between 1832 and 1906, 80 were M.P.s at the time of their nomination; 11 others had been candidates for Parliament. Of those 80, 63 were appointed by their own party while in office.[93] Lord Halsbury, Unionist Lord Chancellor for three periods,[94] was criticised for making bad appointments of Tory M.P.s.[95] Lord Salisbury, the Prime Minister for most of Halsbury's time as Lord Chancellor, "would never apologise for the practice of making [legal promotions] a reward for political

---

[83] Sir Edward Ridley (1897). The fact that he held office was regarded as counting against him rather than for him. He was the brother of the Home Secretary, and was subsequently thought to be a poor judge: See Heuston, *Lives*, pp. 49–52.

[84] The first was Sir Edward Acton (1920), the Nottingham county court judge. Ten more were elevated between 1945 and 1971.

[85] 16 were elevated between 1973 and 1990.

[86] Butler Sloss J. (1979).

[87] 20 out of 150 appointments between 1970 and 1990.

[88] Warner J. (1981).

[89] The youngest in the last 50 years were Lords Hodson and Devlin who were 42 when appointed High Court judges in 1937 and 1948 respectively.

[90] C. P. Harvey Q.C., *The Advocate's Devil* (1958), pp. 33–34, comparing the fifties with the twenties; Lord Devlin, *The Judge* (1979), p. 24; D. Pannick, *Judges* (1987), p. 15.

[91] Lord Hailsham, *The Door Wherein I Went* (1975), p. 257.

[92] See A. Paterson, (1974) 1 B.J.L.S. 118. Party politics continues to play a larger role in the appointment of judges in Scotland. This has given rise to adverse criticism: I. D. Willock, 1969 J.R. 193; C. M. Campbell, 1973 J.R. 254.

[93] H. Laski, (1926) 24 Michigan L.R. 529.

[94] 1885–86; 1886–92; 1895–1905.

[95] See Heuston, *Lives*, pp. 36–66.

'right thinking,' "[96] although he expressed the need for caution following public criticism of some of the early appointments.[97] There was contemporary criticism of the appointments of Grantham, J.C. Lawrence, Bruce, Darling, Ridley and Kekewich, all of whom turned out to be poor judges,[98] although each had his defenders. The first four were Conservative M.P.s at the time of their appointment. Ridley had briefly been a Conservative M.P. nearly 20 years before, although that did not seem to have influenced the choice, and Kekewich had been a Conservative candidate. Heuston argues that the last two appointments were unlucky and that "four dubious appointments out of 30 during a tenure of the woolsack lasting 17 years should not weigh too heavily in the scales when making a final judgment."[99]

Lord Haldane, when Lord Chancellor between 1912 and 1915, introduced a policy of appointing "only on the footing of high legal and professional qualifications,"[1] and this position, as regards puisne judgeships, has more or less been maintained since. The only political tradition that took significantly longer to die was the idea that the Attorney-General and Solicitor-General had a special claim should one of the higher judicial offices fall vacant.[2] The Attorney's claim on the position of Lord Chief Justice was supposed to be particularly strong.[3]

Between 1873 and 1945 only four of the 23 holders of the office of Attorney-General did not go on to hold one of the higher judicial offices.[4] All those appointed Lord Chief Justice, with one exception,[5] were former Attorneys. Nine of the 17 men who were Solicitor-General without becoming Attorney-General also progressed to one of the higher judicial offices.[6]

---

[96] G. Cecil (Lord Salisbury's daughter and biographer) cited by Heuston, *Lives* p. 36.

[97] *Ibid.* p. 57.

[98] Grantham J. attracted severe criticism in Parliament for his partisan trial of two election petitions in 1906: see H. Cecil, *Tipping the Scales* (1965), pp. 194–208; Darling J. was described by C. P. Harvey as a "real shocker" (*The Advocate's Devil* (1958), pp. 32–33) and renowned for his "jokes"; MacKinnon L.J. wrote that J.C. Lawrance J. was "a stupid man, a very ill-equipped lawyer and a bad judge. He was not the worst judge I have appeared before: that distinction I would assign to Mr. Justice Ridley. Ridley had much better brains than Lawrance, but he had a perverse instinct for unfairness that Lawrance could never approach." ((1944) 60 L.Q.R. 324).

[99] *Lives*, p. 66.

[1] R. B. Haldane, *An Autobiography* (1929), p. 253.

[2] J.Ll.J. Edwards, *The Law Officers of the Crown* (1964), pp. 309–334.

[3] Eighteen of the 42 Chief Justices of the Common Pleas between 1600 and 1873 were ex-Attorneys, 16 appointed directly. Between 1725 and 1873 all but two of the Chief Justices of the King's Bench were ex-Attorneys, four appointed directly: Edwards (1964), pp. 320–21.

[4] Lord Chancellor (8), L.C.J. (5), M.R. (2), Lord of Appeal (4), L.J. (4): four held two of these offices. The exceptions were Karslake (1874) who suffered a complete physical breakdown in 1875, Walton (1905–8) who died in office and Patrick Hastings (1924), Attorney-General in the first Labour Government, who apparently "had no wish to be made a judge" (Lord Birkett, *Six Great Advocates* (1961), p. 37). Sir Henry James (1880–85) was given a peerage and often sat in the House of Lords.

[5] Lord Trevethin (1921).

[6] Lord Chancellor (4); L.J. (3); President of the P.D.A. (2); Lord of Appeal (1: Lord Davey, promoted from Lord Justice). Of the other eight, four held other ministerial offices (Harcourt (1873–74), Gorst (1885–86), Cripps (1930–31) and Monckton (1945)), three died in office or shortly after leaving it (Lockwood (1894–95), Melville (1929–30) and O'Connor (1936–40)), and the other, Clarke (1886–92), refused the position of Master of the Rolls in 1897.

However, much controversy surrounded the appointment of Sir Gordon Hewart as Lord Chief Justice.[7] In 1921 it was arranged that Lord Reading C.J. was to become Viceroy of India. Hewart, as Attorney-General, pressed his claim to the position of Lord Chief Justice but could not be spared from the Commons. Lloyd George appointed a 77-year-old Queen's Bench judge, A.T. Lawrence J., on the understanding that he would retire when called upon, although neither Lord Birkenhead L.C. nor Hewart approved of the plan. Nevertheless, in 1922 Lord Trevethin (as Lawrence became) read of his own resignation in *The Times*, and Hewart duly succeeded him. To add injury to insult, Hewart proved to be "perhaps the worst Lord Chief Justice of England since the seventeenth century. Although no imputation of corruption or dishonesty could be brought against him, as against Scroggs and Jeffreys, on the bench he rivalled them in arbitrary and unjudicial behaviour."[8]

Since 1945 the position seems to have changed significantly. In 1946, Viscount Caldecote C.J. was succeeded by a Lord of Appeal, Lord Goddard, after the post had been declined by Sir Hartley Shawcross, the Attorney-General.[9] Lord Goddard and his successors have not had political careers.[10] Lord Goddard was followed by Lord Parker,[11] who subsequently commented that the non-political nature of the appointment, made clear by the appointments of Lord Goddard, himself and Lord Widgery, was of "vital importance for the administration of justice in this country."[12] The only Law Officers subsequently appointed to the bench have been Lynn Ungoed-Thomas[13] and Sir Jocelyn Simon,[14] and only two of the others have become Lord Chancellor.[15] The appointment of Lord Chief Justices from amongst the ranks of the judiciary has been generally welcomed.

It has become progressively more difficult to combine membership of the Commons with a successful practice at the Bar. Lord Hailsham regretted that he was unable to appoint a single High Court judge from among M.P.s.[16] There is something of a vicious circle in that the lack of a reasonable prospect of elevation to the Bench may discourage the ablest lawyers from seeking a political career. Political experience has been regarded by some as an asset for an appointee. Lord Simon has argued that:

"although no one would wish to see a predominantly political Bench, a seasoning of judges with experience of politics and administration is

---

[7] See R. Jackson, *The Chief* (1959), Chap. 9; J. Campbell, *F. E. Smith, First Earl of Birkenhead* (1983), pp. 479–481.

[8] Heuston, *Lives*, pp. 603–604; *Cf.* C. P. Harvey, *The Advocate's Devil* (1958), p. 32.

[9] See F. Bresler, *Lord Goddard* (1977), pp. 112–115. Shawcross had opposed the idea that there was a "right" of succession, and preferred a political career.

[10] Goddard had stood unsuccessfully as an Independent Conservative in the 1929 General Election, a brief and "ill-starred political venture": Bresler (1977), pp. 60–62.

[11] The then Attorney-General, Sir Reginald Manningham-Buller, did not actively seek the post, but would apparently have liked to have been asked: Bresler (1977), pp. 295–298.

[12] Bresler (1977), p. 297.

[13] Labour M.P. 1945–62; Solicitor General 1951; High Court judge 1962–72.

[14] Conservative M.P. 1951–62; Solicitor-General 1959–62; President of the Probate, Divorce and Admiralty Division 1962–71; Lord of Appeal 1971–77. Two previous Presidents had formerly been Solicitor-General: Sir Samuel Evans (1910–1919) and Sir Frank (later Lord) Merriman (1934–1962).

[15] Viscount Dilhorne (formerly, Sir Reginald Manningham-Buller) and Lord Elwyn-Jones. Between 1945 and 1990 there have been 18 holders of one or both of the Law Offices.

[16] *The Door Wherein I Went* (1975), p. 256.

far from disadvantageous; constituency duties, for example, are calculated to develop a social awareness which ordinary forensic work is not
apt to inculcate."[17]

The social and educational background of the judges has been examined
in a number of surveys.[18] These show that the judges are overwhelmingly
upper or upper middle class in origin, with over three-quarters having
attended public school, and a similar proportion either Oxford or Cambridge University. Only four women have reached the High Court bench,
and no members of the ethnic minorities.[19]

The process of socialisation at the Bar tends to mean that those from other
backgrounds do not seem markedly different, if different at all, from the
majority.[20] The extent to which judicial attitudes can be related to the social
background of the judges is a large and debatable question.[21] Given the
continuance for the foreseeable future of the policy of appointing judges
largely from the Bar, it is unlikely that there will be any significant change in
the background of the people appointed. What is more plausible is that the
attitudes of successive generations may gradually change.[22]

Other countries have adopted different methods of appointment. In civil
law systems there is normally a career judiciary, which is part of the general
civil service and separate from the legal profession. In the United States
there are two basic methods of selection, *appointment* and *election*, although
a compromise between the two methods is commonly applied.[23] All federal
judges are appointed by the President, subject to confirmation by the
Senate.[24] An appointment can in practice be vetoed by one of the candidate's home state Senators and candidates are also evaluated by the
American Bar Association's influential Committee on Federal Judiciary,
which makes its views known to the President and the Senate. In 1970, 82 per
cent. of state and local judges were elected, although real contests were
rare.[25] In a number of states elections are used to confirm in office judges

---

[17] (1965) 81 L.Q.R. 289, 295.

[18] *The Economist*, December 15, 1956, pp. 946–947; K. Goldstein-Jackson, *New Society*, May
14, 1970; H. Cecil, *The English Judge* (Revised ed., 1972), Chap. 1; J. Brock (M.Phil.
dissertation, quoted in the JUSTICE Sub-Committee Report on the Judiciary (1972)); F. L.
Morrison, *Courts and the Political Process in England* (1973), Chap. 3. The background of
the Lords of Appeal appointed betwen 1876 and 1969 is examined in L. Blom-Cooper and G.
Drewry, *Final Appeal* (1972), pp. 158–169. The results of these surveys are summarised by J.
A. G. Griffith, *The Politics of the Judiciary* (3rd ed., 1985) pp. 25–29.

[19] Elizabeth Lane J., Booth J., Butler-Sloss J. (now L.J.) and Bracewell J. There is one Circuit
judge from an ethnic minority (Mota Singh Q.C.). Lord Mackay has rejected suggestions
that a "fast-track" appointment mechanism be considered: see (1990) 87 L.S.Gaz., June 27,
p. 4; Sir F. Lawton, (1990) 134 S.J. 1255; T. Holland, *ibid.* p. 1286.

[20] As to the social background of barristers, see above, pp. 166–171.

[21] See below, pp. 232–239.

[22] See P. McAuslan, (1983) 46 M.L.R. 1, 19.

[23] See H. Abraham, *The Judicial Process* (5th ed., 1986), pp. 22–95 and *Justices and Presidents*
(2nd ed., 1985).

[24] The most recent example of a presidential nominee for the Supreme Court failing to obtain
confirmation is Judge Robert Bork: see R. Hodder-Williams, (1988) xxxvi *Political Studies*,
613–637; Essays on the Supreme Court Appointment Process (symposium) 101 Harv.L.R.
1146–1229 (1988).

[25] Abraham (1986), p. 35. In recent years a number of state judges (including Chief Justice
Rose Bird and two associate justices of the California Supreme Court) have failed to obtain
re-election following sustained political campaigns by opponents: see R. Reidinger, "The
politics of judging" A.B.A. Journal, April 1 1987, p. 52.

who have been in office for a limited period following appointment by the governor, a separate Commission, or the two together.[26] It is highly unlikely that any of these methods will be introduced here,[27] although some have favoured the formal establishment of a Judicial Commission to evaluate and advise on appointments.[28]

5. PROMOTION

The traditional view has been that there is no system of "promotion" of judges. The fear is that holders of judicial office might allow their promotion prospects to affect their decision-making; care might be taken to avoid offending the senior judges or the politicians responsible for making or influencing judicial appointments. Nevertheless, the trend seems to be for judges to be elevated from the Circuit Bench more regularly, and for appointments to the House of Lords and Court of Appeal to be made from the court below. It is uncommon for appointments to be made direct from the Bar to the Court of Appeal[29] or the House of Lords,[30] or direct from the High Court to the House of Lords.[31] Three Lord Chancellors, Maugham, Simonds and Dilhorne, have been appointed Lords of Appeal, but the first two of these were simply reverting to an office previously held. At first, elevation to the Court of Appeal from the High Court carried no increase in salary, although membership of the Privy Council was always conferred. The salary of a Lord Justice is now roughly halfway between that of a High Court judge and a Lord of Appeal, although the differentials are small.[32] Apart from the prestige of a higher judicial office, promotion means that there is no longer the disadvantage of having to spend time away from home on circuit. There is, however, no evidence that judges are affected by "promotion sickness."

[26] The "Missouri plan" is favoured by the A.B.A. A non-partisan Commission selects three candidates, one of whom the governor must then appoint. After one year in office he or she must be approved by the electorate, running unopposed in a separate, non-partisan judicial ballot: Abraham (1986), pp. 38–40.

[27] An argument that the Law Lords, the Lord Chief Justice and the Master of the Rolls, but not the other judges, should be elected, under a plan similar to the "Missouri Plan" is presented by D. Pannick, (1981) 131 N.L.J. 1064.

[28] Report of JUSTICE Sub-Committee on *The Judiciary* (1972), pp. 30–31, 61. This Commission would also act as a complaints tribunal and be involved in the processes of removing judges. The conferral of the power of *appointment* on a Judicial Service Commission is advocated by C. Harlow, in Harlow (ed), *Public Law and Politics* (1986), Chap. 10, and R. Brazier, "Government and the Law" [1989] P.L. 64, 88–91; Brazier also advocates the establishment of Circuit Judicial Committees to advise on the appointment of the lower judiciary. A Law Society discussion document has made similar proposals: (1991) 88 L.S. Gaz., February 20, pp. 6–7.

[29] The only examples have been Slesser L.J. (1929), Scott L.J. (1935) and Somervell L.J. (1946) (all Law Officers), Duke L.J. (1918; Chief Secretary for Ireland 1916–18) and Greene L.J. (1935: leader of the Chancery bar, and subsequently Master of the Rolls). Lord Denning has written that experience as a trial judge is valuable for an appeal judge: *The Family Story* (1981), pp. 169–170.

[30] Eleven examples: five Scots, two English, two Irish. The only two since 1930 have been Lord Reid (1948) and Lord Radcliffe (1949) each of whom was an outstanding judge.

[31] Seven examples: Lords Parker (1913), Tomlin (1929), Wright (1932), Porter (1938), Simonds (1944), Uthwatt (1946) and Wilberforce (1964).

[32] See below, p. 226. The introduction of a differential was recommended by the Top Salaries Review Body, "in recognition of the promotion which is involved in appointment to the Court of Appeal from the High Court Bench:" Report No. 6, Cmnd. 5846, 1974, p. 31.

6. TENURE[33]

Every judge of the Supreme Court, other than the Lord Chancellor, who holds office "during the pleasure" of (in effect) the Prime Minister:

> "shall hold that office during good behaviour, subject to a power of removal by Her Majesty on an address presented to Her by both Houses of Parliament."[34]

Similarly:

> "Every Lord of Appeal in Ordinary shall hold his office during good behaviour but he may be removed from such office on the address of both Houses of Parliament."[35]

These arrangements date from the Act of Settlement 1700.[36] Before then judicial tenure was not regulated by statute. The King appointed on his own terms, which were usually, although not invariably, "during pleasure."[37]

The Stuarts removed or suspended a number of judges who did not conform to their expectations, James II being particularly enthusiastic in this regard.[38] From 1688, William III's appointments were made during good behaviour: the Act of Settlement took away the monarch's right to choose otherwise, although it seems that William was reluctant to see the legal position changed.[39]

It is generally accepted that under these provisions a judge may be removed from office either (1) for breach of the requirement of good behaviour or (2) by the Crown on an address by both Houses of Parliament, irrespective of whether he or she has been of good behaviour. The "address" procedure is, theoretically, neither the exclusive procedure for removal, nor restricted to cases of misbehaviour. In cases of misbehaviour, there are indeed a number of alternative procedures for removing a judge, which do not seem to be excluded by the Supreme Court Act 1981 or any of its antecedents:

(1) Proceedings in the Queen's Bench Division commenced by the writ of *scire facias* for the repeal of the letters patent by which the office was granted.
(2) Proceedings in the Queen's Bench Division for an injunction to restrain the judge from continuing to act in an office to which he or she is no longer entitled.[40]
(3) Conviction for a criminal offence.

---

[33] See Shetreet (1976), pp. 1–12, 85–159; Sir Kenneth Roberts-Wray, *Commonwealth and Colonial Law* (1966), pp. 484–491.

[34] Supreme Court Act 1981, s.11(3).

[35] Appellate Jurisdiction Act 1876, s.6, as amended.

[36] Section 3. This section was to take effect should the arrangements for ensuring the Protestant succession become operative: accordingly, the section came into operation in 1714 with the accession of George I.

[37] See C. H. McIlwain, *Constitutionalism and the Changing World* (1939), pp. 294–307.

[38] See J. H. Baker, *Introduction to Legal History* (3rd ed., 1990), pp. 189–193; A. Havighurst, (1950) 66 L.Q.R. 62, 229; (1953) 69 L.Q.R. 522.

[39] D. Rubini, (1967) 83 L.Q.R. 343.

[40] S. A. de Smith and R. Brazier, *Constitutional and Administrative Law* (6th ed., 1989), p. 380.

In these cases the "misbehaviour" must either be connected with the performance or non-performance of official duties, or, if not so connected, must involve the commission of a criminal offence of moral turpitude. Furthermore, a judge can be removed on any ground by an Act of Parliament, or for "high crimes and misdemeanours" by impeachment.[41] Neither would be used in preference to an address: the latter, in addition, is regarded as obsolete in the United Kingdom.[42]

Today, it is likely that the address procedure would be used in any case where a judge was to be removed, and, further, that this would only be done in a case of misbehaviour,[43] although a rather wider view might be taken of "misbehaviour" for this purpose, in particular to include private immoral conduct.[44] There have been many statements to the effect that this would be the "proper" way to proceed, notwithstanding the other possibilities.[45]

Conviction for a criminal offence does not inevitably lead to resignation or removal from office. Six judges[46] have been convicted of driving with excess alcohol, but have continued in office.

The other methods by which a judge may leave office are:

(1) resignation[47];
(2) reaching the retiring age of 75[48];
(3) under the procedure whereby the Lord Chancellor may remove a judge who is disabled by permanent infirmity from the performance of his or her duties and is incapacitated from resigning his or her office.[49]

If a judge were, for example, to bury a meat cleaver in someone's head the address procedure for removal from office would work swiftly and surely. Judges, however, do not indulge in acts of misbehaviour that are clearly inconsistent with their remaining in office. Where matters are not clear cut, the address procedure is complex, and uncertain in some matters of detail. Charges have been presented on a number of occasions, but only one judge has been removed as a consequence. Sir Jonah Barrington, a judge of the

---

[41] A trial by the House of Lords at the instigation of the Commons. This procedure has not been used since the trials of Warren Hastings (1788) and Lord Melville (1805). Among judges who were impeached were two Lord Chancellors, Bacon (1620) and Macclesfield (1725): see H. Cecil, *Tipping the Scales* (1964), pp. 99–126.

[42] The procedure is not obsolete in the U.S.A.: President Nixon resigned rather than face impeachment.

[43] It seems that the address procedure can be used in cases of incapacity: see Shetreet (1976), p. 274. However, resignation would be secured by informal pressure or a judge would be removed by the Lord Chancellor: see below, n. 49.

[44] *Kenrick's case* (1826): Cecil (1964), pp. 165–170.

[45] See Shetreet (1976), pp. 96–103.

[46] A Lord Justice in 1969, a Circuit judge in 1973, a High Court judge in 1975, two circuit judges in 1985 and a High Court Registrar in 1989: see R. Light (1989) 139 N.L.J. 783. The Registrar was severely reprimanded by the Lord Chancellor: *The Times*, June 17, 1989.

[47] Supreme Court Act 1981, s.11(7); Appellate Jurisdiction Act 1876, s.6.

[48] Supreme Court Act 1981, s.11(2). This limitation did not apply to persons who held office on December 17, 1959 (when a retiring age was introduced by the Judicial Pensions Act 1959): s.11(1). One of those to escape was Lord Denning M.R., who retired in 1982 aged 83. A judge may retire on full pension (half the last annual salary, index-linked) (1) after 15 years service; or (2) after attaining the age of 70; or (3) if he or she is disabled by permanent infirmity: Judicial Pensions Act 1981, s.2.

[49] Supreme Court Act 1981, s.11(8) (9). See A. Paterson, "The Infirm Judge" (1974) 1 B.J.L.S. 83.

High Court of Admiralty in Ireland, was removed in 1830 for the embezzlement of sums of money paid into court.

7. DISCIPLINE AND CRITICISM

The mechanisms for disciplining judges who misbehave are more significant in practice than the procedures for removal. Judges may be criticised in Parliament. An extreme case is that of Lord Westbury L.C., who resigned in 1865 following votes of censure passed in both Houses concerning certain appointments he had made.

Judges are often criticised in the press. "Scurrilous abuse" of a judge may, however, be punished as contempt for "scandalising the court."[50] This head of contempt must be distinguished from that concerned with publications likely to interfere with the administration of justice in particular proceedings, by, for example, influencing juries. The former head was thought to be obsolete in 1899.[51] However, proceedings were taken against the editor of the *Birmingham Daily Argus* for a spirited attack on Darling J. (an "impudent little man in horsehair, a microcosm of conceit and empty headedness").[52] He apologised, and was fined £100, with £25 costs. According to Abel-Smith and Stevens[53] "within a decade the criticism of judicial behaviour which had been so outspoken was replaced in the press by almost unbroken sycophantic praise for the judges." Similar proceedings were taken on a number of occasions in the 1920s and 1930s. Since then, press criticism of the judiciary has become more commonplace, without matching the personal insults expressed by Mr. Gray. Proceedings against Quintin Hogg (as he then was), arising out of criticisms of the Court of Appeal published in *Punch*, were dismissed.[54] Salmon L.J. said[55]:

> "The authority and reputation of our courts are not so frail that their judgments need to be shielded from criticism, even from the criticism of Mr. Quintin Hogg. . . . [N]o criticism of a judgment, however vigorous, can amount to contempt of court, provided it keeps within the limits of reasonable courtesy and good faith."

Judges are from time to time rebuked in appellate courts. Censure may be coupled with the setting aside of a conviction or the reversal of a judgment. Thus, judges have been censured for excessive interruptions,[56] threatening a

---

[50] See S. H. Bailey, D. J. Harris and B. L. Jones, *Civil Liberties: Cases and Materials* (2nd ed., 1985), pp. 297–302; N.V. Lowe, *Borrie and Lowe's Law of Contempt*, (2nd ed., 1983), pp. 226–247; C. J. Miller, *Contempt of Court* (2nd ed., 1989), Chap. 12; C. Walker, "Scandalising in the Eighties" (1985) 101 L.Q.R. 359.

[51] *McLeod* v. *St. Aubyn* [1899] A.C. 549, 561 (a colonial judge was accused of "reducing the judicial character to the level of a clown," and "being narrow, bigoted, vain, vindictive and unscrupulous." The Privy Council held that this did not require committal for contempt).

[52] *R.* v. *Gray* [1900] 2 Q.B. 36. The full passage is printed in 82 L.T. 534. *Cf.* above, p. 216, n. 98. Darling was apparently "rather amused by the vigour of its expression": D. Walker-Smith, *The Life of Lord Darling* (1938), p. 122.

[53] *Lawyers and the Courts* (1967), pp. 126–7.

[54] *R.* v. *Metropolitan Police Commissioner, ex p. Blackburn* (*No. 2*) [1968] 2 Q.B. 150.

[55] *Ibid.* p. 155. Mr. Hogg subsequently became Lord Chancellor as Lord Hailsham of St. Marylebone.

[56] *e.g. Yuill* v. *Yuill* [1945] P. 15; *Jones* v. *N.C.B.* [1957] 2 Q.B. 55. The judge in the latter case was Hallett J., who was seen by the Lord Chancellor and resigned shortly afterwards: Lord Denning, *The Due Process of Law* (1980), pp. 58–62 ("The judge who talked too much"). See generally, A. Samuels, "Judicial Misconduct in the Criminal Trial" [1982] Crim.L.R. 221.

jury,[57] improper behaviour on the Bench,[58] falling asleep,[59] incompetence,[60] and disloyalty to the decisions of superior courts.[61] Lord Hailsham has written that there are judges who become subject to "judge's disease, that is to say a condition of which the symptoms may be pomposity, irritability, talkativeness, proneness to *obiter dicta*, a tendency to take short cuts."[62]

There may be complaints from barristers, solicitors or litigants, either expressed in court or in private to the judge personally, or made in some other quarter. Complaints may be made to the Lord Chief Justice or the Lord Chancellor. They may be channelled through a head of chambers, the Chairman of the Bar Council, the Attorney-General, the Law Society,[63] an M.P., or some other intermediary. There is generally a preference for taking action privately. Confrontations in court between counsel and judge may be to the client's disadvantage; it is impossible to assess the extent to which they may also be, or be feared to be, to the barrister's future disadvantage. The upshot may be correspondence or an interview between the Lord Chancellor and the judge,[64] or even, on occasion, a public rebuke.[65]

It has been doubted whether the informal pressures on judges are sufficient. Over the years there have been a few judges whose conduct has often been criticised, but who have nevertheless remained on the Bench. On the other hand, this small minority seems to have dwindled. The JUSTICE Sub-Committee[66] argued that some form of complaints machinery should be established, probably in the form of a complaints tribunal or judicial commission. Such a reform is unlikely to occur in the foreseeable future, and, on the present evidence, the case for it is not made out.[67] Finally, it must be remembered that criticisms of judges in the popular press are commonly marred by such weaknesses as a failure to report accurately the full facts, a failure to understand basic principles of the conduct of trials and a failure to distinguish defects of the law from the defects of the judge.

---

[57] *R.* v. *McKenna* [1960] 1 O.B. 411 (Stable J. at Nottingham Assizes threatened a jury that if they did not return a verdict within 10 minutes they would be locked up all night. They returned in six minutes with verdicts of guilty, which were quashed on appeal).

[58] *R.* v. *Hircock* [1970] 1 Q.B. 67. The judge in a criminal trial made gestures of impatience, sighed, and several times "observed in a loud voice, 'Oh God,' and then laid his head across his arm and made groaning noises" (p. 71). The court did not condone this conduct but declined to quash the conviction as being unsafe and unsatisfactory.

[59] If the judge thereby misses something of importance: *R.* v. *Edworthy* [1961] Crim.L.R. 325; *R.* v. *Langham* [1972] Crim.L.R. 457.

[60] *Taylor* v. *Taylor* [1970] 2 All E.R. 609.

[61] *Cassell & Co. Ltd.* v. *Broome* [1972] A.C. 1027, below, pp. 380–382.

[62] *The Door Wherein I Went* (1975), p. 255.

[63] It seems that the Bar and the Law Society will only act in cases of misconduct towards barristers and solicitors, respectively: JUSTICE, Sub-Committee Report on *The Judiciary*, pp. 49–50.

[64] Or an interview with the Lord Chief Justice: one such as described by Judge James Pickles in *Straight from the Bench* (1987), pp. 53–57, arising out of his publication of newspaper articles.

[65] *e.g.* the rebuke administered to Judge Pickles by Lord Mackay L.C. for holding a press conference in a pub, and referring to the Lord Chief Justice as a "dinosaur." *Cf. R.* v. *Earnshaw* [1990] Crim.L.R. 53.

[66] *Op. cit.*, pp. 45–61. The case for a Judicial Performance Commission is also made by D. Pannick, *Judges* (1987), pp. 96–104. A Judicial Commission with responsibilities covering the monitoring of sentences, training and complaints has been established in New South Wales by the Judicial Officers Act 1986, criticised by S. Shetreet, (1987) 10 Univ. of N.S.W. L.J. 4.

[67] It was not endorsed by the JUSTICE Committee on *The Administration of the Courts* (1986), Chap. 4.

8. TRAINING[68]

In the late 1970s certain tentative steps were taken to introduce a measure of compulsory training for newly appointed judges. From 1963 onwards a series of conferences and judicial seminars on sentencing were organised by the Lord Chief Justice and the Lord Chancellor's Office. Attendance at these was voluntary. However, a Judicial Studies Board was established in 1979 following the report of a Working Party chaired by Bridge L.J.[69] Since 1981 it has been essential for a recorder or assistant recorder, before first sitting in a criminal case, to have attended a residential induction course (now normally lasting a week) organised by the Board. They are lectured by experienced judges and experts from other disciplines about their duties, the main focus being on sentencing, and they take part in sentencing exercises and a mock trial. Also before sitting on their own they must sit for at least a week (or more if necessary) in court with an experienced Circuit judge and must visit various penal institutions. Voluntary refresher seminars are held for experienced judges, and it is intended that each recorder and Circuit judge will be invited to one such seminar every five years. Additional refresher seminars are organised on a circuit basis and seminars on accountancy principles have been held in conjunction with the Institute of Chartered Accountants.[70] A recent development has been the circulation by the Board to all new assistant recorders of a suggested summing-up structure and to all Circuit judges, recorders and assistant recorders a comprehensive set of specimen directions.[71] A handbook of sentencing guideline cases has been distributed to all Court of Appeal, High Court and Circuit judges, with a smaller version for part-time judges.[72] The Board has also commenced publication of a Bulletin to be distributed to judges, with three issues a year.[73]

From October 1985 the Board has been re-established, with enlarged responsibilities beyond the criminal jurisdiction, namely the provision of training in the civil and family jurisdictions and the supervision of training for magistrates[74] and tribunal chairmen and members.[75] Executive functions are delegated to a Criminal Committee, chaired by a Queen's Bench judge; a Civil and Family Committee, jointly chaired by judges of the Queen's

---

[68] See M. Berlins and C. Dyer, *The Law Machine* (3rd ed., 1989), pp. 68–70; (1983) 147 J.P.N. 466–467; A. Ashworth, *Sentencing and Penal Policy* (1983), pp. 65–67; Judicial Studies Board: report for 1979–82 (H.M.S.O., 1983) and report for 1983–87 (H.M.S.O., 1988).

[69] *Judicial Studies and Information* (H.M.S.O. 1978). The Working Party had received "widely felt and strongly voiced objection" to the use in their working paper of the term "judicial training," on the grounds that "training" might represent a threat to judicial independence, that appointees might resent the implication that they need to be "trained" and that the "public image of the judge" would be impaired. The Working Party accordingly adopted the term "judicial studies" and emphasised that their proposals would not involve "indoctrination" or "conditioning" (*ibid.* pp. 2 and 3). Lord Devlin was caustic in his condemnation of the working paper: *The Judge* (1979), pp. 18–53; *cf.* book review by E. J. Griew, [1980] Crim.L.R. 812.

[70] Judicial Studies Board: Report for 1983–1987, pp. 45–46.

[71] *The Observer*, January 30, 1983 ("Secret guide to stop judges blundering"); L.A.G.Bull., February 1983, p. 7. A revised version was distributed in 1987.

[72] Judicial Studies Board: Report for 1983–1987, p. 45.

[73] (1983) 133 N.L.J. 244.

[74] See above, pp. 190–191.

[75] See above, pp. 204–205.

Bench and Family Divisions; a Magisterial Committee, chaired by a Circuit judge; and a Tribunals Committee, chaired by the President of the Industrial Tribunals for England and Wales.[76] The Civil and Family Committee has begun to establish training arrangements on similar lines as for the criminal jurisdiction, the first priority being induction courses for new deputy district judges and for the 50 per cent. or so of new assistant recorders who intended to sit in civil as well as criminal cases. Guidance notes (for district judges) and Bench notes (for recorders) have been distributed.[77]

There has undoubtedly been a welcome increase in the scope and effectiveness of judicial training. However, as the Board itself makes clear, extra resources in money, manpower and judge time will be required if its activities are to be developed further.[78]

9. INDEPENDENCE[79]

Much importance is attached to the independence of the judiciary. By that is meant independence from improper pressure by the executive, by litigants or by particular pressure groups. Reasons given in support of judicial independence are "(1) that independence is a condition of impartiality and therefore also of fair trials, and (2) that it makes for a separation of powers which enables the courts to check the activities of the other branches of government."[80] As to the first, it has been emphasised that judges must not only be impartial but appear to be impartial. Public confidence is only bolstered by "ostentatious impartiality."[81] As to the second, it has been noted with concern that the public today seem less satisfied that the judges are completely independent of the government in power.[82] An illustration of the dangers that arise when judges are dismissed where their decisions incur the displeasure of the executive is provided by the crisis in Malaysia in 1988.[83]

The appointment and the tenure of judges have already been considered. Party political considerations seem to have been eliminated, although this does not mean that the decisions of judges are not "political" in a wider sense[84]:

---

[76] See Judicial Studies Board: Report for 1983–87, Chap. 2.

[77] Ibid., Chap. 11.

[78] Ibid., Chaps. 6, 9.

[79] See W. Lederman (1956) 36 Can.Bar Rev. 769; G. Borrie (1970) 18 Am.J.Comp.Law 697; and for comparative and international perspectives, S. Shetreet and J. Deschênes, Judicial Independence: The Contemporary Debate (1985).

[80] See T. Eckhoff, (1965) 9 Scandinavian Studies in Law, pp. 11–48.

[81] Ibid. p. 12. It has been argued that this feature has been lacking in the appointment of Scottish judges: see C. M. Campbell, 1973 J.R. 254.

[82] See D. Oliver, "The Independence of the judiciary" (1986) 39 C.L.P. 237 and "Politicians and the Courts" (1988) 41 Parliamentary Affairs 13.

[83] See [1988] N.Z.L.J. 217; F. Narinan, [1988] N.Z.L.J. 266; R. H. Hickling, [1989] P.L. 20; F.A. Trindade, (1990) 106 L.Q.R. 51.

[84] A. Paterson, "Judges: A Political Élite" (1974) 1 B.J.L.S. 118. "Whoever can persuade the members of a society that law is inevitable or to take 'law as a given,' and that the legal interpretation of a particular social situation is the only possible one, controls an important if not vital source of power in that society. In my contention British Judges are in precisely this position and that is why it is legitimate to characterize them as involved in the realm of politics": ibid. p. 129. See also R. J. Wilson, "British Judges as Political Actors" (1973) 1 Int. Journal of Criminology and Penology 197.

"Judges are part of the machinery of authority within the State and as such cannot avoid the making of political decisions."[85]

We consider here some other factors relevant to the independence of the judiciary.

(a) Remuneration

Judges are paid large salaries, which are a charge on the Consolidated Fund and so not subject to an annual vote in Parliament. The current salaries are as follows: Lord Chief Justice: £104,750; Master of the Rolls, Lord of Appeal: £97,000; President of the Family Division, Vice-Chancellor, Lords Justices: £93,000; High Court judges: £84,250.[86] They can be increased, but not reduced, by the Lord Chancellor, with the consent of the Prime Minister as Minister for the Civil Service.[87] From the time salaries became a charge on the Consolidated Fund,[88] they could only be changed by statute, or, between 1965 and 1973, by ministerial order.[89] Under the National Economy Act 1931, the salaries of "persons in His Majesty's service," which term was taken to include the judges, were reduced by 20 per cent. The need to secure the independence of the judiciary was placed at the forefront of their arguments both that the Act did not apply to them as a matter of interpretation, and that it should not apply in principle.[90] The government restored the cuts. This argument has, however, not figured so prominently in the recent reports of the Top Salaries Review Board on judicial salaries, in which more important considerations seem to have been the need to attract barristers with the right qualities and experience and the need to maintain the judges' status in the community. Thus the Board has taken into account both barristers' earnings and the salaries payable to Permanent Secretaries as "cross-checks," although there are no formal links with either. The written answer announcing the 1982 increases stated simply that it is "in the national interest to ensure an adequate supply of candidates of sufficient calibre for appointment to judicial office."[91] Indeed, there have been no allegations of corruption against English judges for some centuries, and it is not plausible that it is the level of salary alone that is responsible. Even attempts to bribe judges are rare.

It is an accepted convention that judges may not hold paid appointments such as directorships, or carry on any profession or business. Indeed, the holders of full-time judicial appointments are now expressly barred from legal practice.[91a] Even the few cases of

---

[85] J. A. G. Griffith, *The Politics of the Judiciary* (3rd ed., 1985), p. 195.
[86] H.C.Deb. Vol. 184, cols. 578–579, January 31, 1991, written answer. In effect from April 1, 1991, subject to staging. These figures implement the recommendations of the Top Salaries Review Body: Report No. 30, Cm. 1413, 1991. As to pensions, see above, p. 221, n. 48.
[87] Supreme Court Act 1981, s.12.
[88] Judges appointed after 1786. There was no change between 1851 and 1954 (Judges' Remuneration Act 1954).
[89] Judges' Remuneration Act 1965.
[90] See Heuston, *Lives*, pp. 513–519; W. Holdsworth, (1932) 48 L.Q.R. 25 and 173 L.T. 336; E. C. S. Wade, (1932) 173 L.T. 246, 267. The judges were "in a mutinous mood": Lord Sankey L.C., quoted by Heuston, *op. cit.*, p. 514.
[91] H.C.Deb. Vol. 23, cols. 257–261, written answer, May 12, 1982.
[91a] Courts and Legal Services Act 1990, s.75 and Sched. 11.

judges taking business appointments on leaving the bench have attracted criticism.[92]

(b) Judges and the legislature

Judges of the Supreme Court and Circuit judges are disqualified from membership of the House of Commons.[93] The judges that are members of the House of Lords may contribute to its debates, but by a convention established comparatively recently do not take part in political controversy.[94] They tend to confine their contributions to technical questions of a legal nature. The position in the twenties was not so clear cut. In 1922 Lord Carson attacked the proposals for the establishment of the Irish Free State. He was rebuked for doing so by his former supporter, Lord Birkenhead L.C., but was defended by others.[95]

(c) Judges and the executive

It is generally accepted that judges other than the Lord Chancellor should not hold ministerial office or sit in the Cabinet. Both Lord Mansfield and Lord Ellenborough served in the Cabinet while Chief Justice of the King's Bench, but both cases attracted much criticism. Lord Reading C.J. performed various executive tasks for the government during the First World War, but that can be regarded as an anomalous exception to a well-established principle, which has indeed been strengthened by the recent practice of making non-political appointments to the position of Lord Chief Justice.

One matter that has caused some controversy is the common practice of using judges as chairmen or members of Royal Commissions, Departmental Committees and Tribunals of Inquiry.[96] Indeed, judges are prominent in the ranks of "the Good and the Great."[97] This is both expected and unexceptionable where "lawyers' law" is concerned. However, the subject matter of an

---

[92] In 1970, Fisher J. resigned at the age of 52 after 2½ years on the Bench in order to join a merchant bank. This provoked some criticism: see (1970) 114 S.J. 593. On the other hand, it was pointed out that a reluctant judge was unlikely to be a good one. The position of Lord Chancellor is arguably different, given the precariousness of office. Both Lord Birkenhead and Lord Kilmuir were criticised for taking business appointments, although the latter declined to draw the pension to which he was entitled. Lord Birkenhead defended his rights to take the pension, but assigned it to the benefit of certain hospitals (see Heuston, *Lives*, pp. 396–8; J. Campbell, *F. E. Smith, First Earl of Birkenhead* (1983), pp. 812–814).

[93] House of Commons Disqualification Act 1975, s.1 and Sched. 1. There is no disqualification applicable to recorders. In 1989 there were 11 recorder/M.P.s.

[94] See generally L. Blom-Cooper and G. Drewry, *Final Appeal* (1972), pp. 196–215.

[95] H.L.Debs. Vol. 49, cols. 686–698, March 21, 1922; 715–727, March 22, 1922 and cols. 931–974 March 29, 1922.

[96] See D. G. T. Williams, *Not in the Public Interest* (1965), pp. 188–191; P. Hillyard, (1971) 6 I.J. (N.S.) 93; G. Zellick, [1972] P.L. 1; T. J. Cartwright, *Royal Commissions and Departmental Committees in Britain* (1975); G. Rhodes, *Committees of Inquiry* (1975); Griffith (1985), Chap. 2.

[97] Judges chaired 118 of the 358 committees between 1945 and 1969: Cartwright (1975), p. 72. There is a list of some 4,500 names of people used for these purposes, which "these days . . . is a very swish affair, all floppy discs and visual display terminals, run by a staff of nine and lubricated by a budget of £250,000 a year" (*The Times*, January 22, 1983, p. 9).

inquiry may well be politically controversial. The judge concerned may be called upon to explain or justify the report, and indeed to argue in public the case for or against reform. The topics covered include public disorders (Red Lion Square,[98] Brixton[99]); security matters (security procedures in the public service,[1] the Vassall case,[2] the Profumo affair,[3] the D Notice affair[4]); mismanagement in the public service (the collapse of the Vehicle and General Insurance Company,[5] the Crown Agents[6]); events in Northern Ireland (disturbances in 1969,[7] interrogation methods,[8] legal procedures for dealing with terrorists,[9] the "Bloody Sunday" deaths in Londonderry,[10] the working of anti-terrorist legislation,[11] and police interrogation procedures[12]); the interception of communications[13]; and industrial disputes (electricity supply,[14] miners,[15] and Grunwick[16]). The appointment of a committee is often thought to be a political delaying tactic or a mechanism for shuffling off responsibility for a controversial decision: whether or not either of these criticisms is in fact true, in a particular case it may be unfortunate for a judge to be associated with them. Moreover, the judge may find himself or herself in the midst of political controversy. He or she may be criticised for producing what is perceived by certain sections of the community, rightly or wrongly, to be a "whitewashing report,"[17] or by the government for not producing such a report.[18] It is arguable that a judge is a suitable person to preside over a process for ascertaining the facts of particular incidents such as the Aberfan disaster and the Summerland fire disaster on the Isle of Man, the fire at Bradford City Football Club and the Hillsborough disaster, where

---

[98] Cmnd. 5919, 1975: Lord Scarman.
[99] Cmnd. 8427, 1981: Lord Scarman (Inquiry under the Police Act 1964).
[1] Cmnd. 1681, 1962: Lord Radcliffe (Departmental Committee). The Security Commission is also headed by a judge; the function of this standing commission, first set up in 1964, is to investigate at the Prime Minister's request, breaches of security in the public service, and to report and advise generally on security arrangements.
[2] Cmnd. 2009, 1963: Lord Radcliffe (Tribunal of Inquiry).
[3] Cmnd. 2152, 1963: Lord Denning. See Lord Denning, *The Due Process of Law* (1980), pp. 67–73; "It was a best-seller": *ibid.* p. 68.
[4] Cmnd. 3309, 1967: Lord Radcliffe (Committee of Privy Counsellors).
[5] 1971–72 H.C. 133: James J. (Tribunal of Inquiry).
[6] 1981–82 H.C. 364: Croom-Johnson J. (Tribunal of Inquiry).
[7] Cmnd. 566 (N.I.), 1972: Scarman J. (Tribunal of Inquiry).
[8] Cmnd. 4801, 1972: Lord Parker (Committee of Privy Counsellors).
[9] Cmnd. 5185, 1972: Lord Diplock (Departmental Committee).
[10] 1971–72 H.C. 220: Lord Widgery C.J. (Tribunal of Inquiry).
[11] Cmnd. 5847, 1975: Lord Gardiner (Departmental Committee).
[12] Cmnd. 7497, 1979: Judge Bennett (Departmental Committee).
[13] Cmnd. 283, 1957: Birkett L.J. (Committee of Privy Counsellors).
[14] Cmnd. 4594, 1971: Lord Wilberforce (Court of Inquiry under the Industrial Courts Act 1919).
[15] Cmnd. 4903, 1972: Lord Wilberforce (Court of Inquiry).
[16] Cmnd. 6922, 1977: Scarman L.J. (Court of Inquiry).
[17] *e.g.* the adverse reaction to Lord Widgery's report on the Londonderry shootings: K. Boyle, T. Hadden and P. Hillyard, *Law and State* (1975), pp. 126–129.
[18] *e.g.* the report of the Nyasaland Commission of Enquiry led by Devlin J. (H. Macmillan, *Riding the Storm* (1971), pp. 736–8); and the refusal of Harold Wilson to accept the Radcliffe Report on the D Notice Affair: see the White Paper on the D Notice System (Cmnd. 3312, 1967).

there are no political overtones. Even here, however, there can be problems.[19]

It is accepted that a judge should not become associated with party political research committees.[20]

A stricter view of the permissible range of extra-judicial activities is taken in the United States of America, where the separation of powers is formally entrenched as a constitutional principle. Even the exceptional cases such as the appointment of Justice Murphy as prosecutor at the Nuremberg trials and Chief Justice Warren to investigate the assassination of President Kennedy were controversial.[21]

Analogous problems have arisen in respect of the appointment of judges as members of the Restrictive Practices Court and the short-lived National Industrial Relations Court (N.I.R.C.). The former court determines whether restrictive agreements are contrary to the public interest.[22] Such determinations involve considerations that are political and economic rather than legal. The functions of the N.I.R.C. were more obviously judicial, but the context was that of industrial relations, where it was, and is, highly controversial whether orthodox legal mechanisms are appropriate in principle and workable. Its successor, the Employment Appeal Tribunal, has inherited its less controversial functions.

Finally, a matter of growing controversy is the relationship between the judiciary and the executive in the administration of the courts. Sir Nicolas Browne-Wilkinson in a public lecture[23] expressed concern that the executive, through the mechanisms for controlling public expenditure, was increasingly taking decisions that affected the conduct of cases in court, without consulting the judges. Indeed there was no formal machinery for the resolution of disputes between the judges and court administrators, below the level of the Lord Chancellor. As a result, the criterion of value for money was not properly balanced against the interests of justice.[24]

(d) Public statements by and about judges

Judges are expected to refrain from making party political statements; it is sometimes said that they should refrain from criticising the policy of Acts of Parliament, but that seems too restrictive. Reasoned, responsible criticism

[19] In New Zealand, Mahon J. was appointed as sole member of a Royal Commission to inquire into the Mt. Erebus aircraft disaster. Certain statements in the report were held by the Supreme Court to have been made in excess of jurisdiction, and an order for costs against the airline was quashed: Re Erebus Royal Commission (No. 2) [1981] 1 N.Z.L.R. 618. Mahon J. resigned: see [1982] N.Z.L.J. 37. An appeal to the Privy Council was dismissed: Re Erebus Royal Commission [1984] A.C. 808; see K. Keith, [1984] N.Z.L.J. 35; D. Currie, [1984] N.Z.L.J. 43; A Beck, "Trial of a High Court Judge for Defamation" (1987) 103 L.Q.R. 461.

[20] Lord Avonside, a judge of the Court of Session, resigned from a Conservative Committee on the constitutional position in Scotland following public criticism, e.g. by the Lord Advocate: see The Times, July 30, 1968, August 8, 1968; R. J. Wilson, "British Judges as Political Actors" (1973) 1 Int. Journal of Criminology and Penology, 197, 199–20.

[21] See A. T. Mason, (1953) 67 Harv.L.R. 193; (1970) 35 Law and Contemporary Problems (Symposium).

[22] See above, pp. 86–88.

[23] "The Independence of the Judiciary in the 1980s" [1988] P.L. 44. See also I. R. Scott, (1988) 7 C.J.Q. 103. Similar concerns have been expressed by Sir John Donaldson: The Times, April 13, 1987.

[24] One possible solution was the establishment of a collegiate body of judges responsible for the management of certain functions of court administration.

is acceptable: disparaging remarks are not. Thus, in 1978, Melford Stevenson J. was reprimanded by the Lord Chancellor, Lord Elwyn-Jones, for referring to the Sexual Offences Act 1967 as a "buggers' charter."[25] Judges were formerly inhibited by the so-called "Kilmuir rules"[26] from broadcasting on radio or television (except on special occasions, such as charitable appeals). However, these "rules" were relaxed by Lord Mackay on assuming office, judges now being left to make their own decisions, after such consultation as they may think necessary.[27]

Members of the executive are similarly expected to refrain from attacking judges, unless provoked. It is a rule of parliamentary practice that reflections must not be cast upon a judge's character or motives except on a substantive motion specifically criticising him or her or leading to an address for his or her removal, although reasoned arguments that a judge has made a mistake or was wrong are acceptable.[28] Matters that are *sub judice* cannot be discussed, unless they relate to a ministerial decision or concern issues of national importance, and discussion would not prejudice the proceedings.[29]

(e) Judicial immunity from suit[30]

At common law, every judge of a superior or inferior court is immune from liability in damages for any act that is either (1) within jurisdiction or (2) honestly believed to be within jurisdiction.[31] The protection in (1) is available even where the judge is malicious.[32] He or she is also protected by absolute privilege in the law of defamation. Every judge:

> "should be able to do his work in complete independence and free from fear. He should not have to turn the pages of his books with trembling fingers, asking himself: 'If I do this, shall I be liable in damages?' "[33]

The rules also prevent the relitigation of the issues determined by the court.[34]

---

[25] *The Times*, July 6, 1978.

[26] A letter from the then Lord Chancellor, Lord Kilmuir, to the Director-General of the B.B.C. in 1955, set out at [1986] P.L. 384–386. The Lord Chancellor disclaimed any disciplinary jurisdiction over judges, but stated that it was generally undesirable for judges to broadcast (it would, for example, "be inappropriate for the Judiciary to be associated with any series of talks or anything which could fairly be interpreted as entertainment . . .").

[27] See A. W. Bradley, [1988] P.L. at p. 166.

[28] *Erskine May's Parliamentary Practice* (21st ed., 1989), pp. 379–380; H.C.Deb. Vol. 865, cols. 1092, 1144, 1200, December 4, 1973 (criticisms of Sir John Donaldson as President of the National Industrial Relations Court; H.C.Deb. Vol. 935, cols. 1381–4, July 19, 1977; H.C.Deb. Vol 34, cols. 123–6, 285–6, December 14, 15, 1982 (description by Mrs. Thatcher of a 12 month sentence for the rape of a 6 year old girl as "incomprehensible" ruled to be in order).

[29] *Erskine May*, pp. 377–379. H.C.Deb. Vol. 681 cols. 1416–17, July 23, 1963; H.C.Deb. Vol. 839 col. 1627, June 28, 1972; H.C.Deb. Vol. 916 cols. 882–4, July 29, 1976.

[30] See M. Brazier, [1976] P.L. 397.

[31] *Sirros* v. *Moore* [1975] Q.B. 118, Lord Denning M.R. and Ormrod L.J. Buckley L.J. held that if an act were outside jurisdiction a judge would only be immune if he or she had so acted as a result of a reasonable mistake of fact. See also *Rajski* v. *Powell* (1987) 11 N.S.W.L.R. 522. (The attempt of majority of the court in *Sirros* v. *Moore* to equate the position of judges of inferior and superior courts has been disapproved: see above, pp. 193–194).

[32] *Anderson* v. *Gorrie* [1895] 1 Q.B. 668.

[33] *Per* Lord Denning M.R., in *Sirros* v. *Moore*, *supra*, at p. 136.

[34] *Cf.* the immunity of advocates, above, pp. 162–166.

Deliberate misconduct such as corruption could lead to prosecution for a criminal offence[35] and removal from office.

(f) Disqualification for interest or bias

A judge is disqualified from hearing a case in which he or she has a direct pecuniary or proprietary interest, or in circumstances where there is a reasonable suspicion or a real likelihood that he or she would be biased.[36] This rule applies to judges of the superior courts as much as it does to magistrates and tribunal members. Indeed, the leading case on disqualifying interests[37] concerned decrees made by Lord Cottenham L.C. in favour of a canal company in which he held shares. The House of Lords set aside these decrees. Lord Campbell emphasised that:

> "No one can suppose that Lord Cottenham could be in the remotest degree influenced by the interest . . . but . . . it is of the last importance that the maxim that no man is to be a judge in his own cause should be held sacred."[38]

The matters that may give rise to a suspicion or likelihood of bias include personal hostility, friendship, family relationship or acquaintance with a party or with a witness. The parties may waive the objection. Where a judge is not technically disqualified, he or she may well refuse to act in a case where one of the parties raises an objection. Objections, however, are not commonly made. Lord Denning M.R. withdrew from a case concerning the Church of Scientology of California as the Church felt that "there was an unconscious influence operating adversely to it" in Lord Denning's previous judgments.[39] The Church had been before Lord Denning's Court on eight previous occasions, and noted that his Lordship had doubted whether it was right to call scientology a "religion" and whether the Church was entitled to call itself a church. Shaw L.J. said that it was almost impossible to resist the application for the appeal to be transferred "even though the grounds were not merely slight but non-existent." Conversely, no objection was taken to Lord Denning's acting in a case concerning the Church Commissioners, he being one of the Commissioners,[40] or to the fact that all the members of the Court of Appeal hearing the appeal in the London Transport "fares" case were both users of public transport in London and London ratepayers.[41]

---

[35] Cf. R. v. Llewellyn-Jones [1967] 3 All E.R. 225 (misbehaviour in a public office: misuse of funds by a county court registrar).

[36] See J. M. Evans, de Smith's Judicial Review of Administrative Action (4th ed., 1980), Chap. 5; P. Jackson, Natural Justice (2nd ed., 1979), Chap. 2; R. Cranston, [1979] P.L. 237.

[37] Dimes v. Grand Junction Canal Proprietors (1852) 3 H.L. Cas. 759.

[38] Ibid. p. 793. Dimes was a "crazy attorney" who had "embarked upon interminable litigation" against the Canal company. Cottenham died before judgment was given in the House of Lords: "it was a common belief that Dimes had killed Lord Cottenham": J.B. Atlay, The Victorian Chancellors (1906), Vol. 1, p. 415.

[39] Ex p. Church of Scientology of California, The Times, February 21, 1978. Lord Lane C.J. stood down in Moss v. McLachlan [1985] 149 J.P. 167: Pannick (1987), p. 41.

[40] Hanson v. Church Commissioners [1978] Q.B. 823, 831. The actual management of the estate of the Church Commissioners was vested in a separate board of governors. Various "dignitaries," including the Lord Chief Justice, the Master of the Rolls and the Lord Mayor of London were "merely titular commissioners."

[41] Bromley London Borough Council v. Greater London Council [1983] 1 A.C. 768, 771–77. For an argument that the Lord Chancellor ought not to sit in public law cases, see A. W. Bradley, [1988] P.L. 165.

10. THE JUDICIAL FUNCTION

In the course of legal proceedings, judges may be called upon to perform one
or more of the following tasks: presiding over a trial (*e.g.* controlling the
course of proceedings; keeping order; ruling on questions of the admissibility of evidence; deciding when to adjourn for lunch); presiding over an
appeal[42]; determining a disputed question of fact; determining a disputed
question of law; directing a jury on the evidence and the law; deciding what
remedy to award or punishment to impose; and giving reasons for such
decisions as are theirs. With the marked decline in the use of the jury in civil
cases over the last 60 years, the judicial task of determining disputed
questions of fact has correspondingly grown in significance. When considering the "nature of the judicial function," however, it is usual to concentrate
on the ways in which judges approach the determination of disputed
questions of law. Furthermore, attention is directed in particular to the
appeal courts,[43] as a higher proportion of time is spent on such questions, as
the arguments are more likely to be evenly balanced, and because the
decisions of courts at the top of the hierarchy carry most weight. In Chapters
6 and 7 we consider the principles that are applicable to the interpretation of
statutes and the handling of precedent cases. We shall see that there is
considerable room for flexibility. Moreover, even where there is no directly
relevant precedent and no applicable legislation the judge must still give an
answer to any legal questions that arise.

The extent to which a judge is prepared to innovate depends upon the
respective weight attached to a number of factors[44]: the need for stability and
certainty in law (which suggests consistency with established principles and
precedents); the wish to do justice as between the parties; the need not to
usurp the role of Parliament; the need to justify a decision by reasoned
argument and not merely compromise between the parties; and the need to
base a decision on at least one of the issues raised by the parties. Differences
in approach reflect different weight attached to these factors—in particular
the first two.

Debates as to the nature of the judicial function have taken place in two
different, but related fields: legal theory and socio-legal studies. Important
contributions to the theoretical debate have come from some of our leading
judges, speaking both extra-judicially and in decided cases. The judges' own
perceptions of the proper judicial role are equally of importance as one of
the important influences on judicial decision-making identified in empirical
studies.

Historically, the theory that held sway for the longest time was the
"declaratory theory" expounded by William Blackstone and others. Blackstone wrote[45] that:

---

[42] The president of an appellate court can have a significant influence on the course of
proceedings, although his or her role is more muted than that of a trial judge sitting alone: see
above, p. 93, n. 64.

[43] There have been three studies of the House of Lords: L. Blom-Cooper and G. Drewry, *Final
Appeal* (1972); R. Stevens, *Law and Politics* (1979); A. Paterson, *The Law Lords* (1982).
The nature of the judicial function is analysed in J. Bell, *Policy Arguments in Judicial
Decisions* (1983).

[44] See Paterson (1982), pp. 122–127.

[45] *Commentaries*, Vol. 1, pp. 69–70.

"it is an established rule to abide by former precedents, where the same points come again in litigation ... [the judge] being sworn to determine, not according to his private sentiments: he being sworn to determine, not according to his own private judgment, but according to the known laws and customs of the land: not delegated to pronounce a new law, but to maintain and expound the old one. Yet this rule admits of exception, where the former determination is most evidently contrary to reason; much more if it be clearly contrary to divine law. But even in such cases the subsequent judges do not pretend to make a new law, but to vindicate the old one from misrepresentation. For if it be found that the former decision is manifestly absurd or unjust, it is declared not that such a sentence was *bad law*, but that it was *not law*, that is, not the established custom of the realm, as has been erroneously determined."

Thus the role of the judge is to declare what the law is, not to make it. This theory was not easy to square with the unconcealed law-making activities of particular judges such as Lord Mansfield,[46] and was abused by writers such as Bentham.[47] Nevertheless, judges in the nineteenth and early twentieth centuries generally maintained (with increasing enthusiasm) the position that their function was not to make law and, indeed, that they were not concerned with the policy implications of their rulings.[48] However, this view was held less strongly in the House of Lords than in the lower courts, some of the Law Lords, with equity or Scottish backgrounds, being more concerned with principles than precedent and more likely to advert to the likely consequences of their decisions.

After 1912, the Law Lords, who tended now to be chosen from the professional judiciary, with less regard for political affiliation:

"exhibited an increasing tendency to articulate a declaratory theory of law and to insist that the judicial function, even in the final appeal court, was primarily the formalistic or mechanical one of restating existing doctrines."[49]

At the same time there were still some judges, such as Lord Atkin and Lord Wright, who were prepared to develop private law doctrines significantly while maintaining the facade of the declaratory theory. However, there followed what Stevens terms the "era of substantive formalism" in the House of Lords:

[46] Chief Justice the King's Bench, 1756–1788. See C. H. S. Fifoot, *Lord Mansfield* (1936).
[47] *A Comment on the Commentaries* (eds. J. H. Burns and H. L. A. Hart, 1977), pp. 192–206. Bentham's objections were based in part on his opposition to theories of "natural law." Moreover, he disapproved of law-making by judges, taking the view that this was a matter for Parliament.
[48] See, *e.g.* Parke B. in *Egerton* v. *Brownlow* (1853) 4 H.L.C. 1, 124: "It is the province of the statesman, and not the lawyer, to discuss, and of the legislature to determine, what is the best for the public good, and to provide for it by proper enactments. It is the province of the judge to expound the law only; the written from the statutes: the unwritten or common law from the decisions of our predecessors and of our existing courts, from text-writers of acknowledged authority, and upon the principles to be clearly deduced from them by sound reason and just inference; not to speculate upon what is the best, in his opinion, for the advantage of the community."
[49] Stevens (1979), p. 196.

"For the 1940s and for much of the 1950s there were no obvious signs that the Law Lords had developed rules out of broader principles of the common law or the liberal state. Indeed, there was virtually no acceptance of an element of discretion, let alone a utilitarian balancing of interests. The process, at best fell into Karl Llewellyn's category of judicial formalism, with opinions written 'in deductive form with an air of expression of single-line inevitability.'[50] At worst, the process was a restatement of the declaratory theory in such extreme form that it denied any purpose for a second appeal court. Legal rationality became an end in itself. The literal meaning of words was to be the only criterion of statutory interpretation."[51]

Deference to the executive in public law cases was to be expected in wartime: strong judicial challenges to the Labour government elected in 1945 with a large majority would obviously have been unwise. This approach was associated particularly with Lord Jowitt, the Labour Lord Chancellor, and Lord Simonds, a Law Lord between 1944 and 1962, apart from his period as Lord Chancellor from 1951 to 1954. A few judges stood out against this approach, notably Lord Denning,[52] but to little avail. The only developments could come with the application of established principles to novel factual situations.

Since the mid-1950s the position has changed. It has become generally accepted by the Law Lords that they may properly exercise a limited law-making function.[53] Lord Radcliffe argued that it was best if judges went about this task "on the quiet."[54]

"Would anyone now deny that judicial decisions are a creative, not merely an expository, contribution to the law? There are no means by which they can be otherwise, so rare is the occasion upon which a decision does not involve choice between two admissible alternatives. . . . We cannot run the risk of finding the archetypal image of the judge confused in men's minds with the very different image of the legislator. . . . [T]he image of the judge, objective, impartial, erudite and experienced declarer of the law that is, lies deeper in the consciousness of civilisation than the image of the lawmaker, propounding what are avowedly new rules of human conduct. . . . Personally, I think that judges will serve the public interest better if they keep quiet about their legislative function. No doubt they will discreetly contribute to changes in the law, because . . . they cannot do otherwise, even if they would. The judge who shows his hand, who advertises what he is about, may indeed show that he is a strong spirit, unfettered by the past; but I doubt very much whether he is not doing more harm to general confidence in the law as a constant, safe in the hands of the judges than he is doing to

---

[50] Karl Llewellyn, *The Common Law Tradition* (1960), p. 38.
[51] Stevens (1979), pp. 319–320.
[52] See below, p. 236.
[53] See generally A. Paterson, *The Law Lords* (1982).
[54] See Lord Radcliffe, *Not in Feather Beds* (1968), pp. 265–277. Professor Atiyah has argued that most of the judges "would prefer to shelter behind the declaratory theory in public, and to confine discussion of the nature and use of the creative judicial function amongst the *cognoscenti*" (1980) 15 Israel L.R. 346, 360.

the law's credit as a set of rules nicely attuned to the sentiments of the day."[55]

The dominant influence in the House of Lords in this period was Lord Reid. In his well-known address entitled "The Judge as Law Maker" he swiftly disposed of the declaratory theory:

"We do not believe in fairy tales any more. So we must accept the fact that for better or worse judges do make law, and tackle the question how do they approach their task and how they should approach it."[56]

Where public opinion was sharply divided, whether or not on party lines, no judge should lean to one side or the other if it can be avoided; if it cannot:

". . . we must play safe [and] decide the case on the preponderance of existing authority. Parliament is the right place to settle issues which the ordinary man regards as controversial."[57]

It was also improper for judges to disregard or innovate on settled law in areas where people rely on the certainty of the law in settling their affairs, in particular in making contracts or settlements. A problem might be too complex for it to be appropriate for the judges to change some aspect of it: the only proper way forward would be for there to be legislation following a wide survey of the whole field.[58] Nevertheless, there was considerable scope for judges to mould the development of the common law, which should be done having regard to "common sense, legal principle and public policy in that order."[59] The judges did not have so free a hand when interpreting statutes as when dealing with the common law.

In the late 1950s and early 1960s there were some indications that the House of Lords was taking a freer attitude to precedents. These led to the Practice Statement in 1966 in which the Law Lords announced that they would no longer regard themselves as bound by their own previous decisions.[60] Since then, the criteria for exercising the power to overrule have been analysed in some detail. Lord Reid's views have been especially influential,[61] as they have on the wider issues concerning judicial law-making. Similarly, in the field of statutory interpretation the judges have shown a greater inclination to look at the context of the words in a statute, rather than to adopt a narrow literal approach.

Paterson shows that of the 19 Law Lords who were active between 1967 and 1973 at least 12 considered that the Law Lords had an obligation to develop the common law to meet changing social conditions. An even greater proportion of the sample of barristers interviewed by him shared this view, as did at least three of the six Law Lords appointed between 1973 and

---

[55] Radcliffe (1968), pp. 271–272, 273.
[56] (1972) 12 J.S.P.T.L. 22. For other important contributions to the debate see Diplock L.J., "The Courts as Legislators," in B. W. Harvey (ed.), *The Lawyer and Justice* (1978), p. 263; Lord Edmund-Davies, "Judicial Activism" (1975) 28 C.L.P. 1; Lord Devlin, *The Judge* (1981), Chap. 1.
[57] (1972) 12 J.S.P.T.L. 22, 23.
[58] See *Myers* v. *D.P.P.* [1965] A.C. 1001, 1022.
[59] (1972) 12 J.S.P.T.L. 22, 25.
[60] See A. Paterson, *The Law Lords* (1982), pp. 143–153, and below, pp. 392–397.
[61] See Paterson (1982), pp. 153–169, and below, p. 396.

1979.[62] Ten of 11 Law Lords interviewed accepted that they ought to be concerned with the possible social and legal consequences of their decisions, at least within the acknowledged limitations of the information available to them.[63] A majority of the Law Lords considered that there were cases coming to the Lords to which there was no single correct solution on the basis of existing legal rules and principles, and in which they had a measure of choice.[64]

In the same period, the Court of Appeal was dominated by Lord Denning M.R., who showed a greater preference for innovation than the Law Lords, albeit coupled with varying success in persuading colleagues in the Court of Appeal to agree with him.[65]

The approach of appellate judges varies according to the context. For example, continued importance has been attached by the House of Lords to the "certainty" factor in commercial and property cases, and, to a lesser extent, in criminal law cases. By contrast, there has been a marked extension of liability in such aspects of the tort of negligence as negligent misstatement,[66] omissions,[67] nervous shock,[68] economic loss,[69] and injury to trespassers,[70] although in some of these areas, most notably economic loss, the extension of liability has been followed by retrenchment.[71] In public law, there has been a whole series of cases in which the courts have analysed, refined and sometimes extended the grounds upon which administrative and judicial decisions of government institutions can be challenged under the *ultra vires* doctrine. In some of these, the challenges have been successful.[72]

---

[62] Paterson (1982), pp. 173–4. But note the view expressed by Lord Scarman in *McLoughlin* v. *O'Brian* [1983] 1 A.C. 410, that where "principle" requires a decision which entails a degree of "policy risk", the court's function is to adjudicate according to "principle," leaving "policy curtailment" to Parliament. The policy issue as to where to draw the line in "nervous shock" cases is "not justiciable. The problem is one of social, economic and financial policy. The considerations relevant to a decision are not such as to be capable of being handled within the limits of the forensic process": pp. 430–431. See, *contra*, Lord Edmund-Davies, pp. 427–428.

[63] Paterson (1982), pp. 177–8.

[64] *Ibid*. pp. 192–5. This runs counter to the theory developed by R.M. Dworkin that there is a right answer in all hard cases and that the judges have no discretion to make law: *Taking Rights Seriously* (1977); "No Right Answer" in P. Hacker and J. Raz (eds.), *Law, Morality and Society* (1977); J. W. Harris, *Legal Philosophies* (1980), Chap. 14; Bell (1983), Chap. VIII.

[65] See Stevens (1979), pp. 488–505; Lord Denning *The Discipline of Law* (1979), Parts 1 and 7.

[66] *Hedley Byrne & Co.* v. *Heller & Partners* [1964] A.C. 465.

[67] *Home Office* v. *Dorset Yacht Co.* [1970] A.C. 1004; *Anns* v. *London Borough of Merton* [1978] A.C. 728.

[68] *McLoughlin* v. *O'Brian* [1983] 1 A.C. 410.

[69] *Junior Books Ltd.* v. *Veitchi Co. Ltd.* [1983] 1 A.C. 520.

[70] *British Railways Board* v. *Herrington* [1972] A.C. 877.

[71] See, *e.g. Leigh and Sillavan Ltd.* v. *Aliakmon Shipping Co. Ltd.* [1986] A.C. 785; *Yuen Kun Yeu* v. *Att.-Gen. of Hong Kong* [1988] A.C. 175; *D. & F. Estates Ltd.* v. *Church Commissioners for England* [1989] A.C. 177; *Murphy* v. *Brentwood District Council* [1990] 3 W.L.R. 414 (over-ruling *Anns*).

[72] *e.g. Ridge* v. *Baldwin* [1964] A.C. 40 (dismissal of a chief constable held void for breach of natural justice); *Anisminic Ltd.* v. *Foreign Compensation Commission* [1969] 2 A.C. 147 (decision of the Commission struck down for misinterpretation of the relevant legislation notwithstanding a statutory clause purporting to exclude judicial review); *Padfield* v. *Minister of Agriculture* [1968] A.C. 997 and *Laker Airways* v. *Department of Trade* [1977] Q.B. 643 (ministerial decisions held to be abuses of discretion); *Bromley London Borough Council* v. *Greater London Council* [1983] 1 A.C. 768 (substantial cuts in fares held to be *ultra vires*).

In others, the judges have shown restraint in circumstances where it was not obvious why restraint was any more appropriate.[73]

It is also interesting to contrast the willingness of Sir Robert Megarry V.-C. to extend the field of liability in negligence for economic loss[74] with his unwillingness to create an "altogether new right" in a case where it was claimed that there was a right to hold a telephone conversation in the privacy of one's home without molestation[75]:

> "No new right in the law, fully-fledged with all the appropriate safeguards, can spring from the head of a judge deciding a particular case: only Parliament can create such a right. . . . The wider and more indefinite the right claimed, the greater the undesirability of holding that such a right exists."[76]

There are some apparently formidable arguments in favour of judicial restraint in law-making. The making of new law through the legislative process[77] rather than judicially is often said to be more in accordance with democratic theory[78] and is more likely to be based on a proper examination of all the relevant information. English civil procedure generally prevents anyone but the parties to litigation giving evidence[79] and enables the parties to choose what evidence to present. Moreover, there are difficulties in presenting *evidence* as distinct from *argument* about the possible social and economic implications of decisions. Conspicuous creativity in judicial law making is difficult to square with the "ostentatious impartiality" that is also regarded as desirable.[80] The judges have no written constitution to look to as a source of power.[81]

A more pragmatic reason sometimes advanced in favour of restraint is that:

> "if people and Parliament come to think that the judicial power is to be confined by nothing other than the judge's sense of what is right (or, as Selden put it, by the length of the Chancellor's foot), confidence in the judicial system will be replaced by fear of it becoming uncertain and arbitrary in its application. Society will then be ready for Parliament to

---

[73] *R.* v. *Secretary of State for the Home Department, ex p. Zamir* [1980] A.C. 930 (but *cf. R.* v. *Secretary of State for the Home Department, ex p. Khawaja* [1984] A.C. 74); *Bushell* v. *Secretary of State for the Environment* [1981] A.C. 75.

[74] *Ross* v. *Caunters* [1980] Ch. 297.

[75] *Malone* v. *Metropolitan Police Commissioner (No. 2)* [1979] Ch. 344.

[76] *Ibid.* pp. 372, 373. Compare also the extension of police powers of *seizure* by the Court of Appeal in *Chic Fashions Ltd.* v. *Jones* [1968] 2 Q.B. 299 and *Ghani* v. *Jones* [1970] 1 Q.B. 693 with the refusal of the court to create a new common law power of *search*: *McLorie* v. *Oxford* [1982] Q.B. 1290.

[77] See Chap. 5.

[78] But see Atiyah, (1980) 15 Israel L.R. 362–365.

[79] The rules could, of course, be changed. By contrast, in the United States interest groups are much more able to institute litigation, or to present arguments in cases involving other parties.

[80] See above, p. 225.

[81] Although here it should be noted that the power of judicial review exercised by the Supreme Court in the United States is not expressly created by the Constitution, but is itself judge-made: see *Marbury* v. *Madison* (1803) 1 Cranch 137.

cut the power of the judges. Their power to do justice will become more restricted by law than it need be, or is today."[82]

Nevertheless, restraint is not the same as complete withdrawal from the field. "Law reform" does not rank high in the list of priorities in the struggle for a place in the legislative timetable: if one always waited for Parliament, one would often wait in vain.

In his book, *The Politics of the Judiciary*[83] Professor Griffith argues that the discussion about how creative judges should be:

> "has been and is a somewhat unreal discussion.... What is lacking ... is any clear and consistent relationship between the general pronouncements of judges on this matter of creativity and the way they conduct themselves in court."[84]

Moreover, the appellate judges:

> "have by their education and training and the pursuit of their profession as barristers, acquired a strikingly homogenous collection of attitudes, beliefs and principles, which to them represents the public interest.... The judicial conception of the public interest ... is three-fold. It concerns first, the interests of the State (including its moral welfare) and the preservation of law and order broadly interpreted; secondly, the protection of property rights; and thirdly, the promotion of certain political views normally associated with the Conservative Party."[85]

They are thus concerned to preserve and protect the existing order, to serve the prevailing political and economic forces, this being generally true of all societies today, whether capitalistic or communist. This is not regarded by Griffith as a matter for recrimination: his main concern is simply to dispel the myth that the judges are "neutral."

In relation to Griffith's view that the appellate judges have acquired a homogenous collection of attitudes, Lord Devlin commented[86]:

> "Since he is writing of men in their sixties and seventies whose working life has given them a common outlook on many questions, by no means all political, I have very little doubt that he is right. I have very little doubt either that the same might be written of most English institutions, certainly of all those which like the law are not of a nature to attract the crusading or rebellious spirit."

---

[82] *Per* Lord Scarman in *Duport Steels Ltd.* v. *Sirs* [1980] 1 All E.R. 529, 551. When Roger Parker Q.C. made a similar prediction in his submissions to the Court of Appeal in *Congreve* v. *Home Office* [1976] Q.B. 629, Lord Denning M.R. stated "We trust that this was not said seriously, but only as a piece of advocate's licence." Mr. Parker subsequently apologized if anything he said had sounded like a threat. (See *The Times*, December 6 and 9, 1975).

[83] (3rd. ed., 1985.) For similar studies of particular areas see J. I. Reynolds, "Statutory Covenant of Fitness and Repair" (1974) 37 M.L.R. 377 (and the rejoinder by M. J. Robinson, (1976) 39 M.L.R. 43); J. Hackney, "The Politics of the Chancery" (1981) 34 C.L.P. 113.

[84] p. 185. Paterson, *The Law Lords* (1982), pp. 187–189, argues that the Law Lords have been more consistent than Griffith suggests.

[85] *Ibid*. pp. 198, 199.

[86] (1978) 41 M.L.R. 501, 505–506.

However, he suggested that whether one agrees that the application of the law has been distorted depended on whether one:

"looks at them from right or from the left. . . . To my mind none of the evidence, general or specific adds much to the inherent probability that men and women of a certain age will be inclined to favour the *status quo*."[87]

He, and others, have, for instance, pointed out that in many of the cases discussed by Griffith there has been a division of opinion both between the Court of Appeal and the House of Lords, and within each court.[88]

Griffith does not suggest that anything can be done to change judicial attitudes. Lord Devlin notes that for a known bias allowance can be made:

"[W]here novel measures are imposed by a minister or by Parliament, they must be expressed in language which is emphatic enough and clear enough to penetrate the bias against them of those who are set in their ways: it is no use praying for the rejuvenation of the elderly."[89]

What these contributions to the debate do seem to suggest is that caution should be used in contemplating any dramatic extension of the powers of the judiciary, such as by the creation of a Bill of Rights on the American pattern with entrenched guarantees of civil liberties, expressed in general language, which override both legislation and administative action. Moreover, one can be a little sceptical about claims such as those of Lord Denning[90]:

"May not the Judges themselves sometimes abuse or misuse their power? It is their duty to administer and apply the law of the land. If they should divert it or depart from it—and do so knowingly—they themselves would be guilty of a misuse of power. So we come up against Juvenal's question, '*Sed quis custodiet ipsos custodes?*' (But who is to guard the guards themselves?). . . . Suppose a future Prime Minister should seek to pack the Bench with judges of his own extreme political colour. Would they be tools in his hand? To that I answer 'No.' Every judge on his appointment discards all politics and all prejudices. You need have no fear. The Judges of England have always in the past—and always will—be vigilant in guarding our freedoms. Someone must be trusted. Let it be the Judges."

---

[87] *Ibid.* pp. 507, 509.
[88] B. Roshier and H. Teff, *Law in Society* (1980), p. 67.
[89] (1978) 41 M.L.R. 501, 511.
[90] *Misuse of Power* (*The Richard Dimbleby Lecture 1980*), pp. 18–19. Reprinted in *What Next in the Law?* (1982).

CHAPTER 5

LEGISLATION

A. INTRODUCTION[1]

IN medieval England there was no clear distinction between legislation and other forms of governmental action, and there was no settled procedure for enactment that had to be followed. The terminology was confusing: well-known early statutes include the "Constitutions" of Clarendon 1164, the "Great Charter" 1215, the "Statute" of Merton 1235 and the "Provisions" of Oxford 1258:

"A statute in the region of Edward I simply means something established by royal authority; whether it is established by the King in Council, or in a Parliament of nobles, or in a Parliament of nobles and commons as well is completely immaterial."[2]

By the fifteenth century the consent of the Commons to a statute was regarded as necessary and in early Tudor times the procedure for enactment took on something like its modern form:

"Legislation ... was no longer the Government's vague reply to vaguely worded complaints, but rather the deliberate adoption of specific proposals embodied in specific texts emanating from the Crown or its officers."[3]

In the seventeenth century, Coke wrote that "There is no Act of Parliament but must have the consent of the Lords, the Commons and the Royal assent of the King."[4] The constitutional struggles of that century saw the end of serious attempts by the Crown to assert a legislative competence rivalling that of Parliament.[5] In the *Case of Proclamations*[6] the judges resolved that "the King by his proclamation cannot create any offence which was not an offence before" and "that the King hath no prerogative, but that which the law of the land allows him." However, the courts subsequently upheld the

---

[1] See generally on legislation, D. R. Miers and A. C. Page, *Legislation* (2nd ed., 1990) and F. A. R. Bennion, *Statute Law* (3rd ed., 1990). On the history of legislation see J. H. Baker, *Introduction to Legal History* (3rd ed., 1990), pp. 234–243; C. K. Allen, *Law in the Making* (7th ed., 1964), pp. 435–469.
[2] T. F. T. Plucknett, *Concise History of the Common Law* (5th ed., 1956), p. 322.
[3] Plucknett, (1944) 60 L.Q.R. 242, 248.
[4] 4 Coke's *Institutes of the Laws of England*, p. 25.
[5] See S. A. de Smith and R. Brazier, *Constitutional and Administrative Law* (6th ed., 1989), pp. 70–73.
[6] (1611) 12 Co.Rep. 74.

Crown's claim to a power to impose taxation incidentally to the exercise of prerogative powers such as those to conduct foreign affairs, regulate trade and take emergency measures for the defence of the realm,[7] and a power to "dispense" with the operation of a statute for the benefit of an individual.[8] James II also claimed the power to "suspend" the general operation of statutes, his target being statutes that discriminated against Dissenters and Roman Catholics. The reassertion of such claims to prerogative power after the Civil War and the Restoration led to the "Glorious Revolution" of 1688 and the Bill of Rights. The latter measure, declared to be a statute by the Crown and Parliament Recognition Act 1689, provided (*inter alia*).

"That the pretended power of suspending of laws or the execution of laws by regall authority without consent of Parlyament is illegall. . . .

That the pretended power of dispensing with laws or the execution of laws by regall authoritie as it hath been assumed and exercised of late is illegall. . . .

That levying money for or to the use of the Crowne by pretence of prerogative without grant of Parlyament for longer time or in other manner than the same is or shall be granted is illegal."

The prerogative powers of the Crown were in general restricted, and not abolished, but it was now clear that they could be modified or extinguished according to Parliament's wishes. Other possible rivals have also been unable to maintain any challenge to the dominance of Parliament. The Reformation Parliament established legislative supremacy over the Church.[9] In more recent times, the courts have refused to accept that a resolution of the House of Commons may alter the law of the land.[10]

Certain periods of our history have been noted for increases in legislative activity, and complaints of the difficulty of keeping abreast of the changes. Parliament passed 677 statutes in the reign of Henry VIII and these occupied almost as much space as the whole statute book had done in 1509.[11] Between 1711 and 1811 the annual number of Acts passed increased from 74 to 423. The bulk of the increase was in the number of local and private Acts. The 1811 figures included one for change of name, two for divorce, six for the settlement of private estates, 33 for inclosure and about 150 concerning local matters such as turnpike roads, canals and bridges.[12] The most dramatic increase in legislative activity has, however, been the product of the vast expansion of the activities of the state during the nineteenth and twentieth centuries, and associated factors such as the extensive reforms in the civil service and the administrative machinery, the increasingly representative nature of Parliament, the development of political parties and the strengthening of the role of the Cabinet. The balance as regards Acts of Parliament has also shifted from private legislation to public general legislation.[13]

---

[7] *Case of Impositions*: *Bate's Case* (1606) 2 St.Tr. 371; *Case of Ship Money*: *R.* v. *Hampden* (1637) 3 St.Tr. 825.

[8] *Thomas* v. *Sorell* (1674) Vaughan 330; *Godden* v. *Hales* (1686) 11 St.Tr. 1165.

[9] J. H. Baker, *The Reports of Sir John Spelman Vol. II*, Introduction (1978), pp. 64–70.

[10] See *Stockdale* v. *Hansard* (1839) 9 A. & E. 1, where the Court of Queen's Bench held that the scope of Parliamentary privilege could not be extended by a resolution; *Bowles* v. *Bank of England* [1913] 1 Ch. 57.

[11] See Baker, *op. cit.* note 9, at pp. 43–46.

[12] S. Lambert, *Bills and Acts* (1971), p. 52.

[13] See below, pp. 243–245.

Having established its legislative supremacy, Parliament was reluctant to delegate its powers.[14] In the eighteenth century, public general Acts tended "to be either overloaded with detail or to be directed to specific instances rather than to general rules."[15] However, some law-making powers had from the time of Henry VIII been entrusted to institutions such as the Commissioners of Sewers and the Justices of the Peace, and new powers were from time to time delegated by Parliament. In the eighteenth century, for example, extensive powers were granted to the Commissioners of Customs and Excise, and the Crown was given almost exclusive disciplinary powers over the Army. The following century saw a significant increase of social legislation, and a related extension of powers delegated to local and central government, but the real explosion of delegated legislation has been in the twentieth century.[16] In addition the accession of the United Kingdom to the European Communities has meant that a large body of Community legislation has become applicable in this country. We consider in turn the various forms of legislation: Acts of Parliament, subordinate or delegated legislation and European legislation.

B. ACTS OF PARLIAMENT

1. PARLIAMENTARY SOVEREIGNTY

One of the distinctive features of the constitution of the United Kingdom is the doctrine of Parliamentary sovereignty.[17] A measure which has received the assent of the Queen, Lords and Commons, that assent being given separately and in the two Houses of Parliament by simple majorities, is accepted to have the force of law as an Act of Parliament. Its validity cannot be questioned in the courts and any earlier inconsistent legislation is repealed. Parliament (strictly the "Queen in Parliament") may pass any kind of law without restriction, except that an attempt to bind its successors either as to the content of legislation or the manner and form of its enactment cannot succeed. Acts of Parliament, thus defined, are the supreme form of law; the rule of judicial obedience to them is the "ultimate *political* fact upon which the whole system of legislation hangs."[18] The definition of "Parliament" can be altered, but the process by which that can be achieved is political rather than legal. For example, there is no reason why the British people should not be able to adopt a written constitution, perhaps incorpo-

---

[14] C. K. Allen, *Law and Orders* (3rd ed., 1965), Chap. 2.

[15] *Ibid.* p. 28.

[16] In 1988 there were 55 Public General Statutes (4469 pages: 2170 excluding Consolidation and Scottish Acts); 4 General Synod measures (46 pages); 34 local and personal Acts. In 1987 there were 2279 statutory instruments (6266 pages of those printed).

[17] See S. A. de Smith and R. Brazier *Constitutional and Administrative Law* (6th ed., 1989), Chap. 4; E. C. S. Wade and A. W. Bradley, *Constitutional and Administrative Law* (10th ed., 1985), Chap. 5; Sir William Wade, *Constitutional Fundamentals* (2nd ed., 1989), Chap. 3; C. R. Munro, *Studies in Constitutional Law* (1987); O. Hood Phillips and P. Jackson, *O. Hood Phillips' Constitutional and Administrative Law* (7th ed., 1987), Chaps. 3, 4.

[18] H. W. R. Wade, [1955] C.L.J. 172, 188.

rating a Bill of Rights, which limits the powers of both government and legislature. What is unclear is how this would be done. The people of the United States did so in 1787–88 by means of a Constitutional Convention whose proposals were ratified by specially elected state conventions; the American "Bill of Rights" was added subsequently as a series of constitutional amendments. The judges would have to be satisfied that such a change was generally accepted; a constituent assembly might provide sufficient evidence. They would look to the realities of the situation, as they did at the commencement and conclusion of the Interregnum in the seventeenth century, when they adjusted first to the absence and then to the restoration of the monarchy. It seems unlikely, however, that the "ultimate political fact" will be altered in the near future.

The foregoing represents the orthodox view of Parliamentary sovereignty. It has of course been argued that the definition of "Parliament" is a matter of law rather than politics, and that as such it can be altered by the existing legislative process. Parliament as at present defined could then bind its successors as to the manner and form of legislation by redefining itself either generally or for specific purposes.[19] This view, however, has had more academic support than judicial. The constitutional adviser to the House of Lords Select Committee on a Bill of Rights clearly preferred the orthodox view,[20] and this seemed to be accepted by the Committee. Moreover, the "new view" suffers from the weakness that it would enable a redefinition of "Parliament" to be effected too easily; in effect by a small partisan majority in the House of Commons.[21] For the present, Coke's definition of an Act of Parliament holds good.

It should be noted that while the concept of "Parliamentary sovereignty" is a doctrine of great technical legal significance it should not be taken as a guide to the reality of the legislative process. First, there have always been external influences which have imposed practical restraints on the kinds of legislation which can be passed. Second, the legislative process is today dominated by the government and not by members of Parliament acting independently. Legislation is initiated and formulated outside Parliament, the functions of Parliament are limited to those of scrutiny and legitimisation, and governments normally enjoy a secure party majority. Third, within "Parliament" the House of Commons is the dominant element.[22] Finally it must not be thought that legislation is the only method by which the government can secure its aims; much is achieved by, for example, exhortation, bargaining and the exercise of its economic power.[23]

2. PUBLIC AND PRIVATE ACTS

A distinction is drawn between public and private Acts. The former are those measures that are intended to alter the general law or deal with the

[19] See R. F. V. Heuston, *Essays in Constitutional Law* (2nd ed., 1964), Chap. 1.
[20] Evidence, 1977–78 H.L. 276, pp. 1–10 (D. Rippengal); Report: 1977–78 H.L. 176, of May 24, 1978.
[21] Given that the House of Lords can be by-passed and that the royal assent by convention cannot be withheld (see below p. 255).
[22] See below, pp. 253–254.
[23] See J. J. Richardson and A. G. Jordan, *Governing under Pressure* (1979), Chap. 6.

public revenue or the administration of justice.[24] The latter are of local[25] or personal[26] concern. The procedure for enactment differs in some respects[27]; a person who wishes to rely on a private Act in court must produce a Queen's Printer's copy or an examined or certified copy of the original whereas judicial notice is taken of public Acts[28]; and a private Act may be construed strictly against the interest of the promoter, although this approach is not always followed today.[29]

An important class of private legislation is that promoted by local authorities. Section 262 of the Local Government Act 1972 provided that all local legislation (with some exceptions), in force immediately before April 1974, would cease to have effect at the end of 1979 in metropolitan counties and at the end of 1984 elsewhere.[30] These dates were subsequently postponed by, respectively, one year and two years.[31] Local authorities wishing to preserve particular provisions were required to promote Bills to that end. Many authorities did so,[32] although the rationalisation process proved to be less straightforward and more expensive than had been anticipated.[33]

In 1983, the Statute Law Committee[34] established a Local Legislation Working Party to examine the problems of local statute law and to report on the options for advancing the process of rationalising and reforming it. The Working Party has made recommendations to the Committee concerning the section 262 scheme and has given consideration to the legislation of

---

[24] *Halsbury's Laws of England* (4th ed.) Vol. 34, para. 1223. For a useful analysis of the kinds of public Bills according to their content see I. Burton and G. Drewry, *Legislation and Public Policy* (1981), pp. 32–45. The authors draw a broad distinction between innovatory "policy" Bills and non-innovatory "administration" Bills to remedy anomalies, with further sub-categories of "minor policy" Bills dealing with restricted issues within an area of public policy not otherwise intended to be changed, and "administrative reform" Bills which reorganise administrative support for an existing policy. Session-by-session surveys of legislation by Burton and Drewry appear in the journal *Parliamentary Affairs*.

[25] Bills dealing with the constitution or election of local governing bodies must be introduced as public Bills: *Halsbury, ibid.*; below, note 33 on p. 258. See *e.g.* the London Government Act 1963; the Charlwood and Horley Act 1974.

[26] *i.e.* a "private bill relating to the estate, property, status or style, or otherwise relating to the personal affairs of an individual" (H.L. Standing Order 151). These include Bills affecting estates, and Bills to authorise a marriage between persons within the prohibited degrees of affinity: in the case of the latter, the details are now considered by a Select Committee of the House of Lords, and not on the floor of the House: 2nd Report from the Select Committee on Procedure, 1985–86 H.L. 152, approved by the House (H.L. Deb. Vol. 475, cols. 709–711, June 3 1986).

[27] See below, pp. 253–257 and 257–259.

[28] The line between "public" and "private" Acts is drawn rather differently in this context: see *Halsbury's Laws of England* (4th ed.) Vol. 17, para. 150. For this purpose an Act passed after 1850 is deemed to be a public Act and "to be judicially noticed as such unless the contrary is expressly provided by the Act": Interpretation Act 1978, s.3 and Sched. 2, para. 2. For the definition of "judicial notice" see above p. 11, n. 30.

[29] *Maxwell on Interpretation of Statutes* (12th ed., 1969), pp. 262–3. See, *e.g. Allen* v. *Gulf Oil Refining Ltd.* [1981] A.C. 1001, H.L.

[30] C. A. Cross, *Encyclopedia of Local Government Law*, paras. 1–30 to 1–35; D. Foulkes, [1976] P.L. 272; E. D. Graham, (1979) XLVII *The Table* 109; R. J. B. Morris, [1987] Stat.L.R. 2.

[31] S.I. 1979 No. 969; S.I. 1983 No. 619.

[32] An alternative approach, permitted in a few cases, was for the Secretary of State for the Environment to exercise the power conferred by s.262(9)(*a*) to exempt particular provisions from the general cesser: see S.I. 1986 No. 1133; Morris, *op. cit.* pp. 26–27.

[33] Foulkes, *op. cit.*; Morris, *op. cit.*

[34] See below.

statutory undertakings, the Companies Clauses Consolidation Acts 1845 to 1888 and the local statutory instruments system.[35]

The scope and procedures for enactment of private legislation were considered by the Joint Committee on Private Bill Procedure in 1987–88.[36] The committee's recommendations would reduce the range of private legislation by diverting matters that could be pursued by other, non-Parliamentary procedures. The government expressed reservations about these recommendations but supported other recommendations on matters of detail and procedure.[37]

Public Bills which are found to affect private interests in a manner different from the way in which they affect other private interests in the same category are known as "hybrid" Bills and are subject to an amalgam of the procedural rules applicable to public and private Bills.[38]

3. GOVERNMENT BILLS AND PRIVATE MEMBERS' BILLS

A separate distinction, within the class of public general statutes, is drawn between government and "Private Members' " Bills.[39] Most of the Bills that are successful are introduced by the government of the day,[40] but Bills may also be introduced by individual M.P.s or "Private Peers." In the House of Commons certain days are set aside for Private Members' Bills and a ballot is held each session to determine which M.P.s may take priority on these days. A list of 20 names is drawn up; those near the top have some chance of success, although in practice a Bill will not get through without the support, or at least the benevolent neutrality, of the government. There are other methods by which a private member may introduce a Bill,[41] but such Bills

---

[35] See 20th Annual Report of the Law Commission 1984–85 (1985–86 H.C. 247), pp. 37–38; 21st Annual Report 1985–86 (1986–87 H.C. 342), p. 15; 22nd Annual Report 1986–87 (1987–88 H.C. 13), p. 13.

[36] 1987–88 H.L. 9, H.C. 625.

[37] H.C. Deb. Vol. 151, cols. 474–548, April 20 1989: debate on the Joint Committee Report.

[38] P. Norton, *The Commons in Perspective* (1981), p. 104. In 1976 problems were caused for the government when the Speaker ruled that the Aircraft and Shipbuilding Industries Bill, which had completed its Committee stage, was *prima facie* hybrid: I. Burton and G. Drewry, (1978) 31 *Parliamentary Affairs* pp. 151–6.

[39] On Private Members' Bills see P. G. Richards in S. A. Walkland (ed.) *The House of Commons in the Twentieth Century* (1979), Chap. VI; P. Norton, *The Commons in Perspective* (1981), pp. 99–102; P. G. Richards, *Parliament and Conscience* (1970); D. Marsh and Read, *Private Members' Bills* (1988); J. Gray, [1978] P.L. 242 (case study of the Unsolicited Goods and Services Acts 1971 and 1975); S. M. Cretney, "The Forfeiture Acts 1982—the Private Member's Bill as an Instrument of Law Reform (1990) 10 O.J.L.S. 289; Sir Henry de Waal, [1990] Stat. L.R. 18.

[40] The number per session is generally between 45 and 80; in the average session fewer than 20 will be of major political importance, the rest amending earlier legislation to take account of administrative difficulties, revising "technical law" or consolidating earlier measures: T. C. Hartley and J. A. G. Griffith, *Government and Law* (2nd ed., 1981), p. 210.

[41] (1) After Question Time, on notice given under S.O. No. 58, or (2) under the "ten minute rule," which allows time for brief speeches for and against a Bill. Examples of the former that were ultimately successful include the Protection of Birds (Amendment) Bill 1976 (which went through all its Commons stages in 67 seconds) and the Prohibition of Female Circumcision Bill 1985 (which had been presented and had made some progress in previous sessions: see E. A. Sochart, (1988) 41 *Parliamentary Affairs* 508). Examples of the latter include the Solvent Abuse (Scotland) Bill 1983 and the Rent (Amendment) Bill 1985.

rarely proceed because of lack of time.[42] Some important measures have commenced life as Private Members' Bills, including the Public Bodies (Admission to Meetings) Act 1960 (sponsored by Margaret Thatcher M.P.), the Abortion Act 1967 (David Steel M.P.) and the Indecent Displays (Control) Act 1981 (Timothy Sainsbury M.P.). Governments tend to prefer to leave matters of conscience to Private Members' legislation: the risks generally outweigh any possible political advantages. One result is that such legislation, once in place, can become difficult to repeal or reform, as shown by the many unsuccessful attempts over the years by anti-abortionists to secure the amendment of the Abortion Act 1967.[43] A Private Members' Bill that fails may, however, provide the impetus for subsequent public legislation.[44] The special features of "private Acts" mentioned above do not apply to those "public general statutes" that happen to start their life as Private Members' Bills.

4. Consolidation Acts and Statute Law Revision Acts[45]

On occasion, the law in a particular area is *codified*; the relevant rules as derived from both case-law and existing statutory provisions are set out afresh in one statute. The leading examples are the Bills of Exchange Act 1882, the Sale of Goods Act 1893 (now consolidated in the Sale of Goods Act 1979) and the Theft Act 1968. The Law Commission's objects include that of the codification of areas of English law, but it found that this kind of work could pose great problems and could require the allocation of resources on a scale which was regarded as impossible.[46] Much greater progress has, however, been made by the project on codification of criminal law.[47]

The *consolidation* of statutory provisions on a particular topic is a process that is more modest in aim, and much more commonly achieved.[48] Here, the

---

[42] For example, in 1977–78 there were 20 Bills introduced through the ballot procedure (6 enacted), 80 by other Commons procedures (2 enacted) and 8 Private Peers' Bills (3 enacted). In the same session only two government Bills failed, both consolidation measures enacted the following session: I. Burton and G. Drewry, (1980) 33 *Parliamentary Affairs* 173, 196. The statistics for the 1950–1985 period are given in Marsh and Read (1988), pp. 22–23. The Select Committee on Procedure has recommended changes to prevent the employment of various procedural devices to obstruct the passage of private members' Bill: Second Report, 1988–89 H.C. 330, *Private Members' Time*.

[43] See D. Marsh and J. Chambers, *Abortion Politics* (1981); Marsh and Read (1988), Chap. 6.

[44] *e.g.* the Home Buyers' Bill sponsored by Austin Mitchell in 1983–84 (see above pp. 117–118 and Mitchell, (1986) 39 *Parliamentary Affairs* 1).

[45] See Lord Simon of Glaisdale and J. V. D. Webb, [1975] P.L. 285; I. Burton and G. Drewry, *Legislation and Public Policy* (1981), pp. 205–213; Lord Simon of Glaisdale, [1985] Stat. L.R. 352. On the interpretation of consolidation legislation see below, pp. 343–344.

[46] Law Commissions Act 1965, s.3(1); Law Commission's 13th Annual Report 1977–78 (Law Com. 92), para. 2.34 (codification of the law of landlord and tenant); *cf.* 15th Annual Report 1979–80 (Law Com. 107), para. 1.4 (codification of general principles of liability in criminal law). See above, p. 23.

[47] See above, p. 23, n. 26.

[48] *Report of a Committee appointed by the Lord President of the Council on the Preparation of Legislation* (The Renton Report: Cmnd. 6053, 1975), pp. 17–18 and Chap. XIV; F. A. R. Bennion, *Statute Law* (3rd ed., 1990), Chap. 6.

relevant provisions are re-enacted in one or more consolidating statutes. There are four kinds of consolidation Bill. First, there are straight consolidation Bills that simply re-enact the existing texts. Second, Bills presented under the Consolidation of Enactments (Procedure) Act 1949 may include "corrections and minor improvements,"[49] which must be approved by a Joint Committee of both Houses on Consolidation Bills. Third, improvements designed to facilitate the satisfactory consolidation, but beyond the scope of the 1949 Act may be proposed by the Law Commission; these are also considered by the Joint Committee.[50] Fourth, consolidation with substantial amendments may be prepared by an *ad hoc* expert committee, or as an ordinary departmental Bill.[51] Where the consolidation process requires some amendments of substance these may be included in an ordinary Bill (normally in a Schedule)[52]; once these "pre-consolidation amendments" have been passed one of the first three kinds of consolidation measure can be brought forward.[53] Recent large scale consolidations include those of the Housing legislation and the Companies legislation in 1985, the Income and Corporation Taxes Act 1988,[54] and the Planning legislation in 1990.

Various Statute Law Revision Acts have been passed at intervals from 1856 for the repeal of statutory provisions that are "obsolete, spent, unnecessary or superseded." Since 1969 the Law Commissions have prepared Statute Law (Repeals) Bills for the repeal of enactments that in their opinion are "no longer of practical utility." These are wider in scope. One was passed each year between 1973 and 1978 (inclusive) and further ones in 1981, 1986 and 1989.[55] Statute Law Revision Acts are no longer promoted except in relation to Northern Ireland legislation. Both kinds of Bills are considered by the Joint Committee, and make an important contribution to the tidying up of the statute book.

The main advantage of the kinds of measures considered in this section, other than Bills for consolidation with substantial amendments, is that the

---

[49] *i.e.* "amendments of which the effect is confined to resolving ambiguities, removing doubts, bringing obsolete provisions into conformity with modern practice, or removing unnecessary provisions or anomalies which are not of substantial importance, and amendments designed to facilitate improvements in the form or manner in which the law is stated. . . .": 1949 Act, s.2.

[50] The Law Commission report will also cover any necessary "corrections and minor improvements." Law Commission consolidations are separate from their general law reform proposals.

[51] For an example of the former see the *Report of the Committee on Consolidation of Highway Law* (Cmnd. 630) which led to the Highways Act 1959; (the Highways Act 1980 followed the Law Commission procedure.) For an example of the latter, see the Local Government Act 1972.

[52] Section 116 of the Companies Act 1981 enabled amendments, desirable to enable a satisfactory consolidation to be produced, to be made by Order in Council on the recommendation of the Law Commission and the Scottish Law Commission: see 19th Annual Report of the Law Commission 1983–84 (1984–85 H.C. 214), p. 34. This device was used as part of the massive consolidation of companies legislation in 1985.

[53] See, *e.g.* the Limitation Amendment Act 1980 and the subsequent consolidation measure, the Limitation Act 1980, and the Mental Health (Amendment) Act 1982 and the Mental Health Act 1983.

[54] The longest consolidation produced by the Law Commission and the longest Bill ever introduced.

[55] Provisions identified by the Law Commission as redundant may alternatively be repealed by ordinary legislation: see the 20th Annual Report of the Law Commission 1984–85 (1985–86 H.C. 247), pp. 15–16; 25th Annual Report, 1990 (1990–91 H.C. 249), p. 12.

Parliamentary stages, apart from consideration by the Joint Committee, are taken without debate on matters of substance.

5. PROVISIONAL ORDERS AND SPECIAL PROCEDURE ORDERS[56]

In the nineteenth century, the Provisional Order procedure was introduced as a short cut to local legislation. Many statutes provided that a Minister could make a Provisional Order granting certain powers to a local authority or statutory body, following the completion of certain prescribed formalities. Where there were objections there would normally be a local inquiry. One or more such Orders would then be placed before Parliament to be ratified by a Confirmation Act. Petitions against a Confirmation Bill could be submitted and they would be dealt with in the same manner as objections to a private Bill.[57] There are still some examples of Provisional Order powers on the statute book,[58] but the device has largely been superseded by the use of Orders subject to "special parliamentary procedure" under the Statutory Orders (Special Procedure) Act 1945.[59] This procedure also involves an opportunity for objections to be the subject of a local inquiry, and for petitions either against an Order generally or for amendment to be submitted to Parliament.[60] However, an Order against which no petitions are received comes into effect without a Confirmation Act; an Act is only required when a joint committee of both Houses amends the Order in a way unacceptable to the Minister or reports against the Order as a whole.[61]

6. GENERAL SYNOD MEASURES[62]

The General Synod of the Church of England may pass legislative proposals ("Measures") concerning the Church. A Measure is considered by the Ecclesiastical Committee,[63] which comprises 15 members of each House nominated, respectively, by the Lord Chancellor and the Speaker. The

---

[56] C. K. Allen, *Law and Orders* (3rd ed., 1965), pp. 76–81.
[57] See below, pp. 257–259.
[58] See, *e.g.* Local Government Act 1972, ss.240, 254(8), 262(10).
[59] As amended by the Statutory Orders (Special Procedure) Act 1965, and see S.I. 1949 No. 2393; S.I. 1962 Nos. 409 and 2791. The operation of the procedure was considered by the Joint Committee on Private Bill Procedure (Report, (1987–88) H.L. 9, H.C. 625), pp. 10, 50–51.
[60] For an example of a case where a minister wrongfully refused to accept a memorial from a local authority objector requiring an order to be subjected to special Parliamentary procedure, see *R.* v. *Ministry of Agriculture, Fisheries and Food, ex p. Wear Valley D.C.* (1988) 152 L.G. Rev. 849 (the minister held erroneously that the authority was not "adversely affected" by the order).
[61] This has been done twice: the Mid-Northamptonshire Water Board Order Confirmation (Special Procedure) Act 1949 and the Okehampton Bypass (Confirmation of Orders) Act 1985. The latter was especially controversial as the Joint Committee had reported against the Orders: see the Report of the Joint Committee on Private Bill Procedure, *supra*; H.C. Deb. Vol. 87, cols. 140–224, November 19, 1985, and H.L. Deb. Vol. 468, cols. 1412ff, December 5, 1985.
[62] Church of England Assembly (Powers) Act 1919; Synodical Government Measure 1969. See *Halsbury's Laws of England* (4th ed.) Vol. 14, paras. 399–411.
[63] Established by the 1919 Act, s.2.

Committee reports to Parliament. A Measure approved by each House[64] is then submitted for royal assent, and when this is signified the Measure has the force and effect of an Act of Parliament.

7. PREPARATION AND DRAFTING

The process by which proposals for legislation are converted into a form suitable for enactment is complex.[65] A government Bill originates from the relevant ministry or department, although the ideas may be put forward from many sources including party election manifestos, civil servants, reports of official committees and outside interest groups, whether established to defend some sectional interest or promote some cause. Occasionally, a pre-legislative Select Committee may be appointed by one or both of the Houses to examine a subject with a view to legislation. These are, however, uncommon and not particularly successful.[66] There is normally a considerable measure of consultation. The government may issue a "Green Paper"[67] which sets out tentative proposals, and may suggest alternatives. Legislative proposals are occasionally considered by the relevant departmental select committee[68] but the Select Committee on Procedure has concluded that these committees should not be used principally for that purpose.[69]

Once the appropriate committee of the Cabinet has approved proposals in principle,[70] and provisionally allotted a place in the legislative programme, "Instructions" to draft are prepared by the departmental lawyers[71] and sent to the Parliamentary draftsmen: the "Parliamentary Counsel to the Treasury." The Parliamentary Counsel's office was established in 1869; there are

---

[64] Parliament must either accept or reject a Measure: it has no power to amend: *ibid.*, s.4. In 1927 and 1928 Parliament rejected proposed Measures for the revision of the Prayer Book: other rejected Measures have been the Incumbents (Vacation of Benefices) Measures 1975 and the Appointment of Bishops Measure 1984 (see H.C. Deb. Vol. 64, cols. 126–144, July 16 1984).

[65] See S. A. Walkland, *The Legislative Process in Great Britain* (1968); M. Zander, *The Law Making Process* (3rd ed., 1989), pp. 1–50; and *A Matter of Justice* (1988), pp. 236–252; D. Johnstone, [1980] Stat.L.R. 67 and *A Tax Shall Be Charged* (H.M.S.O., 1975) (preparation of VAT legislation); Miers and Page (1990), Chaps. 2–4; E. A. Dreidger, *The Composition of Legislation* (2nd ed., 1976); G. C. Thornton, *Legislative Drafting* (3rd ed., 1987); A. Graham, [1988] Stat.L.R. 4. See also B. W. Hogwood, *From Crisis to Complacency?* (1987), Chap. 5 (setting the legislative process within the wider context of the shaping of public policy in Britain).

[66] See P. Norton, *The Commons in Perspective* (1981), p. 85; *First Report of the Select Committee on Procedure*, 1977–78 H.C. 588, Vol. 1, p. xiii; Miers and Page (1990), pp. 43–46.

[67] On white paper with green covers.

[68] *e.g.* Abolition of the "sus" law (power under the Vagrancy Act 1824, ss.4, 6 to arrest a "suspected person or reputed thief" loitering in a public place with intent to commit an arrestable offence) following Reports of the Home Office Affairs Committee, 1979–80 H.C. 559, 744. See S. H. Bailey, D. J. Harris and B. L. Jones, *Civil liberties: Cases and Materials* (2nd ed., 1985), p. 55.

[69] First Report, 1977–78 H.C. 588, p. xiii; Second Report, 1984–85 H.C. 49, p. vi.

[70] This work may be done by the Legislation Committee (see below, p. 253) rather than by a separate committee: Sir Harold Wilson, *The Governance of Britain* (1976), p. 129n; see Miers and Page (1990), pp. 30–34.

[71] Instructions for legislation concerning the Inland Revenue are drafted by an Assistant Secretary.

at present 25 counsel, with chambers in Whitehall.[72] Parliamentary counsel are either barristers or solicitors. They normally work in pairs, each Bill being allocated to one of the Senior Counsel working with a Junior Counsel. As well as the drafts of a Bill, the counsel prepare government amendments and relevant motions, give advice on Parliamentary procedure, and attend conferences 'with ministers as well as sittings of both Houses and their committees. They may also assist with the drafting of Private Members' Bills supported by the government or otherwise likely to become law.[73] "The hours are unpredictable and the work arduous, but correspondingly rewarding."[74] A Bill may well go through a whole series of drafts before it is presented to Parliament, clauses being revised in the light of consultation between the draftsmen and the department. Other departments including the Treasury and outside groups may also be consulted at this stage. Firm proposals may be incorporated in a government "White Paper," and this may be debated in Parliament. The actual drafts of legislation are not, however, normally circulated outside the Whitehall machine before they have been presented to Parliament.

F. A. R. Bennion, formerly one of the Parliamentary counsel, has identified a number of "drafting parameters" which the draftsman must bear in mind, and which affect the form of Bills.[75] Some of these considerations relate to the process of enactment; others to the operation of the law once it has been enacted. The "preparational" parameters include compliance with the pre-Parliamentary and Parliamentary requirements as to the form of Bills and the stages through which they must pass (*procedural legitimacy*); strict conformity with the government's timetable for legislation and other time pressures such as those imposed by emergency legislation (*timeliness*); *comprehensibility* to members of Parliament; the need to structure a Bill in such a way that the main points of policy can be debated in a rational order (*debatability*)[76]; the choice of language that will minimise objections from those involved in the legislative process (*acceptability*)[77]; and *brevity*. The "operational parameters" include the need for the text of the Bill to carry out the government's intentions (*legal effectiveness*); the desirability that the text be open to one construction only (*certainty*)[78]; *comprehensibility* to the users of the statute, who will normally be practising lawyers (judge, barrister or solicitor), public officials or non-legal professional advisers[79]; and *legal compatibility* with the rest of the statute book, so that inconsistent provisions are specifically repealed and that the same words mean the same thing even

---

[72] Five more work with the Law Commission. Some appointments are part-time. On drafting in the nineteenth century see F. Bowers, "Victorian Reforms in Legislative Drafting" (1980) 48 *Revue D'Histoire Du Droit* 329–348. The working of the office in the 1930s and 1940s is described in Sir Harold Kent, *In on the Act* (1979).

[73] Private Bills are generally drafted by Parliamentary Agents. Scottish Bills are drafted by members of the Lord Advocate's Department: see Lord Mackay of Clashfern, [1983] Stat.L.R. 68.

[74] Civil Service Commission, *Lawyers: Civil Service Careers* (1980), p. 27.

[75] *Statute Law* (3rd ed., 1990), pp. 28–40. See also G. Engle, [1983] Stat.L.R. 7.

[76] The government may, however, wish a Bill to be drawn in such a way as to restrict opportunities for debate or amendment, for example by drawing the long title narrowly.

[77] "The red-blooded terms of political controversy are toned down. The prose style is flat." (Bennion (1990), p. 34).

[78] The government may, however, intend a provision to be ambiguous.

[79] Bennion (1990), pp. 37–38.

though they appear in different statutes.[80] These parameters frequently conflict. The most important are procedural legitimacy, timeliness and legal effectiveness, and these may well take priority over comprehensibility and legal compatibility. "The task of making legislative proposals understood by non-lawyer politicians while securing their legal effectiveness is one of the most formidable faced by the Parliamentary draftsmen."[81]

The report of the Renton Committee on the Preparation of Legislation[82] recognised that draftsmen had to work under pressures and constraints that made it very difficult to produce simple and clear legislation. Many statutes were well drafted, but there was cause for concern that difficulty was being encountered by statute-users. They had received complaints about the use of obscure and complex language, over-elaboration of detail in the quest for "certainty," the illogical structure of some statutes and problems created by the arrangement of the statute book in a chronological series of separate Acts. There was also criticism of the use of the "non-textual" method of amendment, whereby the amending Act set out the substance of the change proposed to be made without altering the text of the Act being amended. The Renton Committee endorsed the recent change in practice whereby statutes were amended "textually" by adding words to or deleting words from the original provision whenever convenience permitted.[83] The "non-textual" method eases the task of members of Parliament when examining an amending Bill, by enabling them to comprehend its meaning without having to "look beyond the four corners of the Bill."[84] Nevertheless, the Renton Committee thought that the needs of the user should be given priority over those of the legislator, particularly now that there was an official "loose-booklet" publication in which statutes are printed as amended (*Statutes in Force*). It seems that it is now settled practice to make the maximum possible use of textual amendment.[85]

The Renton Committee made a number of other proposals for reform. For example, all available methods should be used to recruit and train more draftsmen as a matter of high priority; the use of statements of principle should be encouraged, with additional guidance given where necessary in Schedules; more use could be made of examples showing how a Bill is intended to work in particular situations; statements of purpose should be used where they are the most convenient method of clarifying the scope and effect of legislation; long un-paragraphed sentences should be avoided; a statute should be arranged to suit the convenience of its ultimate users; the typographical production should be improved, and there should be more consolidation. They rejected suggestions that there should be a "crash" programme of consolidation and that it should be on a "one Act, one subject basis."[86] Under the latter proposal, each subject would have a principal Act

---

[80] "Contrary to most people's belief, however, there are no books of precedents in the Parliamentary Counsel's Office." (*ibid.*, p. 39).

[81] *Ibid.*, p. 33.

[82] Cmnd. 6053, 1975.

[83] *Ibid.* Chap. XIII; Statute Law Society, *Statute Law: the Key to Clarity* (1972), pp. 7–18 and *Renton and the Need for Reform* (1979), pp. 27–40.

[84] Lord Thring, *Practical Legislation* (2nd ed., 1902), p. 8, cited in Bennion (1990), p. 32.

[85] D. Johnstone, [1980] Stat.L.R. 112.

[86] Renton Report, Chap. XIV.

and future legislation on the subject would be effected by textual amendment to that Act. In 1978, Sir David Renton, in an address to the Statute Law Society entitled "Failure to implement the Renton Report,"[87] noted that there had been a small increase in the number of draftsmen and increased momentum in the consolidation process, but that Parliament had continued to pass enormous quantities of legislation, with no diminution in the amount of detail and scarcely any use of statements of purpose. The government's response to the Report had been guarded.[88] The Lord President of the Council (Michael Foot) stated in 1977 that the government regarded the recommendations concerning drafting practice:

> "as a comprehensive and valuable summary of the best drafting practice, and they are being taken into account in the drafting of all current Government legislation. It is considered essential, however, that parliamentary draftsmen should retain discretion to apply the recommendations in accordance with the requirements of particular legislation."[89]

Subsequent governments have not shown any greater enthusiasm for further reforms based on the Renton Report.[90]

There is a recurrent debate on the issue whether there should be a move from the British style of "common-law" drafting to the "continental" or "civil law" method of drafting. The latter is said to be more lucid and succinct, with more emphasis on basic principles and purposes and less on detail. Proponents of such a move include Sir William Dale[91] and J. A. Clarence Smith[92]; opponents include F. A. R. Bennion[93] and Geoffrey Kolts.[94] It is claimed that civilian texts are shorter, better arranged and more easily understood by laymen; common law drafting may by contrast be "a writhing torrent of convoluted indigestion."[95] Others have argued that "civilian" texts produce a considerable degree of uncertainty, which then has to be resolved by the judges; in effect legislative power is delegated to non-elected judges and officials. "Civilian" texts can be as lengthy and complex as British statutes, and can be badly drafted.[96] Of course, the ability of each side to point to examples where the other's preferred method has gone astray proves little; generalisations as to virtues and vices are easy to make but difficult to support. It is, however, unlikely in the present climate of opinion that many English judges would wish to deal with legislative provisions that were significantly more open-textured than at present, and

---

[87] Statute Law Society, *Renton and the Need for Reform* (1979), pp. 2–8.

[88] *Ibid.* pp. 97–98.

[89] H.C. Deb. Vol. 941, col. 329 written answer, December 15, 1977.

[90] Lord Simon of Glaisdale, "The Renton Report—Ten Years On" [1985] Stat.L.R. 133; H.L. Deb. Vol. 489, cols. 1417–1449, summarised at [1988] Stat.L.R. 1.

[91] *Legislative Drafting: A New Approach* (1977); (1981) 30 I.C.L.Q. 141; [1988] Stat.L.R. 15.

[92] Proceedings of the Ninth International Symposium on Comparative Law (1972), pp. 155–178; [1980] Stat.L.R. 14.

[93] *Statute Law* (1990), pp. 23–26; [1980] Stat.L.R. 61.

[94] Second Parliamentary Counsel, Canberra, Australia, [1980] Stat.L.R. 144.

[95] J. A. C. Smith, *op. cit.* note 92, at pp. 158–9.

[96] See, *e.g.* the criticisms of a proposed directive of the European Commission on commercial agents expressed by the Law Commission in 1977 (Law Com. No. 84). The text was described as badly drafted, unclear, ambiguous and internally inconsistent.

equally unlikely that they would be regarded by many in the community as well suited to undertake that role.[97]

8. PARLIAMENTARY PROCEDURE[98]

(a) Public Bills

The legislative timetable of Parliament is managed by the government. Detailed government Bills are examined and placed in the timetable by the Cabinet's Legislation Committee, and may be considered by the full Cabinet or the appropriate policy committee. A Bill may generally be introduced in either the House of Commons or the House of Lords, although money Bills must be introduced in the Commons, and politically controversial Bills are normally introduced there.

A government Bill introduced in the Commons is presented by a minister. It receives a formal *first reading*, when only the title is actually read out, and is ordered to be printed. A day is fixed for the *second reading*. A Bill as printed is accompanied by an "Explanatory Memorandum" which explains in non-technical language the content and object of the Bill. If expenditure is involved a "Financial Memorandum" is also attached. At the second reading stage the principles of the Bill are debated on the floor of the House.[99] If the Bill entails public expenditure or taxation this must be authorised by a *financial resolution* moved by a minister.[1] After receiving a second reading[2] the Bill proceeds to the *committee stage*, either at a Standing Committee of between 15 and 60 M.P.s that reflects the party composition of the House, or in Committee of the Whole House. The latter step is taken for Bills that are either straightforward or urgent, or, at the other extreme, politically contentious or of major constitutional significance. The committee examines the Bill clause by clause, first considering amendments and then the motion that

---

[97] See above, pp. 232–239.

[98] S. A. de Smith and R. Brazier, *Constitutional and Administrative Law* (6th ed., 1989), pp. 272–281; S. A. Walkland (ed.), *The House of Commons in the Twentieth Century* (1979), Chap. V; P. Norton, *The Commons in Perspective* (1981), Chap. 5; I. Burton and G. Drewry, *Legislation and Public Policy* (1981); D. Englefield, *Whitehall and Westminster* (1985), Chap. 7; P. Silk, *How Parliament Works* (2nd ed., 1989), Chap. 6; the following Reports from the Select Committee on Procedure: Second Report, 1970–71 H.C. 538, *The Process of Legislation*; First Report, 1977–78 H.C. 588; Second Report, 1984–85 H.C. 49, *Public Bill Procedure*; Second Report, 1985–86 H.C. 324, *Allocation of Time to Government Bills in Standing Committee*; Second Report, 1986–87 H.C. 350, *The Use of Time on the Floor of the house*; Second Report, 1988–89 H.C. 330, *Private Members' Time*; G. Drewry, (1972) 35 M.L.R. 289 and (1979) 42 M.L.R. 80; T. St. J. Bates, [1987] Stat.L.R. 44; D. R. Miers, [1989] Stat.L.R. 26.

[99] Non-controversial Bills may be referred to a Second Reading Committee of between 16 and 50 M.P.s and Scottish Bills to the Scottish Grand Committee (members for Scottish constituencies plus between 10 and 15 others). Subsequent stages may also be taken by standing committees.

[1] In the case of some Bills, such as Finance Bills, Ways and Means resolutions are passed before the Bill is introduced. Private Members' Bills rarely include provisions involving public expenditure.

[2] Only three government Bills have failed at second reading since 1905, although it is more than a mere formality and ministers do not always approach debates with closed minds: Norton (1981), pp. 86–87. The bills were the Rent Restrictions Bill in 1924, the Reduction of Redundancy Rebates Bill in 1977 (during the period of the minority Labour government) and the Shops Bill in 1986 (following a rebellion by 72 government backbenchers: see P. Regan, (1988) 41(2) *Parliamentary Affairs* 218).

the clause, as amended, "stand part of the Bill." Amendments may be proposed by the minister in charge, backbenchers or the opposition; those to be taken are selected by the chairman. Proposed new clauses are then taken, followed by the Schedules, proposed new Schedules, the preamble (if any) and the long title.[3] A recent innovation has been to send some Bills to a "Special Standing Committee" with the power to question witnesses and request the submission of evidence.[3a] This procedure has been used on only a few occasions,[4] but virtually all the evidence received by the Select Committee on Procedure on its operation was enthusiastic[5] and it was enshrined permanently in Standing Orders from 1986.[6] Next, the House considers the Bill again at the *report stage*.[7] Any aspect of the Bill can be raised and new clauses and further amendments can be proposed. Debate is, however, confined to the contents of the Bill. Normally, the *third reading* immediately follows the conclusion of the report stage. Only minor verbal amendments can be made; if material amendments are necessary the Bill has to be considered again in committee.

The Bill then proceeds to the House of Lords where the stages are repeated, with some minor procedural differences. Any amendment proposed may be moved; there is no selection. The committee stage, if not dispensed with, is normally taken by a Committee of the Whole House, although a Public Bills Committee is sometimes used.[8] If amendments are made, the Bill is returned to the Commons for them to be agreed. The Commons respond with a message to the Lords which either signifies their agreement, gives reasons for disagreement or proposes other amendments. Further messages may be exchanged until either final agreement is reached, the Bill lapses at the end of a session[9] or the Commons resorts to the Parliament Acts procedure.[10]

In recent years, significant features of the work of the House of Lords have included longer hours, a higher regular attendance, an increase in the proportions of the House's time devoted to legislative business and an increase in the self confidence of peers.[11] Claims that they have demonstrated a new independence and a new professionalism[12] have, however,

[3] See below, pp. 259–261.

[3a] *First Report from the Select Committee on Procedure*, 1977–78 H.C. 588, pp. xviii–xix; H.C. Deb. Vol. 991, cols. 716–834, October 30, 1980.

[4] Proceedings in the 1980–81 session on the Criminal Attempts Bill, the Education Bill and the Deep Sea Mining (Temporary Provisions) Bill; in the 1981–82 session on the Mental Health (Amendment) Bill; and in the 1983–84 session on the Matrimonial and Family Proceedings Bill. See H. J. Beynon, [1982] P.L. 193; A. Samuels, [1989] Stat. L.R. 208.

[5] *e.g.* memorandum from Sir Patrick Mayhew, the Attorney-General (Second Report from the Select Committee on Procedure, 1984–85 H.C. 49–II, Appendix 2); and see generally the Report, 1984–85 H.C. 49–I, pp. viii–x.

[6] See H.C. Deb. Vol. 92, February 27 1986, cols. 1083–1136.

[7] There is no report stage if a public Bill considered in Committee of the Whole House is unamended.

[8] An experiment with a Public Bill Committee on the Pilotage Bill in 1986–87 did not lead to a significant saving of time: *Report by the Group on the Working of the House*, 1987–88 H.L. 9, pp. 9–10.

[9] Public Bills that have not been passed lapse at the end of the session: private Bills (see below) may be carried forward.

[10] See below.

[11] N. Baldwin in P. Norton (ed.), *Parliament in the 1980s* (1985), Chap. 5; A. Adonis, "The House of Lords in the 1980s" (1988) 41 *Parliamentary Affairs* 380; *Report by the Group on the Working of the House* (1987–88 H.L. 9).

[12] Baldwin, *op. cit.*

been challenged.[13] Defeats of the government on important questions are still unusual.

A Bill passed in its entirety by both Houses is presented for the *royal assent*.[14] The monarch is expected by convention to give that assent; the last occasion on which it was refused was in 1707 when Queen Anne refused her assent to a Militia Bill. Assent may be signified (1) by the monarch in person (this was last done in 1854); (2) by Lords Commissioners in the presence of both Houses[15]; or (3) as is normally the case today, by separate notification to each House in accordance with the Royal Assent Act 1967. The third method, unlike the others, does not involve the interruption of proceedings in the Commons. The second method is only used where royal assent coincides with prorogation.

The Parliament Acts 1911–1949 lay down special procedures whereby a Bill may be presented for royal assent when it has been passed only by the Commons.[16] A money Bill may be so presented where the Lords have failed to pass it without amendment after it has been before them for one month; a non-money Bill may be presented where it has been passed by the Commons in two consecutive sessions and the Lords have failed to pass it in each of those sessions; one year has elapsed between the Commons second reading in the first session and third reading in the second session; the Bill has been sent to the Lords at least one month before the end of each session and the Speaker certifies that the requirements of the Parliament Acts have been complied with. The certificate is conclusive for all purposes and may not be questioned in a court of law. These procedures may not be employed in respect of Bills to prolong the maximum duration of a Parliament beyond five years, to Provisional Order Confirmation Bills or private Bills. Objections by the House of Lords are normally dropped without the necessity of recourse to the Parliament Acts; the procedure has only been used three times.[17]

For the draftsman, the first publication of the Bill after first reading is an important deadline as changes thereafter have to be made by formal amendments. Indeed most of the amendments that are made are government amendments, and these tend to reflect second thoughts by the civil servants rather than the persuasive arguments of members. Amendments of substance proposed by backbenchers or opposition and actually agreed are few

[13] Adonis, *op. cit.*
[14] See F. A. R. Bennion [1981] Stat.L.R. 133.
[15] Under the Royal Assent by Commission Act 1541; this was originally part of the Bill of Attainder against Catherine Howard, which did not receive the King's assent in person to spare his hearing once more the "wicked facts of the case." The Bill actually received the assent on February 11, 1542. The Reading Clerk reads out the title of the Bill; the Commissioners raise their hats; and the Clerk of the Parliaments pronounces "La Reyne le Veult." In the case of money Bills the expression is "La Reyne remercie ses bons sujets, accepte leur benevolence, et ainsi le veult"; for personal private Acts, "Soit fait comme il est désiré." If assent were refused the expression would be "La Reyne s'avisera."
[16] S. A. de Smith and R. Brazier, *Constitutional and Administrative Law* (6th ed., 1989), pp. 304–308.
[17] Welsh Church Act 1914 (disestablishment); Government of Ireland Act 1914 (Home Rule: the Act was not implemented); Parliament Act 1949.

in number, and are more likely to be accepted in the Lords.[18] More amendments than usual were carried against the government during the passage of the Scotland and Wales Bills in 1977/78. These were controversial constitutional measures, and the Labour government was then in a minority in the Commons.[19] "Parliament's exposure of the successive Bills' inherent defects and illogicalities was impressive."[20] However, "the debates were poorly attended and the debating was done by a few stalwarts, with most M.P.s (though a smaller proportion than usual) content to live up to their image as lobby fodder."

The pressure on the Parliamentary timetable is such that where legislation is particularly contentious governments may secure the placing of limits on the time available for debate (timetable or "guillotine" motions); this may mean that, as in the case of the Scotland and Wales Bills, important clauses are not scrutinised by the Commons, although they will normally be considered by the Lords. The House of Commons Select Committee on Procedure reported in 1978 that:

> "the balance of advantage between Parliament and Government in the day to day working of the Constitution is now weighted in favour of the Government to a degree which arouses widespread anxiety and is inimical to the proper working of our parliamentary democracy."[21]

The Select Committee on Procedure has made proposals, as yet unimplemented, for the earlier timetabling of controversial Bills in Standing Committee by a Legislative Business Committee[22] or by a business sub-committee of the relevant Standing Committee.[23]

The apparent limitations on the effectiveness of Parliamentary scrutiny have led to suggestions for the scrutiny of legislation by other bodies, particularly from the technical standpoint. Sir William Dale has proposed[24] the establishment of a "Law Council" to advise the government on draft Bills. "Its duty would be to examine them from the point of view of coherent and orderly presentation, clarity, conciseness, soundness of legal principle, and suitability for attaining the Government's objective," a function performed in France by the Conseil d'Etat. It would not concern itself with matters of policy, and its advice could be rejected by the government. Its membership would include judges, lawyers (practising and academic) and laymen. The Renton Committee, however, rejected proposals for formal machinery for the scrutiny of the drafting of Bills, either before or after their

---

[18] See J. A. G. Griffith, *Parliamentary Scrutiny of Government Bills* (1974); P. Norton, (1976) 57 *The Parliamentarian* 17. Where the government accepts or is unsuccessful in resisting an amendment, the version proposed in debate is usually replaced at a later stage by one drafted by a parliamentary draftsman: T. Millett, [1988] Stat.L.R. 70.

[19] I. Burton and G. Drewry, "Public Legislation: A Survey of the Sessions 1977/8 and 1978/9" (1980) 33 *Parliamentary Affairs* 173, 174–186. These sessions provided "significant evidence for the power that still belongs to backbenchers in the House of Commons," although "only in a minority Parliament may the fate of Government Bills be in serious doubt. Even then, most legislation, being inevitable whatever the Government in power, is secure, protected by the close rapport between the two front benches" (p. 199).

[20] *Ibid.* p. 186.

[21] First Report, 1977–78 H.C. 588, Vol. 1, p. viii.

[22] Second Report, 1984–85 H.C. 49, Part III: this proposal was defeated in the House of Commons (92 H.C. Deb., February 27, 1986, cols. 1083–1136; Minutes of Evidence of the Select Committee on Procedure (1985–86 H.C. 324-i)).

[23] Second Report from the Select Committee on Procedure, 1985–86 H.C. 324.

[24] *Legislative Drafting: A New Approach* (1977), pp. 336–337.

formal introduction in Parliament.[25] Before introduction, it was for govern-ment departments to decide what advice they should obtain as to the drafting of their Bills; after introduction, a new scrutiny stage would "impose undue strain on a Parliamentary machine which is already under great pressure, and . . . add to the labour of the draftsmen who have more than enough to do as it is to keep pace with the legislative programme."

The Committee did recommend new Parliamentary procedures (1) for incorporating improvements (including the correction of obvious inaccu-racies) certified by the Speaker and the Lord Chancellor to be of a drafting nature, after the passage of a Bill by both houses and before royal assent[26]; and (2) for the re-enactment of statutes, in whole or in part, with drafting improvements.[27] In addition they suggested that the Statute Law Commit-tee[28] should keep the structure and language of statutes under continuous review, monitor the implementation of the Renton Committee's recommen-dations and publish reports. None of these proposals has been accepted, the third being rejected by the Cabinet apparently on the grounds that the Committee was not an "appropriate body" to discharge these functions and that the proposal to keep the statute book under continuous review was not "likely to lead to any worthwhile improvements in the drafting of legislation."[29]

(b) Private Bills[30]

Standing Orders of each House lay down a complicated series of proced-ural requirements that must be observed before a private Bill is introduced, including the giving of public notice. In practice, a promoter needs the professional assistance of a Parliamentary Agent,[31] who drafts the Bill and acts on behalf of the promoter thereafter. Petitions for private Bills must normally be deposited by November 27 each session.[32] A local authority that

[25] Cmnd. 6053, pp. 129–133.
[26] This was endorsed in principle by the House of Commons Select Committee on Procedure, 1977–78 H.C. 588, Vol. 1, p. xxvii. A proposed procedure for the correction of errors *after* royal assent did not find favour with the House of Lords (Acts of Parliament (Correction of Mistakes) Bill [Lords], session 1976–77, withdrawn) and was not supported by the Select Committee (*ibid.*). See A. Samuels, "Errors in Bills and Acts" [1982] Stat.L.R. 94. This is to be distinguished from the correction of printing errors in H.M.S.O. copies of statutes: see below, p. 265 n. 84.
[27] This would be modelled on the present procedure for consolidation Bills.
[28] A committee appointed by the Lord Chancellor and first established in 1868. Its membership includes M.P.s, draftsmen, judges, Permanent Secretaries, the Treasury Solicitor and the Chairmen of the Law Commissions. It meets once a year and supervises the Statutory Publications Office, the form of Acts and the production of *Statutes in Force*. Most of its functions in the field of consolidation and statute law revision passed to the Law Commis-sions in 1965.
[29] *Renton and the Need for Reform*, pp. 7–8; H.L. Deb. col. 776, March 7, 1978. The Select Committee supported the third proposal, and urged the government to reconsider its attitude: 1977–78 H.C. 588, Vol. 1, pp. xxvii–xxviii.
[30] F. Clifford, *History of Private Bill Legislation* (1887); O. C. Williams, *Historical Develop-ment of Private Bill Procedure* (1948); The Study of Parliament Group, "Private Bill Proce-dure; A Case for Reform" [1981] P.L. 206; Joint Committee on Private Bill Procedure, 1987–88 H.L. 97, H.C. 625.
[31] See D. L. Rydz, *The Parliamentary Agents: A History* (1979).
[32] Personal Bills can be deposited at any time, are customarily presented first to the House of Lords and are considered by the Personal Bills Committee of the Lords before first reading. The other stages are similar to those for other private Bills.

wishes to promote a Bill must resolve to do so by a majority of the whole number of council members at a meeting of which 30 days' notice has been given in the local press; a second meeting must confirm the decision after the deposit of the Bill in Parliament.[33] The promoters must prove to the two "examiners," one appointed by each of the Houses, that the formalities have been observed, and this may be challenged by opponents of the Bill.

Private Bills normally proceed first in the House of Lords. The first reading is a formality; the second reading is normally so, but may be opposed. A Bill that passes the second reading is regarded as having received the conditional approval of the House. If the Bill passes the second reading opposed clauses are then referred to a Select Committee of five Lords. The House may agree to an Instruction to the Committee to the effect that the Committee should have regard to or be satisfied of certain matters before passing a particular provision. Procedure here is largely modelled on judicial proceedings: the case for and against the clause is put by counsel for the promoters and for the objectors; witnesses may be called and examined on oath; government departments may make representations and previous decisions of the Committee may be cited. Unopposed clauses are normally considered by the "Committee on Unopposed Bills," an informal meeting conducted by the Lord Chairman of Committees or his Counsel. The promoters, usually represented here by a Parliamentary Agent rather than counsel, must prove a need for the clauses. Unopposed clauses in local Bills promoted as a consequence of the Local Government Act 1972[34] were referred instead to more formal Select Committees. These have applied the principles (1) that the promoters had to prove a current need in their area that could only be met by legislation; (2) that the legislation would deal effectively with the problem; and (3) that provisions to meet a need common to all or a great number of authorities should not be included in a private Bill where the government had given a firm undertaking to introduce general legislation to meet that need.[35] Model clauses were prepared.[36] The House of Lords Select Committee on Practice and Procedure[37] recommended, inter alia, that further Local Government (Miscellaneous Provisions) Bills should be introduced as public legislation to cover matters currently being included in local Acts, and that consideration should be given to the possibility of making such Bills subject to a special procedure for non-controversial Bills.

After the committee stage, the report stage is usually a formality although the Bill may be amended. The Bill is given a third reading and sent to the other House where the various stages are repeated, with some differences in detail.[38]

These procedures have been described as "cumbersome and expensive"; proceedings of private Bill committees "can be casual and their decisions unpredictable" and opposed Bill committees "tend to be legalistic and

---

[33] Local Government Act 1972, s.239. A Bill may not be promoted to change a local government area, its status or electoral arrangements: *ibid.* s.70.

[34] See above, p. 244.

[35] See C. A. Cross, *Encyclopedia of Local Government Law*, para. 1–31.

[36] *Ibid.* para. 1–32.

[37] First Report, 1977–78 H.L. 155.

[38] There are, for example, separate committees for opposed and unopposed *Bills* rather than *clauses*.

time-consuming."[39] Generally, private members take little interest in private legislation; when they do take an interest, however, their influence may be greater than in relation to public legislation as the whips are rarely applied and normally the government simply offers advice.[40]

9. ARRANGEMENT OF ACTS OF PARLIAMENT[41]

The elements of a public general statute are normally arranged in the following order.

(a) Short title

This is the title by which the statute is generally known (*e.g.* the "Interpretation Act 1978"). The practice of including a section providing for the citation of an Act by a short title developed in the nineteenth century; the Short Titles Act 1896[42] conferred short titles on many statutes passed before this practice became established.

(b) Year and chapter number

A statute passed today is cited by reference either to its short title or to the calendar year in which it is passed and its "chapter number" within that year. Statutes are numbered in the order in which royal assent is given. Until 1963[43] statutes were regarded as chapters of the legislation passed in the relevant *session* rather than *calendar year*, and were numbered accordingly. Thus the Interpretation Act 1889 can be cited as "52 & 53 Vict. c. 63" (chapter 63 of the session that fell in the fifty-second and fifty-third years of the reign of Queen Victoria) and its replacement, the Interpretation Act 1978 as "1978 c. 30" (Chapter 30 of 1978).

(c) Long title

This describes the scope of the Act; if a Bill is amended so as to go beyond the long title as printed in the Bill the long title must be amended as well.

(d) Date

The date, given in square brackets, is that on which royal assent was signified.

---

[39] The Study of Parliament Group [1981] P.L. 206, 221. For reform proposals see *ibid.* pp. 218–227; Report of the Joint Committee on Private Bill Procedure, 1987–88 H.L. 97, H.C. 625, debated at H.C. Deb. Vol. 151, cols. 474–548, April 20 1989; Government response, Cm. 1110, 1990.

[40] P. Norton, (1977) 30 *Parliamentary Affairs* 356.

[41] See F. A. R. Bennion, *Statute Law* (3rd ed., 1990), Chap. 3.

[42] Replacing the Short Titles Act 1892. See also the Statute Law Revision Act 1948, Sched. 2.

[43] The practice was changed by the Acts of Parliament Numbering and Citation Act 1962.

(e) Preamble

Public Acts formerly[44] included a preamble, which could be lengthy, explaining why the Act was passed. They are still necessary for private Acts, and begin with the word "Whereas." For example the Parliament Act 1911 includes the following:

"Whereas it is expedient that provision should be made for regulating the relations between the two Houses of Parliament:

And whereas it is intended to substitute for the House of Lords as it at present exists a Second Chamber constituted on a popular instead of hereditary basis, but such substitution cannot be immediately brought into operation:

And whereas provision will require hereafter to be made by Parliament in a measure effecting such substitution for limiting and defining the powers of the new Second Chamber, but it is expedient to make such provision as in this Act appears for restricting the existing powers of the House of Lords:"

(f) Enacting formula

This normally runs:

"Be it enacted by the Queen's most Excellent Majesty, by and with the advice and consent of the Lords Spiritual and Temporal, and Commons, in this present Parliament assembled, and by the authority of the same, as follows:—"

The formula is slightly different for money Bills and Bills passed under the Parliament Acts procedures.

(g) Sections and Schedules

The body of an Act is divided into *sections* (equivalent to the *clauses* of the Bill) and *subsections*, a practice introduced by Lord Brougham's Act of 1850.[45] Each section is printed with a *marginal note* indicating its content. Occasionally, errors may creep in. For example in the Married Women (Maintenance in Case of Desertion) Act 1886, a subsection (section 1(2)), which provided that a wife who had committed adultery could not claim alimony where her husband had deserted her, was printed with the marginal note "custody of children." A long Act may be divided into *Chapters* or *Parts*. Sections dealing with related subject matter may be grouped under *headings*. Matters of detail are commonly included in *Schedules* at the end of the Act. Each schedule is linked to one of the preceding sections and may be divided into *Parts*, *paragraphs* and *sub-paragraphs*. There may also be *marginal notes* and *cross-headings*. A *Schedule* may be used to set out the provisions of an earlier Act as amended.[46]

[44] Preambles are occasionally found in modern public Acts, particularly those which implement international conventions (*e.g.* the Oil in Navigable Waters Act 1963), public Acts of a local nature (*e.g.* the Towyn Trewan Common Act 1963) or legislation of a formal or ceremonial character (*e.g.* the John F. Kennedy Memorial Act 1964). Another example is the Canada Act 1982, which provided for the patriation of the Canadian Constitution.
[45] Interpretation of Acts Act 1850, 13 & 14 Vict. c. 21, s.2.
[46] Known as a "Keeling schedule." Examples include the Cinematograph Films Act 1948, Sched. 2; *cf.* Education Act 1980, Sched. 5.

The body of the Act may include the following kinds of provision: "definitions, principal provisions, administrative provisions, miscellaneous clauses, penal clauses, clauses dealing with the making of rules or byelaws, saving clauses, temporary and transitory clauses, repeals and savings, date of coming into operation (if specified)" and the duration of the Act if it is limited.[47] "Common-form" clauses, those dealing with geographical extent, commencement, short title, citation and interpretation, are normally found at the end of the statute.

(h) Extent[48]

There is a presumption that an Act applies throughout the United Kingdom[49] and not beyond.[50] "Extent clauses" are used to negative that presumption.[51] Acts which apply only to Scotland or Northern Ireland usually include the country in brackets in the short title.[52] Statutes may expressly be made to apply to transactions abroad. For example, the English courts may exercise jurisdiction in respect of murders committed by British subjects abroad[53] and some Acts extend to the territorial waters adjacent to the United Kingdom.[54]

(i) Commencement[55]

Until 1793 each Act of Parliament was deemed to come into operation from the first day of the session in which it was passed, unless a commencement date was specified. The element of retrospectivity was seen to be unjust and the rule was changed[56]; an Act now comes into effect at the beginning of the day on which royal assent is given unless some other commencement date is specified.[57] Today, it is commonly provided that the Act shall come into effect on a specified date, or on a day to be appointed, and, in the latter event, that different days may be appointed for different provisions, different purposes or different areas. The advantages of delayed commencement are that it gives those affected time to prepare, and gives ministers and departments time to draw up the necessary regulations and orders after due consultation with interested parties. The main disadvantage

[47] Statute Law Society, *Statute Law Deficiencies* (1972), p. 6. (based on Sir Alison Russell's analysis of the general frame of a Bill.).
[48] See F. A. R. Bennion, *Statutory Interpretation* (1984), Part IX.
[49] *i.e.* England, Scotland, Wales and Northern Ireland but not the Channel Islands or the Isle of Man.
[50] See *R.* v. *Jameson* [1896] 2 Q.B. 425, 430; *Draper & Son Ltd.* v. *Edward Turner & Son Ltd.* [1965] 1 Q.B. 424; *Air-India* v. *Wiggins* [1980] 1 W.L.R. 815.
[51] Extent clauses normally indicate expressly that an Act applies to Northern Ireland even though this is not strictly necessary.
[52] The Renton Committee recommended that where an Act affects only England and Wales this too should be indicated in the short title: Cmnd. 6053, p. 124. This has not been implemented.
[53] Offences against the Person Act 1861, s.9.
[54] *e.g.* Wireless Telegraphy Act 1949, ss.1, 6; Marine, etc., Broadcasting (Offences) Act 1967, s.1; *Post Office* v. *Estuary Radio Ltd.* [1968] 2 Q.B. 740. See generally the Law Commission's *Report on the Territorial and Extraterritorial Extent of the Criminal Law* (Law Com. No. 91, 1978) and *Jurisdiction over Offences of Fraud and Dishonesty with a Foreign Element* (Law Com. No. 180, 1989).
[55] See Bennion (1984), pp. 409–417.
[56] Acts of Parliament (Commencement) Act 1793.
[57] Interpretation Act 1978, s.4.

is that it may be difficult for users to establish whether a particular provision is in force.[58] There may be many commencement orders in respect of one statute,[59] and some provisions may never be implemented, for reasons such as a lack of resources[60] and governmental second thoughts about the desirability of particular provisions.[61] Complaints have been voiced about the present position and various improvements proposed.[62] Governments have been exhorted to refrain from promoting legislation unless its implementation within a reasonable time can be foreseen.

In 1982 the Management and Personnel Office (the successor to the Civil Service Department) issued new guidance on the commencement of legislation.[63] Acts which do not provide for a commencement date to be appointed by order should provide for commencement not less than two months after royal assent (three months for consolidation Acts). Commencement provisions should be grouped at the end of any Bill in which that is practicable, if appropriate in a separate clause or Schedule; alternatively, a full list of commencement provisions should be published with the Act or in a press notice. Commencement dates should be specified in the Act where possible and appropriate; otherwise, every effort should be made to minimise the number of commencement orders and to rationalise their issue and the dates of commencement.

In interpreting statutes there is a presumption that statutes do not operate retrospectively so as to affect an existing right or obligation, except as regards matters of procedure.[64] Parliament may, however, use words in a statute which clearly show an intention that it should so operate.[65]

(j) Definitions

Modern statutes commonly include "definition sections" in which the meaning of words and phrases found in the statute are explained, either comprehensively (X "means" ABC) or partially (X "includes" ABC). The qualification "unless the contrary intention appears" is usually added. The Interpretation Act 1978 gives definitions of a large number of words and expressions. These are applicable where the words are found "in any Act, unless the contrary intention appears."[66] For example, "Secretary of State"

---

[58] A most useful publication with this information is *Is it in force?*, an annual cumulative publication published in conjunction with the 4th edition of *Halsbury's Statutes of England*.

[59] See, *e.g.* the Consumer Credit Act 1974 and the Control of Pollution Act 1974.

[60] Examples include various provisions concerning legal advice and law centres (see below, p. 435).

[61] Examples include provisions of the Children and Young Persons Act 1969 and the Health and Safety at Work etc. Act 1974, s.71: see J. R. Spencer, (1981) 131 N.L.J. 644.

[62] A. Samuels, (1979) *The Magistrate* pp. 173–4; Statute Law Society Working Party on the Commencement of Acts of Parliament, [1980] Stat.L.R. 40.

[63] (1982) 79 L.S.Gaz. 968.

[64] *Re Athlumney* [1898] 2 Q.B. 547, 551–2 *per* R. S. Wright J.; *Att.-Gen.* v. *Vernazza* [1960] A.C. 965. See below, pp. 357–358.

[65] *e.g.* the War Damage Act 1965, which reversed the decision of the House of Lords in *Burmah Oil Co.* v. *Lord Advocate* [1965] A.C. 75; the Northern Ireland Act 1972, which retrospectively removed limitations on the power of the Parliament of Northern Ireland to legislate for the armed forces: see S. H. Bailey, D. J. Harris and B. Jones, *Civil Liberties: Cases and Materials* (2nd ed. 1985), p. 204.

[66] Interpretation Act 1978, s.5 and Sched. 1. They may also apply to subordinate legislation: see *ibid.* s.23.

means "one of Her Majesty's Principal Secretaries of State."[67] The 1978 Act also provides generally that:

"In any Act, unless the contrary intention appears—
(a) words importing the masculine gender include the feminine;
(b) words importing the feminine gender include the masculine;
(c) words in the singular include the plural and words in the plural include the singular."[68]

There are also general provisions covering such matters as references to service by post, distance, time of day and the Sovereign, and the construction of subordinate legislation.[69]

(k) Amendments and repeals

Statutes commonly amend or repeal earlier enactments. Repeals are normally set out in a Schedule, although important changes may be included in the body of the Act. A power may be conferred to repeal or modify Acts of Parliament by statutory instrument. An earlier statute may also be amended or repealed by implication where the provisions of a later Act are so inconsistent that the two cannot stand together, although the courts seek to reconcile apparently inconsistent provisions where possible. At common law a repealed Act was treated as if it had never existed, except in relation to transactions past and closed, but this rule was changed in 1889.[70] For example, where an offence is committed against an existing statutory provision, criminal proceedings may now be instituted even after that provision is repealed, unless the repealing enactment provides otherwise.[71] There was also a common law rule that where statute A was repealed by statute B and statute B was subsequently repealed by statute C, statute A was regarded as reviving unless the contrary intention appeared. This rule was abolished in 1850: repealed statutes stay repealed unless expressly revived.[72] Unlike the Scots, the English have never had a rule that a statute can be disregarded on

---

[67] Many statutory functions are entrusted to "the Secretary of State." This device enables these functions to be switched between departments without the need for the statute to be amended. Where amendment is necessary, as where a function is given to a particular minister, it is usually effected by a statutory instrument under the Ministers of the Crown (Transfer of Functions) Act 1946. The "Secretary of State" device makes it more difficult to discover where responsibility for a particular function commonly lies.

[68] Section 6. See, *e.g. Annicola Investments* v. *Minister of Housing and Local Government* [1968] 1 Q.B. 631, where the word "houses" was held to include a single house. Examples of cases where the "contrary intention" has appeared are those where the terms "every man" or "any person" have been held not to include women: *e.g. Chorlton* v. *Lings* (1868) L.R. 4 C.P. 374; *Bebb* v. *The Law Society* [1914] 1 Ch. 286, above, p. 112, n. 56.

[69] 1978 Act, ss.7–11.

[70] Interpretation Act 1889, s.38(2); see now the Interpretation Act 1978, s.16.

[71] See *Bennett* v. *Tatton* (1918) 88 L.J.K.B. 313; *Postlethwaite* v. *Katz* (1943) 59 T.L.R. 248; *R.* v. *West London Stipendiary Magistrate, ex p. Simeon* [1983] 1 A.C. 234 (repeal of the "sus" law held not to affect a prosecution for an offence committed before the repeal came into effect).

[72] See now the Interpretation Act 1978, s.15. Similarly, the repeal of an Act does not revive anything not in force or existing at the time of the repeal: *ibid.* s.16(1)(*a*). Hence, if statute B modifies statute A by partial repeal or substitution of words, statute A continues in effect subject to the modification notwithstanding the repeal of statute B.

the ground that it is obsolete[73]; such provisions have to be repealed by a subsequent statute.[74]

10. ENROLLMENT AND PUBLICATION[75]

In medieval times a systematic official record of parliamentary statutes was not kept. An incomplete statute roll was started in the Chancery for internal purposes in 1299 and continued to the middle of the 15th century. *Rotuli Parliamentorum* ("Rolls of Parliament") were kept between 1290 and 1503; they contained a general record of parliamentary proceedings, but only included some of the Acts. From 1483 "Inrollments of Acts" (records of each Act "engrossed" on parchment) were certified by the Clerk of the Parliaments and delivered to the Chancery; the officers of the Chancery commonly termed them the "Parliament Rolls" although they are distinct from the *Rotuli Parliamentorum*. From the middle of the nineteenth century two copies of each Act have been printed on vellum; one copy is kept in the House of Lords, the other in the Public Records Office.[76]

Lawyers at first relied on private manuscript collections of statutes. These formed the basis of unofficial printed collections that began to appear from 1481 onwards. From 1483 *Sessional Volumes of Statutes* were printed and published; these came to be issued by the King's or Queen's Printer but were not technically an official series published by royal or parliamentary authority. Useful collections of *Statutes at Large* appeared in the late eighteenth century, with various editors (*e.g.* Pickering (1762), Ruffhead and Runnington (1786) and Tomlins and Raithby (1811)). These covered statutes from Magna Carta to date; continuation volumes, sometimes covering several sessions, and based on the King's Printer's copies, were produced in the eighteenth and nineteenth centuries under the titles of *Statutes of the United Kingdom* or *Public General Statutes*. The Controller of Her Majesty's Stationery Office was appointed as the Queen's Printer in 1886. From 1940 the King's or Queen's Printer's copies of statutes have been published on an annual rather than a sessional basis, with *Public General Acts and Measures*[77] issued separately from *Local and Personal Acts*; each Act is also published individually by H.M.S.O.

The first official collection of statutes was the edition of *Statutes of the Realm* prepared by the Record Commissioners and published in nine volumes between 1810 and 1828. This gave texts and translations of statutes between 1235 and 1713, excluding the Commonwealth period,[78] and while a considerable improvement on what was otherwise available, was in various respects incomplete and inaccurate.[79] Later in the century, the Statute Law

---

[73] Under the doctrine of desuetude, Acts of the Scottish Parliament may become obsolete and repealed by a long period of contrary practice by the community: *M'Ara* v. *Magistrates of Edinburgh* 1931 S.C. 1059; *Brown* v. *Magistrates of Edinburgh* 1913 S.L.T. 456, 458; *Earl of Antrim's Petition* [1967] A.C. 691.

[74] See above, p. 247.

[75] F. A. R. Bennion, *Statutory Interpretation* (1984), pp. 119–124.

[76] See S. A. de Smith and R. Brazier, *Constitutional and Administrative Law* (6th ed., 1989), p. 85. A third print is made of Measures of the General Synod.

[77] These also appear in the *Law Reports Statutes* series.

[78] As to which see C. H. Firth and R. S. Rait, *Acts and Ordinances of the Interregnum* (1911).

[79] See T. F. T. Plucknett, *Statutes and their Interpretation in the Fourteenth Century* (1922), Chap. II.

Committee[80] supervised the publication of the first edition of *Statutes Revised*, which comprised the public Acts in force at the end of 1878, as amended, given in chronological order. Two further editions were produced between 1888 and 1929 and in 1950. This series has been superseded by *Statutes in Force*, which is published in loose booklet form rather than in bound volumes to facilitate the substitution of revised copies of statutes that are heavily amended; there are also regular supplements. The volumes are arranged in 124 (originally 131) groups according to subject-matter and are printed by computer-assisted typesetting. These official collections are supplemented by the *Index to the Statutes* and the *Chronological Table of the Statutes*.[81] As a matter of citation, references to another Act in a statute passed after 1889 are, unless the contrary intention appears, to be read as referring to (a) any revised edition of the statutes printed by authority, (b) if it is not printed there, to the *Statutes of the Realm*; or (c) in other cases, to the Queen's Printer's copy.[82] Occasionally it may be necessary to go behind the published version and check its authenticity against the original source.[83] Where through a printing error a statute as printed by H.M.S.O. does not reflect the version of the vellum print, the Clerk of the Parliament authorises the issue of a correction slip. This is sometimes done where the vellum print does not reflect the version assented to by Parliament.[84]

There are various departmental compilations of statutes and regulations published by H.M.S.O. and regularly revised, such as *The Taxes Acts* (for the Inland Revenue) and several works on the law of social security (for the Department of Social Security). The most important current commercial collections are *Halsbury's Statutes of England* (4th ed.: a revised edition arranged by subject matter) and *Current Law Statutes Annotated* (arranged in chronological order). There are also many collections on particular topics published in loose-leaf encyclopedias. An important advantage of these commercial publications is that the statutes are given in annotated form. Statutes and statutory instruments are included in the *Lexis* computer database.

11. VALIDITY

The validity of an Act of Parliament may not be questioned in an English court; there is no Bill of Rights or other constitutional limitation to which legislation must conform as there is, for example, in the United States of

---

[80] See above, p. 257.
[81] This covers public and general legislation; editions since 1974 have also recorded the effect of local and personal legislation enacted since then. A limited edition of a *Chronological Table of Local Legislation*, covering the effect of all local legislation passed between 1925 and 1973, was distributed in 1985 to those particularly concerned with local statute law, and to selected libraries and record offices (20th Annual Report of the Law Commission 1984–85 (1985–86 H.C. 247), p. 38). It is to be amalgamated with further work concerning earlier periods and with the information concerning local legislation contained in the *Chronological Table of the Statutes* since 1974 (22nd Annual Report of the Law Commission 1986–87 (1987–88 H.C. 319), p. 14). It will eventually cover the period 1797–1930 (25th Annual Report 1990 (1990–91 H.C. 249), p. 13).
[82] Interpretation Act 1978, s.19.
[83] See, *e.g. R.* v. *Casement* [1917] 1 K.B. 98, 134, in relation to the Treason Act 1351, where the *Rotuli Parliamentorum* and the Statute Rolls were consulted.
[84] F. Bennion, *Statutory Interpretation* (1984), pp. 120–121; J. J. Rankin, [1987] Stat.L.R. 53.

America.[85] This point has arisen in cases where it has been claimed that a private Act is invalid on the ground that parliamentary standing orders have not been observed,[86] or that Parliament has been misled by fraudulent misrepresentations[87]: such claims have failed. In 1982, a taxpayer argued that the change in the status of M.P.s from self-employed meant that they had become employees of the Crown and so disqualified from membership. As a result, the Social Security Act 1975, which imposed on him certain obligations to pay national insurance contributions, was invalid. His argument was emphatically and summarily rejected by Nourse J.: "the court can only look at the Parliamentary roll."[88] Of much more importance was the claim of a group of Canadian Indian Chiefs that the Canada Act 1982 was *ultra vires* on the ground that the consent of the "Dominion" of Canada had not been obtained as required by section 4 of the Statute of Westminster 1931, merely the consent of the Senate and House of Commons of Canada. Sir Robert Megarry V.-C. held[89] that he owed "full and dutiful obedience" to every Act of Parliament, and that the Canada Act 1982 was such an Act. The Court of Appeal held[90] that even on the assumption that Parliament could bind its successors by a provision such as section 4, the application failed as there had been compliance with that section. Attempts to impugn statutes on the ground that they are contrary to international law have also failed.[91]

There were in the seventeenth century dicta that Acts of Parliament "against common right and reason, or repugnant, or impossible to be performed,"[92] or contrary to natural justice by making a man judge in his own cause[93] could be held by the judges to be void. However, these dicta were controversial even at that time, were not acted upon, and are not accepted today: "since the supremacy of Parliament was finally demonstrated by the Revolution of 1688 any such idea has become obsolete."[94] This position was reaffirmed by Lord Scarman in *Duport Steels Ltd.* v. *Sirs*[95]:

> ". . . [I]n the field of statute law the judge must be obedient to the will of Parliament as expressed in its enactments. In this field Parliament makes and unmakes the law: the judge's duty is to interpret and to apply the law, not to change it to meet the judge's idea of what justice requires. Interpretation does, of course, imply in the interpreter a power of choice where differing constructions are possible. But our law

---

[85] See above, pp. 242–243. The question of possible conflict with European legislation is considered below, pp. 299–308. As to whether a court may exercise a jurisdiction to determine whether an *ostensibly* authentic Act of Parliament is *in fact* authentic see S. A. de Smith and R. Brazier, *Constitutional and Administrative Law* (6th ed., 1989), pp. 106–108.

[86] *Edinburgh and Dalkeith Rly.* v. *Wauchope* (1842) 7 Cl. & F. 710.

[87] *Lee* v. *Bude and Torrington Junction Railway* (1871) L.R. 6 C.P. 576; *Pickin* v. *British Railways Board* [1974] A.C. 765.

[88] *Martin* v. *O'Sullivan* [1982] S.T.C. 416, 419, affirmed [1984] S.T.C. 258.

[89] [1983] Ch. 77.

[90] *Ibid.*

[91] *Mortensen* v. *Peters* 1906 S.L.T. 227; *Cheney* v. *Conn* [1968] 1 W.L.R. 242.

[92] *Dr. Bonham's Case* (1610) 8 Co.Rep. 114, 118, *per* Coke C.J.; Coke subsequently expressed a different view extrajudicially: 4 *Coke's Institutes* 37, 41.

[93] *Day* v. *Savadge* (1614) Hob. 85, 87 *per* Hobart C.J.; *cf.* Holt C.J. in *City of London* v. *Wood* (1701) 12 Mod. 669, 686–8.

[94] *Pickin* v. *British Railways Board* [1974] A.C. 765, 782 *per* Lord Reid.

[95] [1980] I.C.R. 161, 189–190.

requires the judge to choose the construction which in his best judgment meets the legislative purposes of the enactment. If the result be
unjust but inevitable, the judge may say so and invite Parliament to
reconsider its provision. But he must not deny the statute.... Only if a
just result can be achieved without violating the legislative purpose of
the statute may the judge select the construction which best suits his
idea of what justice requires."

C. SUBORDINATE LEGISLATION[96]

1. DELEGATION

Each year the output of subordinate[97] legislation vastly exceeds that of Acts
of Parliament. Law-making powers have been delegated by Parliament to a
wide variety of public authorities, including the Crown, ministers, local
authorities and public corporations. Procedural rules may be made for the
courts by Rule Committees consisting of judges and lawyers.[98] In addition,
the Crown retains certain powers to legislate by virtue of the royal prerogative. There have been examples of the delegation of rule-making powers by
Parliament for as long as Parliament has been acknowledged as the supreme
law-making body. However, the nineteenth and twentieth centuries have
seen an enormous increase, albeit "wayward and unsystematic,"[99] in the
extent of delegation, matching the extension of the powers and functions of
government. Each of the world wars saw the creation of a complex system of
statutory powers, mostly contained in delegated legislation made, respectively, under the Defence of the Realm Acts 1914–15 and the Emergency
Powers (Defence) Acts 1939–40; every aspect of national life was closely
regulated.

The developments were at first welcomed on the ground that Parliament
was thereby able to deal with the issues of importance while the details could
be settled departmentally. Certain judges and academic commentators were
less enthusiastic. The most extreme of the criticism was expressed by the
then Lord Chief Justice, Lord Hewart, in a book entitled "The New Despotism" (1929). The main objections articulated were that wide powers were
given to the executive, and that the safeguards against abuse, particularly
Parliamentary safeguards, were inadequate. Some people held the view that
the delegation of legislative power was unwise and might be dispensed with
altogether. However, it was difficult to disentangle general objections to the
extension of state power from objections to the particular form that the
extension took. Delegated legislation was one of the issues considered by

[96] See C. K. Allen, *Law and Orders* (3rd ed., 1965); Sir William Wade, *Administrative Law* (6th
ed., 1988), Chap. 22; B. L. Jones, *Garner's Administrative Law* (7th ed., 1989), Chap. IV; S.
A. de Smith and R. Brazier, *Constitutional and Administrative Law* (6th ed., 1989), Chap.
18; K. Puttick, *Challenging Delegated Legislation* (1988); Cabinet Office (Management and
Personnel Office), *Statutory Instrument Practice* (2nd ed., 1987).
[97] Strictly, the term "subordinate" legislation covers "all legislation, permitted as well as
authorised, that is inferior to statute law"; "delegated" legislation is that "authorised by Act
of Parliament": H.M.S.O., *Access to Subordinate Legislation* (House of Commons Library
Document No. 5).
[98] Rules of the Supreme Court; County Court Rules; Crown Court Rules.
[99] Allen (1965), p. 32.

the Committee on Ministers' Powers, which reported in 1932.[1] The Committee expressed the view that "whether good or bad" the practice of delegation was inevitable[2]:

> "the system of delegated legislation is both legitimate and constitutionally desirable for certain purposes, within certain limits, and under certain safeguards."[3]

It pointed to the pressure on parliamentary time, the technicality of the subject matter of modern legislation, the difficulty of working out administrative machinery in time to insert all the required provisions in the Bill, the flexibility of a system which allowed for adaptation to unknown future conditions without the necessity of an amending Act, and for the opportunity for experiment, and the need on occasion for emergency action. The Committee made a number of suggestions for improving the terminology, publication and scrutiny of delegated legislation. One of the members of the Committee, Ellen Wilkinson M.P., thought that certain passages gave:

> "the impression that the delegating of legislation is a necessary evil, inevitable in the present state of pressure on parliamentary time, but nevertheless a tendency to be watched with misgiving and carefully safeguarded."[4]

Nevertheless, since then the constitutional propriety of delegation has not seriously been questioned, although concern has been expressed at the growing tendency in recent years for statutory instruments to deal "no longer . . . with means but with principles."[5]

2. THE FORMS OF SUBORDINATE LEGISLATION

The nomenclature of nineteenth century subordinate legislation was varied and confusing. Different procedures were followed for making and issuing the different kinds of rules. Some kind of regularity was created by the Rules Publication Act 1893, and the position was further improved by its replacement, the Statutory Instruments Act 1946.[6] Today, most subordinate legislation takes the form of *statutory instruments* made under the procedure laid down by the 1946 Act or *byelaws* made under the Local Government Act 1972, although other forms are possible. Different names are still used for different kinds of statutory instruments; these names merely indicate the general nature of the instrument and no longer reflect any difference as to

---

[1] Cmnd. 4060. The first chairman was the Earl of Donoughmore; he was succeeded as chairman by Sir Leslie Scott.

[2] *Ibid.* p. 5.

[3] *Ibid.* p. 51.

[4] *Ibid.* p. 137. She felt that in the conditions of the modern state the practice "instead of being grudgingly conceded ought to be widely extended, and new ways devised to facilitate the process."

[5] Andrew Bennett, M.P., Chairman of the Joint Committee on Statutory Instruments, in evidence to the Select Committee on Procedure: Second Report, 1986–87 H.C. 350, *The Use of Time on the Floor of the House*, pp. vii, 6. The Committee noted this view "with concern." Examples of recent legislation where the statute merely creates a framework for regulations include the Legal Aid Act 1988 and the Local Government Finance Act 1988 (on the latter, see the notes by M. Grant in *Current Law Statutes Annotated 1988*, pp. 41–12—41–13). See also K. Puttick, *Challenging Delegated Legislation* (1988), Chap. 3.

[6] See below, pp. 270–274.

the procedure whereby they are made and promulgated. The selection of a particular title is a matter of departmental practice.

The following are the main kinds of subordinate legislation. *Orders in Council* are made by the Queen with the advice of the Privy Council (the "Queen in Council"). They may be made under the royal prerogative[7]; more commonly they are made under a statutory power, in which case they are normally statutory instruments. *Proclamations* are notices given by the Queen to her subjects; again, they may be made under the royal prerogative[8] or statute[9] and are published in the *London Gazette*. *Royal Warrants* are made under the royal prerogative and normally concern the pay and pensions of members of the armed forces. *Regulations, Rules, Orders, Schemes* and *Warrants* are usually statutory instruments. The usage of these terms is imprecise although "Rules" are usually[10] the procedural rules of a court or tribunal, and the term "Warrant" is used to describe some Treasury instruments which confer an authority or an entitlement to money. *Directions* may occasionally have to be promulgated as statutory instruments.

3. PREPARATION OF SUBORDINATE LEGISLATION

Subordinate legislation is generally drafted by lawyers in the government department concerned, in the Treasury Solicitor's office where the department has no legal branch, or, in cases of exceptional importance or difficulty, by one of the Parliamentary draftsmen. The "division of labour" between the Parliamentary counsel responsible for statutory drafting and departmental lawyers has been described as "a basic weakness of the system,"[11] although any significant change would obviously require a large increase in the number of counsel. The "preparational parameters" mentioned above[12] in relation to statutes are not applicable to nearly the same extent, although the draftsman has to take care to ensure that the instrument is *intra vires*[13]; the "operational parameters" are, however, equally important.[14] Prior consultation between the department and advisory bodies and interest groups is a well established practice[15]; consultation requirements may be imposed in the parent Act.[16] Local authority byelaws are prepared by the authority concerned but must normally conform to the models issued by government departments to stand much chance of being confirmed. Important statutory instruments may be examined by the Cabinet's Legislation Committee.

---

[7] *e.g.* an Order altering the constitution of a colony. An Order in Council under the prerogative may not alter the common law or statute law: *The Zamora* [1916] 2 A.C. 77, 90.

[8] *e.g.* coinage proclamations.

[9] *e.g.* proclamations of a state of emergency under the Emergency Powers Act 1920.

[10] Not invariably: see the Immigration Rules.

[11] F. A. R. Bennion, *Statute Law* (3rd ed., 1990), p. 57.

[12] At pp. 250–251.

[13] See below, pp. 275–278.

[14] Bennion (1990), pp. 57–58.

[15] See J. F. Garner, [1964] P.L. 105; A. D. Jergesen, [1978] P.L. 290.

[16] A statutory duty to consult is regarded as mandatory (see below p. 275). However, a court will not imply an obligation to consult if there is no express provision: *Bates* v. *Lord Hailsham* [1972] 1 W.L.R. 1373.

4. Procedures for Making Subordinate Legislation

(a) Statutory instruments

The "statutory instrument" procedure applies to delegated legislation (1) made, confirmed or approved under a power conferred on the Crown after 1947 by statute[17] and expressed to be exercisable "by Order in Council"[18]; (2) made, confirmed or approved under a power conferred on a minister after 1947 by statute[19] and expressed to be exercisable "by statutory instrument"[20]; (3) made under a power contained in a statute passed before 1948 to make "statutory rules"[21] within the meaning of the Rules Publication Act 1893,[22] or (4) confirmed or approved under certain powers contained in pre-1948 statutes.[23]

The procedural requirements for statutory instruments are prescribed partly by the parent Acts and partly by the 1946 Act. The parent Act may require that the instrument[24] be laid[25] before Parliament.[26] If it does it has to be laid "before it comes into operation," unless it is essential that it comes into operation sooner, in which case the Lord Chancellor and the Speaker must be informed of the reason.[27] This process merely brings the instrument to the attention of Parliament. An instrument may have to be laid in draft[28] or after it has been made. In addition, the instrument may be made subject to the "affirmative resolution" or the "negative resolution" procedure. Under the former, the instrument can only come into effect if a resolution approving it is passed, within the period (if any) specified in the parent Act.

---

[17] Sub-delegated legislation made under a power conferred by statutory instrument is thus not normally within the scope of the 1946 Act.

[18] Statutory Instruments Act 1946, s.1(1).

[19] See note 17 above.

[20] Statutory Instruments Act 1946, s.1(1).

[21] Provided, in most cases, that the rule is of a "legislative" and not an "executive" character: Statutory Instruments Regulations 1947 (S.I. 1948 No. 1), reg. 2(1).

[22] Statutory Instruments Act 1946, s.1(2). There are certain exceptions: see S.I. 1948 No. 1, reg. 2(3) and Schedule.

[23] Statutory Instruments Act 1946, s.9(1); S.I. 1948 No. 1, reg. 2(2); Statutory Instruments (Confirmatory Powers) Order 1947 (S.I. 1948 No. 2). The rule has to be legislative rather than executive in character and subject to the requirement that it be laid before Parliament.

[24] *i.e.* "any document by which" a power to make orders etc. is "exercised": Statutory Instruments Act 1946, s.1(1). A document referred to in regulations need not be laid provided that it is not part and parcel of the regulations: *R.* v. *Secretary of State for Social Services, ex p. Camden London Borough Council* [1987] 1 W.L.R. 819; and see A. I. L. Campbell, [1987] P.L. 328.

[25] As to the meaning of "laying," see the Laying of Documents before Parliament (Interpretation) Act 1948. It normally involves delivery of copies to the Votes and Proceedings Office of the Commons and the Office of the Clerk of the Parliaments. Subordinate legislation other than statutory instruments may also have to be laid before Parliament, *e.g.* under the Immigration Act 1971: see *R.* v. *Immigration Appeals Tribunal, ex p. Joyles* [1972] 1 W.L.R. 1390.

[26] Sometimes just the House of Commons: *e.g.* orders prescribing maximum rates under the Rates Act 1984: *R.* v. *Secretary of State for the Environment, ex p. Greenwich London Borough Council, The Times*, December 19, 1985; *R.* v. *Secretary of State for the Environment, ex p. Leicester City Council* (1985) 25 R.V.R. 31 (references in section 4(1) to "Parliament" to be read in context as to a reference to the House of Commons only).

[27] Statutory Instruments Act 1946, s.4(1).

[28] See *ibid.* s.6(1). The instrument may not be made within 40 days, and either House may resolve that it shall not be made.

Under the latter, which is a much more common requirement,[29] but which is less efficacious in ensuring Parliamentary scrutiny, either House may within 40 days of its being laid resolve that the instrument should be annulled.[30] Since 1973 it has been possible for proceedings on statutory instruments to be taken in Commons Standing Committees rather than on the floor of the House. Nevertheless, Parliamentary scrutiny of the merits of instruments under these procedures is not particularly effective in either forum.[31]

An instrument may also be scrutinised by the Joint Committee on Statutory Instruments. This committee was first appointed in 1973, and replaced the separate committees of each House that had formerly undertaken this work.[32] The Chairman is an Opposition M.P. The Committee examines instruments laid before either House and subject to either form of resolution procedure, other instruments of a general character and special procedure orders. It may draw the attention of Parliament to a particular instrument on any of a number of specified grounds, or on any other grounds not impinging on the merits of or policy behind the instrument. The specified grounds are that:

  (i) it imposes a charge on the public revenues;
 (ii) it is made under an enactment excluding it from challenge in the courts;
(iii) it purports to have retrospective effect where the parent Act does not so provide;
 (iv) it has been unjustifiably delayed in publication or being laid before Parliament;
  (v) it has not been notified in proper time to the Lord Chancellor and the Speaker where it comes into effect before being presented to Parliament;
 (vi) it may be *ultra vires*;
(vii) it appears to make an unusual or unexpected use of the powers conferred by the parent Act;
(viii) it requires elucidation as to its form or purport; or
 (ix) it is defective in drafting.

Instruments subject to House of Commons proceedings only are examined by the Commons members of the Joint Committee acting as a Commons Select Committee on Statutory Instruments. No formal steps have to be taken in either House following an adverse report by one of these committees, although such reports may be referred to in other Parliamentary proceedings concerning the instruments, and the work of these

[29] In 1976–77 there were 127 instruments subject to affirmative procedure, 669 subject to negative procedure, 37 general instruments only required to be laid, and 197 general instruments not so required: *First Report from the Select Committee on Procedure*, 1977–78 H.C. 588 Vol. 1, p. xxxi; an increasing proportion of instruments have been made subject to the first two procedures.

[30] Statutory Instruments Act, 1946 s.5(1). This takes the form of an address to Her Majesty praying that the instrument be annulled, and is commonly termed a "prayer."

[31] See *First Report from the Select Committee on Procedure*, 1977–78 H.C. 588, Vol. 1, pp. xxix–xxxix; J. Beatson, (1979) 12 Cornell Int. L.J. 199; P. Norton, *The Commons in Perspective* (1981), pp. 95–99; P. Byrne, (1976) 29 *Parliamentary Affairs* 366; A. Beith M.P. (1981) 34 *Parliamentary Affairs* 165.

[32] See the *Report from the Joint Committee on Delegated Legislation*, 1971–72 H.C. 45, H.L. 184.

committees and their predecessors seem to have played a part in reducing delays and improving drafting.[33] A recent survey has concluded that the technical process of scrutiny now appears to work as effectively as a parliamentary committee can be expected to function. Nevertheless, the increasing use of delegated legislation for major policy implementation, the lack of parliamentary time for debate, the increase in decisions taken before the Committee's report is published and the emphasis on political rather than legal points in debates on the merits have led to "the reality that parliamentary scrutiny of delegated legislation is not effective democratic control."[34]

Once a statutory instrument is made it must be sent to the Queen's Printer and copies must as soon as possible be printed and sold.[35] The requirements as to printing and sale do not apply to instruments classified as "local"[35a]; to general instruments otherwise regularly printed and published; to temporary instruments; to schedules whose printing and sale "is unnecessary or undesirable having regard to the nature or bulk of the document" and to any other steps taken to publicize them; and to confidential instruments not yet in operation.[36] The requirements may, however, be imposed by the Statutory Instruments Reference Committee appointed by the Lord Chancellor and the Speaker.[37] The Queen's Printer allocates statutory instruments received to the series for the calendar year in which they are made, and numbers them consecutively as near as may be in the order in which they are received.[38] They are cited by their number and year.[39]

H.M.S.O. also publishes (1) periodical lists of the titles of instruments issued; (2) an Annual Edition with full texts of instruments issued, an appendix of prerogative legislation and relevant lists, tables and indices; (3) the annual *Table of Government Orders*, a chronological list showing which instruments are still in force, amended or revoked; and (4) the *Index to Government Orders*, issued every two years, which lists existing powers to make delegated legislation and current exercises of those powers according to subject matter. Butterworth & Co. publishes *Halsbury's Statutory Instruments*, which lists and summarises delegated legislation in force according to subject matter, gives the annotated text of the "more important orders, rules and regulations, selected on the basis of the likely requirements of subscribers,"[40] and includes a regular updating service. Regulations are avail-

---

[33] See S.A. de Smith and R. Brazier, *Constitutional and Administrative Law* (6th ed., 1989), pp. 342–344.

[34] J. D. Hayhurst and P. Wallington, "The Parliamentary Scrutiny of Delegated Legislation" [1988] P.L. 547, 573–576. The conclusions are Professor Wallington's. For proposals for minor procedural changes, see Hayhurst and Wallington, pp. 575–576; 2nd Report from the Select Committee on Procedure, 1986–87 H.C. 350, *The Use of Time on the Floor of the House*, pp. vi–xi. See also T. St. J. Bates, [1986] Stat.L.R. 114.

[35] Statutory Instruments Act 1946, s.2.

[35a] See generally on local statutory instruments, R. J. B. Morris, [1990] Stat. L.R. 28.

[36] Statutory Instruments Regulations 1947 (S.I. 1948 No. 1), regs. 3–8. These matters have to be "certified" by the responsible authority (*i.e.* minister) in each case. This must be done in proper form: *Simmonds* v. *Newell* [1953] 1 W.L.R. 826.

[37] S.I. 1948 No. 1, reg. 11. The Committee has power to determine certain other questions which may arise as to numbering, publication, classication, etc. It consists of the Lord Chairman of Committees (Lords), the Chairman of Ways and Means (Commons) and six senior officers of both Houses: *Erskine May's Parliamentary Practice* (21st ed., 1989), p. 541.

[38] S.I. 1948 No. 1, reg. 3.

[39] Statutory Instruments Act 1946, s.2(2).

[40] *Halsbury's Statutory Instruments*: *A User's Guide*, p. 5.

able on *Lexis* and also normally included in encyclopedias on particular topics.

Rules and Orders made before 1949 are included in the series *Statutory Rules and Orders and Statutory Instruments Revised to Dec. 31st 1948*, which is arranged according to subject matter.[41]

The position as to the commencement of subordinate legislation is unclear. The subordinate legislation in question may expressly provide for its own commencement.[42] If it does not, there is some authority that an order can only come into effect when it is *made known*.[43] In a later case,[44] however, Streatfeild J. directed a jury as follows:

"I do not think that it can be said that to make a valid statutory instrument it is required that all of these stages should be gone through; namely, the making, the laying before Parliament, the printing and the certification of that part of it which it might be unnecessary to have printed. In my judgment the making of an instrument is complete when it is first of all made by the Minister concerned and after it has been laid before Parliament."[45]

The defendant was prosecuted for breach of a schedule to a statutory instrument that had not been printed as required by the Act. Streatfeild J. held that it was not invalid for lack of publication.

Section 3(1) of the Statutory Instruments Act 1946 provides that regulations should be made for the publication by H.M.S.O. of lists showing the dates of issue of instruments printed and sold by the Queen's Printer; in any legal proceedings, "an entry therein shall be conclusive evidence of the date on which any statutory instrument was first issued" by H.M.S.O.

Section 3(2) provides that in criminal proceedings for a contravention of "any such statutory instrument" it is:

"a defence to prove that the instrument had not been issued by Her Majesty's Stationery Office at the date of the alleged contravention unless it is proved that at that date reasonable steps had been taken for the purpose of bringing the purport of the instrument to the notice of the public, or of persons likely to be affected by it, or of the person charged."[46]

It is not, however, clear whether this defence is available (1) in respect of any instrument which has not been issued, including those exempted from publication requirements; or (2) in respect of an instrument which has not been issued in breach of a publication requirement; or (3) in respect only of

---

[41] Earlier editions were published in 1896 and 1904. Up to and including 1960 the Annual Editions were also arranged by subject-matter rather than chronologically.

[42] From 1947 all statutory instruments required to be laid before Parliament after being made must show the dates on which they come into operation; this does not, however, cover the whole field as not all instruments must be laid. Where a day is specified, the instrument comes into effect at the beginning of that day: Interpretation Act 1978, ss.4(a), 23.

[43] Bailhache J. in *Johnson* v. *Sargant* [1918] 1 K.B. 101. *Cf. Jones* v. *Robson* [1901] 1 Q.B. 673 where a requirement to give *notice* of certain orders was held to be directory (but in this case the order had been published, and the defendant knew of it).

[44] *R.* v. *Sheer Metalcraft Ltd.* [1954] 1 Q.B. 586.

[45] *Ibid.* p. 590. (There may of course be no "laying" requirement).

[46] It has been suggested that a similar defence should be created in respect of Acts of Parliament: Statute Law Society Working Party on Commencement of Acts of Parliament, [1980] Stat.L.R. 40, 51–52. The defence failed on the facts in *R.* v. *Sheer Metalcraft Ltd., supra.*

the period between the making of an instrument and its issue in circumstances where such issue does subsequently take place.[47] Moreover, the statutory defence does not apply to subordinate legislation other than statutory instruments. There is much to be said for the principle of *Johnson* v. *Sargant*:[48] "To bind a citizen by a law, the terms of which he has no means of knowing,[49] is the very essence of tyranny."[50]

(b) Local authority byelaws[51]

District and London borough councils have a general power to make byelaws for the "good rule and government" of the area "and for the prevention and suppression of nuisances" therein[52]; in addition there are numerous specific byelaw making powers.[53] The procedure for making byelaws, to be followed in all cases unless specific provision is otherwise made, is laid down by section 236 of the Local Government Act 1972. Byelaws cannot take effect until they are confirmed by the appropriate minister. Public notice must be given at least one month before application is made for confirmation, and a copy must be available for inspection. The confirming authority may fix the date on which a byelaw is to come into effect; if no date is so fixed, it comes into effect one month after it is confirmed. When confirmed, a copy must be printed and deposited at the authority's offices; it must be open to public inspection without payment at all reasonable hours, and copies supplied on payment of such sum, not exceeding 20p per copy, as the authority may determine.[54]

5. ARRANGEMENT OF STATUTORY INSTRUMENTS

A statutory instrument is normally arranged in the following order:[55]

(i) Year and number of the instrument.
(ii) An indication of the subject matter; this corresponds to the categories in the lists published periodically by H.M.S.O.
(iii) Title.
(iv) The dates when the instrument was made, laid before Parliament and is due to come into operation.
(v) A recital naming the person making the instrument and the relevant enabling powers.

---

[47] The difficulty is created by the word "such": see D. Lanham, (1974) 37 M.L.R. 510, 521–523. The *Sheer Metalcraft* case (1) is not inconsistent with the first interpretation, but the point as to whether the defence can apply in respect of *exempted* instruments did not arise as the minister had not certified that the instrument should be exempt; (2) is inconsistent with the second interpretation; and (3) is inconsistent with the third, as there was no suggestion that the schedule was ever published.
[48] [1918] 1 K.B. 101. Lanham (*ibid.*) argues that even where a date of commencement is specified, an instrument can only come into effect when published.; *contra*: A.I.L. Campbell, [1982] P.L. 569; response by Lanham, [1983] P.L. 395.
[49] Ignorance of a published instrument would probably not be regarded as a defence: ignorance of the law is no excuse.
[50] *Per* Barwick C.J. in *Watson* v. *Lee* (1980) 54 A.L.J.R. 1, 3.
[51] Sometimes spelt "by-laws."
[52] Local Government Act 1972, s.235(1).
[53] See C.A. Cross, *Encyclopedia of Local Government Law*, Appendix 6.
[54] Local authorities do not always seem to be aware of these obligations.
[55] See Bennion (1990), pp. 55–57.

(vi) The main provisions of the instrument. These are termed *articles* (in an Order), *regulations* or *rules* as the case may be. Subdivisions are called *paragraphs*. The instrument may be divided into *Parts* and may include a *Schedule*. Common form provisions as to title, definitions and commencement are placed at the beginning.

(vii) An indication of the minister by whom the instrument was signed.

(viii) An "Explanatory Note" stated to be "not part of" the instrument.

6. VALIDITY OF SUBORDINATE LEGISLATION[56]

All delegated legislation must conform to the limits laid down expressly or impliedly in the enabling Act; if those limits are exceeded the validity of the instrument[57] may be challenged in the courts.[58] Challenges may be made directly, for example by an action in the High Court for a declaration that the legislation is *ultra vires*; or indirectly, for example by raising the argument that an instrument is *ultra vires* as a defence to enforcement proceedings, such as a prosecution for contravening the instrument.[59] An instrument may be *ultra vires* if there has been a failure to comply with a "mandatory" procedural requirement. Some requirements are merely "directory"; the authorities are "directed" to comply with them, but compliance is not a pre-condition to the validity of the instrument. It is not easy to predict whether a court will hold a particular requirement to be mandatory or directory. In this context the duty to consult affected parties has been held to be mandatory,[60] but requirements as to publication[61] and laying[62] have been held to be directory. The scope of a consultation requirement was described

---

[56] See generally Sir William Wade, *Administrative Law* (6th ed., 1988), pp. 863–878; K. Puttick, *Challenging Delegated Legislation* (1988). Successful challenges to the *vires* of statutory instruments between 1914 and 1986 are summarised by J. D. Hayhurst and P. Wallington, [1988] P.L. 547, 566–573.

[57] Or other form of delegated legislation.

[58] The courts may also ensure that prerogative legislation falls within the scope of an existing prerogative power.

[59] Resort to this latter mode of proceeding is well established and in *R.* v. *Reading Crown Court, ex p. Hutchinson* [1988] Q.B. 384, D.C. (pet. dis. [1988] 1 W.L.R. 308, H.L.) the Divisional Court affirmed that its availability had not been affected by the principle of *O'Reilly* v. *Mackman* [1983] 2 A.C. 237 that matters of *vires* should normally be raised directly on an application for judicial review. A different view had previously been expressed in *Quietlynn Ltd.* v. *Plymouth City Council* [1988] Q.B. 114, D.C. (pet. dis. [1987] 1 W.L.R. 1080, H.L.).

[60] *Agricultural etc. Training Board* v. *Aylesbury Mushrooms Ltd.* [1972] 1 W.L.R. 190.

[61] *R.* v. *Sheer Metalcraft Ltd.* [1954] 1 Q.B. 586; see above, pp. 273–274.

[62] See *Bailey* v. *Williamson* (1873) L.R. 8 Q.B. 118; *Starey* v. *Graham* [1899] 1 Q.B. 406, 412; *Springer* v. *Doorly* (1950) L.R.B.G. 10 (W. Indian Court of Appeal); A.I.L. Campbell, [1983] P.L. 43; but see J. M. Evans, *de Smith's Judicial Review of Administrative Action* (4th ed., 1980), p. 148, for the argument that laying requirements should be regarded as mandatory; *cf. Bain* v. *Thorne* (1916) 12 Tas.L.R. 57 (Sup.Ct. of Tasmania). In 1981 Ronald Biggs escaped extradition from Barbados to the U.K. because the Barbados High Court held that regulations designating the U.K. as a country to which a fugitive could be extradited should have been laid before the Barbados Parliament: *The Times*, April 24, 1981: *Biggs* v. *Commissioner of Police* [1982 May] W.I.L.J. 121. Note, however, that the decision turned on a provision of the Interpretation Act of Barbados to the effect that the term "shall" [*i.e.* in "shall ... be laid] was "to be construed as imperative" (*ibid.*). In *R.* v. *Secretary of State for the Environment, ex p. Camden London Borough Council* (Unreported, February 26, 1986) Macpherson J. held that a requirement that supplementary benefit regulations "shall not be made" unless a draft had been laid before Parliament and approved by each House imposed a mandatory requirement. On appeal, the Court of Appeal assumed this to be so without deciding the point ([1987] 1 W.L.R. 819).

as follows by Webster J. in *R.* v. *Secretary of State for Social Services, ex p. Association of Metropolitan Authorities*:[63]

". . . in any context the essence of consultation is the communication of a genuine invitation to give advice and a genuine receipt of that advice. In my view it must go without saying that to achieve consultation sufficient information must be supplied by the consulting to the consulted party to enable it to tender helpful advice. Sufficient time must be given by the consulting to the consulted party to enable it to do that, and sufficient time must be available for such advice to be considered by the consulting party. Sufficient, in that context, does not mean ample, but at least enough to enable the relevant purpose to be fulfilled. By helpful advice, in this context, I mean sufficiently informed and considered information or advice about aspects of the form or substance of the proposals, or their implications for the consulted party, being aspects material to the implementation of the proposal as to which the Secretary of State might not be fully informed or advised and as to which the party consulted might have relevant information or advice to offer."

An instrument may be *ultra vires* if its subject matter lies beyond the scope of the enabling power. For example, in *Hotel and Catering Industry Training Board* v. *Automobile Proprietary Ltd.*[64] the House of Lords held that a power to make an order establishing a Training Board for persons employed "in any activities of industry or commerce" did not enable an order to be made in respect of members' clubs.

The established grounds upon which byelaws may be struck down are usually said to be those of *ultra vires*, uncertainty, unreasonableness and repugnancy to the general law,[65] although the last three grounds may also be regarded as facets of the *ultra vires* doctrine. For example, in *Staden* v. *Tarjanyi*[66] a district council made a byelaw in respect of a pleasure ground which provided:

"A person shall not in the pleasure ground . . . take off, fly or land any glider, manned or unmanned, weighing in total more than four kilogrammes. . . ."

The respondent flew a hang glider over the pleasure ground and was prosecuted under the byelaw. It was conceded that "in" meant "in or over." The Divisional Court held that the byelaw was invalid for uncertainty:

". . . anyone engaged upon the otherwise lawful pursuit of hang gliding must know with reasonable certainty when he is breaking the law and when he is not breaking the law. . . . [T]o be valid the byelaw must set some lower level below which the glider must not fly."[67]

[63] [1986] 1 W.L.R. 1, 4–5.
[64] [1969] 1 W.L.R. 697. See also *R.* v. *Customs and Excise Commissioners, ex p. Hedges and Butler Ltd.* [1986] 2 All E.R. 164 (power to demand production of the whole of the records of a business (including records concerning non-dutiable goods) held not to be "incidental" or "supplementary" to powers concerning the regulation of excise warehouses and dealings in dutiable goods); *R.* v. *Secretary of State for Social Services, ex p. Cotton, The Times,* December 14, 1985; *R.* v. *Inland Revenue Commissioners, ex p. Woolwich Equitable Building Society* [1987] S.T.C. 654.
[65] See C. A. Cross, *Encyclopedia of Local Government Law*, paras. 1–249—1–254.
[66] (1980) 78 L.G.R. 614.
[67] *Ibid.* p. 623.

The leading authority on the meaning of "unreasonableness" in the context of byelaws is *Kruse* v. *Johnson*[68] where Lord Russell of Killowen C.J. stated[69] that local authority byelaws ought to be supported if possible and "benevolently" interpreted, but might be struck down if unreasonable:

"But unreasonable in what sense? If, for instance, they were found to be partial and unequal in their operation as between different classes; if they were manifestly unjust; if they disclosed bad faith; if they involved such oppressive or gratuitous interference with the rights of those subject to them as could find no justification in the minds of reasonable men, the Court might well say, 'Parliament never intended to give authority to make such rules; they are unreasonable and ultra vires'. . . . A by-law is not unreasonable merely because particular judges may think that it goes further than is prudent or necessary or convenient, or because it is not accompanied by a qualification or an exception which some judges may think ought to be there."

Successful challenges on this ground are rare. It is not clear whether a statutory instrument, as distinct from a byelaw, can be challenged for unreasonableness. In *Maynard* v. *Osmond*[70] regulations which did not allow police officers to be legally represented in disciplinary proceedings were challenged on this ground[71]; the members of the Court of Appeal did not express any doubt as to the court's jurisdiction to entertain such a challenge, but dismissed the application on the merits.

In *R.* v. *Secretary of State for the Environment, ex p. Nottinghamshire County Council*,[72] the council challenged the 1985–86 guidance on expenditure limits given by the Secretary of State to local authorities, under section 59 of the Local Government, Planning and Land Act 1980, *inter alia* on the ground of unreasonableness. The guidance was required to be laid before, and approved by resolution of, the House of Commons. Lord Scarman in the House of Lords said[73]

". . . I cannot accept that it is constitutionally appropriate, save in very exceptional circumstances, for the courts to intervene on the ground of 'unreasonableness' to quash guidance framed by the Secretary of State and by necessary implication approved by the House of Commons. . . ."

The challenge failed on the merits. It is to be noted that the possibility of a challenge for unreasonableness was not completely ruled out. Indeed, the

---

[68] [1898] 2 Q.B. 91.
[69] At pp. 99–100.
[70] [1977] Q.B. 240.
[71] The Police (Discipline) Regulations 1965 (S.I. 1965 No. 543); the regulations applicable to Deputy Chief Constables, Assistant Chief Constables and Chief Constables did permit legal representation (S.I. 1965 No. 544). The court did not accept that this constituted "unfair discrimination."
[72] [1986] A.C. 240. *Cf. City of Edinburgh District Council* v. *Secretary of State for Scotland* 1985 S.L.T. 551.
[73] [1986] A.C. 240, 287.

suggestion that Parliamentary approval would properly restrict the permissible scope of such a challenge has been doubted.[74] It is clearly the case that Parliamentary approval, other than in an Act of Parliament, does not render delegated legislation immune from challenges based on other aspects of the *ultra vires* doctrine.[75] In *R.* v. *Secretary of State for the Environment, ex p. Hammersmith and Fulham London Borough Council*[76] the House of Lords unanimously approved Lord Scarman's view, although the list of grounds of challenge said to be permissible is so lengthy[77] that it is difficult to see what kind of challenge is ruled out.[78]

Even where there are grounds for holding delegated legislation *ultra vires*, a remedy may still be refused in the exercise of the court's discretion.[79] The court may be able to hold that an invalid part of an order can be "severed," leaving the remaining part intact.[80] Finally, the court may in an appropriate case hold that an order is invalid only in so far as it affects a particular applicant.[81]

7. QUASI-LEGISLATION[82]

In recent years, greater attention has been paid to "administrative quasi-legislation"[83]: administrative rules that do not have direct legal force. There has been:

[74] Sir William Wade, *Administrative Law* (6th ed., 1988), pp. 29, 410–411, 868; C. M. G. Himsworth, 1985 S.L.T. 369; A. I. L. Campbell, 1986 S.L.T. 101; C. T. Reid, [1986] C.L.J. 169. A provision in the Immigration Rules was held to be unreasonable in *R.* v. *Immigration Appeal Tribunal, ex p. Manshoora Begun* [1986] Imm. A.R. 385. The Rules are "administrative instructions from the Home Secretary to immigration officers and statements of policy and practice" (Wade (1988), p. 226). They are subject to Parliamentary disapproval but are not published as statutory instruments.

[75] *R.* v. *H.M. Treasury, ex p. Smedley* [1985] Q.B. 657, 666–669 (per Sir John Donalson M.R., in relation to an Order in Council); *R.* v. *Secretary of State for the Environment, ex p. Greater London Council* (Unreported, April 3, 1985): discussed in the articles cited in f.n. 74, and in M. Grant, *Ratecapping and the Law* (2nd ed., 1986), pp. 12–13; *R.* v. *Secretary of State for the Environment, ex p. Nottinghamshire County Council* [1986] A.C. 240, 247–251 (per Lord Scarman).

[76] [1990] 3 W.L.R. 898, 960–963.

[77] That the exercise of discretion frustrates the policy of the statute, that legally relevant considerations have been ignored or irrelevant considerations taken into account, that there is bad faith, improper motive, or manifest absurdity: see Lord Bridge at p. 962F and H. *Cf.* below, p. 873.

[78] A challenge to the merits of an exercise of discretion cannot in any event be based on the *ultra vires* doctrine. See below, p. 873.

[79] *e.g. R.* v. *Secretary of State for Social Services, ex p. Association of Metropolitan Authorities* [1986] 1 W.L.R. 1.

[80] *Dunkley* v. *Evans* [1981] 3 All E.R. 285; *cf. R.* v. *Secretary of State for Transport, ex p. Greater London Council* [1985] 3 All E.R. 300.

[81] *e.g. Agricultural etc. Training Board* v. *Aylesbury Mushrooms Ltd.* [1972] 1 W.L.R. 190 (where an order was only held to be invalid in respect of a particular organisation that had not been consulted).

[82] G. Ganz, *Quasi-Legislation: Recent Developments in Secondary Legislation* (1987); R. E. Megarry, (1944) 60 L.Q.R. 125; Lord Campbell, "Codes of Practice as an Alternative to Legislation" [1985] Stat.L.R. 127; A. Samuels, "Codes of Practice and Legislation" [1986] Stat.L.R. 29; T. St. J. Bates, [1986] Stat.L.R. 114, 120–123; Vol. 469 H.L. Deb., cols. 1075–1104, January 15, 1986 (debate on codes of practice); R. Baldwin and J. Houghton, "Circular arguments: The Status and Legitimacy of Administrative Rules" [1986] P.L. 239; R.B. Ferguson, "The Legal Status of Non-Statutory Codes of Practice" [1988] J.B.L. 12.

[83] A term coined by Megarry, *op. cit.*

"an exponential growth of statutory and extra-statutory rules in a plethora of forms. Codes of practice, guidance, guidance notes, guidelines, circulars, White Papers, development control policy notes, development briefs, practice statements, tax concessions, Health Service Notices, Family Practitioner Notices, codes of conduct, codes of ethics and conventions are just some of the guises in which the rules appear."[84]

(a) Statutory rules

There are many variables in the structure and operation of such rules: the overall picture is arguably more confused than the arrangements for delegated legislation were before the Statutory Instruments Act 1946. These variables include the following:

— By whom they are made: a minister; a non-governmental statutory agency; a non-statutory body.
— To whom they are directed: officials; local authorities; courts and tribunals; private organisations and citizens.
— Whether they are subject to Parliamentary scrutiny: there may be a requirement for a code to be laid before Parliament (in draft or in a final version), subject to affirmative or negative procedures.
— How they are published: by H.M.S.O., by a government department or otherwise.
— Their legal effect: there are several forms. In the case of some codes, no effect is stated, although it does not follow that they are entirely devoid of legal effect. There may be a requirement that provisions of the code be taken into account, if relevant, by a local authority, tribunal or court. It may be provided that breach of a code may be relied upon as tending to establish civil or criminal liability, and compliance as tending to negative such liability: indeed in one case as establishing liability unless the contrary is proved.
— The content: McCrudden[85] distinguishes four types of codes, although any one code may contain elements of them all:

"Codes may include provisions (i) to codify existing non-legal practice; (ii) to codify the already existing law of the courts and/or the previous legal interpretations on a particular issue of the body making the code; (iii) to set out recommended good industrial practice; and (iv) to interpret independently those statutory provisions for which the body making the code has some responsibility."

An alternative typology is suggested by Baldwin and Houghton,[86] who distinguish: (i) procedural rules; (ii) interpretative guides; (iii) instructions to officials; (iv) prescriptive/evidential rules; (v) commendatory rules; (vi) voluntary codes; (vii) rules of practice, management or operation; and (viii) consultative devices and administrative pronouncements.

[84] Ganz (1987), pp. 1–2.
[85] (1988) 51 M.L.R. 409, 431.
[86] [1986] P.L. 239, 240–245.

Examples include the Immigration Rules,[87] the PACE Codes of Practice,[88] the Code of Guidance concerning Homelessness,[89] the Highway Code,[90] the Sex Discrimination Code of Practice,[91] the Code of Practice on Picketing,[92] and the Approved Documents giving guidance with respect to the requirements of building regulation.[93]

The position as to Parliamentary scrutiny is different in a number of respects from that for statutory instruments. On the one hand, particular codes have been examined by the appropriate departmental select committee, which does not normally happen with other forms of legislation. On the other, the Joint Committee on Statutory Instruments only has jurisdiction to examine documents, other than statutory instruments, that require Parliamentary approval; there is no provision for the merits to be debated in Standing Committee; and the likelihood of a merits debate in the Chamber is low.[94]

The perceived advantages of codes of practice and the like include the use of informal, non-technical, language; flexibility; and the promotion of uniformity of practice, particularly in the public sector.[95] Their "fundamental rationale" is the adoption of a voluntary approach rather than compulsion.[96]

While there is much to be said for this where codes are based on widespread consultation and consensus, there are nevertheless difficulties.[97] Sometimes they are introduced as an unhappy compromise between statutory regulation and inaction. In some areas the voluntary approach has broken down and compulsion has replaced persuasion. There has been criticism of the use of codes with controversial provisions that go beyond

---

[87] Immigration Act 1971, ss.3(2), 19: made by the Secretary of State, issued as a House of Commons paper, subject to annulment by Parliament and binding on adjudicators and the Immigration Appeal Tribunal, no consultation requirements.

[88] See below, p. 597.

[89] Housing Act 1985, s.71: made by the Secretary of State, published as a Circular, authorities to have regard to guidance, no laying or consultation requirements.

[90] Road Traffic Act 1988, s.38: made by the Secretary of State, who must consult such representative organisations as he thinks fit, issued via H.M.S.O., subject to annulment by Parliament, may be relied on in legal proceedings as tending to establish or negative liability.

[91] Sex Discrimination Act 1975, s.56A: made by the Equal Opportunities Commission (with the approval of the Secretary of State), which must consult appropriate organisations, issued via H.M.S.O., draft subject to annulment by Parliament, to be taken into account by Industrial Tribunal if appears relevant.

[92] Employment Act 1980, s.3, as amended: made by the Secretary of State, who must consult ACAS, draft to be approved by Parliament, to be taken into account by Industrial Tribunal if appears relevant.

[93] Building Act 1984, ss.6, 7: made by Secretary of State or designated body, issued via H.M.S.O., no laying or consultation requirement, breach tends to establish and compliance to negative liability in legal proceedings.

[94] Baldwin and Houghton, [1986] P.L. 239, at pp. 26–32.

[95] In the public sector, codes of practice and other forms of guidance may be used to provide a framework for the exercise of discretionary powers, so as to promote uniformity in decision-making. However, power to give guidance will not normally authorise the issue of binding directions (*Laker Airways Ltd.* v. *Department of Trade* [1977] Q.B. 643) and the recipient of such guidance must not fetter its discretion by regarding it as binding (*R.* v. *Police Complaints Board, ex p. Madden* [1983] 1 W.L.R. 447). Conversely, such guidance is likely to be a legally relevant consideration and must at least be taken into account.

[96] Ganz (1987), pp. 96–98.

[97] *Ibid.*, pp. 98–108.

existing legislation,[98] particularly given the limited effectiveness of Parliamentary scrutiny. The haphazard variety of forms and procedures is indefensible. Proposals have been made for the strengthening of Parliamentary scrutiny, a "code of practice regulating codes of practice" and the establishment of a body "to advise on the creation of quasi-legal or voluntary rules instead of legal rules and evolve criteria for their use."[99] In December 1987, the government issued Guidance on Codes of Practice and Legislation, primarily for the use of parliamentary draftsmen, and those framing legislative proposals.[1]

(b) Voluntary guidance[2]

There are many examples of codes of practice, guidance and the like without any statutory backing. In the public sector, for example, guidance may be given by central government departments to local authorities in circulars and other forms of communication, and instructions are commonly given to officials within departments.[3] The effect varies widely: the legal effect may be indirect, but the practical implications of great significance.[4] In the private sector such codes have in some circumstances been adduced as evidence, for example of proper professional or technical standards, and may be incorporated into a contract.[5] They may also be recognised as appropriate by government, even without express legislative endorsement.[6] Difficulties as to their accessibility and uncertainties as to legal effect are even more pronounced here.

D. COMMUNITY LEGISLATION

1. INTRODUCTION

The accession of the United Kingdom to membership of the European

---

[98] Highlighted by the decision of Scott J. in *Thomas* v. *National Union of Mineworkers* [1986] Ch. 20 to limit by injunction the number of pickets outside particular premises to six, in line with a provision of the Code of Practice on Picketing made under section 3 of the Employment Act 1980.

[99] Ganz (1987), Chap. 6; A. Samuels, [1986] Stat.L.R. 29.

[1] [1989] Stat. L.R. 214.

[2] Ganz (1987), pp. 59–65, 75–95; Ferguson, [1988] J.B.L. 12.

[3] *e.g.* the government's policy to reduce the number of school places in the light of falling school rolls; the use of circulars in town and country planning to state planning policy; extra-statutory tax concessions; standing order and circular instructions governing the management of prisons.

[4] It has been held that even non-statutory guidance, if erroneous in law, can be challenged on an application for judicial review: *Royal College of Nursing* v. *Department of Health and Social Security* [1981] A.C. 800; *Gillick* v. *West Norfolk Area Health Authority* [1986] A.C. 112.

[5] R.B. Ferguson, [1988] J.B.L. 12.

[6] *e.g.* the codes of practice for residential care homes (Centre for Policy on Ageing, *Home Life* (1984)) and nursing homes (National Association of Health Authorities, *Registration and Inspection of Nursing Homes: A Handbook for Health Authorities* (1985)). The Secretaries of State for Social Services and for Wales asked local authorities to regard *Home Life* "in the same light" as guidance issued under section 7 of the Local Authority Social Services Act 1970 (which suggests that it is not technically guidance under the Act). The codes are in practice taken into account by local authorities, inspectors and registered homes tribunals: see D. Carson, [1985] J.S.W.L. 67, 69–70; R. Brooke Ross, [1985] J.S.W.L. 85; R. M. Jones (ed.), *Encyclopedia of Social Services Law and Practice* (1981), para. 1–1534.

Communities (the European Economic Community, the European Coal and Steel Community and the European Atomic Energy Community) has meant that the vast and ever-increasing body of Community law has become applicable in this country.[6a] The system of Community law is founded on the provisions of the various Treaties whereby the Member States agreed to establish the Communities, new members joined, ("Accession Treaties") and aspects of the original Treaties were changed.[7] The Treaty provisions are sometimes termed the *primary* legislation of the Communities. The Treaties give various powers to the Council of Ministers and the Commission to make laws by *regulation*, *directive* or *decision*, the resulting body of law being termed *secondary* legislation. Secondary legislation must conform to the express or implied limits set by the relevant treaty provisions. Under Community law, a further distinction is drawn between laws (both primary and secondary) that have *direct application* or *effect* without any act of implementation by Member States and laws that require such implementation.

Under United Kingdom law, rules of international law such as treaty provisions can only take effect within our domestic legal system if expressly implemented by Act of Parliament. Accordingly, the government secured the passage of the European Communities Act 1972 to enable Community law to take effect within the United Kingdom.

In this section we consider, first, the main Community institutions, second, the different kinds of Community legislation and the extent to which it may be directly applicable or effective, third, the question of the supremacy of Community law, fourth, the implementation of Community law in the United Kingdom, and fifth, the methods by which the validity of Community legislation may be challenged.

2. THE COMMUNITY INSTITUTIONS[8]

The four main institutions of the European Communities, established by the Treaties, are the Commission, the Council of Ministers and the European Parliament (the political institutions) and the Court of Justice. The political institutions will be considered here.[9]

(a) The Commission[10]

The Commission comprises 17 members "appointed by common accord of the governments of Member States." They must be nationals of Member States, with either one or two members from each Member State. In prac-

---

[6a] See L. Collins, *European Community Law in the United Kingdom* (4th ed., 1990), Chaps. 1 and 2; J. Usher, *European Community Law and National Law, The Irreversible Transfer?* (1981); T. C. Hartley, *The Foundations of European Community Law* (2nd ed., 1988); J. Temple Lang, [1989] Stat.L.R. 37.

[7] Most notably the Single European Act of 1986, which had the objectives of "unblocking the Community's decision making process, thereby hastening the completion of a genuine common market," enhancing the role of the Parliament in the legislative process, and establishing a formal basis for European Political co-operation: A. Arnull, (1986) 11 E.L. Rev. 358; see also H.-J. Glaesner, (1986) 6 Y.E.L. 283; Symposium, (1986) 23 C.M.L. Rev. 743–840; M. A. McElhenny, (1988) 39(1) N.I.L.Q. 54.

[8] See Hartley (1988), Chap. 1; D. A. C. Freestone and J. S. Davidson, *The Institutional Framework of the European Communities* (1988), Chap. 3.

[9] The Court of Justice is considered above, pp. 96–101.

[10] Merger Treaty (1965), Arts. 9–19. This treaty provided for the merger of the separate High Authority (E.C.S.C.) and Commissions (E.E.C., Euratom) for the three communities.

tice, the five largest countries (France, West Germany, Italy, Spain and the United Kingdom) have two each, the rest one each.[11] Each Commissioner is in effect nominated by his or her national state, but must be acceptable to all the Member States, and is not a "representative" of his or her own country. Article 10(2) of the Merger Treaty provides:

> "The members of the Commission shall, in the general interest of the Communities, be completely independent in the performance of their duties.
>
> In the performance of these duties, they shall neither seek nor take instructions from any Government or from any other body. They shall refrain from any action incompatible with their duties. Each Member State undertakes to respect this principle and not to seek to influence the members of the Commission in the performance of their tasks. . . ."

The term of office is four years, and may be renewed. All the Commissioners retire together. The Member States appoint one Commissioner as President, and six as Vice-Presidents, for (renewable) two year terms. Individual Commissioners can be compulsorily retired by the European Court, on the application of the Council or Commission, if they are guilty of serious misconduct or no longer fulfil the conditions required for performance of their duties. Otherwise, individual Commissioners cannot be dismissed, although the whole Commission must resign if a motion of censure is passed by the Parliament. Each Commissioner is allocated special responsibility for one or more subjects, by agreement amongst themselves. The Commissioners are supported by over 10,000 staff, organised into twenty Directorates General, with a number of specialised services, including a Legal Service.

The main activities of the Commission are:

> "formulating proposals for new Community policies, mediating between the Member States to secure the adoption of these proposals, co-ordinating national policies and overseeing the execution of existing Community policies."[12]

Under the E.E.C. Treaty, its task is "to ensure the proper functioning and development of the common market."[13] The Commission meets in private and makes decisions by a simple majority vote. Its commitment to the furtherance of Community interests provides a balance to the Council of Ministers, which tends to reflect national interests.

(b) The Council of Ministers[14]

The Council of the European Communities comprises representatives of the Member States, each government sending a minister as its delegate. The Presidency is held by each Member State in turn for a term of six months.

---

[11] The United Kingdom has adopted the practice of nominating one with a Conservative and one with a Labour political background. The U.K. Commissioners have been Sir Christopher Soames and George Thomson (1973–77); Roy Jenkins (1977–81); Christopher Tugendhat (1977–85); Ivor Richard (1981–85); Lord Cockfield and Stanley Clinton Davis (1985–89); Sir Leon Brittan and Bruce Millan (1989–).

[12] Hartley (1988), p. 8.

[13] Art. 155/EEC; *cf.* the broader objective of the Council: below, p. 284.

[14] Merger Treaty (1965), Arts. 1–8. This treaty provided for the merger of separate Councils for each Community.

The Council is attended by different ministers according to the business to be dealt with. General matters are normally considered by foreign ministers; agriculture matters by agriculture ministers, financial matters by finance ministers and so on. The Council meets periodically, and in private. It is supported by a General Secretariat, which is organised on similar lines to the Commission, but is much smaller. The Council's business is prepared by the Committee of Permanent Representatives (COREPER), which itself meets at two levels: COREPER II, comprising the heads of permanent delegations (ambassadors), which deals with matters of political importance, and COREPER I, comprising deputies, which deals with day-to-day business and technical matters. In turn there are many committees and expert working groups.

The Council

"takes the final decision on most E.E.C. legislation, concludes agreements with foreign countries and, together with the Parliament, decides on the Community budget."[15]

Under the E.E.C. Treaty, its task is "to ensure that the objectives set out in the Treaty are attained," and to that end "ensure co-ordination of the general economic policies of the Member States" and "have power to take decisions."[16] The more important decisions are reserved to the Council rather than the Commission.[17]

The Treaties specify different voting arrangements for different kinds of Council decision. Some acts must be unanimous. Most require a "qualified majority."[18] Here the votes of Member States are weighted:

France, Germany, Italy, United Kingdom	:	10 votes each
Spain	:	8 votes
Belgium, Greece, Netherlands, Portugal	:	5 votes each
Denmark, Ireland	:	3 votes each
Luxembourg	:	2 votes

A "qualified majority" is 54 of these 76 votes, where the act is based on a Commission proposal; 54 votes with eight Member States in favour, otherwise. The arrangements mean that the five largest countries cannot outvote the smaller states.

In many important areas the original requirement specified in the Treaties was for unanimity, the qualified majority regime only coming into effect from January 1, 1966. Even then, a convention developed whereby unanimity would be required as a matter of practice (albeit no longer as a matter of law) where "very important interests" of one or more Member States were at stake.[19] In the 1980s, this convention was applied with less force, and matters are now decided by majority votes. The Single European Act 1986 amends various Treaty provisions by substituting a qualified majority procedure for a requirement of unanimity.

[15] Hartley (1988), pp. 13–14.
[16] Article 145/EEC.
[17] See further below, p. 287.
[18] Article 148(2)/EEC.
[19] This was reflected in the so-called "Luxembourg Accords" of January 1966: a press release enshrining the part agreement/part truce that ended a dispute between France and the, then five, other Member States.

(c) The European Parliament[20]

The Parliament consists of "representatives of the peoples" of the Member States. Since 1979, the members have been directedly elected, in the following proportions[21]:

France, Germany, Italy and the United Kindom	81 each
Spain	60
Netherlands	25
Belgium, Greece and Portugal	24 each
Denmark	16
Ireland	15
Luxembourg	6
	518

This does not reflect populations: in those terms the smaller states are over-represented. Members sit in political groupings rather than by country. Much of the work is done by committees.

The Parliament exercises the "advisory and supervisory powers"[22] conferred by the Treaties. It functions

"relate to the communication of ideas, the gathering of information and, to some extent, the formation and expression of public opinion on Community matters. It holds debates and passes resolutions on a variety of topics but, though these generate publicity, they have in general no legal effect."[23]

It puts Questions to the Council and the Commission, and is involved in a consultation capacity in the legislative process, its role here having been strengthened by the Single European Act 1986.[24] Under that Act, it now has a veto over the admission of new Member States and the conclusion of association agreements with other states. It has also had a progressively greater say in the determination of the Community's Budget.[25]

(d) Other institutions

Other organs of the Communities include the Economic and Social Committee,[26] with members from each Member State representing employers, workers and others (e.g. consumers, farmers and the professions), which advises both Council and Commission; the Court of Auditors,[27] which assists the Council and the Parliament in monitoring implementation of the budget; and the European Investment Bank.

Finally, the foreign policy of the different Member States is co-ordinated through the process of European Political Co-operation. This was formerly

---

[20] Articles 137–144/EEC. The Parliament was referred to as the Assembly in the Treaties. It resolved to call itself the "European Parliament" in 1962, and that title was recognised in the Single European Act.

[21] Decision and Act of the Council Concerning Direct Elections 1976, Art. 2, as amended by the Acts of Accession of Greece, Art. 10, and of Spain and Portugal, Art. 10.

[22] Art. 137/EEC.

[23] Hartley (1988), pp. 29–30.

[24] See below, pp. 287–288.

[25] Hartley (1988), pp. 39–44.

[26] Arts. 193–198/EEC.

[27] Arts. 206, 206A/EEC.

kept apart from the operation of the Communities, but a legal framework is now provided by Part III of the Single European Act 1986. This provides for quarterly meetings of the foreign ministers, attended by representatives of the Commission. It is supported by a Political Committee comprising Political Directors from the Foreign Ministries of the Member States, a European Correspondents' Group comprising foreign ministry officials, and by a Secretariat.

At the apex of both the European Communities and European Political Co-operation structures, is the European Council—regular conferences of the Heads of State or of Government and the foreign ministers of the Member States. These were informal meetings, attended by representatives of the Commission, but a regular constitution for them has now been provided by Article 2 of the Single European Act 1986. When discussing Community matters, the European Council acts as the Council of Ministers, but the two are technically distinct.

3. THE KINDS OF COMMUNITY LEGISLATION

(a) Treaty provisions concerning Community legislation

The different kinds of Community acts are described in Article 189 of the EEC Treaty[28]:

> "In order to carry out their task the Council and the Commission shall, in accordance with the provisions of this Treaty, make regulations, issue directives, take decisions, make recommendations or deliver opinions.
>
> A regulation shall have general application. It shall be binding in its entirety and directly applicable in all Member States.
>
> A directive shall be binding, as to the result to be achieved, upon each Member State to which it is addressed, but shall leave to the national authorities choice of form and methods.
>
> A decision shall be binding in its entirety upon those to whom it is addressed.
>
> Recommendations and opinions shall have no binding force."

Recommendations and opinions cannot be regarded as legislative as they do not have binding effect; it has also been suggested that decisions directed to individuals, as distinct from Member States, are administrative rather than legislative in character.[29]

The Treaties require that regulations, directives and decisions state the reasons on which they are based and refer to any proposals or opinions that

---

[28] See also Art. 14/ECSC and Art. 161/Euratom. The terminology of E.C.S.C. acts is different:

EEC Euratom	ECSC
Regulations ⎫ Decisions ⎬	Decisions
Directives	Recommendations
Recommendations ⎫ Opinions ⎬	Opinions

The following discussion is generally confined to EEC legislation.

[29] Case 19/77, *Miller* v. *Commission* [1978] E.C.R. 131, 161 *per* A. G. Warner.

were required to be obtained pursuant to other Treaty provisions.[30] Regulations must be published in the Official Journal.[31] They enter into force on the date specified in them, or, if no date is specified, on the twentieth day following their publication.[32] Directives and decisions must be notified to those to whom they are addressed and take effect upon such notification.[33]

(b) Legislative powers[34]

Under the E.E.C. and Euratom Treaties, the major policy decisions and legislative powers are reserved to the Council; the Commission being involved with (in most cases) the formulation of legislative proposals and with the implementation of decisions. However, the Commission does have some legislative powers conferred upon it by the E.E.C. Treaty.[35] Furthermore, its position has been strengthened in two ways.

First, procedures have been developed for the delegation of functions from the Council to the Commission. A distinction is drawn between the laying down of general principles and detailed implementation. Only the latter process may be delegated, but that may involve rule-making by the Commission. Such arrangements were held to be lawful by the European Court.[36] Express authority is now provided for them by Article 10 of the Single European Act, amending Article 145/EEC. Acts adopted by the Council must confer power for the implementation of the rules laid down therein by the Commission, unless ("in specific cases") the Council reserves the right to exercise directly implementing powers itself. The Council may impose certain requirements in respect of the exercise of these delegated powers, in conformity with procedures prescribed by a Council Decision. The Decision was adopted in 1987,[37] and corresponded for the most part to the previous informal arrangements. Other than in the "specific cases" mentioned above, the Council may select one of a series of procedures set out in the Decision.[38]

Each procedure requires the Commission to consult a committee comprising representatives of the Member States, and chaired by a representative of the Commission. The committee must deliver its opinion within a time limit laid down by the Chairman according to the urgency of the matter.

Procedure I involves an "advisory committee." As the name suggests, the Commission must "take the utmost account of the opinion delivered by the committee" but is not bound by it. Procedure II involves a "management committee," which forms an opinion acting by a qualified majority. The Commission may proceed to adopt the measure in question, but where it is not in accordance with the committee's opinion, the Council must be

---

[30] Art. 190/EEC.
[31] Other secondary legislation is in practice also published there: see below, pp. 296–297.
[32] Art. 191/EEC.
[33] Art. 192/EEC.
[34] See Hartley (1988), pp. 12–13, 102–117.
[35] See T. C. Hartley, (1988) 13 E.L. Rev. 122–123; Cases 88–90/80, *France, Italy and the United Kingdom* v. *Commission* [1982] E.C.R. 2545.
[36] Case 25/70, *Ein fuhr—und Vorratsstelle* v. *Köster* [1970] E.C.R. 1161; Case 41/69, *Chemiefarma* v. *Commission* [1970] E.C.R. 661; Case 23/75, *Rey Soda* v. *Cassa Conguaglio Zuchero* [1975] E.C.R. 1279; *cf.* Case 264/86, *France* v. *Commission* [1989] 1 C.M.L.R. 13.
[37] Dec. 87/373, O.J. 1987, L 197/33.
[38] The Decision also prescribes a procedure that may be applied where the Council confers on the Commission the power to decide on "safeguard measures": Article 3.

informed. There is then a period within which the Council, acting by a qualified majority, may substitute a different decision: under "Variant (a)," a period, determined by the Commission, not exceeding one month; under "Variant (b)," a period not exceeding three months specified by the Council in the original act. Procedure III involves a "regulatory committee," again acting by a qualified majority. The Commission can only adopt the measures forthwith if they are in accordance with the opinion of the committee. If they are not, or if no opinion is delivered, the Commission has to submit to the Council a proposal relating to the measures to be taken, the Council responding by a qualified majority. Then, under "Variant (a)," if the Council has not acted within a period (not exceeding three months) specified in the original act, the proposed measures are to be adopted by the Commission. "Variant (b)" is the same as "Variant (a)," except that the Council can block the measure acting by a simple majority, without formulating its own measures.

The Commission has expressed reservations concerning these procedures, and has complained that the Council has only infrequently adopted the advisory committee procedure, preferring to use "delegation procedures which allow the national authorities to block legislation."[39] The Parliament sought to have the Decision annulled under Article 173, but the European Court held that it did not have capacity to bring such an action.[40]

The second means by which the Commission's powers have been strengthened is by the recognition by the European Court that it enjoys certain *implied* legislative powers. In *Germany* v. *Commission*[41] the European Court held that

"where an Article of the E.E.C. Treaty—in this case Article 118—confers a specific task on the Commission it must be accepted, if that provision is not to be rendered wholly ineffective, that it confers on the Commission necessarily and *per se* the powers which are indispensible in order to carry out that task."[42]

It then proceeded to hold that the Commission enjoyed all "necessary" powers (rather than "indispensible") and took a generous view of what was "necessary."[43] It has been noted that

"Since the E.E.C. Treaty confers many tasks on the Commission, including such wide-ranging functions as that of ensuring that the provisions of the Treaty are applied,[44] this judgment is potentially very significant and could herald an era of increased Commission law-making."[45]

(c) Direct applicability and direct effect

A distinction is sometimes drawn between the terms *direct applicability*

---

[39] See Commission, 21st General Report on the Activities of the European Communities, 1987, point 4; 22nd General Report, 1988, point 9.
[40] Case 302/87, *European Parliament* v. *Council* [1988] E.C.R. 5615.
[41] Cases 281, 283–285, 287/85, [1987] E.C.R. 3203.
[42] *Ibid.*, p. 3253.
[43] T. C. Hartley, (1988) 13 E.L. Rev. 122.
[44] Art. 155/EEC.
[45] Hartley (1988), p. 104. See also the "supplementary means of action" available to the Council under Art. 235/EEC: Hartley (1988), pp. 104–109.

and *direct effect.*[46] Article 189 of the EEC Treaty provides that regulations are "directly applicable" in all Member States; they come into force without any act of implementation by Member States. No other form of Community law is expressly stated in the treaties to be directly *applicable*, and it was at first thought that those other forms of law could only take *effect* within Member States if there was an act of implementation. However, the European Court developed the view that treaty provisions could in principle confer rights and impose obligations directly upon individuals irrespective of any act of implementation. In the *Van Gend en Loos* case[47] the plaintiff claimed before a Dutch tribunal that there had been an increase in import duties which was rendered illegal by Article 12[48] of the EEC Treaty. The European Court, on a reference from the tribunal, held that Article 12 was indeed directly effective, and could be relied upon by the plaintiff in this case. The court stated[49]:

"To ascertain whether the provisions of an international treaty extend so far in their effects it is necessary to consider the spirit, the general scheme and the wording of those provisions.

The objective of the EEC Treaty, which is to establish a Common Market, the functioning of which is of direct concern to interested parties in the Community, implies that this Treaty is more than an agreement which merely creates mutual obligations between the contracting states. This view is confirmed by the preamble to the Treaty which refers not only to governments but to peoples. It is also confirmed more specifically by the establishment of institutions endowed with sovereign rights, the exercise of which affects Member States and also their citizens. Furthermore, it must be noted that the nationals of the states brought together in the Community are called upon to co-operate in the functioning of this Community through the intermediary of the European Parliament and the Economic and Social Committee.

In addition the task assigned to the Court of Justice under Article 177, the object of which is to secure uniform interpretation of the Treaty by national courts and tribunals, confirms that the states have acknowledged that Community law has an authority which can be invoked by their nationals before those courts and tribunals.

The conclusion to be drawn from this is that the Community constitutes a new legal order of international law for the benefit of which the states have limited their sovereign rights, albeit within limited fields, and the subjects of which comprise not only Member States but also their nationals. Independently of the legislation of Member States, Community law therefore not only imposes obligations on individuals but is also intended to confer upon them rights which become part of

---

[46] See J. A. Winter, (1972) 9 C.M.L.R. 425; J.-P. Warner, (1977) 93 L.Q.R. 349; A. Dashwood, (1977–78) 16 J. of Common Market Studies 229; J. Steiner, (1982) 98 L.Q.R. 229 and (1990) 106 L.Q.R. 144; P. Pescatore, (1983) 8 E.L. Rev. 155; N. Green, (1984) 9 E.L. Rev. 295.

[47] Case 26/62, *Van Gend en Loos* v. *Nederlandse Administratie Der Belastingen* [1963] E.C.R. 1.

[48] "Member States shall refrain from introducing between themselves any new customs duties on imports or exports or any charges having equivalent effect, and from increasing those which they already apply in their trade with each other."

[49] pp. 12–13.

their legal heritage. These rights arise not only where they are expressly granted by the Treaty, but also by reason of obligations which the Treaty imposes in a clearly defined way upon individuals as well as upon the Member States and upon the institutions of the Community."

Article 12 imposed a clear and unconditional negative prohibition, "ideally adapted to produce direct effects in the legal relationship between Member States and their subjects."

In this and subsequent cases the European Court has elaborated the criteria by which those *treaty provisions* that are regarded as directly effective are to be distinguished from those that are not. As more provisions have come before the court for consideration, the overall picture has become clearer.[50] The criteria[51] are:

"— the provision must impose a clear and precise obligation on Member States;
— it must be unconditional, in other words subject to no limitation; if, however, a provision is subject to certain limitations, their nature and extent must be exactly defined;
— finally, the implementation of a Community rule must not be subject to the adoption of any subsequent rules or regulations on the part either of the Community institutions or of the Member States, so that, in particular, Member States must not be left any real discretion with regard to the application of the rule in question."

A provision may, exceptionally, be held to have direct effect prospectively only.[52]

The European Court has subsequently invoked these criteria to hold that *decisions* addressed to Member States,[53] *directives*[54] and agreements between the communities and non-Member States[55] can be directly effective. *Van Duyn* v. *Home Office* concerned Article 48 of the EEC Treaty, which

[50] A useful table is given in Collins (1990), pp. 122–126.
[51] As formulated by A. G. Mayras in Case 41/74, *Van Duyn* v. *Home Office* [1974] E.C.R. 1337, 1354. See *e.g. Application des Gaz* v. *Falks Veritas* [1974] Ch. 381 (Articles 85 and 86/EEC); *Rio Tinto Zinc Corporation* v. *Westinghouse Electric Corporation* [1978] A.C. 547 (Article 85).
[52] Case 43/75, *Defrenne* v. *Sabena* (*No. 2*) [1976] E.C.R. 455. This case concerned the direct effect of Art. 119/EEC (equal pay for men and women). The court stated: "As the general level at which pay would have been fixed cannot be known, important considerations of legal certainty affecting all the interests involved, both public and private, make it impossible in principle to reopen the question as regards the past" (p. 481). See T. Koopmans, [1980] C.L.J. 287; M. Waelbroeck, [1981] 1 Y.E.L. 115. This principle was applied in Case 309/85, *Barra* v. *Belgium and City of Liege* [1988] 2 C.M.L.R. 409; Case 24/86, *Blaizot* v. *University of Liege* [1989] 1 C.M.L.R. 57; A. Arnull, (1988) 13 E.L. Rev. 260.
[53] See Case 9/70, *Grad* v. *Finanzamt Traunstein* [1970] E.C.R. 325: this concerned a decision which prohibited member states from applying specific taxes concurrently with the common turnover tax (VAT) system due to be implemented by directive.
[54] See Case 41/74, *Van Duyn* v. *Home Office* [1974] E.C.R. 1337; Case 148/78, *Pubblico Ministero* v. *Ratti* [1979] E.C.R. 162; Case 102/79, *Commission* v. *Belgium* [1980] E.C.R. 1473; Case 8/81, *Becker* v. *Finanzamt Münster-Innenstadt* [1982] E.C.R. 53. In Case 131/79, *R.* v. *Secretary of State for the Home Department, ex p. Santillo* [1980] E.C.R. 1585, 1610–11, A. G. Warner argued that the conditions for the direct effectiveness of Treaty provisions were subject to some qualification when applied to directives. In particular, there will nearly always be some element of discretion which will not, however, prevent a directive being held to be directly effective. See generally, P. Curtin, (1990) 15 E.L. Rev. 195.
[55] Case 104/81, *Kupferberg* [1982] E.C.R. 3641.

provided for the "freedom of movement" of workers, including the right to enter and stay in any Member State "subject to limitations justified on grounds of public policy, public security or public health." The scope of these limitations was further regulated by Council Directive 64/221 which provided in art. 3(1) that, "Measures taken on grounds of public policy or of public security shall be based exclusively on the personal conduct of the individual concerned." Miss Yvonne Van Duyn, a Dutch national, was refused leave to enter the United Kingdom on the ground that she was intending to work for the Church of Scientology. The government regarded scientology as socially harmful, and although it had no power to prohibit its practice it had decided to take steps, within its powers, to curb its growth. Accordingly it decided that foreign nationals such as Miss Van Duyn should be refused entry. She claimed that the refusal was not based on her "personal conduct" and challenged its validity in the High Court. Several questions were referred to the European Court, which held (1) that Article 48 was directly effective; (2) that the relevant provision of directive 64/221 was also directly effective; but (3) that a Member State was entitled to take into account as a matter of personal conduct that the individual was associated with an organisation whose activities were considered by the state to be socially harmful.

There are, however, limitations:

"the European Court has held that directives can only confer rights on individuals (against the state); they cannot impose obligations on individuals (in favour of the state or other individuals). This means that directives are capable of only 'vertical' direct effect; unlike regulations and Treaty provisions, they are not capable of 'horizontal' direct effect."[56]

The leading case here is *Marshall* v. *Southampton and South West Hampshire Area Health Authority* (*Teaching*).[57] Miss Marshall was dismissed by the Authority from her post as a dietician when she was 62, although she wished to continue to 65. It was the Authority's policy that the normal retiring age for its employees was the age at which state retirement pensions became payable. For women, this was 60. (The Authority had waived its policy for two years in respect of Miss Marshall.) The Court held that Article 5(1) of Council Directive 76/207 (the "Equal Treatment Directive") was to be interpreted as meaning that a general policy involving the dismissal of a woman solely because she had attained or passed the qualifying age for state pension, which age was different under national legislation for men and for women, constituted discrimination on the ground of sex, contrary to that directive. It could be relied upon against a state authority acting in its capacity as employer: the principle was not confined to governmental acts. It was for the national court to determine whether the Health Authority was a "state authority" for this purpose, although the Court noted that in the order for reference the Court of Appeal had referred to it as a "public authority."

[56] Hartley (1988), p. 208.
[57] Case 152/84, [1986] Q.B. 401, [1986] E.C.R. 723. See A. Arnull, (1986) 35 I.C.L.Q. 939 and [1987] P.L. 383; T. Millett, (1987) 36 I.C.L.Q. 616; N. Foster, (1987) 12 E.L. Rev. 222. For further proceedings, see *Marshall* v. *Southampton and South-West Hampshire Area Health Authority* (*No. 2*) [1990] I.R.L.R. 481 (Court of Appeal held that the Directive did not override the statutory limit to compensation under the Sex Discrimination Act 1975, s.65).

The Court stated that as Art. 189/EEC provides that a directive is binding "upon each Member State to which it is addressed," it followed

> "that a directive may not of itself impose obligations on an individual and that a provision of a directive may not be relied upon as such against such a person."[58]

Accordingly, the European Court has held that a Member State cannot base criminal proceedings against an individual on the provisions of an unimplemented directive.[59]

The ruling against "horizontal direct effect" has been criticised as having "serious consequences for the rights of the individual."[60] It has been suggested that it can be seen as a compromise between, on the one hand, the desire to give maximum effectiveness to directives and, on the other, the argument based on the wording of Article 189 and doubts expressed by courts in France (the *Conseil d'Etat*) and Germany (the *Bundesfinanzhof*) to the effect that directives should not be regarded as having *any* direct effect.[61]

Three consequences can be noted. First, it has become necessary to determine what amounts to a "state authority."[62] The English courts have taken a narrow view, holding that Directives can give rise to legal rights

> "in employees of the State itself and of any organ or emanation of the State, an emanation of the State being understood to include an independent public authority charged by the State with the performance of any of the classic duties of the State, such as the defence of the realm or the maintenance of law and order within the realm."[63]

This did not cover the British Gas Corporation,[64] and Rolls Royce plc[65] in the period before privatisation. Conversely, a woman police officer who was a member of the Royal Ulster Constabulary Reserve was entitled to rely on the Equal Treatment Directive (76/207) against the Chief Constable,[66] and a regulatory agency acting on behalf of local authorities has been held to be an emanation of the State.[67] The European Court has, however, taken a broader view.[68]

---

[58] [1986] Q.B. 401, 422.
[59] Case 14/86, *Pretore di Salo* v. *Persons Unknown* [1987] E.C.R. 2545, 2569–2570: A. Arnull, (1988) 13 E.L. Rev. 40; Case 80/86, *Kolpinghuis* [1987] E.C.R. 3969: A. Arnull, (1988) 13 E.L. Rev. 42.
[60] Arnull, (1986) 35 I.C.L.Q. 939, 943.
[61] Hartley (1988), pp. 208–210, 225–227, 230–235.
[62] The European Court in Case C188/89, *Foster* v. *British Gas plc.* [1990] 2 C.M.L.R. 833 held that the Court had jurisdiction in a preliminary ruling to determine the categories of persons against whom the provisions of a directive may be relied on, and that it was for national courts to determine whether a party before them fell into one of the categories so defined. The categories include "a body, whatever its legal form, which has been made responsible, pursuant to a measure adopted by the state, for providing a public service under the control of the State and has for that purpose special powers beyond those which result from the normal rules applicable in relations between individuals" (p. 857).
[63] *per* Lord Donaldson in *Foster* v. *British Gas plc* [1988] I.R.L.R. 354, 356.
[64] *Foster* v. *British Gas plc, supra.*
[65] *Rolls Royce plc* v. *Doughty* [1988] 1 C.M.L.R. 569, E.A.T.
[66] Case 222/84, *Johnston* v. *Chief Constable of the Royal Ulster Constabulary* [1986] E.C.R. 1651, [1987] Q.B. 129; A. Arnull, (1987) 12 E.L. Rev. 56;
[67] *R.* v. *London Boroughs Transport Committee, ex p. Freight Transport Association Ltd.* [1990] 1 C.M.L.R. 229.
[68] Case C188/89, *Foster* v. *British Gas plc* [1990] 2 C.M.L.R. 833, n.62, *supra.*

Secondly, it was of course still necessary for the United Kingdom to take legislative steps to implement the directive in question, so as to extend its benefits to all employees. This was done by the Sex Discrimination Act 1986,[69] which took effect from November 7, 1987.

Thirdly, the courts have considered whether the unamended U.K. legislation[70] could be interpreted in accordance with the Equal Treatment Directive so as to render differential retirement ages for men and women unlawful. The House of Lords in *Duke* v. *Reliance Systems Ltd.*[71] held that it could not.

This leads on to the point that even where a directive does not have direct effects,

"in applying the national law and in particular the provisions of a national law specifically introduced in order to implement Directive 76/207, national courts are required to interpret their national law in the light of the wording and purpose of the directive in order to achieve the result referred to in the third paragraph of Article 189."[72]

This is so whether or not the time for implementing the directive has expired.[73] It was suggested by A. G. Slynn in *Marshall* v. *Southampton and South West Hampshire Area Health Authority (Teaching)*[74] that this principle did not apply to require a national court to interpret legislation so that it accords with a *later* directive, "unless it is clear that the legislation was adopted with a proposed directive in mind."[75] This has been criticised as too restrictive an approach,[76] but it was adopted by the House of Lords in *Duke* v. *Reliance Systems Ltd.*[77]

Overall, Member States have tended to present arguments to the European Court against direct effectiveness; Community institutions have tended, not surprisingly, to argue in favour, given that it strengthens their position at the expense of individual Member States, and helps ensure that Community law applies uniformly throughout the Member States. It enables individuals to take action to enforce the requirements of Community law without having to rely on Community institutions to act. It has also been stressed that it is inappropriate for a Member State that has failed to implement a directive or decision addressed to it to rely, in proceedings between itself and an individual, on its own failure to comply with that directive or decision on the basis that it is not directly effective.[78]

[69] ss.2, 3. See B. Fitzpatrick, (1987) 50 M.L.R. 934.

[70] Sex Discrimination Act 1975, ss.1, 6.

[71] [1988] A.C. 618. See below, pp. 305–307.

[72] Case 14/83, *Von Colson and Kamann* v. *Land Nordrhein-Westfalen* [1984] E.C.R. 1891, 1909. This passage appears in the Court's reasoning: the operative part of the judgment refers only to legislation adopted for the implementation of the directive. The principle was invoked in the narrower context in Case 262/84, *Beets-Proper* v. *Van Lanschot Bankiers N.V.* [1986] E.C.R. 782; A. Arnull (1987) 12 E.L. Rev. 229. However, the Court repeated the wider formulation in Case 80/86, *Kolpinghuis Nijmegen B.V.* [1987] E.C.R. 3969; A. Arnull, (1988) 13 E.L. Rev. 42.

[73] *Kolpinghuis, supra.*

[74] [1986] Q.B. 401.

[75] *Ibid.*, p. 411.

[76] A. Arnull, [1988] P.L. 313, 317.

[77] [1988] A.C. 618, *supra*, criticised by Arnull, *op. cit.* See also *Organon Laboratories Ltd.* v. *D.H.S.S.* [1990] 2 C.M.L.R. 49.

[78] Case 148/78, *Pubblico Ministero* v. *Ratti* [1979] E.C.R. 1624, 1650: A. G. Reischl; *Marshall* [1986] Q.B. 401, 421–422.

It has been argued that the

"granting of direct effect to directives has probably done more than any other initiative by the European Court to enhance the effectiveness of Community Law."[79]

Although a regulation is "directly applicable" by virtue of Article 189, it will not necessarily create rights and obligations which may be enforced in national courts. This depends on the wording of the regulation in question[80]: it has been argued that regulations only have "direct effect" if the criteria applicable to treaty provisions and other kinds of Community secondary legislation are fulfilled.[81]

Finally, it should be noted that in these and other cases in this area the European Court has not been consistent in its use of the *terms* "directly applicable" and "direct effect," but has tended to use them interchangeably.[82]

(d) Treaty provisions

The main treaties concerning the Communities are:

(1) the Treaty establishing the European Coal and Steel Community (Paris, 1951);
(2) the Treaties establishing the European Economic Community and the European Atomic Energy Community (Rome, 1957);
(3) the Treaty establishing a Single Council and a Single Commission of the European Communities (Brussels 1965; the "Merger Treaty");
(4) the Treaties amending certain Budgetary Provisions of the Treaties (Luxembourg, 1970 and Brussels, 1975);
(5) the Accession Treaties (Brussels, 1972: Denmark, Ireland, Norway,[83] and the United Kingdom (with effect from January 1, 1973); Athens, 1979: Greece (with effect from January 1, 1981); Madrid and Lisbon, 1985: Spain and Portugal (with effect from January 1, 1986));
(6) the Treaty providing for the withdrawal of Greenland[84] (Brussels, 1984 (with effect from February 1, 1985));
(7) the Single European Act (Luxembourg and The Hague, 1986 (with effect from July 1, 1987)).

Several of the treaties have extensive Annexes and Protocols. The treaties are published by HMSO[85] and in various unofficial collections. There is also a series of treaties entered by the Community with non-Member States.

---

[79] Hartley (1988), p. 206.
[80] Usher (1981) *op. cit.* p. 282, n. 6a, pp. 18–19.
[81] A. G. Warner in Case 31/74, *Galli* [1975] E.C.R. 47 and Case 74/76, *Iannelli* v. *Meronia*; *Steinike and Weinlig* v. *Germany* [1977] E.C.R. 557, 583; A. G. Reischl in *Ratti, supra.*
[82] But see A. G. Warner in *Iannelli* v. *Merioni* [1977] E.C.R. 557 at 583 and A. G. Slynn in Case 8/81, *Becker* [1982] 1 C.M.L.R. 499, 504–5; in *Ratti, supra,* A. G. Reischl argued that the term "direct applicability" should only be used in respect of *regulations*.
[83] Norway subsequently did not ratify the Treaty.
[84] Greenland had not been a Member State, but had been part of the Community through its association with Denmark: see F. Weiss, (1985) 10 E.L. Rev. 173.
[85] Cmnd. 5189; 5179–I; 5179–II.

(e) Regulations, Directives and Decisions

Regulations are the most important form of Community secondary legislation. Under Article 189 of the EEC Treaty they are directly applicable without any act of implementation by Member States. Indeed, such acts of implementation are normally prohibited, in case they have the effect of altering the scope of the regulation in question. Member States may not, for example, enact measures which purport to interpret provisions contained in a regulation[86]; such interpretations might vary from state to state, and the regulation would no longer be uniform in application. This prohibition also ensures that provision of a regulation can clearly be perceived to be of Community origin and so subject to the judicial remedies available under Community law, and avoids any ambiguity as to the date of entry into force.[87] Domestic legislation may, however, make supplementary provision, for example by imposing a sanction for breach of a regulation[88] or by prescribing a limitation period for claims based on Community law.[89] Exceptionally, a regulation may itself expressly require Member States to introduce implementing measures.[90]

Directives are used where the approximation or harmonisation of national laws is sought rather than strict uniformity. They may only be addressed to Member States. Choice of method is left to the Member States, although a time limit for implementation is commonly set.

Decisions may be addressed to Member States, to corporations or to individuals. The European Court has held that:

"a decision must appear as an act originating from the competent organisation intended to produce judicial effects, constituting the ultimate end of the internal procedure of this organisation and according to which such organisation makes its final ruling in a form allowing its nature to be identified."[91]

(f) Preparation of Community secondary legislation[92]

The treaties do not lay down a uniform legislative process to be adopted in all cases. Usually, the Commission first formulates a proposal after consulting national officials, experts and representatives of interest groups (the *avant-projet* stage). The draft proposal is then sent to the Council of Ministers; Member States may at this stage refer it to their national parliaments. A

[86] Case 40/69, *Hauptzollamt Hamburg* v. *Bollman* [1970] E.C.R. 69; classification of products (turkey rumps) under an agricultural regulation; Case 34/73, *Variola* v. *Italian Minister of Finance* [1973] E.C.R. 981.

[87] Usher (1981), p. 17. Member States may not adopt "any measure which would conceal the Community nature and effects of any legal provision from the persons to whom it applies": Case 50/76, *Amsterdam Bulb* v. *Produktschap Voor Siergewassen* [1977] E.C.R. 137, 151.

[88] *Amsterdam Bulb* case, *supra*.

[89] Case 33/76, *Rewe* v. *Landwirtschaftkammer Saarland* [1976] E.C.R. 1989. The periods must be reasonable and non-discriminatory.

[90] See Hartley (1988), pp. 196–200; Case 128/78, *Commission* v. *United Kingdom* [1979] E.C.R. 419.

[91] Case 54/65, *Compagnie des Forges de Châtillon Commentry et Neuves Maison* v. *High Authority* [1966] C.M.L.R. 525, 538.

[92] L. S. Adler in D. M. Palmer (ed.), *Sources of Information on the European Communities* (1979), pp. 20–28; T. St. J. N. Bates, "The Drafting of European Community Legislation" [1983] Stat.L.R. 24; Hartley (1988), pp. 37–39; D. Gordon-Smith, [1989] Stat.L.R. 56.

copy is sent to the European Parliament so that a preliminary unofficial study can be commenced in committee. The Council may, and in some cases must[93] consult the European Parliament and the European Economic and Social Committee (a consultative body representing the various categories of economic and social activity, including industry, workers and consumers). The European Parliament debates the report of its committee in plenary session. The opinions of the Parliament and the E.S.C. are transmitted to the Council. The Council may consider the proposal in three stages: (1) in a Working Group of national experts convened by the Council secretariat; (2) in the Committee of Permanent Representatives (COREPER); and (3) in the Council of Ministers itself.

The Single European Act[94] introduced a new "co-operation procedure"[95] applicable to some of the instances in which the EEC Treaty requires the Parliament to be consulted.[96] This procedure commences at the final stage of the standard legislative process. Instead of adopting the proposal forthwith, the Council takes a "common position," acting by a qualified majority.[97] The proposal is sent to the Parliament for a second time, and the Parliament (acting within three months[98]) can approve or reject it, or propose amendments.[99] If the proposal is approved, or no action is taken within three months,[1] the act will be adopted by the Council. If it is rejected, the Council (acting within three months[2]) can only adopt it by unanimity. Proposed amendments are considered by the Commission (acting within one month) and then returned to the Council. If they are approved by the Commission, the Council (acting within three months[3]) can adopt them by a qualified majority. Amendments not approved by the Commission, and any Council amendments, can only be adopted by unanimity. These arrangements constitute "a real, though small," increase in the power of the Parliament, in so far as it can, in alliance with a Member State, block a measure; as regards amendments, the arrangement in essence enshrines existing practice in legal form.[4]

(g) Publication of Community secondary legislation

Regulations, directives and decisions are published in the *Official Journal*

[93] A requirement to consult will be regarded as an essential procedural requirement: Case 138/79, *Roquette* v. *Council* [1980] E.C.R. 3333; Case 139/79, *Maizena* v. *Council* [1980] E.C.R. 3393: see T. C. Hartley, (1981) 6 E.L. Rev. 181. It is not sufficient that the opinion of the European Parliament is sought; an opinion must be received.

[94] Articles 6 and 7. See J. Fitzmaurice, (1988) 26 J. of Common Market Studies 389.

[95] Substituted Art. 149(2)/EEC. See R. Bieber, (1988) 25 C.M.L. Rev. 711.

[96] *e.g.* in respect of rules designed to prohibit discrimination on the ground of nationality (Art. 7/EEC); directives on regulations concerning free movement of workers (Art. 49/EEC); directives concerning freedom of establishment (Art. 54(2)/EEC); directives concerning exceptions to the right of establishment on the grounds of public order, public safety and public health (Art. 56/EEC); directives for the mutual recognition of diplomas etc. (Art. 57(1)/EEC).

[97] No time limit is specified for this, unlike for the later stages.

[98] The period may be extended by up to one month, by common accord between the Council and the Parliament: Art. 149(2)(g)/EEC.

[99] The Parliament can only reject or propose amendments by an absolute majority of its members: Art. 149(2)(c)/EEC.

[1] See footnote 98.

[2] *Ibid.*

[3] See footnote 98.

[4] Hartley (1988), pp. 33–34.

of the European Communities ("L Series").[5] An English edition has been published from January 1973; English texts of pre-1972 secondary legislation were published in Special Editions of the *Official Journal* covering the pre-accession period, and by H.M.S.O. in a 42-volume work entitled *Secondary Legislation of the European Communities: Subject Edition* (1973). H.M.S.O. supplemented this series with an annual Subject List and Table of Effects up to the end of 1979. Users must now rely on the monthly and annual indices and lists published as supplements to the *Official Journal*. The European Communities also publish periodically a *Directory of Community Legislation In Force*.[6]

(h) Arrangement and citation of Community secondary legislation

The heading of a regulation indicates the authority by which it is made, the Treaty under which it is made and its number.[7] The date on which it is made is given, followed by an indication of the subject matter. (*e.g.* "Council Regulation (EEC) No. 2194/81 of July 27, 1981 laying down the general rules for the system of production aid for dried figs and dried grapes.")

A *preamble* including an explanation of the purposes of the regulation precedes its main provisions. These comprise numbered *articles*, which may be subdivided into *paragraphs*, and grouped under *Titles*. An *annex* may be attached. Directives and decisions are similar to regulations in form.[8] There is a Manual of Precedents.[9]

The correct forms of citation have changed several times.[10] At present they are as follows: Reg. (EEC) 1629/70; Dec. 70/381/EEC; Dir. 72/182/Euratom.

4. SUPREMACY OF COMMUNITY LAW[11]

It is well established in terms of Community law that on a matter regulated by binding Community law, that law takes precedence over the municipal law of a Member State.[12] It is immaterial whether the municipal law is enacted before or after the relevant Community law,[13] and whether it forms

---

[5] Since 1968 the *Official Journal* has appeared in two series, one publishing secondary legislation (the "L Series") and the other giving general information, including drafts of proposed legislation (the "C series").

[6] Volume I: Analytical Register; Volume II: Chronological Index; Alphabetical Index. See also Sweet & Maxwell's *Encyclopedia of European Community Law* and the C.C.H. *Common Market Law Reporter*.

[7] From 1958 to 1967 there were separate series of regulations for the EEC and Euratom; from 1968 there has been a single series. Regulations were numbered in a continuous sequence until 1963; from that time a new sequence has been started each calendar year.

[8] From 1968 they have been numbered in a single series with recommendations, opinions and financial regulations.

[9] *Manual of Precedents drawn up by the Legal/Linguistic Experts of the Council of the European Communities* (2nd ed., 1983).

[10] *Secondary legislation of the European Communities: Subject Edition* (H.M.S.O., 1973) Vol. 42, pp. vii–viii.

[11] See Hartley (1988), Chaps. 7, 8; O. Hood Phillips and P. Jackson, *O. Hood Phillips' Constitutional and Administrative Law* (7th ed., 1987), pp. 71–82; C. Munro, *Studies in Constitutional Law* (1982), pp. 127–132; J. W. Bridge, "Abstract Law and Political Reality in the Post-European-Accession British Constitution" [1987] Denning L.J. 23.

[12] Case 26/62, *Van Gend en Loos* v. *Nederlandse Administratie der Belastingen* [1963] E.C.R. 1.

[13] Case 6/64, *Costa* v. *ENEL* [1964] E.C.R. 585.

part of that state's fundamental or constitutional law.[14] Thus in the *Van Gend en Loos* case[15] the European Court spoke of the creation of a "new legal order . . . for the benefit of which the states have limited their sovereign rights."

Costa v. *ENEL*[16] concerned the nationalisation of Italian electricity undertakings. Costa, a shareholder in one of the undertakings (Edison Volta) refused to pay an invoice for electricity sent by ENEL, and claimed that the nationalisation was contrary to prior Community law (various articles of the EEC Treaty). The European Court, on a reference from the Italian magistrate (the Guidice Conciliatore of Milan), dealt firmly with the submission of the Italian government that a national court was obliged to apply the domestic law in preference to Community law[17]:

"By creating a Community of unlimited duration, having its own institutions, its own personality, its own legal capacity and capacity of representation on the international plane and, more particularly, real powers stemming from a limitation of sovereignty or a transfer of powers from the States to the Community, the Member States have limited their sovereign rights, albeit within limited fields, and have thus created a body of law which binds both their nationals and themselves.

The integration into the laws of each Member State of provisions which derive from the Community, and more generally, the terms and the spirit of the Treaty, make it impossible for the States, as a corollary, to accord precedence to a unilateral and subsequent measure over a legal system accepted by them on a basis of reciprocity. Such a measure cannot therefore be inconsistent with that legal system. The executive force of Community law cannot vary from one State to another in deference to subsequent domestic laws, without jeopardizing the attainment of the objectives of the Treaty set out in Article 5(2) and giving rise to the discrimination prohibited by Article 7. . . .

The precedence of Community law is confirmed by Article 189, whereby a regulation 'shall be binding' and 'directly applicable in all Member States.' This provision, which is subject to no reservation, would be quite meaningless if a State could unilaterally nullify its effects by means of a legislative measure which could prevail over Community law.

It follows from all these observations that the law stemming from the Treaty, an independent source of law, could not, because of its special and original nature, be overridden by domestic legal provisions, however framed, without being deprived of its character as Community law and without the legal basis of the Community itself being called into question.

The transfer by the States from their domestic legal system to the Community legal system of the rights and obligations arising under the Treaty carries with it a permanent limitation of their sovereign rights,

---

[14] Case 11/70, *Internationale Handelsgesellschaft* v. *Einfuhr-und Vorratsstelle für Getreide* [1970] E.C.R. 1125; Case 106/77, *Amministrazione delle Finanze dello Stato* v. *Simmenthal* [1978] E.C.R. 629.

[15] Above, pp. 289–290.

[16] Ente Nazionale Energia Elettrica (National Electricity Board), formerly the Edison Volta undertaking.

[17] pp. 593–594.

against which a subsequent unilateral act incompatible with the concept of the Community cannot prevail. Consequently Article 177 is to be applied regardless of any domestic law, whenever questions relating to the interpretation of the Treaty arise."

In the *Simmenthal* case[18] an Italian judge was faced with a conflict between a Council regulation and Italian laws, some of which were enacted after the regulation. Under Italian law domestic legislation contrary to Community law was unconstitutional. However, only the Constitutional Court had jurisdiction to make such a ruling; the ordinary courts could not. The European Court, on a reference by the judge, held that:

> "every national court must in a case within its jurisdiction apply Community law in its entirety and protect rights which the latter confers on individuals and must accordingly set aside any provision of national law which may conflict with it, whether prior or subsequent to the Community rule.... [I]t is not necessary for the court to request for or await the prior setting aside of such provisions by legislative or other constitutional means."[19]

The position from the point of view of Community law is thus clear; we now consider it from the standpoint of United Kingdom law. The key provisions of the European Communities Act 1972 are contained in sections 2 and 3:

> "2.—(1) All such rights, powers, liabilities, obligations and restrictions from time to time created or arising by or under the Treaties, and all such remedies and procedures from time to time provided for by or under the Treaties, as in accordance with the Treaties are without further enactment to be given legal effect or used in the United Kingdom shall be recognised and available in law, and be enforced, allowed and followed accordingly; and the expression 'enforceable Community right' and similar expressions shall be read as referring to one to which this subsection applies.
>
> (2) Subject to Schedule 2 to this Act, at any time after its passing Her Majesty may by Order in Council, and any designated Minister or department may by regulations, make provision—
>> (a) for the purpose of implementing any Community obligation of the United Kingdom, or enabling any such obligation to be implemented, or of enabling any rights enjoyed or to be enjoyed by the United Kingdom under or by virtue of the Treaties to be exercised; or
>> (b) for the purpose of dealing with matters arising out of or related to any such obligation or rights or the coming into force, or the operation from time to time, of subsection (1) above;
>
> and in the exercise of any statutory power or duty, including any power to give directions or to legislate by means of orders, rules, regulations or other subordinate instrument, the person entrusted with the power or duty may have regard to the objects of the Communities and to any such obligation or rights as aforesaid.

[18] [1978] E.C.R. 629.
[19] *Ibid.* pp. 644, 645–646.

In this subsection 'designated Minister or department' means such Minister of the Crown or government department as may from time to time be designated by Order in Council in relation to any matter or for any purpose, but subject to such restrictions or conditions (if any) as may be specified by the Order in Council. . . .

(4) The provision that may be made under subsection (2) above includes, subject to Schedule 2 to this Act, any such provision (of any such extent) as might be made by Act of Parliament, and any enactment passed or to be passed, other than one contained in this Part of this Act, shall be construed and have effect subject to the foregoing provisions of this section; but, except as may be provided by any Act passed after this Act, Schedule 2 shall have effect in connection with the powers conferred by this and the following sections of this Act to make Orders in Council and regulations.

3.—(1) For the purposes of all legal proceedings any question as to the meaning or effect of any of the Treaties, or as to the validity, meaning or effect of any Community instrument, shall be treated as a question of law (and, if not referred to the European Court, be for determination as such in accordance with the principles laid down by and any relevant decision of the European Court).

(2) Judicial notice shall be taken of the Treaties, of the Official Journal of the Communities and of any decision of, or expression of opinion by, the European Court on any such question as aforesaid; and the Official Journal shall be admissible as evidence of any instrument or other act thereby communicated of any of the Communities or of any Community institution."[20]

Thus, directly applicable and directly effective Community laws are given effect in the United Kingdom under section 2(1); other matters are to be dealt with by statute, or by statutory instruments under section 2(2); any question as to the meaning or effect of the treaties is to be determined in accordance with Community law of which judicial notice is to be taken (section 3). There is, however, no attempt to entrench the European Communities Act itself against repeal. It is unlikely that a court would accept that the "ultimate political fact"[21] has been redefined so as to deny effect to a statute deliberately enacted by Parliament as at present constituted which conflicts with existing Community law. It is even more unlikely that the courts would decline to recognise the express repeal of the 1972 Act.[22] Where a provision of a United Kingdom statute is followed by an inconsistent provision of Community law that is directly applicable or effective, the latter is given precedence by section 2 of the European Communities Act 1972. The position is less clear where the chronology is reversed and the U.K. statute is enacted after the inconsistent provision of Community law. If

[20] Section 2(3) authorises the necessary expenditure; section 2(5) concerns Northern Ireland; section 2(6) concerns the Channel Islands, the Isle of Man and Gibraltar. Section 3(3)–(5) makes further provision for proof of community instruments.

[21] See above, pp. 242–243.

[22] For the contrary argument that there has been a binding transfer of powers see Usher (1981), pp. 30–38; J. D. B. Mitchell, (1967–68) 5 C.M.L.Rev. 112, (1971) *Europarecht* 97, (1979) 56 *International Affairs* 33. A withdrawal from the Communities would, however, be negotiated; the arrangements would be enshrined in a treaty which could be construed as a transfer back from the Communities of those powers: Usher (1981), p. 38.

both laws were made before the 1972 Act, Community law is again given precedence by section 2. If the United Kingdom law is more recent, there are a number of possible situations and the position appears to be as follows:

(1) The United Kingdom legislation may be unclear, in which case an English court will endeavour to interpret it so as to comply with Community law, given the established presumption that Parliament does not intend the United Kingdom to be in breach of its international obligations (the "interpretation" issue).[23] In *Garland* v. *British Rail Engineering Ltd.*,[24] Lord Diplock said[25]:

> "My Lords, even if the obligation to observe the provisions of article 119 were an obligation assumed by the United Kingdom under an ordinary international treaty or convention and there were no question of the treaty obligation being directly applicable as part of the law to be applied by the courts in this country without need for any further enactment, it is a principle of construction of United Kingdom statutes, now too well established to call for citation of authority, that the words of a statute passed after the Treaty has been signed and dealing with the subject matter of the international obligation of the United Kingdom, are to be construed, if they are reasonably capable of bearing such a meaning, as intended to carry out the obligation, and not to be inconsistent with it. A fortiori is this the case where the Treaty obligation arises under one of the Community treaties to which section 2 of the European Communities Act 1972 applies."

(2) If the United Kingdom legislation is clear and unambiguously conflicts with prior Community law, an English court will then determine whether that conflict was intended by Parliament. In the case of inadvertent conflict, the Community legislation will be given priority. Where conflict is intentional, the courts will give effect to the United Kingdom legislation, and the United Kingdom will be in breach of its Treaty obligations (the "sovereignty" issue).

There have been several judicial statements which support the primacy of subsequent inconsistent Acts of Parliament, without drawing a distinction between inadvertent and intentional conflicts. Some preceded accession.[26] In *Felixstowe Dock and Railway Co.* v. *British Transport Docks Board*[27] it was argued that the proposed promotion by the Board of a private Bill to take over the plaintiff company would be an abuse of a dominant position by the Board contrary to Article 86 of the EEC Treaty. Lord Denning M.R. said that there was no evidence of such an abuse and added, *obiter*[28]:

> "It seems to me that once the Bill is passed by Parliament and becomes a Statute, that will dispose of all this discussion about the

---

[23] See below, pp. 302–308, 347–350.
[24] [1983] 2 A.C. 751.
[25] At p. 771.
[26] *e.g.* Salmon L.J. in *Blackburn* v. *Attorney-General* [1971] 1 W.L.R. 1037, 1041. Lord Denning M.R. left the point open.
[27] [1976] 2 C.M.L.R. 655.
[28] At pp. 664–5.

Treaty. These courts will then have to abide by the Statute without regard to the Treaty at all."

Both the "interpretation" and "sovereignty" issues were subsequently raised in *Macarthys Ltd.* v. *Smith*.[29] A man was paid £60 a week for managing a stockroom. Four and a half months after he left a woman was appointed in his place at £50 a week. She claimed that she was entitled to equal pay under provisions of the Equal Pay Act 1970 that had been inserted by the Sex Discrimination Act 1975. The Court of Appeal majority[30] held that Equal Pay Act provisions were confined to cases where a man and a woman were in the same employment at the same time. The words had to be given their natural and ordinary meaning and were clear; the terms of Article 119 of the EEC Treaty[31] could therefore not be used as an aid to construction. The question whether Article 119 was so confined was referred to the European Court.

Lord Denning took a different view of the proper approach to construction of the English statute and then considered the sovereignty issue[32]:

"Under section 2(1) and (4) of the European Communities Act 1972 the principles laid down in the Treaty are 'without further enactment' to be given legal effect in the United Kingdom: and have priority over 'any enactment passed or to be passed' by our Parliament. So we are entitled—and think bound—to look at article 119 of the Treaty because it is directly applicable here: and also any directive which is directly applicable here: see *Van Duyn* v. *Home Office* [1975] Ch. 358. We should, I think, look to see what those provisions require about equal pay for men and women. Then we should look at our own legislation on the point—giving it, of course, full faith and credit—assuming that it does fully comply with the obligations under the Treaty. In construing our statute, we are entitled to look to the Treaty as an aid to its construction: and even more, not only as an aid but as an overriding force. If on close investigation it should appear that our legislation is deficient—or is inconsistent with Community law—by some oversight of our draftsmen—then it is our bounden duty to give priority to Community law. Such is the result of section 2(1) and (4) of the European Communities Act 1972.

I pause here, however, to make one observation on a constitutional point. Thus far I have assumed that our Parliament, whenever it passes legislation, intends to fulfil its obligations under the Treaty. If the time should come when our Parliament deliberately passes an Act—with the intention of repudiating the Treaty or any provision in it—or intentionally of acting inconsistently with it—and says so in express terms—then I should have thought that it would be the duty of our courts to follow the statute of our Parliament. I do not however envisage any such situation. As I said in *Blackburn* v. *Attorney-General* [1971] 1 W.L.R. 1037, 1040: 'But, if Parliament should do so, then I say we will consider

---

[29] [1979] I.C.R. 785, [1981] Q.B. 180; P. Schofield, (1980) 9 I.L.J. 173; T. R. S. Allan, (1983) 3 O.J.L.S. 22. See also *Shields* v. *E. Coomes (Holdings) Ltd.* [1978] 1 W.L.R. 1408.

[30] Lawton and Cumming-Bruce L.JJ., Lord Denning M.R. dissenting on this point.

[31] "Each Member State shall during the first stage ensure and subsequently maintain the application of the principle that men and women should receive equal pay for equal work . . . ." This was amplified by article 1 of a Council directive (Dir. 75/117/EEC).

[32] [1979] I.C.R. 785, at p. 789.

that event when it happens.' Unless there is such an intentional and express repudiation of the Treaty, it is our duty to give priority to the Treaty."

On the sovereignty issue Lawton L.J. said[33]:

"I can see nothing in this case which infringes the sovereignty of Parliament. If I thought there were, I should not presume to take any judicial step which it would be more appropriate for the House of Lords, as part of Parliament, to take. Parliament by its own Act in the exercise of its sovereign powers has enacted that European Community law shall 'be enforced, allowed and followed' in the United Kingdom of Great Britain and Northern Ireland: see section 2(1) of the European Communities Act 1972, and that 'any enactment passed or to be passed ... shall be construed and have effect subject to' section 2: see section 2(4) of that Act. Parliament's recognition of European Community law and of the jurisdiction of the European Court of Justice by one enactment can be withdrawn by another. There is nothing in the Equal Pay Act 1970, as amended, to indicate that Parliament intended to amend the European Communities Act 1972, or to limit its application."

Cumming-Bruce L.J. indicated that if

"the terms of the Treaty are adjudged in Luxembourg to be inconsistent with the provisions of the Equal Pay Act 1970, European law will prevail over that municipal legislation. But such a judgment in Luxembourg cannot affect the meaning of the English statute."[34]

The European Court subsequently held that Article 119 was not restricted to cases of contemporaneous employment,[35] and the plaintiff's claim was duly conceded in the English proceedings. The matter came before the Court of Appeal again on the question of costs.[36] Lord Denning M.R. said[37]:

"the provisions of article 119 of the EEC Treaty take priority over anything in our English statute on equal pay which is inconsistent with article 119. That priority is given by our own law. It is given by the European Communities Act 1972 itself. Community law is now part of our law; and, whenever there is any inconsistency, Community law has priority. It is not supplanting English law. It is part of our law which overrides any other part which is inconsistent with it."

The other members of the court agreed that the Community legislation prevailed.[38] Cumming Bruce L.J. emphasised that his comment at the

---

[33] At p. 796.
[34] At p. 798.
[35] [1981] Q.B. 180 (C.J.E.C.).
[36] [1981] Q.B. 199 (C.A.). *Cf. Re an Absence in Ireland* [1977] 1 C.M.L.R. 5, where a national insurance commissioner allowed a claimant's appeal on two grounds, one of which involved the application of Council Regulation (EEC) No. 1408/71 in preference to the provisions of the Social Security Act 1975. See also *Re Medical Expenses Incurred in France* [1977] 2 C.M.L.R. 317.
[37] At p. 200.
[38] Professor Hood Phillips suggested that even in cases of inadvertent conflict, an English court should give effect to a subsequent, unambiguous United Kingdom Act of Parliament: (1980) 96 L.Q.R. 31; *cf.* O. Hood Phillips and P. Jackson, *O. Hood Phillips' Constitutional and Administrative Law* (7th ed., 1987), pp. 74–79.

earlier stage[39] had to be read in the context of his view (shared by Lawton
L.J.) that the English statute was unambiguous. Had he been of the view
that it was ambiguous, it would have been "appropriate to look at article 119
in order to assist in resolving the ambiguity."[40]

Accordingly, it appears that both Lord Denning M.R. and Lawton L.J.
distinguish between cases of inadvertent and intentional conflict: it would
seem that there is no room in the case of inadvertent conflict for the
application of an "implied repeal rule" as there is between two inconsistent
statutes, and in the case of intentional conflicts the English statute will
prevail. Furthermore, even in the case of intentional conflicts it may be that
effect would only be given to the English statute if it amended or repealed
the European Communities Act 1972: it would not be sufficient merely that
the substantive law prescribed by statute was different from that prescribed
by Community law. Lawton L.J., but not Lord Denning M.R., appears to
support this view.[41]

As to the issues raised in *Macarthys Ltd.* v. *Smith*,[42] it is arguable that
although the Court of Appeal approached them as if there was a *conflict*
between the Equal Pay Act 1970 and Article 119, the better view is that there
was simply a difference between them.

> "Article 119 is directly effective, and Community law applies in the
> industrial tribunals; to the extent that it gave rights to Mrs Smith more
> extensive than the Equal Pay Act 1970 (as amended by the Sex Dis-
> crimination Act 1975), there was nothing in the 1970 Act forbidding the
> court from giving effect to those rights. It should follow that Mrs Smith
> would be entitled to rely on whichever legal rule, art. 119 or the 1970
> Act, gave her more extensive rights."[43]

This approach was echoed by the Court of Appeal in *Pickstone* v. *Freemans
plc*,[44] where it was held that while the relevant provision of the Equal Pay
Act 1970[45] was unambiguous and could not be construed in conformity with
the requirements of Community law, a claim to equal pay (for work of equal
value) could instead be based directly on Article 119.[46] Similarly, the House
of Lords in *R.* v. *Secretary of State for Transport, ex p. Factortame Ltd. (No.
2)*,[47] following a reference to the European Court,[48] has accepted that
Community law imposes an obligation on national courts to provide an
effective interlocutory remedy to protect rights having direct effect under
Community law. Accordingly, interlocutory orders should be granted

---

[39] Set out above.
[40] [1981] Q.B. 180, 201.
[41] This view is endorsed in *Halsbury's Laws of England*, 4th ed., Vol. 51, para. 3.14.
[42] *Supra*.
[43] L. Collins, *European Community law in the United Kingdom* (4th ed., 1990), p. 32.
[44] [1989] A.C. 66.
[45] Section 1(2)(*c*).
[46] The House of Lords took a different approach: see below.
[47] [1990] 3 W.L.R. 856.
[48] Case C213/89, *R.* v. *Secretary of State for Transport, ex p. Factortame Ltd. (No. 2)* [1990] 3
W.L.R. 818, E.C.J.

against the Crown disapplying Part II of the Merchant Shipping Act 1988[49] and restraining the Secretary of State from enforcing it and related regulations against the applicants, pending the final determination by the European Court of questions concerning the compatability of these provisions with Community law. This was so notwithstanding that, as a matter of domestic law, interlocutory injunctions cannot be granted against the Crown.[50]

Cases since *Macarthys Ltd.* v. *Smith*[51] have for the most part raised the "interpretation issue" rather than the "sovereignty issue." The dictum of Lord Diplock in *Garland* v. *British Rail Engineering Ltd.*[52] cited above[53] has been regarded as endorsing Lord Denning's approach in *Macarthys Ltd.* v. *Smith*[54] rather than that of the majority.[55] Lord Diplock's approach was purportedly followed in two, contrasting, decisions of the House of Lords.

In *Duke* v. *Reliance Systems Ltd.*,[56] Mrs. Duke was dismissed by her private sector employers shortly after attaining 60, in accordance with their policy that men should retire at 65 but women at 60. She claimed that this constituted discriminatory treatment under the Sex Discrimination Act 1975, s.6(2), but her claim was dismissed on the ground that section 6(4) preserved the right of the employer to operate discriminatory retirement ages. This said that section 6(2) did not apply to "provision in relation to death or retirement." It was clear that the later Council Directive Dir. 76/207/EEC (the Equal Treatment Directive) did outlaw discriminatory retirement ages,[57] but (1) this did not have "horizonal direct effect" between individuals,[58] and (2) the U.K. legislation implementing the directive, the Sex Discrimination Act 1986, did not apply retrospectively so as to apply to Mrs. Duke's claim. She argued, therefore, that the expression "provision in relation to ... retirement" should be interpreted as "provision consequent upon retirement," and therefore not apply to protect discriminatory retirement ages. This would enable English law to conform with the Equal Treatment Directive. The argument was rejected.[59] Lord Templeman, with whom the other members of the House of Lords agreed, said:

---

[49] The 1988 Act and associated regulations (Merchant Shipping (Registration of Fishing Vessels) Regulations 1988 (S.I. 1988 No. 1926) were designed to narrow the conditions under which fishing vessels can be registered as British (and thus entitled to fish against the U.K. quotas): vessels would have to have "a genuine and substantial" connection with the U.K. (1988 Act, s.14(3)). The applicants were Spanish nationals, who controlled companies that owned ships registered as British, and which would lose that registration under the new rules.

[50] *R.* v. *Secretary of State for Transport, ex p. Factortame Ltd.* [1990] 2 A.C. 85, H.L. See N. P. Gravells, [1989] P.L. 568.

[51] *Supra.*

[52] [1983] 2 A.C. 751, 771.

[53] At p. 301.

[54] *Supra.*

[55] A. W. Bradley, in J. Jowell and D. Oliver, *The Changing Constitution* (2nd ed., 1989), p. 41.

[56] [1988] A.C. 618. Applied by the House of Lords in *Finnegan* v. *Clowney Youth Training Programme Ltd.* [1990] 2 A.C. 418.

[57] Case 151/84, *Roberts* v. *Tate & Lyle Industries Ltd.* [1986] E.C.R. 703, [1986] I.C.R. 371; Case 152/84, *Marshall* v. *Southampton and South-West Hampshire Area Health Authority* (*Teaching*) [1986] E.C.R. 723, [1986] Q.B. 401.

[58] *Marshall, supra* and see pp. 291–292.

[59] It had previously been rejected by the Employment Tribunal and the Court of Appeal in *Roberts* v. *Cleveland Area Health Authority* [1978] I.C.R. 370, [1979] 1 W.L.R. 754.

"Of course a British court will always be willing and anxious to conclude that United Kingdom law is consistent with Community law. Where an Act is passed for the purpose of giving effect to an obligation imposed by a decision or other instrument a British court will seldom encounter difficulty in concluding that the language of the Act is effective for the intended purpose. But the construction of a British Act of Parliament is a matter of judgment to be determined by British courts and to be derived from the language of the legislation considered in the light of the circumstances prevailing at the date of enactment,"[60]

However, the 1975 Act was not passed in order to give effect to the (later) Equal Treatment Directive, and the words of section 6(4)

"are not reasonably capable of being limited to the meaning ascribed to them by the appellant. Section 2(4) of the European Communities Act 1972 does not in my opinion enable or constrain a British court to distort the meaning of a British statute in order to enforce against an individual a Community directive which has no direct effect between individuals. Section 2(4) applies and only applies where Community provisions are directly applicable."[61]

It is clearly the case that the 1975 Act was intended at the time to preserve differential retirement ages. Indeed the United Kingdom's position was that the Equal Treatment Directive did not prohibit discriminatory retirement ages, an argument ultimately rejected by the European Court in *Marshall*.[62]

The reasoning in *Duke* has been cogently criticised by commentators on a variety of grounds.[63] First, it is not obvious that the narrow reading of "in relation to" was a "distortion": it was certainly a less natural reading, but one that was arguably supportable given the requirements of the directive, and the obligation under Community law (via sections 2(4) and 3(1) of the European Communities Act 1972) to interpret national legislation where possible to conform with relevant directives. Secondly, it was incorrect to say that section 2(4) only applied to Community provisions that were "directly applicable."[64] Third, it gave insufficient weight to the presumed continuing intention of the United Kingdom to comply with the requirements of Community law: it is not clear that this was properly subordinated to the contemporary intention in 1975 to preserve discriminatory retirement ages. It is important, however, to see the *Duke* decision in its context. Had Mrs. Duke's argument prevailed, the position would have been as if the Sex Discrimination Act 1986 had retrospective effect, and this would undoubtedly have caused severe practical difficulties. It is to be hoped that the rather doubtful reasoning employed to secure that result is not used in subsequent cases so as to undermine proper implementation by the United Kingdom of the requirements of Community law.

[60] [1988] A.C. 618, 638.
[61] *Ibid.*, pp. 639–640.
[62] *Supra.*
[63] E. Ellis, (1988) 104 L.Q.R. 379; A. Arnull, [1988] P.L. 313; N. Foster, (1988) 51 M.L.R. 775 and (1988) 25 C.M.L. Rev. 629; B. Fitzpatrick, (1989) 9 O.J.L.S. 336.
[64] The European Court in Case 262/84, *Beets-Proper* v. *Van Lanschot Bankiers N.V.* [1986] E.C.R. 782 held that national legislation, designed to implement a directive that was *not* directly effective, should be interpreted so as to conform to it: See above, p. 293. This obligation would apply to U.K. courts via ss.2(4) and 3(1) of the 1972 Act.

The decision of the House of Lords in *Pickstone* v. *Freemans plc*[65] is accordingly to be welcomed. Here, the House placed renewed emphasis on the need to interpret English law, where possible, so as to comply with Community law. The context of the case was significantly different from that in *Duke*. Here, the question concerned the interpretation of amendments to the Equal Pay Act 1970 specifically designed to bring English law into conformity with Community law. Prior to amendment, the Act took effect where the woman was employed (a) "on like work" or (b) on work "rated as equivalent" on a job evaluation study, with a man in the same employment.[66] The European Court held that this was inadequate to comply with Article 119/EEC and Council Directive Dir. 75/117/EEC (The "Equal Pay Directive"), which imposed a requirement of equal pay for the same work or *work of equal value*. The latter element was not fully implemented by (b), which depended on the employer having consented to a job evaluation[67] study. Accordingly, the Equal Pay (Amendment) Regulations 1983[68] introduced a new para. (*c*), which allowed an "equal value" claim to be made "where a woman is employed on work, not being work in relation to which paragraph (*a*) or (*b*) above applies. . . ." Mrs. Pickstone, a "warehouse operative," made a claim under para. (*c*), claiming her work was of equal value to that of a man employed as a "checker warehouse operative." There happened to be one man also employed as a "warehouse operative." The industrial tribunal and the Employment Appeal Tribunal[69] accepted the employer's argument that para. (*a*) applied to Mrs. Pickstone's work, and that the words "not being work. . . ." accordingly barred her claim under para. (*c*). The Court of Appeal[70] held that this was indeed the position under the Equal Pay Act 1970, but that Mrs. Pickstone could base her claim directly on Article 119/EEC. The House of Lords interpreted the 1970 Act in such a way as to allow her claim to proceed under it: the exclusionary words in para. (*c*) were intended to have effect only where the particular man with whom she sought comparison was employed on the same work. Here, her comparator was employed on different work.

"The opposite result would leave a large gap in the equal work provision, enabling an employer to evade it by employing one token man on the same work as a group of potential women claimants who were deliberately paid less than a group of men employed on work of equal value with that of the women. This would mean that the United Kingdom had failed yet again fully to implement its obligations under article 119 of the Treaty and the Equal Pay Directive, and had not given full effect to the decision of the European Court in *Commission* v. *U.K.*[71] It is plain that Parliament cannot possibly have intended such a failure."[72]

---

[65] [1989] A.C. 66. See A. W. Bradley, [1988] P.L. 485. *Cf. J. Rothschild Holdings* v. *Commissioners of Inland Revenue* [1989] 2 C.M.L.R. 612.
[66] Section 1(2)(*a*), (*b*).
[67] Case 61/81, *Commission* v. *United Kingdom* [1982] E.C.R. 2601, [1982] I.C.R. 578; S. Atkins, [1983] P.L. 19 and (1983) 8 E.L. Rev. 48.
[68] S.I. 1983 No. 1794.
[69] [1986] I.C.R. 886.
[70] [1989] A.C. 66. See A. W. Bradley, [1988] P.L. 485, 489–491.
[71] *Supra.*
[72] *per* Lord Keith of Kinkel at pp. 111–112.

A purposive, rather than a literal construction was necessary.[73] There is room for argument how far this result involves a "distortion" of the statutory language.

Finally, in the *Factortame* litigation[74] it was accepted by both the parties and the courts that if the European Court were to rule finally that the relevant provisions of the Merchant Shipping Act 1988 were incompatible with Community law, English courts would have to give effect to the latter, whether as a matter of interpretation of the 1988 Act[75] or by disapplying it as invalid.[76]

5. IMPLEMENTATION OF COMMUNITY LAW IN THE UNITED KINGDOM

As has been seen, Community law that is directly applicable or effective takes effect in the United Kingdom under section 2(1) of the European Communities Act 1972.[77] In appropriate cases,[78] such law may give rise to defences that can be relied on in English litigation.[79] Alternatively, it may form the basis of an award of damages, (*e.g.* for breach of statutory duty[80] or the tort of misfeasance in a public office[81]) or the grant of an injunction,[82] as a

---

[73] See below, pp. 327–329.
[74] See above, pp. 304–305.
[75] *per* Lord Bridge in *R.* v. *Secretary of State for Transport, ex p. Factortame Ltd.* [1990] 2 A.C. 85, 140, referring to s.2(1) and (4) of the 1972 Act: "This has precisely the same effect as if a section were incorporated in Part II of the Act of 1988 which in terms enacted that the provisions with respect to registration of British fishing vessels were to be without prejudice to the directly enforceable Community rights of nationals of any member state of the E.E.C." Although this can be labelled as an approach based on interpretation, this would seem to be "interpretation" of a kind more radical than adopted hitherto; the words read into the statute have a very substantial modifying effect.
[76] The Court of Appeal in *Factortame*: [1989] 2 C.M.L.R. 353, 396 (Lord Donaldson M.R.), 403–404 (Bingham L.J.), 408 (Mann L.J.).
[77] Above, pp. 299–300.
[78] See generally J. Steiner, "How to make the action suit the case: domestic remedies for breach of EEC law" (1987) 12 E.L. Rev. 102; P. Oliver, "Enforcing Community rights in the English courts" (1987) 50 M.L.R. 881; N. Green and A. Barav, "Damages in the national courts for breach of Community law" [1986] 6 Y.E.L. 55, 83–114; J. S. Davidson, (1985) 34 I.C.L.Q. 178.
[79] *e.g.* a defence to criminal proceedings: Case 63/83, *R.* v. *Kirk* [1985] 1 All E.R. 453; Case 121/85, *Conegate* v. *Commissioners of Customs and Excise* [1987] Q.B. 254; or Euro-defences" based on E.E.C. competition law arising in civil actions: *cf. Lansing Bagnall Ltd.* v. *Buccaneer Lift Parts Ltd.* [1984] 1 C.M.L.R. 224; *Ransburg-Gema AG* v. *Electrostatic Plant Systems Ltd.* [1989] 2 C.M.L.R. 712.
[80] *e.g.* for a breach of Art. 86/EEC (abuse of a dominant position): *per* Lord Diplock in *Garden Foods Ltd.* v. *Milk Marketing Board* [1984] A.C. 130, 141: see K. Banks, (1984) 21 C.M.L. Rev. 669; F. G. Jacobs, (1983) 8 E.L. Rev. 353; M. Friend and J. Shaw, (1984) 100 L.Q.R. 188; but not a breach of Art. 30 (prohibition of quantitative restrictions on imports and measures having equivalent effect): *Bourgoin S.A.* v. *Ministry of Agriculture, Fisheries and Food* [1985] Q.B. 716, C.A.; or a breach of Art. 10 of Council Reg. 1422/78: *An Bord Bainne* v. *Milk Marketing Board* [1988] 1 C.M.L.R. 605, C.A.
[81] An action that lies where loss is caused by *ultra vires* acts committed maliciously (*i.e.* with intent to injure the plaintiff) or with knowledge of its illegality: *Bourgoin, supra*: the parties settled for £3.5 M (Vol. 102 H.C. Deb. July 23, 1986, col. 116, written answer).
[82] *Garden Cottage Foods, supra*; *Cutsforth* v. *Mansfield Inns Ltd.* [1986] 1 C.M.L.R. 1.

matter of private law, or the grant of public law remedies against the Crown or other public authority.[83]

Primary legislation has been enacted to give effect to major changes, such as those consequent on the accession of new Member States,[84] major budgetary matters[85] and the Single European Act.[86] Specific Community obligations may also be implemented by Act of Parliament.[87] Section 2(2) of the 1972 Act[88] authorises the making of subordinate legislation (1) to implement other Community laws that are not directly applicable or effective; or (2) to deal with matters related to Community laws that take effect under section 2(1).[89] Subordinate legislation may not, however, (1) provide for the imposition or increase of taxation; (2) be retrospective; (3) confer the power to enact sub-delegated legislation; or (4) create any new criminal offence punishable with more than two years imprisonment, or three months on summary conviction, or a fine of more than £1,000, or £100 a day.[90] It is subject to the negative resolution procedure.[91]

Arrangements have been made for the scrutiny of Community legislation by the Select Committee of the House of Lords on the European Communities and the Select Committee of the House of Commons on European Legislation.[92] These committees consider draft Community legislation and other documents prepared by the Commission for submission to the Council of Ministers. Detailed explanatory memoranda are prepared by the government. The Commons committee concentrates on political implications,

---

[83] e.g. Van Duyn v. Home Office [1974] 1 W.L.R. 1107, Ch.D., and Case 41/74, [1985] Ch. 358 E.C.J. (action for a declaration); R. v. Attorney-General, ex p. I.C.I. [1987] 1 C.M.L.R. 72 and R. v. Intervention Board for Agricultural Produce, ex p. The Fish Producers' Organisation Ltd. [1988] 2 C.M.L.R. 661 (applications for judicial review).

[84] European Communities (Greek Accession) Act 1979; European Communities (Spanish and Portuguese Accession) Act 1985.

[85] European Communities (Finance) Act 1985.

[86] European Communities (Amendment) Act 1986.

[87] e.g. the Companies Acts 1980 and 1981, which implemented directives on the harmonisation of company law; the Importation of Milk Act 1983, passed in response to a judgment of the European Court which held that U.K. restrictions on the importation of U.H.T. milk were contrary to Community rules on the free movement of goods (Case 124/81, Commission v. United Kingdom [1983] E.C.R. 203); the Sex Discrimination Act 1986.

[88] Sections 5 and 6 of the 1972 Act confer powers to make subordinate legislation concerning customs matters and the common agricultural policy. Statutory instruments implementing Community obligations have been made under other statutes.

[89] Note, however, the limits on such legislation in respect of Community regulations: above, p. 295.

[90] European Communities Act 1972, Sched. 2, as amended by the Criminal Law Act 1977, s.32 and the Criminal Justice Act 1982, ss.37, 40, 46.

[91] Ibid. See above pp. 270–271.

[92] Established in 1974. See 1972–73 H.C. 143 and 463–I ("Foster Committee": Commons); 1972–73 H.L. 194 ("Maybray-King Committee": Lords). See also the First Report from the Select Committee on Procedure, 1977–78 H.C. 588 Vol. I, pp. xl–xlvi; First Special Report of the Select Committee on European Legislation 1983–84 (1983–84 H.C. 527): Government response, Vol. 65 H.C. Deb., October 29, 1984, cols. 800–802, written answer); Second Special Report 1985–86 (1985–86 H.C. 400): Government observations, Cm. 123, 1987; Fourth Report from the Select Committee on Procedure (1988–89 H.C. 622): Government response, Cm. 1081, 1990; P. Norton, The Commons in Perspective (1981), pp. 160–164; Lord Fraser of Tullybelton in St. John Bates, et al., (eds.) In Memoriam J. D. B. Mitchell (1983), pp. 29–37; T. St. J. Bates in M. Ryle and P. G. Richards (eds.), The Commons Under Scrutiny (1988), pp. 205–211.

although the merits cannot be considered; the Lords deal more with technical legal and administrative implications.[93] The Lords committee has a number of sub-committees, including one customarily chaired by one of the Law Lords on legal aspects, and each of the rest considering Community proposals within a particular subject area. The committees decide, *inter alia*, whether a particular proposal should be considered further by the respective Houses. In the Commons, a debate may be held on the floor of the House or in a standing committee.[94] The government has undertaken that it will normally[95] provide time for such consideration where recommended by the Select Committee prior to a proposal being discussed by the Council of Ministers. However, the scrutiny of European secondary legislation is indirect in effect, given that Parliament can at best influence only one of the twelve members of the Council of Ministers, especially now that more Council decisions are reached by qualified majorities and that the legislative process is likely to be quicker.[96] Moreover, it can be difficult to keep abreast of changes in draft proposals as they progress through the Community legislative process.

6. VALIDITY OF EUROPEAN SECONDARY LEGISLATION

(a) Article 173; the action for annulment

The validity of acts of Community institutions that are binding in law, and whether legislative or not, may be challenged directly by an *action for annulment* brought in the European Court of Justice[97] under Article 173 of the EEC Treaty[98]:

---

[93] Joint meetings are occasionally held.

[94] From 1981 the Standing Committee on European Community Documents has been able to consider a substantive, amendable motion rather than a neutral motion to the effect that the document has been "considered." In 1990, three European Standing Committees were established in order to shift debates away from the floor of the House: see 1988–89 H.C. 622 and Cm. 1081, *supra*; First Special Report from the Select Committee on European Legislation 1989–90 (1989–90 H.C. 512) and Vol. 178 H.C. Deb., October 24, 1990, cols. 375–401.

[95] The strength of the undertaking has varied from time to time. In 1980, the Commons resolved that no minister should agree to a proposal for Community legislation recommended by the Select Committee for consideration by the House before the House had given it that consideration unless (a) the Committee has indicated that agreement need not be withheld or (b) the Minister decides there are special reasons; in the latter case the reasons should be explained to the House at the first opportunity: H.C. Deb. Vol. 991, col. 844, October 30, 1980. Agreement to a common position under the co-operation procedure is treated as "agreement to a proposal" for these purposes: First Special Report from the Select Committee on European Legislation 1988–89 (1988–89 H.C. 533), pp. iv, v. This was recognised formally, and the resolution was extended to include documents awaiting scrutiny by the Select Committee, in a revised version approved on October 24, 1990: H.C. Deb. Vol. 178, col. 400.

[96] See the reports on the Single European Act and Parliamentary Scrutiny: First Special Report from the Select Committee on European Legislation 1985–86 (1985–86 H.C. 264) and the First Special Report 1988–89 (1988–89 H.C. 533); Twelfth Report from the Select Committee on the European Communities 1985–86 (1985–86 H.L. 149).

[97] See above pp. 96–101: national courts may not rule acts of Community institutions invalid (Case 314/85, *Foto-Frost* v. *Hauptzollamt Lübeck-Ost* [1987] E.C.R. 4199.) The approach adopted by the European Court to the interpretation of Community Law is considered below pp. 361–367.

[98] See also Art. 33(2)/ECSC; Art.146(2)/Euratom.

"(1) The Court of Justice shall review the legality of acts of the Council and the Commission other than recommendations or opinions.[99] It shall for this purpose have jurisdiction in actions brought by a Member State, the Council or the Commission[1] on the grounds of lack of competence, infringement of an essential procedural requirement, infringement of this Treaty or of any rule of law relating to its application, or misuse of powers.

(2) Any natural or legal person[2] may, under the same conditions, institute proceedings against a decision addressed to that person or against a decision which, although in the form of a regulation or a decision addressed to another person, is of direct and individual concern to the former.

(3) The proceedings provided for in this Article shall be instituted within two months of the publication of the measure, or of its notification to the plaintiff, or, in the absence thereof, of the day on which it came to the knowledge of the latter, as the case may be."

Thus the range of acts that can be challenged by an individual is narrower than those that can be reviewed under Article 173(1). First, the act must be a "decision" in that it must have legal effect[3] and must not be a regulation, in the sense of an act which applies to objectively determined situations and has legal effects on classes of persons defined in a general and abstract manner.[4] Second, the act must be of "direct and individual concern" to the applicant.[5] If the action is successful, the act challenged is declared by the Court to be void,[6] and the matter is remitted to the institution concerned.

---

[99] This covers any act intended to have legal effect, and not merely regulations, directives and decisions: Case 22/70, *Commission* v. *Council* [1971] E.C.R. 263 (action for annulment of a Council resolution concerning negotiations leading to an international agreement between the Member States and third countries). The principle has also been extended to acts of the Parliament, notwithstanding their exclusion from Art. 173(1): Case 294/83, *Parti Ecologiste 'Les Verts'* v. *European Parliament* [1986] E.C.R. 1339.

[1] But not the Parliament: Case 302/87, *European Parliament* v. *Council* [1988] E.C.R. 5615: see B. Harris and R. Greaves, (1989) 139 N.L.J. 23; J. Weiler, (1989) 14 E.L. Rev. 334. This decision was surprising given the decision that the Parliament's acts may be subject to an action for annulment: above, n. 99.

[2] This term includes a Member State: Case 25/62 *Plaumann* v. *Commission* [1963] E.C.R. 95.

[3] Cases 8–11/66, *Cimenteries* v. *Commission* (the *Noordwijks Cement Accoord case*) [1967] E.C.R. 75: a notification by the Commission that certain agreements were prohibited under Article 85/EEC, which had the effect of removing a temporary immunity from fines, was held to be reviewable even though such fines could only be imposed if further steps were taken by the Commission.

[4] Collins *op. cit.* p. 282, n. 6a, pp. 232–234, 236–240. The Court looks to the substance and not the form; the fact that the act has been promulgated as a regulation is not conclusive. See, *e.g.* Cases 113, 118–121/77, *Japanese Ball Bearings Cases* [1979] E.C.R. 1185 where four Japanese ball-bearing manufacturers were held to be entitled to challenge a regulation imposing an import duty in general terms, but which on the facts was aimed at them.

[5] There are a number of cases on this point, which are not always easy to reconcile: Collins, pp. 234–256; Hartley (1988), Chap. 12; R. Greaves, (1988) 11 E.L. Rev. 119.

[6] Article 174/EEC.

Preliminary decisions can only be challenged if they affect the applicant's rights independently of the final decision: otherwise, the applicant must await the final decision and challenge that.[7]

The grounds for challenge are set out in Article 173(1).[8] Although they are based upon the grounds for review in continental, particularly French, administrative law, arguments may be based on principles of administrative law derived from the legal systems of any Member State. The grounds may overlap in the sense that a particular set of facts may involve infringements under more than one heading.

Lack of competence corresponds to the English concept of substantive *ultra vires*[9] and the French concept of *excès de pouvoir* or *incompétence*. It may not be easily distinguishable from an allegation of *infringement of the Treaties or any rules of law relating to their application*. An example is *Meroni* v. *High Authority*[10] where certain decisions under the Coal and Steel Treaty were held to be improperly delegated to certain subordinate bodies.

Infringement of an essential procedural requirement corresponds to the English doctrine of procedural *ultra vires* and the French concept of *vice de forme*. Only requirements of substantial importance are mandatory: for example, requirements to hold a hearing,[11] to consult the European Parliament,[12] to give reasons[13] and to state the provision under which the measure is adopted.[14] Minor irregularities are ignored; for example, notification of a decision to a subsidiary rather than to the applicants where the latter had full knowledge of the decision in time to institute proceedings,[15] and the reporting of a decision in the *Official Journal* under an inaccurate title.[16]

Misuse of powers broadly corresponds to the abuse of discretion aspect of the *ultra vires* doctrine and the French concept of *détournement de pouvoir*. It covers, for example, the use of a power for an improper purpose.

---

[7] Compare Case 60/81, *I.B.M.* v. *Commission* [1981] E.C.R. 2639 (decision to institute proceedings for abuse of a dominant position not separately challengeable) with Case 53/85, *A.K.Z.O. Chemie* v. *Commission* [1986] E.C.R. 1965 (decision to show documents, claimed by the applicant to contain confidential information, to the complainant, challengeable).

[8] Hartley (1988), Chap. 15.

[9] On the English *ultra vires* doctrine see below, pp. 871–874.

[10] Case 9/56, [1957–8] E.C.R. 133; see also Case 48/69, *I.C.I.* v. *Commission* (the *Dyestuffs* case) [1972] E.C.R. 619.

[11] Case 41/69, *ACF Chemiefarma* v. *Commission* [1970] E.C.R. 661; the challenge failed on the merits: see also the *Dyestuffs* case *supra*. A hearing may be necessary even though it is not expressly required by Community legislation: Case 17/74, *Transocean Marine Paint Association* v. *Commission* [1974] E.C.R. 1063.

[12] See above, p. 296.

[13] See Art. 190 above, pp. 286–287. Case 24/62, *Germany* v. *Commission* [1963] E.C.R. 63. The reasons must be adequate: the act must "set out, in a concise, but clear and relevant manner, the principal issues of law and of fact upon which it is based and which are necessary in order that the reasoning which has led the Commission to its Decision may be understood" (*ibid.* p. 69). See also Case 166/78, *Italy* v. *Council* [1979] E.C.R. 2575. A Council directive was annulled where the statement of reasons was altered by the Council's secretariat, in a way that went beyond simple corrections of spelling and grammar: Case 131/86, *United Kingdom* v. *Council* [1988] E.C.R. 905.

[14] Case 45/86, *Commission* v. *Council* [1987] E.C.R. 1493; A. Arnull, (1987) 12 E.L. Rev. 448. These cases may also raise questions of competence: see generally K. St. C. Bradley, "The European Court and the Legal Basis of Community Legislation" (1988) 13 E.L. Rev. 379.

[15] *Dyestuffs* case, *supra*.

[16] Case 6/72, *Europemballage & Continental Can* v. *Commission* [1973] E.C.R. 215.

(b) Article 184: the plea of illegality[17]

Article 184 of the EEC Treaty provides that:

"Notwithstanding the expiry of the period laid down in the third paragraph of Article 173, any party[18] may, in proceedings in which a regulation[19] of the Council or of the Commission is in issue, plead the grounds specified in the first paragraph of Article 173, in order to invoke before the Court of Justice the inapplicability of that regulation."

An individual may not challenge a *regulation* under Article 173 (*supra*); if, however, he or she happens to be a party to proceedings before the European Court he or she (and any other party) may do so under Article 184. Article 184 may be invoked where proceedings are brought under some other provision of the Treaty which concern the party making the plea of illegality; it does not give that party an independent cause of action.[20]

(c) Article 175: remedy against inaction[21]

Article 175 of the EEC Treaty provides that:

"(1) Should the Council or the Commission, in infringement of this Treaty, fail to act, the Member States and the other institutions of the Community[22] may bring an action before the Court of Justice to have the infringement established.

(2) The action shall be admissible only if the institution concerned has first been called upon to act. If, within two months of being so called upon, the institution concerned has not defined its position, the action may be brought within a further period of two months.

(3) Any natural or legal person may, under the conditions laid down in the preceding paragraphs, complain to the Court of Justice that an institution of the Community has failed to address to that person any act other than a recommendation or an opinion."

The European Court has built in some limitations to actions under this article. An action can only be brought where the institution in question has failed to define its position within two months. In *Lütticke* v. *Commission*[23] the Commission had declined to take action against France on the ground that it had in fact complied with the Treaty, and stated as much within the two months period; the court held that an action could therefore not be brought. An individual may not use Article 175 to circumvent the restrictions that prevent him bringing an action directly against a Member State for

---

[17] Hartley (1988), Chap. 14.
[18] This includes Member States: Case 32/65, *Italy* v. *Council and Commission* [1966] E.C.R. 389.
[19] But not a *decision*: Case 156/77, *Commission* v. *Belgium* [1978] E.C.R. 1881. The court again looks to substance rather than form: Case 92/78, *Simmenthal* v. *Commission* [1979] E.C.R. 777.
[20] Case 31/62, *Wohrmann* v. *Commission* [1962] E.C.R. 501.
[21] Hartley (1988), Chap. 13.
[22] This includes the Council, the Commission and the Parliament: Case 13/83, *European Parliament* v. *Council* [1985] E.C.R. 1513: See P. Fennell, (1985) 10 E.L. Rev. 264.
[23] Case 48/65, [1966] E.C.R. 19.

breach of a Treaty provision,[24] or an action outside the limits of Article 173,[25] by attempting to bring an action against the Commission (respectively) (1) for failing to take action against the Member State or (2) failing to revoke a decision not in fact open to challenge under Article 173.

(d) Articles 177 and 215

The validity of Community legislation may also be considered by the European Court on a reference under Article 177 of the EEC Treaty,[26] or on an action for damages under Article 215 of the EEC Treaty.[27] In such cases the restrictions built in to Article 173 do not necessarily apply.

---

[24] Under Articles 169 and 170/EEC such actions can only be brought by a Member State or the Commission: See the *Lütticke* case, *supra*.
[25] See above, pp. 310–312; Cases 10 and 18/68, *Eridania* v. *Commission* [1969] E.C.R. 459.
[26] See below, pp. 879–887.
[27] See above, p. 99, n. 17.

CHAPTER 6

STATUTORY INTERPRETATION

A. INTRODUCTION

WHILE the enactment of a statute is the culmination of Parliament's legislative process, it is merely the starting point for what may be many years of existence, in some cases posing problems for generations of users. If it is to have its proper effect it must be read and understood, although there are many other factors which govern the extent to which a particular measure is successful. There are various kinds of statute-user and many matters which may cause them difficulty.[1] It cannot realistically be assumed that all statutes are directed at the general public and are therefore designed to be understood by them. It is argued that statutes are complicated:

"... because life is complicated. The bulk of the legislation enacted nowadays is social, economic or financial; the laws they [*i.e.* statutes] must express and the life situations they must regulate are in themselves complicated, and these laws cannot in any language or in any style be reduced to kindergarten level, any more than can the theory of relativity."[2]

The user tends to be the public official charged with the duty of implementation, the lawyer or the non-legal professional adviser, and statutes tend to be drafted accordingly: by experts for experts. Lay people[3] who wish to use statutes thus have to become acquainted with statute-handling techniques, or rely on explanatory material, such as textbooks or government leaflets, written by experts, or consult an expert personally. This is seen by some as a vicious circle: they doubt whether statutes need to be as complicated as experts who earn a living by explaining them to the rest of us would have us believe.

Some of the problems of the user, even the professional user, relate to the discovery of the relevant provisions and the establishment of an authentic, up-to-date text. The provisions may be spread among a number of statutes and statutory instruments which have to be read together. The uninstructed lay person may well not accomplish even this stage. Once established, the text also has to be understood or "interpreted."[4] The task of interpretation may vary in difficulty. Some provisions can be understood automatically,

---

[1] See F. A. R. Bennion, *Statute Law* (3rd ed., 1990), Part II (pp. 83–205); *cf.* W. Twining and D. Miers, *How To Do Things With Rules* (2nd ed., 1982), Chaps. 4–6.

[2] E. A. Dreidger, cited in Bennion (1990), pp. 209–210.

[3] Or, indeed, lawyers and other professionals in matters outside their expertise.

[4] The O.E.D. definitions of this term include both "to expound the meaning of" and "to make out the meaning of, explain to oneself."

without the conscious perception of any "problem" of interpretation: some problems may be easy to solve after a moment's thought. At the other extreme, a problem may be highly complex, enough to make the reader weep. Printing or drafting errors can turn a provision into gibberish.

F. A. R. Bennion[5] has identified a number of factors that may cause doubt. Some of these doubt-factors are inevitable and even desirable: others are avoidable. First, there is what he terms the technique of *ellipsis*. Here, the draftsman refrains from using certain words that he or she regards as necessarily implied: the problem is that the users may not realise that this is the case. The unexpressed words may normally be implied in statutes of a particular kind unless Parliament expressly provides to the contrary: many of the principles of judicial review of administrative action rest on this basis,[6] as do certain principles of criminal liability.[7] Alternatively the implication may arise from the words that actually are used. The judges on occasion exercise a limited power (in practice but not in theory) to rewrite statutes, although it can be difficult to predict in any particular case whether a judge will be prepared to act in that way.[8]

Second, the draftsman may use a *broad term* ("a word or phrase of wide meaning") and leave it to the user to judge what situations fall within it. Most words can be said to have a core of certain meaning surrounded by a penumbra of uncertainty. A standard example is the term "vehicle." This clearly covers motor cars, buses and motor cycles, but it is less clear whether it covers an invalid carriage, a child's tricycle, a donkey-cart or a pair of roller-skates.[9] Examples from decided cases include whether the routine oiling and maintenance of points apparatus on the railway fell within the term "relaying or repairing" the permanent way[10]; whether an accident arose "out of and in the course of [the victim's] ... employment"[11]; and whether a car from which the engine had been stolen and a car which could not move under its own power as parts were missing or rusted were "mechanically propelled vehicles" for which a licence was required.[12] Sir Rupert Cross described this sort of case as "part of the daily bread of judges and practitioners."[13] One difficulty here may be that the meaning of a

---

[5] *Op. cit.* n. 1 above, Chaps. 15–19.

[6] *e.g.* breach of natural justice, abuse of discretionary powers: see below, p. 873.

[7] *e.g.* the effect of mistake and insanity on criminal liability. A major defect of the drafting of many statutes creating offences is that they do not make it clear whether *mens rea* is a necessary ingredient: see, *e.g. R.* v. *Warner* [1969] 2 A.C. 256. Another common defect is that statutes imposing duties do not indicate whether breach of a duty can give rise to a civil action: see, *e.g., Lonhro Ltd.* v. *Shell Petroleum Co. Ltd. (No. 2)* [1982] A.C. 173.

[8] See below, pp. 331–334.

[9] Twining and Miers (1982), pp. 205–206; *cf.* H. L. A. Hart, (1958) 4 J.S.P.T.L. (N.S.) 144–145.

[10] *London and North-Eastern Railway* v. *Berriman* [1946] A.C. 278.

[11] See, *e.g. R.* v. *Industrial Injuries Commissioner, ex p. A.E.U. (No. 2)* [1966] 2 Q.B. 31. (accident befalling an employee overstaying a tea-break). There have been many cases on this expression: see A. I. Ogus and E. Barendt, *The Law of Social Security* (3rd ed., 1988), pp. 261–278; P. F. Smith, *Industrial Injuries Benefit* (1978), pp. 24–45.

[12] *Newberry* v. *Simmonds* [1961] 2 Q.B. 345; *Smart* v. *Allan* [1963] 1 Q.B. 291: the answers were, respectively, yes and no, the main difference being that in the latter case there was no reasonable prospect of the vehicle ever being made mobile again.

[13] J. Bell and Sir George Engle, *Cross, Statutory Interpretation* (2nd ed., 1987), p. 76. Another good illustration is provided by the refusal of Parliament to define "disposal" and "disposition" for the purposes of, respectively, capital gains tax and capital transfer tax: see J. Tiley, *Revenue Law* (3rd ed., 1981), paras. 20–01 and 42–02.

statutory expression may change with the passage of time.[14] A further technical point that may arise when it has to be decided whether a set of facts conforms to a statutory description is whether that decision is one of fact or one of law. This governs whether it should be decided by the jury (if there is one) or the judge, and the extent to which the decision can be upset by an appellate court.[15]

Third, there may be *politic uncertainty:* ambiguous words may be used deliberately, for example where a provision is politically contentious, or where departments wish to minimise the risk of legal challenge.[15a]

Fourth, there may be *unforeseeable developments.* These the draftsman cannot be expected to cover, although he or she may use language that is capable of extension. A well-known example of such extension is *Attorney-General* v. *Edison Telephone Co.*[16] where the Telegraph Act 1869, passed before the telephone was invented, was held to confer on the Postmaster General certain powers concerning telephone messages. However, extension may not be possible, and fresh legislation may be necessary. For example, new provisions of revenue law are regularly passed to meet novel tax avoidance schemes developed by smart lawyers and accountants precisely to exploit unforeseen loopholes.

Fifth, there are many ways in which the wording may be inadequate. There may be a printing error.[17] There may be a drafting error such as the use of a word with two or more distinct meanings without a sufficient indication from the context or by a definition of which is meant, or grammatical or syntactic ambiguity. Examples of the latter include "ambiguous modification," where it is unclear which words are limited, restricted or described by a "modifier,"[18] and the faulty reference of pronouns.[19] There may be an erroneous reference to another statute.[20] The draftsman may be

---

[14] See, for example, the "public good" defence in section 4 of the Obscene Publications Act 1959: *R.* v. *Jordan* [1977] A.C. 699, 718, *per* Lord Wilberforce: "[the phrase 'other objects of general concern'] is no doubt a mobile phrase; it may, and should, change in content as society changes." *Cf. Dyson Holdings Ltd.* v. *Fox* [1976] Q.B. 503 on whether the term "family" includes a "common law" spouse, criticised by D. J. Hurst, (1983) 3 L.S. 21.

[15] See above, pp. 8–12 and below, pp. 857–858.

[15a] Bennion (1990), Chap. 17; A. S. Miller, "Statutory language and the purposive use of ambiguity" 42 Va.L.Rev. 23 (1956); V. Sacks, "Towards Discovering Parliamentary Intent" [1982] Stat.L.R. 143, 157 (research on the background to a number of cases of interpretative difficulty showed that "unintelligible legislation was being added to the statute book because the Government either lacked clear objectives, or, had deliberately intended to obfuscate in order to avoid controversy").

[16] (1880) 6 Q.B.D. 244. *Cf. Royal College of Nursing* v. *DHSS* [1981] A.C. 800.

[17] *e.g.* the presence of the word "upon" at the end of section 6 of the Statute of Frauds Amendment Act 1828: *Lyde* v. *Barnard* (1836) 1 M. & W. 101; Local Government Act 1972, s.262(12) (reference to subsection (10) rather than subsection (9) in the Queen's Printer's copy, corrected in *Statutes in Force*); the presence of the word "convenient" in the Prescription Act 1832, s.8, apparently a misprint for "easement": Sir Robert Megarry and H. W. R. Wade, *The Law of Real Property* (5th ed., 1984), p. 885.

[18] G. C. Thornton, *Legislative Drafting* (3rd ed., 1987), pp. 23–29. *e.g.* "public hospital or school" (does "public" modify "school" as well as "hospital"?). A statute of Charles II disqualified those who lacked certain property qualifications "other than the son and heir apparent of an esquire, or other person of higher degree." In *Jones* v. *Smart* (1784) 1 Term Rep. 44 the court held that the words "son and heir apparent of" governed "person of higher degree" as well as "esquire."

[19] Thornton, pp. 29–32. *e.g.* "and when they arose early in the morning, behold, they were all dead corpses": 2 Kings XIX 35.

[20] *e.g.* War Damage Act 1943, s.66(2)(*b*), corrected by the Universities and College Estates Act 1964, s.4(1) Sched. 3.

mistaken about the law that is being altered[21] or the factual situation with which he or she is dealing. The statutory provision may be narrower[22] or wider[23] than the object of the legislation. The provision may fail to indicate an important element, such as the time at which conditions of eligibility for some benefit are to be judged.[24] There may be the type of error described as "defective deeming, or asifism gone wrong."[25] There may be conflict within a statute or between different statutes. Overall, Bennion states that "it is extremely common for draftsmen to produce a text which raises doubt unnecessarily."[26]

As mentioned already, various people may have to interpret statutes for their own purposes. Some may take action based on their own view of a statutory provision. For example, in *R.* v. *Adams*[27] police officers decided that they could rely on a search warrant in respect of certain premises which had already been used once. The statute did not deal expressly with the question whether a warrant could be used more than once: the court held that it could not. Tax assessments may well be based on the Inland Revenue's interpretation of a doubtful provision of tax law: it will be for the Commissioners of Taxes or the courts to rule on the matter if the Revenue view is challenged. The courts stand in a rather different position from other statute users in that they have the power to resolve authoritatively disputes concerning the meaning of statutory provisions: their decisions are binding on the parties and may constitute binding precedents for the future.

It is notable that the general methods of statutory interpretation are not themselves regulated by Parliament, but have been developed by the judges. The Interpretation Act 1978, which from its title might seem to fulfil such a function, has the comparatively unambitious aim of providing certain standard definitions of common provisions,[28] and thereby enables statutes to be drafted more briefly than otherwise would be the case. Where Parliament or, more realistically, the executive has been dissatisfied with judicial interpretation of particular provisions the response has been to pay close attention to the future drafting of specific provisions in that area rather than to attempt to introduce legislation giving general directions to the judiciary. In the remainder of this chapter we consider the general approaches taken by judges to the interpretation of statutes, various internal and external aids to interpretation, the main presumptions which may be invoked and proposals for reform.

---

[21] *e.g. Inland Revenue Commissioners* v. *Ayrshire Employers' Mutual Insurance Association.* [1946] 1 All E.R. 537.

[22] *e.g. Adler* v. *George* [1964] 2 Q.B. 7: the Official Secrets Act 1920, s.3 prohibited obstruction "in the vicinity of" a prohibited place; the Divisional Court held that this was to be read as "in or in the vicinity of."

[23] *e.g.* the Criminal Law Act 1977, ss.1 and 5, which on a literal interpretation preserved a much wider range of common law conspiracies than was obviously intended; in *R.* v. *Duncalf* [1979] 1 W.L.R. 918 the Court of Appeal declined to give a literal reading "when the effect of so doing would be so largely to destroy the obvious purpose of this Act" (*per* Roskill L.J. at p. 923). *R.* v. *Duncalf* was approved by the House of Lords in *R.* v. *Ayres* [1984] A.C. 447. See now the Criminal Justice Act 1987, s.12.

[24] *Jackson* v. *Hall* [1980] A.C. 854, concerning the Agriculture (Miscellaneous Provisions) Act 1976.

[25] Bennion (1990), pp. 274–275; R. E. Megarry, *Miscellany-at-law* (1955), pp. 361–362 ("there is too much of this damned deeming": *per* (A. P. Herbert's) Lord Mildew).

[26] *Ibid.* p. 279.

[27] [1980] Q.B. 575.

[28] See above, pp. 262–263.

B. GENERAL APPROACHES TO STATUTORY INTERPRETATION

Judicial attitudes to legislation have changed with the passage of time. One of the important factors has been the part played by statutes in the general scheme of the law: a related factor has been the conception held by judges as to the proper scope of the judicial function. Three "rules" of statutory interpretation have been identified: the "mischief rule," the "golden rule" and the "literal rule," each originating at different stages of legal history. To call them "rules" is somewhat misleading: it is better to think of them as general approaches. They were analysed by Professor John Willis in his influential article "Statute Interpretation in a Nutshell."[29] He suggested that:

> "a court invokes whichever of the rules produces a result that satisfies its sense of justice in the case before it. Although the literal rule is the one most frequently referred to in express terms, the courts treat all three as valid and refer to them as occasion demands, but, naturally enough, do not assign any reasons for choosing one rather than another."[30]

Thus, on some occasions the "literal rule" would be preferred to the "mischief rule": on others the reverse would be the case. It was impossible to predict with certainty which approach would be adopted in a particular case.[31] More recently, Sir Rupert Cross suggested that the English approach involves not so much a choice between alternative "rules" as a progressive analysis in which the judge first considers the ordinary meaning of the words in the general context of the statute, a broad view being taken of what constitutes the "context," and then moves on to consider other possibilities where the ordinary meaning leads to an absurd result. This unified "contextual" approach is supported by dicta in decisions of the House of Lords where general principles of statutory interpretation have been discussed. However, generalisations as to what judges actually do are difficult to substantiate: Sir Rupert Cross made it clear that his propositions were stated "with all the diffidence, hesitancy and reservation the subject demands."[32]

It is important to appreciate that this analysis of the approach of judges to statutory interpretation operates at a high level of generality. It provides a framework for the solution of interpretative problems, but is not and cannot itself provide the solution. Where a problem of statutory interpretation comes before a court, counsel for each side will advance detailed arguments, based on such matters as the nuances of language, the purpose of the statute, the particular aids and presumptions discussed below, and previously decided cases in the area. Different readings of the text will be examined to see which fits best into the statutory scheme. The practical consequences of the different possible interpretations will be compared. Indeed, the discussions in the House of Lords of general approaches to interpretation, on which Sir Rupert Cross's propositions were based, are not commonly cited in argument in decided cases.

[29] (1938) 16 Can. Bar Rev. 1.
[30] *Ibid.* p. 16.
[31] This situation can be unkindly described as the "today's a day for the golden rule" approach. The tone of Professor Willis' article was one of scepticism.
[32] J. Bell and Sir George Engle, *Cross, Statutory Interpretation* (2nd ed., 1987), p. 46.

The most recent major work on the subject is F. A. R. Bennion's *Statutory Interpretation*.[33] In his introduction, the author writes:

"The natural and reasonable desire that statutes should be easily understood is doomed to disappointment. Thwarted, it shifts to an equally natural and reasonable desire for efficient tools of interpretation. If statutes must be obscure, let us at least have simple devices to elucidate them. A golden rule would be best, to unlock all mysteries.

Alas, there is no golden rule. Nor is there a mischief rule, or a literal rule, or any other cure-all. Instead there are a thousand and one interpretative *criteria*. Fortunately, not all of these present themselves in any one case; but those that do yield factors that the interpreter must figuratively weigh and balance."[34]

The book comprises a Code, with a critical Commentary, in which various detailed interpretative criteria are enumerated, illustrated, and criticised. It is a valuable source of the many kinds of detailed arguments that might be advanced before a court, and relies to a much greater extent than the established practitioners' manuals[35] on recent case law. This is particularly important "given the changes in judicial attitudes to statutory interpretation that have occurred in the past two-to-three decades. . . ."[36] There seems to be a greater willingness to attempt to identify and to consider the purpose of the provision in question, and less of an inclination to adhere strictly to the supposed literal meaning of words irrespective of the context and the consequences of such a reading.

In cases of doubt or difficulty, judges often say that it is necessary to discover the "intention of Parliament" as to either the meaning or the scope of a particular word or phrase, or the general purpose that was to be achieved by the statute.[37] This concept causes difficulty for a number of reasons.[38] It cannot mean the intention of "all the members of both Houses" as some may not have been aware of the measure, and others may have opposed it. If it is taken to mean "all the members of both Houses who voted for it" there may be problems in that the majority "will almost certainly have been constituted by different persons at the different stages of the passage of the Bill,"[39] and might have had different views as to its meaning or purpose. A vote in favour of a Bill may reflect loyalty to the party whip rather than an understanding or even half-hearted approval of the measure. Even assuming that there is a "collective intention" it is difficult to see how it could be ascertained. Would it be by reference to the debates or by canvassing the opinions of the legislators individually, possibly years after the event? The former would limit the "sample" to the minority who happened to speak: the

---

[33] (1984). For full reviews, see D. R. Miers, [1986] P.L. 160; J. Bell, (1986) 6 O.J.L.S. 288.

[34] *Ibid.*, pp. xxvii–xxviii.

[35] P. St. J. Langan, *Maxwell on the Interpretation of Statutes* (12th ed., 1969); S. G. G. Edgar, *Craies on Statute Law* (7th ed., 1971). These works are regularly cited in court: this is not as yet the case with Bennion (1984).

[36] D. R. Miers, [1986] P.L. 160, 162.

[37] Termed respectively "particular legislative intent" and "general legislative intent" by G. C. MacCallum Jr., (1966) 75 Yale L.J. 754.

[38] See Cross (1987), pp. 22–30; M. Radin, (1930) 43 Harv. L.R. 863, 869–872; J. M. Landis, *ibid.* pp. 886–893; D. Payne, (1956) 9 C.L.P. 96; R. Dworkin, "How to read the Civil Rights Act," *New York Review of Books,* December 20, 1979, pp. 37–43.

[39] Cross (1987), p. 23.

latter would be a research task which might just produce usable results in respect of a provision requiring interpretation soon after enactment, but with the passage of time it would rapidly become hopeless. In any event it is questionable whether even if it is possible it would be appropriate for the meaning of a particular provision to be determined by an opinion poll of the original legislators. In fact, the courts are not allowed to consider reports of Parliamentary proceedings, or the opinions of the legislators expressed elsewhere,[40] and so references to the "intention of Parliament" may simply involve speculation as to what view might have been taken by the average member of Parliament. The judge's guess is presumably as good as anyone else's and the exercise may at least discourage him or her from simply deciding the issue according to his or her own preferences. In the case of government Bills the people who devote most thought to the purpose and wording of the statutory provisions are the ministers who steer them through Parliament, the civil servants who advise them and the draftsmen who have converted their instructions into a draft Bill. However, it would be incorrect to regard them as "Parliament" and a fiction to regard them as the agents of Parliament. As a result the judges tend to affirm that the best if not the only evidence of the "intention of Parliament" is the wording of the statute:

> "We often say that we are looking for the intention of Parliament, but that is not quite accurate. We are seeking the meaning of the words which Parliament used. We are seeking not what Parliament meant but the true meaning of what they said."[41]

If Lord Reid is right, judicial references to seeking the intention of Parliament are not so much indications of a method of solving a problem of interpretation as restatements of the problem. Such references do serve to emphasise the orthodox position as to the separation of powers whereby Parliament legislates and the judges interpret.[42] They may also conceal the fact that judges on occasion legislate when they exercise their limited power to treat statutes as if their wording were modified.

Variants of references to the "intention of Parliament" are judicial references to the purpose or object of a statute. As we shall see, the words of a statute are to be considered in the light of the object which it is intended to achieve, and interpretations that facilitate the achievement of the object are to be preferred.[43] The "intention" used in this sense approximates most closely to the intentions of the Bill's promoters.

1. THE "MISCHIEF RULE"

The classic statement of the "mischief rule" is contained in the resolutions of the Barons of the Exchequer in *Heydon's Case*[44]:

[40] See below, pp. 350–352.
[41] *Per* Lord Reid in *Black-Clawson International Ltd.* v. *Papierwerke Waldhof-Aschaffenburg A.G.* [1975] A.C. 591, 613.
[42] This important constitutional point was emphasised by Lord Scarman in *Duport Steels Ltd.* v. *Sirs* [1980] I.C.R. 161, 189–190, above, pp. 266–267.
[43] See below.
[44] (1584) 3 Co.Rep. 7a, 7b.

"that for the sure and true interpretation of all statutes in general (be they penal or beneficial, restrictive or enlarging of the common law,) four things are to be discerned and considered:—

1st. What was the common law before the making of the Act.

2nd. What was the mischief and defect for which the common law did not provide.

3rd. What remedy the Parliament hath resolved and appointed to cure the disease of the commonwealth.

And, 4th. The true reason of the remedy; and then the office of all the Judges is always to make such construction as shall suppress the mischief, and advance the remedy, and to suppress subtle inventions and evasions for continuance of the mischief, and *pro privato commodo*, and to add force and life to the cure and remedy, according to the true intent of the makers of the Act, *pro bono publico.*"

These resolutions were the product of a time when statutes were a minor source of law by comparison with the common law, when drafting was by no means as exact a process as it is today[45] and before the supremacy of Parliament was firmly established. The "mischief" could often be discerned from the lengthy preamble normally included.[46]

The "mischief rule" was regarded by the Law Commissions, which reported on statutory interpretation in 1969,[47] as a "rather more satisfactory approach" than the other two established "rules." This was so even though the formulation in *Heydon's Case* was archaic in language, reflected a very different constitutional balance between the executive, Parliament and the people than would now be acceptable, failed to make clear the extent to which the judge should consider the actual language of the statute, assumed that statutes were subsidiary or supplemental to the common law and predated rules which prevented judges considering certain material which might throw light on the "mischief" and the "true reason of the remedy."[48] Seemingly, therefore, it was the best of a bad lot.

It came to be accepted that the "mischief rule" should only be applied where the words were ambiguous[49]; one of the improvements of the "contextual approach" discussed below is that the purpose of the statute should be considered as part of the context of the statutory words, and not merely as a last resort where the words are ambiguous.

2. The "Literal Rule"

The eighteenth and nineteenth centuries saw a trend towards a more literal approach. Courts took an increasingly strict view of the words of a statute: if the case before them was not precisely covered they were not prepared to countenance any alteration of the statutory language. For example, in *R. v. Harris*[50] a statute[51] which made it an offence for someone "unlawfully and maliciously" to "stab, cut, or wound any person" was held not to apply

---

[45] Some statutes were well drafted, such as the Statute of Uses 1535.
[46] *Black-Clawson International Ltd.* v. *Papierwerke Waldhof-Aschaffenburg A.G.* [1975] A.C. 591 *per* Lord Diplock at pp. 637–638. See below, pp. 336–337.
[47] Law Com. No. 21; Scot. Law Com. No. 11.
[48] *Ibid.* pp. 19–20. See below, pp. 345–352.
[49] See the *Sussex Peerage Case,* below, p. 323.
[50] (1836) 7 C. & P. 446.
[51] 9 Geo. IV c. 31 s.12.

where the defendant bit off the end of the victim's nose; the words indicated that for an offence to be committed some form of instrument had to be used.[52]

One of the leading statements of the "literal rule" was made by Tindal C.J. in advising the House of Lords in the *Sussex Peerage* case[53]:

"My Lords, the only rule for the construction of Acts of Parliament is, that they should be construed according to the intent of the Parliament which passed the Act. If the words of the statute are in themselves precise and unambiguous, then no more can be necessary than to expound those words in their natural and ordinary sense. The words themselves alone do, in such case, best declare the intention of the lawgiver. But if any doubt arises from the terms employed by the Legislature, it has always been held a safe means of collecting the intention, to call in aid the ground and cause of making the statute, and to have recourse to the preamble, which, according to Chief Justice Dyer (*Stowel* v. *Lord Zouch,* Plowden, 369) is 'a key to open the minds of the makers of the Act, and the mischiefs which they intended to redress.' "

This was taken to mean that the "mischief rule" was only applicable where the words were ambiguous.

The literal rule was favoured on a variety of grounds. It encouraged precision in drafting. Should any alternative approach be adopted, an alteration of the statutory language could be seen as a usurpation by non-elected judges of the legislative function of Parliament,[54] and other statute users would have the difficult task of predicting how doubtful provisions might be "rewritten" by the judges. On the other hand judges were criticised on the ground that:

"they have tended excessively to emphasise the literal meaning of statutory provisions without giving due weight to their meaning in wider contexts. . . ."[55]

"To place undue emphasis on the literal meaning of the words of a provision is to assume an unattainable perfection in draftsmanship; . . . [and] ignores the limitations of language, which is not infrequently demonstrated even at the level of the House of Lords when Law Lords differ as to the so-called 'plain meaning' of words."[56]

Moreover, the literal approach is not helpful where the court is resolving a doubt as to the applicability of a "broad term."

Much has been made of a few post-war cases where literalism has perhaps been taken too far. For example, in *Bourne* v. *Norwich Crematorium*[57] the

---

[52] The judge indicated that the defendant would be indicted for aggravated assault and thus "would not escape punishment if she was guilty." *Cf. Jones* v. *Smart,* above, p. 317, n. 18.

[53] (1844) 11 Cl. & Fin. 85, 143.

[54] Conversely, it might be argued that a judge could conceal that his or her role was not as impersonal and objective as he or she would like it to appear by paying lip-service to the literal rule.

[55] Law Com. No. 21; Scot. Law Com. No. 11, p. 5.

[56] *Ibid.* p. 17. For example, in *London and North Eastern Railway* v. *Berriman* [1946] A.C. 278 (below p. 329) members of the House of Lords who came to opposite conclusions on the meaning of "repairing" nevertheless each claimed to be applying the "fair and ordinary" (Lord Macmillan at p. 295) or the "natural and ordinary" meaning (Lord Wright at p. 301).

[57] [1967] 1 W.L.R. 691. See also *L.N.E.R.* v. *Berriman,* below, p. 329.

question was whether a capital allowance could be claimed in respect of expenditure on a new furnace chamber and chimney tower of a crematorium, as expenditure on "buildings and structures" in use "for the purpose of a trade which consists of the manufacture of goods or materials or the subjection of goods or materials to any process." Stamp J. held that it could not: it would be "a distortion of the English language to describe the living or the dead as goods or materials."[58] However, it is unlikely that either the draftsman or Parliament thought specifically of cremation in connection with capital allowances and the policy of the provisions on capital allowances would seem to cover the "trade" of cremation.[59]

The "contextual approach" discussed below is based on the literal approach, but requires greater attention to be paid to the context in which the words appear.

3. THE "GOLDEN RULE"

Some judges have suggested that a court may depart from the ordinary meaning where that would lead to absurdity. In *Grey* v. *Pearson*[60] Lord Wensleydale said:

"I have been long and deeply impressed with the wisdom of the rule, now, I believe, universally adopted, at least in the Courts of Law in Westminster Hall, that in construing wills and indeed statutes, and all written instruments, the grammatical and ordinary sense of the words is to be adhered to, unless that would lead to some absurdity, or some repugnance or inconsistency with the rest of the instrument, in which case the grammatical and ordinary sense of the words may be modified, so as to avoid that absurdity and inconsistency, but no farther."

This became known as "Lord Wensleydale's golden rule" following a dictum of Lord Blackburn in *River Wear Commissioners* v. *Adamson*[61]:

"I believe that it is not disputed that what Lord Wensleydale used to call the golden rule is right, *viz.*, that we are to take the whole statute together and construe it all together, giving the words their ordinary signification, unless when so applied they produce an inconsistency, or an absurdity or inconvenience so great as to convince the Court that the intention could not have been to use them in their ordinary signification, and to justify the Court in putting on them some other signification, which, though less proper, is one which the Court thinks the words will bear."

One controversial aspect of this "rule" was whether it could only apply where the words were ambiguous, or whether it could also be used where the ordinary meaning was clear but "absurd." In so far as it was confined to the former situation it was a statement of the blindingly obvious: that where statutory words are ambiguous an interpretation that is not absurd is to be preferred to one that is. In so far as the "rule" could be applied in the latter

---

[58] *Ibid.* p. 695.
[59] See Law Com. No. 21, pp. 5–6; Cross (1987), pp. 70–71. The decision has not, however, been reversed by statute.
[60] (1857) 6 H.L.Cas. 61, 106 (a case concerning the construction of a will). *Cf.* the same judge when he was Parke B. in *Becke* v. *Smith* (1836) 2 M. & W. 191, 195.
[61] (1877) 2 App.Cas. 743, 764–765.

situation it was clear that it should be used sparingly.[62] Some judges argued it could not be used in such a case at all. Lord Esher said[63]:

> "If the words of an Act are clear, you must follow them, even though they lead to a manifest absurdity. The Court has nothing to do with the question whether the legislature has committed an absurdity."

Another point of doubt was whether the concept of "absurdity" was confined to cases where a provision was "absurd" because it was "repugnant" to or "inconsistent" with other provisions of the statute, or whether it extended to "absurdity" for any reason. The Law Commissions noted that the "rule" provided no clear means to test the existence of the characteristics of absurdity, inconsistency or inconvenience, or to measure their quality or extent.[64] As it seemed that "absurdity" was in practice judged by reference to whether a particular interpretation was irreconcilable with the general policy of the legislature "the golden rule turns out to be a less explicit form of the mischief rule."[65] The ideas behind the "golden rule" are reflected in the second and third aspects of the contextual approach discussed below.

4. THE UNIFIED "CONTEXTUAL" APPROACH

Sir Rupert Cross set out a unified approach to statutory interpretation as follows[66]:

> "1. The judge must give effect to the [grammatical and][67] ordinary or, where appropriate, the technical meaning of words in the general context of the statute; he must also determine the extent of general words with reference to that context.
>
> 2. If the judge considers that the application of the words in their [grammatical and][68] ordinary sense would produce [a result which is contrary to the purpose of the statute],[69] he may apply them in any secondary meaning which they are capable of bearing.
>
> 3. The judge may read in words which he considers to be necessarily implied by words which are already in the statute and he has a limited power to add to, alter or ignore statutory words in order to prevent a provision from being unintelligible or absurd or totally unreasonable, unworkable, or totally irreconcilable with the rest of the statute.

---

[62] Lord Mersey in *Thompson* v. *Goold & Co.* [1910] A.C. 409, 420; Lord Loreburn in *Vickers, Sons, and Maxim Ltd.* v. *Evans* [1910] A.C. 444, 445.

[63] *R.* v. *Judge of the City of London Court* [1892] 1 Q.B. 273, 290. *Cf.* Lord Atkinson in *Vacher & Sons Ltd.* v. *London Society of Compositors* [1913] A.C. 107, 121–122.

[64] Law Com. No. 21; Scot. Law Com. No. 11, p. 19.

[65] *Ibid.* Sir Rupert Cross regarded the "golden rule" as a "gloss upon the literal rule": Cross *Statutory Interpretation* (1976), p. 170. *Cf.* E. A. Dreidger, (1981) 59 Can. Bar Rev. 781.

[66] Cross (1976), p. 43; second edition by J. Bell and Sir George Engle (1987), p. 47. The label "contextual" was not attached by Cross, but is used here for convenience of reference. Rules 1 and 2 were expounded by Lord Simon in *Maunsell* v. *Olins* [1975] A.C. 373, 391; rule 3 by Lord Reid in *Federal Steam Navigation Co. Ltd.* v. *Department of Trade and Industry* [1974] 1 W.L.R. 505, 508–509. The "aids" and "presumptions" are discussed in Chapters 5 to 7 of Cross's book.

[67] These words were added by the editors of the 2nd edition of *Cross*.

[68] *Ibid.*

[69] These words replace "an absurd result which cannot reasonably be supposed to have been the intention of the legislature" from the 1st edition. See pp. 92–96 of the 2nd edition for discussion of the change.

4. In applying the above rules the judge may resort to [certain] aids to construction and presumptions. . . ."

(a) Rule 1

Under this approach a broader view is taken of the context than under previous approaches. The importance of context was discussed in *Attorney-General* v. *Prince Ernest Augustus of Hanover*.[70] A statute of Queen Anne's reign[71] provided that Princess Sophia of Hanover "and the Issue of Her Body and all Persons lineally descending from Her born or hereafter to be born be and shall be . . . deemed . . . natural born Subjects of this Kingdom." The preamble recited that in order that they might be encouraged to become acquainted with the laws and constitutions of this realm "it is just and highly reasonable that they in Your Majesties Lifetime" be naturalised.[72] The respondent, who was born in 1914 and was a lineal descendant of Sophia, was granted a declaration that he was a British subject. The enacting words were clear and could not be restricted by the words in the preamble. Viscount Simonds said[73]:

"[W]ords, and particularly general words, cannot be read in isolation; their colour and content are derived from their context. So it is that I conceive it to be my right and duty to examine every word of a statute in its context, and I use context in its widest sense which I have already indicated as including not only other enacting provisions of the same statute, but its preamble, the existing state of the law, other statutes *in pari materia,* and the mischief which I can, by those and other legitimate means, discern the statute was intended to remedy. . . .

"[N]o one should profess to understand any part of a statute or of any other document before he has read the whole of it. Until he has done so, he is not entitled to say that it, or any part of it, is clear and unambiguous."

Lord Normand said[74]:

"In order to discover the intention of Parliament it is proper that the court should read the whole Act, inform itself of the legal context of the Act, including Acts so related to it that they may throw light on its meaning, and of the factual context, such as the mischief to be remedied. . . . It is the merest commonplace to say that words abstracted from context may be meaningless or misleading."

Even after the context had been considered it could not be said that the enacting words were unclear; the preamble itself was ambiguous; three of their Lordships also held that there was no inherent absurdity, judged at the time when the statute was passed, in the fact that all lineal descendants would be naturalised.[75]

[70] [1957] A.C. 436.
[71] 4 & 5 Anne c. 16.
[72] On the death of Queen Anne without issue the Crown of England would descend on Sophia and her heirs; Sophia's son became King George I.
[73] At pp. 461, 463. Lord Tucker expressed his "complete agreement" with Viscount Simonds' opinion (p. 472).
[74] At p. 465. See also Lord Somervell at pp. 473–474.
[75] Most of the royal heads of Europe in the early twentieth century, including the Kaiser, were lineal descendants of Sophia.

That the object of the statute is to be considered as part of the context was emphasised in *Maunsell* v. *Olins*.[76] The plaintiff owned the freehold of a farm. The farm's tenant had sublet a cottage to the Olins. If the cottage formed "part of premises which had been let as a whole on a superior letting" the Olins were entitled to the continued protection of the Rent Acts after the tenant's death. The House held by 3 to 2[77] that the word "premises" was to be limited to dwelling-houses[78] and as the Olins were not the subtenants of part of premises in that limited sense they were not protected. Lord Wilberforce expressly endorsed Viscount Simonds' dictum in the *Hanover* case.[79] Lord Simon, with whom Lord Diplock entirely agreed, held that the term "premises" was to be construed more widely as in ordinary legal parlance as "the subject-matter of a letting" or, more technically, as "the subject-matter of the habendum clause of the relevant lease." He did, however, make certain general observations as to interpretation, which were not controverted in the speeches of the majority[80]:

"The rule in *Heydon's Case*, 3, Co.Rep. 7a itself is sometimes stated as a primary canon of construction, sometimes as secondary (*i.e.* available in the case of an ambiguity): *cf. Maxwell on the Interpretation of Statutes* (12th ed., 1969), pp. 40, 96, with *Craies on Statute Law*, 7th ed. (1971) pp. 94, 96. We think that the explanation of this is that the rule is available at two stages. The first task of a court of construction is to put itself in the shoes of the draftsman—to consider what knowledge he had and, importantly, what statutory objective he had—if only as a guide to the linguistic register. Here is the first consideration of the 'mischief.' Being thus placed in the shoes of the draftsman, the court proceeds to ascertain the meaning of the statutory language. In this task 'the first and most elementary rule of construction' is to consider the plain and primary meaning, in their appropriate register, of the words used. If there is no such plain meaning (*i.e.*, if there is an ambiguity), a number of secondary canons are available to resolve it. Of these one of the most important is the rule in *Heydon's Case*. Here, then, may be a second consideration of the 'mischief.' "

In 1980, Lord Scarman said in a lecture in Australia that, "In London, no one would now dare to choose the literal rather than a purposive construction of a statute: and 'legalism' is currently a term of abuse."[81] This should not, however, be taken too far. It is clearly the case that reference is now

---

[76] [1975] A.C. 373. See also *Stock* v. *Frank Jones (Tipton) Ltd.* [1978] 1 W.L.R. 231, 236.
[77] Lord Reid, Lord Wilberforce and Viscount Dilhorne; Lord Simon and Lord Diplock dissented.
[78] Viscount Dilhorne thought the term might mean "buildings."
[79] Above.
[80] p. 395. Other recent examples of interpretation in the light of the mischief include *Marshall* v. *British Broadcasting Corporation* [1979] 1 W.L.R. 1071; *Maidstone B.C.* v. *Mortimer* [1980] 3 All E.R. 552 and *Royal College of Nursing of the United Kingdom* v. *DHSS* [1981] A.C. 800.
[81] (1981) 55 A.L.J. 175. *Cf.* Glanville Williams, "The Meaning of Literal Interpretation" (1981) 131 N.L.J. 1128, 1149, who argues that the primary question should be "What was the statute trying to do?" followed by "Will a particular proposed interpretation effectuate that object" and lastly, "Is the interpretation ruled out by the language?"

frequently made by judges to the concept of "purposive"[82] statutory construction. Sometimes the term is used broadly to describe the general approach to the construction of statutes. As such, it is misleading as the legislative purpose is but one of the factors that should be considered as part of the context.[83] More commonly, it is used in a narrower sense, in the course of comparing readings based on the literal or grammatical meaning of words with readings based on a purposive approach. It may be used even more narrowly to denote a construction that involves straining the words of the statute in order to fulfil the legislative purpose.[83a] The increased frequency in the use of the term by judges coincides with a discernible change in emphasis,[84] but the magnitude of the change should not be exaggerated.

First, it should not be assumed that a purposive approach will lead to a different result than a literal approach. Indeed, the opposite is normally the case:

"This correspondence is not surprising; indeed it is what we would expect. Parliament, having a certain purpose, naturally seeks to express this in the words used. If it did otherwise to any great extent, the legislature would be using an inefficient method."[85]

Accordingly, in a number of cases a purposive approach to construction has been adopted alongside a literal approach, each being regarded as leading to the same result.[86] The choice between different possible readings of the provision in question will commonly be influenced by a consideration of which reading best fulfils the legislative purpose.[87] On occasion, a purposive approach has been adopted where a literal approach would have led to absurdity or would have clearly defeated the purposes of the Act.[88] However, a purposive interpretation may only be adopted if judges "can find in the statute read as a whole or in material to which they are permitted

---

[82] *i.e.* one that will "promote the general legislative purpose underlying the provisions": *per* Lord Denning M.R. in *Nothman* v. *London Borough of Barnet* [1978] 1 W.L.R. 220, 228, based on the Law Commissions' Report: see below, p. 359.

[83] See above, p. 326.

[83a] Bennion ((1984), p. 664) suggests that the term "purposive construction" is usually intended by judges to bear this meaning. *Sed quaere.*

[84] Lord Diplock in *Carter* v. *Bradbeer* [1975] 1 W.L.R. 1204, 1206–1207.

[85] Bennion (1984), p. 662.

[86] *Suffolk County Council* v. *Mason* [1979] A.C. 705 (by both majority and minority judges): effect of designation of a footpath on a definitive map prepared under the National Parks and Access to the Countryside Act 1949; *Gardner* v. *Moore* [1984] A.C. 548: Motor Insurers Bureau liable to compensate victim of international criminal act; *Leverton* v. *Clwyd County Council* [1989] A.C. 706: woman and man employed at different establishments under the same collective agreement held to be employed under "common terms and conditions of employment."

[87] See, *e.g. Bank of Scotland* v. *Grimes* [1985] Q.B. 1179; *In re Smalley* [1985] A.C. 622; *Greater London Council* v. *Holmes* [1986] Q.B. 989; *Ferguson* v. *Welsh* [1987] 1 W.L.R. 1553: see below.

[88] *R.* v. *Ayres* [1984] A.C. 447, modified in *R.* v. *Cooke* [1986] A.C. 909; *cf.* Lord Diplock in *Jones* v. *Wrotham Park Settled Estates* [1980] A.C. 74, 105: *cf.* "rule 2" below.

by law to refer as aids to interpretation an expression of Parliament's purpose or policy,"[89] and the power to read in words is limited.[90]

In a number of cases the task of the court is to determine whether a particular expression, often of some generality, applies to certain facts.[91] The decision may be reached as a matter of common sense, often with the assistance of dictionaries,[92] but here, as elsewhere, consideration of the legislative purpose may be helpful. Recent examples include decisions that discrimination on the ground of nationality was not prohibited as being discrimination on the ground of "national origins,"[93] that painting was "construction or maintenance work,"[94] that a newspaper competition card was a "literary work,"[95] that demolition work falls within the expression "work of construction" for the purposes of the Occupiers' Liability Act 1957,[96] that the provision of a daily continental breakfast constitutes "board" under the Rent Act 1977,[97] that a ship of any size provided by an employer for the purposes of his business constituted "equipment" under the Employer's Liability (Defective Equipment) Act 1969,[98] and that a miscellaneous variety of items (including ceramic tiles, creosote, curtain railing, roofing felt and wallpaper) were not "motor accessories."[99]

Cases where a court has had to choose between different "ordinary meanings" include *London and North Eastern Railway Co.* v. *Berriman,*[1] where the issue was whether a railwayman was "relaying or repairing" the permanent way while oiling and cleaning points apparatus. He had been knocked down and killed by a train. If he had been so engaged, his widow was entitled to damages and the company's failure to provide an adequate warning system would be a criminal offence. By 3 to 2 the House of Lords held that "relaying or repairing" involved putting right something that was wrong and not merely maintenance work of the kind the railwayman had been doing. The object of the statute seemed to cover workmen in this

---

[89] *Per* Lord Scarman in *R.* v. *Barnet London Borough Council, ex p. Nilish Shah* [1983] 2 A.C. 309, 348 (the test was not satisfied here). For examples of cases where judges have found it impossible to discern a legislative purpose, see Harman J. in *Re Potters Oils Ltd.* [1985] B.C.L.C. 203, 207–208; Lloyd L.J. in *Hemens (Valuation Officer)* v. *Whitsbury Farm and Stud Ltd.* [1987] Q.B. 390, 401 (the House of Lords did not advert to this point on appeal, [1988] A.C. 601); Lloyd L.J. in *I.R.C.* v. *Mobil North Sea Ltd.* [1987] 1 W.L.R. 389, 398, disapproved on appeal by Lord Templeman [1987] 1 W.L.R. 1065, 1071; Mann J. in *Hadley* v. *Texas Homecare Ltd.* and other cases (1987) 86 L.G.R. 577, 582 (list of items that may be sold on Sunday).

[90] *Per* Lord Diplock in *Jones* v. *Wrotham Park Settled Estates*, *supra*; *cf.* "rule 3" below.

[91] See above, p. 316.

[92] Below, p. 341.

[93] *Ealing London Borough Council* v. *Race Relations Board* [1972] A.C. 342.

[94] *Wilkinson* v. *Doncaster Metropolitan Borough Council* (1985) 84 L.G.R. 257.

[95] *Express Newspapers* v. *Liverpool Daily Post and Echo* [1985] 1 W.L.R. 1089.

[96] *Ferguson* v. *Welsh* [1987] 1 W.L.R. 1553, 1560.

[97] *Otter* v. *Norman* [1989] A.C. 129.

[98] *Coltman* v. *Bibby Tankers Ltd.* [1988] A.C. 276. This was so, notwithstanding a statutory definition of "equipment" to the effect that it "includes any plant and machinery, vehicle, aircraft and clothing" (1969 Act, s.1(3)): this was held to be "for the purpose of clarity" and not to cut down the general meaning of "equipment." The House of Lords could not think of any rational explanation for the exclusion of "ship" from the definition section (although this was probably deliberate: Sir Denis Dobson, [1988] Stat. L.R. 126).

[99] *Hadley* v. *Texas Homecare Ltd.* and other cases (1987) 96 L.G.R. 577.

[1] [1946] A.C. 278.

situation, but there was also a presumption that penal statutes should be strictly construed.[2]

Similarly, a narrow interpretation of the provision that a decision of the Crown Court on a matter "relating to trial on indictment" cannot be questioned by an appeal by case stated or on an application for judicial review[3] was preferred to a broad interpretation in *In re Smalley*.[4] It was not possible to discern any legislative purpose which would be served by giving the words any wider operation than in respect of decisions "affecting the conduct of"[5] the trial. An order estreating the recognisance of a surety for a defendant who failed to surrender to his bail at the Crown Court when committed for trial was not such a decision, and so could be challenged by judicial review. By contrast, in *Greater London Council* v. *Holmes*,[6] a purposive approach to the interpretation of the right to a home loss payment, following compulsory acquisition of land, was held to be better served by a broad rather than a narrow interpretation. It should be noted that it has become increasingly common for judges to duck interpretative difficulties by classifying words as "ordinary English words."[7]

Examples of words used in a statute in a technical rather than an ordinary sense include "fettling" (trimming up of metal castings as they come from the foundry rather than "to put into good fettle" generally[8]); "crawling boards" (special boards with battens rather than simply boards for crawling on[9]); "offer for sale" (held not to cover the placing of a flick-knife in a shop window as this was in the law of contract merely an invitation to treat[10]); and "acceptance" (held to be used in its technical, commercial meaning, derived from the Bills of Exchange Act 1882, and not in its ordinary colloquial meaning).[11] Conversely, the majority in *Maunsell* v. *Olins*[12] preferred what they regarded to be the popular meaning of "premises" to the technical legal meaning.

(b) Rule 2

A court may choose a "secondary meaning" where the primary meaning is productive of injustice, absurdity, anomaly or contradiction or a result contrary to the purpose of the statute.[13] Thus, provisions giving a power of

---

[2] See further, below, pp. 356–357. *Cf. Ealing London Borough* v. *Race Relations Board* [1972] A.C. 342, where the House of Lords held by 4 to 1 that discrimination on the ground of *nationality* was not prohibited as being discrimination on the ground of "national origins."

[3] Supreme Court Act 1981, ss.28(2), 29(3).

[4] [1985] A.C. 622: see below, p. 878. See also *Cooper* v. *Motor Insurers Bureau* [1985] Q.B. 575. Contrast the statement by May L.J. in *R.* v. *Broadcasting Complaints Commission, ex p. Owen* [1985] Q.B. 1153, 1174.

[5] *per* Lord Bridge at pp. 642–643.

[6] [1986] Q.B. 989. See Oliver L.J. at p. 995.

[7] See above, pp. 11–12.

[8] *Prophet* v. *Platt Brothers & Co. Ltd.* [1961] 1 W.L.R. 1130: See Harman L.J. at p. 1133. The word "fettle" has other meanings, as in "Tom offered to . . . fettle him over the head with a brick" quoted in O.E.D.

[9] *Jenner* v. *Allen West and Co. Ltd.* [1959] 1 W.L.R. 554.

[10] *Fisher* v. *Bell* [1961] 1 Q.B. 394; *cf. Partridge* v. *Crittenden* [1968] 1 W.L.R. 1204, *British Car Auctions* v. *Wright* [1972] 1 W.L.R. 1519.

[11] *R.* v. *Nanayakkara* [1987] 1 W.L.R. 265.

[12] See above, p. 327.

[13] *Cf.* the "golden rule," above, pp. 324–325; *Stock* v. *Frank Jones (Tipton) Ltd.* [1978] 1 W.L.R. 231; *R.* v. *Pigg* [1983] 1 W.L.R. 6, below p. 812.

arrest in respect of an "offender" or "a person found committing an offence" have been held to cover *apparent* offenders[14]: police officers had to act on the facts as they appeared at the time and were not to be exposed to the risk of actions for damages merely because the suspect was subsequently acquitted. A provision of the Factories Act 1937 requiring the fencing of dangerous parts of a machine while the parts were "in motion" was held not to apply where a workman turned the machine by hand in order to repair it. The machine could not have been repaired while it was fenced.[15]

A court was held entitled to grant relief to a mortgagor under an endowment mortgage, notwithstanding that the words did not strictly apply to that form of mortgage.[16] The legislative purpose of providing relief to mortgagors in temporary financial difficulties applied whatever the kind of mortgage. The notion of "absurdity" here seems not to be confined to cases where a provision is repugnant to or inconsistent with the rest of the statute.[17]

(c) Rule 3

A judge may read in words necessarily implied by the words actually used.[18] The line between cases of "necessary implication" and cases where the statutory language is modified to prevent an anomaly arising is, however, a fine one. It is clear that such modification should be a rare event. In *Stock* v. *Frank Jones (Tipton) Ltd.*[19] Lord Scarman said[20]:

"If the words used by Parliament are plain, there is no room for the 'anomalies' test, unless the consequences are so absurd that, without going outside the statute, one can see that Parliament must have made a drafting mistake. If words 'have been inadvertently used,' it is legitimate for the court to substitute what is apt to avoid the intention of the legislature being defeated: *per* MacKinnon L.J. in *Sutherland Publishing Co. Ltd.* v. *Caxton Publishing Co. Ltd.*[21] This is an acceptable exception to the general rule that plain language excludes a consideration of anomalies, *i.e.* mischievous or absurd consequences. If a study of the statute as a whole leads inexorably to the conclusion that Parliament had erred in its choice of words, *e.g.* used 'and' when 'or' was clearly intended, the courts can, and must, eliminate the error by interpretation. But mere 'manifest absurdity' is not enough; it must be an error (of commission or omission) which in its context defeats the intention of the Act."

---

[14] *Barnard* v. *Gorman* [1941] A.C. 378; *Wiltshire* v. *Barrett* [1966] 1 Q.B. 312; *Wills* v. *Bowley* [1983] 1 A.C. 57 (but note the strong dissenting speeches of Lord Elwyn-Jones and Lord Lowry, who took the view that it was not proper to depart from the literal interpretation of a statute where that would prejudice the liberty of the subject).

[15] *Richard Thomas and Baldwin's Ltd.* v. *Cummings* [1955] A.C. 321.

[16] *Bank of Scotland* v. *Grimes* [1985] Q.B. 1179. See also *Paterson* v. *Aggio* (1987) 19 H.L.R. 551.

[17] See Cross (1987), pp. 92–96. *Cf.* above, p. 325.

[18] *Federal Steam Navigation Co.* v. *Department of Trade and Industry* [1974] 1 W.L.R. 505, 508–9. *Cf.* the concept of "ellipsis": above, p. 316; *Adler* v. *George,* above, p. 318, n. 22; *Wiltshire* v. *Barrett, Barnard* v. *Gorman,* and *Wills* v. *Bowley,* above.

[19] [1978] 1 W.L.R. 231.

[20] At p. 239.

[21] [1938] Ch. 174, 201.

In the same case Lord Simon said that:

> "a court would only be justified in departing from the plain words of
> the statute were it satisfied that: (1) there is clear and gross balance of
> anomaly; (2) Parliament, the legislative promoters and the draftsman
> could not have envisaged such anomaly, could not have been prepared
> to accept it in the interest of a supervening legislative objective; (3) the
> anomaly can be obviated without detriment to such legislative objec-
> tive; (4) the language of the statute is susceptible of the modification
> required to obviate the anomaly."[22]

There are a number of cases where the word "and" has been substituted
for "or," and (? or) "or" for "and." *Federal Steam Navigation Co. Ltd.* v.
Department of Trade and Industry[23] concerned section 1(1) of the Oil in
Navigable Waters Act 1955, which provided that where oil was discharged
from a British ship in a prohibited sea area "the owner or master of the ship
shall be guilty of an offence." The House of Lords held that where the owner
and the master were separate persons both could be convicted, the provision
being treated as if it read "the owner and/or the master." In *R.* v. *Oakes*[24] the
Divisional Court treated section 7 of the Official Secrets Act 1920, which
made it an offence where a person "aids or abets and does any act preparatory to the commission of an offence" under the Official Secrets Act as if
it read "aids or abets *or* does any act preparatory." If read literally the result
would have been "unintelligible."[25]

In *Re Lockwood*[26] Harman J. ignored certain words of a provision[27] which
would have had the effect on an intestacy of preferring more distant relations to nephews and nieces.

In *R.* v. *Central Criminal Court, ex p. Francis & Francis (A firm)*,[28] the
House of Lords held that files of conveyancing documents in the possession
of solicitors were "items held with the intention of furthering a criminal
purpose" and therefore not "items subject to legal privilege"[29] protected
from production to the police.[30] The solicitors had no such intention, but the
majority of the House of Lords[31] held that it was sufficient that the documents were intended by a third party to be used to further the criminal
purpose of laundering the proceeds of illegal drug-trafficking. This interpre-

---

[22] [1978] 1 W.L.R. 231, p. 237. See also the similar remarks of Lord Diplock in *Jones* v.
Wrotham Park Settled Estates [1980] A.C. 74, 105, applied in *I.R.C.* v. *Trustees of Sir John
Aird's Settlement* [1984] Ch. 382, and note the cautious remarks of Sir John Donaldson M.R.
in *Carrington* v. *Therm-A-Stor Ltd.* [1983] 1 W.L.R. 138.

[23] [1974] 1 W.L.R. 505. *Cf. R. F. Brown & Co. Ltd.* v. *T. & J. Harrison* (1927) 43 T.L.R. 394,
633, where the Court of Appeal suggested that "or" could sometimes be construed conjunc-
tively; *cf.* MacKinnon L.J. at first instance and in *Sutherland Publishing Co. Ltd.* v. *Caxton
Publishing Co. Ltd.* [1938] Ch. 174, 201: "That is a cowardly evasion. In truth one word is
substituted for another. For 'or' can never mean 'and.' "

[24] [1959] 2 Q.B. 350.

[25] *Per* Lord Parker C.J. at p. 354. See also *R.* v. *Corby Juvenile Court, ex p. M* [1987] 1 W.L.R.
55, where Waite J. indicated *obiter* that he would have been prepared in effect to rectify a
drafting error, in the light of the legislation's manifest purpose.

[26] [1958] Ch. 231.

[27] Administration of Estates Act 1925, s.47(5), as amended.

[28] [1989] A.C. 346.

[29] Police and Criminal Evidence Act 1984, ss. 10(1), (2).

[30] Under the Drug Trafficking Offences Act 1986, s.27.

[31] Lords Brandon, Griffiths and Goff.

tation accorded with the purpose of the legislation. However, in the view of the minority[32] this could not be the grammatical meaning of the words, and such a widening of the ambit of the subsection could not be justified by any legitimate process of implication of terms.[33]

> "It is one thing to abstain from giving to the language of a statute the full effect of its ordinary grammatical meaning in order to avoid some positively harmful or manifestly unjust consequence. This I would describe as a legitimate process of construction to avoid a positive absurdity. But it is quite another thing to read into a statute a meaning which the language used will not bear in order to remedy a supposed defect or shortcoming which, if not made good, will make the statutory machinery less effective than the court believes it ought to be in order to achieve its proper purpose. Even if the lacuna appears to the court as absurd, this is what I describe, inelegantly but in order to point the contrast, as a negative absurdity. I know of no legitimate principle of construction which permits such a negative absurdity to be remedied by implying words which the court thinks necessary to enhance the operation of the statutory machinery."[34]

Lord Oliver regarded the words as clear, concise, unequivocal and unambiguous: "there is no difficulty about giving the subsection a perfectly sensible operation." It might be said to be "anomalous and incomplete" but was not necessarily "absurd."[35] By contrast, Lord Griffiths regarded an interpretation that confined the application of the exception to cases where the solicitors were party to the requisite intention as "such an extraordinary result that I would only adopt such a construction if driven to it."[36]

In some cases, however, defective statutory provisions are regarded as beyond judicial redemption. For example, in *Inland Revenue Commissioners* v. *Hinchy*[37] section 55(3) of the Income Tax Act 1952 provided that a person who failed to submit an accurate tax return should forfeit £20 plus "treble the tax which he ought to be charged under this Act." Hinchy failed to declare some interest upon which the tax due would have been £14 5s. The Commissioners claimed £438 14s. 6d. (three times Hinchy's total tax bill for the year plus £20). The House of Lords upheld their claim; their Lordships recognised that the result was absurd, but the words actually used were not capable of a more limited interpretation.

It may be that judges are less inhibited in reading statutory provisions as if the language were modified where they are contained in subordinate legislation. In *R.* v. *Stratford-on-Avon District Council, ex p. Jackson*,[38] the Court of Appeal held that the words "an application for judicial review shall be made promptly" in R.S.C. Order 53, s.4(1) were to read as if they referred to the application for leave to apply for judicial review. This was the "only

---

[32] Lords Bridge and Oliver.
[33] *Per* Lord Bridge at pp. 371, 374.
[34] *Ibid.*, p. 375.
[35] *Ibid.*, p. 389.
[36] *Ibid.*, p. 383. For other examples of "rectification", see *Deria* v. *General Council of British Shipping* [1986] I.C.R. 172 and *McMonagle* v. *Westminster City Council* [1990] 2 A.C. 716 (words regarded as surplusage to avoid absurd result).
[37] [1960] A.C. 748. See also *Inland Revenue Commissioners* v. *Ayrshire Employers' Mutual Insurance Association Ltd.* [1946] 1 All E.R. 637.
[38] [1985] 1 W.L.R. 1319.

sensible construction"[39] which could be given to the rule, and the construction that had been adopted in practice.[40] Similarly, in *Pickstone* v. *Freemans plc*[41] the House of Lords held that regulations amending the Equal Pay Act 1970 so as to enable the United Kingdom to comply with European Community law should be interpreted so as to achieve that result.

> "It may be that, in order to ... [do so], some necessary implication falls to be made into their literal meaning. The precise terms of that implication do not seem to me to matter. It is sufficient to say that the words must be construed purposively in order to give effect to the manifest broad intention of the maker of the regulations and of Parliament."[42]

Lord Oliver agreed:

> "... a construction which permits the section to operate as a proper fulfilment of the United Kingdom's obligation under the Treaty involves not so much doing violence to the language of the section as filling a gap by an implication which arises, not from the words used, but from the manifest purpose of the Act and the mischief it was intended to remedy."[43]

Finally, in *Porter* v. *Honey*[44] the House of Lords held that the deemed consent conferred by regulations[45] for the display of one estate agent's sale board extended by necessary implication to cover the first board displayed notwithstanding the unlawful display of subsequent boards by other agents. The result suggested by the grammatical construction of the regulation was that the first agent would be guilty of an offence where another agent, without the former's knowledge or consent, placed a second board upon the same property. Such a result would be "unjust and absurd."[46]

> "We are dealing here with delegated legislation which does not receive the scrutiny of primary legislation and if in the interests of administrative convenience such an apparently unjust rule is to be introduced it should be in the clearest possible language so that the purport of the legislation can be readily recognised and the need for such a measure can be carefully considered before it is approved."[47]

C. THE CONTEXT: INTERNAL AIDS TO INTERPRETATION

There is a wide range of material that may be considered by a judge both (1) in determining the primary meaning of the statutory words and (2) where

---

[39] *Ibid.*, p. 1322.
[40] The drafting error was subsequently corrected by S.I. 1987 No. 1423, r. 63, Schedule.
[41] [1989] A.C. 66.
[42] *Per* Lord Keith of Kinkel at p. 112.
[43] *Ibid.*, p. 125. *Cf.* Lord Oliver's remarks in the *Francis & Francis* case, above. In the *Pickstone* case, his Lordship regarded the words as "reasonably capable of bearing" the secondary meaning contended for [1989] A.C. at p. 128; in *Francis & Francis*, he did not.
[44] [1988] 1 W.L.R. 1420.
[45] The Town and Country Planning (Control of Advertisements) Regulations 1984 (S.I. 1984 No. 421).
[46] *Per* Lord Griffiths at p. 1422.
[47] *Ibid.*, pp. 1426–1427.

there is ambiguity, in pointing the way to the interpretation that is to be preferred. Some of these aids may be found within the statute in question, or in certain "rules of language" commonly applied to statutory texts: others are external to the statute. We deal first with "internal aids."

It is commonly observed that statutes must be read as a whole.[48] It may perhaps be doubted whether every word of a long and complicated statute will be examined with care, but a judge may well be presented with arguments based on (1) a comparison with enacting words elsewhere in the statute or (2) one of the non-enacting parts of the statute listed in the previous chapter.[49] There is an important distinction between these two kinds of aid. Non-enacting words of a statute may be consulted as a guide to the meaning of the provision in question; however, if the words of the provision, considered in their context, are regarded as clear, any conflict between them and any of the non-enacting parts must be disregarded. Where a conflict between enacting words cannot be resolved by interpretation, the later provision takes precedence.

1. OTHER ENACTING WORDS

An examination of the whole of a statute, or at least those Parts which deal with the subject matter of the provision to be interpreted, should give some indication of the overall purpose of the legislation. It may show that a particular interpretation of that provision will lead to absurdity when taken with another section.[50] Moreover, there is at least a weak presumption that a word or phrase is to be accorded the same meaning wherever it appears in the statute. For example, in *Gibson* v. *Ryan*[51] the court had to decide whether an inflatable rubber dinghy and a fish basket came within the term "instrument" in section 7(1) of the Salmon and Freshwater Fisheries (Protection) (Scotland) Act 1951. It held that they did not in the light of section 10, which drew a distinction "between instruments on the one hand, boats on the other hand and baskets on, if there is such a thing, the third hand."[52] A court may, however, be satisfied that different meanings are intended.[53] There may, of course, be a definition section.[54]

2. LONG TITLE

It became established in the nineteenth century that the long title could be considered as an aid to interpretation,[55] once it was accepted that it could be amended as a Bill passed through Parliament. The long title should be read, as part of the context, "as the plainest of all the guides to the general

[48] See, *e.g.* pp. 326–327 above.
[49] See above, pp. 259–260.
[50] See, *e.g. R.* v. *Prince* (1875) L.R. 2 C.C.R. 154 and cases establishing that a court could not order the forfeiture of real property used in relation to the commission of criminal offences: *R.* v. *Beard (Graham)* [1974] 1 W.L.R. 1549 and *R.* v. *Khan (Sultan Ashraf)* [1982] 1 W.L.R. 1405.
[51] [1968] 1 Q.B. 250.
[52] Diplock L.J. at p. 255.
[53] *e.g.* "whosoever being married, shall marry" in section 57 of the Offences Against the Person Act 1861, considered in *R.* v. *Allen* (1872) L.R. 1 C.C.R. 367: "being married" meant "being validly married" whereas "shall marry" meant "go through a marriage ceremony."
[54] Above, pp. 262–263.
[55] *Fielding* v. *Morley Corporation* [1899] 1 Ch. 1, 34.

objectives of a statute"[56] although "it will not always help as to particular provisions."[57] In *Fisher* v. *Raven*[58] the House of Lords held that the term "obtained credit" in section 13 of the Debtors Act 1869 (which made it an offence to obtain credit under false pretences) was limited to the obtaining of credit in respect of the payment or repayment of money only and did not extend to cover the receipt of money on a promise to render services or deliver goods in the future. The Act's long title:

> "An Act for the Abolition of Imprisonment for Debt, for the Punishment of Fraudulent Debtors, and for other purposes"

was regarded as supporting the view that the Act concerned debtors in the ordinary sense of the word. However, in *Ward* v. *Holman*[59] the Divisional Court held that section 5 of the Public Order Act 1936, which made it an offence to use in any public place or meeting, *inter alia*, insulting behaviour likely to cause a breach of the peace, was not restricted to conduct at public meetings, processions and the like, notwithstanding the Act's long title. The relevant part of the long title read:

> "An Act to ... make ... provision for the preservation of public order on the occasion of public processions and meetings and in public places"

but the court regarded the enacted words as wide and "completely unambiguous"[60] and, accordingly, applicable to disputes between neighbours. The position appears to be that:

> "once their full context is considered in the light of the purposes of the Act, it is the unambiguous words of a section which will prevail over the long title."[61]

3. PREAMBLE

The use of preambles[62] was considered in *Attorney-General* v. *Prince Ernest Augustus of Hanover*.[63] The position was summarised by Lord Normand[64]:

> "When there is a preamble it is generally in its recitals that the mischief to be remedied and the scope of the Act are described. It is therefore clearly permissible to have recourse to it as an aid to construing the enacting provisions. The preamble is not, however, of the same weight as an aid to construction of a section of the Act as are other relevant enacting words to be found elsewhere in the Act or even in related Acts. There may be no exact correspondence between preamble and enactment, and the enactment may go beyond, or it may fall

---

[56] Not all long titles are as helpful in this regard as Lord Simon's words suggest.
[57] *Per* Lord Simon in *Black-Clawson International Ltd.* v. *Papierwerke Waldhof Aschaffenburg A.G.* [1975] A.C. 591, 647.
[58] [1964] A.C. 210. See also *Watkinson* v. *Hollington* [1944] K.B. 16; *R.* v. *Wheatley* [1979] 1 W.L.R. 144.
[59] [1964] 2 Q.B. 580.
[60] *Per* Lord Parker C.J. at p. 587.
[61] Cross (1987), p. 125; *R.* v. *Bates* [1952] 2 All E.R. 842, 844, *per* Donovan J.; *R.*v. *Galvin* [1987] Q.B. 862.
[62] The long title is on occasion referred to erroneously as the preamble.
[63] [1957] A.C. 436, see above p. 326.
[64] At p. 467. See also Viscount Simonds at pp. 462–464, and see *The Norwhale* [1975] Q.B. 589.

short of the indications that may be gathered from the preamble. Again, the preamble cannot be of much or any assistance in construing provisions which embody qualifications or exceptions from the operation of the general purpose of the Act. It is only when it conveys a clear and definite meaning in comparison with relatively obscure or indefinite enacting words that the preamble may legitimately prevail."

The preamble cannot prevail over clear enacting words.

4. SHORT TITLE

It seems that the short title should not be used to resolve a doubt as it is given "solely for the purpose of facility of reference" or as a "statutory nickname."[65] Some judges, however, have questioned whether it should always be ignored.[66]

5. HEADINGS

Unlike the previous three parts of a statute, headings, side-notes and punctuation are not voted on in Parliament. They may nevertheless be considered as part of the context. In *Director of Public Prosecutions* v. *Schildkamp*[67] Lord Reid said:

"The question which has arisen in this case is whether and to what extent it is permissible to give weight to punctuation, cross-headings and side-notes to sections in the Act. Taking a strict view, one can say that these should be disregarded because they are not the product of anything done in Parliament. . . .

But it may be more realistic to accept the Act as printed as being the product of the whole legislative process, and to give due weight to everything found in the printed Act. I say more realistic because in very many cases the provision before the court was never even mentioned in debate in either House, and it may be that its wording was never closely scrutinised by any member of either House. In such a case it is not very meaningful to say that the words of the Act represent the intention of Parliament but that punctuation, cross-headings and side-notes do not.

So, if the authorities are equivocal and one is free to deal with the whole matter, I would not object to taking all these matters into account, provided that we realise that they cannot have equal weight with the words of the Act. Punctuation can be of some assistance in construction. A cross-heading ought to indicate the scope of the sections which follow it but there is always a possibility that the scope of

---

[65] Lord Moulton in *Vacher & Sons Ltd.* v. *London Society of Compositors* [1913] A.C. 107, 128. Section 4(1) of the Trade Disputes Act 1906 was held to confer upon trade unions immunity from tort actions generally and not just in trade dispute cases. See also *R.* v. *Crisp and Homewood* (1919) 83 J.P. 121, where Avory J. held that the broad enacting words of s.2 of the Official Secrets Act 1911 were not to be altered or limited by reference to the short title (*Cf. R.* v. *Galvin* [1987] Q.B. 862).

[66] Scrutton L.J. in *Re Boaler* [1915] 1 K.B. 21, 40; but *cf.* Buckley L.J. at p. 27. In *British Amusement Catering Trades Association* v. *Westminster City Council* [1990] 1 A.C. 147, Lord Griffiths stated (at p. 157) that he had "given weight to the title of the [Cinematograph] Acts" in holding that a video game was not a "cinematograph exhibition." Many other considerations pointed to the same conclusion (see below, p. 345).

[67] [1971] A.C. 1, 10.

one of these sections may have been widened by amendment. But a side-note is a poor guide to the scope of a section, for it can do no more than indicate the main subject with which the section deals."

This case concerned section 332(3) of the Companies' Act 1948, which makes it an offence knowingly to be a party to the carrying on of a business with intent to defraud creditors or for a fraudulent purpose. However, it appeared among a group of sections grouped under the cross-heading "Offences Antecedent to and in course of Winding-Up," and section 332(1), a parallel provision making the officers of a company personally responsible for its debts in similar circumstances, included the words "in the course of the winding-up." The House of Lords held by a majority that an offence under section 332(3) could only be committed after a winding-up order had been made.[68]

It also seems that reference may be made to a heading to resolve a doubt where the enacted words are ambiguous. However, it may not be used to change the meaning of enacted words where they are regarded as clear. Thus, a woman was convicted of an indecent assault upon a boy notwithstanding that the relevant section appeared under the heading of "Unnatural Offences."[69] The words "any indecent assault" were not regarded as ambiguous so as to justify consideration of the heading.

6. SIDE-NOTES

There is no sensible reason why side-notes should be ignored, as Lord Reid noted in *Director of Public Prosecutions* v. *Schildkamp*.[70] However, the same judge had stated in an earlier case, *Chandler* v. *Director of Public Prosecutions*,[71] that "side-notes cannot be used as an aid to construction" as they were inserted by the draftsman, altered if necessary during the passage of a Bill by an officer of the House, and were not considered by Parliament.[72] In *Chandler* the defendants were charged under section 1(1) of the Official Secrets Act 1911, which makes it an offence to approach a prohibited place for a purpose prejudicial to the safety of the state, in respect of a demonstration at a military airfield in favour of nuclear disarmament. The marginal note read "Penalties for spying" and it was accepted that the defendants had not engaged in "spying." Nevertheless, the House of Lords held that the defendants were rightly convicted. In so far as this case indicates that a side-note cannot change the meaning of clear enacted words it is consistent with other cases; in so far as it would prohibit any consideration of a side-note it is inconsistent.

7. PUNCTUATION

Punctuation in statutes was considered by Lord Reid in *Inland Revenue Commissioners* v. *Hinchy*[73]:

---

[68] The effect of this decision was reversed by the Companies Act 1981, s.96 (now the Companies Act 1985, s.458): see *R.* v. *Kemp* [1988] Q.B. 645.
[69] Offences Against the Person Act 1861, s.62; *R.* v. *Hare* [1934] 1 K.B. 354. See also *R.* v. *Surrey (North-Eastern Area) Assessment Committee* [1948] 1 K.B. 28, 32–33.
[70] Above.
[71] [1964] A.C. 763.
[72] *Ibid.* p. 789.
[73] [1960] A.C. 748, 765.

"[B]efore 1850 there was no punctuation in the manuscript copy of an Act which received the Royal Assent, and it does not appear that the printers had any statutory authority to insert punctuation thereafter. So even if punctuation in more modern Acts can be looked at (which is very doubtful), I do not think that one can have any regard to punctuation in older Acts."

In modern statutes, it does now seem that punctuation will be considered to the same extent as non-enacting words, although it may be altered or ignored where necessary to give effect to the purpose of the statute.[74] In *Hanlon* v. *The Law Society*[75] Lord Lowry said:

"I consider that not to take account of punctuation disregards the reality that literate people, such as Parliamentary draftsmen, punctuate what they write, if not identically, at least in accordance with grammatical principles. Why should not literate people, such as judges, look at the punctuation in order to interpret the meaning of the legislation as accepted by Parliament."

D. THE CONTEXT: RULES OF LANGUAGE

There are a number of so-called "rules of language" commonly referred to in the context of statutory interpretation by Latin tags. They are not legal rules, but "simply refer to the way in which people speak in certain contexts."[76] Moreover, they are not as precise in their operation as would be expected from their label as "rules."

1. EJUSDEM GENERIS

General words following particular ones normally apply only to such persons or things as are *ejusdem generis* (of the same *genus* or class) as the particular ones. For example, the Sunday Observance Act 1677 provided that "no tradesman, artificer, workman, labourer or other person whatsoever, shall do or exercise any worldly labour, business, or work of their ordinary callings upon the Lord's Day." In a series of cases the prohibition was held to be restricted to "other persons" following callings of a similar kind to those specified.[77] There must normally, and perhaps invariably, be more than one species mentioned to constitute a "genus,"[78] and it must be possible to construct a "genus" out of the list of specific words. In *Allen* v. *Emmerson*[79] it was held that the phrase "theatres and other places of entertainment" in section 33 of the Barrow-in-Furness Corporation Act 1872 did not constitute a genus. Accordingly, a fun fair required a licence under the section even though no charge was made for admission.

---

[74] *Alexander* v. *Mackenzie* 1947 J.C. 155, 166; *R.* v. *Brixton Prison Governor, ex p. Naranjansingh* [1962] 1 Q.B. 211; *Luby* v. *Newcastle upon Tyne Corporation* [1965] 1 Q.B. 214.

[75] [1981] A.C. 124, 198. *Cf.* Lord Reid in *D.P.P.* v. *Schildkamp* above, pp. 337–338.

[76] Cross (1987), p. 132.

[77] Not, therefore, a coach proprietor (*Sandeman* v. *Beach* (1827) 5 L.J. (o.s.) K.B. 298), farmer (*R.* v. *Cleworth* (1864) 4 B. & S. 927) or barber (*Palmer* v. *Snow* [1900] 1 Q.B. 725).

[78] *Alexander* v. *Tredegar Iron and Coal Co. Ltd.* [1944] K.B. 390; *Quazi* v. *Quazi* [1980] A.C. 744, 807–808 (*per* Lord Diplock): the term "other" in the expression "judicial or other proceedings" was held not to be confined to quasi-judicial proceedings.

[79] [1944] K.B. 362.

The *ejusdem generis* rule may be displaced where the general words should be interpreted widely to accord with the object of the statute. *Skinner* v. *Shew*[80] concerned a provision which enabled a person to obtain an injunction against someone claiming to be the patentee of an invention who threatened him or her with any legal proceedings or liability "by circular advertisement or otherwise," unless he or she instituted those proceedings promptly. The Court of Appeal held that the desire of Parliament was "that threats of patent actions shall not hang over a man's head" and that it would be wrong to read the section as not applying to threats sent by private letter. In *Flack* v. *Baldry*[81] the Divisional Court held that electricity, discharged[82] from an electric stun gun, fell within the description "any noxious liquid, gas or other thing" in the Firearms Act 1968.[83] Such a weapon as an electric stun gun came within the mischief of the Act.

2. Noscitur a Sociis

This tag refers to the fact that words "derive colour from those which surround them."[84] For example, the word "floors" in the expression "floors, steps, stairs, passages and gangways," which were required to be kept free from obstruction, was held not to apply to part of a factory floor used for storage rather than passage.[85] The wider context may, however, negative any such "colouration." The "*ejusdem generis* rule" can be regarded as an application of this wider principle.

3. Expressio Unius est Exclusio Alterius

"Mention of one or more things of a particular class may be regarded as silently excluding all other members of the class. . . . Further, where a statute uses two words or expressions, one of which generally includes the other, the more general term is taken in a sense excluding the less general one: otherwise there would have been little point in using the latter as well as the former."[86]

For example, a provision that imposed a poor rate on the occupiers of "lands," houses, tithes and "coal mines" was held not to apply to mines other than coal mines, although the word "lands" would normally cover all kinds of mine.[87] However, a court may be satisfied that the "exclusio" was accidental, particularly where an application of the maxim would lead to absurdity.[88]

[80] [1893] 1 Ch. 413. *Cf.* Lord Scarman in *Quazi* v. *Quazi, supra,* at p. 824.
[81] [1988] 1 W.L.R. 214.
[82] The House of Lords held, overruling the Divisional Court on this point, that the electricity was "discharged": [1988] 1 W.L.R. 393.
[83] s.5(1)(*b*).
[84] *Per* Stamp J. in *Bourne* v. *Norwich Crematorium Ltd.* [1967] 1 W.L.R. 691.
[85] Factories Act 1961, s.28(1): *Pengelley* v. *Bell Punch Co. Ltd.* [1964] 1 W.L.R. 1055.
[86] *Maxwell on Interpretation of Statutes* (12th ed., 1969), p. 293. See J. M. Keyes, [1989] Stat.L.R. 1.
[87] Poor Relief Act 1601, s.1: *R.* v. *Inhabitants of Sedgley* (1831) 2 B. & Ad. 65.
[88] *Colquhoun* v. *Brooks* (1888) 21 Q.B.D. 52, 65; *Dean* v. *Wiesengrund* [1955] 2 Q.B. 120.

E. THE CONTEXT: EXTERNAL AIDS TO INTERPRETATION

1. Historical Setting

A judge may consider the historical setting of the provision that is being interpreted. In *Chandler* v. *Director of Public Prosecutions*[89] the defendants sought to argue that disarmament would be beneficial to the State, and that their purpose was thus not "prejudicial to the safety or interests of the State." Lord Reid said[90]:

> "Even in recent times there have been occasions when quite large numbers of people have been bitterly opposed to the use made of the armed forces in peace or in war. The 1911 Act was passed at a time of grave misgiving about the German menace, and it would be surprising and hardly credible that the Parliament of that date intended that a person who deliberately interfered with vital dispositions of the armed forces should be entitled to submit to a jury that Government policy was wrong and that what he did was really in the best interests of the country, and then perhaps to escape conviction because a unanimous verdict on that question could not be obtained."

The Victorian attitude of sympathy towards insurgents against continental governments has been considered as part of the background of the Extradition Act 1870.[91]

2. Dictionaries and Other Literary Sources

Dictionaries are commonly consulted as a guide to the meaning of statutory words.[92] As words are to be read in their context, as already discussed, this should only be a starting point:

> "Sentences are not mere collections of words to be taken out of the sentence, defined separately by reference to the dictionary or decided cases, and then put back into the sentence with the meaning which one has assigned to them as separate words so as to give the sentence or phrase a meaning which as a sentence or phrase it cannot bear without distortion of the English language."[93]

Textbooks may also be consulted.[94]

---

[89] [1964] A.C. 763: see above p. 338.
[90] At p. 791.
[91] *Schtraks* v. *Government of Israel* [1964] A.C. 556, 582, 583; *R.* v. *Governor of Pentonville Prison, ex p. Cheng* [1973] A.C. 931. See now the Extradition Act 1989.
[92] See, *e.g. R.* v. *Peters* (1886) 16 Q.B.D. 636 (definitions of "credit" in Dr. Johnson's and Webster's dictionaries); *Re Ripon (Highfield) Confirmation Order 1938, White and Collins* v. *Minister of Health* [1939] 2 K.B. 838 (definition of "park" in O.E.D.); *Eglen (Inspector of Taxes)* v. *Butcher* [1988] S.T.C. 782 (definitions of "infirmity" in O.E.D.: third definition, with connotations of illness or congenital defect, preferred to first, "a weakness or want of strength," with the result that a dependent relative allowance could not be claimed under income tax legislation in respect of a healthy infant).
[93] *Per* Stamp J. in *Bourne* v. *Norwich Crematorium Ltd.* [1967] 1 W.L.R. 691, 696.
[94] *e.g. Re Castioni* [1891] 1 Q.B. 149 where Stephen J. referred to his own *History of the Criminal Law* on the meaning of "political crime"; a work by John Stuart Mill was also consulted.

3. PRACTICE

The practice followed in the past may be a guide to interpretation. For example, the "uniform opinion and practice of eminent conveyancers has always had great regard paid to it by all courts of justice."[95] This is the case where the technical meaning of a word or phrase used in conveyancing is in issue.[96] Commercial usage may also be considered. In *United Dominions Trust Ltd.* v. *Kirkwood*[97] the Court of Appeal had to apply the phrase "any person bona fide carrying on the business of banking."[98] Lord Denning M.R. said[99]:

> "In such a matter as this, when Parliament has given no guidance, we cannot do better than look at the reputation of the concern amongst intelligent men of commerce."

In these cases the usage or practice precedes the enactment of related technical legislation. The *subsequent* practice of those who are involved in the implementation of a statute is not generally regarded as a permissible aid.[1] A different view may be taken in respect of old statutes:

> "It is said that the best exposition of a statute . . . is that which it has received from contemporary authority. . . . *Contemporanea expositio est fortissima in lege.* Where this has been given by enactment or judicial decision, it is of course to be accepted as conclusive. But, further, the meaning publicly given by contemporary or long professional usage is presumed to be the true one, even where the language has etymologically or popularly a different meaning."[2]

This principle cannot be applied to modern statutes.[3]

4. OTHER STATUTES IN PARI MATERIA

Related statutes dealing with the same subject matter as the provision in question may be considered both as part of the context and to resolve ambiguities.[4] A statute may indeed provide expressly that it should be read as one with an earlier statute or series of statutes. *Later* statutes *in pari materia* cannot be regarded as part of the context of the enactment but may

---

[95] *Per* Lord Hardwicke L.C. in *Bassett* v. *Bassett* (1744) 3 Atk. 203, 208.

[96] See *Jenkins* v. *Inland Revenue Commissioners* [1944] 2 All E.R. 491; *cf. Pilkington* v. *Inland Revenue Commissioners* [1964] A.C. 612, 634.

[97] [1966] 2 Q.B. 431.

[98] Moneylenders Act 1900, s.6(*d*).

[99] At pp. 454, 455.

[1] *e.g.* practice notes provided by the Central Land Board for the guidance of its staff in the administration of the Town and Country Planning Act 1947: *London County Council* v. *Central Land Board* [1958] 1 W.L.R. 1296.

[2] *Maxwell on Interpretation of Statutes* (12th ed., 1969), p. 264 cited in *R.* v. *Casement* [1917] 1 K.B. 98, where the court declined to take the Statute of Treasons 1351 "and read it as though we had seen it for the first time." See D. J. Hurst, "The problem of the elderly statute" (1983) 3 L.S. 21, 23–30, who notes that the term *contemporanea expositio* should (1) be confined to exposition by commentators at or near the time of enactment, and (2) be distinguished from continuous usage and custom.

[3] *Campbell College, Belfast (Governors)* v. *Commissioners of Valuation for Northern Ireland* [1964] 1 W.L.R. 912 (strictly, a case concerning usage rather than *contemporanea expositio*: Hurst, *op. cit.*).

[4] See Viscount Simonds in the *Hanover* case, above, p. 326.

be considered where a provision is ambiguous, "to see the meaning which Parliament puts on the self-same phrase in a similar context, in case it throws any light on the matter."[5]

Occasionally an argument may be based on a comparison with a statute not *in pari materia,* although such a statute will not be considered as part of the context.[6]

Where a later Act amends an earlier Act the position as to interpretation is not clear. In *Lewisham London Borough Council* v. *Lewisham Juvenile Court JJ.*[7] Viscount Dilhorne stated[8] that it was wrong to construe an *unamended* section of the earlier Act in the light of amendments made by the later Act, unless there was an ambiguity. Lord Salmon, however, said[9] that:

> "the whole Act as amended should be taken into consideration when construing any section in the Act. A section of an Act, whether or not it is amended, must in my view be construed in the context of the whole Act as it stands."

The other judges did not express their views unequivocally on this point, although Lord Keith seemed to incline to Viscount Dilhorne's position and Lord Scarman to Lord Salmon's.[10] Lord Salmon's view may create difficulties for the draftsman of subsequent amendments if he or she is to be required to judge the effect of the amendments on the interpretation of unamended provisions.

Where a later Act inserts a new provision in an earlier Act, it may be held that this provision is to be interpreted by reference to the later Act.[11]

5. LEGISLATIVE ANTECEDENTS

A slightly different situation from those considered in the previous section arises when the provision in question has been re-enacted in the same or similar form in a succession of statutes. For example, the origins of section 56 of the Law of Property Act 1925[12] were considered in *Beswick* v. *Beswick,*[13] where the House of Lords held that the term "other property" did not apply to personalty. However, the legislative antecedents should not be considered as part of the context of a consolidation measure, and reference

---

[5] *Per* Lord Denning M.R. in *Payne* v. *Bradley* [1962] A.C. 343, 357; *cf. Re MacManaway* [1951] A.C. 161; *Lewisham London Borough Council* v. *Lewisham Juvenile Court JJ.* [1980] A.C. 273, 281–2, 291.

[6] See, *e.g. R.* v. *Westminster Betting Licensing Committee, ex p. Peabody Donation Fund* [1963] 2 Q.B. 750.

[7] [1980] A.C. 273.

[8] At pp. 281–2.

[9] At p. 291.

[10] See pp. 302 and 310.

[11] *R.* v. *Secretary of State for the Home Department, ex p. Margueritte* [1983] Q.B. 180; see A. Samuels, [1983] Stat.L.R. 111.

[12] "A person may take an immediate or other interest in land or other property, or the benefit of any condition, right of entry, covenant or agreement over or respecting land or other property, although he may not be named as a party to the conveyance or other instrument."

[13] [1968] A.C. 58. See also *Pierce* v. *Bemis* [1986] Q.B. 384.

to them should only be made if the words are unclear.[14] In interpreting consolidation Acts there is a presumption that Parliament does not intend to alter the existing law.[15] As with all presumptions it may be rebutted by clear language.[16]

Where other statutes are considered, arguments may be based on similarities or dissimilarities in the statutory language itself, or on judicial decisions concerning provisions subsequently re-enacted. It is sometimes suggested that Parliament, or more realistically, the draftsman, must have had such decisions in mind during the preparation of consolidation legislation,[17] that there is at least a rebuttable presumption that re-enactment without alteration amounts to the Parliamentary endorsement of the decisions and that, for example, a decision of a High Court judge thus "endorsed" would have to be applied by the Court of Appeal and the House of Lords.[18] The theory of "Parliamentary endorsement" was doubted by Lord Wilberforce and Lord Simon in *Farrell* v. *Alexander*.[19] Moreover, in *R*. v. *Chard*[20] the House of Lords held that there might be such a presumption where the judicial interpretation is well settled and well recognised, but that it would yield to the fundamental rule that the ordinary sense of statutory words should be adhered to unless it led to some absurdity. The re-enactment of words in a consolidation Act subject to one of the special parliamentary procedures precluding debate on the merits would not have an effect on the construction of those words.

In the case of *codifying* statutes,[21] "the proper course is in the first instance to examine the language of the statute and to ask what is its natural meaning, uninfluenced by any considerations derived from the previous state of law."[22] The application of any presumption that the law is unaltered would destroy the utility of codification. However, the previous state of the law

---

[14] *Farrell* v. *Alexander* [1977] A.C. 59: Lord Wilberforce at pp. 72–73, Lord Simon at pp. 82–85 and Lord Edmund-Davies at p. 97; *R*. v. *West Yorkshire Coroner, ex p. Smith* [1983] Q.B. 335; *R*. v. *Heron* [1982] 1 W.L.R. 451; *Champion* v. *Maughan* [1984] 1 W.L.R. 469; *Prior (Valuation Officer)* v. *Sovereign Chickens Ltd.* [1984] 1 W.L.R. 921; *Di Palma* v. *Victoria Square Property Co. Ltd.* [1986] Ch. 150; *Morton* v. *The Chief Adjudication Officer* [1988] I.R.L.R. 444 (construction of consolidating regulations). Indeed, "it is particularly useful to have recourse to the legislative history if a real difficulty arises," whatever the form of the consolidation measure (see above, pp. 246–248) (*per* Lord Scarman in *R*. v. *Heron* [1982] 1 W.L.R. 451, 459, 460; *cf.* Lord Simon at p. 455 who stressed the point that the statute in issue here was not (unlike that in *Farrell* v. *Alexander*), a "modern consolidation Act," but was a "pure" consolidation, with verbatim reproduction of the existing enactment "with all its blemishes and imperfections"; accordingly, it was more likely to be necessary to look at the legislative history). See generally, A. F. Newhouse, "Constructing and Consolidating" [1980] B.T.R. 102.

[15] *R*. v. *Governor of Brixton Prison, ex p. De Demko* [1959] 1 Q.B. 268, affirmed [1959] A.C. 654.

[16] *e.g. Re A Solicitor* [1961] Ch. 491.

[17] See Lord Evershed in *Ex p. De Demko* [1959] 1 Q.B. 268, 281.

[18] *Re Cathcart, ex p. Campbell* (1869) 5 Ch. App. 603, 706 (James L.J.); *Barras* v. *Aberdeen Fishing and Steam Trawling Co. Ltd.* [1933] A.C. 402, 411–412 (Lord Buckmaster).

[19] [1977] A.C. 59, 74, 90–91. See also Denning L.J. in *Royal Crown Derby Porcelain Ltd.* v. *Raymond Russell* [1949] 2 K.B. 417, 429; *R*. v. *Bow Road JJ*. (*Domestic Proceedings Court*), *ex p. Adedigba* [1968] 2 Q.B. 572, 583; E. A. Marshall, (1974) 90 L.Q.R. 170; C. J. F. Kidd, (1977) 51 A.L.J. 256.

[20] [1984] A.C. 279.

[21] See above, p. 246.

[22] *Bank of England* v. *Vagliano Brothers* [1891] A.C. 107, 144, 145 (Lord Herschell).

may be considered where a technical expression is used or a provision of the code is ambiguous.

6. STATUTORY INSTRUMENTS

The extent to which a regulation may be used in interpreting a provision in the Act under which it was made was considered in *Hanlon* v. *The Law Society*,[23] where Lord Lowry formulated the following propositions[24]:

"(1) Subordinate legislation may be used in order to construe the parent Act, but only where power is given to amend the Act by regulations or where the meaning of the Act is ambiguous.

(2) Regulations made under the Act provide a Parliamentary or administrative *contemporanea expositio* of the Act but do not decide or control its meaning: to allow this would be to substitute the rule-making authority for the judges as interpreter and would disregard the possibility that the regulation relied on was misconceived or *ultra vires*.

(3) Regulations which are consistent with a certain interpretation of the Act tend to confirm that interpretation.

(4) Where the Act provides a framework built on by contemporaneously prepared regulations, the latter may be a reliable guide to the meaning of the former.

(5) The regulations are a clear guide, and may be decisive, where they are made in pursuance of a power to modify the Act, particularly if they come into operation on the same day as the Act which they modify.

(6) Clear guidance may also be obtained from regulations which are to have effect as if enacted in the parent Act."

Propositions (3) and (4) were cited by Lord Griffiths in *British Amusement Catering Trades Association* v. *Westminster City Council*,[25] in the course of holding that a video game was not a "cinematograph exhibition," and that, accordingly, an amusement arcade did not have to be licensed under the Cinematograph Act 1909, s.1. His Lordship noted that relevant safety regulations[26] only made sense

"if the 'cinematograph exhibitions' referred to in the regulations are understood in the sense of a show to an audience; for example, there are frequent references to the auditorium...."[27]

7. GOVERNMENT PUBLICATIONS

Legislation may be preceded by a report of a Royal Commission, the Law Commissions or some other official advisory committee. This kind of material may be considered as evidence of the pre-existing state of the law and the "mischief" with which the legislation was intended to deal. However, the recommendations contained therein may not be regarded as evidence of

---

[23] [1981] A.C. 124.

[24] At pp. 193–4.

[25] [1989] A.C. 147, 158.

[26] The Cinematograph (Safety) Regulations 1955 (S.I. 1955 No. 1129).

[27] [1989] A.C. 147, 158. *Cf.* the unwillingness of Wood J. in *R.* v. *Bolton Metropolitan Borough Council, ex p. B.* (1985) 84 L.G.R. 78 to use the Code of Practice made under s.12G of the Child Care Act 1980 as a guide to the meaning of ss.12A to 12G.

Parliamentary intention as Parliament may not have accepted the recommendations and acted upon them.[28] The first of these propositions is generally accepted: the second proposition only survived in the *Black-Clawson* case by 3 to 2. The question was whether a judgment in a German court dismissing the plaintiff's claim for money due, on the ground that it was brought out of time, barred such a claim in an English court. It did not have this effect at common law,[29] and the House of Lords held by 4 to 1 that this had not been altered by section 8 of the Foreign Judgments (Reciprocal Enforcement) Act 1933. Section 8 had been enacted in a form identical to clause 8 of a draft Bill attached to the report of a departmental committee of "eminent lawyers," and the report indicated that the draft Bill was not thought to change the common law. Of the majority, Lords Reid and Wilberforce held that the report could not be considered as a guide to Parliament's intention. Lord Reid thought that the rule against the citation of expressions of intention in Parliament excluded *a fortiori* such expressions in pre-Parliamentary reports. Lord Wilberforce stated that if reports were admissible as evidence of the meaning of the enacted words there would simply be two documents to construe instead of one, that it was the function of the courts to declare the meaning of enacted words, and that "it would be a degradation of that process if the courts were to be merely a reflecting mirror of what some other interpretation agency might say."[30] Viscount Dilhorne and Lord Simon of Glaisdale thought, however, that reports should be admissible as a guide to Parliament's intention; at least in a case such as this where a draft Bill had been enacted without material alteration.[31] To forbid this "would be to draw a very artificial line which serves no useful purpose."[32] "Why read the crystal when you can read the book? Here the book is already open; it is merely a matter of reading on."[33] Lord Diplock dissented as to the meaning of section 8 but agreed with Lords Reid and Wilberforce on the use of official reports.

In *J. H. Rayner Ltd.* v. *Department of Trade*,[34] Staughton J. held that Cabinet and department documents from the 1950s, obtained from the Public Record Office under the 30-year rule,[35] were not admissible as an aid to the interpretation of Order in Council concerning the International Tin Council.

"It would be quite extraordinary to construe either parliamentary or delegated legislation by reference to the secret deliberations of depart-

---

[28] *Eastman Photographic Materials Co. Ltd.* v. *Comptroller General of Patents* [1898] A.C. 571; *Assam Railways and Trading Co. Ltd.* v. *Inland Revenue Commissioners* [1935] A.C. 445; *Black-Clawson International Ltd.* v. *Papierwerke Waldhof-Aschaffenburg A.G.* [1975] A.C. 591; *R.* v. *Allen* [1985] A.C. 1029, (but *cf. R.* v. *Anderson* [1986] A.C. 27, where the House of Lords adopted a doubtful reading of the Criminal Law Act 1977, s.1 (statutory conspiracy) that might have been avoided had reference been made to the relevant Law Commission Report: see Commentary by J. C. Smith, [1985] Crim.L.R. 651); *Arnold* v. *Central Electricity Generating Board* [1988] A.C. 288. On examination, the mischief identified in a report may turn out to be narrower than that dealt with by Parliament: *R.* v. *Kemp* [1988] Q.B. 645.

[29] *Harris* v. *Quine* (1869) L.R. 4 Q.B. 653.

[30] p. 629.

[31] pp. 621–623 and 651–652 respectively.

[32] Viscount Dilhorne at p. 622.

[33] Lord Simon at p. 652.

[34] [1987] BCLC 667.

[35] Public Records Act 1958, s.5.

mental officials or of the Cabinet. One cannot, after all, even look at the deliberations in Parliament recorded by Hansard, which ought at least in theory to be a more immediate guide to the meaning of legislation than the intentions of ministers and their officials."[36]

8. TREATIES AND INTERNATIONAL CONVENTIONS[37]

Problems of statutory interpretation relating to treaties (or international conventions) may arise in four main ways. In the background are two principles: first, that a treaty cannot have effect in English law unless incorporated by statute; and second, that there is a presumption that Parliament does not legislate in such a way that the United Kingdom would be in breach of its international obligations.

(1) An Act of Parliament may implement a treaty and expressly enact that it shall be part of English law. The text will normally be given in a schedule. Here, a broad purposive construction should be adopted rather than a literal one.[38] Textbooks, dictionaries, expert opinion and the judgments of foreign courts may be consulted[39]; *travaux préparatoires*, such as the proceedings of the conferences at which the treaty was prepared, may also be used, albeit with caution.[40]

(2) An Act of Parliament may implement a treaty by enacting substantive provisions of English law but without expressly incorporating the text of the treaty as part of English law. Three questions may arise concerning the use of the treaty as an aid to the interpretation of the statute.

(i) Can the treaty only be considered if it is expressly referred to in the Act? The intention to implement the treaty may, for example, be mentioned in the preamble or long title.[41] In *Salomon* v. *Commissioners of Customs and Excise*[42] the Court of Appeal held that a relevant treaty could be consulted even if not expressly referred to in the statute. *Per* Diplock L.J.:

"If from extrinsic evidence it is plain that the enactment was intended to fulfil Her Majesty's Government's obligations under a particular convention, it matters not that there is no express reference to the convention in the statute. One must not presume that Parliament

---

[36] [1988] BCLC 667, 689, *per* Staughton J.

[37] See F. A. Mann, *Foreign Affairs in English Courts* (1986), Chap. 5; R. Higgins in F. G. Jacobs and S. Roberts (eds), *The Effect of Treaties in Domestic Law* (1987), Chap. 7; L. Collins (ed.), *Dicey and Morris on the Conflict of Laws* (11th ed., 1987), pp. 8–15.

[38] *Stag Line Ltd.* v. *Foscolo Mango & Co. Ltd.* [1932] A.C. 328, 350; *James Buchanan & Co. Ltd.* v. *Babco Forwarding and Shipping (U.K.)* Ltd. [1978] A.C. 141: *cf.* below, p. 367, n. 83 and R. J. C. Munday, (1978) 27 I.C.L.Q. 450; *Fothergill* v. *Monarch Airlines Ltd.* [1981] A.C. 251; *Rothmans Ltd.* v. *Saudi Airlines* [1981] Q.B. 368; *The Hollandia* [1983] 1 A.C. 565: see F. A. Mann, "Uniform Statutes in English Law" (1983) 99 L.Q.R. 376, who argues that the purposive approach has been carried too far.

[39] See, *e.g., Swiss Bank Corporation* v. *Brink's M.A.T. Ltd.* [1986] Q.B. 853.

[40] See the *Fothergill* case, *supra*; *Gatoil International Inc.* v. *Arkwright-Boston Manufacturers Mutual Insurance Co.* [1985] A.C. 255, 263–265. The material must be "public and accessible" and "clearly and indisputably point to a definite legislative intention" (*ibid.*).

[41] See, *e.g.*, Recognition of Divorces and Legal Separations Act 1971; Arbitration Act 1975; State Immunity Act 1978.

[42] [1967] 2 Q.B. 116.

intends to break an international convention merely because it does not say expressly that it is intending to observe it."[43]

(ii) Can the treaty only be considered if the words of the statute are on their face ambiguous, or is the treaty to be read as part of the context of the statute *before* it is determined whether the words are ambiguous? The first, more restrictive, approach is supported by authority.[44] However, the courts have not been astute to hold statutory words to be clear, without consideration of the treaty,[45] and, in any event, the better view is that the treaty should be considered as part of the context of the enacting words.[46] This would be in conformity with the modern trend towards a broader view of "context" in statutory interpretation.[47]

(iii) If the enacted words are unambiguous, can they be read as if they were modified, by reference to the treaty? The answer here is clearly no. If the enacted words are unclear, but are reasonably capable of more than one meaning, a meaning that is consonant with treaty obligations is to be preferred to one that is not, in accordance with the presumptions mentioned above.[48] However,

> "If the terms of the legislation are clear and unambiguous, they must be given effect to, whether or not they carry out Her Majesty's treaty obligations, for the sovereign power of the Queen in Parliament extends to breaking treaties (see *Ellerman Lines Ltd.* v. *Murray*[49]), and any remedy for such a breach of an international obligation lies in a forum other than Her Majesty's own courts."[50]

---

[43] *Ibid.*, p. 144. *Cf.* Lord Denning M.R. (in more general terms) at p. 141; Russell L.J. at p. 152. *In re Westinghouse Uranium Contract* [1978] A.C. 547; *In re State of Norway's Application* [1987] Q.B. 433. The decision of the House of Lords in *Ellerman Lines Ltd.* v. *Murray* [1931] A.C. 126 had been thought to support a requirement of express reference, but Diplock L.J. in *Salomon* expressed the view that it was not authority for that proposition: [1967] 2 Q.B. 116, 144.

[44] Diplock L.J. in *Salomon* v. *Commissioners of Customs and Excise* [1967] 2 Q.B. 116, 145. References having recourse to the terms of a treaty as aids to the construction of provisions that are "ambiguous or vague" are frequent: *e.g.*, *Quazi* v. *Quazi* [1980] A.C. 744, 808 (Lord Diplock); *Fothergill* v. *Monarch Airlines Ltd.* [1981] A.C. 251, 299 (Lord Roskill); *Minister of Public Works* v. *Sir Frederick Snow* [1984] A.C. 426, 435 (Lord Brandon). The principle has been formulated by Lord Diplock without *express* reference to "ambiguities" or "vagueness" but it is unlikely that he intended a different result: *The Eschersheim* [1976] 1 W.LR. 430, 436; *Garland* v. *British Rail Engineering Ltd.* [1983] 2 A.C. 751, 771.

[45] Brandon J. in *The Annie Hay* [1968] P. 341; Lane J. in *The Banco* [1971] P. 137; Warner J. in *National Smokeless Fuels Ltd.* v. *I.R.C.* [1986] S.T.C. 300 (emphasising that a broad view is to be taken in this context of what constitutes an "ambiguity").

[46] I. Brownlie, *Principles of Public International Law* (4th ed., 1990), p. 49; Bennion (1984), p. 537. Lord Denning M.R. appeared to support this position in *Salomon* v. *Commissioners of Customs and Excise* [1967] 2 Q.B. 116, 141.

[47] Above, pp. 326–330.

[48] *Per* Diplock L.J. in *Salomon's* case, [1967] 2 Q.B. 116, 143; *Post Office* v. *Estuary Radio Ltd.* [1968] 2 Q.B. 740, 757.

[49] [1931] A.C. 126. It was not "proper to resort to the draft convention for the purpose of giving to the section a meaning other than that which . . . is its natural meaning," (*per* Lord Tomlin at p. 147).

[50] *Per* Diplock L.J. in *Salomon's* case, [1967] 2 Q.B. 116, 143.

Statutory words cannot be interpreted in order to produce conformity with a treaty if the words are not reasonably capable of bearing that meaning.[51]

(3) It may be argued that a statute should be interpreted in the light of an international convention such as the European Convention on Human Rights. In *Birdi* v. *Secretary of State for Home Affairs*[52] Lord Denning M.R. said that if an Act of Parliament contradicted the Convention "I might be inclined to hold it invalid." However, he retracted this in *Ex p. Bhajan Singh*.[53] In *R.* v. *Chief Immigration Officer, ex p. Salamat Bibi*[54] it was said that a court could look to the Convention "if there is any ambiguity in our statutes, or uncertainty in our law."[55] It clearly cannot prevail over clear words in a statute.[56] However, it has also been held that the Secretary of State is not under any legal obligation to take the Convention into account when exercising statutory discretionary powers,[57] and the fact that a right is protected by the Convention does not itself mean that it will be a "legitimate expectation" protected by principles of English administrative law.[58] It is difficult to square this restrictive approach with more positive dicta elsewhere.[59] Indeed, there is much to be said for encouraging consideration of Convention provisions, given that cases involving alleged breaches of the Convention can be taken to the European Court of Human Rights.[60] This last consideration was not present in a recent decision in which the Court of Appeal held that a court was entitled to take account of the provisions of a treaty in interpreting a statute, even where the statute was not passed to *implement* any particular treaty obligation:

> "The principle . . . requires that domestic legislation should be construed so as to be in conformity with an international obligation of this country if it is clear that the legislation was intended by Parliament to be in conformity with that obligation and if such a construction is one

---

[51] *Cf.* Lord Diplock in *The Eschersheim* [1976] 1 W.L.R. 430, 436. However, it is not obvious that the courts should not be able in this context to employ their limited power to read statutes as if modified: above pp. 331–333.

[52] Unreported, referred to in *R.* v. *Secretary of State for the Home Department, ex p. Bhajan Singh* [1976] Q.B. 198.

[53] *Ibid.*

[54] [1976] 1 W.L.R. 979.

[55] *Ibid.* p. 984 *per* Lord Denning M.R. See, to similar effect, Lord Fraser in *Attorney-General* v. *B.B.C.* [1981] A.C. 303, 352; Sir Robert Megarry V.-C. in *Trawnik* v. *Lennox* [1985] 1 W.L.R. 532, 541; Lord Goff in *Attorney-General* v. *Guardian Newspapers (No. 2)* [1990] 1 A.C. 109, 283: ". . . I conceive it to be my duty, when I am free to do so, to interpret the law in accordance with the obligations of the Crown under this treaty." *Waddington* v. *Miah* [1974] 1 W.L.R. 683 and *R.* v. *Deery* [1977] Crim.L.R. 550, where the presumption against retrospective legislation was reinforced by prohibitions against the retrospective application of criminal penalties contained in the European Convention and the U.N. Covenant on Civil and Political Rights: S. H. Bailey, D. J. Harris and B. Jones, *Civil Liberties: Cases and Materials* (2nd ed., 1985), pp. 4–6; O. Hood Phillips and P. Jackson, *Constitutional and Administrative Law* (7th ed., 1987), pp. 429–433.

[56] *R.* v. *Greater London Council, ex p. Burgess* [1978] I.C.R. 991; *Kynaston* v. *Secretary of State for Home Affairs* (1981) 73 Cr.App.R. 281.

[57] *Fernandes* v. *Secretary of State for the Home Department* [1981] Imm. A.R. 1. *Cf.* the powerful argument that standards derived, *inter alia*, from the Convention should be used to structure the inherently vague concept of *Wednesbury* unreasonableness: J. Jowell and A. Lester, [1987] P.L. 368.

[58] *R.* v. *Immigration Appeal Tribunal, ex p. Chundawadra* [1988] Imm. A.R. 161.

[59] See the cases cited in f.n. 55, *supra*.

[60] Above, pp. 102–104.

which is and was properly applicable to the terms of the legislation when
first enacted. International obligations cannot alter the clear meaning
of statutes. They may, however, be permitted to make clear which of
more than one reasonable meaning was intended by Parliament."[61]

Finally, it may be noted that a much more restrictive approach has been
adopted in Scotland, where it has been held that regard cannot be had to a
treaty even as an aid to construction, except in cases concerning a statute
designed to give effect to provisions of the treaty.[62]

(4) The special case of the interpretation of Community legislation is
considered below.[63]

9. PARLIAMENTARY MATERIALS

It has been reaffirmed by the House of Lords that a court may not refer to
Parliamentary materials for any purpose whatsoever connected with the
interpretation of statutes. The prohibition covers such materials as reports
of debates in the House and in committee, the explanatory memoranda
attached to Bills and successive drafts of Bills. Lord Denning M.R.
expressed his disagreement with this rule in the Court of Appeal in *Davis* v.
Johnson[64]:

> "In some cases Parliament is assured in the most explicit terms what
> the effect of a statute will be. . . . In such cases I think the court should
> be able to look at the proceedings. . . . And it is obvious that there is
> nothing to prevent a judge looking at these debates himself privately
> and getting some guidance from them. Although it may shock the
> purists, I may as well confess that I have sometimes done it. I have done
> it in this very case. It has thrown a flood of light on the position."

In earlier cases, Lord Denning had himself cited extracts from *Hansard*,[65]
and passages from textbooks that happen to have contained such extracts.[66]
Lord Upjohn referred to the proceedings of the Joint Committee on Consolidation Bills in *Beswick* v. *Beswick*.[67] Nevertheless, the prohibition was

---

[61] *Per* Ralph Gibson L.J. in *J. H. Rayner Ltd.* v. *Department of Trade* [1989] Ch. 72, 230–231;
see to similar effect, Kerr L.J. at pp. 164–166; with whom Nourse L.J. agreed on this point: p.
222. The court approved a dictum of Scarman L.J. in *Pan-American World Airways Inc.* v.
Department of Trade [1976] 1 Lloyd's Rep. 257, 261.

[62] Lord Ross in *Kaur* v. *Lord Advocate* 1980 S.C. 319; *Moore* v. *Secretary of State for Scotland*
1985 S.L.T. 38. See A. C. Evans, 1984 J.R. 41; P. R. Beaumont, A. I. L. Campbell and J. J.
Rankin, 1986 S.L.T. 61. Lord Ross cited the views of Professor O. Hood Phillips in
Constitutional and Administrative Law (6th ed., 1978), p. 446 (see now the 7th ed., 1987, p.
433).

[63] pp. 361–368.

[64] [1979] A.C. 264, 276–7.

[65] *e.g. Sagnata Investments Ltd.* v. *Norwich Corporation* [1971] 2 Q.B. 614.

[66] *R.* v. *Local Commissioner for Administration, ex p. Bradford Metropolitan City Council*
[1979] Q.B. 287, 311: reference to the "Crossman catalogue" of examples of
maladministration.

[67] [1968] A.C. 58, 105. In *Re C., An Infant* [1937] 3 All E.R. 783, Luxmoore J. referred to a
passage in *Hansard*, although this reference did not appear in [1938] Ch. 121.

unanimously reaffirmed by the House of Lords in *Davis* v. *Johnson*.[68] Various reasons have been given in support of this position:

"For purely practical reasons we do not permit debates in either House to be cited: it would add greatly to the time and expense involved in preparing cases involving the construction of a statute if counsel were expected to read all the debates in Hansard, and it would often be impracticable for Counsel to get access to at least the older reports of debates in select committees of the House of Commons; moreover, in a very large proportion of cases such a search, even if practicable would throw no light on the question before the court. . . ."[69]

What is said in Parliament:

"is an unreliable guide to the meaning of what is enacted. . . . The cut and thrust of debate and the pressures of executive responsibility are not always conducive to a clear and unbiased explanation of the meaning of statutory language."[70]

The Law Commissions reported in favour of the prohibition, after rehearsing the doubts about the reliability and availability of legislative material.[71] They did suggest that in the case of some Bills a detailed explanatory statement should be specially prepared by the promoters for use in Parliament, amended to take account of changes in the Bill during its passage, and made available for statute users after enactment.[72] This would be fuller than a preamble, or the brief explanatory memoranda used at present. (The detailed "Notes of Clauses" prepared for ministers by their civil servants could not be used: they might contain confidential information

---

[68] [1979] A.C. 264. Lord Denning M.R. took no notice, and was reproved unanimously by the House of Lords in *Hadmor Productions* v. *Hamilton* [1983] 1 A.C. 191, 232–233. Lord Diplock pointed out that counsel were under a duty not to cite *Hansard* and a judge who cited a passage on his or her own initiative was acting in breach of natural justice, here, the right of each party to be informed of any point adverse to him or her and to be given the opportunity to comment (*ibid*). Lord Denning's citations from *Hansard* here have been criticised as selective: V. Sacks, [1982] Stat.L.R. 143, 155–156. Notwithstanding these clear expressions, references to *Hansard* are still occasionally made: *e.g. McVeigh* v. *Beattie* [1988] Fam. 69, 84; *Hampson* v. *Department of Education and Science* [1988] I.C.R. 278, (argument that the word "justifiable" in s.1(1)(*b*)(ii) of the Race Relations Act 1976 was to be read as "necessary" rejected, an express amendment to that effect having been defeated in Parliament; on appeal, the Court of Appeal regarded this as an "impermissible" argument: [1989] I.R.L.R. 69, 76). See generally, D. Miers, [1983] Stat.L.R. 98; M. Rawlinson, [1983] B.T.R. 274; S. J. Gibbs, [1984] Stat.L.R. 29; Vincent J. G. Power, [1984] Stat.L.R. 38; and Lord Mackay of Clashfern, [1989] Stat.L.R. 15.

[69] *Per* Lord Reid in *Beswick* v. *Beswick* [1968] A.C. 58, 73–74. The last point has been supported by an analysis of a series of cases where problems of interpretation arose but reference to *Hansard* would not have assisted: V. Sacks, *op. cit.*; but *cf.* Cross (1987), p. 157; H. W. Wiggin, (1983) 80 L.S.Gaz. 461, on *Leedale* v. *Lewis* [1982] 1 W.L.R. 1319; I. B. McKenna, (1983) 46 M.L.R. 759, 763–764, on *Mandla* v. *Dowell-Lee* [1983] 2 A.C. 548; J. Dignan, (1983) 99 L.Q.R. 605–624, on *Bromley London Borough Council* v. *Greater London Council* [1983] 1 A.C. 768; *L'Oreal's Application* [1986] R.P.C. 19.

[70] *Per* Lord Scarman in *Davis* v. *Johnson* [1979] A.C. 264, 350.

[71] Law Com. No. 21, Scot.Law Com. No. 11 (1969), pp. 31–37. The matter has also been debated in the House of Lords, with, amongst others, Lords Goff, Griffiths and Templeman speaking in favour of change, and Lords Donaldson and Ackner against. The Lord Chancellor, Lord Mackay, also supported the present position, although he did not rule out the possibility of exceptions: H.L.Deb. Vol. 503, cols. 278–307, January 18, 1989.

[72] *Ibid.*, pp. 38–43.

and were not intended for publication.) No action has been taken upon the Law Commissions' recommendation.

Legislative materials are used in many foreign jurisdictions, including the United States of America and many European countries, where they tend to be more accessible and concise. There have, however, been criticisms that the practice of referring to legislative history has been abused.[73]

By way of contrast, it is permissible to cite the terms in which delegated legislation is presented to Parliament by ministers as a guide to the intention of Parliament in approving the legislation in question, and thus as an aid to the interpretation of the legislation.[74] The regulations in question,[75] as is almost universally the case,[76] were not subject to the Parliamentary process of consideration and amendment in Committee as a Bill would have been.

F. PRESUMPTIONS

1. PRESUMPTIONS OF GENERAL APPLICATION

There are various presumptions that may be applied in doubtful cases. These are to be distinguished from the "presumptions of general application" whereby certain basic legal principles are presumed to apply unless excluded by express words or necessary implication.[77] These principles modify even unambiguous provisions. Examples include aspects of the *ultra vires* doctrine, such as natural justice and abuse of discretion, general principles of criminal liability, and the principle that no-one shall be allowed to gain an advantage from his or her own wrong. Striking illustrations of this last principle include *Re Sigsworth*,[78] where Clawson J. held that apparently unambiguous provisions as to the distribution of the residuary estate on an intestacy were not to be applied so as to enable a murderer to benefit from the victim's estate, and *R. v. Secretary of State for the Home Department, ex p. Puttick*,[79] where Astrid Proll, who had achieved a marriage with a citizen of the United Kingdom and Colonies by the crimes of fraud, forgery and perjury, was held not to be entitled to registration as a United Kingdom citizen, notwithstanding the absolute terms of section 6(2) of the British Nationality Act 1948. She had entered the country under a false identity, and she had committed these crimes in satisfying the Registrar General that in her assumed identity she had been divorced and there was no impediment to the marriage, and in obtaining a marriage licence.

---

[73] *Ibid.*, pp. 32–34. The rules against reliance on legislative materials have been relaxed in Australia (by statute: Acts Interpretation Act (Cwlth) s.15 AB, added in 1984) and New Zealand (by the judges: see J. F. Burrows, [1989] N.Z.L.J. 94).
[74] *Pickstone v. Freemans plc* [1989] A.C. 66, H.L.: see A. I. L. Campbell, 1989 S.L.T. 137. See also *Conerney v. Jacklin* [1985] Crim.L.R. 234, where *Hansard* was cited as a guide to the purpose of regulations, as distinct from their interpretation.
[75] The Equal Pay (Amendment) Regulations 1983 (S.I. 1983 No. 1794), amending section 1(2)(c) of the Equal Pay Act 1976, so as to comply with requirements of community law.
[76] See above, pp. 270–272, on Parliamentary scrutiny.
[77] See above, p. 316.
[78] [1935] Ch. 89.
[79] [1981] Q.B. 767. See also *R. v. Chief National Insurance Commissioners, ex p. Connor* [1981] Q.B. 758 and the Forfeiture Act 1982. Cf. *R. v. Registrar-General, ex p. Smith* [1991] 2 W.L.R. 782 (similar principle applied to prevent future crime).

2. PRESUMPTIONS FOR USE IN DOUBTFUL CASES

These have been termed "policies of clear statement"[80]; or "in effect announcements by the courts to the legislature that certain meanings will not be assumed unless stated with special clarity."[81] The courts have created a measure of protection for certain values by establishing a requirement that Parliament use clear words if they are to be compromised or overridden. There are many difficulties. The Law Commissions pointed out that there was no established order or precedence in the case of conflict between different presumptions; that the individual presumptions were often of doubtful status or imprecise in scope; that reference to a presumption was unnecessary where a court decided that the words are clear; and that there was no accepted test for resolving a conflict between a presumption, such as the presumption that penal statutes should be construed restrictively, and giving effect to the purpose of a statute, for example the purpose of factory legislation to secure safe working conditions.[82]

It is impossible to produce a definitive list of presumptions which may be applied. As the Law Commissions noted, particular presumptions may be "modified or even abandoned with the passage of time, and with the modification of the social values which they embody."[83] There is room for debate as to why certain values and not others are selected for protection, and differences of view among the judges as to the strength of the protection that ought to be accorded. For example, the presumptions concerned with protecting the existing property or money of individuals have been contrasted with the absence of any presumptions in favour of individuals claiming state benefits.[84] While there are authorities stressing in general terms the importance of protecting individual liberty,[85] and particular freedoms such as freedom of speech,[86] freedom of assembly[87] and freedom from physical restraint,[88] there are comparatively few cases outside the last of these categories where full effect has been given to these factors.[89] Some of the principles of interpretation that have already been mentioned are sometimes put in the form of a presumption, for example presumptions against "intending what is inconvenient or unreasonable" or "intending injustice or absurdity."[90] On the other hand, it has been suggested that now that there is

[80] H. M. Hart and A. M. Sacks, cited in Law Com. No. 21, p. 21.
[81] Law Com. No. 21, p. 21.
[82] *Ibid*. p. 22.
[83] *Ibid*. p. 21. *Cf.* section (d) below.
[84] Cross (1987), pp. 183–184; *Presho* v. *Department of Health and Social Security* [1984] A.C. 310; *Chief Adjudication Officer* v. *Brunt* [1988] A.C. 711; *Riley* v. *Chief Adjudication Officer* (*Note*) [1988] A.C. 746, C.A.
[85] "Parliament is presumed not to enact legislation which interferes with the liberty of the subject without making it clear that this was its intention": *per* McCullough J. in *R.* v. *Hallstrom, ex p. W.* [1986] Q.B. 1090, 1104 (in the context of detention for treatment under the Mental Health Act 1983: see M. J. Gunn, [1986] J.S.W.L. 290)).
[86] *e.g.* Lord Reid in *Cozens* v. *Brutus* [1973] A.C. 854, 862; Scarman L.J. in *In re F.* (*orse. A.*) (*A Minor*) (*Publication of Information*) [1977] Fam. 58, 99.
[87] *Cf. Beatty* v. *Gillbanks* (1892) 9 Q.B.D. 308; Lord Denning M.R. (dissenting) in *Hubbard* v. *Pitt* [1976] Q.B. 142, 178–179; *Hirst* v. *Chief Constable of West Yorkshire* (1986) 85 Cr.App.R. 143.
[88] *e.g. R.* v. *Hallstrom, ex p. W., supra*; *Collins* v. *Wilcock* [1984] 1 W.L.R. 1172.
[89] Compare the above cases with, *e.g.*, *Duncan* v. *Jones* [1936] K.B. 218; *Thomas* v. *Sawkins* [1935] 2 K.B. 249; *Liversidge* v. *Anderson* [1942] A.C. 206.
[90] See *Maxwell on Interpretation of Statutes* (12th ed., 1969), pp. 199–212.

a greater willingness to adopt a purposive approach to interpretation and that a wider view is taken of the context of particular provisions, "the role of presumptions in interpretation is necessarily less important than in the days of more literal interpretation."[91]

(a) Presumptions against changes in the common law

This is one of the more controversial presumptions, given that modern legislation may often be intended to change the common law or may deal with matters with which the common law was unconcerned, such as the "welfare state." Lord Reid formulated the presumption as follows in *Black-Clawson International Ltd.* v. *Papierwerke Waldhof-Aschaffenburg A.G.*[92]:

> "In addition to reading the Act you look at the facts presumed to be known to Parliament when the Bill which became the Act in question was before it, and you consider whether there is disclosed some unsatisfactory state of affairs which Parliament can properly be supposed to have intended to remedy by the Act. There is a presumption which can be stated in various ways. One is that in the absence of any clear indication to the contrary, Parliament can be presumed not to have altered the common law further than was necessary to remedy the 'mischief.' Of course it may and quite often does go further. But the principle is that if the enactment is ambiguous, that meaning which relates the scope of the Act to the mischief should be taken rather than a different or wider meaning which the contemporary situation did not call for."

In *Leach* v. *R.*[93] a provision that a spouse of a defendant "may" be called as a witness was held not to overturn the common law rule that a wife was not *compellable*; it merely made her a *competent* witness. In *Beswick* v. *Beswick*[94] the House of Lords refused to interpret section 56 of the Law of Property Act 1925 in such a way as to overturn the doctrine of privity of contract. A more doubtful use of the presumption was made in *Chertsey Urban District Council* v. *Mixnam's Properties Ltd.*[95] where the House held that a power for a local authority to attach "such conditions as . . . [it] may think it necessary or desirable to impose" to a caravan site licence could only be used to impose conditions relating to the use of the land: conditions by which the authority sought to protect the interests of tenants were held to be *ultra vires*.

(b) Presumption against ousting the jurisdiction of the courts

The courts have generally looked with disfavour upon Parliament's attempts to oust their jurisdiction. Such attempts have been particularly common in the administrative law context,[96] where "exclusion clauses" have

---

[91] Cross (1987), p. 187.
[92] [1975] A.C. 591, 614.
[93] [1912] A.C. 305; Criminal Evidence Act 1898, s.4(1). See now the Police and Criminal Evidence Act 1984, s.80.
[94] [1968] A.C. 58, See above, p. 343.
[95] [1965] A.C. 745.
[96] See J. M. Evans, *de Smith's Judicial Review of Administrative Action* (4th ed., 1980), pp. 364–376; Sir William Wade, *Administrative Law* (6th ed., 1988), pp. 719–733.

been construed narrowly[97] or evaded.[98] It is notable that where the courts have given effect to an "exclusion clause" the clause has only purported to oust their jurisdiction after a six-week period.[99]

(c) Presumption against interference with vested rights

If there is any ambiguity it is presumed that, "the legislature does not intend to limit vested rights further than clearly appears from the enactment."[1] There is an associated presumption that proprietary rights are not to be taken away without compensation.[2] It has been suggested that where the words are ambiguous, they should be construed in such a way as will cause less interference with existing rights notwithstanding that it appears that Parliament intended a more "stringent" meaning.[3]

However,

"judges are bound to administer the law as it is, not as they would like it to be. If Parliament, in its wisdom, chooses to legislate in a way which clearly does infringe individual rights, the court is bound to give effect, however unwillingly, to such legislation."[4]

In *Secretary of State for Defence* v. *Guardian Newspapers Ltd.*[5] the House of Lords unanimously rejected the narrow interpretation of section 10 of the Contempt of Court Act 1981[6] adopted by Scott J., who had held that the section had no application to a case where the order being sought was to enforce a property right. Lord Scarman stated that this was not

"an appropriate guide to the true interpretation of a section which has constitutional significance in that its purpose is to support for the benefit of the public the existence of 'a truly effective press.' Specifically, it is my view that, since it is 'in the interests of all of us that we

---

[97] *e.g.* where a statute provides that a decision shall be "final," that is read as meaning only that there is no right of *appeal*: the remedy of certiorari is not excluded: *R.* v. *Medical Appeal Tribunal, ex p. Gilmore* [1957] 1 Q.B. 574; *cf. Ex p. Waldron* [1986] Q.B. 824.

[98] *e.g.* a provision that a "determination by the Commission . . . shall not be called in question in any court of law" was held not to exclude proceedings for judicial review where the "determination" was *ultra vires* and a nullity, and thus not a "determination" at all: *Anisminic Ltd.* v. *Foreign Compensation Commission* [1969] 2 A.C. 147 (Foreign Compensation Act 1950, s.4(4)); *cf. Att.-Gen.* v. *Ryan* [1980] A.C. 718.

[99] *Smith* v. *East Elloe Rural District Council* [1956] A.C. 585; *R.* v. *Secretary of State for the Environment, ex p. Ostler* [1977] Q.B. 122; Wade (1988), pp. 733–747. Rather inconsistently, effect in excluding judicial review has been accorded to a "conclusive evidence" provision: *R.* v. *Registrar of Companies, ex p. Central Bank of India* [1986] Q.B. 1114.

[1] *Per* Ungoed-Thomas J. in *Re Metropolitan Film Studios Application* [1962] 1 W.L.R. 1315, 1323.

[2] *Belfast Corporation* v. *O.D. Cars Ltd.* [1960] A.C. 490; *cf. Westminster Bank Ltd.* v. *Beverley Borough Council* [1971] A.C. 509.

[3] *Per* Winn L.J. *obiter* in *Allen* v. *Thorn Electrical Industries Ltd.* [1968] 1 Q.B. 487.

[4] *Per* Sir Nicolas Browne-Wilkinson in *E.M.I. Records Ltd.* v. *Spillane* [1986] 1 W.L.R. 967, 973, in the course of holding that the Customs and Excise Commissioners had wide powers under the V.A.T. legislation to require the production of documents, which powers were "distasteful to those trained in the law" (*ibid*).

[5] [1985] A.C. 339.

[6] "No court may require a person to disclose . . . the source of information contained in a publication for which he is responsible, unless it be established to the satisfaction of the court that disclosure is necessary in the interests of justice or national security or for the prevention of disorder or crime."

should have a truly effective press,"[7] rights of property have to yield pride of place to the national interest which Parliament must have had in mind when enacting the section. I would, however, add that there certainly remains a place in the law for the principle of construction which the judge applied, namely, that the courts must be slow to impute to Parliament an intention to override property rights in the absence of plain words to that effect. But the principle is not an overriding rule of law: it is an aid, amongst many others, developed by the judges in their never ending task of interpreting statutes in such a way as to give effect to their true purpose."[8]

(d) Strict construction of penal laws in favour of the citizen

Laws which impose criminal or other penalties are strictly construed, so that if the words are ambiguous and there are two reasonable interpretations, the more lenient one will be given.[9] Thus, the provision that "all lotteries are unlawful" was not interpreted as creating a criminal offence.[10] A provision penalising the personation at an election of "any person entitled to vote" was held not to apply to a person who personated a deceased voter.[11] Other examples are *R.* v. *Harris*[12] and *London and North Eastern Railway Co.* v. *Berriman.*[13] It has, however, been suggested that while the courts still pay lip service to this principle, it is rarely applied in practice if there are social reasons for convicting.[14] In *Anderton* v. *Ryan*[15] the House of Lords adopted a restrictive, and purportedly "purposive," reading of section 1 of the Criminal Attempts Act 1981, so that it would not apply to some forms of impossible attempts. In so doing they took insufficient account of the Law Commission Report that led to the 1981 Act,[16] and introduced "confusion and uncertainty."[17] Their Lordships regarded some results of a broad reading of the section as absurd, and Lord Bridge found it surprising that Parliament, if intending to do so, "should have done so by anything less

---

[7] *Per* Griffiths L.J., [1984] Ch. 156, 167.

[8] [1985] A.C. 339, 362–363. The House of Lords (by 3 to 2) dismissed an appeal against an order that the *Guardian* return a leaked document to the Secretary of State, in the interests of national security. The identity of the "leaker," Sarah Tisdall, was thereby discovered.

[9] *Per* Lord Esher in *Tuck & Sons* v. *Priester* (1887) 19 Q.B.D. 629, 638; *R.* v. *Allen* [1985] A.C. 1029, 1034; *R.* v. *Clarke* [1985] A.C. 1037, 1048, 1053; but *cf. R.* v. *Caldwell* [1982] A.C. 341 where the House of Lords majority held that the word "reckless" was to be construed as an "ordinary English word" notwithstanding that this was contrary to: (1) the interests of the defendant; (2) the views of the Law Commission and (3) established decisions of lower courts, and that it would cause great complexity in the law: see J. C. Smith, [1981] Crim.L.R. 393.

[10] Betting and Lotteries Act 1934: *Sales-Matic Ltd.* v. *Hinchcliffe* [1959] 1 W.L.R. 1005.

[11] Poor Law Amendment Act 1851, s.3: *Whiteley* v. *Chappell* (1868) L.R. 4 Q.B. 147.

[12] Above, pp. 322–323.

[13] Above, pp. 329–330.

[14] Glanville Williams, *Textbook of Criminal Law* (2nd ed., 1983), pp. 12–18; *cf. Fisher* v. *Bell* (p. 330, above); *R.* v. *Ottewell* [1970] A.C. 642, 649; *R.* v. *Bloxham* [1983] 1 A.C. 109, 114; *Attorney-General's Reference* (*No. 1 of 1988*) [1989] A.C. 971, 991.

[15] [1985] A.C. 560.

[16] Law Com. No. 102.

[17] J. C. Smith, [1985] Crim.L.R. 504.

than the clearest express language."[18] Following devastating academic criticism,[19] the House of Lords overruled *Anderton* v. *Ryan* in *R.* v. *Shivpuri*.[20]

Statutes giving the police a power of arrest are not regarded as "penal laws" for this purpose[21]:

"no one doubts that a prime factor in the process of construction [of statutes conferring arrest powers] is a strong presumption in favour of the liberty of the innocent subject. But it is clear from the authorities at least that a statute may be held to have rebutted the presumption by something falling short of clear express language."[22]

(e) Presumption against retrospective operation

"Perhaps no rule of construction is more firmly established than this—that a retrospective operation is not to be given to a statute so as to impair an existing right or obligation, otherwise than as regards matter of procedure, unless that effect cannot be avoided without doing violence to the language of the enactment. If the enactment is expressed in language which is fairly capable of either interpretation, it ought to be construed as prospective only."[23]

Furthermore,

"it seems to me entirely proper, in a case where some retrospective operation was clearly intended, equally to presume that the retrospective operation of the statute extends no further than is necessary to give effect either to its clear language or to its manifest purpose."[24]

In *Yew Bon Tew* v. *Kenderaan Bas Maria*[25] the Privy Council emphasised that the expression "procedural" in this context could be misleading. An apparently "procedural" alteration, such as a change in a limitation period, could in some circumstances affect existing rights or obligations. Here, a statute extending a limitation period came into operation, (1) after the plaintiff's claim was statute-barred under the existing law, but (2) so that the claim would not be barred according to the new law: it was held not to

---

[18] [1985] A.C. 560, 583.
[19] Most notably by Glanville Williams, "The Lords and Impossible Attempts or *Quis Custodiet Ipsos Custodes*?" [1986] C.L.J. 33, acknowledged by Lord Bridge in *R.* v. *Shivpuri* [1987] A.C. 1, 23. See below, pp. 394–395.
[20] [1987] A.C. 1: see J. R. Spencer, [1986] C.L.J. 361; P. R. Glazebrook, [1986] C.L.J. 363 (noting that the decision in *Shivpuri* involves modification of the statutory language).
[21] See above, p. 331, n. 14.
[22] *Per* Lord Bridge in *Wills* v. *Bowley* [1983] 1 A.C. 57, 101. It is difficult to see how such a presumption can be regarded as either "strong" or even much of a "presumption."
[23] R. S. Wright J. in *Re Athlumney* [1898] 2 Q.B. 547, 551–2. See above, p. 262.
[24] *Per* Lord Bridge in *Arnold* v. *Central Electricity Generating Board* [1988] A.C. 228, 275, in the course of holding that while the Limitation Act 1975 modified retrospectively the position as to limitation in respect of actions governed by the Law Reform (Limitation of Actions, etc.) Act 1954, as amended, it did not apply so as to defeat a right to plead a time bar that had accrued under the Limitation Act 1939. See also *Pearce* v. *Secretary of State for Defence* [1988] A.C. 755.
[25] [1983] 1 A.C. 553. For other examples of cases where retrospective effect has been denied, see *Bonning* v. *Dodsley* [1982] 1 W.L.R. 279; *Lewis* v. *Lewis* [1986] A.C. 828. Retrospective effect was given to procedural changes in *Thompson* v. *Thompson* [1986] Fam. 38.

operate retrospectively so as to affect the defendant's accrued right to plead a time bar.

In *Waddington* v. *Miah*[26] the House of Lords held that certain offences created by the Immigration Act 1971 were not intended to operate retrospectively. Lord Reid stated[27] that in view of the prohibitions contained in the Universal Declaration of Human Rights and the European Convention on Human Rights, "it is hardly credible that any government department would promote or that Parliament would pass retrospective criminal legislation."

On the other hand, in *Chebaro* v. *Chebaro*[28] the Court of Appeal held that the right conferred by the Matrimonial and Family Proceedings Act 1984, section 12(1), to apply for financial relief where a marriage "has been dissolved" by proceedings overseas, applied to a decree pronounced before the commencement of the Act. The meaning of the words used, importing a retrospective effect, was "plain and unequivocal."[29]

(f) Presumption that statutes do not affect the Crown

It is presumed that the Crown is not bound by a statute unless reference is made to it expressly or by necessary implication:

> "Since laws are made by rulers for subjects a general expression in a statute such as 'any person,' descriptive of those upon whom the statute imposes obligations or restraints is not to be read as including the ruler himself."[30]

Questions may arise as to whether a particular institution is a servant or agent of the Crown and so within the "shield of the Crown."[31]

(g) Others

Other presumptions that may be invoked include the presumption that Parliament does not intend to violate international law,[31a] and that a statute does not apply to acts committed abroad.[32]

G. REFORM

As mentioned above,[33] Parliament has refrained from intervening to give

---

[26] [1974] 1 W.L.R. 683.

[27] At p. 694.

[28] [1987] Fam. 127.

[29] *Per* Balcombe L.J. at p. 131. See also *Williams* v. *Williams* [1971] P. 271; *Powys* v. *Powys* [1971] P. 340; *Hewitt* v. *Lewis* [1986] 1 W.L.R. 444.

[30] *Per* Diplock L.J. in *B.B.C.* v. *Johns* [1965] Ch. 32, 78; *cf.* Wrottesley J. in *Att.-Gen.* v. *Hancock* [1940] 1 All E.R. 32, 34. *Lord Advocate* v. *Dumbarton District Council* [1990] 2 A.C. 580 (noted by J. Wolffe, [1990] P.L. 14); O. Hood Phillips and P. Jackson, *Constitutional and Administrative Law* (7th ed., 1987), pp. 613–616. The Crown may rely on any statutory defence that would be available to a private party: Crown Proceedings Act 1947, s.31(1). See generally, P. W. Hogg, *Liability of the Crown* (2nd ed., 1990).

[31] See, *e.g. Tamlin* v. *Hannaford* [1950] 1 K.B. 18; *Town Investments Ltd.* v. *Department of the Environment* [1978] A.C. 359; *British Medical Association* v. *Greater Glasgow Health Board* [1989] A.C. 1211.

[31a] See above, pp. 347–350.

[32] See above, p. 261.

[33] p. 318.

general directions to the judges as to methods of statutory interpretation. The Law Commissions saw their report on *The Interpretation of Statutes*[34] as a contribution to the process of educating judges and practitioners, and only proposed a limited degree of statutory intervention. They appended draft clauses, of which these were the first two[35]:

"1.—(1) In ascertaining the meaning of any provision of an Act, the matters which may be considered shall, in addition to those which may be considered for that purpose apart from this section, include the following, that is to say—

(a) all indications provided by the Act as printed by authority, including punctuation and side-notes, and the short title of the Act;

(b) any relevant report of a Royal Commission, Committee or other body which had been presented or made to or laid before Parliament or either House before the time when the Act was passed;

(c) any relevant treaty or other international agreement which is referred to in the Act or of which copies had been presented to Parliament by command of Her Majesty before that time, whether or not the United Kingdom were bound by it at that time;

(d) any other document bearing upon the subject-matter of the legislation which had been presented to Parliament by command of Her Majesty before that time;

(e) any document (whether falling within the foregoing paragraphs or not) which is declared by the Act to be a relevant document for the purposes of this section.

(2) The weight to be given for the purposes of this section to any such matter as is mentioned in subsection (1) shall be no more than is appropriate in the circumstances.

(3) Nothing in this section shall be construed as authorising the consideration of reports of proceedings in Parliament for any purpose for which they could not be considered apart from this section.

2.—The following shall be included among the principles to be applied in the interpretation of Acts, namely—

(a) that a construction which would promote the general legislative purpose underlying the provision in question is to be preferred to a construction which would not; and

(b) that a construction which is consistent with the international obligations of Her Majesty's Government in the United Kingdom is to be preferred to a construction which is not."

Clause 1 would clarify, and in some respects relax the strictness of the rules which excluded altogether, or excluded when the meaning was otherwise unambiguous, certain internal and external aids from consideration by a court. Clause 1(1)(e) would also encourage the preparation in selected cases of explanatory material for use by the courts, which might "elucidate the

---

[34] Law Com. No. 21; Scot. Law Com. No. 11 (1969).
[35] Clause 3 provided for the application of the first two clauses to subordinate legislation; Clause 4 provided for a presumption that breach of a statutory duty should be actionable at the suit of any person who sustains damage.

contextual assumptions on which legislation has been passed."[36] Clause 2 emphasised the importance in interpretation of a provision of the general legislative purpose underlying it (clause (2)(*a*)) and the fulfilment of international obligations (clause 2(*b*)).[37]

The Renton Committee[38] approved the whole of clauses 1 and 2 except paragraphs (*b*) and (*d*) of clause 1: unrestricted admission of such materials would place too great a burden on litigants, their advisers and the courts, would do nothing to make statutes more immediately intelligible to the lay public and might greatly lengthen court proceedings. They doubted the value of clause 1(*e*) as it was already open to Parliament to do this.[39] Clause 2 was regarded as reflecting current practice. No opinion was expressed on the other two clauses. The Committee proposed in addition the enactment of a provision that "In the absence of any express indication to the contrary, a construction that would exclude retrospective effect is to be preferred to one that would not." It should also be made clear that a court in interpreting legislation intended to give effect to a provision of a Community treaty or instrument should take the relevant provisions of Community law into account.

Lord Scarman, who had been chairman of the Law Commission at the time of the 1969 report, introduced the Commissions' proposals as a draft Bill in 1980. The following year he introduced a Bill based on those proposals modified largely to take account of the Renton Committee's suggestions. The first Bill failed on second reading in the Lords; the second passed the Lords but was the subject of objections on the motion for second reading in the Commons, and as a Private Peer's Bill without government support did not proceed further.[40]

In so far as the proposed provisions reflect current practice they seem superfluous; the few that go beyond it, such as the use of official reports and White Papers, are highly controversial.[41] Clause 1(*c*)[42] would have the effect of disapproving the restrictive approach adopted in *Ellerman Lines* v. *Murray*,[43] and as such would be useful, but that decision has been largely outflanked, and might well be reconsidered by the House of Lords if the occasion were to arise. Overall, the enactment of these proposals would probably make little difference in practice.

The Renton Committee's recommendation that the preparation of a new Interpretation Act should be put in hand eventually led to the Interpretation Act 1978, a consolidation measure with minor changes incorporating Law Commission proposals. This is an aid to drafting rather than interpreta-

---

[36] See above. pp. 351–352.
[37] Law Com. No. 21; Scot. Law Com. No. 11, pp. 49–50.
[38] Cmnd. 6053, 1975 pp. 139–148. See above, pp. 251–252.
[39] Clauses in the Matrimonial Proceedings and Properties Bill 1970 and the Animals Bill 1970, which provided that regard could be had to relevant, specified Law Commission reports, were successfully opposed in the House of Commons.
[40] Interpretation of Legislation Bill (1979–80 H.L. Bill 141); Interpretation of Legislation Bill (1980–81 H.C. Bill 120); F. A. R. Bennion, (1981) 131 N.L.J. 840; Miers and Page (2nd ed., 1990), pp. 176–180.
[41] See above, pp. 345–347.
[42] Clause 1(*b*) of the 1980–81 Bill.
[43] [1931] A.C. 126; above, p. 348, n. 43.

tion.[44] "At the more exalted level of general principles the subject does not lend itself to legislation."[45]

H. THE INTERPRETATION OF COMMUNITY LEGISLATION

1. Methods of Interpretation

Close attention has been paid to the methods of interpretation of Community legislation adopted by the Court of Justice of the European Communities.[46] A number of different techniques have been identified, to which commentators have attached a variety of labels. The Court has consistently shown that it is more likely to be influenced by the *context*[47] and *purposes*[48] of a legislative provision than its exact *wording*[49] or the subjective intentions of those who promulgated the legislation.[50] The extent to which the Court's overall approach differs from the so-called "common law" approach of English judges is debatable. It has also probably been exaggerated.[51] Certainly the ideas underlying the various techniques of interpretation adopted by the Court are more familiar than some of the labels. It should also be noted that the techniques tend to be employed cumulatively rather than as alternatives.[52]

The process of interpretation must obviously commence with an analysis of the text. However, literal interpretation, in so far as that implies an exclusive or predominant concern with wording and grammar, is not favoured. The Court has shown little inclination to hold that words carry one "plain," "ordinary" or "clear" meaning so that considerations of context and purpose are rendered irrelevant. There are several reasons for this.

(a) The method of drafting

Many of the key provisions of the EEC and Euratom Treaties are drafted in general terms, and with no "definition sections." For example, Article 9/EEC refers to the prohibition between member states of customs duties and "all charges having equivalent effect." Article 86/EEC prohibits the "abuse by one or more undertakings of a dominant position within the common market or in a substantial part of it." It gives four examples of an "abuse" but no indication of what is meant by "dominant position." These

---

[44] Above, pp. 319–320.
[45] Cross (1987), p. 188. Courts of Commonwealth countries where declarations of general principles of interpretation have been enacted seem rarely to refer to them in practice: W. A. Leitch, [1980] Stat.L.R. 5, 8.
[46] See the *Reports of the Judicial and Academic Conference,* Court of Justice of the European Communities, September 27–28, 1976; A. Bredimas, *Methods of Interpretation and Community Law* (1978); L. N. Brown and F. G. Jacobs, *The Court of Justice of the European Communities* (3rd ed., 1989), Chap. 14; R. Plender, "The Interpretation of Community Acts by Reference to the Intentions of the Authors" [1982] 2 Y.E.L. 57; T. Millett, [1989] Stat.L.R. 163.
[47] "Contextual" or "schematic" interpretation.
[48] "Purposive" or "teleological" interpretation.
[49] "Literal" interpretation.
[50] "Historical" or "subjective" interpretation.
[51] P. Dagtoglou, "The English Judges and European Community Law" [1978] C.L.J. 76.
[52] There is, for example, no place for a "today's the day for the teleological rule" approach.

concepts are left to be developed by the Community institutions, including the Court. The ECSC Treaty and Community secondary legislation are in general more tightly drafted, but they still, inevitably, employ broad terms.

(b) Languages

The texts of the EEC and Euratom Treaties and all Community secondary legislation are published in several languages, each of which is equally authentic.[53] Arguments based on the exact wording of any one version are accordingly less compelling; it can never have been intended that Community law applies differently in different Member States. In cases of doubt it may be necessary to consider all the versions, in the light, as ever, of context and purposes. For example, in *Stauder* v. *City of Ulm*[54] the Court considered a decision of the Commission on the sale of butter at reduced prices to persons in receipt of welfare benefits. The German and Dutch versions provided that the butter had to be exchanged for a "coupon indicating [the recipients'] names." A German citizen argued that this was an infringement of fundamental rights. The Court found that the French and Italian versions referred to a "coupon referring to the person concerned," and preferred this more liberal wording. The objective of the decision could be achieved by methods of identification other than names.

(c) The status of the Court

The Court is in a stronger position in relation to the other Community institutions than a national court in relation to its national parliament. Legislation is not promulgated by an elected body, but by the nominated Commission and Council of Ministers. The European Parliament is now directly elected, but its role in law making is essentially consultative. The Court is expressly enjoined to "ensure that in the interpretation and application of this Treaty the law is observed"[55] and is expressly empowered to review the legality of acts of the Council and Commission.[56] It is placed on an equal footing with the other institutions in Article 4/EEC. Moreover, it has proved more difficult than expected for the Council to agree upon legislative proposals placed before it by the Commission. The resultant "legislative short-fall" has compelled the Court to determine questions of interpretation, and to fill gaps, in the light of the general aims of the Community and general principles of law. To an extent it has been forced to adopt a legislative role, and has not felt the need to disguise it.[57]

The Court's position in relation to the Member States is more problematic. There is an inevitable tension between the Community's harmonisation aims and the interests of individual Member States. The Court could have adopted a position of neutrality; instead it has chosen to take a "partisan" line in favour of the achievement of the aims of the Community,

---

[53] The only authentic text of the ECSC Treaty is French. The other two basic Treaties and the Single European Act are authentic in Danish, Dutch, English, French, German, Greek, Irish, Italian, Portuguese and Spanish and the secondary legislation in all these except Irish.
[54] Case 29/69, [1969] E.C.R. 419.
[55] Article 164/EEC.
[56] Article 173/EEC. Above, pp. 310–312.
[57] Note, for example, the enunciation of a rule with *prospective* effect only in the second *Defrenne* case: Case 43/75 [1976] E.C.R. 455.

as a kind of counterweight to the Council of Ministers, which has tended more to reflect state interests. Member States are indeed expressly required by Article 5/EEC to take all appropriate measures to fulfil obligations arising out of the Treaty or acts of Community institutions, to facilitate the achievement of the Community's tasks and to abstain from any measure that could jeopardise the attainment of the objectives of the Treaty.

(d) Community purposes

The freedom of the Court to adopt a purposive approach is naturally facilitated by the express statement of the Community's aims and objectives included in the Treaties (including their preambles). Articles 2 and 3/EEC provide:

"ARTICLE 2

The Community shall have as its task, by establishing a common market and progressively approximating the economic policies of Member States, to promote throughout the Community a harmonious development of economic activities, a continuous and balanced expansion, an increase in stability, an accelerated raising of the standard of living and closer relations between the States belonging to it.

ARTICLE 3

For the purposes set out in Article 2, the activities of the Community shall include, as provided in this Treaty and in accordance with the timetable set out therein:

(a) the elimination, as between Member States, of customs duties and of quantitative restrictions on the import and export of goods, and of all other measures having equivalent effect;
(b) the establishment of a common customs tariff and of a common commercial policy towards third countries;
(c) the abolition, as between Member States, of obstacles to freedom of movement for persons, services and capital;
(d) the adoption of a common policy in the sphere of agriculture;
(e) the adoption of a common policy in the sphere of transport;
(f) the institution of a system ensuring that competition in the common market is not distorted;
(g) the application of procedures by which the economic policies of Member States can be co-ordinated and disequilibria in their balances of payments remedied;
(h) the approximation of the laws of Member States to the extent required for the proper functioning of the common market;
(i) the creation of a European Social Fund in order to improve employment opportunities for workers and to contribute to the raising of their standard of living;
(j) the establishment of a European Investment Bank to facilitate the economic expansion of the Community by opening up fresh resources;

(k) the association of the overseas countries and territories in order to increase trade and to promote jointly economic and social development."

Moreover, the reasons on which regulations, directives and decisions are based are stated in a preamble. The Court has attached much more importance to these express statements of purpose than to attempts to discern from other sources the subjective intentions of the authors of Community legislation.[58] Indeed, the details of the negotiations leading up to the Treaties and of debates within the Council and Commission concerning secondary legislation have not been published. There have been occasional references by Advocates General to a statement made by the government of a Member State to the national parliament in the course of a ratification debate, but not to the exclusion of other considerations.[59]

In relation to purposive interpretation reference has been made to the so-called "rule of effectiveness" (règle de l'effet utile), a concept borrowed from international law. This means that, "preference should be given to the construction which gives the rule its fullest effect and maximum practical value."[60] This concept has been used as a justification for holding that the Community or one of its institutions has certain "implied powers," such as the power to require the repayment of a state aid granted in breach of the Treaty.[61] Similarly, in the E.R.T.A. Case[62] it was held that the Community had the implied power to establish treaty relations with non-Member States. The Court argued that it was the "necessary effect" or "consequence" of the making of a regulation on the harmonisation of provisions in the road transport field that the Community assume the exclusive right to conclude international agreements relating to the same subject matter.

(e) Context

References by the Court to the purposes of the Community are commonly closely associated with arguments that seek to place the provision to be interpreted in the context of relevant rules of Community law. The Court may refer to the "general scheme of the Treaty," or to other treaty provisions in the relevant Part or to general principles of Community law. In the case of secondary legislation reference will be made to the enabling provisions in the Treaty.

(f) Examples

Striking examples of the Court's dynamic approach to interpretation are provided by its decisions already discussed on the direct effectiveness of treaty provisions and secondary legislation, and the supremacy of Com-

---

[58] In Case 136/79, *National Panasonic (U.K.) Ltd.* v. *Commission* [1980] E.C.R. 2033, A. G. Warner argued that statements by individual members of the Council, the European Parliament, the Commission or the Commission's staff could not be relied upon for guidance as to the meaning of a Council Regulation (pp. 2066–7). See generally Plender (1982), *op. cit.* n. 46 above.

[59] See, *e.g.*, Case 6/60, *Humblet* v. *Belgium* [1960] E.C.R. 559.

[60] H. Kutscher, *Conference Reports* (see p. 361, n. 46, above), I–41.

[61] *e.g.* Case 70/72, *Commission* v. *Germany* [1973] E.C.R. 829.

[62] Case 22/70, *Commission* v. *Council (E.R.T.A.)* [1971] E.C.R. 263.

munity law.[63] Another good example is the *Continental Can* case.[64] A New York company (Continental Can) held, through a German subsidiary (SLW), what the Commission determined to be a dominant position over a substantial part of the common market in meat tins, fish tins and metal closures for glass jars. Subsequently, acting through a Belgian subsidiary (Europemballage), Continental Can acquired a Dutch firm (TDV) which specialised in similar products. The Commission decided that the merger amounted to an abuse of the dominant position mentioned above, as the effect was practically to eliminate competition in the relevant products. The ECSC treaty expressly provided for merger control (Article 66); the EEC Treaty did not. Nevertheless, the Court held that a merger could in principle amount to an abuse of a dominant position contrary to Article 86/EEC, although it did not do so on the facts of the case. In so deciding the Court stated that it was necessary "to go back to the spirit, general scheme and wording of Article 86, as well as to the system and objectives of the Treaty."[65] It referred to Article 2 and 3(f),[66] and to Article 85, which prohibited:

> "all agreements between undertakings, decisions by associations of undertakings and concerted practices which may affect trade between Member States and which have as their object or effect the prevention, restriction or distortion of competition within the common market. . . ."

The Court observed[67]:

> "[I]f Article 3(f) provides for the institution of a system ensuring that competition in the common market is not distorted, then it requires *a fortiori* that a competition must not be eliminated. This requirement is so essential that without it numerous provisions of the Treaty would be pointless. Moreover, it corresponds to the precept of Article 2 of the Treaty. . . .
> . . . Articles 85 and 86 seek to achieve the same aim on different levels, that is, the maintenance of effective competition within the common market. The restraint of competition which is prohibited if it is the result of behaviour falling under Article 85, cannot become permissible by the fact that such behaviour succeeds under the influence of a dominant undertaking and results in the merger of the undertaking concerned."

In other words, the prohibition of certain acts when done in concert by separate undertakings was not to be evaded by merger of those undertakings.

(g) Restrictive interpretation

Interpretation in the light of purposes and context does not necessarily mean that such interpretation is "broad" or "liberal." Exceptions to general

---

[63] The *Van Gend en Loos* case, above, pp. 289–290; *Costa* v. *E.N.E.L.*, above, pp. 298–299.
[64] Case 6/72, *Europemballage Corporation and Continental Can Co. Inc.* v. *Commission* [1973] E.C.R. 215.
[65] *Ibid.* p. 243.
[66] Above, p. 363.
[67] p. 244.

Community rules and derogations to Treaty obligations are restrictively interpreted. For example, the principle of the free movement of workers is subject to "limitations justified on grounds of public policy, public security or public health."[68] These limitations are strictly construed.[69] Restrictions may not be imposed unless the person's presence or conduct "constitutes a genuine and sufficiently serious threat to public policy,"[70] and the requirements of public policy must affect "one of the fundamental interests of society,"[71] although it is for the national authorities to determine whether the facts of a particular case fall within these principles.

2. GENERAL PRINCIPLES OF LAW[72]

The Court often refers to "general principles of law" derived from the national laws of Member States.[73] These are regarded as part of "the law" of which the Court is to ensure observance.[74] They can be employed in the interpretation of Treaty provisions but cannot override them. In relation to secondary legislation and other acts of the institutions they are not so confined: a challenge to the legality of a measure may be based on breach of one of these principles.[75]

Examples include:

—the principle of *proportionality*, which requires that:
  "the individual should not have his freedom of action limited beyond the degree necessary for the public interest"[76];
—the *audi alteram partem* principle of natural justice, which requires that persons affected by an adverse decision be given an opportunity to make representations[77];
—the principle of *equality*:
  "whereby differentiation between comparable situations must be based on objective factors"[78];

[68] Article 48(3)/EEC; Directive 64/221/EEC.
[69] Case 41/74, *Van Duyn* v. *Home Office* [1974] E.C.R. 1337, above, pp. 290–291; Case 67/74, *Bonsignore* v. *Oberstadtdirektor Cologne* [1975] E.C.R. 297; Case 36/75, *Rutili* v. *French Minister of the Interior* [1975] E.C.R. 1219; Case 30/77, *R.* v. *Bouchereau* [1977] E.C.R. 1999.
[70] *Rutili* [1975] E.C.R. 1219, 1231.
[71] *Bouchereau* [1977] E.C.R. 1999, 2014.
[72] L. N. Brown and F. G. Jacobs, *The Court of Justice of the European Communities* (3rd ed., 1989), Chap. 15; D. Wyatt and A. Dashwood, *The Substantive Law of the E.E.C.* (2nd ed., 1987), pp. 59–71; T. C. Hartley, *The Foundations of European Community Law* (2nd ed., 1988), Chap. 5.
[73] They may also be derived from Treaty provisions.
[74] Article 164/EEC, above, p. 362. See also Article 173/EEC, above, p. 311 which provides expressly that a community act may be annulled for infringement of "any rule of law relating to its application." *Cf.* Article 215(2).
[75] See above, pp. 310–314.
[76] A. G. de Lamothe in Case 11/70, *Internationale Handelsgesellschaft* v. *EVSt.* [1970] E.C.R. 1125, 1147; *cf. R.* v. *Barnsley Metropolitan Borough Council, ex p. Hook* [1976] 1 W.L.R. 1052 and the *Rutili* case, above (requirement of a *genuine and sufficiently serious* threat to public policy to justify interference with freedom of movement).
[77] Case 11/74, *Transocean Marine Paint Association* v. *Commission* [1974] E.C.R. 1063; *cf.* Case 136/79, *National Panasonic Ltd.* v. *Commission* [1980] E.C.R. 2033 (no need to give prior warning of an investigation by Commission inspectors).
[78] Wyatt and Dashwood (1987), p. 64. See Case 20/71, *Sabbatini* v. *European Parliament* [1972] E.C.R. 345 (Council Regulation concerning expatriation allowances for employees of the Parliament held invalid on the ground of sex discrimination.)

—the related principles of *legal certainty* and *legitimate expectation*, which require, respectively, that:

"those subject to the law should not be placed in a situation of uncertainty as to their rights and obligations" and "those who act in good faith on the basis of the law as it is or seems to be should not be frustrated in their expectations."[79]

These "general principles" include respect for "fundamental rights,"[80] derived from national constitutions or from international conventions concerning human rights, such as the European Convention on Human Rights.[81] This does not mean that the Convention is part of Community law and so directly enforceable under the European Communities Act 1972: "the European Court does not deal with fundamental rights in the abstract; it only deals with them if they arise under Treaties and have a bearing on Community law questions."[82]

3. INTERPRETATION BY ENGLISH COURTS

The approach that should be taken by English judges was considered by Lord Denning M.R. in *Bulmer* v. *Bollinger*[83]:

"Beyond doubt the English courts must follow the same principles as the European court. Otherwise there would be differences between the countries of the nine. . . . It is enjoined on the English courts by section 3 of the European Community Act 1972. . . .

No longer must they examine the words in meticulous detail. No longer must they argue about the precise grammatical sense. They must look to the purpose or intent. To quote the words of the European court in the *Da Costa* case [1963] C.M.L.R. 224, 237, they must deduce 'from the wording and the spirit of the Treaty the meaning of the community rules.' They must not confine themselves to the English text. They must consider, if need be, all the authentic texts. . . . They must divine the spirit of the Treaty and gain inspiration from it. If they find a gap, they must fill it as best they can. They must do what the framers of the

---

[79] Wyatt and Dashwood (1987), p. 61.

[80] T. C. Hartley, (1975–76) 1 E.L.Rev. 54; M. Dauses, (1985) 10 E.L.Rev. 398; the *International Handels* case (n. 76, above).

[81] Case 4/73, *Nold* v. *Commission* [1974] E.C.R. 491; the *Rutili* Case (n. 70, above); Case 118/75 *Watson and Belmann* [1976] E.C.R. 1185; Case 136/79, *National Panasonic (U.K.) Ltd.* v. *Commission* [1980] E.C.R. 2033 (no infringement of the right of privacy guaranteed by article 8(1) of the European Convention: an investigation of a company's books without prior warning was held to be justified as "necessary in a democratic society in the interests of . . . the economic well-being of the country," within the one of the exceptions specified in article 8(2)); Case 63/83, *Kirk* [1984] E.C.R. 2689 (application of the principle that penal provisions may not have retrospective effect): see N. Foster, (1985) 10 E.L.Rev. 276.

[82] *Kaur* v. *Lord Advocate* 1980 S.C. 319, 333 (Lord Ross, Court of Session (Outer House)).

[83] [1974] Ch. 401, 425–426. See also the similar views expressed by Lord Denning M.R. in *Buchanan & Co. Ltd.* v. *Babco Forwarding & Shipping (U.K.) Ltd.* [1977] Q.B. 208, 213–214. His Lordship's attempt to apply the "European Method" of "filling gaps" to the interpretation of an international convention on the carriage of goods by road was resisted by the House of Lords: [1978] A.C. 141, 153 (Lord Wilberforce), 156 (Viscount Dilhorne) and 160 (Lord Salmon); *cf.* above, p. 347. See also the doubts as to the propriety of "gap-filling" expressed by Nolan J. in *Yoga for Health Foundation* v. *Customs and Excise Commissioners* [1984] S.T.C. 630.

instrument would have done if they had thought about it. So we must do the same. Those are the principles, as I understand it, on which the European court acts."

The dangers of applying a strict literal interpretation to provisions of Community law are illustrated by *R. v. Henn*.[84] Article 30/EEC prohibits the imposition of "quantitative restrictions on imports and all measures having equivalent effect." The Court of Appeal (Criminal Division) held that the ban on the importation of indecent or obscene material imposed by section 42 of the Customs Consolidation Act 1876 did not fall within Article 30 as it imposed a total prohibition rather than a mere restriction "measured by quantity." This view was, not, however, relied upon by counsel on appeal to the House of Lords, or in argument before the European Court, as it was clearly contrary to a number of earlier decisions of the European Court, and inconsistent with the purposes of the Community. As a matter of common sense, a complete prohibition on the free movement of goods is likely to be more questionable under Community law than a partial restriction. Lord Diplock said that this showed "the danger of an English court applying English canons of statutory construction."[85] It is submitted that the Court of Appeal's interpretation was excessively "literalist" even by English standards.

---

[84] [1978] 1 W.L.R. 1031, C.A.; [1981] A.C. 850, E.C.J., H.L.; Case 34/79 [1979] E.C.R. 3795.
[85] [1981] A.C. at p. 904. See also *R. v. Licensing Authority, ex p. Smith, Kline & French Laboratories Ltd.* [1990] 1 A.C. 64, 75 (Dillon L.J.), 84 (Balcombe L.J.) and 87 (Staughton L.J.) (need to adopt a purposive and not a semantic approach to the interpretation of E.C. directives). An appeal to the House of Lords was dismissed, the matter being determined by reference to English law: [1990] 1 A.C. 64, 90. See to the same effect the House of Lords in *Litster* v. *Forth Dry Dock & Engineering Co. Ltd.* [1990] 1 A.C. 546.

CHAPTER 7

JUDICIAL PRECEDENT

A. INTRODUCTION[1]

ONE of the hallmarks of any good decision-making process is consistency: like cases should be treated alike. Consistency is not, however, always appropriate, as, for example, where a case is seen with the passage of time and changes of circumstance no longer to offer a just solution to a recurring problem. Moreover, there are always difficulties in determining whether two cases are truly "like." Nevertheless, unjustifiable inconsistency may lead to a sense of grievance on the part of those affected and to a reasonable suspicion that the people making the decisions do not know what they are about. One of the main functions of the superior courts of law is the authoritative determination of disputed questions of law. A court's decision is expected to be consistent with decisions in previous cases and to provide certainty for the future so that the parties and others may arrange their affairs in reliance on the court's opinion. These considerations are reflected in the English system of judicial precedent.

The decisions of judges must be reasoned, and the reasons will include propositions of law. A judge in a later case is bound to consider the relevant case law and will normally accept the propositions stated as correct unless there is good reason to disagree; in some circumstances he or she is required to accept them even if they are in his or her view obviously wrong. So all relevant precedents are to a greater or lesser extent "persuasive," and some of them may be "binding" under what is termed the doctrine of *stare decisis*.[1a] The characteristic that an individual precedent may be binding is distinctive of common law systems. In continental systems based upon codes that are theoretically complete, judicial decisions are not, technically, sources of legal rules. They may, however, carry great persuasive weight, particularly where there is a trend of cases to the same effect, and they have been of great importance in the development of certain areas of the law.[2]

---

[1] See generally Sir Rupert Cross, *Precedent in English Law* (3rd ed., 1977); L. Goldstein (ed.), *Precedent in Law* (1987) (note the bibliography at pp. 249–273).

[1a] "Keep to what has been decided previously:" Cross (1977), p. 4. The term is most commonly used to refer to the common law notion of *binding* precedent (Cross (1977), p. 105: "the general orthodox interpretation of *stare decisis* . . . is stare *rationibus decidendis* ('keep to the *rationes decidendi* of past cases')."). Alternative possible usages are (1) broader: referring to the general desirability of conformity with past precedents (*cf.* Cross (1977), p. 4), and (2) narrower: referring to the obligation to follow the *decision* (*i.e.* order of the court) in a past case that is not reasonably distinguishable, as distinct from the principle of law on which the decision was based (Cross (1977), pp. 105–106).

[2] *Ibid.* pp. 12–17. R. David and J. Brierley, *Major Legal Systems in the World Today* (3rd ed., 1985), pp. 133–149; R. David, *English Law and French Law* (1980), pp. 21–26.

Under the English system, a proposition stated in or derived from case A is binding in case B if (1) it is a proposition of law; (2) it forms part of the *ratio decidendi* of case A (the reason or ground upon which the decision is based); (3) case A was decided in a court whose decisions are binding on the court that is deciding case B; and (4) there is no relevant difference between cases A and B which renders case A "distinguishable." A precedent which is not binding may nevertheless be persuasive. These points are developed below. As we shall see, judges faced with a precedent that they do not like have a number of possible escape routes to explore, and there is for the litigant who can afford it the possibility of recourse to a higher court for a bad precedent to be overruled. The system seeks to balance the general benefits of consistency and certainty against the requirement of justice in individual cases.

On one view judges are seen as picking their way through dusty old volumes of law reports and loyally following the precedents without too much regard for the justice of the case. On another they are seen as paying lip service to the system, and "loyally" following all the precedents that they agree with; those that they do not agree with are distinguished on spurious grounds, or just ignored. These views lie at the extremes and contain elements of caricature as well as truth. It is not possible to make a useful generalisation about judicial behaviour in practice; there are variations in approach from judge to judge, and the same judge may even vary his or her position according to the nature of the case to be decided.[3]

The notion that judges ought generally to abide by relevant precedents developed over several centuries.[4] Blackstone wrote in the eighteenth century that it was "an established rule to abide by former precedents, where the same points come again in litigation . . . unless flatly absurd or unjust,"[5] and Parke J. said in 1833[6]:

> "Our common-law system consists in the applying to new combinations of circumstances those rules of law which we derive from legal principles and judicial precedent; and for the sake of attaining uniformity, consistency and certainty, we must apply those rules, where they are not plainly unreasonable and inconvenient, to all cases which arise; and we are not at liberty to reject them, and to abandon all analogy to them, in those to which they have not yet been judicially applied, because we think that the rules are not as convenient and reasonable as we ourselves could have devised."

The practice of relying on precedents in equity was also established by the eighteenth century. The modern strict rules whereby a single precedent can be binding, and precedents can be binding even if "unreasonable and inconvenient," developed in the nineteenth and twentieth centuries. Important factors were the regularisation of and improvements in law reporting following the establishment of the Incorporated Council of Law Reporting[7]

---

[3] See further above, pp. 232–239.
[4] See C. K. Allen, *Law in the Making* (7th ed., 1964), pp. 187–235, 380–382; T. Ellis Lewis, (1930) 46 L.Q.R. 207, 341, (1931) 47 L.Q.R. 411, (1932) 48 L.Q.R. 230; W. H. D. Winder, (1941) 57 L.Q.R. 245 (precedent in equity); G. J. Postema, "Some roots of our notion of precedent" and J. Evans, "Changes in the doctrine of precedent during the nineteenth century" in Goldstein (1987), Chaps. 1, 2.
[5] 1 *Blackstone's Commentaries* 69, 70.
[6] *Mirehouse* v. *Rennell* (1833) 1 Cl. & F. 527, 546.
[7] See below, p. 406.

and the reorganisation of the courts with a clear hierarchical structure in the latter part of the nineteenth century.[8] The rule that appellate courts are normally bound by their own previous decisions was clearly established for the House of Lords in 1898[9] and for the Court of Appeal in 1944.[10]

B. PROPOSITION OF "LAW"

Decisions on questions of fact may not be cited as precedents.[11] The line between "law" and "fact" may, however, be difficult to draw. An issue is one of fact where it turns on the reliability or credibility of direct evidence, or on inferences from circumstantial evidence. For example, the fact that someone was driving at a high speed may be established by the testimony of a witness, or by inference from such evidence as tyre marks. More difficult are cases which raise an issue whether the facts found conform to a legal description. Such issues are sometimes classified as issues of fact. For example, whether conduct is "unreasonable," and so a breach of the duty of care for the purposes of the tort of negligence, is a question of fact. In *Baker* v. *E. Longhurst & Sons Ltd.*[12] Scrutton L.J. stated[13] that "if a person rides in the dark he must ride at such a pace that he can pull up within the limit of his vision...." This was treated as a proposition of law until the Court of Appeal ruled that it was not.[14] In *Qualcast (Wolverhampton) Ltd.* v. *Haynes*[15] the House of Lords held that a county court judge could not be bound by precedent to hold that an employer who failed to give instructions to an employee as to the use of protective clothing had been negligent.

Where a legal description contained in a statute is "an ordinary word of the English language" its application to the facts found is a question of fact, and it may not be the subject of judicial definition or interpretation.[16] The judges are particularly inclined to classify questions as questions of fact where they wish to avoid the proliferation of authorities.[17] However, where words are used in an unusual sense, or a statute has to be "construed" or "interpreted" before it can be applied, a question of law is raised.[18] The construction of particular words in a contract similarly does not give rise to a binding decision on a point of law.[19]

[8] See above, p. 32.
[9] See below, pp. 392–397. It was changed in 1966.
[10] See below, pp. 380–390.
[11] *Qualcast (Wolverhampton) Ltd.* v. *Haynes* [1959] A.C. 743. Otherwise, "the precedent system will die from a surfeit of authorities" (*per* Lord Somervell at p. 758), or the judges might be "crushed under the weight of our own reports" (*per* Lord Denning at p. 761).
[12] [1933] 2 K.B. 461.
[13] At p. 468.
[14] *Tidy* v. *Battman* [1934] 1 K.B. 319; *Morris* v. *Luton Corporation* [1946] 1 K.B. 114; Lord Greene hoped that this "suggested principle" would "rest peacefully in the grave" (p. 116). *Cf. Worsfold* v. *Howe* [1980] 1 W.L.R. 1175.
[15] [1959] A.C. 743.
[16] See above, pp. 11–12.
[17] *e.g. R.* v. *Industrial Injuries Commissioner, ex p. A.E.U. (No. 2)* [1966] 2 Q.B. 31, 45, 48–49, *per* Lord Denning M.R., in relation to the expression "arising out of and in the course of his employment."
[18] Denning L.J. in *British Launderers' Association* v. *Borough of Hendon Rating Authority* [1949] 1 K.B. 462, 471–472; Lord Reid in *Cozens* v. *Brutus*, above, pp. 11–12.
[19] *per* May L.J. in *Ashville Investments Ltd.* v. *Elmer Contractors Ltd.* [1989] Q.B. 488, 495 (construction of an arbitration clause); *Clarke* v. *Newland* (Unreported, December 21, 1988) (interpretation of restrictive covenant in a partnership agreement).

C. DETERMINING THE RATIO DECIDENDI

1. RATIO AND DICTUM

A proposition of law can only be binding if it forms part of the *ratio decidendi*[20] (commonly shortened to *ratio*) of the case.

Sir Rupert Cross, in the leading English monograph on precedent, gives this description[21]:

> "The *ratio decidendi* of a case is any rule of law expressly or impliedly treated by the judge as a necessary step in reaching his conclusion, having regard to the line of reasoning adopted by him, or a necessary part of his direction to the jury."[22]

He also points out that a judge may adopt more than one line of reasoning leading to the same result, in which case there may be more than one *ratio*. A proposition of law stated by a judge that is not necessary for his or her conclusion is termed an *obiter dictum* or *dictum*.[23] It may, for example, be a proposition wider than is necessary for the facts of the case, or a proposition concerning some matter not raised in the case. Statements of law on points which are fully argued by counsel and considered by the judge, but which do not technically play any part in determining the result, are sometimes termed "judicial *dicta*."[24]

Conversely, where a court *assumes* a proposition of law to be correct without addressing its mind to it, the decision of that court is not binding authority for that proposition.[25]

2. THE PRINCIPLE ENUNCIATED BY THE JUDGE

The task of determining the *ratio* of a case can be complicated, and writers on the subject are not agreed as to how that task is approached by the judges

---

[20] Usually pronounced "rayshio," although variants may be encountered in practice.

[21] *Precedent in English Law* (3rd ed., 1977), p. 76.

[22] *Cf.* the narrower definition proposed by N. MacCormick (in L. Goldstein (ed.), *Judicial Precedent* (1987), Chap. 6, p. 170): "A *ratio decidendi* is a ruling expressly or impliedly given by a judge which is sufficient to settle a point of law put in issue by the parties' arguments in a case, being a point on which a ruling was necessary to his justification (or one of his alternative justifications) of the decision in the case." It is narrower in that it refers to a "ruling" by the judge (so as to cover the interpretation of a statute rather than the statute itself where one is involved), and a requirement that it be necessary for the *justification* for the decision, rather than the decision itself.

[23] Not "an *obiter*." The plural is *obiter dicta*. For examples of cases where it has been held that a particular proposition was not necessary for the decision, see *Penn-Texas Corporation* v. *Murat Anstalt* (*No. 2*) [1964] 2 Q.B. 647, 661 (Lord Denning M.R.); *In re State of Norway's Application* (*No. 2*) [1988] 3 W.L.R. 603, 618–620 (May L.J.), 629–631 (Balcombe L.J.), 646–649 (Woolf L.J.); *Rickless* v. *United Artists Corp.* [1988] Q.B. 40.

[24] Megarry J. in *Brunner* v. *Greenslade* [1971] Ch. 993, 1002–3.

[25] *Per* Warner J. in *Barrs* v. *Bethell* [1982] Ch. 294, 308, relying on Lord Diplock in *Baker* v. *The Queen* [1975] A.C. 774, 788 and Russell L.J. in *National Enterprises Ltd.* v. *Racal Communications Ltd.* [1975] Ch. 397, 406; *Pritchard* v. *J. H. Cobden Ltd.* [1988] Fam. 22, 38, 49; *In re Hetherington* [1990] Ch. 1. This principle, however, is not always observed, *e.g.* in respect of the *Havana* case: see below, pp. 386–387. It has been suggested that the matter turns on whether the court in the earlier case had "turned its mind to the point" and not on whether the point has been argued: *R.* v. *Charles* (1975) 63 Cr.App.R. 252, 259 (Bridge L.J.); *Meer* v. *London Borough of Tower Hamlets* [1988] I.R.L.R. 399, 402 (Balcombe L.J.).

in practice, or how, in theory, it should be approached.[26] It is impossible to assert with confidence that there is any one method of approach which is invariably adopted by the judges. The obvious starting point is the wording of the judgment in question. A judge in giving the reasons for his or her decision will normally indicate the proposition[27] of law upon which he or she regards the decision as based. He or she will explain why he or she thinks this proposition is correct, usually by referring to earlier authorities and showing that it makes good sense. These "explanations" or "justifications" must be distinguished from the proposition of law which they support, as only the latter can be part of the *ratio*.[28] The proposition as enunciated by the judge has a good claim to be regarded as the *ratio*. For example, the editor of a published law report who endeavours to state the *ratio* in the headnote to the case, will frequently use actual sentences from the judgment. A judge in a later case will commonly summarise the effect of a case by citing a passage from the judgment, and saying that a particular sentence or passage sets out "the *ratio*." In many cases, the judge will be content to leave the matter there. However, it may be necessary for the judgment in the earlier case to be subjected to careful analysis (by academic commentators, by counsel, and ultimately by the judge) for the *ratio* to be determined.

In some cases, the rulings are "so embedded in the reasoning as to require minor grammatical reconstruction in order to obtain more explicitly stated forms of them."[29] There may be differing views as to whether a particular ruling was "necessary for the decision."[30] It may be unclear, where a number of different reasons are given for a decision, whether each is to be regarded as a *ratio*.[31] Further difficulties may arise from the differing levels of generality of language that may be used in the formulation of propositions of law: the *ratio* may subsequently be restated in wider or narrower form.[32]

Then, in "extreme cases, judges may do no more than indicate that it is because the facts of the case are certain facts viewed under certain fact-descriptions that the decision ought to be as it is."[33] Here, the method for determining the *ratio* suggested by A. L. Goodhart[34] can be employed: that

---

[26] See, *e.g.* Cross (1977), Chap. 2; A. L. Goodhart, "Determining the *Ratio Decidendi* of a Case" in *Essays in Jurisprudence and the Common Law* (1931), pp. 1–26; the somewhat acerbic dispute between J. L. Montrose and A. W. B. Simpson: (1957) 20 M.L.R. 124, 413, 587, (1958) 21 M.L.R. 155, A. L. Goodhart, (1959) 22 M.L.R. 117; Simpson, in A. G. Guest (ed.) *Oxford Essays in Jurisprudence* (1961), Chap. VI; N. H. Andrews, (1985) 5 L.S. 205, 209–222; N. MacCormick in L. Goldstein (ed.), *Judicial Precedent* (1987), Chap. 6.

[27] There may be more than one relevant proposition; the singular is used here for convenience.

[28] *Cf.* Goodhart (1931), pp. 3–4: "A bad reason may often make good law."

[29] MacCormick (1987), p. 180.

[30] A good example here is provided by a proposition stated by Lord Bridge in *R.* v. *Secretary of State for the Home Department, ex p. Khawaja* [1984] A.C. 74, 117, to the effect that the Home Secretary could not base a "conducive to the public good" deportation order (Immigration Act 1971, s.3(5)(*b*)) on a ground arising from the circumstances of the original entry of the person concerned. Divergent views were subsequently expressed on (1) what Lord Bridge meant; (2) whether it was necessary for the ultimate decision in *Khawaja*; (3) whether it should anyway be followed even if *obiter*: compare *In re Owusu-Sekyere* [1987] Imm.A.R. 425, C.A., with *R.* v. *Immigration Appeal Tribunal, ex p. Patel* [1988] Imm.A.R. 35, C.A. The matter was ultimately resolved by the House of Lords (through Lord Bridge) holding that the proposition was "simply mistaken": *Ex p. Patel* [1988] A.C. 910, 922.

[31] See below, pp. 375–376.

[32] See below, pp. 374–375.

[33] MacCormick (1987), p. 180.

[34] Goodhart (1931), pp. 1–26.

is, by taking account of (a) the facts treated expressly or impliedly by the judge as material, and (b) the decision as based on them. Other features of Goodhart's theory were (1) that the *ratio* was not found in the reasons given on the rule of law set forth in the opinion (although the opinion might furnish a guide for determining which facts the judge considered material and which immaterial); (2) the inclusion of a series of rules for finding which facts were and were not material; (3) that the judge's view on this question had to be accepted by subsequent courts. The theory was offered as being of general application, and, indeed, as "a guide to the method which I believe most English courts follow."[35] Both claims are doubtful, the first because of the downplaying of the principle as enunciated by the judge,[36] and the second simply because "there seems little or no evidence to support this."[37] Nevertheless, the method remains potentially helpful where, probably through faulty technique, the reasons given for a decision do not include an express indication of the relevant principle of law.

3. The "Interpretation" of Precedents

The judge who is called upon to determine a disputed point of law chooses the generality of the language in which he or she expresses a conclusion. The proposition may be very general, it may be closely tailored to the facts of the case or it may be formulated at some intermediate level. Most, although not all judges are reluctant to make general statements of law, and it is anyway well established that a judgment must be read in the light of the facts of the case in which it was given. In *Quinn* v. *Leathem*,[38] the Earl of Halsbury L.C. said that:

> "every judgment must be read as applicable to the particular facts proved, or assumed to be proved, since the generality of the expressions which may be found there are not intended to be expositions of the whole law, but governed and qualified by the particular facts of the case in which such expressions are to be found."

This point is commonly made where the judge in case B wishes to hold that the *ratio* of case A is narrower than that apparently expounded by the judge or court in case A, and is accordingly not applicable. An example of this is given by the decision of the majority of the Privy Council in *Mutual Life and Citizens' Assurance Co. Ltd.* v. *Evatt*,[39] which sought to restrict the scope of liability in tort for negligent misstatement to cases where the defendant was or claimed to be in the business of giving information or advice of the relevant kind. The speeches in the leading case, *Hedley Byrne & Co. Ltd.* v. *Heller and Partners Ltd.*[40] were interpreted to support the incorporation of such a condition, notwithstanding the dissent of Lord Reid and Lord Morris

[35] A. L. Goodhart, (1959) 22 M.L.R. 117, 124.
[36] *Cf.* Cross (1977), pp. 66–76, criticising Goodhart's "scanty regard to the way in which the case was argued and pleaded, the process of reasoning adopted by the judge and the relation of the case to other decisions" (*ibid.* p. 70).
[37] Lord Lloyd and M. D. A. Freeman, *Lloyd's Introduction to Jurisprudence* (5th ed., 1985), p. 1117.
[38] [1901] A.C. 495, 506. *Cf.* Diplock L.J. in *Miller-Mead* v. *Minister of Housing and Local Government* [1963] 2 Q.B. 196, 235–236.
[39] [1971] A.C. 793. On the Privy Council and precedent, see below, pp. 387, 397–398.
[40] [1964] A.C. 465.

of Borth-y-Gest, who had taken part in the *Hedley Byrne* decision and who said that they were "unable to construe the passages from our speeches cited in the judgment of the majority in the way in which they are there construed."[41] Conversely, a proposition stated by a judge may be regarded as too restrictive. A well known example is *Barwick* v. *The English Joint Stock Bank*,[42] where Willes J. said:

> "The general rule is, that the master is answerable for every such wrong of the servant or agent as is committed in the course of the service and for the master's benefit, though no express command or privity of the master be proved."[43]

It had previously been doubted whether a master was vicariously liable in respect of the fraud, as distinct from the non-deliberate wrongdoing, of a servant. On the facts of the case the master had benefited, albeit unwittingly, from the fraud. Subsequently, in *Lloyd* v. *Grace, Smith & Co.*[44] the House of Lords held that an employer could be vicariously liable for the fraud of an employee committed in the course of employment, notwithstanding that the employer received no benefit. The reference to the "master's benefit" was not to be regarded as part of the *ratio* of *Barwick's* case in the light of Willes J.'s judgment when read as a whole and of judgments in other cases both before and after *Barwick*. These are examples of the *ratio* of a case being reformulated *by a court not bound by it*. It has indeed been doubted whether courts "exercise any power of correcting statements of law drawn from binding decisions."[45]

4. CASES WHERE NO REASONS ARE GIVEN

The report of an old case may simply contain a statement of the facts, the arguments of counsel and an order of the court based on those facts. Here, the *ratio* has, if possible, to be inferred, but its authority is understandably very weak.[46] It would be most unusual for such a case to be decisive in modern litigation.

5. JUDGMENTS WITH MORE THAN ONE RATIO

A number of distinct points of law may be at issue in a case, each of which taken separately would be sufficient to determine the case in favour of one side (say the plaintiff). The judge may be content to take one point only, give judgment for the plaintiff, and decline to comment on the other points. Instead, he or she may express an opinion on these points, while making it clear that the decision is to rest on the first point and that the other remarks are *dicta*. Yet again, he or she may state a conclusion on each point without any distinction, resolving them all in favour of the plaintiff. In the third

---

[41] [1971] A.C. 793, 813. The minority position has been preferred by several English judges: see *Esso Petroleum Co. Ltd.* v. *Mardon* [1975] Q.B. 819, 830 (Lawson J.) and [1976] Q.B. 801, 827 (Ormrod L.J.); *Howard Marine and Dredging Co. Ltd.* v. *Ogden & Sons Ltd.* [1978] Q.B. 574, 591 (Lord Denning M.R.), 600 (Shaw L.J.).
[42] (1866) L.R. 2 Ex. 259.
[43] *Ibid*. p. 265.
[44] [1912] A.C. 716.
[45] See A. W. B. Simpson, (1959) 22 M.L.R. 453, 455–457.
[46] Cross (1977), p. 48.

situation, each conclusion is a separate *ratio*, and in principle, each *ratio* is binding.[47]

6. THE RATIO DECIDENDI OF APPELLATE COURTS[48]

Determining the *ratio* of the decision of an appellate court where separate judgments are given can be a difficult task. Some principles are reasonably clear. Where all the members of the court are agreed as to the result of the case, any *ratio* that commands the support of a majority is binding.[49] For example, in a three-member court where two judges support ground A and the third ground B, ground A is the *ratio*. If three judges support ground A and two ground B, there are two *rationes*. Where a judge dissents as to the result, his or her views must technically be disregarded for the purpose of ascertaining the *ratio* on the ground that his or her reasons cannot be "necessary" for a decision he or she opposes. Dissenting judgments may, however, carry persuasive weight. Where there is no majority in favour of any particular *ratio*, a later court may hold that the case has no discernible *ratio* which has to be followed, although it may not adopt any reasoning which would show the decision itself to be wrong.[50] In some cases there may be much time and effort spent in the search for a *ratio* which is as elusive as the holy grail.[51]

A further complication arises where the Court of Appeal bases a decision on point A, but the case proceeds to the House of Lords, which (1) dismisses the appeal, but (2) bases its decision on point B, (3) holds that on a proper analysis point A does not arise and (4) expresses no view on the soundness of point A. In *R. v. Secretary of State for the Home Department, ex p. Al-Mehdawi*[52] the Court of Appeal held that the previous decision of the Court of Appeal[53] is no longer binding authority for point A, although it remains of "powerful persuasive influence."[54] Counsel for the Secretary of State had argued that this was so either (1) because point A had been replaced by point

---

[47] *Jacobs* v. *London County Council* [1950] A.C. 361, 369 (Lord Simonds); *Behrens* v. *Bertram Mills Circus Ltd.* [1957] 2 Q.B. 1, 24–25 (Devlin J.); *Miliangos* v. *George Frank (Textiles) Ltd.* [1975] Q.B. 487, 502–503 (Lord Denning M.R.); R. E. Megarry, (1958) 74 L.Q.R. 350. On other occasions Lord Denning argued that the Court of Appeal is not necessarily bound by both or all the *rationes* of an earlier *Court of Appeal* decision: *Hanning* v. *Maitland (No. 2)* [1970] 1 Q.B. 580; *Ministry of Defence* v. *Jeremiah* [1980] 1 Q.B. 87. On this he stood alone: see Hazel Carty, (1981) 1 L.S. 68, 71–72.

[48] Cross (1977), pp. 90–102; G. Paton and G. Sawer, (1947) 63 L.Q.R. 461; A. M. Honoré, (1955) 71 L.Q.R. 196.

[49] *e.g. Amalgamated Society of Railway Servants* v. *Osborne* [1910] A.C. 87. A statement "I agree" may simply indicate concurrence with the order proposed in the leading judgment and not necessarily all the reasoning: Lord Russell of Killowen (then Russell L.J.), Address to the Holdsworth Club of the University of Birmingham 1968–69, reprinted in B. W. Harvey (ed.), *The Lawyer and Justice* (1978).

[50] See the analysis of the decision of the House of Lords in *Central Asbestos Ltd.* v. *Dodd* [1973] A.C. 518 by the Court of Appeal in *In re Harper* v. *National Coal Board (Intended Action)* [1974] Q.B. 614.

[51] See, for example, the decision of the House of Lords in *Chaplin* v. *Boys* [1971] A.C. 356. First-year law students are not recommended to read this case; it should, however, be one of the party pieces of students of Conflict of Laws.

[52] [1990] 1 A.C. 876.

[53] Here, *R. v. Diggines, ex p. Rahmani* [1985] Q.B. 1109, C.A., on appeal: [1986] A.C. 475.

[54] *per* Taylor L.J., [1990] 1 A.C. 876, 883. Taylor L.J. had, indeed, been a party to the Court of Appeal decision in *ex p. Rahmani*, and ultimately, here, remained of the same opinion. The decision on the point in question was, however, ultimately reversed by the House of Lords: *ibid.*

B as the *ratio* of the decision, or (2) as an additional exception to the rule in *Young* v. *Bristol Aeroplane Co.*[55] The Court of Appeal seemed to accept the first of these arguments, but did not expressly reject the second.

D. THE HIERARCHY OF THE COURTS AND THE RULES OF BINDING PRECEDENT

Broadly speaking, a court is only *obliged* to follow the decisions of courts at a higher or the same level in the court structure, and there are a number of exceptions even to that requirement. For the purposes of the following discussion it must be assumed that all the other factors mentioned in Section A above are present which combine to make a precedent binding in a particular case.

1. MAGISTRATES COURTS AND COUNTY COURTS

Decisions of these courts are rarely reported outside the pages of local newspapers, but even if they were properly reported they would not constitute precedents binding on anyone. They do not bind themselves, although it is to be expected that an individual magistrate or county court judge will attempt to be consistent in his or her own decision-making. A magistrates' court may also be reminded by the clerk of the practice of the local bench, and other benches in the area. The matter upon which a "local view" may develop will rarely be a point of law; more commonly it will relate to a procedural requirement or the exercise of discretion, as in sentencing or the granting of bail.[56] Magistrates' courts and county courts are bound by decisions of the High Court, Court of Appeal and House of Lords.

2. THE CROWN COURT

Decisions of judges in the Crown Court are reported rather more frequently than those of magistrates' and county courts. This is partly because the judge may be a High Court judge whose pronouncements are inevitably more authoritative, and partly because reports of cases on points of criminal law, even at this level, find an outlet in the pages of publications such as the Criminal Law Review and the Criminal Appeal Reports. However, there is no regular reporting, and it has been suggested that Crown Court decisions are merely persuasive authorities whatever the status of the judge.[57] The Crown Court is bound by decisions of the Court of Appeal and the House of Lords. It has been asserted that it is not bound by decisions of the Divisional Court,[58] but this is hard to square with the rule that Divisional Courts are normally bound by their own previous decisions.[59]

[55] [1944] K.B. 718. See below, pp. 382–390.
[56] See, *e.g. R.* v. *Nottingham JJ., ex p. Davies* [1981] 1 Q.B. 38 where the practice of the City of Nottingham bench of refusing to hear full argument on a third or subsequent application for bail, unless there were "new circumstances," was endorsed by the Divisional Court.
[57] A. Ashworth, "The Binding Effect of Crown Court Decisions" [1980] Crim.L.R. 402–403; *cf.* Cross (1977), pp. 7, 122. Some cases are reported in the regular law reports: see, *e.g. R.* v. *Bourne* [1939] 1 K.B. 687, where the summing up of Macnaghten J. on the pre-Abortion Act 1967 law of procuring an abortion was generally accepted as authoritative (*cf.* [1938] 3 All E.R. 615).
[58] *R.* v. *Colyer* [1974] Crim.L.R. 243 (Judge Stinson).
[59] See below, pp. 378–380.

3. THE HIGH COURT

The decision of a High Court judge is binding on inferior courts, but not technically on another High Court judge, and certainly not on a Divisional Court (*i.e.* a court of two or more judges). High Court judges are reluctant to depart from the decisions of other High Court judges,[60] Chancery judges being particularly loath to disagree with their colleagues for fear of upsetting transactions affecting property rights and the like.[61] There are, however, examples of judicial disagreement, one of the most notable in recent years being on the question whether failure to wear a seat-belt in a car can amount to contributory negligence. This had to be settled by the Court of Appeal.[62] However, it has been stated that where there are conflicting decisions of judges of co-ordinate jurisdiction, the later decision should thereafter be preferred, provided that it was reached after full consideration of the first decision: the only, rare, exception would be where the third judge was convinced that the second judge was wrong in not following the first, for example where some binding or persuasive authority had not been cited in either of the first two cases.[63] This view has been cited with approval on a number of occasions,[64] although it has been emphasised that the matter remains one of judicial comity: there is no new head of binding precedent.[65]

4. DIVISIONAL COURTS

A Divisional Court is bound by decisions of the Court of Appeal and the House of Lords. In *Huddersfield Police Authority* v. *Watson*[66] and *Young-husband* v. *Luftig*,[67] Divisional Courts of the King's Bench Division, in each case presided over by Lord Goddard C.J., held that they were bound by previous Divisional Court decisions to the same extent that the Court of Appeal was bound by its own previous decisions.[68]

The matter was reconsidered by the Divisional Court in *R.* v. *Greater Manchester Coroner, ex p. Tal.*[69] It was held that the position was different where a Divisional Court was exercising the supervisory jurisdiction of the High Court on an application for judicial review,[70] and was faced by a previous decision of the Divisional Court acting in the same capacity. Its position was analogous to that of a judge at first instance faced with a

---

[60] See *Police Authority for Huddersfield* v. *Watson* [1947] K.B. 842, 848, where it is explained by Lord Goddard C.J. to be a matter of "judicial comity."
[61] There are also many fewer Chancery judges than Queen's Bench judges and so they are more likely to meet each other; whether this boosts "judicial comity" is a matter for speculation.
[62] *Froom* v. *Butcher* [1976] Q.B. 286 answered the question in the affirmative.
[63] *Colchester Estates (Cardiff)* v. *Carlton Industries plc.* [1986] Ch. 80.
[64] *Taylor Woodrow Property Co. Ltd.* v. *Lonrho Textiles Ltd.* [1985] 2 E.G.L.R. 120, B. Hytner Q.C., sitting as a deputy High Court judge (in respect of two conflicting decisions of the Court of Appeal); *Elite Investments Ltd.* v. *T. I. Bainbridge Silencers Ltd.* [1986] 2 E.G.L.R. 43, Judge Paul Baker Q.C., sitting as a judge of the High Court; *Glofield Properties Ltd.* v. *Morley* [1988] 1 E.G.L.R. 113, Hutchison J.
[65] *Forsikringsaktieselskapet Vesta* v. *Butcher* [1986] 2 All E.R. 488, Hobhouse J.
[66] [1947] K.B. 842: on an appeal from quarter sessions in a civil case concerning police pensions.
[67] [1949] 2 K.B. 354: on an appeal by case stated from justices in a criminal case.
[68] Under *Young* v. *Bristol Aeroplane Co. Ltd.*, *infra*. The possibility of the Divisional Court applying one of the *Young* v. *Bristol Aeroplane* exceptions was acknowledged by Lord Goddard in the latter case: [1949] 2 K.B. 354, 361.
[69] [1985] Q.B. 67. See P. Jackson, (1985) 101 L.Q.R. 157.
[70] See below, pp. 874–878.

previous decision of another judge of first instance: here, the judge in the later case would follow the earlier decision

> "unless he is convinced that that judgment is wrong, as a matter of judicial comity; but he is not bound to follow a judge of equal jurisdiction."[71]

The same principle of *stare decisis* was applicable where two Divisional Court decisions were involved:

> "We have no doubt that it will be only in rare cases that a divisional court will think it fit to depart from a decision of another divisional court exercising this jurisdiction."[72]

Ex p. Tal was one of these "rare cases,"[73] the Divisional Court holding that any error of law made by an inferior court or tribunal caused it to act outside its jurisdiction.[74] It declined to follow *R. v. Surrey Coroner, ex p. Campbell*,[75] where it had been held that this principle applied only to *tribunals*, and not *courts*, such as a coroner's court.[76] The court in *Ex. p. Tal*[77] also expressed doubts, *obiter*, as to whether the strict approach to precedent in cases where the Divisional Court was acting in an appellate capacity was still appropriate. Robert Goff L.J. noted that at the time of *Younghusband* v. *Luftig*,[78] the Divisional Court was the final court of appeal in criminal cases tried summarily,[79] and the House of Lords, in most cases the final court of appeal, regarded itself as bound by its own previous decisions (subject to narrow exceptions).[80] Neither of these points remained true in 1984. In criminal cases at least, his Lordship[81] could see no reason why the Divisional Court should not adopt the more flexible approach of the Criminal Division of the Court of Appeal,[82] in preference to the narrower approach of the Civil Division based on *Young* v. *Bristol Aeroplane Co.*[83]

---

[71] *Ibid.*, at p. 81, *per* Robert Goff L.J., citing *Police Authority for Huddersfield* v. *Watson* [1947] K.B. 842, 848, *per* Lord Goddard C.J.

[72] [1985] Q.B. 67, 81, *per* Robert Goff L.J.

[73] Another is *R. v. Chief Metropolitan Stipendiary Magistrate, ex p. Secretary of State for the Home Department* [1988] 1 W.L.R. 1204.

[74] Under the principle of *Anisminic Ltd.* v. *Foreign Compensation Commission* [1969] 2 A.C. 147.

[75] [1982] Q.B. 661.

[76] In accordance with *dicta* of Lord Diplock in *In re Racal Communications Ltd.* [1981] A.C. 374.

[77] *Supra.*

[78] *Supra.*

[79] See below, p. 829. It had also been the final court of appeal under the police pensions legislation in *Huddersfield Police Authority* v. *Watson, supra.*

[80] See below, p. 392.

[81] [1985] Q.B. 67, 78, 79.

[82] See below, pp. 390–392. A more flexible approach had also been adopted in two nineteenth century Divisional Court cases, both concerning criminal appeals: *Fortescue* v. *Vestry of St. Matthew, Bethnal Green* [1891] 2 Q.B. 170; *Kruse* v. *Johnson* [1898] 2 Q.B. 91. These cases were not cited in *Huddersfield Police Authority* v. *Watson* and *Younghusband* v. *Luftig*.

[83] Below, pp. 382–390.

In subsequent cases, the approach to precedent of the Divisional Court in *Ex p. Tal*[84] has been cited with approval,[85] although the judges seem happier to disregard a previous Divisional Court decision if this can be done by reference to a "*Young* v. *Bristol Aeroplane Co.* exception."[86] It has also been emphasised that *Ex p. Tal*

"was not intended to provide freedom to parties to re-argue points simply on the ground that they might persuade the Court to reach a different conclusion. Before a point may be re-argued, the party must be able to indicate, at the outset of the argument, specific material on the basis of which it might properly be submitted that the Court may be convinced that the previous decision was plainly wrong."[87]

Divisional Court decisions are binding on High Court judges sitting alone[88] and inferior courts, but not the Employment Appeal Tribunal.[89]

5. THE COURT OF APPEAL (CIVIL DIVISION)

(a) The general position

Decisions of the Court of Appeal are binding on the Divisional Court, the Employment Appeal Tribunal, High Court judges[90] and inferior courts. The Court of Appeal is bound to follow decisions of the House of Lords. On occasion, the House has felt it necessary to remind the Court of Appeal of this. In 1970, Captain Jack Broome R.N. (retd.) brought a libel action against David Irving and Cassell & Co. Ltd., respectively author and publisher of a book entitled *The Destruction of Convoy P.Q.17*. The case was heard over 17 days by Lawton J. and a jury.[91] The jury awarded £15,000 "compensatory damages" and £25,000 "exemplary damages." The situations in which exemplary damages could be awarded had been listed by Lord Devlin in *Rookes* v. *Barnard*,[92] a decision of the House of Lords, and the

---

[84] *Supra*.
[85] *Hornigold* v. *Chief Constable of Lancashire* [1986] Crim.L.R. 792 (appeal in a criminal case); *R.* v. *Chief Metropolitan Stipendiary Magistrate, ex p. Secretary of State for the Home Department* [1988] 1 W.L.R. 1204 (application for judicial review); *cf. Rogers* v. *Essex County Council* [1985] 1 W.L.R. 700, where the Divisional Court on an appeal in a criminal case preferred to distinguish an earlier decision (on doubtful grounds: see P. Jackson, (1985) 101 L.Q.R. 486): *Ex p. Tal* was cited for the proposition that as the court was acting in an "appellate capacity" it was "prima facie bound" by a previous decision (p. 706).
[86] *R.* v. *Plymouth JJ., ex p. Driver* [1986] Q.B. 95, 123–124 (*per incuriam*); *R.* v. *Plymouth JJ., ex p. Hart* [1986] Q.B. 950 (conflicting decisions); *R.* v. *Weston-super-Mare JJ., ex p. Shaw* [1987] Q.B. 640, 648 (conflicting decisions): all applications for judicial review.
[87] *Hornigold* v. *Chief Constable of Lancashire* [1986] Crim.L.R. 792.
[88] *Police Authority for Huddersfield* v. *Watson* [1947] K.B. 842, 848; *Ettenfield* v. *Ettenfield* [1939] P. 377, 380; *contra: Elderton* v. *United Kingdom Totalisator Co. Ltd.* (1945) 61 T.L.R. 529 where a judge of the Chancery Division declined to follow the decision of a Divisional Court of the Queen's Bench Division.
[89] *Portec (U.K.) Ltd.* v. *Mogensen* [1976] I.C.R. 396, 400; *Breach* v. *Epsylon Industries Ltd.* [1976] I.C.R. 316, 320.
[90] Even an *ex parte* decision of the Court of Appeal: *The Alexandros P.* [1986] Q.B. 464. In *Lane* v. *Willis* [1972] 1 W.L.R. 326, 332, Davies L.J. rebuked Lawson J. for expressing the opinion, though accepting he was bound by it, that a Court of Appeal decision was wrong.
[91] It survived an interruption by Welsh language demonstrators: *Morris* v. *Crown Office* [1970] 2 Q.B. 114.
[92] [1964] A.C. 1129. The other members of the House expressly concurred with Lord Devlin's statement on exemplary damages.

principles subsequently applied by the Court of Appeal to the tort of defamation.[93] Not surprisingly, Lawton J. had directed the jury accordingly in the *P.Q.17* case. Both author and publisher appealed against the award of exemplary damages. The Court of Appeal, after a nine-day hearing, rejected the appeal.[94] The case fell within one of the situations in which Lord Devlin had held that exemplary damages could be awarded,[95] the judge's direction had been adequate and the jury's award was not perversely large. The Court of Appeal was not, however, content with that. The members of the court (Lord Denning M.R., Salmon and Phillimore L.JJ.) took the view that the law on exemplary damages as expounded by Lord Devlin was "unworkable." Lord Denning M.R. said that the common law on exemplary damages had been well settled before 1964, that there were two House of Lords cases[96] which had approved that settled doctrine and which Lord Devlin must have "overlooked" or "misunderstood," that *Rookes* v. *Barnard* had not been followed in Commonwealth courts, and that the new doctrine was "hopelessly illogical and inconsistent." He concluded:

> "I think the difficulties presented by *Rookes* v. *Barnard* are so great that the judges should direct the juries in accordance with the law as it was understood before *Rookes* v. *Barnard*. Any attempt to follow *Rookes* v. *Barnard* is bound to lead to confusion."[97]

Surprisingly, there was no discussion of the question whether Lord Devlin's statement formed part of the *ratio decidendi* of *Rookes* v. *Barnard*.

Cassells appealed to the House of Lords; a 13-day hearing was held before seven Law Lords. The Court of Appeal's decision to uphold the jury's verdict was affirmed by a majority.[98] Lord Devlin's approach to exemplary damages was endorsed, with varying enthusiasm, by a majority. The approach of the Court of Appeal to *Rookes* v. *Barnard* was roundly condemned. Lord Hailsham L.C.:

> "[I]t is not open to the Court of Appeal to give gratuitous advice to judges of first instance to ignore decisions of the House of Lords in this way and, if it were open to the Court of Appeal to do so, it would be highly undesirable....
>
> "The fact is, and I hope it will never be necessary to say so again, that, in the hierarchical system of courts which exists in this country, it is necessary for each lower tier, including the Court of Appeal, to accept loyally the decisions of the higher tiers. Where decisions manifestly conflict, the decision in *Young* v. *Bristol Aeroplane Co. Ltd.* offers guidance to each tier in matters affecting its own decisions. It does not entitle it to question considered decisions in the upper tiers with the same freedom."[99]

---

[93] *McCarey* v. *Associated Newspapers Ltd.* [1965] 2 Q.B. 86; *Broadway Approvals Ltd.* v. *Odhams Press Ltd.* [1965] 1 W.L.R. 805.

[94] *Broome* v. *Cassell & Co. Ltd.* [1971] 2 Q.B. 354.

[95] See W.U.H. Rogers, *Winfield and Jolowicz on Tort* (13th ed., 1989), pp. 601–606.

[96] *E. Hulton & Co.* v. *Jones* [1910] A.C. 20 and *Ley* v. *Hamilton* (1935) 153 L.T. 384.

[97] [1971] 2 Q.B. 354, 381, 384.

[98] *Cassell & Co. Ltd.* v. *Broome* [1972] A.C. 1027. It has been described as "what may well be the most hostile *affirmation* of a Court of Appeal decision in our history": Julius Stone, "On the Liberation of Appellate Judges—How not to do it!" (1972) 35 M.L.R. 449.

[99] [1972] A.C. 1027, 1054.

Other members of the House of Lords added their voices to the chorus of disapproval.[1] They pointed out that the parties had been put to much expense in litigating broad legal issues unnecessary for the disposal of their dispute.[1a] Lord Devlin had not overlooked the two House of Lords cases (*Ley* v. *Hamilton* was discussed at length in his speech) and, on proper analysis, they were not binding authorities on the award of exemplary damages.[2]

The House of Lords similarly found it necessary to assert its authority over the Court of Appeal in *Miliangos* v. *George Frank (Textiles) Ltd.*[3]

(b) Young v. Bristol Aeroplane Co. Ltd.

In *Young* v. *Bristol Aeroplane Co. Ltd.*[4] the Court of Appeal[5] held that it was bound by its own previous decisions, and by decisions of courts of co-ordinate jurisdiction such as the Courts of Exchequer Chamber. Three exceptions were identified. First a decision of the Court of Appeal given *per incuriam* need not be followed. Secondly, where the court is faced by previous conflicting decisions of the Court of Appeal or a court of co-ordinate jurisdiction, it may choose which to follow. Thirdly, where a previous decision of the Court of Appeal, although not expressly overruled, cannot stand with a subsequent decision of the House of Lords, the decision of the House must be followed. Since *Young's* case further light has been thrown on the scope of these three exceptions and suggestions have been made for additional ones. Lord Denning M.R. fought, almost single-handed, against the notion that the Court of Appeal should be bound by its own previous decisions at all. In addition, it has been unclear whether the grounds upon which the Court of Appeal may question one of its own decisions may be employed by a court lower in the hierarchy in respect of a decision of a higher court. These matters are considered in turn.

(c) Accepted exceptions to Young v. Bristol Aeroplane Co. Ltd.

(i) *Decisions given per incuriam*

If interpreted and applied literally the *per incuriam* doctrine could be used to evade the effect of any decision thought to have been reached "through want of care." However, the term in this context is interpreted narrowly. A decision will not be regarded as *per incuriam* merely on the ground that another court thinks it wrongly decided, that it has been inadequately argued[6] or that the decision contains points which are not derived from the arguments of counsel.[7] In *Morelle* v. *Wakeling*, Sir Raymond Evershed

---

[1] See Lord Reid at pp. 1084, 1091–3; Lord Wilberforce at pp. 1112–3; Lord Diplock at pp. 1131–2; Lord Kilbrandon at pp. 1132, 1135.

[1a] *Cf.* below, p. 864, n. 91.

[2] Viscount Dilhorne dissented on this last point: [1972] A.C. at pp. 1109–11.

[3] [1976] A.C. 443, discussed below, pp. 385–387.

[4] [1944] K.B. 718.

[5] A "full court" consisting of Lord Greene M.R., Scott, MacKinnon, Luxmoore, Goddard and du Parcq L.JJ. Note that it was held in this case a "full court" is bound by previous Court of Appeal decisions to the same extent as a court ordinarily constituted. See further below p. 391.

[6] *Morelle* v. *Wakeling* [1955] 2 Q.B. 379, 406; *Miliangos* v. *George Frank (Textiles) Ltd.* [1975] Q.B. 487, 503 (Lord Denning M.R.); *cf. Chief Adjudication Officer* v. *Brunt* [1988] A.C. 711, 724, 726, C.A.

[7] *Per* Lord Diplock in *Cassell & Co. Ltd.* v. *Broome* [1972] A.C. 1027, 1131.

M.R. said that as a general rule the *per incuriam* doctrine could only apply to:

> "decisions given in ignorance or forgetfulness of some inconsistent statutory provision or of some authority binding on the court concerned: so that in such cases some part of the decision or some step in the reasoning on which it is based is found, on that account to be demonstrably wrong."[8]

In *Dixon* v. *British Broadcasting Corporation*[9] a decision on the construction of a statutory provision was regarded as *per incuriam* on the ground that other relevant provisions which threw light on the words in question had not been brought to the attention of the court. A clearer example is *Bonulami* v. *Home Secretary*.[10] An order was obtained under the Bankers' Books Evidence Act 1879 for the inspection of bank accounts to obtain evidence in criminal proceedings. The Court of Appeal (Civil Division) held that it had no jurisdiction to entertain an appeal as this was a "criminal cause or matter,"[11] notwithstanding that in an earlier[12] case it had heard such an appeal. The point as to jurisdiction had not been taken or considered by counsel or any member of the court:

> "Failure to consider a statutory provision is one of the clearest cases in which, on the principles laid down in *Young* v. *Bristol Aeroplane Co.*, this court is not bound to follow its own decisions."[13]

The exact scope of the *per incuriam* doctrine has been thrown into some doubt by three judgments of Sir John (subsequently Lord) Donaldson M.R. In *Duke* v. *Reliance Systems Ltd.*[14] he put it in narrow terms, as applying where the court *must* (not *might*) have reached a different conclusion had a statute or binding precedent been drawn to its attention. In *Williams* v. *Fawcett*,[15] the Court of Appeal disapproved one of the grounds of a number of decisions[16] in which it had been held that a notice to show cause why the respondent should not be committed to prison for breach of a non-molestation order had to be signed by the "proper officer" of the county court. There was no warrant for this requirement in the statute or procedural rules. Sir John Donaldson M.R. recognised the dangers of treating a decision as given *per incuriam* simply on the ground that it could be demonstrated to be wrong, but argued that this was an "exceptional" case for various reasons: (1) the clearness with which the growth of the error could be detected if the decisions were read consecutively; (2) the cases were concerned with the

---

[8] [1955] 2 Q.B. 379, 406. See generally, P. Wesley-Smith, (1980) 15 J.S.P.T.L. (N.S.) 58. In *Industrial Properties Ltd.* v. *A.E.I.* [1977] Q.B. 580 *dicta* in a Court of Appeal decision were held to have been made *per incuriam* on the ground that the court had misunderstood a decision of the Court of Exchequer Chamber; they had only been referred to an inadequate report of that decision.

[9] [1979] Q.B. 546.

[10] [1985] Q.B. 675. See also *White* v. *Chief Adjudication Officer* [1986] 2 All E.R. 905; *Pearce* v. *Secretary of State for Defence* [1988] A.C. 755, 785, C.A.; *Rakhit* v. *Carty* [1990] 2 Q.B. 315.

[11] Supreme Court Act 1981, s.18(1)(*a*): see below, p. 849.

[12] *R.* v. *Grossman* (1981) 73 Cr.App.R. 302.

[13] *Per* Stephenson L.J. at [1985] Q.B. 675, 682.

[14] [1988] Q.B. 108. See above, pp. 305–306.

[15] [1988] Q.B. 604.

[16] *Lee* v. *Walker* [1988] Q.B. 1191 and several unreported decisions.

liberty of the subject[17]; (3) they were by no means unusual; and (4) they were "most unlikely to reach the House of Lords, which, if we do not act is alone able to correct the error which has crept into the law."[18]

Subsequently, in *Rickards* v. *Rickards*[19] the Court of Appeal declined to follow its own previous decision in *Podberry* v. *Peak*,[20] in which it had been held that the Court of Appeal had no jurisdiction to entertain an appeal against the refusal of a judge to grant leave to appeal out of time. The court in *Rickards*, which included Lord Donaldson M.R., was satisfied that the decision in *Podberry* v. *Peak* was wrong, but noted that in practice it was unlikely that litigants would incur the cost of appealing to the House of Lords on this point.[21] Further considerations that justified treating *Podberry* v. *Peak* as a decision given *per incuriam* were (1) that it related to a procedural rule rather than substantive law (erroneous decisions as to procedural rules affecting only the parties engaged in the relevant litigation); and (2) that it involved the jurisdiction of the court, errors on matters of jurisdiction being "particularly objectionable."[22] It was stated that this extended approach to the *per incuriam* doctrine should only be adopted in "rare and exceptional" cases.[23] It remains to be seen how common they will be.

(ii) *Conflicting decisions*

Decisions in the Court of Appeal may conflict. The decision in case A may not be cited to the court in case B whereas both cases A and B are cited in case C[24]; case A may not have been reported,[25] or may simply have been overlooked. Cases A and B may be decided by different divisions of the Court of Appeal at roughly the same time. Case A may be cited in case B but, in the view of the court in case C, erroneously interpreted. The resulting confusion may be settled by the Court of Appeal choosing which case or line of cases to follow and overruling any cases that conflict.[26] It has been argued that the court should be bound by the earlier case, case A (as the court in case B was not entitled to depart from it[27]) and, alternatively, that it should follow case B (as the later case[28]) but neither argument has prevailed.

---

[17] Although it was noted that the present decision would not be beneficial to the contemnors, who would be deprived of a technical ground of challenge to their imprisonment; *Williams* v. *Fawcett* is therefore not to be equated with the "special exception" recognised in the Criminal Division of the Court of Appeal: see below, pp. 390–392.

[18] [1988] Q.B. 604, 616–617.

[19] [1989] 3 W.L.R. 748.

[20] [1981] Ch. 344.

[21] Leave was granted in *Bokhari* v. *Mahmood* (Unreported, 1988) for the point to be taken to the House of Lords, but the appeal was not pursued.

[22] "either because it will involve an abuse of power if the true view is that the court has no jurisdiction or a breach of the court's statutory duty if the true view is that the court is wrongly declining jurisdiction": *per* Lord Donaldson M.R. at p. 755.

[23] Lord Donaldson M.R. at p. 755; Balcombe L.J. at p. 758; Nicholls L.J. at p. 761.

[24] See the cases discussed in *Fisher* v. *Ruislip-Northwood Urban District Council* [1945] K.B. 584. The decision in case B may be regarded as given *per incuriam*: see *W. A. Sharratt Ltd.* v. *John Bromley Church Stratton Ltd.* [1985] Q.B. 1038.

[25] E.g. *Cathrineholm A/S* v. *Norequipment Trading Ltd.* [1972] 2 Q.B. 314.

[26] *Ibid.; Ross-Smith* v. *Ross-Smith* [1961] P. 39; *Ashburn Anstalt* v. *Arnold* [1989] Ch. 1; *cf. Midland Bank Trust Co. Ltd.* v. *Hett, Stubbs & Kemp* [1979] Ch. 384.

[27] A. L. Goodhart, (1947) 9 C.L.J. 349.

[28] R. N. Gooderson, (1950) 10 C.L.J. 432.

(iii) *Decisions impliedly overruled by the House of Lords*

In *Young* v. *Bristol Aeroplane Co.*[29] Lord Greene M.R. stated that the Court of Appeal was not bound by a previous decision which "although not expressly overruled, cannot stand with a subsequent decision of the House of Lords."[30] This principle was relied upon by Oliver J. in *Midland Bank Trust Co. Ltd.* v. *Hett, Stubbs & Kemp*[31] where he declined to follow the decision of the Court of Appeal in *Groom* v. *Crocker*[32] on the ground that it was inconsistent with the subsequent decision of the House of Lords in *Hedley Byrne & Co. Ltd.* v. *Heller & Partners Ltd.*[33]

(iv) *Decisions on interlocutory appeals*

In *Boys* v. *Chaplin*[34] the Court of Appeal held that it was not bound by a previous decision of the Court of Appeal where that court comprised two Lords Justices hearing an interlocutory appeal.

(d) Possible exceptions to Young v. Bristol Aeroplane Co. Ltd.

(i) *Inconsistency with an earlier House of Lords decision*

Lord Greene M.R.'s summary of conclusions in the *Young* case and the headnotes of most of the reports indicate that a Court of Appeal decision which is inconsistent with *any* House of Lords case, whether prior or subsequent, does not bind the Court of Appeal. The relevant passage from the main body of Lord Greene's judgment,[35] however, includes the word "subsequent." Moreover, in *Williams* v. *Glasbrook Bros.*[36] Lord Greene expressly asserted that the exception was so limited; if the Court of Appeal misinterprets an earlier House of Lords decision "nobody but the House of Lords can put that mistake right."[37] This position has been supported by Lord Denning M.R.[38] and Lord Simon,[39] and is to be preferred "in the interests of certainty."[40] Against these authorities, and in favour of a more widely drawn exception to *Young's* case, are the decision of the Court of Appeal in *Fitzsimons* v. *The Ford Motor Co.*[41] and the opinion of Lord Cross in *Miliangos* v. *George Frank (Textiles) Ltd.*[42]

[29] [1944] K.B. 718.
[30] *Ibid.* p. 722.
[31] [1979] Ch. 384. The case concerned the liability of a solicitor for negligence: see above pp. 162–164.
[32] [1939] 1 K.B. 194. Authorities following *Groom* v. *Crocker* and decided after *Hedley Byrne* were regarded as inconsistent with the decision of the Court of Appeal in *Esso Petroleum Co. Ltd.* v. *Mardon* [1976] Q.B. 801.
[33] [1964] A.C. 465.
[34] [1968] 2 Q.B. 1.
[35] Above, p. 382.
[36] [1947] 2 All E.R. 884.
[37] *Ibid.* p. 885. If the House of Lords decision had not been cited, the Court of Appeal decision would be *per incuriam*: see above.
[38] *Miliangos* v. *George Frank (Textiles) Ltd.* [1975] Q.B. 416, 502.
[39] *Ibid.* [1976] A.C. 443, 478–479.
[40] Cross (1977), p. 143.
[41] [1946] 1 All E.R. 429. This was not cited in *Williams* v. *Glasbrook Bros.*
[42] [1976] A.C. 443, 496.

The *Miliangos* case illustrates some of the difficulties that can arise. In 1960 the House of Lords in the *Havana* case[43] made a decision which was based on the unchallenged assumption that a judgment in an English court could only be given in sterling. The actual point in issue was the date at which a debt payable in U.S. dollars had to be converted to the equivalent in sterling for the purposes of proceedings in England to enforce payment. In *Schorsch Meier G.m.b.H.* v. *Hennin*[44] the Court of Appeal[45] held (1) that the operation of the *Havana* case had been limited by Article 106 of the EEC Treaty, which was regarded as enabling EEC nationals to obtain judgments in a foreign currency and (2) (Lawton L.J. dissenting) that in any event the *Havana* rule could be disregarded as the fact that sterling was no longer a stable currency meant that the rationale behind the rule no longer stood. On the latter point, the majority founded themselves on the maxim *cessante ratione legis cessat ipsa lex* (if the reason for a law ceases to be valid the law itself ceases). In *Miliangos* v. *George Franks (Textiles) Ltd.* a plaintiff who was not an EEC national sought to take advantage of the second *ratio* of *Schorsch Meier*. Bristow J.[46] held that he was obliged to follow the House of Lords decision in *Havana* in preference to that of the Court of Appeal in *Schorsch Meier*, notwithstanding the fact that it had been cited to the court in *Schorsch Meier*. The *Havana* rule could only be altered by statute or another decision of the House. On appeal, the Court of Appeal[47] then held that *Schorsch Meier* was binding (1) on courts beneath the Court of Appeal in the hierarchy and (2) on the Court of Appeal itself, the relevant exception to *Young* v. *Bristol Aeroplane Co. Ltd.* being confined to inconsistent *subsequent* House of Lords decisions. The House of Lords held (1) that the Court of Appeal had acted incorrectly in *Schorsch Meier* in failing to follow *Havana*; but (2) (Lord Simon dissenting) that the *Havana* case should be overruled. As to the dilemma facing the trial judge and the Court of Appeal in *Miliangos*, Lord Cross[48] took the view that *Schorsch Meier* should not have been followed (endorsing Bristow J.'s approach), Lord Simon[49] thought that the Court of Appeal in *Miliangos* had acted correctly, and the other members of the House of Lords expressed no definite opinion.[50] The position taken by Bristow J. and Lord Cross assumes that:

> "the *Schorsch Meier* majority decision was not law in any proper sense, since it was reached in total disregard of the proper law as it then existed in a rule of the House of Lords, and which . . . bound the Court of Appeal to reach a decision contrary to that actually reached."[51]

However, the analogous argument is not accepted in cases of "horizontal conflict" between decisions in the same court. Thus, where Court of Appeal

---

[43] *In re United Railways of Havana and Regla Warehouses Ltd.* [1961] A.C. 1007.
[44] [1975] Q.B. 416.
[45] Lord Denning M.R., Lawton L.J. and Foster J.
[46] [1975] Q.B. 487, 491.
[47] [1975] Q.B. 487, 499.
[48] [1976] A.C. 443, 496.
[49] [1976] A.C. 443, 470.
[50] Professor Cross thought the desirability of contradictory statements on this point to be "highly questionable" and that there was "something to be said for the discreet silence" of the other three members of the House: P. M. S. Hacker and J. Raz (eds.), *Law, Morality and Society* (1977), p. 153.
[51] C. E. F. Rickett, (1980) 43 M.L.R. 136, 141.

decisions conflict, the Court of Appeal in a subsequent case may choose which to follow.[52]

(ii) *Inconsistency with a Privy Council decision*

In *Worcester Works Finance Ltd.* v. *Cooden Engineering Co. Ltd.*[53] Lord Denning M.R. said[54]:

> "Although decisions of the Privy Council are not binding on this Court, nevertheless when the Privy Council disapproves of a previous decision of this Court or casts doubt on it, we are at liberty to depart from the previous decision."

This statement can be seen as part of Lord Denning's battle against the rule that the Court of Appeal is bound by its own previous decisions, and it is not clear whether it is still authoritative in the light of the strictures of the House of Lords in *Davis* v. *Johnson*.[55]

(iii) *Other possibilities*[56]

In *B.* v. *B.*[57] the Court of Appeal held that section 1(1) of the Domestic Violence and Matrimonial Proceedings Act 1976 did not give a county court jurisdiction to grant an injunction excluding a spouse[58] from the "matrimonial home" where that spouse had a proprietary interest in the home. A few days later this decision was followed by the Court of Appeal in *Cantliff* v. *Jenkins*.[59] These cases caused some consternation as the plain words of the statute seemed to give the county court that jurisdiction. The point was raised again in *Davis* v. *Johnson*, and a five-member Court of Appeal was assembled.[60] Only Cumming-Bruce L.J. held that the earlier cases were correctly decided. Goff L.J. held that they were binding even though they were wrong. The other three members of the court held that they were wrong, and, on a variety of grounds, not binding. Lord Denning said that:

> "while the court should regard itself as normally bound by a previous decision of the court, nevertheless it should be at liberty to depart from it if it is convinced that the previous decision was wrong."[61]

Either the Court of Appeal should take for itself guidelines similar to those taken by the House of Lords,[62] or this should be regarded as an additional exception to *Young* v. *Bristol Aeroplane Co. Ltd.*[63] Lord Denning had long

[52] See above, p. 384.
[53] [1972] 1 Q.B. 210.
[54] At p. 217.
[55] Below. On the Privy Council and precedent see further below, pp. 397–398 and 400–401.
[56] See also *R.* v. *Secretary of State for the Home Department, ex p. Al-Mehdawi* [1990] 1 A.C. 876, above, pp. 376–377.
[57] [1978] Fam. 26, decided on October 13, 1977 by Bridge, Waller and Megaw L.JJ.
[58] Whether real, or for want of a better expression, "common law."
[59] [1978] Fam. 47, decided on October 20, 1977 by Stamp, Orr and Ormrod L.JJ. The couple were joint tenants.
[60] [1979] A.C. 264. Lord Denning M.R., Sir George Baker P., Goff, Shaw and Cumming-Bruce L.JJ.: described by Lord Denning as "a court of all the talents" [1979] A.C. 264, 271.
[61] [1979] A.C. 264, 278–282.
[62] See below, pp. 392–397.
[63] [1944] K.B. 718.

argued for such a change,[64] but had been unable to convince either his colleagues or the House of Lords.

Sir George Baker P. was prepared to distinguish *B.* v. *B.* on the ground that the welfare of a child was not involved as it was in *Davis* v. *Johnson*. If that distinction were not acceptable,[65] a new exception to *Young* v. *Bristol Aeroplane Co. Ltd.* should be created:

"The Court is not bound to follow a previous decision of its own if satisfied that that decision was clearly wrong and cannot stand in the face of the will and intention of Parliament expressed in simple language in a recent statute passed to remedy a serious mischief or abuse, and further adherence to the previous decision must lead to injustice in the particular case and unduly restrict proper development of the law with injustice to others."[66]

Shaw L.J. suggested a new exception to *Young's* case that was even narrower:

"in some such terms as that the principle of *stare decisis* should be relaxed where its application would have the effect of depriving actual and potential victims of violence of a vital protection which an Act of Parliament was plainly designed to afford to them, especially where, as in the context of domestic violence, that deprivation must inevitably give rise to an irremediable detriment to such victims and create in regard to them an injustice irreversible by a later decision of the House of Lords."[67]

The House of Lords unanimously dismissed an appeal; *B.* v. *B.* and *Cantliff* v. *Jenkins* were overruled.[68] However, the House strongly re-affirmed the rule that the Court of Appeal was bound by its own previous decisions, subject to clearly defined exceptions which did not include those advanced in the Court of Appeal. The argument in favour of *Young's* case was summarised by Lord Diplock[69]:

"In an appellate court of last resort a balance must be struck between the need on the one hand for the legal certainty resulting from the binding effect of previous decisions, and, on the other side the avoidance of undue restriction on the proper development of the law. In the case of an intermediate appellate court, however, the second desideratum can be taken care of by appeal to a superior appellate court, if

[64] *The Discipline of Law* (1979), pp. 297–300; *Gallie* v. *Lee* [1969] 2 Ch. 17, 37; *Hanning* v. *Maitland* (*No.* 2) [1970] 1 Q.B. 580, 587; *Barrington* v. *Lee* [1972] 1 Q.B. 326, 338. He temporarily conceded defeat in *Tiverton Estates Ltd.* v. *Wearwell Ltd.* [1975] Ch. 146, 160–161, but raised the point again in *Davis* v. *Johnson* and suffered a "crushing rebuff" (*The Discipline of Law* (1979), p. 299).
[65] That this distinction was not acceptable was subsequently conceded in the House of Lords.
[66] [1979] A.C. 264, 290.
[67] [1979] A.C. 264, 308.
[68] Lord Diplock alone thought that *B.* v. *B.* had been correctly decided, making the overall division of appellate judicial opinion eight all: [1979] A.C. 264, 323. That case had concerned the situation where the man was sole tenant. However, his Lordship held that an injunction could be awarded where both parties were joint tenants: as the facts of *Davis* v. *Johnson* fell into that category he was in favour of dismissing the appeal.
[69] [1979] A.C. 264, 326. Viscount Dilhorne, Lord Kilbrandon, and Lord Scarman expressly agreed with Lord Diplock's views on precedent: [1979] A.C. 264, 336, 340, 349. See also Scarman L.J. in *Tiverton Estates Ltd.* v. *Wearwell Ltd.* [1975] Ch. 146, 172–173 and in *Farrell* v. *Alexander* [1976] Q.B. 345, 371.

reasonable means of access to it are available; while the risk to the first desideratum, legal certainty if the court is not bound by its own previous decisions grows even greater with increasing membership and the number of three-judge divisions in which it sits . . . ."

The argument against is that "the House of Lords may never have an opportunity to correct [an] error; and thus it may be perpetuated indefinitely, perhaps for ever."[70] Litigants may be unable to finance a further appeal; the case may be settled; an insurance company or big employer who wins in the Court of Appeal may "buy off an appeal to the House of Lords by paying ample compensation to the appellant."[71] Lord Diplock responded by pointing out that in view of *Cantliff* v. *Jenkins* there had been no need for anything but the briefest of hearings in the Court of Appeal, and an appeal to the House could have been heard and decided quickly. The argument of delay and expense could also be used to justify any High Court or county court judge in refusing to follow a decision of the Court of Appeal that he thought was wrong. There is also the possibility of using the "leap-frog" procedure under the Administration of Justice Act 1969.[72]

Lord Salmon expressed some sympathy for Lord Denning's views, but said that "until such time, if ever, as all his colleagues in the Court of Appeal agree with those views, *stare decisis* must still hold the field."[73] In view of the large number of Lord Justices, keeping to *stare decisis* might be "no bad thing." He suggested that where the Court of Appeal gave leave to appeal from a decision it felt bound to make by authority and with which it disagreed, it should have the statutory power to order that the costs of the appeal be paid from public funds. This would be a very rare occurrence, and the cost minimal.

According to the Court of Appeal *stare decisis* does not prevent an English court giving effect to a change in a rule of international law notwithstanding the existence of English precedents based on the old rule.[74] It also seems that the Court of Appeal is not bound by its own previous decisions where it is the court of last resort, with no possible appeal to the House of Lords.[75]

(e) Can lower tiers rely on the exceptions to Young v. Bristol Aeroplane Co. Ltd.?

This question was answered in the negative by Lord Hailsham L.C. in *Cassell & Co. Ltd.* v. *Broome*,[76] but there have been cases where the

---

[70] *Per* Lord Denning M.R. in *Davis* v. *Johnson* [1979] A.C. 264, 278.

[71] *Ibid.* p. 278.

[72] See below, pp. 863–864. Lord Diplock [1979] A.C. 264, 324–325.

[73] [1979] A.C. 264, 344.

[74] *Trendtex Trading Corporation* v. *Central Bank of Nigeria* [1977] Q.B. 529, 554 (Lord Denning M.R.), 579 (Shaw L.J.) (a case on the scope of the doctrine of state immunity). Stephenson L.J. dissented on this point. The Court of Appeal's decision was followed by Robert Goff J. and the Court of Appeal in *I Congreso del Partido* [1978] Q.B. 500 and [1981] 1 All E.R. 1092, and Lloyd J. in *Planmount Ltd.* v. *Republic of Zaire* [1981] 1 All E.R. 1110; but not by Donaldson J. in *Uganda Co. (Holdings) Ltd.* v. *Government of Uganda* [1979] 1 Lloyd's Rep. 481. The House of Lords in *I Congreso del Partido* endorsed the general approach of the Court of Appeal in *Trendtex* but did not advert to the "precedent" aspect: [1983] 1 A.C. 244.

[75] Lord Denning M.R. in *Davis* v. *Johnson* [1979] A.C. 264, 282.

[76] [1972] A.C. 1027, 1054; above, pp. 381–382. In *Baker* v. *The Queen* [1975] A.C. 774, 788, Lord Diplock stated that a lower court could not rely on the *per incuriam* rule in relation to the decision of a higher court, but could choose between conflicting decisions.

Divisional Court or a trial judge has declined to follow a decision of the Court of Appeal on the ground that it was inconsistent with a House of Lords decision,[77] and the point cannot be regarded as settled. It is difficult, for example, to see that a trial judge should follow a decision of a higher court given in ignorance of a binding statutory provision. According to Lord Denning M.R., where decisions of the same court conflict, lower courts should follow the later case[78]; Donaldson J. disagreed.[79]

6. THE COURT OF APPEAL (CRIMINAL DIVISION)[80]

This court is obviously bound by decisions of the House of Lords. It is also generally bound by its own previous decisions and those of its forerunners, the Court of Criminal Appeal and the Court for Crown Cases Reserved. However, as the liberty of the subject is involved, *stare decisis* is not applied with the same rigidity as in the Civil Division. A decision may not be followed if it falls within one of the established exceptions to *Young* v. *Bristol Aeroplane Co. Ltd.*[81] An example is *R.* v. *Gould*[82] where the Court of, Appeal (Criminal Division) followed a decision of the Court of Crown Cases Reserved in 1889[83] in preference to a later conflicting decision of the Court of Criminal Appeal in 1921,[84] on the question whether *mens rea* was an essential ingredient of the offence of bigamy. In addition, Diplock L.J. stated in *Gould* that:

> "if upon due consideration we were to be of opinion that the law had been either misapplied or misunderstood in an earlier decision of this court or its predecessor, the Court of Criminal Appeal, we should be entitled to depart from the view as to the law expressed in the earlier decision notwithstanding that the case could not be brought within any of the exceptions laid down in *Young* v. *Bristol Aeroplane Co. Ltd.*"[85]

It has been uncertain whether this power is available wherever the court is convinced that the earlier decision is wrong, as this *dictum* suggests, or only

---

[77] *R.* v. *Northumberland Compensation Appeal Tribunal, ex p. Shaw* [1951] 1 K.B. 711, where the Divisional Court declined to follow the decision of the Court of Appeal in *Racecourse Betting Control Board* v. *Secretary for Air* [1944] Ch. 114 on the ground that it was inconsistent with the views expressed by the House of Lords in *Walsall Overseers* v. *L.N.W. Ry. Co.* (1878) 4 App.Cas. 30 and the Privy Council in *R.* v. *Nat. Bell Liquors Ltd.* [1922] 2 A.C. 128, which cases had not been cited. The *Shaw* case was not cited in *Cassell & Co. Ltd.* v. *Broome*. See also *Midland Bank* v. *Hett, Stubbs & Kemp*, above, p. 163; *The Alexandros* P. [1986] Q.B. 464.

[78] *Davis* v. *Johnson* [1979] A.C. 264, 279. See to the same effect *Taylor Woodrow Property Co. Ltd.* v. *Lonrho Textiles Ltd.* [1985] 2 E.G.L.R. 120, B. Hytner Q.C. (sitting as a deputy High Court judge); Warner J. in *Re Smith* (*a bankrupt*) [1988] Ch. 457.

[79] *Uganda Co. (Holdings) Ltd.* v. *Government of Uganda* [1979] 1 Lloyd's Rep. 481, 485: a trial judge should "seek to anticipate how the Court of Appeal itself would ... resolve the conflict."

[80] See G. Zellick, [1974] Crim.L.R. 222; R. Pattenden, [1984] Crim.L.R. 592.

[81] [1944] K.B. 718. See above, pp. 382–390. For an example of an application of the *per incuriam* doctrine, see *R.* v. *Ewing* [1983] Q.B. 1039, disapproving *R.* v. *Angeli* [1979] 1 W.L.R. 26 on the ground that it could not stand with the decision of the House of Lords in *Blyth* v. *Blyth* [1966] A.C. 643; and *R.* v. *El-Gazzar* (1986) 8 Cr.App.(S) 182.

[82] [1968] 2 Q.B. 65. Other examples are *R.* v. *Preece*, *R.* v. *Howells* (1976) 63 Cr.App.R. 28; *R.* v. *Maginnis* [1986] Q.B. 618.

[83] *R.* v. *Tolson* (1889) 23 Q.B.D. 168.

[84] *R.* v. *Wheat* [1921] 2 K.B. 119.

[85] [1968] 2 Q.B. 65, 69.

where overruling is in the interests of the defendant. The preponderance of authority supports the latter, narrower view. A clear statement was made by the court in *R.* v. *Spencer*[86]:

> "As a matter of principle we respectfully find it difficult to see why there should in general be any difference in the application of the principle of *stare decisis* between the Civil and Criminal Divisions of the Court, save that we must remember that in the latter we may be dealing with the liberty of the subject[87] and if a departure from authority is necessary in the interests of justice to an appellant, then this court should not shrink from so acting."[88]

This restriction does not apply to decisions on matters of sentencing. In *R.* v. *Newsome, R.* v. *Browne*[89] the Court of Appeal (Criminal Division) over-ruled two earlier decisions of the court[90] to the effect that a judge could not increase a sentence of imprisonment once passed to ensure that it would not be suspended even if this were to be done immediately. Widgery L.J. said[91] that if a court of five members is constituted:

> "to consider an issue of discretion and the principles upon which discretion should be exercised, that court ought to have the right to depart from an earlier view expressed by a court of three, especially where it was a matter in which the court did not have the opportunity of hearing argument on both sides."

The view that a "full court"[92] has greater power to overrule than an ordinarily constituted court was also held by the Court of Criminal Appeal,[93] although it has been rejected by the Divisional Court[94] and the Court of Appeal.[95] It seems in practice that a full court is not necessary where one of the exceptions to *Young* v. *Bristol Aeroplane Co. Ltd.* is applied, but is thought appropriate where overruling is contemplated on wider grounds.[96]

---

[86] [1985] Q.B. 771.

[87] The defendant's "liberty" appears not to be at stake where he or she has been fined but not imprisoned: *R.* v. *Burke* [1988] Crim.L.R. 839, C.A.

[88] *Ibid.*, p. 779, *per* May L.J. See, to the same effect, Lord Goddard C.J. in *R.* v. *Taylor* [1950] 2 K.B. 368, 371 (Court of Criminal Appeal), referring to the "bounden duty" of the court to reconsider an erroneous decision, on the strength of which "an accused person has been sentenced and imprisoned"; Lord Diplock, *obiter*, in *D.P.P.* v. *Merriman* [1973] A.C. 584, 605: the liberty of the court "to depart from a precedent which it is convinced was erroneous is restricted to cases where the departure is in favour of the accused": this *dictum* was applied by the court in *R.* v. *Jenkins* (1983) 76 Cr.App.R. 313, 318 (the better view here is that the consideration was irrelevant as the court was choosing between conflicting decisions and not overruling a single decision: J. C. Smith, [1983] Crim.L.R. at pp. 388–389), and in *R.* v. *Howe* [1986] Q.B. 626, 642.

[89] [1970] 2 Q.B. 711, decided in July 1970.

[90] *R.* v. *Corr, The Times*, January 16, 1970 and *R.* v. *Maylam* (unreported) decided on February 26, 1970. In *Newsome* and *Browne*, the actual sentences were suspended as it was "the only fair thing to do" (a form of prospective overruling: see below, p. 397).

[91] At p. 717.

[92] A term which usually denotes a court of more than the usual number of judges (*e.g.* five or seven for the Divisional Court, five for the Court of Appeal and seven in the House of Lords) and not a court of all the judges eligible to sit.

[93] *R.* v. *Taylor* [1950] 2 K.B. 368.

[94] *Younghusband* v. *Luftig* [1949] 2 K.B. 354: curiously, a criminal case.

[95] In the exercise of its civil jurisdiction: *Young* v. *Bristol Aeroplane Co. Ltd.* [1944] K.B. 718, 725.

[96] *Gould* was decided by a three-member court: see Zellick [1974] Crim.L.R. 222, 231–232.

In *Newsome* Widgery L.J. stressed that the court would be more reluctant to depart from an earlier decision where guilt or innocence was involved as distinct from the exercise of the court's discretion. In practice, the court seems reluctant to depart from its own previous decisions, even where it regards them as doubtful, and overruling would be in the accused's interests. Instead, the matter is left for the House of Lords.[97]

It is uncertain whether the Court of Appeal (Criminal Division) is bound by decisions of the Court of Appeal (Civil Division), and *vice versa*. Before reorganisation the Court of Appeal and Court of Criminal Appeal seemed not to be bound by each other's decisions.[98]

A decision of the court is treated as a binding authority notwithstanding that the appellant who has won the argument on the point of law has had his or her appeal dismissed under the proviso to section 2 of the Criminal Appeal Act 1968.[99]

7. THE HOUSE OF LORDS

Decisions of the House of Lords are[1] binding on courts lower in the hierarchy, including, if not especially, the Court of Appeal. In *London Tramways* v. *London County Council*[2] the House of Lords held that it was bound by its own previous decisions in the interests of finality and certainty in the law. It was accepted that a decision could be questioned where it conflicted with another decision of the House or was made *per incuriam*.[3] Other exceptions were suggested. However, as the House was the final court of appeal the correction of error was normally dependent on the vagaries of the legislative process. In 1966 Lord Gardiner L.C. made the following statement on behalf of himself and the Lords of Appeal in Ordinary[4]:

"Their Lordships regard the use of precedent as an indispensable foundation upon which to decide what is the law and its application to individual cases. It provides at least some degree of certainty upon which individuals can rely on the conduct of their affairs, as well as a basis for orderly development of legal rules.

Their Lordships nevertheless recognise that too rigid adherence to precedent may lead to injustice in a particular case and also unduly

---

[97] See the cases discussed by R. Pattenden, [1984] Crim.L.R. 592, 599–602. Pattenden's argument that the "special exception" in criminal cases no longer survives predates the reaffirmation of its existence in *R.* v. *Spencer*, *supra*.

[98] See *Hardie & Lane* v. *Chilton* [1928] 2 K.B. 306, C.A. versus *R.* v. *Denyer* [1926] 2 K.B. 258, C.C.A. and the statement of Lord Hewart C.J. in the Court of Criminal Appeal at 20 Cr. App. Rep. 185.

[99] See below, pp. 834, 837. Here the distinction between *ratio* and *dictum* is "meaningless in practice:" Cross (1977), p. 85; above, pp. 372–374.

[1] The dismissal by the House of Lords of a petition for leave to appeal against a decision of a lower court does not constitute implied approval of that decision by the House: *In re Wilson* [1985] A.C. 750, 756.

[2] [1898] A.C. 375: not "London Street Tramways" see the list of errata at the start of the [1898] A.C. volume (Cross (1977), p. 107, n. 4).

[3] See above, pp. 382–384.

[4] *Practice Statement (Judicial Precedent)* [1966] 1 W.L.R. 1234. Lord Denning M.R. and Lord Parker C.J. were also present. See R. W. M. Dias, [1966] C.L.J. 153; R. Stone, [1968] C.L.J. 35; J. Stone, (1969) 69 Columbia L.R. 1162. The circumstances surrounding the introduction of the Statement and the way in which it has been used are examined by A. Paterson in *The Law Lords* (1982), Chap. 6 and pp. 154–169 and G. Maher, [1981] Stat.L.R. 85. See also below, pp. 398–399.

restrict the proper development of the law. They propose, therefore, to modify their present practice and, while treating former decisions of this House as normally binding, to depart from a previous decision when it appears right to do so.

In this connection they will bear in mind the danger of disturbing retrospectively the basis on which contracts, settlements of property and fiscal arrangements have been entered into and also the especial need for certainty as to the criminal law.

This announcement is not intended to affect the use of precedent elsewhere than in this House."

A press notice issued at the same time[5] indicated that the statement was of great importance although it should not be supposed that it would frequently be applied. An example of a case where it might be used would be where an earlier decision was "influenced by the existence of conditions which no longer prevail, and that in modern conditions the law ought to be different." The change would also enable the House to pay greater attention to Commonwealth decisions critical of the House. As predicted the power has been used sparingly. Members of the House seem reluctant to state expressly that an earlier decision is "overruled" even where that appears to be the case.

The decision in *The Aello*[6] on a point of shipping law[7] was overruled in the *Johanna Oldendorff*.[8] As we have seen, the *Havana* case,[9] or at least the assumption upon which it was based, was overruled in *Miliangos* v. *George Frank (Textiles) Ltd.*[10] The decision in *Congreve* v. *Inland Revenue Commissioners*[11] was overruled in *Vestey* v. *Inland Revenue Commissioners (Nos. 1 and 2)*[12] on the ground that the earlier decision, on a point of construction of a Finance Act, had led to unforeseen results that were "arbitrary, potentially unjust and fundamentally unconstitutional."[13] The law as to the liability of the occupiers of land towards trespassers was restated by the House, with some differences of formulation among their Lordships, in *British Railways Board* v. *Herrington*.[14] The law as expounded, more restrictively, by the House in *Robert Addie & Sons (Collieries) Ltd.* v. *Dumbreck*[15] was, accord-

---

[5] See M. Zander, *The Law-Making Process* (3rd ed., 1989), pp. 181–182.
[6] [1961] A.C. 135.
[7] The test for determining when a ship has "arrived" in port. The expense of delay in discharging cargo from an "arrived" ship caused, for example, by congestion at the berths, normally falls on the charterer and not on the owners of the vessel.
[8] *E. L. Oldendorff* v. *Tradax Export* [1974] A.C. 479. This was the first occasion when the statement was clearly used. It has been argued that it had already been used in *Conway* v. *Rimmer* [1968] A.C. 910 and *British Railways Board* v. *Herrington* [1972] A.C. 879: see Paterson (1982), p. 164. On *Conway* v. *Rimmer*, see J. Stone, *op. cit.* n. 4 above.
[9] [1961] A.C. 1007: see above, p. 386.
[10] [1976] A.C. 443. In the same year the Statement was used in the Scottish case of *Dick* v. *Burgh of Falkirk* 1976 S.L.T. 21.
[11] [1948] 1 All E.R. 948.
[12] [1980] A.C. 1148.
[13] *Per* Lord Wilberforce at p. 1176.
[14] [1972] A.C. 879.
[15] [1929] A.C. 358.

ing to the headnote in the Law Reports, "reconsidered."[16] Then, the House in *R. v. Secretary of State for the Home Department, ex p. Khawaja*[17] overruled the recent decision in *R. v. Secretary of State for the Home Department, ex p. Zamir*,[18] holding that a person could only be removed as an "illegal immigrant" if the *court* was satisfied that the entry was illegal: it would no longer be sufficient that the *immigration officer* was satisfied and had some evidence for that belief. The issue concerned the liberty of the subject and did not fall into any of the categories in which the *Practice Statement* indicated the need for special caution.

Most spectacularly, the House of Lords in *R. v. Shivpuri*[19] overruled its earlier decision in *Anderton v. Ryan*,[20] which had misinterpreted the Criminal Attempts Act 1981 in holding that a defence of impossibility in the criminal law had to an extent survived the Act. *Anderton v. Ryan* had been adversely criticised by almost all the academic commentators, most notably by Professor Glanville Williams in an article in the Cambridge Law Journal.[21] Among the grounds for Professor Williams' criticism were that the House disregarded (1) the bulk of the relevant academic literature, (2) the Law Commission report that led to the 1981 Act[22] and (3) the plain words of the Act. Lord Bridge, who had been a party to the decision in *Anderton v. Ryan*, delivered the main speech in *R. v. Shivpuri*. He acknowledged that the earlier decision was wrong, that there was no valid ground on which it could be distinguished, and that it should be overruled, notwithstanding the "especial need for certainty in the criminal law."[23] He was undeterred by the consideration that *Anderton v. Ryan* was recent: "If serious error is embodied in a decision of this House has distorted the law, the sooner it is corrected the better."[24] He could not see how anyone could have acted in reliance on *Anderton v. Ryan* in the belief that he or she was acting innocently, and now find that, after all, he or she was to be held to have committed a criminal offence. A decision to follow *Anderton v. Ryan* would "be tantamount to a declaration that the Act of 1981 left the law of criminal attempts unchanged following the decision in *R. v. Smith (Roger)*."[25] He concluded by referring to Professor Williams' article:

"The language in which he criticises the decision in *Anderton v. Ryan* is not conspicuous for its moderation, but it would be foolish, on that

---

[16] Lord Reid's word at p. 879. Lord Reid (p. 898) and Lord Morris did, however, say that *Addie's* case was "wrongly decided." Lord Pearson regarded the *Addie* formulation as an "anomaly" which "should be discarded" (p. 930). Lord Diplock rejected it "as amounting to an exclusive or comprehensive statement" of the duty owed to a trespasser (p. 941). Lord Wilberforce spoke of "developing" the law in *Addie's* case (p. 921). See now the Occupiers' Liability Act 1984.

[17] [1984] A.C. 74.

[18] [1980] A.C. 930.

[19] [1987] A.C. 1.

[20] [1985] A.C. 560.

[21] "The Lords and Impossible Attempts, or *Quis Custodiet Ipsos Custodes*? [1986] C.L.J. 33.

[22] *Attempt, and Impossibility in relation to Attempt, Conspiracy and Incitement* (Law Com. No. 102, 1980).

[23] A reference to the 1966 *Practice Statement*, above p. 393.

[24] [1987] A.C. 1, 23.

[25] [1975] A.C. 476, also known as *Haughton v. Smith* [1973] 3 All E.R. 1109, H.L. Criticism of this decision had led to the 1981 Act.

THE HIERARCHY OF THE COURTS

account, not to recognise the force of the criticism and churlish not to acknowledge the assistance I have derived from it."[26]

Nine months later, in *R. v. Howe*[27] the House of Lords again departed from an earlier decision in a criminal law case, overruling *D.P.P. for Northern Ireland* v. *Lynch*.[28] In *Howe*, it was held that duress can never be a defence to murder: in *Lynch* it had been held that it could be raised as a defence by a principal in the second degree, albeit not the actual killer. Here, the arguments in favour of overruling were significantly weaker than in *R. v. Shivpuri*.[29] Finally, in *Murphy* v. *Brentwood District Council*,[30] the House overruled its decision in *Anns* v. *Merton London Borough Council*,[31] and held that a local authority owes no duty of care in tort to protect the purchaser of a house from economic losses caused by defects in the house. *Anns* was contrary to established principle, and overruling would restore certainty to the law.

Other invitations to the House to overrule a past decision have not been accepted. A remarkable example is *Jones* v. *Secretary of State for Social Services*[32] where four out of seven members of the House held that the earlier decision of the House in *Re Dowling*[33] on a point of national insurance law[34] was incorrect, but only three thought that *Re Dowling* should be overruled. The main "defector" was Lord Simon of Glaisdale, who stated[35] that the 1966 declaration should be used most sparingly; that a variation of view on a matter of statutory construction would rarely provide a suitable occasion for its use unless it could be convincingly shown that a previous, erroneous, construction was causing administrative difficulties or individual injustice; that the House should be reluctant to encourage litigants to reopen arguments once concluded; that there was much to be said for each side of

---

[26] [1987] A.C. 1, 23. Professor Williams' campaign on this issue has stretched over decades: see P. S. Atiyah, *Pragmatism and Theory in English Law* (1987), pp. 180–183. On *Shivpuri*, see J. R. Spencer, [1986] C.L.J. 361; P. R. Glazebrook, [1986] C.L.J. 363; [1986] Crim.L.R. 536, commentary by J. C. Smith; E. M. Clare Canton, (1987) 137 N.L.J. 491, also commenting on *Howe*, below.

[27] [1987] A.C. 417.

[28] [1975] A.C. 653.

[29] *Supra*. See [1987] Crim.L.R. 480, commentary by J. C. Smith; C. Gearty, [1987] C.L.J. 203; H. P. Milgate, "Duress and the Criminal Law: Another about turn by the House of Lords" [1988] C.L.J. 61; L. Walters, "Murder under duress and judicial decision-making in the House of Lords" (1988) 8 L.S. 61.

[30] [1990] 3 W.L.R. 414.

[31] [1978] A.C. 728.

[32] [1972] A.C. 944. Alternatively entitled *R. v. National Insurance Commissioners, ex p. Hudson*. See J. Stone, (1972) 35 M.L.R. 449, 469–477.

[33] *R. v. Deputy Industrial Injuries Commissioner, ex p. Amalgamated Engineering Union, In re Dowling* [1967] 1 A.C. 725.

[34] Whether a decision by a National Insurance Commissioner (adjudicating a claim for industrial injuries benefit) that injuries were caused by an industrial accident, was binding on a Medical Appeal Tribunal (adjudicating a subsequent claim for industrial disablement benefit).

[35] At pp. 1024–5. Lord Wilberforce would not have favoured overruling *Re Dowling* if its *ratio* had been narrowly interpreted (see pp. 995–996). Lord Diplock was in favour of overruling but recognised he was in the minority and so he reluctantly agreed that the appeal should be allowed (p. 1015). *Cf.* Lord Reid in *R. v. Knuller* [1973] A.C. 435, 455–456, where he expressed the view that the House should not overrule *Shaw* v. *D.P.P.* [1962] A.C. 220, notwithstanding that he had dissented in *Shaw* and still thought that it had been wrongly decided *cf.* Lord Hailsham and Lord Edmund-Davies in *R. v. Cunningham* [1982] A.C. 566, 581, 582. See R. Brazier, [1973] Crim.L.R. 98.

this case; and that *Re Dowling* was not unworkable and could in any event be altered more appropriately by Parliament.[36] In *Fitzleet Estates Ltd.* v. *Cherry*[37] the House refused to review a 1965 majority decision on a point of tax law, in the absence of any new argument, any change of circumstances or any suggestion that it was productive of injustice. In *Hesperides Hotels Ltd.* v. *Muftizade*[38] the House declined to modify the long established rule that the High Court has no jurisdiction to entertain an action for damages for trespass to land situated abroad.[39] The rule was accepted in other jurisdictions, a change might involve conflict with foreign jurisdictions and there had been no change of circumstances. Finally, in *President of India* v. *La Pintada Compania Navigacion S.A.*[40] the House declined to depart from an earlier decision[41] that the common law does not award general damages for delay in payment of a debt. Much of the injustice caused by this decision had been removed by a combination of legislative and judicial intervention; Parliament had declined to accept a recommendation from the Law Commission[42] that would have covered the case here, while accepting other recommendations in the area; and reversal of the common law rule would have the effect of overriding restrictions in the statutory provisions that had been enacted.

Paterson[43] has identified seven criteria relating to the proper use of the *Statement* which were articulated by Lord Reid, and which reflected the dominant consensus of the Law Lords in the mid-seventies both in what they said and in how they acted. The freedom to depart from a previous decision should be exercised sparingly. A decision should not normally be overruled if that would upset the legitimate expectations of people who had regulated their affairs in reliance on it; or if it concerned the construction of a statute or document; or if it was impracticable to foresee the consequences of overruling; or if there ought to be a comprehensive reform by legislation. A decision ought not to be overruled merely because it was wrong; there should be additional reasons justifying that step. Conversely, a decision should be overruled if it gave rise to great uncertainty, or was unjust or outmoded.

---

[36] It was so altered: see A. I. Ogus and E. M. Barendt, *The Law of Social Security* (3rd ed., 1988), pp. 284–285.

[37] [1977] 1 W.L.R. 1345. Similarly, in *Paal Wilson & Co.* v. *Partenreederei Hannah Blumenthal* [1983] 1 A.C. 854 the House declined to overrule the recent decision in *Bremer Vulkan* v. *South India Shipping Corp.* [1981] A.C. 909, which had "provoked serious disquiet among the whole commercial community" (*per* Lord Goff in *Food Corporation of India* v. *Antclizo Shipping Corporation (The Antclizo)* [1988] 1 W.L.R. 603, 606). One point was "the special need for certainty, consistency and continuity in the field of commercial law" (*per* Lord Brandon at p. 913). In *The Antclizo*, Lord Goff stated that the earlier refusal to reconsider *Bremer Vulkan* would not necessarily prevent the House from doing subsequently: he was "strongly inclined" to do so, but this was not an appropriate case as on the facts, the outcome of the review would have no effect on the disposition of the appeal (p. 607). See B. J. Davenport, (1988) 104 L.Q.R. 493.

[38] [1979] A.C. 508.

[39] *British South African Co.* v. *Companhia de Moçambique* [1893] A.C. 602.

[40] [1985] A.C. 104. See P.M.N., [1984] 3 LMCLQ 365.

[41] *London, Chatham and Dover Railway Co.* v. *South Eastern Railway Co.* [1893] A.C. 429.

[42] Law Com. 88 (Cmnd. 7229, 1978) Report on Interest: see the Administration of Justice Act 1982, Sched. 1. The relevant recommendation had indeed been rejected by the government: see P.M.N., *op. cit.*, p. 366.

[43] *The Law Lords* (1982), pp. 156–167.

In *Jones* v. *Secretary of State for Social Services*,[44] Lord Simon of Glaisdale suggested that consideration should be given to the introduction, preferably by statute, of a power for the House of Lords to overrule a decision "prospectively" (*i.e.* for future cases only). Such a power is exercised by the United States Supreme Court[45] and in several states in the U.S.A. This involves the express recognition that the notion that judges do not make law is a fiction, but avoids the undesirable consequences of retrospectively upsetting established arrangements.[46] There are difficulties in choosing the date of transition: for example, should the litigant who has successfully argued that a case should be overruled be entitled to the retrospective effect of that decision, notwithstanding the general determination that the rule should be changed prospectively? If the answer is no, litigants will have little incentive to mount the necessary arguments. Lord Devlin has opposed the general idea of prospective overruling on the ground that it "turns judges into undisguised legislators."[47] The House of Lords changed a rule of *practice* (as distinct from a rule of *law*) prospectively in *Connelly* v. *D.P.P.*[48]

In practice a decision of the House of Lords on an appeal from Scotland or Northern Ireland will be regarded as binding on English courts lower in the hierarchy on points where the law of the two countries is the same.[49]

8. The Privy Council

Decisions of the Judicial Committee of the Privy Council are not technically binding on English courts except in respect of matters where an appeal lies from such a court to the Privy Council.[50] They may, however, be highly persuasive.[51] The Privy Council will normally follow its own previous decisions, but is not bound to do so.[52] It is not bound to follow decisions of the House of Lords on common law issues, although the latter have great persuasive authority: the common law may develop differently in different parts of the Commonwealth.[53] A House of Lords decision on the interpreta-

---

[44] [1972] A.C. 944, 1026–7. See also his Lordship's statement in *Miliangos* v. *George Frank (Textiles) Ltd.* [1976] A.C. 443, 490, and Lord Diplock, [1972] A.C. 944, 1015.

[45] See, *e.g. Mapp* v. *Ohio* 367 U.S. 643 (1961); *Linkletter* v. *Walker* 381 U.S. 618 (1965); *Miranda* v. *Arizona* 384 U.S. 436 (1966).

[46] See generally W. Friedmann, (1966) 29 M.L.R. 593; M. D. A. Freeman, (1973) 26 C.L.P. 166; A. Nichol, (1976) 39 M.L.R. 542; Cross (1977), pp. 229–233.

[47] Lord Devlin, "Judges and Lawmakers" (1976) 39 M.L.R. 11, 20: reprinted in *The Judge* (1979), p. 12.

[48] [1964] A.C. 1254.

[49] Cross (1977), p. 20; *Heyman* v. *Darwins Ltd.* [1942] A.C. 356, 401 (Lord Porter); *Glasgow Corporation* v. *Central Land Board* 1956 S.C. (H.L.) 1: where the law of "crown privilege" was held to be different in the two countries; *Re Tuck's Settlement Trusts, Public Trustee* v. *Tuck* [1978] Ch. 49, 61 (Lord Denning M.R.).

[50] *e.g.* in ecclesiastical and prize matters: *Combe* v. *Edwards* (1877) 2 P.D. 354. In *Port Line Ltd.* v. *Ben Line Steamers Ltd.* [1958] 2 Q.B. 146, Diplock J. declined to follow a Privy Council decision that was in his view wrongly decided.

[51] See, *e.g.* above, p. 387, below, pp. 400–401.

[52] *Gideon Nkambule* v. *R.* [1950] A.C. 379; *Fatuma Binti Mohamed Bin Salim* v. *Mohamed Bin Salim* [1952] A.C. 1; *Baker* v. *The Queen* [1975] A.C. 774, 787–788.

[53] *e.g.* on the right to punitive damages in tort: the Privy Council in *Australian Consolidated Press Ltd.* v. *Uren* [1969] 1 A.C. 590 did not follow the House of Lords decision in *Rookes* v. *Barnard* [1964] A.C. 1129.

tion of recent legislation common to England and another part of the Commonwealth will however, be treated as binding.[54]

9. The Court of Justice of the European Communities

The decisions of this court on matters of Community law are binding on English courts up to and including the House of Lords.[55] It tends to follow its own previous decisions, although it is not bound to do so.[56]

10. Tribunals

Where there is a hierarchy of tribunals, the decisions of the appellate tribunals will bind lower tribunals. For example, social security appeal tribunals must follow decisions of the social security commissioners (formerly known as the national insurance commissioners).[57] Tribunals are not permitted to lay down precedents binding on themselves,[58] the emphasis, in theory at least, being on deciding each case on its own facts. However, the case law of some tribunals is systematically reported[59] and general principles tend to become established,[60] and the "essential differences in practice from, say, the House of Lords or the Court of Appeal . . . are not as marked as one might think."[61] In the context of social security appeals, a Tribunal of Commissioners has held[62] that in determining whether to be bound by a decision of a previous Tribunal, it should adopt and adapt the principles laid down in the 1966 *Practice Statement*[63] concerning the House of Lords, and not the principles laid down in *Young* v. *Bristol Aeroplane Co.*[64]

11. The Nature of Rules of Binding Precedent

Apart from the 1966 *Practice Statement*, propositions as to the binding effects of previous decisions have been contained in the judgments of

---

[54] *de Lasala* v. *de Lasala* [1980] A.C. 546.

[55] See above, pp. 297–308; European Communities Act 1972, s.3(1).

[56] *Da Costa en Schaake NV* v. *Nederlandse Belasting-administratie* (Cases 2, 8, 29, 30/62) [1963] E.C.R. 31; L. N. Brown and F. G. Jacobs, *The Court of Justice of the European Communities* (3rd ed., 1989) Chap. 16; T. Koopmans in D. O'Keefe and H. G. Schermers (eds.), *Essays in European Law and Integration* (1982); A. G. Toth, "The authority of judgments of the European Court of Justice: binding force and legal effect" (1984) 4 Y.E.L. 1.

[57] *R.(I) 12/75* (Tribunal of Commissioners); A. I. Ogus and E. M. Barendt, *The Law of Social Security* (3rd ed., 1988), pp. 583–584. A single Commissioner should follow a decision of a Tribunal of Commissioners on a point of legal principle unless there are compelling reasons why he should not: *ibid.*; *R.(U) 4/88(T)*.

[58] *Merchandise Transport Ltd.* v. *British Transport Commission* [1962] 2 Q.B. 173, C.A., in relation to the Transport Tribunal.

[59] In the context of social security, the Commissioners have emphasised that adjudicating officers and tribunals are bound by unreported Commissioners' decisions as well as reported: *R.(I) 12/75; R.(SB) 22/86*.

[60] J. A. Farmer, *Tribunals and Government* (1974), Chap. 3, pp. 171–180.

[61] *Ibid.* p. 175.

[62] *R.(U) 4/88.*

[63] Above, pp. 392–393.

[64] Above, p. 382.

decided cases. It has been pointed out that such propositions cannot form part of the *ratio* of a case as they are "necessarily irrelevant to the issues of law and fact that have to be decided by the court."[65] Professor Cross[66] has argued that this only seems applicable to statements of higher courts about the way in which lower courts should behave,[67] but that in any event statements about the rules of precedent are statements about the courts' own practice which fall outside the *ratio-obiter* distinction. The 1966 *Practice Statement* owed its validity "to the inherent power of any court to regulate its own practice."[68] The possibility that the Court of Appeal might change the rule that it is bound by its own previous decisions by a similar practice statement has been mooted.[69] However, Lord Simon of Glaisdale asserted that any change would require legislation,[70] Cumming-Bruce L.J. accepted loyally that the constitutional functions of the House of Lords include that of declaring with authority the extent to which the Court of Appeal is bound by its previous decisions,[71] and Lord Denning in any event failed to persuade his colleagues that a change would be desirable.[72]

E. PERSUASIVE AUTHORITIES[73]

Precedents that are not technically binding may be cited as persuasive authorities. The extent to which a precedent will be persuasive may depend on a variety of factors including the status of the court, the country in which it was located, the reputation of the judge, whether the relevant proposition formed part of the *ratio*, whether the judgment was considered or *ex tempore*[74] and whether the judge in the later case agrees with it. Thus the attention of the court may be drawn to the *ratio* of a decision of an English court lower in the hierarchy, to *obiter dicta*, to a dissenting judgment, to a decision of the Privy Council or to a court abroad.

Great weight will be attached to considered statements by the House of Lords whatever their technical standing. For example, in *Hedley Byrne & Co. Ltd.* v. *Heller and Partners Ltd.*,[75] the House of Lords held that the

---

[65] Glanville Williams, (1954) 70 L.Q.R. 469, 471; *cf.* Diplock L.J. in *Boys* v. *Chaplin* [1968] 2 K.B. 1, 35.

[66] "The House of Lords and the Rules of Precedent" in P. M. S. Hacker and J. Raz (eds.), *Law, Morality and Society* (1977), pp. 144–160. For the contrary argument that pronouncements on precedent do indeed establish rules of law, see P. J. Evans, [1982] C.L.J. 162, criticised by L. Goldstein, [1984] C.L.J. 88, with a reply by Evans, *ibid.* p. 108. For the argument that they establish rules of *customary* law, see P. Aldridge, (1984) 47 M.L.R. 187. For the argument that the 1966 *Practice Statement* established, or modified, a constitutional convention, see Lord Simon of Glaisdale in *R.* v. *Knuller* [1973] A.C. 435, at p. 485 and A. R. Blackshield, in L. Goldstein (ed.), *Judicial Precedent* (1987), Chap. 5.

[67] *Ibid.* p. 154.

[68] *Ibid.* p. 157; Salmon L.J. in *Gallie* v. *Lee* [1969] 2 Ch. 17, 49; Lord Denning M.R. in *Davis* v. *Johnson* [1979] A.C. 264, 281; Lord Salmon in *Davis* v. *Johnson* (above p. 389).

[69] *Ibid.*

[70] *Miliangos* v. *George Frank (Textiles) Ltd.* [1976] A.C. 443, 470.

[71] *Davis* v. *Johnson* [1979] A.C. 264, 311.

[72] See above, pp. 388–389.

[73] See R. Bronaugh, "Persuasive precedent" in L. Goldstein (ed.), *Judicial Precedent* (1987), Chap. 8.

[74] Lord Russell of Killowen has suggested that unreserved judgments should be approached with "great caution:" *op. cit.* p. 376, n. 49; *cf.* Lord Reid in *Haley* v. *London Electricity Board* [1965] A.C. 778, 792.

[75] [1964] A.C. 465.

existence of a special relationship could give rise to a duty to take care in giving information or advice; breach of the duty could in turn lead to an action for damages in respect of purely economic losses. The Court of Appeal had held that such a duty could not arise, following its earlier decision in *Candler* v. *Crane, Christmas & Co.*[76] The House overruled the *Candler* decision and endorsed the dissenting judgment in that case by Denning L.J. Having found that a duty of care *did* arise as the plaintiffs claimed, the House nonetheless found for the *defendants* on the ground that they had effectively disclaimed responsibility for the statements in question. There was much debate on the issue whether the observations concerning the duty of care were *obiter*.[77] Cairns J. in *W.B. Anderson and Sons Ltd.* v. *Rhodes*[78] regarded such a suggestion as "unrealistic":

> "When five members of the House of Lords have all said, after close examination of the authorities, that a certain type of tort exists, I think that a judge of first instance should proceed on the basis that it does exist without pausing to embark on an investigation whether what was said was necessary to the ultimate decision."[79]

Similarly, it became accepted that solicitors acting as advocates were entitled to the same immunity from legal action as barristers, notwithstanding that the view had been expressed in decisions of the House of Lords concerning barristers.[80]

The "neighbour principle" expounded by Lord Atkin in *Donoghue* v. *Stevenson*[81] can be regarded as part of the *ratio* of his speech, but not as part of the *ratio* of the House of Lords as a whole.[82] Nevertheless the principle was influential in subsequent decisions which extended the scope of the tort of negligence,[83] although the most recent decisions in the area have emphasised that it should be used cautiously and is not the sole determinant of the existence of a duty of care.[84] Decisions of the Privy Council may be strongly persuasive, particularly now that membership of the Judicial Committee is mainly drawn from Lords of Appeal.[85] The Privy Council decision in *The Wagon Mound (No. 1)*[86] is accepted to be the leading authority on remote-

---

[76] [1951] 2 K.B. 164.
[77] See W. V. H. Rogers, *Winfield and Jolowicz on Tort* (13th ed., 1989), p. 275, n. 7.
[78] [1967] 2 All E.R. 850.
[79] *Ibid.* p. 857.
[80] For the present position, see above, pp. 162–166.
[81] [1932] A.C. 562, 580.
[82] Two of the five members dissented and the other two did not expressly concur with Lord Atkin's formulation: see R. F. V. Heuston, (1957) 20 M.L.R. 1, 5–9.
[83] See, *e.g. Hedley Byrne & Co. Ltd.* v. *Heller and Partners Ltd.* [1964] A.C. 465.
[84] See, *e.g. Murphy* v. *Brentwood District Council* [1990] 3 W.L.R. 414.
[85] Similarly, decisions of the House of Lords and Court of Appeal are of high persuasive authority in the courts of the Isle of Man, given that the Privy Council is the final court of appeal from a Manx court: *Frankland* v. *The Queen* [1987] A.C. 576, P.C.
[86] *Overseas Tankship (U.K.) Ltd.* v. *Morts Dock Engineering Co. Ltd.* [1961] A.C. 388.

ness of damage in the tort of negligence, and has been applied in preference to the decision of the Court of Appeal in *Re Polemis*.[87]

The desirability of uniformity between Scottish and English courts on points common to both systems has often been stressed, particularly on the construction of statutes and revenue and taxation matters.[88] The citation of overseas authorities seems to be increasingly common.[89] Lord Denning would not, however, in practice have followed a decision of the deputy magistrate of East Tonga in preference to six decisions of the House of Lords.[90] There have been complaints that counsel, particularly in busy appellate courts, cite too many authorities both English and foreign[91]; at the same time, counsel owes a duty to the court to cite all relevant authorities whether for or against him.

Textbooks may be cited as authorities although they can never be binding.[92] Some treatises have long been accepted as authoritative guides to the law in previous centuries, including the Abridgments of the Year Books[93] compiled by Fitzherbert and Brooke, the treatise known as "Glanvill" dating from the late twelfth century, Bracton's *De Legibus et Consuetudinibus Angliae* from the thirteenth, Littleton's *Tenures* from the fourteenth, Fitzherbert's *Nature Brevium*, Coke's *Institutes of the Laws of England* first published in 1628, eighteenth century works on criminal law by Hale, Hawkins and Foster[94] and Blackstone's *Commentaries on the Laws of England* first published in 1765–69. These works are not cited often today, the ones on criminal law perhaps being referred to most commonly.[95] It used to be convention that living authors could not be cited as authorities, although their words could be adopted by counsel as part of his or her argument,[96] on the doubtful ground that while alive the author might change his or her mind.[97] This convention is no longer observed,[98] and books and

---

[87] *Re Polemis and Furness, Withy & Co. Ltd.* [1921] 2 K.B. 560: see *Doughty* v. *Turner Manufacturing Co. Ltd.* [1964] 1 Q.B. 518, C.A.; *Smith* v. *Leech Brain & Co. Ltd.* [1962] 2 Q.B. 405, 415, where Lord Parker C.J. indicated *obiter* that the *Wagon Mound* case enabled a trial judge to follow other decisions of the Court of Appeal prior to *Polemis*. The test for remoteness is now whether the kind of damage was reasonably foreseeable: the former test was whether the damage was the direct consequence of the defendant's conduct. *Cf.* Robert Goff J. in *I Congreso del Partido* [1978] Q.B. 500, 517–519.

[88] See, *e.g. Abbott* v. *Philbin (Inspector of Taxes)* [1960] Ch. 27, rvsd. [1961] A.C. 352; *Westward Television Ltd.* v. *Hart (Inspector of Taxes)* [1969] 1 Ch. 201, 212; *Secretary of State for Employment and Productivity* v. *Clarke, Chapman & Co. Ltd.* [1971] 1 W.L.R. 1094, 1102.

[89] See R. J. C. Munday, (1978) 14 J.S.P.T.L. (N.S.) 201, 203–207.

[90] See the (regrettably) fictional report of *Grenouille* v. *National Union of Seamen* reproduced in Denning, *The Family Story* (1981), pp. 219–220.

[91] See, *e.g.* Lawton L.J., (1980) 14 L.T. 163, 166.

[92] *Cordell* v. *Second Clanfield Properties Ltd.* [1969] 2 Ch. 9, 16: Megarry J. in relation to Sir Robert Megarry and H. W. R. Wade, *The Law of Real Property*.

[93] See below, p. 405.

[94] Sir Matthew Hale, *The History of the Pleas of the Crown*, published posthumously in 1736 but written in the previous century; William Hawkins, *Pleas of the Crown* (1716); Sir Michael Foster, *Crown Cases* and *Crown Law* (1762).

[95] See, *e.g. Button* v. *D.P.P.* [1966] A.C. 591; *R.* v. *Merriman* [1973] A.C. 584 (*Hale* and *Hawkins*).

[96] See, *e.g.* Vaughan Williams L.J. in *Greenlands Ltd.* v. *Wilmshurst* (1913) 29 T.L.R. 685, 687.

[97] Lord Reid, (1972) 12 J.S.P.T.L. (N.S.) 22. This convention was the basis of somewhat leaden jokes to the effect that certain celebrated works were "fortunately" not works of authority.

[98] See *Halsbury's Laws of England* (4th ed.) Vol. 26, para. 587.

articles by authors both living and dead are commonly cited.[99] In appropriate cases reference may also be made to principles of Roman law, and especially, in that regard, Justinian's *Digest*.[1]

F. DISTINGUISHING

A precedent, whether persuasive or binding, need not be applied or followed if it can be "distinguished:" *i.e.* there is a material distinction between the facts of the precedent case and the case in question. What counts as a "material" distinction is obviously crucial. The judge in the later case is expected to explain why the distinction is such as to justify the application of a different rule. If the distinction is spurious, the judge may be criticised or reversed or, if the case distinguished is generally regarded as a bad precedent, applauded for his or her boldness. There is no test or set of tests for whether a distinction is legally relevant; it all depends upon the circumstances of the case.

An example is provided by *R.* v. *Secretary of State for the Environment, ex p. Ostler*.[2] In 1956, the House of Lords in *Smith* v. *East Elloe R.D.C.*[3] ruled that a provision[4] that the validity of a compulsory purchase order should not be questioned in any legal proceedings, other than a statutory application to quash made within six weeks, meant what it said: an action to impugn an order on the ground of fraud could not be brought some six years later. However, in *Anisminic Ltd.* v. *The Foreign Compensation Commission*[5] the House held that section 4 of the Foreign Compensation Act 1950, which provided that a determination by the Commission "shall not be called in question in any court of law," was not effective to render immune from judicial review a purported determination that was in truth a nullity and thus not a "determination" at all. The decision in *Smith* v. *East Elloe R.D.C.* was adversely criticised but not overruled. In *Ostler* the Court of Appeal was faced with an ouster clause of the kind at issue in *Smith* v. *East Elloe R.D.C.*, and it followed *Smith* in preference to *Anisminic*, which was distinguished on a variety of grounds. For example, the point was taken that section 4 of the 1950 Act purported to exclude judicial review altogether whereas the provision in *Ostler* was more akin to a limitation period in that it excluded review only after a six-week period. It was said that *Anisminic* concerned a "judicial" decision and *Ostler* an "administrative" one. Their Lordships were not, however, unanimous as to their reasons, and Lord Denning M.R. subsequently indicated extra-judicially that he no longer regarded most of his own as sound.[6]

---

[99] For example, in criminal law cases references to books by Glanville Williams and J. C. Smith and B. Hogan are frequent; in administrative law, Sir William Wade, *Administrative Law*, (6th ed., 1988) and J. M. Evans, *de Smith's Judicial Review of Administrative Action* (4th ed., 1980) are similarly authoritative. See the splendid story by A. Arden, [1980] Conv. 454, 458 (review of *de Smith*).

[1] See, *e.g. Coggs* v. *Bernard* (1703) 2 Ld. Raym. 909 and *Dalton* v. *Angus* (1881) 6 App.Cas. 740.

[2] [1977] Q.B. 122.

[3] [1956] A.C. 736.

[4] Acquisition of Land (Authorisation Procedure) Act 1946, Sched. 1, Part IV, paras. 15, 16.

[5] [1969] 2 A.C. 147.

[6] *The Discipline of Law* (1979), pp. 108–109.

G. PRECEDENT AND STATUTORY INTERPRETATION

A decision on a question of the construction of a statute is binding to the same extent as a decision on other kinds of question.[7] Thus it is applicable in cases concerning the same words in the same Act and "in all cases which do not provide substantial relevant differences."[8] The same words appearing in a different statute may be interpreted differently, although a decision on the construction of a particular set of words may be used as a guide when other statutes dealing with the same or a similar subject-matter are considered.[9] If words which have been the subject of construction by a court are re-enacted by Parliament without alteration, a court will be very slow to overrule that decision but not always unwilling to do so.[10] Moreover Lord Wilberforce has stated that[11]:

> "Self-contained statutes, whether consolidating previous law, or so doing with the amendments, should be interpreted, if reasonably possible, without recourse to antecedents,[12] and that recourse should only be had when there is a real and substantial difficulty or ambiguity which classical methods of construction cannot resolve."

H. RATIO DECIDENDI AND RES JUDICATA

In its wider meaning the term "judgment" is used to cover the whole of the judge's pronouncement after the arguments of each side have been heard (e.g. as in "I will deliver my judgment after lunch"). In its narrower meaning it is used to cover the order of the court as distinct from the reasons for it (e.g. "There will be judgment for the plaintiff for £500"). Assuming the order lies within the judge's jurisdiction it is binding on the parties (res judicata). They may not reopen the issue that has just been determined, unless a statute has provided for an appeal.[13] Thus the court's order is binding on the parties under the res judicata doctrine; the ratio decidendi is binding on other courts in accordance with the principles outlined above under the doctrine of binding precedent. A startling illustration of the distinction was provided by the following series of cases. A testator, John Arkle Waring, left annuities to Mr. Howard and Mrs. Louie Burton-Butler "free of income tax." In 1942 the Court of Appeal in In re Waring, Westminster Bank Ltd. v. Awdry,[14] on an appeal in which Howard was a party, held that income tax had to be deducted. Louie was not a party as she was in an enemy occupied country. Leave to appeal to the House of Lords was

---

[7] Per Lord Reid in Goodrich v. Paisner [1957] A.C. 65, 88 and London Transport Executive v. Betts [1959] A.C. 211, 232.

[8] Goodrich v. Paisner, ibid.

[9] Ibid.; Lord Upjohn in Ogden Industries Pty. Ltd. v. Lucas [1970] A.C. 113, 127; R. v. Freeman [1970] 1 W.L.R. 788 (meaning of "firearm" in successive Firearms Acts).

[10] Royal Crown Derby Porcelain Ltd. v. Raymond Russell [1949] 2 K.B. 417, 429, per Denning L.J.; cf. R. v. Bow Road JJ., ex p. Adedigba [1968] 2 Q.B. 572.

[11] Farrell v. Alexander [1977] A.C. 59, 73. Lord Simon and Lord Edmund-Davies agreed with this approach cf. above pp. 343–344.

[12] i.e. the history of the provisions and the cases decided on them.

[13] See Chap. 17. In the case of courts and tribunals with a jurisdiction limited by statute there is also the possibility of judicial review under the ultra vires doctrine where the jurisdiction has been exceeded or abused.

[14] [1942] Ch. 426.

refused. Four years later the House of Lords in *Berkeley* v. *Berkeley*[15] overruled the *Awdry* case. Subsequently, Jenkins J. held that the *Awdry* case was *res judicata* so far as Howard was concerned notwithstanding that its *ratio* had been overruled in *Berkeley* v. *Berkeley* and that Louie's annuity would be dealt with in accordance with the latter case.[16]

I. LAW REPORTS[17]

(a) Introduction

Any legal system that is based to any significant extent upon judicial precedent requires an effective system whereby those precedents are reported and indexed. In theory, a case may be cited as a precedent even it if has not been reported. In practice, comparatively few cases are referred to in textbooks or cited in court unless they have been reported in one of the series of published law reports, although such references seem to be becoming more common.[18] Occasionally a judge has referred to an unreported case with which he was concerned as counsel or judge.[19] Indexed transcripts of all unreported cases in the Court of Appeal (Civil Division) are kept in the Supreme Court Library[20] and some are listed in *Current Law* and copies of unreported House of Lords decisions are kept in the House of Lords Records Office. Thousands of unreported cases decided since January 1, 1980, including all decisions of the House of Lords and Court of Appeal (Civil Division), are included on *Lexis* (Butterworths' computer-assisted legal research service). Until recently, the only condition for admission of a report has been that it has been vouched for by a barrister present during the whole time when the judgment was given.[21] However, in *Roberts Petroleum Ltd.* v. *Kenny Ltd.*,[22] the House of Lords stated that in future it would

---

[15] [1946] A.C. 555.

[16] *Re Waring, Westminster Bank* v. *Burton-Butler* [1948] Ch. 221.

[17] See generally Sweet & Maxwell's *Guide to Law Reports and Statutes* (4th ed., 1962); J. Dane and P. A. Thomas, *How to use a law library* (2nd ed., 1987), Chap. 2; W. W. S. Breem, in E. M. Moys (ed.), *Manual of Law Librarianship* (2nd ed., 1987), Chap. 4: "Primary sources: law reports."

[18] R. J. C. Munday, (1978) 14 J.S.P.T.L. (N.S.) 201, 207–216.

[19] *e.g. Wilkinson* v. *Downton* [1897] 2 Q.B. 57, 61; *Harling* v. *Eddy* [1951] 2 K.B. 739, 746 (Denning L.J.).

[20] From 1951, an official note has been made of all Court of Appeal (Civil Division) decisions (see (1951) 95 S.J. 266). A microfiche edition of the transcripts 1951–1980 is available from H.M.S.O. (see V. Tunkel, (1986) 136 N.L.J., 1045). Transcripts of decisions of the Court of Appeal (Criminal Division) from 1960 are held by the Criminal Appeal Office in the Royal Courts of Justice (Breem, in Moys (1987), p. 143). The arrangements for transcribing cases are considered by Breem, *op. cit.*, pp. 144–146, and S. Cole, (1988) 19 *The Law Librarian* 89.

[21] See *Parkinson* v. *Parkinson* [1939] P. 346, 348, 351–352; *Birtwistle* v. *Tweedale* [1954] 1 W.L.R. 190n: *Estates Gazette* report not admitted. *Cf. Baker* v. *Sims* [1959] 1 Q.B. 114 and *Smith* v. *Wyles* [1959] 1 Q.B. 164. A report by a person who is a solicitor or has a Supreme Court qualification (*i.e.* a right of audience in relation to all proceedings in the Supreme Court) has the same authority as if it had been by a barrister: Courts and Legal Services Act 1990, s.115.

[22] [1983] 2 A.C. 192. See R. J. C. Munday, (1983) 80 L.S.Gaz 1337; N. H. Andrews, (1985) 5 L.S. 205. Note the critical response of F. A. R. Bennion (*ibid.* p. 1635) and N. Harrison (Managing Director of the company which markets *Lexis*), (1984) 81 L.S.Gaz. 257. It is uncertain whether the Court of Appeal will adopt a similar stance, but note the remarks of Sir John Donaldson M.R. in *Stanley* v. *International Harvester Co. of Great Britain Ltd.*, *The Times*, February 7, 1983.

decline to allow transcripts of unreported judgments of the Court of Appeal (Civil Division) to be cited in the House without leave; such leave would only be granted on counsel giving an assurance that the transcript contained some relevant principle of law that was binding on the Court of Appeal and of which the substance, as distinct from the mere choice of phraseology, was not to be found in any judgment of that court that had appeared in one of the generalised or specialised series of reports.

(b) A modern law report

A full law report today commonly includes the following information:

The names of the parties[23]; the court in which the case was decided; the name of the judge or judges; the date or dates of the hearing; the headnote (a summary of the decision prepared by the reporter)[24]; lists of the cases discussed and cited; the previous history of the litigation, including a summary of the claims made and the result of proceedings in lower courts; the facts[25]; the names of counsel; the arguments of counsel[26]; an indication of whether judgment is reserved by the inclusion of the expression *Cur. adv. vult*[27]; the judgment or judgments[28]; the order of the court and an indication of whether leave to appeal is granted or refused; the names of the solicitors; the name of the barrister who reports the case.

(c) Law reporting[29]

The earliest law reports were contained in the "Year Books" compiled annually between the thirteenth and sixteenth centuries. These reports concentrated upon points of procedure and pleading rather than the final decisions of the courts, and were written first in Norman French and later in "law French" (an amalgam of English, French and Latin).[30] These are today mainly of interest to legal historians. Between the sixteenth and nineteenth centuries a large number of "private" or "nominate" reports appeared. Most were named after the reporter. They varied widely in their style and content, their accuracy and their reputation.[31] Some, such as those of Coke, Plowden and Saunders were of high authority. Others were regarded as of little

---

[23] Appeals to the House of Lords have since 1974 carried the same title as in the court of first instance: *Procedure Direction* [1974] 1 W.L.R. 305. Previously, the name of the appellant appeared first.

[24] The headnote may be inaccurate (see, *e.g. Young* v. *Bristol Aeroplane Co. Ltd.* above, p. 385) although modern headnotes are generally reliable. It may include a summary of the facts or simply be the reporter's version of the *ratio decidendi*.

[25] The facts stated in the judgments may be left unedited or the reporter may set out the facts separately.

[26] These are only regularly printed in a few sets of reports such as The Law Reports and Lloyds' Law Reports. Interjections from the bench may also be included.

[27] *Curia advisari vult*: "the court wishes to consider the matter."

[28] In full reports these are printed verbatim, in some, such as in the Criminal Law Review and the Solicitors' Journal, only summaries are given.

[29] See J. H. Baker, *An Introduction to English Legal History* (3rd ed., 1990), pp. 204–214; L. W. Abbott, *Law Reporting in England 1485–1585* (1973), reviewed by Baker, [1974] C.L.J. 156; P. Reeves, (1989) 86 L.S.Gaz. July 26.

[30] See J. H. Baker, *Manual of Law French* (1979).

[31] C. K. Allen, *Law in the Making* (7th ed., 1964), pp. 221–232.

value.[32] Some were in law French; most were in English. The focus of attention switched from the pleadings to the Court's decision and the best reports included the full reasons. The first to be published in more or less the form we have today, although not verbatim reports, were Burrow's reports of the eighteenth century. The first that regularly published reports of newly decided cases were Durnford and East's "Term Reports." The private reports are cited by the name, usually abbreviated, of the reporter or the reports, the volume and the page.[33] The year is not technically part of the reference but is normally included.[34] Most of the cases in the private reports were reprinted in *The English Reports* published in 176 volumes between 1900 and 1930. There was also a series entitled *The Revised Reports* edited by Sir Frederick Pollock and included such cases reported between 1785 and 1865 as were "still of practical utility."[35]

The patchwork coverage of private enterprise law reports was seen to be unsatisfactory.[36] In 1865 a council consisting of the Attorney-General, the Solicitor-General, two barristers from each of the inns of court, two serjeants and two solicitors was formed; in 1870 it was incorporated as "The Incorporated Council of Law Reporting for England and Wales" with as its primary object:

> "the preparation and publication in a convenient form, at a moderate price, and under gratuitous professional control of Reports of Judicial Decisions of the Superior and Appellate Courts of England."

The Council is not funded by the state and is non-profit-making.[37] Its reports are semi-official in that judgments appearing in the Law Reports are revised by the judges, and that this series should be 'cited in preference to any alternative.[38] The corrections may make the report conform to what was actually said; on occasion a report is changed to conform to what the judge meant to say, which is rather more controversial.[39] There have been three series of the Law Reports: the first from 1865 to 1875,[40] the second from 1875 to 1890[41] and the third from 1891 to date.[42] The Incorporated Council also publishes the (unrevised) "Weekly Law Reports" and the "Industrial Cases Reports." There are a number of series of specialist official reports including

---

[32] *e.g.* Barnardiston: see R. G. Logan, (1987) 18 *The Law Librarian* 87.

[33] *e.g.* Coggs v. *Bernard* (1703) 2 Ld. Raym. 909 (Lord Raymond).

[34] In round brackets. Where the year is part of a reference it is given in square brackets.

[35] See R. G. Logan, (1982) 13 *The Law Librarian* 23.

[36] See W. T. S. Daniel, *The History and Origin of "The Law Reports"* [1884].

[37] *Incorporated Council of Law Reporting v. Att.-Gen.* [1972] Ch. 73. The Court of Appeal held that the Council's purposes were charitable.

[38] *Westminster Bank Executors and Trustee Co. (Channel Islands) Ltd.* v. *National Bank of Greece S.A. (Practice Note)* [1970] 1 W.L.R. 1400; *Bray* v. *Best* [1989] 1 W.L.R. 167, 169; *Practice Direction (Law Reports: Citation)* [1991] 1 W.L.R. 1.

[39] See, *e.g. Ghani* v. *Jones* [1970] 1 Q.B. 693; R. M. Jackson, [1970] C.L.J. 1, 3; (1969) 119 N.L.J. 1011; (1970) 120 N.L.J. 423.

[40] *e.g. Osgood* v. *Nelson* (1872) L.R. 5 H.L. 636. A reference to this series normally includes the year of the decision (in round brackets as it is not technically part of the reference); the letters "L.R."; the volume number of the relevant series; the abbreviation for that series (there were 11 in all, running concurrently); and the page number.

[41] *e.g. Huth* v. *Clarke* (1890) 25 Q.B.D. 391. A reference no longer includes the letters "L.R." and there are six series: one for Appeal Cases and one for each of the five divisions of the High Court (reduced to three in 1888).

[42] *e.g. Ridge* v. *Baldwin* [1964] A.C. 40. A reference includes the year of the *report*, not the decision, in square brackets; the series (A.C.; Q.B.; Ch.; Fam.) and the page number.

the "Reports of Tax Cases" published under the direction of the Inland Revenue, the "Reports of Patent, Design and Trade Mark Cases" published by the Patent Office and the "Immigration Appeal Reports" published by H.M.S.O. There are also a number of series associated more obviously with private enterprise, of which the "All England Law Reports" is a general series rivalling the Weekly Law Reports.[43] The trend is for an increasing number of cases to be reported and for new series of reports to be started,[44] with concomitant problems of expense for law libraries and practitioners, duplication[45] and pressure on research time. Brief law reports also appear in an increasing number of daily newspapers.[46] These are usually printed shortly after judgment has been given, and are compiled by barristers and are so citable in court.[47]

The system of law reporting was examined by a committee which reported in 1940.[48] The committee did not favour any radical change, such as giving the Incorporated Council a monopoly of reporting or the licensing of reporters. The majority rejected the proposals of A.L. Goodhart, who wrote a dissenting report, that a shorthand writer should take down the text of every judgment, that a transcript be sent to the judge for correction and that the corrected report be filed in the court records and made available to any reporter or member of the public for a small fee. The reasons put forward were the cost, the extra burden on the judges and the fact that almost every decision of importance was already reported: "What remains is less likely to be a treasure house than a rubbish heap in which a jewel will rarely, if ever, be discovered."[49]

Decisions of the Court of Justice of the European Communities are reported in the *European Court Reports*, an official series, and in the *Common Market Law Reports*, a private enterprise series, which includes in addition reports of the decisions of national courts on Community law matters.

The most significant developments in the near future may lie in the field of the computerisation of statutes, statutory instruments and law reports.[50] Butterworths offer the American *Lexis* system, which includes English, Scottish and American materials[51]; and some European and Commonwealth materials.

---

[43] The criteria for the selection of cases for reporting in the Law Reports and the All England Law Reports are considered by N. H. Andrews, "Reporting Case Law" (1985) 5 L.S. 205, 225–231, based on information supplied by the editors of these series. See also, F. D. Cumbrae-Stewart, "The aim and form of law reports" (1985) 59 A.L.J. 616.

[44] R. J. C. Munday, (1978) 14 J.S.P.T.L. (N.S.) 201–203. See also D. Milman, (1987) 8 Co. Law. 242, noting several new series of company law reports.

[45] A glance at Sweet & Maxwell's *Current Law Citator* will confirm this.

[46] *The Times* has printed law reports for over 100 years. It has now been joined by the *Financial Times*, *Guardian*, *Independent* and *Daily Telegraph*: see M. Findlay, *The Law Magazine*, March 18, 1989, p. 31. These reports are indexed in the *Daily Law Reports Index* published by Legal Information Resources Ltd., which commenced publication in 1988 (with fortnightly, quarterly and annual cumulations).

[47] They must be distinguished from summaries of cases in the "news" pages of "The Sun" (etc.).

[48] Report of the Law Reporting Committee (H.M.S.O., 1940).

[49] *Ibid.* p. 20.

[50] See generally G. Bull, (1980) 11 *The Law Librarian* 34–40; *Poly Law Review*, Vol. 5, No. 2, Spring 1980; C. M. Campbell (ed.), *Data Processing and the Law* (1984) (introduction); and "Computers in Legal Work" (1988) 39 N.I.L.Q. 1.

[51] (1979) 130 N.L.J. 507.

PART II

SOLVING LEGAL PROBLEMS

CHAPTER 8

PROBLEMS ABOUT PROBLEMS

WE encounter a difficulty at the beginning of this part of the book by directing our attention to the solution of "legal" problems. How should such problems be defined? Are there distinctions to be drawn between legal problems and social problems? How effective are lawyers in solving legal problems? How far should lawyers be "creating" problems by identifying malpractice and abuse and making the victims aware of it? What is a problem?

These are issues which have been the subject of research and discussion in the last two decades reflecting the growing awareness of the existence of an unmet need for legal assistance with problems and the development of law centres and other agencies to meet it. They are central to the debate over the provision of legal services and the response to these issues will affect the formulation of policy.

This chapter explores some of these issues and Chapter 9 assesses the strengths and weaknesses of the major agencies currently involved in giving advice and solving problems. Throughout both chapters we shall be particularly concerned with the role of lawyers.[1]

A great deal of emphasis is placed on the role of courts in settling disputes. The law student learns much of his or her law from decided cases,[2] public attention is inevitably focused upon the adversarial contest, civil and criminal procedure is lengthy and complex, books on the English legal system (including ours) devote a considerable amount of space to litigation, and English procedure tends to individualise grievances and tailor them to the adversarial model.[3] Yet it remains true that only a tiny fraction of legal

---

[1] In the long run such concern may have to change depending upon the effect the Courts and Legal Services Act 1990 has on widening the types of people who provide legal services, see pp. 117–140, 144–149 above.

[2] Through the doctrine of *stare decisis*, see Chap. 7 above.

[3] It is, of course, true that a successful individual action will have an effect on the rights and duties of other people through the definition of the law, but there is no general provision as yet in the English legal system for a group or class action except in matters of company law. This can make things difficult, *e.g.*, in environmental matters where the residents of a whole area are disadvantaged. The Civil Justice Review recommended that there should be a separate study of the case for extending the availability of representative or class actions: *Civil Justice Review: Report of the Review Body on Civil Justice* (Cm. 394, 1988), paras. 274–276. As one means of fulfilling that recommendation, consideration is being given to the ways in which legal aid funding might support multi-party actions: *Legal Aid Board: Report to the Lord Chancellor* (Cm. 688, 1989), pp. 15–16 and 35–41. The potential of class actions and their use elsewhere is discussed in M. Zander, *Legal Services for the Community* (1978), pp. 227–232.

matters end up in court.[4] If it were otherwise the court system would simply collapse under the strain.

This is partly explained by the ability of lawyers to advise on and negotiate settlements to the mutual satisfaction of the parties to the dispute. Such settlements are an acceptable part of English civil procedure.[5] Again, some legal matters are non-contentious and would not, in any event, come to court. Other matters may be resolved simply by the giving of information or advice about the law.

However, it is now clear that many legal matters never emerge even for legal assistance, let alone litigation, because they are never identified as legal problems by the sufferers, or never reach lawyers, or, having reached lawyers, are not recognised as problems within the purview of the law.[6] This situation is not acceptable and the success of any scheme to provide legal services to the public should be judged on its ability to bridge this gap by involving lawyers in the resolution of all matters that require their assistance.

A. WHAT IS A PROBLEM?

This may appear to be an odd question to pose, but it has a bearing on our approach to the provision of legal services and the involvement of lawyers. Does a situation only become a problem when the sufferer identifies it as something about which he or she can do something? If the mood is one of resigned acceptance, that the situation represents one's life difficulties, that there is no help to be obtained in dealing with the matter, should we consider that such a person has a problem?

This is not confined to legal problems (although in many situations there may be an unrecognised legal problem) but has its effects in other areas as well. The failure on the part of the sufferer to appreciate that solutions might exist may be the result of a combination of factors including ignorance,[7] apathy,[8] complexity of the situation,[9] generality of the problem and the extent of financial or physical resources required to rectify matters.[10] When the need for assistance is not even recognised, there is considerable difficulty for any advice agency in providing assistance. The role of the lawyer or adviser in taking the initiative in identifying problems with which help can

---

[4] See pp. 494–496, below.

[5] The general question of settlements and the factors which may influence the parties are discussed in Chap. 10.

[6] This general difficulty has been termed "unmet legal need" and has been the subject of much study. See, *e.g.*, B. Abel-Smith, M. Zander and R. Brooke, *Legal Problems and the Citizen* (1973); P. Morris, R. White and P. Lewis, *Social Needs and Legal Action* (1973); Law Society, "Law Society's Memo No. 2—Unmet Need" (1976) 73 L.S. Gaz. 1061; A. Byles and P. Morris, *Unmet need: the case of the neighbourhood law centre* (1977); H. Genn, *Meeting Legal Needs?* (1982); D. Harris, *et al, Compensation and Support for Illness and Injury* (1984); The Committee on the Future of the Legal Profession, *A Time for Change* (1988), Chair: Lady Marre, ch. 7 (hereafter, the Marre Committee).

[7] Ignorance of the criminal law does not excuse from liability for its breach—ignorance of the civil law on the part of the public seems almost to be assumed. See pp. 417–418 below.

[8] See below, p. 417.

[9] H. Genn, "Who Claims Compensation: Factors Associated with Claiming and Obtaining Damages" in Harris, *et al* (1984), esp. pp. 70–76.

[10] The sufferer may recognise a problem but see no realistic opportunity of solving it, see *ibid.*, esp. pp. 73–76. See also the Marre Committee (1988), para. 7.15.

be provided becomes important, and it is in this type of work that the law centres have been particularly successful. The identification of the problem then is made by the adviser rather than the sufferer and the relationship between the *need* for legal services and the *demands* actually made by clients is exposed.[11]

If the provision of legal services is to be limited to those matters in which the sufferer realises that there is a situation of difficulty for which the law provides a means of solution and with which a lawyer can be of assistance much of the pioneering work of law centres would be nullified.[12]

B. WHEN IS A PROBLEM "LEGAL"?

The attribution of a particular "legal" character to certain problems underlies the research which has been done into "unmet legal need" for it is by no means every problem which requires the assistance of a lawyer in its resolution. Equally, not every problem with which a lawyer is asked to deal is a legal one since many lawyers are proud of their reputation as sound advisers on general financial and property matters. In any event, it would be pointless to define as legal problems only those which are *actually* dealt with by lawyers for that would exclude all those problems which never reach them, but perhaps should.

However, would it be realistic to define legal problems as those with which the private practitioner normally deals? This definition involves the combination of two factors—the selection of appropriate problems by potential clients[13] and, on presentation, their acceptance by the solicitor as appropriate for him or her to handle. The combination of these factors establishes a pattern of work to be regarded as normally appropriate for a solicitor and, arguably, a definition of legal problems. In fact, this definition would be highly restrictive because it depends upon the subjective views of both client and practitioner. If a client does not identify a failure on the part of a landlord to make repairs to a rented house as a problem appropriate to a solicitor, or if a solicitor considered such a matter outside his or her field, it

---

[11] For an analysis of this particular problem, see Adamsdown Community Trust, *Community Need and Law Centre Practice* (1978), pp. 36–37. The Marre Committee stated that it might be suggested that ". . . legal services could be divided into those which are needed (and so should, presumably, be guaranteed to all) and those relative luxuries for which there is simply a 'demand'. We do not believe that there is such a distinction. Access to legal services is a pre-requisite of a just society and we believe that this access should be provided to the extent that private and public funding is available to meet it": Marre Committee (1988), para. 7.9.

[12] It can be extremely difficult to draw the line between intervention on behalf of those suffering in the local community and the mounting of "campaigns." This has been one of the most sensitive issues in the development of law centres and is still unresolved. See R.C.L.S., Vol. 1, pp. 83–84 and the Law Centres Foundation, "A response to the Royal Commission on Legal Services" (1980). For the problems encountered by NACAB, see *Review of the National Association of Citizens Advice Bureaux* (Cmnd. 9139, 1983). See below, p. 422.

[13] This should change over the years in response to increasing awareness of legal services through, *e.g.*, advertising by lawyers and education in schools.

would not, under such a definition, be a legal problem. This cannot be right.[14]

There have certainly been criticisms of the relatively narrow view which private practitioners have taken of their work (a failing which results partly from the type of legal education currently provided) and it is true that the introduction of the legal advice and assistance scheme in 1973 was intended to give solicitors the opportunity to take a wider range of work. It did not succeed in this objective.[15]

An alternative approach is to attempt an objective definition of problems which have a legal component by reference to a list or catalogue of types of problem. This approach does not place the emphasis upon the problems with which solicitors *do* deal, but upon those with which they *could* deal. The list is composed of a variety of types of problem including those traditionally accepted as legal by both lawyer and client, those regarded as legal by lawyers but not necessarily by clients and those not normally viewed by either as legal. This approach was adopted by Abel-Smith, Zander and Brooke in their research into unmet legal need, published as *Legal Problems and the Citizen*. Their approach led them to choose 17 specific and common situations as the basis of a questionnaire.[16]

This approach was adopted because of the differing perceptions of what is a legal problem and the consequent inadequacy of a questionnaire which simply sought information on "legal problems." It is important to note what the purpose of the definition was before being too critical of the notion that legal problems can be objectively defined by reference to specific situations. The authors acknowledged that ". . . new needs will come to be recognised and new legal remedies will come to be developed," but asserted that ". . . at any time there will be some problems which are clearly perceived by lawyers or lay [people] as more 'legal' than others."[17]

An objective definition of this nature is inevitably open to criticism on the grounds of particular exclusions from, or inclusions in, the categories on the list and as to the extent of the categories themselves. However, there is a more fundamental objection. Such a definition involves the construction of categories within the general scope of the law and, though they may be widely drawn, is open to the same objection as a definition based upon the perceptions of solicitors. It tends to be *exclusive* rather than *inclusive*, in that our thinking may be confined to those matters which fall within accepted categories rather than accepting that all situations to which the law pertains

---

[14] If this definition were acceptable there would, presumably, be no unmet legal need except where a client could not afford to seek advice on a matter accepted as "legal" (see, generally, Genn (1984)). Despite the strange results of such a definition there is a good deal of evidence that the range of problems on which the public would expect to seek the advice of a solicitor is even narrower than the range of problems with which solicitors recognise that they can manage. See P. Morris, R. Cooper and A. Byles, "Public Attitudes to Problem Definition and Problem Solving: A Pilot Study" (1973–74) 3 Brit. J. Social Work 301, 309–310; Adamsdown Community Trust (1978), p. 44.

[15] See below, pp. 455–456.

[16] The situations were: taking a lease, repairs undone, attempted eviction of the client (a tenant), attempted eviction by the client (a landlord), buying a house, defective goods, instalments arrears, unpaid debt owed, taken to court for debt, death in the family, making a will, accidents, social security benefits, employment problems, matrimonial problems, court proceedings, and juvenile court proceedings. See *Legal Problems and the Citizen*, Chap. 8.

[17] *Legal Problems and the Citizen,* p. 110.

can give rise to legal problems despite the fact that there is no immediately available legal framework for their solution.

A definition of a legal problem as "an unresolved difficulty to which the law is relevant," may appear to be far too vague and begging too many questions.[18] However, it may form the basis of a new approach to problems in which lawyers and advisers will not seek to establish the legal nature of the problem and then find the relevant law, but will rather seek to establish the nature of the problem and then contemplate whether any part of the law might be relevant. Such a definition tries to indicate an approach, an attitude, rather than provide a litmus-paper test.

Three potential advantages of such an approach have been demonstrated by research projects and other developments in recent years. First, it diminishes the tendency to distinguish between legal problems and, for example, social problems.[19] Even in some official reports there are discussions of social need *or* legal need and the likelihood of overlapping problems is too often ignored. Any definition which helps to recognise that there may be substantial overlapping of legal and social issues, and that neither can be adequately dealt with in isolation is to be commended. Consequently, the call in the Report of the Marre Committee for a response to the unmet need in relation to social welfare law (including housing law, immigration law and the law of debt) is to be welcomed.[20] Secondly, the inclusive approach may act as a positive encouragement to clients to make use of legal services. It is often the case that a stumbling-block for those needing advice is how to identify the "correct" agency to approach.[21] The legal profession seems to have a distinct image and the number of matters which are identified by the public as appropriate to a solicitor is relatively narrow.[22] The adoption of a more broadly-based approach would help. Finally, the acceptance of a problem and consequent search for any law which might be relevant may disclose a novel application of the law or a new remedy.[23] It is certainly an approach which encourages the lawyer to use imagination in the solution of the problem.

We have considered alternative definitions of a legal problem and indicated what we consider to be the best working definition to adopt, but this discussion will remain largely academic (save in estimating the extent of unmet legal need) unless there is some effective way of ensuring that those who have legal problems, however defined, secure legal assistance.

[18] This sort of definition was adopted both by the R.C.L.S. (Vol. 1, para. 2.2), and by the Marre Committee (1988), para 7.3.

[19] This dichotomy is considered and criticised in Morris, Cooper and Byles (1973–74).

[20] The Marre Committee (1988), paras. 7.10–7.13.

[21] See, *e.g.*, Adamsdown Community Trust (1978), p. 41 and the Marre Committee (1988), para. 7.15 and Chap. 9.

[22] J. Jenkins, E. Skordaki, C.F. Willis, *Public Use and Perception of Solicitors' Services* (1989), Chap. 5; Adamsdown Community Trust (1978), p. 55; Abel-Smith, Zander and Brooke (1973), pp. 156–160; R.C.L.S., Vol. II, Part B, pp. 195–206; Research Surveys of Great Britain, *Report on Awareness, Usage and Attitudes towards the Professional Services and Advice Provided by Solicitors* (1986). See also G. Chambers and S. Harwood, *Solicitors in England and Wales: Practice, Organisation and Perceptions* (1990). See also, with regard to personal injuries, S. Burman, H. Genn and J. Lyons, "The Use of Legal Services by Victims of Accidents in the Home—A Pilot Study" (1977) 40 M.L.R. 47; Genn (1982); Harris, *et al* (1984). The research all relates to a period prior to important changes such as advertising by solicitors.

[23] See the Marre Committee (1988), paras. 7.9–7.14. An example of such imaginative use of the law is the application of the law of trusts to give an unmarried partner an interest in a shared home: *Cooke* v. *Head* [1972] 1 W.L.R. 518.

C. LEGAL PROBLEMS AND THE USE OF LAWYERS

Some writers would not accept the proposition that the best people to assist with legal problems are always lawyers. In an important article, Titmuss suggested that lay people are better advocates than lawyers in certain tribunals[24] and the Consumer Council doubted the wisdom of allowing lawyers to practise in the new small claims courts which it proposed.[25] These arguments are based on the disadvantages of applying established legal techniques in situations where speed, flexibility and informality are the objectives of the tribunal.[26] Of course, the Courts and Legal Services Act 1990 is designed to extend the types of people who may offer at least certain forms of legal services, but it remains to be seen whether this will make a dramatic difference by demystifying the provision of advice.[27]

However, whilst noting that view, we are primarily concerned with the passage of legal problems through to lawyers and the reasons why that passage may become obstructed.

1. WHO USES SOLICITORS?

The survey of what the private profession do and for whom, conducted on behalf of the Royal Commission on Legal Services,[28] reinforced the results of earlier, more limited, surveys[29] and has largely been confirmed by more recent surveys.[30] The range of problems on which solicitors are consulted is quite narrow, and of 27 categories adopted in the survey, seven accounted for over 80 per cent. of all matters taken to solicitors. These seven were domestic conveyancing (30 per cent.); dealing with the estate of a dead person (11 per cent.); making or altering wills (10 per cent.); divorce and matrimonial (12 per cent.); motoring and other offences (7 per cent.); personal injuries compensation (7 per cent.); and domestic property matters (5 per cent.).[31]

In the 1989 Law Society survey, it was shown that the public associate solicitors most closely with conveyancing and property matters (68 per cent.), divorces and legal separations (35 per cent.), wills and trusts (38 per cent.), and law and order and criminal convictions (30 per cent.).[32] Following prompting, the respondents in the survey also associated solicitors with disputes between individuals, matters involving claims and compensation, debt and motoring offences.[33]

[24] "Welfare 'Rights', Law and Discretion" (1971) 42 *Political Quarterly*, 113.
[25] The Consumer Council, *Justice Out of Reach* (1970).
[26] R. Lawrence, "Solicitors and Tribunals" [1980] J.S.W.L. 13.
[27] See Chap. 3, above.
[28] Survey of Users and Non-users of legal services in England and Wales, R.C.L.S., Vol. 2, s.8, pp. 173–298. The sample was based on 2026 consultations in 1977 which involved 1770 people out of 7941 households interviewed. Some 15 per cent. of adults used a lawyer's service in some matter in 1977: R.C.L.S., Vol. 2, p. 183. A more rudimentary analysis is published annually in the *Legal Aid Annual Reports* and now the *Annual Report of the Legal Aid Board*.
[29] *e.g.* M. Zander, "Who goes to solicitors" (1969) 66 L.S. Gaz. 174; Morris, Cooper and Byles, (1973–74); Abel-Smith, Zander and Brooke (1973); Adamsdown Community Trust (1978).
[30] Research Surveys of Great Britain (1986); Jenkins, Skordaki & Willis (1989), Chap. 5.
[31] R.C.L.S., Vol. 2, p. 197.
[32] Jenkins, Skordaki and Willis (1989), p. 14. See also the information relating to the use made by the respondents of solicitors: *ibid.*, Chap. 6.
[33] *Ibid.*, p. 15.

Whether this pattern of usage of solicitors is evidence of a restricted perception of the sorts of matters with which solicitors deal or of a failure of people to approach solicitors knowing that they could help is unclear. The Royal Commission survey showed that a number of people were aware that a solicitor could help, but, for a variety of reasons, failed to approach one. Other surveys have found a much more limited perception of the solicitor's role.[34] The 1989 Survey revealed that many people are aware of other sources of advice[35] and may well pursue them.[36]

Care needs to be taken in assessing most of these figures in the present situation as there are two important recent changes. First, more people are now permitted to undertake domestic conveyancing, which may mean that fewer people will see solicitors and this may cause solicitors to encourage greater use of their other services.[37] Secondly, solicitors are now permitted to advertise their services.[38]

It seems to be clear that not enough use is made of solicitors for the solution of legal problems. The reasons for this seem to fall into three categories: ignorance of what solicitors can do on the part of potential clients and a lack of preparedness in pursuing legal action, that is apathy; the public image of lawyers; and barriers against use, in particular cost and accessibility.

2. IGNORANCE AND APATHY

The problem created by people generally not knowing what services solicitors can provide is well documented. In the context of claims for personal injuries, it is clear that ignorance of the law dissuades potential claimants from seeking advice, and most people only seek legal advice after first obtaining advice from other services, which may be ill-informed and thus cause a person with a claim not to pursue it.[39] More generally, the Marre Committee was convinced by the evidence which it received that ignorance was a major cause of people not seeking legal advice when it was appropriate.[40] An aspect of the problem related to ignorance is that of apathy in the sense that a person says "it's not worth pursuing it" or "let's just forget about it" or "it's just one of those things." The Oxford Study shows that apathy is a major reason in explaining why people do not seek legal advice.[41]

The Marre Committee suggested that the solutions lie in four areas.[42] The first area is the teaching of legal awareness in schools, now being

---

[34] See the surveys cited at n. 29, above.

[35] Jenkins, Skordaki and Willis (1989), Table 19 showing, *e.g.* in connection with conveyancing, the alternative sources of estate agents, building societies and banks and, in settling disputes, the alternatives of accountants and financial advisers and, primarily, Citizens' Advice Bureaux.

[36] *Ibid.*, Table 20 showing, *e.g.* in connection with conveyancing, that expertise is the most important factor in determining the source of professional help and that solicitors were the preferred source to estate agents. In connection with settling disputes there was not so obvious a prime reason although the choice primarily appears to be between the perceived expertise of solicitors and the cheapness of CABx.

[37] This is one of the motivations behind the 1989 Survey and one of its conclusions: *ibid.*, p. 33.

[38] For further consideration of these changes, see Chap. 3, above.

[39] Genn (1984), esp. pp. 75–76, 65–67.

[40] The Marre Committee (1988), paras. 7.17–7.39.

[41] Genn (1984).

[42] The Marre Committee (1988), paras. 7.20–7.39.

undertaken through a collaborative project between the Law Society and the School Curriculum Development Committee on Law in Education.[43] The second area is that of public relations, by which is meant that good public relations exercises, as opposed to advertising, on the part of both individual lawyers and the professional bodies themselves should be encouraged. The third area is that of media advertising by individual firms on the basis of the Solicitors' Publicity Code, which would be of advantage not just to the firms but to potential clients as well. The fourth area concerns information from the professional bodies, directed to specific areas,[44] rather than generalised campaigns, which tend to be both expensive and ineffective.

3. THE PUBLIC IMAGE

It has been convincingly argued that the image of an advice-giving agency is crucial because it is at the stage of identification of the appropriate agency that most people are obstructed on the way to the solution of their problem.[45] A strong image will assist in this identification, although it can act negatively as well as positively. The Marre Committee made it clear that the image of lawyers is a particular problem. The Committee identified two aspects of the problem. First, there is a fear of lawyers. The Committee took the view that lawyers are unapproachable because of the inaccessibility of premises and their unwelcoming nature, because the methods of work do not tie in with the needs of clients, and because of a lack of response to the needs of linguistic minorities. Thus they recommended greater use of shop floor premises, encouraged innovative work practices, emphasised the need for interpreters and encouraged the professional bodies to assist people from different ethnic and cultural backgrounds to become established as lawyers.[46] Secondly, there is dissatisfaction with laywers. It did not appear that this was a major problem.[47] Nevertheless, the occasional problems of delay, inefficiency or incompetence, overcharging, unhelpfulness, inconsiderateness and lack of communication were felt to be of sufficient concern to demand redress by the professions.[48]

The 1989 Law Society survey showed that "the image of solicitors amongst the general public is good but not outstanding."[49] In comparison with accountants, bank managers, NHS doctors and estate agents, they were found to be as easy to talk to as bank managers and easier to talk to than all the others bar NHS doctors, to be easier to understand than accountants and estate agents, to be more efficient than accountants and estate agents, to be

---

[43] See A. Phillips, "A new approach to law" (1988) 138 N.L.J. 742.

[44] e.g. the Accident Legal Advice Scheme, see, p. 442, below; see chapters 3 and 9, generally, for further consideration. There is some evidence that these are successful: Jenkins, Skordaki and Willis (1989), Chap. 7.

[45] In the report of the Adamsdown Community Trust (1978), pp. 41–46.

[46] The Marre Committee (1988), paras. 7.40–7.47. Addressing the response of the law to the needs of people from different cultural backgrounds is only just beginning and the research is scarce. See, however, Jenkins, Skordaki and Willis (1989), Chap. 10.

[47] 7 per cent. of people who had used a solicitor for personal business during the previous three years were very dissatisfied and 7 per cent. were somewhat dissatisfied, which is broadly the same as shown by other surveys: ibid., p. 12.

[48] The Marre Committee (1988), paras. 7.48–7.93. See, further, Chap. 3, above. The 1989 Survey found that the main reason for dissatisfaction was delay, followed by inefficiency, expense, poor advice and lack of communication: Jenkins, Skordaki and Willis (1989), p. 12.

[49] Ibid., p. 9.

more hardworking than accountants, bank managers and estate agents, to be as dependable as bank managers and more dependable than accountants and estate agents, to be as up-to-date as accountants and more up-to-date than estate agents.[50] Solicitors were found to be "mainly on the make" or "after your money" only less so than estate agents and to be regarded as reasonably honest.[51] In conclusion, the Survey indicated that its results demanded an emphasis on improvements in practice management and that the service could be faster and more responsive to users' needs.[52]

It is interesting to note the different sorts of problems brought to lawyers in law centres and other advice agencies. They do not seem to be burdened with the same difficulties as the private profession, presumably partly because of the different image of the agency involved and the different expectations of the client involved.[53]

4. BARRIERS

We have identified difficulties which may be encountered in realising that a problem has a legal dimension and in connecting that problem to the sort of work with which lawyers are commonly understood to deal. There are, however, further barriers in the way of those needing legal advice, notably its cost and its accessibility.

The bodies and researchers which have considered the problem of access to lawyers all conclude that cost has a deterrent effect on seeking legal advice initially and then pursuing a claim.[54] This is not surprising in view of the apparent ignorance of the legal aid scheme.[55]

The second barrier is that of the accessibility of lawyers. If there are not enough lawyers, or they are not in the right place, knowing that a solicitor can be of assistance is of no value.[56]

It is inappropriate simply to throw money at these problems in the hope that they will be consequently solved, since the resources available for deployment are necessarily limited. Consequently, the recommendations made by, for example, the Marre Committee are much more specific in their treatment of the problem. Whilst assistance with cost and redeployment of lawyers is part of the answer to the failure of many people to use lawyers, they are clearly not the whole answer. Indeed, public education about the nature of legal problems and the role of lawyers in solving them might be much more effective in the long run.

D. UNMET LEGAL NEED

It may appear that we consider that every problem with a legal component

---

[50] *Ibid.*, Table 2.

[51] *Ibid.*, Table 2.

[52] *Ibid.*, p. 33.

[53] This is the experience of the Adamsdown Community and Advice Centre (1978) and has been one of the strengths of Citizens' Advice Bureaux—they have a very strong *generalist* image. For a broad analysis of the comparative problems taken to solicitors, CABx and law centres, see *33rd Legal Aid Annual Report* [1982–3], p. 57.

[54] R.C.L.S., Vol. 1, pp. 48–49; Vol. 2, p. 262; Genn (1984), esp. pp. 73–74; Marre Committee (1988), paras. 7.15 and Chaps. 8 and 10; *Civil Justice Review* (1989), Chap. 6.

[55] Genn (1984), esp. p. 67.

[56] See the Marre Committee (1988), paras. 7.94–7.108, and see, further, Chap. 3, above.

requires legal assistance, for we have not proposed any other criterion for the provision of legal services than that a legal problem exists. This may seem a profligate approach, yet just as there are difficulties in defining legal problems so there are difficulties in defining when an individual *needs* assistance. It is obvious that the circumstances, financial resources and personal competence of individuals differ, as will the subjective importance of the matter. How can a general proposition of need be formulated when there are so many personal variables? Should any such proposition even be attempted?

In conducting their pioneering survey,[57] Abel-Smith, Zander and Brooke were faced with this problem. The solution they adopted was to assess, in respect of each category of problems identified,[58] what would constitute ". . . a risk of substantial loss or disadvantage which would be important for the individual concerned."[59] This standard differed for each category and it is difficult to see how it could be translated into a more general form. Zander later acknowledged that the decisions as to what amounted to a need for advice in each category were conservative, highly artificial and suitable only for research purposes, and he described the test as ". . . necessarily crude and inadequate."[60] Such comments illustrate the exceptional difficulty of defining need. Others have not made the attempt.[61]

In respect of the provision of legal aid, the test of need (usually described as a "merit" test) is based upon whether a solicitor would advise a private client, with sufficient means to pay the costs, to assert or dispute the claim.[62] A similar test can hardly be applied to legal advice.

The Royal Commission on Legal Services recommended that an initial half-hour's worth of advice should be provided free of charge to anyone who requests it, despite the possibilities of abuse by those who have adequate financial resources.[63] This recommendation, which has not been implemented, appears to accept that legal need can be defined by reference to the existence of a legal problem on which an individual wishes to be advised, albeit that part of the half-hour would be used to examine the case and determine the "need" for further advice. At least the individual concerned would have got to the solicitor who might then be able to satisfy those further needs.

If it be conceded that the need for legal advice arises from the existence of a legal problem, the difficulties in meeting that need would appear to have been exposed earlier in the chapter. However, studies demonstrate that obstructions on the way of obtaining legal advice have different effects on different sorts of people.

The most obvious differential obstruction is cost. Some studies show that it is those in the higher socio-economic groups that use lawyers more often

---

[57] *Legal Problems and the Citizen* (1973).
[58] The categories are listed in n. 16 above.
[59] *Ibid.*, p. 12.
[60] *Legal Services for the Community* (1978), p. 280.
[61] See, *e.g.* the Marre Community (1988), para. 7.10.
[62] This is an interpretation of the statutory provision contained in the Legal Aid Act 1988, s.15(2), used in deciding eligibility. See further pp. 509–510 below.
[63] R.C.L.S., Vol. 1, pp. 134–135. The Marre Committee (1988), para. 7.35, comments favourably on the adoption of such schemes by individual firms.

than those in the lower groups.[64] On the basis of this evidence, it has been suggested that poverty is the primary cause of the failure to seek legal advice,[65] and it has been proposed that the failure is due to a lack of "legal competence" among the less affluent who suffer not only from lack of money, but also from lack of influence, lack of energy and lack of awareness.[66]

One important study, the Oxford Study suggests, however, that people from the higher socio-economic groups are *less* likely to make a claim for damages consequent upon personal injury being suffered.[67] The most important factor in determining whether an accident victim obtains damages for injuries was found to be access to advice, both pre-legal and legal, which may be offered without it even being sought.[68] The importance of pre-legal advice was considerable. Such advice came from a number of sources, not all of them well informed. It came from the following advisers: trade union, medical, employer, police, potential defendant, AA/RAC, the advisee's own insurance company, workmate or fellow patient, friend, relative.[69] This finding confirms the need for considerable attention to be paid to general public education, to the various existing advice agencies and to such people as counter clerks, court officials, doctors and others in official agencies.[70] Taking in part a similar line, the Civil Justice Review has recommended staff training to enable court staff to give direct assistance to members of the public in the handling of their cases.[71]

Needless to say, the answer to the problem of unmet legal need does not lie solely in the development of advice agencies. Not all recipients of damages in the Study received "pre-legal advice." The evidence of the Users' Survey of the Royal Commission on Legal Services suggested that three quarters of the people who sought legal advice had received no help from people outside their household on the matter in question.[72] Further it suggested that of those people who did not go to a lawyer, a higher proportion had received help from outside the household, and of that group only one-quarter had received advice to go to a lawyer which they had ignored.[73]

---

[64] Amongst the studies which have demonstrated this factor are Abel-Smith, Zander and Brooke (1973) (U.K.); M. Cass and R. Sackville, *Legal Needs of the Poor* (1975) (Australian Government Commission of Inquiry into Poverty); B. Curran, *The Legal Needs of the Public: The Final Report of a National Survey* (1977) (American Bar Association—American Bar Foundation study); *Survey of Users and Non-users of Legal Services in England and Wales*, R.C.L.S., Vol. 2, s.8; Jenkins, Skordaki and Willis (1989), Table 12. The 1989 Law Society Survey showed that skilled manual workers "have an unfavourable image [of solicitors] compared with other social classes. Not surprisingly the higher social classes award solicitors the best association scores for 'easy to talk to' and 'easy to understand' ": *ibid.*, p. 11.

[65] Partly, according to Zander, because the researchers concentrated on the poor, without extending the survey to the whole population: *Legal Services for the Community*, p. 288.

[66] J. Carlin and J. Howard, "Legal Representation and Class Justice" (1965) 12 U.C.L.A. Law Review 381.

[67] Genn (1984), esp. pp. 51–56, Table 2.6.

[68] *Ibid.*, pp. 65–67, 76.

[69] *Ibid.*, Table 2.11. Similar conclusions may be drawn from the 1989 Law Society Survey: Jenkins, Skordaki and Willis (1989), p. 19.

[70] See also M. Zander, *Legal Services for the Community* (1978) pp. 288–290; A. Phillips, "Social Work and the Delivery of Legal Services" (1979) 42 M.L.R. 29.

[71] *Civil Justice Review* (1989), para. 363.

[72] R.C.L.S., Vol. 2, p. 207, para. 8.127.

[73] R.C.L.S., Vol. 2, p. 262, para. 8.395.

Such contrary evidence does not denigrate the value of pre-legal advice, but suggests that, as would be expected, it is not the only significant factor in determining whether, and if so why and how, people seek legal advice.

The Oxford Study pointed out other significant factors in assessing the kinds of people who do not seek legal advice for a claim for damages for personal injuries. Of particular interest, is the finding that, proportionately, women were less likely to seek damages, although, if they did, they were more likely to be successful. Two other groups which were under-represented in terms of making such claims were the young and the elderly.[74] The needs here may well be partly dealt with by educational improvements and the importance of changing work practices and the image of lawyers.

It is quite possible that the extent of unmet legal need can never be ascertained and that which can be ascertained cannot adequately be explained. The barriers are clear enough, what remains unclear is why some people are able to surmount them when others fail miserably.

E. INTERVENTION OF LAWYERS—THE "CREATING" OF LEGAL PROBLEMS

Lawyers have not usually been slow in their individual involvement with causes and with legal reform, but questions have arisen over the extent to which it is proper to intervene in socio-legal problems as part of a professional service. The law centre, in particular, has taken a broad view of its obligation to service the local community and some have been active in stimulating and articulating local protest. Is this proper?

The Royal Commission on Legal Services concluded that this sort of work should *not* be part of the responsibilities of the citizens' law centres that were proposed.[75] What was identified as ". . . general community work . . . organising groups to bring pressure to bear . . . becoming a focus in the neighbourhood for campaigns,"[76] was said to be inappropriate for a legal service. The Commission took the view that the responsibility of a legal service was the provision of legal advice and assistance to individuals, that community action tends to involve only one section of the community, and that the independence of a centre is compromised if it becomes a base for campaigns. Consequently, they recommended that "campaigning" should be funded from elsewhere and not undertaken by law centres.

The Report was published after a very interesting and well-argued case was made by the Adamsdown Community Trust[77] for precisely the sort of intervention which the Report proscribed.[78] Independence was not compromised, it was stated, and although the identification of causes deserving of

---

[74] Genn (1984), esp. pp. 51–56, 58–65, Table 2.12. The 1989 Law Society Survey shows that the above average users of solicitors for personal matters were 25–34 year olds, people in professional/managerial jobs, and people from the South East outside London and from the South West. The below average users were people 55+, people in unskilled manual jobs, single people, and people from the North and East Midlands: Jenkins, Skordaki and Willis (1989), Table 12.

[75] R.C.L.S., Vol. 1, pp. 83–84. See p. 461 below.

[76] *Ibid.*, p. 83, para. 8.19.

[77] Adamsdown Community Trust (1978).

[78] The projects described in the survey concerned a provisional slum clearance programme and roads and pavements in disrepair in the Adamsdown area.

support and finance from the advice agency might be questionable, in practice only those problems which gave real cause for community concern could be pursued successfully because of the need for public support. It was also noted that interventionist action could include leafletting in the area, talks to local groups and the preparation of kits and materials as well as the organisation of pressure groups and similar activities.

There may be difficulties in particular law centres in finding the right balance between assisting clients in individual cases and taking on group work or projects, but it seems unduly restrictive to deny that the latter was a proper role for lawyers to play.

CHAPTER 9

INFORMATION AND ADVICE SERVICES

By discussing in the preceding chapter the ways in which the public may perceive a problem as a "legal" problem and the steps which the profession might take to assist in the identification of problems which require legal advice for their solution we have already indicated that we are concerned, in the main, with the provision of information and advice by lawyers. However, legal advice is not provided solely by lawyers and it is certainly not restricted to those operating within the professional structure described in Chapter 3.[1] In this chapter we shall deal with the major advice-giving agencies prior to a discussion of the arrangements under which the private profession and the law centres provide legal advice and assistance.

A. THE SPECIAL FEATURES OF INFORMATION AND ADVICE PROVISION

A person may seek advice for one or more purposes and it is important to distinguish those who may need help in establishing whether they have a problem, those who need help in establishing what action they can take and those who need help in pursuing a remedy. Even when the problem has been identified as having a legal perspective it is by no means certain that the client will conclude that a solicitor is the most appropriate source of advice. Different agencies may assist in different situations and lawyers still labour under the handicap of their public image.[2]

1. WHICH AGENCY?

What are the factors which influence the choice of a particular agency? Whilst there may be circumstances which influence individuals in their selection of an adviser,[3] it seems likely that the crucial factors are availability, cost and reputation.

The distribution of advice agencies around the country leaves large areas (especially the rural districts) without some of the basic agencies,[4] and even

---

[1] See particularly pp. 120–149 above.
[2] R.C.L.S., Vol. 1, pp. 33–36, 45.
[3] For example, previous contact with a particular agency; personal knowledge of existing agencies; recommendations from friends.
[4] See the maps taken from various sources collected in *The Fourth Right of Citizenship*, a National Consumer Council Discussion Paper (1977), pp. 47–55. For an analysis of the especial problems of rural areas, see *Rural Advice and Information*, NACAB Occasional

within urban areas it is unusual to find solicitors, in particular, located in the districts with the greatest density of population.[5] Advice needs to be locally available.

The cost of obtaining advice becomes significant when a client considers using professional agencies. Cost is obviously a factor which is balanced against the need for special skill or expertise, but it was an appreciation of the fears of the public about the financial consequences of visiting a solicitor which led the Royal Commission on Legal Services to recommend the "free initial half-hour" despite the possibilities of abuse.[6] Many of the statutory and voluntary agencies provide advice without charge.

The reputation of a particular agency will depend on the public perception of its efficiency, its impartiality, its independence and its approachability. That there is concern over the indifferent public image of the legal profession is evident—other agencies place varying degrees of emphasis upon different features of their reputation, some stressing their independence, others their approachability.

2. WHAT HELP?

Information and advice may be different and may require different communication skills on the part of the adviser. Again, advice and assistance may be different with the latter requiring some positive action on behalf of the client. Most of the agencies that we shall be describing in the following sections would claim to offer information, advice and assistance but some are dubious as to the extent to which they *should* take action on behalf of a client[7] and some will refer a matter on to specialists when they reach the limits of their competence. This raises the question of the role of the specialist agency in relation to the generalist and the development of a referral system. Co-ordination of generalist and specialist advice services is of prime importance and the National Consumer Council identified as a fundamental objective of a national advice system:

> "... the achievement of a proper mix of specialist and voluntary services and of working links and effective referral systems for the handling of people's problems where more than one agency needs to be involved."[8]

Paper No. 2, (1978); *36th Legal Aid Annual Reports* (1985–86), pp. 208–214; K. Economides and M. Blacksell, "Access to Justice in Rural Britain: Final Report" (1987) 16 Anglo-Am.L.R. 353 (and associated working papers); M. Blacksell *et al.*, *Legal Action*, April 1986, p. 7 and August 1986, p. 7; M. Slatter and M. Moseley, (1986) 136 N.L.J. 626; E. Kempson, *Legal Advice and Assistance* (1989) (comparative study of services in Cornwall, Oldham and Newham).

[5] See above, p. 122.

[6] R.C.L.S., Vol. 1, pp. 45, 134–135. This recommendation was not accepted by the Government: see p. 462, below.

[7] See, for example, the Chairman's statement in the National Association of Citizens Advice Bureaux Annual Report and Accounts, 1979–80, at p. 5.

[8] *The Fourth Right of Citizenship*, p. 65, cited with approval in R.C.L.S., Vol. 1, p. 72. The National Consumer Council have long expressed concern about the lack of a national policy for generalist advice provision. See *Ordinary Justice* (1989), pp. 108–114.

We have already noted that lawyers can be expected to provide a whole range of help which would certainly include information, advice and assistance.[9]

3. GIVEN BY WHOM?

Some agencies we shall be discussing rely solely upon one type of adviser so that there is no dispute about suitability. In others, however, there can be tensions over the relative desirability of volunteers and professionals. Citizens' Advice Bureaux, for example, rely heavily upon volunteers with few paid advisers and it is argued that this gives the organisation a positive strength and a particularly good claim to independence and impartiality. On the other hand, professional advisers (including lawyers) tend to lay emphasis upon the skill and expertise which are supposed to come with professional status and training.

The dispute between the volunteer and the professional is likely to continue[10] but it should not be allowed to obscure the fact that the skills of the good adviser are not necessarily professional skills, nor are they especially lawyerly skills. The client wants an adviser who can interview sympathetically, ascertain the facts, analyse the problem and suggest a course of action. The expertise of the adviser in the particular problem which emerges will doubtless influence the proposed course of action (which might include a referral) but the preliminary *advisory* skills may be possessed by a volunteer as by a professional. We shall return to these points later in the chapter but should now describe the range of information and advice agencies which will offer help with legal problems.

4. THE OVERALL PICTURE

One point clearly illustrated in this chapter is that there is no overall strategy for the provision, co-ordination and funding of advice services. There are many forms that such services may take; there is excessive reliance on the charity of volunteers to provide services that ought in principle to be publicly funded; funding problems seem to be chronic. An attempt to look at the overall picture was made by the Royal Commission on Legal Services: its recommendations were widely criticised and largely ignored.[11] More recently, attention has been focused on the statutory legal advice scheme (and, indeed, legal aid generally), prompted, it seems, more by government concern at rising public expenditure costs than any serious wish that those who need but cannot afford legal services obtain them. In 1986, the Legal Aid Efficiency Scrutiny, conducted by four civil servants from the Treasury and the Lord Chancellor's Department, made radical proposals for change. Some, but not all, of its recommendations were implemented in the Legal

---

[9] Above, p. 413.

[10] If only because the evidence in other areas of social work is of increased professional involvement. 90 per cent. of the staff of Citizens Advice Bureaux are volunteers: NACAB Annual Report 1988–89. The proportion of paid workers has increased, and there can be tensions between paid workers and volunteers: see Citron (*op. cit.*, fn. 14 below), pp. 64–66, and disputes about their respective merits: see V. Macnair, *Legal Action*, May 1989, p. 8; responses, June 1989, p. 28; July 1989, pp. 25–26.

[11] See below, pp. 460–462.

Aid Act 1988 (which also consolidated legal aid legislation). The administration of the legal advice and assistance and civil legal aid schemes was transferred to a new Legal Aid Board, whose remit included that of considering fundamental changes in the administration of the schemes.[12]

For a recent overview of the provision of legal services, it is necessary to look, outside the mainstream of governmental activity, to the National Consumer Council.[13]

B. GENERALIST AGENCIES OFFERING LEGAL ADVICE

1. THE CITIZENS' ADVICE BUREAUX[14]

It is somehow ironic that the major generalist agency owes its existence to wartime necessity. The CAB service has its origins in the combined operation set up in 1938 by the Ministry of Health, the National Council for Social Service and the Family Welfare Association to provide advice and information in an emergency. The outbreak of war was the emergency and a centrally-funded national service came into being. At the end of the war government assistance was withdrawn and local Bureaux were left to scrape along on what they could glean from local authorities and other sources. Many disappeared.

The service was revived at the beginning of the 1960s by the injection of government funding and was stimulated by honourable mention from two major inquiries. In 1962 the Molony Committee on Consumer Protection declared itself to be strongly in favour of the service and recognised its potential:

> "The aggrieved consumer needs an accessible local service to which he can take his troubles and where he will receive a realistic appraisal, a measure of help in presenting his case, or a pointer to the next step. This need cannot be better filled than by the Citizens Advice Bureaux."[15]

In 1980 the Royal Commission on Legal Services reported that it had:

> ". . . identified a particular national advice service, provided by the citizens' advice bureaux, which together form the largest and, in our view, the best placed organisation to provide a primary or first tier service."

The central body, the National Association of Citizens' Advice Bureaux was the subject of a review[16] initiated by Dr. Gerard Vaughan, as Minister for Consumer Affairs, which described the C.A.B. service as, ". . . an invaluable national asset."

---

[12] See below, pp. 462–467.

[13] N.C.C., *Ordinary Justice: Legal services and the courts in England and Wales: a consumer view* (H.M.S.O., 1989).

[14] J. Citron, *Citizens Advice Bureaux: For the Community, by the Community* (1989); J. Richards, *Inform, Advise and Support: 50 Years of the Citizens Advice Bureau* (1989).

[15] *Final Report of the Committee on Consumer Protection*, (Cmnd. 1781, 1962), Recommendation 108, relating to paras. 481, 491–3.

[16] *Review of the National Association of Citizens' Advice Bureaux* (the Lovelock report: Cmnd. 9139, 1984). The review dismissed concerns about the alleged party political activities of CAB workers: see Richards (1989), pp. 15–23.

At the present time there are 709 Bureaux[17] in the United Kingdom which are registered with the National Association of Citizens' Advice Bureaux (NACAB). All these Bureaux are required to conform with national standards in their operation and to conform to the training requirements adopted by NACAB. The advantage of membership of the national association is the receipt of the NACAB monthly information service and access to other support services.[18]

The aims of the Citizens' Advice Bureaux service are:

"— to ensure that individuals do not suffer through ignorance of their rights and responsibilities or of the services available; or through an inability to express their needs effectively;
— to exercise a responsible influence on the development of social policies and services, both locally and nationally.

The service therefore provides free to all individuals a confidential, impartial and independent service of information, guidance and support, and makes responsible use of the experience so gained."[19]

There is strong evidence that greater and greater use is being made of the CAB service. In 1989–90 the service handled 6,959,276 enquiries, an increase of 38 per cent. over 1982–83.[20] In the categorisations adopted by NACAB the greatest number of enquiries were concerned with social security (22.9 per cent.), consumer and debt (20.2 per cent.), housing (11.6 per cent.), employment (10.2 per cent.), family and personal (9.9 per cent.), and administration of justice (7.5 per cent.).[21]

In relation to those enquiries which have a legal content, a Citizens' Advice Bureau may adopt one of a number of approaches. It may train its advisers sufficiently to be able to give para-legal advice in those cases which do not require professional assistance; it may refer the client to a solicitor[22]; it may arrange a rota scheme whereby a solicitor attends at the CAB office to see clients[23]; it may try to appoint its own solicitor.[24]

The Royal Commission on Legal Services gave a firm indication of how it considered the CAB should resolve the conflict between its generalist role and the inclination to become involved in specialist areas:

"... the functions to be fulfilled by the CAB service [must] be defined with care. There is sometimes a tendency for a generalist service to expand into specialisms with which it is in daily contact. If this were to happen in the case of the CABx, they would have lost their primary purpose as first tier advisory agencies; there would be duplication of effort, waste of public money and, in all probability, deterioration in the quality of specialised advice provided."[25]

[17] 1,313 outlets altogether: NACAB Annual Report, 1989–90, inside cover.
[18] See Citron (1989), Chap. 5.
[19] Ibid., p. 204.
[20] NACAB Annual Reports, 1989–90, p. 6, and 1982–83, p. 6.
[21] Ibid., p. 9. The most significant change in recent years has been the rise in the proportion of social security cases, with a bulge in inquiries arising out of the changes in April 1988.
[22] There is general guidance from NACAB as to the principles to be followed in making referrals, but much is left to the discretion of CAB managers: J. Baldwin, (1989) 8 C.J.Q. 24, 33–36.
[23] See below, pp. 441–442.
[24] In 1988, seven CABs had resource lawyers attached: see A. Grosskurth, Legal Action, October 1988, pp. 6–7 for a discussion of their work.
[25] Ibid. p. 75. These views were echoed in the Lovelock review (Cmnd. 9139, 1984).

In 1989–90 the financial assistance from central government amounted to £9M.[26] Three quarters of the money goes to maintain the national organisation and to provide central services for Bureaux. The remainder is used to set up new bureaux or develop existing ones, with grant tapering down by year 3 or 4.[27] The running expenses of the actual Bureaux are met mainly from local sources. Almost all local authorities now fund a CAB, with total funding near £23M,[28] although there is growing evidence that difficulties for local authorities arising from the community charge may in turn put pressure on CAB funding.[28a]

2. NEIGHBOURHOOD ADVICE CENTRES[29]

These are informal groups operating in a wide diversity of localities and conditions, with very different structures and objectives. In general they offer assistance with all types of problem but are often to be found in the areas of urban development and rehousing which are likely to expose housing, welfare benefit and educational problems.[30] About two-thirds provide a generalist advice service, and about one third, general assistance to a specific group of users, (e.g. women, the elderly, ethnic minority communities).[31] These centres may attract finance from a variety of sources, mainly local authorities, and there has been some government funding.[32]

3. YOUNG PEOPLE'S ADVISORY AND COUNSELLING SERVICES

There are over 70 generalist agencies providing information, advice and counselling to young people. They are federated nationally to the National Association of Young People's Counselling and Advisory Services (NAYPCAS), which has a small secretariat funded by the Home Office. The largest proportion of funds is received through local authorities.[33]

4. THE MEDIA

It is impossible to ignore the increasing use of the media as a source of

[26] NACAB Annual Report, 1989–90, p. 4. See generally on funding and publicity Citron (1989), Chap. 9.
[27] See Efficiency Scrutiny of Government Funding of the Voluntary Sector (H.M.S.O., 1990), pp. 73–74.
[28] NACAB Annual Report, 1989–90, p. 4.
[28a] Legal Action, November 1990, p. 4.
[29] There is a comparative dearth of material charting the activities of centres of this kind. An early appraisal was contained in Leissner, Family Advice Centres, National Bureau for Co-operation in Child Care (1967), and particular studies include Bond, The Hillfields Information and Opinion Centre—the Evolution of A Social Agency Controlled by Local Residents, CDP Occasional Paper (1972); Report, Evaluation and Recommendations from Cumbria CDP, Dept. of Soc. Admin., York University (1975); N.C.C., Information and Advice Services in the U.K. (1983). The Federation of Independent Advice Centres (FIAC) Directory of Independent Advice Centres (ed., A. Thackeray and M. Jones, 1988) lists about 390 such centres in England and Wales. They rely more on paid staff than do CABx. Guidance on the establishment of advice centres is given in C. Thornton, Managing to Advise (1989), published by FIAC.
[30] The Fourth Right of Citizenship.
[31] R. Berthoud et al., Standing Up for Claimants (PSI Research Report 663, 1986), pp. 78–79, based on a survey by E. Kempson.
[32] Notably from the Home Office Community Development Project 1968–78 (hence CDP in n. 29): see M. Loney, Community against Government (1983).
[33] R. Berthoud, et al., (1986), pp. 79–80.

information and advice. Quite apart from the communication of information of all kinds which is the function of radio, television and the press, more and more time is being devoted to the provision of general and specific advice, usually at the request of individuals. This development is not unconnected with the development of local radio and the popularity of the phone-in programme.

Depending on resources, the media can respond to enquiries in much the same way as any other agency. The particular organisation can build up its own expertise[34]; it can acquire answers which are then relayed[35]; it can refer the enquirer to another agency; it can bring in specialists to answer the enquiries direct.[36] Legal advice frequently forms the basis of specific programmes or articles, no doubt because of the inherent fascination of legal problems for the lay people.[37] There is also some credit to be gained by radio, television or the press where an individual's problem is solved and (as it is normally represented) the forces of darkness are vanquished.[38]

C. SPECIALIST AGENCIES OFFERING LEGAL ADVICE TO THE PUBLIC

1. CONSUMER ADVICE CENTRES

The high percentage of enquiries to the CABx concerning consumer, trade and business affairs[39] demonstrates the particular need for specialist advice in the field. Before 1970 it was largely left to the Weights and Measures Departments of local authorities to enforce those statutes which gave protection to the consumer of goods and they often took the view that they had no competence to deal with complaints which did not indicate a possible breach of the criminal law.

It was a combination of pressure from the Consumers' Association; the introduction of more consumer protection legislation; the injection of national government funding[40] and the reorganisation of local government in 1974 that led to the establishment of some 110 Consumer Advice Centres run by local authorities by the end of 1976. These centres provided both pre-shopping advice on quality, fitness and "value for money"[41] and a complaints service for disgruntled consumers. In most places they were very closely integrated with the (newly-named) Trading Standards Department.

---

[34] As where a particular phone-in presenter gains local knowledge and experience, or where a presenter researches problems raised by listeners and makes them into a programme through his or her own investigation, e.g. Roger Cook in "Checkpoint," a BBC Radio 4 programme: see J. Wilson, *Roger Cook's Checkpoint* (1983).

[35] By getting those who have the answers, for example local authority departments or welfare agencies, to take part in the programme by telephone.

[36] To answer questions on particular topics specified in advance either in print or on radio/television.

[37] So long as they are well-presented, e.g. Jimmy Young and his "legal beagle" on BBC Radio 2: see B. Thomas, (1989) 139 N.L.J. 810.

[38] e.g. "That's Life," BBC Television; "Action Desk," *Nottingham Evening Post*.

[39] See above p. 428.

[40] £1·4 million in December 1975 and a further £3 million in November 1976, see *The Fourth Right of Citizenship* (1977), National Consumer Council.

[41] By comparative testing with the justification that the consumer can often be better protected by buying wisely than by complaining vigorously.

They attracted criticism from a number of quarters and only 29 remain, run by the Trading Standards Departments of 20 local authorities[42]; the remainder fell victim to a political change in the relevant local authority coupled with the withdrawal of central government funding.[43] It is unfortunate that the CACs were seen as a political football and they provide an interesting indication of what might possibly happen were all legal services to be funded from local or central government.[44] There were advantages for the consumer in the close links between the centres and the enforcement mechanisms of Trading Standards Departments.

2. Housing Advice

Housing advice centres were coming into existence at about the time that the first law centre was being opened,[45] and it is not unrealistic to attribute their inception to the generally increased awareness of the need for advice services. However, the direct impetus came from the Seebohm Report[46] in 1968, which recommended the establishment of an official housing advice agency to give assistance with, *inter alia*, landlord and tenant problems, public health legislation and rent fixing. The obligation to provide such a service should rest, it was said, with the local authority.

In the event the first two centres demonstrated the dual approach to much advisory work in that one was set up by a local authority (in Lambeth) and one by voluntary bodies (in South Kensington).[47] That pattern has continued: a majority of the centres now in operation are run by the local authority, and the rest are independent, many either run by or associated with Shelter.[48] Financial assistance from the Urban Aid programme acted as an inducement to many local authorities and Department of the Environment schemes fund some centres directly. One obvious limitation of local authority-run centres is that unlike the independent centres they cannot help local authority tenants and homeless applicants fight legal battles against the authority.[49]

A separate development has seen the establishment of a variety of arrangements offering advice and perhaps representation to defendants to possession actions in the county court. There are about 20 at present; they offer a valuable service, and are generally welcomed by the judiciary. Models include a permanent welfare officer available at the county court,[50]

---

[42] N.C.C., *Ordinary Justice* (1989), pp. 52–53.

[43] But that was not the only reason. The CAC in Nottingham attracted strong criticism when it embarked upon a survey of the level of professional fees. The criticism came from the professions, not the consumers.

[44] *Cf.* below pp. 439–440.

[45] See below p. 437.

[46] *Report of the Committee on Local Authority and Allied Personal Social Services* (Cmnd. 3703, 1968).

[47] The bodies concerned were Shelter and the Catholic Housing Aid Society.

[48] In 1986 there were 55 access points operating independently of the local authority: N.C.C., *Ordinary Justice* (1989), p. 51.

[49] *Ibid.*

[50] This scheme has run at the Birmingham County Court for the last 10 years funded by the CAB: A. Grosskurth, *Legal Action*, April 1990, pp. 7–8. See also *34th Legal Aid Annual Reports* [1983–84], pp. 348–350; *35th Annual Reports* [1984–85], pp. 230–232; Lee Burrows, *Rent Arrears and the Courts: A Report by the Lay Advisory Service* (1986). The Legal Aid Board has proposed pilot schemes for county court duty advisers: (1990) 87 L.S. Gaz., October 3, 1990, p. 8.

rota schemes for duty lay advisers from local advice agencies, and duty schemes staffed by private practitioners.[51] The major stumbling block to the last of these is that solicitors can only be remunerated for advice under the green form scheme. The regulations governing assistance by way of representation (ABWOR) in county courts were tightened in 1989 to exclude arranged schemes.[52]

3. MONEY ADVICE CENTRES

The provision of specialist money advice expanded significantly in the 1980s. In 1982, the National Consumer Council identified 16 money advice centres in Britain.[53] By 1986 there were over a hundred specialist money advice services, all but four in England and Wales, taking the form either of individual advisers within a larger unit or of separate units. The majority were based in CABx, some in local authorities, (e.g. in social services departments or to support rent officers), and there were six voluntary sector money advice centres.[54] NACAB have established five Money Advice Support Units, with funding from private sector credit agencies.[55] A Policy Studies Institute report[56] concluded that specialist money advice was helpful to debtors, particularly multiple debtors. Advisers had skills in negotiating with individual creditors and in planning an overall strategy of negotation among several creditors, arising out of their knowledge of the legal position, experience of previous negotiations, the ability to communicate in a businesslike way, and their position as independent third parties. The location of money advice services is, however, haphazard. The case for expansion is strong, with debt "one of the fastest growing problems of the 1980s,"[57] but they are as much a victim of the lack of a coherent overall strategy as other advice services.

4. WELFARE RIGHTS UNITS

In 1986, 65 local authorities, usually in urban areas and Labour controlled, employed specialist welfare rights workers. There might be a single worker employed by the council or a team. Their work comprises the provision of direct advice services to claimants, including casework and tribunal representation, the promotion of benefits through campaigns, publicity and work with local groups, support and training for other advice givers, both among

---

[51] *Ibid.*
[52] See below, pp. 446–447, 452.
[53] N.C.C., *Money Advice: debt counselling and money advice services training and publications* (1982). The first was the Birmingham Settlement Money Advice Centre established in 1971: see J. Blamire and A. Izzard, *Debt Counselling* (1987).
[54] T. Hinton and R. Berthoud, *Money Advice Services* (PSI Research Report 669, 1988), Chap. 1.
[55] NACAB Annual Report, 1988–89, p. 17. See M. Wolfe, *Legal Action*, November 1989, p. 25, emphasising the need for caution about credit industry funding.
[56] Hinton and Berthoud (1988), Chap. 7.
[57] N.C.C., *Ordinary Justice* (1989), p. 116. The N.C.C. estimate that there is a need for over 4,000 specialist money advisers compared with current numbers of about 200: *ibid.*, p. 119.

council staff and in the voluntary sector, and influencing the policy and practice of public agencies.[58]

5. CHARITIES AND PRESSURE GROUPS

Organisations with charitable status operating in a particular field often acquire knowledge and expertise which can prove extremely valuable to individuals who may be in need of that sort of advice. The housing charity, Shelter, was in at the beginning of the Housing Advice Centre movement and the Child Poverty Action Group has been extremely active in the field of welfare rights.[59] DIAL (Disablement Information and Advice lines) give a great deal of assistance to people who are disabled or who have a disabled relative,[59a] and Gingerbread, the charity concerned with one-parent families, does much educative and advisory work.

The Claimants Union has been active in the field of social security and welfare benefits and, in some areas of the country, offers advice and representation at tribunals to those in need.

D. SPECIALIST AGENCIES OFFERING LEGAL ADVICE TO MEMBERS

One of the benefits of membership of some organisations is that specialist legal advice is made available, normally connected with the main business of the organisation. This may be done through the employment of lawyers within the organisation or by the engagement of lawyers in private practice at the expense of the organisation. It is not proposed to list all the groups providing this sort of service, merely to select three examples.

1. THE TRADE UNIONS[60]

Legal services provided through a trade union have been, and remain, a significant factor in the recruitment and retention of members. It appears that most, if not all, trade unions offer some form of legal advice service to members although it is likely to be restricted to those matters which touch

---

[58] R. Berthoud, S. Benson and S. Williams, *Standing Up for Claimants: Welfare Rights Work in Local Authorities* (PSI Research Report No. 663, 1986). There has been some debate as to whether welfare rights work has a proper place in social work: see G. Fimister, *Welfare Rights Work in Social Services* (1986) (Fimister argues persuasively that it does).

[59] Especially in publications, notably the *National Welfare Benefits Handbook*, and the monthly *Welfare Rights Bulletin*, and in the establishment of the Citizens' Rights Office handling telephone enquiries from advisers from all over the country.

[59a] In 1988 there were 65 centres affiliated to Dial U.K. Some concentrate on a telephone service, others also have a centre where people can call. See N.C.C., *Ordinary Justice* (1989), pp. 49–50.

[60] See generally, G. Latta and R. Lewis, "Trade Union Legal Services" (1974) XII *British Journal of Industrial Relations* 561; R. Lewis and G. Latta, "Union Legal Services" (1973) 123 N.L.J. 386; M. Zander, *Legal Services for the Community* (1978), pp. 305–308; R. Lewis, "Legal Services in the Trade Unions," in, *Advice Services in Welfare Rights* (ed. Brooke), Fabian research series 329 (1976). Much of the work is based on the survey conducted by Lewis and Latta at the L.S.E. See also D. Harris *et al.*, *Compensation and Support for Illness and Injury* (1984), pp. 66–70, 80–81, 119–120; L. Dickens, *et al.*, *Dismissed* (1985), pp. 43–48.

directly on employment.[61] The unions have been heavily involved in the development of industrial injuries law; common law claims arising out of accidents at work; employment law; and health and safety standards. Additionally, they provide representation at Social Security Appeal Tribunals and at Industrial Tribunals.

This has placed trade unions in something of a dilemma. Whilst their representatives might wish to see a general extension of legal services in the public sector, they would not wish the value of their own legal services to members to diminish. The TUC evidence to the Royal Commission on Legal Services appeared to place greater emphasis upon the preservation of the union role in advice-giving than on a general expansion of legal services.[62] This position was reaffirmed by the exclusion of employment-related matters from the Unionlaw scheme launched in 1989.[63]

The unions provide advice in a variety of ways, some using legal staff engaged for the purpose and others relying on the general full-time officials supported by recourse to the private practitioner.

The professional associations will normally offer a legal advice service in exactly the same way as trade unions and in the medical profession specific groups have been established to provide insurance cover and assist members who are sued.[64]

2. THE MOTORING ORGANISATIONS

The Automobile Association and the Royal Automobile Club provide a variety of benefits for their members which includes legal advice. Naturally, this is confined to motoring but can include the cost of representation in summary proceedings as well as advice on claims and general motoring law, disputes with garages, and claims arising out of accidents.

The benefits offered by the AA are not as substantial as they may, at first sight, appear since the free legal representation scheme may be withheld altogether at the discretion of the Association; the AA will not negotiate in respect of the defence of claims made against members; the AA cannot give advice or act where the Association or any of its subsidiary companies may be involved.[65] Notwithstanding these limitations, members must be reassured by such a scheme and it must be an aid to recruitment.

3. THE CONSUMERS' ASSOCIATION

The CA began in 1957 as a small group publishing a magazine with the results of the comparative testing of aspirins and kettles and has since then

---

[61] Taken from the results of a 1976 questionnaire sent out by the T.U.C. and forming the basis of evidence to the Royal Commission. Of 55 unions who replied, *all* provided advice on employment but only 9 provided general legal advice to members.
[62] For a critical analysis of the T.U.C. position, see G. Bindman, "Trade Unions and Legal Services," *LAG Bulletin*, March 1979, p. 56.
[63] (1988) 138 N.L.J. 640; (1990) 87 L.S. Gaz., September 19, p. 6. The scheme, available to members of T.U.C.-affiliated unions, provides access lists to solicitors participating in the scheme, free diagnostic interviews (without use of the green form), free estimates of the cost of further work, fixed priced conveyancing and wills, and a Code of Practice.
[64] The Medical Defence Union, the Medical Protection Society and the Medical Practitioners' Defence Society. The role of these societies has changed now that damages claims involving the N.H.S. are met wholly by health authorities (from January 1, 1990).
[65] *Automobile Association Members' Handbook* 1988/89, p. 19.

become a multi-million pound operation with influence over manufacturers and retailers as well as those responsible for the formulation of consumer policy.

The information function is performed through the magazine *Which?* available to subscribers but having a general impact because of its availability in libraries and the extent to which it is referred to and talked about. The value of the information lies in its comparative nature and in the reputation for thoroughness which the CA has acquired. Unfavourable mention in *Which?* is regarded as a major problem for well-known manufacturers.[66]

On the legal advice side, the CA operates a legal service for individual members on payment of a separate subscription. Legal advice, in the form of answers to readers' questions, is also contained in the magazines, and there are statements of law in other CA publications.[67]

E. LAW CENTRES[68]

One of the most significant developments in the provision of legal advice and assistance over the last 20 years has been the emergence of law centres. Drawing some inspiration from the American system of neighbourhood law firms but adapting themselves to local conditions and the rules of the legal profession in this country, the law centres now provide a local base for the dissemination of legal services outside the private profession.

1. THE BEGINNINGS

Some provision was made for the giving of legal advice by salaried solicitors outside the ambit of private practice in the Legal Aid and Advice Act 1949, but the part of the Act which would have established full-time paid solicitors located at the Legal Aid Area Headquarters and travelling to smaller places was never brought into force.[69] An alternative scheme for the provision of advice was proposed and adopted after 10 years of pressure had failed to get the original scheme implemented.[70]

The real origins of the law centre movement are usually attributed to the publication of pamphlets by the lawyers of the Conservative and Labour parties and the individual initiative of pioneers who became impatient at the

---

[66] As exemplified by the critical report of the B.L. Metro in the July 1981 *Motoring Which?* and the responses of the manufacturer and users, *Sunday Times*, June 28, 1981, *The Times*, June 29, 1981.

[67] *The Good Food Guide* attempts to set out the law about eating in a restaurant.

[68] For a comprehensive survey of the origins and development of the law centre movement, see M. Zander, *Legal Services for the Community* (1978), Chaps. 2 and 3; R.C.L.S., Vol. 1, Chap. 8; Law Centres Federation, *The Case for Law Centres* (3rd ed., 1989); R. Widdison, (1988) L.S.Gaz., March 16, pp. 35–37. See also G. Burke and G. Cole, [1985] J.S.W.L. 274 (evaluation of Holloway Neighbourhood Law Centre); J. Morton, "Liverpool, 8: Anatomy of a Law Centre" (1988) 138 N.L.J. 141.

[69] s.7 contains the appropriate provisions. The significance of the failure to implement the proposals should not be underestimated. This part of the scheme was, ". . . an essential part of the total Scheme without which it would lack the necessary impact." The failure to implement it ". . . was a fatal mistake from which the inevitable consequences are now being reaped": *Legal Aid and Advice, Report of The Law Society* 1973–74 (24th Report), Special Appendix 18, "Legal aid at the cross-roads."

[70] The "statutory" and the "voluntary" scheme introduced in 1959, see below, p. 443.

slowness of the official bodies to respond to the pressure for change. *Justice for All*[71] analysed the unmet need for professional legal services and proposed the establishment of local legal centres in places of deprivation, to be staffed by salaried lawyers and to exist with and be supplemental to the private profession. It was suggested that the type of work undertaken by the centres should be restricted but that they should be free of those rules of professional etiquette (*e.g.* advertising and touting for business) which would inhibit their work.[72] It is not, perhaps, surprising that the solution of the Conservative lawyers in their pamphlet, *Rough Justice*,[73] to the same problem of unmet legal need was the introduction of subsidies for practitioners operating privately in deprived areas and an extension of the assistance given by lawyers to voluntary advice agencies. However, they were prepared to countenance the appointment of salaried lawyers as a last resort.

The Law Society was striking various poses in 1968 and 1969,[74] but from apparently implacable opposition to the original scheme of salaried solicitors contemplated in the 1949 Act (to depart from the alternative system adopted in 1959 would be "a serious mistake"[75]) and the proposals of *Justice for All*[76], it moved to acceptance of salaried solicitors as part of its own proposals for an Advisory Liaison Service.[77] This Service would provide legal help to CABx and other social agencies, similar to that hitherto provided by solicitors to CABx on an honorary basis; would establish close liaison between the local profession and CABx and other social services; would provide oral advice for the public in cases that could be readily disposed of; would maintain permanent advisory centres where necessary, offering advice and assistance short of proceedings or representation in court; and would set up permanent local centres offering representation in magistrates' courts and county courts and the conduct of litigation so far as this could not be absorbed by solicitors' firms.

Part II of the Legal Advice and Assistance Act 1972 contained provisions which appeared to be designed to give the Law Society power to carry out these proposals. The Lord Chancellor's Legal Aid Advisory Committee had already indicated that the Law Society should be given these powers,[78] but it, and the Law Society, were then frustrated[79] by the failure of successive governments to bring this part of the Act into force. In fact, the Law Society had minimal involvement in projects connected with the Advisory Liaison Service.[80]

---

[71] A report of the Society of Labour Lawyers, Fabian research series 273 (1968). Quite apart from the well-argued and well-documented proposals the report contains references to most of the written material then available about law centres and a helpful description of the American experience.

[72] *Ibid.*, pp. 61–62.

[73] Society of Conservative Lawyers, *Rough Justice* (1968).

[74] These are fully explored and possible explanations offered in M. Zander, *Legal Services for the Community* (1978), pp. 64–76.

[75] *Legal Advice and Assistance*, Memorandum of the Council of The Law Society, February 1968, para. 21.

[76] (1968) 65 L.S.Gaz. 655: Inaugural address of Mr. H. E. Sargant.

[77] *Legal Advice and Assistance*, Memorandum of the Council of the Law Society, July 1969.

[78] *Report of the Advisory Committee on the better provision of Legal Advice and Assistance*, (Cmnd. 4249, 1970).

[79] See, *e.g. 23rd and 24th Annual Reports on Legal Aid*, 1972–73 and 1973–74.

[80] *Cf.* below, p. 459.

2. DEVELOPMENT

Impatient of the slow progress made through the "official channels" local lawyers and community workers set up a law centre in North Kensington in 1970.[81] After a lapse of three years a variety of centres emerged in 1973/74; by October 1982 there were 38 centres around the country,[82] and by 1987–88, 61.[83]

The struggle for most of the centres has been for funds. There are a variety of sources ranging from the Urban Programme of the Department of the Environment[84] to charities[85] but there has been much uncertainty about funding, the Legal Aid Annual Reports regularly referring to the financial problems of particular centres. Law centres can, of course, earn money through taking on work financed under the statutory legal advice scheme.

The other problem which affected some law centres was the necessity to obtain exemption (a "waiver") from the professional rules of etiquette imposed by the Law Society. The particular rules in question related to advertising and touting and became the focus for the antagonism which some established members of the profession displayed towards the new centres. After much acrimony[86] an agreement was reached in 1977 about the conditions under which the Law Society would grant waivers to law centres[87] and it was thereafter no longer a source of difficulty. The objective of the operation of the power to grant waivers was to produce harmonious relations between all lawyers and to ensure that the roles of the "public" and "private" sectors of the profession continued broadly to complement one another.

3. WORK

As there are many centres, so there are many different ways of operating, but in a survey conducted for the Royal Commission[88] an extract from a document prepared by the Legal Action Group was found helpful, not only for the description of law centres, but also for the distinction it drew between their function and that of *legal advice centres*.

"Legal advice centres are staffed by volunteer lawyers (solicitors, barristers and articled clerks) and have limited opening hours. The centres are essentially for advice and usually offer only a limited

---

[81] It has managed to survive: see C. Robinson *et al.*, *Coming of Age: North Kensington Law Centre 1970–1988*; R. Smith, *Legal Action*, August 1988, pp. 6, 23 (interview with Peter Kandler, one of its founders).

[82] As at October 1982, *31st Legal Aid Annual Reports* [1980–81], pp. 128–129. The early stages of development are chartered by M. Zander and P. Russell, "Law Centres Survey" (1976) 73 L.S. Gaz. 208; R.C.L.S., Vol. 2, Part B, Section 3.

[83] *38th Legal Aid Annual Reports* (1987–88), pp. 102–103.

[84] *e.g.* for projects in Lambeth, Hounslow, North Manchester, Sandwell and South Islington. For a breakdown of the sources of funding see R.C.L.S., Vol. 2, Part B, Section 3.17, Table 3.4.

[85] The North Kensington Law Centre started on funds from the City Parochial Foundation and the Pilgrim Trust.

[86] M. Zander, "Waivers—the end of a long story?" (1977) 127 N.L.J. 1236, and *Legal Services for the Community* (1978), pp. 89–93.

[87] See now, *The Law Society, The Guide to the Professional Conduct of Solicitors* (1990), Chap. 5.

[88] R.C.L.S., Vol. 2, Part B, Section 3.1.

amount, if any, of further assistance. There is no charge for the service. . . . The telephone, where there is one, may be staffed only during
advice sessions. . . .

Law centres employ full-time staff, including lawyers, and will handle
a client's case from beginning to end, including representation in court
or at a tribunal. The service is free unless the centre explains otherwise.
Law centres vary in the services that they provide for individual clients.

> (a) They are all restricted to acting for clients living (or sometimes
>   working) within a limited geographical area round the centre.
> (b) They all operate on a very broad restriction against acting for
>   clients who can afford to pay solicitors' fees.
> (c) They are restricted in the kind of work they undertake. This
>   varies from centre to centre but most specialise in landlord/
>   tenant, juvenile crimes and care cases, employment and wel-
>   fare benefits.
> (d) Some centres concentrate on group work and do little indivi-
>   dual case work.

All centres may be prepared to give preliminary advice to clients
falling outside these categories. . . ."[89]

It is important to point out the major differences between the work of law
centres and that of the private profession. The subject-matter of the problems dealt with by a law centre will tend to reflect local community conditions and housing, employment, social security and consumer problems are
likely to be predominant. These problems may be sought out by a law centre
with a view to running "campaigns" to benefit all those in the local community who may be in similar difficulties. It is in the nature of a law centre that
the test case strategy will be utilised more extensively because the perception of community need will be greater and because limited resources may
best be deployed through group work.[90]

The division of work between the private profession and the law centre
has not been based entirely on the choice of clients in deciding which
problems to bring in to the law centre. Until 1990, the waiver agreement
required that a law centre should not normally deal in particular matters,
save in an emergency or for the provision of initial advice, or for other
carefully circumscribed reasons.[91] Conveyancing, divorce, probate and criminal matters concerning adults were all in this category. Thus, the profession was protected against competition from law centres in these matters but
was not required to refrain from dealing in those matters which "normally"
go to law centres. This overlap has raised some difficulty about the extent to
which a client should be expected to contribute to the cost of the services
received.

---

[89] LAG directory of legal advice and law centres.
[90] *Community Need and Law Centre Practice*, Adamdown Community Trust (1978); R. Campbell, *Legal Action*, February 1989, pp. 7–8; *cf.* K. Hatton, *Legal Action*, June 1989, p. 10.
[91] See the Law Society, *Guide to the Professional Conduct of Solicitors* (1990), Appendix B,
para. 7. The expressed object was to ensure that law centres did not duplicate the services
provided by solicitors in private practice. In practice, they had no wish to do so. The
restrictions were removed from the Solicitors Practice Rules 1990: see Rule 4 and the
Employed Solicitors Code 1990, para. 7.

Traditionally, the law centres have not levied any charges on those using the service. This means that there is financial discrimination operating between those clients who use a law centre and those who may go to a solicitor with the same problem and who will then have to pay fees or a contribution towards the cost under the Legal Aid or Legal Advice schemes.[92] Should the law centres operate a means test? Or should certain classes of work be reserved exclusively for law centres? Or should we continue to accept the anomaly?[93]

In practice, research on the overall provision of legal services in particular areas shows that CABx, law centres and private practitioners tend to establish co-operative and complementary relationships.[93a] The establishment of a law centre may lead to the development of local legal aid solicitors' practices, to some extent relying on referrals from the law centre.[94]

4. THE FUTURE

It is clear that law centres have played a significant part in the provision of legal advice, but there are contrasting indications about their future well-being. Some have run into considerable financial and political difficulty. The long and bitter dispute in Hillingdon which culminated in the closure of the centre in April 1979[95] and the closure of the three Wandsworth law centres in January 1980[96] illustrate the problems faced by law centres. Others have had to rely on government funding to keep going, although funding from the Department of the Environment through the Urban Programme has been restricted and only seven centres have been funded on a continuing basis by the Lord Chancellor's Department, and (for the time being) the Legal Aid Board.[97] Following the abolition of the G.L.C. and the metropolitan county councils under the Local Government Act 1985 there were difficulties in securing funding from successor councils,[98] and there were further difficulties from 1988 with the rate-capping or charge-capping of particular local authorities.[99] On the other hand, there is the evidence of new law centres opening.[1]

---

[92] Unless, on the operation of the means test, a nil contribution is calculated. See below, pp. 445–446, 508–510.

[93] For a full discussion of the various possibilities, see M. Zander, *Legal Services for the Community* (1978), pp. 94–100.

[93a] E. Kempson, *Legal Advice and Assistance* (1989), p. 71; J. Baldwin, "The role of CABx and law centres in the provision of legal advice and assistance" (1989) 8 C.J.Q. 24.

[94] R. Widdison, (1989) 86 L.S. Gaz. 35, 37; and see J. Baldwin, *op. cit.*

[95] "The Lessons of Hillingdon," *LAG Bulletin*, November 1978, p. 250 and August 1979, p. 176.

[96] "Wandsworth Law Centre," *LAG Bulletin*, August 1979, p. 177 and January 1980, p. 4. In both Hillingdon and Wandsworth, "Legal Resource Centres" were established by those who wished to continue the provision of legal advice on a voluntary basis. In 1988, the Hillingdon centre was in existence with local authority funding: *38th Legal Aid Annual Reports* (1987–88), p. 129. In 1990, centres in Wandsworth were again under threat: (1990) 87 L.S. Gaz., September 12, p. 3, September 19, p. 4; *Legal Action*, February 1991, p. 4.

[97] See below, pp. 440, 464–467.

[98] *Legal Action*, April 1986, pp. 4–5.

[99] *Legal Action*, March 1988, p. 4. There were reprieves, with grants cut but closure averted: *Legal Action*, May 1988, p. 4. Centres have survived political difficulties in Bradford (with the help of Judge Pickles) and Gloucester: see (1989) 139 N.L.J. 102, 318; *Legal Action*, January 1990, p. 6. See also, *The Lawyer*, April 3, 1990.

[1] *e.g.* in Luton: G. Sargeant, *Legal Action*, December 1988, p. 9; in Rochdale and Chesterfield: *Legal Action*, April 1989, p. 4.

The Lord Chancellor's Advisory Committee has argued in vain that law centres should be treated as an essential part of the national network of legal services and that the Lord Chancellor should take on responsibility for their core funding.[2] The Legal Aid Board has said itself to be impressed with the contribution of law centres to the provision of legal services in the areas they serve. However, it intends to continue general funding for its seven in the short term only. Future funding from the Board to law centres would be for cases done under the green forms and legal aid schemes, including any new arrangements that might be developed,[3] "and possibly grants for specific types of work where the law centres could demonstrate that they would provide a better and more efficient service in ways that did not lend themselves to payment on a case by case basis."[4] Beyond that, law centres would be expected to look to local authorities and other sources to fund work arising out of other needs of the communities they serve.[5]

F. SOLICITORS IN PRIVATE PRACTICE

For all the varieties of advice agency that have flourished in the past decade it is still the established legal profession which is the major purveyor of legal advice. The role of the private practitioner has, however, been called into question in respect of two of the requirements of an advice agency discussed at the beginning of this chapter, namely the cost and availability of the service.

Evidence that the cost of a solicitor's advice (together with fear about cost) and the relative inaccessibility of many offices combined to deter large sections of the community from using a solicitor led to speculation about the degree of "unmet legal need" which exists.[6] It was that speculation and accompanying doubts about the ability of the private practitioner to meet this need which led to the rapid growth of interest in alternative means of providing legal advice. Other agencies have already been described—we are now concerned with the response of the private profession to these problems of cost and access.

If clients are able to pay the bill they can get advice from a solicitor as often as they desire and on whatever topic they choose. If they cannot pay the bill they must rely on the services provided voluntarily by solicitors and barristers; or a law centre; or come within the statutory advice scheme; or use another agency; or do without.

---

[2] *34th Legal Aid Annual Reports* [1983–84], pp. 338–346; *35th Annual Reports* [1984–85], pp. 225–226; *38th Annual Reports* (1987–88), pp. 102–103. See also, Law Centres Federation, *The Case for Law Centres* (3rd ed., 1989), pp. 16–17; (1990) 87 L.S. Gaz., July 4, p. 4.

[3] See below, pp. 466–467.

[4] *Legal Aid Board: Report to the Lord Chancellor* (Cm. 688, 1989), Section 5.

[5] See R. Smith, *Legal Action*, August 1989, p. 7, noting, *inter alia*, the dilemma for law centres that acceptance of grant aid from the Board would be likely to endanger their campaigning role.

[6] The best examination of this problem is to be found in B. Abel-Smith, M. Zander and R. Brooke *Legal Problems and the Citizen*, (1973). See also a memorandum of the Law Society, "Unmet Need" (1976) 73 L.S. Gaz. 1061. See further, Chap. 8.

1. VOLUNTARY SCHEMES

It is unnecessary to go too far back in history to discover the origins of some of the voluntary schemes for the provision of legal advice which now exist. Lawyers have traditionally been generous with their time and talents, more so than any other profession except, perhaps, medicine, and they are accustomed to rendering assistance to those who are genuinely unable to afford professional fees. This help took the form of the poor persons' procedure in litigation[7] but it was realised that procedures were no good unless those who might need them were aware of them. From the beginning of this century there was a growing awareness of the need for legal advice.[8]

However, in 1944 the Rushcliffe Committee[9] were still able to conclude that there was no organised provision for legal advice throughout the country. Amongst the disorganised provision were to be found examples of clients who would never be charged by solicitors; advice-giving by stipendiary magistrates, magistrates' clerks, and county court registrars; a Poor Man's Lawyer service in London and the provinces staffed by volunteers; trade union legal advice and Citizens' Advice Bureaux.[10]

Of these the Poor Man's Lawyer scheme involved the greatest number of solicitors and barristers, having begun at Toynbee Hall in 1893 and spread from there. Cambridge House Legal Advice Centre and Mary Ward Settlement Centre flourished on either side of the Thames. These are the direct forerunners of the legal advice centres now to be referred to and all such centres relied exclusively on volunteer professional legal personnel.

(a) Legal advice centres

These have already been compared with law centres earlier in this chapter[11] and it was noted then that they are staffed by volunteer lawyers, have limited opening hours, offer only advice, and make no charge for the service provided. There are 100 or so such centres and they can attribute their origins to the individual legal and charitable initiatives of members of the profession.[12] They operate to give advice and to act as a referral agency for the private profession.

(b) Rota schemes

The CAB service has taken the initiative in setting up a system of advisory sessions in which local solicitors, operating on a rota, give free legal advice to clients who have been "booked in" to a special session by a local CAB. These sessions are particularly appropriate where the bureau worker is of the opinion that the problem can be dealt with in one interview with a

---

[7] Below, p. 506.

[8] See the description in B. Abel-Smith and R. Stevens, *Lawyers and the Courts* (1978), pp. 148–149.

[9] *Report of the Committee on Legal Aid and Advice* (Cmd. 6641, 1945).

[10] *Ibid.*, pp. 17–21.

[11] Above, pp. 437–438.

[12] R.C.L.S., Vol. 1, p. 76; LAG Report, *Legal Advice Centres—an explosion* (1972), referred to in *LAG Bulletin*, October 1972, p. 11. The assistance and advice provided through Toynbee Hall, the Mary Ward Settlement and Cambridge House, three London charities, was the model for much of what followed.

solicitor, but it is permissible for the solicitor taking the session to accept the interviewee as his or her own client if further advice is needed.[13] More and more Bureaux are establishing this arrangement with the consent and encouragement of the Law Society and the goodwill of very many members of the profession.

The importance of the rota scheme should not be underestimated. It ensures that the solicitor only sees those clients who have been identified by a volunteer worker as being in need of professional advice; it provides a free initial interview to encourage those who may be worried about cost; and it permits the solicitor to take on those clients who may need more extensive legal assistance. The drawback, inevitably, is that everything is dependent upon the existence of a CAB in the area, its willingness to set up the scheme, and the co-operation of the local profession.

The development of such schemes ought to be assured since they were commended by the Royal Commission,[14] are greatly valued by NACAB[15] and has the support of the Law Society. However, in 1988 over 300 bureaux still lacked schemes.[16]

(c) General

There is some evidence that solicitors also provide a form of gratuitous legal advice by waiving their charges in respect of a short initial consultation which does not require action on their part or a further interview. This is partly philanthropic and partly economic—it may cost more to process the bill and collect the money than to write off the charge! Needless to say, this service is not advertised but nonetheless appreciated. More formally, solicitors may offer a "£5 fixed fee interview." This is an initial interview for up to half an hour for which the maximum charge will be £5. There is also an Accident Legal Advice Service (ALAS!), whereby solicitors offer a free interview to accident victims. Solicitors willing to offer either of these services are indicated in the Solicitors Regional Directory.

The fixed fee interview scheme has not been successful.[17] Although many solicitors offer fixed fee interviews they are given little publicity beyond referral lists and notices in some solicitors' offices. Most clients who seek them in fact qualify for green form assistance and they are comparatively uncommon. Most participating solicitors seem unenthusiastic.

An accident leaflet scheme was started in 1978 in the North West. Leaflets were distributed which gave information about personal injury claims, suggested various sources of help and also offered a free interview with a solicitor. The scheme was regarded as successful in encouraging victims to claim who would not otherwise have done so.[18] About a third of local law

---

[13] This formerly required a waiver from the Law Society in respect of the Solicitors' Practice Rules, rule 1, but all that is required now is compliance with the Solicitors' Introduction and Referral Code 1988: see the Law Society, *The Guide to the Professional Conduct of Solicitors* (1990), Chap. 5 and Appendix B5, and above, p. 140.

[14] R.C.L.S., Vol. 1, p. 73.

[15] NACAB Annual Report, 1981–82, p. 8.

[16] NACAB Annual Report, 1988–89, p. 14.

[17] J. Baldwin and S. Hill, *The Operation of the Green Form Scheme in England and Wales* (1988), pp. 119–121.

[18] See H. Genn, *Meeting Legal Needs?* (1982); C. Schofield, *Legal Action*, August 1987, pp. 8, 23.

societies started similar schemes but many gave up following opposition from doctors. The scheme was relaunched in June 1987 on a national basis under the title ALAS! It has been much better publicised and early results have been encouraging.[19]

2. THE GREEN FORM SCHEME[20]

We have already noted that the Legal Aid and Advice Act 1949 made provision for the establishment of a statutory system of legal advice, but that the appropriate part of the Act was never brought into force.[21] After 10 years of effort to get some form of advice scheme started the Law Society settled for the introduction, in 1959, of two schemes designed to alleviate the growing problem.[22] Both relied heavily upon the goodwill of the private profession because the payment involved was minimal. The Statutory Advice Scheme (the "pink form" scheme) was means-tested with the top limit for eligibility set very low, involved an initial payment of half-a-crown by the client and permitted the solicitor to claim £1 per half-hour from the Law Society up to a maximum of £3. The scheme was not greatly used and was complemented by a Voluntary Advice Scheme under which solicitors would give up to half-hour's advice for a flat fee of £1 paid by the client irrespective of means.

The current "green form" scheme came into existence with the passing of the Legal Advice and Assistance Act 1972,[23] and a fixed fee interview scheme was resurrected in 1977.[23a]

(a) Administration

As the Legal Aid scheme was given to the Law Society to administer in 1949 and it had also been responsible for the voluntary and statutory schemes in 1959 it was quite logical that the Law Society should also run the new advice scheme and that it should use the local and regional structure which already existed to administer the legal aid scheme. Indeed, the basis of the new scheme had been proposed by the Law Society itself in a memorandum published in 1968.[24] Administration of the scheme passed to the Legal Aid Board on April 1, 1989, under the Legal Aid Act 1988.

However, it is notable that the individual practitioner has far more discretion in legal advice than legal aid, and need only refer to the Area Director where he or she requires an extension to the financial limit placed on the amount of advice which can be given.[25] He or she also has power to refuse for good cause to accept an application or to decline to give advice.[26]

---

[19] N.C.C., *Ordinary Justice* (1989), p. 143.

[20] See Baldwin and Hill (1988), a research study commissioned by the Lord Chancellor's Department. Aspects are summarised by Baldwin and Hill, (1986) 5 C.J.Q. 247; Baldwin, (1988) 138 N.L.J. 631, 664, 928 and (1989) 8 C.J.Q. 24; O. Hansen, *Using Civil Legal Aid: the 1989 Scheme* (1989), Chap. 2.

[21] Above, p. 435.

[22] See generally S. Pollock, *Legal Aid—the first 25 years* (1975), pp. 79–81.

[23] Now consolidated in the Legal Aid Act 1988, and regulations made thereunder.

[23a] See above.

[24] *Legal Advice and Assistance* (1968).

[25] Legal Aid Act 1988, s.10(1)(*b*); Legal Advice and Assistance Regulations 1989 (S.I. 1989 No. 340), reg. 21.

[26] *Ibid.*, reg. 18.

(b) Scope

The object of the green form scheme is to make readily available a cheap and effective source of legal advice for those who would otherwise be unable to afford it. To that end, a solicitor may give oral or written advice on the application of English law to any particular circumstances in relation to the person seeking the advice, and on any steps which he or she might appropriately take.[27] The client may also be given "assistance" in taking those steps.[28] If necessary, the solicitor may seek the advice of counsel[29] but this may be difficult because of the financial limits imposed.

It will be observed that although the range of matters which fall within the scheme is very wide, the solicitor is limited to the giving of advice and assistance and not representation. Since legal aid is also unavailable for representation at the vast majority of tribunals,[30] the scheme was immediately criticised for leaving out of its scope those who needed the services of an advocate at a tribunal. This was alleged to be a very serious omission, and a great handicap to the efficacy of the scheme.

In fact, various techniques and a belated statutory intervention have combined to lessen the effect of the omission. It is, of course, possible for a solicitor's written advice to include a "brief" for the client to read out at a tribunal hearing. Alternatively, the solicitor may accompany the client to the hearing and advise him or her orally as a McKenzie adviser[31] in the course of the hearing. This can be very tiresome for the tribunal with the constant interruptions and the solicitor may end up as advocate. Provided that the tribunal does not object to the "representation" of the client, and the Area Director has approved an application for any extension,[32] the solicitor can in practice act as advocate for the client and get paid. Finally, the Legal Aid Act 1979 made special provision for "assistance by way of representation" in certain situations and this development is considered further below.[33]

---

[27] Legal Aid Act 1988, s.2(2).

[28] *Ibid.*, s.2(3).

[29] *Ibid.*, s.2(6). This would involve seeking an extension to the financial limit, see below p. 445.

[30] Below, pp. 507–508.

[31] A "McKenzie adviser" is an adviser who accompanies a party to proceedings before a court or tribunal and gives advice on the conduct of the case, and is so called as a result of *McKenzie* v. *McKenzie* [1971] Ch. 33, where an Australian barrister (not called McKenzie) was held to have been wrongly excluded from the hearing of the action. The Court of Appeal adopted the words of Lord Tenterden C.J. in *Collier* v. *Hicks* (1831) 2 B.A. 663 at p. 669: "Any person, whether he be a professional man or not, may attend as a friend of either party, may take notes, may quietly make suggestions, and give advice; but no one can demand to take part in the proceedings as an advocate, contrary to the regulations of the court as settled by the discretion of the justices." There is, however, no *right* to a McKenzie adviser: *R.* v. *Leicester City JJ.*, *ex p. Barrow, The Times*, January 9, 1991, in the context of proceedings to enforce payment of the community charge. See O. Hansen, (1991) 141 N.L.J. 122.

[32] See the *Legal Aid Handbook 1990*, pp. 31–32: criteria specified by the Legal Aid Board are that it will normally be unreasonable to grant an extension (a) where full legal aid is available and the client will be better served by full representation; and (b) unless the solicitor can satisfy the Area Office that by reason of either the difficulty of the case, or the importance to the client or the inability of the client to act without legal help it is necessary for the client to have the services of a McKenzie adviser.

[33] At pp. 446–447, 452. The general question of the desirability of legal representation at tribunals is considered below at pp. 742–746.

Another limitation placed upon the scheme is the amount of advice which a solicitor is permitted to give without reference to the Area Director. From March 1973 (when the scheme started) until October 1980 this figure stood at £25 worth of advice.[34] It was subsequently raised to £40 in October 1980 and £50 in November 1983. The limit in respect of advice in relation to undefended divorce proceedings had been raised to £45 in April 1977 when legal aid ceased to be available for such proceedings and that figure was subsequently raised to £55 in 1979, £75 in 1981 and £90 in 1985. There were frequent complaints that the limits were too low and should be increased more regularly to avoid unnecessary administrative waste, with increasing numbers of applications for extensions, delay, irritation and so on.[35] From April 1, 1989, the limit for advice and assistance provided to a petitioner for divorce or judicial separation has been three times the sum for preparation for magistrates' court criminal proceedings; and in other cases, two times that sum.[36] Accordingly, in future the limit will rise with increase in the hourly remuneration rates,[37] which should ease the position.

Further limitations were introduced in 1989 when considerable restrictions were placed on the use of the scheme for conveyancing and wills. Conveyancing services are now only covered where they are necessary to implement a court order, or an agreement made in matrimonial proceedings, or where the client is proposing to enter a rental purchase agreement or conditional sale agreement. Advice and assistance in making a will can only be given to a client who is over 70, or disabled or suffering from a mental disorder (or a parent or guardian wishing to provide for such a person), or a single parent wishing to appoint a testamentary guardian.[38] The exclusion of wills and conveyancing originated in a recommendation of the Legal Aid Scrutiny that public money should be directed towards the enforcement or defence of rights and not simply to enable clients to arrange their own affairs.[39] The recommendation, and its ultimate partial acceptance, have been criticised on the grounds that lack of legal advice at an early stage may simply lead to disputes later on, to be resolved with the support of legal aid, and that the cost savings were unlikely to be substantial.[40]

(c) Eligibility

Would-be recipients of advice under the green form scheme must demonstrate their eligibility by complying with a means test. The result of the application of the test will establish entitlement to advice free of charge; or

[34] Legal Advice and Assistance Act 1972, s.3; Legal Aid Act 1974, s.3(2).
[35] *e.g. 30th Legal Aid Annual Report* [1979–80], p. 5; below, p. 457.
[36] Legal Advice and Assistance Regulations 1989 (S.I. 1989 No. 340), reg. 4(1)(*b*)(*c*). The limit does not apply to urgent advice and assistance at police stations or to duty solicitor arrangements: *ibid.*, reg. 4(2); a £90 limit normally applies to advice and assistance at police stations: *ibid.*, reg. 4(1)(*a*).
[37] The figure for preparation for magistrates' courts criminal proceedings is found in the Legal Aid in Criminal and Care Proceedings (Costs) Regulations 1989 (S.I. 1989 No. 343), Sched. 1, Part I, para. 1(1)(*a*), as amended. In 1990–91 it was £42 per hour (£44.50p. for London).
[38] Legal Advice and Assistance (Scope) Regulations 1989 (S.I. 1989 No. 550), regs. 3, 4.
[39] *Legal Aid Scrutiny* (1986), Vol. 2, Pt. IV, para. 24.
[40] *36th Legal Aid Annual Reports* (1985–86), p. 154 (the Law Society); *37th Annual Reports* (1986–87), p. 156 (Lord Chancellor's Advisory Committee); *Legal Action*, December 1988, p. 4 (L.A.G.).

entitlement subject to a contribution; or disentitlement. The test is administered by the solicitor who will require information about the "*disposable capital*" and "*disposable income*" of the applicant. An applicant in receipt of income support or family credit is automatically entitled to advice without payment of contribution provided that his or her capital does not exceed the prescribed limits. The financial criteria are altered from time to time by regulations.

A client who has *disposable capital* in excess of the prescribed limit is not entitled to assistance at all; a client who has *disposable income* in excess of the lower limit is liable to pay a contribution towards the cost of the advice. A person who has disposable income in excess of the higher limit becomes disentitled.[41]

The solicitor calculates entitlement by use of the "Key Card' and the green form itself. The Key Card and the green form are intended to be placed side by side and are reproduced on pages 448–451. The card discloses the financial limits, the range of contributions and the advice given to the solicitor on the completion of the form. One further point to note is that the Legal Aid Board may exercise a statutory charge on any money or property recovered or preserved by the client in respect of unpaid fees.[42] Even though there are both specific and general exemptions from this provision[43] it is so important to the client that the solicitor must be at pains to explain its effect very carefully to an applicant for legal advice.

(d) Assistance by way of representation[44]

The Legal Aid Act 1979,[45] extended the scope of legal advice and assistance so as to include within the ambit of the scheme, "assistance by way of representation" (ABWOR) at certain designated proceedings.

Whilst the new provisions appeared to create a very wide power to use the scheme for representation in all manner of courts, tribunals or statutory inquiries, the detailed implementation of the section was left to regulations to be made by the Lord Chancellor, whose approach has been cautious. From April 18, 1980, the green form scheme became available for domestic proceedings in magistrates' courts, transferring the cost of representation from civil legal aid to legal advice.[46] The Supplementary Benefits Commission (who then carried out the means assessment in legal aid) were released from 50,000 assessments a year, but the overall effect was minimal. Indeed, there was some inconsistency in the provisions since the capital limits for legal advice and legal aid were different and some applicants might still be

---

[41] Legal Advice and Assistance Regulations 1989 (S.I. 1989 No. 340), regs. 11–13, Sched. 3.

[42] Legal Aid Act 1988, s.11.

[43] Legal Advice and Assistance Regulations 1989, regs. 32 and 33, and Schedule 4. See also below, pp. 512–513.

[44] O. Hansen, *Using Civil Legal Aid: the 1989 Scheme* (L.A.G., 1989), Chap. 3; *35th Legal Aid Annual Reports* [1984–85], pp. 248–261; *Legal Aid Handbook 1990*, pp. 36–44.

[45] s.1, amending the Legal Aid Act 1974, s.2. See now the Legal Aid Act 1988, s.2(4) (definition of "representation"), 8(2); Legal Advice and Assistance (Scope) Regulations 1989 (S.I. 1989 No. 550), Part III; Legal Advice and Assistance Regulations 1989 (S.I. 1989 No. 340), regs. 5, 7, 22, 27.

[46] See now the Scope Regulations, Schedule, as amended by S.I. 1990 No. 1477. The Schedule also now applies to appeals against prohibition notices under s.10A of the Fire Precautions Act 1971: *ibid.*

forced to apply for legal aid.[47] Since 1980, ABWOR has been made available in Mental Health Review Tribunals (from 1982)[48]; prison disciplinary proceedings before a board of visitors where legal representation has been granted (from 1984)[49]; and in respect of applications for warrants of further detention (or extensions) under the Police and Criminal Evidence Act 1984 (from 1986).[50] There is also provision for ABWOR to be provided at the request of a magistrates' court or a county court by a solicitor within the precincts of the court for purposes other than the provision of ABWOR, where the court considers that the case should proceed the same day and that the client would not otherwise receive representation. The client must not have previously been refused representation.[51]

ABWOR would only be highly significant if it were to be used for a much wider range of proceedings, especially those for which legal aid is not available. One critic expressed fears that it might "... become a new kind of legal aid on the cheap,"[52] yet others were concerned lest it be thought that the green form was appropriate for anything other than low-cost proceedings. The Law Society conceded that it might "... be suitable for some tribunal proceedings or even some criminal proceedings in magistrates' courts," but remained "firmly convinced of the necessity for retaining the certificate [legal aid] procedure for cases which are likely to be lengthy and costly."[53]

At least the powers are there in the statute and have been used in some cases. ABWOR is a useful peg for piecemeal extensions of publicly-funded representation.

A solicitor is required to obtain authority to use the green form scheme in such proceedings.[54] An application must be made to the Area Director, and there is a right to appeal against a refusal to the area committee.[55] Eligibility depends on the client's resources[56]: the income limits and contributions are the same as for the ordinary green form scheme, but the capital limit is different.[57] Counsel may be briefed with the approval of the Area Director; assistance may be withdrawn in certain circumstances; costs may be awarded out of the legal aid fund to an unassisted party; the statutory charge operates

---

[47] *30th Legal Aid Annual Reports* [1979–80], p. 12. Conversely, an application for legal aid will be refused if the applicant is eligible for ABWOR: see the Legal Aid Act 1988, s.15(3)(*b*). In 1986 the capital limit for ABWOR was aligned with the lower limit for civil legal aid.

[48] The Law Society has set up a panel of solicitors with experience in MHRT work.

[49] This followed the decision of the Divisional Court in *R.* v. *Secretary of State for the Home Department, ex p. Tarrant* [1985] Q.B. 251 that boards had a discretion to allow legal representation in the light of such factors as the seriousness of the case, whether a point of law was involved, the capacity of the prisoner, procedural difficulties in the way of a prisoner preparing his or her own case, and the need for reasonable speed and fairness.

[50] See now the Legal Advice and Assistance (Scope) Regulations 1989 (S.I. 1989 No. 550), regs. 7(1)(*a*), (*c*), 9. On warrants of further detention, see below, p. 606.

[51] Scope Regulations, reg. 7(1)(*b*), 8. These provisions are narrower than those replaced (Legal Advice and Assistance Regulations (No. 2) 1980 (S.I. 1980 No. 1898), reg. 19): See D. Burrows, (1989) 139 N.L.J. 1348. The provision of advice and representation by duty solicitors under reg. 7(2) and (4) is considered separately, below.

[52] Lord Gifford, in the debate on the Legal Aid Act 1979 (H.C.Deb., Vol. 398, col. 919).

[53] *30th Legal Aid Annual Reports* [1979–80], p. 12.

[54] Except in respect of warrants of further detention and the precincts provisions.

[55] Legal Advice and Assistance Regulations 1989 (S.I. 1989 No. 340), regs. 22, 26–27.

[56] Except in respect of warrants of further detention.

[57] The disposable capital limit is £3,000, and a person on income support is deemed not to have capital over that limit: Legal Advice and Assistance Regulations 1989, regs. 11(2), 13(3).

GF 1

LEGAL AID BOARD
LEGAL AID ACT 1988

GREEN FORM

Key Card

PLEASE USE BLOCK CAPITALS

Surname	Forenames	Male/Female	AREA REF. No.

Address

CAPITAL		CLIENT	£
TOTAL SAVINGS and OTHER CAPITAL		SPOUSE OR COHABITEE	£
		TOTAL	£

Ⓐ

INCOME

State whether in receipt of Income Support or Family Credit

YES/NO   If the answer if YES ignore the rest of this Section.

Ⓑ

NOTES FOR SOLICITORS

1. Advice and assistance may only be given in relation to the making of **wills** in the circumstances set out in The Legal Advice and Assistance (Scope) Regulations 1989. In such circumstances your client must complete **Form GF 4**

2. Where advice and assistance are being given in respect of **divorce or judicial separation proceedings** and the work to be carried out includes the preparation of a petition, the solicitor will be entitled to ask for his claim for costs and disbursements to be assessed up to an amount referred to in The Legal Advice and Assistance Regulations 1989.

Total weekly Gross Income

Client	£
Spouse or Cohabitee	£
TOTAL	£

Allowances and Deductions from Income

Income tax	£	Ⓒ
National Insurance Contributions, etc.	£	Ⓓ
Spouse	£	Ⓔ

Dependent children and/or other dependants	Number	
Under 5		£
5 but under 11		£
11 „ „ 13		£
13 „ „ 16		£
16 „ „ 18		£
18 and over		£

Ⓕ

LESS TOTAL DEDUCTIONS	→	£
TOTAL WEEKLY DISPOSABLE INCOME		£

TO BE COMPLETED AND SIGNED BY CLIENT

I am over the compulsory school-leaving age.

I have/have not previously received help from a solicitor about this matter under the Legal Aid and Advice Schemes.

I am liable to pay a contribution not exceeding   ... ... £

Ⓖ

I understand that any money or property which is recovered or preserved for me may be subject to a deduction if my contribution (if any) is less than my Solicitor's charges.

The information on this page is to the best of my knowledge correct and complete. I understand that I may be prosecuted for giving false information.

Date ....   Signature ....

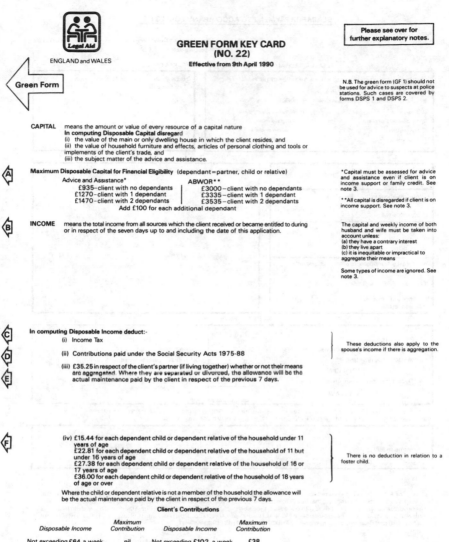

ENGLAND and WALES

GREEN FORM KEY CARD
(NO. 22)
Effective from 9th April 1990

Please see over for further explanatory notes.

Green Form

N.B. The green form (GF 1) should not be used for advice to suspects at police stations. Such cases are covered by forms DSPS 1 and DSPS 2.

CAPITAL means the amount or value of every resource of a capital nature
In computing Disposable Capital disregard
(i) the value of the main or only dwelling house in which the client resides, and
(ii) the value of household furniture and effects, articles of personal clothing and tools or implements of the client's trade, and
(iii) the subject matter of the advice and assistance.

A **Maximum Disposable Capital for Financial Eligibility** (dependant=partner, child or relative)

Advice and Assistance*	ABWOR**
£935 – client with no dependants	£3000 – client with no dependants
£1270 – client with 1 dependant	£3335 – client with 1 dependant
£1470 – client with 2 dependants	£3535 – client with 2 dependants
Add £100 for each additional dependant	

*Capital must be assessed for advice and assistance even if client is on income support or family credit. See note 3.

**All capital is disregarded if client is on income support. See note 3.

B **INCOME** means the total income from all sources which the client received or became entitled to during or in respect of the seven days up to and including the date of this application.

The capital and weekly income of both husband and wife must be taken into account unless:
(a) they have a contrary interest
(b) they live apart
(c) it is inequitable or impractical to aggregate their means

Some types of income are ignored. See note 3.

C **D** **E** **In computing Disposable Income deduct:-**

(i) Income Tax

(ii) Contributions paid under the Social Security Acts 1975-88

(iii) £35.25 in respect of the client's partner (if living together) whether or not their means are aggregated. Where they are separated or divorced, the allowance will be the actual maintenance paid by the client in respect of the previous 7 days.

These deductions also apply to the spouse's income if there is aggregation.

F (iv) £15.44 for each dependent child or dependent relative of the household under 11 years of age
£22.81 for each dependent child or dependent relative of the household of 11 but under 16 years of age
£27.38 for each dependent child or dependent relative of the household of 16 or 17 years of age
£36.00 for each dependent child or dependent relative of the household of 18 years of age or over

Where the child or dependent relative is not a member of the household the allowance will be the actual maintenance paid by the client in respect of the previous 7 days.

There is no deduction in relation to a foster child.

Client's Contributions

Disposable Income	Maximum Contribution	Disposable Income	Maximum Contribution
Not exceeding £64 a week	nil	Not exceeding £102 a week	£38
„ £72 „	£5	„ £108 „	£45
„ £78 „	£12	„ £114 „	£51
„ £84 „	£19	„ £120 „	£58
„ £90 „	£25	„ £125 „	£64
„ £96 „	£32	„ £130 „	£70
		„ £135 „	£75

G Where the initial green form limit is two hours' worth of work (the green form rate is currently £39.25 per hour or £41.75 in London), a client's contribution in excess of this amount can only be called for if a financial extension has been obtained from the legal aid area office.

Note The green form must be signed by the client at the initial interview as soon as his/her eligibility has been determined except in the case of an authorised postal application.

INFORMATION AND ADVICE SERVICES

CLAIM FOR PAYMENT TO ACCOMPANY FORM G F 2

Name of Client

Has a Legal Aid Order been made?   Yes/No.

If so, give date ....

PLEASE ATTACH ANY AUTHORITIES GIVEN BY THE AREA OFFICE.

TICK THE APPROPRIATE LETTER TO INDICATE THE NATURE OF THE PROBLEM

A. Divorce or judicial separation (see note on page 1)

B. Other family matters (Specify in Summary)   G. Accident/injuries

C. Crime   H. Welfare benefits/tribunals

D. Landlord/tenant/housing   J. Immigration/Nationality

E. H.P. and Debt   K. Consumer problems

F. Employment   L. Other matters (Specify in Summary)

Has any money or property been recovered?
If so, give details.

No. of letters written	
No. of telephone calls Made Received	
Time otherwise spent: Specify in Summary	

Summary of work done:

Has a legal aid certificate or order been granted?
          Yes/No.

If not, is one being applied for?   Yes/No.

Certificate or Order No.
if appropriate:

PARTICULARS OF COSTS

£   £

1. Profit costs   Details of disbursements: –

2. Disbursements (including Counsel's fees)   Counsel's fees (if any)

3. Add VAT as appropriate   Other disbursements (listed)

          TOTAL CLAIM

4. Deduct maximum contribution (if any)

          NET CLAIM

Have you previously made a claim for legal advice and assistance for your client in respect of divorce or judicial separation
proceedings or matters connected therewith.   YES/NO   If Yes, how much was allowed   £ ....

Signed .... Solicitor Date .... Solicitor's ref. ....

Firm name (in full) ....

Address ....

Date ....   NOTICE OF ASSESSMENT

The Area Director has assessed your costs in this matter as set out below. In view of the fact that the sum assessed is less than that claimed, you may appeal in writing to the Area Committee in support of your claim as originally submitted or on any item in it, if you wish. These representations must be received within 14 days of the date hereof. I have deleted this matter from the consolidated claim form G.F.2 with which it was sent and I should be obliged if you would do the same. If you accept the assessment, please include this matter on your next consolidated claim form as assessed below AND RE-SUBMIT THIS FORM WITH IT.

Authorised Signatory Legal Aid Area No.

£

1. Profit costs

2. Disbursements

3. Add VAT as appropriate

          TOTAL CLAIM

4. Deduct maximum contribution (if any)

          NET CLAIM

NOTE. –You are advised to keep a copy of this page because if in the same matter your client obtains a L.A. Certificate or Order, you may on taxation of your costs and disbursements be required to produce to the Taxing Officer a copy of this form indicating work done and quantum of payment. You may also require a copy of this page if after submitting your claim for payment you apply to the Area Office for a financial extension to enable you to give further advice and assistance to your Client.

Oakley Press Ltd   April 1989

GREEN FORM KEY CARD (NO. 22)
EXPLANATORY NOTES

1. General
Your attention is particularly drawn to *The Legal Advice and Assistance Regulations 1989* ("the regulations") and to *The Legal Advice and Assistance (Scope) Regulations 1989* ("the scope regulations").

2. Conveyancing and Wills
You should note that it is not permitted to give advice and assistance in respect of conveyancing matters or the making of a will except in those circumstances set out in *regulations 3* and *4* of the scope regulations. Form GF4 must be signed by the client in respect of advice and assistance in the making of a will.

3. Financial Eligibility
(a) The responsibility for determining eligibility is placed upon the solicitor under *Schedule 2* of the regulations.

(b) *Schedule 2* of the regulations sets out the method of assessment of resources of the client. The only deductions and allowances which can be made are those referred to in *Schedule 2*. Built-in deductions have already been made for miscellaneous expenditure such as rent, mortgage repayments and hire-purchase repayments etc.

(c) When considering a client's means it may be useful to have the following points in mind:-

(i) If part of the main dwelling is let and the client lives in the remaining part, although the capital value of the main dwelling house should be left out of account in computing capital, the rent should be included in computing income.

(ii) Capital means the amount or value of every resource of a capital nature so that capital derived from a bank loan or borrowing facilities should be taken into account.

(iii) There is no power to disregard income in self-employed cases merely because the client may have incurred unspecified expenses at an earlier date.

(iv) A cohabitee should be included within the definitions of a spouse.

(v) Income means the total income from all sources which the client received or became entitled to during or in respect of the seven days up to and including the date of application. It will include child benefit.

(vi) Fostering allowances received in respect of fostered children should not be taken into account in assessing the financial eligibility of the client.

(vii) Mobility Allowance should be disregarded when computing income.

(viii) Because different capital limits apply for advice and assistance and ABWOR, clients may be eligible for ABWOR when not eligible for advice and assistance.

(ix) Clients in receipt of income support will always be eligible for ABWOR regardless of capital but not necessarily for advice and assistance.

4. Solicitor and Client relationship
(a) A solicitor may, for reasonable cause, either refuse to accept an application for legal advice and assistance or, having accepted it, decline to give advice and assistance without giving reasons to the client. He may however be required to give reasons to the legal aid area office.

(b) Once financial eligibility has been established, a client should be told the amount of the contribution due (if any), and arrangements should be made for payment either outright or by instalments. Any contribution paid should be retained on client account until the matter for which advice and assistance has been given has been concluded.

(c) If the contribution exceeds the costs payable and VAT, the excess should be returned to the client.

5. Remuneration
(a) The initial financial limit of expenditure (at present two hours' worth of work, or three hours' worth of work in the case of an undefended divorce or judicial separation petition) is exclusive of VAT as is any financial extension granted.

(b) The financial limit of three hours' worth of work in undefended divorce or judicial separation cases is only applicable where a petition has been drafted. It need not, however, have been filed.

(c) The legal aid fund is only responsible for paying to solicitor and counsel such of their costs as are not covered by the client's contribution (if any), party and party costs awarded and the charge which arises in the solicitor's favour on any property recovered or preserved. *Schedule 4* of the regulations sets out the circumstances when the charge does not apply. Application may be made to the area committee for authority not to enforce the charge where (a) it would cause grave hardship or distress to the client, or (b) it could be enforced only with unreasonable difficulty.

(d) Costs for work done under *regulation 7* or *regulation 8* of the scope regulations, together with any advice and assistance, should not exceed the financial limit.

6. Court Proceedings
A solicitor may not take steps in court proceedings unless either approval is given by the legal aid area office for ABWOR in a magistrates' court or a solicitor is acting according to the other conditions detailed in *regulation 7* and *regulation 8* of the scope regulations.

7. Authorities
(a) The authority of the legal aid area office is required before accepting an application from a child, a person on behalf of a child or a patient, such person not falling within the categories referred to in *regulation 14* of the regulations, a person residing outside England and Wales, or a person who has already received advice and assistance from another solicitor on the same matter.

(b) Approval of the legal aid area office is required for ABWOR. Even if approval is given, the prior permission of the legal aid area office is required to obtain a report, or opinion or an expert, to tender expert evidence or to perform an act which is either unusual in its nature or involves unusually large expenditure. Thus the prior permission of the legal aid area office would be required before obtaining a blood test.

Printed by Oakley Press Plc

subject to specified exceptions.[58] All these provisions indicate the hybrid nature of assistance by way of representation. Legal advice in form—legal aid in substance.

(e) Duty solicitor schemes[59]

The first duty solicitor scheme was initiated by the Bristol Law Society in 1972 with the objective of discovering whether there were defendants appearing before Bristol Magistrates who were in need of legal advice but not receiving it.[60] Experienced solicitors took turns in seeing defendants in custody and those referred to them by the court so that they could advise (not represent) an appropriate course of action. This could involve an adjournment for legal aid application, social welfare report, referral to another solicitor, bail application or simply suggestions for a plea in mitigation. All those involved in the Bristol scheme (local law society, magistrates, magistrates' clerks and police) expressed themselves to be satisfied with the result and this scheme provided the model for others which followed.

Since the development of schemes was left to local initiative and was dependent upon the co-operation of the local magistrates' court, national coverage was patchy and the services offered were variable. By mid-1975 there were 29 duty solicitor schemes operating[61] and the Law Society, in consultation with other interested parties, prepared and published a guide for the assistance of local law societies.[62] This document listed such matters as the functions of a duty solicitor, the scope of the scheme, remuneration,[63] emergency services and waivers.[64]

These schemes were well received and had extended considerably by the end of the 1970s. The Royal Commission on Legal Services described them as ". . . indispensable in a number of ways: they provide pre-trial advice to defendants who are often confused or ignorant and who have not previously obtained it, they encourage the adequate preparation of bail applications and help to reduce the number of ill-advised pleas, whether of guilt or innocence, and the number of remands required."[65]

The Legal Aid Act 1982[66] enabled the Law Society, under scheme-making powers contained in the Legal Aid Act 1974,[67] to formulate a uniform scheme for the provision of duty solicitor services. The first statutory scheme was the Legal Aid (Duty Solicitor) Scheme 1983.[68] This provided for a three-tier committee structure. Overall responsibility was exercised by the

[58] *Ibid.*, regs. 23, 25, 27, 32, 33, Sched. 4.
[59] A. Blake *et al.*, *The Duty Solicitors' Handbook* (1988).
[60] The pilot scheme was described in (1972) 69 L.S. Gaz 819.
[61] *25th Legal Aid Annual Reports* [1974–75], pp. 6–7.
[62] (1975) 72 L.S. Gaz. 577–579.
[63] The Law Society's Guide advised that neither the green form nor criminal legal aid was ideal, but that the former should where possible be used for advice and the latter for representation.
[64] A waiver of Rule 1 of the Solicitors' Practice Rules was required for voluntary schemes as in law centres and legal advice centres.
[65] R.C.L.S. Vol. 1, p. 93.
[66] s.1.
[67] s.15.
[68] Set out as Appendix 4P to the *34th Legal Aid Annual Reports* [1983–84], pp. 185–197, discussed at pp. 37–43, *ibid.* See S. Hillyard, (1983) 80 L.S. Gaz. 2649 and (1984) 81 L.S. Gaz. 1184. It was replaced, successively, by the Legal Aid (Duty Solicitor) Schemes 1985, 1987 and 1988, and the Duty Solicitor Arrangements 1989 (see below).

Law Society's Legal Aid (Duty Solicitor) Committee.[69] There were 24 regional duty solicitor committees,[70] whose functions included those of deciding at which courts duty solicitors should be in attendance, and establishing and appointing the members of the local committees. Local schemes were run by a local duty solicitor committee,[71] whose functions included that of considering applications from those wishing to act as duty solicitors. Selection criteria were specified, including the requirements that the solicitor's office be reasonably accessible to the appropriate magistrates' court and that the solicitor have sufficient criminal advocacy experience during the previous 18 months.[72] An unsuccessful applicant could appeal to the regional committee.

Under the scheme "advice and representation" was available without a means test or the payment of a contribution. A duty solicitor had an obligation to provide advice to persons in custody and, if desired, to make a bail application; he or she had a discretion to provide advice and representation to defendants, whether or not in custody, in cases involving imprisonable offences, and even in connection with non-imprisonable offences in exceptional cases. Representation could not, however, be provided for contested cases or committal proceedings. The Scheme emphasised the right of defendants to choose their own solicitor, and required the duty solicitor to check whether the defendant already had one. Remuneration was claimed from the appropriate area legal aid committee.[73]

The first task of the regional committees was to bring the existing voluntary schemes within the scope of the statutory Scheme and to establish new local schemes so as to secure coverage of "busy" courts.[74] The next stage involved the establishment of schemes for "less busy" courts.[75] For the former, the normal requirement would be for the duty solicitor to attend the court; for the latter the predominant arrangement would be a "call-in" scheme based on either a list or a rota of duty solicitors. Coverage has progressively been extended, with 88 per cent. of courts covered by 1990.[76]

A parallel development, which started in 1983 in anticipation of implementation of what became the Police and Criminal Evidence Act 1984, saw the planning and introduction of the "24-hour duty solicitor scheme" for the

[69] The Law Society's Legal Aid Committee and three nominees of the Lord Chancellor.
[70] Including a representative of each local duty solicitor committee and of the legal aid area committee, a J.P., a justices' clerk, and two lay persons, and perhaps representatives of the probation service, police and prosecuting solicitors and, in London, stipendary magistrates. A police member became a requirement (following the development of the 24-hour scheme for advice at police stations: see below).
[71] With at least three solicitors with criminal advocacy experience, and perhaps a J.P., a justices' clerk and not more than three lay persons; a *requirement* that there be at least one lay member was introduced in 1987.
[72] Provision was subsequently made for an alternative requirement of 12 months experience with a compulsory interview.
[73] Initially under the Legal Advice and Representation (Duty Solicitor) (Remuneration) Regulations 1983 (S.I. 1983 No. 1451). Remuneration is based on the time spent at court (plus travel costs where a duty solicitor is called in by the court or attends court at weekends or Bank Holidays). The current regulations are the Legal Advice and Assistance (Duty Solicitor) (Remuneration) Regulations 1989 (S.I. 1989 No. 341), as amended.
[74] Defined as those dealing with more than 1,250 new (non-motoring) defendants per annum or 10 per sitting; there were estimated to be about 225: *34th Legal Aid Annual Reports* [1983–84], pp. 40–41.
[75] *35th Legal Aid Annual Reports* [1984–85], pp. 36–37.
[76] *Legal Aid Board Annual Reports* (1989–90), p. 33.

provision of legal advice to suspects and others in police stations. As we discuss elsewhere,[77] the 1984 Act introduced a new statutory right to legal advice, as part of a detailed legal regime governing the detention and interrogation of suspects. Both this and the 24-hour Scheme were implemented as from January 1, 1986.[78] Administration of this Scheme was passed to the committee structure already established for court duty solicitor schemes, and indeed provided an additional impetus for the establishment of new local court schemes.

A local 24-hour scheme can take one of three forms. First, there can be a rota scheme, where all the member solicitors are on duty in turn. During the duty period the solicitor has to be available all the time to provide advice over the telephone or at the police station, and receives a standby payment, up to half of which is deducted if advice is provided up to that level of work. Secondly, there can be a panel scheme where the member solicitors are asked in turn to provide advice; as no one is obliged to give the advice there is no standby payment. Thirdly, there may be a combined rota/panel scheme where a panel normally operates but there is a rota at certain times, such as at night, weekends or bank holidays. Panel schemes are more appropriate where the volume of work is low. Solicitors are contacted by telephone, with calls channelled through a service provided by Air Call plc. The proportion of police stations covered has increased steadily to 95 per cent., the majority of the rest being small stations where there are likely to be few suspects.[79]

The Scheme has been successful in contributing to the increase in the proportion of suspects who receive legal advice at the police station, although that proportion is still relatively low.[80] As would be expected, own solicitors are less available than duty solicitors and rota schemes perform better than panels.[81] There have, however, been difficulties. On the one hand, the rates of remuneration are regarded by solicitors as low.[82] The withdrawal of solicitors from a scheme can lead to increasingly unacceptable burdens on the rest, and a number of local schemes have collapsed or come near to collapse.[83] On the other, a research report commissioned by the Lord Chancellor's Department was critical of the quality of service provided by duty solicitors, with a high proportion relying on telephoned advice rather than attendance at the police station. It suggested that standards of recruit-

---

[77] Below, pp. 607–608, 672–675.
[78] Only just: the revised Legal Aid (Duty Solicitor) Scheme 1985 was only approved on December 10, 1985; much ill-will was generated by the L.C.D.'s delay in providing information, especially about remuneration, until late 1985: see the *36th Legal Aid Annual Reports* (1985–86), pp. 15–19.
[79] *Legal Aid Board Annual Reports* (1989–90), p. 33.
[80] See below, pp. 673–674. Duty solicitors give over one-third of all police station advice: A. Sanders *et al.*, *Advice and Assistance at Police Stations and the 24-Hour Duty Solicitor Scheme* (L.C.D. 1989), p. 185.
[81] Sanders, *et al.*, (1989), p. 185.
[82] See the Legal Advice and Assistance at Police Stations (Remuneration) Regulations 1989 (S.I. 1989 No. 342), as amended by S.I. 1990 No. 487 and S.I. 1991 No. 527. Advice provided by a suspect's own solicitor is also remunerated under these regulations, with less favourable rates for unsocial hours and travelling and waiting.
[83] See Sanders *et al.*, (1989), pp. 160–161. The collapse of the St. Albans scheme was well documented: see *Legal Aid Board Annual Reports* (1989–90), pp. 33–34.

ment and discipline appeared to be rather low and that there was a reluctance to scrutinise service delivery.[84]

From April 1, 1989, responsibility for both aspects of the duty solicitor scheme has passed to the Legal Aid Board. The 1988 Scheme was replaced by the Duty Solicitor Arrangements 1989,[85] and the Legal Aid (Duty Solicitor) Committee of the Law Society by the Duty Solicitor Committee appointed by the Legal Aid Board. This Committee comprises three members of the Board, two lay and two solicitor members from regional duty solicitor committees, two nominees from the Law Society, and one each from the Justices' Clerks Society, the Magistrates' Association and the Association of Chief Police Officers. The regional and local committees remain, but are now responsible to the Duty Solicitor Committee. The new Arrangements are very similar to the 1988 Scheme, the main, and welcome, change being the removal of the lower tier in what had previously been a two-tier system for remuneration for advice at police stations: a solicitor could undertake up to £90 of work, extendable retrospectively, where the client was in custody for an arrestable offence, but only up to £50 (nonextendable) otherwise. The distinction had been criticised by both the Law Society and the Lord Chancellor's Advisory Committee from its inception.[86]

The Board has decided to change the rules to require duty solicitors to attend the police station where a suspect is to be questioned about an arrestable offence, when an identity parade is to be held, or the suspect complains of serious maltreatment by the police; unless the solicitor can show exceptional circumstances justifying non-attendance. Attendance is strongly recommended where the suspect is a juvenile or a person at risk.[87]

(f) Green form usage

It was quite clear in 1973 that the new advice scheme was intended to bring into solicitors' offices problems of a kind which had not hitherto surfaced. The analysis of the unmet need for legal services identified types of problem which were not being dealt with as well as types of people. Since the advice scheme now permitted access to a solicitor on *any* question of English law and the advertising campaign which launched it stressed the "social welfare" problems now within the scheme, it was disappointing that the first evidence of usage showed little deviation from the traditional pattern.[88] The absence of legal aid for tribunal representation was advanced as a reason for the very

---

[84] Sanders *et al.*, (1989), Chap. 10 (summarised at (1989) 86 L.S. Gaz. December 6, p. 12). For a lay member's view of the monitoring of schemes, see A. Galbraith, *Legal Action*, January 1988, p. 8. The role of regional and local committees is considered generally in Sanders *et al.*, (1989), Chap. 8.

[85] Made under the Legal Advice and Assistance Regulations 1989 (S.I. 1989 No. 340), regs. 6–8. See E. Cape and A. Blake, *Legal Action*, August 1989, p. 11 and (1989) 86 L.S.Gaz. September 6, p. 19.

[86] See *35th Legal Aid Annual Reports* [1984–85], pp. 246–247; *36th Reports* (1985–86), p. 16; *37th Reports* (1986–87), pp. 166–167. Other changes included a broader power to represent fine defaulters and persons in breach of court orders under the court duty solicitor scheme.

[87] Duty Solicitor Arrangements 1990, discussed by E. Cape, *Legal Action*, March 1991, pp. 21–23.

[88] *24th Legal Aid Annual Reports* [1973–74], Appendix 4, Part II, 2. The analysis, based on a sample of 10 per cent. of claims for payment under the scheme in 1973–74, showed that the largest categories were matrimonial, 60 per cent.; criminal, 10 per cent.; and landlord and tenant, 5 per cent.: the remaining 25 per cent. was spread among the remaining categories, with only 1 per cent. for tribunals.

low percentage of cases concerned with tribunals, as well as the expectation that cases categorised under other headings (e.g. "employment," "landlord and tenant") might have included tribunal work.

In fact, the statistics on the type of problems on which advice is sought have remained remarkably constant since 1973/74. Over the years, the proportion of family cases has settled at just over 40 per cent.; crime at around 22 per cent.; landlord and tenant and housing, and hire purchase and debt, at around 6 per cent. each; accidents and injuries at around 5 per cent.; employment and consumer at around 2 per cent. each; immigration just under 1 per cent. and the rest around 11 per cent.[89] The main features have been a decrease in the proportion of family cases; an increase in the proportion of criminal cases; and, over the last few years, a slight increase in the proportion of welfare benefits cases.[90]

It may be that difficulty in getting people with problems to consult a solicitor is more to do with their perception of the problem and the ability of a solicitor to help than with the cost and availability of the advice service. The Law Society is left to reflect that ". . . the types of problem on which advice and assistance was sought during the past year is surprisingly, and perhaps regrettably, consistent with the experience of previous years . . . people who are eligible for advice and assistance are still accustomed to consult solicitors for a comparatively narrow range of problems."[91]

Apart from questions of the *pattern* of usage, the overall amount of usage has steadily increased,[92] as has the cost.[93] There are, however, considerable regional variations, with variations among solicitors as to their policy in using the green form scheme, and variations in the practice of area offices.[94]

(g) Green form deficiencies

Some would argue that the major deficiency in the green form scheme is that it is administered through solicitors and must, therefore, share the same unattractiveness to some members of the public. The arguments about the location, availability, approachability and cost of the solicitors' offices emerge again in this context. The evidence to support these contentions is equivocal. On the one hand it would appear that only the traditional prob-

---

[89] *Legal Aid Annual Reports*: in recent years, Appendix 1F to the Law Society's, now the Legal Aid Board's, Annual Report. This general picture was confirmed by the Baldwin and Hill (1988) research study, Chap. 2. For surveys of the extent of social welfare work in Newham, Oldham and Cornwall, see E. Kempson, *Legal Advice and Assistance* (1989), Chap. 3, showing considerable geographical variations.

[90] The number of bills rose from 21,833 in 1985–86 to 44,073 in 1989–90 (an increase from 2 per cent. to 4 per cent. of the total bills).

[91] *30th Legal Aid Annual Reports* [1979–80], p. 6.

[92] From 438,519 bills in 1979–80 to 1,077,454 in 1987–88 and 1,029,018 in 1989–90: there was an increase of at least 10 per cent. each year between 1979–80 and 1984–85, smaller increases but some decreases (probably associated with declining eligibility) thereafter: *Legal Aid Annual Reports*: Appendix 1A to the Law Society's Annual Report; Appendix 1A to the *Legal Aid Board Annual Reports*.

[93] Payments totalled £12.3M in 1979–80, compared with £60.4M in 1987–88, £58.1M in 1988–89 and £66.5M in 1989–90.

[94] *e.g.* in deciding whether to pursue a legal aid application or stay with the green form scheme: see Baldwin and Hill (1988), Chap. 2.

lems are being brought in (see above), on the other, the fact that 90 per cent. of green form assessments require no contribution from the client despite the strict financial criteria suggests that the scheme is serving the least well-off.[95] Is it that the "right" people are reaching solicitors with the "wrong" problems?

Four other major criticisms of the scheme have been advanced—that the initial limit is too low; that the financial criteria are too strict; that the scheme is not sufficiently well-known to attract those who need it; and that the system is open to abuse by solicitors.

The first of these criticisms was by far the strongest made by solicitors interviewed for the research study by Baldwin and Hill.[96] The consequences of a low initial limit was that a solicitor would either have to stop work at an early stage and wait for an extension to be authorised, which "is time-consuming, causes delay and raises difficulties with clients," or work on without an extension. In any event it might not be worthwhile seeking an extension where the sum over the limit is relatively small. Work might also be unremunerated given the difficulties of extracting contributions from clients.[97] The move to limits based on hours[98] may help, but the periods of two and three hours specified have still been criticised as too low.[99]

The financial criteria are contained on the Key Card reproduced earlier in the chapter[1] and the substantial changes in eligibility introduced in 1979 took away most of the grounds for the criticism that they were pitched too low. However, the position worsened again in the late 1980s so that less than half the population appear to be eligible.[2]

The advertising of the scheme and the consequent level of public awareness has been a constant source of concern. Two targets have been identified. One, the general public, can really only be reached by direct advertising in the media—the other, the "gate-keepers," those who work in the social field and in advice agencies, need to be approached much more selectively. They are the people who can refer clients on to solicitors and it is highly likely that the "Advisory Liaison Service" and the proposed liaison officers[3] could have played a significant part in making and fostering those contacts. In their absence, the information circulating about the green form scheme can be haphazard depending upon the enthusiasm of voluntary and statutory advice agencies and the activities of local law societies. Advertising campaigns have been sporadic and their effect is extremely difficult to assess.[4]

---

[95] *33rd Legal Aid Annual Reports* [1982–83], p. 55; *Legal Aid Board Annual Reports* (1989–90), p. 78.

[96] Baldwin and Hill (1988), p. 62, Table 14. This criticism was over 10 times more common than complaints that the rates of remuneration were too low.

[97] *Ibid.*, pp. 54–64.

[98] Above, p. 445.

[99] *38th Legal Aid Annual Reports* (1987–88), p. 105 (Lord Chancellor's Advisory Committee).

[1] Above, pp. 447–451.

[2] C. Glasser, (1989) 86 L.S. Gaz. April 5, 1989, pp. 9, 11. There is an analogous problem with eligibility rates for legal aid: see below, pp. 516–517.

[3] Above, pp. 435, 436.

[4] Some have been specific, such as that to launch the £25 scheme, in 1973 and that directed at the North-East, others more general, such as the "Don't Trust Whatsisname" campaign. See above p. 137.

As to abuse of the scheme by solicitors, the research study by Baldwin and Hill[5] found that officials in area legal aid offices "tended to view members of the legal profession with considerable suspicion,"[6] but more on the basis that solicitors might make full or excessive use of the scheme[7] than that there was malpractice or dishonesty. The checks that were carried out were not particularly rigorous and did not in fact tend to reveal abuse. Indeed "evidence of serious abuse of the green form scheme has always proved elusive."[8] There was a case for the introduction of much more systematic and thorough random checks: these might detect or deter wrongdoers, although the vast majority of solicitors would be unlikely to risk their livelihoods for trifling amounts; "more importantly they would . . . allay public concern and offical suspicion about improper use of the green form scheme."[9]

Notwithstanding the various deficiencies, mentioned in this section, the overall view of the green form scheme expressed by Baldwin and Hill was encouraging:

> ". . . we have found ourselves at the end of the research thoroughly persuaded of its merits. Notwithstanding the serious criticisms we have made in the report about certain aspects of the scheme, the results, taken as a whole, demonstrate that the green form scheme represents an invaluable social service and provides a source of immediate legal advice to those who need it. . . . [Many] more people are assisted under the . . . scheme than are assisted under all other forms of legal aid put together. This is remarkable given that the . . . scheme makes up only about a fifth of the total legal aid budget."[10]

G. ADMINISTRATION AND POLICY MAKING

Until 1989, the green form scheme and the duty solicitor scheme were administered by the Law Society, as an adjunct to its responsibilities for civil legal aid.[11] The annual reports of the Law Society, and the comments and advice of the Lord Chancellor's Advisory Committee on Legal Aid[12] have been a valuable source of information and of recommendations for changes in policy (whether accepted or not).[13] Other sources of informed comment are the various national bodies with an interest in legal services: the Legal Action Group, NACAB, the Law Centres Federation, the Advice Services Alliance (an umbrella organisation for advice services), the National Con-

---

[5] Baldwin and Hill (1988), Chap. 4.
[6] *Ibid.*, p. 67.
[7] *e.g.* "We found in one firm, for instance, that every client seemed to come out with a will regardless of what the original problem was": statement by an officer cited at p. 68.
[8] *Ibid.*, p. 79.
[9] *Ibid.*, p. 80.
[10] *Ibid.*, pp. 128, 129. A more sceptical view has been expressed by A. Sanders and L. Bridges, (1990) 140 N.L.J. 85, arguing by analogy with their findings on the 24 Hour Duty Solicitor Scheme (above, pp. 454–455); for a critical response see S. Hill, (1990) 140 N.L.J. 323, reply by Sanders and Bridges, (1990) 140 N.L.J. 496.
[11] Below, pp. 506–507.
[12] Constituted under the Legal Aid Act 1974, s.21, and now the Legal Aid Act 1988, s.35. The future of this committee is uncertain.
[13] See the *Legal Aid Annual Reports*; *Legal Aid Board Annual Reports*.

sumer Council and so on.[14] The decisive voice is, as one would expect, that of the Lord Chancellor's Department and the Treasury, given the resource implications of most proposals for change.

The Greater Manchester Legal Services Committee was established in April 1977. It originally consisted of various types of lawyer and representatives of volunteer and statutory organisations, with the common objective of co-ordinating and improving legal services in Manchester.[15] It extended its boundaries in 1985, becoming the North Western Legal Services Committee, covering Greater Manchester, Cumbria and Lancashire. The progress of the Committee has been charted in the Legal Aid Annual Reports[16] and it has an impressive list of achievements. It has stimulated duty solicitor schemes, including schemes at prisons; encouraged law centres; monitored the grant and refusal of legal aid in magistrates' courts; provided training for volunteer workers at advice agencies; published a leaflet aimed at those who have suffered accidents; produced directories of advice agencies; and taken on other responsibilities connected with the stimulation and co-ordination of legal services. Most importantly, it has shown what advances are possible given enthusiasm, goodwill and a full-time secretary paid for out of the Legal Aid Fund.[17]

A North East Legal Services Committee was established in 1982. To the disappointment of the Law Society and the Lord Chancellor's Advisory Committee, the Lord Chancellor declined to fund a full-time secretariat, claiming that it should be left to local or charitable sources.[18] As a result, its activities have been more limited than its counterpart in the North-West.

The Lord Chancellor's Advisory Committee has proposed that a committee should be established for each circuit[19]: "we remain convinced that these could inexpensively and effectively contribute to securing improvements across the country in the co-ordination and standard of legal services."[20] The Legal Aid Board's attitude has been non-committal.[21]

---

[14] The Lord Chancellor's Advisory Committee has regularly convened a Legal Services Conference, with representatives of these and other organisations.

[15] The original members included members of both branches of the legal profession, the Legal Aid Area Secretary, the Director of the local law centre, the clerk to the Bury Magistrates and representatives of the C.A.B., the Child Poverty Action Group, the probation services, the local Social Services Department, the local trades council and other groups.

[16] They are mentioned annually. For fuller treatment, see *32nd Legal Aid Annual Reports* [1981–82], pp. 121–124; *36th Annual Reports* (1985–86), pp. 214–218. See also C. Schofield and V. Hereward, *L.A.G. Bulletin*, June 1979, p. 127 and R. Smith, *Legal Action*, October 1987, pp. 6–7.

[17] The full-time official has undoubtedly played a major part in the success of the experiment. This was a liaison officer appointment authorised by the Lord Chancellor and demonstrates how useful the provisions of the Legal Advice and Assistance Act 1972 (see above, p. 436) could have been if applied nationally.

[18] *34th Legal Aid Annual Reports* [1983–84], pp. 54–55, 346–347, and subsequent Reports. There is a project for the establishment of a committee in South Wales, subject to similar funding difficulties: *37th Annual Reports* (1986–87), pp. 26–27; *39th Annual Reports* (1988–89), p. 3.

[19] *38th Annual Reports* (1987–88), pp. 101–102.

[20] *39th Annual Reports* (1988–89), p. 88.

[21] *Legal Aid Board: Report to the Lord Chancellor* (Cm. 688, 1989), p. 14.

H. REFORM

"In the last analysis, therefore, it is for Parliament to decide the extent to which legal services are to be provided at public expense to meet the needs of the majority of the population. But, unless legal services are provided, the full benefit of our legal rights and safeguards cannot be realised."[22]

The preceding parts of the chapter have shown that the present diversity of sources for legal information and advice has resulted from piecemeal development, partly by lawyers, partly by non-lawyers, without any coherent structure or philosophy. There is legal advice from non-lawyers, from salaried lawyers and from the private profession paid for by the client, the State, local government, charities or provided gratuitously—or a combination of them.

The case for the establishment of a coherent overall strategy for the provision of publicly-funded legal services is overwhelming. An attempt to provide such a strategy was made by the Royal Commission on Legal Services, which reported in 1979.[23] Many of its recommendations were criticised and the government's response was dismissive. Another was made by the Legal Aid Efficiency Scrutiny, a team of civil servants which reported to the Lord Chancellor in 1986. Some of its recommendations were accepted[24] and found their way into the Legal Aid Act 1988. Major changes were, however, left to the new Legal Aid Board, to which responsibility for the management of the legal aid and advice schemes was transferred from the Law Society, and are still in the pipeline. We will consider these in turn. The other source of change in the provision of legal services is the fundamental reform of the legal profession effected by the Courts and Legal Services Act 1990; that is dealt with in Chapter 3.

1. THE ROYAL COMMISSION ON LEGAL SERVICES

(a) Principles[25]

The three basic principles identified by the Commission were unexceptionable. They were all related to the general principle, said to have been established with the introduction of legal aid in 1950, that ". . . legal services should be available to those who need them but cannot afford to pay for them." Despite the acceptance of this principle the Commission found that a large number of people were not obtaining adequate legal services and set out the principles that should, in future, govern the provision of legal services:

(i) Financial assistance out of public funds should be available for every individual (not corporations) who, without it, would suffer an undue financial burden in properly pursuing or defending his or her legal rights;

(ii) All those who receive legal services are entitled to expect the same standard of legal service irrespective of their personal circumstances;

[22] R.C.L.S., Vol. 1, p. 58.
[23] Chaired by Lord Benson (Cmnd. 7648, 1979): see above pp. 25–26.
[24] White Paper, *Legal Aid in England and Wales: A New Framework* (Cm. 118, 1987).
[25] R.C.L.S., Vol. 1, pp. 50–54.

(iii) The client, whether supported out of public funds or fee-paying, should always have a free choice among available lawyers and should not be required to retain an assigned lawyer.

In turning these principles into the means by which legal services were to be provided the Commission did not recommend any radical departure from the present "mixed economy" in legal advice and information. There would still be a place for amateurs, for salaried professionals and for private professionals, all of them supported in varying degrees by government funds.

(b) Proposals

The Commission's main proposals were

  (i) the establishment of an advisory council for Legal Services to keep under review the provision of all forms of legal services;
 (ii) the establishment of regional committees modelled on the Greater Manchester Legal Services Committee (as it then was);
(iii) the encouragement of CABx as first-tier generalist advice agencies, with the development of rota schemes; they should not become over-specialised and required adequate government funding;
 (iv) the establishment of a new species of law centre, "Citizens' Law Centres," financed out of public funds, without involvement in general community work such as the mounting of campaigns or political or social work, with clients paying on the same basis as legally-aided clients of private practitioners, managed by a central agency and advised by a local advisory committee;
  (v) assimilation of the green form scheme with legal aid when the levels of eligibility and contribution could be made the same, with eligibility limits raised;
 (vi) provision for a free initial half-hour interview with a solicitor, available irrespective of means.

(c) Responses

The public response to the Royal Commission Report was largely predictable. Particularly in its treatment of legal services the Report was alleged to be unduly supportive of the private profession and insufficiently imaginative in its proposals for the development of the public sector.

However, the critical response of organisations heavily involved in the current provision of legal services should be noted. The Legal Action Group attacked the Report on all fronts,[26] making particularly strong comment about the failure to recommend significant changes in the private profession and the ineffectual role assigned to the proposed Council for Legal Services. Only a Legal Service Commission with executive powers could do the necessary research and co-ordination job. The Law Centres Federation,[27] not surprisingly, were entirely hostile to the proposed Citizens' Law Centres and their response was directed mainly to that topic. The Federation was

[26] "Legal Services—A new start" LAG (1980).
[27] *A response to the Royal Commission on Legal Services*, Law Centres Federation (1980).

especially opposed to the means-testing of clients and the prospect of central control. Following this pattern, the Greater Manchester Legal Services Committee was also critical of the particular proposals which affected its area of concern and took the view that the regional committees proposed in the Report would not achieve what was required. Despite receiving warm commendation from the Commission, the Committee's response was cool with further criticism of the proposals on law centres and practice in deprived areas. The NACAB responses[28] were less strident in tone but contained detailed criticisms of many aspects of the Report, again, with particular reference to its own area of operation. The professions, by contrast, welcomed the majority of the recommendations with more than a hint of relief.

The Government response was belated and almost insulting.[29] The two volumes of the Commission's Report were dismissed in a very short document. In particular:

(a) the case for the creation of a Council for Legal Services was rejected;

(b) the role of generalised agencies was endorsed, but with no additional funding;

(c) the recommendations on Citizen's Law Centres were still under consideration;

(d) eligibility limits for legal aid were to be retained, and the contributions currently payable are not unreasonable;

(e) the "free half-hour" of advice would not be introduced;

(f) extension to the scheme for assistance by way of representation would be made when necessary.

2. THE LEGAL AID EFFICIENCY SCRUTINY

Following the Benson Report, the Lord Chancellor's Advisory Committee continued to stress the desirability of an overall strategy for the provision of legal services. It noted that the government's response to the Royal Commission "singularly lacked any commitment to a unified approach" and that "lack of clear ministerial responsibility and direction for legal services is a chronic problem.[30] In January 1986, the government appointed a team of officials "to consider the determinants of expenditure on the legal aid scheme by looking at its operation and administration in practice, and make recommendations." The team reported in June 1986.[31] It concluded that there was a pressing need for action in four main areas:

(i) legal aid procedures for handling applications, contributions and payments needed to be redesigned;

---

[28] Memoranda in response to the Report published by NACAB in August 1980 and March 1981.

[29] The Government Response to the Report of the Royal Commission on Legal Services (Cmnd. 9077, 1983).

[30] 34th Legal Aid Annual Reports [1983–84], p. 334.

[31] Legal Aid Efficiency Scrutiny (L.C.D., 1986), Vols. 1 and 2. There had come and gone, meanwhile, with comparatively little result, a management scrutiny by Coopers & Lybrand, a substantial study of eligibility by the Lord Chancellor's Advisory Committee (34th Legal Aid Reports [1983–84], pp. 239–333), and a National Audit Office enquiry (1985–86 H.C. 128) and associated Public Accounts Committee Report (1985–86 H.C. 330).

(ii) improved value for money should be obtained by cutting down on unnecessary procedures, (*e.g.* committals, remand hearings), strengthening controls on the progress of legally aided proceedings, changing listing practices, and restricting legal aid to solicitors who have demonstrated competence by membership of an appropriate panel;

(iii) the arrangements for legal advice represented a wasteful use of resources and did not guarantee a reasonable service to all who need it;

(iv) the administration of the legal aid system should be reorganised to ensure that the systems were simple, that there were clear lines of responsibility and that one organisation had clear overall responsibility for the operation of legal aid and advice.

Many (but not all) of the specific recommendations under (i) and (ii) were accepted and have led or will lead to changes in law or practice.[32] They are dealt with, as appropriate, in the sections on legal aid.[33]

As to the question of overall responsibility for the system, the Scrutiny team recommended that there should be a nationally based Legal Services Board responsible for all aspects of legal aid and advice, controlling all the necessary operations through the existing area offices directly and through agents in the courts.[34] The ensuing White Paper[35] paid tribute to the work of the Law Society but proposed to transfer its responsibilities to a new Legal Aid Board. Provision would be made for the possible transfer of other functions at a later date, (*e.g.* the assessments of means, decisions on the grant of criminal legal aid, and at least some of the determinations of bills now carried out in the courts). The constitution and functions of the Board, established by the Legal Aid Act 1988, are considered below.

The Scrutiny team's proposals for legal advice were the most controversial.[36] Its diagnosis of existing weaknesses was unexceptional, with reference to the lack of co-ordination in the provision of advice agencies, overlap in the service provided by advice agencies and private practitioners and difficulties in obtaining advice in an emergency. The proposals were startling. In essence, the existing green form scheme should be abolished and replaced by a system of advice based on a much greater involvement of advice agencies. Except in criminal areas, initial advice should be given by an advice agency, such as a CAB, rather than a private practitioner, and criminal cases would be limited to one hour's work. Family cases should be only referred to a solicitor where detailed advice and negotiation about the arrangements to be made for financial provision and for the children were needed; other civil cases should only be referred once it was clear that court proceedings should be initiated. The Area Directors should be made responsible for the effective and co-ordinated provision of legal advice and tribunal representation in their areas. The Scrutiny team estimated that this

---

[32] See Vol. 2, Chaps. II and III of the *Scrutiny*; the White Paper, *Legal Aid in England and Wales: A New Framework* (Cm. 118, 1987), Chaps. 5 and 6, and Annex B.
[33] Below, pp. 507–517, 675–680. Committal proceedings and remand hearings are considered at pp. 651, 657–664 and 692–694.
[34] See Vol. 2, Chap. V.
[35] Cm. 118, Chap. 3.
[36] Vol. 2, Chap. IV.

would generate a need for an additional 500 lay advisers and 125 lawyers for the advice agencies.

The proposals were widely regarded as unrealistic, with adverse criticism (at varying strengths) from the Law Society, the Lord Chancellor's Advisory Committee on Legal Aid, NACAB, the Legal Action Group and others.[37] The strong reservations of NACAB were particularly noteworthy given the proposal to switch responsibilities to CABx and other generalist advice agencies. The 1986 NACAB AGM overwhelmingly passed a resolution expressing concern that the proposals might change the fundamental character of the CAB sevice and might prejudice its independence, would cut legal services and reduce freedom of choice of legal service to the poor and would damage working relationships between CABx and legal aid practitioners, other advice agencies and law centres.

The White Paper[38] accepted that there was force in some of the objections that had been made, and expressed the belief that the existing Green Form Scheme could be "improved to provide better service at lower cost."[39] The only changes that would be put into effect immediately would be the removal of wills and conveyancing from the ambit of the scheme.[40] The government was, however, "attracted to the principle of using the skills of advice agencies, especially to deal with those areas of work in which their special experience is likely to be greater than that of many solicitors in private practice.[41] The new Legal Aid Board would accordingly be given power to make alternative arrangements for the provision of particular categories of work. For example, the Board might contract with advice agencies for the provision of advice on welfare benefits, which would then be removed from the scope of the green form scheme. However, it would be left to the Board to consider whether and how this might be done. The immediate threat to the green form scheme was thus lifted, with a question mark left hanging over at least aspects of it.

3. THE LEGAL AID BOARD

(a) The Board

The Legal Aid Board was established by Part II of the Legal Aid Act 1988.[42] It formally commenced operations in August 1988 after some three

---

[37] See, respectively, *Legal Aid Efficiency Scrutiny: The Law Society's Response* (October 1986); *36th Legal Aid Annual Reports* (1985–86), pp. 198–208 (Lord Chancellor's Advisory Committee); NACAB Annual Report 1986–87, pp. 20–21, 26; *Legal Action*, October 1986, pp. 4–9. See also J. Baldwin and S. Hill, (1986) 5 C.J.Q. 283, indicating that their research project (above, pp. 457–458) provided no evidence to support such a restructuring.

[38] Cm. 118, Chap. 4.

[39] *Ibid.*, para. 24. " 'It was never a living duck,' said Lord Hailsham of the proposal ... to transfer green form advice to the voluntary sector": quoted in *Legal Action*, May 1987, p. 4.

[40] Above, p. 445.

[41] Cm. 118, para. 24. This point was taken up in a debate conducted through the pages of *Legal Action* in 1988 as to the desirability of transferring welfare benefit and housing work from solicitors to advice agencies; following an article by A. Blake and D. Beale, *Legal Action*, December 1987, p. 6.

[42] See *Current Law Statutes 1988*, annotations by I. Storey; D. Matheson, *Legal Aid: The New Framework* (1988).

months' shadow existence, and assumed the Law Society's legal aid and advice responsibilities on April 1, 1989.

It comprises between 11 and 17 members appointed by the Lord Chancellor (one appointed by him as chairman), with at least two solicitors and two barristers (appointed after consultation with, respectively, the Law Society and the General Council of the Bar).[43] Its general function is that of securing that advice, assistance and representation are available in accordance with the Act and of administering the Act.[44] Some specific functions can only be conferred by an order made by the Lord Chancellor.[45] It has power to secure the provision of advice, assistance or representation by entering contracts, but only if the Lord Chancellor directs.[46] It is to publish information as to the discharge of its functions, supply information to the Lord Chancellor as and when required, make annual reports, and "have regard, in discharging its functions, to such guidance as may from time to time be given by the Lord Chancellor."[47] A major focus of concern among commentators was how independent of the Lord Chancellor the Board would be.[48]

The first Board had 12 members. Its chairman (John Pitts) and five members had backgrounds in industry or commerce; there were two solicitors (both legal aid practitioners), two barristers, one person with an advice agency background and one academic lawyer.[49]

The initial concerns of the Board were with the transfer of responsibilities from the Law Society and their subsequent management.[50] The Board took over the legal aid scheme's administrative structure and most of the staff. It also took over all aspects of the duty solicitor scheme.[51] The Board reported that it had established management objectives and expressed confidence that the introduction of new management techniques, in many cases building on work in hand, would lead to significant improvements in the speed and quality of service and efficiency.[52] Among its aims are increasingly to devolve responsibility to area offices, to set performance targets and to secure that policies on the grant and continuation of legal aid are applied consistently.

The Board also has started considering matters where there might be change in the longer term. It does not for the moment wish to take on additional responsibilities in respect of criminal legal aid, means assessments and determinations and taxations of costs, given that it is not at

[43] Legal Aid Act 1988, s.3(5)–(8). The Lord Chancellor must have regard to the desirability of including members with knowledge of the provision of legal services, the work of the courts and social conditions and management: *ibid.*, s.3(9).

[44] *Ibid.*, s.3(2).

[45] *Ibid.*, s.3(4): these include determining the costs of representation under civil legal aid; functions as regards representation under criminal legal aid (other than determining costs of representation in magistrates' courts); determining the financial resources of persons for the purposes of the Act.

[46] *Ibid.*, s.4(2)(a), (4).

[47] *Ibid.*, s.5.

[48] *e.g.* R. Smith, *Legal Action*, April 1988, p. 6.

[49] Profiles of the members were given in *Legal Action*, June 1988, p. 4.

[50] *Legal Aid Board: Report to the Lord Chancellor* (Cm. 688, 1989), sections 1–3. See also the interview with Stephen Orchard, the Board's Chief Executive, in *Legal Action*, December 1989, p. 8.

[51] The Council of the Law Society decided by a small majority not to seek to retain responsibility for the vetting and appointment of duty solicitors: see *Legal Action*, October 1988, p. 3 and December 1988, p. 5.

[52] Cm. 688, p. 4.

present in a position to do the work more effectively.[53] Rather more attention has been paid to the future of the green form scheme and to multi-party actions.[54] The latter are considered elsewhere.[55]

(b) The future of the green form scheme

Amongst the early tasks indicated for the Board by the Lord Chancellor was to consider whether the best use was being made of resources devoted to advice and assistance, whether better arrangements might be made by using advice agencies and other organisations, and whether any further exclusions from the green form scheme would be appropriate.[56]

The Board gave indications of its thinking in its first Report to the Lord Chancellor and in a consultation paper issued in May 1989.[57] It was impressed with the usefulness and flexibility of the scheme, but needed to consider whether there could be a more effective use of resources. It confirmed that the scheme should remain demand-led, with payment on a case-by-case basis. Specific ideas on which it sought views were that preparatory advice given before the granting of a legal aid order should be claimed and paid for under that order and not the green form scheme, and that welfare benefit entitlement work[58] should either be limited to a fixed fee or excluded altogether. As to more general options for change, the Board referred to the possibilities of exclusive or semi-exclusive "contracting," and of "franchising." The idea of "contracting," with tendering for contracts, had been floated in the 1987 White Paper. However, the Board was unenthusiastic: there would be either limited or no consumer choice, and restricted access for the public would cause difficulties arising out of conflicts of interest between parties; the Board was "far from satisfied that there is generally a sufficient spread of the skills to make any form of competitive tendering a realistic or worthwhile exercise now or in the near future."[59]

Instead, the favoured option was "franchising." This would involve identifying those who could satisfy criteria or competence and reliability, and encouraging them by removing some of the administrative restrictions now applying.[60] It would be open to any solicitors' firms, and (although there were difficulties, *e.g.* about funding) advice agencies and law centres, that satisfied the criteria. The green form scheme would continue alongside franchise outlets until the access objective was met, with the aim of concentrating the majority of legal advice work on franchises. Moreover, franchising had the potential of extending beyond the green form scheme to civil and criminal legal aid. There could be two kinds, "general practice" and "specialist" franchises. The former, covering all or most categories of legal aid

---

[53] *Ibid.*, section 7.
[54] *Ibid.*, section 4 and Annex C, section 6 and Annex D.
[55] Below, p. 483.
[56] Letter from the Lord Chancellor to the Board, cited in the Board's Report, (Cm. 688, 1989, pp. 10–11).
[57] *Ibid.*, 4 and Annex C; *Second Stage Consultation on the Future of the Green Form Scheme* (1989).
[58] Advice and assistance relating to the assessment of an entitlement to benefits, including negotiations with the D.S.S.
[59] Consultation Paper, p. 7.
[60] Delegation of power to exceed the green form limits; a system of monthly payments on account; simplified administration; ability to advertise that a franchise is held.

work, would almost always be provided by solicitors' firms; the latter could be provided by solicitors' firms, law centres, advice agencies and national organisations giving advice to individual clients. Prospective franchisees would need to demonstrate substantial involvement in the relevant work (in the case of general practice franchise, receipt of at least £40,000 p.a. from the Legal Aid Fund). There would be mechanisms to enable the Board to monitor the quality of service provided.

Responses were mixed.[61] There was wide support for the continuation of the scheme, in the light of the endorsements provided by the Baldwin and Hill research project, and that it should operate on a demand-led basis. Contracting was unanimously rejected.[62] Welfare benefit work should not be excluded from the scheme; on the contrary, it should be accorded a high priority. There was some support for specialist but not for general practice franchising. Respondents other than the Law Society thought that the supposed difficulties of including advice agencies in franchising had been exaggerated; their involvement should indeed be encouraged, and would require additional resources. Any changes should only be introduced after proper research and costing, and after an initial experiment. A number of respondents noted that franchising would probably be as, if not more, suitable for legal aid administration than the green form scheme. The Law Society had greater reservations about franchising than the other bodies, except that it liked the administrative advantages and thought that they should be extended to all legal aid practitioners who satisfied quality control criteria developed by the Board and the Law Society.

In the light of the various responses, the Board has decided to concentrate on specialist franchising.[63] An 18-month pilot project is to be established, in an area of Birmingham, starting in July 1990. All solicitors in that area will have the opportunity to apply for franchises, and the project will be subject to independent research. Franchisees will have devolved powers on all green form matters except waiving the green form charge, ABWOR, and emergency certificates, and payments on account will apply to both green form and legal aid work.[64]

Overall, the picture is less gloomy than might have been feared. The flaws in some of the ideas put forward by the Board have been cogently exposed, but it has shown a welcome willingness to take account of criticisms and alter its position accordingly.

4. CONCLUSION

We conclude this chapter as we started it. It does not seem that we are any nearer the integrated approach to legal services long advocated by the Lord Chancellor's Advisory Committee. In recent years, the Committee has noted, with disappointment, that the new Legal Aid Board was not "a Legal

---

[61] See the Law Society, *Franchising Legal Aid* (1989); NACAB, *Response to the Consultation Paper on the Future of the Green Form Scheme* (1989); N.C.C., *Franchising and the Future of the Green Form Scheme* (1989); *39th Legal Aid Annual Reports* (1988–89), pp. 95–98 (Lord Chancellor's Advisory Committee).

[62] An impressive catalogue of criticisms is set out in the NACAB paper at p. 13.

[63] S. Orchard and A. Blake, "Franchising: the next steps" (1989) 86 L.S. Gaz. December 20, pp. 12–13; S. Hillyard and L. Storey, (1991) 88 L.S. Gaz. January 30, pp. 25–26.

[64] The Law Society declined, initially, to endorse the experiment: (1990) 140 N.L.J. 618, but subsequently relented: (1990) 87 L.S. Gaz. June 13, p. 4.

Services Board with overall responsibility for legal aid and legal services"[65]; that the present system could not be said to constitute a "comprehensive system of legal services offering good early advice"[66]; and that in considering reform to the legal profession, there had been a failure by government "to examine the place that lawyers' services should occupy in the field of legal services as a whole."[67] The Committee has expressed concern that these reforms, particularly those concerning conveyancing and the Bar, may lead to a breakdown in the network of solicitors' offices, especially in rural areas, and a diminution in the quality of service to legally aided clients.[68]

There are blueprints available for the comprehensive provisions of legal services. One is provided by the National Consumer Council in its report *Ordinary Justice*, with a proposed network of general advice centres with access both to specialist advice agencies, with salaried staff and volunteers, and the legal profession.[69] In the end, it comes down to resources. The argument is often heard that problems are not necessarily solved by throwing money at them; how are they solved if you don't?

[65] *37th Legal Aid Annual Reports* (1986–87), p. 155.
[66] *38th Legal Aid Annual Reports* (1987–88), p. 98.
[67] *39th Legal Aid Annual Reports* (1988–89), p. 100.
[68] *Ibid.*, pp. 98–101.
[69] (H.M.S.O., 1989), Chap. 4. The Council had previously issued a discussion document (*Good Advice for All* (1986)) setting out guidelines on standards for local advice services. These were adopted by the Advice Services Alliance (which includes NACAB, the Federation of Independent Advice Centres, the Law Centres Federation, DIAL, Shelter and U.K.I.A.S.) in its "Go for Advice" manifesto in 1987 (but note the comments of R. Smith, *Legal Action*, August 1987, p. 6).

PART III

PRE-TRIAL PROCEDURE

CHAPTER 10

FEATURES OF LITIGATION

IN Part II we looked at advice and information. Now we begin a Part called Pre-trial Procedure and it may appear that we are progressing inexorably towards the courtroom. Yet between the recognition of a dispute which may end in a trial and its actual arrival before the judge lies a lengthy period of negotiation before or during the operation of the formal pre-trial procedure. An understanding of the significance of these negotiations, which may sometimes more accurately be described as bargaining, and the resulting settlements is fundamental to civil litigation. We concentrate on civil matters, even though in the criminal context there is the analogous feature of "plea bargaining."[1] The other two topics we consider in this chapter, costs and delay, have significance in both civil and criminal litigation, and are inter-related with pre-trial negotiations.

Influencing both civil and criminal procedure before and at trial, the English *adversarial* approach permits the parties to dictate the issues to be resolved and to settle the pace of the action. In civil cases, the court has had no role in directing the course of the proceedings except on the application of one or other party. It has always been able to impose penalties on parties who break the rules without permission, by the award of costs against them,[2] but it has not been able to enforce the rules of its own volition. This all changes with the introduction consequent upon the Civil Justice Review of court management of litigation.[3]

The parties select the issues on which to fight and the evidence with which to support their case. Whilst it may be in the interests of the court and a "fair result" for as much as possible to be disclosed in the early stages so that the matters really in dispute can be identified and the strength of the evidence assessed, it will often be in the interests of the parties to conceal what they know. For them, negotiation, in the form of bargaining, can proceed more effectively through a process of bluff and ambush, which is inimical to the demands of justice. Consequently, the Civil Justice Review recommends that there be greater openness in pre-trial procedure.[4]

---

[1] "Plea bargaining" is dealt with in Chapter 16 on the Criminal Trial. On the point of comparison between criminal and civil matters, see H. Genn, *Hard Bargaining* (1987), esp. at Chap. 2.

[2] See below, p. 474. There are other possible sanctions, see Sir Jack I.H. Jacob, *The Fabric of English Civil Justice* (1987), Chap. 2.

[3] *Civil Justice Review, Report of the Review Body on Civil Justice* (Cm. 394, 1988), paras. 220–228, see pp. 491 and 536–537 below.

[4] See p. 491, below.

A. COSTS

1. CIVIL CASES[5]

The costs involved in civil litigation are of the utmost importance to the parties—they may prevent an action ever being brought,[6] they may render a victory in court Pyrrhic when damages are swallowed up in costs,[7] they may prevent a meritorious appeal and they will always be a factor in the risk of litigation.[8]

Costs have to be looked at in two respects, first, the costs which may be ordered to be paid by one of the parties to the other in litigation, and, secondly, the costs which a client is obliged to pay the solicitor. It is not necessarily the case that the successful party will receive costs from the losing party which will cover the whole of the solicitor's bill.

Costs payable in litigation

In deciding whether to begin or continue litigation, one major factor is whether a party will have to pay the costs or be able to recover them from the other party.

The principles in relation to the taxation of costs[9] after a trial do not prevent the parties reaching their own agreement about costs where a settlement is effected before trial. Indeed, in the majority of cases costs are agreed between the parties. Nevertheless the taxation rules remain significant in providing the framework within which the parties can negotiate.[10]

The steps are, first, that the judge must decide who should pay costs and on what basis, and, secondly, a "taxing officer"[11] must determine exactly what costs are to be paid. The basic rule is that "costs follow the event," that is to say the successful party can expect the judge to order the loser to pay some or all of his or her solicitor's bill.[12]

---

[5] This topic is dealt with more fully in J. O'Hare and R.N. Hill, *Civil Litigation* (5th ed., 1990), Chap. 23. See also *The Supreme Court Practice 1991*, pp. 987–1089; *The County Court Practice 1989*, pp. 777–832; R. Blackford, *County Court Practice Handbook* (9th ed., 1989); E. Owen, *County Court Litigation* (1988).

[6] See pp. 500–501 above.

[7] See pp. 479–480 below.

[8] See pp. 485 and 501–502 below.

[9] *i.e.* the procedure whereby the exact sum to be paid is determined.

[10] Since the taxation of costs is both expensive and time consuming, O'Hare & Hill (1990), p. 530, recommend that solicitors should, where possible, try to avoid taxation by agreeing costs with each other.

[11] A "taxing officer" is a taxing master (or, in minor matters, a principal clerk of the taxing office) in the High Court in London; a district judge of the High Court outside London; and a district judge in the county court.

[12] The award of costs is a discretionary matter: Supreme Court Act 1981, s.51; R.S.C. Ord. 62, r. 2, but the discretion is exercised within the rules that have been established: R.S.C. Ord. 62, which impose no real limit on the exercise of judicial discretion: *Aiden Shipping Ltd.* v. *Interbulk Ltd.* [1986] A.C. 965. A successful plaintiff who receives more than nominal damages should, in normal circumstances, be granted a costs order against the defendant: *Gupta* v. *Klito, The Times*, November 23, 1989. In some cases it is known that costs do not follow the event: R.S.C. Ord. 62, r. 6. Certain matters must be taken into account in exercising the discretion, such as payments into court, and "Calderbank" letters: R.S.C. Ord. 62, r. 9, below at p. 476. See, further, O'Hare & Hill (1990), pp. 513–516 and Jacob (1987), pp. 45–46, 275–276. The costs of and incidental to all proceedings in a county court

A judge may order that costs are to be taxed on one of two bases.[13]

(a) *Standard basis*, where ". . . a reasonable amount in respect of all costs reasonably incurred" is allowed. Any doubts as to questions of reasonableness in either respect are resolved in favour of the paying party.[14] As the terminology suggests, this is the usual basis upon which costs will be taxed.

(b) *Indemnity basis*, where "all costs . . . except insofar as they are of an unreasonable amount or have been unreasonably incurred" will be allowed. Any doubts as to questions of reasonableness in either respect are to be resolved in favour of the receiving party.[15]

Thus it is only in cases of debate about the reasonableness of costs incurred that the different bases of taxation produce any difference in the actual costs received. From the point of view of the receiving party, the indemnity basis is the preferred basis, since then the burden of establishing that the expenditure was unreasonable lies upon the other party. It appears that costs are awarded on the indemnity basis only in exceptional cases, for example "major test cases" and "cases in which the paying party's conduct is considered to have been wholly unmeritorious, oppressive or in contempt of court"[16] and the court must expressly direct that costs be awarded on such a basis.[17]

The subsequent procedure is for the solicitor to compile a bill of costs and send it to the appropriate officer of the court for "taxing."[18] The preparation of a bill of costs for a taxation hearing is a very skilled and detailed task.[19] Specialists exist who undertake the drafting of the bill, usually for a commission calculated on the total amount of the bill or for a salary if employed by a large firm of solicitors. This payment is allowable on taxation and so may be recoverable from the losing party.[20]

The taxing officer hears the parties and decides any issues in dispute,[21] either allowing the item in the bill to stand or disallowing or reducing it. The total arrived at by this process is the total of "taxed costs" and is that amount which the loser is required to pay.[22] Taxation is designed to ensure that the losing party only has to pay those expenses properly incurred and is not saddled with the cost of unnecessary or unduly expensive work. The taxing officer must consider the directions of the court.

---

are at the discretion of the court: C.C.R., Ord. 38, r. 1(2). The issue of costs is an example of the complexity produced in civil procedure by two sets of rules, one applicable to High Court procedure, the other to county court procedure. This complexity is why the Civil Justice Review has recommended that there be a common core of procedural rules: *Civil Justice Review* (1988), paras. 277–280. See p. 491, n. 60 below. See also Jacob (1987), p. 50–67, 260.

[13] As to the position prior to new rules introduced in April 1986, see the first edition of this work at p. 363.

[14] R.S.C. Ord. 62, r. 12(1); C.C.R. Ord. 38, r. 19A.

[15] R.S.C. Ord. 62, r. 12(2); C.C.R. Ord. 38, r. 19A.

[16] O'Hare & Hill (1990), p. 508.

[17] R.S.C. Ord. 62, r. 3(4); C.C.R. Ord. 38, r. 1.

[18] "Taxing" is the term given to the procedure which is conducted by taxing officer, see n. 11 above.

[19] See the specimen bill of costs reproduced in O'Hare & Hill (1990), pp. 519–527.

[20] R.S.C. Ord. 62, r. 27; C.C.R., Ord. 38, r. 2.

[21] Where a hearing is held.

[22] In some circumstances, in addition to there being agreed costs between the parties, which avoids this process, there might also be "assessed costs" that is a fixed sum specified by the court at trial: R.S.C. Ord. 62, r. 7; C.C.R. Ord. 38, r. 19; or "fixed costs": R.S.C. Ord. 62,

In a High Court action, the taxing officer, in exercising his or her discretion must have regard, amongst other factors, to the complexity, difficulty and novelty of the case, the skill, specialised knowledge and responsibility required of, and the time and labour expended by, solicitor and counsel, the number and importance of documents, the importance of the matter to the client, and the amount of money or value of property involved.[23] In a county court action, on the other hand, the amount of costs awarded, in general, is determined by the application of one of four scales with fixed costs.[24]

Complexity is necessarily produced by such an approach. Further, there is a natural desire to ensure that the case is a High Court action, since the recoverable costs will be greater. Consequently, the Civil Justice Review recommended that there should be a single costs regime for High Court and County Court actions, except for county court actions below £3,000, since in such smaller cases fixed costs should be attractive and there would be less desire to seek to take such actions in the High Court.[25] This proposal is to be implemented by section 4 of the Courts and Legal Services Act 1990. A more radical approach would have been to introduce scales of costs into the High Court.[26]

The costs which may be ordered to be paid are limited to "fees, charges, disbursements, expenses and remuneration and, in relation to proceedings ..., also ... costs of or incidental to those proceedings."[27] Such costs are unlikely to cover all the work that a solicitor has undertaken on behalf of a client.[28]

There are some circumstances in which costs are *not* awarded to the successful party. For example, in the various stages of pre-trial procedure the party who is ultimately successful may have caused undue delay or not followed the proper procedure and been penalised at that time by the award of costs against him or her in respect of a particular hearing.[29] These will eventually be disallowed on taxation.

Two other related matters should be mentioned. First, the successful unassisted party in an action where the opponent is legally aided may be awarded costs against the Legal Aid Board where certain statutory conditions are met.[30] Secondly, since 1975, people who conduct their own litigation have become entitled to costs in respect of their own time and effort spent preparing and presenting the case.[31] In addition to costs incurred by such a person which would also have been incurred by a solicitor acting on

---

Appendix 3; C.C.R., Appendix B; see, O'Hare & Hill (1990), pp. 530–531; *County Court Practice 1989*, pp. 246–247.

[23] R.S.C. Ord 62, Appendix 2, Part 1, para. 1.

[24] Fixed costs do not apply to two items in the top scale; here the High Court criteria apply. The items are counsel's fees and costs involved with preparation for trial. See, further, C.C.R., Ord. 38 and Owen (1988), pp. 254–266.

[25] *Civil Justice Review* (1988), paras. 287–293.

[26] Jacob (1987), p. 275.

[27] R.S.C. Ord. 62, r. 1(4) and see O'Hare & Hill (1990), pp. 506–507.

[28] See *ibid* p. 507. As to the bill which a solicitor may present to a client, see below.

[29] *e.g.* the failure to observe specified time limits, see below, p. 543.

[30] See below, pp. 514–515.

[31] The Litigants in Person (Costs and Expenses) Act 1975. This is one of those rare statutes which started life as a Private Member's Bill. See R.S.C. Ord. 62, r. 18; C.C.R., Ord. 38, r. 17.

his or her behalf, the court can allow on taxation a sum not more than two-thirds of that which a solicitor would have been allowed for profit costs. If the litigant in person has not actually suffered pecuniary loss in the preparation of the case (which this sum would compensate) the court will only allow up to £7.50 per hour for the time reasonably spent in preparation.[32]

Costs payable to solicitor[33]

The successful party will often receive money in payment of costs from the losing party. However, it has to be considered whether this payment will actually cover what the successful party must pay to his or her solicitor. Further, since most cases never end up in court, it may be that what the client will have to pay the solicitor will not be covered by the other party as agreed costs.

The obligation on the client of a solicitor is to pay the bill presented.[34] The relationship between solicitor and client is a contractual one and the solicitor can sue the client for "proper costs."[35] What costs are proper may ultimately be determined independently by the process of "taxation."[36]

The costs payable by a client to a solicitor in a civil matter will depend upon whether or not the matter is classified as "contentious," that term only applying where an action has begun.[37] The negotiation of a settlement in a civil matter where no writ is issued counts as "non-contentious" business.

If a client objects to the bill submitted by the solicitor in a *contentious* matter an application may be made to the High Court for an order for taxation of the bill.[38] If granted,[39] taxation is carried out on the "indemnity basis" but it is presumed that the costs (a) have been reasonably incurred, if they were incurred with the express or implied approval of the client; (b) have been reasonable in amount, if their amount was expressly or impliedly approved by the client; (c) have been unreasonably incurred, if in the circumstances of the case they are of an unusual nature, unless the solicitor satisfies the taxing officer that prior to their being incurred the client was informed that they might not be allowed on taxation of costs.[40] It appears

[32] R.S.C. Ord. 62, r. 18; C.C.R., Ord. 38, r. 17. In 1987 the average amount at which taxed bills were allowed for litigants in person in the Queen's Bench Division (other than District Registry cases) was £1,946, although there appear to have been no such litigants in 1989; there were two bills taxed for litigants in person in the Family Division, Principal Registry, in 1989: *Judicial Statistics 1989* (Cm. 1154, 1990), Table 10.2. In 1989 in county court jurisdiction as a whole, 141 bills were taxed for litigants in person, the average amounts being for general jurisdiction £1,082, for divorce jurisdiction £2,256 and for insolvency jurisdiction £1,210. In 1989 in District Registry cases 28 bills were taxed for litigants in person, the average amounts being for Queen's Bench jurisdiction £326 and for Chancery jurisdiction £1,337: *ibid.* Table 10.3.
[33] See F.T. Horne, *Cordery's Law relating to Solicitors* (18th ed., 1988), pp. 155–189.
[34] A more detailed bill than the initial brief one may be demanded: Solicitors Act 1974, s.64.
[35] See O'Hare & Hill (1990), p. 538.
[36] See below.
[37] The definition is contained in the Solicitors Act 1974, s.87.
[38] Solicitors Act 1974, s.70.
[39] An order must be granted if the request is made within one calendar month of delivery of the bill, otherwise the court has a discretion: Solicitors Act 1974, s.70, and see O'Hare & Hill (1990), p. 539.
[40] R.S.C. Ord. 62, r. 15(2).

that this procedure is rarely used because of the ignorance and fear of disgruntled clients and because there appears to be a generally high level of satisfaction with the services provided.[41]

As we have seen, where the business is contentious, the client is assisted in paying what is owed to the solicitor if he or she wins, since costs are then likely to be obtained from the losing party.

In *non-contentious* civil matters the client may be charged such sum as is fair and reasonable having regard to the circumstances of the case and, *inter alia*, its complexity, the skill and responsibility involved, the time spent, the number and importance of the documents, the amount or value of money or property involved, and the importance of the matter to the client.[42] The client must be informed of the rights to require the solicitor to obtain a certificate from the Law Society and to seek "taxation."[43] If the client is dissatisfied, the right to request certification by the Law Society may be pursued.[44] The Law Society will peruse the bill and documents and certify that the sum charged is fair and reasonable or that a lower sum should be charged. The client may then pursue the right to apply to the High Court for an order to have the bill taxed.[45] If granted, the taxing officer assesses the costs on the same basis as for costs in contentious matters.

Costs and settlement

The doubts as to whether costs will be available to a party and the possibility that what costs are payable by the other party will not cover the full costs of seeking legal assistance are powerful factors in decisions as to whether and when to settle.[46]

There are also two procedures which can place a plaintiff in further difficulties. The first procedure is the *payment into court*.[47] At any stage after an action has begun in the High Court or the county court, the defendant may make a payment into court in satisfaction of the plaintiff's claim. The plaintiff may accept the payment in settlement or may continue the action. If a sum greater than that paid in is not recovered at the trial, the plaintiff will be liable for the defendant's taxed costs from the time of the payment in, even though he or she has "won" the action. The judge in making an award of damages will know that a payment into court has been made, but will not know in what sum and so cannot ensure that the damages awarded are high enough to beat the payment into court, if minded to make an award similar

---

[41] These conclusions were arrived at in the R.C.L.S. Report which preceded the 1986 changes in costs rules, but there seems no reason to suspect that the conclusions are no longer valid; see also O'Hare & Hill (1990), p. 538. This conclusion is confirmed by Jenkins, Skordaki & Willis, *Public Use and Perception of Solicitors' Services* (1989), Chap. 4. See above pp. 149–150.

[42] Solicitors Remuneration Order 1972, art. 2.

[43] The provision of information was one method whereby the Royal Commission on Legal Services felt that challenge to improper bills could be improved: R.C.L.S. Report, pp. 546–547.

[44] Solicitors Remuneration Order 1972, art. 3.

[45] Solicitors Act 1974, s.70.

[46] See below, pp. 500–501.

[47] For the place of payment into court in pre-trial procedure, see below, p. 563; for its effect in the settlement process, see below, p. 501. The procedure is considered in some detail in O'Hare & Hill (1990), Chap. 16.

to that which the defendant has offered. This rule has been criticised[48] and adds considerably to the "risk" element in litigation.[49]

The second procedure is the use of *Calderbank letters*.[50] The defendant makes a written offer to compromise the claim, making that offer "without prejudice save as to costs." The court is unaware of the offer until the question of costs falls to be decided. This procedure is not to be used if a payment into court would have protected the defendant's position.[51]

2. CRIMINAL CASES[52]

To what extent can the "loser pays costs" rule apply in criminal matters? This rule is of lesser significance because of the existence of criminal legal aid[53] and because prosecutions brought by the Crown Prosecution Service are funded by government.[54] Further, the defendant does not have the option of minimising the cost by deciding not to go ahead with the case! Criminal courts do, however, have powers to make orders about costs in various circumstances.

A defendant's costs order may be made in favour of an *acquitted defendant* by the Crown Court or a magistrates' court.[55] These costs are awarded out of central funds. The award covers what the court considers is reasonably sufficient to compensate the defendant for any expenses properly incurred by him or her in the proceedings.[56] Such an order should usually be made, unless there are positive reasons for not so doing, such as the defendant's own conduct in bringing suspicion on himself or herself or in misleading the prosecution, or where there is ample evidence supporting a conviction, but the defendant is acquitted on a technicality.[57]

In many cases the acquitted defendant will have been receiving legal aid. The principles for the making of a defendant's costs order still apply, although it would be simpler for the court to achieve the same object in those cases by ordering that no contribution need be made by the defendant to his or her own costs.[58]

A defendant's costs order may also be made in the following circumstances: (1) by a magistrates' court where an information has been laid before magistrates but not proceeded with; or where the magistrates' court

---

[48] See *e.g.* P. Cane, *Atiyah's Accidents, Compensation and the Law* (4th ed., 1987), pp. 268–270.

[49] See below, pp. 501–502.

[50] So called after the Court of Appeal decision in *Calderbank* v. *Calderbank* [1976] Fam. 93, and now codified in and extended by R.S.C. Ord. 22, r. 14; C.C.R., Ord. 12, r. 10.

[51] R.S.C. Ord. 62, r. 14(2); C.C.R. Ord. 12, r. 10(2). See O'Hare & Hill (1990), pp. 369–372. Note the requirement that the court take the offer into account has been removed from R.S.C. Ord. 22, r. 14 by S.I. 1990, No. 1689.

[52] The governing statute is the Prosecution of Offences Act 1985; see *Halsbury's Laws of England*, Vol. 11(2), paras. 1527–1540.

[53] See pp. 672–680, below.

[54] See pp. 623–626, below.

[55] Prosecution of Offences Act 1985, s.16(1), (2) and *Practice Note* [1989] 2 All ER 604; see *Halsbury's Laws of England*, Vol. 11(2), para. 1527. For doubts about the award of defendant's costs under the old law, see M. Zander, *Cases and Materials on the English Legal System* (5th ed., 1988), pp. 462–463.

[56] Prosecution of Offences Act 1985, ss.21(1), 16(6) and *Practice Note* [1989] 2 All ER 604.

[57] *Practice Note* [1989] 2 All E.R. 604.

[58] See below, pp. 675–680 for the rules governing criminal legal aid.

inquiring into an indictable offence as examining justices determines not to commit the accused for trial; (2) by the Crown Court where the defendant is not tried for an offence for which he or she had been indicted or committed for trial; or the defendant who has been convicted of an offence before a magistrates' court appeals against conviction or sentence and, in consequence of that appeal, the conviction is set aside or a less severe punishment is awarded; (3) by the Divisional Court where it deals with any criminal appeal; (4) by the Court of Appeal where it allows an appeal against conviction or sentence or on such an appeal finds the defendant guilty of a different offence or imposes a different sentence; (5) by the House of Lords where it determines a criminal appeal, or application for leave to appeal.[59]

Costs may be awarded to a successful private prosecutor[60] out of central funds.[61] The costs awarded may not be the full costs incurred by the prosecutor, only such costs as are just and reasonable.[62] Such an order should be made save where there is good reason for not doing so, for example, where the proceedings have been instituted or continued without good cause.[63]

An award of costs may be made *against* a convicted defendant.[64] The costs awarded will be those that the court considers just and reasonable.[65] The judge has a discretion to exercise in determining whether to make such an order, taking account of whether the defendant chose to contest a strong case against him or her and if the defendant must have known the real truth of the matter.

3. TRIBUNALS

We shall repeat elsewhere that it is difficult to generalise about tribunals. Broadly, the parties to a dispute which is settled by a tribunal will bear their own costs, subject to any specific rules applicable to a particular tribunal. We can merely give a number of examples.

In Social Security Appeal Tribunals,[66] the claimant will receive only compensation for loss of earnings (if any) and travelling expenses. These are payable whatever the outcome of the hearing. No costs can be awarded against the claimant.

In Industrial Tribunals, the tribunal will not normally make an award of costs. There is a power to make an award only where a party has acted frivolously, vexatiously or otherwise unreasonably, either for a fixed sum or for taxed costs.[67]

---

[59] Prosecution of Offences Act 1985, s.16 and *Practice Note* [1989] 2 All ER 604. See, further, *Halsbury's Laws of England*, Vol. 11(2), para. 1527.

[60] *i.e.* not a public authority or a person acting on behalf of a public authority: Prosecution of Offences Act 1985, s.17(2).

[61] Prosecution of Offences Act 1985, s.17, and see *Halsbury's Laws of England* Vol. 11(2), para. 1528.

[62] Prosecution of Offences Act 1985, s.17(3).

[63] *Practice Note* [1989] 2 All ER 604.

[64] Prosecution of Offences Act 1985, s.18, and see *Halsbury's Laws of England*, Vol. 11(2), para. 1529.

[65] Prosecution of Offences Act 1985, s.18(2), as amended by the Criminal Justice Act 1987, see also *Practice Note* [1989] 2 All E.R. 604.

[66] The same rules apply to appeals to the Social Security Commissioners: Social Security Act 1975, Sched. 10, para. 3.

[67] Industrial Tribunals (Labour Relations) Regulations 1985 (S.I. 1985 No. 16), Rules of Procedure, Rule 11. Similar provisions apply to the Employment Appeal Tribunal.

In the Lands Tribunal, costs are within the discretion of the tribunal[68] and it is interesting to note that of the 21 Lands Tribunal bills taxed in 1989, the average amount allowed on taxation was £18,385.[69]

The last example is highly unusual. Legal aid is not generally available for tribunals,[70] they are intended to be cheap and both sides are clearly expected to bear their own costs.[71]

4. Civil Proceedings—What do they Actually Cost?

As a part of the Civil Justice Review, the Inbucon Study examined the question of costs and the relationship between costs and damages.[72] The existence of a research study is significant, because in the past critics of the high cost of going to law have tended to support their views with horror stories.[73] The Inbucon Study analysed 232 cases by cost bands, separately for county courts, District Registries and the Royal Courts of Justice. Consequently, the following results were discovered for plaintiffs' costs.[74]

Court	Cases in band	Plaintiffs' costs
County Courts (54 cases)	61% of cases cost between	£500 and £1,500
	24% of cases cost between	£1,500 and £2,500
	87% of cases costs less than	£2,500
District Registries (90 cases)	38% of cases cost between	£500 and £1,500
	28% of cases cost between	£1,500 and £2,500
	19% of cases cost between	£2,500 and £5,000
	89% of cases cost less than	£5,000
Royal Courts of Justice (88 cases)	10% of cases cost between	£500 and £1,500
	14% of cases cost between	£1,500 and £2,500
	33% of cases cost between	£2,500 and £5,000
	24% of cases cost between	£5,000 and £8,000
	88% of cases cost less than	£8,000

In some cases costs will be significantly higher than the bands above. Even though these cases may be comparatively rare, it would still appear that such high costs present a problem needing resolution if people are to have access to justice as and when needed.

---

[68] Lands Tribunal Rules 1975 (S.I. 1975 No. 299), r. 56.

[69] *Judicial Statistics 1989* (Cm. 1154, 1990), Table 10.2, p. 99. The figure is quite startling in comparison with the much lower figure for actions in the Queen's Bench Division, see p. 480, below.

[70] See below, pp. 507–508.

[71] There are some examples of money being made available to agencies providing a representation and advice service for those using tribunals, *e.g.* government grants are made to the United Kingdom Immigrants Advisory Service, by virtue of Immigration Act 1971, s.23. The Royal Commission on Legal Services advocated that this approach should be adopted more widely.

[72] Inbucon International Consultants, *Civil Justice Review: Study of Personal Injury Litigation* (1986), Chap. 5.

[73] One such horror story was reproduced in the first edition of this book, see pp. 368–369.

[74] Inbucon (1986), para. 5.2.1. These figures are not significantly different, once inflation is borne in mind, from those obtained by M. Zander, "Costs of Litigation—A Study in the Queen's Bench Division" (1975) 72 L.S. Gaz 679. Beware of printing errors, see M. Zander, *Cases and Materials on the English Legal System* (5th ed., 1988), pp. 448–449.

The Judicial Statistics contain a statement of the average amount at which bills are taxed in a particular year. In 1989 the average amount of bills taxed in the 4,553 Queen's Bench actions or matters was £3,695, compared with £4,833 for 1988.[75] These are the costs of the successful party only. These figures may be compared with both the average District Registry taxed bill at £3,083 where a solicitor was involved and £326 where there was a litigant in person and the average county court taxed bill at £1,261 where a solicitor was involved and £1,082 where there was a litigant in person.[76]

It is not sufficient merely to know what costs are incurred by the plaintiff, even though such costs may be a deterrent to litigation.[77] It must also be ascertained what percentage of damages received is represented by the costs to be paid. Consequently, it can be determined whether relatively the costs of litigation are too high when compared with the amount of damages awarded. It is likely that the plaintiff will have to satisfy such costs from the damages award, subject to recovering some of the costs from the other party.[78] The Inbucon Study shows that, in their sample, in county court cases plaintiffs' costs were 98.8 per cent. of the damages, in District Registry cases plaintiffs' costs were 23.9 per cent. of damages and in Royal Courts of Justice cases plaintiffs' costs were 26.5 per cent. of damages.[79]

5. CIVIL PROCEEDINGS—CAN LITIGATION BE AFFORDABLE?

Clearly civil litigation is often very expensive. We want to examine possible ways of making litigation affordable, perhaps by diverting the cost from the parties (at least initially) so that those who would otherwise find payment difficult, impossible or off-putting might be enabled to bring or defend an action.[80] There are, broadly, three possible approaches.

Jurisdictional, procedural and administrative reforms

The first, with which we are not primarily concerned, is by undertaking jurisdictional, procedural and administrative reforms, as recommended by the Civil Justice Review, which are expressly designed to reduce delay, cost and complexity.[81]

Parties enabled to pay more easily

The second approach is by examining ways in which the parties pay, but

---

[75] *Judicial Statistics 1989* (Cm. 1154, 1990), Table 10.2, which provides figures for actions in all civil proceedings, both first instance and appellate.
[76] *Ibid*. Table 10.3.
[77] See p. 500 below.
[78] See above, pp. 472–475.
[79] Inbucon (1986), para. 5.2.3.
[80] As to the effect of costs on seeking legal action, see p. 419 above.
[81] *Civil Justice Review* (1988). As to the relevant reforms, see Chap. 11 *passim*. Prior to the Civil Justice Review, Jacob had expressed the view that "mere changes in practice and procedure are unlikely to produce any substantial reduction of the costs of litigation": Jacob (1987), pp. 273–274.

without having to find such large sums at the time of the litigation. One method is through support by an organisation. Such support occurs either through membership of an organisation which happens to provide support for litigation, such as a trade union, or through membership of, or support by a pressure group, which is interested in dealing with only one issue, but which will support litigation if that litigation furthers the objectives of the group.

Of more importance presently is the possibility of *legal expenses insurance*. The provision of such insurance is a recent innovation. It defrays the cost of litigation by providing cover for individuals and members of families or groups. Such insurance is common in Europe, particularly West Germany, and it has been launched in this country with the support of the Law Society. As with other insurance policies, cover varies according to the company and according to the premium paid, but the approach favoured by the Law Society, and exemplified by Sun Alliance, is a blanket cover subject to specified exclusions. It has been marketed through the profession but there was only a small response.[82] Currently, Sun Alliance provides such insurance through the Legal Protection Group, which advertises its services to the public.

A second method is through a *contingency fee* system[83] whereby a lawyer agrees to act for a client on the basis that he or she will receive an agreed proportion of any damages recovered. If no damages are recovered, there is no fee. This is the way in which many accident cases are conducted in the United States. There is in Scotland a long tradition of a lawyer acting on a "speculative" basis, whereby the lawyer will be paid the normal fee if the case is successful, but if the case is lost he or she will be paid nothing.[84] Evidence was given to the Royal Commission on Legal Services advocating the introduction of a contingency fee system in England and Wales. It was argued that it allows litigation which would otherwise not be brought, that the lawyers involved act more conscientiously on behalf of their client because of the mutual financial interests, and that it is a simpler method of payment.[85]

The alleged undesirable consequences of the introduction of a contingency fee scheme would include an open invitation to unprofessional conduct,[86] a tendency for lawyers to refuse to take on weaker cases, and increased pressure to accept an early settlement (when actual costs will have

---

[82] See M. Berlins and C. Dyer, *The Law Machine* (3rd ed., 1989), pp. 176–177; P.J. Purton, "Legal Expenses Insurance" (1982) 79 L.S. Gaz. 1341, (1984) 81 L.S. Gaz 1196; M. Zander, *Cases and Materials on the English Legal System* (5th ed., 1988), pp. 469–470; M. Zander, *A Matter of Justice* (Revised edn. 1989), pp. 53–55; National Consumer Council, *Ordinary Justice* (1990), pp. 171–183. The Royal Commission on Legal Services preferred the option of extending legal aid eligibility, but supported the idea of legal expenses insurance: R.C.L.S., Report, p. 179.

[83] See M. Zander, *Legal Services for the Community* (1978), Chap. 7; R. White, "Contingent Fee: a Supplement to Legal Aid?" (1978) 41 M.L.R. 286; M. Zander, *Cases and Materials on the English Legal System* (5th ed., 1988), pp. 467–468; Jacob (1987), pp. 278–280; *Ordinary Justice* (1990), pp. 183–190. For the doubts expressed by a judge see (1989) 139 N.L.J. 1622.

[84] *Royal Commission on Legal Services in Scotland* (Cmnd. 7846, 1980). This is not a contingency fee system: (1989) 139 N.L.J. 138.

[85] R.C.L.S., Report, p. 176.

[86] In particular, the allegation of "ambulance-chasing" lawyers seen most graphically at the time of the Bhopal disaster in India: Zander (1989), pp. 55–56.

been relatively low) rather than press on to trial and incur the heavy costs involved.[87] The Royal Commission accepted these arguments and recommended that the contingency fee arrangement should continue to be prohibited, as well as rejecting a related proposal from JUSTICE.[88]

The JUSTICE proposal[89] advocated the establishment of a Contingency Legal Aid Fund, financed by contributions from successful litigants, which would pay lawyers on a normal basis but recoup costs on a contingency basis. Consequently, the lawyer would be paid whatever the outcome of the case. Zander indicated that the major problem with such a scheme is the initial funding, particularly if the fund were to be established on a voluntary basis.[90]

Zander was more sceptical about the rejection of contingency fee schemes, refusing, in particular, to believe that professional standards would be lost completely.[91] The Civil Justice Review, on examining the arguments, recognised the need to assist people who do not qualify for legal aid funding, drew attention to the major advances that had been made in regulation policy so as probably to be able to control a contingency fee system and, on the basis of competition policy, considered whether it would be more desirable to devise more limited schemes under which lawyers would have a stake in the outcome of a case as an incentive.[92] It recommended that the prohibition on contingency fees and other forms of incentive should be re-examined.[93]

The outcome of this consideration is that section 58 of the Courts and Legal Services Act 1990 introduces conditional fee agreements. Such an agreement is an agreement in writing between a person providing advocacy or litigation services and the client, which is not concerned with certain matrimonial and children proceedings; provides for that person's fees and expenses, or part of them, to be payable only in specified circumstances; complies with any requirements imposed by the Lord Chancellor; and is not a contentious business agreement.[94] The agreement may provide for the amount of any fees to which it applies to be increased, but only if a

---

[87] Because of the pressure to win. Among techniques mentioned by the Royal Commission were the construction of evidence, the coaching of witnesses and competitive touting for work: R.C.L.S., Report, p. 177. These views are echoed by the majority in *Wallersteiner* v. *Moir (No. 2)* [1975] Q.B. 373. Lord Denning M.R., in the minority, put in a strong plea for the contingency fee in a particular type of company law action brought by a shareholder.

[88] R.C.L.S., at p. 177. Until the Criminal Law Act 1967 a contingency fee arrangement would have involved the commission of the criminal offences of maintenance and champerty. Now it would merely be an unenforceable contract and contrary to the professional rules of conduct.

[89] *Trial of Motor Accident Cases* (1966), criticised by R.C.L.S., Report, pp. 177–178. Zander sees some merit in it: Zander (1989), p. 219. JUSTICE has reiterated its call for such a scheme: JUSTICE, *Memoranda on the Green Papers issued by the Lord Chancellor's Department: Contingency Fees* (1989). See also *Ordinary Justice* (1990), pp. 191–193. The Law Society's Contentious Business Committee has put forward a similar proposal: *Improving Access to Civil Justice* (1987), which has some advantages over CLAF: *Ordinary Justice* (1990), pp. 193–196.

[90] Zander (1989), p. 56.

[91] Zander (1978), p. 218. For an even more spirited defence, see White (1978).

[92] *Civil Justice Review* (1988), para. 389. The significance of competition in a free-market society influencing opinions as to the desirability of such a system was anticipated in the first edition of this book, see p. 372.

[93] *Ibid.* paras. 384–389.

[94] The excluded proceedings are listed at s.58(10). A "contentious business agreement" is defined in s.59 of the Solicitors Act 1974.

percentage is specified. Such an agreement is not unenforceable by reason only of its being a conditional fee agreement.[95]

A third method of making it easier on the parties is through the *Fixed Costs Scheme* proposed by the Law Society.[96] Zander describes this scheme as meaning that solicitors would pay a premium to an insurance company and the client would pay a fixed amount to cover the costs in the event of the case being lost.[97]

A fourth method is to examine again the appropriateness of the rules restricting *actions brought by groups of plaintiffs*, which would mean that the costs were spread amongst a number of people. At present English procedure only permits representative actions, whereby members of a group must have the same interest in the same proceedings; the action cannot seek damages, but only some other form of relief.[98] The Civil Justice Review recommended that the suggestion of Lord Donaldson M.R.[99] that the subject be looked at in the round be taken up.[1]

As an aspect of this approach, and recognising in particular the problems involved for victims of disasters or defective medicines, the Legal Aid Board, encouraged by the government, is examining how to fund multiparty actions through the legal aid scheme by directing legal aid cases to a single firm or small group of firms of solicitors.[2] The conduct of the case would then be the responsibility of the co-ordinating solicitor, whilst the solicitor first approached by the client would deal with the client on a day-to-day basis. The Legal Aid Board is of the view that the disadvantages of such a scheme, that is the restriction on the applicants' choice of solicitor to have the main conduct of the case and a weakening of the direct link between the legally aided plaintiff and the solicitor, are far outweighed by the advantages. The advantages would include

"—a high quality of legal advice, experience and competence in conducting and managing cases of this sort;

—the greater likelihood that all potential plaintiffs would be brought in from the outset, assisting the conduct of the case and giving greater certainty to defendants;

—the co-ordinated organisation of claims, research, expert opinions and pre-trial procedures."[3]

Public funding of litigation

The current method of public funding is the *civil legal aid* scheme which already exists to assist litigants who fall within its limits. It is discussed at the beginning of the following chapter.[4] It alleviates the burden of costs by

[95] Courts and Legal Services Act 1990, s.58(3). If the percentage for an increase is too great, it then becomes unenforceable, s.58(6).

[96] Law Society's Contentious Business Committee, *Improving Access to Justice* (1987): see Zander (1989), pp. 56–57.

[97] *Ibid.* p. 57.

[98] R.S.C. Ord. 15, r. 12, see *The Supreme Court Practice 1991*, pp. 216–226.

[99] In *Davies (Joseph Owen)* v. *Eli Lilly & Co. and others* [1987] 3 All E.R. 94 at p. 96h.

[1] *Civil Justice Review* (1988), paras. 274–276.

[2] Legal Aid Board, *Report to the Lord Chancellor* (Cm. 688, 1989), pp. 15–16, 35–41.

[3] *Ibid*, p. 16, see also *Legal Aid Board Annual Report 1989–90*, pp. 45–46.

[4] See below, pp. 506–517.

providing financial assistance to litigants who can satisfy a means test,[5] and a merits test[6] and provide the contribution towards their own costs which may be required under the rules of eligibility.[7] This scheme does not always divert costs away from the assisted litigant to the Legal Aid Fund—far from it. More often it works as a way of postponing the cost to the successful assisted litigant until damages and costs are received from the opponent. The costs incurred by the Fund on behalf of a successful assisted party are defrayed from costs awarded against the loser.[8] Any further outstanding amount is taken from the contribution levied on the assisted party (if any), and any amount still outstanding will normally be taken from any damages awarded in the action.[9] In the end the successful assisted party probably often pays the same amount as a private client would have done.

The benefits of the scheme are two-fold. The responsibility for payment is assumed by the Fund, and if the total costs of the assisted party cannot be covered by costs awarded, contribution and damages, the liability of that party to the Fund is nonetheless limited to the original assessed contribution. More importantly, liability is similarly limited in the event of the assisted party being unsuccessful.[10] The Legal Aid Fund bears the costs risk rather than the litigant.[11]

Thus the legal aid scheme permits those eligible to take the risk of litigation at the possible expense of the Fund. People who could not afford litigation (because they could not pay the difference between their costs and the taxed costs recoverable) or who could not afford the risk of litigation (because costs awarded might not be recoverable or because they might lose) might be assisted by the scheme. However, the two substantial hurdles which protect the Fund mean many people will not benefit. If an applicant fails to satisfy the means test, he or she will be totally ineligible, and the applicant must satisfy the Area Director that the case merits assistance. The proposal to abolish the financial criteria made by the Royal Commission on Legal Services has not met with the agreement of the Government.[12] However, the Lord Chancellor wishes the Legal Aid Board to keep the arrangements governing eligibility and contributions for legal aid under review so as to fulfil the Board's overall aim, which is to ensure that legal advice, assistance and representation is made available to those who need it.[13] The Legal Aid Board is undertaking this review.[14]

[5] Taking into account both the income and capital of the applicant. For the current figures, see below, p. 509.

[6] Broadly, "Would a solicitor advise a private client to bring (or defend) this action?" See below p. 510.

[7] Above the lower limit of financial eligibility (below which no contribution is required), the contribution is 1/4 of disposable income and all disposable capital. See below, pp. 509–512.

[8] i.e. taxed costs awarded on the normal basis (see above, p. 472). This is on the assumption that these costs can actually be recovered from the loser.

[9] The so-called "statutory charge" on the proceeds of the action. There are certain exceptions, see below, pp. 512–514.

[10] The unsuccessful assisted party may find an order for costs against him or her, but most successful unassisted litigants realise that they are not likely actually to recover very much from an opponent who was sufficiently poor to be eligible for legal aid.

[11] Since the Fund is only substantially at risk where the assisted party loses, the object is, naturally, only to back winners.

[12] R.C.L.S. Report, pp. 120–121.

[13] The overall aim is set out in the letter from the Lord Chancellor, see Legal Aid Board (1989), Annex A.

[14] Ibid. p. 20. As to the working group on financial contributions, see p. 517 below.

A further proposal which appears to have little, if any, current support, is for litigation to be financed from *public funds* irrespective of the means of the parties. In particular this would support litigation which is not the fault of the parties to it, yet involves them in cost. The Royal Commission on Legal Services considered a *suitors' fund* which would indemnify litigants against the additional costs resulting from a successful appeal, the death or illness of a trial judge and the determination of an unsettled point of law of public importance.[15]

The recommendation that costs thrown away as a result of the death or illness of a judge in the course of a trial should be paid out of public funds has been given effect by the Administration of Justice Act 1985.[16] It provides that the Lord Chancellor may "if he thinks fit" reimburse the litigant's costs which are thrown away in these circumstances.[17]

The possibility of funding actions which determine important points of law is particularly interesting, since civil justice has two possibly opposed objectives. First, it is to assist people to resolve their disputes as easily as possible[18] and, secondly, it should enable the making or declaring of law that applies in those disputes.[19] Considerable service is done by the taking of actions which resolve points of law, but public officials can rarely bring actions[20] and the legal aid scheme will not support an action unless the case also passes the merits test.[21] Support for such a fund goes back to the Evershed Committee[22] in 1953, which recommended that a fund should be available for actions at first instance and on appeal, certified by the Attorney-General as raising a question of law of exceptional public interest which it is in the public interest to clarify. The Committee further proposed that the Attorney-General should be able to act on his or her own initiative and apply to intervene in an action or to pursue an appeal even where the parties had settled their differences. The Law Society put forward rather wider proposals in 1964,[23] which would have included cases in which on appeal it appears that the inferior court was precluded from reaching a just decision by virtue of the doctrine of precedent. The Royal Commission on Legal Services supported the proposals of the Evershed Committee, with the proviso that the judge at trial or on appeal should also be able to determine eligibility in cases where the point at issue does not emerge until later.[24]

---

[15] R.C.L.S., Report, p. 179.

[16] s.53.

[17] The Commission recognised that it is possible to insure against this possibility, but felt that it was not the parties' responsibility even to provide such a premium: R.C.L.S., Report, p. 180. See also JUSTICE, *A Proposal for a Suitors' Fund* (1969).

[18] Which may well be best served by not going to court, see below pp. 493–499.

[19] Jacob draws attention to this dichotomy in his Hamlyn Lectures, *The Fabric of English Civil Justice* (1987), see *e.g.* p. 8.

[20] The Attorney General has limited powers, see J.Ll.J. Edwards, *The Attorney General, Politics and the Public Interest* (1984), Chap. 6 and above p. 18 and below p. 876.

[21] *R.* v. *Legal Aid Committee No. 1 (London) Legal Aid Area, ex p. Rondel* [1967] 2 Q.B. 482.

[22] *Committee on Supreme Court Practice and Procedure* (Cmd. 8878, 1953), Chair: Lord Evershed M.R.

[23] The Law Society, "The Indemnity Rule" *Annual Report*, 1963–64.

[24] This modification was suggested in a JUSTICE report, *Lawyers and the Legal System* (1977). In America considerable attention has been given to the development of public interest litigation by individuals and groups, see Zander (1978), pp. 228–232. In this country there is no comparable development. Litigation is the responsibility of an individual and the possibilities for group actions are limited, although this is likely to change in the future, see above p. 483.

In general these proposals have not been implemented, indeed the government has stated that it is not convinced that it is right to fund litigation out of public funds, other than through the legal aid scheme, where points of law of general importance are involved.[25] There have though been four related developments. The Administration of Justice Act 1969[26] introduced the leap-frog appeal so that cases could go straight from first instance to the House of Lords when the Court of Appeal would be bound by precedent, thereby saving considerable costs.[27] The Criminal Justice Act 1972[28] provides for the Attorney-General to be able to refer a case to the Court of Appeal when he or she is concerned with the law applied by the Crown Court. The defendant's acquittal is not affected.[29] The Criminal Justice Act 1988[30] provides for a similar Attorney-General's reference where a sentence which is thought to be too lenient is imposed.[31] In a different way, the Equal Opportunities Commission and the Commission for Racial Equality are empowered by the Sex Discrimination Act 1975[32] and the Race Relations Act 1976[33] respectively to render assistance to individuals alleging discrimination. This assistance can include the provision of legal services. Similar assistance is given to those who might become involved with Immigration Appeal Tribunals by U.K.I.A.S., who receive Government money for the purpose.[34]

The JUSTICE report, *A Proposal for a Suitors' Fund*, advocates a more radical reform by suggesting that public funds should be used to indemnify litigants against "faults in the system" amongst which it included appeals on fact or law. At the moment it is the ultimate loser who pays the costs even if he or she happens to have won at first instance and in the Court of Appeal. The report suggested that it was not the ultimate loser's fault that the judge at first instance and the Court of Appeal did not get the right answers, and that the loser should not be liable for the appellate costs. The loser should remain liable for the first instance costs, which would have been incurred in any event. This proposal was rejected outright by the Royal Commission, primarily on the grounds that the risk of a decision being overturned on an appeal is a risk inherent in all litigation and "should be taken into account by all who embark on it."[35]

B. DELAY

Delay causes problems in both civil and criminal matters despite the exis-

---

[25] Cmnd. 9077, 1983, p. 19.
[26] ss. 12, 13.
[27] As to leap frog appeals, see pp. 863–864 below.
[28] s.36.
[29] See pp. 843–844 below.
[30] s.36.
[31] See pp. 838–841 below.
[32] s.75.
[33] s.66.
[34] By virtue of the Immigration Act 1971, s.23.
[35] R.C.L.S., Report p. 180.

tence of time-limits which are intended to expedite cases. The reasons for delay differ in civil and criminal procedure, not least because in civil matters the conduct of the action lies in the hands of the parties, who may agree through their lawyers to delays in proceedings. It is largely for the problems of delay that the Civil Justice Review recommended greater court involvement through court management of litigation.[36]

1. CIVIL MATTERS

"Delay in the conduct of civil proceedings occurs at three main stages, namely:

   (i) before proceedings are commenced;
  (ii) between the commencement of proceedings and the point where the case is either settled or is ready for trial; and
 (iii) between readiness for trial and the trial itself."[37]

The reasons for the slow progress of actions at these stages are diverse. At the outset, the plaintiff may be slow to contact a solicitor,[38] negotiations for a settlement may drag on,[39] the extent of the plaintiff's injuries may not become clear until the end of a lengthy period of treatment, investigations may have to be carried out to ascertain the evidence, expert opinions may have to be obtained, communication and action by both sides may be poor and slow, the advice of counsel may be taken, pleadings are often extended, the length of time spent waiting for the trial to begin can be substantial, and errors may be made by the professionals involved.[40] The problem of delay tends to be greater with regard to High Court proceedings, whether at the Royal Courts of Justice or not, than county court proceedings.

The Inbucon Study into Personal Injury Litigation[41] concluded that the three principal causes of delay were: (1) the medical circumstances of the case; (2) the long waits for trials in the Royal Courts of Justice and provincial

---

[36] *Civil Justice Review* (1988), paras. 220–228. See also, Jacob (1987), p. 106.

[37] *Civil Justice Review* (1988), para. 49.

[38] The time taken from an incident causing personal injury to advice first being sought was found in the Inbucon Study to be, expressed as medians (that is half the cases took more than the time and half took less), 3·4 months for cases ultimately at the Royal Courts of Justice, 1·6 months for cases ultimately at District Registries (for provincial High Court cases) and 1·9 months for county court cases: Inbucon (1986), Appendix 1. The figures only relate to those cases where writs or summons were actually issued. The reasons why people may take so much time to see a solicitor are, in part, explored in Chap. 8 above.

[39] The Inbucon Study showed that the median period from incident to settlement, where a writ or summons had been issued, for the various types of case, were 43·7 months (Royal Courts of Justice cases), 37·5 months (District Registry cases), 22·0 months (county court cases): Inbucon (1986), Appendix 1.

[40] The Inbucon Study found that, in cases where writs or summons were issued in personal injuries cases, the major component of elapsed time was the period between the issue of writ or summons and the settlement or trial: *ibid.* para. 4.2. See also, Jacob (1987), p. 69, and Chap. 2 generally. As to resolving such errors, see J. Hern, "Court v. solicitor errors" (1990) L.S. Gaz., May 2, p. 32.

[41] The Study, undertaken as a part of the Civil Justice Review, only provides evidence with regard to those cases where a writ or summons, that is the procedure for instigating an action, is issued.

trial centres,[42] and (3) a lack of clear or prompt response from the other side.[43]

Delay created by these reasons, both human and procedural, can prove extremely frustrating to the parties, most particularly to the plaintiff who will feel that delay amounts to a denial of justice.[44]

The complexities of the law can add to the amount of time taken to resolve a case. *Saif Ali* v. *Sydney Mitchell and Co.*[45] provides an example of a remarkably prolonged action, complicated by the expiry of the limitation period.[46] It is clearly an unusual case, but there was still a considerable lapse of time while the normal procedures were being followed. The timetable was as follows[47]:

March 26, 1966	Mr Saif Ali, a passenger in a car driven by his friend Mr Akram, was injured in a collision with a car driven by Mrs Sugden.
October 16, 1966	Mrs Sugden was convicted of driving without due care and attention.
1967	Mr Ali and Mr Akram consulted a solicitor with a view to making a claim. The solicitor took counsel's opinion.
October 1968	The solicitor instructed the barrister to draft the pleadings and to advise.
November 14, 1968	A writ and statement of claim was issued claiming damages against Mr Sugden only, alleging that his wife was driving as his agent at the time of the accident. Mr Sugden was the owner of the car and he had insured it.
Later	A meeting was held between Mr Ali's solicitor and the insurance company at which the company indicated that the agency question might be disputed, and that contributory negligence might be alleged against Mr Akram.
March 26, 1969	The limitation period expired[48] without any

---

[42] The problem created by having to wait for trial is not new; the Winn Committee on Personal Injuries Litigation (Cmnd. 3691, 1968) drew attention to it, considering that such delay was deplorable. The Inbucon Study found that the mean waiting periods from setting down until trial were 10·2 months for Royal Courts of Justice cases, 5·1 months for District Registry cases and 1·9 months for county court cases: Inbucon (1986), Appendix 1.

[43] Inbucon (1986), para. 4.8.1. For a consideration of the various factors relevant to delay, see *ibid*. pp. 19–26.

[44] Because the onus is very largely on the plaintiff to keep the action moving, it is he or she who is most likely to become frustrated by delay. Various writers refer to a recognisable medical condition, "litigation neurosis," which can afflict those enmeshed in an unfinished action.

[45] [1978] Q.B. 95, C.A.; [1980] A.C. 198, H.L.

[46] Jacob states that the Limitation Acts have "operated in a sort of blind, mathematical way, without regard to the merits of the claim or the circumstances of the parties or any other consideration": Jacob (1987), p. 268. He makes certain recommendations for reform: *ibid*. pp. 269–270.

[47] The timetable is culled from the judgments in both the Court of Appeal and the House of Lords. There are, unfortunately, some discrepancies in the dates given in the two courts—naturally, the House of Lords' version has been accepted!

[48] In a personal injuries action such as this, the writ must be issued within three years of the cause of action arising.

amendment to the writ, and without Mr Ali issuing proceedings against either Mr Akram or Mrs Sugden, the actual drivers in the collision.[49]

August 29, 1969	The writ was served on Mr Sugden.
October 16, 1969	Mr Sugden entered a defence denying his wife's agency.
November 1969	The barrister advised that Mr Ali should be separately represented.[50]
June 24, 1971	Mr Sugden amended his defence and admitted that his wife *was* acting as his agent.
January 21, 1972	Mr Sugden applied to the court for leave to withdraw his admission of agency with consent of the plaintiff's solicitors. Leave was granted.
May 9, 1972	The House of Lords decision in *Launchbury* v. *Morgans*[51] led Mr Ali's advisers to believe that it was impossible to continue the action.
April 22, 1974	The action against Mr Sugden was discontinued and Mr Ali's impregnable claim had disappeared.
September 19, 1974	Freshly advised, Mr Ali issued a writ against the solicitors who had represented him until November 1969 alleging negligence.
May 29, 1975	The defendant solicitors issued a third party notice[52] against the barrister whose advice they had taken, asking that he should indemnify them on the grounds that they had acted on his advice.
July 26, 1976	The barrister successfully applied to have the third party notice struck out on the grounds that it disclosed no cause of action.
February 24, 1977	The solicitors successfully appealed to Kerr J. and the third party notice was restored. The barrister successfully appealed to the Court of Appeal and the third party notice was again struck out.[53]
November 2, 1978	The solicitors successfully appealed to the House of Lords and the third party notice was restored.[54]
	N.B. The third party action between the solicitors and the barrister did not decide that

---

[49] There would appear to have been good cases against both the actual drivers—presumably, Mr Ali was advised to proceed against Mr Sugden because he was the insured person, and Mr. Akram was his friend.

[50] It was perceived too late that Mr. Ali's interests and Mr. Akram's interests were not identical!

[51] [1973] A.C. 127. A case in which the House of Lords held that a husband who had borrowed his wife's car to go on a "pub-crawl" was not her agent for the purpose of fixing her with liability for his negligent driving.

[52] *i.e.* joining the barrister in Mr Ali's action.

[53] [1968] Q.B. 95. The court relied heavily on *Rondel* v. *Worsley* [1969] A.C. 191, see above, p. 164.

[54] [1980] A.C. 198.

> he *was* negligent merely that *if* he was
> negligent he *would* be liable to the solic-
> itors. The question of whether he *was*
> negligent remained for trial if disputed
> by the barrister.

Prior to the Civil Justice Review, which considered the problem of delay generally in civil proceedings, two official committees[55] had considered the incidence and causes of delay with particular reference to personal injuries litigation. Much of the work of these Committees informed the work of the Civil Justice Review, which made numerous proposals to alleviate the problem.

Steps were taken before the Report of the Civil Justice Review to deal with the problem of waiting for trial with regard to the general list cases in the Queen's Bench. In 1988 a High Court judge was given charge of the list. Cases which had been settled or withdrawn were removed from it and sanctions for non-compliance were announced. Non-personal injury cases involving claims below £20,000 were identified for transfer to the county court and three extra Circuit judges sat in the High Court for three months to take Queen's Bench cases.[56] It appears that in relation to non-jury trial cases these steps have had success.[57]

The Civil Justice Review recommended that delay should be dealt with in a number of ways. The first, since introduced by the Courts and Legal Services Act 1990 Part I,[57a] is by a re-examination of the relationship between the High Court and the county court. This involves increasing the number of cases heard in the county courts, thereby maintaining High Court hearings for public law cases, specialist cases and general list cases of importance, complexity and substance.[58] This is achieved by limiting the range of cases heard by the High Court, by extending the jurisdiction of the county court, ensuring that, in most cases, the same remedies are available in the county court as in the High Court, amending the transfer system, reviewing the costs sanction system that applies when a case is taken inappropriately in the High Court, improving the trial facilities at county courts by concentrating trials at centres where continuous trial facilities are available, providing new centres, creating a new tier of Circuit judges to take additional civil jurisdiction burdens, and increasing the number of people eligible for appointment as county court and district registrars or district judges.[59] The general concern expressed about the approach is whether the county courts are going to be able to cope with the significant extra workload.

---

[55] *Report of the Committee on Personal Injuries Litigation* (Cmnd. 3691, 1968), Chair: Winn L.J.; *Report of the Personal Injuries Litigation Working Party* (Cmnd. 7476, 1979), Chair: Cantley J. For a brief consideration of their proposals, see the 1st edition of this book, pp. 376–378.

[56] So summarised in *Civil Justice Review* (1988), para. 55.

[57] *Listing Statement* (*Queen's Bench Non-Jury and Judge in Chambers Lists*), *The Times*, November 24, 1990.

[57a] Ss.1 and 5 came into force on November 1, 1990, and ss.6, 8, 11 and 16 on January 1, 1991.

[58] *Civil Justice Review* (1988), para. 124. For further consideration of the jurisdiction of the two courts, see Chap. 2, above.

[59] *Civil Justice Review* (1988), Chap. 3.

The second approach is to amend civil procedure. The Review proposed many changes to particular aspects of standard procedure which will speed up and streamline that procedure.[60] Detailed proposals were also made with regard to procedures in the area of personal injuries, small claims and the work of the Commercial Court.[61] In addition, a number of major themes of change were identified. One major theme was that a system of court management of litigation, that is court control over the progress of cases, should be introduced.[62] Courts would be involved in pre-trial procedure much more actively than at present in attempting to keep the parties to proposed new timetables, whilst allowing for a realistic degree of relaxation by the court, and permitting the parties to vary particular time limits by agreement, subject always to the obligation to have the case ready for trial and set down within the overall timetable. The Review recommended that there be a fixed period within which the parties would be required to set down the case for trial or to report to the court. Standard periods would be prescribed for different types of business, although it would be possible to apply for a special timetable at an early stage and for detailed variations of the timetable. Consequently, there would have to be an efficient case monitoring system. This, implicitly at least, demands the use of major computer systems, otherwise it would not be possible easily to carry out the necessary regular checks as to whether the various procedures have been undertaken within the prescribed time period. If there is no good reason for delay, the sanction available would be the issue of a summons to the solicitors on one or both sides to come to the registrar or master to explain matters. Once the parties had been heard, the master or registrar would have the power either to make an "unless" order, that is that the case would be struck out unless particular steps were taken within a particular time, or the case would be set down for trial. Ultimately the court would be able to strike out a case. Such changes have major implications for judicial administration and training.[63]

Further procedural changes should include improving the exchange of information between the parties,[64] encouraging the issue of specific written

---

[60] e.g. (1) the recommendation that the normal period between issue and service of process should be four months: ibid., e.g. paras. 201–204. This recommendation has already been followed, see p. 538, below; (2) with some exceptions, all proceedings should be commenced by a writ: ibid. paras. 213–216; (3) standard pre-trial directions should be devised, with the possibility of applying for additional or different directions, since in practice standard directions are provided through the summons for directions procedure even though it was not intended to be used for that purpose, and consequently the present system takes more time than a standard procedure: ibid. paras. 237–254; (4) the system of a pre-trial hearing in the High Court should be expanded on a trial basis: ibid. paras. 255–260; (5) there should be a common core of procedural rules in the High Court and the county court: ibid. paras. 277–280.

[61] As to such changes, see Civil Justice Review (1988), Chap. 7 (personal injuries), Chap. 8 (small claims) and Chap. 11 (the Commercial Court).

[62] Ibid. paras. 220–228. The recommendations broadly follow those made by the Cantley Committee (1979). See also, Jacob (1987), pp. 264–265.

[63] Civil Justice Review (1988), Chap. 5, see pp. 536–537.

[64] By providing for the exchange of witness statements, requiring more informative pleading, introducing an automatic right to administer interrogatories and imposing a costs sanction where specified facts are not admitted: see Civil Justice Review (1988), paras. 229–236 and, introducing these recommendations, Rules of the Supreme Court (Amendment No. 4) Rules 1989 (S.I. 1989 No. 2427), and County Court (Amendment No. 4) Rules 1989 (S.I. 1989 No. 2426), and see pp. 550–558 below. The Inbucon Study had found that the failure to communicate between the parties was a major reason for delay, see p. 488 above.

Professional Standards relating to the conduct of all principal types of litigation by the Bar and the Law Society combined with schemes to foster competence and experience,[65] introducing new arrangements for trials, particularly so that the judge can read the case papers (including witness statements) before the hearing, and so be much better prepared when the hearing begins,[66] and, in cases where there are many documents, providing a bundle of key documents, abuse of which would be checked by a personal costs sanction against the solicitors involved.[67]

As has already been indicated, delay can be caused by professional errors. Indeed the Lord Chancellor's Department figures draw attention to the fact that solicitors make mistakes in court documentation and evinces the hope that improvements can be made in this respect.[68] The Courts and Legal Services Act 1990, s.110 has begun to address this by providing a right of complaint against court maladministration to the Parliamentary Commissioner of Administration.[69]

2. CRIMINAL MATTERS

Although the delay in criminal cases is of a different order of magnitude, it still gives rise to concern. The concern is expressed on behalf of defendants in custody because they may ultimately be acquitted or given non-custodial sentences, and on behalf of defendants on bail because of the uncertainty and unpleasantness of a pending criminal trial. In addition there are difficulties associated with trials relating to incidents which happened in times long gone by. Witnesses forget.

There is, in theory, an 8-week time limit between committal and trial on indictment,[69a] but that rule may be dispensed with by the Crown Court and the following figures indicate the present position. In England and Wales in 1989, of the 89,316 defendants committed for trial who pleaded guilty 52 per cent. were dealt with in less than eight weeks; of the 34,539 who pleaded not guilty only 24 per cent. were dealt with in less than eight weeks. Indeed, of this latter group ("not-guilty pleas"), 41 per cent. had to wait longer than 16 weeks for trial.[70]

Delays for defendants in trials on indictment were giving cause for concern in 1975, when the James Committee reported, but at that stage over 70

---

[65] Professional Standards were also recommended by the R.C.L.S., Vol. 1, paras. 22.57–22.60, to which the Law Society and the Bar have both begun to respond. In addition the Law Society has already set up specialist panels for child care and mental health review tribunal work and is considering the establishment of further panels, see The Law Society, *Specialisation: The Way Forward* (1990) and Chap. 3, above.

[66] The recommendation is not for wholesale adoption of that procedure, which is already used in the Commercial Court; it is argued that the change, whilst interfering with the principle of orality, should be conducive to justice as well as to economy and effectiveness: *Civil Justice Review* (1988), paras. 261–265.

[67] *Ibid.* para. 303. In addition, the introduction of split trials in personal injuries actions will reduce delay, see below p. 497.

[68] *Ibid.*

[69] This section came into force on January 1, 1991. The divide between "judicial" and "administrative" activity may cause problems: J. Hern (1990), p. 33.

[69a] See below, p. 661.

[70] *Judicial Statistics 1989*, Cm. 1154, Table 6.15.

per cent. of cases were disposed of within eight weeks.[71] The overall figure for 1989 would now appear to be 45 per cent.[72]

Those defendants awaiting trial in custody might seem to be the most seriously disadvantaged by delay and they do tend to take priority. In 1989, 57 per cent. of this group waited less than eight weeks for trial, and 84 per cent. less than 16 weeks. The figures for those defendants on bail were 41 per cent. and 73 per cent. respectively.[73]

The situation differs around the country and the *average* length of time between committal and trial varies from 7·9 weeks on the Wales and Chester circuit to 17·4 weeks in London. The national average is 12·4 weeks.[74]

There is little information on waiting times in magistrates' courts.[75] The Royal Commission on Criminal Procedure noted research which suggests that only 15 per cent. of contested cases were dealt with in less than six weeks, and further noted the delay that can occur between the defendant's first contact with the police and the issue of the summons. It concluded that, "The speed with which cases are brought to trial is in our view determined almost entirely by the volume of business and the resources available to deal with it."[76] This distinguishes the criminal problem from the civil, but it sounds like a counsel of despair. If there were more judges, more lawyers and/or less criminals, and/or more guilty pleas then the problem would diminish. Indeed it would, but there may be more imaginative solutions to be commended. The widespread adoption of a rigorous and effective pre-trial review?[77]

C. SETTLEMENT

Cost and delay are just two of the factors which persuade the great majority of those in dispute to effect a compromise and settle their differences without trial. The then Lord Chief Justice in 1980 commented that, "If it were not that a high proportion of cases are compromised long before they reach court the administration of justice would soon grind to a halt; the courts would be overwhelmed by the volume of work."[78] Indeed Jacob values settlements sufficiently to suggest that a power, or perhaps even a duty, should be imposed on the court to promote a settlement or compromise between the parties.[79]

[71] *The Distribution of Criminal Business between the Crown Court and the Magistrates' Courts*, Cmnd. 6323 (1975), para. 23.
[72] *Judicial Statistics 1989*, Table 6.14.
[73] *Ibid*. Table 6.16.
[74] *Ibid*. Table 6.14.
[75] *Criminal Statistics England and Wales 1988*, Table 6.2, gives the percentage of cases dealt with on first appearance, the average number of times a case is listed and average days from offence to disposal, but does not distinguish between contested and uncontested cases.
[76] *The Royal Commission on Criminal Procedure, Report*, Cmnd. 8092 (1981), para. 8.25.
[77] See below, pp. 668–670.
[78] In the course of the Foreword to the 1st edition (1980) of D. Foskett, *The Law and Practice of Compromise* (2nd ed., 1985). This is a practitioner's work which gathers together the technical law on compromise. Since the question to be asked in this section is whether the process of settlement is fair, this quote may suggest a fundamental dilemma when considering civil procedure.
[79] Jacob (1987), p. 267.

1. Who Settles When?

The settlement of a dispute is achieved by an agreement between the parties to abandon any further claim in respect of the subject of the dispute. It takes the form of a legally binding contract and the normal rules of contract apply to establish the existence, meaning and effect of the agreement.[80] In general the parties are completely free to negotiate the terms of the settlement.[81] A settlement may be arrived at more usually before proceedings have begun, but may also be arrived at after proceedings have begun.[82] Once agreement is reached, the settlement is just as final as a judgment and, unless the agreement has been improperly procured, the issues of fact and law raised in the original claim may not be the subject of further litigation.[83]

There is no source of official information on settlements, since court formalities are rare, and thus deductions have to be made from the information available in the judicial statistics, supported by the available research.

Information from the judicial statistics

The judicial statistics inevitably provide an incomplete picture since the only information available relates to matters where a writ has been issued and many disputes may already have been settled by then.[84] The following figures[85] are culled from the Judicial Statistics for 1989,[86] and relate to the Queen's Bench Division:

WRITS ISSUED	288,287
JUDGMENT GIVEN WITHOUT HEARING	111,405
CASES SET DOWN FOR TRIAL	11,565
CASES DISPOSED OF:	12,859
Comprising:	
Determined after trial	1,565
Settled during trial or hearing	540
Approval of prior settlement	900
Settlement without notice after court attendance	610
Settled with consent order before hearing	2,030
Withdrawn before hearing, settled without court order, or struck out	7,220

Clearly these figures are not entirely comparable because they relate to cases at different stages in the procedure. Most of the cases determined after a trial would have been begun by a writ issued in 1985 or 1986. However, the

---

[80] Foskett (1985), Chap. 3.
[81] There are some exceptions, *e.g.* settlements involving infants and mental patients: Foskett (1985), Chap. 21.
[82] Usually a court order is not necessary, although it may, in some circumstances, be thought to be a good idea, see O'Hare & Hill (1990), pp. 35–39 and 382–384.
[83] Foskett (1985), Pt. I.
[84] See below, p. 496.
[85] Some of the figures are estimates, which is why they do not always quite add up.
[86] Cm. 1154, Chap. 3, esp. Tables 3.1, 3.2, 3.3, 3.4.

figures do give an indication of the proportion of cases resolved by settlement rather than trial.

It will be seen that a high proportion of cases disappear after the issue of a writ, presumably either settled or discontinued. A similarly high proportion end in a swift judgment because the defendant is in default or has no real defence.[87] About one case in 25 goes through all the pre-trial procedure and is set down for trial. Even then, a large proportion are withdrawn, many settled, before a hearing. A surprisingly high number of cases are settled "at the door of the court" with the parties in attendance ready for trial.[88] A number of settlements require the formal approval of the court.[89] A high proportion of trials which begin will end in settlement rather than judgment. By the end, we find that for every 184 writs that were issued in 1989, one case was determined by trial. In 1988 about one case in 19 was set down for trial and for every 94 writs issued one case was determined by trial.[90]

These statistics relate to all actions in the Queen's Bench Division. A slightly different picture emerges if we sift out the figures relating to *personal injury negligence actions alone*—the category most discussed in relation to the efficacy of settlements. Again from the Judicial Statistics 1989,[91] the table now looks like this:

WRITS ISSUED	56,219
JUDGMENT GIVEN WITHOUT HEARING	Not specified
CASES SET DOWN FOR TRIAL	Not specified
CASES DISPOSED OF:	9,820
Comprising:	
Determined after trial	1,150
Settled during trial or hearing	390
Approval of prior settlement	720
Settlement without notice after court attendance	500
Settled with consent order before hearing	1,510
Withdrawn before hearing, settled without court order, or struck out	5,560

From these figures we can see that a high proportion of the cases disposed of in 1989 were personal injury actions (9,820 out of 12,859) hence the attention paid to this category of cases, and that in such cases for every 49 writs issued in 1989, one case was determined by trial. In 1988 for every 25 writs issued, one case was determined by trial.[91a]

[87] See pp. 543 and 550 below for judgment in default and "Order 14" procedure.
[88] The prospect of immediate trial concentrates the minds of the parties and the advisers wonderfully. The action brought by four firemen who attended the King's Cross fire against London Underground was settled just before their claims were to be heard: *The Times*, December 19, 1990.
[89] *e.g.* settlements involving infants and mental patients.
[90] *Judicial Statistics 1988* (Cm. 745), Chap. 3.
[91] Cm. 1154, Tables 3.2, 3.3.
[91a] Cm. 745, Tables 3.2, 3.3

Research information

The Judicial Statistics figures tend to confirm the conclusions of the Winn Committee, which reported in 1968[92] that "... of all personal injury claims asserted about 20–25 per cent. reach the stage of proceedings being started, and only about 10 per cent. of these reach the doors of the court, of which between one-third and one-half are then settled without trial." In the 1989 figures, 56,219 actions were started, 2,760 reached the doors of the court of which 1,610 were settled. The studies conducted for the Pearson Commission produced figures of 86 per cent. of cases settled without proceedings being started.

The Oxford Study[93] reveals that of 169 people who reported receiving damages as a consequence of an accident suffered, only four received them as a result of a court order. Of the 165 cases in which damages were received without a court order, 104 were on the basis of the acceptance of the first offer that was made.[94]

We should by now have demonstrated to your satisfaction the enormous importance of the process of settlement. It is the normal procedure in the vast majority of cases. Is it fair?

2. NEGOTIATIONS FOR A SETTLEMENT

"The settlement process is very much a matter of bargaining, and it is bargaining of a difficult and expensive character. As economists would say, the case involves a bilateral monopoly, since the plaintiff has to 'sell' his claim to one potential buyer—the insurer—and the insurer has to 'buy' the claim from only one potential seller—the plaintiff."[95]

Having taken pains in Part II to point out that there are a number of non-legal sources of advice and assistance, we do not now wish to give the impression that the negotiation of settlements is exclusively the province of lawyers. Other agencies are quite heavily involved, some in the capacity of mediator or arbitrator,[96] others representing the interests of members in a more specialised field.[97]

Settlements can best be examined by considering personal injury claims, in which they play a major role, and which have been the subject of research and critical assessment.[98] In such actions, it is clear that the analysis in the first paragraph holds good, whoever the parties actually are. The plaintiff cannot shop around for the best offer, the two parties must deal with each other and strike an acceptable bargain through their own negotiating skill.

---

[92] *Report of the Committee on Personal Injuries Litigation* (Cmnd. 3691, 1968), para. 59.

[93] D. Harris, *et al.*, *Compensation and Support for Illness and Injury* (1984).

[94] D. Harris, "Claims for Damages: Negotiating, Settling or Abandoning" in Harris, *et al.* (1984), Table 3.3. The same study shows that the vast majority of accident victims do not make a claim at all, a factor supported by the Pearson Commission.

[95] Cane (1987), p. 266.

[96] See below, pp. 502–504.

[97] Primarily the trade unions, but also the motoring organisations. Advice agencies also involve themselves on behalf of clients, from time to time taking an active part in negotiation and settlement.

[98] See, in particular, Harris *et al.* (1984); H. Genn, *Hard Bargaining* (1987); see also Cane (1987).

The defendant in a personal injuries action is likely to be represented by an insurance company, which takes complete control of and financial responsibility for the claim. If the defendant is not insured, he or she is not likely to be worth suing.[99] The staff in the claims department of an insurance company will be skilful and experienced negotiators, with adequate resources to deal with claims.[1]

The plaintiff in a personal injury action is the person hurt as a result of an accident. He or she is unlikely to have any skill or previous experience in seeking compensation for injury and is, therefore, largely dependent on the legal advice sought and received.[2] The routes to seeing a solicitor vary.[3] Some accident victims seek legal advice through an agency, such as their trade union, who will place them in touch with an experienced solicitor.[4] Other plaintiffs will adopt the common, often haphazard, methods of seeking legal advice, which may result in a plaintiff seeing a solicitor who is not experienced in the field.[5]

Once the plaintiff has found a solicitor, the problems that may face the plaintiff in the initial stages of negotiation must be discussed. Two questions arise: first, the liability question, *i.e.* is the defendant liable in law? secondly, the quantum question, *i.e.* if the defendant is liable, how much should the damages be?[6]

Proving liability will depend, if it is denied by the defendant, upon three factors. First, there is the information which the client has about the accident. It is likely that the client will see the solicitor some time after the accident, when memory may already have begun to fade. Indeed there is evidence which shows that the longer the delay in seeing a solicitor, the less likely damages will be obtained.[7] Secondly, more may be discovered about the accident. Research has shown that it is often the case that a plaintiff's solicitor either does not have the resources to undertake investigations or is loath to seek out all available reports.[8] On the other hand, much information may be available, from accidents reports and other sources.[9] Some help is given by section 33 of the Supreme Court Act 1981. This section establishes a

---

[99] Unless rich, either personally or because the defendant is a large company or other organisation (*e.g.* considerable sums of health service finance fund legal actions against health authorities and their employees).

[1] There would appear to be considerable value in being experienced negotiators, see Genn (1988), pp. 7–8 and *passim*. The availability of resources places the insurance company at an advantage with regard to at least some plaintiffs, *ibid.* pp. 7, 50–52, 63.

[2] See H. Genn, "Who Claims Compensation: Factors Associated with Claiming and Obtaining Damages" in Harris, *et al.* (1984), p. 76.

[3] *Ibid.* pp. 65–67.

[4] It is clear from the evidence about trades unions' solicitors provided in *ibid.* that there is considerable value in seeing a solicitor through this route since the solicitors engaged by trades unions are experienced in the field of personal injury litigation.

[5] As to seeking legal advice, see Chap. 9, above.

[6] The separateness of these issues is reflected in the fact that is is possible for split trials to be ordered so that, for example, liability can be established whilst waiting for the medical condition of the plaintiff to be diagnosed adequately before the quantum issue is determined: R.S.C. Ord. 33, r. 4(2A); C.C.R. Ord. 13, r. 2(2A) and see *Civil Justice Review* (1988), para. 452.

[7] D. Harris, "Claims for Damages: Negotiating, Settling or Abandoning" in Harris, *et al.* (1984), p. 104 and Table 3.7.

[8] Genn (1987), pp. 67–69.

[9] See, on methods recommended to solicitors for investigating a claim, Pritchard, *Personal Injuries Litigation* (5th ed., 1986), Chap. 4.

procedure whereby a plaintiff may seek an order requiring a defendant to disclose any documents which may become the subject matter of subsequent proceedings.[10] Unfortunately, the plaintiff must specify the documents believed to be in the possession of the defendant, but the power is still useful in assisting the plaintiff to evaluate the case. Thirdly, there is the question of how good the witnesses will be when, and if, it comes to establishing a case in court. Any witnesses will need to be contacted and the quality of their evidence assessed. Overall, it may be difficult to discover whether there is enough evidence to pursue a claim.[11] If a possible action does emerge from the evidence available an attempt will be made to put a monetary valuation on the injuries suffered by the plaintiff. At this stage negotiations are likely to begin.

The defendant, however, may well be in a much better position to assess liability, because insurance companies are often able to anticipate possible claims and have considerable resources available to investigate the circumstances of an accident fairly soon after its occurrence.[12]

To establish the quantum of damages that may be available, it is necessary to obtain as much information as possible about the injuries which the client suffered, and the future effect of such injuries, in particular upon the client's earning capacity. The client will, therefore, need a medical report.[13] Evaluating quantum is particularly difficult. In an American experiment, 20 pairs of practising lawyers negotiated on identical information about a case. The highest outcome was $95,000; the lowest $15,000; and the average was just over $47,000![14] Since negotiation over figures is difficult, a practical suggestion is to "[l]eave it to the insurers to put forward figures in settlement. . . . [T]he insurer's representative . . . should be left to initiate the discussions, for it is not the plaintiff's role to make settlement proposals."[15] One main reason for the difficulties considered here is that a settlement usually involves payment of one lump sum in the same way that damages consequent upon a successful court action are also paid in a lump sum.[16] It is, however, possible for the injured party and the insurance company to agree on a "structured settlement." Under such a scheme sums of money are paid over periodically either for a fixed period or until the death of the injured party. These sums can then be varied over time to reflect changes consequent upon the damage caused to the injured party.[17]

The orthodox view of civil pre-trial procedure is that the more the two parties know about the real issues between them the more likely it is that a "realistic" settlement can be reached.[18] In the early stages, however, it may

---

[10] R.S.C. Ord. 29, r. 7A; and see Pritchard (1986).

[11] See also Genn (1987), p 72–75. For the role of the Bar, see *ibid.* pp. 78–81.

[12] *Ibid.* pp. 62–66.

[13] *Ibid.* pp. 75–78. For the role of the Bar, see *ibid.* pp. 78–81.

[14] G.R. Williams, *Legal Negotiation and Settlement* (1983), referred to in Genn (1987), p. 77.

[15] Pritchard (1986), p. 29.

[16] See below, p. 709.

[17] The payments are financed by the purchase of an annuity by the liability insurer, and, by an Inland Revenue concession, are not taxable as income. See M.A. Jones, *Textbook on Torts* (2nd ed., 1989), pp. 380–381; R. Lewis, (1988) 15 J.L.S. 392; D.K. Allen, (1988) 104 L.Q.R. 448.

[18] This is the especial function of pleadings, see below, pp. 550–558; discovery, see below pp. 558–563; and interrogatories, see below, p. 563. All these procedures take place well after the start of the action and, as we have already seen, a considerable time after the accident.

not be in the plaintiff's interests to disclose too much. As good a bargain must be struck as possible. In setting out general guidelines for a solicitor negotiating on behalf of a plaintiff, Pritchard counsels caution. Do not provide too much detailed information; do not disclose medical reports; do not indicate the financial status of the client or his or her willingness and ability to litigate. This advice, along with other hints,[19] emphasises that negotiations are conducted in an atmosphere of pressure.

The desire not to reveal too much information to the other side is, however, a major reason for delay in the civil justice system,[20] as well as causing expense. Consequently, the Civil Justice Review made a number of recommendations which will ensure greater openness in pre-trial proceedings.[21]

The quality of the negotiators and their approach consequently plays a significant role in the settlement that is achieved. Insurance company representatives are almost invariably skilled, but the levels of skill and experience of the plaintiff's solicitor varies considerably, and the research evidence suggests that this is a highly significant factor in the settlement process.[22] Further, there is a debate as to whether the best method of approach by the plaintiff's solicitor is confrontation or co-operation. On the whole, the evidence[23] and advice[24] suggests that a combative approach is best, making clear that the plaintiff is prepared to litigate, and doing so swiftly by the issue of proceedings.

Clearly there is considerable pressure on the various parties to the negotiations. Since the plaintiff is a prime contributor, it must be realised that whilst it is important to utilise what advantages are possessed, there is considerable pressure on him or her as well.

3. PRESSURES

The pressure to conclude a settlement is almost always on the plaintiff who is placed at a considerable disadvantage against the skilled defendant.[25] Broadly, the pressures are attributable to delay, cost and the risk of litigation.

We have considered the *delay* likely to occur in a personal injury action which goes to trial in the High Court.[26] The incentive to settle and clear the matter up quickly is significant. The plaintiff may be urgently in need of the money. It is he or she who will be incurring additional expenses as a result of the accident and whose earning power may have been impaired. Social

[19] Ask for an interim payment before proceedings commence, leave it to the insurers to put forward the settlement figure, the time to negotiate is when the other side is under pressure. Pritchard (1986), pp. 27–30.

[20] See above, p. 488.

[21] See above, p. 491.

[22] See Genn (1987), *passim*. Increasingly, skills training forms a part of legal professional education, see N. Gold, K. Mackie and W. Twining, *Learning Lawyers' Skills* (1989), Chap. 7, which is concerned with negotiation.

[23] See Genn (1987), esp. pp. 46–50, 53.

[24] See Pritchard (1986), pp. 27–30.

[25] Whilst the defendant is skilled if represented by an insurance company (see above), the company may be under pressure not to stretch out negotiations too far, especially when it becomes obvious that the plaintiff has a strong case.

[26] See above pp. 487–492; see also, Genn (1987), pp. 100–108.

security payments are unlikely to be adequate compensation for loss of earnings and injuries. Interest is payable on damages from the date of the cause of action to the date of judgment in all personal injury cases (unless there are special reasons to the contrary) and the court *may* order interest on that basis in other cases,[27] but the plaintiff may still prefer to have the money in hand. An interim payment may be ordered by the court on application, but an order will only be made when it is clear that the defendant will be held liable at trial.[28]

There is some evidence that delay and associated anxiety can cause a recognisable psychological state of "litigation neurosis,"[29] a complaint which disappears on the resolution of the dispute. It is almost inevitable that the circumstances associated with a legal dispute will cause worry and upset, but long delays weaken the spirit as well as the claim.[30]

The plaintiff has little to gain by delay. It may be that the injuries are such that their full effects will not become apparent for some time and a hasty settlement might lead to an underestimation of the damage,[31] but generally delay is on the side of the defendant. Apart from the interest charges involved, the longer a defendant can spin out the negotiations the better. American evidence cited by Phillips and Hawkins demonstrates that delay can be used as a deliberate tactic either against unmeritorious or unreasonable claims, or to alleviate the cash-flow problems of smaller insurance companies.[32]

Plaintiffs have cash-flow problems as well. It is cash flowing on *costs* as the case progresses which provides another incentive to settle. We need not elaborate on our earlier discussion of costs,[33] save in two respects. The rule that costs follow the event is important in negotiations because it adds another factor to the equation. The more unsure the plaintiff is about winning the case, the more significant the possibility of a costs claim becomes,[34] and the calculation of costs which would ultimately be awarded to the successful party complicates the estimation of the total value of the claim. Secondly, the costs pressure can be greatly increased by a judicious

---

[27] Supreme Court Act 1981, s.35A (and County Courts Act 1984, s.69).

[28] Supreme Court Act 1981, s.32. An order may be made after an interlocutory hearing if the Master is satisfied that the defendant has admitted liability *or* the plaintiff has obtained judgment with damages to be assessed *or* the plaintiff will win on liability at trial without substantial contributory negligence AND the defendant is insured *or* a public authority *or* has the means to pay: R.S.C. Ord. 29, r. 11, see also C.C.R., Ord. 13, r. 12.

[29] See the material cited by Cane (1987), p. 151 and footnotes thereto.

[30] The circumstances of the plaintiff are also important. An elderly, infirm person might want to receive money quickly in order to enjoy it.

[31] The problem is alleviated by the power of the court to award provisional damages in an action for personal injuries in which there is proved or admitted to be a chance that in the future the injured person will develop some serious disease or suffer some serious deterioration caused by the wrongful act or omission of the defendant: Supreme Court Act 1981 s.32A. This power is unlikely to assist the *settlement* process, since it only applies to judgments. Indeed, it may encourage plaintiffs to go to court to take advantage of the power. It will not be possible to reopen settlements on this account so that the plaintiff will now have an additional choice to make in deciding on settlement or action. On the other hand, it may give the plaintiff greater bargaining power with the defendant, since a settlement may now be in the defendant's interests.

[32] J. Phillips and K. Hawkins, "Economic aspects of the settlement process" (1976) 39 M.L.R. 497 at pp. 502–503. There is also some English evidence, see *Report of the Committee on Personal Injuries Litigation* (Cmnd. 3691, 1968), paras. 46–62.

[33] Above pp. 472–477. See also, Genn (1987), pp. 109–119.

[34] *Ibid*. Chap. 5 and pp.109–119.

payment into court.[35] The mechanics of the payment in have been explained.[36] The tactical advantages to the defendant are considerable. They accrue mainly from the uncertainty which surrounds the calculation of damages. Solicitors and barristers experienced in personal injury litigation will have to estimate a sum for loss of amenity and pain and suffering based on awards in similar cases, their own practice and the published awards contained in specialist books.[37] A rather gruesome list emerges which indicates the value of a leg, arm or toe—but not a precise value. The figure is almost always expressed as a range which will expand according to the seriousness of the injury.[38] When pecuniary losses are added the outcome of an assessment of the plaintiff's damage may be that it is worth, say, between £8,000 and £10,500. If the defendant makes a payment into court of £8,250, the gamble is obvious. Either the plaintiff will receive £8,251 + costs (if the judge's estimate tallies with that of the plaintiff's advisers) or a much lower figure (if it does not, and he or she has to pay costs). Clearly this procedure could impose considerable pressure on plaintiffs.

Zander found that a large number of payments in were accepted and that it was a tactic well used by defendants.[39] However, the Oxford Study showed that in many cases it was not a factor, since very little use was made of this procedure, despite its obvious advantages to the defendant.[40]

Does a payment in place unfair pressure on a plaintiff? Both sides are gambling because the defendant may be paying more than a judge would award at trial. The plaintiff is playing with higher stakes because the cost penalty is likely to be bigger than the amount by which the defendant might overestimate the claim.

Even if it is not used much the trenchant criticisms of it would appear to demand reform, as it appears to be a blunt instrument which "should be honed down to produce a greater quality of justice."[41] However, the Civil Justice Review recommended no change, since the evidence suggested that, despite its bluntness, most people were broadly satisfied with payments into court.[42] The procedure saves costs and time and though it has been criticised, no better procedure has been proposed.

The third factor is the *risk* of litigation. The onus lies on the plaintiff, if the dispute goes to trial, to prove the case on a balance of probabilities.[43] Uncertainties abound. It may be unsettled whether the defendant is liable at law for the plaintiff's damage.[44] In the absence of a settlement the parties

[35] Similarly also the use of *Calderbank* letters, see above, pp. 476–477.

[36] Above, p. 476.

[37] *Kemp and Kemp on The Quantum of Damages*. The monthly parts of *Current Law* also contain details of the latest awards categorised anatomically.

[38] The more serious the injury, the more difficult the estimate. One of the highest damages award in a personal injury action is the £1,571,282 awarded to J. Lambert, 42, an airline pilot injured in a motorcycle accident, see *The Independent*, July 28, 1990.

[39] M. Zander, "Payment into Court" (1975) 125 N.L.J. 638.

[40] Genn (1987), pp. 111–113.

[41] Jacob (1987), p. 118. The Winn Committee described it as, ". . . rather a hit-and-miss affair; it is not sufficiently discriminating to achieve the object which it sets out to achieve; and it may work injustice.": *Winn Committee* (1968), para. 512.

[42] *Civil Justice Review* (1988), paras. 271–273.

[43] This is the standard of proof in a civil action. It means, "Is it more likely than not?"

[44] The case of the unborn children injured by the drug thalidomide illustrates the difficulty. At the time it was by no means certain that there was any liability towards unborn children. That point has now been resolved by the Congenital Disabilities (Civil Liability) Act 1976 for children born after July 22, 1976.

have to litigate to find out. Even if the law is clear, the case may be difficult because of lack of evidence.[45] Evidence depends upon witnesses and, to some extent, their credibility is dependent upon their performance in the witness box.[46] Some witnesses perform very badly. Some witnesses are unavailable at the time of trial.[47] Assuming the case is proved, the judge's estimate of the injuries and the consequent amount of the award is uncertain. After trial, there could be *two* appeals.[48] Looming large over all these doubts is the spectre of costs.

The plaintiff as an individual will feel the pressures much more keenly than the defendant, backed by the insurance company.

No one can be surprised that only one writ in a hundred comes to trial.

D. SETTLEMENT AND ALTERNATIVE DISPUTE RESOLUTION

Since settlement is a contractual matter, one wonders what can be done to achieve equality of bargaining power in the settlement process. The option of settling a dispute rather than resolving it by going to trial can be described as a form of alternative dispute resolution,[48a] meaning methods of resolving a variety of disputes in ways alternative to court hearings. The advantages of settling are clear. So also are the disadvantages. In particular, a difficulty stressed above in relation to settling personal injuries claims is the imbalance which often exists between the parties. The defendant, through an insurance company, is often in a much stronger bargaining position than the plaintiff. It was for this reason that it was made clear that the negotiations leading to a settlement might best be described as bargaining hence suggesting a somewhat aggressive method of resolving the matter.

The imbalance between the parties does not mean that all disputes ought to be resolved in court, rather it suggests that there may be methods of organising dispute resolution which are fairer for the parties involved. A particular example of this approach is that of mediation or conciliation in family disputes, particularly in relation to custody of children upon divorce.[49] Other forms of alternative dispute resolution, some of which arise out of Government initiatives, include the involvement of the Advisory, Conciliation and Arbitration Service in many industrial disputes,[50] the work of the Equal Opportunities Commission and the Commission for Racial

---

[45] See above pp. 497–498. The plaintiff is aided by discovery and other pre-trial procedures, but it is still up to him or her to find the evidence. The evidence may no longer exist, *e.g.* the alleged defective machine may no longer exist, or the allegations may be hard to prove, *e.g.* the witnesses may not give accurate or complementary evidence as to how the road traffic accident happened, and expert evidence to support a claim, *e.g.* to establish for how long someone will be unable to work or work less well, is expensive.

[46] Any inherent difficulties will be greatly exacerbated by the problem of delay. Witnesses are often giving evidence about incidents which happened some years before the trial.

[47] Abroad, ill, dead. All things are possible.

[48] Creating further delay and potential costs.

[48a] A major development in the field of alternative dispute resolution is the establishment of the Centre for Dispute Resolution: see J. Harris, (1990) 134 S.J. 1427.

[49] For a summary of and references to some of the literature, see A. Ogus, M. Jones-Lee, W. Cole and P. McCarthy, "Evaluating Alternative Dispute Resolution: Measuring the Impact of Family Conciliation on Costs" (1990) 53 M.L.R. 57 and R. Dingwall and J. Eekelaar, *Divorce Mediation and the Legal Process* (1988).

[50] See I.T. Smith and Sir J.C. Wood, *Industrial Law* (4th ed., 1989), pp. 31–38.

Equality in the settlement of disputes in their fields of interest,[51] the role of "ombudsmen" to deal with disputes in the banking and insurance worlds,[52] as well as complaints against central and local administration and the National Health Service,[53] the various alternative methods for resolving consumer disputes,[54] and the use of arbitration to resolve commercial dispute in private.[55]

Mediation or conciliation in such a context is frequently made available to a divorcing couple. There are many models, some court connected others independent.[56] The object of mediation or conciliation is to achieve a resolution of the dispute by the parties agreeing on who should have custody and what access rights the other should have, as well as how to make decisions for the up-bringing of the children. The function of the impartial mediator or conciliator may be described[57] as to act as a catalyst to ensure that negotiation does take place and that the issues are confronted and as a facilitator to enable an agreement which both parties can perceive to be fair.

The prime advantage of a form of alternative dispute resolution such as family mediation or conciliation is that the parties are in charge of resolving their dispute in an atmosphere conducive to avoiding domination by one party or another.[58] If the view is taken that "civil disputes are a matter of private concern of the parties involved, and may even be regarded as their private property ... and that the parties are themselves the best judges of how to pursue and serve their own interests in the conduct and control of their respective cases, free from the directions of or intervention by the court,"[59] forms of alternative dispute resolution must be considered as worth pursuing for the control that is provided to the parties over their dispute.

Such idealism is not the only reason why methods of alternative dispute resolution are supported. It is often suggested that they are cheaper. At first glance it might be assumed that this would always be the case. If an expensive court, barristers and pre-trial procedure do not have to be paid for, it must be the case that permitting the parties to agree between themselves is cheaper. Such an analysis might well apply where the court system is an expensive one and where little expenditure has to be spent on the method of

---

[51] See K. O'Donovan and E. Szyszczak, *Equality and Sex Discrimination Law* (1988), pp. 219–221; D. Pannick, *Sex Discrimination Law* (1985), Chap. 10.

[52] See R. Thomas, "Alternative Dispute Resolution—Consumer Disputes" (1988) 7 C.J.Q. 206, pp. 209–211 and R.B. Ferguson, (1980) 7 B.J.L.S. 141.

[53] See B.L. Jones, *Garner's Administrative Law* (6th ed., 1989), pp. 90–106.

[54] See Thomas (1988).

[55] The description is adapted from P.M.B. Rowland, *Arbitration: Law and Practice* (1988), p. 1. Arbitration is regulated by legislation, primarily now the Arbitration Acts 1950, 1975 and 1979. It is in relation to the resolution of commercial disputes that the mini-trial has been used, *e.g.* presentation of the various issues by in-house lawyers in front of senior executives from each side: *ibid.* p. 2, see also J. Lieberman and J. Henry, "Lessons from the Alternative Dispute Resolution Movement" (1986) 53 U. Chicago L.R. 424 and K.J. Mackie, *Lawyers in Business and the Law Business* (1989).

[56] See The University of Newcastle upon Tyne, Conciliation Project Unit, *Report to the Lord Chancellor on the Costs and Effectiveness of Conciliation in England and Wales* (1989). For a critique of the Report, see S. Roberts, "A Blueprint for Family Conciliation?" (1990) 53 M.L.R. 88.

[57] See M. Roberts, *Mediation in Family Disputes* (1988), Chap. 6. Properly understood, these two terms are not indicating the same form of involvement by the third party. The conciliator is more active than a mediator.

[58] See *ibid.* esp. Chap. 11. See also Thomas (1988), pp. 212–216.

[59] Jacob (1987), p. 8 and pp. 267–268.

resolution. This may be the case with personal injuries actions. However, the relevant court system is not always so expensive and the methods adopted to enable the fair resolution of the dispute may not always be cheap. The Conciliation Project Unit discovered that general adoption of a form of conciliation in family disputes would be more expensive than resolution through the various courts with family jurisdiction.[60]

Undoubtedly many further proposals will be made for the use of forms of alternative dispute resolution[61] in which case it will be important to assess their strengths and weaknesses on the basis of proper and specific evidence, if possible, and not rely upon anecdotal evidence or assumed propositions, in particular in relation to cost.[62]

---

[60] See Conciliation Project Unit (1989), Chaps 13–19, see also Ogus, et al. (1990). The difference in costs would be less if full account could be taken of the capital costs involved in the provision of the courts.

[61] For an overview of American developments, see Lieberman & Henry (1986).

[62] The objective of the Conciliation Project Unit was to provide such evidence, see Conciliation Project Unit (1989). The Office of Fair Trading is undertaking a project in this regard with respect to consumer disputes: Thomas (1988), p. 216.

CHAPTER 11

PRE-TRIAL CIVIL PROCEDURE

AT this stage, we move from a comparative approach, taking account of civil, tribunal and criminal procedure, and concentrate on civil procedure. The procedures which must be followed before a trial in the High Court or county court should be used by the parties to expose the real area of difference between them and concentrate attention upon it. Issues which are not in dispute should be eliminated and the scope of the disagreement narrowed. Using the procedures in this way has the dual effect of preparing the case as precisely as possible for the trial judge and of encouraging a settlement by revealing to the parties the exact nature of their dispute. It has been equally possible to operate the procedures in such a way as to leave all the issues open and so reveal very little to the other party about the case he or she would have to meet. Such obstructionism is a major contributor to delay and the high cost of litigation.

The complexity of pre-trial procedure, particularly in the High Court, has been said to act not only as a deterrent to all but the most determined litigant, but also as a weapon for the recalcitrant defendant who may manipulate it so as to place the pressure of delay upon the plaintiff. It may have been a factor in leading a plaintiff to sue in the county court rather than the High Court when his or her claim lay within its jurisdiction.[1] It was certainly used as an argument in support of the establishment of special courts with simplified procedure to deal with small claims.[2]

The problems identified here of delay, cost and complexity have long been recognised as requiring to be redressed. Indeed the terms of reference of the Civil Justice Review directed attention to these problems:

"To improve the machinery of civil justice in England and Wales by means of reforms in jurisdiction, procedure and court administration and in particular to reduce delay, cost and complexity."[3]

It is hoped that implementation of the recommendations of the Civil Justice Review will make significant improvements in the machinery of civil justice. The Courts and Legal Services Act 1990 has provided much of the statutory basis for many of the reforms and others are being introduced through changes in civil procedure rules.[4]

---

[1] See above, pp. 67–70. This is very much a matter of judgment. Where the sum in dispute is substantial, there are highly detailed procedural provisions in the county courts.
[2] See below, p. 531.
[3] *Civil Justice Review, Report of the Review Body on Civil Justice* (Cm. 394, 1989), para. 1.
[4] See, *e.g.*, County Court (Amendment No. 3) Rules 1990 (S.I. 1990 No. 1764) and Rules of the Supreme Court (Amendment No. 4) 1989 (S.I. 1989 No. 2427).

Nevertheless, certain procedural complexities will remain and continue to necessitate the services of a lawyer[5] in the pursuit of a claim. The legal advice scheme may be invoked for initial advice and assistance,[6] but the litigant who requires the services of a lawyer in civil proceedings must rely on the provisions of the representation element of the legal aid scheme or meet the cost himself or herself. Since many people are unable to meet the costs of litigation from their own resources, the availability of representation under the legal aid scheme will often be the crucial factor in deciding whether the case goes on at all. Therefore, we consider first the operation of the legal aid scheme.

A. OBTAINING LEGAL AID REPRESENTATION

1. THE DEVELOPMENT OF THE SCHEME[7]

The modern legal aid scheme, which provides financial assistance (subject to eligibility) in connection with proceedings in most of our civil courts, has come a long way since 1495 when statute provided for poor people, at the discretion of the Lord Chancellor, to sue without payment to the Crown, and to have lawyers assigned to them without fee.[8] A more formal Poor Persons Procedure was established in 1914[9] and was put under the control of the Law Society in 1925.[10] The Law Society provided the necessary administrative structure. Further, its involvement made more likely the necessary free provision by solicitors of their services. Government money was only made available to meet the cost of the administrative work involved.

The Poor Persons Procedure, dependent upon the charity of the legal profession, could not cope with the increasing pressure of work in the 1930s and was supplemented in 1942 by a Services Divorce Department. This department, consisting of salaried solicitors employed by the Law Society with government funds, dealt with the matrimonial problems occasioned by the Second World War. It must have been in the minds of the members of the Rushcliffe Committee as they took evidence. The committee was set up, with Lord Rushcliffe in the chair, in 1944, to review the provision of professional help for those who were unable to afford it, in both civil and criminal matters. The Committee's report[11] provided the basis upon which the Law Society was invited by the Lord Chancellor to undertake the task of organising a legal aid scheme, which resulted in the Legal Aid and Advice Act 1949 and the regulations made thereunder. The legislation, later amended by the Legal Aid Act 1974, relied heavily upon the decisions of the

---

[5] Or other person providing the appropriate legal service, see Chap. 3.
[6] As discussed above at p. 443.
[7] For a full consideration of the origins of the legal aid scheme, see S. Pollock, *Legal Aid, the first 25 years* (1975), and R. Egerton, "Historical Aspects of Legal Aid" (1945) 61 L.Q.R. 87.
[8] "An Act to admit such persons as are poor to sue *in forma pauperis*."
[9] Described as ". . . the first regular scheme for legal aid in the Supreme Court": H. Kirk, *Portrait of a Profession* (1976), p. 164.
[10] After it had fallen into complete chaos and on the recommendation of a committee under Mr. Justice P.O. Lawrence (The Poor Persons' Rules Committee (Cmd. 2358, 1925)).
[11] *Report of the Committee on Legal Aid and Advice* (Cmd. 6641, 1945). This report also contains a good review of the then existing facilities for legal aid and advice.

Rushcliffe Committee. Subsequently, the major concern perceived with the system of legal aid was that confusion and inefficiency were created by too many people having the ability to decide whether or not to grant help.[12] Consequently, the administration of the scheme has been removed from the Law Society and placed in the hands of the Legal Aid Board by the Legal Aid Act 1988.[12a] The 1988 Act otherwise maintains the same basic structure, but with some reforms.

2. THE SCOPE OF THE SCHEME[13]

The scope of the legal aid scheme is restricted in four respects. It only applies in specified *courts*, for specified *proceedings*, and to those who fall within the *financial conditions* and have *reasonable grounds* for taking, defending or being party to an action. If all the requirements are fulfilled, civil legal aid consists of *representation* for the purposes of proceedings, and it includes all such assistance as is usually given by a solicitor or counsel in the steps preliminary or incidental to any proceedings and all such assistance as is usually given by a solicitor or counsel in civil proceedings arriving at or giving effect to a compromise to avoid or bring to an end any proceedings.[14] The cost of such representation is met by the Legal Aid Fund, which is administered by the Legal Aid Board,[15] although a contribution may be required from the assisted party in accordance with the rules discussed below.

Taking the first two restrictions, section 14 and Schedule 2 of the Legal Aid Act 1988 prescribe the courts and the proceedings for which representation is available. Representation is currently available for almost all cases[16] in the House of Lords, the Court of Appeal, the High Court and county courts; the Employment Appeal Tribunal; the Lands Tribunal; the Restrictive Practices Court;[17] and certain proceedings in a magistrates' court.[18] The excepted proceedings, which are specified,[19] are actions in defamation, relator actions, certain proceedings for the recovery of a penalty,[20] election petitions, actions relating to judgment summons in the county court, actions in the county court where the only question is the time and mode of payment of a debt, and any incidental proceedings.

[12] See *Legal Aid Efficiency Scrutiny* (Lord Chancellor's Department, 1986), followed by the White Paper, *Legal Aid in England and Wales: A New Framework* (Cm. 118, 1987). See pp. 462–464.

[12a] See above, pp. 464–466.

[13] For further information, see *Legal Aid Handbook 1990*; D. Burrows, *Civil Legal Aid* (1989); D. Matheson, *Legal Aid: The New Framework* (1988). For a view that civil legal aid should be abolished, see C. Ellison, "Is civil legal aid necessary?" (1990) 134 S.J. 249.

[14] Legal Aid Act 1988, s.2(4).

[15] *Ibid.*, s.6.

[16] In addition to proceedings in the courts mentioned, provision is made for representation in connection with care proceedings: Legal Aid Act 1988, ss.27 and 28; and representation will be available in contempt proceedings where it appears to the court to be desirable to provide it in the interests of justice: Legal Aid Act 1988, s.29.

[17] When the proceedings in that court are taken under the Fair Trading Act 1973, Part III.

[18] *e.g.* proceedings under the Children Act 1989: Legal Aid Act 1988, s.14, Sched. 2, Part I, para. 2, as amended by the Children Act 1989, Sched. 13.

[19] Legal Aid Act 1988, Sched. 2, Part II.

[20] *i.e.* where those proceedings may be taken by anybody and the penalty is payable to whoever happens to take the proceedings.

Representation is not available for most tribunals. However, the advice and assistance scheme can be extended to provide some form of representation through the *advice by way of representation scheme* (ABWOR) which extends to certain domestic proceedings in a magistrates' court, urgent court applications, and other proceedings, that is hearings before Mental Health Review Tribunals and prison boards of visitors.[21]

3. MAKING APPLICATION—THE MEANS AND MERITS TEST

The overall administration of the legal aid scheme rests with the Legal Aid Board. The Board operates, according to the Legal Aid Act 1988, through 15 Area Directors and area committees[22] who work from area offices.[23] An application for a representation certificate is made to an Area Director.[24] It is recommended that a solicitor should assist in the completion of the appropriate application form, for which green form assistance[25] is available.[26]

On receipt of such an application, the Area Director will consider the *financial conditions* of the applicant and the *merits* of the applicant's case.

The assessment of the applicant's resources, which determines financial eligibility for representation, is undertaken by an "assessment officer" at the Department of Social Security.[27] The two significant assessments are of the

---

[21] Legal Advice and Assistance (Scope) Regulations 1989 (S.I. 1989, No. 550), regs. 7, 8, 9 [hereafter "the Scope Regulations], and see pp. 446–452 above.

[22] Area committees hear appeals from a refusal to grant legal aid by the Director.

[23] The Legal Aid Board has the power to introduce radical changes in such administration: see Civil Legal Aid (General) Regulations 1989 (S.I. 1989, No. 339), reg. 4 [hereafter "the General Regulations"]. The Legal Aid Board is undertaking a major review of administrative functions and controls within clearly defined management objectives which, in essence, are to secure effectiveness and efficiency: Legal Aid Board, *Report to the Lord Chancellor* (Cm. 688, 1989), pp. 4–8. For a description of the administration under the old legislation, see the first edition of this work at pp. 389–390. The Legal Aid Board works through a management structure which involves a Chief Executive and five Group Managers. Group Managers are responsible for two or three Area offices. An Area office is headed by a Group or Area Manager (known by the Act as an Area Director) and the office is divided into a number of sections to ensure that enquiries get a prompt and proper response. As to the administration of the scheme see *Legal Aid Board Annual Reports* (1989–90 H.C. 489), pp. 7–10.

[24] The application may be made to any Area Director where the applicant lives in the United Kingdom: the General Regulations, reg. 10(*a*). However, the application may be passed on to another area office, if it appears to the Area Director who received the application, that the application "could, without prejudice to the applicant, be more conveniently or appropriately dealt with" elsewhere: *ibid.* reg. 17. As to applications by people resident outside the United Kingdom, see Burrows (1989), para. 5.12. Forms are provided for the making of such applications: the relevant form for an application for a representation certificate is CLA1; if it is for matrimonial proceedings—CLA2; if for an emergency certificate—CLA3.

[25] See pp. 444–446, above.

[26] Burrows (1989), para. 5.5.

[27] As to how to calculate eligibility for civil legal aid, see *Legal Action*, April 1990, p. 22 and *Legal Aid Handbook 1990*, pp. 9–10. The procedure for the assessment of resources has been criticised, for example by the Law Society in the *31st Legal Aid Annual Reports* (1980–81), at p. 7, partly on the grounds of delay, partly because 74 per cent. of assisted parties made no contribution and of them between one-third and one-half were on supplementary benefit (the precursor to income support). The administrative cost to the then D.H.S.S. was almost £4,000,000 p.a. The last Annual Report of the Law Society indicated an average wait of 95.47 calendar days, (*i.e.* over 13 weeks) for a contributory certificate, and 48.08 calendar days (*i.e.* over six weeks) for a non-contributory certificate: *39th Legal Aid Annual Reports* (1988–89), Appendix 2E. The average wait reported in the 33rd Report for a contributory certificate was

applicant's *disposable income* and *disposable capital*. These are calculated by reference to the regulations[28] and allowance is made for dependants, income tax, national insurance, housing costs, and work expenses.[29] As from April 9, 1990, the levels of eligibility[30] for actions other than personal injury cases,[30a] are as set out in the following table:

	Disposable income	
(a)	more than £6350 p.a.	: ineligible
(b)	£2645–£6350 p.a.	: eligible subject to a contribution of one-quarter of the sum by which the disposable income exceeds £2645[31]
(c)	less than £2645 p.a.	: eligible without contribution
	Disposable capital	
(a)	more than £6310	: ineligible, if it appears that the applicant could afford to proceed without legal aid
(b)	£3000–£6310	: eligible subject to a contribution of the sum by which the disposable capital exceeds £3000
(c)	less than £3000	: eligible without contribution

The applicant must be eligible both in respect of income and capital. These specific figures appear in the Assessment of Resources Regulations and not in the Act, and so can be easily uprated as necessary.[32]

If an applicant is financially eligible, the Area Director must further be satisfied that he or she "has reasonable grounds for taking, defending or

12 weeks: *33rd Legal Aid Annual Reports* [1982–83], p. 70. The *Legal Aid Board Annual Reports* (1989–90), Appendix 2E suggests that improvement has been achieved in reducing the time taken to process applications for civil legal aid, but that the targets set by the Board are still not being achieved. In recognition of this problem, the Legal Aid Board has been given the power to carry out assessment of resources through its own staff: Legal Aid Act 1989, s.3(4)(d). Burrows (1989) describes this, at para. 4.29, as a controversial aspect of the Act. The Legal Aid Board has concluded that it would not be appropriate to transfer the assessment procedure to the Board, but is involved in streamlining and simplifying the procedure: *Report to the Lord Chancellor* (1989), pp. 18–19; *Legal Aid Board Annual Reports* (1989–90), Chap. 6. The report in relation to the scheme to assess streamlining means assessment has been completed, see *Legal Aid Board Annual Reports* (1989–90), Appendix 5E. The Legal Aid Board has concluded that national adoption of the Manchester Pilot Scheme would be proper, see *ibid.* para. 6.5. In consequence, solicitors will be provided with more forms which will enable the D.S.S. to determine eligibility more speedily.

[28] *i.e.* The Civil Legal Aid (Assessment of Resources) Regulations 1989 (S.I. 1989 No. 338) [hereafter known as the Assessment of Resources Regulations].

[29] See the Assessment of Resources Regulations, reg. 4, and Sched. 2 and 3, as amended by S.I. 1990 No. 484.

[30] If a person is on income support, he or she is automatically eligible.

[30a] Where the subject matter of the discretion includes a claim in respect of personal injuries, legal aid is available to a person whose income does not exceed £7,000 a year, but a person may be refused legal aid where his or her disposable capital exceeds £8,000 and it appears to the Area Director that he or she could afford to proceed without legal aid: Assessment of Resources Regulations, reg. 4, as amended by S.I. 1990 No. 484.

[31] Such contribution is payable in instalments over one year.

[32] Indeed, the 1990 figures are an uprating on those of 1989: see The Civil Legal Aid (Assessment of Resources) (Amendment) Regulations 1990 (S.I. 1990 No. 484). The 1991 uprating has increased, from April 8, 1991, the lower income level from £2,645 to £2,860: S.I. 1991 No. 635.

being a party to the proceedings."[33] This *merits* test is often expressed by asking the following question: "If this applicant were the private client of a solicitor would he or she be advised to take or defend the action?" The regulations give some guidance by directing that an application may be refused where it appears that any advantage accruing would only be trivial, where the simple nature of the proceedings would not normally require the assistance of a solicitor, or where funds from another source were available but not pursued.[34] However, a good deal of discretion is left in the hands of the Area Director to determine the merits of the application, having considered ". . . all questions of fact or law arising out of the action, cause or matter to which the application relates and the circumstances in which it was made."[35] Concern has been expressed about the delays in determining the merits test, especially as delay and refusal of legal aid appear to be related.[36]

4. THE REPRESENTATION CERTIFICATE AND THE APPLICANT'S CONTRIBUTION

If the application is approved by the Area Director, a representation certificate is issued, subject to the acceptance by the applicant of any conditions attached to it. The certificate is likely to specify the extent of the aid available and will often be limited to the taking of particular steps in the action. In the first instance, the certificate may be limited to the taking of counsel's opinion and another application may have to be made to the Area Director to amend the certificate for further action if counsel's opinion appears to warrant it. In this way, the Area Director can keep an action under review at all the crucial stages.[37]

If the application is successful and no contribution is payable, the Area Director issues a representation certificate to the applicant's solicitor, and a copy is sent to the applicant, now known as the "assisted person." If the applicant is successful but there are conditions attached or there is a contribution to pay, an offer of a certificate with a requirement to accept the conditions or pay the contribution is made. The applicant has 28 days in which to signify acceptance of any conditions attached. He or she must also make any capital contribution, which is normally payable forthwith, and pay the first instalment of any contribution from income, so that the whole sum will be paid off within 12 months.[38] Once payment is confirmed, a certificate is issued and forwarded to the solicitor.[39]

---

[33] Legal Aid Act 1988, s.15(2). It is also a requirement that an Area Director consider whether any other person has an interest in the proceedings, see *Legal Aid Handbook 1990*, pp. 50–51.

[34] The General Regulations, regs. 29, 30.

[35] *Ibid*. reg. 28. Guidance as to the exercise of the discretion is provided in the *Legal Aid Handbook 1990*, pp. 48–50. This discretion may be exercised overly conservatively, see, *e.g.* in relation to the "Opren litigation," *R.* v. *Legal Aid Area No. 8 Area Committee, ex p. Parkinson*; *Legal Aid Board Annual Reports* (1989–90), p. 152.

[36] *39th Annual Report of the Lord Chancellor's Advisory Committee on Legal Aid* (1988–89), para. 22. See also National Consumer Council, *Ordinary Justice* (1989), pp. 81–82 and *Civil Justice Review* (1988), paras. 378–379.

[37] In particular, certificates in matrimonial and personal injury proceedings are likely to be limited to part of the proceedings: see the General Regulations, reg. 46 and Burrows (1989), para 6.4.

[38] The General Regulations, reg. 45.

[39] Burrows (1989), para. 6.3.

The contributions payable are significant financial burdens, particularly for an applicant towards the top end of the financial eligibility range, and probably lead to rejection of the offered certificate by a number of applicants who cannot afford the contribution. In addition, where the contribution is payable from disposable income, the limits set out above apply strictly, whereas there is a discretion to permit the grant of a certificate even if the applicant's disposable capital is over the financial eligibility limit. "Curiously for a legal aid system, this may favour the person with capital as against the person with income, the wage earner."[40] Given that the level of eligibility for free legal aid is so low, it is interesting to note that in 1989–90, 79 per cent. of the certificates issued granted legal aid without any contribution. This figure may suggest that the requirement of a contribution acts as a serious deterrent. The analysis of maximum contributions determined during 1988–89 contained in the first Legal Aid Board Annual Report (1989–90)[41] contains the following figures relating to all courts:

Contribution required	Number	%
Nil	205,740	79.29
Under £30	3,113	1.20
£30 to under £50	2,098	0.81
£50 to under £75	2,420	0.93
£75 to under £100	2,438	0.94
£100 to under £150	4,489	1.73
£150 to under £300	11,903	4.59
£300 to under £500	12,832	4.95
£500 and over	14,432	5.56
Total	259,465	100

Once a certificate has been issued there are wide powers vested in the Area Director to amend it.[42] The Area Director also has power to discharge or revoke it upon the happening of specified events including a request from the applicant so to do, or where the aid has been abused, or where the applicant is in arrears with contributions, or where the applicant's financial position improves so that he or she is able to afford to fund legal action.[43]

There is a right of appeal to an area committee against a refusal to grant a representation certificate or upon discharge or revocation of a certificate.[44]

Obviously there may be circumstances in which the normal procedure of application and issue cannot be followed because of the urgency of the

[40] *Ibid.* para. 5.22; see also *16th Legal Aid Annual Reports*, 1965–66, p. 30.
[41] Appendix 2H. Appendix 2H provides a five year summary of the maximum contributions which shows that the pattern of contributions in the text is representative.
[42] The General Regulations, Part VII, and see Burrows (1989), pp. 63–66.
[43] The General Regulations, Part X, and see Burrows (1989), Chap. 8.
[44] The General Regulations, regs. 35–39, 81(2). As to appeals against refusal to remove a limitation upon application to amend, see Burrows (1989), para. 6.31. In 1989–90, 48.80 per cent. of the 22,855 appeals against the refusal of legal aid were successful: *Legal Aid Board Annual Reports* (1989–90), Appendix 2F.

matter and a procedure exists for obtaining an emergency representation certificate in such cases.[45]

5. THE LIABILITIES OF THE ASSISTED CLIENT

When the provision of legal services for those who could not afford the normal fees was dependent upon the charity of the profession, the relationship between client and lawyer must have been somewhat awkward. The object of the legal aid scheme is to ensure that the relationship between solicitor and assisted client is on exactly the same basis as that between solicitor and private client.[46] To that end, a client's financial obligations are to the Legal Aid Fund and the solicitor receives payment from the Fund.[47]

The full financial obligations of an assisted party will, inevitably, depend upon the outcome of the case. As has been seen, the assisted party is under no obligation to pay any costs to the solicitor whatever the result; but may be under a liability to pay costs to a successful opponent.

If the assisted party is *successful*, costs may be payable by the opponent in the normal way.[48] These costs are paid straight into the Legal Aid Fund and go to defray the actual costs of the action in the accounts rendered to the Fund by solicitors and counsel acting for the assisted party. If the costs recovered are *not* sufficient to cover the cost to the Fund, the difference is recouped from the contribution made by the assisted party. Any balance remaining from the contribution is returned.[49]

However, where the contribution, if any, is not sufficient to make up the difference, the Legal Aid Board has a first charge on any property, including money, recovered or preserved by the assisted party in the proceedings.[50] This is the "statutory charge." The charge means that the Board is entitled to recover the shortfall on its expenditure out of the property that has been recovered or preserved by the assisted party in the proceedings. Consequently, the assisted party will not receive the full amount of a money award, the Board retaining sufficient to cover the shortfall,[51] or other property will come subject to a charge, which may be enforced by the Board.[52] However, the charges on both money and other property may be postponed or other property substituted, especially where the money or property is required to

---

[45] The General Regulations, Part III, and see Burrows (1989), Chap. 11. In 1989–90, 121, 247 applications for an emergency certificate were received, 88, 782 (73.22 per cent.) certificates were issued: *Legal Aid Board Annual Reports* (1989–90), Appendix 2B(i)(a).

[46] Legal Aid Act 1988, s.31.

[47] To that end a solicitor or barrister may not take any payment for work except from the Board in relation to work covered by the certificate: Legal Aid Act 1988, ss.15(6), 31(3); the General Regulations, r. 64; see *Littaur* v. *Steggles Palmer* [1986] 1 W.L.R. 287, *Legal Aid Handbook 1990*, pp. 73–75 and Burrows (1989), paras. 6.47–6.55, 9.61.

[48] For an explanation of costs, see above, pp. 472–477, 479–480.

[49] The General Regulations, reg. 92.

[50] Legal Aid Act 1988, s.16(6). See *Legal Aid Handbook 1990*, pp. 51–56. The charge on property can be registered so as to prevent anyone taking the property without notice of the charge, and so ensuring that the Legal Aid Fund can obtain the money unless the charge is transferred to the new property. At 31.3.90, 54,615 charges were protected by registration: *Legal Aid Board Annual Reports* (1989–90), Appendix 2N(ii)(a). It may be some time before the Fund obtains its money: in 1989–90, 367 charges were satisfied which had been originally registered before 1983–84: *ibid*. Appendix 2N(ii)(b).

[51] The General Regulations, reg. 92, and see Burrows (1989), para. 9.39.

[52] The General Regulations, reg. 95, and see Burrows (1989), para. 9.42.

provide somewhere for the assisted person to live.[53] It is, therefore, very important to establish whether the property was recovered or preserved in the proceedings, since only then does the statutory charge apply. The Legal Aid Board will be concerned to resist any attempt to defeat the charge.[54] Further, there are certain exceptions to the charge, the best known being the first £2,500 recovered or preserved in certain matrimonial proceedings.[55] The charge generally ensures that the Legal Aid Board is not out of pocket. This is particularly so when it is remembered that certificates are only granted in those cases where there are reasonable grounds for taking action.

In 1989–90, a statutory charge was imposed in 38,196 non-matrimonial cases, resulting in £5,316,286 being retained to satisfy the net liability of the Legal Aid Fund. The average amount retained was £139.18, which, on average, was 2 per cent. of the award made to the successful assisted party.[56] In matrimonial cases in 1989–90, a statutory charge was imposed in 22,431 cases, resulting in £24,230,968 being retained to satisfy the net liability of the Legal Aid Fund. The average amount retained was £1,080.24, which, on average, was 7.73 per cent. of the award made to the successful assisted party.[57] The figures for average amount and average percentage retained are slightly misleading because the average is arrived at by taking into account those cases where no monies are retained for the benefit of the fund. Thus the averages would be higher in those cases where money was retained.

The statutory charge can be harsh,[57a] but account must be taken of the justification for its existence. It is justified as "an important and essential part of a publicly funded legal aided system to prevent unreasonable conduct of legally aided litigation and to prevent assisted persons profiting at the expense of public funds."[58]

If the assisted party is *unsuccessful*, his or her liability to the Legal Aid Board is limited to the amount of his or her contribution and, in that respect, the Board bears the financial risk of litigation. However, it is possible for the court to order an assisted party to pay the opponent's costs in the action. The court must first consider whether, on normal grounds, an awards for costs should be so made.[59] If an award should be made, it can only order the assisted party to pay such of those costs as are reasonable having regard to all

---

[53] The General Regulations, regs. 90, 96, 97, 98. See *Legal Aid Handbook 1990*, pp. 54–56, Burrows (1989), paras. 9.36–9.37, 9.40–9.50 and see also *Hanlon* v. *Law Society* [1981] A.C. 124. Postponement extending to money removes the effect of *Simpson* v. *Law Society* [1987] A.C. 861.

[54] As to whether property has been recovered or preserved, see Burrows (1989), paras. 9.12–9.26; *Legal Aid Handbook 1990*, pp. 52–53; *Hanlon* v. *Law Society* [1981] A.C. 124 (property is recovered or preserved if it was in issue in the proceedings, recovered by the claimant if the subject of a successful claim, preserved by the respondent if the claim fails); *Curling* v. *Law Society* [1985] 1 W.L.R. 470 (property recovered where possession of property obtained through proceedings); see also *Van Hoorn* v. *Law Society* [1985] Q.B. 106. Burrows' example, at paras. 9.24–9.26, is particularly instructive. As to the castigation by the courts of any attempts to defeat the charge, see *Manley* v. *Law Society* [1981] 1 W.L.R. 335 and Burrows (1989), paras. 9.57–9.59.

[55] See the General Regulations, reg. 94; *Legal Aid Handbook 1990*, pp. 53–54 and Burrows (1989), paras. 9.8–9.10.

[56] *Legal Aid Board Annual Reports* (1989–90), Appendix 2N(i)(*b*).

[57] *Ibid*. Appendix 2N(i)(*a*).

[57a] See, *e.g.* National Consumer Council, *Ordinary Justice* (1989), pp. 92–94.

[58] *Legal Aid Handbook 1990*, p. 51.

[59] See pp. 472–475, above.

the circumstances, particularly the financial resources of the parties and their conduct in connection with the dispute.[60] This is not likely to be an especially serious problem for the assisted party, since if no contribution has been expected, he or she is not likely to be able to pay much in the way of costs to the opponent. This leaves successful unassisted parties in a rather unfortunate position.

6. THE COSTS OF SUCCESSFUL UNASSISTED PARTIES

It is only since 1964 that a successful unassisted party has been able to obtain costs from the Legal Aid Fund at all. It is not easy to obtain such an award. Section 18 of the Legal Aid Act 1988 permits a court, on the application of a successful unassisted party,[61] to award costs to be paid by the Legal Aid Board if:

  (i) an order for costs would be made on normal principles;
  (ii) the proceedings are finally decided in favour of the unassisted party[62];
  (iii) it is just and equitable that provision for those costs should be made out of public funds;
  (iv) as respects the costs incurred in a court of first instance, the proceedings were instituted by the assisted party[63];
  (v) the court has considered the personal liability for costs of the assisted party; and
  (vi) with regard to first instance proceedings, the unassisted party would otherwise suffer severe financial hardship.

The initial approach of the courts was to adopt a highly restrictive interpretation of these provisions, meaning that trifling sums were awarded in costs.[64] It took a bold decision of the Court of Appeal in *Hanning* v. *Maitland* (*No. 2*)[65] to admit the error of the earlier interpretation and relax the application of the conditions. In that case, Lord Denning M.R. said that the "severe financial hardship" condition, applying to courts of first instance only, should not be construed so as "to exclude people of modest income or modest capital who find it hard to bear their own costs."[66] The courts have gone further than might be suggested by this statement. They accept that, in principle, it is possible for private and public companies to suffer severe

---

[60] Legal Aid Act 1988, s.17(1).
[61] As to the detailed provisions relating to the making of an application, see the General Regulations, regs. 134–147.
[62] This requirement is satisfied if that party has substantially succeeded in the action: *Kelly* v. *London Transport Executive* [1982] 1 W.L.R. 1055.
[63] The meaning of "court of first instance" and of "proceedings" can cause trouble, see *Megarity* v. *Law Society* [1982] A.C. 81; *R.* v. *Leeds City Council, ex p. Morris & Morris*; *Legal Aid Board Annual Reports* (1989–90), p. 151 and see Burrows (1989), paras. 10.31–10.33, 10.41–10.43.
[64] See *Nowotnik* v. *Nowotnik* [1967] P. 83. The fact that the husband had not had to restrict his activities on account of his solicitor's bill led the court to conclude that there was no severe financial hardship. The costs awarded were, according to the court in *Hanning* v. *Maitland* [1970] Q.B. 580, at p. 587: 1964–5, £74; 1965–6, £838; 1966–7, £243; 1967–8, £251; 1968–9, £239.
[65] [1970] Q.B. 580. *Nowotnik* v. *Nowotnik* was also a Court of Appeal decision.
[66] *Ibid.* p. 588.

financial hardship.[67] The courts look at the effect that costs will have on that person's financial position and decide on the facts whether severe financial hardship will be suffered.[68]

In all cases, whether in courts of first instance or not, an award of costs must be "just and equitable." The courts have found that this requirement was satisfied by a building society,[69] a person indemnified by the Automobile Association,[70] an insurance company[71] and a county police authority.[72]

This relaxation of attitude has led to a significant increase in the annual amount paid out of the fund to the successful unassisted parties,[73] but it still remains perilous to be sued by an assisted person. This places an additional responsibility on an Area Director in deciding whether an applicant for legal aid has reasonable grounds for bringing an action as plaintiff—the Director may be protecting unassisted defendants as well as the public purse.

7. THE LEGAL AID SCHEME—A CRITIQUE

The legal aid scheme is kept under constant review by the Legal Aid Board, which is required to report annually to the Lord Chancellor on the discharge of its functions. The scheme has also been kept under review by the Lord Chancellor's Legal Aid Advisory Committee. In the past, the Advisory Committee appended a report to that of the Law Society in which it commented upon the report and added comments of its own about the provision of legal services generally. The two documents were published together and helped to ensure that attention was focussed upon any alleged defects in the scheme and its administration. However, since the establishment of the Board, the future of the Advisory Committee has been uncertain.

A major concern is whether the *financial conditions of eligibility* for representation are too restrictive.[74] First, there is the question whether the limits when set are sufficiently generous. Secondly, whether the eligibility levels are then allowed to drift downwards, thereby eliminating many people from the scheme. The first matter is difficult to assess, since a judgment has to be made as to how many people *ought* to be in receipt of

---

[67] *Kelly* v. *London Transport Executive* [1982] 1 W.L.R. 1055; *Thew (R. & T.) Ltd.* v. *Reeves* [1982] Q.B. 1283.

[68] As in *Adams* v. *Riley* [1988] Q.B. 372 where the spouse's income was not simply aggregated to that of the successful unassisted party in determining whether he would suffer severe financial hardship, but regard was had to the wife's means only to the extent that they diminished his financial responsibilities.

[69] *Gallie* v. *Lee (No. 2)* [1971] A.C. 1039.

[70] *Lewis* v. *Averay (No. 2)* [1973] 1 W.L.R. 510.

[71] *Davies* v. *Taylor (No. 2)* [1974] A.C. 225.

[72] *Maynard* v. *Osmond (No. 2)* [1979] 1 W.L.R. 31. The observations by the Court of Appeal on the procedure to be adopted by the court in the case of an application by a successful unassisted party must be read in the light of *Din* v. *Wandsworth London Borough Council (No. 2)* [1982] 1 All E.R. 1022, H.L.

[73] From the Annual Reports 1984–85 to 1989–90, it can be seen that the payments to successful unassisted parties have been: 1983–84, £232,130; 1984–85, £239,248; 1985–86, £208,503; 1986–87, £280,092; 1987–88, £227,436; 1988–89, £445,999; 1989–90, £524,381.

[74] Further major concerns are with performance of the scheme, which is measured differently by the person seeking legal advice, the legal profession, the judiciary and the government, see *Legal Aid Board Annual Reports* (1989–90), pp. 7–8 and 13–17; the administration of the scheme (see p. 508 above) and knowledge of the scheme. See above, p. 457 and *Ordinary Justice* (1989), pp. 80–81.

representation. This depends upon many factors, amongst them political and moral viewpoints. However, in assessing whether the limits are in principle too low, it may be worth considering the gross income of people entitled to representation. This information is provided in the *Legal Aid Handbook 1990* in tabular form:

Table illustrating the Gross Income of Persons Entitled to Legal Aid, either Free or on Payment of Contributions, taking into account the change in Income Tax rates from April 6, 1990 and the Social Security uprating from April 9, 1990

Type of Applicant	Income from all sources before deduction of Income Tax, NI Contribution and housing costs	
	Maximum permitting free legal aid (DI £2,515)	Minimum which makes applicant ineligible for legal aid (DI £6,350)
	Gross income incl. child benefit	Gross income incl. child benefit
	£	£
1. Single non-householder	4,992 (96 pw)	10,608 (204 pw)
2. Single non-householder with 2 children aged 4 and 12	6,812 (131 pw)	12,428 (239 pw)
3. Couple non-householders	7,696 (148 pw)	13,312 (256 pw)
4. Couple non-householders with 2 children aged 4 and 12	10,296 (198 pw)	15,912 (306 pw)
5. Single householder	10,192 (196 pw)	15,808 (304 pw)
6. Single householder with 2 children aged 4 and 12	12,012 (231 pw)	17,628 (339 pw)
7. Couple householders	12,896 (248 pw)	18,460 (355 pw)
8. Couple householders with 2 children aged 4 and 12	15,236 (293 pw)	20,852 (401 pw)

Notes: The examples in the above tables are intended to be illustrative only and are based upon the following assumptions:

(1) The national average for rented accommodation (including water rates of £1,212.12 per annum (£23.31 per week) has been given in examples 1 to 4 inclusive. In addition an allowance of £7.12 per person per week is allowed in respect of the Community Charge.

(2) The national average for owner-occupied accommodation, subject to an endowment mortgage, (including water rates) of £4,439.24 per annum (£85.37 per week) has been given in examples 5 to 8 inclusive. In addition, an allowance of £7.12 per person per week is allowed in respect of the Community Charge.

[From Legal Aid Handbook 1990, p. 10]

The second concern is easier to assess. The starting position is that of eligibility set at a particular time. It can then be shown whether or not fewer people are eligible for representation at some later stage. Unfortunately, the legal aid statistics have not provided the direct evidence that the levels have been allowed to drift. Nevertheless, the Lord Chancellor's Advisory Committee was convinced by the indirect evidence that there was such a drift.[75] Independent analysis of Government statistics supports this view,[76] as do the claims of one commentator, Cyril Glasser.[77] In response, the Lord Chancellor established a review of the financial conditions for legal aid in November 1989, which is expected to take three years to complete its work.[78]

The Royal Commission on Legal Services took a more fundamental view with regard to financial conditions, which has not been accepted. It took the view that the upper limit is arbitrary, and might operate unfairly, since a person just above the limit receives no assistance,[79] whereas a person just below it might have to make a substantial contribution but would have the security of knowing that that contribution represents the maximum liability[80] for costs regardless of the actual cost or the outcome of the case. Some people are exposed "to a choice between abandoning their legal rights and accepting the risk of suffering an undue financial burden."[81] Consequently, it recommended that the financial limits should be abolished.[82]

B. THE COUNTY COURT[83]

The county court has a wide jurisdiction,[84] but most of the actions brought in the county court are claims based upon contract and tort. 2,615,508 plaints were entered in 1989. 2,358,583 (90 per cent.) of these were "money" plaints.[85]

In order to reduce delay, cost and complexity in the civil justice system, the Civil Justice Review recommended that the county court should be retained as a court separate from the High Court, but that the upper limit of county court jurisdiction should be abolished, that all civil proceedings, with a few exceptions, should be commenced by a document called a writ, which would be issued in either the High Court or a county court, and that there should be an improved system of transfer of cases between county court and

---

[75] *39th Annual Report of the Lord Chancellor's Advisory Committee on Legal Aid* 1988–9, (1989–90 H.C. 154), 88. See also *Ordinary Justice* (1989), pp. 83–91.

[76] M. Murphy, "Civil legal aid eligibility," *Legal Action*, October 1989, p. 7. As to an indication of the results of more recent research by Murphy see M. McKeone, (1991) 88 L.S.Gaz., March 27, p. 4.

[77] C. Glasser, "Legal aid eligibility," (1988) 85 L.S.Gaz., March 9, p. 11; C. Glasser, "Financing legal services" (1988) 85 L.S.Gaz., April 20, p. 11; C. Glasser, "Legal Services and the Green Papers" (1989) 86 L.S.Gaz., April 5, p. 9.

[78] The working group consists of officials from the Lord Chancellor's Department and the Legal Aid Board: H.C. Debates, Vol 158, col. 3, November 13th, 1989, written answer.

[79] Except in relation to the discretion with regard to disposable capital over the limit where the costs are expected to be particularly high, see p. 511, above.

[80] Subject to the statutory charge on any property recovered or preserved in the proceedings, see p. 512, above.

[81] R.C.L.S., para. 12.32.

[82] *Ibid.*, Vol. 1, paras. 12.29–12.32. Any adjustment would be made by fixing contribution at an appropriate level.

[83] *The County Court Practice 1989*. See also R. Blackford, *County Court Practice Handbook* (9th ed., 1989); E. Owen, *County Court Litigation* (1988).

[84] See Chap. 2.

[85] *Judicial Statistics 1989*, Cm. 1154, Tables 4.1 and 4.2 The remaining 256,925 plaints were entered for possession of land. In addition, 253,000 further proceedings were instituted in the county court of which, *e.g.*, 190,165 were concerned with family matters (primarily divorce, nullity and judicial separation petitions), and 7,474 were bankruptcy petitions: *ibid.*, Table 4.2.

High Court.[86] In consequence, the High Court would handle and try public law cases, other specialist cases and general list cases of importance, complexity and substance.[87] In order to achieve such a streamlined system, the Review also recommended that there should be a single costs regime for High Court and county court cases, subject to an exception for county court cases below £3,000,[88] that trial facilities should be improved at county courts,[88a] that remedies in county courts and the High Court should be harmonised,[89] and that there should be a common core of procedural rules.[90] To the extent that statutory changes were necessitated by these recommendations, they have largely been made by the Courts and Legal Service Act 1990, Part I. Consequently, the relationship between the jurisdiction and procedure of the county courts and High Court will change over the next few years.[91]

Before commencing an action in the county court under the existing system, the potential plaintiff must consider whether the claim is within the jurisdiction of the court and whether there are factors which might justify use of the High Court instead. The jurisdiction of the respective courts is set out in Chapter 2[91a] and it will have been observed that there is an overlap between them. If an action is begun in the wrong court,[92] that court may transfer it to the court with appropriate jurisdiction. There are also advantages in a county court action, even though the core rules are being harmonised.[93] County court procedure may be simpler and, although there are some difficult aspects, the unrepresented litigant can handle it more easily than High Court procedure. Special procedures have been devised to deal with small claims, that is those for below £500, encouraging use of what is known as the small claims court.[94] A county court action is likely to provide a quicker hearing and one which is more convenient to the parties than a High Court hearing.[95]

[86] Civil Justice Review, Report of the Review Body on Civil Justice (Cm. 394, 1988), paras. 82–126, 213–216 and 159–172.
[87] Ibid. paras. 117–124.
[88] Ibid. paras. 287–293 and see above, p. 70.
[88a] Ibid. paras. 174–181. Other related recommendations will assist in dealing with the increased county court workload and improve court administration. These include proper resourcing (ibid. para. 314), changes in judicial personnel (see above, p. 70), general improvements in judicial administration (ibid. Chap. 5), and improvements in pre-trial procedures (referred to below).
[89] Ibid. paras. 186–191 and see below, p. 708.
[90] Ibid. paras. 277–286. There is an on-going commitment to achieving the common core.
[91] The Civil Justice Review also recommended particular changes with regard to particular key areas: personal injuries (ibid. Chap. 6), small claims (see below, pp. 531–535), debt enforcement (see below, p. 714), housing cases (ibid. Chap. 10), and the Commercial Court (ibid. Chap. 11). Apart from small claims, these aspects of the Review are not considered further.
[91a] See pp. 64–67, 79–80.
[92] As to the allocation of business, see Chap. 2 above. Most cases begun in the county court have been concerned with small claims, when High Court action is clearly inappropriate. In 1989 of 2,615,508 actions entered in the county court for the recovery of sums or value, 1,574,130 were for sums up to £500: Judicial Statistics 1989 (Cm. 1154, 1990), Table 4.3.
[93] In pursuit of the recommendation of the Civil Justice Review that there should be a common core of procedural rules in the High Court and the county court: Civil Justice Review (1988), paras. 277–280.
[94] See below, pp. 531–535.
[95] Since most county court actions can be instituted in the court of the plaintiff's choice, the old problems relating to venue have largely ceased to exist. Housing possession and liquidated claims for not over £5,000 should still be commenced in the defendant's local court or the

Whilst there may still be a feeling that a High Court writ will have a greater threatening effect on a recalcitrant defendant than a county court summons, inducing him or her to settle the claim, the changes to the costs rules,[96] and the harmonisation of remedies,[97] will lessen the attractiveness of such action. However, it may still be the case that higher damages will be awarded in the High Court and that enforcement procedures are better, and will remain so.

1. COURT MANAGEMENT OF LITIGATION

In an attempt to reduce the delay common in civil litigation, the Civil Justice Review recommended that there should be court management of litigation.[98] Since the problem of delay was considerably greater in High Court than county court actions,[99] this proposal is discussed in relation to High Court actions.

2. COMMENCING AN ACTION[1]

A county court action is classified as a fixed date action or a default action, depending upon the nature of the claim. A claim for any relief other than the payment of money must be brought as a fixed date action—any claim for money as a default action.[2] The procedure for the two actions, though initially similar, is different, so it is important to observe the distinction.

To begin either action, the plaintiff must file at the court office a formal request to the registrar, now the district judge, to issue a summons to commence the action together with the particulars of claim.[3] There are different forms of the request available from the county court depending upon the nature of the action.[4] The forms require information to be provided which will establish that the court has jurisdiction. There is no specific form for the particulars of claim, even though the object of the particulars is to inform the defendant with sufficient particularity of the claim against him or her. The plaintiff must supply them. If legal help is sought, the lawyer is likely to rely on the precedents which are published.[5] The litigant in person may just concoct a statement, in which case assistance as to the sort of things to say is provided in a booklet entitled *Small Claims in the County Court*. A request for a summons against a defendant in a default action and the basic particulars of claim in the (imaginary) case of *Wilkinson* v. *Walkertronic Super Hi-Fi-Vid* are set out below.

court with whose district the case is most closely connected: *Civil Justice Review* (1988), paras. 217–219. As to the problems created by having to sue in a county court where either the defendant resided, or carried on business, or the cause of action wholly or in part arose, see the 1st edition of this book, pp. 398–399; Blackford (1989), pp. 18–21; Owen (1988), pp. 70–73.

[96] See above p. 474.
[97] See below p. 708.
[98] *Ibid.* paras. 220–228.
[99] See above p. 487.
[1] Note the recommendation of the Civil Justice Review referred to above as to the intention to introduce a system of commencing all civil proceedings by writ.
[2] C.C.R., Ord. 3, r. 2.
[3] C.C.R., Ord. 3, r. 3; Ord 6, r. 1. The summons may not be prepared by the plaintiff rather than the court office: *ibid.* Ord. 3, r. 3(2).
[4] *Ibid.* Ord. 6.
[5] *Atkin's Encyclopedia of Court Forms in Civil Proceedings* (2nd ed., 1983).

Request for Issue of Default Summons

For court use only	
Case Number	

- Please read the notes over the page before filling in this form. You will find it useful to read the booklet "Small Claims in the County Court" which is available from any county court office.

Summons in form
N1 ☐
N2 ☐

Service by:
Post ☐
Plaintiff('s solr) ☐

1 Plaintiff's full name Address

CYRIL JACK WILKINSON,
24 ACACIA AVENUE,
NADDLEBOROUGH,
NOTTINGHAM

2 Name and address for service and payment *(if different from above)* **Ref/Tel No.**

POPP, LEES AND STONE,
23 HALTERGATE,
NOTTINGHAM
Solicitor's Ref. No. SP 123

3 Defendant's name Address

WALKERTRONIC SUPER HI-FI-VID LTD.,
37 GRINLING STREET,
NOTTINGHAM

- Please be careful when filling in the request form. Do not write outside the boxes.
- Type or write in BLOCK CAPITALS using **black ink**.
- If the details of the claim are on a separate sheet you must also give the court a copy for each defendant.
- You can get help to complete this form at any county court office or citizens' advice bureau.

4 What the claim is for

Give brief description of the type of claim

Price of goods supplied not of merchantable quality and/or fit for purpose, and consequent damage to television, curtains and redecoration

5 If the defendant does not live in the district of the court, the plaintiff states that the cause of action arose:

6 Particulars of the plaintiff's claim

SEE ENCLOSED PARTICULARS OF CLAIM

7

Plaintiff's claim	£	875	00
Court fee	£	43	00
Solicitor's costs	£	85	00
Total amount		£1003	00

for court use Issued on

Small Claims Procedure

Any defended claim for £500 or less will be automatically dealt with by arbitration. If you do not want the claim to be dealt with by arbitration you will have to apply to the court. The court office can give you more details.

9 If the claim exceeds £500 and you would like it to be dealt with by arbitration, please tick the box below.

The claim exceeds £500 and I would like it to be dealt with by arbitration ✓

8 Signed POPP, LEES AND STONE
Plaintiff('s solicitor)
(or see enclosed particulars of claim)

N201   Request for default summons (Order 3, rule 3(1))

Printed in the UK for HMSO D.8156124 1,000m 1/90 36625

Notes

1 Plaintiff *the person making the claim*

Enter the plaintiff's full name and address or place of business.
If the plaintiff is

- a **company registered under the Companies Act 1985,** give the address of the registered office and describe it as such.
- a **person trading in a name other than his own,** give his own name followed by the words "trading as" and the name under which he trades.
- **Two or more co-partners suing in the name of their firm,** "A Firm".
- an **assignee,** say so and give the name, address and occupation of the assignor.
- a **minor required to sue by next friend,** state this, and give the full names, addresses or place of business, and occupation of next friend. You will also need to complete and send in Form N235 (which you can get from the court office).
- **suing in a representative capacity,** say in what capacity.

2 Address for service and payment

If the request is completed by a solicitor or by the plaintiff's legal department, the name, address and reference of the solicitor or legal department should be in Box 2. The court will use this address for sending documents to you (service). A plaintiff who is not represented by a solicitor or legal department should use Box 2 for the address where payment is to be made. (If the address is the same as shown at Box 1, please write "as above" in Box 2.)

3 Defendant *the person against whom the claim is made*

Enter the defendant's surname and (where known) his or her initials or names in full. **It is essential that the defendant should be identified as fully and as accurately as possible.** Also give the defendant's address or place of business (if the owner of a business). Say whether defendant is male or female and, if under 18, state "minor".
If the defendant is:

  a **company registered under the Companies Act 1985,**
- the address given can be the registered office of the company (you must describe it as such) or its place of business. However, if the summons is not sent to the registered office, there is a risk that it will not come to the notice of an appropriate person in the company. As a result, the court may be asked to set aside any judgment or order that has been made.

  a **person trading in a name other than his own who is**
- **sued under that name,** add "A Trading Name".

  two or more co-partners sued in the name of their firm,
- add "A Firm".

  sued in a representative capacity, say in what capacity.

-

4 What the claim is for

Put a brief description of your dispute in the box (eg price of goods sold and delivered, work done, money due under an agreement).

5 Jurisdiction

If the defendant or one of the defendants does not live or carry on business within the district of the court, you must show that the cause of action (ie what gives rise to the claim) arose wholly or partly within the district of the court. The court can deal with the action, if, for instance, the claim arises out of:

- a contract made at an address in the district;
- a contract under which payment is to be made at an address in the district;
- an accident which happened in the district.

If any of these apply, you must enter the address in the box. The defendant is entitled to apply to the court to have the case transferred to his local court.

6 Particulars of the plaintiff's claim

Give a brief statement of the facts of your claim and the amount for which you are suing. Include any relevant dates and sufficient details to inform the defendant of the nature of your claim against him. He is entitled to ask for further details. If there is not enough space or the details of your claim are too complicated, you should enclose a separate sheet for the court and a copy for each defendant. The court can help you in setting out your particulars of claim.

7 Amount claimed

Enter the total amount you are claiming. The court fee and solicitor's costs are based on this and you should enter these too. A leaflet setting out the current fees is available from the court.

8 Signature

The person filling in the form should sign and date it unless enclosing separate details of claim, in which case the enclosed sheet should be signed.

9 Claims exceeding £500

If your claim exceeds £500, you can ask for it to be dealt with by arbitration. The grounds for setting aside an arbitrator's award are strictly limited.

10 Personal injury claims *issued after 4 June 1990*

In these cases you must include a medical report for the court and for each defendant. If you are also claiming special damages (eg loss of income, medical expenses etc), an up to date statement, to include details of any future expenses or losses, must also be included for the court and for each defendant. If you cannot provide these you should apply to the court for directions.

To be completed by the court	
Served on:	
By posting on:	
Officer:	

IN THE NOTTINGHAM COUNTY COURT

CASE NO.

Between

CYRIL JACK WILKINSON

Plaintiff

and
WALKERTRONIC
SUPER HI-FI-VID LTD

Defendant

PARTICULARS OF CLAIM

1. The Plaintiff purchased for the sum of £75.00 from the Defendant on February 1st 1990 at the Defendant's place of business, a Magivid electronic football game ("the game") for use in conjunction with a television owned by the Plaintiff.

2. At all material times the Defendant was an electrical retailer and the game was sold in the course of the Defendant's business.

3. It was an implied term of the agreement ("the agreement") that the goods supplied to the Plaintiff would be of merchantable quality.

4. Further, or alternatively, the Defendant was aware of the Plaintiff's purpose in purchasing the game, namely for use in conjunction with the Plaintiff's television and it was an implied term of the agreement that the game would be fit for such purpose.

5. The Plaintiff used the game on three occasions, but whilst in use on February 5th 1990 it exploded ("the explosion") causing damage to the Plaintiff's television and setting fire to a pair of curtains. Decorations in the same room were damaged by smoke and scorching.

6. The explosion was caused by the Defendant's breach of contract.

7. In breach of the contract the goods supplied to the Plaintiff were not of merchantable quality and/or were not fit for their purpose.

PARTICULARS

(When operated the game malfunctioned causing it to explode.)

8. By reason of matters aforesaid the Plaintiff has suffered loss and damage.

9. Further the Plaintiff claims interest pursuant to section 69 of the County Courts Act 1984 on the amount found to be due to the Plaintiff at such rate and for such period as the Court thinks fit.

PARTICULARS OF SPECIAL DAMAGE

1.	refund of price paid	£75.00
2.	value of the television	£250.00
3.	replacement of curtains	£60.00
4.	redecoration	£390.00

AND the Plaintiff claims:

(1) Damages

(2) The aforesaid interest pursuant to section 69 of the County Courts Act 1984.

Dated this .... day of 1990

To the Registrar of the
Nottingham County Court and
to the Defendant

Popp, Lees and Stone,
Solicitors,
Haltergate,
Nottingham
where they will accept service of
proceedings on behalf of the Plaintiff

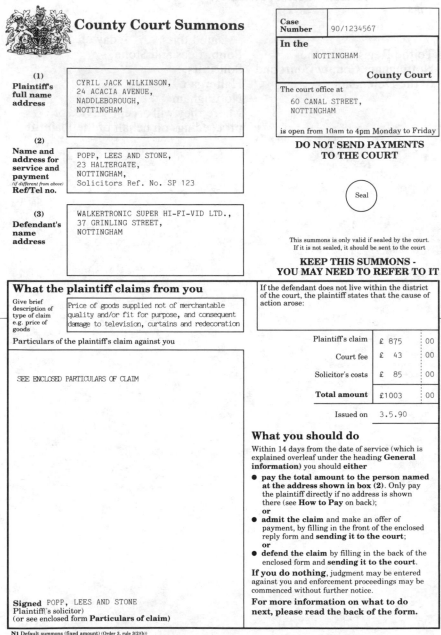

County Court Summons

Case Number	90/1234567

In the

NOTTINGHAM

County Court

The court office at

60 CANAL STREET, NOTTINGHAM

is open from 10am to 4pm Monday to Friday

(1) Plaintiff's full name address

CYRIL JACK WILKINSON, 24 ACACIA AVENUE, NADDLEBOROUGH, NOTTINGHAM

(2) Name and address for service and payment *(if different from above)* **Ref/Tel no.**

POPP, LEES AND STONE, 23 HALTERGATE, NOTTINGHAM, Solicitors Ref. No. SP 123

DO NOT SEND PAYMENTS TO THE COURT

Seal

(3) Defendant's name address

WALKERTRONIC SUPER HI-FI-VID LTD., 37 GRINLING STREET, NOTTINGHAM

This summons is only valid if sealed by the court. If it is not sealed, it should be sent to the court

KEEP THIS SUMMONS - YOU MAY NEED TO REFER TO IT

What the plaintiff claims from you

Give brief description of type of claim e.g. price of goods

Price of goods supplied not of merchantable quality and/or fit for purpose, and consequent damage to television, curtains and redecoration

If the defendant does not live within the district of the court, the plaintiff states that the cause of action arose:

Particulars of the plaintiff's claim against you

SEE ENCLOSED PARTICULARS OF CLAIM

Plaintiff's claim	£ 875	00
Court fee	£ 43	00
Solicitor's costs	£ 85	00
Total amount	£1003	00
Issued on	3.5.90	

What you should do

Within 14 days from the date of service (which is explained overleaf under the heading **General information**) you should **either**

- **pay the total amount to the person named at the address shown in box (2)**. Only pay the plaintiff directly if no address is shown there (see **How to Pay** on back); or
- **admit the claim** and make an offer of payment, by filling in the front of the enclosed reply form and **sending it to the court**; or
- **defend the claim** by filling in the back of the enclosed form and **sending it to the court**.

If you do nothing, judgment may be entered against you and enforcement proceedings may be commenced without further notice.

For more information on what to do next, please read the back of the form.

Signed POPP, LEES AND STONE
Plaintiff's solicitor)
(or see enclosed form **Particulars of claim**)

N1 Default summons (fixed amount) (Order 3, rule 3(2)(b))

Please read this page: it will help you deal with the summons

If you admit owing all the claim

either pay the total amount - see **How to Pay** on this page; **or**, if you require time to pay, fill in the part of the enclosed form for admitting the claim and return it to the court. Give details of how you propose to pay the claim.

If your offer of payment is accepted, the court will enter judgment and send an order telling you how to pay.

If your offer is not accepted, the court may **either**
- enter judgment and tell you how to pay; **or**
- arrange a hearing which you should attend.

You will be told what the court has decided.

If you dispute all or part of the claim

You may be entitled to help with your legal costs. Ask about the legal aid scheme at any county court office, citizens' advice bureau, legal advice centre or firm of solicitors displaying the legal aid sign.

- Say how much you dispute in the part of the enclosed form for defending the claim and return it to the court. The court will arrange a hearing and will tell you when you should attend.
- If you dispute only part of the claim, you should also fill in the part of the form for admitting the claim and pay the amount admitted to the address for payment.
- If you have paid the amount of the plaintiff's claim since the summons was issued, fill in the part of the form for defending the claim. Say when you paid the claim. Then pay the costs to the address for payment unless you dispute having to pay them. Explain your reasons.
- If the court named on the summons is not your local county court, you may write to the court named, asking for the case to be transferred to your local county court and explaining your reasons. However, if the case is transferred and you later lose the case, you may have to pay more in costs.
- A claim for £500 or less will normally be dealt with by arbitration under the small claims procedure. A free booklet about the small claims procedure is available from any county court office.

If you want to make a claim against the plaintiff

This is known as a counterclaim
Fill in the part of the enclosed form headed **Counterclaim**. If your claim is for more than the plaintiff's claim, you may have to pay a fee - the court will let you know. Unless the plaintiff admits your counterclaim there will be a hearing. The court will tell you when to attend.

To be completed on the court copy only
Served on:
By posting on:
Officer:

N1 Default summons (fixed amount)

Registration of judgments

If the summons results in a judgment being made against you, your name and address may be entered in the Register of County Court Judgments.

This may make it difficult for you to get credit
- If the money is paid in full <u>within one month</u> of the date of judgment, you can ask the court to remove the entry and for a certificate proving payment. You will have to pay a fee for this.
- If you pay in full <u>after one month</u>, you can ask the court to mark the entry in the register as satisfied and for a certificate proving payment. You will have to pay a fee for this.

General information

- If you received this summons through the post, the date of service will be 7 days (for a limited company at its registered office, the second working day) after the date of posting as shown by the postmark. You have 14 days from this date to pay or reply to the summons.
- You can get help to complete the enclosed form at any county court office or citizens' advice bureau.
- If the total amount is not paid in full within 14 days after the date of service of this summons, you may have to pay more costs.
- When corresponding with the court, please address forms or letters to the Chief Clerk.
- Always quote the whole of the case number which appears at the top right corner of the front of this form; the court is unable to trace this summons without it.

How to Pay

- **PAYMENT(S) MUST BE MADE to the person named at the address for payment quoting their reference and the court case number.**

- **DO NOT bring or send payments to the court. THEY WILL NOT BE ACCEPTED.**

- You should allow <u>at least</u> 4 days for your payment to reach the plaintiff or his representative.

- Make sure that you keep records and can account for all payments made. Proof may be required if there is any disagreement. It is not safe to send cash unless you use registered post.

- A leaflet giving further advice about payment can be obtained from the court.

- If you need more information, you should contact the plaintiff or his representative.

This summons was returned by the Post Office marked 'Gone Away' on:

Printed in the UK for HMSO Dd 8155939 C20000 28312 11/89

Once the request and the particulars of claim have been filed and the appropriate fee paid,[6] the district judge must enter a plaint in the court record and, for a fixed date action, fix a return day on which the pre-trial review is to take place or the action is to be heard.[7] The district judge must also prepare and issue a summons, together with the particulars of claim, and this is normally served by a court officer on the defendant. Service of the summons does not have to be effected in person; postal service is likely to be sufficient and there are special rules for violent or threatening defendants![8]

Together with the summons, the defendant receives a form for admission, defence and counterclaim[9] which must be returned to the court within 14 days of service. In a default claim and some fixed date actions, failure to submit a defence will permit the plaintiff, on submission of the appropriate form, *to have judgment entered against the defendant immediately*.[10] Therein lies the advantage of the default action. If the defendant in a default action does submit a defence in the prescribed time, the district judge fixes a date for the preliminary hearing, and the action proceeds in the same way as a fixed date action. The defendant in a fixed date action is permitted to submit a defence at any point before the return day,[11] but if it is outside the 14 day period he or she may have to meet any costs incurred as a result of the delay.[12]

3. THE DEFENCE

A defendant to any action may wish to dispute all or part of the liability asserted by the plaintiff, or may disagree with the amount claimed whilst admitting liability, or may wish to dispute the claim and make a counterclaim against the plaintiff.[13] The form served on the defendant permits all these possibilities and is much easier to follow than the old forms, which were criticised as being too complicated. It is not necessary to use the form to make a defence, the defendant only needs to submit some document indicating that the claim is disputed.[14]

The district judge must send a copy of the defence to the plaintiff.[15] The case will then proceed to pre-trial review. As already mentioned, the defendant[16] may submit a defence up to the return day and even at the pre-trial review if he or she is prepared to risk costs being awarded against him or her. However, if a defendant delays submitting a defence unduly, the court has

---

[6] On a scale in proportion to the amount of damages claimed, see *County Court Practice 1989*, pp. 835–836. Where the claim is relatively small it will be advantageous to place a limit on the amount of general damages claimed so as to minimise the court fee.

[7] See below, p. 530. The date must be notified to the defendant along with the summons, but if it is inconvenient an application may be made for adjournment.

[8] C.C.R., Ord. 7, r. 5.

[9] The form does not have to be used in making a defence.

[10] C.C.R., Ord. 9, r. 6 and 4A, as inserted by S.I. 1990 No. 1764.

[11] Or the day on which judgment was entered for failure to submit a defence.

[12] *Ibid*. Ord. 9, r. 9, as amended by S.I. 1990 No. 1764.

[13] It is possible that the defendant's only dispute will be with either the mode of payment of the damages claimed by the plaintiff or with the quantum, the total amount of damages. These possibilities are not dealt with in the text, see the works on county court practice at n. 83 above.

[14] *Ibid*. Ord. 9, r. 2(1).

[15] *Ibid*. Ord. 9, r. 2(2).

[16] *i.e.* a defendant where the plaintiff does not seek a judgment in default upon failure by the defendant to submit a defence.

power to order him or her to deliver a defence or risk being debarred from defending the action at all.[17]

The defendant may request further and better particulars of the claim and the court has the power to require the plaintiff to supply them on pain of having the action dismissed.[18]

In our imaginary case, Walkertronic needs no further information and indicates an intention to defend in the following terms. The case will now proceed to pre-trial review.

[17] C.C.R., Ord. 9, r. 11; Ord. 13, r. 2(2).
[18] C.C.R., Ord. 6, r. 7; Ord. 13, r. 2(2).

Form for Replying to a Summons

- Read the notes on the summons before completing this form
- Tick the correct boxes and give the other details asked for
- Send or take this completed and signed form immediately to the court office shown on the summons
- You should keep your copy of the summons unless you are making full payment
- **For details of where and how to pay see the summons**

In the NOTTINGHAM **County Court**

Case Number *Always quote this* 90/1234567

Plaintiff CYRIL JACK WILKINSON *(including Ref.)* Ref. SP 123

Defendant WALKERTRONIC SUPER HI-FI-VID LTD.

What is your full name? (BLOCK CAPITALS)

Surname WALKERTRONIC SUPER HI-FI-VID LTD

Forenames ....

Mr ☐   Mrs ☐   Miss ☐   Ms ☐

How much of the claim do you admit?

☐ **All of it** *(complete only sections 1 and 2)*
☐ **Part of it** *(sections 1, 2, 3, 4, 5)* **Amount £**   :
☑ **None of it** *(complete sections 3, 4 and 5 overleaf)*

Section 1   Offer of payment

I offer to pay the amount admitted on (date) ....

or for the reasons set out below

I cannot pay the amount admitted in one instalment

but I can pay by monthly instalments of   **£**   :

Fill in the next section as fully as possible. Your answers will help the plaintiff decide whether your offer is realistic and ought to be accepted. Your answers will also help the court, if necessary, to fix a rate of payment that you can afford.

Section 2   Income and outgoings

a. Employment   I am

☐ Unemployed
☐ A pensioner
☐ Self employed as ....
☐ Employed as a ....

My employer is ....

Employer's address:

b. Income   *specify period: weekly, fortnightly, monthly, etc.*

My usual take home pay	£	:
Child benefit(s) total	£	:
Other state benefit(s) total	£	:
My pension(s) total	£	:
Other people living in my home give me	£	:
Other income *(give details)*	£	:

c. Bank account and savings

☐ I do not have a bank account
☐ I have a bank account with ....

(branch) ....

The account is ☐ *in credit* ☐ *overdrawn* £   :

☐ I do not have a savings account
☐ I have a savings account with ....

(branch) ....

The amount in the account is   £   :

d. Dependants *(people you look after financially)*

Number of dependants
(give ages of children) ....

e. Outgoings

I make regular payments as follows:

	weekly	monthly		
Mortgage		☐	£	:
Rent	☐	☐	£	:
Mail order	☐	☐	£	:
TV Rental/licence	☐	☐	£	:
HP repayments	☐	☐	£	:
Court orders	☐	☐	£	:

specify period: yearly, quarterly, etc.

Gas	....	£	:
Electricity	....	£	:
Community charge	....	£	:
Water rates	....	£	:

Other regular payments *(give details below)*

£   :

Credit card and other debts *(please list)*

£   :

Of the payments above, I am behind with payments to

£   :

continue on a separate sheet if necessary – put the case number in the top right hand corner

---

Give an address to which notices about this case should be sent to you

Post code ☐

Signed

(to be signed by you or by your solicitor)

Dated

N9   Form of admission, defence and counterclaim to accompany Forms N1, 2, 3 and 4   (Order 3, rule 3(2)(c))   Dd 8155932 1,000M 12/89 Ed(273057)

Case No 90./.1.2.3.4.5.6.7...............................

Section 3 Defending the claim: defence	Section 4 Making a claim against the plaintiff: counterclaim

Section 3   Defending the claim: defence

Fill in this part of the form only if you wish to defend the claim or part of the claim

a.   How much of the plaintiff's claim do you dispute?

All of it   ☑

Part of it   ☐ *give amount*   £......................

If you dispute only part of the claim, you must complete sections 1 and 2 overleaf and part b. below

b.   What are your reasons for disputing the claim?

I do not owe Mr. Wilkinson anything and he has been pestering me for three months.

1. I did not sell the game to him (it was his son).
2. The game was in perfectly good condition when I sold it because I tested it in the shop.
3. I think that somebody probably wired it up wrong which was not my fault. Whoever did it probably couldn't understand the instructions.
4. I do not think that there is any proper claim against me.

Section 4   Making a claim against the plaintiff: counterclaim

Fill in this part of the form only if you wish to make a claim against the plaintiff

If your claim against the plaintiff is for more than his claim against you, you may have to pay a fee. Ask at the court office whether a fee is payable

a.   What is the nature of the claim you wish to make against the plaintiff?

b.   If your claim is for a specific sum of money, how much are you claiming?

£......................

c.   What are your reasons for making the claim?

continue on a separate sheet if necessary – put the case number in the top right corner

Section 5   Arbitration under the Small Claims Procedure

(This involves an informal hearing taking place in private instead of a formal trial held in public)

Fill in this part if the claim against you or the amount you claim is more than £500

Do you want the case to be dealt with by arbitration?   Yes ☐   No ☐

Notes
- If you defend a claim for £500 or less it will be referred to arbitration automatically. If you do not want the claim to be dealt with by arbitration you will have to apply to the court. The court office can give you more details.
- When a defended claim is arbitrated the decision of the arbitrator is final. There are only very limited circumstances in which a judge can set aside an arbitration decision.

Give an address to which notices about this case should be sent to you	**Signed** J. WALKER
37 GRINLING STREET, NOTTINGHAM	*(to be signed by you or by your solicitor)*
Post code	**Dated** 10.5.90

4. THE PRE-TRIAL REVIEW

This stage of county court procedure was introduced in 1972 and was part of the response to criticism that the county court did not cater adequately for the resolution of small claims.[19] The review can be used either (i) to give judgment for the plaintiff if the district judge thinks fit where the defendant admits the plaintiff's claim[20] or fails to appear,[21] or (ii) to give instructions for the future conduct of the action.[22]

The function of the pre-trial review is made clear by the instructions to the district judge whereby he or she is required to ". . . give all such directions as appear to be necessary or desirable for securing the just expeditious and economical disposal of the action or matter."[23] Also, the district judge ". . . should endeavour to secure that the parties make all such admissions and agreements as ought reasonably to be made by them. . . ."[24] Further, the notice to the parties in relation to the pre-trial review indicates that the hearing is informal and in private and that "its purpose is to:

(a) make sure that all the parties and the court understand what the case is about;
(b) see if there is any possibility of settling the dispute, and if not, decide how it is going to be heard and how long the hearing will last;
(c) decide what documents or other evidence is needed from both sides."[25]

The approach of the district judge at this stage of the proceedings is clearly crucial, although, whatever approach may be adopted in practice towards the parties, the review does at least give them the opportunity to meet and survey the relative strength of their cases. Applebey[26] concluded that, whilst useful to lawyers, the pre-trial review in the county court civil action has not been of enormous assistance to the ordinary person trying to conduct his or her own case.

The plaintiff or defendant may, at the pre-trial review, ask for any necessary interlocutory order or any other direction or may request arbitration rather than trial.[27]

As soon as practicable after the pre-trial review, a date for trial is fixed,[28] if a hearing is necessary.

[19] The criticisms were most cogently expressed in Consumer Council, *Justice Out of Reach* (HMSO, 1970) and T.G. Ison, "Small Claims" (1972) 35 M.L.R. 18.
[20] C.C.R., Ord. 17, r. 6.
[21] Where the defendant has not delivered either an admission or a defence and fails to appear the powers is to be found in C.C.R., Ord. 17, r. 7. Where the defendant has delivered a defence but fails to appear, judgment can be given for the plaintiff, on proof of facts entitling him or her to relief: *ibid*. Ord. 17, r. 8.
[22] *Ibid*. Ord, 17, rr. 1, 9; Ord. 19, rr. 2, 7. This function of the district judge is similar to that of a master in the High Court on a summons for directions.
[23] *Ibid*. Ord. 17, r. 1.
[24] *Ibid*. Ord. 17, r. 2.
[25] Practice Form N. 233, see *County Court Practice 1989*, p. 677.
[26] G. Applebey, *Small Claims in England and Wales* (1978).
[27] Except in cases where a sum not exceeding £500 is involved (see below) the case cannot be referred to arbitration unless both parties agree.
[28] C.C.R., Ord. 17, r. 9.

5. SPECIAL PROCEDURES FOR SMALL CLAIMS

About 68 per cent. of money claims in the county court in 1989 were for less than £500, the small claims limit.[29] It is hardly surprising that special procedures have been devised to make provision for claims of this size, and that the way in which the county court handles such claims has been the subject of close scrutiny and criticism, not least during the recent Civil Justice Review.[30]

The county court owes its establishment to the cost and complexity of civil procedure, which persuaded the government of the day to pass the County Courts Act 1846 against much opposition from parts of the legal profession.[31] With an original jurisdiction of £20, the court was intended to provide a cheap, accessible and simple forum for the recovery of small debts and demands. It was the criticisms of costs and complexity in small claims, put most convincingly by the Consumer Council in *Justice Out of Reach*, which led to the procedural reforms of the early 1970s. Further published evidence[32] and public pressure have provoked more changes in recent years, in particular through the establishment of the Review Body on Civil Justice.[33]

The changes in the early 1970s were modifications of existing procedure and did not represent a major shift in emphasis. They were intended to make the procedure more attractive and less expensive than before. The changes included the introduction of the pre-trial review (see above) with the object, in part, of assisting the litigant in person,[34] the encouragement of the use of arbitration rather than trial to resolve the dispute at the request of one of the parties,[35] and the introduction of a rule that solicitor's costs would not be awarded to the successful party where the claim was for less than £100.[36]

More changes in 1981 were designed to facilitate further the procedures so that they could be used by the general public,[37] making arbitration the normal method of settling disputes where the amount of the claim was less

---

[29] *Judicial Statistics 1989*, Cm. 1154, Tables 4.1 and 4.3. In the first edition, the figures for 1982 produced a figure of just over 75 per cent., the reduction being a reason for increasing the limit.

[30] See pp. 532–535 below.

[31] The Bar was particularly strongly opposed, mainly on the grounds that it was proposed to give solicitors the right of audience in the new court. The history of initial and continuing opposition to the county court is chronicled in B. Abel-Smith and R. Stevens, *Lawyers and the Courts* (1967) and in W. Holdsworth, *History of English Law*, Vol. 1, pp. 187ff.

[32] *e.g.* Applebey (1978); National Consumer Council/Welsh Consumer Council, *Simple Justice* (1979).

[33] See, *e.g.*, Applebey (1978), National Consumer Council/Welsh Consumer Council, *Simple Justice* (1979) for changes since the early 1970s and *Civil Justice Review* (1988), Chap. 8.

[34] "The pre-trial review was designed primarily to help small claimants and their opposite numbers, the defendants to small claims, particularly litigants in person whether plaintiffs or defendants": from a speech by Lord Hailsham L.C. made on March 2, 1973 at the opening of the Wandsworth County Court. See J. Neville Turner, "Small Claims and the County Court in England—a contrast to the Australian approach" (1980) 9 Anglo-Am.L.R. 150 at pp. 160–162. The pre-trial review was introduced in March 1972.

[35] Arbitration had always been available, but was rarely used. The Lord Chancellor encouraged its use by registrars through a *Practice Direction* [1973] 1 W.L.R. 1178, see now Blackford (1989), Chap. 13.

[36] The rule was introduced in 1973. For an analysis of the objectives of the rules, see *Hobbs* v. *Marlowe* [1978] A.C. 16 and Applebey (1978), pp. 35–38.

[37] County Court (Amendment No. 3) Rules (S.I. 1980 No. 1807), consolidated in the County Court Rules 1981 (S.I. 1981 No. 1687), see *The County Court Practice 1989*.

than £500, amending the "no costs" rule[38] and amending the terms of reference for the conduct of arbitration.[39]

The Civil Justice Review recommended that the small claims limit be increased to £1,000.[40] Whilst this change has not yet been made, the £500 limit is now calculated without reference to any sum claimed or amount involved in a counterclaim.[41]

Further major changes were recommended by the Civil Justice Review, although these did not extend to the creation of a small claims court separate from the county court.[42] The recommendations were intended to ensure that the small claims court would be well used, especially by people without legal representation. It recommended that the preliminary hearing be abolished, that the district judge be required to conduct the hearing on an interventionist basis, that he or she be required to give reasons for a decision and explain the rules of law and that specific guidance should be provided on the expenses recoverable for small claims.

The plaintiff must follow the initial procedure outlined above. If the claim is for less than £500, the district judge of the county court will automatically refer the matter to arbitration, unless there are good reasons why the matter should go to trial instead.[43] The arbitrator, who may be the district judge, a judge or an "outside arbitrator,"[44] sets the date for the single substantive hearing of the dispute.[45] There is a standard set of terms for the conduct of an arbitration.[46] Representation under the legal aid scheme is not available for an arbitration hearing[47] although the plaintiff and defendant may obtain legal advice and assistance if they meet the eligibility conditions.[48] It is expected that the parties will appear in person, but legal representation is not prohibited. No solicitor's costs, nor costs allowed to a litigant in person in lieu, will be allowed in an arbitration except for those stated on the summons, those incurred in enforcing the award, and those incurred through the unreasonable conduct of the opposing party.[49] (If the case goes for trial rather than arbitration, solicitor's costs *will* be allowed subject to the normal rules).

---

[38] The rule was further amended in 1984, for the current rule, see below.

[39] See, G. Applebey, "Small Claims in Birmingham County Court" (1985) 4 C.J.Q. 203, at p. 204. As to the current position with regard to arbitration, see County Courts Act 1984, s.64 and C.C.R., Ord. 19.

[40] *Civil Justice Review* (1988), para. 162.

[41] C.C.R., Ord. 19, r. 2(3), as amended by S.I. 1990 No. 1764.

[42] *Civil Justice Review* (1988), Chap. 8.

[43] C.C.R., Ord. 19, r. 2(3), see below. Of course, this only happens where a defence to the claim has been entered.

[44] *Ibid.* An "outside arbitrator" is neither a judge nor a district judge (C.C.R., Ord. 19, r. 1), but is some suitable person. Outside arbitrators are rarely used. There is debate as to the value of using a non-lawyer, even if he or she is a member of the Chartered Institute of Arbitrators: G. Applebey, "Justice within Reach?—A Review of the Progress in Reforming Small Claims" (1987) 6 C.J.Q. 214, at p. 223.

[45] C.C.R., Ord. 19, r. 5(2).

[46] C.C.R., Ord. 19, rr. 5(1), 9(a)–(e).

[47] Since it is not a proceeding in the county court, for which, in general, representation is available: Legal Aid Act 1988, s.14 and Sched. 2, Part I, para. 1(d).

[48] See above, pp. 445–446.

[49] C.C.R., Ord. 19, r. 6 as amended by S.I. 1990 No. 1764. If a reference to arbitration is rescinded, costs incurred thereafter are recoverable. These provisions do not preclude the award of witnesses' allowances.

Why arbitration? The object of providing for arbitration rather than trial in small claims is to allow litigants to represent themselves at a hearing where their ignorance of procedure and adversarial techniques will not be a handicap. It is intended that the hearing should be informal, and this is indicated by the following standard terms of reference.[50]

The formal rules of evidence and procedure do not apply. The arbitrator must conduct the hearing according to the circumstances of each case and will in the future be required to adopt an interventionist role.[51] This will mean that he or she will be able to assume the control of the questioning of the parties and their witnesses, requiring questions to be directed through him or her. The arbitrator will be able, with the consent of the parties, to get in an expert witness or procure an expert report. Hearings should normally be in private. It is anticipated that this type of hearing will be much more appropriate for small claims and will prove to be fairer, simpler and cheaper.

The automatic reference to arbitration of a dispute involving a sum of less than £500 can be rescinded on the application of either party or on the motion of the district judge, but only on one (or more) specified grounds. The district judge can order a trial instead of arbitration, if satisfied that a difficult question of law or exceptionally difficult questions of fact are involved, that fraud is alleged, that both parties agree to trial, or that it would be unreasonable to order arbitration in the particular case having regard to the subject matter, the size of any counterclaim, the circumstances of the parties or the interests of other persons likely to be affected by the claim.[52] *Pepper* v. *Healey*[53] shows that arbitration may not always be the ideal solution in small claims and provides an example of an arbitration being rescinded.

In that case, Mrs. Pepper alleged that Mrs. Healey had driven into her car causing damage amounting to £133. Mrs. Healey denied that there had been any collision and proposed to call expert evidence to prove that any damage to the plaintiff's car could not have been done by her car. Mrs. Healey, comprehensively insured, would have had her legal expenses met by her insurance company. Mrs. Pepper, insured only against third-party claims, would not. The registrar rescinded the automatic reference to arbitration on the grounds that the plaintiff needed legal representation in order to present her case properly and the costs burden on her in an arbitration would therefore be unfair. Because the insurance company was paying the defendant's costs, the contest would be unequal. The Court of Appeal upheld this view. (It may seem ironical that the initial question of whether the case should go to arbitration or trial involved three hearings—two in the county court and one in the Court of Appeal.)

6. REVIEW OF SMALL CLAIMS PROCEDURE

The small claims procedure is designed to ensure a relatively informal, inexpensive and speedy form of resolving civil disputes. A review of the

[50] C.C.R., Ord. 19, r. 5(2).
[51] As to the debate about an interventionist or non-interventionist role, see *Civil Justice Review* (1988), paras. 488–493, 509, 526–527. See also *Ordinary Justice* (1989), pp. 294–296, 297–300.
[52] C.C.R., Ord. 19, r. 2(4), as amended by S.I. 1990 No. 1746.
[53] [1982] R.T.R. 411.

procedure demands an assessment of whether these objectives are achieved, and, if they are not, a consideration of what reforms of the present procedure are necessary or whether a more radical approach is required. Most of this was undertaken during the course of the Civil Justice Review, although the nature of the review excluded consideration of the possibility of a radical approach in the form of a new Small Claims Court. The recommendations of the Review are being implemented and a consideration of the basis upon which those recommendations were made is appropriate.

Many of the recommendations of the Civil Justice Review[54] relied upon the results of a factual study undertaken by Touche Ross Management Consultants.[55] Whilst the factual study produced considerable valuable information, there are gaps and some errors in methodology which mean that its conclusions cannot be relied on exclusively in an assessment of the present procedure.[56]

On the positive side, the factual study indicated that, in general, the small claims procedure provided a suitable forum for use by the general public, although the comments on the procedure tended to be about details rather than an overall critique. Sight should not be lost of the calls for a separate small claims court (see below) and care must be taken in considering the use to which the procedure is put by the private citizen, as distinct from businesses and other organisations. On the face of it, the *Judicial Statistics* suggest that the procedure is extensively used. In 1989, 1,574,130 money plaints valued under £500 were entered.[57] Whilst this suggests that a large number of people make use of the procedure, the recent research figures reveal that it is not only private citizens, but also "large organisations"[58] and other "small litigants,"[59] who make extensive use of the procedure.[60] Even if a large number of private citizens do use the procedure, what is unknown is how many more people with a small claim never take legal proceedings.[61] Indeed, it is often suggested that a major problem with the procedure is its lack of accessibility to the private citizen.[62]

The problem of accessibility arises in a number of different ways, but primarily in the general difficulty that the private citizen has in undertaking

---

[54] *Civil Justice Review* (1988), Chap. 8.

[55] *Civil Justice Review: Study of The Small Claims Procedure* (1986).

[56] For a critique see C.J. Whelan, "The Role of Research in Civil Justice Reform: Small Claims in the County Court" (1987) 6 C.J.Q. 237. See also Applebey (1987), pp. 216–218.

[57] *Judicial Statistics 1989* Cm. 1154, Table 4.1.

[58] *i.e.* Large and medium to large companies, banks, building societies, H.P. companies, national or public bodies, and public utilities: Touche Ross Management Consultants (1986), at p. 18.

[59] *i.e.* small businesses and local professional companies: Touche Ross Management Consultants (1986), at pp. 18–19. Unfortunately, the Touche Ross research failed for most purposes to distinguish between private citizens and other small litigants, see Whelan (1987), at pp. 243–244 noting the weaknesses that consequently existed in that research.

[60] Touche Ross Management Consultant (1986), p. 20, shows that, in their sample, 38 per cent. of plaintiffs were private citizens and 58 per cent. of defendants were private citizens. So extensive was the use made of the small claims procedure by one large organisation, Severn Trent Water Authority, that in Birmingham County Court special provision was made in 1982: Applebey (1985), at p. 205.

[61] The failure to examine this question properly is a major criticism of the Touche Ross Management Consultants (1986): see Whelan (1987), at pp. 238–239.

[62] See, *e.g.*, Tamara Goriely, Legal Officer of the N.C.C. quoted in Applebey (1987), p. 227: "It is one of the failures of the small claims procedure that the greater majority of potential small claimants do not make use of it." See also *Ordinary Justice* (1989), pp. 286–294, 300.

litigation without representation, even though this is the intention behind the procedure. Consequently, it is suggested that private citizens have difficulty with the forms, both in understanding what they say and in how they should be filled in, and with the hearings, which can be legalistic.[63] On the other hand, there is some evidence that comprehension of the various aspects of small claims procedure is quite high.[64]

A number of specific problems have been identified which suggest that the objectives are not attained fully or consistently. One of the criticisms is of the variations in approach adopted by the various county courts, court staff and registrars, resulting in a difficulty in providing advice of a consistent nature.[65] On the other hand, there may be real value in divergence of approach not only in terms of flexibility, but also in encouraging experimentation which may lead to overall advances being made, which might otherwise not be possible.[66]

Consequently, it must be questioned, with Sir Jack Jacob, whether the present small claims procedure provides "a procedure which is simple, inexpensive and fair."[67] Is it simple? The experience of the Birmingham County Court when it established a separate office to deal with litigants in person would suggest that the answer is that it is not. The office was established because court staff found it extremely time-consuming to assist litigants in person with processing a claim, and, in particular, with providing help with summonses.[68]

C. THE HIGH COURT

The process of settlement or compromise referred to in Chapter 10 can continue throughout a civil action in the High Court, so that the procedural steps necessary to bring an action to trial may be taken in the knowledge that a hearing may yet be averted. Indeed, some parts of pre-trial High Court procedure have the effect of increasing the possibilities for compromise at the same time as preparing the issue for hearing by a judge.[69] Much of the court involvement through the pre-trial procedures is through masters rather than judges.[70]

Whilst the Civil Justice Review, as its recommendations are introduced, will produce considerable changes to the current High Court procedure in an

---

[63] See, e.g. Applebey (1987), pp. 225, 227–228, 233.
[64] Touche Ross Management Consultants (1986), p. 84.
[65] See, e.g., Civil Justice Review (1988), para. 509, and Applebey (1987), p. 221.
[66] Applebey (1987), p. 234, quoting from National Center for State Courts, Small Claims Courts: A National Examination (1978).
[67] Opening Address to the "Reforming Small Claims" conference organised by the Institute of Judicial Administration, University of Birmingham held in 1987, reported in Applebey (1987), p. 227.
[68] See Applebey (1985), p. 206. The evidence showed that the changed administrative procedure also produced costs savings, improved relationships with users who understood the procedure and in training for court staff. See also Ordinary Justice (1989), pp. 296–297.
[69] In particular, properly drawn pleadings can have this effect by disclosing more clearly the precise areas of disagreement between the parties and the procedure whereby the defendant can make a payment into court may greatly increase the pressure on the plaintiff if the amount of the payment is shrewdly calculated. See p. 501, above.
[70] See Sir Jack I.H. Jacob, The Fabric of English Civil Justice (1987), pp. 109–114.

effort to reduce delay, cost and complexity, the current procedure nevertheless provides an insight to what happens to civil actions prior to trial. We,
therefore, provide an outline of the Queen's Bench Division procedure,
indicating the changes that have taken place and specific recommendations
for change made by the Review. We begin, however, with an examination of
a recommendation which, when introduced, will take much of the control of
pre-trial procedure out of the hands of the parties and place it under the
control of the court.

1. COURT MANAGEMENT OF LITIGATION

The Civil Justice Review recommended that a system of court control of case
progress should be introduced in an effort to reduce the delay produced by
pre-trial procedure, which is the major area of delay.[71] Consequently the
parties to an action will not be as free to use pre-trial procedure to their own
ends, delaying trials where that is advantageous.[72] Once an action becomes
defended there is to be a fixed period within which the parties will be
required either to set the case down for trial, on the assumption that it has
not been settled or been otherwise disposed of, or to report to the court.
Standard periods will be prescribed for different types of business. It will be
possible to apply, at an early stage, for a special timetable, although applications to the court for detailed variations of the standard timetable will be
permitted.

The court will have an effective monitoring system, building upon the
introduction of computerised methods of instituting actions.[73] The monitoring will be applied at either the commencement of the case or at the point
where it becomes defended, and will require notice of the defendant's
intention to defend. The court record will show the date by which the case is
due to be set down for trial. The court file will record that setting down
within the prescribed period if it takes place. Plaintiffs will also be required
to give the court notice of disposal by settlement or otherwise before that
date, subject to a fixed penalty for failing to give such notice, which will be
payable by the plaintiff's solicitor. Three months before the due date for
setting down the court will issue reminder cards to parties in live cases stating
the date by which their case is due to be set down.

Regular record checks will enable courts to identify cases not set down or
disposed of within the prescribed period. In any such case the plaintiff's
solicitor will be sent a reminder of the requirement to set down and will be
invited to fill in a standard report form on the state of the case. If no reply is
received within 14 days, a further reminder will be sent to the plaintiff's
solicitor. If the second reminder produces no result or the reply to either

[71] As to the recommendations, see *Civil Justice Review* (1988), paras. 220–228. As to the causes
of delay, see pp. 487–490 above. Numerous recommendations are also made with regard to
judicial administration, see *ibid.*, Chap. 5. Of direct relevance are the recommendations
relating to the training of court staff (*ibid.*, para. 313), training of case listing officers (*ibid.*,
paras. 315–316), the introduction of a five-hour sitting day, five days a week as the normal
objective (*ibid.*, paras. 329–335), and the limitation of the long vacation to August (*ibid.*,
paras. 337–342).
[72] See above p. 505.
[73] For some time forms have been available in connection with county court proceedings which
are designed for use with a computerised system of dealing with summonses. See *Civil Justice
Review* (1988), para. 317.

reminder seems to indicate the need for court intervention the matter will be referred to a master or district judge, who will have the power to issue a summons for the solicitors of one or both sides to come and explain matters. Having given an opportunity to the parties to be heard, the master or district judge will be able to make an "unless" order to the effect that the case be struck out unless particular steps are taken within a particular time, or will be able to set the case down for trial.

Intervention by the court will normally cure delay or give rise to an acceptable explanation. In the last resort, however, the court will have the power, of its motion and after hearing the parties if they wish, to strike out a case, leaving it to the parties to resolve the matter themselves. Failure to comply with a court summons, or to comply with an "unless" order, will constitute grounds for striking out. In such cases the court will, when giving reasons for striking out and after hearing the parties' representatives if they wish, indicate who in its view is to blame for the delay, thus assisting the process of professional disciplinary sanctions and the pursuit of compensation by litigants.

The new timetables will relate to the overall periods up to setting down for trial. Within that period there will continue to be stated periods for exchange of pleadings[74] and other interlocutory steps since these provide a guide to parties and a means by which they can keep one another up to schedule. There is, however, room for a realistic degree of relaxation in the system and the present 14 day periods allowed for exchange of pleadings will be increased to 28 days, subject to compliance with the overall timetable. It will also be permissible for parties to vary particular time limits by agreement, subject always to the obligations to have the case ready for trial and set down within the overall timetable.

2. COMMENCING AN ACTION

We concentrate on the plaintiff beginning an action by way of writ of summons, rather than an originating summons, originating motion or petition.[75] In order to engender simplicity and reduce delay, the Civil Justice Review proposed that all actions be instituted by a writ.[76] A writ is a formal document containing details of the parties, the plaintiff's claim, an instruction to the defendant to acknowledge the writ within a specified time and a warning to the defendant that he or she must acknowledge the summons and indicate an intention to contest the case or risk the plaintiff proceeding directly to a judgment.[77]

On the back of the writ the plaintiff must set out ("indorse") the nature of the claim against the defendant either in a brief, general statement (a "general indorsement")[78] or in a full statement (a "special indorsement").[79]

---

[74] See below, p. 554.
[75] R.S.C. Ord. 5
[76] *Civil Justice Review* (1988), paras. 213–216.
[77] Every writ must be in the established form: R.S.C., Ord. 6, r. 1. See generally as to issue and service of a writ, J. O'Hare and R. N. Hill, *Civil Litigation* (5th ed., 1990), pp. 209–210, 215–221.
[78] See, *e.g. Hacker* v. *Reliable Nag Supply Stables*, below.
[79] See, *e.g. Maserati* v. *Lagonda*, below. Special indorsement would normally only be used where the claim is for a liquidated sum, that is a specific sum of money due, in this case, to the plaintiff, or the plaintiff is very anxious to hurry the matter along.

If the writ contains a general indorsement and the defendant wishes to contest the case, a full statement of claim by the plaintiff will become a necessary part of the pleadings which will follow in due course and then the defendant will at least know the outline of the case against him or her.[80]

The plaintiff (or solicitor) must draw up the writ. The writ must then be "issued" and "served." The "issue" of the writ is the process by which it is made a formal document with the authority of the court. This is achieved by the presentation of sufficient copies of the writ to allow one to be filed at the Writ Department of the Central Office of the High Court[81] and one to be served on each defendant. Forms of Acknowledgements of Service for each defendant must also be handed in. The court officer stamps the writs and assigns a reference number, that is a year, letter and number to the action.[82]

As a consequence of the Civil Justice Review "service" of the writ must take place within four months of the date of issue of the writ.[83] It is expected that this will help in reducing the problem of delay.[84] Service is normally effected by sending it by first-class post to the usual address of the defendant or to his or her solicitor who will accept service on the defendant's behalf.[85] Personal service, where the plaintiff or his or her agent actually gives to or leaves with the defendant a copy of the writ, is still possible, but postal service is obviously less onerous.[86] Service of documents may also be made through a document exchange or by fax.[86a]

The following are two examples of a writ of summons. The first, in the imaginary case of *Hacker* v. *Reliable Nag Supply Stables* (*a firm*) is a claim for damages for breach of contract, the writ being generally indorsed. The second in the imaginary case of *Maserati* v. *Lagonda*, is a claim for the price of goods sold and delivered, the writ being specially indorsed.

---

[80] See below, p. 551.
[81] Or at a convenient District Registry.
[82] *e.g.* 1990-A-No. 789, where A is the initial of the plaintiff's surname or family name.
[83] R.S.C., Ord. 6, r. 8(2), as amended by the Rules of the Supreme Court (Amendment No. 4) 1989 (S.I. 1989, No. 2427), r. 2. Exceptions are permitted to this rule: *ibid.*
[84] *Civil Justice Review* (1988), paras. 201–204 and recommendation R.17(i).
[85] R.S.C., Ord. 10, r. 1 and Ord. 65, r. 5, as amended by S.I. 1990 No. 2599.
[86] Postal service was introduced in 1980 and was described in the 1988 White Book as "... a landmark in the procedure and practice of the Chancery and Queen's Bench Divisions of the High Court"; *Supreme Court Practice 1988*, para. 10/1/6. Thus there is now little scope for the athletic and ingenious defendant to avoid service of the writ by keeping out of the way of the plaintiff.
[86a] R.S.C., Ord. 65, r. 5, as amended by S.I. 1990 No. 2599.

Writ indorsed
with Statement
of Claim
[Unliquidated
Demand]
(O. 6, r.1)

IN THE HIGH COURT OF JUSTICE

Queen's Bench Division

19₈₈ .**H** .—No. 179

[NOTTINGHAM **District Registry]**

Between

PETER GEORGE MARTIN HACKER Plaintiff

AND

RELIABLE NAG SUPPLY STABLES (sued as a firm)

Defendant

(1) Insert name.

(2) Insert address.

To the Defendant (¹) RELIABLE NAG SUPPLY STABLES

of (²) THE WIDE PADDOCKS, LEAK AVENUE, GROATHAM, NOTTINGHAMSHIRE .

This Writ of Summons has been issued against you by the above-named Plaintiff in respect of the claim set out on the back.

Within 14 days after the service of this Writ on you, counting the day of service, you must either satisfy the claim or return to the Court Office mentioned below the accompanying **Acknowledgment of Service** stating therein whether you intend to contest these proceedings.

If you fail to satisfy the claim or to return the Acknowledgment within the time stated, or if you return the Acknowledgment without stating therein an intention to contest the proceedings, the Plaintiff may proceed with the action and judgment may be entered against you forthwith without further notice.

(3) Complete
and delete as
necessary.

Issued from the (³) [Central Office] [Admiralty and Commercial Registry]
[NOTTINGHAM District Registry] of the High Court
this FIRST day of DECEMBER 19 88

NOTE:—This Writ may not be served later than 4 calendar months *(or, if leave is required to effect service out of the jurisdiction, 6 months)* beginning with that date unless renewed by order of the Court.

IMPORTANT

Directions for Acknowledgment of Service are given with the accompanying form.

Statement of Claim

The Plaintiff's claim is for

Damages for breach of an implied term in the contract for sale
of a piebald gelding by the Defendant to the Plaintiff on the
25th day of June 1988 and for interest thereon.

(Signed)   George Washington

(1) If this Writ
was issued out of
a District Registry,
this indorsement
as to place where
the cause of
action arose
should be
completed.

(2) Delete as
necessary.

(3) Insert name
of place.

(4) For phrase-
ology of this
indorsement where
the Plaintiff sues
in person, see
*Supreme Court
Practice*, Vol. 2,
para. 1.

(1) [(2) [The cause] [one of the causes] of action in respect of which the Plaintiff
claim   relief in this action arose wholly or in part at (3)
in the district of the District Registry named overleaf.]

(4) **This Writ** was issued by Popp, Lees and Stone

of 23 HALTERGATE, NOTTINGHAM

[Agent   for

of   ]

Solicitor   for the said Plaintiff   whose address   (2) [is] [are]

19 Long Road, Pegworth, Nottinghamshire

Solicitor's Reference   MB 456   **Tel. No:** 0602-000000

High Court A3A

COURT FEES ONLY

Writ indorsed with
Statement of Claim
[Liquidated
Demand]
(O.6, r. 1)

IN THE HIGH COURT OF JUSTICE   19 88 . $\frac{M}{}$.—No. *792*

QUEEN'S BENCH   **Division**

[Group   ]

[*NOTTINGHAM*   District Registry]

Between

ALFONSO FREDERICO MASERATI   Plaintiff

AND

WILLIAM DANIEL HENRY LAGONDA

(1) Insert name.   **To the Defendant(¹)** *WILLIAM DANIEL HENRY LAGONDA*   **Defendant**

(2) Insert
address.   **of(²)** *423, TALBOT GARDENS, MORGAN-CUM-MIDGET, NOTTINGHAMSHIRE*

This Writ of Summons has been issued against you by the above-named Plaintiff in respect of the claim set out overleaf.

Within 14 days after the service of this Writ on you, counting the day of service, you must either satisfy the claim or return to the Court Office mentioned below the accompanying **Acknowledgment of Service** stating therein whether you intend to contest these proceedings.

If you fail to satisfy the claim or to return the Acknowledgment within the time stated, or if you return the Acknowledgment without stating therein an intention to contest the proceedings the Plaintiff may proceed with the action and judgment may be entered against you forthwith without further notice.

(3) Complete
and delete as
necessary.   Issued from the(³) [~~Central Office~~] [*NOTTINGHAM*   District Registry]
of the High Court this   *FIRST*   day of   *DECEMBER*   1988

NOTE:—This Writ may not be served later than 12 calendar months beginning with that date unless renewed by order of the Court.

IMPORTANT
Directions for Acknowledgment of Service are given with the accompanying form.

Statement of Claim

The Plaintiff's claim is for

the sum of £3990 being the price of goods sold and delivered to the Defendant and interest amounting to [£ total by date of writ] and continuing at a rate of [£] per day until payment or judgement.

Particulars

A motorcar, registered number ABC 123, sold to the defendant under contract contained in letters dated the 29th day of June 1988 and delivered to the defendant at his house by the plaintiff on the 30th day of June 1988.

£3990

(Signed)   *George Washington*

If, within the time for returning the Acknowledgment of Service, the Defendant pay the amount claimed and £300 for costs and, if the Plaintiff obtain an order for substituted service, the additional sum of £10.00 , further proceedings will be stayed. The money must be paid to the Plaintiff , *his* Solicitor or Agent

(1) If this Writ was issued out of a District Registry, this indorsement * as to place where the cause of action arose should be completed.

(2) Delete as necessary.

(3) Insert name of place.

(4) For phraseology of this indorsement where the Plaintiff sues in person, see *Supreme Court Practice,* Vol 2, para 3.

(1) [(2) [The cause] [One of the causes] of action in respect of which the Plaintiff claims relief in this action arose wholly or in part at(3) *MORGAN-CUM-MIDGET* in the district of the District Registry named overleaf.]

(4) **This Writ** was issued by *POPP, LEES AND STONE*

of *23, HALTERGATE, NOTTINGHAM*

[Agent for

of]

Solicitor for the said Plaintiff whose address (2) [is] [are]

423, TALBOT GARDENS, MORGAN-CUM-MIDGET

NOTTINGHAMSHIRE

3. THE ACKNOWLEDGEMENT OF SERVICE—AND THE CONSEQUENCES OF FAILURE[87]

As noted, the plaintiff is required to serve on the defendant, as well as a writ, a form on which service of the writ can be acknowledged. Normally an acknowledgement is required within 14 days. The acknowledgement must indicate whether the defendant intends to contest the claim.[88] If the claim is to be contested and the writ has been specially indorsed, a defence must be served on the plaintiff within 14 days after the time for acknowledging service.[89] If the writ is generally indorsed, a defence need not be served until after a full statement of claim has been served by the plaintiff.

The defendant may wish to contest the claim and the form makes provision for that response. If the defendant simply fails to indicate an intention to contest the action (by not acknowledging service at all) the plaintiff is entitled to enter *final* judgment for the amount claimed, interest and costs, if the claim is for a liquidated amount[90] and *interlocutory* judgment, if the claim is for an unliquidated amount.[91] In the latter case the defendant will still be able to appear and dispute the amount of damages when they fall to be assessed by a master prior to final judgment being entered for the plaintiff. In both cases, the judgment in favour of the plaintiff can, by order of the court, be set aside[92] if the defendant has a reasonable excuse for the default and also has some merit in his or her case.[93] If a judgment is set aside in this way, the defendant is likely to bear some penalty in costs.

Acknowledgments of service to the two writs are set out below. The stables wish to dispute the claim, Mr. Lagonda does not.

---

[87] See O'Hare and Hill (1990), pp. 221–222, 227–230, 233–235.
[88] See example in the text, question 2 on the Acknowledgment of Service.
[89] *Ibid.* Directions for Acknowledgment of Service.
[90] R.S.C., Ord. 13, r. 1. A "liquidated" amount is where the damages claimed is a specified sum.
[91] R.S.C., Ord. 13, r. 2.
[92] R.S.C., Ord. 13, r. 9.
[93] This is not the only ground for setting aside the judgment, there may have been formal irregularities.

Acknowledgment
of Service
of Writ
of Summons
(Queen's Bench)
(O. 12, r. 3)

Directions for Acknowledgment of Service

1.   The accompanying form of **ACKNOWLEDGMENT OF SERVICE** should be detached and completed by a Solicitor acting on behalf of the Defendant or by the Defendant if acting in person. After completion it must be delivered or sent by post to the Central Office, Royal Courts of Justice, Strand, London WC2A 2LL.

2.   A Defendant who states in his Acknowledgment of Service that he intends to contest the proceedings **MUST ALSO SERVE A DEFENCE** on the Solicitor for the Plaintiff (or on the Plaintiff if acting in person).

If a Statement of Claim is indorsed on the Writ (i.e. the words "Statement of Claim" appear at the top of the back of the first page), the Defence must be served within 14 days after the time for acknowledging service of the Writ, unless in the meantime a summons for judgment is served on the Defendant.

If a Statement of Claim is not indorsed on the Writ, the Defence need not be served until 14 days after a Statement of Claim has been served on the Defendant. If the Defendant fails to serve his defence within the appropriate time, the Plaintiff may enter judgment against him without further notice.

3.   **A STAY OF EXECUTION** against the Defendant's goods may be applied for where the Defendant is unable to pay the money for which any judgment is entered. If a Defendant to an action for a debt or liquidated demand (i.e. a fixed sum) who does not intend to contest the proceedings states, in answer to Question 3 in the Acknowledgment of Service, that he intends to apply for a stay, execution will be stayed for 14 days after his Acknowledgment, but he must, within that time, **ISSUE A SUMMONS** for a stay of execution, supported by an affidavit of his means. The affidavit should state any offer which the Defendant desires to make for payment of the money by instalments or otherwise.

4.   **IF THE WRIT IS ISSUED OUT OF A DISTRICT REGISTRY** but the Defendant does not reside or carry on business within the district of the registry and the writ is not indorsed with a statement that the Plaintiff's cause of action arose in that district, the Defendant may, in answer to Question 4 in the Acknowledgment of Service, apply for the transfer of the action to some other District Registry or to the Royal Courts of Justice.

See over for Notes for Guidance

Notes for Guidance

1.   Each Defendant (if there are more than one) is required to complete an Acknowledgment of Service and return it to the appropriate Court Office.

*Not applicable if the Defendant is a Company served at its Registered Office.

*[2.   For the purpose of calculating the period of 14 days for acknowledging service, a writ served on the Defendant personally is treated as having been served on the day it was delivered to him and a writ served by post or by insertion through the Defendant's letter box is treated as having been served on the seventh day after the date of posting or insertion unless the contrary is shown.]

3.   Where the Defendant is sued in a name different from his own, the form must be completed by him with the addition in paragraph 1 of the words "sued as (*the name stated on the Writ of Summons)*".

4.   Where the Defendant is a **FIRM** and a Solicitor is not instructed, the form must be completed by a **PARTNER** by name, with the addition in paragraph 1 of the description "partner in the firm (...)" after his name.

5.   Where the Defendant is sued as an individual **TRADING IN A NAME OTHER THAN HIS OWN,** the form must be completed by him with the addition in paragraph 1 of the description "trading as (..............................)" after his name.

6.   Where the Defendant is a **LIMITED COMPANY** the form must be completed by a Solicitor or by someone authorised to act on behalf of the Company, but the Company can take no further step in the proceedings without a Solicitor acting on its behalf.

7.   Where the Defendant is a **MINOR** or a **MENTAL** Patient, the form must be completed by a Solicitor acting for a guardian *ad litem*.

8.   A Defendant acting in person may obtain help in completing the form either at the Central Office of the Royal Courts of Justice or at any District Registry of the High Court or at any Citizens' Advice Bureau.

9.   A Defendant who is NOT a Limited Company or a Corporation may be entitled to Legal Aid. Information about the Legal Aid Scheme may be obtained from any Citizens' Advice Bureau and from most firms of Solicitors.

10.   These notes deal only with the more usual cases. In case of difficulty a Defendant in person should refer to paragraphs 8 and 9 above.

Acknowledgment
of Service of Writ
of Summons
(Queen's Bench)

IN THE HIGH COURT OF JUSTICE
Queen's Bench Division

19 88.ᴴ   .—No. 179

Between

*The adjacent
heading should
be completed by
the Plaintiff*

PETER GEORGE MARTIN HACKER   Plaintiff

AND

RELIABLE NAG SUPPLY STABLES
(sued as a firm)   Defendant

**If you intend to instruct a Solicitor to act for you, give him this form
IMMEDIATELY. Please complete in black ink.**

IMPORTANT. Read the accompanying directions and notes for guidance carefully before completing
this form. If any information required is omitted or given wrongly, THIS FORM MAY HAVE TO BE
RETURNED. Delay may result in judgment being entered against a Defendant whereby he or his solicitor
may have to pay the costs of applying to set it aside.

*See Notes 1, 3,
4 and 5*

1   State the full name of the Defendant by whom or on whose behalf the service of
the Writ is being acknowledged. ALICE MARY ARKLE, partner in the firm
of RELIABLE NAG SUPPLY STABLES

2   State whether the Defendant intends to contest the proceedings (*tick
appropriate box*)   ✔ yes   ☐ no

See Direction 3

3   If the claim against the Defendant is for a debt or liquidated demand, AND
he does not intend to contest the proceedings, state if the Defendant intends
to apply for a stay of execution against any judgment entered by the Plaintiff
(*tick box*)   ☐ yes

See Direction 4

4   If the Writ of Summons was issued out of a District Registry and

(*a*)   the Defendant's residence, place of business or registered office (if a
limited company) is NOT within the district of that District Registry
AND

(*b*)   there is no indorsement on the Writ that the Plaintiff's cause of action
arose wholly or in part within that district,

state if the Defendant applies for the transfer of the action (*tick box*)   yes

If YES, state—   ☐   to the Royal Courts of Justice, London:
(*tick appropriate box*)   OR

**State which
Registry*   ☐   to the*   District Registry

Service of the Writ is acknowledged accordingly

(*Signed*) Alice Mary Arkle

†*Where words
appear between
square brackets,
delete if
inapplicable.
Insert "Defendant
in Person" if
appropriate*

†[Solicitor] [Agent for   Defendant in Person   ]

Address for service **(*See notes overleaf*)**
The Wide Paddock,
Leak Avenue,
Groatham, Nottinghamshire

Please complete overleaf

Indorsement by Plaintiff's solicitor (or by Plaintiff if suing in person) of his name address and reference, if any, in the box below.

```
POPP, LEES AND STONE,
23 HALTERGATE,
NOTTINGHAM

Solicitor's Reference MB 456
```

Notes as to Address for Service

Solicitor. Where the Defendant is represented by a Solicitor, state the Solicitor's place of business in England or Wales. If the Solicitor is the Agent of another Solicitor, state the name and the place of business of the Solicitor for whom he is acting.

Defendant in person. Where the Defendant is acting in person, he must give his residence OR, if he does not reside in England or Wales, he must give an address in England or Wales where communications for him should be sent. In the case of a limited company, "residence" means its registered or principal office.

IN THE HIGH COURT OF JUSTICE

QUEEN'S BENCH **Division**

[Group   ]   19 88 .—$\frac{M}{}$.—No. *792*

Between

ALFONSO FREDERICO MASERATI   Plaintiff

AND

WILLIAM DANIEL HENRY LAGONDA

Defendant

If you intend to instruct a Solicitor to act for you, give him this form IMMEDIATELY. Please complete in black ink.

IMPORTANT. Read the accompanying directions and notes for guidance carefully before completing this form. If any information required is omitted or given wrongly, THIS FORM MAY HAVE TO BE RETURNED. Delay may result in judgment being entered against a Defendant whereby he or his solicitor may have to pay the costs of applying to set it aside.

See Notes 1, 3, 4 and 5

1   State the full name of the Defendant by whom or on whose behalf the service of the Writ is being acknowledged.   *WILLIAM DANIEL HENRY LAGONDA*

2   State whether the Defendant intends to contest the proceedings *(tick appropriate box)* ☐ yes   ☑ no

See Direction 3

3   If the claim against the Defendant is for a debt or liquidated demand, AND he does not intend to contest the proceedings, state if the Defendant intends to apply for a stay of execution against any judgment entered by the Plaintiff *(tick box)*   ☐ yes

See Direction 4

4   If the Writ of Summons was issued out of a District Registry and

     (*a*)   the Defendant's residence, place of business or registered office (if a limited company) is NOT within the district of that District Registry AND

     (*b*)   there is no indorsement on the Writ that the Plaintiff's cause of action arose wholly or in part within that district,

state if the Defendant applies for the transfer of the action (*tick box*) ☐ yes

*State which Registry

If YES, state—   ☐ to the Royal Courts of Justice, London:
(*tick appropriate box*)   OR
                 ☐ to the*   District Registry

Service of the Writ is acknowledged accordingly

(*Signed*)   Furlong and Co.

†*Where words appear between square brackets delete if inapplicable. Insert "Defendant in Person" if appropriate*

†[Solicitor] [Agent for   ]

Address for service *(See notes overleaf)*

    43, BRIDLE LANE, NOTTINGHAM

Please complete overleaf

Indorsement by plaintiff's solicitor (or by plaintiff if suing in person) of his name address and reference, if any, in the box below.

```
    POPP, LEES AND STONE,
    23 HALTERGATE,
    NOTTINGHAM.
```

Notes as to Address for Service

Solicitor. Where the Defendant is represented by a Solicitor, state the Solicitor's place of business in England or Wales. If the Solicitor is the Agent of another Solicitor, state the name and the place of business of the Solicitor for whom he is acting.

Defendant in person. Where the Defendant is acting in person, he must give his residence OR, if he does not reside in England or Wales, he must give an address in England or Wales where communications for him should be sent. In the case of a limited company, "residence" means its registered or principal office.

Indorsement by defendant's solicitor (or by defendant if suing in person) of his name address and reference, if any, in the box below.

```
    FURLONG AND CO.,
    43 BRIDLE LANE,
    NOTTINGHAM.
```

Oyez Publishing Limited, Norwich House, 11/13 Norwich Street, London EC4A 1AB, a subsidiary of The Solicitors' Law Stationery Society, Limited.   F376—4-80

High Court E22 (PR)   ★ ★ ★ ★

4. SUMMARY JUDGMENT[94]

It would obviously be an unacceptable delaying tactic for a defendant to indicate an intention to defend when there was no real defence, thus gaining time in which to pay a debt or damages which could not seriously be disputed. The procedure by which a plaintiff is permitted to request the court to enter judgment for him or her summarily is clearly very important, but it is equally important to ensure that a power given to a judge or master to award a case to the plaintiff who can show that there is no real answer to the claim should not be exercised lightly. The provisions of Order 14 of the Rules of the Supreme Court seek to achieve this balance.[95]

A plaintiff may apply to the court to enter judgment on his or her behalf for the whole or part of the claim if the application can be supported with an affidavit swearing the truth of the facts of the case and stating that the plaintiff believes there to be no defence to the claim.[96] The defendant may be given leave to seek to refute the plaintiff's contention by affidavit or otherwise[97] and demonstrate, at least, that there is an issue to be tried, but he or she is not obliged to prove a defence.[98]

At the hearing, the Master has the task of balancing the rights of plaintiff and defendant, but must allow the defendant to go on if the issue is triable, even if the defendant's chances of success are thought to be slender. However, there are a number of options open to the master and conditions may be attached to the leave to defend.[99] Conditions may have the effect of discouraging the defendant, or at least inducing careful consideration of the strength of the case. The Master may give judgment for the plaintiff and thus greatly speed up the process of litigation.

5. THE PLEADINGS[1]

Since the adversarial system depends upon the two parties selecting the issues for resolution and acquiring the evidence to support them, it is necessary that the parties should communicate to each other the elements of their case. The system of pleadings amounts to a formal exchange of allegations so as to define with clarity and precision the matters which are in dispute. They also reduce the possibility of one party being surprised by the case of the other at trial.[2] Pleadings can offer an opportunity to narrow down the issue between the parties. The way in which the pleadings are conducted

[94] See Jacob (1987), pp. 122–124 and O'Hare and Hill (1990), pp. 235–237, 241–246.
[95] The summary judgment procedure is commonly referred to as "Order 14 procedure." This procedure is not available in certain actions, including defamation, malicious prosecution, false imprisonment and fraud, all of which are triable by jury as of qualified right: R.S.C., Ord. 14, r. 1(2), and see pp. 703–704, below. A court may, at any stage in proceedings, determine a question of law or construction of a document where the matter can be suitably and finally determined: R.S.C., Ord. 14A as inserted by S.I. 1990 No. 2599.
[96] R.S.C., Ord., 14, r. 2.
[97] It is, however, unusual to allow oral examination of the parties at an Order 14 hearing.
[98] R.S.C., Ord., 14, rr. 3, 4.
[99] The order most favourable to the defendant is an order for unconditional leave to defend, but the Master may require money to be paid in by the defendant, or only give leave to defend as a "short cause" (a special list to cater for actions which can be tried in a short time—up to 4 hours).
[1] See Jacob (1987), pp. 87–92 and O'Hare and Hill (1990), pp. 247–251.
[2] See, further, Jacob (1987), p. 90.

is largely a matter for the parties, although this aspect of pleadings is constantly being eroded in an effort to produce a fair and efficient system of civil justice. The objective of the Civil Justice Review to encourage openness has partly been achieved by the introduction of the requirement of more informative pleadings.[3]

If the plaintiff has served a generally indorsed writ on the defendant, the first document to be prepared and served is the statement of claim. In the statement of claim the plaintiff's claim against the defendant must be set out, with the facts which will be relied upon for support, the injury/loss that has been suffered and the remedy which is sought.[4] The statement needs to be sufficiently full to allow the defendant to ascertain the case against him or her and to prepare a defence.

The basic rule governing all pleading is contained in R.S.C., Ord., 18, r. 7(1):

> "... [E]very pleading must contain, and contain only, a statement in a summary form of the material facts on which the party pleading relies for his claim or defence, as the case may be, but not the evidence by which the facts are to be proved, and the statement must be as brief as the nature of the case admits."

The art of drafting pleadings is therefore very important. Pleadings must state facts only, not law or evidence, they must state only the material facts and those material facts must be pleaded with sufficient detail but without excessive detail. Drawing that latter balance is where the real skill lies.[5]

In *Hacker* v. *Reliable Nag Supply Stables*[6] the statement of claim could be set out as follows.

IN THE HIGH COURT OF JUSTICE   1988 H. No. 179
QUEEN'S BENCH DIVISION
NOTTINGHAM DISTRICT REGISTRY.
WRIT ISSUED THE 1st DAY OF DECEMBER 1988

Between

PETER GEORGE
MARTIN HACKER   *Plaintiff*
and
RELIABLE NAG SUPPLY
STABLES   *Defendants*
(SUED AS A FIRM)

STATEMENT OF CLAIM

1. The Plaintiff and the Defendants entered into an oral contract ("the

---

[3] R.S.C., Ord. 18, r. 12, as amended by the Rules of the Supreme Court (Amendment No. 4) 1989. See *Civil Justice Review* (1988), para. 236. The other recommendations related to introducing an automatic right to administer interrogatories (see p. 554, below); and a penalty for failure to admit specified facts (see p. 554, below). These have been introduced through the Rules of the Supreme Court. In addition there is a recommendation that there should be provision of for the exchange of witness statements: *ibid.* paras. 229–235.

[4] R.S.C., Ord. 18, r. 15.

[5] See O'Hare and Hill (1990), Chap. 9.

[6] The imaginary case which we began by writ of summons at p. 539 above.

contract") on June 25th 1988 at the Defendant's place of business for the sale of a piebald gelding, known as Skipper, ("the horse") by the Defendants to the Plaintiff for the price of £65,000 which was paid by the Plaintiff to the Defendants on that day.

2. At all material times the Defendants were horse traders and the horse was sold in the course of the Defendant's business.

3. The Plaintiff took delivery of the horse from the Defendant on June 26th 1988.

4. There was an implied term in the contract that the horse was sound and in good health.

5. Further or alternatively the Plaintiff made known to the Defendants before and at the time of the contract that he required the horse for general hacking and for jumping at the local gymkhanas and accordingly it was an implied term of the said contract that it would be fit for such purposes.

6. In breach of the contract the horse supplied by the Defendants to the Plaintiff was not of merchantable quality and/or was not fit for its purpose.

PARTICULARS

The horse was found to be suffering from Bastard Strangles and in consequence thereof was entirely useless and worthless to the Plaintiff.

7. By reason of the matters aforesaid the plaintiff has suffered loss and damage.

PARTICULARS OF SPECIAL DAMAGE

Cost price of horse	£65,000
Fees paid to Sutton Riding Enterprises for the care of alternative horse from July 1st to August 20th	£290

8. Further the plaintiff claims interest pursuant to section 35A of the Supreme Court Act 1981 on the amount found to be due to the Plaintiff at such rate and for such period as the Court thinks fit.

AND the Plaintiff claims:

(1) Damages
(2) The aforesaid interest pursuant section 35A of the Supreme Court Act 1981.

Served this 12th day of January 1989
by Popp, Lees and Stone, 23 Haltergate, Nottingham.
Solicitors for the Plaintiff.

The defendant may consider that the information given in the statement of claim is defective, or insufficient to allow a defence to the claim to be prepared. The defendant is entitled to request from the plaintiff any further information required and this is done by way of request for what are known as "further and better particulars."[7] This procedure may be used in different ways—it may be a genuine request for information so that the defendant may better understand the case, or it may be another delaying tactic

---

[7] R.S.C., Ord. 18, r. 12. See O'Hare and Hill (1990), pp. 202–205.

designed to increase the pressure on the plaintiff who is anxious to get damages. In future both parties will have to adhere to the overall timetable.[8] In the case of *Hacker*, the defendant wishes to know more...

IN THE HIGH COURT OF JUSTICE   1988 H. No. 179
QUEEN'S BENCH DIVISION
NOTTINGHAM DISTRICT REGISTRY

Between

PETER GEORGE
MARTIN HACKER   *Plaintiff*
and
RELIABLE NAG SUPPLY
STABLES   *Defendants*
(SUED AS A FIRM)

REQUEST BY THE DEFENDANTS FOR FURTHER AND BETTER PARTICULARS OF THE STATEMENT OF CLAIM

The Plaintiff and Defendant entered into an oral Contract on June 25th 1988 at the Defendant's place of business for the Sale of a piebald gelding, known as Skipper, by the Defendants to the Plaintiff for the price of £65,000 which was paid by the Plaintiff to the Defendant on that day.
Under paragraph 1

> Give full particulars of all facts and matters relied on in support of the allegation that an oral contract was made between the Plaintiff and the Defendants on June 25th 1988.

Under paragraph 5

> Give full particulars of all facts and matters relied upon in support of the allegation that the Plaintiff made known to the Defendants that he required the horse for general hacking and jumping at local gymkhanas, and of the allegation that there was an implied term that the horse would be fit for such purpose.

Under paragraph 6

> State at which time it is alleged that the said horse was discovered to be suffering from Bastard Strangles and for how long it is alleged that the condition had existed.

---

[8] See above, p. 536. In addition the adoption by the Bar and the Law Society of specific written Professional Standards relating to the conduct of all principal types of litigation and schemes fostering specialisation by practitioners based on objective criteria of competence and experience (*Civil Justice Review* (1988), paras. 205–212 and see p. 492 above) are designed to lessen misuse of this aspect of pre-trial procedure.

Under paragraph 7

> Give full particulars of the stabling provided for the alternative horse at
> Sutton Riding Enterprises and a detailed analysis of the fees charged.

Martin Martinson

Served this 18th day of February 1989,
By Furlong and Co., 43 Bridle Lane, Nottingham
Solicitors for the Defendants.

In due course the defendant must serve a defence on the plaintiff.[9] There
are specified time limits for the conduct of pleadings,[10] but these are often
dispensed with by the consent of the parties or by order of the court.[11] The
possibility of creating delay in the whole procedure will be lessened by the
introduction of the overall timetable.

Having been given the necessary information about the plaintiff's case,
the defendant must settle on his or her tactics. In the defence, he or she may
choose to refute the whole of the plaintiff's claim and the facts on which it is
based,[12] or may admit the whole case whilst pleading an explanation which
allows liability to be avoided,[13] or may admit the whole case but object that it
discloses no cause of action,[14] or may adopt a combination of these
approaches, or may adopt them as alternatives.[15] Naturally, the wider the
defence, the wider the issues that remain for resolution at the trial and the
greater must be the plaintiff's preparations. If the defendant is not prepared
to admit any of the facts pleaded by the plaintiff they may all have to be
proved in court with a consequent increase in the length and cost of the case.
However, either party may serve notice under R.S.C., Ord. 27 requiring the
admission of facts with a penalty in costs for refusal.[16] If the defendant does
make substantial admissions, the defence will have the effect of disclosing
and narrowing the issue between the parties so that they are both aware of
precisely what remains in dispute. In order that the pleadings should disclose
clearly what remains in dispute, any issue of fact in a pleading must be
specifically denied or it will be deemed to have been admitted.[17]

---

[9] And every other party to the action who may be affected thereby: R.S.C., Ord. 18, r. 2 as
amended by S.I. 1990 No. 2599.

[10] Contained in the provisions of Ord. 18. Technically the current time limit, which is often not
observed by agreement, is 14 days, but this, as part of the proposals on court management of
litigation, will be increased to 28 days: see p. 537, above.

[11] R.S.C., Ord. 3, r. 5. The advantage of obtaining the consent of the other party to an
extension of time limits is that it saves the cost of an application to the court.

[12] Known as a "traverse."

[13] Known as a "confession and avoidance."

[14] Known as "objection in point of law."

[15] Pleadings in the alternative can sometimes appear extremely confusing. Hence, "(1) The
Defendant denies that she was present at the time alleged and that she hit the plaintiff
(traverse); (2) If, which is not admitted, the defendant was present and did hit the plaintiff,
she did so in self-defence (confession and avoidance); (3) If, which is not admitted, the
defendant was present and hit the plaintiff and did not act in self-defence, the statement of
claim discloses no cause of action (objection in point of law)."

[16] R.S.C., Ord. 27 has been amended (by S.I. 1989 No. 2427), in line with the recommendations
of the Civil Justice Review (1988), para. 236, in an attempt to encourage openness in pre-trial
procedure to reduce delay and cost.

[17] R.S.C., Ord. 18, r. 13. Since the aim is to produce the real controversy between the parties
which requires to be determined, there are liberal powers of amendment: R.S.C., Ord. 20, r.
8.

So far we have omitted consideration of one important possibility. The defendant may wish to make a claim against the plaintiff in addition to defending the plaintiff's claim. It is not necessary to begin a separate action. It is possible to add a *counterclaim*[18] to the defence. Set out below is the defence and counterclaim of the Reliable Nag Supply Stables.

IN THE HIGH COURT OF JUSTICE   1988 H. No. 179
QUEEN'S BENCH DIVISION
NOTTINGHAM DISTRICT REGISTRY

Between

PETER GEORGE
MARTIN HACKER   *Plaintiff*
and
RELIABLE NAG SUPPLY
STABLES   *Defendants*
DEFENCE AND COUNTERCLAIM

DEFENCE

1. It is admitted that by a contract made on June 25th 1988, the Defendants sold to the Plaintiff a piebald gelding for the price of £65,000, which price was paid by the Plaintiff. Save as aforesaid the first paragraph of the Statement of Claim is denied.
2. Paragraphs 2 and 3 of the Statement of Claim are admitted.
3. It is admitted that the said horse was found to be suffering from Bastard Strangles after it had been delivered to the Plaintiff. Save as aforesaid, the implied terms and each and every fact and matter alleged in the fourth, fifth, sixth and seventh paragraphs of the Statement of Claim are denied, and it is denied that the Defendants were in breach of contract as alleged or at all.
4. Further or alternatively, it was an express term of the said agreement that the Defendant would exchange the said horse for another if the same should within 14 days prove unsuitable to the Plaintiff.
5. By a further agreement made at or about the beginning of July 1988 between the Defendants and the Plaintiff, pursuant to the express term referred to in paragraph 4 hereof, the Plaintiff agreed to exchange the said horse for another and to take delivery of a suitable bay mare owned by the Defendants pending his decision to retain the said piebald gelding or the said bay mare.
6. In breach of contract, the Plaintiff failed to make any decision as to which of the said horses he would retain, and, on or about August 21st 1988 returned the said bay mare to the Defendants thereby repudiating the said agreement.
7. If and to the extent, if at all, which is denied, that the Defendants are liable to the Plaintiff they will seek to set off the damages and sums counter-claimed herein to extinguish or diminish such liability.

[18] R.S.C., Ord. 18, r. 18.

COUNTERCLAIM

8. The Defendants repeat paragraphs 1 to 6 of their defence herein.
9. It was an implied term of the agreement pursuant whereto the Defendants delivered the said bay mare to the Plaintiff that the Plaintiff would take reasonable care of the said bay mare whilst in his custody.
10. In breach of the said implied term the Plaintiff failed to take reasonable care of the said bay mare.

PARTICULARS

When the Plaintiff returned the said bay mare to the Defendants its ribs were protruding, its hooves were broken, its coat was dull and ungroomed, 3 shoes were missing and it was in poor health.
11. By reason of the said breaches and each of them, the Defendants suffered loss and damage.
12. Further the Defendant claims interest pursuant to section 35A of the Supreme Court Act 1981 on the amount found to be due to the Plaintiff at such rate and for such period as the Court thinks fit.

PARTICULARS OF DAMAGE

(1)	Loss of profit on the sale of a horse	300.00
(2)	Transport costs on delivery and collection	50.00
(3)	Veterinary costs for said bay mare	120.00
(4)	Farrier's fees for said bay mare	90.00
(5)	Loss of value of said bay mare	400.00
		960.00

AND the Defendants counterclaim
   (1) Damages under paragraph 12 hereof.
   (2) The aforesaid interest pursuant to section 35A of the Supreme Court Act 1981.

William Naseby

Dated this 28th day of March 1989

Where a defence raises new facts the plaintiff may wish to enter a reply[19] and where a counterclaim has been made it is usual for the plaintiff to enter a defence. These can conveniently be combined and will usually be the final document in the pleadings. The defendant is, however, permitted to seek the leave of the court[20] to enter a *Rejoinder*, the plaintiff a *Surrejoinder*, the defendant a *Rebutter*, the plaintiff a *Surrebutter*. Despite these delightful names, the White Book comments "None of these names for pleadings occurs in the former or present rules. All except rejoinder are rare to the point of extinction; and even rejoinder is seldom seen."[21] In the light of the

[19] R.S.C., Ord. 18, r. 3.
[20] R.S.C., Ord. 18, r. 4.
[21] *Supreme Court Practice 1991*, para. 18/4/1.

development of court management of litigation, especially in relation to delay, they are likely to become extinct.[22]

Below we set out a reply and defence to counterclaim in *Hacker's* case:

IN THE HIGH COURT OF JUSTICE   1988 H. No. 179
QUEEN'S BENCH DIVISION
NOTTINGHAM DISTRICT REGISTRY

Between

PETER GEORGE
MARTIN HACKER   *Plaintiff*
and
RELIABLE NAG SUPPLY
STABLES   *Defendants*
(SUED AS A FIRM)

REPLY AND DEFENCE TO COUNTERCLAIM

REPLY

1. The Plaintiff joins issue save insofar as paragraphs 1 to 3 of the Defence and Counterclaim are concerned.

DEFENCE TO COUNTERCLAIM

2. It is admitted that the further agreement referred to in paragraph 4 of the Defence and Counterclaim was made, but it is denied that the Defendants offered a suitable horse in exchange.
3. The Plaintiff paid employees of Sutton Riding Enterprises to attend to the said substitute horse and informed the Defendants at all times of the poor condition of the said horse.
4. The Plaintiff denies that the said horse was in the condition described in paragraph 10 of the Defence and Counterclaim.
5. Whereas the Plaintiff had been informed and believed that the said horse was ill when returned to the Defendants the said illness was a direct result of the poor condition of the said horse at the time of its delivery to the Plaintiff by the Defendants.
6. Each and every claim for damages in paragraph 12 of the Defence and Counterclaim is denied by the Plaintiff.

George Washington

Dated this 25th day of April 1989

"It has become fashionable in these days to attach decreasing importance to pleadings, and it is beyond doubt that there have been times when an insistence on complete compliance with their technicalities put justice at risk. . . . But pleadings continue to play an essential part in civil action . . . the

[22] See above, pp. 536–537.

primary purpose of pleadings remains and it can still prove of vital importance. That purpose is to define the issues and thereby to inform the parties
in advance of the case they have to meet and so enable them to take steps to
deal with it."[23]

6. THE SUMMONS FOR DIRECTIONS[24]

Within one month of the close of pleadings, the plaintiff must take out a
"summons for directions."[25] This procedure is designed to bring the action
before a Master who may give directions to resolve any outstanding matters
between the parties which should be dealt with by an interlocutory application and directions about the future course of the action designed to "secure
the just, expeditious and economical disposal thereof."[26] The summons can,
therefore, operate as a time-saving and cost-saving device in that its object is
to ensure that the action is fully prepared for trial. It may also provide an
opportunity for the parties to indicate to the Master and to each other that
points formerly in issue will not be pursued at trial. In that way, like the
preliminary hearing in the county court, it may serve to assist the process of
settlement and compromise.

Prior to the Civil Justice Review, in theory different directions were given
dependent upon the particular action. In fact, as Jacob pointed out, the
general summons for directions had become "virtually a non event," with
the master knowing little or nothing about the case, except what was
revealed in the pleadings. Consequently, "in summons after summons, the
orders and directions follow[ed] substantially the same pattern, with more
repetition than variation."[27]

In consequence a system of automatic directions is being introduced.
Currently, automatic directions are provided for in personal injury actions[28]
and in county court actions.[29] In the future standard directions will be
provided for High Court actions, but it will be open to the parties to apply to
the court for additional or different directions, for a general stock-taking
and for directions as to the conduct of the case.[29a] Where, exceptionally, no
standard directions have been devised there should be a summons for
directions.

7. DISCOVERY OF DOCUMENTS[30]

So that each party may be aware of documents relating to issues in the case,

---

[23] *Per* Lord Edmund Davies in *Farrell* v. *Sec. of State for Defence* [1980] 1 W.L.R. 172 at p. 179.
    See also observations on the importance of pleadings by Scarman L.J. in *Fulham* v. *Newcastle
    Chronicle* [1977] 1 W.L.R. 651 at 659c and Megaw L.J. in *Commission for Racial Equality* v.
    Ealing London Borough Council [1978] 1 W.L.R. 112, at pp. 117–118. See also Jacob (1987),
    p. 90.
[24] See Jacob (1987), pp. 102–109 and O'Hare and Hill (1990), pp. 448–462.
[25] R.S.C., Ord. 25, r. 1. If the plaintiff fails to take out the summons, the defendants may do so
    or apply to have the action dismissed.
[26] R.S.C., Ord. 25, r. 1(1)(*b*).
[27] Jacob (1987), p. 104.
[28] R.S.C., Ord. 25, r. 8 and see O'Hare and Hill (1990), pp. 462–464.
[29] See County Court (Amendment No. 3) Rules 1990 (S.I. 1990 No. 1764) and *Civil Justice
    Review* (1988), paras. 255–260.
[29a] *Civil Justice Review* (1988), paras. 237–254.
[30] See Jacob (1987), pp. 92–102 and O'Hare and Hill (1990), Chap. 18.

rules requiring "discovery" of those documents place an obligation on the litigants to disclose their existence and, possibly, to disclose their content.[31] Discovery is automatic in actions where the pleadings are closed, with the possibility of using the summons for directions to require additional information.[32]

Each party must produce a list of documents ". . . which are or have been in his possession, custody or power relating to any matter in question . . . in the action."[33] The list must be in a prescribed form[34] and the documents are divided into three categories—those which the plaintiff or defendant has in his or her possession, custody or power and is willing to produce; those which he or she has, but is not willing to produce; and those which he or she has had, but has no longer. Objections to the production of documents for inspection will be based on one or more of the privileges[35] to which a litigant is entitled.

A list of documents in *Hacker* v. *Reliable Nag Supply Stables* is set out below.

[31] R.S.C., Ord. 24.
[32] *Ibid*. r. 2.
[33] *Ibid*. r. 2(1).
[34] See below.
[35] There are certain recognised privileges—the legal privilege; the privilege against self-incrimination; "without prejudice" documents; Crown privilege or public interest immunity.

List of
Documents
(O.24 r.5)

IN THE HIGH COURT OF JUSTICE 19 88 .H .—No. 179

QUEEN'S BENCH **Division**

NOTTINGHAM DISTRICT REGISTRY

Between

    PETER GEORGE MARTIN HACKER

Plaintiff

AND

    RELIABLE NAG SUPPLY STABLES (SUED AS A FIRM)

Defendant

LIST OF DOCUMENTS

The following is a list of the documents relating to the matters in question in this action which are or have been in the possession, custody or power of the

(1) Plaintiffs (or Defendant(s)) A.B.

above-named (¹) plaintiff PETER GEORGE MARTIN HACKER

and which is served in compliance with Order 24, rule 2 [or the order herein dated the   day of   , 19].

(2) Plaintiff(s) or Defendant(s).

1. The (²) plaintiff has in his possession, custody or power the documents relating to the matters in question in this action enumerated in Schedule 1 hereto.

2. The (²) plaintiff objects to produce the documents

(3) State ground of objection.

enumerated in Part 2 of the said Schedule 1 on the ground that (³) they are privileged documents as between solicitor and client.

3. The (²) plaintiff has had, but has not now, in his possession, custody or power the documents relating to the matters in question in this action enumerated in Schedule 2 hereto.

4. Of the documents in the said Schedule 2, those numbered 1 and 2

(4) Plaintiff's or Defendant's.

(5) State when.

(6) Here state what has become of the said documents and in whose possession they now are.

in that Schedule were last in the (⁴)plaintiff'spossession, custody or power on (⁵) 19th May 1987 and the remainder on (⁵)

(⁶) They are now in the possession of the defendant's solicitors

(2) Plaintiff(s) or
Defendant(s).
5. **Neither** the (²)plaintiff nor h is Solicitor nor any other person on h is behalf, ha s now, or ever had, in h is possession, custody or power any document of any description whatever relating to any matter in question in this action, other than the documents enumerated in Schedules 1 and 2 hereto.

SCHEDULE 1.—Part 1.

(Here enumerate in a convenient order the documents (or bundles of documents, if of the same nature, such as invoices) in the possession, custody or power of the party in question which he does not object to produce, with a short description of each document or bundle sufficient to identify it.)

Description of Document	Date
1. Copy letters between Plaintiff's solicitors and Defendant's solicitors	Various
2. Receipts for £100 signed by Alice Arkle	25th June 1988
3. Account of Sutton Riding Enterprises	22nd August 1988
4. Letter from Plaintiff to Defendants	20th August 1988
5. Letter from Defendants to Plaintiff	21st August 1988
6. Copy letter from Plaintiff to Defendants	3rd September 1988

SCHEDULE 1.—Part 2.

(Here enumerate as aforesaid the documents in the possession, custody or power of the party in question which he objects to produce.)

Description of Document	Date
Correspondence between Plaintiff's solicitor and Plaintiff	
Notes and documents related solely to the preparation of the Plaintiff's case	

SCHEDULE 2.

(Here enumerate as aforesaid the documents which have been, but at the date of service of the list are not, in the possession, custody or power of the party in question.)

		Date
1.	Copy letters to Defendant's solicitors	
2.	Copy letters from Plaintiff to Defendants	20th August 1988

Dated the 20th   **day of**   May   , 1988 .

NOTICE TO INSPECT

Take notice that the documents in the above list, other than those listed in Part 2 of Schedule 1 [and Schedule 2], may be inspected at [the office of the Solicitor of the above-named (⁷) POPP, LEES AND STONE, 23 HALTERGATE,NOTTINGHAM
]

(*7*) Plaintiff(s) *or* Defendant(s) *(insert address) or as may be.*

on the   20th   **day of**   June   , 1988   , between the hours of 9.30 a.m. and 5.00 p.m.

(8) Defendant(s) *(or Plaintiff(s))* C.D.

To the (⁸) Defendant

and his   Solicitor

Served the   20th   **day of**   May   **1988** ,
by POPP, LEES AND STONE
of 23 HALTERGATE, NOTTINGHAM
Solicitor   for the Plaintiff

The objects of discovery are further assisted by the procedure known as "discovery by interrogatories."[36] Interrogatories are methods of eliciting information relevant to the action. Some interrogatories may be served without a court order, that is those relating to any matter in question between the parties which are necessary either for disposing fairly of the case or for saving costs.[37] Further, a party may apply to the court for an order giving him or her leave to serve any interrogatories on the other party relating to any matter in question between the parties.[38] Interrogatories are to be answered within 28 days of service.[39]

Objections may be made to such requests for information. The person on whom interrogatories without order are served may apply to the court within 14 days of service to have them varied or withdrawn, the court on such an application making whatever order it thinks fit.[40] A copy of the proposed ordered interrogatories must be served on the other party with the summons by which the application is made.[41] It is at the stage of hearing objections that issues relating to privilege will be considered. If the answers to the interrogatories are provided, but are insufficient, the request can be renewed. If an order is not complied with, the court has the power, if it thinks fit, to order that the action is dismissed or that the defence is struck out and judgment entered accordingly.[42]

A new power was given to the courts in 1970 to assist a party who wished to discover whether or not he or she had a case by acquiring information from the potential defendant. Now contained in the Supreme Court Act 1981 s.33(2), this provision permits a person who appears to be likely to be a party to a personal injuries claim to request the court to order discovery of any documents relevant to the issue held by another potential party.[43]

8. Payment into Court[44]

At any stage of the action after the issue of a writ, a defendant may pay money to the court in attempted satisfaction of the plaintiff's claim. The plaintiff may then choose whether to accept the amount paid in and discontinue the action, or carry on the action in the hope of obtaining a greater sum at trial. The penalty for the plaintiff is that he or she will normally bear all the costs of the action from the date of the payment in unless awarded a sum in excess of the amount the defendant has paid in.[45]

This is a very useful procedure for a defendant who may use it either to protect himself or herself from a zealous plaintiff who wants to have the "day in court" or to apply pressure to accept a sum in settlement rather than risk a heavy bill in costs. It is important to stress two points. First, that the plaintiff

---

[36] R.S.C., Ord. 26, as amended by the Rules of the Supreme Court (Amendment No. 4) Rules 1989 (S.I. 1989, No. 2427).

[37] *Ibid*. r. 1(1).

[38] *Ibid*. r. 1(2).

[39] *Ibid*. r. 2(1).

[40] *Ibid*. r. 3(2).

[41] *Ibid*. r. 4(1).

[42] *Ibid*. rr. 5, 6.

[43] Further, plaintiffs in personal injuries actions must have provided with their statement of claim a medical report and a statement of the special damages claimed: R.S.C., Ord. 18, r. 12.

[44] See pp. 476, 501 above; Jacob (1987), pp. 117–119 and O'Hare and Hill (1990), Chap. 16.

[45] The matter of costs is within the discretion of the court, see above, p. 472.

must "take it or leave it"—the sum cannot be accepted and the action continued. Second, the judge is not told of the payment in until the questions of liability and damages have been settled.[46]

In the case of a claim for a liquidated sum, the plaintiff's decision is not likely to be difficult. Where the sum is unliquidated the inherent uncertainties of the value of the claim, the difficulties of proof, the desirability of money in hand will all combine to make the choice much harder.

D. PRE-TRIAL REMEDIES[47]

Pre-trial remedies are "designed to deal with the position of the parties pending the trial, to maintain as far as possible the *status quo ante* and to preserve, protect and where necessary enhance the rights and interests of the parties in the inevitable interval between the start of the proceedings and the trial."[48] There are many remedies available, but perhaps the three most significant are the interlocutory injunction, the Mareva injunction and Anton Piller orders.

Interlocutory injunction[49]

The significance of the interlocutory injunction is not only that it is a speedy and effective method of preserving the *status quo* prior to a trial, but also that the decision of the judge on the granting of an injunction is often taken by the parties as an indication of what the trial judge would do, and therefore the proceedings may go no further.[50]

An interlocutory injunction is usually negative in form, that is to restrain the defendant from doing something, rather than mandatory, that is requiring an act to be done.[51] It is effective because a breach of an injunction is a contempt of court, which is punishable by imprisonment, fine and sequestration of property, as appropriate. Further, the injunction does not just affect the parties to the action, it also applies to anyone knowing of it and its terms. Third parties then are under an obligation to observe its terms at least so that steps amounting to a breach are not taken, under the penalty of contempt of court.[52]

Such an injunction can be granted in either High Court or county court proceedings.[53] It is usually applied for on the basis of the other party being informed and thus able to challenge the issue of the injunction. However, in an emergency it may be applied for and granted *ex parte*.[54]

---

[46] R.S.C., Ord. 22, r. 7. If the judge is told inadvertently he or she must decide whether to continue the case or order a retrial.

[47] See Jacob (1987), pp. 132–147 and O'Hare and Hill (1990), Chap. 14.

[48] Jacob (1987), p. 132.

[49] The jurisdiction for the grant of such an injunction arises under the Supreme Court Act 1981, s.37, and see R.S.C., Ord. 29.

[50] See O'Hare and Hill (1990), p. 318.

[51] *Bonner* v. *G.W. Railway* (1883) 24 Ch.D. 1; *Locabail International Finance Ltd.* v. *Agroexport* [1986] 1 All E.R. 901.

[52] *Hubbard* v. *Woodfield* (1913) 57 S.J. 729; *Seaward* v. *Paterson* [1897] 1 Ch. 545.

[53] Supreme Court Act 1981, s.37; County Court Act 1984, s.38; R.S.C., Ord. 29; C.C.R, Ords. 13, 29. The procedure in county court cases is slightly different from that in the High Court, see Blackford (1989), pp. 81–82.

[54] R.S.C., Ord. 29, r. 1(1), (2). An injunction can usually only be applied for after the issue of a writ, except in cases of urgency: R.S.C., Ord 29, r. 1(3).

An interlocutory injunction will be granted if the principles laid down in *American Cyanamid Co.* v. *Ethicon Ltd.*[55] are satisfied. First the plaintiff must establish that there is a good arguable claim to the right which is to be protected. Secondly, the plaintiff must show that there is a serious question to be tried. Thirdly, the grant depends upon which way the balance of convenience lies.[56]

Mareva injunctions

The Mareva injunction[57] is a specialised form of interlocutory injunction used to prevent not only a foreign defendant transferring assets abroad and thus out of the jurisdiction and defeating an action, but also to prevent a defendant within the jurisdiction transferring assets abroad or concealing them in England and Wales.[58]

The injunction is effective because it is swift and secret and not only does it act against the defendant, who would be in contempt of court for breach, but also against innocent third parties. The main advantage of this is that it applies to banks through which transfer of assets is most likely to take place, especially in an age of the computerised transfer of funds.[59] The third party has a right to be entitled to be paid all reasonable expenses and costs, thus having a right of set-off in connection with an account which has become the subject of a Mareva injunction.[60]

Such an injunction may be granted in either the High Court or the county court.[61] A Mareva injunction is usually applied for *ex parte*, so that the opponent cannot defeat its effect consequent upon notice of an application. The plaintiff must then show a good arguable case, must make full and frank disclosure of all the facts that the judge will need to know, including in particular information of the existence of assets that are desired to be the object of the injunction, and must make clear the grounds for believing that without an injunction there is a real risk of any judgment in his or her favour not being satisfied. As with all injunctions, the plaintiff must provide an

---

[55] [1975] A.C. 396.

[56] The balance of convenience means that: (1) if damages are an adequate remedy and the defendant is able to pay them, no injunction will be granted; (2) if the plaintiff's undertaking as to damages, that is the promise to pay the opponent's expenses if he or she fails to establish a right to the injunction, is adequate and payable by the plaintiff, the injunction will be granted; (3) the court will desire to maintain the *status quo*, thus an injunction may well issue; (4) the court will take other factors, including social and economic factors, into account in determining whether it is appropriate to grant an injunction; (5) the relative strength of the parties' cases is a factor of last resort: see O'Hare and Hill (1990), pp. 319–320. There are exceptions to the principles established in *American Cyanamid*, see *ibid.* pp. 320–324.

[57] So called after the second case in which it was granted: *Mareva Compania Naviera S.A.* v. *International Bulk Carriers S.A., The Mareva* [1975] 2 Lloyd's Rep. 509.

[58] *The Supreme Court Practice 1991*, para. 29/1/20, and Jacob (1987), pp. 136–138, at 137. It may be issued post trial. There are also analogous powers in criminal proceedings, that is confiscation orders under the Drug Trafficking Offences Act 1986 and the Criminal Justice Act 1988, see *Halsbury's Law of England*, Vol. 11(2), paras. 1284–1325 and D. Feldman, *Criminal Confiscation Orders—The New Law* (1988).

[59] For the full effect, see *The Supreme Court Practice 1991*, para. 29/1/22.

[60] Jacob (1987), p. 138.

[61] Supreme Court Act 1981, s.37; County Courts Act 1984, s.38; R.S.C., Ord. 29; C.C.R., Ords. 13, 29; see also Matrimonial Causes Act 1973, s.37.

undertaking as to damages, that is the ability to cover the expenses of the defendant should the plaintiff's case ultimately fail.[62]

Anton Piller orders

The Anton Piller order,[63] which is a special form of mandatory injunction, derives from the inherent power of the court to make an order for the detention or preservation of property which is the subject matter of a cause, and of documents and articles relating to it.[64] The order often empowers the plaintiff to enter the defendant's premises and search for and seize material documents and articles, but, as it is not a search warrant,[65] no force may be used in entering premises. The sanction for failure to obey is contempt of court.

Such an order may be granted in High Court or county court proceedings. The application is *ex parte*, that is without notice to the defendant, for obvious reasons. The plaintiff must provide evidence describing the premises and the relevant property or documents and showing some strong evidence that serious harm or serious injustice will be done if the order is not made.[66] As usual, the plaintiff must make an undertaking as to damages.

Other pre-trial remedies

Other remedies include[67] the High Court power to make interlocutory receivership orders,[68] the High Court or county court power to make interlocutory orders relating to property relevant to an action,[69] the limited power to prevent a defendant leaving the jurisdiction,[70] and the High Court or county court power to make an order requiring an interim payment on account of any damages, debt or other sum which a defendant may be held liable to pay.[71]

---

[62] O'Hare and Hill (1990), p. 319. As to applications for discharge or variation, see, *ibid*. pp. 283–284.

[63] So called after the case which approved the order: *Anton Piller K.G.* v. *Manufacturing Processes Ltd.* [1976] Ch. 55.

[64] *The Supreme Court Practice 1991*, pp. 516–520, at p. 516 and Jacob (1987), pp. 139–141, at p. 139 and see R.S.C., Ord. 29, rr. 2, 3; C.C.R., Ord. 13, r. 7.

[65] See below p. 602.

[66] O'Hare and Hill (1990), p. 333.

[67] For further remedies, see Jacob (1987), pp. 143–147 and O'Hare and Hill (1990), pp. 335–345.

[68] Supreme Court Act 1981, s.37, see O'Hare and Hill (1990), pp. 335–336.

[69] As mentioned as part of the jurisdictional background to Anton Piller orders, see R.S.C., Ord. 29, rr. 2, 2A, 3; C.C.R., Ord. 13, r. 7.

[70] See Jacob (1987), pp. 141–142.

[71] O'Hare and Hill (1990), pp. 338–345; Jacob (1987), pp. 142–143.

CHAPTER 12

PRE-HEARING: TRIBUNALS

IN the preceding chapter we used the actions in the county court and the Queen's Bench Division as examples of civil procedure. For this chapter there is no standard model. Generalisation about tribunal procedure is almost impossible in the face of widely divergent practice in different tribunals[1] and there is no accepted pattern. However, there are certain common principles and objectives in tribunal adjudication and there are common procedural problems to be solved. This chapter sets out to examine these objectives and the way in which they influence procedure prior to a tribunal hearing; the common problems which procedural rules must attempt to solve; the amount of legal advice or help which is available; and finally, the pre-hearing procedure adopted in two particular tribunals as illustrative of the various solutions designed to meet the needs of individual claimants and individual tribunals.

A. THE COMMON OBJECTIVES

The starting point of any discussion must be the Franks Report[2] and its assertion that tribunals should display three common characteristics: openness, fairness and impartiality.[3] It is clear that the attainment of each of these objectives will have implications for the procedural rules adopted.

In requiring that tribunals should be open, the Committee intended that the proceedings should be given sufficient publicity so that they were known to those who might need to make use of them. In addition, it was stated that the essential reasoning underlying decisions should be made known to the parties.[4]

Openness means more than the adoption of a rule of procedure that, save where the personal interests of the claimant would be prejudiced, tribunal hearings should be conducted in public. It signifies rather a notion of availability or accessibility—that tribunal adjudication is open to all those who might have a problem lying within the jurisdiction of a particular tribunal. In order that a tribunal is *accessible* to the public, each citizen needs to be aware of his or her right to use the tribunal where appropriate[5]; the

---

[1] The various types of tribunal and their jurisdiction are discussed above, pp. 34–40.

[2] Report of the Committee on Administrative Tribunals and Enquiries (Cmnd. 218, 1957).

[3] *Ibid*. In particular, paras. 23–25, 41–42.

[4] *Ibid*., para. 98.

[5] This goes back to the question of ensuring that problems are recognised and identified accurately, see Chap. 8.

information given in official publications and forms must be comprehensible; tribunal hearings need to be conveniently located; advice and assistance needs to be available either through the legal advice scheme or through other agencies; and the procedure to be followed both prior to and during the hearing should be sufficiently clear that the claimant can follow it and understand the implications of seeking a tribunal hearing. Establishing the right procedural rules is but one aspect of making tribunals accessible to the public.

The objectives of fairness and impartiality are closely linked, and are especially important to a system which does not have the weight and authority enjoyed by the courts in the public esteem. Naturally, the claimant must be assured that the adjudication is even-handed or he or she will dismiss the whole proceedings as unfair, but the procedure to be followed is also crucial. Every claimant will judge the fairness of the tribunal (and hence assess its credibility and reputation) by reference to the way in which the case has progressed and the extent to which he or she has been able to put his or her own side of the argument in the knowledge of the case that has to be met. Procedural fairness—the feeling induced in the claimant that he or she has had "a fair crack of the whip"—is absolutely essential and, according to the Franks Committee, depends upon, ". . . the adoption of a clear procedure which enables parties to know their rights, to present their case fully and to know the case which they have to meet."[6]

As well as displaying these three characteristics, tribunals are also expected to offer informal, cheap and quick adjudication, providing a contrast to the procedures of the High Court.[7] The problem lies in achieving an acceptable standard of decision-making based on adequate information and argument, without rendering tribunals as formal, expensive and slow as the civil courts.

Before a tribunal case reaches a hearing it must be prepared for adjudication and the parties must be in a position to participate fully at the hearing. There are, broadly, three stages in pre-hearing procedure which might be termed, "knowing your rights," "knowing the ropes," and "knowing the case."

B. "KNOWING YOUR RIGHTS"—IDENTIFYING THE TRIBUNAL

Courts do not have to advertise. There is a general awareness that civil courts are the venue for settling disputes, (although there may be some difficulty for individuals in perceiving that they have a problem capable of legal settlement), and as to criminal courts, defendants have little choice about whether they wish to avail themselves of the court's jurisdiction! In respect of tribunals, the first difficulty for the parties may lie in realising that there is a body with jurisdiction over their grievance whose assistance might be invoked. The various tribunals need to be sufficiently well publicised so as to alert people to their existence and powers.

In general, individuals may take their case to a tribunal as a result of a decision of a Government department which affects them (a citizen/state

---

[6] Franks Report (1957) para. 42.
[7] For a comparison between courts and tribunals, see R. E. Wraith and P. G. Hutchesson, *Administrative Tribunals* (1973), Chap. 10. *Cf.* above, pp. 39–40.

dispute), or as a result of experiencing an event or series of events which the law places within the jurisdiction of a particular tribunal (normally a citizen/citizen dispute). Into the former category would fall appeals to Social Security Appeal Tribunals[8]; to the General Commissioners of Income Tax[9]; to Vaccine Damage Tribunals[10]; to the Immigration Appeal Tribunal[11] and many others. Into the latter category would fall applications to an Industrial Tribunal[12]; to a Family Practitioner Committee[13]; to a Rent Assessment Committee.[14] This division is significant because in a citizen/state dispute the individual concerned may be notified of the existence of the tribunal and of the right of appeal at the time that the decision is notified. Thus, the claimant knows of the right of appeal and, usually, how to make application. He or she may not know what are the implications of an appeal or precisely how to go about preparing the case, but he or she is given a start.

In respect of citizen/citizen disputes it is for the applicant to realise that if he or she is unfairly dismissed, or maltreated by a doctor, or the rent is too high, that there is an opportunity to pursue the grievance in a tribunal. Some tribunals must, therefore, give special consideration to how they can make the public aware of their jurisdiction.

1. The Availability of Legal Advice

With very limited exceptions, legal aid is not available for *representation* at tribunal hearings.[15] The legal advice scheme, however, was intended to provide a source of advice for the public on matters relating to tribunals and how to use them.[16] The legal advice scheme has already been considered in detail,[17] but you will recall that a solicitor is permitted to give advice under the scheme to any suitably qualified applicant, "on the application of English law to any particular circumstances which have arisen in relation to the person seeking the advice and as to the steps which that person might appropriately take. . . ."[18]

It has been a source of regret to the Lord Chancellor's Advisory Committee on Legal Aid that the green form scheme is not used more extensively for

---

[8] Where the original decision is made by an adjudication officer at the Department of Social Security, see above, pp. 60–63.

[9] Against an income tax assessment, the tribunal being arranged in accordance with the Taxes Management Act 1970.

[10] Against the decision of an adjudication officer that the claim of a person under the Vaccine Damage Payments Act 1979 is disallowed.

[11] Either against the decision of an immigration adjudicator or, in certain cases, directly against decisions of an immigration officer under the Immigration Act 1971.

[12] See above, pp. 57–59.

[13] Where complaints may be made about services provided by a general practitioner to his or her patients.

[14] Rent Assessment Committees exercise jurisdiction under Part I of the Housing Act 1988 in determining rents for assured periodic tenancies; this is to replace its jurisdiction under the Rent Act 1977 to review the decisions of rent officers as to fair rents for protected tenancies. They have also exercised the jurisdiction formerly exercised by rent tribunals: Housing Act 1980, s.72.

[15] See above, pp. 507–508.

[16] In 1969, the Law Society asserted that the introduction of a legal advice scheme would encourage solicitors to operate in areas of unmet legal need and ensure that adequate legal services would be provided. See also, above, pp. 455–456.

[17] In chap. 9, above, pp. 443–458.

[18] Legal Aid Act 1988, s.2(2).

advice on tribunal matters,[19] but that is part of the wider problem of encouraging those who could benefit from the green form scheme to get along to a solicitor's office.[20] There was some evidence that claims for payment by solicitors who had undertaken welfare benefits work on the green form scheme were refused by officials in some legal aid area offices.[21] The Attorney-General subsequently confirmed that matters affecting entitlement to welfare benefits were matters of law to which the scheme applied.[22]

It is difficult to quantify precisely the number of tribunal cases dealt with by solicitors under the green form scheme. The study by Genn and Genn of representation at tribunals found that solicitors were consulted by 4 per cent. of appellants before Social Security Appeal Tribunals, 27 per cent. of appellants to Immigration Adjudicators, 36 per cent. of applicants to Industrial Tribunals and over 60 per cent. of patients applying to Mental Health Review Tribunals.[23] It is Social Security Appeal Tribunals that have by far the highest case load,[24] and the contribution of solicitors here under the green form scheme or otherwise is clearly very limited.

2. Other Sources of Advice

The agencies discussed in Chapter 9 (CABx, independent advice centres, neighbourhood law centres, Trade Unions, etc.) are available to offer help to individuals, but their work has been supplemented by the growth of specialist groups. Some of these are attached to large, generalist agencies, some exist independently.[25]

Although Citizens Advice Bureaux have been prominent in developing tribunal assistance and representation, no standard pattern of organisation has emerged. Instead, individual schemes have grown up according to the particular circumstances in different parts of the country. Inevitably, the availability of resources has had a great influence on the type of provision made and its effectiveness. In the West Midlands, a specially funded scheme set up an individual tribunal unit independent of the bureaux in the area, but offering training and support to them and their clients.[26] In Newcastle upon Tyne, a smaller unit was situated within the bureau dealing specifically with cases referred on to it through the bureau. In Chapeltown, Leeds, a Tribunal

---

[19] See, *e.g. 26th Legal Aid Annual Reports* [1975–76], p. 58.
[20] See above, pp. 416–419.
[21] *LAG Bulletin*, July 1983, pp. 1, 5.
[22] H.C. Deb. Vol. 45, col. 604, July 11, 1983; *LAG Bulletin*, August 1983, p. 5. See *Legal Aid Handbook 1990*, p. 32.
[23] H. Genn and Y. Genn, *The Effectiveness of Representation at Tribunals* (L.C.D., 1989), pp. 15, 30, 39, 56. See further on this study, below, pp. 571–572, 736–748. Only 14 per cent. of green forms relate to the subjects of landlord and tenant, housing, employment, welfare benefits and immigration and nationality: *39th Legal Aid Annual Reports* [1988–89], Appendix 1F, p. 20.
[24] See above, pp. 45–49.
[25] A survey of some of these specialist groups is contained in, R. Lawrence, *Tribunal Representation, The Role of Advice and Advocacy Services* (1980).
[26] The original project was jointly funded by the National Association of Citizens Advice Bureaux and the EEC Action Against Poverty Programme. The report on the project and its significance for tribunal advice and advocacy services generally is E. Kessler, *et al.*, *Combatting Poverty: CABx, Claimants and Tribunals* (1980). The unit now acts as a support unit for West Midland CABx, but organises training courses more widely and provides a national information service through a telephone hotline, *The Adviser* magazine and the Lawtel data base: see J. Citron, *Citizens Advice Bureaux* (1989), pp. 54–56.

Assistance Unit offered a service to claimants through the local bureau.[27] In other areas, salaried welfare rights workers have been appointed to provide expertise for a group of bureaux. The universal experience has been that contact with any form of expertise, however provided, has raised the general level of advice-giving in respect of tribunal matters by the ordinary volunteer in the bureau.[28] This, together with the greatly increased demand for assistance with social security and employment problems, has enhanced the value of the CAB service to the general public.

The Free Representation Unit is an independent group, now based in Gray's Inn, which offers an advocacy service in cases referred to it by other advice agencies. In fact, this Unit may not be involved at the pre-hearing stage and relies heavily on the referring agency for the initial advice to the claimant and preparation of the case. The Unit employs two salaried case workers, one for social security cases and one for employment cases, and there is an Administrator, whose salary is paid directly by the Bar Council. These support a hundred or so volunteer representatives, many of whom are Bar students or pupil barristers, some qualified lawyers.[29]

Other independent groups[30] have based themselves in advice centres offering a service to clients of that centre and those referred by other statutory or voluntary agencies.

The advice available is, therefore, dependent partly upon local initiatives and there is certainly no national coverage.

3. SEEKING ADVICE

A study of tribunal representation conducted for the Lord Chancellor's Department[31] looked at the proportion of appellants before four tribunals (Social Security Appeal Tribunals, Immigration Adjudicators, Industrial Tribunals and Mental Health Review Tribunals) who sought advice before the hearing. From information drawn from case files,[32] it appeared that only 22 per cent.[33] of S.S.A.T. appellants sought advice before the hearing.[34] The corresponding figures for the other three were much higher: 80 per cent. for

---

[27] *Tribunal Assistance, the Chapeltown Experience* (NACAB Occasional Paper No. 14, 1982), describes and evaluates the scheme.

[28] See Lawrence, *op. cit.* at p. 75. *Chapeltown Citizens' Advice Bureau, Leeds, Tribunal Assistance Unit, Progress Report—First Two years* (NACAB Occasional Paper No. 6. 1979), at pp. 7–8.

[29] *FRU Prospectus*, see also the FRU's Annual Reports; M. Westgate, *Counsel*, Vol. 2, No. 1, Michaelmas/Autumn 1986, p. 12; H. Brooke Q.C. and P. Leaver, *ibid.* p. 13; General Council of the Bar, *Quality of Justice: The Bar's Response* (1989), pp. 72–76 (indicating the Bar Council's wish for FRU services to be expanded); N. Lieven, *Counsel*, February 1991, p. 22. FRU work has also been developed in Birmingham.

[30] *e.g.* Birmingham Tribunal Representation Unit; Walsall Advice and Representation Project; South Wales Anti-Poverty Action Centre.

[31] H. Genn and Y. Genn, *The Effectiveness of Representation at Tribunals* (L.C.D., 1989), discussed by R. Young (1990) 8 C.J.Q. 16 and T. Mullen (1990) 53 M.L.R. 230.

[32] Likely to understate the position.

[33] Of these, 31 per cent. went to a C.A.B., 16 per cent. a solicitor, and the rest a wide variety of sources including trade unions, tribunal units, law centres, welfare rights centres, social workers, general advice centres, unemployment centres, pressure groups and church groups.

[34] Genn and Genn (1989), pp. 13–15. There were considerable variations according to region and type of case: *ibid.* pp. 15–18.

Immigration Adjudicators,[35] 70 per cent. for Industrial Tribunals,[36] and 64 per cent. for M.H.R.T.s,[37] again with regional and other variations. The study suggested that failure to seek advice (or representation) often stemmed from ignorance about the nature of appeals (ranging from over-confidence to bewilderment). In other cases, appellants who recognised a need for advice either did not know where to go or could not obtain or pay for representation.[38]

C. "KNOWING THE ROPES"—MAKING APPLICATION TO A TRIBUNAL

Rules of procedure begin to take effect when an applicant decides to invoke the jurisdiction of the tribunal by making an application for a hearing. Prior to that he or she may have tried to effect a settlement of the grievance in the same way as would have been done in a civil matter, but because a significant proportion of tribunal matters concern the correctness of a decision made by a Government department the scope of settlement is fairly limited.[39] The means of expressing disagreement with such a decision is not to complain about it to the individual responsible but to commence an appeal to the appropriate tribunal. In other cases, particularly where an application to an Industrial Tribunal may be in prospect, there are pre-hearing procedures designed to secure a mutually acceptable resolution of the problem.[40]

In relation to the making of an application there are three procedural aspects to be considered. What form should the application take? What information should it contain? Within what time limit, if any, should it be made? These are questions which have been considered and answered in the civil courts, and they are obviously questions which are common to all tribunals. It would be tempting to assume that a Code of Procedure could be devised to encompass all tribunals and make specific provision for these and other points. The Franks Committee[41] moved towards this position with a recommendation that a Council on Tribunals should formulate the procedural rules for each tribunal, based on principles common to all tribunals but tailored to suit the needs of the particular tribunal.[42] In the event, the Tribunals and Inquiries Act 1958 merely provided that the Council on Tribunals (established by the Act) should be consulted when procedural

---

[35] *Ibid.* pp. 29–32; the main sources were U.K.I.A.S. and solicitors.

[36] *Ibid.* pp. 38–43; the main sources were solicitors and trade unions (appellants), outside or in-house lawyers (respondents).

[37] *Ibid.* pp. 56–57; dominated by solicitors.

[38] *Ibid.* pp. 59–62, 221–222.

[39] This is dependent upon the procedures of the Department concerned. In social security matters an application to a tribunal ensures an initial review of the decision by an adjudication officer, and there is some evidence to suggest that the intervention of an advice agency can get "mistakes" straightened out without recourse to a tribunal: Chapeltown Tribunal Assistance Unit, *Progress Report—First Two Years* (see above, n. 26), at pp. 11, 12; Genn and Genn (1989), pp. 136–137.

[40] In the Industrial Tribunal procedure, emphasis is placed upon conciliation and the mediating role of the Advisory Conciliation and Arbitration Service, although this usually occurs after the application has been made.

[41] Report of the Committee on Administrative Tribunals and Enquiries (Cmnd. 218, 1957).

[42] *Ibid.*, paras. 63–64.

rules were made in respect of certain specified tribunals.[43] We shall return to the role of the Council on Tribunals in procedural matters later in the chapter.

What form should an application to a tribunal take? Many tribunals require the completion of a printed form—a method of application which can either assist or hinder the applicant. He or she may be deterred from pursuing the case by the complexity or unintelligibility of the questions, but will at least be shown the information required and sometimes directed towards a source of help and advice.[44] Again, the nature of the dispute may have an effect on procedure in that in citizen/state disputes the jurisdiction is likely to be automatic and the applicant will not have to show the grounds which bring the matters within the tribunal's jurisdiction. In citizen/citizen disputes the applicant's first job will be to establish that the case falls within the tribunal's jurisdiction and a printed form with appropriate questions will be helpful both to tribunal and applicant.

The different procedural approaches of Social Security Appeal Tribunals and Industrial Tribunals are illustrated later in the chapter.[45] In many cases the applicant has the opportunity of including matters for the consideration of the tribunal in the application, or in a subsequent statement. Ultimately, he or she may make representations at the hearing (if one is held)[46] and it is likely to be the style and conduct of the hearing which determines how much advance information is required by the tribunal.

All tribunals find it necessary to impose time limits within which an application must be submitted, and some impose limits on later stages of the procedure.[47] The balance has to be struck between allowing a tribunal to make a speedy determination in a dispute (based on evidence which is not too far distant in time) and ensuring that an applicant is not unduly prejudiced by the limit. The Council on Tribunals have taken a particular interest in this matter and have welcomed the extension of time limits in some tribunals.[48] In addition it is desirable that there should be a procedural rule allowing for applications to be made out of time where there is good cause.[49]

---

[43] Now Tribunals and Inquiries Act 1971, s.10. Procedural rules are normally contained in a statutory instrument made by the Minister whose Department is responsible for the particular tribunal. The Council has published Model Rules of Procedure (Cm. 1434, 1991) for the guidance of those who draft such rules.

[44] e.g. the form of originating application to an Industrial Tribunal states that a Trade Union or C.A.B. may be able to give advice, information, and help in filling the form. D.S.S. and S.S.A.T. leaflets include similar advice (see Leaflets N.I. 245, *How to Appeal* and N.I. 260, *A Guide to Reviews and Appeals*).

[45] See below, pp. 576–594.

[46] Not all tribunals will hold an oral hearing. The Social Security Commissioner may determine an appeal without a hearing, as may a Rent Assessment Committee. Needless to say, where there is to be no hearing the written submissions have to be much fuller.

[47] An application to a Social Security Appeal Tribunal must be made within three months of the decision appealed against (to 1986 it had been 28 days); an application to an Industrial Tribunal in respect of unfair dismissal within three months of dismissal. Unfortunately there are no time limits on the hearings and the Council on Tribunals has regularly expressed disquiet at the long backlog of cases awaiting hearing by various tribunals.

[48] The Annual Report of the Council on Tribunals, 1980/81, at p. 23.

[49] e.g. for industrial tribunals, the claim can be presented "within such further period as the tribunal considers reasonable in a case where it is satisfied that it was not reasonably practicable for the complaint to be presented before the end of the period of three months": Employment Protection (Consolidation) Act 1978, s.67(2). See, e.g. *Palmer* v. *Southend-on-Sea Borough Council* [1984] I.C.R. 372 (question what is reasonably practicable essentially

D. "KNOWING THE CASE"—THE PRE-HEARING EXCHANGE OF INFORMATION

"... citizens should know in good time the case which they will have to meet, whether the issue to be heard by the tribunal is one between citizen and administration or citizen and citizen. ... We do not suggest that the procedure should be formalised to the extent of requiring documents in the nature of legal pleadings. What is needed is that the citizen should receive in good time beforehand a document setting out the main points of the opposing case. It should not be necessary ... to require the parties to adhere rigidly at the hearing to the case as previously set out, provided always that the interests of another party are not prejudiced by such flexibility."[50]

The amount of pre-hearing activity and the precision with which the parties are required to formulate and disclose their respective cases can vary very considerably from tribunal to tribunal. Before 1984, the applicant was given the greatest latitude in Social Security Appeal Tribunals. He or she was not required to produce any specific grounds of appeal or indicate what his or her argument might be. This was then changed, and the appeal now must "contain particulars of the grounds on which it is made or given."[51] It is not clear how much detail is necessary.[52] The applicant will receive from the adjudication officer a full statement of facts, submissions, statutory authorities and Commissioner's decisions.[53] This document will also be sent to members of the tribunal and is likely to form the basis of the hearing.

Disclosure in social security tribunals certainly ensures that the applicant knows the case to be met, but it can to an extent leave the adjudication officer in the dark.

The parties before a Rent Assessment Committee are more likely to have had a full opportunity of finding out about the case.[54] Where the issue concerns the determination of a fair rent for a protected tenancy, before the matter can come before a Rent Assessment Committee, application must be made to a rent officer. This application can be made by either landlord or tenant or both jointly, but if the application is not joint, the other party is invited to take part in consultations with the rent officer and the applicant to consider what rent should be registered.[55] Only if one party is dissatisfied with the rent which is registered can he or she appeal to the Rent Assessment Committee, who then invite both parties to make written or oral representa-

---

one of fact for the tribunal); *Machine Tool Industry Research Association* v. *Simpson* [1988] I.C.R. 558.

[50] Report of the Committee on Administrative Tribunals and Enquiries (Cmnd. 218, 1957), at pp. 17–18.

[51] Social Security (Adjudication) Regulations 1986 (S.I. 1986 No. 2218), reg. 3(5). It must also include sufficient particulars to enable the decision appealed against to be identified: S.I. 1990 No. 603, amending reg. 3(5).

[52] see *C.P.A.G.'s Income Support, The Social Fund and Family Credit: The Legislation*, Commentary by J. Mesher (1989), pp. 341–342. Mesher notes that "the instructions given to Adjudication Officers are that if some reasons, however poorly expressed, are given for an appeal it should be accepted." If the claimant refuses to do so, the matter is put before a chairman of tribunals.

[53] See below, p. 578, where an example is reproduced.

[54] See generally R. E. Megarry, *The Rent Acts* (1988), Vol. 1, Chaps. 24 and 25, Vol. 3, Chaps. 16 and 17; J. E. Martin, *Residential Security* (1989), Chaps. 11 and 15.

[55] Rent Act 1977, Sched. 11, para. 3, as amended.

tions. By the time of the hearing, both parties will have had the opportunity to familiarise themselves with all the circumstances and the representations made by each of them. Subject to a few exceptions, no new protected tenancies can be granted after the commencement of the Housing Act 1988. The Rent Assessment Committee does, however, have jurisdiction under Part I of the Act to fix the rent of an assured tenancy where the landlord proposes a rent increase.[56] Here, the tenant applies directly to the committee, and the committee then serves a notice on both parties specifying a period of not less than seven days during which either written representations or a request to make oral representations may be made by that party to the committee. The committee may make such inquiry (if any) as it thinks fit.[57] The tenant must complete an application form providing factual details about the premises,[58] but there is no requirement for the tenant to indicate why he or she objects to the proposed rent increase. Accordingly, the parties here may be less well-informed by the time of the hearing than in cases where the committee's function is that of reviewing the decision of a rent officer.

A third approach is adopted in the Industrial Tribunal. The forms by which an applicant makes the application and the respondent indicates an intention to defend the case, require a certain minimum amount of information. In particular, the applicant is required to state the grounds of the application and particulars thereof.[59] This ensures at the outset that both sides will have some idea of the case to be met. Thereafter there are opportunities for both formal and informal exchange of information.[60]

Formal procedures exist whereby the tribunal may, at the request of one of the parties or of its own volition, require either side to provide further particulars of its case or risk losing the case.[61] These formal procedures reinforce informal requests for information which either party may make of the other. In addition, the tribunal has the power to order discovery of documents.[62] In race and sex discrimination cases there is also a "question-and-answer procedure," analogous to interrogatories in civil procedure.[63] Standard questionnaires are available for the purposes of this procedure.[64]

A new procedure was introduced in 1980 which has the effect of disclosing information to the parties. The pre-hearing assessment is an attempt to reduce the number of cases going to a hearing by bringing the parties

[56] Housing Act 1988, s.13(4)(a), 14. There are certain other matters also within its jurisdiction under Part I.
[57] Rent Assessment Committee (England and Wales) Regulations 1971 (S.I. 1971 No. 1065), reg. 2A, inserted by S.I. 1988 No. 2200.
[58] Prescribed by the Assured Tenancies and Agricultural Occupancies (Forms) Regulations 1988 (S.I. 1988 No. 2203).
[59] Strictly speaking, there is no requirement that the printed forms be used so long as the required information is given in another form, e.g. a letter. However, it is crucial that the grounds and particulars are given, so the form is usually regarded as helpful.
[60] For procedure in Industrial Tribunals generally see, I. T. Smith and J. C. Wood, Industrial Law (4th ed., 1989), Chap. 6, pp. 251–264; M. J. Goodman, Industrial Tribunals' Practice and Procedure (4th ed., 1987); Tribunal practice and procedure (I.D.S. Employment Law Handbook, 45, 1989).
[61] Industrial Tribunal (Rules of Procedure) Regulations 1985 (S.I. 1985 No. 16), r. 4(1)(b)(i).
[62] Ibid. r. 4(1)(b)(ii).
[63] Sex Discrimination Act 1975, s.74; Race Relations Act 1976, s.65.
[64] Sex Discrimination (Questions and Replies) Order 1975 (S.I. 1975 No. 2048); Race Relations (Questions and Replies) Order 1977 (S.I. 1977 No. 842).

together, without witnesses, to undergo a review of the application. This obviously operates to expose the case to both sides and although there is no power to strike out an unworthy case there is a possible penalty on costs at the hearing if the tribunal indicates, at the pre-hearing assessment, that there is no reasonable prospect of a successful application or defence.[65] These procedures owe more to the High Court and county court than to other tribunals, but have not overall proved to be a success,[66] and JUSTICE has recommended its abolition.[67] The government intends that they should be replaced by "pre-hearing reviews" which will include a new power for the person or tribunal conducting the review to require a party to pay a deposit of £150 if he or she wishes to continue the proceedings.[68] This last step was opposed by the Council on Tribunals, without success.[69]

Informally, there may be an exchange of information because of the involvement of conciliation officers. All applications and subsequent documents are sent to ACAS[70] and a conciliation officer is under an obligation to attempt a conciliation either at the request of one of the parties, or of his or her own volition.[71] This conciliation may be rejected by the parties but it is likely to lead to some informal exchange of information unless the conciliation officer never even gets his foot in the door. Could this process usefully be adapted to assist settlements in the High Court?

These examples of pre-hearing procedure, necessarily selective, are intended to illustrate three different approaches to the objective set out by the Franks Committee. Full obligatory disclosure by one side; opportunity to disclose by both sides, but no obligation and no penalty for non-disclosure; limited obligatory disclosure by both sides, with opportunities for further disclosure supported by sanctions. Each tribunal would say that it had developed a procedure suited to its own needs.

E. PRE-HEARING PROCEDURE IN TWO TRIBUNALS

We have already contrasted some of the procedural aspects of social security tribunals and industrial tribunals in making general points about procedure. Below we set out two cases which illustrate the progress of a case towards a hearing in a Social Security Appeal Tribunal and an Industrial Tribunal. It was noted at the outset that it is difficult to produce "typical" tribunals for consideration, and it is no easier to produce "typical" cases from a single tribunal. One of the alleged virtues of the tribunal system is its flexibility in dealing with differing circumstances. These examples at least demonstrate the documentation involved and indicate the normal procedure.

---

[65] *Ibid.*, r. 6.
[66] See Smith and Wood (1989), pp. 258–259. There has been a decline in their use; they may make conciliation more difficult.
[67] JUSTICE Report, *Industrial Tribunals* (1987), para. 2.34.
[68] Employment Act 1989, s.20, giving the Secretary of State power to make regulations for pre-hearing reviews.
[69] Annual Report of the Council on Tribunals for 1987–88 (1988–89 H.C. 102), pp. 36–38; Annual Report for 1988–89 (1989–90 H.C. 114), pp. 33–34.
[70] The Advisory Conciliation and Arbitration Service.
[71] Employment Protection (Consolidation) Act 1978, ss.133, 134. See Smith and Wood (1989), pp. 256–258; L. Dickens *et. al.*, *Dismissed* (1985), Chap. 6. In 1988, 68 per cent. of applications notified to conciliation officers were settled or withdrawn without a hearing: ACAS Annual Report 1988, p. 71, Table 13.

1. A SOCIAL SECURITY APPEAL TRIBUNAL

Facts: Mr. Hussein was unemployed, and had back trouble. He was refused invalidity benefit on the ground that, although incapable of his normal occupation, he was capable of light work. He appealed to the Gumby Social Security Appeal Tribunal. The schedule of documents prepared for the hearing comprised—

(1) Form SC1, on which Mr. Hussein claimed invalidity benefit on 21.6.89.

(2) A medical report from an Examining Medical Officer, dated 1.8.89.

(3) A statement taken from Mr. Hussein at the local DSS Office on 5.10.89 in which he stated in part

"I disagree with the medical people's findings because I am still having difficulty with my back and since the medical my condition has got worse. There is nothing at all that I think I can do as I am having difficulty standing and walking and bending."

(4) Job descriptions, provided by the Department of Employment, for (1) Light Labourer/Factory Worker (General), (2) Fee Collection (Toll, Parking) and (3) Garage Forecourt Attendant (Console Operator).

The description for the first of these was as follows:

LIGHT LABOURER/FACTORY WORKER (GENERAL)

Performs one or more manual tasks requiring a minimum of training, little or no previous experience and little physical effort.

Performs one or more of the following or similar tasks in relation to work of a light nature; conveys materials, equipment, goods, etc. about work areas and stacks materials or goods; opens bales, crates or other containers manually; assists in setting up machinery or equipment; prepares equipment such as tools, laboratory apparatus and lamps for use; assists in loading materials onto or into, and unloading finished or processed materials or products from, machinery or equipment; provides general assistance to craftsmen, operators, machine minders, etc. as required; washes or cleans parts, components or finished articles, or crates or similar containers manually; paints or fixes identification markings, labels, etc. on products or containers; clears machine blockages and cleans machinery, equipment and tools; loads and unloads vehicles, trucks, trolleys, etc., keeps work areas tidy and clears waste materials and spillages; disposes of waste materials by bailing, tipping on waste heap, burning, etc.; sweeps and cleans paths, roadways, parking areas, etc.; performs routine tasks in the maintenance of premises and grounds such as rough painting, washing windows and cutting grass.

(5) A second medical report, dated 16.11.89.

(6) Form AT2, which sets out the full facts and the Adjudication Officer's Submission.

At the hearing, unusually, the presenting officer was absent, but the tribunal proceeded nevertheless. The Tribunal allowed the appeal. The record of proceedings was made by the Chairman on Form AT3, which, for convenience, is reproduced here rather than in Chapter 15 on the Tribunal Hearing.

We reproduce Forms AT2 and AT3 below.

Form AT2:

SOCIAL SECURITY APPEAL TRIBUNAL

For hearing on 10.5.90
Appeal Reg No

IN CONFIDENCE

Sheet 30 Line 4

Appeal or Reference to Appeal Tribunal

Benefit: Income Support   Tribunal: DERBY

	Title	Surname	Other Names
Name of Claimant:	Mr.	HUSSEIN	AHMED

Address: 3 WORTLEY STREET, GUMBY

NI No AA 00 00 01 A

1	Appeal received on 30.1.90 against the following decision of the Adjudication Officer (Code No 19513) which was issued on 15.12.89

ADJUDICATION OFFICER'S DECISION

I have reviewed the decision of the Adjudication Officer awarding invalidity benefit from and including 17.10.89. The decision awarded benefit for days after the date of claim and the requirements for entitlement are not satisfied. This is because he is capable of work.

My revised decision is as follows:—

Invalidity benefit is not payable from and including 29.11.89. This is because Mr. Hussein has not proved that he was incapable of work by reason of some specific disease or bodily or mental disablement.

2	Provisions in Acts and Regulations considered by the Adjudication Officer to be relevant

Social Security (Claims and Payments) Regulations, reg. 17(4); Social Security Act 1975, Section 15(1) and 17(1)(a)(ii) and the Social Security (Unemployment, Sickness and Invalidity Benefit) Regulations, reg. 3.

Blue Volume 2.161–2.174 and 1.6426

| 3 | Reported decisions of the Commissioner considered by the Adjudication Officer to be relevant |

R(S) 11/51; R(S) 20/52; R(S) 1/53; R(S) 7/60; R(S) 12/78; R(S) 2/82.

Form AT2 Originals of any documents which are copied in whole or in part will be available at the hearing

Person concerned: HUSSEIN, A

| 4 | Claimant's grounds of appeal dated 29.1.90 |

I wish to appeal against the RMO's decision not to find me entitled to IVB. I hope to supply you with medical evidence to bind up my case.

| 5 | SUMMARY OF FACTS |

1. Mr. Hussein is a 55 year old labourer who became incapable of work on 16.6.88 and received sickness benefit until 28.9.88 and invalidity benefit from 29.9.88. The cause of incapacity was stated by his doctor to be lumbago and hypertension.

2. On 1.8.89 Mr. Hussein was examined by an Examining Medical Officer of the Divisional Medical Office, Department of Social Security. The officer reported that the claimant has had backache on and off for two years and has high blood pressure. No other complaints were found. He was of the opinion that whilst Mr. Hussein was incapable of his normal occupation, he was capable of work within certain limits. These limits were specified as any work which does not involve arduous and physical work. He was found to have full function in his shoulders, arms, hands, slight impairment on climbing stairs, walking, standing, with substantial impairment on bending and climbing ladders.

3. On 18.8.89 Mr. Hussein was advised of the outcome of the examination and asked to see his doctor to discuss the Examining Medical Officer's findings. He was also informed that the Disablement Resettlement Officer at the Job Centre/Employment Office would be available to help him in finding suitable employment. Mr. Hussein failed to call at the Unemployment Benefit Office on the grounds that he did not feel able to do any work.

4. On 5.10.89 Mr. Hussein was interviewed at the local office of the Department of Social Security to obtain full details of his employment and educational background, together with his own assessment of his limitations and reasons why he considered that he was incapable of all work. At this interview the claimant stated that he regards himself as unfit to work.

5. The Adjudication Officer, having considered all the available evidence, concluded that Mr. Hussein was capable of various alternative occupations. As examples she indicated that he was, in her opinion, capable of undertaking the duties of a light labourer, fee collector and garage forecourt attendant.

6. On 8.11.89 Mr. Hussein was examined by a different Medical Officer who was also asked to give an opinion as to the claimant's capacity to undertake the duties involved in the jobs identified by the Adjudication Officer as being suitable alternative occupation.

The Examining Medical Officer was of the same opinion as the first, that Mr. Hussein was capable of work within previously defined limits. He felt that the claimant was capable of performing all the duties in the first job descriptions provided, *e.g.* light labourer.

7. On 4.12.89 the Adjudication Officer disallowed the claim to invalidity benefit from and including 29.11.89.

6	ADJUDICATION OFFICER'S SUBMISSION

1. It is a condition of entitlement to invalidity benefit that a claimant is incapable of work (Social Security Act 1975 Sections 15(1) and 17(1) Section 17(1)(a)(ii) of the Act provides that a day shall not be treated in relation to any person as a day of incapacity unless on that day he is, or is deemed in accordance with regulations to be, incapable of work by reason of some specific disease or bodily or mental disablement. This section of the Act defines work in this context as work which the person can reasonably be expected to do. Regulation 3 of the Social Security (Unemployment, Sickness and Invalidity Benefit) Regulations 1975 provides the circumstances in which a person may be deemed to be incapable of work but it does not assist the claimant in the present case.

2. In decision R(S) 1/53 the Commissioner held that whether a person is incapable of work is a question of fact to be determined bearing in mind Commissioner's decisions as to what that expression means. The certificates of the claimant's own doctor, the reports of the medical officers of the (then) Ministry of Health and any other relevant evidence must be taken into account. There is no question of the Insurance, now Adjudication Officer, being bound to decide in the same way as any particular doctor certifies. In decision R(S) 11/51, a tribunal of three Commissioners explained that "a person is incapable of work within the meaning of the National Insurance Act 1946, Section 11(2)(a)(ii) (now re-enacted as Section 17(1)(a)(ii) of the Social Security Act 1975) if, having regard to his age, education, experience, state of health and other personal factors, there is no work or type of work which he can reasonably be expected to do. By 'work' in this connection we mean remunerative work, that is to say, work whether part-time or whole-time for which an employer would be willing to pay or work as a self-employed person, in some gainful occupation."

In decision R(S) 4/56 the Commissioner held that where doctors disagree, the statutory tribunals have to decide on the balance of probability which of the contrasting opinions is more probably correct.

3. In this case Mr. Hussein had been continuously incapable of work since 16.6.88. By 4.12.89 it was clear that incapacity for his normal occupation of labourer would continue for a prolonged period. In view of his age, previous experience and education, I submit that he could reasonably be expected to adapt to some new form of employment. I therefore submit that by 4.12.89 the point had been reached where it was no longer sufficient to consider incapacity for work solely in relation to his normal occupation.

4. In decision R(S) 2/82 which concerned a 52 year old man with back trouble, who was considered to be capable of work within certain limitations, a tribunal of Commissioners held that in some cases, "... it is necessary to explore more specifically whether or not medical views ... do in fact correspond with 'actualities'—not as we again stress as to the prospects of obtaining a particular employment, but as to capacity to meet the job requirements of an identifiable character of employment which is to be found in real life. ..." Earlier in that decision the Commissioners had held that the local level of employment is not a relevant consideration and that the correct approach in determining the question of incapacity is whether the claimant is capable of work and not whether he can obtain work.

In decision R(S) 6/85 the Commissioner referred to cases in which, having regard to the medical and general circumstances he was not prepared to find against the claimant "without forming an affirmative conclusion, within reasonably precise and practical parameters, as to what work, within the overall sphere of employments for which an employer would pay, it is of which he is properly to be considered to have been capable (as distinct from holding the claimant capable of work upon more abstract assumption that there 'must be something') by way of work which he could reasonably have been expected to do and for which an employer would have paid." He went on to say "in those circumstances and without in any way departing from the principle that the burden of proof lies upon the claimant, I am much assisted if provided with evidence ... of job descriptions—not job vacancies—which are submitted and relied upon by (the Adjudication Officer) as descriptive of work of which the particular claimant was capable at the material time."

In decision R(S) 7/85 the Commissioner cited with approval decision R(S) 2/82 and held that there were cases in which it is necessary "to examine more carefully the question whether medical views expressed in general terms correspond with the 'actualities'." In these circumstances he said that the Adjudication Officer should put forward suggested occupations for consideration.

5. The Medical Officer who examined Mr. Hussein on 8.11.89 was asked for his opinion as to whether Mr. Hussein could undertake the various duties of jobs which the Adjudication Officer had identified as being suitable for him. He decided that Mr Hussein could undertake both of these jobs.

6. Full descriptions of the occupations quoted are given in an appendix to this submission (item 4 on RHS). These have been supplied by the Department of Employment and are official descriptions of jobs which are in existence. The suggested jobs should not be taken to be job vacancies, neither are they intended to be an exhaustive list of those which the claimant could do; they are an indication in more specific terms of the claimant's capacity to work having regard to his accepted limitations.

7. It is my submission that Mr. Hussein is capable of undertaking the job which have been identified as being suitable for him and that he has failed to prove that for the period from 29.11.89 he was incapable of all work. I therefore submit that the claim for invalidity benefit for the period from and including 29.11.89 is for disallowance.

8. Should the tribunal decide that invalidity benefit is payable for any of the period at issue, they are respectfully requested to direct that any unemployment benefit already paid during the period should be treated as having been paid on account of invalidity benefit now available.

Form AT3 (Heading)

IN CONFIDENCE

Record of proceedings of .... Social Security Appeal Tribunal held on 10.5.1990

	(Surname)	(Other names)
Full name of Appellant	HUSSEIN	AHMED

Local Office: HIGH ST

Case List No.	:	714/02
Tribunal Reg. No.	:	54/7

CONSTITUTION OF TRIBUNAL

*Full/Chairman and one member

Names of Tribunal Chairman and members
MR SMITH
MRS JONES
MR BROWN

Appellant notified of hearing on 25.4.1990

Appellant— *present ~~absent~~

NAMES OF OTHERS PRESENT (WRITE "NONE" WHERE APPROPRIATE)

Appellant's representative *(state organisation if any)*
MR WISE (CAB)

Witness(es)
NONE

Others *(state capacity)*
CLERK—MISS ROBINSON
INTERPRETER—MR SHAH

Adjudication Officer
NOT PRESENT

Consent to hearing by less than full tribunal

* Appellant's consent given on tear-off portion AT6.   Yes/No

I consent to this case being proceeded with in the absence of a member of the Tribunal other than the Chairman.
I understand the Chairman will have a casting vote if required.

Appellant's signature ....

Form AT3 (Continuation)

1. Chairman's note of evidence (*i.e. concise details of all oral and written details put before the tribunal*).

No Presenting Officer had attended. The Adjudication Officer had been advised of the hearing 25.4.90. Clmt. and Rep. content to proceed in absence of a Presenting Officer. Tribunal decide to proceed. Mr. Wise refers to R(S) 7/83 re burden of proof—on a review decision burden is on Dept. Also to R(S) 85 re test for incapacity—current capability without retraining.

Letter from clmt.'s doctor produced. Clmt. has back pain—cannot stand for long. Lives alone—daughter-in-law does housekeeping for him and prepares meals. Cannot walk far without resting—was driven here by car today.

Mr. Wise refers to summary of facts in Adjudication Officer's statement—also adds clmt. walks with a stick—difficulty climbing stairs. Refers to job description for "light labourer." Suggests cannot do "conveying materials, stacking materials, opening bales" etc.—all involve lifting and bending. Suggests that setting up machinery would involve following written instructions—clmt. cannot read English—same would apply to labelling etc. Cleaning machinery and general cleaning and sweeping would require greater dexterity and flexibility of movement than clmt. is capable of. Loading and unloading again requires lifting and carrying. Even Department's doctors have said no lifting or bending, or carrying weights.

Refers to R(S) 7/85—Test is work of a sort for which employer would be willing to pay normal rates of pay.

Mr. Hussein through the interpreter confirms his back pain and limited physical capability. Also says has had stroke. Two further strokes this year since the Department's doctors saw him. First stroke was about a year ago. Now gets giddy if he stands for some time.

Clmt. has signed on to receive I.S.—was advised to do so pending this decision.

Form AT3   *Delete as necessary*   **OVER**

APPELLANT

---

2. Findings of Tribunal on questions of fact material to decision (*i.e. the relevant facts accepted from the evidence available*).

1. Mr. Hussein is 55 years old. His usual occupation was that of factory worker.

2. He has been unemployed since 1980. Became incapable of work on 16.6.88 and received sickness benefit until 28.9.88 followed by Invalidity Benefit from 29.9.88.

3. Mr. Hussein was examined by two doctors from DSS on 1.8.89 and 8.11.89. They both found lumbar spine disorder with pain in his back and right leg. They both found him fit for light work. One doctor said he should avoid lifting, bending and carrying weights, the other said he should avoid walking, climbing stairs, lifting and bending.

4. The clmt. has also suffered from strokes which now leave him giddy and unable to stand.

5. The clmt.'s Invalidity Benefit was suspended from 29.11.89, he has since that time been in receipt of Income Supplement. He has been signing on as fit for work pending the outcome of these proceedings.

3. Full text of *unanimous/*majority decision on the *Appeal/*Reference *(including amounts and effective date(s) as appropriate).*

The appeal is allowed. Invalidity Benefit is payable from and including 29.11.89. Any Income Support paid to the clmt. from and including that date is to be treated as paid on account of the IVB payable as a result of this decision.

4. Reasons for decision *(i.e. an explanation of why, when applying the facts to the statutory provisions and case-law, a particular conclusion is reached. And why, if it is not clear from Box 2, certain evidence has been accepted or rejected).*

The Tribunal decided that this case could be heard and determined in the absence of the Presenting Officer because a full and detailed submission had been included in the case papers. The Tribunal also finds that the effect of Reg. 17(1) of Claims and Payments Regs. 1987 is to make Mr. Hussein's claim one for an indefinite period. This means that he became entitled to IVB indefinitely until a decision to review was made by the Adjudication Officer. That being so the onus of proof is on the Adjudication Officer to show that the clmt. was fit for work. (This is not the same as a new claim for benefit when it is accepted that the onus is on the clmt. to show that he is incapable of work.)

The time at which the decision to review was taken was November 1989. The clmt.'s condition may have worsened since that date as a result of further strokes but we are deciding this case only on the basis of the information then available.

The test to be applied by the Tribunal is whether the clmt. is capable of doing a real job that does exist (though not necessarily as a vacancy) and for which an employer would be willing to pay him. The DSS doctors have said that he could do the job of a light labourer and a copy of that job description was included in the case papers. They also said that he should avoid lifting and bending.

In our opinion the client's ability to perform the job would be so curtailed by those restrictions that no employer would be willing to pay him in that job. We cannot think of any other job for which the clmt. would be fitted given his physical and educational limitations.

*Reasons for dissent if Tribunal not unanimous

Date 10.5.90 .... Chairman's signature ....

For clerk's use only   Form AT22 noted   ☐
SSAT decision notified to
parties to the proceedings on   Typing checked   ☐

.../ .../19....   Initials .... Date 19
Delete as necessary

This is not an outrageously difficult case, and the documentation provided by the DSS certainly gives Mr. Hussein the fullest possible notice of the case. However, the material is laid out in such a way and in such detail that it might be very difficult for the average person to comprehend without the help of a knowledgable adviser. The problem of setting out the case clearly is compounded in social security matters by the complexity of the law.

2. AN INDUSTRIAL TRIBUNAL[72]

Facts: Mr. Seamer had been employed by Convoy Carriers as a lorry driver for nearly 10 years. One day in May 1990 he was called into the office of the Managing Director where there were four bottles of gin on the table. The Managing Director said that they had been found in Mr. Seamer's car and accused him of stealing them. In the presence of Mr. Seamer he telephoned the Police and reported the alleged theft. An argument ensued in which Mr. Seamer protested his innocence. Both men lost their temper and abused each other. Eventually, the Managing Director told Mr. Seamer that he was sacked, with immediate effect, and that he could collect a week's wages from the Accounts Department.

Mr. Seamer subsequently went to the Department of Employment where he obtained an application form to send to the Industrial Tribunal. He filled in the form and sent it off, having been told by a friend that his Union might help him.

Mr. Seamer submitted the form to the central office of the Industrial Tribunals. To help him he was given an explanatory leaflet and a small booklet, "Industrial Tribunals Procedure."[73]

On receipt of an application (Form IT1) the Central Office attempt to ensure that it discloses a cause of action within the jurisdiction of the tribunal.[74] Given that the information on the form can be very sparse this is not always an easy job. If it appears that there is no jurisdiction, the application is returned to the applicant[75] otherwise it is sent to the respondent with Form IT2, "Notice of Originating Application," which requires the respondent to enter an appearance within 14 days. In this case the company wishes to dispute the application. It gives "notice of appearance," by completing and returning Form IT3. Forms IT1 and IT3 are reproduced below.

---

[72] The jurisdiction of the tribunal is set out above, pp. 57–59. The rules of procedure governing the tribunal are to be found in the Industrial Tribunals (Rules of Procedure) Regulations 1985 (S.I. 1985 No. 16), as amended.

[73] Published by the Department of Employment and available free.

[74] This is done by a vetting section at the Central Office.

[75] With a letter pointing out why it appears that the application is outside the jurisdiction. This does not prevent the applicant making a further application and, if it is accepted, the original defective application is not disclosed to the respondent.

Application to an Industrial Tribunal

Notes for Guidance

Before filling in this form please read:
- **these GUIDANCE NOTES**
- **LEAFLET ITL1 which you were given with the form**
- **the correct BOOKLET for your type of case**

Information: There are many things you can complain to a Tribunal about. LEAFLET ITL1 tells you what they are, which law (an Act of Parliament) covers your complaint, and which booklet you should get. Each of the BOOKLETS explains the law in simple terms. You can get the booklets free from any employment office, Jobcentre, or Unemployment Benefit Office. If you are in doubt, your Trade Union or a Citizens' Advice Bureau may be able to give you further advice or information.

Time limits: You must send in your application form so that it arrives at the Central Office of the Industrial Tribunals within the time limit. The time limit depends on which complaint you are making; for example, for unfair dismissal complaints it is three months beginning with the date of dismissal. So if you were dismissed on 10th January, the form must arrive by 9th April.

Qualifying periods: There are rules about how long you have to work for an employer before you can bring a case to a Tribunal. These rules are explained in the BOOKLETS.

If you are in any doubt about the time limits or qualifying periods, please contact your local employment office, Jobcentre, or Unemployment Benefit Office; or get in touch with the Advisory Conciliation and Arbitration Service (ACAS) - see the LEAFLET ITL1 for addresses and telephone numbers.

Representatives: You can present your own case at the Tribunal. If you want someone else to present your case, try to consult him or her before you complete your application form, but remember your form must arrive within the TIME LIMIT. If you name a representative, all future dealings will be with him or her and not with you. If you name a representative, you should ask him or her any questions you have about the progress of your case and when the Tribunal hearing will be.

If your complaint concerns EQUAL PAY or SEX DISCRIMINATION, you may wish to contact the Equal Opportunities Commission for advice or representation. If your complaint is about RACIAL DISCRIMINATION, you may wish to contact the Commission for Racial Equality for advice or representation.

Application to an Industrial Tribunal

Filling in the form

Help: Your Trade Union or local Citizens' Advice Bureau may be able to help you fill in the form if you have any problems, but make sure your form arrives within the TIME LIMIT.

Questions to answer: Try to complete all the boxes that apply in your case. You MUST answer the questions in boxes 1, 2, 4 and 10.

Be clear: This form has to be photocopied, so please use black ink, or type your answers, and use CAPITAL LETTERS for names and addresses.

Box 1
Put here the type of complaint you want the Tribunal to decide (for example, unfair dismissal, redundancy payment, equal pay, etc.). A full list of types of complaint is given in the leaflet ITL1. If there is more than one complaint you want the Tribunal to decide, please say so. Give the details of your complaints in Box 10.

Box 2
Give your name and address and date of birth, and if possible a telephone number where the Tribunal or ACAS can contact you during the day about your application.

Box 4
Put here the name and address of the employer, person or body (the "respondent") you wish to complain about. In the second box, give also the place where you worked or applied for work, if different from that of the respondent you have named. (For example, complete both boxes if you have named a liquidator, the Secretary of State for Employment, or your employer's Head Office as the respondent).

Box 10
Give full details of your complaint. If there is not enough room on the form, continue on a separate sheet, and attach it to the form. Do NOT send any other documents or evidence in support of your complaint at this stage. Your answer may be used in an initial assessment of your case, so make it as complete and accurate as you can. (See **Help** above).

When you have finished:

- **Sign and date the form**
- **Keep these Guidance Notes and a copy of your answers**
- **Send the form to: The Secretary of the Tribunals,**
  Central Office of the Industrial Tribunals
  93 Ebury Bridge Road
  London SW1W 8RE
  Tel: 01-730 9161

FOR OFFICIAL USE ONLY

Received at COIT

Case No.	12345/90		Code	U D L
Initials	H P B		ROIT	I I

Application to an Industrial Tribunal

Please read the notes opposite before filling in this form.

1 Say what type of complaint(s) you want the tribunal to decide *(see note opposite).*

Unfair dismissal

2 Give your name and address etc. in CAPITALS *(see note opposite).*

Mr/~~Mrs~~
~~Miss/Ms~~   BARRY SEAMER

Address
          23 WOOD LANE
          DARBYVILLE
          NOTTS

Telephone

Date of birth   23.9.50

3 Please give the name and address of your representative, if you have one.

Name   NOT YET, BUT I AM GOING TO THE UNION

Address

Telephone

4 Give the name and address of the employer, person or body (the respondent) you are complaining about *(see note opposite).*

Name   CONVOY CARRIERS PLC

Address
          23 LONDON ROAD
          DARBYVILLE
          NOTTS

Telephone   DARBYVILLE 1249

Give the place where you worked or applied for work, if different from above.

Name

Address

Telephone

5 Please say what job you did for the employer (or what job you applied for). If this does not apply, please say what your connection was with the employer.

DRIVER (HGV)

IT 1 (Revised August 1986)   Please continue overleaf

6 Please give the number of normal basic hours you worked per week.

Hours | 45 | per week

7 Basic wage / salary | £ 125 | per | week

Average take home pay | £ 220 | per | week

Other bonuses / benefits | £ 1.73 night allowance | per | week

8 Please give the dates of your employment *(if applicable)*

Began on | 1 FEBRUARY 1980

Ended on | 1 MAY 1990

9 If your complaint is **not** about dismissal, please give the date when the action you are complaining about took place (or the date when you first knew about it).

Date

10 Give the full details of your complaint *(see note opposite)*.

My boss (Mr Hacker) told me that some bottles of gin that were missing from the depot had been found on the back seat of my car. The car was at the depot. He told me not to come back to work and gave me a week's wages. He called me a thief. I told him that I hadn't pinched the gin and that I had been fitted up, but he didn't believe me. I did not pinch the gin. I have been interviewed by the Police, but they have not told me whether they will prosecute me.

11 Unfair dismissal claimants only (Please tick a box to show what you would want if you win your case).

☑ Reinstatement: to carry on working in your old job as before

☐ Re-engagement: to start another job, or a new contract, with your old employer

☐ Compensation: to get an award of money

You can change your mind later. The Tribunal will take your preference into account, but will not be bound by it.

Signature: *B. Seamer*   Date: 1 June 1990

Dd 8040082 100m 11.86 H.D.B. Ltd. 3657

Industrial Tribunals

Case number: 12345/90

Notice of Appearance by Respondent

1 Please give the following details

Mr ☐   Mrs ☐   Miss ☐   Ms ☐

Other title _____

(Or give the name of the company or organisation)

Name   CONVOY CARRIERS PLC

Address   23 LONDON ROAD

           DARBYVILLE

           NOTTS

Telephone   DARBYVILLE 1249

---

2 Do you intend to resist the application made by

_____

YES ☑   NO ☐

---

3 Was the applicant dismissed?

YES ☑   NO ☐

If 'YES' what was the reason?

He stole goods belonging to a client of the company.

---

4 Are the dates of employment given by the applicant correct?

YES ☑   NO ☐

If 'NO', please give the correct dates

Began on _____

Ended on _____

---

5 If a representative is acting for you, please give his/her name and address (NOTE: *All further communications will be sent to him or her, not to you*)

Name   POPPLE, LEES AND STONE

Address   83 MAIN STREET

           GUMBY

           NOTTS

Telephone _____

Reference _____

---

6 Are the details given by the applicant about wages/salary or other payments or benefits correct?

YES ☑   NO ☐

If 'NO', or if details were not given, please give the correct details:

Basic wage/salary

£ _____   per _____

Average take home pay

£ _____   per _____

Other bonuses/benefits

£ _____   per _____

---

7 Maternity rights cases only

When the applicant's absence began did you have more than five employees?

YES ☐   NO ☐

Please continue overleaf ▶

IT 3

8 If you answered 'YES' to question **2**, please give below sufficient details to show the grounds on which you intend to resist the application: *(continue on a separate sheet if there is not enough space for your answer)*

(a) The applicant was fairly and properly dismissed on May 1 1983 for stealing goods belonging to a client of the company.

(b) The goods in question were found by a security officer in the back of the applicant's car.

(c) When questioned the applicant failed to give a satisfactory answer to the Managing Director, Mr P J R Hacker.

(d) Honesty is of the utmost importance amongst our staff.

(e) The matter is in the hands of the Police.

9

Signed   P. M. Hacker

Date

10 Please send this form to:
The Assistant Secretary
Regional Office of the Industrial
  Tribunals
London South
93 Ebury Bridge Road
LONDON SW1W 8RE

For official use

Date received   Initials

IT 3 (Reverse)

HQR.12.87

At the same time as the originating application is sent to the respondent it is also sent to a conciliation officer.[76] He receives a copy of the notice of appearance in due course. He is obliged to assist the parties in reaching a conciliation if he is requested to do so, or if he thinks there is a reasonable prospect of success.[77] In this case he sees both parties individually. Mr. Seamer wants his job back. Convoy Carriers will not give it to him. Mr. Seamer has sought the assistance of his Union and they ask the company for more information. The company refuses but is ordered to give further particulars after an application to the Tribunal by the applicant. A standard form direction would be:

Regional Office of the Industrial Tribunals
(address)

> To: Convoy Carriers PLC,
> 23 London Road,
> Darbyville,
> Notts.
> Case No. 12345/90 Seamer *v.* Convoy Carrier PLC

1. An application has been received from the Applicant for further and better particulars of the grounds on which you rely. This application has been referred to the Chairman of Tribunals who by virtue of the powers conferred upon him under rule 4(1)(*a*) of the Rules of Procedure has granted an order as follows.
2. The particulars requested in the letter dated September 4, 1990 (copy enclosed) should be furnished to Mr. D. York, National Union of Lorrymen, York Row, Darbyville by October 30, 1990 and a copy sent to this office.
3. Your attention is drawn to the fact that rule 4(5) provides that if an order under rule 4(1)(*a*) is not complied with, a tribunal, before or at the hearing, may, where the order relates to an originating application, dismiss the application, or where the order relates to a notice of appearance strike out the whole or part of the notice of appearance and, where appropriate, direct that a respondent shall be debarred from defending altogether.

	A. Bowler
Dated 1, October 1990	Assistant Secretary of the Industrial Tribunals

Mr. York (Mr. Seamer's Union representative) had asked for further particulars of the company's normal security procedures; a list of other employees dismissed on the grounds of dishonesty in the preceding five years; and reasons why the company considered it reasonable to dismiss Mr. Seamer immediately without awaiting the outcome of police investigations. The neces-

---

[76] An employee of ACAS.
[77] The evidence points to a considerable number of cases settled without a tribunal hearing (see above, p. 576). The conciliation officer is in a position to assist in negotiations leading to any result—compensation, reinstatment or the withdrawal of the application.

sary information was supplied. No pre-hearing assessment was held[78] and the case was listed for hearing on December 10, 1990. Mr. Seamer lost.

This example demonstrates a relatively straightforward case where the issue between the parties is clear and unlikely to be resolved in advance of the hearing. Much more documentation can be generated, but this is essentially under the control of the parties and is dependent upon the amount of information that is requested. This is in contrast with the Social Security Appeal Tribunal where the appellant receives the full documentation whether he or she wants it or not. Again, even in this simple case, the advisability of securing skilled assistance can be appreciated.

F. THE ROLE AND INFLUENCE OF THE COUNCIL ON TRIBUNALS[79]

"Our most important contribution over the years has, we believe, been our constant effort to translate the general ideals of the Franks Committee into workable codes of principles and practice, accepted and followed by all those who are responsible for setting up administrative tribunals, devising their manner of operation and, indeed, serving upon them as chairmen and members."[80]

The Franks Committee proposed a significant role for the Council on Tribunals in controlling and overseeing all aspects of tribunal operation[81] but, in the event, the Council was given only limited powers by the Tribunals and Inquiries Act 1958.[82] It emerged as an advisory body with the primary function of keeping under review the constitution and working of certain tribunals specified in a Schedule to the Act.[83] This function is assisted by a requirement that the Council should be consulted before any procedural rules or regulations are made in respect of the specified tribunals,[84] but there is no corresponding requirement of consultation on primary legislation affecting tribunals. Nor is there a requirement that the views expressed by the Council on consultation should be made known when the appropriate legislation is laid before Parliament.

In a review of the functions of the Council[85] other limitations were exposed. The terms of reference do not permit the Council to operate as a general advisory body on all matters pertaining to tribunals, including their overall pattern and organisation. The Council is hampered in dealing with complaints by the lack of any statutory power of investigation. Members of the Council should be specifically empowered to be present at private

---

[78] The assessment is only held where it is requested by one of the parties or where the Tribunal itself considers that the application or response is lacking in merit. In this case, both sides would appear to have a chance and the issue is primarily one of fact to be determined by the tribunal.

[79] See also above, pp. 36–37.

[80] *The Functions of the Council on Tribunals.* Special Report by the Council (Cmnd. 7805, 1980), para. 6.3.

[81] Franks Report, *op. cit.* paras. 43, 49, 57, 63–64, 131–134.

[82] Now the Tribunals and Inquiries Act 1971.

[83] Tribunals and Inquiries Act 1971, s.1(1)(*a*) and Sched. 1.

[84] Tribunals and Inquiries Act 1971, s.10.

[85] *The Functions of the Council on Tribunals*, see above, n. 80. The particular frustrations of the Council are expressed in Chaps. 5, 7 and 8.

hearings of tribunals and remain present during the deliberations of the tribunal. Despite these hindrances to the work that the Council would wish to do, there is no doubt that it has exerted a considerable influence in procedural and other matters.

There are a number of examples of procedural changes being effected as a result of the advice of the Council.[86] This advice is based not only on the expertise of the individual members, but also on the experience of other tribunals and other countries. The framing of procedural rules is still the obligation of the Ministry which is responsible for the tribunal and it is not easy for the civil servants in that Ministry to be aware of the procedural pitfalls discovered in other tribunals.[87]

[86] They are discussed in the Annual Reports which also contain lists of the procedural regulations considered by the Council each year.

[87] This is particularly true where new tribunals are established. See *e.g.* the reference to the rules of procedure for the Vaccine Damage Tribunal in, *The Functions of the Councils on Tribunals, op. cit.*, at pp. 20–21.

CHAPTER 13

PRE-TRIAL CRIMINAL PROCEDURE

IN this chapter we consider the stages in the process of dealing with those suspected of having committed criminal offences that take place before trial. A trial (whether contested or not) is a necessary pre-condition for the imposition of a formal criminal sanction.[1] However,

> "[t]here are few who would now propound the view that the centre-piece of the English criminal process is the trial, and that the few earlier procedures are merely designed to ensure that no one is put on trial unless there is a good case against them and that dangerous people are kept in custody before trial."[2]

This change of view has resulted from research into the operation of the criminal justice system, which has developed particularly strongly from the 1970s onwards.[3] Attention has been paid to the various pressures that lead to pleas of guilty and the avoidance of contested trials. "It has become a commonplace that early decisions in the criminal process seem strongly associated with and determinative of later decisions. . . ."[4] For example, a confession made by a suspect to the police may well be crucial, given the difficulties that will thereafter arise in challenging it or explaining it away in court.[5] A defendant who is remanded in custody will have to overcome a host of practical problems in the organisation of a defence that do not arise if bail is granted.[6] Moreover, the whole system would break down were it not that a very high proportion of those who are prosecuted for an offence plead guilty. In 1989–90, there were guilty pleas in 72.9 per cent. of cases handled by the Crown Prosecution Service in the Crown Court, and 61.5 per cent. of cases in the magistrates' courts.[7] Accordingly the outcome of the vast

---

[1] Which is why fixed penalty charges for certain motoring offences do not technically constitute "fines."

[2] A. Ashworth, "Criminal Justice and the Criminal Process" (1988) 28 Brit. J. Criminol. 111, 112.

[3] For general surveys see A. Ashworth, *op. cit.* and *The English Criminal Process: a Review of Empirical Research*, Centre for Criminological Research, Occasional Paper No. 11 (1984). Important contributions have been made by among others, the Home Office Research and Planning Unit (which publishes separate series of Research Studies and Papers) and the Institute of Judicial Administration at the University of Birmingham.

[4] Ashworth, *op. cit.* n. 2, p. 113.

[5] See below, pp. 608–615.

[6] See below, pp. 645–657.

[7] *Annual Report of the Crown Prosecution Service 1989–90* (1989–90 H.C. 305), pp. 37, 38. The proportion of guilty pleas in all Crown Court cases is given in the *Judicial Statistics* Annual Volume.

majority of cases is determined by the processes considered in the present chapter, and only a minority by the trial process considered in chapter 16.

The material in the present chapter falls into three broad parts. First, we consider the process of investigation of offences (section A); secondly, the process whereby a decision is taken whether a prosecution should be instituted (sections B and C); and thirdly, the pre-trial procedures in criminal cases (sections D to J). We conclude with an attempt to evaluate some of the basic features of the system (section K).

A. INVESTIGATION

1. THE ROLE OF THE POLICE

Only a small proportion of the criminal offences committed lead ultimately to a criminal prosecution. Many offences will be undetected, or if detected not reported to the police,[8] or if reported not recorded as an offence by the police.[9] Of the offences that do come to the attention of the police, it seems that about 85 per cent. are reported by members of the public and only about 15 per cent. discovered by the police themselves.[10] About a third of the "members of the public" are in fact organisations, store detectives or security firms.[10a]

Once offences have come to the attention of the police,

"the clear message that emerges from practically all recent empirical studies . . . is that the police are rarely faced with the classic situation of detective fiction, that of the search for the unidentified perpetrators of known offences."[11]

In most cases the process of detection is straightforward as the offender is, for example, caught red-handed, identified by the victim or other witnesses or found by the police at or near the scene of the crime, or is one of a few people with ready access or an obvious motive, or gives himself or herself up.[12] In a significant number of cases an offence is admitted during an interview concerning other offences,[13] or the offender is identified as such

---

[8] The *British Crime Survey* (H.O. Research Study No. 76, 1983, p. 10) suggested that less than a quarter of offences are reported. The *1988 British Crime Survey* (H.O. Research Study No. 111, 1989) gives an overall reporting rate of 37 per cent. for crimes of violence against the person and theft of and damage to private property (p. 11). There are considerable variations according to the offence. Reporting rates have been increasing.

[9] See generally A. K. Bottomley and K. Pease, *Crime and Punishment: Interpreting the Data* (1986), pp. 34–41.

[10] Ashworth (1984), p. 12, based, *inter alia*, on D. Steer, *Uncovering Crime* (RCCP Research Study No. 7, H.M.S.O., 1980); A. K. Bottomley and C. Coleman, *Understanding Crime Rates* (1981); J. Burrows, "How Crimes Come to Police Notice," H.O. Research Bulletin No. 13, pp. 12–15 (1982).

[10a] Burrows, *op. cit.*

[11] Bottomley and Pease (1986), p. 46, based on R. Mawby, *Policing the City* (1979) and Steer (1980).

[12] In Steer's study (1980) of indictable offences dealt with by the Oxford police, these accounted for 47 per cent. of a random sample and 71 per cent. of a sample of serious cases: p. 73, Table 3.4. See generally pp. 71–78, 96–116.

[13] Many offences thereby come to the attention of the police for the first time. Such admissions are commonly made with a view to the other offences being "taken into consideration" during sentencing. See below, p. 795.

following a search of his or her property, or by someone in police custody.[14] In only a minority of cases[15] are special detection skills used (*e.g.* involving informants, fingerprint search, local police knowledge, police records). Given the limitations on police manpower and the seemingly ever-increasing crime rate, it is unsurprising that most effort will be directed on investigations where a result is most likely, and on the more serious cases.[16]

To facilitate the process of investigation, the law provides the police with a series of powers to interfere with the legal rights of members of the public: powers of arrest and detention, powers to enter and search land and buildings and to search persons, and powers to seize property. The law also establishes a framework for controlling the exercise of such powers by setting conditions as to who may exercise the power and the circumstances in which it may be exercised, and by providing for supervision or periodic reviews. It also provides remedies for a breach of legal requirements. Given that most police powers authorise the commission of what would otherwise be torts or crimes (*e.g.* assault, false imprisonment, trespass to land, trespass to goods), exceeding the limits of a particular power may well expose the officers concerned (and the chief constable, who is vicariously responsible in tort[17]) to an action for damages or a criminal prosecution. The police are also subject to disciplinary regulations which may be contravened even where no tort or crime is committed.

The key statute in this area is the Police and Criminal Evidence Act 1984.[18] This Act extended the formal powers of the police in certain significant respects but narrowed them in others. It also strengthened the controls over the exercise of police powers in general and clarified and strengthened the rights of defendants in custody. Many of these controls are, however, found not in the Act itself but in Codes of Practice made by the Secretary of State.[19] The sanctions for breach of a Code tend to be more indirect than for breach of the substantive law.[20] The intention was to strike a satisfactory balance between police powers and the rights of subjects, but it remains controversial whether that has been achieved.[21] There is not the space here for more than a brief survey.[22]

[14] 41 per cent. and 20 per cent. respectively: *ibid.*
[15] 13 per cent. and 11 per cent. respectively: *ibid.*
[16] *Ibid.* pp. 71 72.
[17] Police Act 1964, s.48.
[18] This followed the Report of the Royal Commission on Criminal Procedure (Cmnd. 8092, 1981) but differed in some important matters from its recommendations. For an evaluation, see below, pp. 680–687.
[19] Under ss.66, 67. There are at present five codes: Code A on Powers of Stop and Search; Code B on Search and Seizure; Code C on the Detention, Treatment and Questioning of Persons; Code D on the Identification of Persons; and Code E on Tape Recording, Codes A to D were issued in 1985, and revised with effect from April 1, 1991; Code E was issued in 1988.
[20] Breach of a Code by a police officer is a disciplinary offence; other persons who investigate offences must have regard to any relevant provision (see *R. v. Twaites and Brown* [1990] Crim.L.R. 863) and the Codes are admissible in evidence and if relevant to civil or criminal proceedings are to be taken into account by the court or tribunal. However, breach of a Code by a person does not of itself render him or her liable to any civil or criminal proceedings (s.67(8)–(11)). Breach of a Code may give rise to the exclusion of evidence: see below, pp. 611–615.
[21] For a sceptical view, see A. Sanders, "Rights, Remedies and the Police and Criminal Evidence Act" [1988] Crim.L.R. 802.
[22] For fuller treatment see J. Benyon and C. Brown (eds), *The Police: Powers, Procedures and Proprieties* (1986); L. Leigh, *Police Powers in England and Wales* (2nd ed., 1985); R. Clayton

2. POLICE POWERS

(a) Arrest

Powers of arrest can be grouped in five categories:

(i) *Arrest with a warrant*

In some cases an arrest is authorised by a warrant issued by a justice of the peace under section 1 of the Magistrates' Courts Act 1980, as an alternative to the issue of a summons.[23] The issue of an arrest warrant or a summons follows the laying of an information on oath to the effect that the person named has, or is suspected of having, committed an offence. A warrant should not be issued where a summons would be equally effectual, but may, for example, be employed where the defendant fails to answer to a summons.[24]

(ii) *Arrest without a warrant for "arrestable offences"*

Section 24 of the Police and Criminal Evidence Act 1984 gives the police and members of the public general powers to arrest without a warrant in respect of the more serious offences classified as "arrestable offences."[25] These are:

— offences for which the sentence is fixed by law (murder, treason, piracy with violence and genocide);
— offences for which a person of 21 or over (not previously convicted) may be sentenced to five years' imprisonment;
— certain other offences specified in section 24(2) that would not otherwise be arrestable offences (*e.g.* some offences under the Customs and Excise Acts, offences under the Official Secrets Act 1989, indecent assault on a woman, taking a motor vehicle without authority) and related offences (conspiracy, attempt, aiding and abetting etc.).

The offences may be in the present, the past or the future. Thus, any person may arrest anyone who is in the act of committing an arrestable offence or whom he or she has reasonable grounds for suspecting to be committing such an offence. Where an arrestable offence has been committed, any person may arrest anyone who is guilty of it, or whom he or she has

and H. Tomlinson, *Civil Actions Against the Police* (1987); V. Bevan and K. Lidstone, *A Guide to the Police and Criminal Evidence Act 1984* (1985); M. Zander, *The Police and Criminal Evidence Act 1984* (2nd ed., 1990); D. Feldman, *The Law of Entry and Seizure* (1986); R. T. H. Stone, *Entry, Search and Seizure* (2nd ed., 1989); H. Levenson and F. Fairweather, *Police Powers: a practitioner's guide* (2nd ed., 1990); Symposia, [1985] P.L. 388ff, [1985] Crim.L.R. 535ff and [1990] Crim.L.R. 452ff; S. Jones, (1985) 48 M.L.R. 679.
[23] See below, pp. 642–645.
[24] *Ibid.*
[25] This replaced similar provisions in the Criminal Law Act 1967, s.2, which in turn had replaced common law powers of arrest for felonies.

reasonable grounds for suspecting to be guilty. (Here, the offence must have been committed by someone.) Where a constable has reasonable grounds for suspecting that an arrestable offence has been committed, he or she may arrest anyone whom he or she has reasonable grounds for suspecting to be guilty of it. A constable may arrest anyone who is about to commit an arrestable offence or whom he or she has reasonable grounds for suspecting to be about to commit such an offence. It will be seen that the powers of the police here are wider than those of private citizens.

(iii) *Arrest without a warrant by virtue of "general arrest conditions"*

A novel feature of the 1984 Act was the introduction in section 25 of general arrest powers exercisable by the police in respect of all offences other than arrestable offences. These are available where for some reason or another an arrest is necessary notwithstanding that the offence in question is comparatively trivial. Where a constable has reasonable grounds for suspecting such an offence has been or is being committed or attempted, he or she may arrest the relevant person "if it appears to him [or her] that service of a summons is impracticable or inappropriate because any of the general arrest conditions are satisfied." The "general arrest conditions" are:

(a) that the name of the relevant person is unknown to, and cannot readily be ascertained by the constable;

(b) that the constable has reasonable grounds for doubting whether a name furnished is the real name;

(c) that the relevant person has failed to furnish a satisfactory address for service, or the constable has reasonable grounds for doubting whether an address furnished is a satisfactory one;
that the constable has reasonable grounds for believing that an arrest is necessary

(d) to prevent the relevant person causing physical injury to himself or herself or any other person; suffering physical injury; causing loss of or damage to property; committing an offence against public decency; or causing an unlawful obstruction of the highway; or

(e) to protect a child or other vulnerable person from the relevant person.

(iv) *Arrest without warrant under specific statutory powers*

The 1984 Act repealed many specific statutory powers of arrest, while preserving powers under some 21 Acts listed in Schedule 2. These include powers under the Immigration Act 1971 and the Mental Health Act 1983. Other specific powers have been created since.[26]

(v) *Arrest at common law*

At common law, there is a power to arrest for breach of the peace where a

---

[26] *e.g.* Sporting Events (Control of Alcohol etc.) Act 1985, s.7(2); Public Order Act 1986, s.3(6) (affray), 4(4) (fear or provocation of violence), 5(4) (harassment, alarm or distress), 12(7), 13(10) and 14(7) (processions and assemblies); Prevention of Terrorism (Temporary Provisions) Act 1989, s.15.

breach of the peace is taking place or reasonably anticipated.[27] This power is not confined to constables and was not modified by the 1984 Act.

(vi) Common requirements

There are a number of conditions that must be fulfilled for an arrest to be valid, apart from the existence of a relevant power of arrest. Some are derived from the common law and some from statute. Very commonly, the arrestor is required to have "reasonable grounds" to believe or suspect the arrested person to be guilty of an offence. If the validity of the arrest is challenged in legal proceedings the onus lies on the arrestor to establish to the satisfaction of the court that objectively reasonable grounds existed: it is insufficient that the arrestor honestly believed that he or she had such grounds.[28] The concept of reasonable suspicion lies between that of suspicion without any proof and that of prima facie proof based on admissible evidence (i.e. evidence that if not controverted would be sufficient for a conviction).[29] Whether it exists in a particular case is a question of fact not law, and it is unusual for an arrest to be held unlawful for lack of reasonable grounds.[30] As well as possessing the requisite reasonable grounds, the arrestor must in fact suspect the arrestee.[31]

The arrestor must make it clear that the arrestee is under compulsion either by physical means, such as taking him or her by the arm, or by using words of compulsion to which the arrestee accedes.[32] The arrestee must be informed that he or she is under arrest, and of the ground for arrest, at the time of the arrest or as soon as practicable thereafter,[33] except where the arrestor is a private citizen and the fact or ground of arrest is obvious. There is a further, general, exception where it is not reasonably practicable to impart the information before the arrestee escapes from arrest.[34] The arrestor must regard his or her action as an arrest in the sense of a possible first step in the criminal process: if, for example, he or she simply detains someone for questioning with no thought of arrest it cannot be a valid

---

[27] R. v. Howell (Erroll) [1982] Q.B. 416, D.C.; Albert v. Lavin [1982] A.C. 546. The court in Howell stated that "there is breach of the peace whenever harm is actually done or is likely to be done to a person or in his presence to his property or a person is in fear of being so harmed through an assault, an affray, a riot, unlawful assembly or other disturbance" (per Watkins L.J. at p. 427).

[28] R. v. Inland Revenue Commissions, ex p. Rossminster Ltd. [1980] A.C. 952, 1011, per Lord Diplock.

[29] Dumbell v. Roberts [1944] 1 All E.R. 326; Hussein v. Chong Fook Kam [1970] A.C. 942.

[30] See generally S. H. Bailey and D. J. Birch, [1982] Crim.L.R. 475–477. An arrest may be based on hearsay evidence: Erskine v. Holland [1971] R.T.R. 199; R. v. Evans [1974] R.T.R. 232. See also the Code of Practice for the Exercise by Police Officers of Statutory Powers of Stop and Search (1990 ed.), paras. 1.5–1.7.

[31] Castorina v. Chief Constable of Surrey (1988) 138 N.L.J. 180; Chapman v. D.P.P. (1988) 153 J.P. 27.

[32] Alderson v. Booth [1969] 2 Q.B. 216.

[33] See Nicholas v. Parsonage [1987] R.T.R. 199 (arrest under s.25); D.P.P. v. Hawkins [1988] 1 W.L.R. 1166 (arrest not retrospectively unlawful if the ground is not given when it first becomes practicable); Abbassy v. Commissioner of Police of the Metropolis [1990] 1 W.L.R. 385 (no need to specify a particular crime or give a technical definition of the offence; sufficient to use commonplace language).

[34] Police and Criminal Evidence Act 1984, s.28. The requirements as to giving the ground of arrest were based on the common law: Christie v. Leachinsky [1947] A.C. 573. See Gelberg v. Miller [1961] 1 W.L.R. 153; R. v. Telfer [1976] Crim.L.R. 562.

arrest.[35] Finally, as the power is a statutory discretion exercisable (normally) by a public official, a particular exercise may be challenged as an *ultra vires* abuse of discretion.[36]

(b) Stop and search

The 1984 Act extended the general powers of the police to stop and search persons and vehicles. Under section 1 a constable may stop and search a person or vehicle in a public place if he or she has reasonable grounds to believe he or she will find stolen goods, an offensive weapon, articles adapted for use in burglary, theft, obtaining by deception or taking a vehicle without authority, or a knife or other bladed or sharply pointed article.[37] There are similar powers under other statutes, authorising searches, for example, for drugs, for firearms and for intoxicating liquor at sporting events.[38] All these powers are now subject to the safeguards set out in section 2 of the 1984 Act, which, *inter alia*, require the constable, before commencing a search, to give his or her name and that of his or her police station, the object of the proposed search, the grounds for the search, and, if out of uniform, documentary evidence that he or she is a constable. The person searched may not be required to remove any clothing in public other than an outer coat, jacket or gloves, and only a constable in uniform may stop a vehicle. A record must be made of the search unless it is not practicable to do so.[39]

The exercise of stop and search powers has been controversial, particularly in the light of evidence that black people are more likely to be stopped and searched than white.[40] The Home Secretary has issued a Code of Practice under the 1984 Act regulating their use, emphasising, *inter alia*, that a person's colour, dress or hairstyle can never itself be a reasonable ground for suspicion,[41] but it is still doubted whether the reasonable ground standard is generally met.[42]

There is also a power to carry out general road checks on the authority of a police superintendent.[43] The aim must be to find a person who has committed or is intending to commit an offence, a witness to an offence or a person unlawfully at large. In each case the offence must be a "serious arrestable offence." This concept is defined in section 116 of the 1984 Act, and is employed in respect of several of the powers in the Act. It covers (1) a group

---

[35] *Kenlin* v. *Gardiner* [1967] 2 Q.B. 510; *R.* v. *Brown* (1976) 64 Cr.App.R. 231.
[36] *Holgate-Mohammed* v. *Duke* [1984] A.C. 437 (where the challenge failed on the merits): *cf.* below, p. 873.
[37] Police and Criminal Evidence Act 1984, s.1, as amended by the Criminal Justice Act 1988, s.140.
[38] See the list in Annex A to the *Code of Practice for the Exercise by Police Offices of Statutory Powers of Stop and Search* (H.M.S.O., 1990) (Code A).
[39] 1984 Act, s.3.
[40] C. F. Willis, *The Use, Effectiveness and Impact of Police Stop and Search Powers* (H.O. Research and Planning Unit Paper 15, 1983); M. McConville, [1983] Crim.L.R. 605.
[41] 1984 Act, s.66; Code A.1.5–1.7.
[42] D. Dixon *et al.*, "Reality and Rules in the Construction and Regulation of Police Suspicion" (1989) 17 Int. Jo. Sociology of Law 185.
[43] 1984 Act, s.4.

of arrestable offences that are always "serious,"[44] and (2) any other arrestable offences that have led or are intended or likely to lead to specified consequences.[45]

(c) Entry, search and seizure

The police have a wide variety of powers to enter and search premises, and seize property, either with or without a warrant. A large number of statutes enable a judge or magistrate to issue a warrant authorising the entry to and search of specified premises. For example, warrants may be granted to search for stolen goods, obscene publications, drugs and a host of other items.[46] The 1984 Act introduced a new general power for justices of the peace to issue warrants authorising entry and search for evidence relating to a serious arrestable offence,[47] other than "items subject to legal privilege,"[48] "excluded material"[49] or "special procedure material."[50] Existing powers to grant search warrants were thereafter also subject to the restriction that they could not authorise searches for such material.[51] Instead, an order granting access to excluded material or special procedure material may be granted by a Circuit judge, in limited circumstances. The material must either relate to a serious arrestable offence or, apart from the restriction mentioned, fall within the scope of an existing search warrant power.[52] In the last resort, a Circuit judge may issue a warrant authorising a constable to enter and search

---

[44] These are specified in Sched. 5 and include, *inter alia*, treason, murder, manslaughter, rape, kidnapping, certain sexual offences, certain firearms offences and causing death by reckless driving. They also include drug trafficking offences: Drug Trafficking Offences Act 1986, s.36.

[45] 1984 Act, s.116(6), (7). Serious harm to the security of the State or public order; serious interference with the administration of justice or the investigation of offences; death; serious injury; substantial financial gain or serious financial loss to any person (loss being serious if "having regard to all the circumstances, it is serious for the person who suffers it"). See *R. v. McIvor* [1987] Crim.L.R. 409 (Sheffield Crown Court) (theft of 28 beagles worth £880, collectively owned by a hunt, held not to involve serious financial loss); *R. v. Eric Smith* [1987] Crim.L.R. 579 (Stafford Crown Court) (robbery of two video recorders and £116 cash held not to be a SAO).

[46] Theft Act 1968, s.26; Obscene Publications Act 1959, s.3; Misuse of Drugs Act 1971, s.23; for a full account, see R. T. H. Stone, *Entry Search and Seizure* (2nd ed., 1989), Chap. 4.

[47] 1984 Act, s.8.

[48] *Ibid.* s.10: generally, communications involving legal advice between professional legal adviser and client, communications concerning legal proceedings, and items enclosed with or referred to in such communications. Items held with the intention of furthering a criminal purpose are not covered (s.10(2)), regardless of whether the intention is that of the holder or another person (*R. v. Central Criminal Court, ex p. Francis & Francis* [1989] A.C. 346); although such items are likely to be special procedure material: *R. v. Guildhall Magistrates' Courts, ex p. Primlaks Ltd.* [1990] 1 Q.B. 261 (see below)).

[49] *Ibid.* s.11. This covers confidential personal records, human tissue or tissue fluid taken for medical purposes and confidential journalistic material ("personal records" and "journalistic material" being further defined in ss.12 and 13).

[50] *Ibid.* s.14. This covers confidential and journalistic material falling outside the definition of "excluded material."

[51] *Ibid.* s.9(2).

[52] *Ibid.*, s.9(1) and Sched. 1. Non-compliance with an order is a contempt of court. The application is made *inter partes*, prior notice being given to the person holding the material. The material in question must be specified, either in the notice of application or otherwise: *R. v. Central Criminal Court, ex p. Adegbesan* [1986] 1 W.L.R. 1292; *R. v. Manchester Crown*

for such material.[53] The 1984 Act also clarified and strengthened the safe-guards governing the issue and execution of all search warrants.[54]

The 1984 Act also set out a series of powers for the police to enter premises without a warrant; to execute an arrest warrant; to arrest for an arrestable offence or certain other specified offences; to pursue and recapture a person unlawfully at large; to save life or limb or prevent serious damage to property.[55] The constable must have reasonable grounds for believing that the person sought is there. All common law powers of entry were abolished, save that of entry to deal with or prevent a breach of the peace.[56]

Where a person is arrested by a constable away from a police station, that person may be searched on arrest if the constable has reasonable grounds to believe that he or she may present a danger to self or others, or has something which might be used to assist an escape, or which might be evidence relating to an offence. In addition, the constable may enter and search any premises in which the person was at the time of or immediately before the arrest, for evidence relating to the offence in question, if he or she has reasonable grounds to believe that such evidence is there.[57] In the case of arrestable offences, a constable may be authorised by an officer of the rank of inspector or above to enter and search any premises occupied or controlled by a person under arrest if the constable has reasonable grounds to suspect that there is evidence relating to the offence in question or a similar or related arrestable offence.[58]

(d) Detention[59]

Part IV of the 1984 Act introduced for the first time detailed arrangements regulating the length of time persons may be kept in custody by the police before a court appearance. The provisions replaced[60] had merely required

---

Court, ex p. Taylor [1988] 1 W.L.R. 705; but the evidence on which the application is based need not: *R.* v. *Inner London Crown Court, ex p. Baines & Baines* [1988] Q.B. 579. The suspect need not be notified if he or she is not the holder of the material: *R.* v. *Leicester Crown Court, ex p. D.P.P.* [1987] 1 W.L.R. 1371. The judge may hold the hearing in open court or in chambers: *R.* v. *Central Criminal Court, ex p. D.P.P., The Independent*, March 31, 1988. See generally R. T. H. Stone, [1988] Crim.L.R. 498 and A. A. S. Zuckerman, [1990] Crim.L.R. 472.

[53] *Ibid.*, Sched. 1, paras.12–14. This is available, *e.g.* where use of the order procedure might seriously prejudice the investigation.

[54] ss.15, 16. See also the *Code of Practice for the Searching of Premises by Police Officers and the Seizure of Property found by Police Officers on Persons or Premises* (H.M.S.O., 1990) (Code B). For example, entry and search must be within one month of the date of the warrant; it must be at a reasonable hour and the officer in charge must first attempt to communicate with the occupier, unless it appears that would frustrate the object of the search; before the search commences (not before entry: *R.* v. *Longman* (1988) 88 Cr.App.R. 148), the officer must identify him- or herself and state the purpose of the search and the grounds for undertaking it; a copy of the warrant must be given to the occupier or left at the premises.

[55] s.17.

[56] As to which see *Thomas* v. *Sawkins* [1935] 2 K.B. 249.

[57] 1984 Act, s.32.

[58] *Ibid.* s.18. This power, unlike s.32, is not limited to cases where the person was there at the time of or immediately before the arrest. The authorisation must be contained in an independent document: a record of oral authority included in a notebook is insufficient: *R.* v. *Badham* [1987] Crim.L.R. 202 (Wood Green Crown Court).

[59] See generally D. Feldman, [1990] Crim.L.R. 452.

[60] Magistrates' Courts Act 1980, s.43(4).

the police to bring detainees to court "as soon as practicable." If this was not practicable within 24 hours, the police had to consider whether to grant bail, and had indeed to grant bail unless the offence appeared to be "serious" (a term that was not defined). Under the new arrangements, a person arrested by a constable must be taken to a police station as soon as practicable.[61] This should normally be a "designated police station" (*i.e.* one of the stations designated by the chief officer of police as having enough accommodation for detained prisoners[62]). In some circumstances any station may be used, but no-one may be kept longer than six hours at a non-designated station.

(i) *The Custody Officer*

An important feature of the arrangements is the division of function between the "custody officer" and the officers concerned with the investigation. One or more custody officers (usually sergeants) must be appointed for each designated police station, and a variety of duties are imposed directly on that officer once a person has been brought to the station. Subject to a few exceptions, the custody officer must not be involved in the investigation.[63]

Thus,

— The custody officer (CO) must determine, as soon as practicable, whether there is sufficient evidence to charge the person arrested (D);
— If in the CO's view there is not sufficient evidence, D must be released (with or without bail), unless the CO has reasonable grounds for believing that D's detention without charge is necessary to secure or preserve evidence relating to an offence for which D is under arrest, or to obtain such evidence by questioning him or her. In that case the CO may authorise D to be kept in police detention, and, if this is done, must open a "custody record" in respect of D, *i.e.* a written record of the various stages and incidents of the period in detention;
— If in the CO's view there is sufficient evidence, D must be (1) charged or (2) released without charge, either with or without bail;
— If at any time the CO becomes aware that the grounds of detention have ceased to apply, and he or she is not aware of any other grounds on which continued detention under the Act could be justified, he or she must order D's immediate release. This is to be without bail unless it appears to the CO (1) that there is need for further investigation of any matter in connection with which D was detained, or (2) that proceedings may be taken against D in respect of any such matter[64];
— Once D is charged with an offence, the CO must order his or her release (with or without bail) unless (1) D's name and address cannot be ascertained satisfactorily; or the CO has reasonable grounds for believing (2) that D's detention is necessary for his or her own protection, or to prevent D from causing physical injury or loss of or damage to property; or (3) that D will fail to appear in court to answer to bail or

[61] 1984 Act, s.30.
[62] *Ibid.* s.35.
[63] *Ibid.* s.36. An officer of any rank may perform the functions of a custody officer if such an officer is not readily available: s.36(4).
[64] *Ibid.* s.37.

that D's detention is necessary to prevent him or her from interfering with the administration of justice or with the investigation of offences. In any of these circumstances, the CO may authorise D to be kept in police detention[65];

— The CO also has general responsibilities for the welfare of those in detention (including ensuring that the requirements of the Act and the Code of Practice governing Detention are observed) and for maintaining the custody records.[66]

These various responsibilities may lead a CO into conflict with an officer of higher rank involved in the investigation. Such matters must be referred to an officer of the rank of superintendent or above.[67]

(ii) *Periodic reviews*

Provision is made for there to be periodic reviews of a person's continued detention in custody. Thus a "review officer" (the CO if D has been arrested and charged, otherwise an inspector or above not directly involved in the investigation) must carry out a review not later than six hours after the detention was first authorised, and then at intervals not longer than nine hours, although these can in some circumstances be postponed. If D has not been charged by the time of the review, the review officer considers again the matters considered by the CO when initially processing D. If D has been charged by then, the review officer performs the functions of the CO arising after an arrested person is charged. Before authorising D's continued detention the review officer must give D (unless asleep), or any solicitor representing D who is available, an opportunity to make representations about the detention.[68]

(iii) *Time limits for detention without charge*

As to the periods of detention, a person cannot be kept in police detention for more than 24 hours without being charged. The "detention clock" normally starts (the "relevant time") when D arrives at the first police station to which he or she is taken after arrest, or, if D is arrested at a police station after attending voluntarily, at the time of arrest. There are special provisions governing persons brought from another police area or outside England and Wales. After the 24-hour period, a person who is not charged must be released, either with or without bail.[69] Exceptionally, however, a longer period of detention without charge may be authorised. This requires the authority of an officer of the rank of superintendent or above, who must have reasonable grounds of believing that D's continued detention is necessary to secure or preserve evidence relating to the offence for which D is

[65] *Ibid.* s.38. In the case of an arrested juvenile (generally persons between 10 and 17) there is a further ground; i.e. that the CO has reasonable grounds for believing that D ought to be detained in his or her own interests: s.38(1)(*b*).

[66] *Ibid.* s.39. See the *Code of Practice for the Detention, Treatment and Questioning of Persons by Police Officers* (H.M.S.O., 1990) (Code C).

[67] *Ibid.* s.39(6).

[68] *Ibid.* s.40.

[69] *Ibid.* s.41. The time the "clock" starts is termed the "relevant time" by s.41(2) and time limits are generally calculated from then.

under arrest, or to obtain such evidence by questioning him or her; that the offence in question is a serious arrestable offence; and that the investigation is being conducted diligently and expeditiously. The period of detention can be extended by a further 12 hours beyond the initial 24. Authorisation cannot be given by the superintendent after the expiry of the 24-hour period or before the second review.[70]

Detention can only be extended beyond the 36 hour period on the authority of a warrant of further detention granted by a magistrates' court.[71] The criteria for the grant of a warrant are the same as for authorisation of continued detention by a superintendent. D must be brought before the court and is entitled to legal representation. The application must be made within the 36-hour period, or, if it is not practicable for a court to sit at the expiry of 36 hours, within six hours thereafter.[72] The warrant may extend the detention for such period as the court thinks fit, up to a maximum of 36 hours.[73] Fresh applications may be made to the court, on the same basis, for the warrant to be extended for further periods not exceeding 36 hours, up to a maximum of 96 hours.[74] If an application for a warrant or an extension is refused, and in any event at the expiry of the 96 hour period, D must be charged or released, with or without bail. Release may, however, be postponed until the expiry of any period of detention that has already been authorised.[75] Full details of the various steps involved in extending periods of detention must be entered in the custody record.

(iv) *Detention after charge*

Where D is kept in detention after charge, he or she must be brought before a magistrates' court as soon as is practicable. If this is to be a local court this must be on the day D is charged or the following day; if this is to be a court in a different petty sessions area, D must be removed to that area as soon as practicable and brought before the court on the day of his or her arrival in the area or the following day. If necessary, the clerk to the justices must make special arrangements for a court to sit.[76]

(e) Treatment of persons in custody

Part V of the 1984 Act and the Code of Practice on Detention (Code C), give the police certain powers to obtain evidence from persons in custody but, more importantly, make detailed provisions as to the conditions in which such persons are kept.

---

[70] *Ibid.* s.42.

[71] *i.e.* a court of two or more justices sitting otherwise than in open court: s.45(1).

[72] If an application is made after the 36-hour period, the court must dismiss it if it appears that it would have been reasonable for the police to make it within that period: s.43(7); see *R.* v. *Slough Magistrates' Court, ex p. Stirling* (1987) 151 J.P. 603.

[73] 1984 Act, s.43.

[74] *Ibid.* s.44.

[75] *e.g.* by a superintendent where a warrant of further detention is refused (see s.43(15), (16)), or by a warrant if an extension is refused (see s.44(7)(8)).

[76] *Ibid.* s.46. The clerk has a discretion to arrange for a local court or for a court in another division, in accordance with the wishes of the local justices: *R.* v. *Avon Magistrates' Courts Committee, ex p. Broome* [1988] 1 W.L.R. 1246.

The Custody Officer (CO) must make a record of everything the person detained (D) has with him or her and if necessary D may be searched to enable this to be done.[77] An officer of the rank of superintendent or above may authorise an intimate search if he or she has reasonable grounds for believing D may have concealed on him or her anything which he or she could use to cause physical injury, or a Class A drug (possessed with criminal intent).[78] Such an officer may also authorise D's fingerprints to be taken without consent if he or she has reasonable grounds for suspecting D's involvement in a criminal offence and that the fingerprints will tend to prove or disprove that involvement.[79] He or she has a similar power to authorise a "non-intimate sample"[80] to be taken without consent, but only where D is suspected of involvement in a serious arrestable offence.[81] An "intimate sample"[82] may only be taken in such a case if there is *both* authorisation by a superintendent *and* written consent.[83]

A person held in custody is normally entitled to have someone informed[84] when arrested and to have access on request to legal advice.[85] The latter comprises a right to consult a solicitor[86] privately at any time. Delay in the exercise of these rights can only be authorised by an officer of the rank of superintendent and above in respect of a person in custody for a serious

[77] *Ibid.* s.54, as amended by the Criminal Justice Act 1988, s.147. Clothes and personal effects may only be seized if the CO (a) believes that D may use them use them to cause injury or damage, to interfere with evidence or to assist him or her to escape, (b) has reasonable grounds for believing that they may be evidence relating to an offence: s.54(4). D may be searched at any time in order to ascertain whether he or she has anything which could be used for the purposes set out in (a). The Code of Practice or Detention only permits the CO to order a strip search if he or she considers it necessary to remove an article which D would not be allowed to keep: Code C, Annex A.

[78] *Ibid.* s.55, as amended by the 1988 Act, Sched. 15, para. 99. Items may be seized on the same grounds as those set out in s.54(4): s.55(12).

[79] *Ibid.* s.61. No such authorisation is necessary if D has been charged with, informed that he or she will be reported for, or convicted of, a "recordable offence" (*i.e.* an offence specified in the National Police Records (Recordable Offences) Regulations 1985 (S.I. 1985 No. 1941): all imprisonable offences and a few others). Fingerprints may be taken at any time with consent. Broadly similar provisions govern the photographing of persons arrested: Code D. 4.

[80] *i.e.* a sample of hair other than pubic hair; a sample taken from or from under a nail; a swab taken from any part of the body orifice; a footprint or similar impression of any part of the body other than a hand: s.65.

[81] *Ibid.* s.63.

[82] *i.e.* "a sample of blood, semen or any other tissue fluid, urine, saliva or pubic hair, or a swab taken from a person's body orifices": s.65, as amended by the 1988 Act, Sched. 15, para. 100.

[83] *Ibid.* s.62. A court or jury may draw such inferences as appear proper from a refusal without good cause, and a refusal may constitute corroboration: s.62(10). For the destruction of fingerprints and samples after use, see *ibid.* s.64, as amended by the 1988 Act, s.148.

[84] *Ibid.* s.56. This replaced the Criminal Law Act 1977, s.62. In addition, the person responsible for the welfare of an arrested child or young person must, if practicable be informed: Children and Young Persons Act 1933, s.34(2)–(11), substituted by the 1988 Act, s.57.

[85] *Ibid.* s.58. This express legal right replaced the much weaker statement in the Preamble to the Judges Rules that a person under investigation should be able to consult a solicitor privately, even if he or she was in custody, provided no unreasonable delay or hindrance was caused to the investigation or the administration of justice. This was not a legal requirement: in practice few suspects asked to see a solicitor and many requests were refused: see below, p. 673.

[86] This extends to cover a clerk or legal executive, who is to be admitted unless an officer of the rank of inspector or above considers that such a visit will hinder the investigation of crime: Code C.6.9. See *R.* v. *Chief Constable of the Avon and Somerset Constabulary, ex p. Robinson* [1989] 1 W.L.R. 793.

arrestable offence: the officer must have reasonable grounds for believing that exercise of the right will lead to interference with evidence connected with a serious arrestable offence; interference with or injury to other persons; or the alerting of others suspected of such an offence but not yet arrested; or will hinder the recovery of any property obtained as the result of such an offence, or the value of the suspect's proceeds of drug trafficking.[87] In any event, D must be allowed to exercise these rights within 36 hours of the "relevant time."[88]

Code C sets out in some detail requirements as to the physical conditions in which detainees are kept,[89] the handling of any complaints[90] about treatment in custody and medical treatment,[91] the welfare of detainees being the basic responsibility of the custody officer.

(f) Questioning

Detailed provision is made in Code C governing the questioning of persons in custody. This replaced the non-statutory Judges' Rules and Administrative Directions to the Police, which had previously provided guidance as to the proper conduct of interrogations.[92] A central feature of the position of a person under interrogation (at least in theory) is the so-called "right to remain silent" or "right of silence."

In general, the police may ask any person such questions as they think appropriate. However, the person asked is normally under no duty to answer.[93] A mere refusal to answer cannot constitute the offence of obstructing a police officer in the exercise of his or her duty.[94] The jury at a trial may not normally be expressly invited to draw any adverse inferences from the silence of the accused before the trial (although they cannot be stopped from doing so in the privacy of the jury room).[95] Code C requires a person to be

---

[87] "will" not "might": R. v. Samuel [1988] Q.B. 615: see below, p. 614.
[88] 1984 Act, ss.56(2)–(9); 58(5)–(11), as amended by the Drug Trafficking Offences Act 1986, s.32; Code C, Annex B(A). Access may not be delayed on the ground that the solicitor might advise the person not to answer any questions: ibid. Part (A).3. Access may only be delayed by reference to the specific circumstances of the case: general fears that solicitors will unwittingly carry out messages etc. will not be sufficient: R. v. Samuel, supra; cf. R. v. Alladice (1988) 87 Cr.App.R. 380.
[89] C. 5, covering, e.g. visits, provision of writing materials, and giving an additional right to make one telephone call; C. 8., covering, e.g. the heating, cleanliness and ventilation of cells, bedding, toilet facilities, clothing, meals, exercise and hourly visits.
[90] C. 9.1. Complaints must be dealt with by an officer of at least the rank of inspector not connected with the investigation.
[91] C. 9.2–9.6. Special provision is also made for the treatment in custody of the mentally ill, the handicapped, and overseas nationals: C. 1.4, 1.6, 3.6–3.14.
[92] The Judges' Rules originated in 1906, with revised versions issued in 1964 and 1978 together with related Administrative Directions from the Home Office. Compliance with the Rules would tend to ensure that a confession was admissible. Breach of a particular Rule or Direction might, but in practice normally did not, render the confession inadmissible.
[93] There are some exceptions where a refusal to give information is itself an offence: e.g. the Companies Act 1985, ss.434–436 (investigation of the affairs of a company); Financial Services Act 1986, ss.105 (investigation of investment business) and 177–178 (investigation of insider dealing). Moreover, a refusal to give name and address by a suspect may lead to an arrest under the general arrest conditions—or detention in custody: see above, pp. 599, 604.
[94] If the refusal is combined with positive acts that obstruct the police, such as abuse, threats or misleading answers the position may be different: e.g. Ricketts v. Cox (1981) 74 Cr.App.R. 298 (abuse: although the case is doubtful on its facts: see S. H. Bailey, D. J. Harris and B. L. Jones, Civil Liberties: Cases and Materials (2nd ed., 1985), p. 39).
[95] See J. A. Andrews and M. Hirst, Criminal Evidence (1987), paras.8.10–8.12, 19.86–19.95.

cautioned, if there are grounds to suspect him or her of an offence, before questions are put for the purpose of obtaining evidence which may be given to a court of law. A person must also be cautioned on arrest for an offence, unless that is impracticable by reason of his or her condition or behaviour, or he or she has already been cautioned, and when charged or informed that he or she may be prosecuted. The caution is to be in the terms: "You do not have to say anything unless you wish to do so, but what you say may be given in evidence," or other words to the same effect.[96]

In practice, only a minority of suspects questioned by the police rely on their right of silence.[97] Indeed, commentators have noted the considerable psychological pressures on suspects:

"To remain silent in a police interview room in the face of determined questioning by an officer with legitimate authority to carry on this activity requires an abnormal exercise of will."[98]

It is a matter of some debate how important confessions or admissions are in establishing the prosecution case. The police certainly regard interrogation as a central feature of their work, a very high proportion of suspects who make confessions subsequently plead guilty, with, *inter alia*, a consequent saving of police time, and only a very small proportion of those who confess are ultimately acquitted.[99] On the other hand, the research concerning Crown Court cases conducted by Baldwin and McConville indicated that the prosecution's case would only have been fatally weakened had the accused's statement not been adduced in about 20 per cent. of cases.[1] Whatever the true position, if confession evidence is to be relied upon in court, it is only right that proper attention is paid to ensure the reliability of such evidence. False confessions and police misconduct, usually in the form of the inventing of confessions, have been identified by JUSTICE as two of the five common threads through most of the allegations of miscarriages of justice made over the years.[2]

In various ways, the arrangements under the 1984 Act seem designed to encourage exercise of the right of silence and to improve the reliability of

[96] C. 10.

[97] This was confirmed in the Report of the Royal Commission on Criminal Procedure (Cmnd. 8092, 1981), pp. 83–84, based on research it had commissioned: see P. Softley (Research Study No. 4: confession or admission made by 61 per cent. of the 187 suspects in the study); B. Irving (Research Study No. 2: admissions made by 65 per cent. of the 60 suspects observed). See also J. Baldwin and M. McConville, Research Study 5 (*Confessions in Crown Court Trials*) and *Courts, Prosecution and Conviction* (1981), Chap. 6; J. Vennard, Research Study No. 6. *Contested Trials in Magistrates' Courts* and H.O. Research Study No. 71 (1982); M. Zander, [1979] Crim.L.R. 203; B. Mitchell, [1983] Crim.L.R. 5. See further, below, pp. 687–688.

[98] Irving, *op. cit.* p. 153. On the psychology of the interrogation process, see B. Irving and L. Hilgendorf, Research Study No. 1 (*Police Interrogation: The Psychological Approach*); B. Irving and I. K. McKenzie, *Police Interrogation: the effect of the Police and Criminal Evidence Act 1984* (1989), pp. 17–25, 235–240; G. H. Gudjonsson, "The Psychology of False Confessions" (1989) 57 Medico-legal Jo. 93.

[99] M. McConville and J. Baldwin, *Courts, Prosecutions, and Convictions* (1981), Chap. 5, esp. pp. 106–114.

[1] *Ibid.* Chap. 6. Evaluations of case papers were made by independent assessors. Research concerning contested magistrates' court cases suggested that confession evidence was most influential in cases based on circumstantial rather than direct evidence: Vennard (1980) and (1982).

[2] JUSTICE, *Miscarriages of Justice* (1989), p. 4.

confessions. Thus, a person who asks for legal advice may not be interviewed[3] until he or she has received it unless
(1) exercise of the right of access to such advice can properly be delayed[4]; or
(2) an officer of the rank of superintendent or above has reasonable grounds for believing that
    — delay will involve an immediate risk of harm to persons or serious loss of or damage to property[5];
    — or awaiting the arrival of the solicitor would cause unreasonable delay to the process of investigation; or
(3) the solicitor nominated cannot be contacted or refuses to attend (and D declines to ask for a duty solicitor or the duty solicitor is unavailable); or
(4) D agrees in writing or on tape that the interview may be started at once.[6]
In situations (3) and (4), an officer of the rank of inspector or above must agree for the interview to proceed.

If D is allowed to consult a solicitor, and the solicitor is available, D must be allowed to have him or her present during the interview. The solicitor may only be required to leave the interview if his or her conduct is such that the investigating officer is unable properly to put questions to the suspect, and then only on the authority of an officer of the rank of superintendent or above.[7]

Code C prescribes that an accurate record must be made of each interview with a suspect.[8] Interview must normally take place at a police station and the record must normally be made during the course of the interview, which implies either tape recording the interview or making contemporaneous notes. Eight hours must normally be allowed in any period of 24 hours free from a questioning, travel or other interruptions, if possible at night. Interview rooms must be adequately heated, lit or ventilated. Breaks must normally be made at recognised meal times and at two-hour intervals. Full details must be recorded of the periods and of incidents of the interrogation. Written statements under caution must be taken in accordance with Annex D.

---

[3] In *R.* v. *Absolam* (1988) 88 Cr.App.R. 332, the Court of Appeal held that a series of questions and answers constituted an interview in that "it was a series of questions directed by the police to a suspect with a view to obtaining admissions on which proceedings could be founded" (p. 336); definition applied in *R.* v. *Maguire* (1989) 90 Cr.App.R. This may be too narrow as a definition: see P. Addison, [1989] Crim.L.R. 606 (letter). See also *R.* v. *Matthews* [1990] Crim.L.R. 190; *R.* v. *Manji* [1990] Crim.L.R. 512. A narrow definition has been adopted in Note *11A* of the revised Code C.

[4] Above, pp. 607–608.

[5] It is only on this ground that a person heavily under the influence of drink or drugs can be interviewed at all or an arrested juvenile or a person who is mentally ill or mentally handicapped, a person who has difficulty in understanding English or a hearing disability can be interviewed in the absence, respectively, of an appropriate adult or of an interpreter: Code C. 11.14, 12.3, 13.2, 13.5, and Annex C. See *D.P.P.* v. *Blake* [1989] 1 W.L.R. 432 (estranged father of juvenile not an "appropriate adult": see new Note for Guidance *1C*).

[6] Code C. 6.6.

[7] Code C. 6.8–6.11. The Notes for Guidance state (*6D*) that it is not misconduct for a solicitor to challenge an improper question or the manner in which it is put, or to give further advice, or to advise the clients not to reply to particular questions; *cf. ibid.* Annex B(A)3, above, p. 608, n. 88.

[8] C. 11. The revised Code makes it clear that a written record must be kept of all interviews and other comments by suspects, and, unless impracticable, shown to the suspect. Under the earlier version, the latter requirement was held to apply only to interviews at police stations: *R.* v. *Brezeanu and Francis* [1989] Crim.L.R. 650, C.A.; *R.* v. *Beycan* [1990] Crim.L.R. 185.

It is intended that the tape-recording of interviews should become standard practice by the end of 1991.[9] This will be the culmination of an extraordinarily protracted period of discussion and trials, following the recommendation of the Criminal Law Revision Committee that an experiment should be conducted.[10] Field trials set up by the Home Office showed that, with co-operation from all those involved, tape-recording operated well. There was no evidence that the police were avoiding tape-recording by making greater use of interviews outside the police station, police fears that interviews would be less informative were not borne out, challenges to interview evidence were now infrequent, and (expensive) written transcripts were rarely needed.[11] Indeed, there has been a remarkable change in the police attitude to tape-recording from hostility to support,[12] encouraged further by the P.A.C.E. requirement that contemporaneous notes of interviews be kept if there is no tape-recording. The tape-recording of interviews is regulated by P.A.C.E. Code of Practice E.[13] In the areas where the Code is applied, tape-recording must normally be used for any interview with a person who has been cautioned for an indictable only or either-way offence, other than terrorism and espionage offences.

In addition to these changes to the regime of police interrogation, there has been an important change in the law governing the admissibility of confessions and admissions in evidence. At common law, the test was whether a confession was "voluntary, in the sense that it has not been obtained from him by fear of prejudice or hope of advantage, exercised or held out by a person in authority, or by oppression."[14] The case law was directed more to the technicalities of this definition than the realities of the reliability of confessions.[15]

The key provisions are now section 76 of P.A.C.E., which relates to confessions, and section 78, which concerns the exclusion of all kinds of evidence. The basic test is found in s.76(2):

"(2) If, in any proceedings where the prosecution proposes to give in evidence a confession[16] made by an accused person, it is represented to the court that the confession was or may have been obtained—
    (a) by oppression[17] of the person who made it; or
    (b) in consequence of anything said or done which was likely, in the

[9] See Zander (1990), p. 124.
[10] 11th Report, *Evidence (General)* (Cmnd. 4991, 1972), paras. 50–52. On the ensuring history see P. Mirfield, *Confessions* (1985), pp. 19–40.
[11] C. F. Willis *et al.*, *The Tape-Recording of Police Interviews with Suspects: an Interim Report* (H.O. Research Study 97, H.M.S.O., 1988).
[12] Documented by J. Baldwin, [1985] Crim.L.R. 695.
[13] H.M.S.O., 1988.
[14] Para. (*e*) of the preamble to the Judges' Rules, based on *Ibrahim* v. *R.* [1914] A.C. 599, 609 (basic test for "voluntariness"); and see *R.* v. *Prager* [1972] 1 W.L.R. 260 and *R.* v. *Hudson* (1980) 72 Cr.App.R. 163 (oppression).
[15] See, generally, R.C.C.P. Report (1981), pp. 91–95.
[16] This "includes any statement wholly or partly adverse to the person who made it, whether made to a person in authority or not and whether made in words or otherwise" (s.82(1)); it therefore covers any admission, not just a full confession. However, it seems not to apply to statements which are intended to be exculpatory, but which become damaging at the trial, *e.g.* by then being shown to be evasive or false or inconsistent with the maker's evidence at the trial: *R.* v. *Sat-Bhambra* (1988) 88 Cr.App.R. 55, criticised by Di Birch, [1989] Crim.L.R. 95, 114–116.
[17] This "includes torture, inhuman or degrading treatment, and the use or threat of violence (whether or not amounting to torture)": s.76(8). See below, pp. 612–613.

circumstances existing at the time, to render unreliable any confession which might be made by him in consequence thereof,
the court shall not allow the confession to be given in evidence against him[18] except in so far as the prosecution proves to the court beyond reasonable doubt that the confession (notwithstanding that it may be true) was not obtained as aforesaid."[19]

Section 78(1) provides:

"In any proceedings the court may refuse to allow evidence on which the prosecution proposes to rely to be given if it appears to the court that, having regard to all the circumstances including the circumstances in which the evidence was obtained, the admission of the evidence would have such an adverse effect on the fairness of the proceedings that the court ought not to admit it."

This is applicable to confessions as well as other kinds of evidence.[20]

The courts have employed these sections to exclude confession evidence rather more vigorously than had been anticipated.[21]

The first hurdle is that of "oppression," to which the Court of Appeal in R. v. Fulling[22] accorded its dictionary meaning as the

"Exercise of authority or power in a burdensome, harsh or wrongful manner; unjust or cruel treatment of subjects, inferiors etc., the imposition of unreasonable or unjust burdens."

The court noted, with apparent approval, a quotation in the dictionary under this definition: "There is not a word in our language which expresses more detestable wickedness than oppression," and continued: "We find it hard to envisage any circumstances in which such oppression would not entail some impropriety on the part of the interrogator."[23] This definition is narrower than the concept of "oppression" at common law,[24] but wider than that suggested by the definition section.[25] To date there are very few de-

---

[18] If confession is put before the jury and the judge subsequently has doubts about oppression or reliability, it is too late for exclusion under s.76, although the judge could discharge the jury or direct the jury to disregard the statement under the common law: R. v. Sat-Bhambra, supra.

[19] The court may require this to be proved of its own motion: s.76(3). Facts discovered in consequence of an inadmissible confession are themselves admissible, but evidence that they were discovered as a result of the confession is not unless adduced by D: s.76(4)–(6).

[20] R. v. Mason [1988] 1 W.L.R. 139. The court's common law powers to exclude evidence were preserved by s.82(3). The ambit of these powers was uncertain, although they clearly included power to exclude evidence whose probative value was outweighed by its prejudicial effect: R. v. Sang [1980] A.C. 402. In Matto v. Wolverhampton Crown Court [1987] R.T.R. 337, Woolf L.J. indicated that s.78 was if anything wider than the common law (p. 346).

[21] See generally, Di Birch, "The Pace Hots Up: Confessions and Confusions under the 1984 Act" [1989] Crim.L.R. 95.

[22] [1987] Q.B. 426.

[23] Ibid. p. 432. See also R. v. Hughes [1988] Crim.L.R. 545, C.A. (no police misconduct, so not oppression where, through a misunderstanding, D did not see the Duty Solicitor).

[24] "something which tends to sap, and has sapped, that free will which must exist before a confession is voluntary" (per Sachs L.J. in R. v. Priestly (1967) 51 Cr.App.R. 1); cf. Edmund Davies L.J. in R. v. Prager [1972] 1 W.L.R. 260, 266.

[25] See f.n. 17, supra. The term "includes" in the definition suggests that it was not intended to be exclusive.

cisions[26] in which a confession has been excluded on this ground. It seems clear that breaches of the law or Codes on the part of the police will not necessarily constitute oppression[27]; conversely, it is highly unlikely that oppression will be found in the absence of such breaches. In *Fulling*[28] itself, D confessed while (so she claimed) in distress following the revelation by the interrogator that her boyfriend had for some three years been having an affair with the woman currently held in the next cell: this was held not to constitute oppression.

The second hurdle is that of "unreliability" and has been invoked more frequently. This has been done where a child has been interviewed in the absence of an "appropriate adult"[29]; where there have been doubts about the reliability of a confession by a person of low intelligence[30]; where proper records of the confession have not been kept[31]; where there has been an improper inducement[32]; and, in one case, where a drug addict was held in custody for 18 hours without being allowed the prescribed rest periods.[33] In principle, this hurdle is not limited to breaches of the law or of the Codes, but as most of the requirements are designed to promote reliability, breaches of them are a common factor to many of the cases. One limitation is that the unreliability must arise from something "said or done," and this has been held not to include anything said or done by D himself.[34]

By far the largest number of cases in which confessions have been excluded fall under section 78. This has been employed where the police

---

[26] *R.* v. *Davison* [1988] Crim.L.R. 442 (Central Criminal Court). D was unlawfully detained and there were various breaches of the 1984 Act and Code C; the judge did not expressly find that the police had acted "wickedly" or in deliberate breach of the law but held that the prosecution had not disproved oppression in that the police had acted in a "wrongful manner." The concept of "oppression" was perhaps stretched here, although the circumstances are very similar to other cases where confessions have been excluded under s.78 (see below). See further D. J. Birch, Commentary, [1988] Crim.L.R. 444 and [1989] Crim.L.R. 95, 102. See also *R.* v. *Ismail* [1990] Crim.L.R. 109.

[27] *Cf. R.* v. *Samuel* [1988] Q.B. 615, C.A.; *R.* v. *Hughes* [1988] Crim.L.R. 545, C.A.

[28] *Supra.*

[29] *D.P.P.* v. *Blake* [1989] 1 W.L.R. 432, C.A.

[30] *R.* v. *Harvey* [1988] Crim.L.R. 241 (Central Criminal Court): (psychopathic woman of low intelligence may have confessed after hearing her lover confess in order to protect her); *R.* v. *Everett* [1988] Crim.L.R. 826, C.A. (man of 42 with mental age of 8: judge had taken no account of his mental condition); *R.* v. *Delaney* (1988) 88 Cr.App.R. 338, C.A. (D educationally subnormal and proper records not kept); *R.* v. *Moss* (1990) 91 Cr.App.R. 371 (conviction based on confession of a man of limited intelligence held in custody for 6 days without a solicitor quashed as unsafe and unsatisfactory).

[31] *R.* v. *Doolan* [1988] Crim.L.R. 747, C.A.; *R.* v. *Delaney, supra*; *R.* v. *Waters* [1989] Crim.L.R. 62 (W was also wrongly questioned after charge). In the absence of a proper record, the prosecution may be unable to discharge its onus of proving reliability beyond reasonable doubt: see D. J. Birch, Commentary on *Delaney* [1989] Crim.L.R. 139.

[32] *R.* v. *Phillips* (1987) Cr.App.R. 18, C.A. (statement that if D confessed, offences could be taken into consideration rather than prosecuted); *R.* v. *Howden-Simpson* [1991] Crim.L.R. 49 (threat to pursue more than two charges).

[33] *R.* v. *Trussler* [1988] Crim.L.R. 446 (Reading Crown Court).

[34] *R.* v. *Goldenberg* (1988) 88 Cr.App.R. 285, C.A. (D's argument that his confession was unreliable as his motive was to obtain bail, or credit for helping the police, held not to fall within s.76(2)(*b*)).

have denied access to a solicitor in breach of D's right under section 58[35]; where D has not been advised of the right to legal advice[36]; where a proper record of the interview has not been made[37]; and where a young person has been interviewed in the absence of an appropriate adult.[38] A number of these decisions, particularly at first instance, have been criticised on the ground that the court has concluded too readily that breaches of the Code render it unfair for the confession to be admitted.[39] The Court of Appeal has emphasised that "not every breach or combination of breaches would justify exclusion . . .: they must be significant and substantial."[40] However, "if the police have acted in bad faith, the court will have little difficulty in ruling any confession inadmissible under section 78, if not under section 76."[41] The court has also stated that the main object of section 58 and the Codes was to achieve fairness to a suspect and to the Crown and its officers; that if there were significant and substantial breaches then, prima facie at least, the standards of fairness would not have been met, and to admit evidence thus obtained could not but have an adverse effect on the fairness of proceedings; but that it would still be necessary to consider whether there would be *such* an adverse effect that justice required exclusion of the evidence.[42]

The case which seems to have caused the judges most consternation is *R.* *v. Mason (Carl)*,[43] where D confessed to arson after the interrogators falsely told him, and his solicitor, that they had found at the scene a fragment of a bottle which had contained inflammable liquid and that D's fingerprint was on the fragment. This was described as "reprehensible":

"we hope never again to hear of deceit such as this being practised on an accused person, and more particularly possibly on a solicitor whose duty it is to advise him, unfettered by false information from the police."[44]

---

[35] *R. v. Samuel* [1988] Q.B. 615, C.A. (Confession excluded: "the appellant was denied improperly one of the most important and fundamental rights of a citizen," D would probably not have made incriminating admissions had he had legal advice); *R. v. Parris* (1989) 89 Cr.App.R. 68, C.A. (superintendent's order that D be kept incommunicado under s.56 wrongly assumed to exclude access to a solicitor under s.58); *R. v. Walsh* (1989) 91 Cr.App.R. 161, C.A.; *cf. R. v. Alladice* (1988) 87 Cr.App.R. 380, C.A. (confession not excluded: D was fully aware of his rights and the interviews were found to have been conducted with propriety); *R. v. Dunford* (1990) 91 Cr.App.R. 150, C.A. (D aware of his rights).

[36] *R. v. Absolam* (1988) 88 Cr.App.R. 332, C.A. (see also f.n. 37); *R. v. Beycan* [1990] Crim.L.R. 185.

[37] Commonly, neither contemporaneous notes nor other notes made after the interview and shown to D: *R. v. Absolam, supra* (no caution before questioning, no proper record); *R. v. Keenan* [1990] 2 Q.B. 54, C.A. (officers unaware of Code C); *R. v. Walsh, supra*; *R. v. Ismail, supra*; *R. v. Canale* [1990] 2 All E.R. 187 (*cf. R. v. Matthews, Dennison and Voss* (1989) 91 Cr.App.R. 43; *R. v. Scott* [1991] Crim.L.R. 56 (Code breaches, but confession led to discovery of other evidence)).

[38] *R. v. Delroy Fogah* [1989] Crim.L.R. 141 (Snaresbrook Crown Court).

[39] See Di Birch, [1989] Crim.L.R. 95, 105–106, and Commentary on *R. v. Williams (Violet)* [1989] Crim.L.R. 66 and *R. v. Woodall, ibid.* p. 288 (both Crown Court decisions).

[40] *R. v. Keenan, supra*; *R. v. Parris, supra*; *R. v. Walsh, supra*.

[41] *Per* Lord Lane C.J. in *R. v. Alladice* (1988) 87 Cr.App.R. 380, 386.

[42] *R. v. Walsh, supra*.

[43] [1988] 1 W.L.R. 139.

[44] *Ibid.* p. 144.

The courts' willingness to exclude confessions for breaches of the Act or the Codes does much to make their requirements effective.[45] However, it remains the case that the courts have failed to articulate the principles upon which their decisions are based.[46]

(g) Identification evidence

Identification evidence is recognised as one of the kinds of evidence that must be treated with especial caution:

"Identification, whether by sight or hearing, is evidence which can seem immensely convincing and compelling to a jury but can also, notoriously, be mistaken."[47]

There are, accordingly, special arrangements governing the gathering of such evidence and how it is dealt with at the trial.[48]

The former is now governed by the *Code of Practice for the Identification of Persons by Police Officers* (Code D) made under P.A.C.E. The methods for establishing identifications include, in order of preference, formal identification parades, where the suspect is seen by the witness with others of similar appearance; group identifications, where he or she is simply placed in a group of people, commonly in a public place; video film identifications, where he or she is filmed with others of similar appearance; and confrontations, where the suspect alone is confronted by the witness. These are arranged by an "identification officer," not involved in the investigation and at least of the rank of inspector. A parade must be held in a case which involves disputed identification evidence if the suspect asks for one and it is practicable to hold one, and may be held if the investigation officer considers that it would be useful and the suspect consents. Conversely, one need not be held if the identification officer considers that, whether by reason of the suspect's unusual appearance or otherwise, it would not be practicable to assemble sufficient people who resemble him or her to make it fair. Group identifications are permitted if a parade is impracticable, or if the suspect refuses to attend one or if the investigating officer considers that would be more satisfactory and the suspect consents. Video identifications are permitted if the investigating officer considers that would be more satisfactory. Confrontations do not require the suspect's consent but may only take place

---

[45] See, *e.g.* a general instruction issued by the deputy chief constable of Avon, in part responding to case law, set out in *R.* v. *Chief Constable of the Avon and Somerset Constabulary, ex p. Robinson* [1989] 2 All E.R. 15, C.A.

[46] See Di Birch, *op. cit.* f.n. 39. The relevant principles have been helpfully analysed by commentators, and include, apart from reliability and fairness, the protection of rights and the deterrence of police misconduct. See A. Ashworth, "Excluding Evidence as Protecting Rights" [1977] Crim.L.R. 723.

[47] JUSTICE Report on *Miscarriages of Justice* (1989), p. 10. Well-known cases of miscarriages of justice based on identification evidence include those of Laslo Virag and Luke Dougherty, which led to the Devlin Committee on *Evidence of Identification in Criminal Case* (1975–76 H.C. 338).

[48] On the latter, see below, p. 792.

if a parade or group or video identification is impracticable, for example as a result of the suspect's non-co-operation.[49]

The courts seem willing to exclude identification evidence under section 78 of P.A.C.E. where the identification officer has concluded too readily that a parade is impracticable[50] or where there have been other breaches of Code D.[51]

JUSTICE has made a number of recommendations for improving arrangements, including the improvement of police training, videoing parades and the encouragement of purpose-built centres for parades.[52]

B. THE RESPONSIBILITY FOR INSTITUTING PROSECUTIONS[53]

The historical development of the English prosecution process placed emphasis upon the role of the private individual as prosecutor. As the police forces grew so they began to assume the responsibility for bringing prosecutions (but only exercising individual rather than statutory rights); and practice diverged from that in Scotland where a public prosecutor (the procurator fiscal) became established and the right of private prosecution diminished. In fact, for many years the theory of the private prosecution in England no longer matched the reality of the situation, not only because of the powers of the Director of Public Prosecutions,[54] but also because of restrictions placed by statute upon private prosecutions for many offences.[55] In practice, the majority of prosecutions were brought by the police and almost all the balance by other public agencies. Truly private prosecutions were highly unusual.[56] Furthermore, from 1986 the conduct of most classes of criminal proceedings has been taken over by the Crown Prosecution Service established by the Prosecution of Offences 1985. The fiction that the prosecution is acting in a private capacity is here not maintained.

---

[49] Code D2 and Annexes A (parades and group identifications), B (video identifications) and C (confrontations). Identification from photographs, photofits etc. is confined where possible to the process of investigation: see Annex D. JUSTICE (*supra*) were informed that formal parades are usually held in about 80 per cent. of cases where such evidence was possible (p. 10).

[50] *R.* v. *Gaynor* [1988] Crim.L.R. 242 (Liverpool Crown Court); *R.* v. *Brittain and Richards* [1989] Crim.L.R. 144 (Leeds Crown Court).

[51] *R.* v. *Gall* (1989) 90 Cr.App.R. 64, C.A. (investigating officer took part in the conduct of a parade); *R.* v. *Conway* (1990) 91 Cr.App.R. 143, C.A. (parade not held although requested: no good reason); *R.* v. *Nagah* [1991] Crim.L.R. 55; *cf. R.* v. *Quinn* [1990] Crim.L.R. 581 (evidence of identification of Q while on trial in a Dublin court admitted); *R* v. *Grannell* (1989) 90 Cr.App.R. 149 (breach of Code D, but no unfairness).

[52] Report, *supra*, f.n. 47, pp. 10–11.

[53] See generally, J. Sigler, "Public Prosecution in England and Wales" [1974] Crim. L.R. 642; *The Royal Commission on Criminal Procedure* (Cmnd. 8092, 1980); JUSTICE, *The Prosecution Process in England and Wales* (1970); P. Devlin, *The Criminal Prosecution in England* (1960); M. McConville, "Prosecuting Criminal Cases in England and Wales: Reflections of an inquisitorial adversary" (1984) VI(1) Liverpool L.R. 15; K. de Gama, "Police Powers and Public Prosecutions: Winning by Appearing To Lose?" (1988) 6 Int. J. Sociology of Law 339.

[54] See below, p. 618.

[55] By requiring the consent of the D.P.P., the Attorney-General, a High Court judge or some other authority, to the proposed prosecution. See below, pp. 618, 619.

[56] See further, below, pp. 629–630.

1. Prosecution Arrangements Before the Prosecution of Offences Act 1985

(a) Police Prosecutions

Prior to the establishment of the Crown Prosecution Service, the responsibility of deciding whether or not to prosecute suspects and the conduct of proceedings for less serious offences were regarded as two of the main functions of the police, as aspects of their general duty to enforce the law.[57]

The procedure adopted varied according to the practice of the force concerned but the initial steps were normally taken in the name of the officer who had decided on the prosecution.[58] If there was any legal difficulty, for example in deciding the appropriate charge or assessing the weight of the evidence on a particular charge, the police were able to take advice either from a prosecuting solicitors' department established by the police authority or from a private firm employed for that purpose. The growth of prosecuting solicitors' departments had a significant effect on police prosecutions, but that effect was haphazard since the constitution, size and operation of such departments was entirely a matter for local decision and varied from force to force.

By the 1980s, 31 of the 43 police forces in England and Wales were able to draw on the expertise of their own prosecuting solicitors' department for legal advice and for representation in court.[59] The growth of such departments owed much to the recommendations of the Royal Commission on the Police,[60] but lacked any statutory basis or central model for development. It was, at least, clear that a prosecuting solicitor acted on instructions from the police and was merely an adviser in a solicitor/client relationship, but the line of authority, the budgetary controls, the amount of advocacy undertaken and the degree of "independence" enjoyed varied greatly from force to force.[61]

If the police *did* decide on a prosecution it was quite possible for a police officer to present the case in the magistrates' court. The Royal Commission on the Police suggested that it was undesirable for police officers to act as prosecutors save in minor cases.[62] In practice, the police could not conduct cases in the Crown Court and only prosecuted in the magistrates' court in straightforward cases.[63] In some areas, *all* prosecutions were undertaken by prosecuting solicitors. In serious cases, a measure of control was exerted by the Director of Public Prosecutions and the Law Officers.

---

[57] Final Report of the Royal Commission on the Police (Cmnd. 1782, 1962), para. 59.
[58] Sometimes in the name of the Chief Constable, more often in the name of the head of the appropriate division or subdivision.
[59] The Metropolitan Police and the City of London force had their own special arrangements, leaving 10 forces to rely on private practitioners to provide the necessary service. See *Royal Commission on Criminal Procedure, The Investigation and Prosecution of Criminal Offences in England and Wales: The Law and Procedure* (hereafter R.C.C.P. I) (Cmnd. 8092–1, 1980), Appendix 22.
[60] Cmnd. 1782, para. 380.
[61] An analysis of the system is to be found in, *The Prosecution System, Survey of Prosecuting Solicitors, Departments*, R.C.C.P. Research Study No. 11 (HMSO, 1980).
[62] Cmnd. 1782, para. 381.
[63] R.C.C.P. I, paras. 144–145.

(b) The Director of Public Prosecutions and the Law Officers[64]

The basic functions of the D.P.P. have always included those of under-taking prosecutions of particular importance or difficulty and advising chief officers of police. Indeed, prior to the establishment of the C.P.S. and the D.P.P.'s new role as head of the service, these were his main functions. Regulations 6 and 7 of the Prosecution of Offences Regulations 1978 (which are still in force[65]) required cases in a number of classes to be referred to the D.P.P.[66] These gave the D.P.P. an important co-ordinating function in these cases, which cases tended to be of a serious or sensitive nature. In addition, two further devices strengthened his position.

First, many statutes provided that prosecutions could only be brought in respect of certain offences with the consent of the D.P.P.[67] This has become a popular provision where the offence is controversial, or the statutory provision slightly ambiguous, or public policy considerations are involved, or mitigating factors might be present or where vexatious or trivial private prosecutions might be brought.[68] At the time that the D.P.P. gave evidence to the Royal Commission on Criminal Procedure there were 62 statutes creating offences requiring his consent to prosecution.[69]

Secondly, there was a general power vested in the D.P.P. by sections 2 and 4 of the 1979 Act to take over criminal proceedings and then to deal with them as he wished, including the offering of no evidence if he so chose. This power was equally applicable to private prosecutions and was used, for example, to discontinue a private prosecution brought against a person to whom the D.P.P. had given a promise of immunity from proceedings in return for giving evidence for the prosecution at another trial.[70] In that case it was held that the court had no power to interfere with the Director's exercise of discretion in how he conducted proceedings taken over by him.

All these powers taken together gave the D.P.P. a significant amount of control over prosecution policy in relation to serious criminal offences.

The two important provisions relating to the Attorney-General were[71] his power to enter a *nolle prosequi* in proceedings on indictment[72] and the requirement of his consent to the prosecution of certain offences.[73] (These remain after the Prosecution of Offences Act 1985.)

The grant of a *nolle prosequi* by the Attorney-General stops proceedings on indictment immediately and is entered on the court record. It does not

---

[64] For a general description see above pp. 18–20.

[65] See below, p. 625.

[66] *Ibid.*

[67] Not necessarily *all* the offences in a particular statute.

[68] See the evidence of the D.P.P. to the R.C.C.P., part of which is reproduced at R.C.C.P.-I, para. 159.

[69] R.C.C.P. Report, Appendix 12.

[70] *Turner* v. *D.P.P.* (1978) 68 Cr.App.R. 70. See also statements about the circumstances in which it is proper to grant such immunity in *R.* v. *Turner* (1975) 61 Cr.App.R. 67 (no relation). The matter has been further considered in *Raymond* v. *Att.-Gen.* [1982] Q.B. 839, where the Court of Appeal confirmed that the power to "conduct" proceedings under s.4 included the power to discontinue them, pointing out that control was exercised over the D.P.P. by the Attorney-General who was, in turn, accountable to Parliament.

[71] The Solicitor General acts as the Attorney's deputy, see above, p. 19.

[72] This is a common law power not subject to any control by the courts: *R.* v. *Comptroller of Patents* [1899] 1 Q.B. 909.

[73] *cf.* the powers of the D.P.P. referred to earlier.

actually amount to an acquittal, so the accused may be indicted again on the same charge,[74] but another *nolle prosequi* may then be granted. A request for such a grant may be made by any person and the exercise of the power is equivalent to the D.P.P. taking over proceedings and offering no evidence or a prosecutor offering no evidence, except that in both the latter cases the effect would formally be an acquittal.

The requirement of consent by the Attorney-General to prosecution was to be found in 39[75] statutes at the time of the Royal Commission on Criminal Procedure and included in that category were offences under the Public Order Act 1936,[76] the Hijacking Act 1971 and the Suppression of Terrorism Act 1978. These indicated that the primary responsibility of the Attorney-General in deciding whether to give consent was to weigh factors of national and public significance, conscious that he was the Minister answerable in Parliament for all matters connected with the conduct of criminal proceedings. However, it was clearly established that the Attorney-General's decision should be made on quasi-judicial and not on political grounds.[77]

(c) Criticisms

These arrangements were subjected to close scrutiny, first by JUSTICE in 1970, and then by the Royal Commission on Criminal Procedure in 1982. JUSTICE[78] argued that the responsibility for prosecutions in all but trivial cases should be taken out of the hands of the police and given to a national prosecuting authority. In support of this recommendation it was said that:

(a) a police officer might convince himself of the guilt of a suspect and become psychologically committed to a prosecution;

(b) public policy and the circumstances of the individual were relevant considerations in the decision to prosecute;

(c) the English system was unique in Europe in allowing the whole process from interrogation to prosecution to be effectively under the control of the police in the majority of cases;

(d) investigators found it difficult to achieve the necessary detachment in taking what is essentially a "judicial-type" decision whether or not to prosecute;

(e) police involvement might influence the conduct of the prosecution in

---

[74] Archbold, *Criminal Pleading, Evidence and Practice* (43rd ed.), para. 1–122, relying on *Goddard* v. *Smith* (1704) 3 Salk. 245.

[75] D.P.P.'s evidence to the R.C.C.P., Appendix 11.

[76] Including that created by the Race Relations Act 1976, of incitement to racial hatred, then s.5A of the 1936 Act.

[77] Statement by the Prime Minister to the House of Commons, February 16, 1959 (H.C. Deb., Vol. 600, col. 31), part of which is cited in R.C.C.P. I, para. 164. Questions can be asked in the House and, in one celebrated case, led to the downfall of the first Labour Government following the withdrawal of a prosecution for incitement to mutiny against J. R. Campbell, editor of a Communist publication, *Workers Weekly*: see J.Ll.J. Edwards, *The Law Officers of the Crown* (1964), Chap. 11 and *The Attorney-General, Politics and the Public Interest* (1984), pp. 310–318; F. H. Newark, (1969) 20 N.I.L.Q. 19; N. D. Siederer, (1974) 9 *Jo. of Contemporary History* 143; J. F. Naylor, *A Man and an Institution* (1984), pp. 140–149, 156–157 (biography of Sir Maurice Hankey). The independent role of the Attorney-General is fully considered in the two works by Edwards.

[78] *The Prosecution Process in England and Wales* (1970). See also, J. Sigler, [1974] Crim. L.R. 642; A. S. Bowley, [1975] Crim. L.R. 442.

deciding appropriate charges or otherwise "bargaining" with a suspect, or in putting pressure on counsel at trial to take a particular line;
(f) police officers were not trained as lawyers or advocates and those
tasks involving the expertise of lawyers or advocates should not be
undertaken by the police.

The Royal Commission took account of these and similar arguments, and
also the fact that the "present arrangements have grown gradually and
piecemeal, adapting themselves to changing conditions, over the 150 years
since an organised modern police service was first created. Since the late
1870s, there has been no major legislative attempt to alter them and until
recently little manifestation of public concern about them. It might be
concluded, therefore that by and large the arrangements work and have
worked satisfactorily. . . ."[79] However, the Commission's approach was to
analyse and establish the standards for judging the adequacy of a prosecution system; to measure the existing system by those standards; and then to
recommend any changes necessary to achieve the standards. Put briefly, the
Commission decided that the system should be judged on fairness, openness
and accountability, and efficiency.

"Is the system fair; first in the sense that it brings to trial only those
against whom there is an adequate and properly prepared case and who
it is in the public interest should be prosecuted (that is, tried by a court)
rather than dealt with in another way (by cautioning, for example), and
secondly in that it does not display arbitrary and inexplicable differences in the way that individual cases or classes of case are treated
locally or nationally? Is it open and accountable in the sense that those
who make the decisions to prosecute or not can be called publicly to
explain and justify their policies and actions as far as that is consistent
with protecting the interests of suspects and accused? Is it efficient in
the sense that it achieves the objectives that are set for it with the
minimum use of resources and the minimum delay? Each of these
standards makes its own contribution to what we see as being the single
overriding test of a successful system. Is it of a kind to have and does it in
fact have the confidence of the public it serves?"[80]

In considering the question of *fairness* in existing arrangements the Commission concentrated on the issues of whether the "right" people were
brought to trial, and in a way which demonstrated "consistency" in policy
and practice in the various police forces.

On the former issue, the Commission discussed the extent to which it was
possible or desirable to separate the role of the investigator from that of
lawyer in the prosecution process. In an analysis of the respective functions
of the United States District Attorney, the Scottish Procurator Fiscal and
the Canadian Crown Counsel, the Commission considered that the two roles
there had not been entirely separated.[81] The District Attorney used his staff
in an investigative capacity both to improve the quality of cases presented by
the police and to deal with major fraud, corruption and "white-collar"

[79] R.C.C.P. Rep., para. 6.6.
[80] *Ibid*. para. 6.8.
[81] *Ibid*. paras. 6.30–6.39.

crime.[82] The Procurator Fiscal was directly involved in the investigation of violent deaths and in the most serious cases would see and take statements from police and witnesses before deciding whether to prosecute.[83] By contrast, in the provinces of British Columbia and Ontario, Crown Counsel were responsible entirely for the conduct of prosecutions *once the police had decided to bring a person to trial*. Crown Counsel had no investigative function, but the police retained a part of the lawyer's function in the initial decision to prosecute. The Commission concluded that if any of these systems were more effective in putting the "right" people on trial it was not because they had succeeded in separating the functions of investigator and prosecutor. On the same issue the Commission considered the evidence of acquittal statistics which indicated that a high proportion of acquittals ordered and directed by the judge at the Crown Court were the result of insufficient prosecution evidence.[84] The failure of prosecution witnesses at trial accounted for many of these cases, but there were clearly some cases where it should have been foreseen that the evidence would be inadequate. The lack of fairness demonstrated by such cases was only mitigated by their relative infrequency.[85]

Statistics contained in the Report showed that there was, indeed, a degree of inconsistency in prosecution policy and practice,[86] and that there was no effective machinery for achieving conformity.[87] Although this created unfairness the Commission concluded that it was not the main focus of public concern and that the solution, the strengthening of central control or a national prosecution service, could find better justification on the ground of openness and accountability than on the ground of improved fairness.

The question of *accountability* was complicated because of the implications for the defendant of any public scrutiny of the exercise of the discretion to prosecute. Questioning the decision of the prosecutor after an acquittal might amount to a "retrial" if the prosecutor attempted to defend the decision. If the prosecutor was required to defend a decision not to institute proceedings, unwarranted doubts might be cast on the suspect without the suspect having an opportunity to defend him- or herself.

However, the Commission considered that those problems could be overcome by generalising the issue involved, and that accountability in the

---

[82] See further, J. Sigler, *An Introduction to the Legal System* (1968), p. 79 *et seq.*; H. Mueller, "The Position of the Criminal Defendant in the U.S.A." in J. A. Coutts (ed.), *The Accused* (1966), at pp. 102–104.

[83] The role and powers of the Procurator Fiscal are described in *Criminal Procedure in Scotland and France*, (HMSO Edinburgh, 1975), and by Lord Kilbrandon, "Scotland: Pre-Trial Procedure," in *The Accused, op cit.* See also S. R. Moody and J. Tombs, *Prosecution in the Public Interest* (1982).

[84] R.C.C.P. Rep., para. 6.19. See also M. McConville and J. Baldwin, *Courts Prosecution and Conviction* (1981).

[85] The R.C.C.P. Report suggested that one-fifth of directed acquittals might fall into this category. However, directed acquittals only formed 7 per cent. of all cases disposed of by the Crown Court and the Crown Court only dealt with approximately 15 per cent. of all indictable offences. See R.C.C.P. Rep., para. 6.22.

[86] *Ibid.* para. 6.40. Inconsistency was primarily evident in the statistics relating to the use of the caution for both adults and juveniles.

[87] See above, p. 617.

"explanatory and co-operative mode"[88] to a local supervisory authority was desirable. Additionally, a prosecution agency would clearly be accountable to the body providing it with funds for its economic efficiency and organisation. There was an obligation on the Attorney-General to answer in Parliament questions on the exercise of discretion, and the courts had some limited degree of control, but there was no real local supervision.[89]

The *efficiency* of a prosecuting system was not to be judged solely in terms of the efficient use of resources. Delays in preparation causing adjournments and inadequate preparation causing the collapse of cases certainly cost money, but could also cause injustice, inconvenience and frustration to all those concerned in the process.

At the same time, the concept of efficiency was notoriously difficult to use in relation to the criminal justice system; objectives were hard to define in precise terms and it was accordingly difficult to measure whether they had been achieved. The best the Royal Commission could propose was uniformity in prosecution arrangements, which would make possible the detection of inefficiencies in the system, and assist in achieving nationally such consistency in the application of general prosecution policies as was thought desirable.[90]

The Commission concluded that "... there is a case for some change. Indeed, not a single witness who has addressed this part of our terms of reference in detail has argued that there should be absolutely no change made. The areas of debate are on the direction and extent of change."[91]

Obviously impressed with the Canadian experience, the Commission recommended that the police should retain sole responsibility for the investigation of offences and the initial decision whether to prosecute, and that thereafter the prosecutor should take over the conduct of the case and decide whether to proceed as charged, or modify or withdraw the charges.[92] The major advantage of this proposal appeared to be that it indicated a reasonably clear demarcation of function, but it also would serve to maintain the primary responsibility of the police for investigation whilst enhancing the independent status of the prosecutor. The Commission proposed that the prosecutor should be designated "Crown prosecutor" and that the organisation should be locally based drawing heavily upon the existing prosecuting solicitors' departments. Obviously, every police force would need to have such a department (which would then also offer an advice service to the police) and, consistent with the Commission's declared standards, a local supervisory authority would need to be designated for the purposes of accountability. After examining various possibilities,[93] a majority of the Commission favoured the development of existing police authorities into police and prosecutions authorities with additional powers to

---

[88] The Commission adopted terminology coined by G. Marshall, "Police Accountability Revisited" in *Policy and Politics* (Ed. Butler and Halsey) (1978). The "explanatory and co-operative mode" is described as a type of accountability in which the supervisory authority has no power to bind or to reverse executive decisions, but where a means is provided for challenge, for the requirement of reasoned explanation and the communication of advice and recommendation. R.C.C.P. Rep., para. 6.50.
[89] See pp. 618–619 above for the then current controls.
[90] R.C.C.P. Rep., para. 6.64.
[91] *Ibid.* para. 6.65.
[92] R.C.C.P. Rep., paras. 7.5 *et seq.*
[93] *Ibid.* paras. 7.21 *et seq.*

supervise the functioning of the prosecution service. Central involvement in the prosecution process should continue in the form of the D.P.P.; ministerial responsibility for the new prosecution service should rest either with the Home Secretary or the Attorney-General, and the Minister should be empowered to set national standards for staffing and performance.[94]

These proposals had a mixed reception,[95] but were broadly accepted by the Government, with the exception that the new prosecution service was to be nationally and not locally based.[96] Accountability of a prosecutor to a local body would not be "a proper or efficient arrangement." In matters of prosecution policy the service should be required to conform to guidance from the Attorney-General and not from local authorities; and "to give local authorities responsibility for finance and manpower alone would be to divorce control over policy from control over resources, which would not be conducive to sensible and efficient management of the new service."[97]

2. PROSECUTION ARRANGEMENTS UNDER THE PROSECUTION OF OFFENCES ACT 1985[98]

(a) The Crown Prosecution Service

The 1985 Act established the Crown Prosecution Service. It is headed by the D.P.P., who is now appointed by the Attorney-General and not the Home Secretary.[99] The D.P.P. and the headquarters staff continue to be based in London. England and Wales is divided by the D.P.P. into Areas (in practice based on police areas or combinations of areas).[1] Staff are appointed by the D.P.P. Any member of the C.P.S. who has a "general qualification" may be designated by him as a Crown Prosecutor. The D.P.P. must designate a Chief Crown Prosecutor for each Area, who is responsible to him for supervising the operation of the Service in that Area.[2] Crown Prosecutors, whether barristers or solicitors, are accorded the limited rights of audience enjoyed by solicitors holding practising certificates.[3]

---

[94] *Ibid.* para. 7.60.
[95] See generally, A. F. Wilcox, [1981] Crim.L.R. 482.
[96] *An Independent Prosecution Service for England and Wales* (Cmnd. 9074, 1983). The White Paper included, as an Annex, the report of an inter-departmental Working Party on Prosecution Arrangements.
[97] Cmnd. 9074, p. 9.
[98] See the symposium in [1986] Crim.L.R. 3–44; A. N. Khan, (1986) J.Crim.L. 297; K. W. Lidstone, (1987) 11 Crim.L.J. 296.
[99] 1985 Act s.2. The D.P.P. must possess a 10 year general qualification under the Courts and Legal Services Act 1990, s.71 (*i.e.* a right of audience in any part of the Supreme Court or all proceedings in county courts or magistrates' courts). Recent holders of the office have been Sir Theobald Mathew (1944–64); Sir Norman Skelhorn (1964–77); Sir Thomas Hetherington (1977–87); and Sir Allan Green Q.C. (1987–   ). For short biographies of all the Directors, see J. Rozenburg, *The Case for the Crown* (1987), Chap. 2.
[1] There are 31 Areas, grouped in four Regions (Northern, Midland, London & South East, South & West: see *Crown Prosecution Service Annual Report for 1987–88* (1987–88 H.C. 563), p. 45.
[2] 1985 Act, s.1, as amended by the 1990 Act, Sched. 10, para. 61(1).
[3] *Ibid.* s.4(1). See above, p. 129. The Lord Chancellor was given power to give additional rights of audience to Crown Prosecutors: s.4(3). Sir Robert Andrew in his *Review of Government Legal Services* (H.M.S.O., 1989) recommended that this power should be exercised in respect of suitably qualified members of the C.P.S. (pp. 51–53). See now, s.4(1)–(3E) substituted by the 1990 Act, Sched. 18, para. 51. The D.P.P. proposes to seek extended rights of audience by applying to the Lord Chancellor's Advisory Committee: see pp. 132–133.

Accordingly, the C.P.S. must normally brief counsel in private practice to appear in the Crown Court and higher courts. The C.P.S. also employs unqualified staff.

Arrangements may be made for proceedings to be conducted on behalf of the C.P.S. by any person with a "general qualification," appointed by the D.P.P. Such lawyers have all the powers of a Crown Prosecutor, but exercise them subject to any instructions given by a Crown Prosecutor.[4]

(b) Functions of the Crown Prosecution Service

The 1985 Act is phrased in terms of a set of functions conferred on the D.P.P., acting under the superintendence of the Attorney-General. However, it is also provided that every Crown Prosecutor shall have all the powers of the D.P.P. as to the initiation and conduct of proceedings, acting under his direction.[5] Section 3(2) of the 1985 Act provides that it is the duty of the D.P.P.—

"(a) to take over the conduct of all criminal proceedings, other than specified proceedings, instituted on behalf of a police force (whether by a member of that force or by any other person);
(b) to institute and have the conduct of criminal proceedings in any case where it appears to him that—
  (i) the importance or difficulty of the case makes it appropriate that proceedings should be instituted by him; or
  (ii) that it is otherwise appropriate for proceedings to be instituted by him;
(c) to take over the conduct of all binding over proceedings instituted on behalf of a police force (whether by a member of that force or by any other person);
(d) to take over the conduct of all proceedings begun by summons issued under section 3 of the Obscene Publications Act 1959 (forfeiture of obscene articles);
(e) to give, to such extent as he considers appropriate, advice to police forces on all matters relating to criminal offences;
(f) to appear for the prosecution, when directed by the court,[6] [on appeals to the Court of Appeal or the House of Lords in criminal cases, and appeals against orders under section 12 of the Contempt of Court Act 1981 (contempt of magistrates' courts)]; and
(g) to discharge such other functions as may from time to time be assigned to him by the Attorney-General in pursuance of this paragraph."

The key provision governing the relationship between the C.P.S. and the police is section 3(2)(a). The usual task of the C.P.S. is to take over proceedings instituted by the police. Proceedings are "instituted" for these purposes when an information is laid before a justice of the peace before the issue of a summons or arrest warrant, or when a person charged with an

---

[4] *Ibid.* s.5, as amended by the Courts and Legal Services Act 1990, Sched. 10, para. 61(2).
[5] 1985 Act, s.1(6). Similarly, where the consent of the D.P.P. is required by statute, that consent can be expressed by a Crown Prosecutor: s.1(7).
[6] Defined in s.3(3).

offence after being taken into custody without a warrant is informed of the particulars of the charge, or when a voluntary bill of indictment is preferred before the court.[7] In these cases, the question for the C.P.S. is whether proceedings should be continued or discontinued.[8] Express provision for the discontinuance of proceedings is made by section 23.

In the case of a person taken into custody without a warrant and charged, but where no magistrates' court has been informed of the charge, the prosecutor may discontinue proceedings by giving notice to the person concerned. Where proceedings have otherwise been instituted, but are still in their "preliminary stages" (i.e. before the court commences to hear evidence at a summary trial, or before committal for trial), the prosecutor may discontinue them by giving notice, with reasons, to the clerk of the court. The accused must also be informed, but need not be given reasons, and has the right to require the proceedings to continue. The discontinuance of proceedings under section 23 does not prevent the institution of fresh proceedings in respect of the same offence.[9] If the prosecutor wishes to discontinue at a later stage, the court's consent may be necessary.[10]

There is a limited range of offences which can still be prosecuted to conclusion by the police. These are the "specified proceedings" mentioned in section 3(2)(a), and comprise a number of less serious road traffic offences,[11] some commonly dealt with by the fixed penalty procedures. They remain "specified" provided that there is a written plea of guilty. If the case is contested, it must then be dealt with by the C.P.S. Apart from these offences, *all* proceedings instituted by the police must be taken over by the C.P.S. It is uncertain whether proceedings are "instituted" by the police where their only involvement is that the suspect is charged by the custody officer.[12]

Section 3(2)(b) preserves the right of the C.P.S. to institute proceedings in serious or difficult cases. Regulations made by the Attorney-General under section 8 require the police to inform the D.P.P. whenever there is a prima facie case that offences in a list set out in the regulations have been committed.[13] These include offences in which a prosecution requires the consent of a Law Officer or the D.P.P., homicide offences (except causing death by reckless driving), abortion, treason or sedition offences, offences which may be subject to an application for extradition and offences where it appears to the chief officer of police that the D.P.P.'s advice or assistance is desirable.

---

[7] s.15(2). If more than one of these is applicable, the earliest time is taken.

[8] s.15(3) provides that reference to the conduct of any proceedings include references to their being discontinued.

[9] *Ibid.* s.23(9).

[10] At the Crown Court, the approval of the judge is necessary: *R.* v. *Broad* (1979) 68 Cr.App.R. 281, but at committal proceedings, the consent of the justices is *not* required: *R.* v. *Canterbury and St Augustine's JJ., ex p. Klisiak* [1982] 1 Q.B. 398.

[11] Prosecution of Offences Act 1985 (Specified Proceedings) Order 1985 (S.I. 1985 No. 2010, as amended by S.I. 1988 No. 1121); J. N. Spencer, (1988) 152 J.P.N. 691. See also (1989) 139 N.L.J. 1739.

[12] Yes: *R.* v. *Ealing Magistrates' Court, ex p. Dixon* [1990] 2 Q.B. 91 (prosecution for breach of the Copyright Act 1956 held to be wrongly left to the copyright owner's federation); No: *R.* v. *Stafford JJ., ex p. Commissioners of Customs and Excise* [1990] 3 W.L.R. 656 (held that the Customs and Excise Commissioners could continue a prosecution after charge by the police).

[13] Prosecution of Offences Regulations 1978, as amended by S.I. 1978 No. 1846 and S.I. 1985 No. 243, regs. 6(1), 7. These were made under previous legislation but are thought to take effect under s.8: *Halsbury's Statutes of England*, Vol. 12 (Reissue), p. 940.

In addition, the D.P.P. may specify other cases which the police are to report to him.[14] These include some conspiracies concerning drugs or contravention of immigration laws, criminal libel, certain obscenity cases, and all cases raising questions of Community law.[15]

The 1985 Act also preserves the right of private prosecution by providing that nothing in Part I shall preclude any person from instituting any criminal proceedings, or conducting any proceedings which the D.P.P. is not under a duty to take over. The D.P.P. does, however, still have power to take over private prosecutions at any stage.[16] If a prosecution is taken over, the prosecutor may of course exercise the power to discontinue under section 23.

Crown Prosecutors are given guidance as to the exercise of their powers by the Code for Crown Prosecutors issued by the D.P.P. under section 10.[17]

One organisational problem has concerned the use of unqualified staff within the C.P.S. to review certain categories of cases (most summary offences) to decide whether a prosecution should proceed. A case would only be passed to a Crown Prosecutor where the "case screener's" view was that there was insufficient evidence or a prosecution would be against the public interest, or if he or she considered that that would be helpful. The Divisional Court held that this arrangement was *ultra vires*, there being no express or implied power to delegate such decisions to persons other than Crown Prosecutors and qualified agents.[18] An appeal was taken to the Court of Appeal but the case was settled by agreement. Under that agreement, case examiners will vet a more limited range of cases, and a decision whether or not to proceed will always be taken by a lawyer.[19] Law clerks were also used to respond to bail applications in the Crown Court and High Court, but this practice was stopped in the light of legal advice that it was unlawful in the absence of express authority in the Prosecution of Offences Act 1985.[20] The necessary authority is provided by section 74 of the Court and Legal Services Act 1990. The C.P.S. is also considering the idea that minor summary cases might be presented by unqualified staff, after appropriate training.[21] Legislation would be necessary for such a change.

(c) Relationship between the Crown Prosecution Service and the police

As has been mentioned, the crucial feature of this relationship is that in most cases it is still a matter for the police to determine whether proceedings should be *instituted*. They may obtain the advice of the C.P.S. before so deciding, but this is only done in a minority of cases.[22] As a result, the C.P.S. normally has no involvement in cases where the police decide not to prose-

[14] 1978 regs, reg. 6(2).
[15] See Archbold, *Criminal Pleading, Evidence and Practice* (43rd ed.), para. 1–124.
[16] 1985 Act, s.6.
[17] See below.
[18] *R. v. Director of Public Prosecutions, ex p. Association of First Division Civil Servants* (1988) 138 N.L.J. 158.
[19] *Annual Report of the Crown Prosecution Service for 1988–89* (1988–89 H.C. 411), pp. 17–18.
[20] Evidence of the C.P.S. to the Home Affairs Committee (1989–90 H.C. 118–i), p. 28.
[21] *Ibid.* pp. 28–29.
[22] In 1987–88, 1,444,212 defendants' cases were finalised in the magistrates' courts, of which 108,000 were discontinued. The C.P.S. advised the police before charge in 55,760 cases: National Audit Office, *Review of the Crown Prosecution Service* (1988–89 H.C. 345), p. 10.

cute, including the cases where the caution procedure is adopted. This makes it more difficult for a rational prosecution policy to be worked out,[23] although it is perhaps unlikely that the police will drop a case that the C.P.S. would have been prepared to prosecute.

Furthermore, doubts were expressed as to the effectiveness in principle of a system of review after the initial decision to prosecute has been taken. It was argued that there is a natural tendency for the police, once satisfied as to who is responsible, to consider as mistaken any material that points in another direction,[24] this tendency being present in a number of notorious miscarriages of justice.[25] The prosecutor would be constrained by the information provided by the police, and

> "it would be irrational and indefensible in most cases if the prosecutor did *not* endorse police action, because the file is constructed in order to leave this as the only proper option."[26]

Accordingly, any satisfactory reform would require changes to the investigation process. The prosecutors might be given some powers of direction over investigations and the decision to prosecute might be removed altogether from the police.[27]

In practice, the C.P.S. has shown greater independence than might have been anticipated. While its effectiveness as a filter has been doubted, there is as yet no substantial research evidence. The operation of the C.P.S. is considered further at the end of the chapter.[28]

(d) Role of the Attorney-General and the D.P.P. under the new arrangements

Mention has been made earlier in this chapter[29] of the various powers and duties of the D.P.P. and Law Officers that provided a measure of central co-ordination and control under the old arrangements, including requirements for cases to be reported to the D.P.P., consents to prosecution,[30] the D.P.P.'s general power to take over prosecutions, and the *nolle prosequi*. These all still exist, but are obviously no longer the main vehicle for exerting central control or influence over prosecutions. They may, however, still be of importance in respect of prosecutions brought other than by the police.

---

[23] *cf.* M. McConville, (1984) VI(1) Liverpool L.R. 15, 28.

[24] McConville, *op. cit.* pp. 28–32; A. Sanders, "Constructing the Case for the Prosecution" (1987) 14 J.L.S. 229.

[25] The Evans, Virag and Dougherty and Confait cases: see L. Kennedy, *Ten Rillington Place* (1961); Devlin Report on *Evidence of Identification in Criminal Cases* (H.M.S.O., 1976); Fisher Report on the Confait Case (H.M.S.O., 1977). See also the case of Bruce Lee: below, p. 834.

[26] McConville, *op. cit.*, p. 30. *Cf.* A. Sanders, [1986] Crim.L.R. 16, 27, who argues that the structure gives the prosecutors power to drop cases but little incentive to do so; and K. W. Lidstone, (1987) 11 Crim.L.J. 296, 310–312.

[27] See McConville, Sanders and Lidstone, *ops. cit.*

[28] Below, pp. 689–692.

[29] Above, pp. 618–619.

[30] Some of the consent requirements mentioned above (p. 619) have been re-enacted: see now, *e.g.* Public Order Act 1986, s.27(1) (incitement to racial hatred offences); Aviation Security Act 1982, s.8(1) (offences against safety of aircraft); Official Secrets Act 1989, s.9 (most offences under the Act).

Requirements that proceedings may only be instituted by or with the consent of the Attorney-General or the D.P.P. do not prevent an arrest or the remand in custody or on bail of a person charged with an offence.[31] Accordingly a prosecution may get to the stage of a charge by the police and an initial court appearance without reference to the Attorney-General or the D.P.P. However, a summons should not be issued by a justice of the peace or clerk to the justices unless he or she is satisfied, *inter alia*, that any necessary authority to prosecute has been obtained.[32] This is the only procedure open to non-police prosecutors, unless the police are prepared to charge on their behalf.[32a]

When the consent of the D.P.P. to the prosecution is required, that may now be expressed by a Crown Prosecutor,[33] There are internal arrangements within the C.P.S. governing which cases are to be referred to headquarters.[34]

3. THE SERIOUS FRAUD OFFICE

The Serious Fraud Office[35] was established by the Criminal Justice Act 1987, following the Report of the Roskill Committee on Fraud Trials.[36] Its jurisdiction covers England, Wales and Northern Ireland. The Director of the Serious Fraud Office is appointed by the Attorney-General, and acts under his superintendence.[37] Staff are appointed by the Director.[38] The Director may (i) investigate any suspected offence which appears to him or her on reasonable grounds to involve serious or complex fraud; (ii) institute and have the conduct of any prosecutions which appear to him or her to relate to such fraud; and (iii) take over the conduct of any such proceedings at any stage. He or she may designate any member of the office who is a barrister or solicitor to exercise the Director's powers for the purposes of (ii) and (iii), and such persons have the same rights of audience as Crown Prosecutors.[39] Where the Director has the conduct of a case, the D.P.P.'s responsibilities cease.[40] The main distinctive feature of the Office's work is that it extends to the investigation as well as the prosecution of offences, and it has wide powers to require the person under investigation and any other

---

[31] Prosecution of Offences Act 1985, s.25, re-enacting s.6 of the 1979 Act: see *R.* v. *Elliott* (1985) 81 Cr.App.R. 115 (the Attorney-General's consent to a prosecution under the Explosive Substances Act 1883 was given eight weeks after charge: it was held that, in view of s.6 of the 1979 Act, the proceedings were instituted at the defendant's first court appearance.
[32] *R.* v. *Gateshead J.J.*, *ex p. Tesco Stores Ltd.* [1981] Q.B. 470, 478.
[32a] See below, p. 643.
[33] Prosecution of Offences Act 1985, s.1(7).
[34] See *Crown Prosecution Service Annual Report for 1986–87* (1987–88 H.C. 14), Chap. 8. Only a few offences must always be referred to headquarters, (*e.g.* treason, all prosecutions requiring the Attorney-General's consent, abortion, large scale drug and immigration conspiracies, criminal libel, election petitions and criminal bankruptcies, and substantial fraud cases). Others may be referred if of particular difficulty or exceptional public concern.
[35] J. Wood, "The Serious Fraud Office" [1989] Crim.L.R. 175; Criminal Justice Act 1987 (*Current Law Statutes 1987*: Annotations by I. Leigh); P. Carey, (1989) 139 N.L.J. 1629 (comments on some of the S.F.O.'s early cases).
[36] H.M.S.O., 1986.
[37] Criminal Justice Act 1986, s.1. The first Director was John Wood, formerly a senior member of the C.P.S., and he was succeeded in 1990 by Barbara Mills.
[38] 1987 Act, Sched. 1, para. 2.
[39] *Ibid.* s.1.
[40] *Ibid.* Sched. 1, para. 5. Statutory requirements for the consent of the D.P.P. to a prosecution are not to prohibit the taking of any step by the Director: *ibid.* para. 4.

person whom the Director has reason to believe has relevant information to answer questions or otherwise furnish information, and to require the production of documents.[41] It concentrates on a comparatively small number of the most serious cases: the prosecution of other serious fraud cases continues to be handled by the Fraud Investigation Group within C.P.S. headquarters.

4. OTHER AGENCIES

There are a considerable number of other bodies who institute prosecutions and who should not be left out of account. Government departments, local authorities, nationalised industries and other public bodies may all have cause to institute prosecutions within their particular field. A survey was undertaken on behalf of the Royal Commission on Criminal Procedure[42] which concentrated on particular courts and identified the Post Office, the British Transport Police, the Department of the Environment and local authorities as contributing almost 70 per cent. of the non-police prosecutions in those courts.[43]

5. PRIVATE PROSECUTIONS

"This historical right which goes right back to the earliest days of our legal system, though rarely exercised in relation to indictable offences, and though ultimately liable to be controlled by the Attorney-General (by taking over the prosecution and, if he thinks fit, entering a *nolle prosequi*) remains a valuable constitutional safeguard against inertia or partiality on the part of authority."[44] Lord Wilberforce thus stated the traditional view of the private prosecution.

In fact, the growing practice of requiring the consent of the D.P.P. or Attorney-General to prosecution, the establishment of the C.P.S. and the considerable cost of mounting a private prosecution now combine to minimise the significance of this historical right. We have already noted the requirement of consent,[45] but cost is an even more discouraging factor. Legal aid is not available to a private prosecutor who must meet the cost of investigation, preparation and representation out of his or her own pocket. A court may award costs to a successful private prosecutor[46] but he or she also runs the risk of having them awarded against him or her if he or she is not successful. In addition, if the prosecution was vindictive, the prosecutor risks the possibility of an action in malicious prosecution.[47] A private prosecutor has no right of access to documents, such as police statements, reports and photographs, held by the C.P.S.[48]

---

[41] *Ibid*. s.2. These powers continue to be available after the suspect has been charged: *R*. v. *Director of Serious Fraud, ex p. Saunders, The Independent*, July 29, 1988.

[42] *Prosecutions by Private Individuals and Non-Police Agencies*, R.C.C.P. Research Study No. 10 (HMSO, 1980). See also A. Samuels, [1986] Crim.L.R. 33.

[43] *Ibid*., Table 2.3. at p. 15.

[44] *Gouriet* v. *Union of Post Office Workers* [1978] A.C. 435 at p. 477.

[45] At pp. 627–628 above.

[46] Prosecution of Offences Act 1985, s.17: costs can only be awarded in respect of proceedings for an indictable offence, and proceedings in the Divisional Court or the House of Lords in respect of a summary offence. They cannot cover investigation expenses. See further p. 478.

[47] See *Winfield and Jolowicz on Tort* (13th ed.), pp. 543–551.

[48] *R*. v. *Director of Public Prosecutions, ex p. Hallas* (1987) 87 Cr.App.R. 340.

There have, of course, been some notable private prosecutions,[49] but they have been generally confined to offences of shoplifting and common assault.[50] In some areas supermarkets and other large concerns are encouraged by the police to conduct their own prosecutions for shoplifting. Section 42 of the Offences Against the Person Act 1861 dictated a private prosecution in the majority of cases where common assault occurred,[51] but this section was repealed by the Criminal Justice Act 1988.[52]

C. THE EXERCISE OF DISCRETION IN PROSECUTIONS

Not every criminal offence is prosecuted. The courts could not possibly cope with the workload and, in any event, prosecution may not always be the most effective means of dealing with a violation of the criminal law. If some offenders are to be "let off" whilst others are brought before the courts it is important to know when such a decision may be made, by whom and on what principles. The exercise of this particular discretion has attracted increasing attention.[53]

1. THE POLICE

A choice exists as soon as a police officer discovers that a criminal offence may have been committed. Should an investigation be started if the situation is unclear? If the facts are already clear should action be taken to ensure that the offence is formally considered for prosecution? This problem is faced by every police officer present at an incident and it must be resolved on individual initiative and/or in accordance with instructions received from a superior officer. Although it may be the officer's inclination to warn a motorist driving without lights not to repeat the offence, the Chief Constable may have decided, as a matter of policy, to prosecute all such offenders and issued instructions accordingly. The discretion exercised in this way by the officer concerned is otherwise generally uncontrolled, except where

---

[49] Two cases brought by Mrs. Mary Whitehouse aroused interest—R. v. Lemon [1979] A.C. 617, where the accused was convicted of blasphemous libel and the Crown subsequently took over the case on appeal; and Whitehouse v. Bogdanov, where the accused was acquitted on a charge of procuring an act of gross indecency between males contrary to section 13 of the Sexual Offences Act 1956 which resulted from his producing a play (The Romans in Britain), containing a scene of intercourse between males (one non-consenting). The prosecution was discontinued after the judge had ruled that there was a case to answer and the Attorney-General eventually entered a nolle prosequi. See [1982] P.L. 165. In Scotland, private prosecutions are extremely rare, but not obsolete: see X. v. Sweeney 1982 J.C. 70; R. Harper and A. McWhinnie, The Glasgow Rape Case (1983). An individual aggrieved by the decision of the procurator fiscal not to prosecute must obtain authority to prosecute from the High Court by petitioning by Bill for Criminal Letters.

[50] R.C.C.P. Research Study No. 10 (see above, n. 42), Chap. 5.

[51] The section specified that in cases of common assault the prosecution should be brought "by or on behalf of the party aggrieved."

[52] Common assault and battery were made summary offences by s.39 of the 1988 Act.

[53] The literature is expanding. See A. F. Wilcox, The Decision to Prosecute (1972); N. Osborough, "Police Discretion not to prosecute Juveniles" (1965) 28 M.L.R. 179; D. Steer, Police Cautions—A Study in the Exercise of Police Discretion (1970); D. G. T. Williams, "Prosecution, discretion and the accountability of the police" (in R. Hood (ed.) Crime, Criminology and Public Policy (1974)), and the works cited in fns. 70 and 71 below.

failure to take action may itself amount to a criminal offence or neglect of duty.[54]

Two cases have explored the exercise of discretion at a senior level which would affect the way that the officer on the spot carries out his or her duties. In *R.* v. *Metropolitan Police Commissioner, ex p. Blackburn (No. 1),*[55] Mr. Raymond Blackburn applied for an order of mandamus directed to the Commissioner requiring him to enforce the provisions of the Betting, Gaming and Lotteries Act 1963 in London gaming clubs. It appeared that the Commissioner had sanctioned a force order which effectively stopped observation in gaming clubs by the police and prevented any attempt to enforce the Act.[56] The Court of Appeal held that, whilst the police had a discretion not to prosecute, it was not proper to take a policy decision that certain offences would *never* be prosecuted since that was to negate the exercise of discretion and would amount to a failure in their duty to enforce the law. However, the courts will not interfere in cases where it is alleged that the police are not paying *enough* attention to particular offences or prosecuting in sufficient numbers. Mr. Blackburn again sought an order of mandamus in *R.* v. *Metropolitan Police Commissioner, ex p. Blackburn (No. 3),*[57] this time in respect of the Obscene Publications Act 1959, but the court would not grant it. Whereas in the first case the police had deliberately decided not to prosecute, in this case they were hampered by lack of resources and the uncertainty of the law. "It is no part of the duty of this court to presume to tell the (Commissioner) how to conduct the affairs of the Metropolitan Police, nor how to deploy his all too limited resources. . . ."[58]

Given that an individual officer may be under instructions about how to deal with particular offences and will also have received training for this task, what considerations are likely to be taken into account in the exercise of discretion? Naturally, the gravity of the offence is likely to be uppermost but the officer may also think about the evidence likely to be available in a prosecution; the degree of certainty that the offence has been committed; the attitude of the victim; the personal circumstances of the offender and the efficacy of a prosecution compared with other ways of dealing with the problem. These are, on a local level, not dissimilar to the considerations appropriate to the decisions of the C.P.S. on whether to continue a prosecution.[59] In this case, however, the decision will need to be taken quickly and often without the help and advice of colleagues. If the officer decides not to arrest or report for prosecution he or she might issue a warning to the offender, attempt a conciliation between offender and victim, or even take the offender into preventive arrest.[60]

---

[54] By virtue of the Police (Discipline) Regulations 1985 (S.I. 1985 No. 518), Sched. 1, para. 4. See also *R.* v. *Dytham* [1979] Q.B. 722 (criminal offence of wilful neglect of duty).
[55] [1968] 2 Q.B. 118.
[56] The terms of the relevant instructions are set out in the judgment of Lord Denning M.R. at pp. 134–135. In the event, the instructions in question were withdrawn before the appellate hearing and the Commissioner, through counsel, gave an undertaking to that effect.
[57] [1973] Q.B. 241. For a further instalment in the drama see *R.* v. *Metropolitan Police Commissioner, ex parte Blackburn, The Times,* March 6, 1980. Mr. Blackburn referred to the Master of Rolls in the course of that case as, "the greatest living Englishman"—Lord Denning is reported to have replied, "Tell that to the House of Lords."
[58] *Per* Roskill L.J. at p. 262.
[59] See below, pp. 633–636.
[60] Discussed by Wilcox, *op. cit.* at p. 106.

Assuming that an officer has arrested an offender or reported him or her for prosecution the decision will pass to a more senior officer. At this stage the police may decide to prosecute, not to prosecute or to caution, and they may have the benefit of advice from the C.P.S. If the decision is to prosecute, there is also an exercise of discretion in selecting the particular charge.

The practice differs according to the method of procedure adopted: arrest and charge, or summons. Under the former, the person is arrested (either outside or at the police station) and charged at the police station. After charge the suspect will either be kept in custody and brought by the police before magistrates' court,[61] or, as is more usual, released on bail subject to a duty to attend a magistrates' court on a specified date. Here a decision to charge is made initially by the investigating officer, but must be approved by the custody officer, who must be satisfied that there is sufficient evidence.[62] Where a person is reported for summons, the investigating officer prepares a file and passes it to a more senior officer, who decides whether a prosecution should be instituted. Where a decision not to prosecute is contemplated, the case must be passed up the hierarchy, usually to a Detective Superintendent; a decision to prosecute can be taken at the level of Detective Inspector or Detective Chief Inspector.[63] Overall, the arrest and charge procedure is the normal method used in respect of indictable offences, and the summons procedure the normal method for summary offences,[64] but police forces vary considerably in the respective proportions in which they are used.[65]

The caution, a formal warning issued by the police in circumstances where they are satisfied that the offence is capable of proof but do not intend to prosecute, has only rarely received statutory mention[66] and its use has developed by practice rather than by law. Offenders may only be cautioned if they admit the offence. Cautioning has been much more frequently used in respect of juveniles than adults: there is a presumption that a first-time juvenile offender will be cautioned. A Home Office Circular (59/1990) sets out standard practice.[67] In 1989, about 238,000 offenders were cautioned in respect of all offences other than motoring offences, and of that figure 96,600 offenders were aged under 17. The percentage of offenders cautioned out of the numbers of males 17 and over found guilty or cautioned remained fairly constant at around 4 per cent. for over 20 years, but

---

[61] In accordance with the requirements of s.46 of the Police and Criminal Evidence Act 1984: above, p. 606.

[62] 1984 Act, ss.37(1)(7); *Code of Practice on Detention etc.* C.16.1. The equivalent step prior to P.A.C.E. was the decision of the charge sergeant whether to accept a charge, on the basis of an oral report from the investigating officer. In practice refusals were rare; "charge sergeants (uniformed officers) do not see CID work as their business, so accepting a CID charge is often a mere formality": A. Sanders, "The prosecution process" in D. Moxon (ed.), *Managing Criminal Justice* (1985), pp. 72–73.

[63] Sanders, *op. cit.*, pp. 70–72.

[64] See *Criminal Statistics England and Wales 1989* (Cm. 1322, 1990), Table 8.1 (summons used for 16 per cent. of indictable offences, 68 per cent. of summary (non-motoring) offences and 87 per cent. of summary motoring offences. The proportions have been declining).

[65] See R. Gemmill and R. F. Morgan-Giles, *Arrest, Charge and Summons* (R.C.C.P. Research Study No. 9) (H.M.S.O., 1980), based on figures for 1976 and 1978; R. Tarling, P. Jones and A. Sanders, "Police Bail" (1986) 21 H.O.R.B. 52, 54–55, based on figures for 1980.

[66] The Street Offences Act 1959 s.2; the Children and Young Persons Act 1969, s.5(2) (not in force).

[67] See also R.C.C.P. I, paras. 150–154.

increased sharply between 1985 and 1989 to 14 per cent.[68] (indictable offences) and 16 per cent. (summary offences). The 1985 Circular[69] encouraged the wider use of cautioning for adults. There are still wide variations in the cautioning rates in different police areas.[70] Motoring offences are dealt with differently by the administration of a written caution which is not dependent upon an admission by the offender and may not be referred to in subsequent proceedings for another offence.[70a]

2. THE CODE FOR CROWN PROSECUTORS

Prior to the establishment of the C.P.S., as we have seen, the decision to prosecute would in most cases be taken by the police, in some cases with the advice of a prosecuting solicitor, or by a member of the D.P.P.'s office. It was clear that the police did not adopt a blanket policy of prosecutions, and did take other factors into account, but there was comparatively little formal evidence of what those factors were.[71] More was known of the approach of the D.P.P., particularly through his evidence to the Royal Commission on Criminal Procedure.[72] In February 1983, the Attorney-General issued *Criteria for Prosecution*,[73] setting out the approach of the Attorney and the D.P.P. to the institution of prosecutions in cases for which they were responsible. The intention was, however, that they be taken into account by all those responsible for prosecutions. The *Criteria* subsequently formed the basis of the *Code for Crown Prosecutors* issued by the D.P.P. However, they remain in operation as guidance in respect of the exercise of discretion by the police in instituting proceedings, prior to the case being handed over to the C.P.S.

Section 10 of the Prosecution of Offences Act 1985 requires the D.P.P. to issue a Code for Crown Prosecutors giving guidance on general principles to be applied by them in determining whether to institute or discontinue

---

[68] *Criminal Statistics England and Wales 1989* (Cm. 1322, 1990), Chap. 5. Comparable figures for 1982 were 161,000 and 112,700.

[69] H.O. Circular 14/1985, superseded by the 1990 Circular.

[70] *Ibid.* See also G. Laycock and R. Tarling, "Police force cautioning: policy and practice" in Moxon (ed.) (1985), Chap. 6; H. Giller and N. Tutt, [1987] Crim.L.R. 367 and 587; C. Wilkinson and R. Evans, [1990] Crim.L.R. 165; A. Sanders, "The limits to diversion from prosecution" (1988) 28 Brit. J. Criminol. 513.

[70a] R.C.C.P. I, para. 153.

[71] See, however, the account by a former chief constable: A. F. Wilcox, *The Decision to Prosecute* (1972), and the research project conducted by A. Sanders between 1980 and 1983: Sanders, [1985] Crim.L.R. 4, and "The Prosecution Process" in D. Moxon (ed.), *Managing Criminal Justice* (1985), Chap. 7. Sanders' research illustrates various ways in which weak cases come to be prosecuted: *e.g.* where relevant information about the circumstances is not known or suppressed, where weak cases are prosecuted for policy reasons, and "resource charging" as a justification for a previous arrest, especially in the context of public order; and various situations in which stronger cases are dropped, *e.g.* where the suspect has been generally useful to the police, or is to be used as a witness against others involved in same events.

[72] A useful extract from the evidence submitted is to be found at R.C.C.P. I, Appendix 25. See generally G. Mansfield and J. Peay, *The Director of Public Prosecutions* (1987), the report of a research project on the operation of the D.P.P.'s Office prior to the Prosecution of Offences Act 1985: the case samples studied dated from 1982 and 1983.

[73] (1983) 147 J.P.N. 223; Home Office Circular 26/1983. See A. Sanders, "Prosecution Decisions and the Attorney-General's Guidelines" [1985] Crim.L.R. 4: he doubted that the *Criteria* would generally have much effect in reducing "inconsistency, weak cases and shady practice," but noted that they had led to changes in at least two forces (*ibid.* pp. 17, 18).

proceedings, what charges should be preferred and what representations should be made about mode of trial.[74] The D.P.P. may make alterations in the Code, and the Code, and any alterations, must be published in an Annual Report of the C.P.S.[75] The Code has separate sections on the criteria for prosecution, discontinuance, charging practice, mode of trial and juveniles.

The criteria for prosecution relate to (1) evidential sufficiency and (2) the public interest. As to (1), the Crown Prosecutor "must be satisfied that there is admissible, substantial and reliable evidence that a criminal offence known to the law has been committed by an identifiable person." Moreover, there must be "a realistic prospect of conviction" and not merely "a bare prima facie case." There must be no realistic expectation of an ordered acquittal or a successful submission of no case in the magistrates' court. The prosecutor should "have regard to any lines of defence which are plainly open to, or have been indicated by, the accused," and any other factors affecting the likelihood of a conviction. The Code sets out a series of factors relevant to the evaluation of evidence by the prosecutor, including whether there have been any breaches of P.A.C.E. and the Codes of Practice, whether there are grounds for doubting the reliability of admissions, the availability, competence and credibility of the witnesses and the likely impression they would make, and the cogency of identification evidence.

Once the prosecutor is satisfied that the evidence can justify proceedings, he or she must then consider whether the public interest requires a prosecution.[76] "The factors which can properly lead to a decision not to prosecute will vary from case to case, but broadly speaking, the graver the offence, the less likelihood there will be that the public interest will allow of a disposal less than prosecution, for example, a caution." If an offence is not so serious as plainly to require prosecution, the prosecutor should "strive to ensure that the spirit of the Home Office Cautioning Guidelines is observed." The Code then lists a series of categories: if a case falls into any of them that is an indication that proceedings may not be required, subject to the circumstances of the cases. The categories are—

(i) likely penalty: the prosecutor should consider alternative forms of disposal if the circumstances are not particularly serious, and a purely nominal penalty is likely (especially where the offence is triable on indictment, in which case the length and cost of proceedings should also be weighed against the likely penalty);

(ii) staleness: the prosecutor should be slow to prosecute if the last offence was committed three or more years before the probable date of the trial, unless an immediate custodial sentence is likely to be imposed; less regard should be paid to staleness if it has been contributed to by the accused, or the complexity of the case has necessitated lengthy police investigation or the

---

[74] See A. Ashworth, "The 'Public Interest' Element in Prosecutions" [1987] Crim.L.R. 595; R. K. Daw, (1989) Jo. Crim. Law 485.

[75] The Code, as amended, is published as an Annex to the Annual Reports of the C.P.S.

[76] The D.P.P., and now the C.P.S., are guided by a statement made by a former Attorney-General, Lord Shawcross, in the course of a House of Commons debate. "It has never been the rule in this country—I hope it never will be—that suspected criminal offences must automatically be the subject of prosecution. Indeed, the very first Regulations under which the Director of Public Prosecutions worked provided that he should ... prosecute ... wherever it appears that the offence or the circumstances of its commission is or are of such a character that a prosecution in respect thereof is required in the public interest. That is still the dominant consideration": H. C. Deb. Vol. 483. col. 681, January 29, 1951.

particular characteristics of the offence have themselves contributed to delay in its coming to light;

(iii) youth: the possibility of cautioning a young adult should be carefully considered;

(iv) old age: the older and more infirm the offender, the more reluctant the prosecutor should be to prosecute unless there is a real possibility of repetition, or the offence is grave, or the accused still holds a position of some importance; the accused should also be likely to be fit enough to stand trial;

(v) mental illness and stress: proceedings should be discontinued where a prosecutor is satisfied that the probable adverse effect on the defendant's mental health outweighs the interests of justice in the particular case;

(vi) sexual offences: the prosecutor should take into account each participant's age and whether there was an element of seduction or corruption; sexual assaults upon children and offences such as rape should always be regarded seriously; if the evidence is sufficient, there will seldom be any doubt that the prosecution will be in the public interest;

(vii) complainant's attitude;

(viii) peripheral defendants: in general proceedings should be continued only against those whose involvement goes to the heart of the issue to be placed before the court.

If having weighed such of these factors as are relevant, the prosecutor is still in doubt, the attitude of the local community and the prevalence of the offence should be considered. If doubt remains, the scales will normally be tipped in favour of prosecution.

The Code emphasises that the police decision to institute proceedings (unless itself based on the advice of the C.P.S.) should always be reviewed, and that the discretion to discontinue is a continuing one. It should be normal practice to consult the police before discontinuing. The prosecutor should only accept pleas to lesser offences if the court will be able to pass a proper sentence consistent with the gravity of the defendant's actions.

As regards charging practice, every effort should be made to keep the number of charges as low as possible, using specimen charges if appropriate. Multiplicity of charging should never be used to obtain leverage for the offering of a plea of guilty. The charges should adequately reflect the gravity of the defendant's conduct and will normally be the most serious revealed by the evidence.[77]

In making representations as to mode of trial, the attraction of an expeditious disposal should never be the sole reason for a request for summary trial. However, the prosecutor is entitled to have regard to the delay, additional cost and possible adverse effect on witnesses likely to be occasioned by proceedings on indictment. Where there are co-accused, it will generally be in the interests of justice for all of them to be tried at the same court.

Finally, there is special guidance concerning juveniles, emphasising the requirement fully to consider the juvenile's welfare, the presumption in favour of methods of disposal falling short of prosecution, and consideration of the Home Office Cautioning Guidelines.

In many respects the Code seems eminently reasonable, albeit at a fairly high level of generality[78]: what is important is how it is applied in practice.

[77] Special guidance is given as to the use of conspiracy charges.
[78] See A. Ashworth, [1987] Crim.L.R. 595.

One aspect that has been controversial is the "reasonable prospects of conviction" test.[79] It has been argued that this weighs too heavily against prosecution.[80] To promote consistency in decision-making, the Service has issued the *Crown Prosecution Service: Policy Manual*, and a companion *Practice and Procedure Manual*. These documents are not published.

3. PROSECUTIONS BY OTHER AGENCIES

Most of the prosecutions brought by non-police agencies arise out of the enforcement of regulatory legislation in the context of business, including legislation concerning protection of the health and safety of employees,[81] trading standards[82] and protection of the environment.[83] Those who enforce this kind of legislation tend to prefer other methods of securing compliance, such as advice, negotiation and warning, with prosecution as a last resort. The internal decision-making arrangements tend to make prosecution more difficult than non-prosecution.[84] It has been noted that the potential defendants tend to be middle class (companies, managers, self-employed) rather than working class (who comprise the majority of those dealt with by the police).[85] However, it has been argued that the class bias exhibited by the prosecution patterns arises not from deliberate bias on the part of the law enforcers, but reflects more fundamental economic and social differences between different types of "crime" and "criminal."[86] A similar contrast can be drawn between the rarity of prosecutions for tax evasion by the Inland

---

[79] This test is more stringent than the "prima facie" standard previously applied by the police; under this test, there had to be "enough admissible evidence to prove all the necessary elements of the offence and evidence that does not appear so manifestly unreliable that no reasonable tribunal could safely convict upon it": R.C.C.P. paras. 6–10. It has been expressed in terms of it being more likely that there will be a conviction than an acquittal (labelled, rather to the annoyance of the then D.P.P., as "the 51 per cent. rule"). It was reformulated following criticism by G. Mansfield and J. Peay, *The Director of Public Prosecutions* (1987), pp. 52–54, 217–225.

[80] G. Williams "Letting off the Guilty and Prosecuting the Innocent" [1985] Crim.L.R. 115, criticised by P. Worboys, [1985] Crim.L.R. 764. Prof. Williams proposed that the prosecutor should consider (1) whether he or she believes the suspect to be guilty; (2) whether a prosecution would have a fair chance of success; (3) whether considerations of humanity or public policy stand in the way of proceedings; and (4) whether he or she has the resources to justify bringing a charge.

[81] See W. G. Carson, "White collar crime and the enforcement of factory legislation" (1970) 10 Brit. J. Criminol. 383, and *The Other Price of Britain's Oil* (1982); D. Kloss, [1978] Crim.L.R. 280.

[82] R. Cranston, *Regulating Business* (1979) (enforcement of trading standards); B. Hutter, *The Reasonable Arm of the Law* (1988) (environmental health officers); H. Croall, (1988) 15 J.L.S. 293 and (1989) 29 Brit. J. Criminol. 157.

[83] See G. Richardson, A. Ogus and P. Burroughs, *Policing Pollution* (1982); K. Hawkins, *Environment and Enforcement* (1984); M. Weatt, (1989) 29 Brit. J. Criminol. 57.

[84] See A. Sanders, "Class Bias in Prosecution" (1985) 24 *Howard Journal* 176, comparing the "institutional propensity to prosecute" of the police with the "propensity not to prosecute" of the Factory Inspectorate.

[85] Sanders, *op. cit.*.

[86] *Ibid.* pp. 194–197.

Revenue and the much more common use of prosecutions for social security frauds.[87]

D. THE CLASSIFICATION OF OFFENCES

If a decision is taken to prosecute an offender, the Crown Prosecutor must decide on the appropriate charge.[88] The selection of the charge is important because it may determine the court in which the case will be tried and, hence, the mode of trial. We have already recorded that both the magistrates' court and the Crown Court have original criminal jurisdiction and the work is divided between them according to the seriousness of the charge. In the Crown Court, the trial is "on indictment" with a judge and jury, and in the magistrates' court the trial is summary and conducted by the magistrates. Criminal offences are classified according to the way in which they are to be tried and the number of categories was reduced to three by the Criminal Law Act 1977[89] which was based upon the report of the James Committee on the Distribution of Criminal Business between the Crown Court and the Magistrates' Courts.[90]

Section 14 of the 1977 Act provided that there should be offences triable only on indictment; offences triable only summarily; and offences triable either way.[91] A fourth category has been added by section 40 of the Criminal Justice Act 1988, which provides that, in certain circumstances, a summary offence may be added to an indictment tried at the Crown Court.[92]

1. OFFENCES TRIABLE ONLY ON INDICTMENT

All offences at common law were triable on indictment. The other two categories are the creatures of statute and, therefore, in the absence of any specific provision an offence will be triable on indictment. In practice, this category is reserved for the most serious offences including murder, manslaughter, rape, robbery, causing grievous bodily harm with intent, blackmail and riot. Some offences were "downgraded" by the Criminal Law Act 1977, Schedule 2[93] so as to be triable either way, in recognition of the fact

---

[87] See M. Levi, [1982] B.T.R. 36; Report of the Keith Committee on the *Enforcement Powers of the Revenue Departments* (Cmnd. 8822, 1983); S. Uglow, "Defrauding the Public Purse" [1984] Crim.L.R. 128; R. Smith, "Who's Fiddling? Fraud and Abuse" in S. Ward (ed.) *DHSS in Crisis* (1985); D. Cook, *Rich Law, Poor Law* (1989). The approach of both the police and other agencies to the investigation and prosecution of fraud is considered by M. Levi, *Regulating Fraud* (1987).

[88] He or she can, of course, substitute a different charge for that originally preferred by the police, and can add further charges.

[89] The pertinent parts of this Act have been re-enacted in the Magistrates' Courts Act 1980.

[90] (Cmnd. 6323, 1975). The Committee was chaired by Lord Justice James.

[91] Section 14 was repealed by the Magistrates' Courts Act 1980 and *not* re-enacted but it is a convenient statement of the three categories. The procedures hereafter stated apply to adults. In the case of juveniles summary trial is almost always the mode of trial, even for indictable offences: see Magistrates' Courts Act 1980, s.24. The crucial date is the date of D's appearance before the court on the occasion when the court makes its decision as to the mode of trial. If the defendant is over 17 on that date he or she has the right to jury trial: *R.* v. *Islington North Juvenile Court, ex p. Daley* [1983] 1 A.C. 347; *R.* v. *Nottingham JJ. ex p. Taylor, The Times*, March 26, 1991.

[92] See below, p. 642.

[93] Now to be found in Magistrates' Courts Act 1980, Sched. 1.

that, *inter alia*, appearing to be the keeper of a bawdy house[94]; not providing apprentices or servants with food[95]; assaulting a clergyman at a place of worship[96] and bigamy[97] were no longer regarded as the gravest of offences.

2. OFFENCES TRIABLE ONLY SUMMARILY

Magistrates actually deal with the vast majority of trials in this country and they have exclusive jurisdiction in summary trial. Summary offences must be created by statute and the designation of an offence as summary prevents a jury trial. It was the proposed reclassification of certain offences as triable only summarily which caused much heated criticism of the James Report.[98] The Criminal Law Act 1977 subsequently made provision for the "down-grading" of certain offences which might previously have come before a jury,[99] and no strenuous objection was taken to allocating a number of road traffic offences (including driving with a blood-alcohol concentration above the prescribed limit[1]) assaulting a police constable,[2] threatening behaviour in public places[3] and other offences to the magistrates alone. The major controversy was caused by a proposal about theft.

"We think that small thefts should not be triable on indictment. . . . In the last analysis society has to choose between two conflicting aims. On the one hand is the existing right of the citizen to be tried by a judge and jury on any charge of theft or criminal damage, however small the amount involved. On the other is the right, especially important to anyone defending a serious charge, to be tried as soon as possible. . . . At present, defendants on serious charges are suffering the injustice of long-delayed trial, while the time of the Crown Court is partly occupied with minor cases of low monetary value."[4] The Committee went on to recommend that where a person was charged with theft or a related offence where the value of the property involved did not exceed £20, that offence should be triable only summarily.[5] That was included in the Criminal Law Bill.

This raised squarely the question of what sorts of offence should entitle a defendant to trial by jury and the reactions to the proposal were emotional.[6] The Bill was introduced into the House of Lords and by the time it reached the House of Commons the clause which would have enacted the proposal had been withdrawn by the Government. It is interesting to note that a similar proposal relating to criminal damage where the value of the property damaged is less than £200 was accepted and such an offence is now triable

[94] Disorderly Houses Act 1751, s.8.
[95] Offences Against the Person Act 1861, s.26.
[96] *Ibid.* s.36.
[97] *Ibid.* s.57.
[98] *The Distribution of Criminal Business between the Crown Court and Magistrates' Courts* (Cmnd. 6323, 1975).
[99] 1977 Act, s.15 and Sched. 1.
[1] Now the Road Traffic Act 1988, s.5.
[2] Police Act 1964, s.51(1). Concern was expressed about these changes: see E. J. Griew, *Current Law Statutes Annotated 1977*, General Note to ss.15–17.
[3] Public Order Act 1936, s.5, as substituted by Race Relations Act 1965, s.7: see now the Public Order Act 1936, ss.4, 5.
[4] James Committee Report (see n. 98 above), para. 87.
[5] *Ibid.* para. 100.
[6] See the speeches of members of the House of Lords during the debate on the second reading of the Criminal Law Bill, H. L. Deb. Vol. 378, cols. 801–873, December 14, 1976.

only summarily.[7] The crucial difference was said to be the element of dishonesty inherent in the offence of theft, " . . . people lose a lifetime's reputation for probity by a single action of dishonesty of a material triviality. . . . [Small thefts] remain offences which are serious in the eyes of all honest men."[8]

The offences of taking a motor vehicle without consent and driving while disqualified[9] were changed from triable either way to summary offences by the Criminal Justice Act 1988.[10] Common assault and battery were also made summary offences.[11] The pressure to reclassify other offences, such as small thefts, as summary only, has continued.[12]

3. Offences Triable Either Way

This category is now comprised of (1) those offences specifically mentioned in the First Schedule to the Magistrates' Courts Act 1980[13]; (2) all other offences which prior to the 1977 Act were triable either on indictment or summarily and which were not redesignated[14]; and (3) all offences established since 1977 as triable either way. Amongst the important offences triable either way are all indictable offences under the Theft Acts 1968 and 1978 (save for robbery, blackmail, assault with intent to rob and some burglaries); most of the offences under the Criminal Damage Act 1971, including arson; and certain offences under the Perjury Act 1911, the Sexual Offences Act 1956, the Forgery and Counterfeiting Act 1981, and the Public Order Act 1986.

In respect of offences triable either way it is, of course, necessary to provide a procedure for determining the mode of trial. Save where the prosecution is being carried on by the Attorney-General, the Solicitor-General or the D.P.P. and trial on indictment is required by him,[15] the accused may opt for summary trial or trial on indictment. The court may impose trial on indictment, but may not insist on summary trial if the

---

[7] Magistrates' Courts Act 1980, s.22, as amended, and Sched. 2. The limit was raised to £400 by S.I. 1984 No. 447, art. 2(1) Sched. 1, and then to £2,000 by the Criminal Justice Act 1988, s.38; s.22 of the 1980 Act sets out a special procedure to be adopted in these cases, on which see *R.* v. *Salisbury Magistrates' Court, ex p. Mastin* (1986) 84 Cr.App.R. 248; *R.* v. *Braden* (1987) 152 J.P. 92.

[8] *Per* Lord Edmund-Davies in the debate referred to in n. 6, above.

[9] Theft Act 1968, s.12; Road Traffic Act 1972, s.99 (now re-enacted in the Road Traffic Act 1988, s.103).

[10] s.37. Penalties greater than the maximum applicable in the magistrates' court had been imposed in only a small number of cases: *Consultative Paper on the Distribution of Business between the Crown Court and the Magistrates' Court* (Home Office, 1986), paras. 17–20.

[11] *Ibid.* s.39. It was formerly triable either way, unless, anomalously, the prosecution was brought by or on behalf of the victim, in which case it was triable summarily or on indictment *at the discretion of the justices*: see *R.* v. *Harrow JJ., ex p. Osaseri* [1986] Q.B. 589; E. J. Griew, [1983] Crim.L.R. 710.

[12] See, *e.g.* D. Wolchover, "The Right to Jury Trial" (1986) 136 N.L.J. 530, 576 (critical of the proposal); N. A. McKittrick, "Curbing the Right to Jury Trial" (1988) 152 J.P.N. 515.

[13] Re-enacting Sched. 3 to the Criminal Law Act 1977.

[14] Magistrates' Courts Act 1980, s.17.

[15] *Ibid.* s.19(4). The D.P.P. must obtain the consent of the Attorney-General: *ibid.* s.19(5), inserted by the Prosecution of Offences Act 1985, Sched. 1, Pt. 1, para. 2.

defendant[16] objects. The procedure to be followed by the magistrates is as follows[17]:

(i) the charge is written down and read to the accused;

(ii) the court listens to any representations from the prosecutor and the accused about the most suitable mode of trial;

(iii) the court proceeds to decide on the more suitable mode of trial, taking into account the nature of the case, whether the circumstances make the offence one of serious character, whether the limited powers of punishment of a magistrates' court would be adequate, and any other relevant circumstances;

(iv) if the court considers summary trial more appropriate, that should be explained to the accused, and that he or she need not consent to summary trial but can opt for trial by jury, and that after a summary trial the magistrates have power to send him or her to the Crown Court for sentence;

(v) if the accused consents to summary trial, the case proceeds;

(vi) if the accused opts for trial on indictment, the magistrates proceed with committal proceedings[18];

(vii) if the court considers that trial on indictment is more appropriate it will proceed with committal proceedings and the accused effectively has no choice in the matter.

Finally, it is important to stress that the magistrates must give proper consideration to all the factors and should not be persuaded by the accused (or prosecutor) to allow a summary trial where the offence ought really to be tried on indictment. There are a number of examples of magistrates' courts being severely criticised for allowing serious cases to be tried summarily.[19] The justices are aided somewhat by a provision that they may, during a trial (before the conclusion of the prosecution evidence),[20] decide to change the mode of trial to indictment if the prosecution case reveals the offence to be more serious than might at first have appeared.[21] The reverse change is possible, from committal proceedings to summary trial, subject, in this case, to the consent of the accused.[22]

[16] Or any one of joint defendants: *R.* v. *Brentwood JJ.*, *ex p. Nicholls* [1990] 2 Q.B. 598.

[17] *Ibid.* ss.19–21.

[18] For committal proceedings, see below, pp. 657–664, 692–694.

[19] See *R.* v. *Coe* [1968] 1 W.L.R. 1950, and the statements of principle about the circumstances in which the justices can commit for sentence to the Crown Court after a summary trial in *R.* v. *Kings Lynn JJ.*, *ex p. Carter* [1969] 1 Q.B. 188; *R* v. *Tower Bridge Magistrates' Court*, *ex p. Osman* [1971] 1 W.L.R. 1109; *R.* v. *Lymm JJ.*, *ex p. Brown* [1973] 1 W.L.R. 1039; *R.* v. *Warrington JJ.*, *ex p. Mooney* (1980) 2 Cr.App.R.(S) 40. In general, unless new factors emerge during the trial or afterwards the justices should not consider the evidence which they heard before deciding how to proceed, on the question of whether to commit for sentence: see *R.* v. *Cardiff Stipendiary Magistrate, ex p. Morgan* (1989) 153 J.P. 446 (decision to commit for sentence quashed where the magistrate had misunderstood the material facts at the mode-of-trial enquiry).

[20] Not after a plea of guilty has been accepted: *R.* v. *Dudley JJ.*, *ex p. Gillard* [1986] A.C. 442, H.L.; *R.* v. *Telford JJ.*, *ex p. Darlington* (1987) 87 Cr.App.R. 194; and not prior to the commencement of summary trial: *R.* v. *Southend Magistrates' Court, ex p. Wood* (1986) 152 J.P. 97; *R.* v. *St. Helens Magistrates' Court*, *ex p. Critchley* (1987) 152 J.P. 102. See R. Stevens, (1987) 151 J.P.N. 848.

[21] Magistrates' Courts Act 1980, s.25(2).

[22] *Ibid.*, s.25(3), (3A), (4), as amended by the Prosecution of Offences Act 1985, Scheds. 1, 2. See *R.* v. *Liverpool JJ.*, *ex p. C.P.S.* (1989) 154 J.P. 1.

The defendant should be permitted to change his or her election if he or she has not properly understood the nature and significance of the choice of the mode of trial.[23] In the absence of bad faith on the part of the prosecutor or of unfairness or prejudice to the accused, the prosecutor may substitute a summary offence for an either-way offence even if the purpose is to deprive the accused of the right to jury trial.[24]

In recent years, there has been a steady increase in the number and proportion of triable-either-way cases committed to the Crown Court.[25] Home Office research has indicated that a significant proportion, some 40 per cent. were committed at the discretion of the magistrates rather than at the insistence of the defendant, and that there were considerable variations in practice among the courts surveyed.[26] Guidelines have been formulated in some areas to enhance consistency[27] and magistrates have been in effect encouraged to retain more cases within their jurisdiction.[28] National guidelines were published in October 1990.[29]

Research into defendants' reasons for choosing between summary trial and trial by jury (where a choice is permitted) suggests that the major factor was the intended plea: defendants intending to contest the case commonly regarded trial by jury in the Crown Court as offering a fairer hearing and a better chance of acquittal, in comparison with the magistrates' courts which were said to be biased in favour of the prosecution. A significant number of defendants intending to plead guilty also wished to be dealt with in the Crown Court, notwithstanding its larger sentencing powers, given their greater confidence in sentencing by a judge rather than by magistrates. Reasons cited most frequently for those choosing summary trial were to get the case to court quickly, the chance of a lighter sentence, to avoid lengthy court proceedings and the triviality of the case.[30]

4. SUMMARY OFFENCES IN THE CROWN COURT

The position is further complicated by sections 40 and 41 of the Criminal

[23] R. v. Birmingham JJ., ex p. Hodgson [1985] Q.B. 1131, D.C. (unrepresented defendants had been under the misapprehension that they had no defence; earlier authorities considered); see B. Gibson, (1985) 149 J.P.N. 67. See also R. v. Forest Magistrates' Court, ex p. Spicer (1988) 153 J.P. 81; R. v. Bourne JJ., ex p. Cope (1988) 153 J.P. 161.

[24] R. v. City of Liverpool Stipendiary Magistrate, ex p. Ellison (1988) 153 J.P. 433.

[25] From 55,000 to 80,400, an increase from 15 per cent. to 21 per cent. of all defendants proceeded against for either-way offences: Criminal Statistics 1979, Table 4.5, 1989, Table 6.4. The number peaked in 1987 at 93,500. This has been coupled with an increase in the number of defendants remanded in custody: Criminal Statistics 1989, Table 8.8.

[26] D. Riley and J. Vennard, Triable-Either-Way Cases: Crown Court or Magistrates' Court? (Home Office Research Study No. 98, 1988). See also studies by A. E. Bottoms and J. D. McClean, Defendants in the Criminal Process (1976), Chap. 4, and C. R. Searle, (1989) 153 J.P.N. 526.

[27] N. A. McKittrick, "Considerations in determining mode of trial" (1987) 151 J.P.N. 468, setting out guidelines formulated by the liaison judges in the East Midlands. A revised version is set out at (1989) 153 J.P.N. 314. Cf. the study by Searle, op. cit., of cases in Nottingham, in which he found that the vast majority of committals complied with the local guidelines.

[28] Cf. Letter from the Home Office to the Magistrates' Association summarising the research and suggesting that it was unlikely that the increase in committal rates was accounted for by an increase in the level of the seriousness of offences: (1989) 45 The Magistrate 65.

[29] Practice Note (Mode of Trial: Guidelines) [1990] 1 W.L.R. 1439.

[30] Riley and Vennard (1988), confirming earlier surveys by Bottoms and McClean (1976) and J. Gregory, Crown Court or magistrates' court? (H.M.S.O., 1976).

Justice Act 1988.[31] Under section 41, where a magistrates' court commits a person to the Crown Court for trial of an either-way offence, it may also commit him or her for trial of any summary offence which is (a) punishable with imprisonment or disqualification from driving, and (b) arises out of circumstances which appear to be the same as or connected with those giving rise to the either-way offence. A decision to exercise this power cannot be questioned on appeal or on an application for judicial review. If the defendant is convicted on the indictment, and then pleads guilty to the summary offence, the Crown Court can deal with it then and there, although it can only exercise the sentencing powers that the magistrates' court would have had. If the defendant pleads not guilty, the matter has to be remitted for trial in the magistrates' court, unless the prosecution state that they would not wish to offer evidence in which case the Crown Court must dismiss the charge. If the Court of Appeal allows an appeal against conviction for the associated either-way offence, it must set aside the conviction for the summary offence, and it may direct that no further proceedings be taken in relation to it.

Section 40 applies to a narrower range of summary offences, but enables them to be added to the indictment and actually tried in the Crown Court. The offences are those which were made summary only by sections 37 to 39 of the 1988 Act,[32] and any other offence punishable by imprisonment or a driving disqualification and specified by the Secretary of State. A summary offence in one of these categories can be added to the indictment if it is (a) founded on the same facts or evidence as a count charging an indictable offence, or (b) part of a series of offences of the same or similar character as an indictable offence which is also charged.[33] In either case, the relevant facts or evidence must be disclosed in the committal papers or the depositions. The offence is tried as if it were an indictable offence, but if the person is convicted, the Crown Court (as under section 41) may only exercise the sentencing powers that the magistrates' courts would have had. Where a person is committed for trial for a summary offence under section 41, and the offence falls in one of the section 40 categories, it may be dealt with at the Crown Court under that section rather than under section 41. These sections provide a more convenient procedure for dealing with cases involving both summary and indictable offences but at the cost of adding to the complexity of the law.

E. GETTING THE ACCUSED INTO COURT

If an accused is to be prosecuted for an offence, he or she must actually be brought before a court to have the charge tried or at least to have it determined how and when the trial process should begin. As we have already seen there are two basic methods by which this can be done: by arrest (without warrant) and charge, or by summons.[34] A variant of the

---

[31] See D. Tucker, (1989) L.S.Gaz., 15 March, p. 23.

[32] Common assault, taking a motor vehicle without authority, driving while disqualified, criminal damage not exceeding £2,000.

[33] *Cf.* the Indictment Rules 1971, r. 9: below, p. 784.

[34] See above, p. 632. Not all persons originally arrested without warrant and subsequently proceeded against are charged: a proportion are reported for summons instead. Powers of arrest without a warrant are considered above, pp. 598–600.

second method involves issue of a warrant for the arrest of the accused rather than a summons; these both depend upon the decision of a magistrate after the laying of an information by a named person.[35] The police may be willing to charge a person on behalf of a private prosecutor.[36]

An information is merely a statement of the suspected offence and offender, either written or verbal, in terms specified by the Magistrates Courts Rules 1981,[37] which is placed before a magistrate or the justices' clerk[38] so that a summons or warrant may be issued. If a warrant is required the information must be in writing and on oath,[39] so requiring the attention of a magistrate since a clerk may not act where the information is on oath.[40] A typical information would be set out as follows:[41]

NOTTINGHAM MAGISTRATES COURT

DATE:	March 1st 1991
ACCUSED:	Henry Frederick Smailey
ADDRESS:	32 Woodland Hall Grove, Cripston, Nottingham.
ALLEGED OFFENCE:	Henry Smailey on February 27th 1991, at the Department of Law, University Park, Nottingham, dishonestly stole £5, the property of N. P. Gravells, Esq., contrary to section 1 of the Theft Act 1968.
THE INFORMATION OF:	Gavin Edmunds, Police Constable 1234
ADDRESS:	Cripston Police Station, Jug Road, Cripston, Nottingham.
TELEPHONE:	999999

WHO UPON OATH STATES THAT THE ACCUSED COMMITTED THE OFFENCE OF WHICH PARTICULARS ARE GIVEN ABOVE.

TAKEN AND SWORN BEFORE ME

Cordelia Lear
JUSTICE OF THE PEACE

JUSTICES' CLERK

---

[35] Not, *e.g.* in the name of a police force: *Rubin* v. *D.P.P.* [1990] 2 Q.B. 80 (although the information here was not held invalid as the identity of the relevant constable could easily have been ascertained and the defendant had suffered no injustice).
[36] *R.* v. *Stafford JJ.*, *ex p. Commissioners of Customs and Excise* [1990] 3 W.L.R. 656.
[37] S.I. 1981 No. 552, and the accompanying Magistrates' Courts Forms Rules 1981 (S.I. 1981 No. 553).
[38] Justices of the Peace Act 1979, s.28(1).
[39] Magistrates' Courts Act 1980, s.1(3).
[40] Justices' Clerks Rules 1970 (S.I. 1970 No. 321), r. 3.
[41] Magistrates' Courts (Forms) Rules 1981, Form. 1.

The information procedure does not seem to be used very often to procure a warrant[42] (the conditions for the grant of which are, in any event, carefully prescribed[43]). On the grant of a summons the magistrate, or the clerk, should satisfy him- or herself that the offence is known to the law; that it is not out of time; that the court has jurisdiction and that the informant has the requisite authority to prosecute.[44] A warrant should only be issued if it appears that a summons will be ineffective.[45] The summons, if issued, will not look very different from the information.[46]

NOTTINGHAM MAGISTRATES COURT

DATE: March 1st 1991

TO THE ACCUSED: Henry Frederick Smailey

OF: 32 Woodland Hall Grove, Cripston, Nottingham

YOU ARE HEREBY SUMMONED TO APPEAR ON May 18th 1991, AT 10.30 a.m. BEFORE THE MAGISTRATES' COURT at the Guildhall, Nottingham to ANSWER TO THE FOLLOWING INFORMATION

ALLEGED OFFENCE: You on February 27th 1991 at the Department of Law, University Park, Nottingham dishonestly stole £5, the property of N. P. Gravells, Esq., contrary to section 1 of the Theft Act 1968.

PROSECUTOR: Trevor Gunn, Chief Inspector of Police

ADDRESS: Cripston Police Station, Jug Road, Cripston, Nottingham.

                                        Cordelia Lear
                                JUSTICE OF THE PEACE

The accused should then respond to the summons and attendance at court on a specified day has therefore been secured. The process can be continued on that day. If he or she fails to respond, a warrant may then be appropriate.

The decision to issue a summons or warrant is a judicial decision and cannot be delegated, for example to members of the clerk's staff.[47] In general, magistrates cannot try a summary offence unless the information was laid within six months from the time when the offence was committed. The information is regarded as laid when it is received at the office of the

---

[42] R.C.C.P. I, para. 179.
[43] By the Magistrates' Courts Act 1980, ss.1(4), 13(2). Broadly speaking, the alleged offence must be indictable or punishable with imprisonment, or the accused must have failed to respond to a summons, or his or her address is not sufficiently known for a summons to be served.
[44] R. v. Metropolitan Stipendiary Magistrate, ex p. Klahn [1979] 1 W.L.R. 933.
[45] O'Brien v. Brabner (1885) 49 J.P.N. 227.
[46] Magistrates' Courts (Forms) Rules 1981, Form 2.
[47] R. v. Gateshead JJ., ex p. Tesco Stores Ltd. [1981] Q.B. 470; R. v. Manchester Stipendiary Magistrate, ex p. Hill [1983] 1 A.C. 328, 342–343.

clerk to the justices in the relevant area. For this purpose it is not necessary for it to be considered personally by a justice or justices' clerk; such consideration is only a necessary pre-condition for the issue of a summons or warrant on the basis of the information.[48] The laying of an information before a decision to prosecute has been taken, in order to comply with the time limit, may constitute an abuse of the process of the court, causing the court to decline jurisdiction,[49] as may excessive delay before issuing a summons.[50]

If the accused has been arrested by warrant or without warrant it is the duty of the police then to procure his or her attendance at court. He or she will have been given bail by the police or by the warrant to appear on an appointed day or will have been brought to court in custody. If the accused is in custody after arrest without a warrant he or she must be brought before a magistrates' court in accordance with the requirements of the Police and Criminal Evidence Act 1984.[51]

Technically, when an accused is arrested without warrant and charged at the police station an information is laid when the charge sheet is remitted by the police to the justices' clerk for inclusion on the court list,[52] but this is in reality a fiction and offenders who are brought to court in this way will never have the facts initially scrutinised by a magistrate.

(The Royal Commission concluded that the summons and warrant procedure was a virtual dead letter since the consideration given to the decision to prosecute by the justices' clerk or magistrate was minimal. It was proposed that there should, in future, be a single procedure for getting an accused to court, the making of a formal "accusation" by the police fixing the date and time of the first court appearance.[53] This recommendation was not accepted.)

Where an accused is arrested the question will arise at what stage, if at all, he or she should be released before trial.

F. BAIL OR CUSTODY?[54]

To deprive an accused[55] of liberty pending trial may be to keep in custody an innocent person or one who, though convicted, ultimately receives a non-custodial sentence. To allow an accused liberty pending trial may be to

---

[48] Ex p. Hill, supra, disapproving dicta in the Gateshead case, supra. Informations fed into a computer system within the time limit although printed out after were held to be properly laid in R. v. Pontypridd Juvenile Court, ex p. B. (1988) 153 J.P. 213.

[49] R. v. Brentford JJ., ex p. Wong [1981] Q.B. 445.

[50] R. v. Fairford JJ., ex p. Brewster [1976] Q.B. 600.

[51] See above, pp. 604–606.

[52] The process is described and commented on in R.C.C.P. I, para. 182.

[53] R.C.C.P. Report, para. B.4.

[54] See generally, M. King, Bail or Custody, Cobden Trust (1971); A. K. Bottomley, Decisions in the Penal Process (1973), pp. 93–105, and "The Granting of Bail: Principles and Practice" (1968) 31 M.L.R. 40; M. Zander, "Bail: A Reappraisal" [1967] Crim.L.R. 25, 100, 128; A. Ashworth, The English Criminal Process: a Review of Empirical Research (1984), Chap. 5; M. Winfield, Lacking Conviction (1984); C. Chatterton, Bail: Law and Practice (1986); E. Cape, Legal Action, October 1989, p. 11 and November 1989, p. 21; N. Corre, Bail in Criminal Proceedings (1990).

[55] We use the term "accused" throughout this section to include those arrested, those on trial, and those convicted.

permit him or her to disappear, commit further offences, or interfere with witnesses and obstruct the course of justice. It is a difficult decision. The issue is raised as soon as a person is taken into custody and remains live until trial and, indeed, between conviction and appeal. The procedure by which the accused is released subject to a requirement to surrender to custody again at a specified time and place is termed the granting of bail. Bail may be granted by the police, the magistrates' court, the Crown Court, the High Court and the Court of Appeal under a variety of statutory and common law provisions,[56] but the granting of bail in all criminal proceedings must be in accordance with the principles set out in the Bail Act 1976.

This Act, which came into force in the Spring of 1978, was a response to the widespread disquiet about the operation of the system of bail and resulted from the Report of a Home Office Working Party[57] which had been established in 1971 "to review practice and procedure in magistrates' courts relating to the grant or refusal of bail and to make recommendations."[58] Before considering the general principles it is helpful to define two important terms.

A *surety* is a person who is willing to undertake to secure the surrender of the accused to custody. The grant of bail may be made conditional upon the accused finding a suitable surety or sureties.[59] Whoever is willing to be a surety must enter into a *recognizance*, which is a formal acknowledgment that he or she will owe the Crown a specified sum of money if the accused fails to surrender to custody. No money is payable by the surety unless the accused actually absconds.[60] The amount of the recognizance is a matter for the police officer or court granting bail.

Statutory criteria are now fixed for determining the suitability of persons who may offer to be sureties where the grant of bail is conditional upon finding sureties.[61] In considering the suitability of a proposed surety, regard may be had, *inter alia*, to financial resources, character and any previous convictions, and "proximity" to the accused.[62] If a court or police officer considers a proposed surety to be unsuitable there is provision for appeal.[63]

---

[56] See below, pp. 652–655.

[57] *Bail Procedures in Magistrates' Courts*, Report of the Home Office Working Party (1974).

[58] Although the terms of reference of the Working Party referred specifically to magistrates' courts the provisions of the Bail Act 1976 actually went somewhat wider.

[59] Bail Act 1976, s.3(4).

[60] The recognizance may not be forfeited if the surety has made every effort to secure the appearance of the accused and acted with all due diligence, but the obligation is upon the surety to satisfy the court that all or part of the sum should not be forfeited. Only in exceptional cases will the court order that the recognizance should not be forfeited: Magistrates' Courts Act 1980, s.120; *R.* v. *Southampton JJ.*, *ex p. Green* [1976] Q.B. 11; *R.* v. *Waltham Forest JJ.*, *ex p. Palfrey* (1980) 2 Cr.App.R.(S.) 208; *R.* v. *Knightsbridge Crown Court*, *ex p. Newton* [1980] Crim.L.R. 715; *R.* v. *Ipswich Crown Court*, *ex p. Reddington* [1981] Crim. L.R. 618; *R.* v. *Wells Street Magistrates' Court*, *ex p. Albanese* [1982] Q.B. 333; *R.* v. *Uxbridge JJ.*, *ex p. Heward-Mills* [1983] 1 W.L.R. 56; *R.* v. *Inner London Crown Court*, *ex p. Springall* (1986) 85 Cr.App.R. 214; *R.* v. *York Crown Court*, *ex p. Coleman and How* (1987) 86 Cr.App.R. 151; *R.* v. *Reading Crown Court*, *ex p. Bello, The Times*, December 11, 1990. The courts appear to be becoming more willing to remit the whole or part of the sum due where the surety has acted reasonably or has not been informed of a change in bail conditions.

[61] Bail Act 1976, s.8(2). See generally J. Morton, "Sureties" (1985) 135 N.L.J. 981.

[62] "Proximity" to the accused includes consideration of kinship, place of residence or other matters.

[63] Bail Act 1976, s.8(5).

Prior to the Bail Act it was quite common for the accused to be required to enter into a personal recognizance, but this has now been abolished[64] and the only circumstances in which the accused may be required to provide security is if it appears likely that he or she will leave Great Britain.[65]

1. GENERAL PRINCIPLES RELATING TO THE GRANT OF BAIL

The Bail Act introduced a general right to bail for accused persons and certain others subject to exceptions specified in a Schedule to the Act. In fact, the exceptions are substantial and this has led commentators to speak of a "presumption in favour of bail" rather than a "right to bail." In addition the Act focussed attention upon the need for information about the accused to be available to the court so that the bail decision could be an informed one, and required reasons to be given to the accused where bail was not granted so that he or she might more effectively conduct an appeal against the decision.

Section 4 of the Bail Act 1976 creates the *right to bail*:

> "(1) A person to whom this section applies shall be granted bail except as provided in Schedule 1 to this Act.
> (2) This section applies to a person who is accused of an offence when—
>> (a) he appears or is brought before a magistrates' court or the Crown Court in the course of or in connection with proceedings for the offence, or
>> (b) he applies to a court for bail in connection with the proceedings."

There are additional categories brought within the entitlement and some which are excepted.[66] It is important to note that this section applies to the grant of bail by courts only. The grant of bail by the police, considered below, is not subject to this provision.

Schedule 1 of the Act creates the *exceptions to the right to bail*, and distinguishes between defendants accused or convicted of offences punishable with imprisonment[67] and those not punishable with imprisonment.[68] In respect of the imprisonable offences the accused need not be granted bail if the court is satisfied that there are substantial grounds for believing that the accused would, if released on bail:

(a) fail to surrender to custody, or
(b) commit an offence while on bail, or

---

[64] *Ibid.* s.3(2).

[65] *Ibid.* s.3(5).

[66] Within the entitlement—a person remanded for reports after conviction (Bail Act 1976, s.4(4)); a person brought before the court for breach of a probation or community service order (s.4(3)). Excluded from entitlement—a person convicted of the offence charged (unless remanded for reports) (s.4(2)); a fugitive offender (s.4(2)); a person who the court is satisfied should be kept in custody for his or her own protection or (if a child or young person) his or her own welfare (Sched. 1, Part I, para. 3; Part II, para. 3); a person charged with treason (s.4(7)); a person arrested for absconding or breach of bail granted (Sched. 1, Part I, para. 6; Part II, para. 5).

[67] Sched. 1, Part I.

[68] Sched. 1, Part II.

    (c) interfere with witnesses or otherwise obstruct the course of justice.[69]

The accused need not be granted bail where the court is satisfied that it has not been practicable to obtain sufficient information since the proceedings were instituted to make a proper decision on bail.[70]

    This latter point emphasises that the court must have access to information about the defendant because it is required to have regard to specified matters (as far as they appear relevant) including:

    (a) the nature and seriousness of the offence (and the probable method of dealing with it);
    (b) the character, antecedents, associations and community ties of the defendant;
    (c) the defendant's record in respect of any previous grants of bail;
    (d) the strength of the evidence against him or her.[71]

In respect of non-imprisonable offences the defendant may only be denied bail if it appears to the court that he or she has previously failed to surrender to bail and that the court believes that, if released, he or she would again fail to surrender to custody.[72]

    The court, if it is to refuse bail, must be "satisfied that there are substantial grounds for believing" that one of the specified situations exists. This formulation of the standard of proof is a compromise reached after much debate both in the House of Commons and the House of Lords. The original draft was "satisfied that it is probable"; an amendment in the Lords substituted, "satisfied that there is an unacceptable risk"[73]; and the eventual compromise was thought to pitch the standard of proof somewhere between the two.[74]

    If bail is refused by the court or conditions are imposed on the grant of bail in respect of anyone to whom section 4 of the Act applies, the court must give reasons for withholding bail or imposing the conditions with a view to enabling the accused to make application to another court.[75] This is a logical provision, given that the courts are now directed towards specific considerations in the refusal of bail. The accused is entitled to know in what respect he or she is considered unsuitable for bail. Furthermore, reasons must now be given where the court grants bail to an accused charged with murder, manslaughter, rape, attempted murder or attempted rape.[76]

---

[69] Sched. 1, Part I, para. 2.
[70] *Ibid.* para. 5.
[71] *Ibid.* para. 9.
[72] Sched. 1, Part II, para. 2.
[73] See the speech of Lord Hailsham, H.L. Deb., April 6, 1976, Vol. 369, col. 1544 *et seq*.
[74] H.C. Deb., November 2, 1976, Vol. 918, col. 1323–4, Mr. Brynmor John, then Minister of State, Home Office.
[75] Bail Act 1976, s.5(3).
[76] *Ibid.* Sched. 1, Part I, para. 9A, inserted by the Criminal Justice Act 1988. This provision was passed in view of public concern about bail being too readily granted in cases of serious alleged violence.

The court may attach conditions necessary to secure that he or she

    (a) surrenders to custody;
    (b) does not commit an offence while on bail;
    (c) does not interfere with witnesses or otherwise obstruct the course of justice;
    (d) makes him- or herself available for the purposes of enabling enquiries, or a report to be made to assist the court in dealing with him or her for the offence.[77] In this context, it is not necessary that the court has "substantial grounds": it is sufficient that it perceives "a real and not fanciful risk" of, for example, an offence being committed.[78]

The imposition of conditions on the grant of bail can be a very serious matter. It is not uncommon for the magistrates to require the accused to report regularly to a police station as a condition of bail, or to observe a curfew, or to reside in or keep away from particular places. In serious matters the accused may be required to surrender his or her passport.[79] It is arguable that the conditions attached ought to relate primarily to securing the attendance of the accused in court but they can also be used to curtail potentially criminal activities pending the trial of the alleged offence.[80]

2. APPLICATION OF THE PRINCIPLES

It seems that the Bail Act has not made a substantial difference to the practice of the courts. There were, indeed, two significant reductions in the number of prisoners on remand[81] but such research as there is shows little general change.[82] The most significant factors influencing remand decisions in the magistrates' courts are whether the police have granted bail, the seriousness of the offence and court policy.[83] Furthermore, Home Office

[77] *Ibid.* s.3(6), Sched. 1, para. 8(1). The power to attach conditions extends to both imprisonable and non-imprisonable offences (see *R.* v. *Bournemouth Magistrates' Court, ex p. Cross* (1988) 89 Cr.App.R. 90). For the argument that a surety of good behaviour might be imposed as a condition of bail under the court's binding-over powers, see N. Corre, [1986] Crim.L.R. 162. See also B. P. Block, (1990) 154 J.P.N. 83; P. W. H. Lydiate, *ibid.* p. 132.

[78] *R.* v. *Mansfield JJ.*, *ex p. Sharkey* [1985] Q.B. 613.

[79] Guidance was given by the Home Office in Circular 206/1977 of November 18, 1977. Courts were, *e.g.*, requested to be especially selective in requiring regular reporting to a police station as this can be burdensome for the police and also raise identification problems.

[80] During the 1984–85 miners' strike, striking miners charged with criminal offences were frequently granted bail subject to conditions prohibiting picketing at premises other than the defendant's own place of work: the practice was controversial (see S. McCabe and P. Wallington, *The Police, Public Order, and Civil Liberties* (1988), pp. 97–98), but held to be lawful by the Divisional Court (*R.* v. *Mansfield JJ.*, *ex p. Sharkey* [1985] Q.B. 613). See also *R.* v. *Bournemouth Magistrates' Court, ex p. Cross* (1988) 89 Cr.App.R. 90 (bail conditions prohibiting defendants charged with disturbing a fox hunting meet from attending another hunt meeting held valid).

[81] One after the Home Office Circular (No. 155/1975) which urged the courts to take a more liberal view on bail, and the other after the Bail Act 1976.

[82] See below, p. 656 and M. Zander, "The Operation of the Bail Act in London Magistrates' Courts" (1979) 129 N.L.J. 108. See also, R. Vogler, "The Changing Nature of Bail," *LAG Bulletin*, February 1983, 11; R. East and M. Doherty, "The Practical Operation of Bail," *LAG Bulletin*, March 1984, 12; R. Morgan, "Remands in Custody" [1989] Crim.L.R. 481.

[83] P. Jones, "Remand decisions in magistrates' courts" in D. Moxon (ed.), *Managing Criminal Justice* (1980), Chap. 10. See also P. M. Morgan and R. Pearce, *Remand Decisions in Brighton and Bournemouth* (H.O.R.P.U. Paper 53, 1989); P. M. Morgan, (1990) 29 H.O.R.B. 18.

statistics indicate significant variations in the use of custodial remands among different petty sessional divisions.[84]

An issue which initially concerned the courts was the procedure to be adopted on successive applications for bail. The magistrates' court is given power, prior to the commencement of the hearing, to remand an accused person in custody for a period not exceeding eight clear days[85] and this may be appropriate where the prosecution are not yet ready to proceed with the case. In complex cases this meant a court appearance every eight days for a considerable length of time.[86] At every appearance the accused was entitled to request bail and would normally appear before differently constituted courts each time.[87] In Nottingham, the City justices adopted a policy under which after a second application[88] for bail they would not consider on subsequent applications matters previously before the court unless there had been a change in circumstances.[89] In effect, remand in custody became automatic. A group of Nottingham solicitors organised an application for mandamus by one Clive Edgar Davies, charged with various offences of criminal damage and rape, directing the justices to hear the full facts supporting an application for bail made on April 10, 1980[90] and determine it accordingly. In *R.* v. *Nottingham JJ. ex p. Davies*[91] the Divisional Court refused the application.

It was argued on behalf of Davies that he had a right to bail which was only defeasible on the specified grounds; that the court has a duty to consider the grant of bail on every occasion on which the accused appears; and that the fact of a previous remand could not, of itself, satisfy the justices that one of the specified grounds still existed. The court did not accede to the argument and Donaldson L.J. based his judgment primarily upon a notion of *res judicata*.[92] The finding of the original court that Schedule 1 circumstances existed, "... is to be treated like every other finding of the court. It is *res judicata* or analogous thereto. . . . It follows that on the next occasion when bail is considered the court should treat, as an essential fact, that at the time when the matter of bail was last considered, Schedule 1 circumstances did indeed exist. Strictly speaking, they can and should only investigate whether that situation has changed since then."[93] The court also indicated that the

---

[84] Jones, *op. cit.* Home Office Statistical Bulletin 7/87, discussed by B. Gibson (1987) 151 J.P.N. 520 and B. Rowland, (1987) 151 J.P.N. 651. The Home Office has emphasised the need for consistency: Home Office Circular 25/1988: (1988) 44 *The Magistrate* 173.

[85] Magistrates' Courts Act 1980, s.128(6).

[86] This can clearly be oppressive since the accused is being held in custody without trial, but it is well established that an unreasonable delay on the part of the prosecution will be a good reason for granting bail: *R.* v. *Nottingham Justices, ex p. Davies* [1981] Q.B. 38, at p. 44.

[87] At the time of Davies' application (see note above) the Nottingham bench consisted of 320 justices, with up to 25 courts sitting each day. The chance of getting the same justices two weeks running was negligible.

[88] After the *second* application, because the first is usually made by a duty solicitor (see above, p. 452) who may not be fully briefed so as to make a proper application. On the second application the accused will normally be legally aided and represented by his or her own solicitor who should then be in a position to place all relevant matters before the court.

[89] A policy apparently inspired by certain remarks made by Ackner J. to a meeting of justices' clerks and reported in (1980) 36 *The Magistrate* 34, 97. The actual wording of the Nottingham policy is contained in the report of *Davies*, [1981] Q.B. 38, at p. 41.

[90] The date was significant because that was Davies' third application for bail.

[91] [1981] Q.B. 38.

[92] A final judgment already decided by a competent court on the same question.

[93] [1981] Q.B. 38 at p. 44.

position of the accused is safeguarded by the provision for an application to a High Court judge for bail.[94]

This decision excited both favourable[95] and unfavourable[96] comment, and was in certain respects in need of clarification.[97] It has now been codified by section 154 of the Criminal Justice Act 1988.[98] This provides:

"(1) If the court decides not to grant the defendant bail, it is the court's duty to consider, at each subsequent hearing while the defendant . . . remains in custody, whether he ought to be granted bail.

(2) At the first hearing after that at which the court decided not to grant the defendant bail he may support an application for bail with any argument as to fact or law that he desires (whether or not he has advanced that argument previously).

(3) At subsequent hearings the court need not hear arguments as to fact or law which it has heard previously."

This makes it clear that while the court is not obliged to hear repeated arguments, it has a discretion to do so; the position is, accordingly, a little more flexible than that suggested by Donaldson L.J. in *ex p. Davies*.

The position has also been affected to some extent by the provisions of section 59 and Schedule 9 of the Criminal Justice Act 1982.[99] This enables the court to remand an accused in his or her absence for up to three successive remand hearings provided that he or she consents and is legally represented. This alleviates the problem of constant weekly journeys for the accused who does not wish to contest the remand, but *ex p. Davies* still applies to prevent the non-consenting accused from seeking bail on every remand appearance. Section 155 of the Criminal Justice Act 1988[1] authorises the introduction of a new power for the court to remand in custody for a period up to 28 days without the accused's consent. This is to be exercisable where the accused has previously been remanded in custody and the court has set a date for the next stage in the proceedings.[2]

The only reported case on the application of the relevant considerations when refusal of bail is contemplated is *R. v. Vernege*,[3] where the Court of Appeal regretted that the grant of bail on committal on a charge of murder had prevented the examination of the accused by a prison doctor and, consequently, the early submission of psychiatric evidence. It was noted

[94] See below, pp. 654–655.
[95] Anon. "Bail Applications" (1980) 144 J.P.N. 319; Editorials in (1980) 36 *The Magistrate* 97, 135; K. Polak, "Applications for Bail" (1980) 144 J.P.N. 525.
[96] M. Hayes, "Where Now the Right to Bail" [1981] Crim.L.R. 20. In "Bail—a Suitable Case for Treatment" (1982) 132 N.L.J. 409, J. Burrow analyses other less predictable effects of the decision.
[97] See S. Holdham, (1985) 135 N.L.J. 471; P.W.H. Lydiate, "Bail procedure in magistrates' courts: basic procedures" (1987) 151 J.P.N. 164, 181. See also *R. v. Reading Crown Court, ex p. Malik* [1981] Q.B. 451 and *R. v. Slough JJ., ex p. Duncan and Embling* (1982) 75 Cr.App.R. 384 (different views expressed on whether as a general rule reaching the stage of committal for trial would constitute a change in circumstances: Donaldson L.J. in the *Reading* case indicated *obiter* that it would; Ormrod L.J. in the *Slough* case that it would not necessarily do so).
[98] Inserting a new Part IIA in Sched. 1 to the Bail Act 1976.
[99] Inserting s.128(1A)–(1C), (3A)–(3E) of the Magistrates' Courts Act 1980.
[1] Inserting s.128A of the Magistrates' Courts Act 1980.
[2] The provision is first to be introduced experimentally in specified areas: see Magistrates' Courts (Remands in Custody) Order 1989 (S.I. 1989 No. 970).
[3] [1982] 1 W.L.R. 293.

that on a charge of murder, the obtaining of such reports was a "relevant matter" in relation to bail and it could be in the accused's interests to be remanded in custody, at least until the examinations had been carried out. There is now a power to remand to a hospital for a report on the accused's medical condition.[3a]

3. POLICE BAIL[4]

The Police and Criminal Evidence Act 1984 establishes a number of situations in which a person in police custody may be released on bail. The decision in most cases is taken by the custody officer. Where the custody officer orders a person's release under section 34, this must be without bail unless it appears to the custody officer (1) that there is need for further investigation of any matter in connection with which he or she was detained, or (2) that proceedings may be taken against him or her in respect of any such matter: if it does so appear, the person must be released on bail. In other situations, there is a discretion to release with or without bail, as where a person is released before charge (section 37); after charge (section 38); after 24 hours detention (section 41); after 36 hours detention (section 42); or where a warrant for further detention is refused or expires (sections 43, 44).[5] In each case a release on bail "shall be a release on bail granted in accordance with the Bail Act 1976,"[6] and shall be subject to a duty to appear before a magistrates' court or to return to the police station as directed by the custody officer, who must specify the time and place.[7] The option of requiring the accused to return to the police station can be employed to give the police time to continue their enquiries, and to decide whether they wish to prosecute and if so on what charges.

If the accused is in police custody as the result of a warrant issued by a magistrate or the Crown Court, then the warrant itself will dictate the granting of bail and the previous provisions will not apply. Either the warrant will be "endorsed for bail"[8] in terms which must be observed by the police, or it will require the police to bring the accused before the court immediately.[9] In this case, of course, the grant of bail is, strictly speaking, made by the court and not the police.

The use of police bail is substantial. In 1989, 729,700 persons were arrested and charged of whom 620,800 (85 per cent.) were bailed and the remainder, 108,900 (15 per cent.) held in custody.[10] In general, the more serious the offence, the higher the proportion of those arrested who are held in custody. The highest proportion is in respect of robbery (57 per cent.); and burglary, sexual offences and criminal damage all exceed the average.[11]

[3a] Mental Health Act 1983, s.35.
[4] See R. Tarling, P. Jones and A. Sanders, "Police Bail" (1986) 21 H.O. Research Bulletin 52; J. Wadham, "Bail from Police Stations" Legal Action, December 1988, pp. 24–25.
[5] See ss.37(2), (7)(b); 38(1); 41(7); 42(10); 43(15)(18); 44(7).
[6] Ibid. s.47(1).
[7] Ibid. s.47(3).
[8] Ibid. s.117. The magistrate issuing the warrant will state on the warrant that the person arrested is to be released subject to a duty to appear at a specified court and time.
[9] See the form of warrant set out as Form 4, the Magistrates' Courts (Forms) Rules 1981 (S.I. 1981 No. 553).
[10] Criminal Statistics England and Wales 1989, Chap. 8.
[11] See R. Tarling, P. Jones and A. Sanders, "Police Bail" (1986) 21 H.O.R.B. 52, Table 2, based on 1980 figures.

4. BAIL FROM THE MAGISTRATES' COURT

If the accused has been arrested without warrant, and has not been bailed by the police, or arrested with a warrant which is not endorsed for bail, he or she must be brought before a magistrates' court and will then have an opportunity to request bail. Indeed, the court is under an obligation to consider the question of bail even if no application is made.[12] Only compara-tively minor cases can be disposed of at one appearance in the magistrates' court. The court accordingly has express power to adjourn

(1) an inquiry as examining justices, either before or during the inquiry[13];

(2) a summary trial, either before or during the trial[14];

(3) proceedings to determine mode of trial in the case of offences triable either way[15]; and

(4) the hearing, where the court has begun to try an offence triable either way, but decides to discontinue summary trial and proceed to inquire as examining justices.[16]

On these occasions, the court may, and sometimes must, remand the accused, which simply means a direction that he or she should be held in custody for a specified period, or that he or she should be released on bail with an obligation to appear again before the court on a specified date.[17] The court *must* remand in situation (1); in situations (2) and (3) where the offence is triable either way and either the accused initially attends the court in custody or has at any time been remanded[18]; and where it commits the accused for trial[19] or sentence[20] in the Crown Court. Otherwise the court may either remand the accused or simply adjourn the hearing without remanding, although the latter step is normally only taken in minor cases, usually road traffic matters.[21]

In deciding whether to remand on bail or in custody the magistrates must have regard to the provisions of the Bail Act but may take advantage of section 154 of the Criminal Justice Act 1988[22] to lessen the burden of continuing applications. The position is further eased by the provision for extended remands in custody.[23]

---

[12] Because of the provision in the Bail Act 1976, s.4(1) that a person to whom the Act applies *shall* be given bail except where Schedule 1 applies. See J. N. Spencer, (1986) 150 J.P.N. 724; P. H. W. Lydiate, (1987) 151 J.P.N. 25.

[13] Magistrates' Courts Act 1980, s.5(1).

[14] *Ibid*. s.10(1). This power may be exercised after conviction and before sentence, to enable inquiries to be made: s.10(3). There is also a power to adjourn a trial to enable a medical examination and report to be made; this power is available where the offence is punishable with imprisonment and the court is satisfied that the accused did the act or made the omission charged: s.30.

[15] *Ibid*. s.18(4).

[16] *Ibid*. s.25(2).

[17] *Ibid*. s.128(1).

[18] *Ibid*. ss.10(4), 18(4).

[19] *Ibid*. s.6(3).

[20] *Ibid*. s.38. Or adjourns for medical reports under. s.30.

[21] Emmins (1988), p. 423.

[22] Above, p. 651.

[23] Above, p. 651. Adjournments under ss.10(3) and 30 (see f.n. 14) may be for not more than four weeks at a time (if the accused is on bail) or three weeks at a time (if he or she is in custody); and the accused may be remanded for the period of the adjournment: s.128(6)(*b*). Remands on bail may be for longer than eight days if the accused and the other party consent: s.128(6)(*a*). The accused may be further remanded if he or she is unable to appear by reason of illness or accident: 129(1).

5. Bail from the Crown Court

The Crown Court may grant bail to an accused who is in custody pending a hearing in the Crown Court (after committal for trial or sentence); or pending an appeal against conviction or sentence by the magistrates; or pending the completion of the hearing in the Crown Court; or pending the statement of a case for the High Court or the outcome of an application to have proceedings removed from the Crown Court to the High Court; or pending an appeal to the Court of Appeal where the Crown Court has given a certificate under the Criminal Appeal Act 1968.[24]

If, in any of those cases, the accused is actually before the court then application is made orally to the judge, otherwise the application is in writing in a specified form and the accused is not entitled to be present at the hearing.[25] The jurisdiction of the court is quite separate from that of the justices and the High Court, and prior applications to either of those courts will not diminish the obligation of the Crown Court judge to consider the application on its merits and exercise discretion.[26] However, the accused may not make repeated applications to the Crown Court unless there is a change in circumstances.[27]

An important addition to the powers of the Crown Court is the power to grant bail on an application by a person who has been refused bail by a magistrates' court.[28] The application may only be made where the magistrates have heard full argument before refusal.[29] Legal aid is available for the application.[30] This reform was a response to criticism that there was no effective appeal against refusal of bail by the magistrates other than an expensive and difficult application to the High Court.

6. Bail from the High Court

A judge of the High Court may exercise both the inherent jurisdiction to grant bail and the statutory powers vested in the High Court by the Criminal Justice Act 1967.[31] The application for a writ of habeas corpus has now largely been superseded by a bail application. The ability of the accused to make application to the High Court was specifically mentioned in the *Davies*

---

[24] Supreme Court Act 1981, s.81, as amended by Criminal Justice Act 1982, s.29. See also, *Practice Direction* [1983] 1 W.L.R. 1292. There is also inherent jurisdiction to grant bail during a trial on indictment and for the period of adjournment for reports following conviction. See *Practice Note* [1974] 1 W.L.R. 770.

[25] Crown Court Rules 1982, r.19.

[26] *R. v. Reading Crown Court, ex p. Malik* [1981] 1 Q.B. 451.

[27] There is no specific provision in the Crown Court Rules to this effect, but the Divisional Court in the *Reading* case (above) indicated that simultaneous or immediately consecutive applications to more than one Crown Court judge will not be permitted.

[28] Criminal Justice Act 1982, s.60, amending the Supreme Court Act 1981, s.81. See also, *Practice Direction* (1983) 77 Cr.App.R. 69.

[29] For the certification procedure to be adopted see Criminal Justice Act 1982, s.60(3), inserting new subsections 5(6A), (6B), (6C) in the Bail Act 1976.

[30] Criminal Justice Act 1982, s.60(4), amending the Legal Aid Act 1974, s.30: see now the Legal Aid Act 1988, ss.19, 20.

[31] s.22, as amended by the Bail Act 1976. The court also has jurisdiction under the Criminal Justice Act 1948, s.37, to grant bail where the accused is applying for certiorari to quash a decision of a magistrates' court or the Crown Court, or appealing by case stated from the Crown Court.

case[32] as a check on the accuracy of magistrates' decisions, and an additional safeguard is provided by the application to the Crown Court set out above. Application to the High Court was always a difficult operation because legal aid was rarely granted, forcing applicants to rely on the Official Solicitor.[33]

The accused must apply to a judge in chambers either through his or her own solicitor by summons and affidavit, or by giving written notice to the judge that he or she wants bail.[34] In the latter case, the judge will then appoint the Official Solicitor to act on the accused's behalf. The Official Solicitor will not actually represent the applicant at a hearing in chambers (as his or her own lawyer would) but merely prepares a set of papers for the judge to consider, along with the police submissions. This is widely regarded as an unsatisfactory form of procedure and research demonstrates that the success rate in bail applications made by the Official Solicitor is much lower than in applications made by a lawyer instructed by the applicant.[35] The legally-aided right of appeal referred to above ought to obviate this problem.

7. BREACH OF BAIL

The Bail Act 1976 replaced the defendant's personal recognizance with a new criminal offence of failing to surrender to custody without reasonable cause.[36] If a defendant has reasonable cause for failure to surrender to custody at the appointed time and place, he or she must surrender as soon as reasonably practicable thereafter, or be guilty of an offence.[37] Powers of arrest are attached to the offence. The accused may be fined or imprisoned on summary conviction, or by the Crown Court, where the offence is dealt with as if it were a criminal contempt of court.[38] Where the accused has failed to surrender to bail granted by a magistrates' court, proceedings are initiated by the court by its own motion, following an invitation by the prosecutor, the proceedings then being conducted by the prosecutor.[39] Where the accused

---

[32] *R.* v. *Nottingham JJ., ex p. Davies* [1981] Q.B. 38, see above, pp. 650–651.

[33] It is civil legal aid which is appropriate for these applications and the evidence suggests that it has generally been refused on the basis that applicants can rely on the assistance of the Official Solicitor in presenting a case. This is not, apparently, a procedure that is followed willingly by the Law Society, for it made strong criticisms of the Official Solicitor procedure in a paper, *Report on Legal Aid for Bail Applications* (January 1972). See comment in *LAG Bulletin*, January 1980, p. 28.

[34] R.S.C., Ord. 79, r.9(4), (5).

[35] N. Bases and M. Smith, "A study of bail applications through the Official Solicitor to the judge in chambers" [1976] Crim.L.R. 541.

[36] Bail Act 1976, s.6(1).

[37] *Ibid.* s.6(2).

[38] The maximum penalties are three months imprisonment or a fine not exceeding level 5 on the standard scale; 12 months imprisonment or a fine at the Crown Court (the offence does not constitute a contempt of court (although treated as such), and so the two years' maximum penalty under the Contempt of Court Act 1981 is inapplicable: *R.* v. *Reader* (1986) 84 Cr.App.R. 294).

[39] *Practice Direction (Bail: Failure to Surrender)* [1987] 1 W.L.R. 79. This "clarified" the decision of the Divisional Court in *Schiavo* v. *Anderton* [1987] Q.B. 20, which had raised the possibility of the proceedings being conducted by the justices' clerk rather than the prosecutor (see B. Gibson, (1986) 150 J.P.N. 212; G. J. Bennett and B. Hogan, All E.R. Rev. 1986, p. 112, and note the criticisms expressed in *Murphy* v. *D.P.P.* [1990] 1 W.L.R. 601). As

has failed to surrender to police bail, proceedings should be commenced by charge or the laying of an information.[40]

In the event of failure to surrender, any personal security given by the accused under the limited powers in the Act[41] may be forfeited, as may the sums of money promised by the sureties. Normally those sums would be forfeited in full, but the court must exercise a proper discretion as to whether any part of the sum should be remitted on account of the sureties' behaviour, responsibility or means.[42]

8. NUMBERS OF REMAND PRISONERS

In magistrates' courts the number of persons remanded in custody in respect of indictable offences increased between 1979 (37,900) and 1985 (44,900), fell in 1986 to 36,300, and then rose to 42,000 in 1989.[43] The numbers committed for trial in custody also increased from 13,000 to 21,000 in the same period.[44] There are indications of increases in committal rates for offences such as burglary, theft and handling, which are kinds of offences more likely to involve a remand in custody, and in the rate at which bail is refused in certain kinds of case, especially burglary and drugs.[45]

The increase in the number of remand prisoners has caused severe problems of overcrowding in conditions less favourable than those of convicted prisoners, sometimes involving detention in police, rather than prison, custody.[46] Apart from the Bail Act change to a presumption in favour of bail, other contributions to reducing the pressure have been the establishment of more bail hostels[47] and schemes for the collection of information about the accused that would justify release on bail.[48] New schemes are subject to approval by a Bail Practice Committee of the Association of Chief Officers of Probation. A National Steering Group, chaired by the Home Office, advises on strategic and policy considerations.[49] The schemes have the

---

[40] the proceedings are not commenced by laying an information, the six month time limit in the Magistrates' Court Act 1980, s.127 does not apply: this is helpful where the accused absconds abroad and remains there for some years, as in *Schiavo* v. *Anderton, supra.*

[40] Failure to surrender here is not tantamount to defiance of a court order.

[41] *i.e.* any security taken where it appears likely that the accused will leave Great Britain: Bail Act 1976, s.3(5).

[42] See above, p. 646, n. 60.

[43] *Criminal Statistics England and Wales 1989*, Table 8.5. The percentage of persons proceeded against for indictable offences who were remanded increased from 43 per cent. in 1979 to 58 per cent. in 1989, but the percentage of the remands that were remands in custody fell from 17 per cent. to 13 per cent. in the same period. (Tables 8.4, 8.5).

[44] *Ibid.* Table. 8.7. An increase from 19 per cent. to 21 per cent. of all those committed for trial.

[45] R. Pearce, *Waiting for Crown Court trial: the remand population*, H.O.R.P.U. Paper No. 40 (1987), based on 1980–84 data.

[46] Authorised for periods not exceeding three clear days by the Magistrates' Courts Act 1980, s.128(7), (8). See (1987) 151 J.P.N. 433.

[47] Under the Criminal Justice Act 1982, s.53. See (1987) 151 J.P.N. 831 (plans for nine new bail hostels); H. Lewis and G. Mair, *Bail and Probation Work II: the use of London probation bail hostels for bailees*, H.O.R.P.U. Paper No. 50 (1988); (1990) 154 J.P.N. 60 (plans for 1,000 new places by April 1993).

[48] (1987) 151 J.P.N. 433, 523; G. Mair, *Bail and Probation Work: the ILPS bail action project*, H.O.R.P.U. Paper No. 46 (1988); C. Fiddes and C. Lloyd, (1990) 29 H.O.R.B. 23 (schemes running in 70 magistrates' courts and seven prisons, leading to fewer remands in custody); (1990) 154 J.P.N. 60 (plans to expand to 100 courts by April 1992).

[49] *Bail Information*: Report of the Bail Practice Committee on the expansion of Bail Information Schemes in 1988–89 (1990).

support of all the agencies concerned (probation service, C.P.S., police, Home Office) and monitoring over a six month period showed an overall trend in favour of bail of 13 per cent. where bail information sheets are presented to the C.P.S. compared with cases were they are not.[50] Consideration is being given to the involvement of the private sector.[51] There have also been experiments with electronic monitoring ("tagging") schemes, in which the defendants are remanded on bail subject to conditions prescribing periods of curfew, their continued presence at home during these periods being monitored by means of an electronic device.[52]

G. COMMITTAL PROCEEDINGS[53]

Before an accused can be tried on indictment there must normally be a preliminary inquiry into the case conducted in the magistrates' court in order to establish whether there is a prima facie case. The magistrates, referred to in this context as "examining justices," will be required to decide whether to commit the accused for trial at the Crown Court, or whether to call a halt to the proceedings at that point if there is not "such evidence that, if it be uncontradicted at the trial, a reasonably minded jury may convict on it."[54] However, if the accused is discharged by the magistrates at the end of the committal proceedings this is not the equivalent of an acquittal at trial. He or she may be charged again with the same offence, and be required to undergo committal proceedings again, whereas an acquittal at trial effectively prevents any further proceedings for the same offence.[55] This distinction has an important influence on the conduct of committal proceedings and the defendant's attitude towards them.

Committal proceedings have evolved from the special role of the magistracy as policemen and prosecutors prior to the establishment of police forces,[56] but their object is still said to be the elimination of ill-founded prosecutions for serious offences. The only alternative to committal, outside serious or complex fraud cases, is for the prosecution to seek a voluntary bill of indictment which permits the case to be taken straight to the Crown Court. This procedure is discussed further later in this section.

---

[50] *Ibid.*; (1990) 46 *The Magistrate* 35. See also Fiddes and Lloyd, *op cit.* n. 48, *supra*.

[51] *Private Sector Involvement in the Remand System* (Green Paper, Cm. 434, 1988).

[52] G. Mair and C. Nee, *Electronic Monitoring: The Trials and Their Results* (H.O. Research Study 120, 1990). It is envisaged that the system might be employed in respect of the sentencing of convicted persons, but, in the absence of legislation, an experiment can only involve remand prisoners. See now the Criminal Justice Bill 1991.

[53] See C. E. M. Chatterton and P. K. Brown, *Committals for trial to the Crown Court* (1988).

[54] *R. v. Governor of Brixton Prison, ex p. Bidwell* [1937] 1 K.B. 374.

[55] If re-tried in respect of an offence for which he or she has been acquitted, the accused is entitled to the plea of *autrefois acquit* (see below, p. 763). If he or she is discharged after committal proceedings this plea is not available because there has been no trial for the offence. The prosecutor will have to choose whether to abandon the prosecution, or seek further evidence with a view to beginning proceedings again, or invoke the voluntary bill procedure discussed at p. 664 below. Repeated use of committal proceedings may in an appropriate case be restrained as vexatious or an abuse of process: *R. v. Manchester City Stipendiary Magistrate, ex p. Snelson* [1977] 1 W.L.R. 911.

[56] See above, p. 181.

1. THE FORM OF PROCEEDINGS

The Magistrates' Courts Act 1980, s.6(1) states clearly the obligations of the magistrates' court:

"Subject to the provisions of this and any other Act relating to the summary trial of indictable offences, if a magistrates' court inquiring into an offence as examining justices is of opinion, on consideration of the evidence and of any statement of the accused, that there is sufficient evidence to put the accused on trial by jury for any indictable offence, the court shall commit him for trial; and, if it is not of that opinion, it shall, if he is in custody for no other cause than the offence under inquiry, discharge him."

Until 1968 there was only one form of committal proceedings. This procedure is still available and is termed a "full," "conventional," "long" or "old-style" committal to contrast it with the alternative form introduced by section 1 of the Criminal Justice Act 1967, now termed a "paper" or "new style" committal.

Full committal proceedings consist of the oral presentation of evidence for the consideration of the court. The prosecution must call sufficient of its witnesses to establish a prima facie case against the defendant (although there is no obligation to call every potential prosecution witness[57]) and they will be subject to cross-examination and re-examination, with the whole of their evidence written down, read back to them and authenticated.[58] The defence must, at the close of the prosecution case, select its tactics. A submission may be made that the evidence given discloses no prima facie case. If the court accedes to the submission it will discharge the defendant; if it does not, the charge will be written down (if this has not already been done). If the defendant is unrepresented, the charge is read and explained in ordinary language. The defence will then choose whether to offer any evidence.[59] It it does, which is unusual, the witnesses called and their evidence will be treated in exactly the same way as for the prosecution. The court must make its decision on all the evidence.[60] If the defence does not offer evidence, the magistrates will commit for trial immediately. It is uncertain whether the examining justices' approach to the question whether there is a prima facie case should correspond to the position on submissions of no case in summary trials,[61] or the more restricted position in trials on indictment.[62] The latter approach would prevent the justices declining to

[57] Even the principal prosecution witness: *R.* v. *Epping and Harlow JJ.*, *ex p. Massaro* [1973] 1 Q.B. 433 (victim of alleged sexual assault); and see *R.* v. *Grays JJ.*, *ex p. Tetley* (1979) 70 Cr.App.R. 11: the procedure "is not intended to allow an accused person to explore the evidence as a rehearsal for trial" (*per* Eveleigh L.J. at p. 16). Conversely, if the prosecution offer no evidence, the defendant must be discharged: *R.* v. *Canterbury and St. Augustine JJ.*, *ex p. Klisiak* [1982] 1 Q.B. 398; *R.* v. *Horseferry Road Magistrates' Court, ex p. O'Regan* (1986) 150 J.P. 525.

[58] These are referred to as depositions and, of course, form the basis of the evidence to be given at trial.

[59] The defence has a right to offer evidence even after an unsuccessful submission of no case: *R.* v. *Horseferry Road Stipendiary Magistrate, ex p. Adams* [1977] 1 W.L.R. 1197 and where the defendant does not personally give evidence: *R.* v. *Blyth Valley JJ.*, *ex p. Fawcus, The Times*, April 30, 1986.

[60] Including evidence tendered to establish a defence: *Re Roberts* [1967] 1 W.L.R. 474.

[61] See below, p. 754.

[62] Under *R.* v. *Galbraith* [1981] 1 W.L.R. 1039: see below, pp. 778–779.

commit for trial on the ground that the prosecution evidence has been shown, by cross-examination or by evidence tendered by the defence, to be unreliable. It has been argued that as this would render the defendant's undoubted right to offer evidence largely pointless, the former approach is to be preferred.[63]

The full oral procedure has been varied somewhat by provisions which permit the court to accept written evidence subject to specified conditions.[64] This can lead to a marginally shorter hearing, but the old-style committals tend to take a long time and may be rendered fairly ineffective if the defendant decides to "accept" committal by not contesting the evidence offered by the prosecution. Criticism can also be made of the expense and waste of resources involved. It was, therefore, a welcome relief when the Criminal Justice Act 1967 provided an alternative procedure.

The *paper committal* permits the magistrates to commit a case for trial at the Crown Court without giving any consideration to the prosecution (or defence) evidence provided that certain conditions are fulfilled. So long as all the evidence is in the form of written statements tendered to the court in accordance with section 102 of the Magistrates' Courts Act 1980, the court may commit for trial without considering the contents of the statements unless the accused is not legally represented or the defence submits that the statements disclose insufficient evidence.[65] In effect, if the prosecution request a committal under this procedure, the defendant may simply choose to be committed for trial without further ado.

The obligation will be on the prosecution to select the procedure—the defendant may object to a paper committal but cannot demand one. There are no regular statistics on the number of cases which proceed with a full committal, but the evidence suggests that there are comparatively few.[66] What factors might induce the prosecution or defence to opt for a full hearing?[67] The prosecution, in a complex case, would have to assemble the evidence and arguments which will be pertinent at the trial and would also have an opportunity to observe the behaviour and composure of their witnesses under examination and cross-examination. Additional information may be obtained from the witness which does not appear on the original statements. The defence, if it chooses to put its case at all, will enjoy both those advantages and in addition will be given the opportunity of probing such prosecution evidence as is adduced, ahead of trial. The case to be met by the defendant is likely to emerge more clearly from an oral hearing and

---

[63] D. Wright, "Old Style Committals—R.I.P.?" [1986] Crim.L.R. 660; C. J. Emmins, *A Practical Approach to Criminal Procedure* (4th ed., 1988), pp. 30–31. Chatterton and Brown (1988) suggest that the *Galbraith* rule applies to a submission of no case made at the conclusion of the prosecution case but not to a decision made after consideration of defence evidence (pp. 128–130). Archbold, *Criminal Pleading, Evidence and Practice* (43rd ed., 1988) asserts, without authority, that the *Galbraith* rule applies to both (para. 4–387) and this statement has been influential in practice: see Wright, *op. cit..*

[64] Criminal Justice Act 1967, s.2. Now Magistrates' Courts Act 1980, s.102. The conditions are that the statement is signed; that it contains a declaration that it is true to the best of the maker's knowledge; that a copy is given to the other party; that no party objects.

[65] See now the Magistrates' Courts Act 1980, s.6(2). Section 6(2) was amended by the Criminal Justice Act 1982, s.61, so that "legally represented" meant merely that the accused had a solicitor acting for him or her, not that the solicitor or counsel was present in court. References to "solicitor" and "counsel" were replaced by reference to a "legal representative" by the Courts and Legal Services Act 1990, Sched. 18, para. 25.

[66] R.C.C.P. I, para. 193; below, p. 692.

[67] These are considered more fully in D. Napley, *A Guide to Law and Practice under the Criminal Justice Act 1967* (1967), Chap. 1. See also T. Culver, *Legal Action*, June 1984, p. 63.

there will be an opportunity to make realistic judgments about the strength of the evidence. Evidence established in careful cross-examination may require investigation for which there would be little opportunity if the facts had emerged for the first time at trial.[68] It may even be that press reports of committal proceedings (see below) produce witnesses who have their memories jogged by reading about an incident. Finally, the accused may want to demonstrate at as early a stage as possible that he or she rejects the charges. Even though a discharge after committal proceedings will not prevent further charges, an accused may prefer not to be tried at all than to be tried and found not guilty.

Only the final consideration, the desire to establish innocence/avoid committal, is not related to tactics at trial, and puts committal proceedings in their true context. Their objective may be to filter out trivial and ill-founded cases which should not go to trial, but this is very difficult to achieve where the vast majority of committals are unconsidered by the magistrates and the few that are considered are not necessarily strongly contested on the issue of whether or not to commit.

The *Confait* case illustrates the inadequacy of committal proceedings in their present form. After a fire at 27 Doggett Road, Catford, in April 1972 the body of Maxwell Confait was discovered in a first floor room. Following confessions which they were said to have made, an 18-year-old boy and a 15-year-old boy were charged with the murder of Confait and, jointly with a 14-year-old boy, with setting fire to 27 Doggett Road. They were convicted of murder and manslaughter (diminished responsibility) respectively and all three were convicted of arson. They were refused leave to appeal in July 1973, but after representations by an M.P. the Home Secretary referred the case to the Court of Appeal in June 1975. That court quashed the two homicide convictions because of discrepancies in the evidence so serious that the convictions were unsafe and unsatisfactory. Why had these discrepancies not been revealed at the committal?

A subsequent Inquiry by Sir Henry Fisher[69] revealed that an "old style" committal had been held, but the magistrates received written statements in lieu of oral testimony.[70] The solicitor for the prosecution had not noticed the discrepancies and could not draw them to the attention of the magistrates. The defence were handicapped by the absence of early statements of key witnesses[71] and, presumably, by the general tactic at committal to discover prosecution evidence and then not offer much by way of defence. "There is obviously scope for using committal proceedings to a greater extent to test the prosecution's case. But this will not happen unless there is either a defence submission or the person appearing for the prosecution himself draws the attention of the magistrates to a point of difficulty in the prosecu-

---

[68] Little is seen in English courts of the Perry Mason style of investigative advocacy where crucial facts emerge in the course of cross-examination, are investigated by Della Street in the luncheon adjournment and the results communicated to the intrepid advocate in time to secure another forensic triumph before the credits roll. (For younger readers, "Perry Mason" was an American TV courtroom drama series starring Raymond Burr who re-emerged later as "A Man Called Ironside").

[69] A former High Court judge. *Report of an Inquiry by the Hon. Sir Henry Fisher into the circumstances leading to the trial of three persons on charges arising out of the death of Maxwell Confait and the fire at 27 Doggett Road, London, SE6* (H.M.S.O., 1977).

[70] *Ibid.* Chap. 27.

[71] *Ibid.* para. 27.2.

tion's case. And this will not happen unless there is a careful and dispassionate survey and review of the evidence by the counsel, solicitor or police officer responsible for presenting the case. Committal proceedings cannot therefore act as a safeguard against a failure to perform this duty. Under our system, the magistrates do not take the initiative."[72]

Sir Henry Fisher concluded, on this point, that if there was a serious case for an independent review of every serious case before trial, a *viva voce* hearing was necessary and committal proceedings could not be relied upon unless a full old-style committal with oral testimony was used.[73]

2. OTHER TASKS OF THE MAGISTRATES ON COMMITTAL

On committing an accused for trial the magistrates must select the place and time of trial, the appropriate charge and decide whether to grant bail. All these decisions are guided by established rules and the scope for discretion is, in fact, limited.

The magistrates will commit on the offence charged if there is a paper committal because they have no opportunity to review the evidence, but on a full committal they may substitute a new charge if the evidence fails to support the original one but does indicate another offence.[74]

The place of the trial is determined mainly by the nature of the charge on which the accused is committed. Criminal offences triable on indictment are divided into four classes according to their seriousness[75] and the classes are distinguished by stipulations about the seniority of the judge required to try the case. In the light of these, the magistrates must specify the most convenient location of the Crown Court.

An accused or the prosecutor may make an application to a High Court judge to vary the specified place of trial[76] and such applications are usually made in cases where it is feared that local prejudice and hostility will endanger the prospects of a fair trial.[77]

The committal by the magistrates for trial should ensure that the trial does not begin before the expiration of 14 days or after the expiration of eight weeks from committal.[78]

---

[72] *Ibid.* para. 27.7.
[73] *Ibid.* para. 27.8. See below, p. 833, on other issues arising out of the case.
[74] That will then form the basis of the indictment drafted for the trial at the Crown Court. The magistrates should not reduce the charge unrealistically so as to bring the offence within their summary jurisdiction: *R. v. Coe* [1968] 1 W.L.R. 1950.
[75] *Practice Direction (Crime: Crown Court Business)* [1987] 1 W.L.R. 1671; Supreme Court Act 1981, s.75. See pp. 73–75, above.
[76] Supreme Court Act 1981, s.76.
[77] For example, the trial of Brady and Hindley, the Moors Murderers, was held in Chester rather than the more likely location in Manchester, and the trial of those convicted of the Birmingham pub bombings was held in Lancaster. Prejudice is not the only ground for altering the venue, see *Halsbury's Laws of England* (4th ed.) Vol. 11(2), para. 938.
[78] Supreme Court Act 1981, s.77; Crown Court Rules 1982, r. 19. This requirement is, however, directory and not mandatory: in an appropriate case the Crown Court may grant an extension of time, even after the eight week period has expired: *R. v. Governor of Spring Hill Prison, ex p. Sohi and Dhillon* (1987) 86 Cr.App.R. 382.

A much more complex scheme of time limits for the different stages in the trial process is to be established by regulations made under section 22 of the Prosecution of Offences Act 1985. "Custody time limits" may be imposed to govern the period for which a defendant may be kept in custody before the start of summary trial; and, in cases of trial on indictment, between the first court appearance and committal for trial, and between committal and trial.[79] "Overall time limits" may be set for the same stages. The effect of expiry of a custody time limit is release on bail; and of an overall time limit that the defendant is treated as acquitted. However, the court[80] may extend a time limit where there is good and sufficient cause for doing so[81] and the prosecution has acted with all due expedition. The scheme has been introduced progressively, on an area-by-area basis, and so far is confined to custody time limits.[82]

Finally, the magistrates must decide the question of bail in accordance with the principles discussed above, and should give the accused a warning about the notice required of evidence to be adduced at trial in support of an alibi.[83] If the accused is intending to rely on such a defence he or she must notify the prosecution of the particulars of the alibi not later than seven days after the end of the committal proceedings. If he or she fails to give the requisite notice the alibi defence can only be relied upon at trial with the special permission of the court.[84]

A decision to commit or refuse to commit for trial cannot be the subject of an appeal by case stated to the High Court as it is not a "final" decision.[85] It may be challenged on an application for judicial review,[86] but such an application will only be successful where the examining justices have acted without jurisdiction,[87] and not merely where they have acted on evidence

---

[79] See *R. v. Bristol Crown Court, ex p. Commissioners of H.M. Customs & Excise, The Times*, August 23, 1989 (meaning of "arraignment" for expiry of custody time limit).

[80] The Crown Court if the defendant has been committed for trial or indicted; otherwise the magistrates' court. A decision of a magistrates' court to grant or refuse an extension may be taken on appeal to the Crown Court (s.22(7)(8)); such a decision of the Crown Court may be the subject of an application for judicial review (see s.22(13)). The matter cannot be raised on any appeal against conviction (s.22(10)).

[81] Which may include the defence's need for time: *McKay White* v. *D.P.P.* [1989] Crim.L.R. 375. See also *Re Craig* (1989) 91 Cr.App.R. 7; *R.* v. *Southampton Crown Court, ex p. Roddie, The Times*, February 11, 1991.

[82] Prosecution of Offences (Custody Time Limits) Regulations 1987 (S.I. 1987 No. 299), as amended by S.I. 1988 No. 164, S.I. 1989 Nos. 767 and 1107. Different periods have been specified in different areas. A survey of four areas indicated that compliance was generally high, although variable according to area: P. Morgan and J. Vennard, *Pre-Trial Delay: the implications of time limits* (H.O. Research Study 110, 1989). It has, however, been suggested that the limits are unlikely to have much impact in serious and complex cases: C. Corbett and Y. Korn, [1987] Crim.L.R. 737.

[83] Magistrates' Courts Rules 1981, r. 6(4), 7(9).

[84] Criminal Justice Act 1967, s.11. See *R.* v. *Fields and Adams* [1991] Crim.L.R. 38.

[85] *Atkinson* v. *U.S. Government* [1971] A.C. 197; *Cragg* v. *Lewes District Council* [1986] Crim.L.R. 800; *Cf. Streames* v. *Copping* [1985] Q.B. 920.

[86] See below, pp. 871–878.

[87] *e.g.* where the offence is summary only: *R.* v. *Hatfield JJ., ex p. Castle* [1981] 1 W.L.R. 217; or the defendant is not permitted to offer evidence at the committal proceedings: *R.* v. *Horseferry Road Magistrates' Court, ex p. Adams* [1977] 1 W.L.R. 1197.

that will or may be inadmissible at the trial.[88] An application will not be entertained before the proceedings have been concluded.[89]

3. THE REPORTING OF COMMITTAL PROCEEDINGS

The form of committal proceedings prior to 1968, with full oral testimony, was a great boon to local newspapers in search of material for their columns. The hearing was held in public and there were no restrictions on reporting.[90] This led to certain difficulties for the defendant and, it was said, could prejudice the chances of a fair trial if he or she was committed, by influencing readers who might ultimately be members of the jury in the particular case.

Often the defence would not offer any evidence so that only the prosecution case would be reported, thus distorting the overall impression. The prosecution might call witnesses who were not ultimately called at trial. Reference might be made in the prosecution evidence to matters which were not the subject of charges, or charges on which the accused was committed might not be proceeded with at trial. The result of extensive publicity of the committal might therefore be to influence potential jurors with a one-sided review of the evidence or to provide them with information about matters or charges which would form no part of the eventual trial. The difficulties were exposed by Devlin J. at the trial of Dr. Bodkin Adams in 1957. Dr. Adams was charged with murder and, in the course of the committal proceedings, reference was made to the death of two other patients, whose demise was not the subject of the charge. The trial judge expressed a view that the committal would have been better conducted in private when publicity could not have been given to these potentially prejudicial facts. In the event, Dr. Adams was acquitted.[91]

The Tucker committee[92] subsequently considered the problem and although it could not produce firm evidence of cases where the accused had actually been prejudiced, formed the view that the reporting of committal proceedings should be restricted. Amid great controversy and anguished protests about attacks on the freedom of the press, the Criminal Justice Act 1967 placed a ban on the full reporting of proceedings where the accused is committed for trial, unless a defendant requests that restrictions should be lifted.[93] On committal, all that may be reported are matters of formal record.[94]

---

[88] R. v. Norfolk Quarter Sessions, ex p. Brunson [1953] 1 Q.B. 503; R. v. Ipswich JJ., ex p. Edwards (1979) 143 J.P. 699; R. v. Horsham JJ., ex p. Bukhari (1981) 74 Cr.App.R. 291; R. v. Highbury Corner Magistrates' Court, ex p. Boyce (1984) 79 Cr.App.R. 132. Examining justices do not have the discretion to exclude legally admissible evidence that is available to trial judges: ex p. Boyce, supra. Exceptionally, they are required by s.76(2) of the Police and Criminal Evidence Act 1984 to rule, if requested, on the admissibility of a confession, although a failure to do so will not normally lead to the quashing of the proceedings: R. v. Oxford City JJ., ex p. Berry [1988] Q.B. 507.
[89] R. v. Wells Street Stipendiary Magistrate, ex p. Seillon [1978] 1 W.L.R. 1002.
[90] Other than the general constraints on newspapers which prevent them from publishing proceedings or certain details of proceedings in certain circumstances.
[91] See P. Devlin, Easing the Passing (1985).
[92] The chairman was Lord Tucker, a Lord of Appeal. Proceedings before Examining Magistrates (Cmnd. 479, 1958). See M. Jones, Justice and Journalism (1974), Chap. 7.
[93] Now contained in the Magistrates' Courts Act 1980, s.8.
[94] Ibid. s.8(4).

A defendant may require reporting restrictions to be lifted by order of the court[95] and there are certainly occasions on which a report of a full committal may prove advantageous. If the case is particularly controversial or sensational, more damage may be done by the circulation of gossip and rumour prior to the trial than by the report of the factual statements given in support of the prosecution case at committal.[96] It is possible that additional witnesses may emerge prompted by recognition of the case.[97] The immediate public protestation of innocence may be important to the accused. The desire of one of a number of co-defendants being tried together to have the restrictions lifted caused a problem where the other defendant(s) were not in agreement.[98] The law was changed so that now, where one of two or more accused objects to the court making an order lifting restrictions at the request of a co-accused the court shall only make the order if, after hearing representations, it is satisfied that it is in the interests of justice to do so.[99]

4. The Voluntary Bill Procedure[1]

It is convenient, if somewhat anomalous, to deal with the voluntary bill procedure at this point since it is a way of getting an indictable offence tried *without* committal by the magistrates. At the trial, a bill of indictment must be preferred against a defendant as a preliminary to the trial. A bill may only be preferred if the defendant has been committed for trial, or as directed by the Court of Appeal (*e.g.* where ordering a new trial) or by a High Court judge.[2]

[95] *Ibid.* s.8(2). It will be possible for magistrates to lift reporting restrictions but forbid the publication of particular matters under s.4(2) of the Contempt of Court Act 1981: *R.* v. *Horsham JJ. ex p. Farquharson* [1982] Q.B. 762.

[96] This is argued by Napley, *op. cit.* p. 26. This was certainly the case in respect of the Moors Murderers, Brady and Hindley, from the authors' own experience. Ironically, however, the publication of details of the committal proceedings, gruesome as they were, did not scotch the even more horrific rumours. Local people still chose to believe the rumours on the basis that the truth was too dreadful even to reveal in court.

[97] This is not likely to happen often, but an example was provided at the trial of P.C. Kneale on charges arising out of a demonstration in Liverpool. A witness who had been present only realised that his evidence could be significant on reading press reports of the trial. As a result of his coming forward to give evidence, the defendant was acquitted. See *The Times*, May 9–12, 1984.

[98] The courts had ruled that the desire of one co-defendant to have the restriction lifted was enough, *R.* v. *Russell, ex p. Beaverbrook Newspapers* [1969] 1 Q.B. 342, but the matter was given wide exposure in the Jeremy Thorpe case where the committal proceedings were given publicity against the wishes of three of the defendants. See P. Chippindale and D. Leigh, *The Thorpe Committal* (1979).

[99] Criminal Justice (Amendment) Act 1981, s.1, amending the Magistrates' Courts Act 1980, s.8(2). The magistrates must weigh the balance of interest between defendants who disagree over the reporting of the proceedings: *R.* v. *Leeds JJ., ex p. Sykes* [1983] 1 W.L.R. 132. All co-defendants must have a chance to make representations: *R.* v. *Wirral Magistrates' Court, ex p. Meikle* (1990) 154 J.P. 1035.

[1] See Chatterton and Brown (1988), pp. 232–241; C. Lewis, (1981) 78 L.S.Gaz. 1442; *Practice Direction (Crime: Voluntary Bills)* [1990] 1 W.L.R. 1635.

[2] Administration of Justice (Miscellaneous Provisions) Act 1933, s.2(2). This Act abolished the grand jury, which had had to find a bill of indictment to be a "true bill" before the accused could stand trial: the decision in the case of bills preferred following committal proceedings or with the consent of a High Court judge was a formality; the presentation of a bill by a private person was a rarity. A separate procedure whereby a judge or magistrate could order a prosecution for perjury without committal proceedings under the Perjury Act 1911, s.9, was abolished by the Prosecution of Offences Act 1985, s.28. See also below, p. 837.

Any person may make a written application to a High Court judge for consent to the preferring of a bill of indictment and must state reasons for the application. If committal proceedings have been taken, the application must be accompanied by depositions and certain statements of belief about the truth of the case.[3] The defendant has no right to a hearing, although the judge, may in the exercise of discretion, entertain written or, perhaps, in very exceptional circumstances, oral representations.[4] The decision of a judge to issue a voluntary bill is not susceptible to challenge on an application for judicial review.[5]

This procedure allows an accused to be put on trial at the discretion of a High Court judge and is rarely used, but can be effective in circumventing committal proceedings where unusual problems arise.[6] The use of the voluntary bill procedure can be controversial. Three prison officers were put on trial for murder in this way after a stipendiary magistrate discharged them after committal proceedings, and 15 youths charged variously with murder, affray and riotous assembly were put on trial by voluntary bill after committal proceedings had been in progress for nearly three weeks with no sign of finishing.[7] Both cases excited considerable comment.

H. DISCLOSURE OF EVIDENCE

In a civil case, the pre-trial procedure can be operated so as to allow each party to discover the essentials of the case to be met and to discover the basic issues in dispute between the parties. In a criminal matter, the two sides have much less scope for selecting the ground on which they wish to fight and all issues are likely to be left in dispute until the trial.[8] However, it can be a considerable advantage to prosecution, defence and court if by the time of the trial the two sides have some indication of the evidence to be given and the arguments to be raised. At the very least, this will obviate the necessity for an adjournment of the trial if new matters which require investigation are raised for the first time. What do the two sides currently have to disclose?

[3] The Indictments (Procedure) Rules 1971 (S.I. 1971 No. 2084) govern the procedure. To be valid, the bill must be signed by a proper officer of the court certifying compliance with the requirements: *R.* v. *Morais* (1988) 87 Cr.App.R. 9; *R.* v. *Laming* (1989) 90 Cr.App.R. 450. The applicant (unless the D.P.P. or a Crown Prosecutor: *R.* v. *Liverpool Crown Court, ex p. Bray* [1987] Crim.L.R. 51) must file an affidavit in support of the application.

[4] *R.* v. *Raymond* [1981] Q.B. 910, criticised by G. Harrison, (1986) J. Crim. Law 383. The *Practice Direction* (n. 1 *supra*) refers only to the possibility of written representations.

[5] *R.* v. *Manchester Crown Court, ex p. Williams and Simpson* (1990) 154 J.P. 589.

[6] *e.g.* where the defendant disrupted committal proceedings (*R.* v. *Paling* (1978) 67 Cr.App.R. 299); or to prefer an indictment against two defendants, one of whom has already been committed for trial (see C. Emmins, *A Practical Approach to Criminal Procedure* (4th ed., 1988), pp. 43–44).

[7] The three men were charged with the murder of Mr. Barry Prosser, a prisoner, in Winson Green prison, Birmingham. One of the accused had been the subject of *two* unsuccessful committal proceedings on the same charge. This case provides another example of change of venue, the trial being transferred to Leicester Crown Court because of all the publicity that had been generated. The charges against the youths arose out of the death of Terence May, a motor cyclist, in Thornton Heath, South London.

[8] Although there is a procedure whereby formal admissions can be made under Criminal Justice Act 1967, s.10, thus eliminating the necessity for undisputed evidence to be given orally at trial.

1. DISCLOSURE BY THE PROSECUTION

At the committal proceedings the defendant is likely to get sight of a substantial part, if not all, of the prosecution evidence. Whether the committal is "full" or "paper" the prosecution is required to supply the defence with copies of the depositions or written statements, as the case may be.[9] Additionally, the prosecution normally gives notice to the defence of any further evidence which is to be called at trial and a copy of the evidence.[10] As a result, the defence will know the total extent of the prosecution evidence and, if a full committal has taken place, will have had the opportunity of testing at least some of the prosecution witnesses in cross-examination.

What was less clear was the obligation of the prosecution to tell the defence of any additional material of which they were aware, but which was not actually to be used as part of the prosecution case. Much was left to the discretion of prosecuting counsel and a good deal of information would be communicated on a confidential "counsel to counsel" basis. Some requirements had to be observed by the prosecution including that of notifying the defence of, at least, the name and address of a witness who could give material evidence but would not be called by the prosecution[11]; making expert and technical evidence available; giving the defence a copy of any statements made by a prosecution witness which conflict with the evidence given at trial[12]; making known any convictions affecting the credibility of prosecution witnesses.[13] A Practice Direction now sets out the additional material which must be made available to the defence, with exceptions for especially prejudicial or sensitive information.[14] The Direction extends to all witness statements and documents not included in the committal bundles, the statements of any witnesses to be called at committal and documents referred to therein, and the unedited version(s) of any edited statements or composite statement included in the committal bundle.[15]

This information will be of use to the defence in formulating their case and there is nothing to stop them asking for any other information which may be of assistance. The prosecution, however, is under no obligation to supply it. Prosecuting counsel are often asked to consider, and advise on, the extent of the material which should be disclosed.

All the foregoing relates to trial on indictment. In respect of summary trial there are more limited arrangements for disclosure. The rule about not-

[9] Magistrates' Courts Act 1980, s.102.
[10] Archbold, *Criminal Pleading, Evidence and Practice* (43rd ed.), para. 4–185. There is very little authority for this proposition, but it is clearly accepted practice. A conviction may be quashed for a material irregularity where this is not done: *R.* v. *Phillipson* (1989) 91 Cr.App.R. 226.
[11] There was disagreement between Lord Denning M.R. and Diplock L.J. in *Dallison* v. *Caffery* [1965] 1 Q.B. 348 on the extent of the obligation. The Master of the Rolls was of the opinion that prosecuting counsel should make the witness' statements available to the defence. Diplock L.J. thought it was enough to make the witness available by notifying a name and address. (*cf. R.* v. *Bryant and Dickson* (1946) 31 Cr.App.R. 146; *R.* v. *Lawson* (1989) 90 Cr.App.R. 108).
[12] *R.* v. *Howes*, March 27, 1950, C.C.A. (unreported), cited in Archbold, *op. cit.* para. 4–179.
[13] *R.* v. *Collister and Warhurst* (1955) 39 Cr.App.R. 100.
[14] [1982] 1 All E.R. 734, issued by the Attorney-General.
[15] Prosecuting counsel must consider whether statements have been disclosed in accordance with the guidelines: Code of Conduct (1990 edn.), Annex H (Professional Standards Applicable to Criminal Cases).

ification of witnesses with material evidence applies,[16] and the procedure for pleading guilty by post requires the accused to be given a concise statement of the facts.[17] The identity of the complainant should be revealed at an early stage.[18] Section 48 of the Criminal Law Act 1977[19] provided for the adoption of rules requiring advance disclosure in summary trials, but even partial implementation was delayed until 1985. The Magistrates' Courts (Advance Information) Rules 1985[20] provide that, in the case of offences triable either way, the prosecution must upon request provide the defence either with copies of the prosecution witnesses' written statements or with a summary of the facts and matters of which the prosecutor proposes to adduce evidence. The request should be made before the mode-of-trial hearing and complied with as soon as practicable. The court at the mode-of-trial hearing must satisfy itself that the accused is aware of the right to advance information. If a request is not complied with, the proceedings must be adjourned unless the court is satisfied that the conduct of the case will not be substantially prejudiced.[21]

Prior to the introduction of the rules a wide variety of informal disclosure practices had developed in different areas.[22] There was optimism that such practices led to more guilty pleas, fewer elections for trial and other savings.[23] In practice, although improving the fairness of proceedings, the 1985 Rules have not been as successful in this regard as hoped, and, indeed, are commonly regarded as increasing delays.[24] The burdens on the Crown Prosecution Service have been such that in most areas summaries rather than full statements have been served. The summaries are prepared by the police and have varied widely in quality, the prosecutor normally lacking sufficient time to scrutinise them before disclosure. As disclosure is required at a relatively early stage, widespread reliance on summaries is probably inevitable, the main concern being to see an improvement in their standards. In practice, the summaries are commonly supplemented by copies of the contemporaneous notes of interviews now required under the P.A.C.E. Code of Practice,[25] and by further information at later stages where it becomes clear from the way the case is progressing, (e.g. by being contested) that this is appropriate.[26]

---

[16] Failure to notify the defence, if it is a gross failure, can lead to the decision of the court being quashed: R. v. Leyland JJ. ex p. Hawthorn [1979] Q.B. 283.

[17] Magistrates' Courts Act 1980, s.12: see below, pp. 751–752.

[18] Daventry District Council v. Olins (1990) 154 J.P. 478 (the context was a prosecution for selling food unfit for human consumption).

[19] Following recommendations of the James Committee on the Distribution of Criminal Business (Cmnd. 6323, 1975), pp. 95–103.

[20] S.I. 1985 No. 601; criticised by J. Pugh, (1985) 149 J.P.N. 327 and Anon., ibid., p. 499.

[21] Failure to comply will only exceptionally amount to an abuse of process: King v. Kucharz (1989) 153 J.P. 336.

[22] See J. Baldwin, Pre-Trial Justice (1985) and (1985) 149 J.P.N. 179; F. Feeney, "Advance disclosure of the prosecution case" in D. Moxon (ed.), Managing Criminal Justice (1985), Chap. 9 (describing two pilot schemes established by the Home Office).

[23] Ibid.

[24] J. N. Spencer, (1986) 150 J.P.N. 356; J. Morton, (1988) 152 J.P.N. 104.

[25] See above, p. 610.

[26] J. Baldwin and A. Mulvaney, [1987] Crim.L.R. 315 and 805, (1987) 151 J.P.N. 409; J. Baldwin, (1988) 152 J.P.N. 259.

2. Disclosure by the Defence

The defence is entitled, very largely, to reserve the whole of the defence for the trial and say nothing about their case until then. The only exceptions to this principle are the requirements to disclose an alibi defence[27] and any expert evidence intended to be adduced[28] on a trial on indictment and to give notice of certain specific defences in minor regulatory offences. The standard form returned by the defence to the Crown Court listing officer (with a copy to the prosecution) requires the intended plea to be indicated.[29]

This appears to leave the disclosure requirements very unbalanced as between prosecution and defence and, at various times and in various circumstances, proposals have been made to impose a general requirement of disclosure on the defence after the conclusion of committal proceedings in a trial on indictment, or rather more specific requirement in respect of particular defences.[30] The object of such proposals is to prevent the "springing" of a defence at trial when the prosecution may face the choice of asking for a costly adjournment or meeting the defence unprepared.

3. A Pre-trial Review

A relatively recent development in criminal procedure has been the provision of a hearing between committal and trial designed to fulfil the same objects as the pre-trial review in civil proceedings.[31] The rules for such a hearing were promulgated by the Central Criminal Court[32] and apply to cases to be heard in that court where application is made by either party. The rules provide for a hearing at which both defence and prosecution make stipulated disclosures to the court and the judge may make such orders as may be necessary to secure the proper and efficient trial of the case. Among the matters of which counsel will be expected to inform the court are the pleas to be tendered by the accused; prosecution evidence; points of law arising; agreed exhibits and schedules and other evidentiary matters.

The object of disclosure is to indicate as clearly as possible the likely issues in the case and so save time and money at and before the trial. The costs of such a review can, therefore, only be justified in the more complex cases where the savings in time and money will exceed the amount expended on the review itself. A number of the circuits have adopted the procedure and varied it according to their own needs. One limitation is that the pre-trial review does not have the force of law and nothing decided at it is enforceable at the trial.

---

[27] Criminal Justice Act 1967, s.11. See above, p. 662.

[28] Crown Court (Advance Notice of Expert Evidence) Rules 1987 (S.I. 1987 No. 716); Home Office Circular 35/1987. The obligation applies to both prosecution and defence, but the prosecution would be obliged to disclose the evidence anyway.

[29] See *The Crown Court. A guide to good practice* (1990) published by the Law Society, Appendix I; and p. 8 of the equivalent *Guide* published by the L.C.D. (H.M.S.O., 1990).

[30] The (Butler) *Committee on Mentally Abnormal Offenders* (Cmnd. 6244, 1975), recommended that notice should be given if the defence is to put in issue the mental state of the accused. The Law Commission made a similar proposal in respect of duress (Law Com. No. 83, 1977).

[31] See A. Samuels, (1982) 146 J.P.N. 677, 686.

[32] They are reproduced in Archbold, *Criminal Pleading, Evidence and Practice* (43rd ed.), para. 4–43. They also appear in Appendix 27 of R.C.C.P. I, together with the rules adopted on the North Eastern Circuit.

"Counsel are expected to honour promises and undertakings given in the course of the review; but if they receive contrary instructions from clients thereafter, they must follow them unless circumstances demand withdrawal from the case."[33]

Moreover, nothing said or done at the pre-trial review can be used in evidence at the trial without the consent of the party affected.[34]

A Working Party on the Criminal Trial, chaired by Watkins L.J., proposed a system of forms and, in the last resort, oral-pretrial reviews backed by Crown Court Rules. Under this system, the defence would be required to indicate within 14 days of committal how the defendant intended to plead, and both sides would be required to give details of how the case would proceed at trial (*e.g.* by identifying matters not in dispute, and the questions of law and admissibility of evidence that would arise).[35] Pilot schemes were conducted in six centres in 1983 and 1984,[36] but no changes have as yet resulted. The Roskill Committee on Fraud Trials also examined pre-trial reviews.[37] It noted that there had been no qualitative or quantitative research into their effects, but had the impression that they operated sensibly and efficiently in many but not all of the cases in which they were conducted. They recommended a more formal procedure for serious fraud cases.[38]

In the magistrates' court the same problem occurs before summary trial, but the number of cases in which a formal pre-trial review is beneficial may be more limited. Prior to implementation of section 48 of the Criminal Law Act 1977, the Nottingham justices' clerks instituted a scheme on their own initiative which was alleged to save money as well as reducing delay and frustration caused by the repeated adjournment of trials where the defence had been caught unprepared by the prosecution.[39] In approximately 20 cases each week, prosecution and defence met at an appointed time for "an informal but candid discussion" without a magistrate present. The benefits of such a scheme were said to include a saving of court time by inducing "realistic" pleas; early notification of points of law that may arise; a reduction in the length of contested cases; confirmation of readiness for trial and a general tidying-up to ensure that the case can go ahead when listed. About a dozen other courts introduced similar schemes, some short-lived, and with differences in the details of the arrangements.[40] The schemes were indeed perceived to have advantages in promoting the efficient disposal of cases, but there were doubts as to the adequacy of the safeguards for the accused (who in most schemes was not permitted to be present)[41] and the Law Society emphasised that any disclosure of the defence case could only be

---

[33] *Per* Watkins, L.J. in *R.* v. *Hutchinson* (1985) 82 Cr.App.R. 51, 56.

[34] *R.* v. *Hutchinson* (1985) 82 Cr.App.R. 51.

[35] *Report of Lord Justice Watkins' Working Party on the Criminal Trial* (1982), summarised in the Roskill Report, *infra*, pp. 81–82.

[36] See W. Merricks, (1983) 133 N.L.J. 879.

[37] *Report on Fraud Trials* (H.M.S.O., 1986), pp. 79–86.

[38] *Ibid.* pp. 87–113; below, pp. 671–673.

[39] The scheme is glowingly described and commended in A. Debruslais, "Pre-Trial Disclosure in Magistrates' Courts: Why Wait?" (1982) 146 J.P.N. 384, and was the subject of a study by J. Baldwin: *Pre-Trial Justice* (1985).

[40] See J. Baldwin and F. Feeney, "Defence Disclosure in the Magistrates' Courts" (1986) 49 M.L.R. 593.

[41] Baldwin (1985), Chap. 7.

done with the express or implied authority of the client.[42] The introduction of the requirements for advance disclosure of the prosecution case led to modifications to most although not all of the schemes that remained.[43] The reviews are no longer required as a vehicle for disclosure by the prosecution, and "tend to be held in fewer cases and often are confined to those cases that present particular procedural or evidential difficulties."[44]

I. SPECIAL ARRANGEMENTS FOR FRAUD CASES

The pre-trial procedures discussed in the previous two sections can be replaced in respect of serious and complex fraud cases by arrangements under the Criminal Justice Act 1987.[45] This Act was passed following the Report of the Committee on Fraud Trials, chaired by Lord Roskill,[46] although it differs in some important respects from the Committee's recommendations.[47]

The first modification to normal procedures is that committal proceedings can be replaced by a notice of transfer procedure.[48] This can be put into effect where a person has been charged with an indictable offence, and, in the opinion of the "designated authority"[49] or one of its officers, the evidence would be sufficient for a committal and reveals a case of fraud of such seriousness and complexity that it is appropriate for its management to be taken over by the Crown Court without delay. A "notice of transfer" must be served on the magistrates' court in whose jurisdiction the offence has been charged, before the commencement of committal proceedings. The court's functions thereupon cease, except in respect of such matters as bail, legal aid and witness orders.[50] The notice must specify the proposed place of trial and the charge or charges, and a copy of the notice and a statement of the evidence on which the charge or charges are based must be given to the defendant and to the Crown Court.[51]

A decision to give notice of transfer "shall not be subject to appeal or liable to be questioned in any court," but any person to whom the notice relates may apply to the Crown Court for any charge to be dismissed on the ground that the evidence disclosed would not be sufficient for a jury properly to convict him or her of it.[52] Applications may be made orally or in writing, but in order to prevent oral applications becoming as drawn out as

---

[42] "Pre-Trial Reviews in the Magistrates' Court: Guidance for Defence Solicitors" (1983) 80 L.S.Gaz. 2330.

[43] J. Baldwin, (1987) 151 J.P.N. 611. The schemes in Nottingham and Stockport were not much affected.

[44] *Ibid.* p. 613.

[45] See the annotations to this Act by I. Leigh in *Current Law Statutes Annotated 1987*; N. Addison, (1988) 132 S.J. 436.

[46] H.M.S.O., 1986. See M. Levi, (1986) 13 J.L.S. 117.

[47] In particular, the government rejected a recommendation that trial by jury be replaced in some cases by trial by a fraud trials tribunal: see below, p. 817.

[48] 1987 Act, ss.4–6, as amended by the Criminal Justice Act 1988, s.144 (the amendments are explained by H.O. Circular 84/1988: (1988) 152 J.P.N. 700).

[49] The D.P.P., the Director of the Serious Fraud Office, the Commissioners of Inland Revenue, the Commissioners of Customs and Excise or the Secretary of State.

[50] See The Magistrates' Courts (Notice of Transfer) Rules 1988 (S.I. 1988 No. 1701).

[51] The Criminal Justice Act 1987 (Notice of Transfer) Regulations 1988 (S.I. 1988 No. 1691).

[52] 1987 Act, s.6, substituted by the Criminal Justice Act 1988, s.144; The Criminal Justice Act 1987 (Dismissal of Transferred Charges) Rules 1988 (S.I. 1988 No. 1695).

full committal proceedings, oral evidence may only be given with the leave of the judge, and leave is only to be granted if it appears to him or her that the interest of justice so requires. A discharge has the same effect as a refusal by a magistrates' court to commit for trial, except that no further proceedings may be brought on the charge except by a voluntary bill of indictment. There is no right of appeal at the interlocutory stage against a refusal to dismiss a charge.

The other major modification is that there are formal arrangements for "preparatory hearings" in place of the informal arrangements that exist for pre-trial reviews in the Crown Court.[53] The aims of such a hearing are (a) identifying issues likely to be material to the jury's verdict; (b) assisting its comprehension of such issues; (c) expediting proceedings before the jury; or (d) assisting the judge's management of the trial. A judge of the Crown Court may order a preparatory hearing where it appears that substantial benefits are likely to accrue, on the application of prosecution or defence or of his or her own motion. They are not confined to cases which have been the subject of a notice of transfer. The judge has power to order the prosecution to prepare and serve a "case statement" setting out the principal facts, names of witnesses, exhibits and propositions of law that the prosecution will be relying upon. The prosecution should also indicate any documents or other matters that in their view should be agreed by the defendant. On compliance with such an order, the judge may order the defendant to prepare and serve a written statement setting out in general terms the nature of the defence, and to indicate any objections to the case statement, any point of law which he or she wishes to take, and the extent to which documents or other matters specified by the prosecution are agreed. The defendant need not, however, disclose who will give evidence.[54] The process is similar to the exchange of pleadings and other documents in civil litigation.

The preparatory hearing is regarded as part of the trial and not as a preliminary to it, and accordingly starts with the arraignment[55] of the defendant. The hearing is conducted by the judge who is to preside at the trial proper, and counsel briefed to appear at the trial should take part in the hearing. The judge has the same powers to order disclosure as exist before the hearing, and there is a general duty on each party to inform the court of any significant matter which might affect the proper and convenient trial of the case. More importantly, the judge may determine any question as to the admissibility of evidence and any other question of law relating to the case.[56] Any such order or ruling will take effect at the trial, subject to two qualifications. First, an appeal against the order or ruling can be taken forthwith to the Court of Appeal (Criminal Division), but only with the leave of the judge or the Court of Appeal.[57] The preparatory hearing can continue meanwhile, but the jury cannot be sworn until after the appeal is determined

---

[53] 1987 Act, ss.7–10; The Criminal Justice Act 1987 (Preparatory Hearings) Rules 1988 (S.I. 1988 No. 1699).

[54] Except in relation to an alibi or expert evidence: see p. 668.

[55] See pp. 762–764.

[56] But only questions that accord with the specified aims of preparatory hearings, not, *e.g.* a question whether proceedings should be dismissed as an abuse of process: *In re Gunawardena, Harbutt and Banks* [1990] 1 W.L.R. 703.

[57] The Criminal Justice Act 1987 (Preparatory Hearings) (Interlocutory Appeals) Rules 1988 (S.I. 1988 No. 1700).

or abandoned. Secondly, the order or ruling can be varied or discharged by the judge at the trial.

The requirement that the defence disclose its case at the preparatory hearing was controversial, in that this was required before the prosecution had proved its case.[58] In the Act's final form, the defendant is only required to set out the nature of the defence in general terms, and need not disclose the names of defence witnesses. Moreover, no part of the defence case revealed at the preparatory hearing can be disclosed at the trial proper, unless either the defendant consents, or there has been a departure from the case as indicated at the hearing. Either party is at liberty to depart from the case disclosed at the hearing, but if there is such a departure, or a failure to comply with a requirement imposed at the hearing, the judge (or any other party, with the leave of the judge) may comment, and "the jury may draw such inference as appears proper."[59]

There are reporting restrictions in respect of applications for dismissal, preparatory hearings and related interlocutory appeals, analogous to those for committal proceedings.[60]

J. OBTAINING LEGAL ADVICE AND REPRESENTATION

We stressed the importance of legal aid and advice in civil proceedings by dealing with it at the beginning of the civil procedure chapter. Its availability may determine whether the case goes ahead at all. In criminal proceedings it is not relevant to that issue, but must be made available as a way of ensuring that defendants have what specialist help they need in the presentation of their defence. Different criteria are obviously required for the grant and administration of criminal legal aid.[61]

Legal advice and professional assistance may be required by defendants at two quite different stages. They will initially have to deal with the police and face interrogation by them, the results of which are likely to have a considerable influence on their case at trial. They may wish to be advised how to conduct themselves to the best advantage at this stage of the procedure. Then, if charged, they will want assistance in the preparation and presentation of their case at and before the trial. The extent to which lawyers are involved in these two distinct situations is different. Almost all those charged with serious offences are represented at trial, many fewer are "represented" during interrogation at the police station.

1. LEGAL ADVICE AT THE POLICE STATION

As we have seen, the Police and Criminal Evidence Act 1984 strengthens the right of those being interviewed by the police to have access to legal advice, and the courts have emphasised the importance of these rights in excluding evidence of confessions obtained in breach of them.[62]

---

[58] I. Leigh, *op. cit.*, n. 45, pp. 38–21—38–23.
[59] 1987 Act, s.10(1).
[60] *Ibid.*, s.11, *cf.* above, pp. 663–664.
[61] It was only in 1980 that both schemes were put under the aegis of the same government department. Formerly, criminal legal aid was the responsibility of the Home Office.
[62] See above, pp. 613–614.

The legal advice scheme can be used for the purpose of securing the services of a solicitor at the police station and the eligibility of the accused and the extent of any financial contribution are calculated according to the figures set out earlier in our discussion of the scheme.[63] In theory, the accused has the opportunity, the means and the motive to ensure that he or she is properly advised on the most advantageous way to conduct him- or herself at the police station. In practice, only a minority of accused persons receive that advice.

Prior to the introduction of the Police and Criminal Evidence Act 1984, a number of surveys showed that a minority of suspects at the police station asked to see a solicitor, and most such requests were refused.[64] The requirement in the Administrative Directions that accompanied the Judges' Rules that persons in custody should be informed orally of the rights and facilities available to them was not widely observed.[65] The police were also criticised for simple obstruction of those who got as far as asking to be allowed to contact a solicitor. The Royal Commission on Criminal Procedure took note of these criticisms in their final recommendations,[66] on which the relevant provisions in P.A.C.E. were based. The Commission recognised that the provision of information alone does not ensure that the right to have a lawyer is exercised. This was illustrated by American experience after the decision in *Miranda* v. *Arizona*[67] required every suspect to be told of his or her right to consult a lawyer, and have the lawyer present during interrogation. Studies carried out in the United States still revealed surprisingly small numbers of suspects getting legal advice.[68]

The early indications of the impact of P.A.C.E. on access to legal advice at the police station[69] are that (1) there has been a significant increase in the number of suspects seeking legal advice; (2) that they still only constitute a minority; (3) that a variety of ploys are used by the police to discourage exercise of the right to see a lawyer; (4) that only a small proportion of suspects have a lawyer with them during police investigation; (5) that there may have been a rise in the number of suspects who refuse to make admissions during interrogation.

---

[63] See above, pp. 445–446.

[64] M. Zander, [1972] Crim.L.R. 342 (11 per cent. of 134 appellants to the Court of Appeal had contacted a solicitor; a further 32 per cent. had asked to speak to a solicitor and had been refused); J. Baldwin and M. McConville, [1979] Crim.L.R. 145 (31 per cent. of 352 defendants at Crown Court had asked to see a solicitor, over three quarters of these requests being refused; P. Softley, *Police Interrogation: An Observational Study in Four Police Stations*, R.C.C.P. Research Study No. 4 (H.M.S.O., 1980) (requests from 12 per cent. of 168 suspects being interrogated at a police station, with one third refusals).

[65] Softley (1980), p. 65.

[66] R.C.C.P. Report, paras. 4.81 ff.

[67] 348 U.S. 436 (1966).

[68] See, *e.g.* M. Wald, *et al.*, "Interrogation in New Haven: the Impact of Miranda" 76 Yale L.J. 1519 (1967).

[69] See D. Brown, *Detention at the Police Station under the Police and Criminal Evidence Act 1984* (H.O. Research Study 104, 1989), Chap. 3 and "P.A.C.E. and the right to legal advice" (H.O.R.P.U. Bulletin 26:26); A. Sanders, *et al.*, *Advice and Assistance at Police Stations and the 24 Hour Duty Solicitor Scheme* (L.C.D., 1989), summarised at (1990) 140 N.L.J. 85, and [1990] Crim.L.R. 494; B. L. Irving and I. K. McKenzie, *Police Interrogation* (1989), pp. 53–59, 113–115, 157–164, 199–200.

Brown's study,[70] showed that 25 per cent. of all detainees asked for a solicitor while at the police station, although there was considerable variation (14 per cent. to 41 per cent.) from station to station. As might be expected, take-up rates were higher for more serious offences, again with considerable variations for individual stations.[71] The police contacted a solicitor on behalf of 22 per cent. of detainees, and 21 per cent. had some form of consultation with one whilst at the police station. In over three quarters of these cases, the solicitor attended in person; otherwise, advice was given over the telephone.[72] In 80 per cent. of cases in which solicitors attended advice was given prior to any police interview, but solicitors attended only 12 per cent. of all police interviews with suspects. 50 per cent. of those who requested a solicitor saw one within the hour and nearly 80 per cent. within two hours, but some detainees had to wait much longer. Duty solicitors gave over one third of all advice and assistance provided at police stations.[73] A superintendent permitted access to a lawyer to be delayed in 4 per cent. of cases in which legal advice was requested.

The research by Sanders, et al. sought to examine the factors behind the low take up rates.[74] These include failure in a small proportion of cases to inform suspects of the right to legal advice, either orally or by Home Office notice[75]; failure in a much larger number of cases to inform the suspect that legal advice will be free, under the 24-hour scheme[76]; the use by the police of a wide variety of ploys to discourage exercise of the right of access[77]; "unwillingness of suspects to add to their length of detention; fatalism (legal advice will not help them out of trouble); confidence (legal advice is not needed because their innocence is obvious); triviality of the alleged offence; their feelings about the police; dislike of lawyers."[78] It was suggested that take-up rates will always be low because many suspects are fatalistic, confident or view a quick escape from custody as an overriding priority. However, they might well rise considerably if rights were explained properly, and if P.A.C.E. required a positive decision to *refuse* legal advice to trigger section 58.

The research of Sanders, et al. also raises doubts about the quality of service provided to suspects in police stations, more particularly by duty solicitors, given the high proportion of telephone advice, often perceived as less satisfactory by suspects, and the low rate of attendance at interrogations.[79] As to the nature of the advice given, it seems that "most solicitors appear to advise silence in few cases, although a few give that advice in most

---

[70] *Supra*. Based on a sample of over 5,500 custody records from 32 police stations in 10 forces.
[71] See further, Sanders, *et al.* (1989), Chap. 3.
[72] The research by Sanders, *et al.* showed a higher proportion of cases where telephone advice was given, particularly by duty solicitors: *ibid*. Chap. 6.
[73] *Ibid*. p. 42.
[74] *Ibid*. Chap. 4.
[75] Contrary to the requirements of Code C. 3.1 and C. 3.2: and see above, p. 607.
[76] This became a Code requirement in the revised draft (*ibid*.). Prior to that, Custody Officers had merely been asked in a Note for Guidance (*3E*) to provide suspects with a Law Society leaflet explaining the scheme.
[77] *e.g.* the incomplete or incomprehensible reading of rights; emphasis on delay; "sign here, here and here" with no information given; "you don't want a solicitor do you?"
[78] Sanders, *et al.* (1989), p. 72.
[79] *Ibid*. Chap. 6.

cases . . . . [S]uspects actually remain silent rarely. Nearly half of all suspects confess, and a similar number deny the offence with an explanation."[80]

The actual impact of advice is uncertain. Sanders, *et al.* found that suspects confess less often when they have advice, but that the differences are not dramatic. It might be that solicitors persuade suspects to remain silent or deny the offence or simply that they help suspects to hold firm to their existing intentions to do so. Most officers claimed that advice had little or no effect. Sanders, *et al.* suggested, however, that many suspects who do not receive advice could have been greatly assisted, and found that the police manage to circumvent solicitors in various ways, such as by questioning during the journey to the police station, during processing, and while the suspect is alone in the cell.[81] They also emphasised that solicitors do not only provide legal advice: they can provide less tangible assistance such as by protecting suspects from real or imaginary danger from the police, explaining to suspects what is happening to them, and making representations to the police about charge or bail, or alleged mistreatment.[82] Overall, effort needed to be put into securing more wholehearted police compliance with P.A.C.E. and the Code of Practice; and equal effort into securing better responses from solicitors.[83]

2. ADVICE AND REPRESENTATION AFTER CHARGE

The primary vehicle for the provision of publicly funded legal assistance in criminal cases is the criminal legal aid scheme. Apart from this, however, an accused person may obtain advice and assistance from his or her own solicitor under the green form scheme,[84] or from a duty solicitor at the magistrates' court under the Legal Aid Board Duty Solicitor Arrangements.[85] Apart from receiving legal advice the accused may, for example, be assisted in applying for a legal aid order. Assistance may also include assistance by way of representation (ABWOR).[86] This can cover a bail application; making a plea in mitigation for an accused in custody who pleads guilty; representing a person who is to be dealt with for failure to obey a court order and who may be imprisoned; and representation for any other person not in custody who in the solicitor's opinion requires it.[87] However, ABWOR is not available for committal proceedings or proceedings in which the client pleads not guilty, or, unless the solicitor considers the circumstances exceptional, in connection with a non-imprisonable offence.[88] It is also the case that ABWOR for a hearing can be provided by a solicitor in the precincts of the court at the court's request; the court must be satisfied that the hearing should proceed on the same day and that the party would not

---

[80] *Ibid.* p. 150.
[81] *Ibid.* pp. 150–151.
[82] *Ibid.* p. 186.
[83] *Ibid.* p. 192.
[84] Above, pp. 443–446.
[85] Above, pp. 452–455.
[86] Above, pp. 446–447, 452. Legal advice and ABWOR for criminal cases in the magistrates' courts is provided for by the Legal Advice and Assistance (Scope) Regulations 1989 (S.I. 1989 No. 550), regs. 6, 7, and the Legal Advice and Assistance Regulations 1989 (S.I. 1989 No. 340), esp. regs. 4–13, 22–27; Legal Aid Board Duty Solicitor Arrangements 1989, paras. 51–54.
[87] Scope Regulations, reg. 7(2); Duty Solicitor Arrangements 1989, para. 52.
[88] Respectively, reg. 7(3) and para. 53(1).

otherwise be represented.[89] Where advice and assistance is provided under the Duty Solicitor Arrangements, there is no limit on the cost of advice and assistance, it is available without regard to the client's resources, and the solicitor claims remuneration under the Arrangements.[90] Otherwise, it is funded through the green form scheme, and subject to that scheme's cost limits and conditions of eligibility.[91]

The principles upon which legal aid is granted, and the obligations of the recipient, are established by the Legal Aid Act 1988[92] and the regulations made thereunder.[93] It has been argued that fundamental questions relating to criminal legal aid remain unanswered,[94] but the present system attempts to ensure that every person charged with a serious offence, or an offence which may have particularly serious consequences for him or her, is provided with sufficient professional assistance to allow the case to be properly prepared and presented, subject to a contribution towards the cost according to means.

An application for criminal legal aid is normally made to the magistrates' court, although the Crown Court also has the power to grant it and even the appellate courts in appropriate circumstances.[95] There is also a role for the area committees, appointed by the Legal Aid Board, which administer the civil legal aid scheme, since they constitute the criminal legal aid committees with functions under the Criminal Legal Aid regulations.

In all cases, representation can only be granted to persons if it appears to the court that their financial resources are such as under the regulations make them eligible.[96] If it does, then legal aid is *mandatory* in cases of murder trials; where the prosecutor is seeking to appeal to the House of Lords; where the accused is brought before a magistrates' court in custody, is liable to be remanded in custody, and wishes to be represented; and where the accused is kept in custody after conviction for medical or other reports.[97] In all other cases, the court may make an order for legal aid for a defendant ". . . where it appears desirable to do so in the interests of justice. . . ."[98] Any doubts are to be resolved in the defendant's favour.[99]

---

[89] Scope Regulations, reg. 7(1)(b). This provision is not confined to criminal proceedings. However, the solicitor must not be in the precincts of the court for the purpose of providing ABWOR.

[90] S.I. 1989 No. 550, regs. 4(2)(b)(c), 7(3), 8(2); Legal Advice and Assistance (Duty Solicitors) (Remuneration) Regulations 1989 (S.I. 1989 No. 341).

[91] S.I. 1989 No. 340, reg. 9. The prior approval of the Legal Aid Board is necessary for ABWOR under reg. 7(2) of the Scope Regulations, but not under reg. 7(1)(b).

[92] The Legal Aid Act 1982, s.1, provided for these schemes to be put on a statutory basis under Legal Aid Act 1974, s.15.

[93] Legal Aid in Criminal and Care Proceedings (General) Regulations 1989 (S.I. 1989 No. 344). See generally, A. Samuels, "Criminal Legal Aid: The Issues of Principle" [1983] Crim.L.R. 223, especially the materials noted on p. 223; H. Levenson, "Contributions and the new criminal legal aid" [1984] *Legal Action* 37, and "Appeals and reviews in criminal legal aid" [1984] *Legal Action* 49.

[94] See Samuels, *op. cit.*

[95] Legal Aid Act 1988, s.20.

[96] *Ibid.* s.21(5). The court must require a statement of means from applicants, unless they are incapable of furnishing one by reason of their physical or mental condition, or they have already submitted one and their financial circumstances have not changed: 1989 Regulations, regs. 11 and 23.

[97] *Ibid.* s.21(3).

[98] *Ibid.* s.21(2).

[99] *Ibid.* s.21(7).

A single legal aid order may be made by a magistrates' court to cover the committal proceedings, the trial on indictment (if committed), and advice and assistance as to an appeal (if convicted).[1] There is little disagreement about legal aid for trials in the Crown Court and the statistics show a remarkable degree of consistency. All but a handful of applications for legal aid for trial at the Crown Court are granted and the proportion of legally-aided defendants in the Crown Court has risen from 93 per cent. (in 1972) to 98 per cent. (in 1988).[2] The statutory condition that legal aid should be granted where it is in the interests of justice has been amplified by the "Widgery criteria,"[3] now set out in section 22 of the 1988 Act. If a case exhibits one or more of the following factors, there are grounds for thinking that representation is desirable:

"(a) That the charge is a grave one in the sense that the accused is in real jeopardy of losing his liberty or suffering serious damage to his reputation;
(b) that the charge raises a substantial question of law;
(c) that the accused is unable to follow the proceedings and state his own case because of his inadequate knowledge of English, mental illness or other mental or physical disability;
(d) that the nature of the defence involves the tracing and interviewing of witnesses or expert cross-examination of a witness for the prosecution;
(e) that legal representation is desirable in the interest of someone other than the accused as, for example, in the case of sexual offences against young children where it is undesirable that the accused should cross-examine the witness in person."[4]

There is rarely any difficulty in establishing that an offence to be tried on indictment can be fitted into one or other of the categories.

The problems in the criminal legal aid scheme have related to the application of these principles in magistrates' courts when a defendant seeks legal aid in respect of a summary offence or an either-way offence to be tried summarily. An application for legal aid in magistrates' court proceedings may be made orally to the court (who may then refer it to the justices' clerk to be dealt with) or in writing direct to the justices' clerk.[5] The clerk or the court may grant or refuse the application. If it is refused, the applicant may either renew it or, in certain cases, apply for review to the appropriate area legal aid committee. Only the court (or a justice of the peace to whom the matter has been referred by the justices' clerk) can refuse a renewed application; either the court (or justice of the peace) or the justices' clerk can grant it.[6] The role of the clerk in administering legal aid led to some disquiet about the rate of refusal in certain courts, particularly where it appeared that the

[1] *Ibid.* s.19(2).
[2] *Criminal Statistics England and Wales 1982*, Cmnd. 9048, Chap. 9; *Judicial Statistics 1989*, Cm. 1154, Chap. 10.
[3] Contained in para. 180 of *Legal Aid in Criminal Proceedings* (Cmnd. 2934, 1966) the report of a Departmental Committee chaired by Widgery J., as he then was.
[4] These criteria are incorporated, in the form of questions, into the application form for criminal legal aid which is prescribed by S.I. 1989 No. 344.
[5] The term "justices' clerk" incluces a court official authorised by the clerk to act on his or her behalf: S.I. 1989 No. 344, reg. 3.
[6] S.I. 1989 No. 344, regs. 11–17.

clerks were acting vigorously to implement undisclosed policies or Government directives on cost-saving.[7] The review procedure, originally instituted by the Legal Aid Act 1982, was an attempt to meet some of those criticisms in relation to committal proceedings and the trial of either-way offences. The cases in which legal aid must be granted in the magistrates' court are very few. It is clear from the statistics that very few defendants charged with summary offences receive legal aid, although a significant number of defendants tried for either-way offences do.[8] The magistrates' court, however, does not have an easy task. It has been suggested that the Widgery criteria do not work well because they are complex, imprecise and open to a wide range of interpretations.[9] This inevitably leads to substantial variations in the grant of legal aid, and the refusal figures are further distorted by the unwillingness of solicitors even to apply for aid to courts where they know that the application is likely to be unsuccessful. Financial pressures can add to the uncertainties of interpretation. A circular from the Lord Chancellor's Department to justices' clerks in March 1981 expressed concern that, ". . . legal aid in criminal proceedings should secure value for money . . . every effort must be made to avoid waste . . . legally-aided defendants should be asked to contribute . . . realistic down payments should be required in all suitable cases."[10] The defendant is meant to be given the benefit of the doubt,[11] but the 1981 circular reminded justices' clerks that applicants are not entitled to the benefit of those doubts ". . . on the strength of vague applications . . . a simple statement that the applicant is in danger of losing his liberty or livelihood or, as the case may be, that the charge raises a point of law does not suffice."

What matters to a defendant is the refusal to grant aid, and the possibility of having such a decision reviewed depends upon the type of offence charged. In the case of a *summary* offence, he or she may make a further application, for the court has power to grant aid at any stage of the proceedings,[12] or may seek judicial review in the High Court.[13] Neither course of action is likely to be successful in the majority of cases.[14] In the case of an *either-way* offence which is to be tried summarily, he or she may seek a review by the criminal legal aid committee[15] so long as the application for review is made after the first refusal of legal aid, *and* the refusal was based on lack of merits, *and* the application for legal aid had been made at least 21 days before the date fixed for the trial of the offence.[16] On a review, the

---

[7] L.C.D. Circular 81(3), reproduced in (1981) 131 N.L.J. 359, and see H. Levenson, (1978) 128 N.L.J. 52; (1979) 129 N.L.J. 375; *LAG Bulletin*, January 1980, April 1980, May 1981. Especial attention was paid to Waltham Forest: "What a difference a clerk makes," *LAG Bulletin*, March 1982.

[8] 5 per cent. of defendants in summary trials and 71 per cent. of defendants in the trial of either-way offences in the magistrates' court receive legal aid: *Judicial Statistics 1989*, Cm. 1154, Table 10.8.

[9] The Royal Commission on Legal Services described the evidence to this effect as "compelling": R.C.L.S., Vol. 1, para. 14.7.

[10] L.C.D. Circular 81(3); see n. 7 above.

[11] Legal Aid Act 1988, s.21(7), formerly the 1974 Act, s.29(6).

[12] S.I. 1989 No. 344, reg. 10.

[13] See pp. 871–878, below.

[14] See, *e.g.*, *R.* v. *Macclesfield JJ.*, *ex p. Greenhalgh* (1979) 144 J.P. 142; *cf. R.* v. *Brigg JJ.*, *ex p. Lynch* (1983) 148 J.P. 214.

[15] The area committees functioning under the civil legal aid scheme are designated for this additional purpose: S.I. 1989 No. 344, reg. 9.

[16] *Ibid.*, reg. 15.

criminal legal aid committee may make an order subject to the contribution conditions that will already have been fixed by the court or the justices' clerk.[17] As an alternative to the review, the defendant may renew the application for legal aid or seek judicial review[18] as above. In the case of a refusal of legal aid for *committal proceedings*, the defendant has the same remedies as in respect of either-way offences. When the magistrates refuse legal aid for a *trial on indictment* the simplest course will be to make a fresh application to the Crown Court.[19]

Legal aid in criminal cases may be made subject to a contribution from the defendant. Prior to the Legal Aid Act 1982, the amount of contributions actually collected was not significant when set against the overall cost of criminal legal aid,[20] but the contribution system was then restyled.[21]

The effect of this provision is to require a means test which leads to a fixed contribution. The court appears to have no discretion over whether to order a contribution or over the amount.[22] In applying the means test, the regulations provide for a calculation closely linked to that made in the grant of civil legal aid[23] which results in the assessment of disposable income and disposable capital. In respect of disposable income the defendant must contribute a weekly amount (determined by reference to the Fourth Schedule of the regulations)[24] for a period of six months,[25] and in respect of disposable capital, the whole of the amount in excess of £3,000.[26] In any event, the contribution shall not exceed the actual costs of the defence and any excess will be refunded.[27] In addition, the court has a discretion to remit the contribution where a defendant is acquittted or an appeal against conviction is allowed.[28]

This new system came into operation on March 1, 1984, but does not seem to have led to a significant increase in the level of contributions.[29] It is very different from that proposed by the Royal Commission on Legal Services, which would have involved a statutory right to legal aid save for summary

---

[17] As the court has no discretion to vary the stipulated contribution, neither does the committee.

[18] Again, this is unlikely to be successful: *e.g. R.* v. *Cambridge Crown Court, ex p. Hagi* (1979) 144 J.P. 145.

[19] Legal Aid Act 1988, s.20(2).

[20] In 1982, the total amount spent on criminal legal aid was £108,000,000. Contributions amounted to £1,540,000, collected from 24,000 out of 478,000 defendants who were granted aid: *Criminal Statistics 1982, op. cit.*, Chap. 9, Table 9.5.

[21] See H. Levenson, "Contributions and the new criminal legal aid" [1984] *Legal Action* 37.

[22] Legal Aid Act 1988, s.23.

[23] S.I. 1989 No. 344, regs. 26, 27 and Sched. 3.

[24] Average weekly disposable income, £55.01–£61, contribution £1; £61.01–£65, contribution £2; £65.01–£69, contribution £3; £69.01–£73, contribution £4; £73.01–£77, contribution £5; £77.01–£81, contribution £6; £81.01–£85, contribution £7; increased thereafter at the rate of £1 for every £4 or part of £4 in excess of £85. Thus, the income contribution from a man with an average weekly disposable income of £59, would be £26, and for a man with a disposable income of £100 would be £286. These figures were substituted by S.I. 1990 No. 489.

[25] The "contribution period": S.I. 1989 No. 344, reg. 3.

[26] *Ibid*. Sched. 4.

[27] *Ibid*. reg. 39.

[28] *Ibid*. reg. 35.

[29] In 1989, 47,000 of the 450,000 applications granted in magistrates' courts had contribution orders attached: *Judicial Statistics 1989*, Tables 10.10, 10.12. In 1989–90, expenditure on legal aid in magistrates' courts totalled £141,285,737, and contributions £2,231,866: *ibid*. Table 10.15.

offences and the abolition of contribution orders in magistrates' court proceedings.[30]

The Legal Aid Act 1988[31] gives the Lord Chancellor power to direct the Legal Aid Board to assume responsibility for granting criminal legal aid. The Board in its Report to the Lord Chancellor in May 1989 stated that such a transfer should not be contemplated unless the Board were to improve on or at least match the current levels of service. At present, transfer would not be justified: legal aid applications were dealt with on the day of application as a matter of routine; the present system combined expertise and flexibility; and there was no pressure for transfer from the courts. The Board did, however, indicate that it had a role in collecting information and offering guidance, and in the proper management of criminal legal aid committees.[32]

K. EVALUATIONS

So far in this chapter we have described rather than commented. However, criminal procedure is a subject which excites considerable discussion. The latest major review in the area of criminal procedure was undertaken by a Royal Commission appointed in 1978.

The Royal Commission on Criminal Procedure,[33] under the chairmanship of Sir Cyril Philips, was instructed to examine whether changes are needed in England and Wales, in:

"(i) the powers and duties of the police in respect of the investigation of criminal offences and the rights and duties of suspects and accused persons, including the means by which these are secured;
(ii) the process of and responsibility for the prosecution of criminal offences; and
(iii) such other features of criminal procedure and evidence as relate to the above."[34]

1. P.A.C.E. AND THE INVESTIGATION OF OFFENCES

(a) The "fundamental balance" and the structure of P.A.C.E.

In formulating its recommendations in respect of the matters within its terms of reference, the Royal Commission was required to have regard "both to the interests of the community in bringing offenders to justice and to the rights and liberties of persons suspected of crime," and to take into account the "need for the efficient and economical use of resources."[35]

The Commission regarded the task of reviewing the criminal process with what it termed the "fundamental balance" between the interests of the

---

[30] R.C.L.S.; Vol. 1, paras. 14.9 and 14.30–31.
[31] s.3(4).
[32] Legal Aid Board: Report to the Lord Chancellor (Cm. 688, 1989), pp. 17–18.
[33] Report, (Cmnd. 8092, 1981) The Investigation and Prosecution of Criminal Offences in England and Wales: The Law and Procedure, (Cmnd. 8092–1, 1981). Twelve Research Studies were commissioned.
[34] R.C.C.P. Rep. p. iv.
[35] Ibid.

community and the rights and liberties of individual citizens in mind as the "central challenge" which faced it.[36] Previous official reports on aspects of criminal justice[37] had made no or only passing reference to the concept, although the debate that followed the Eleventh Report of the Criminal Law Revision Committee had revealed the main schools of thought on the nature and role of a possible balance in pre-trial criminal procedure. The most controversial of the recommendations in the Eleventh Report involved the restriction of the suspect's right of silence when interrogated by the police. The supporters of the change took a utilitarian approach: "the law should be such as will secure as far as possible that the result of the trial is the right one."[38] The many improvements in criminal law, procedure and trial over the previous century justified the removal of safeguards that appeared unduly to favour the defence. Leading opponents took a libertarian stance, and argued that

"... in reality the right of silence formed a vital issue in the whole constitutional relationship in a free society between the individual and the state.... Each step in the criminal process, ... including the right of silence, must be judged not only as a means to the goal of reaching a reliable verdict, but also, and equally important, for its coherence with a liberal understanding of how free persons, including suspects in the police station, at all stages ought to be treated."[39]

A third, distinct, approach was to regard some, although not necessarily all, of the individual's rights in pre-trial procedure as negotiable, provided that appropriate checks and safeguards were introduced. Thus a minority of the Criminal Law Revision Committee was prepared to modify the right of silence only if statutory provision was made for the use of tape recorders.[40] In general terms it was the third approach that the Royal Commission on Criminal Procedure purported to adopt, although not simply as a series of compromises between the other main schools of thought. Some commentators on the Report took the view that an appropriate balance had not been struck[41]: others were less sceptical.[42]

The Royal Commission also characterised the "two main opposing groups" in the right of silence debate as "those who gave paramountcy to the principles of the presumption of innocence and the burden of proof, and those who saw the purpose of the criminal justice system as being a means to the end of bringing the guilty to justice."[43] The identification by the Royal

[36] *Ibid.* p. 4.
[37] Royal Commission on Police Powers and Procedure (Cmd. 3297, 1929); Royal Commission on the Police (Cmnd. 1728, 1962); Eleventh Report of the Criminal Law Revision Committee on Evidence (General) (Cmnd. 4991, 1972).
[38] Eleventh Report, p. 15.
[39] R.C.C.P. Rep., pp. 9, 10.
[40] *Ibid.* pp. 10, 11.
[41] *e.g.* D. McBarnet, [1981] Crim.L.R. 445 (noting the wider powers to be given to the police, the removal of traditional safeguards, the weakness and vagueness of the safeguards proposed in their place, and that the research was heavily dependent on police sources, and even then selectively ignored); M. McConville and J. Baldwin, (1982) 10 Int. Jo. Sociology of Law 287.
[42] (albeit with particular reservations): L. H. Leigh (1981) 44 M.L.R. 296; B. Smythe [1981] P.L. 184, 481.
[43] R.C.C.P. Rep., p. 11.

Commission of these two major schools of thought echoes the two theoretical models of the criminal process proposed by Herbert L. Packer as an aid to the evaluation of the criminal justice system in the United States, the Due Process Model and the Crime Control Models.[44] These models represented

> "an attempt to abstract two separate value systems that compete for priority in the operation of the criminal process. Neither is presented as either corresponding to reality or representing the ideal to the exclusion of the other."[45]

Moreover, they did not represent the difference between the law as it should be ("law in the books") and the law as in fact it operated ("law in action"). They were extremes, and reality lay at some point on the spectrum between them. Indeed, there was some common ground in the two models: assumptions (1) that the functions of defining conduct that may be treated as criminal is separate from and prior to the process of identifying and dealing with persons as criminals; (2) that when it appears that a crime has been committed and that there is a reasonable prospect of apprehending and convicting its perpetrator, criminal process ought ordinarily to be invoked; (3) that there are limits to the powers of government to investigate and apprehend persons suspected of committing crimes (*e.g.* the security and privacy of the individual may not be invaded at will); (4) that accused persons may, if they wish, force the operators of the process to demonstrate to an independent authority (the court) that they are guilty. Differences between the models lay in part in the strength and content of these assumptions, particularly the fourth.

Under the Crime Control Model, the most important function of the criminal process is the repression of criminal conduct. To fulfil this purpose, the system must operate efficiently. It must have the capacity to apprehend, try, and convict a high proportion of offenders whose offences become known, and to do so with speed and finality. This leads to an emphasis on informality and uniformity, and on minimising the occasions for challenge. Extra-judicial processes are preferred to judicial: the expertise of police and prosecutors is relied upon to screen out those who are probably innocent; those who are left in should be processed as speedily as possible, preferably with a plea of guilty at the trial stage.

> "The image that comes to mind is an assembly-line conveyor belt down which moves an endless stream of cases, never stopping, carrying the cases to workers who stand at fixed stations and who perform on each case as it comes by the same small but essential operation that brings it one step closer to being a finished product. . . ."[46]

By contrast, the Due Process Model resembles an obstacle course. "Each of its successive stages is designed to present formidable impediments to carrying the accused any further along in the process."[47] This model stresses the dangers of error in informal, non adjudicative fact finding: people are notoriously unreliable observers of disturbing events and confessions to the police may be induced by physical or psychological coercion. Formal, adjud-

---

[44] H. L. Packer, *The Limits of the Criminal Sanction* (1969), Part II.
[45] *Ibid.* p. 153.
[46] *Ibid.* p. 159.
[47] *Ibid.* p. 163.

icative, adversary fact finding processes, in which the case is heard by an impartial tribunal and the accused has a full opportunity to challenge the case against him or her, are necessary to reduce the dangers of error. Mistakes (convicting the innocent, setting the guilty free) should be eliminated to the fullest extent possible. (Under the Crime Control Model, such mistakes are acceptable in so far as they do not interfere with the repression of crime, (*e.g.* by allowing too many guilty people to escape)). Apart from the question of reliability, there is also a concern to prevent official oppression of the individual, and emphasis on the presumption of innocence and on securing compliance with the procedural rules governing the criminal process, perhaps with the exclusion of illegally obtained evidence or reversal of convictions where the rules are breached. On the assumption that the resources made available for the operation of the criminal process are limited, a preference for Due Process values over Crime Control values will lead to a reduction in the quantitative output of the system.

Writing in the late 1960s, Packer concluded that the criminal process as it actually operated in the large majority of cases in the United States probably approximated to the Crime Control Model. On the other hand, judicial decisions based on the U.S. Constitution were pushing the law nearer to the Due Process Model.[48] For McConville and Baldwin, writing in 1981, the English system too in many ways conformed to the Crime Control Model. Although the police-suspect encounter was one of the key exchanges in the criminal process, the safeguards available to suspects in custody were virtually non-existent. Similarly, there was a lack of Due Process safeguards surrounding pleas of guilty, and connected procedures such as plea bargaining; almost 90 per cent. of all defendants charged with serious offences pleaded guilty, and trial by jury (the epitome of the Due Process Model) was used by only 5 per cent. of those eligible to be so tried. The function of the jury was thus "largely symbolic—to uphold due process values in the occasional show trial."[49]

Another commentator, D. J. McBarnet, has stressed the point that it would not be correct to regard the substance of the law as reflecting Due Process Values which are then subverted "by policemen bending the rules, by lawyers negotiating adversaries out of existence, by out-of-touch judges or biased magistrates. . . ." In reality "the law governing the production, preparation and presentation of evidence does not live up to its own rhetoric. . . . Police and court officials need not abuse the law to subvert the principles of justice; they need only use it."[50]

The Royal Commission's recommendations concerning the investigation of offences were implemented, with modifications, in the Police and Criminal Evidence Act 1984. Those concerning the prosecution of offences, also with modifications, were implemented in the Prosecution of Offences Act

---

[48] *Ibid.* p. 239. Major cases included *Miranda* v. *Aryona* 384 U.S. 436 (1966) (suspects in custody must be advised of their rights, which include the right of access to a lawyer before interrogation); *Mapp* v. *Ohio* 367 U.S. 643 (1961) (rule excluding illegally obtained evidence applicable to state as well as federal prosecutions); *Gideon* v. *Wainwright* 372 U.S. 325 (1963) (state must provide counsel for defendants financially unable to provide their own).

[49] M. McConville and J. Baldwin, *Courts, Prosecution and Conviction* (1981), pp. 3–7.

[50] *Conviction* (1981), pp. 154–157. See also McBarnet, "False Dichotomies in Criminal Justice Research" in J. Baldwin and A. K. Bottomley, *Criminal Justice: Selected Readings* (1978), Chap. 2.

1985. How has the "fundamental balance" fared in the light of these and other changes? We consider this question in the context of pre-trial procedures in the following pages, and in the context of the trial in Chapter 16.

Finally, it is important to note that the Due Process and Crime Control Models are not the only ones that have been proposed,[51] although they remain the most helpful for our purposes.

(b) P.A.C.E. in practice

There are two main sources of information: first, the statistics regularly published by the Home Office[52] and, secondly, the findings of a series of research projects on aspects of P.A.C.E.[53] The statistics show that some of the powers enshrined in the Act, such as road checks, detention beyond 24 hours, warrants of further detention and intimate searches are comparatively rarely used.[54] The figures for stops and searches are increasing,[55] in part due to more comprehensive recording. About one in six is followed by arrest.

The research studies, as is to be expected, have produced much more interesting and helpful information on a number of topics.

(i) Use of arrest powers

Irving and McKenzie found some evidence in their study of interrogation practice in Brighton[56] that the level of initial evidence on which arrests are based had become stronger, with greater emphasis on independent evidence, although there was still a proportion of suspects who were arrested on limited evidence.[57]

---

[51] See A. E. Bottoms and J. D. McClean, *Defendants in the Criminal Process* (1976), pp. 226–232, and M. King, *The Framework of Criminal Justice* (1981), Chap. 2. Bottoms and McClean identify a third, Liberal Bureaucratic Model, based on the viewpoint of the "enlightened courts administrator": this purports to prefer Due Process values to Crime Control values, but imposes pressures (*e.g.* in support of summary trials and guilty pleas) to make the system workable, and in so doing in practice reinforces Crime Control. King analyses six models, three based on the perspectives of typical participants: (i) Due Process (defence lawyers), (ii) Crime Control (police), and (iii) Medical (probation officers: emphasis on rehabilitation); and three based on the work of social theorists: (iv) Bureaucratic (emphasising the management of crime and criminals), (v) Status Passage (emphasising the public degradation of the defendant) and (vi) Power (emphasising the maintenance of class domination).

[52] Home Office Statistical Bulletins.

[53] See M. Maguire, "Effects of the 'P.A.C.E.' provisions on detention and questioning: Some preliminary findings" (1988) 28 Brit. J. Criminol. 19; D. Brown, *Detention at the Police Station under the Police and Criminal Evidence Act 1984* (H.O. Research Study 104, 1989) and "P.A.C.E. and the Right to Legal Advice" (H.O.R.P.U. Bulletin 26, p. 26) B. L. Irving and I. K. McKenzie, *Police Interrogation: the effects of the Police and Criminal Evidence Act 1984* (1989) and "Interrogating via Legal Framework" in R. Morgan and D. J. Smith, *Coming to terms with Policing* (1989), Chap. 9; A. Sanders *et al.*, *Advice and Assistance at Police Stations and the 24 Hour Duty Solicitor Scheme* (L.C.D., 1989); I. McKenzie, R. Morgan and R. Reiner, "Helping Police with their Inquiries" [1990] Crim.L.R. 22.

[54] *e.g.* 1988 (1987 figures in brackets): 294 road checks (349); 747 people detained over 24 hours and subsequently released without charge; 446 warrants of further detention applied for (498): only 13 refused; 62 intimate searches (71): H.O. Statistical Bulletin 16/89.

[55] 149,000 in 1988 (26 per cent. up on 1987): *ibid.*

[56] Irving and McKenzie (1989). Irving's original study of 1979 (R.C.C.P. Research Study No. 2, 1980) was replicated in 1986 and again in 1987.

[57] *Ibid.* pp. 64–66, 145–147, 193.

(ii) *The detention process*

Brown's study[58] found considerable variations in the length of detention without charge from station to station, this being strongly linked with the seriousness of the crime in question, but also perhaps with differences in custody officers' approach to P.A.C.E. The mean length of detention was just over five hours and the median three hours, 19 minutes. By 24 hours, only 1 per cent. were still being held without charge. Pre-P.A.C.E. comparisons suggested that detention times were now shorter in some more serious crimes, but slightly longer for less serious offences. 18 per cent. of those charged were detained in custody, the mean length of detention being nearly 16 hours.[59] Powers available to the police in respect of serious arrestable offences were used infrequently.[60] The detainee's premises were searched in 7 per cent. of the sampled cases, (4 per cent. under section 18, 3 per cent. with consent). Strip searches were less common (1 per cent. of the sample) and intimate searches and non-consensual fingerprinting rare (seven and five cases in the sample).

Maguire reported that the levels of complaints about treatment by the police in the charge room or cells were said to have fallen dramatically in three of the four areas studied, and that conditions in charge rooms and cells, although not fully satisfactory, had clearly improved. He was surprised by the relaxed and even polite manner in which the procedures were often carried out.[61] Irving and McKenzie noted that the custody officer role and the record-keeping requirements "have, in Brighton at least, eliminated casual infringement of suspects' welfare rights." Moreover, "the system is now so constituted that if a serious breach of the rules governing the welfare of prisoners does occur, a serious conspiracy would now be necessary to avoid its detection."[62]

On the other hand, it does seem that at least the initial authorisation of detention by the custody officer (based on reasonable grounds for believing that detention is necessary to secure or preserve evidence or obtain evidence by questioning) is in practice a formality. Initial refusals are almost unknown.[63]

(iii) *The interrogation process*

The operation and effect of the right of access to legal advice conferred by P.A.C.E. has already been considered. Here we look at other effects on the interrogation process.

---

[58] Brown (1989). This covered just over 5,500 custody records from three or four stations in each of 10 forces.

[59] *Ibid.* pp. 61–67. See also Maguire (1988), pp. 22–27, Irving and McKenzie (1989), pp. 81–84, 194–196.

[60] *Ibid.* pp. 47–51: detention without charge over 24 hours (46 cases out of 5,519); warrants of further detention (11 cases); extension of warrant (3 cases); delayed legal advice (55 cases); delayed notification (53 cases); intimate samples (20 cases); non intimate sample without consent (5 cases).

[61] Maguire (1988), p. 41.

[62] Irving and McKenzie (1989), pp. 196–198.

[63] I. McKenzie, R. Morgan and R. Reiner, [1990] Crim.L.R. 22, 23–27. They point out that Code C.2.1. oddly requires a custody record to be opened for all persons brought to a police station under arrest, *i.e.* before the question of continued detention arises.

Irving and McKenzie found in their comparative study of interrogations by the Brighton police in 1979 and 1986 that the Act had led to a sharp reduction in the number of suspects interrogated more than once, and in the use of persuasive bargaining tactics to influence suspects into providing information, (e.g. references to police discretion over charging, bail, and the involvement of others; references (as experts in the working of the criminal justice system) to the likely attitude of the court or the likely sentence; references to the consequences of confession to the suspect; suggestions that the suspect really has no choice in the light of the information already in police hands). The requirements that contemporaneous notes be kept made interviews more stiff and formal, to the observed irritation of C.I.D. officers.[64] The typical interview now took longer to complete, but total interviewing time per suspect had decreased. However, there was little effect on the admission rate.[65] By 1987, officers had adapted to contemporaneous note-taking, and there was resurgence in the use of tactics, particularly those which attempted to manipulate the suspect's perception of the consequence of confessing or remaining silent. The researchers also now identified a drop in the admission rate for serious cases.[66]

(c) Overall

Professor Zander, in a review of the first four years of P.A.C.E.,[67] concludes that the Act and accompanying Codes have "given a coherent shape and structure to many of the aspects of the relationship between the police and the suspect—and above all in the police station. . . . This is decidedly a step in the right direction. . . ."[68] The sceptics who doubted whether controls enshrined in Codes of Practice would be sufficient to alter police practice have been proved wrong. Changes in practice indeed predated the indications that the judges were prepared to exclude evidence obtained in breach of the Codes, and could perhaps be explained by the fact that "Police officers by training and, generally, by temperament are rule-orientated. Doing things by the book is the way they instinctively prefer to operate."[69] This is not to say that there are no areas of concern. Zander notes that the proportion of arrests from stops and searches remains disappointingly low; there are doubts as to the reliability of some of the overall statistics (e.g. arising from different interpretations of the concept of "voluntary" stops and searches, attendance at police stations[70] and searches of premises); there are differences of opinion over whether access to legal advice is working satisfactorily; and the controls over stops and searches and strip searches in the police station, based on the making of a record which includes reasons, seem ineffective. Overall, some parts of the Act and accompanying Code have made a distinct impact, some have made little or none and in some the position is unclear. Unsurprisingly, "there are (and

---

[64] Forces which prior to P.A.C.E. had adopted contemporaneous note taking did not experience great difficulties.
[65] Ibid. pp. 74–78, 86–95, 102–113.
[66] Ibid. pp. 167–188. See also Brown (1989), pp. 43–46.
[67] (1989) 40 N.I.L.Q. 319.
[68] Ibid. p. 321.
[69] Ibid. p. 322.
[70] See further, I. McKenzie, R. Morgan and R. Reiner, [1990] Crim.L.R. 22.

will remain) differences of view as to whether particular parts of the new system are working well or as intended."[71]

It can be seen that overall the "fundamental balance" has been drawn rather nearer to the interests of the accused than under the previous arrangements; whether sufficiently so is doubtful. The development discussed in the next section threatens to tip the balance once again more in the direction of crime control.

2. THE RIGHT TO SILENCE

As already mentioned,[72] the suspect in theory at least enjoys the "right to remain silent," which encompasses a right not to answer questions when interviewed by the police; a right not to give any indication of plea or line of defence before trial; and a right not to be compelled to plead or give evidence at the trial. The first two aspects fall within the scope of this chapter.

The Criminal Law Revision Committee in its 11th Report[73] recommended that the suspect's right of silence should be restricted by enabling the jury or magistrates' court to draw whatever inferences were reasonable from the failure of the accused when interviewed or charged to mention a fact which he or she could reasonably have been expected to mention and which is later relied on for his or her defence. The caution would be modified accordingly. Where there was a case to answer, inferences might also be drawn from a refusal to be sworn or to answer questions at trial.

These proposals provoked such a storm of opposition that the whole report, including many useful proposals for reforming the law of evidence, was shelved.[74] The matter was reviewed by the Royal Commission on Criminal Procedure,[75] and the majority, perhaps fearful of a similar reaction as there had been to the 11th Report, proposed no change in the law. The majority noted that a change might increase a risk that innocent people might make damaging statements. Indeed, such a change would only be acceptable if interrogation were to become in effect a quasi-judicial function, with the suspect provided with full knowledge of their rights, complete information about the evidence available to the police and an exact understanding of the consequences of silence.

It is accordingly unfortunate that the Home Secretary, acting on little better than anecdotal police evidence about a fall in admission rates after P.A.C.E., and after six months of public debate in which widely divergent views were expressed, announced that as a matter of principle the case for change was strong and that all that remained was for a Working Group to meet to consider the precise form the change in the law should take.[76] In October 1988 it was announced that there would be changes to the right of

---

[71] (1989) 40 N.I.L.Q. 319, 332.
[72] Above, pp. 608–609, 668.
[73] *Evidence* (*General*) (Cmnd. 4991, 1972). See generally D.J. Galligan, (1988) 41 C.L.P. 69.
[74] See M. Zander, (1974) 71 L.S.Gaz. 954 and "The Right of Silence in the Police Station and the Caution" in P. Glazebrook (ed.), *Reshaping the Criminal Law* (1978), pp. 344–363.
[75] R.C.C.P. Rep. (Cmnd. 8092, 1981), pp. 80–91.
[76] H. C. Deb., Vol. 133, May 18, 1988, Col. 466.

silence in Northern Ireland, and these were put into effect in the Criminal Evidence (Northern Ireland) Order 1988.[77]

The Working Group reported in July 1989.[78] It recommended that the recommendations in the 11th Report should be implemented, with the modifications (1) that there should be statutory guidelines for the courts about the factors to be taken into account in relation to the inferences which may be drawn; (2) that at the Crown Court the judge should be required to direct the jury as to these factors, and magistrates should be required themselves to take them into account. There should be a revised form of caution:

> "You do not have to say anything. A record will be made of anything you do say and it may be given in evidence. So may your refusal to answer any question. If there is any fact on which you intend to rely in your defence in court it would be best to mention it now. If you hold it back until you go to court you may be less likely to be believed."

The majority thought this should be administered at the time of arrest as well as subsequently; one member thought that the suspect should be cautioned on arrest with the first two sentences only, with the full caution given before the commencement of any interview and after access to legal advice. Silence would not itself be evidence of guilt or corroborate other evidence, but merely lead to the adverse inference that a subsequent line of defence is untrue and, perhaps, an adverse effect upon general credibility. There would be no additional requirements placed on the police to disclose details of their case.

As regards advance disclosure of the defence case, the Working Group recommended the introduction of a model based on the procedure applicable to serious and complex fraud cases under section 9 of the Criminal Justice Act 1987.[79] For resource reasons, it should, initially at least, apply only to serious or complex Crown Court cases.

The Working Group's proposals have been roundly criticised.[80] They seem indeed to constitute a significant shift away from due process and towards crime control. While there might be comparatively little danger in the proposals for advance disclosure before trial in serious or complex cases where the accused is legally represented and is invited to respond to a case statement provided by the prosecution, the same cannot be said for suspects in custody on the way to the police station, and for the 80 per cent. or so of suspects who do not in practice have legal advice before or during interrogation, especially where the police case is not disclosed. Admittedly, few suspects in practice rely on the right of silence so as to refuse to answer any questions, and a large number of suspects do make admissions. However, this argument cuts both ways. It might be thought that there is no point in protecting a right that very few rely upon. On the other hand, it also suggests that there is little need for change.

---

[77] S.I. 1988 No. 1987 (N.I. 20). J. D. Jackson, "Recent Developments in Criminal Evidence" (1989) 40 N.I.L.Q. 105.

[78] *Report of the Working Group on the Right of Silence* (Home Office, 1989).

[79] Above, pp. 671–672.

[80] See A. A. S. Zuckerman, "Trial by Unfair Means" [1989] Crim.L.R. 855; J. Wood and A. Crawford, *The Right of Silence: The case for retention* (1989); S. Greer, (1990) 53 M.L.R. 709.

3. THE CROWN PROSECUTION SERVICE

Earlier in the chapter we have described the basic structure and operation of the Crown Prosecution Service. At this point we consider how it has worked in practice.

The picture is mixed. It is generally agreed that the C.P.S. got off to a bad start, many of its problems stemming from lack of resources. Its official complement for staff was inadequate for the work it had to do, and it was unable to recruit up to its complement. Much of its press coverage was adverse. More systematic reviews were conducted by the National Audit Office in 1989 and the House of Commons Public Accounts and Home Affairs Committees in 1990.[81]

The National Audit Office concluded that most C.P.S. Areas had insufficient staff and time for training and preparation to enable them to run an efficient and effective service from the start; that the Home Office had seriously underestimated the resource implications, partly as a result of the lack of information about previous prosecution costs; that manpower requirements and workload continued to rise after the service had started; and that staff shortages continued. Nevertheless, the Service had been able to set up a reasonably sound basis for monitoring and improving their performance, and had been reasonably effective in continuing and conducting prosecutions and keeping unsatisfactory cases out of court.

Similar points were made by the Public Accounts Committee, which noted that the C.P.S. appeared to be costing almost twice as much as the previous prosecution arrangements, with a staff requirement practically double the size originally envisaged. Staff shortages were still a serious problem, although there had been a gradual improvement in recruitment. The Committee was disturbed at the very high cost of employing agent lawyers and the large proportion of discontinued cases not dropped until the court hearing, and was surprised that the C.P.S. undertook no systematic analysis of the reasons for discontinuance.

Many of the organisations which submitted evidence to the Home Affairs Committee supported the concept of an independent prosecution service, but were critical, and in some cases highly critical, of aspects of the operation of the C.P.S. in practice. A recurrent theme was the inadequate preparation of cases, particularly less important cases handled by inexperienced staff, leading to the late service of papers, delays and the unnecessary discontinuance of cases. The police were critical of the discontinuance of cases that they would have prosecuted, the slower feedback to investigating officers, the fact that administrative tasks such as warning witnesses to attend court had not been transferred to the C.P.S. and the insistence of the C.P.S. on a higher standard of file preparation than had been the norm under the

---

[81] Report by the Comptroller and Auditor General, *Review of the Crown Prosecution Service* (1988–89 H.C. 345); Second Report of the Committee of Public Accounts, *Review of the Crown Prosecution Service* (1989–90 H.C. 164); Fourth Report of the Home Affairs Committee, *Crown Prosecution Service* (1989–90 H.C. 118). See also A. Green, (1989) 57 Medicolegal Jo. 77; C. Moiser, (1987) 151 J.P.N. 711; J. V. Bates, *ibid.* p. 864 (reply to Moiser); S. Eysenck, (1989) 153 J.P.N. 620; B. T. McArdle, *ibid.* p. 622 (reply to Eysenck); A. Grosskurth, *Legal Action*, July 1989, 8. The story of the establishment of the C.P.S. is told from the point of view of its first head in Sir Thomas Hetherington, *Prosecution and the Public Interest* (1989); *cf.* J. Rozenberg, *The Case for the Crown* (1987), Chap. 4.

previous arrangements, with full witness statements, reports that were typed and not handwritten and a duplicate copy of the file retained by the police. On the other hand, the C.P.S. voiced criticisms of the quality and late delivery of police files.

Differing views were expressed on the effectiveness of the C.P.S. as a "filter." The C.P.S. noted that in the three years from October 1986, over 250,000 cases were discontinued, and claimed that these figures "show that the C.P.S. has been effective in filtering a considerable number of un-meritorious cases out of the judicial system."[82] Others were critical. The Association of Chief Police Officers stated that:

"There is a widely-held view that the Service will only prosecute where there is little or no likelihood of acquittal. . . . By only pursuing those cases in which they have an obvious chance of winning, the Crown Prosecution Service appear as good advocates and are provided with the sort of statistics which show the organisation in good light."[83]

Other witnesses indicated that there were instances both of the dropping of winnable cases and of the continuation of cases doomed to failure.[84] On the other hand, the C.P.S. was congratulated on having established its independence from the police.[85] Where the truth lies is uncertain. The C.P.S. has acknowledged that there is a wide variation in discontinuance rates across the country, ranging from 4 per cent. to 19 per cent., and has commissioned a study of discontinuance rates in areas with low or high rates.[86] Meanwhile, it has suggested that variations in police practice may be a significant factor:

"It must be appreciated that some forces operate a stricter policy of quality control, while other forces are much more inclined to leave it to the C.P.S. to weed out weak cases, and such practices may largely account for the variations in discontinuance rates between Areas."[87]

Many of these problems can be traced to the problems of staffing, with the particular difficulties of recruiting and retaining experienced lawyers, and of recruiting up to complement. The consequences have included overwork, excessive reliance on inexperienced staff, the need to employ an excessive number of agents (who often have to be paid substantially more than C.P.S. staff to do the same work, with an adverse effect on C.P.S. morale) and the various administrative breakdowns that any overburdened bureaucracy might suffer. Several initiatives have been taken to improve the position.[88] A review of salaries in the Government Legal Service generally led to substantial pay increases, particularly in London[89]; arrangements have been made to offer young lawyers the opportunity to qualify at the expense of the C.P.S. before joining it; and the groups targeted for recruitment have been widened to include undergraduates and part-time and older lawyers. The

---

[82] *Memorandum of Evidence*, p. 10.
[83] *Ibid.* p. 67.
[84] *Ibid.* pp. 56–57 (Midland and Oxford Circuit of the Bar); 58 (Magistrates' Association).
[85] *Ibid.* p. 49 (Criminal Law Committee of The Law Society); *cf.* p. 53: Criminal Bar Association poll of barristers who practise regularly in the Crown Court: 40 per cent. had detected a greater sense of independence from the police.
[86] *Ibid.* p. 10.
[87] *Ibid.*
[88] 2nd Report of the P.A.C., (1989–90 H.C. 164), paras. 10–17.
[89] Andrew Report, see pp. 20–21.

conferment of rights of audience in the Crown Court would not only enhance morale and job satisfaction but could also lead to significant financial savings.[90]

Other problems cannot, however, be explained simply by reference to staffing difficulties. The loss of police control over prosecutions would in any event have led to tensions between the police and the C.P.S., assuming that the new service showed itself willing to act independently and discontinue prosecutions the police would have wished to pursue. In practice there has been a greater degree of hostility between the police and the C.P.S. than anticipated, although the relationship has been much easier in those areas where there was previously an established prosecuting solicitors' department than in the areas where the police conducted their own prosecutions[91] or employed solicitors in private practice. Arrangements for liaison have been established at both national and local levels and the D.P.P. has reported that there has been substantial progress in improving relationships between the C.P.S. and the police, and, indeed, between the C.P.S. and other institutions within the criminal justice system.[92]

The government's objectives in establishing the C.P.S. were that it:

"would promote consistency and fairness; would reduce the proportion of cases pursued despite lack of evidence; would improve the preparation and presentation of cases in court; would provide an attractive career structure for staff; and would lead to greater efficiency and accountability in the use of resources."[93]

Overall, the picture is one of gradual progress in meeting the various difficulties that have arisen. In its Report on the C.P.S.,[94] the Home Affairs Committee stated that it fully shared the view that an independent prosecution service is fairer and more just than the system which existed before. It rejected the suggestion, which it said was to be inferred from some remarks of the D.P.P., that there was a feud or even a gulf of distrust between police and C.P.S. on the principle of the latter's independence. It endorsed steps which were already being taken to promote co-operation and efficiency and made a series of specific recommendations for change. In response,[95] the government announced the establishment of a national inspectorate, operating within the structure of the C.P.S., which would sample cases "to monitor the quality and consistency of lawyer judgement." The government would consider the introduction of an external monitor and a scheme of mandatory time limits. It agreed in principle that the C.P.S. and police should each have a single officer identified as responsible for a case and that

---

[90] See above, p. 624.
[91] As was typically the case in London, where about 80 per cent. of the workload was handled by the police and 20 per cent. by Metropolitan Police Solicitors' Department and the D.P.P.
[92] *Annual Report of the Crown Prosecution Service 1988–89* (1988–89 H.C. 411), pp. 27–29. "Nearly all Areas are now able to report good or excellent relationships with the police at all ranks. ... Even those Areas which initially experienced hostility... have at least been able to establish working relationships with the senior officers and are working hard to improve their relationships with the other ranks" (p. 28).
[93] 2nd Report of the P.A.C. (1989–90 H.C. 164), para. 4.
[94] Fourth Report of the H.A.C., 1989–90, *The Crown Prosecution Service* (1989–90 H.C. 118–I, II).
[95] Government Response (Cm. 1145, 1990).

every Crown Court should have a sufficiently senior C.P.S. officer in attendance.

However, the government rejected the Committee's recommendation that the C.P.S. should adhere rigidly to the Code for Crown Prosecutors in deciding to drop or reduce charges and always explain the decision to the police in writing; that the Code should be subject to parliamentary approval; and that the C.P.S. should take over private prosecutions where magistrates decide there is a case to answer. It agreed with the Committee in rejecting proposals that prosecutions for summary offences be returned to the police, and that the police be entitled to undertake a private prosecution if they disagreed with a decision of the C.P.S. to drop a case.

Accordingly, substantial alterations to the structure or role of the C.P.S. are unlikely at present. The involvement of the C.P.S. at an earlier stage in the prosecution process, with responsibility for the *commencement* of a prosecution and not merely its *continuance*, even if desirable in principle, would require substantial increases in resources for a service apparently under-resourced for its present functions. The present difficulties in the relationship between police and C.P.S. would be magnified and an increase in delays inevitable.

4. Do Committal Proceedings Serve Their Purposes?

There is considerable evidence that committal proceedings do not operate as an effective filter of weak cases. The research undertaken by McConville and Baldwin showed that a proportion of the acquittals at the Crown Court directed by the trial judge occurred in cases which ought not to have been allowed to proceed beyond the committal stage.[96] They recorded the considerable anguish and serious consequences for some of the defendants involving loss of job, loss of business, loss of reputation and, in one case, loss of custody of a child.[97] Doubts had previously been expressed by the James Committee on the Distribution of Criminal Business,[98] the Fisher Report on the Confait case[99] and the Royal Commission on Criminal Procedure.[1]

Are the proceedings themselves ineffective or is it the way in which they are operated? The full committal ought to give a clear opportunity to weigh the evidence and make an effective decision. Two problems have been identified. Comparatively few cases now proceed through a full committal. In a study of all committals in January 1981, it was found that 7.6 per cent. were full committals,[2] although by 1986 the proportion was 13 per cent.[3] The second problem is the alleged unwillingness of magistrates to discharge an accused in any event.[4] It may be easier for the examining justices to dodge

---

[96] *Courts, Prosecution and Conviction* (1981), particularly Chaps. 3 and 4.

[97] *Ibid.* pp. 48–50.

[98] H.M.S.O. 1975, para. 232.

[99] Above, pp. 660–661.

[1] R.C.C.P. Report (Cmnd. 8092, 1981), para. 8.26.

[2] P. Jones, R. Tarling and J. Vennard, "The effectiveness of committal proceedings as a filter in the criminal justice system" in D. Moxon (ed.), *Managing Criminal Justice* (1985), Chap. 8.

[3] *Committal Proceedings: A Consultation Paper* (Home Office, Lord Chancellor's Department, 1989), para. 4.

[4] See the views expressed by B. F. Harrison, [1955] Crim.L.R. 153; C. Allen, [1958] Crim.L.R. 647; E. Goldrein, [1959] Crim.L.R. 273.

the responsibility by ordering committal and letting the jury decide. Even so, the full committal could fulfil the stated objective, as Sir Henry Fisher observed of the Confait case, but at an enormous cost in time and money.[5] In any event the research conducted by Jones, Tarling and Vennard found that a higher proportion of the full committals in their sample (15 per cent.) ended in an acquittal directed by the judge than of the paper committals (5.4 per cent.), although this might be because full committals tend to take place in cases which are more problematic than those normally dealt with in paper committals.[6]

The paper committal procedure has effectively shifted the burden of deciding whether there should be a trial from the magistrates to the lawyers involved.[7] If there is any doubt, it is always possible for the defence to object to a paper committal and demand a full committal. The Royal Commission, relying on evidence provided by McConville and Baldwin, concluded that the reason for the failure to weed out the weak cases which are allowed to go through to the Crown Court under the paper committal procedure is the "lack of effective scrutiny of the case by prosecution and defence (who may often only receive the papers on the day of the hearing)."[8] The James Committee had speculated on the reasons why a defence solicitor may not be able to scrutinise the prosecution case fully before agreeing to committal, identifying lack of time and resources as particular problems.[9]

Recognising that the prevalence of paper committals places the responsibility for weeding out weak cases firmly on the shoulders of the prosecutor and the defence lawyer, the James Committee and the Royal Commission came up with different solutions to the problem. The James Committee recommended the retention of the paper committal procedure with the additional requirement that both the prosecution and defence sign a certificate to the effect that they have examined the witness statements and are satisfied that the case is suitable for committal for trial. The imposition of sanctions for abuse of this procedure would be left to the legal profession.[10] The Royal Commission recommended the abolition of committal proceedings, subject to the provision of a right to make a submission of no case to answer to a magistrates' court if the delay before trial of the offence would exceed a specified period. This procedure would be termed "application for discharge" and would depend partly upon improved provisions for disclosure of prosecution evidence to the defence. The responsibility thus placed upon the Crown Prosecutor was recognised by the Commission and accepted as appropriate.[11]

Since then there has been a series of proposals for reform from various quarters, there being a general consensus that the present arrangement for

---

[5] The 1989 Consultation Paper estimates that the global cost of all full committals is about twice that of all paper committals: Annex C.
[6] *Op. cit.* n. 2, p. 91.
[7] By relieving the magistrates of the obligation even to consider the evidence.
[8] R.C.C.P. Rep., para. 8.26. This echoes the observation of Sir Henry Fisher in his Report on the Confait case: above pp. 660–661.
[9] Cmnd. 6323, 1975, para. 233.
[10] *Ibid.* paras. 235–239.
[11] R.C.C.P. Rep., paras. 8.27–8.31.

committals are a waste of time and money.[12] In serious fraud cases, committal proceedings can now be by-passed by the notice of transfer procedure.[13] Then in 1989 the Home Office and the Lord Chancellor's Department issued a joint Consultation Paper,[14] summarising two options for replacing committal proceedings. Option 1 was modelled on the notice of transfer procedure under the Criminal Justice Act 1987, with the possibility of an application for discharge made to a judge at the Crown Court. The government indicated that it did not favour this option; it would constitute an unjustifiable use of the time of Crown Court judges, which was in any event in short supply. The procedure was justified in serious and complex fraud cases, but not generally.

The government's preference was for Option 2. This involved removing mode of trial decisions from magistrates. In either-way cases, the prosecution would indicate whether it proposed trial in the magistrates' court or in the Crown Court, although the defendant would retain the right to elect for trial in the Crown Court. The prosecution would have to certify that it had sufficient evidence to justify trial. In the case of either-way offences where trial in the Crown Court has been chosen, and in the case of all indictable-only offences, there would be a prescribed period during which the defendant could apply to the magistrates' court to be discharged on the ground that there was insufficient evidence to establish a prima facie case. Such applications should be conducted, save in exceptional circumstances, on the basis of written statements (both witness statements and submissions). Oral applications could be made, with the leave of the court, but oral evidence would not be received. In the absence of a successful application to discharge, the papers would simply be transferred to the Crown Court.

Matters requiring further consideration included the arrangements that should be made for unrepresented defendants, whether prosecutors other than the C.P.S. should have the power to override the defendant's choice of summary trial in either-way cases, and whether a scheme for expedited hearings should be incorporated. Moreover, the resource implications of the proposals would need to be closely examined.

5. THE ROLE OF THE VICTIM

In recent years, increased attention has been paid to the role of the victim. Two paradoxes have been noted.[15] First, there is the contradiction that the victim has a crucial role to play in reporting the offence to the police and as the major agent in detecting the offender, but that little or no account is taken of the victim's attitudes and experiences by the professionals involved in the criminal justice system. Second, "major projects aimed at fulfilling victims' needs have been set up without regard to, or even investigation into, victims' expressed needs."[16] These projects include the Criminal Injuries

---

[12] They are summarised in Annex B to the 1989 Consultation Paper, and emanate from, *inter alia*, the Bar, the Law Society and the Justices Clerks' Society. See also the exchange of views between A. R. Rickard (1986) 150 J.P.N. 52, 293 and D. Napley, *ibid.*, p. 147. Napley argues for the retention of the option of a full committal, with modifications, as "properly used they are an important and essential constitutional safeguard."

[13] Above, pp. 670–671.

[14] *Op. cit.*, n. 3. See (1989) 153 J.P.N. 521.

[15] J. Shapland, J. Willmore and P. Duff, *Victims in the Criminal Justice System* (1985), Chap. 10. See, generally, S. Walkate, *Victimology* (1989).

[16] *Ibid.* p. 178.

Compensation Scheme (a state scheme for compensating the victims of violent crime[17]), schemes for compensation or reparation by offenders,[18] victim support schemes[19] and mediation or conciliation schemes.[20] While such schemes provide some assistance to victims, much more could be done.[21] The police seem to have been rather more responsive to the needs of victims than have magistrates' courts.[22] The government has responded by strengthening the compensation provisions, and by issuing a Victims' Charter which sets out the "rights and entitlements" of crime victims.[23] Among its features are the duty of the police to keep victims informed of all important stages in a case; the duty of the C.P.S. to ensure that full details of injuries or losses have been established before trial and to advise prosecutors to correct statements made in court which denigrate a victim's character; the right of the families of murder victims to be consulted about the timing of the killer's release and whether restrictions should be placed on where he or she lives and works. This all, however, falls short of giving the victim a formal role in the criminal justice process as a party to the prosecution, which some argue is necessary for the problems to be cured.

[17] Established under the royal prerogative in 1964; to be reconstituted as a statutory scheme by the Criminal Justice Act 1988, ss.108–117, and Scheds. 6, 7. The scheme is administered by the Criminal Injuries Compensation Board. See T. Newburn *The Settlement of Claims at the Criminal Injuries Compensation Board* (H.O. Research Study No. 112, 1989).

[18] Criminal courts have power to make compensation orders under the Powers of Criminal Courts Act 1973, ss.35–38, as amended or substituted by the Criminal Justice Act 1988, ss.104, 105. The defendant's means have to be taken into account, and orders have been made less frequently than they could be: see Shapland, *et al.* (1985), Chap. 8; T. Newburn, *The Use and Enforcement of Compensation Orders in Magistrates' Courts* (H.O. Report Study No. 102, 1988). A court must now give reasons if it fails to make an order.

[19] Schemes whereby volunteers visit victims and offer emotional and practical support. The reactions of both victims and police are generally positive: T. Newburn, (1989) 26 H.O.R.B. 22; and see M. Maguire and C. Corbett, *The Effects of Crime and the Work of Victims Support Schemes* (1987); D. Trust, *Help for Victims of Crime and Violence* (1989); M. L. Gill and R. I. Mawby, *Volunteers in the Criminal Justice System* (1990), Chap. 5.

[20] See T. F. Marshall and S. Merry, *Crime and Accountability: Victim/Offender Mediation in Practice* (H.M.S.O., 1990).

[21] See Shapland, *et al.* (1985), Chap. 10.

[22] J. Shapland and D. Cohen, "Facilities for Victims: the Role of the Police and the Courts" [1987] Crim.L.R. 28. See also T. Newman and S. Merry, *Keeping in Touch* (H.O. Research Study No. 116, 1990).

[23] *The Times*, February 23, 1990. The Charter is published by the Home Office.

PART IV

THE HEARING

CHAPTER 14

THE CIVIL TRIAL

FROM the variety of different civil proceedings we take the action in the Queen's Bench Division as our example, as we did in the chapter on pre-trial civil procedure.[1] However, we shall also make reference to the county court and the resolution of issues in that court by the arbitration process.

A. ADVERSARIAL PROCEDURE

Adversarial procedure is the fundamental, characteristic feature of English civil justice.[2]

"You have two adversaries in every civil dispute—someone asserting a right, someone denying it. Someone contending for one thing, someone contending against it."[3]

The trial procedure reflects this view of the conduct of civil cases, as well as the principles of judicial neutrality and unpreparedness. Judicial unpreparedness, however, is not necessarily conducive to effectiveness and efficiency, and consequently the Civil Justice Review recommended that judges should read case papers before the hearing.[4] It is the function of the parties, normally through counsel, to bring the evidence and argue the law which will win the case.[5] However, since there is usually no jury present, there can be significant differences between a civil and criminal trial. In order to improve the machinery of civil justice, the Civil Justice Review recommended that there should be control over the excessive use of documents, particularly by introducing the idea of a core bundle of documents, hence saving time and cost.[6] Further, it was suggested that many of the rules on the admissibility of evidence are not necessary, in particular the rule against hearsay,[7] and that

---

[1] See Chap. 11.

[2] Sir Jack I.H. Jacob, *The Fabric of English Civil Justice* (1987), p. 5. Adversarial procedure can be compared with the inquisitorial system, see *ibid.* pp. 5–19.

[3] Sir Jack I.H. Jacob, "The Adversary System of Civil Litigation" (1983) City of London Law Review 17, 18.

[4] *Civil Justice Review, Report of the Review Body on Civil Justice* (Cm. 394, 1988), paras. 261–265.

[5] This view is reflected right from the stage of pleadings (see above, p. 550) to trial.

[6] *Civil Justice Review* (1988), para. 303. The sanction would be in costs against solicitors personally within R.S.C., Ord. 62, r. 11. This proposal has been adopted in county court trials: C.C.R. Ord. 17, r. 12, as inserted by S.I. 1990 No. 1764.

[7] Following the invitation by the Civil Justice Review (paras. 266–270) that the hearsay rule be reconsidered, the Lord Chancellor referred the matter to the Law Commission which has provisionally recommended that the exclusionary rule be abolished with the addition of some elementary and simple safeguards against abuse of the power to adduce hearsay: Law Commission: *The Hearsay Rule in Civil Proceedings* (L.C. Consultation Paper No. 117, 1991).

"[t]here should be the free admission of evidence and there should be what is called the free evaluation of the evidence by the court. This would carry to its logical conclusion what has been happening in practice, that the rules of evidence play an almost insignificant part in the civil trial process."[8]

At the beginning of a trial, the *opening speech* is made on behalf of the plaintiff. The object of the opening speech is to outline the case with reference to the evidence that is to be called. The opening may be briefer in a civil case than in a criminal case since there will not normally be a jury and, one hopes, counsel will not have to explain the burden and standard of proof to the judge. Counsel has not been able to assume that the judge has any familiarity with the papers in the case[9] so his or her job has been summarised as being: ". . . to explain the whole case to the judge: to read the pleadings, the letters and other documents . . . , to summarise what all the witnesses he is calling will say, and how his client views the issue."[10] Normally any agreed reports or other documentary evidence are put in evidence in the opening speech.[11] In addition to recommending that judges read case papers before the hearing, the Civil Justice Review recommended that, if the judge has had the opportunity to read the relevant papers, it may be indicated to counsel that there is no need to cover all the points in the opening speech. This illustrates the advantage of trial by judge alone—the judge can move counsel on where matters are understood or undisputed without the constraint of ensuring that the jury have grasped the issue, and if the judge is prepared, considerable time and cost can be saved during the trial. At the conclusion of the opening speech for the plaintiff, the first witnesses are called.

It is no accident that there are witnesses *for* the plaintiff and witnesses *for* the defendant. The parties are free to choose the people who can give evidence to support their contentions and the witnesses line up behind the "litigant gladiators,"[12] clearly identified with one side or the other.

Counsel for the plaintiff will call each witness in turn. A witness is questioned to extract testimony which is expected to be favourable to the plaintiff. The plaintiff's solicitor will have prepared in advance a statement of the evidence already given by the witness and counsel will use this "proof of evidence" as the basis of his or her questions. The questioning of a witness by the counsel "on the same side" is termed *examination in chief*.[13] Counsel must observe two rules during the examination. Leading questions[14] must not be asked and the witness's evidence given in court must not be contradicted by reference to a conflicting statement of that witness in the proof of

---

[8] Jacob (1987), p. 266. For an introduction to the law of evidence in civil trials, see J. O'Hare and R. N. Hill, *Civil Litigation* (5th ed., 1990), Chap. 19.

[9] But see now the expectation that judges will have to read case papers, as in the Commercial Court: n. 4 above.

[10] *Going to Law* (1974), a report by JUSTICE, at para. 16. See also D. Barnard, *The Civil Court in Action* (2nd ed., 1985), p. 200.

[11] *e.g.* medical reports or the reports of other experts.

[12] A phrase taken from Jacob (1983).

[13] As to the judge's role in examining witnesses for both the plaintiff and the defence, see p. 784, below.

[14] A leading question is one which suggests to the witness the answer which counsel expects. "What time did the accident occur?" is a proper question. "The accident occurred at 7.30 p.m. did it not?" is a leading question and, therefore, prohibited. It is commonly agreed between counsel that a witness may be "led" on non-contentious issues to save time.

evidence.[15] Because the Code of Conduct prevents a barrister from discussing a case or the evidence to be given with a potential witness other than the lay client, a character witness or an expert witness[15a] and because the "coaching" of witnesses by counsel is forbidden,[16] it is quite possible that there may be variations in testimony when the witness is under examination.

At the conclusion of the examination-in-chief of each witness for the plaintiff, counsel for the defendant is given the opportunity to *cross-examine* in an attempt to shake the testimony of the witness or to extract information useful to the defendant's case. In cross-examination, counsel is at liberty to exploit contradictory statements made by the witness but counsel does not have available the witness's proof of evidence which is the property of the other side.

The case for the defendant is put in exactly the same way with an opening speech and the examination of witnesses.[17] After the defence evidence has been heard, counsel for the defendant may make a closing speech summarising his or her view of the evidence and the law, to which counsel for the plaintiff may reply. Again, the judge has a discretion to indicate to counsel that argument on a particular point which may already have been decided or which is considered to be irrelevant need not be recited. At any point in the proceedings the judge may decide to look at the place in which the events in issue took place.[18] The judge would normally be accompanied at a "view" by the parties and their legal representatives.[19]

Ultimately, the judge is required to give a reasoned judgment, stating the conclusions on the factual issues in dispute and the legal implications of those findings of fact.[20]

B. WITNESSES AND EXPERT EVIDENCE

Witnesses may well be under pressure in giving evidence. It will be for counsel to decide who to call, taking account, for example, of whether they

[15] It is, of course, open to counsel to ask a witness to think again about an answer, but the discrepancy between the answer and the earlier statement may not be suggested. In an extreme case, counsel might seek to have the earlier statement put in as evidence at the end of the examination-in-chief: Civil Evidence Act 1968, s.2(2).

[15a] *Code of Conduct for the Bar of England and Wales* (1990), para. 607.

[16] *Ibid.*; *Written Standards for the Conduct of Professional Work; General Standards*, para. 6.1.

[17] Defence counsel is only permitted an opening speech if he or she is actually calling witnesses: R.S.C. Ord. 35, r. 7(4). In the county court, defence counsel must normally choose between an opening and a closing speech: O'Hare and Hill (1990), p. 495. Before proceeding to case presentation, defence counsel may submit that the plaintiff has failed to make out a case to which a response is required. A judge is unlikely to be prepared to accept such a submission, because the defendant has to agree to give evidence in the event of the submission being rejected: *Alexander* v. *Rayson* [1936] 1 K.B. 169; Barnard (1985), p. 202; O'Hare and Hill (1990), p. 496.

[18] R.S.C., Ord. 35, r. 8. The viewing is not necessarily restricted to places, although that is most common. The rule provides for an inspection of "any place or thing with respect to which any question arises." In *Line* v. *Taylor* (1862) 3 F. & F. 731 it had to be determined whether a dog was vicious. Serjeant Ballantine proposed that the dog be brought into court in the charge of his keeper. His opponent, Chambers, objected "as the experiment would be useless, while the dog was under the control of his keeper, and perilous, if he were not so." The dog was produced; the jury decided it was not vicious.

[19] *Goold* v. *Evans* [1951] T.L.R. 1189; *Salsbury* v. *Woodland* [1970] Q.B. 324.

[20] See below p. 708.

will provide evidence that is convincing enough to be a valuable aid to the presentation of the case.

The pressures on an expert witness will be less, particularly since such a witness will have had time to reflect upon the evidence to be given. In many civil trials part of the evidence is likely to be given by such witnesses. Expert witnesses are those asked to give evidence on technical matters, so that the court may form a proper view on matters of which it will have no other knowledge. Expert evidence is opinion evidence,[21] and opinion evidence is admissible from an expert, though not from an ordinary witness.[22] There are any number of matters on which expert evidence may be relevant: the extent and effect of proper safety procedures; handwriting; questions of the interpretation of foreign law; and many others.

The right of the parties to adduce expert evidence is somewhat restricted by the Civil Evidence Act 1972[23] and the Rules of the Supreme Court[24] and provision is made for pre-trial disclosure of such evidence in most cases. The object of such disclosure is to save expense, where possible, by discovering whether there is a real dispute between the parties and to avoid either party being taken by surprise on a technical matter and being forced to seek an adjournment. A party will not normally be allowed to call expert evidence at trial unless the disclosure procedure has been followed or unless the other party agrees.[25] It is, therefore, possible for the parties to make an explicit agreement that each side may call what expert evidence it wishes at trial, thus getting round the disclosure provisions, but the prospect of savings in time and money both before and at trial may well be a powerful inducement to disclose.

The expert witness may be different from an "ordinary" witness in that evidence is being given on matters within a field of knowledge, often after a prolonged examination. However, the expert witness is examined and cross-examined in just the same way. More importantly, the expert witness is just as much the "property" of one party. There is a temptation for parties to indulge in a battle of experts in court, sometimes hoping to win the point by the sheer volume of evidence or by the eminence of their witness(es). Some have argued[26] that it is unedifying to see leading members of the same profession being forced to disagree under skilful cross-examination, that such disagreement may serve to confuse rather than clarify the issues for the court, and that additional costs are unnecessarily incurred by taking evidence from two or more people on the same point. However, this is an almost inevitable consequence of the adversarial system of procedure and the power of the parties to adduce what relevant evidence they wish.

There is a power in the court to alleviate some of these problems by appointing an independent expert in any matter which is to be tried by judge alone.[27] This may seem to present an ideal solution to the problem of the battle of experts but it is subject to a serious limitation. The court may only make such an order on the application of a party to the action. The *Supreme*

[21] Which would not normally be admissible as evidence.
[22] See Sir R. Cross and C. Tapper, *Cross on Evidence* (7th ed., 1990), Chap. 13.
[23] s.2.
[24] Ord. 38, Part IV.
[25] Ord. 38, r. 36.
[26] See, *e.g.* A. Kenny, "The Expert in Court" (1983) 99 L.Q.R. 197.
[27] R.S.C., Ord. 40, r.1.

Court Practice notes that such applications have been very few in number.[28] Perhaps the court should be given the power to appoint an independent expert on its own authority even though that would begin to erode the adversarial system.

An additional power, which is useful in this context, is contained in the Supreme Court Act 1981, s.70, which allows the appointment of assessors or scientific advisers to assist in the hearing and disposal of the action. These are people who sit with the judge at the trial of the action and their role is considered more fully later in this chapter.

C. THE USE OF THE JURY IN CIVIL CASES

Jury trial is wholly exceptional and confined to a handful of cases. The erosion in the use of juries has been gradual. It appears to have begun with the introduction of the discretionary use of juries in all but six causes of action in 1833,[29] and was continued by the temporary suspension of jury trial beginning during the First World War and ending in 1925.[30]

The current position, now found in section 69 of the Supreme Court Act 1981, was first established in 1933.[31] Section 69 provides, first, for a qualified right to jury trial in some cases, and, secondly, for a discretion to order jury trial in other cases.

The qualified right to jury trial applies in cases of fraud,[32] libel, slander, malicious prosecution and false imprisonment.[33] Jury trial is to be granted unless "the court is of the opinion that the trial requires any prolonged examination of documents or accounts or any scientific or local examination which cannot conveniently be made with a jury. . . ."[34] This qualified right is exercised most frequently in defamation actions (that is libel and slander). The decision whether to permit jury trial depends upon a balance of the desire to grant trial by jury where requested and the need to take a realistic

---

[28] *The Supreme Court Practice 1991*, p. 676. There has been some judicial encouragement for the appointment of a court expert but this has obviously not had any significant effect: *Re Saxton* [1962] 1 W.L.R. 968, *per* Lord Denning M.R. at p. 973.

[29] Rules of the Supreme Court 1883, Ord. XXXVI. The causes of action in which there was a right to jury trial were: libel, slander, malicious prosecution, false imprisonment, seduction and breach of promise of marriage. These provisions formed the basis of the statutory reform in 1933. An analysis of the decline in the use of the jury, on the basis of statistics then available, is contained in R.M. Jackson, "The Incidence of Jury Trial during the Past Century" (1937) 1 M.L.R. 132. Jackson does not advance the view that the 1883 Rules were significant in reducing the number of jury trials, but the figures seem to support that contention. See also, M.G. Buckley, "Civil Trial by Jury" (1966) 19 C.L.P. 63. A good chronological account is provided by Bankes L.J. in *Ford* v. *Blurton* (1922) 38 T.L.R. 801, at pp. 802–803.

[30] The Juries Act 1918 provided for trial by judge alone unless the court ordered otherwise, subject to the right to jury trial in a category of cases slightly wider than that in the 1883 Rules. This provision was continued by the Administration of Justice Act 1920, but repealed by the Administration of Justice Act 1925.

[31] The Administration of Justice (Miscellaneous Provisions) Act 1933, s.6. The number of jury trials declined sharply after 1933.

[32] The meaning of fraud in this context was considered by Sir Robert Megarry V.-C. in *Stafford Winfield Cook* v. *Winfield* [1981] 1 W.L.R. 45. In criminal trials, the recent debate has centred upon the question of whether jury trials in (complex) fraud cases should be retained, see pp. 816–818, below.

[33] Or any other questions or issues prescribed: Supreme Court Act 1981, s.69(1)(c).

[34] Supreme Court Act 1981, s.69(1).

view about the material with which juries can deal in a trial and the length of time which a trial is expected to take or, put another way, the efficient administration of justice.[35] After considerable debate about the outcome of a number of celebrated libel actions,[36] the Court of Appeal now has the power either to order a new trial on the ground that damages awarded by a jury are excessive or inadequate or, without the agreement of the parties, to substitute for the sum awarded by the jury such sum as appears to the court to be proper.[37]

Further, the court has a discretion to order jury trial in other cases.[38] Jury trial should be ordered only in exceptional cases[39] and it will be very difficult to persuade a judge to exercise the discretion to order trial by jury. The factors to be taken into account are: the need for uniformity in the award of damages in personal injury cases, the jury being ignorant of the conventional figures in comparable cases;[40] that in such cases the severity[41] or unusual[42] nature of the injuries are not exceptional circumstances, but if they are unique or nearly so,[43] jury trial may be appropriate; the possibility of dishonesty[44] or deliberate lying; the fact that the honour and integrity of the person applying for jury trial may be at stake;[45] the fact that trial without a jury is speedier and less expensive;[46] the proposition that, in the circumstances, trial by judge alone is "more likely to achieve a just result than trial by jury."[47] Further, Lord Diplock indicated that jury trial should not be ordered either simply because there might be a conflict of evidence, since many cases will involve issues of credibility and that is not a sufficient reason to depart from the "usual rule" of trial by judge alone[48] or simply because a

[35] *Beta Construction Ltd.* v. *Channel Four Television Co. Ltd.*, *The Independent*, November 7, 1989. The national importance of the issues may render jury trial appropriate even if there is considerable documentary evidence: *Rothermere* v. *Times Newspapers* [1973] 1 W.L.R. 448. The case concerned an article written by Bernard Levin in *The Times*, March 19, 1971, entitled "Profit and dishonour in Fleet Street." However, due care must be taken not to overburden the jury, as may have occurred in *Orme* v. *Associated Newspapers Group*, March 31, 1981 (unreported) (Q.B.D.); December 20, 1982 (unreported) (C.A.), where the trial, involving alleged defamation of the Moonies, lasted more than five months and 117 witnesses were called. Lawyers are required to take great care in estimating the length of trials so as to avoid hardship for potential jurors: *Practice Direction* (*Juries: Length of Trials*) [1981] 1 W.L.R. 1129.

[36] *e.g.* the cases brought by Jeffrey Archer, Koo Stark and Sonia Sutcliffe.

[37] Courts and Legal Services Act 1990, s.8 and R.S.C., Ord. 59, r. 11 as amended by S.I. 1990 No. 2599.

[38] Supreme Court Act 1981, s.69(3).

[39] *Ward* v. *James* [1966] 1 Q.B. 273, per Lord Denning M.R., at p. 303. In the event, this case was sent for jury trial but the court was influenced by factors peculiar to it. The point was emphasised in *Williams* v. *Beasley* [1973] 1 W.L.R. 1295, per Lord Diplock at p. 1299H.

[40] *Ward* v. *James* [1966] 1 Q.B. 273, per Lord Denning M.R. at pp. 296–300, 303.

[41] *Sims* v. *William Howard and Son Ltd.* [1964] 2 Q.B. 409.

[42] *Watts* v. *Manning* [1964] 1 W.L.R. 623.

[43] *Hodges* v. *Harland and Wolff Ltd.* [1965] 1 W.L.R. 523. In this highly unusual case the plaintiff was injured whilst using a diesel driven air compressor. The spindle of the machine caught in his trousers and avulsed his penis and scrotal skin. Jury trial was ordered. The observations of Davies L.J. at pp. 1087–1088 are helpful in setting out the difficulties of jury trial.

[44] *Sims* v. *William Howard and Son Ltd.* [1964] 2 Q.B. 409, per Pearson L.J. at p. 419.

[45] *Ward* v. *James* [1966] 1 Q.B. 273, per Lord Denning M.R. at p. 295; *Williams* v. *Beasley* [1973] 1 W.L.R. 1295, per Lord Diplock at p. 1298H.

[46] *Williams* v. *Beasley* [1973] 1 W.L.R. 1295, per Lord Diplock at p. 1299H.

[47] *Ibid.* per Lord Diplock at p. 1299H.

[48] *Ibid.* per Lord Diplock at p. 1298–9.

party has "the mistaken belief . . . that judges as a class are likely to be biased against him or in favour of his opponent" since to decide on that basis would provide such beliefs with credence, whereas the system is based upon "an impartial judiciary."[49]

If a jury trial does take place it, as in criminal proceedings, is controlled by the provisions of the Juries Act 1974. The qualification for service of jurors, the procedure for summoning, the compilation of panels, the ballot and swearing of jurors, and the right to challenge for cause are all exactly the same for civil and criminal trials.[50] Majority verdicts may be accepted in civil cases, although there is greater flexibility than in criminal matters since the parties to the action may proceed by agreement with an incomplete jury.[51] The discretion to exclude a juror from service which may be exercised by the appropriate officer or by the court[52] is likely to be exercised more freely in civil matters where there may be considerable hardship or inconvenience caused by a long trial.[53]

Should the Jury be Retained in Civil Cases?

If the debates on the Supreme Court Bill 1981 are any guide, this is, indeed, an academic question. Parliament showed itself unwilling to countenance any further restriction on the right to jury trial, let alone its abolition.[54]

The disadvantages of jury trial appear to be the additional time, and consequent additional expense, of a jury trial, the variability of jury verdicts, the potential hardship and inconvenience suffered by individual jurors in lengthy cases, the unrealistic expectations that lay people should listen to and comprehend complex and extensive evidence, the unpredictability of jury verdicts and the reluctance of the Court of Appeal to interfere with jury awards, and the additional burden which may be placed on counsel and judge where complex questions of law are in issue.[55]

These reasons are sound pragmatic grounds for the proposition that jury trial is not the "best" mode of trial for all civil actions and that trial by judge alone would normally be preferable. But are any of the reasons sufficiently strong to support the view that trial by jury should not be permissible?

---

[49] *Ibid.* p. 1299H.
[50] See below, pp. 799–809.
[51] Juries Act 1974, s.17.
[52] Juries Act 1974, s.9(2), (4).
[53] *Practice Direction (Juries: Length of Trial)* [1981] 1 W.L.R. 1129.
[54] Jacob (1987), pp. 156–160. Similarities with the argument with regard to the jury in criminal trials will be noted, although the functions and role of the jury in criminal trials may well be different: see pp. 813–819, below.
[55] These defects of the jury as a mode of trial are culled from various sources including: M.G. Buckley, "Civil Trial by Jury" (1966) 19 C.L.P. 63; W.R. Cornish, *The Jury* (1968), Chap. 8; P. Devlin, *Trial by Jury* (1956), pp. 130–135; *Hodges* v. *Harland and Wolff Ltd.* [1965] 1 W.L.R. 523; *Ward* v. *James* [1966] 1 Q.B. 273; and the *Report of the Committee on Defamation* (Cmnd. 5909, 1975) (The Faulks Committee). Some of the disadvantages of jury trial are illustrated by *Orme* v. *Associated Newspapers Ltd.* (see n. 35 above), a case involving the alleged defamation of the director of The Holy Spirit Association for the Unification of World Christianity. The trial began in October 1980 and lasted until the end of March 1981. 117 witnesses were called. Very many documents had to be considered. The closing speeches lasted several days. The original estimate of the length of the trial was six to seven weeks. This case lead to the proposal of an, ultimately unsuccessful, amendment to the Supreme Court Bill which would have meant that trial by jury could be denied where the length of the trial would make it inconvenient for a jury to try the action.

The Faulks Committee on Defamation[56] recommended restrictions on the use of juries in defamation actions whilst rejecting arguments for their total abolition. The Committee concluded that in defamation cases the court should have the same discretion to order jury trial as in other civil cases and that the function of the jury should be limited to deciding issues of liability, leaving the assessment of damages to the judge.[57] The following summarises the view of the Committee:

> "We believe that much of the support for jury trials is emotional, and derives from the undoubted value of juries in serious *criminal* cases, where they stand between the prosecuting authority and the citizen. But the true function of the civil jury is to weigh facts impersonally and recompense the claimant for an injury that he may have sustained— tasks for which the judge is trained by many years of experience and for which jurors have no training at all."[58]

Is it right to describe the support for the jury as "emotional"? Various distinguished judges have declared the constitutional importance of the right to jury trial. For example, Atkin L.J. in *Ford* v. *Blurton* described jury trial as "the bulwark of liberty, the shield of the poor from the rich and the powerful."[59] Although, the argument of Atkin L.J. may appear to be more suited to the jury in criminal trials, there is some truth in it in relation to civil trials. However, if judges are independent of the state and other vested interests,[60] perhaps the argument has lost much of its force. A different argument is that it is desirable to involve as many people as possible in the administration of justice[61] and that the jury stands between the judges and the person in the street to ensure that ordinary standards are applied in the doing of justice.[62]

Even if there may be criticism of the distinction between the five specified causes of action and other civil cases, trial by jury is unlikely to be abolished in civil matters, but responsibility lies with the judges for ensuring that the worst features of jury trial are not often evident.

D. THE ROLE OF THE JUDGE

In civil matters the judge normally sits alone to determine the outcome of the action. The incidence of jury trial has already been explained, but there are a number of situations in which the judge may have the assistance of others sitting with him or her. The composition of the Restrictive Practices

[56] *Report of the Committee on Defamation* (Cmnd. 5909, 1975), Chap. 17 gives a very good account of the role of the jury in defamation actions.
[57] *Ibid.* paras. 455–457.
[58] *Ibid.* para. 496.
[59] (1922) 38 T.L.R. 801 at 805. See also, to similar effect, Bankes L.J. in the same case. The same point was made by Mr. Frank Dobson M.P. in the debates on the Supreme Court Bill when he said: "Jury service is more important to the preservation of individual liberty and the preservation of our judicial system than all the scurvy race of lawyers put together."
[60] See above, pp. 225–231.
[61] See, *e.g.* the evidence of Sir Peter Rawlinson Q.C. and Viscount Dilhorne given to the Faulks Committee (1975), para. 477.
[62] On a pragmatic level, Lord Denning M.R. supported the jury for the protection of a person's honour and integrity or to discover when one party may be lying: *Ward* v. *James* [1966] 1 Q.B. 273, at p. 295.

Court,[63] with lay members and High Court judges, exemplifies the formal introduction of lay expertise into the judicial process, but there is a general power vested in the High Court to call in the aid of one or more assessors or scientific advisers in particular cases.[64]

Assessors are used especially in admiralty proceedings in the Queen's Bench Division,[65] but there is nothing to prevent a judge using an assessor in other cases. It may cause expense and inconvenience to the parties if the hearing has to be adjourned so that the judge may find and appoint an appropriate expert, but there is strong support for that course of action,[66] in preference to obtaining assistance from an expert after the hearing has concluded and before judgment is given.[67]

Scientific advisers may be appointed in an action for the infringement of a patent and will render similar assistance to the judge.[68] The role of both assessor and scientific adviser is to listen to the evidence and give the judge such assistance as may be required in formulating the judgment and, if an opinion is given on the outcome, that opinion and the reasons for it may be taken into account by the Court of Appeal in the event of an appeal.[69]

In a civil action it may prove difficult for the judge to refrain from intervening with questions and observations. However, the judge does not have to attain the standards of objectivity and neutrality as appertain in a criminal trial, since usually no jury is present. The procedure is relatively flexible in a civil trial and the absence of the jury enables the judge to take a more positive line over matters which may be considered to be irrelevant or uncontentious. However, the judge must not take such an active part in the case that it appears that counsel is deprived of the conduct of the action. Denning L.J. put the judge's role as follows:

"The judge's part . . . is to hearken to the evidence, only himself asking question of witnesses when it is necessary to clear up any point that has been overlooked or left obscure; to see that the advocates behave themselves seemly and keep to the rules laid down by law; to exclude irrelevancies and discourage repetition; to make sure by wise intervention that he follows the points that the advocates are making and can assess their work; and at the end to make up his mind where the truth lies."[70]

If sitting alone, a judge may take time to decide where the truth lies or, more accurately, whether the plaintiff has satisfied the burden of proof,[71] and give a reserved judgment at a later date, or an extempore judgment may be given at the conclusion of the hearing. If sitting with a jury, the judge must sum up the evidence and direct on the law as would be done in a trial on indictment.[72] Ultimately judgment will be given.

---

[63] A further example is the Employment Appeal Tribunal. For the composition of these courts, see pp. 86–88, 59–60, above.
[64] Supreme Court Act 1981, s.70 and R.S.C., Ord. 33, 1.6.
[65] Where the assessor is normally one or more of the Elder Brethren of Trinity House.
[66] From Devlin J. in *Esso Petroleum Co. Ltd.* v. *Southport Corporation* [1956] A.C. 218 at pp. 222–223. His view was supported by the House of Lords in the same case.
[67] *Ibid.* at p. 223.
[68] Supreme Court Act 1981, s.70. See also *Supreme Court Practice 1991*, p. 577.
[69] *Hettersley and Sons* v. *G. Hodgson Ltd.* (1905) 21 T.L.R. 178.
[70] *Jones* v. *National Coal Board* [1957] 2 Q.B. 55 at p. 64.
[71] *i.e.* whether the plaintiff has proved his or her case on a balance of probabilities.
[72] See below pp. 789–794.

E. THE JUDGMENT AND REMEDIES

A judgment is a reasoned decision in which the judge will normally set out the facts of the case as he or she has decided, and give the conclusions on the law applicable to them. Some of the arguments put by counsel may be rehearsed so as to set the decision in context,[73] and an opinion is likely to be given on all matters relating to the action which might be relevant if the losing party were to appeal. In particular, there may be findings of fact which are not crucial to the judgment given at first instance but which might become relevant if the Court of Appeal were to take a different view of the law. The trial judge will be attempting to avoid the expense and difficulty of a new trial if the appellate court changes a part of the judgment.[74]

The remedies available in civil proceedings are various, dependent upon the action being sought by the plaintiff.[75] There is an important adage worthy of repetition. It states that where there is a legal right there is, or ought to be, a legal remedy and where there is no remedy there is no right. There is consequently an extensive range of remedies, which may be added to or varied[76] by judicial decision or the Rules Committee establishing the Rules of the Supreme Court.[77] The remedies that are available have varied according to whether the action is one in the High Court or the county court. This will be changed when section 3 of the Courts and Legal Services Act 1990 comes into force. Section 3 provides that county courts may make the same remedial orders as the High Court.[78] The real significance of this change for present purposes is with regard to the enforcement of judgments, considered in section F below. In addition to damages, the most likely remedy sought in an action in the Queen's Bench as considered here and in Chapter 11, students should be aware that other remedies are available. In particular, the plaintiff may be seeking the recovery or restitution of property,[79] one of the many equitable remedies, such as an order for specific performance[80] or an injunction,[81] or a declaration.[82]

---

[73] Because it is the responsibility of the parties to advance argument on the issues which they wish to be decided it is always important to know whether a particular line of argument has been canvassed or not when assessing a judgment. In respect of appellate decisions reported in the Law Reports series, the major arguments of counsel are normally set out as part of the report.

[74] *e.g.* although a judge may find against a plaintiff on the question of the defendant's liability in negligence, the quantum of damages will be determined lest the Court of Appeal reverses on the liability point. If no finding had been made on quantum the issue would have to be the subject of another trial.

[75] See, generally, F.H. Lawson, *Remedies of English Law* (2nd ed., 1980) and M. Tilbury, M. Noone and B. Ketcher, *Remedies* (1988) (this is an Australian work drawing on considerable English material).

[76] If a new remedy affects the substantive law, it can only be created by Act of Parliament.

[77] See Jacobs (1987), pp. 170–172.

[78] County courts will not have the power to order mandamus, certiorari or prohibition or orders of kinds to be prescribed by the Lord Chancellor.

[79] As to recovery of land, see Lawson (1980) and A.M. Prichard, *Squatting* (1981). Specific recovery of chattels is possible, although an order may provide the defendant with an option of retaining the property and paying its value instead.

[80] Available to enforce contractual obligations.

[81] The prime form of injunction is prohibitory since it forces a defendant to desist from wrongful conduct or forbids wrongful conduct when it has not even started, *i.e.* the *quia timet* injunction. A mandatory injunction requires the doing of some act.

[82] R.S.C., Ord. 15.

Damages is the common law term for an order requiring payment of money. An award of damages may be made in relation to a vast range of wrongs and indebtedness.[83] The traditional division of damages is into liquidated and unliquidated damages: liquidated where the plaintiff specifies a set sum of money as owed at law in the original claim; unliquidated where the court must calculate the sum to be paid if liability is established, unless there is agreement on the quantum of damages between the parties. The method by which unliquidated damages are assessed is of most concern.

Damages can be claimed primarily on a contract or tort claim, and the basis for awarding damages will be slightly different dependent upon the action. The basic theory of damages for contract is that they should provide a sum that will, financially at least, fulfil the claimant's expectation under the promise made. The basic theory of tort damages is that the claimant, so far as money can, should be returned to the pre-existing position before the wrong was done. However, it would appear that, despite the theoretical differences, modern law is taking a more pragmatic attitude.

In practice, High Court judges are most commonly called upon to assess damages in cases where the defendant has negligently inflicted personal injuries upon the plaintiff.[84] Damages are usually awarded in a lump sum[85] and, as the action lies in tort, are designed to compensate the plaintiff for his or her losses. There are normally two basic aspects of an award: (i) compensation for non-pecuniary losses, and (ii) compensation for pecuniary or economic losses. Under the first head there may be damages for pain and suffering and loss of amenity[86] or, where the part of a body injured has no apparent function, the injury itself.[87] Damages for loss of amenity are awarded roughly in accordance with a tariff dependent on the seriousness of the injury or injuries.[88] Under the second head fall damages for such items as lost earnings[89] and medical expenses.

For example, in *Lim Poh Choo* v. *Camden and Islington Area Health Authority*[90] the plaintiff, an N.H.S. registrar, suffered serious brain damage

[83] Whilst the chapter concentrates on actions in contract and tort, an award of damages can be made in relation to an action in quasi-contract, in certain equity actions, *e.g.*, where recission is allowed for innocent misrepresentation, or where a trustee commits a breach of trust. Further, certain tribunals may also make awards of compensation, *e.g.*, an industrial tribunal for unfair dismissal.

[84] See W.V.H. Rogers, *Winfield and Jolowicz on the Law of Tort* (13th ed., 1989), Chap. 23; M. A. Jones, *A Textbook on Torts* (2nd ed., 1989), pp. 373–397. See also above, pp. 497–498, 501.

[85] *Ibid.* There are exceptions to this general rule: (1) there is now a procedure for the award of provisional damages in personal injuries actions where there is a possibility that there will be a serious deterioration in the plaintiff's condition, thus a sum can be awarded without regard to that eventuality but, if it occurs, the plaintiff may return to court, see s.32A of the Supreme Court Act 1981 and Jones (1989), pp. 379–380; (2) the private arrangement of a "structured settlement" that is payment of damages in periodic payments, which can take account of related losses as they occur, either for a fixed period of time or until the death of the plaintiff, see Jones (1989), pp. 380–381. For other exceptions, see, *ibid.* pp. 377–381.

[86] *e.g.* damages for the loss of a leg, which may be increased where the plaintiff was a keen sports player whose enjoyment of life is thus substantially impaired.

[87] *e.g.* a spleen: *Forster* v. *Pugh* [1955] C.L.Y. 741.

[88] Details of damages awarded in personal injury cases are given in *Kemp and Kemp on the Quantum of Damages* (Revised ed., 1982).

[89] In the most serious cases there will be the difficult task of estimating the loss of earnings in the future.

[90] [1980] A.C. 174.

after a minor operation. She was ultimately awarded £229,298.64. This included £20,000 for pain and suffering and loss of amenities; £3,956 for expenses to the date of trial; £16,500 for the cost of care in Malaysia; £1,923 for travelling expenses; £4,226.64 for the cost of care in the United Kingdom to date; £14,213 for loss of earnings to the date of trial; £76,800 for the cost of future care and £92,000 for the loss of future earnings including pension rights.

At the end of the judgment, counsel for the successful party must ask formally for judgment to be entered for the client in the terms which the judge has indicated. Counsel may ask for "judgment for the plaintiff for £229,298.64," or "judgment for the defendant and that the plaintiff's claim be dismissed." At this stage the question of any interest payable on a money judgment will be raised by counsel, who will also ask for costs.[91] Traditionally, money judgments were expressed in sterling, but since 1975 it has been possible for a court to give judgment in a foreign currency.[92]

The final responsibility rests with the successful party, who relies upon his or her solicitor. He or she must draw up the terms of the judgment on a special form and have it entered in the judgment book kept in the Judgment Office.[93] Having obtained judgment, the successful party must go on to enforce it. Contrary, perhaps, to expectations, that party's troubles may only just be beginning![94]

F. ENFORCING JUDGMENT: EXECUTION[95]

"[T]he machinery of the enforcement of the judgments and orders of the court constitute the very foundation of the judicial process. It represents the coercive power of the court in the exercise of its judicial authority. It expresses the will of the state to buttress the judiciary ... and makes their judgments and orders authoritative and obligatory, binding and conclusive."[96]

If judgment is obtained, the order of the court may be declaratory or constitutive[97] and nothing more need be done. In most instances, however,

---

[91] See pp. 472–475 above.

[92] *Miliangos* v. *George Frank (Textiles) Ltd.* [1976] A.C. 443, not following the previous authority, *Re United Railways of Havana and Regla Warehouses Ltd.* [1961] A.C. 1007. On the precedent implications of this decision, see above pp. 386–387.

[93] R.S.C., Ord. 42, r.5. See *Supreme Court Practice 1991*, pp. 697–701.

[94] One of the considerations which a plaintiff must have in mind at the commencement of an action is whether the defendant will be able to satisfy any judgment that may be given against him or her.

[95] Jacob (1987), pp. 185–210; Sir Jack I.H. Jacob, "The Enforcement of Judgment Debts" in *The Reform of Civil Procedural Law* (1982); J. O'Hare and R. N. Hill, *Civil Litigation* (5th ed., 1990), Chaps. 24, 25. As to the enforcement of foreign judgments and the enforcement of judgments outside England and Wales, see O'Hare & Hill (1990), pp. 558–561.

[96] Jacob (1987), pp. 185–186.

[97] "Constitutive" orders are extremely various and extend across many areas of law. Examples in the civil law are: adoption and legitimation orders, award of custody and guardianship, divorces, appointment of trustees, dissolution of partnerships, liquidation of companies, adjudication in bankruptcy. Sometimes the order merely records a fact, an example being the declaration that a seeming marriage was in fact always null and void. See Lawson (1980), Chap. 17.

the order will require the performance of some further act or acts or the abstention from acts. The law appears to lean heavily in favour of inducement rather than direct compulsion. The form of the court order will frequently demonstrate this: thus the normal order in an action for damages requires the defendant to pay the plaintiff the specified figure.[98]

Many defendants obey court orders out of law-abiding motives. Others will be influenced by the appreciation that practical procedures exist to secure performance or obedience. These procedures might be said to form a system of enforcement, which Jacob, however, has described as being

> "an unplanned, unsystematic, haphazard, complex system. It operates, especially in relation to money judgments, largely on a hit-or-miss basis. In relation to both money and non-money judgments, it is in part effective, but in part it is ineffective, inefficient, somewhat random and sometimes oppressive."[99]

The procedures that exist are variously derived from the common law, equity and statute. They are primarily aimed at specific forms of judgment, but they are capable of being used for any type of judgment if they can be effective. Thus sequestration, authorising the seizure of all or any property of the defendant within the jurisdiction, imposition of a fine and committal to prison are all drastic sanctions suitable for flagrant breaches of orders such as injunctions, but in extreme circumstances they can be used to enforce other types of judgment where there has been a civil contempt of court.[1] Imprisonment for a few civil debts may also be imposed, separately from a finding of contempt of court.[2]

A brief description of the main execution orders available follows, but prior to seeking such an order it may be necessary to discover the debtor's means. This can be achieved by an oral examination of the judgment debtor in the High Court or a county court.[3]

(1) Enforcement of money judgments[4]

(a) *Fieri facias or warrant of execution*

These forms of enforcement operate against the debtor's chattels and

---

[98] R.S.C., Appendix A, Forms Nos. 39–51. In the ordinary procedure for recovering land, the modern formula is that the defendant "do give" possession to the plaintiff: R.S.C., Appendix A, Forms 42, 44, 45 and C.C. Form 134.

[99] Jacob (1987), p. 188.

[1] *Ibid.* pp. 205–210.

[2] *Ibid.* pp. 198–202. Since the Administration of Justice Act 1970, s.11, imprisonment, through the issue of a judgment summons, has been retained only for debtors on maintenance orders, debtors for the payment of taxes and certain specified statutory contributions and liabilities: see O'Hare and Hill (1990), p. 558 and R. Blackford, *County Court Practice Handbook* (9th ed., 1989), Chap. 23. The *Report of the Committee on One-Parent Families* (Cmnd. 5629, 1974) recommended that imprisonment for maintenance defaulters be abolished. Jacob recommends that imprisonment for all classes of debt should be abolished ((1987), p. 202) although it appears that some Circuit judges would welcome the restoration of imprisonment for civil debt (*ibid.*, p. 250, n. 7).

[3] See O'Hare & Hill (1990), pp. 544–546 and Blackford (1989), pp. 143–145.

[4] See O'Hare and Hill (1990), Chap. 24 and Blackford (1989), Chaps. 20, 22 and 24.

goods. The High Court form is the writ of *fieri facias*. This writ is issued to the sheriff of the county where the defendant's goods are located and the sheriff's officers enforce the writ by seizing goods sufficient to cover in value the amount owed under the judgment, the costs of execution and expenses.

The county court form is the warrant of execution which requires the court bailiff to carry out the order. The seized goods must be expected to cover only the amount owed under the judgment and the costs of execution.

The exercise of this concurrent jurisdiction is vast. In 1989, 80,010 writs of *fieri facias* were issued and 1,230,063 warrants of execution were issued.[5] It has been suggested that the debtor's goods "which are exempt from seizure in execution are woefully inadequate both in their description and their value."[6] The Courts and Legal Services Act has since amended the list.[6a] The writ of *fieri facias* would appear to be overused, but the real vice is that the concurrent jurisdiction creates inequality in civil procedural law, because there are two different systems of enforcement for the same amount of judgment debt, producing a different quality of justice for litigants in the same situation.[7]

(b) *Garnishee proceedings*

The successful party, the judgment creditor, obtains the judgment debt by "attachment" of a debt owed to the judgment debtor by a third party, *i.e.* a debt owed to the judgment debtor by a third party is automatically paid to the judgment creditor. In 1989, 1,548 garnishee orders were made absolute in the High Court,[8] that is the third party was required to pay the debt to the judgment creditor. Using a slightly different procedure, 4,006 garnishee orders were issued in the county courts.[9]

(c) *Attachment of earnings*

A garnishee order is not available with regard to earnings. The Attachment of Earnings Act 1971 for the first time empowered the courts to enforce employers to make deductions from the earnings of employees to be paid into court to satisfy the employees' debts. This is primarily a jurisdiction of the county court, the High Court only having power to attach for

---

[5] *Judicial Statistics 1989* (Cm. 1154, 1990), Tables 3.10 and 4.16 respectively. 1,125 warrants to enforce High Court judgments and orders were issued by the county courts: *ibid.*, Table 4.16; and see Blackford (1989), Chap. 21.

[6] Jacob (1987), p. 196.

[6a] S.15, following the recommendations of the *Report on the Enforcement of Judgment Debts* (Cmnd. 3909, 1969), para. 675, has provided a new list of goods which are exempt from seizure: "(i) such tools, books, vehicles and other items of equipment as are necessary to that person for use personally by him in his employment, business or vocation; (ii) such clothing, bedding, furniture, household equipment and provisions as are necessary for satisfying the basic domestic needs of that person and his family." See D. Greenberg, "Enforcement Law and the Courts and Legal Services Act 1990" (1990) 140 N.L.J. 1794.

[7] Jacob (1987), pp. 197–198.

[8] *Judicial Statistics 1989*, Table 3.10.

[9] *Ibid.*, Table 4.16.

payment of maintenance orders, and not judgments generally.[10] In 1989, 47,244 orders were made to secure the payment of a judgment debt.[11]

(d) Charging orders

Charging orders are statutory orders whereby charges are created on property.[12] The judgment creditor becomes in effect an equitable chargee with rights to recoup his or her debt from income of the property or from its sale in due course. Consequently, the debtor cannot, for example, sell the property without satisfying the debt or having the order transferred to other property. The principal property so chargeable is land or any interest in land, and the charge is registrable under the Land Charges Act 1972. Government and company stocks, dividends and interest on such stock, and moneys in court may also be subjected to a charging order.[13] In 1989, 39,801 charging orders were made.[14]

(e) Equitable execution: appointment of a receiver

Where none of the other means of execution is likely to be effective, it is possible for a receiver to be appointed to take income due to the judgment debtor and apply it towards the debt owed to the judgment creditor.[15] Because of the effectiveness of the other means of execution and since it is cumbersome, this is a rarely used means of enforcement.[16]

(2) Possession orders[17]

(a) Land

The normal procedure is to apply for a writ of possession in the High Court[18] or a warrant for possession in the county court.[19] The bailiffs acting under the writ clear all people from the premises, whether they were parties to the action or not. This is a very important procedure, because it may well be dangerous for a successful party otherwise to attempt to occupy land which has been awarded by the court. In 1989, 1,711 possession writs were issued by the High Court and 29,287 county court warrants for possession of land were executed.[20]

---

[10] Attachment of Earnings Act 1971, s.1. The procedural amendments introduced by the Courts and Legal Services Act 1990, Sched. 17, will make collection arrangements more flexible and may pave the way for this procedure to be handled by one central office: see Greenberg (1990).

[11] *Judicial Statistics 1989*, Table 4.17. In the same year 1,138 orders were made in the county court to secure the payment of maintenance: *ibid.*

[12] Charging Orders Act 1979, s.1; R.S.C., Ord. 50; C.C.R., Ord. 31. County court orders must be sought where the sum in question is less than £5,000.

[13] Charging Orders Act 1979, s.2; R.S.C., Ord. 50; C.C.R., Ord. 31.

[14] *Judicial Statistics 1989*, Tables 3.10, 4.16, of which 33,147 were made in a county court: *ibid.* Table 4.16.

[15] R.S.C., Ord. 51; C.C.R., Ord. 32. See O'Hare and Hill (1990), p. 557 and Blackford (1989), p. 176.

[16] In 1989, 7 appointments were made by the High Court: *Judicial Statistics 1989,* Table 3.10.

[17] See O'Hare & Hill (1990), pp. 563–564 and Blackford (1989), pp. 140–147.

[18] R.S.C., Ord., 45(3). Special rules under Ord. 88 apply to a mortgage action.

[19] C.C.R., Ord. 25.

[20] *Judicial Statistics 1989*, Tables 3.10, 4.16. The county court issued 85,310 warrants for possession of land.

(b) *Goods*

Judgments for delivery of goods may or may not contain an option in the defendant to pay the value instead of giving up the goods. Where there is no such option, execution is by way of writ of delivery in the High Court which instructs the sheriff to cause the goods to be delivered to the plaintiff.[21] In the county court a similar procedure is undertaken through the warrant of delivery.[22] In 1989, the High Court issued 117 writs for delivery and 2,441 county court warrants for delivery of goods were executed.[23]

(3) Mandatory and prohibitory order[24]

(a) *Specific performance*

A failure by a seller to execute an instrument in response to a judgment for specific performance may be overcome by the appointment of someone else (usually a Chancery master or a registrar, now a district judge) to execute it in the seller's stead.

(b) *Injunction*

The injunctions that may be imposed as a means of execution are the same as those that may be imposed as a remedy consequent upon the trial.[25]

Such enforcement procedures form the largest component of the work of the civil courts, amounting for a substantial proportion of their resources.[26] This is reflected in the figures quoted from the *Judicial Statistics 1989*. For this reason, and for the long expressed concern about the enforcement system, debt enforcement procedures were examined as a part of the Civil Justice Review.[27] As a consequence of the factual study,[28] the Review identified the following considerations which should form the basis of any system of debt recovery through the courts:

"(i) The system should aim to recover as much as possible of the debt quickly, cheaply and simply.
 (ii) Creditors should be able to obtain adequate information about debtors' circumstances.
(iii) Maximum information should be available about debtors on public files.
(iv) There should be machinery for bringing together multiple debts.
 (v) The period for repayment should not last indefinitely and a debtor should be restored to full economic status as soon as possible.
(vi) Debtors and their families should not be subjected to unwarranted hardship, fear or humiliation."[29]

---

[21] R.S.C., Ord. 45.
[22] C.C.R., Ord. 26.
[23] *Judicial Statistics 1989*, Tables 3.10, 4.16. The county courts issued 11,723 warrants for the delivery of goods.
[24] O'Hare & Hill (1990), pp. 564–565 and Blackford (1989), Chap. 33.
[25] See above p. 708.
[26] *Civil Justice Review* (1988), para. 534(i).
[27] *Ibid.* Chap. 9. "Debt enforcement" is not limited to the enforcement of judgment debts: *ibid.*, para. 534.
[28] *Civil Justice Review*; Consultation Paper No. 4 (1986).
[29] *Civil Justice Review* (1988), para. 620.

Based on these considerations, a series of recommendations was made, including: changing the responsibility for executing county court judgments; improving the county court bailiff system by changing its management, particularly by integrating it into the court service, and by redefining its duties; creating a manual setting out the duties of a county court bailiff which should be made publicly available; inviting detailed reform of the law relating to the High Court enforcement officers; and introducing plain English into the terminology.[30] The possibility of requiring all claims to start in the county court was not pursued.[31]

Whilst these reforms, if introduced, would go a considerable way to solving some of the problems with enforcement, they do not address Jacob's central demand which is that the system is so confusing, complex and unfair that radical reform is called for in the form of the creation of a Central Enforcement Authority.[32] Such a system would have the attributes of simplicity and speed, efficiency and effectiveness. The Authority "would operate as an integrated system for the enforcement of judgments and would enjoy exclusive jurisdiction for this purpose and thus it would produce uniformity and equality of treatment for all judgments and eliminate procedural anomalies and differences between the different courts that enforce judgments at present. It would provide the mechanism for enforcing through one office, attached to each of the county courts throughout the country, all the judgments of the civil courts and tribunals."[33]

G. ARBITRATION IN THE COUNTY COURT

The significance of the arbitration procedure in small claims in the county court is growing. In 1989, 52,999 cases were set down for arbitration and 49,829 arbitrations were heard.[34] The number of arbitrations exceeded the number of trials.

The situations in which a small claim will reach arbitration in the county court and the standard terms of reference for the arbitration have been set out in Chapter 11.[35] We only need to remind ourselves at this point of the particular features of the arbitration which distinguish it from the trial procedure we have been considering in this chapter.

The strict rules of evidence do not apply to the hearing[36] and it is intended to be informal. In order to afford a fair and equal opportunity to each party to present their case, the arbitrator is free to adopt whatever form of procedure is thought to be appropriate. This clearly marks a substantial

[30] *Ibid.* paras. 627–651.
[31] *Ibid.* paras. 612–3. At present all applications for charging orders when the judgment debt is within the monetary jurisdictional limits of the county court must be made in the county court and not in the High Court: Charging Orders Act 1979, ss.1(2) and 7, see Jacob (1987), p. 193, which Sir Jack regard as a model principle to apply to all processes for the enforcement of money judgments.
[32] *Ibid.* pp. 271–273. This proposal builds on that of an Enforcement Office made by the Payne Report (1969).
[33] Jacob (1987), p. 271.
[34] *Judicial Statistics 1989*, Table 4.13.
[35] See above, pp. 532–533.
[36] Unless the court on making the reference to arbitration determines otherwise: C.C.R., Ord. 19, r. 5.

deviation from the adversarial procedure of trial, although quite how flexibly the procedures are operated will depend upon the district judge who is likely to be the arbitrator.

In one respect the rules for the arbitration seem to be narrower than the rules in the High Court. There is a power given to the arbitrator to consult an expert, or call for an expert report, or invite an expert to attend the hearing as an assessor, *but only with the consent of the parties*.[37] As against the power of the High Court to appoint an assessor of its own volition,[38] this is a surprising limitation and, although the arbitrator's own initiative may be used in suggesting expert evidence (in the High Court it must be on the application of a party[39]), either party may frustrate the arbitrator's objective. It is presumably to prevent additional cost being forced on the parties that the arbitrator does not have the power to call evidence of his or her own motion, but that problem might be circumvented by a requirement that the arbitrator gain the agreement of the parties to a reasonable fee for the evidence, rather than to the obtaining of the evidence.

However, this restriction does not seem to be affecting the growth of arbitration in the county court and it will be interesting to see whether the apparent popularity of the procedure has any effect on the adversarial procedure adopted in other courts.

[37] This power may be exercised at any time before the decision of the arbitrator is given, and either before or after the hearing: C.C.R., Ord. 19, r. 5.
[38] Supreme Court Act 1981, s.70; see p. 707 above.
[39] R.S.C., Ord. 40, r. 6.

CHAPTER 15

THE TRIBUNAL HEARING

AT the hearing, the chairman of the tribunal has the difficult task of ensuring that a sufficient level of informality is achieved so that the parties do not feel inhibited in putting their respective cases, whilst maintaining some procedural and evidentiary safeguards so that the rights of the parties are not prejudiced in an unacceptable way.

We made the point in the previous chapter on tribunals that it is scarcely possible to choose a "typical" tribunal and the observations hereafter draw on a variety of sources. However, just as there are common problems to be solved in devising an appropriate pre-hearing procedure, so there are common problems in the conduct of hearings. What procedural rules, if any, should be followed? What evidence will be admitted? What role should the chairman play and what responsibilities does he or she have? What sort of representation, if any, should be permitted/encouraged, and how should it be funded?

A. PROCEDURE

Differing approaches to the achievements of procedural fairness may be observed, but in most tribunals much is left to the chairman in determining the form of the hearing. Three illustrations may demonstrate that the amount of guidance given by the appropriate rules is often minimal.

1. THE SOCIAL SECURITY APPEAL TRIBUNAL

The Social Security Appeal Tribunal came into being in April 1984, as a result of the merger of National Insurance Local Tribunals and Supplementary Benefit Appeal Tribunals. New procedural rules were made but did not differ substantially from those previously applicable. The new regulations still contain the following general provision:

> "Subject to the provisions of the Act and of these regulations—... in the case of a tribunal ... the procedure shall be such as the chairman of the tribunal shall determine."[1]

This general power is qualified in certain respects by other provisions. Representation is permitted[2]; witnesses may be called[3]; every person who

[1] Social Security (Adjudication) Regulations 1986, (S.I. 1986, No. 2218), reg. 2(1).
[2] *Ibid.*, reg. 2(1)(*b*).
[3] *Ibid.*, reg. 4(9).

717

has the right to be heard shall be given an opportunity of putting questions directly to any witnesses called at the hearing and of addressing the tribunal[4]; the hearing shall be in public unless the claimant requests a private hearing or the chairman directs that the hearing shall be private on the grounds that intimate personal or financial circumstances may have to be disclosed or that public security is involved[5]; any party to the proceedings is entitled to be present and to be heard.[6]

It is the chairman who decides how these requirements should be fulfilled and it is to be expected that there will be variations in procedure from chairman to chairman. There is, however, a guide which sets out general principles.[7] The Social Security Commissioners[8] may correct procedural irregularities on appeal, but it will be apparent that the provisions are so widely drafted that such an irregularity will have to be very serious before it will be regarded as material.[9]

The standard procedure[10] is for the claimant (or his or her representative) to state the case and call witnesses[11]; the claimant and his witnesses may then be questioned by the chairman, and/or the members, and/or the presenting officer[12]; the presenting officer then makes a submission and is subject to questioning; the claimant is asked for any final observations. The *Guide to Procedure* makes it clear, however, that

> "There is . . . no hard and fast rule about this and it may be courteous, and help to dispel any feeling on his part that matters have been taken out of his hands, to offer the choice of sequence to the claimant or his representative."[13]

---

[4] *Ibid.*, reg. 4(9).

[5] *Ibid.*, reg. 4(4).

[6] *Ibid.*, reg. 4(5). "Party to the proceedings" is defined in reg. 1(2), and in the case of appeals to an appeal tribunal includes the claimant, the adjudication officer (the D.S.S. Officer whose job is to make the original decision on entitlement to benefit), the Secretary of State and any other person appearing to the chairman to be interested in the proceedings.

[7] *Social Security Appeal Tribunals: a guide to procedure* (H.M.S.O., 2nd ed., 1988).

[8] See above, p. 62. The Commissioners constitute an appeal body from the decisions of Social Security Appeal Tribunals.

[9] In practice the most important ground of appeal is failure to state the reasons for a decision adequately: A. Ogus and E. Barendt, *The Law of Social Security* (3rd ed., 1988), p. 581.

[10] Suggested in the *Guide to Procedure*, pp. 24–25. However, it is not just the order of events which is significant but the attitude and appearance of the tribunal members. One of the authors, representing a nervous claimant at a N.I.L.T., had been at pains to explain in advance the informality of the procedure and distinguish it from court procedure as seen in "Crown Court" on television. The opening remarks of the chairman of the tribunal were, "Good afternoon, I must warn you, Mrs. X, that you must tell the truth in these proceedings—we are just like a court." If the claimant had been unrepresented, the niceties of procedure would have mattered little after that!

[11] This assumes that the claimant attends or is represented. The tribunal has a discretion to proceed with the hearing in the absence of the claimant: Adjudication Regulations, reg. 4(3); and if a claimant fails to attend without giving a reasonable explanation "it will usually be right to proceed with the hearing": *Guide to Procedure*, p. 18.

[12] The presenting officer is an officer of the D.S.S. specifically assigned to present cases before tribunals. Some presenting officers, therefore, become very experienced "advocates" and well known to their local tribunal. This job may not, however, occupy all the time of an officer, in which case he or she may also carry out the duties of an adjudication officer.

[13] p. 24.

At the conclusion of the hearing, the members of the tribunal consider their decision in private.[14]

The procedure is similar to that adopted in one of the Tribunal's ancestors, the National Insurance Local Tribunal. There was no substantial criticism of procedure in N.I.L.T.s although the ancillary arrangements were said to deter claimants from making an appeal,[15] or to give an impression that the tribunal was part of the departmental machinery rather than an independent review body.[16] It was certainly the case that attendance at the hearing improved, and representation greatly improved, the chances of success for the claimant.[17]

In the S.B.A.T., the presenting officer was normally allowed to go first and the wide variations in procedure which were observed raised serious doubts about the quality of the decision-making.[18]

The parties to the proceedings must be informed, in writing, of the decision as soon as may be practicable after the case has been decided.[19] The written decision must include a statement of the grounds of the decision, a record of the material facts found and, where the decision is not unanimous, that one of the members dissented and the reasons for that dissent.[20]

The role of the presenting officer in the procedure of the S.S.A.T. is interesting in that he or she is expected to put forward the view of the officer who made the decision against which the claimant is appealing, but is also expected to exercise individual judgment and assist the tribunal in reaching a proper resolution of the case.[21] This may require him or her to advance arguments on behalf of the appellant if he or she thinks that they should be brought to the attention of the tribunal, although there have been differing views expressed about the enthusiasm with which presenting officers have fulfilled that function.[22] The tribunal and the claimant may be assisted insofar as it is unlikely that a presenting officer will be defending at a hearing

[14] The clerk to the tribunal is permitted to remain with the members during their deliberations: Adjudication Regulations, reg. 2(2).

[15] The apparent complexity of the pre-hearing procedure; fears about the hearing; the inaccessibility of some tribunal venues; see K. Bell *et al.*, "National Insurance Local Tribunals: A Research Study" (1975) 4 *Journal of Social Policy* 1, at pp. 5–6.

[16] The independence of N.I.L.T.s was always difficult to establish. The Department of Health and Social Security did all the administration and the hearing was often held in a "government" building. The chairman often stressed at the hearing that the tribunal was independent but the claimant might find it hard to believe!

[17] Bell, *op. cit.* at pp. 11–21.

[18] M. Herman, *Administrative Justice and Supplementary Benefits* (1972); J. Fulbrook *Administrative Justice and the Unemployed* (1978); M. Adler, E. Burns and R. Johnson, "The Conduct of Tribunal Hearings," in M. Adler and A. Bradley, *Justice, Discretion and Poverty* (1976); K. Bell, *Research Study on Supplementary Benefit Appeal Tribunals, Review of Main Findings: Conclusions: Recommendations* (D.H.S.S. 1975).

[19] Adjudication Regulations, reg. 25(3).

[20] *Ibid*. reg. 19(2).

[21] For a lawyer's analysis of this role, see Diplock L.J. in *R.* v. *Deputy Industrial Injuries Commissioner, ex p. Moore* [1965] 1 Q.B. 456 at p. 486. A claimant would not necessarily take the same view, even if he knew what was meant by *lis inter partes* and *amicus curiae*!

[22] Herman, *op. cit.* and Bell, *op. cit.*, above, n. 18. The *Adjudication Officers' Guide* (Vol. 1, para. 05287) states that "The role of the AO is most closely analogous to that of *amicus curiae* ... and not as an advocate. The AO should not put questions to any claimant or witness in a hostile manner and it is entirely inappropriate for the AO to think in terms of 'winning' the case." Despite this, during observations of hearings for the study by Genn and Genn (1989) "many Presenting Officers were seen to argue their cases forcefully and to display pleasure when their decision was ultimately confirmed" (p. 161).

his or her own decision on an original claim and objectivity may be easier to display in those circumstances.[23] The unusual practice of allowing adjudication officers to defend their own decisions as presenting officers is likely to emphasise the adversarial nature of the proceedings at the expense of the inquisitorial.

It is legitimate to ask to what extent an inquisitorial mode is adopted in the hearing. It is true that the tribunal members are more involved in the direct questioning of both sides than a judge would be, and the informal structure of the proceedings allows particular points, once raised, to be followed through to a conclusion immediately if that appears convenient.[24] The functions of the statutory authorities (adjudication officer, tribunal, Commissioner) have been described as

> "investigatory or inquisitorial. A social security appeal tribunal is exercising quasi-judicial functions and forms part of the statutory machinery for investigating claims . . . . Its investigatory function has as its object the ascertainment of the facts and the determination of the truth . . . ."[25]

As an aspect of this

> "It is open to a tribunal and indeed it is the members' duty, whenever they identify a point in favour of the claimant, notwithstanding that it has not been taken by the claimant, to consider it and to reach their decision in the light of it."[26]

Moreover, the adjudication officer should attempt to present a balanced view. However, there are limits. A tribunal is not expected to question facts presented by a claimant just in case after further investigation they might prove to be materially different in the claimant's favour, especially where there is no suggestion that the claimant is unsure of the facts as presented.[27]

> ". . . [T]he primary duty for making out his case falls on the claimant,[28] and he must not expect to rely on the tribunal's own expertise. We would be slow to convict a tribunal of failure to identify an uncanvassed factual point in favour of the claimant in the absence of the most obvious and clear cut circumstances."[29]

---

[23] The *Adjudication Officers' Guide* states (Vol. 1, para. 05271) that "The AO who made the decision under appeal can attend the hearing and present the case personally. However, more often the AO will be represented by the presenting officer."

[24] One of the authors experienced a N.I.L.T in which he was interrupted in the midst of representations by comments from the claimant's husband who was attending the hearing as a "member of the public" and was sitting at the back of the room. The chairman encouraged him to speak up and proceeded to deal with the point he raised by questioning both the claimant and the insurance officer. Having dealt with it to his satisfaction the chairman asked if the husband had any further observations . . .

[25] R.(S) 1/87, pp. 6–7 (Commissioner V. G. H. Hallett); *Guide to Procedure*, p. 8.

[26] R.(SB) 2/83, p. 557 (Tribunal of Commissioners).

[27] *Ibid.*, p. 558. It was contended on behalf of the claimant that the local tribunal should, of its own motion, have investigated the origin and nature of funds in a personal account in a building society, in order to determine whether they truly represented business assets and not personal monies. That contention was rejected.

[28] But see pp. 725–727, on the burden of proof in S.S.A.T.s.

[29] R.(SB) 2/83, p. 558.

Moreover, exhortations that an inquisitorial approach should be adopted do not necessarily reflect the actual practice.[30]

An example of a Form AT3, which records the proceedings at a particular S.S.A.T. hearing, is reproduced in Chapter 12.[30a]

2. THE INDUSTRIAL TRIBUNAL

The rules of procedure for a hearing at an Industrial Tribunal are, in some respects, more explicit. The objectives to be attained at the hearing are included as part of the rules. In respect of the S.S.A.T., we noted that the normal provision is simply for the chairman to determine the procedure; for the Industrial Tribunal, the rules specify that:

"The tribunal shall conduct the hearing in such manner as it considers most suitable to the clarification of the issues before it and generally to the just handling of the proceedings; it shall so far as appears to it appropriate seek to avoid formality in its proceedings. . . ."[31]

Although those may be the implicit objectives of other tribunals, it is interesting that they should be explicit for the Industrial Tribunal, and consequently ironic that the Industrial Tribunal is generally reckoned to be one of the more formal and legalistic of the tribunals.

The hearing takes place in public unless the tribunal is of the opinion that a private hearing is appropriate on the grounds of national security or other specified grounds[32]; any person entitled to appear at the hearing is entitled to give evidence, call witnesses, question any witness and address the tribunal.[33] If a party has failed to attend the hearing, any documents that he or she has submitted may be treated as written representations, but subject to that provision, the hearing may proceed or may be adjourned, or the application may be dismissed, at the discretion of the tribunal.[34]

The order of events at a hearing is likely to differ with the nature of the claim.[35] In the ordinary unfair dismissal case the burden of proof lies with the employer to show that the dismissal was not unfair and the employer will normally be called on first. If the employee alleges constructive dismissal, or the employer otherwise disputes the fact of dismissal, then it will be for the employee to begin and make out his or her case. Whoever has the first word, the procedure thereafter is, in form, similar to court procedure with the calling, examination and cross-examination of witnesses leading to final statements on both sides. The chairman and members of the tribunal may ask more questions and become more involved in the proceedings than a

---

[30] The study by Genn and Genn (1989) found that while S.S.A.T. chairs consistently expressed the belief that proceedings were inquisitorial, this was denied by many experienced representatives, whose views were "often based on the perception that tribunals did not have the time to delve in sufficient detail into appellants' cases:" pp. 159–163.

[30a] See above, pp. 582–584.

[31] The Industrial Tribunals (Rules of Procedure) Regulations 1985 (S.I. 1985 No. 16), reg. 8(1).

[32] *Ibid.*, reg. 7(1).

[33] *Ibid.*, reg. 8(2).

[34] *Ibid.*, regs. 7(3), 8(3).

[35] For Industrial Tribunal procedure generally, see S. Anderman, *The Law of Unfair Dismissal* (2nd ed., 1985), Appendix IV; I. T. Smith and J. C. Wood, *Industrial Law* (4th ed. 1989), pp. 235–265; B. A. Hepple and P. O'Higgins, *Encyclopaedia of Labour Relations Law*, Parts 1A, Chap. 8 and Part 4A. by M. J. Goodman; *Tribunal Practice and Procedure* (I.D.S. Handbook 45, 1989).

judge would, and the rules about the correct form of examination and cross-examination are relaxed along with the rules of evidence,[36] but an observer at a hearing would receive a strong impression of adversarial procedure and formality.

3. RENT ASSESSMENT COMMITTEES

The Rent Assessment Committee[37] exercises jurisdiction of three main kinds. It receives and determines objections against the fixing and registration (or confirmation) of a fair rent by a rent officer[38]; it fixes the rent of an assured tenancy where the landlord proposes a rent increase[39]; and, when exercising the powers of a rent tribunal, it controls rent and security of tenure in respect of "restricted contracts."[40] Some potential confusion was created by the Housing Act 1980 in the abolition of the rent tribunal and the reallocation of its functions to a Rent Assessment Committee[41] but we shall attempt to distinguish the two by reference to R.A.C. and R.A.C. (R.T.).

The R.A.C. and R.A.C. (R.T.) share a feature which distinguish them from the other tribunals we have so far considered, in that they do not need to hold a hearing. The obligation lies on the landlord and the tenant to request the opportunity to make oral representations and there are provisions for the disposal of the matter on written representations in the absence of an application for a hearing.[42] It should be emphasised that the absence of a hearing does not relieve the tribunal of considering the matter, indeed it points up the inquisitorial role because the committee then have an obligation to make such inquiry as they think fit and consider any information supplied or representation made by the parties.[43] This demonstrates the necessity for procedural safeguards throughout the determination of an issue—they are not confined to a hearing.

If the landlord or tenant requests the opportunity to make oral representations then the R.A.C. or the R.A.C. (R.T.), as appropriate, will arrange a hearing. For the hearing, the procedural rules are slightly different in

[36] S.I. 1985, No. 16, reg. 8(1) (see n. 31 above), and see pp. 723–731 below for further discussion.
[37] See generally R. E. Megarry, *The Rent Acts* (1988), Vol. 1, Chaps. 24 and 25, Vol. 3, Chaps. 16 and 17; J. C. Martin, *Residential Security* (1989), Chaps. 11 and 15.
[38] Under the provisions of the Rent Act 1977 Part IV.
[39] Under the Housing Act 1988, Part I.
[40] As defined in Rent Act 1977, ss.19–21.
[41] s.72. The provisions of the section are, at first sight, so startling that they may properly be set out in full:
    "(1) Rent tribunals, as constituted for the purposes of the 1977 Act, are hereby abolished and section 76 of the 1977 Act (Constitution, etc. of rent tribunals) is hereby repealed.
    (2) As from the commencement of this section the functions which, under the 1977 Act, are conferred on rent tribunals shall be carried out by rent assessment committees.
    (3) A rent assessment committee shall, when constituted to carry out functions so conferred, be known as a rent tribunal."
    The object appears to be to achieve a uniformity of appointment for the two bodies, without diminishing their functions.
[42] Rent Act 1977, Sched. 11, paras. 6, 7(1)(b), 9 and Rent Assessment Committee (England and Wales) Regulations 1971 (S.I. 1971 No. 1065), reg. 6 (R.A.C.s); Rent Act 1977 s.28(1), (2); Rent Assessment Committees (England and Wales) (Rent Tribunal) Regulations 1980 (S.I. 1980 No. 1700), reg. 4 (R.A.C. (RT)).
[43] 1977 Act, Sched. 11, paras. 7(1)(a), 9(1) (R.A.C.s); Rent Act 1977, s.78(2) (R.A.C. (RT)).

respect of the R.A.C. and R.A.C. (R.T.) but it is unlikely that the formal differences are reflected in the actual procedure adopted by the chairman.

The R.A.C. rules provide that, ". . . the parties shall be heard in such order, and . . . the procedure shall be such as the committee shall determine" and "a party may call witnesses, give evidence on his own behalf and cross-examine any witnesses called by the other party."[44] Each party may be heard in person "or by a person authorised by him in that behalf," whether or not a solicitor or barrister.[44a] The rules specify that the hearing shall be in public unless the committee decide otherwise "for special reasons."[45]

In respect of the R.A.C. (R.T.), "the procedure at a hearing shall be such as the rent tribunal may determine" and a party may appear in person or be represented by anyone he or she wishes.[45a] The tribunal may if they think fit, and at the request of either party shall, unless for some special reason they consider it undesirable, allow the hearing to be held in public.[46] There is no specific provision for the calling of witnesses, giving of evidence, or cross-examination.

These formal differences may not actually affect the *style* of the hearing but it is odd that there should be discrepancies in the procedural rules, particularly where the same members are involved in each type of hearing. The R.A.C. (R.T.) rules are the later and there are echoes in them of the rules which have been developed in social security tribunals, yet the allocation of the functions of the rent tribunal to the R.A.C. in 1980 ought to have provided an opportunity for standardisation. If there can be no accepted procedural criteria in this case, what hope is there for establishing uniform procedure across the wide range of tribunals?

B. EVIDENCE

In civil and criminal trials there are clear rules about the sort of evidence which may be given; the location of the burden of proof; and the standard of proof. Such clear rules are not to be found in tribunal adjudication. In the adversarial procedure of the civil or criminal trial the burden of proof is readily identified, but where there is an inquisitorial atmosphere in tribunals it is more difficult to locate. Some of the rules which render relevant evidence inadmissible at a trial rely heavily for their justification on the inability of a jury to decide the proper weight to be given to potentially prejudicial evidence.[47] An experienced tribunal chairman, it is said, ought to be able to attribute the correct amount of weight to almost every piece of relevant information. Further, it is always argued that the absence of "strict" rules of evidence enhances the informality of tribunal procedure and makes it more comprehensible to the lay person.

[44] S.I. 1971 No. 1065, reg. 4.
[44a] Rent Act 1977, Sched. 11, para. 8.
[45] S.I. 1971 No. 1065, regs. 3(1), 4.
[45a] S.I. 1980 No. 1700, regs. 6, 7(1).
[46] *Ibid.*, reg. 7(1).
[47] A detailed consideration of rules of evidence is outside the scope of this book, but an example of the exclusionary rules referred to is that which prevents the admission of evidence of the defendant's previous convictions in a criminal trial. Though possibly highly relevant, that particular evidence needs to be weighed carefully in arriving at a conclusion about whether the accused has committed a crime on *this* occasion.

However, a balance needs to be maintained between the requirements of informality and the interests of the parties to the tribunal. It may be assumed that some rules of evidence are specifically designed to prevent a conclusion being reached on unreliable information,[48] so that it would not be acceptable to abandon the principles of evidence altogether in tribunal adjudication. We shall hope to illustrate how tribunals cope with the problems of onus and standard of proof, relevance and admissibility.

1. GENERAL PRINCIPLES[49]

There is an important difference between courts and tribunals in that many tribunals rely on the expertise of the chairmen and members in determining questions of fact.[50] It is interesting to note that the jury, at its inception, was intended to rely upon the collective knowledge of its members, although such knowledge could now constitute a reason for excusal or challenge.[51] The justification for tribunal adjudication rests partly on the expertise of the adjudicators in the appropriate field, and there is ample authority for the proposition that they may rely on their own specialist knowledge to interpret evidence given to them by the parties or to fill in gaps where evidence has not been given.[52] Were this not the case there would be no possibility of an appeal succeeding in a social security matter where the appellant chose not to appear, was unrepresented and made no written representations. The chances of success for such an appellant are slender but they do exist![53]

Those tribunals which are not merely administrative bodies but exercise a judicial function are bound to conform to the rules of natural justice.[54] The way in which a tribunal deals with evidence must accord with those rules which require, broadly, that the proceedings must be fair in all the circumstances. In respect of the giving of evidence it seems that every party to a hearing must be given an opportunity to put his or her case and to call relevant evidence in support.[55] That right is supported by the rules of procedure of some tribunals[56] and although there was a discretion on the part of the chairman of Supplementary Benefit Appeal Tribunals to exclude evidence which was clearly irrelevant or immaterial, that discretion had to be exercised with care and with a due regard to the necessity of allowing

---

[48] The exclusion of hearsay evidence is based mainly on its unreliability, and such evidence is treated with considerable caution in tribunal proceedings although it is admissible, see pp. 729–731, below.

[49] There is little available material about the use of evidence in tribunals, but see R. E. Wraith and P. G. Hutchesson, *Administrative Tribunals* (1973), pp. 265–273; J. Fulbrook, *Administrative Justice and the Unemployed* (1978), pp. 268–276; C. Yates, [1980] J.S.W.L. 273 (supplementary benefit appeals) and [1980] Conv. 136 (rent tribunals); J. G. Logie and P. Q. Watchman, (1989) 8 C.J.Q. 109 (S.S.A.T.s).

[50] Indeed, expertise is a criterion for the appointment of members in many tribunals, see above, p. 203.

[51] See below, pp. 798, 805.

[52] J. A. Smillie, "The Problem of 'Official Notice'—Reliance by Administrative Tribunals on the Personal Knowledge of their Members" [1975] P.L. 64.

[53] There are reported instances in K. Bell *et al*, "National Insurance Local Tribunals: A Research Study" (1975) 4 *Journal of Social Policy* 1.

[54] See Sir William Wade, *Administrative Law* (6th ed., 1988), Chap. 15. All the tribunals we have so far considered have a judicial function.

[55] R. v. *Hull Prison Board of Visitors, ex p. St. Germain (No. 2)* [1979] 1 W.L.R. 1401.

[56] See above, pp. 717–718, 721, 722–723.

justice to be seen to be done.[57] In the Industrial Tribunal it has been suggested that there is no discretion to exclude evidence which would be admissible; there is clearly a discretion to include evidence which would be inadmissible.[58] Such a discretion is often referred to as a discretion to disregard the "strict" rules of evidence.[59]

2. THE STANDARD OF PROOF AND THE BURDEN OF PROOF

Proof beyond reasonable doubt is the standard adopted in the trial of criminal matters, and in civil cases the party bearing the burden of proof must establish the case on a balance of probabilities.[60] It is the latter standard that is adopted in tribunal proceedings, although some writers suggest that in particular tribunals the chairman and members may not always identify the standard as clearly as that.[61] The standard of proof is closely linked in reported decisions of tribunals with the question of the burden of proof and who bears it. In an early decision of a National Insurance Commissioner the formulation of Lord Birkenhead L.C. in *Lancaster* v. *Blackwell Colliery Co.*[62] was adopted:

"If the facts which are proved gave rise to conflicting inferences of equal degrees of probability, so that the choice between them is a mere matter of conjecture, then of course the applicant fails to prove his case, because it is plain in these matters the onus is on the applicant. But where the known facts are not equally balancing probabilities as to their respective value, and where a reasonable man might hold that the more probable conclusion is that for which the applicant contends, then the arbitrator is justified in drawing an inference in his favour."

The question of which party, if any, bears the burden of proof in tribunal proceedings really needs to be examined in respect of each individual tribunal,[63] starting from the assumption that it will normally be the party

---

[57] Although this proposition is taken from R(SB) 6/82 and related to Supplementary Benefit Appeal Tribunals, it is likely to have wider application as an expression of one of the requirements of natural justice. The dilemma for a tribunal chairman is that he or she may not be able to take a view about the relevance of evidence until it has been heard.

[58] *Rosedale Mouldings Ltd.* v. *Sibley* [1980] I.C.R. 816. The first part of the proposition was doubted in *Snowball* v. *Gardner Merchant Ltd.* [1987] I.C.R. 719, where the E.A.T. suggested that an industrial tribunal might properly "decide not to admit evidence which would be admissible under the strict rules of evidence, if, for example, it considered it to be unfair to do so or, as in the field of criminal law, its prejudicial effect outweighed its probative value" (p. 722).

[59] This is a significant phrase because it embodies the notion that some basic rules of evidence must still apply, even in tribunals. The phrase is also to be found in the standard terms of reference to arbitration under the small claims procedure in the county court, see above, pp. 531–535.

[60] For a full consideration of the standard of proof in civil and criminal matters, see *Cross on Evidence* (7th ed., 1990), pp. 145–159.

[61] There was particular doubt about S.B.A.T.s.: J. Fulbrook, *Administrative Justice and the Unemployed* (1978), p. 272. There are isolated examples where a higher standard of proof has been required, *e.g. Judd* v. *Minister of Pensions and National Insurance* [1966] 2 Q.B. 580, where the Divisional Court held that the Minister must establish his or her case beyond reasonable doubt in certain matters before the Pensions Appeal Tribunal.

[62] (1919) 12 B.W.C.C. 400 at p. 406, cited in C.I. 401/50.

[63] We have already made the point that it is impossible to generalise about tribunals. The examples which follow are from tribunals which we have described elsewhere.

making the assertion who must prove it. That assumption, which derives from the position in the civil or criminal trial,[64] may not be appropriate where the proceedings are conducted on a truly inquisitorial basis with the tribunal reaching an evaluation of the information presented, yet it exercises a powerful influence.

It may not, of course, be necessary to rely on an assumption. Provision may have been made by statute,[65] or by procedural rules,[66] or in the decisions of particular tribunals,[67] stipulating where the burden of proof will lie. Where the jurisdiction of the tribunal is original, rather than appellate, it will also usually be clear where the burden lies, even if it may shift during the hearing. In the Industrial Tribunal, for example, when the applicant alleges that he or she has been unfairly dismissed it will be for the *employer* to prove that the dismissal was not unfair. If the employer disputes that there has been a dismissal the onus lies with the *employee* to prove that there has.[68]

In respect of some tribunals, no importance attaches to the question of burden of proof because the tribunal is arriving at a valuation rather than establishing a right or claim. The Rent Assessment Committee provides an example in that it is the obligation of the committee to arrive at its own judgment of a fair rent in the light of any representations made by the landlord and/or tenant.[69] Neither has the burden of proof—the committee must make its own decision which may not reflect the contentions of either party.

As regards Social Security Appeal Tribunals, the general position appears to be[70] that it is for the claimant to make out his or her entitlement[71]; that where there are exceptions from basic entitlements it is for those who assert

---

[64] See *Cross on Evidence* (7th ed., 1990), pp. 110–143.

[65] Employment Protection (Consolidation) Act 1978, ss.91(2), 151(2), providing that on a reference to a tribunal a person's employment during any period shall be deemed to have been continuous unless the contrary is proved, and that a dismissal shall be presumed to have been on account of redundancy, unless the contrary is proved. *Cf. Secretary of State for Employment* v. *Globe Elastic Thread Co. Ltd.* [1980] A.C. 506. See also, Social Security Act 1975, s.19(1), excusing from disqualification for unemployment benefit those who can prove that they were not directly interested in the relevant trade dispute, and Employment Protection (Consolidation) Act 1978, s.57(3), which is interpreted as imposing no burden of proof on either party in respect of the reasonableness of a dismissal: *Post Office (Counters) Ltd.* v. *Heavey* [1990] I.C.R. 1.

[66] *e.g.* The Immigration Appeals (Procedure) Rules 1984 (S.I. 1984 No. 2041), r. 31, which deals specifically with the burden of proof and locates it on the appellant or the Secretary of State depending on the fact in issue.

[67] *e.g.* The decision of the National Insurance Commissioner that the burden of proof on the allegation of cohabitation should lie with the insurance officer, R(G) 1/53. This decision has been consistently followed.

[68] See above, p. 721.

[69] See above, pp. 722–723.

[70] See J. Mesher in A. Kiralfy (ed.), *The Burden of Proof* (1987), Chap. 11, "Social Security Law." Before amalgamation, the position was less clear in S.B.A.T.s than N.I.L.T.s: see C. Yates, [1980] J.S.W.L. 273, 274–276.

[71] *R.* v. *National Insurance Commissioner, ex p. Hudson and Jones* [1970] 1 Q.B. 477; *R.* v. *National Insurance Commissioner, ex p. Viscusi* [1974] 1 W.L.R. 646; see also, *e.g.* R.(I) 32/61; R.(S.B.) 15/81; R.(S.B.) 8/84 ("It is for the claimant to establish his title to a single payment . . ." (p. 882)).

that the exceptions apply to prove that they do[72]; and that once a decision has been made awarding benefit for a particular period, the onus of proving that grounds exist for reviewing the decision lies on those who assert that the existing decision is wrong.[73] However, the basic principle that it is for the claimant to establish entitlement is modified to the extent that the tribunal conforms to the rhetoric of adopting an inquisitorial rather than accusatorial approach.[74]

Thus, in *R.* v. *National Insurance Commissioner, ex p. Viscusi,*[75] which concerned a claim for industrial disablement benefit, Buckley L.J. had this to say:

> "As regards the burden of proof, as Lord Denning M.R. has pointed out, these are not adversary proceedings: they are inquisitorial proceedings; and in such proceedings questions of burden of proof do not arise in the same way in which they would in proceedings between parties in a law suit. It is for the medical board or the medical appeal tribunal, as the case may be, to investigate the case inquisitorially and to decide whether the claimant is entitled to benefit under the Act. But, of course, the fact remains that the medical board or the medical appeal tribunal, as the case may be, must be satisfied that the claimant is entitled to benefit: and so, in a sense, and subject to such statutory assumptions as are prescribed by the Act itself, it does rest with the claimant in the end to make out his claim."

3. RELEVANCE AND ADMISSIBILITY

Detailed exclusionary rules have been developed in civil and criminal matters which render certain evidence inadmissible on the grounds that it would be unduly prejudicial or unreliable. Inevitably, the operation of such rules can lead to the exclusion of evidence which is highly relevant to the facts in issue. In tribunal proceedings the test of *relevance* is given priority with the consequence that very little evidence is likely to be excluded altogether from consideration. It may be that particular sorts of evidence are treated with some circumspection by the chairman and members, but it is expected that they will be able to assess the value and reliability of the evidence given and accord it appropriate weight in their deliberations. Many of the strict exclusionary rules of evidence result from a fear that a jury will be unable to judge satisfactorily how much significance to attach to inherently unreliable or prejudicial evidence,[76] and that fear should not be present when it is tribunal members who are adjudicating. Consequently, the strict rules of evidence are normally disregarded in favour of a much wider test of admissibility:

---

[72] *e.g.* disqualifications for unemployment benefit under s.20, Social Security Act 1975: R.(U) 2/60 (for the insurance officer (now adjudication officer) to prove that the claimant lost her job through misconduct); R.(U) 20/64 (for the insurance officer to prove that claimant left employment voluntarily; if this is done, it is for the claimant to prove that he or she did not leave without just cause): Mesher (1987), pp. 220–222. Another example is discontinuance of benefit on the ground of cohabitation: R.(SB) 17/81; *Crake* v. *Supplementary Benefits Commission* [1982] 1 All E.R. 498.

[73] R.(I) 1/71; Mesher (1987), pp. 225–227.

[74] Mesher (1987), pp. 214–218. See above, pp. 720–721.

[75] [1974] 1 W.L.R. 646.

[76] That is why the rules are stricter in criminal cases, but have been relaxed in civil cases where it is now highly unusual to have a jury, see pp. 703–705, above.

"... technical rules of evidence, however, form no part of the rules of natural justice. The requirement that a person exercising quasi-judicial functions must base his decision on evidence means no more than it must be based upon material which tends logically to show the existence or non-existence of facts relevant to the issue to be determined, or to show the likelihood or unlikelihood of the occurrence of some future event the occurrence of which would be relevant. It means that he must not spin a coin or consult an astrologer, but he may take into account any material which, as a matter of reason, has some probative value in the sense mentioned above. If it is capable of having any probative value, the weight to be attached to it is a matter for the person to whom Parliament has entrusted the task of deciding the issue."[77]

This statement of Diplock L.J. has been cited with approval on a number of occasions and applied to different adjudications. The judge was actually dealing with the decision of a deputy Industrial Injuries Commissioner on a claim for industrial injury benefit, but his words have also been held to apply to an appeal to the Minister under the Town and Country Planning Act 1962[78]; an adjudication by a prison Board of Visitors under the Prison Rules 1964[79]; and a formal investigation of a complaint of unlawful discrimination under the Race Relations Act 1976.[80] This general rule, that evidence is admissible in tribunal proceedings if it is of some "probative value", even though it would be inadmissible in court, has been embodied in procedural rules[81] and adopted in tribunal decisions.[82] It would appear that probative means relevant.

This rule of admissibility has been formulated in the context of the principles of natural justice and it is still the case that there is an obligation to ensure that each party has a full and fair hearing. In the Industrial Tribunal the general rule has been expressed in a slightly modified way to permit the exclusion of evidence where its admission, "... could in some way adversely affect the reaching of a proper decision in the case."[83] In R. v. *Hull Prison Board of Visitors, ex p. St. Germain (No. 2)*,[84] Geoffrey Lane L.J. held that there may be circumstances in which a Prison Board of Visitors should not admit hearsay evidence unless the prisoner accused was given the opportunity to cross-examine the maker of the statement. The powers of the tribunal to dispense with the strict rules of evidence must always be subject to the overriding obligation to provide a fair hearing. In social security tribunals the general rule was followed and many reported decisions expressed the power of the tribunals to admit any relevant evidence.[85]

---

[77] R. v. *Deputy Industrial Injuries Commissioner, ex p. Moore* [1965] 1 Q.B. 456 at p. 488.

[78] *T. A. Miller Ltd.* v. *Minister of Housing and Local Government* [1968] 1 W.L.R. 992.

[79] R. v. *Hull Prison Board of Visitors, ex p. St. Germain (No. 2)* [1979] 1 W.L.R. 1401.

[80] R. v. *Commission for Racial Equality, ex p. Cottrell* [1980] 1 W.L.R. 1580.

[81] *e.g.* The Immigration Appeals (Procedure) Rules 1984 (S.I. 1984 No. 2041 r. 29). "An appellate authority may receive oral, documentary or other evidence of any fact which appears to the authority to be relevant to the appeal, notwithstanding that such evidence would be inadmissible in a court of law."

[82] See below, n. 85.

[83] *Coral Squash Clubs Ltd.* v. *Matthews* [1979] I.C.R. 607, at p. 611. The Employment Appeal Tribunal in that case held that it was "... clear that an Industrial Tribunal is not bound by the strict rules of evidence but should exercise its good sense in weighing matters which come before it" (*ibid.*)

[84] [1979] 1 W.L.R. 1401.

[85] *e.g.* R.(I) 36/61, R.(I) 13/74, R.(U) 12/56, R.(U) 5/77.

The weight that is to be attached to relevant evidence is a matter for the tribunal and it is instructive to consider the approach of various tribunals in respect of hearsay evidence—the sort of evidence which tribunals have most often been invited to exclude.

4. HEARSAY

A hearsay statement is one which is made, orally or in writing, by a person other than the witness testifying and which is offered to prove a fact asserted in the statement.[86] An adjudication officer, investigating the question of whether a person in receipt of unemployment benefit is actually working, states that he has interviewed the claimant's next door neighbours who have told him that they saw the claimant leave his house every morning with a bag of tools, and that the claimant has admitted to them that he is "making a bit on the side." The statement of the adjudication officer, when put to the tribunal by the presenting officer at the hearing of the claimant's appeal against disqualification from benefit, would constitute hearsay.

The rules restricting the admissibility of hearsay evidence in civil courts are much less stringent than they were,[87] but the rules in criminal matters remain strict and their justification is said to be that hearsay evidence cannot properly be tested in court because of the absence of the maker of the statement; and depends upon the potentially inaccurate repetition of the statement by the witness.[88] Set against those difficulties is the undeniable fact, recognised by tribunals, that, "If tribunals were obliged to reject hearsay evidence ... many claimants would find it quite impossible to establish their claims."[89]

The solution adopted by tribunals in most circumstances is to admit the evidence whilst expressing caution as to the weight to be attached to it, and stressing the desirability of having other evidence available as well. Hearsay evidence may well be unreliable and some consideration has recently been given to safeguards that may be appropriate. It is useful first to look at the particular case and then to consider the extent to which it may influence other tribunals in their treatment of hearsay.

R. v. Hull Prison Board of Visitors, ex p. St. Germain (No. 2)[90] dealt with the propriety of disciplinary proceedings conducted by the Board of Visitors of Hull Prison in the aftermath of a serious riot at the prison in 1976. The proceedings were conducted under the Prison Rules 1964[91] and it was later alleged, in the course of an application to the Divisional Court for an order of certiorari,[92] that the board had admitted and acted on hearsay evidence in that it had heard evidence from the governor of the prison about the contents of reports made by prison officers who did not give evidence to the board in person. It was argued before the Divisional Court that the admission of such evidence constituted a breach of the rules of natural justice. In

---

[86] This is a very abbreviated definition. Interested students should consult *Cross on Evidence* (7th ed., 1990), Chap XIV.
[87] Reforms were effected by the Civil Evidence Act 1968. See Cross, *op. cit.* Chap. XV.
[88] See Law Reform Committee, 13th Report, *Hearsay Evidence in Civil Proceedings* (Cmnd. 2964, 1966); Criminal Law Revision Committee, 11th Report, *Evidence (General)* (Cmnd. 4991, 1972), pp. 132–154.
[89] R.(U) 12/56.
[90] [1979] 1 W.L.R. 1401.
[91] S.I. 1964 No. 388.
[92] See below, p. 877.

dealing with this argument, Geoffrey Lane L.J. referred to the statement of Diplock L.J. in *Moore's* case which is set out above.[93] He reaffirmed the general rule that hearsay evidence is admissible but stated that it should be subject to the overriding obligation to provide a fair hearing.[94]

The provision of a fair hearing may oblige the board, depending upon the circumstances of the case and the nature of the evidence, not only to give the accused an opportunity to know of and comment on the evidence, but also to cross-examine the maker of the original statement. The court recognised the enormous burden which might be placed on the board by a requirement that the witness be made available for cross-examination, but also noted that hearsay evidence would not be resorted to in the total absence of direct evidence and therefore directed that where the problem of producing the witness is insuperable the hearsay evidence should not be admitted or, if admitted already, should be dismissed from consideration. The court found support for this view in a Home Office report on Adjudication Procedure in Prisons.[95]

This may fairly be regarded as an unusual case and, perhaps, of limited application. The proceedings involved were akin to criminal proceedings; the procedural irregularities were clear[96]; the Home Office report had also concluded that unsupported hearsay should not be admitted. However, it may provide a basis on which other tribunals can decide a clearer policy about the circumstances in which hearsay will be admitted. The crucial disadvantage in the admission of hearsay is the denial of the opportunity of cross-examination with its twin objectives of eliciting information, and testing the memory, veracity and credibility of a witness.[97]

In the Industrial Tribunal the policy merely seems to be to require the members of the tribunal to consider carefully what *weight* to attach to admitted hearsay evidence. In *Coral Squash Clubs Ltd.* v. *Matthews*,[98] the Industrial Tribunal had refused to admit hearsay evidence about alleged licensing offences by the manager of a squash club, on the grounds that where the allegation was of a criminal offence and where the witnesses could have been located and produced the strict rule of exclusion should be applied. Their decision was reversed by the Employment Appeal Tribunal who ruled the evidence to be admissible, holding that the question of criminality was not in issue before the tribunal and that the failure to produce witnesses merely went to the weight of the evidence. The E.A.T. stated that a tribunal should, ". . . exercise its good sense in weighing the matters that come before it."[99]

Social security tribunals have taken much the same view. In an early decision, a Commissioner warned that the value of evidence which would be inadmissible in a court of law must be carefully considered and may be of very little weight,[1] and that phrasing has been adopted in subsequent decisions.[2] A particular type of hearsay which social security tribunals have

---

[93] *R.* v. *Deputy Industrial Injuries Commissioners, ex p. Moore* [1965] 1 Q.B. 456. See above, p. 728.
[94] [1979] 1 W.L.R. 1410 at p. 1409D.
[95] *Ibid.* at p. 1401.
[96] The board of visitors had also refused to call certain witnesses requested by the accused.
[97] See Cross, *op. cit.* at pp. 513–515.
[98] [1979] I.C.R. 607.
[99] *Ibid.*, at p. 611.
[1] C.I. 97/49.
[2] R.(G) 1/51; R.(U) 12/56; R.(U) 5/77.

been unwilling to accept is the statements of claimants' representatives. The Commissioner has said that such statements are not evidence and that where questions of fact are in issue on which a claimant or other qualified witness can speak they should be called to give evidence.[3] It has indeed been suggested that

"In practical terms, the result would seem to be that the use of hearsay is so severely restricted that it is virtually inadmissible. Indeed there is no reported case known to the authors in which a Commissioner has upheld the decision of an appeal tribunal which acted solely or principally on the basis of hearsay evidence."[4]

What is lacking is a clear policy on the criteria to be applied in determining the admissibility and reliability of hearsay evidence.[5] Our tribunals have contented themselves so far with the broadest of exhortations to weigh such evidence carefully, and the *Hull Prison* case is likely to be regarded as of specific, rather than general, application. Even where the matter has been considered and included in procedural rules, the tribunal is given no guidance.

5. WITNESSES

The requirement of natural justice that a party should be given a fair hearing is normally taken to comprehend the right to put his or her own case and correct or contradict statements that have been made by the other party.[6] This is likely to be achieved by the calling of witnesses. The right to call witnesses is set out in the procedural rules for the tribunals we have so far considered in detail.[7] However, the right appears to be subject to the discretion of the chairman. The chairman's obligation is to ensure a fair hearing, but he or she is not required to hear every witness that one of the parties might wish to call.

In the *Hull Prison*[8] case, where this point was also in issue, Geoffrey Lane L.J. held that it was not inconsistent with the principles of natural justice that the chairman of the board of visitors should have a discretion to refuse to allow evidence to be given.

"However, that discretion has to be exercised reasonably, in good faith, and on proper grounds .... A more serious question was raised whether the discretion could be validly exercised where it was based on considerable administrative inconvenience being caused if the request to call a witness or witnesses was permitted ... mere administrative difficulties, simpliciter, are not in our view good enough. Convenience and justice are often not on speaking terms."[9]

[3] R.(I) 36/61. The same principle applies to the adjudication officer's representative: R.(SB) 10/86.
[4] J. G. Logie and P. Q. Watchman, (1989) 8 C.J.Q. 109, 116.
[5] An Australian commentator put it thus: "... English administrative case law has taken the question very little further than merely saying that hearsay can be admitted. It is therefore to the U.S. experience that we must turn ...." G. A. Flick, "The Opportunity to Controvert Adverse Testimony in Administrative Proceedings: A Search for Criteria" (1978) 28 U. Toronto L.J. 1.
[6] See generally Sir William Wade. *Administrative Law* (6th ed., 1988), Chap. 15.
[7] See above, pp. 717–723.
[8] [1979] 1 W.L.R. 1401, see above, p. 728.
[9] *Ibid.*, at p. 1406.

The Divisional Court concluded that the exclusion of witnesses because the chairman considered there to be ample evidence against the accused, or because he misunderstood the nature of the prisoners' defence, would clearly be wrong, but that this may be justifiable where the accused is merely trying to render the hearing impracticable or where it would be unnecessary to call so many witnesses to establish the point at issue.[10]

Again, as with the hearsay point, the decision of the Divisional Court may be rather narrower than the current practice in other tribunals and may be restricted to its own facts if its principles were to be argued in general. The position in Social security tribunals was stated recently by a Commissioner in R(SB)6/82. The decision related to a S.B.A.T., but the principles are presumably equally applicable to the S.S.A.T.s. In that decision, the chairman of a S.B.A.T. had refused to hear a witness whom the claimant wished to call. On the facts, the Commissioner concluded that there had been an error of law since the witness appeared to have relevant and material evidence to give, and the case was remitted for re-hearing. On the general point the Commissioner said:

"Tribunals are not bound to hear evidence which is clearly irrelevant or immaterial, whether it be from a witness actually giving evidence before the tribunal or from a proposed witness. The discretion to stop or curtail such evidence should, however, always be exercised with care, and in its exercise due regard should in my view always be paid to the necessity of allowing justice to be seen to be done."[11]

Industrial Tribunals would, no doubt, adopt similar criteria. Other aspects of the law of evidence relating to witnesses have been held to be applicable to tribunal adjudications, including the principles that a witness's testimony can be accepted even though not corroborated,[12] and that a witness's answers to questions concerning his or her credibility must be accepted as final (to avoid undue preoccupation with side-issues).[13]

C. THE ROLE OF THE CHAIRMAN

The references to the chairman in the last two sections of this chapter will already have demonstrated the significance of his role. The task of any chairman, whatever the nature of the tribunal, is to ensure that:

"... the proceedings are conducted with scrupulous fairness to all parties and that the proper balance is struck between formality and informality. In particular, he must make sure at the outset that the parties fully understand the issue, especially when they are not legally represented; and he must ensure that they have an opportunity to present their cases adequately."[14]

Different chairmen may quite properly take different views about how to conduct tribunal hearings whilst pursuing the objectives referred to in the

[10] *Ibid.*, at p. 1406.
[11] R.(SB) 6/82, para. 5, a decision of Mr. J. S. Watson.
[12] R.(I) 2/51; R.(SB) 33/85; R.(SB) 12/89 (social security tribunals).
[13] *Aberdeen Steak Houses Group plc* v. *Ibrahim* [1988] I.C.R. 550, E.A.T. (Industrial Tribunals); *cf. Snowball* v. *Gardner Merchant Ltd.* [1987] I.C.R. 719, E.A.T.
[14] *Report of the Council on Tribunals 1959*, p. 6.

preceding paragraph, and the chairman's discretion is substantial. Since so much depends on the chairman it is important briefly to examine three issues—the appointment and qualification of chairmen; training provision; the adequacy of judicial and other safeguards intended to ensure procedural fairness. The first and last of these issues also fall to be considered elsewhere in the book but it is important to review them here in the context of the tribunal hearing.

1. APPOINTMENT AND QUALIFICATION

The formal position on appointment and qualification is set out in Chapter 4.[15] The involvement of the Lord Chancellor in the appointment of the majority of tribunal chairmen is intended to demonstrate, and preserve, their independence of the relevant government department. As to qualification, the controversy is over the desirability of requiring that a chairman should be legally qualified.

The inherent difficulty in tribunal adjudication will by now have become apparent. It is desirable to achieve a high standard of decision-making coupled with demonstrable procedural fairness, whilst retaining the informality, cheapness and speed which are meant to be the hallmarks of the tribunal. Lawyer-chairmen seem to have less difficulty in achieving the former than the latter. Two examples will suffice.

When the Industrial Tribunal was created, the procedural rules specifically required the chairman, in setting the procedure, to seek to avoid formality so far as it was appropriate to do so.[16] All chairmen of Industrial Tribunals are lawyers of not less than seven years' standing[17] and the appellate body is presided over by a High Court judge.[18] The Industrial Tribunal has become formal, with predictable procedure and a growing body of case-law.[19] That can hardly be a coincidence.

The Supplementary Benefit Appeal Tribunal was accustomed to non-lawyer chairmen. There was no prohibition on the appointment of lawyers but by 1980, after 14 years of existence,[20] only one chairman in four was legally qualified.[21] Kathleen Bell's research,[22] published in 1975, was not especially complimentary to the existing chairmen: ". . . generally speaking, they did not fully comprehend the complexities of the work . . . too often

---

[15] Above, pp. 201–204.
[16] Now contained in the Industrial Tribunals (Rules of Procedure) Regulations 1985 (S.I. 1985 No. 16), reg. 8(1).
[17] Above, p. 203, n. 71.
[18] For the composition of the Employment Appeal Tribunal, see above, pp. 59–60.
[19] It has begun to attract both judicial and academic criticism on that account. The criticism reflects a particular view of the functions of an I.T. See the observations of Lord Denning M.R. in *Walls Meat Co. Ltd.* v. *Khan* [1979] I.C.R. 52, at p. 56; Lawton L.J. in *Clay Cross (Quarry Services) Ltd.* v. *Fletcher* [1979] I.C.R. 1, at p. 8; Ormrod L.J. in *National Vulcan Engineering Insurance Group Ltd.* v. *Wade* [1978] I.C.R. 800, at p. 808; Dunn L.J. in *Methven* v. *Cow Industrial Ltd.* [1980] I.C.R. 463, at p. 470.
[20] S.B.A.T.s were created by the Ministry of Social Security Act 1966 as the successor to national assistance appeal tribunals.
[21] N. Harris, "The Appointment of Legally Qualified Chairmen for S.B.A.T.s" (1982) 132 N.L.J. 495.
[22] *Research Study on Supplementary Benefit Appeal Tribunals, Review of Main Findings: Conclusions: Recommendations* (H.M.S.O., 1975).

proceedings were unsystematic, inconsistent and over-influenced by sympathy or otherwise. Separate deliberations were frequently non-existent when the appellant was absent, and in other instances were quite often somewhat rambling and of rather poor quality. We examined a large number of official Reports of Proceedings, the majority of which did not adequately record a reasoned decision."[23] This view was supported by other commentators.[24] Following the Bell Report there was a determined effort to appoint more lawyers as S.B.A.T. chairmen. Following the merging of S.B.A.T.s and N.I.L.T.s into Social Security Appeal Tribunals,[25] the chairmen of the S.S.A.T.s are all lawyers of at least five years' standing,[26] and a regional and national structure of full-time chairmen has been created.[27]

S.S.A.T.s are obviously more closely modelled on the N.I.L.T. than the S.B.A.T., and are expected to achieve the standards set by the N.I.L.T. The N.I.L.T. certainly achieved a reputation as one of the best models of an informal tribunal with a qualified chairman.[28] In the view of Professor Lewis, who had some harsh criticism of S.B.A.T.s, N.I.L.T.s [were] ". . . usually a model of balancing informal expertise with order and legality."[29]

The debate over the desirability of lawyer-chairmen involves many of the same arguments that are deployed in respect of legal representation at tribunals.[30] The skills of the lawyer are thought to lie in order, objectivity and procedure rather than speed, informality and expertise. The Franks Committee were early advocates of the legally-qualified chairman. "Objectivity in the treatment of cases and the proper sifting of facts are most often best secured by having a legally qualified chairman."[31] The Committee also noted that there had been substantial agreement on this matter among witnesses. Later writers have advanced further arguments[32]: the ability of lawyers to uphold basic legal principles in the field of administrative adjudications[33]; the maintenance of firm control over tribunals bred out of confidence and expertise[34]; the natural inclination of lawyers to control bias and prejudice in the presentation of cases; and the grasp of legal questions which is relevant in most areas of tribunal work.[35]

---

[23] Ibid., at p. 6.
[24] A. Frost and C. Howard, Representation and Administrative Tribunals (1977); M. Herman, Administrative Justice and Supplementary Benefits (1972); N. Lewis, "Supplementary Benefits Appeal Tribunals" [1973] P.L. 257.
[25] Above, p. 61. These arrangements came into effect in April 1984 and there were transitional provisions which have now eliminated all non-lawyer chairmen.
[26] Ibid. The period was formerly seven years.
[27] There is a President of Social Security tribunals and a number of Regional Chairmen with supervisory and training responsibilities.
[28] There appears to have been no specific requirement that chairmen of N.I.L.T.s should be qualified lawyers, but it was an almost unbroken rule of practice.
[29] N. Lewis, "Supplementary Benefit Appeal Tribunals" [1973] P.L. 275.
[30] See below, pp. 742–746.
[31] Report of the Committee on Administrative Tribunals and Enquiries (Cmnd. 218, 1957), para. 55.
[32] They are collected and analysed by J. Fulbrook, Administrative Justice and the Unemployed (1978), pp. 215–219.
[33] H. W. R. Wade, Towards Administrative Justice (1963), p. 43.
[34] H. L. Elcock, Administrative Justice (1969), pp. 50–53.
[35] Especially in the Industrial Tribunals, and in the determination of claims for industrial injuries.

These views have not gone unopposed,[36] and even the advocates of lawyer-chairmen have not usually gone so far as to suggest that chairmanship should be the exclusive province of lawyers,[37] yet the recent developments have been along that line. It is unfortunate that other very suitable people may be excluded from chairmanship.

2. TRAINING

Arrangements for the training of tribunal chairman and (especially) members have long been recognised to be inadequate. In recent years steps have been taken to improve the position, but the matter is yet to receive the attention and the resources that are necessary.[38]

3. CORRECTION OF PROCEDURAL IRREGULARITIES

In the major tribunals we have so far considered there is a provision for a right of appeal to an appellate body who have the power to correct procedural irregularities.[39] Where there is no appellate body[40] or where the appeal does not properly deal with the defect alleged judicial review may be sought. That remedy is considered in Chapter 17.[41] Both the existence of the appellate body and the ultimate oversight of the courts provide the safeguard against the wrongful exercise of chairman's considerable discretion.

D. THE ROLE OF THE "WINGMEN"

It is a distinctive feature of the tribunal system that it gives considerable scope for lay participation in adjudication. Some of the alleged disadvantages of lawyer-chairmen may be moderated by the presence of lay people as members of the tribunal.

The appointment of the lay members has already been described,[42] and there is little in the way of research work into how the laymen approach their task and the nature of their relationship with the chairman.[43] At least in relation to social security tribunals there is doubt about the extent of their participation in the hearing and the adjudication, although it is recognised that a lack of participation may result from the absence of training and guidance.

---

[36] R. M. Titmuss, "Welfare 'Rights', Law and Discretion" (1971) 42 *Political Quarterly*, pp. 113–132.

[37] The Franks Committee (above, n. 31) recommended that, ". . . the appointment of persons without legal qualification should not be ruled out when they are particularly suitable." (para. 55).

[38] See above, pp. 204–205.

[39] The Employment Appeal Tribunal for Industrial Tribunals, and the Social Security Commissioners for S.S.A.T.s.

[40] *e.g.* there is no appeal from the Immigration Appeal Tribunal.

[41] pp. 871–878.

[42] Above, pp. 202, 203.

[43] See J. Fulbrook, *Administrative Justice and the Unemployed* (1978), pp. 226–229.

E. REPRESENTATION BEFORE TRIBUNALS

"... it is desirable that every applicant before any tribunal should be able to present his case in person or to obtain representation."[44]

In order to achieve this objective, the Royal Commission on Legal Services asserted that tribunal procedure would need to be simplified wherever possible; the existing schemes for representation by lay persons would need to be developed and funded; and legal aid would need to be made available for certain cases.[45] These findings were based on a significant amount of evidence received by the Commission[46] which was in addition to the published research already available.[47] An important study has more recently been commissioned by the Lord Chancellor's Department, covering Social Security Appeal Tribunals, Industrial Tribunals, Mental Health Review Tribunals and Immigration Adjudicators.[48] The whole question of tribunal representation is one which has continued to attract much attention, especially because of the large numbers of cases currently being determined by tribunals.[49]

In this section we consider six related issues, the first three relating to the present position and the second three to possible future provision of representation. What are the rules about representation? Who are the representatives? What do they do? Should lawyers be involved in representation less often, more often, or not at all? Should legal involvement be funded under the Legal Aid Scheme? In what way, if at all, should schemes of representation by lay persons be developed?

1. THE RULES

Whether or not there is an absolute right to legal representation protected by the principles of natural justice,[50] it is rare for such a right to be specifically denied by tribunal rules.[51] However, a right to legal representation is only useful if the applicant has sufficient funds to pay a lawyer[52]; can find one who is competent in the field; and if the case is one in which the skills of a

---

[44] R.C.L.S. Vol. 1 para. 15.11, p. 169.

[45] Ibid.

[46] The Commission received evidence from both lawyers and non-lawyers active in the tribunal representation field. Its own research is contained in Vol. 2. Section 4, pp. 91–101.

[47] Notably the studies carried out by Professor Kathleen Bell, Research Study on Supplementary Benefit Appeal Tribunals, Review of Main Findings: Conclusions: Recommendations (D.H.S.S. 1975): "National Insurance Local Tribunals," Journal of Social Policy, Vols. 3.4 and 4.1 (1974/5). Other studies include R. Lawrence. Tribunal Representation (1980); E. Kessler et al., Combatting Poverty; C.A.Bx., Claimants and Tribunals (NACAB Occasional Paper No. 11, 1980); R. Lawrence, "Solicitors and Tribunals" [1980] J.S.W.L. 13; Tribunal Assistance, the Chapeltown experience (NACAB Occasional Paper, No. 14, 1982).

[48] H. Genn and Y. Genn, The Effectiveness of Representation at Tribunals (L.C.D., 1989), discussed by R. Young, (1990) 9 C.J.Q. 16 and T. Mullen, (1990) 53 M.L.R. 230.

[49] See Chap. 2, pp. 45–49.

[50] See Sir William Wade, Administrative Law (6th ed., 1988), at p. 546.

[51] The only exception seems to be the service committee to the Family Practitioner Committee, which hears complaints against general practitioners made by their patients. Before that Tribunal paid representation by a lawyer is not permitted, he or she may only appear as a "friend": National Health Service (Service Committees and Tribunal) Regulations 1974 (S.I. 1974 No. 455), reg. 7 (substituted by S.I. 1974 No. 907).

[52] Save in exceptional circumstances, see pp. 738–739, below.

lawyer will be significant. As we shall see, representation by lawyers in tribunals is not generally common.

Some tribunals place restrictions on representation by persons other than lawyers,[53] but the usual provision is for an unfettered right to representation.[54] The ability of the applicant to select an appropriate representative has resulted in the appearance before tribunals of a wide variety of representatives.

2. Who are the Representatives?

Some distinctions must be made between the different tribunals in that they attract different representatives.

The study by Genn and Genn showed that Citizens Advice Bureaux were the most frequent representatives at S.S.A.T.s (closely followed by family or friends); the U.K.I.A.S. before Immigration Adjudicators; lawyers and trade unions at Industrial Tribunals; and solicitors at M.H.R.T.s.[55] The proportion of all appellants represented at the hearing varied considerably. 16 per cent. of S.S.A.T. appellants were represented, but only 12 per cent. by agencies or individuals with experience of representation or with any special expertise.[56] In contrast, 90 per cent. of appellants at immigration hearings, 58 per cent. of applicants and 73 per cent. of respondents at Industrial Tribunals, and 61 per cent. of applicants at M.H.R.T.S were represented by someone other than a relative or friend.[57]

Although there will always be some who defy categorisation, it is possible to discern five groupings from amongst those people who undertake representation.

First, there are those who represent at tribunals as a result of a *professional interest in their members or clients*. Lest that definition would appear to include lawyers we would stress that we are referring here principally to trade union representatives, employers' organisation representatives and social workers who go to a tribunal with a client. Representation has been a significant feature of the legal services supplied by trade unions to their members,[58] and this is particularly marked in the field of national insurance, industrial injuries and employment issues. This has resulted in the trade unions taking a cautious view over the future development of lay or legal representation. They are not anxious to have competitors providing alternative services to their members![59] Social workers have been involved in the work of S.B.A.T.s and S.S.A.T.s. This group of representatives should be in a position to offer effective representation as a result of skill and experience acquired in particular tribunals.

---

[53] For example, representation by non-lawyers is only permitted at the discretion of the Performing Rights Tribunal, the Lands Tribunal and the Commons Commissioners, see R.C.L.S. Vol. 1, para. 15.3.

[54] See the procedural rules of the tribunals considered at pp. 717–723, above.

[55] Genn and Genn (1989), pp. 19, 33, 46, 58. R.C.L.S. Vol. 2, Section 4, Tables 4.7; Bell, *Research on S.B.A.T.s*, at pp. 15–16 (see n. 47, above).

[56] Genn and Genn (1989), pp. 19–22.

[57] *Ibid.*, pp. 32–35, 43–53, 56–59.

[58] G. Latta and R. Lewis, "Trade Union Legal Services" (1974) *XII British Journal of Industrial Relations* 561; R. Lewis and G. Latta, "Union Legal Services" (1973) 123 N.L.J. 386.

[59] See G. Bindman, "Trade Unions and Legal Services" *LAG Bulletin*, March 1979, 56.

The second group consists of representatives provided by *voluntary organisations* for the benefit of their members. The Benson Commission noted the work done by the Royal British Legion in Pensions Appeal Tribunals,[60] and the Claimants' Unions have specialised in the area of social security tribunals.[61]

The third group consists of representatives provided by *generalist or specialist advice agencies* for the benefit of anyone who wishes to consult the agency and accept an offer of help. The Citizens Advice Bureaux have provided such a service to the public,[62] and there are other examples of advice agencies becoming involved in representation as an incidental part of their general service. Specialist agencies, like the Child Poverty Action Group, provide representation in their own field[63] and there are many local examples of advice agencies which offer representation as part of their services.[64] The United Kingdom Immigration Advisory Service (U.K.I.A.S.) provides an interesting example of a specialist agency set up with public funds to deal with enquiries on a particular topic. It was described by the Benson Commission as, ". . . a unique counselling and advocacy service dealing with one field of tribunal work and manned by a full time salaried staff."[65]

The fourth group consists of representatives provided by various specific *tribunal representation projects*. The C.A.B. service has been associated with major schemes in Birmingham, Leeds, Sheffield, Newcastle and Wolverhampton and has also provided the stimulus for other local initiatives.[66] The Free Representation Unit provides representation before tribunals in London and is staffed by young barristers and bar students.[67] The various tribunal representation schemes have come under close scrutiny, since they may provide a model for the development of lay representation. They are all organised on a different basis and attract funds from different sources but this variety may prove fruitful in the evaluation of alternative models. We consider their organisation further, at a later point in this chapter.

The fifth group consists of *lawyers*. We have already noted that lawyers do provide some representation in tribunals, but this is normally at the expense of the client. Very few tribunals have rules as to costs which would allow the recovery of legal expenses.[68] Some representation is funded publicly but it is

---

[60] R.C.L.S., Vol. 1, para. 15.16.

[61] On the role of the Claimants' Unions, see H. Rose, "Who Can de-label the Claimant," in M. Adler and A. Bradley, *Justice, Discretion and Poverty* (1976).

[62] Although it is fair to point out that much has depended on the ability and willingness of volunteers in a particular bureau to undertake the task of representation, and there is considerable pressure and CABx resources. The coverage has consequently been patchy. A majority of CABx provide a representation service of some sort, although not necessarily for more than the occasional case: interview with a NACAB representative cited by J. Baldwin, (1989) 8 C.J.Q. 24, 36.

[63] CPAG can take up a limited number of more complex cases such as appeals to the Commissioners, and then only if referred by local advisers: *National Welfare Benefits Handbook* 1988–89, para. 1.1.6.

[64] *e.g.* in Hull, welfare rights advice was dispensed from a market stall every Friday. Representation was also offered in appropriate cases.

[65] R.C.L.S. Vol. 1 para. 15.17. For the role of U.K.I.A.S. see p. 479 above.

[66] See further, below, pp. 746–748.

[67] See above, p. 571.

[68] See above, pp. 478–479.

exceptional. Legal aid is available for representation before the Lands Tribunal, the Commons Commissioners and the Employment Appeal Tribunal, and the legal advice scheme is available for representation at Mental Health Review Tribunals—assuming that the applicant can satisfy the general criteria of eligibility.[69] The legal advice scheme may be used to fund preparatory work for tribunal hearings and to pay for a solicitor to "assist" a client at the hearing.[70] Assistance short of representation can no doubt prove very irritating for the tribunal and it appears that solicitors may have been remunerated for assistance which has spilled over into representation.

There must inevitably be a composite group of "everybody else." Particularly in S.B.A.T.s, the category of friends and relatives as representatives was significant. As we shall shortly demonstrate, the role of a "representative" can be very restricted, and it may be sufficient that his attendance has ensured the attendance of the applicant. That job can be done as well (possibly better) by a friend as by an advocate.

3. WHAT DO REPRESENTATIVES DO?

This may seem to be an odd question. However, we use it to demonstrate that the assistance offered by a representative may range more widely than simply putting the applicant's case at a hearing.

From the outset, the representative is likely to be involved in an advice-giving role whether he or she is an expert in the field or not.[71] It is obvious that those experienced representatives who have gained a thorough knowledge of their subject are able to evaluate the merits, and likely success, of the applicant's case and can act accordingly. This advisory role is significant because it may operate to exclude the weak and unmeritorious cases at an early stage.[72] If the effect of this screening is to allow the representative only to pursue those cases believed to be worthwhile, he or she gains an enhanced reputation with the tribunal in respect of the cases that are pursued through to a hearing. Moreover, the scarce resources of advice agencies and the like should not be used to support hopeless cases.

There are some reservations expressed about the validity of this advisory role, not least because the adviser may be constituting *him-* or *herself* as the adjudicator rather than the tribunal, and coming between the applicant and the tribunal. It is argued that applicants should be given the confidence and expertise to use the system themselves rather than experience the "interference" of another expert who would come to some tidy arrangement with the tribunal leaving the claimant as isolated as ever.[73] This is a minority view, however, and most of the representation schemes that have been established

---

[69] For legal aid, see pp. 506–517 above; for advice by way of representation (ABWOR) see pp. 446–447, 452, above.

[70] See above, p. 444. The legal advice scheme only covers representation if regulations so provide: Legal Aid Act 1988, s.8(2); ABWOR is only available in a limited range of situations.

[71] Even the next-door neighbour might be asked whether or not to appeal!

[72] See Genn and Genn (1989), pp. 134–135.

[73] The Claimants' Union recognises a "right" to be represented whatever the merits of the case might appear to be. See generally, R. Lawrence, *Tribunal Representation* (1980), p. 18; H. Rose, "Who Can De-Label the Claimant?" in M. Adler and A. Bradley, *op. cit.*

place emphasis on the provision of advice by an "expert" at an early stage.[74] There is also the reservation expressed by some about

> "doing the Government's job for them. You are telling someone to leave the country or not to ... claim a benefit. You are the soft police."[75]

A second function of a representative may be to act as a negotiator on behalf of the applicant with a view to effecting a settlement of the problem.[76] We noted the importance of settlements in the civil process in Chapter 10[76a]—they also have their place in the tribunal process. The intervention of a third party on behalf of an applicant may produce a change in the decision which satisfies the claimant. This might be called anti-representation since it has the effect of preventing a tribunal hearing, but it benefits both the applicant and the tribunal.[77]

A third function of representation may be simply to ensure the attendance of the applicant. This is sometimes referred to as a "hand-holding exercise."[78] The published figures demonstrate that an applicant has a higher chance of success at a tribunal if he or she attends, whether or not represented, than if he or she does not attend.[79] Claimants who receive an unfavourable decision on their claim may immediately give notice of appeal without giving thought to how to pursue the appeal.[80] On receipt of the appeal papers they decide not to go along to the hearing because the case is not arguable, or they are frightened, or ignorant of the process, or no longer interested. If they seek advice at all, they may simply need the reassurance that someone will attend the tribunal with them and help them through the procedure—not necessarily as an advocate but as a friend. Once at the hearing, with the presence of a supporter they are able to respond sufficiently to the tribunal to allow the case fully to be considered.

A fourth function is that of preparing the case for the hearing, good preparation being fundamental to the success of appeals. This includes interviewing the client, collecting documentary evidence, arranging for witnesses to attend and researching the law. Most appellants and applicants are likely to have difficulty in identifying the facts relevant to the case and securing the necessary evidence.[81]

---

[74] Some of the tribunal representation schemes operate on a "consultancy" basis whereby volunteer lay representatives themselves receive help and guidance at the early stages of a possible appeal (see, for example, the West Midlands project—*Combatting Poverty*, n. 47, above). Others give a direct service to the claimant but rely heavily on the expertise of the representatives.

[75] Quotation from a Law Centre, cited by Genn and Genn (1989), pp. 134–135.

[76] *Ibid.*, pp. 135–138.

[76a] Above, pp. 493–504.

[77] One of the arguments advanced in favour of the extension of representation is its effect in diminishing the caseload of tribunals.

[78] Particularly by the Citizens Advice Bureaux. See the NACAB Administrative Circular (1974), cited in R. Lawrence, *Tribunal Representation* (1980), p. 59. This circular is no longer current, but the function remains the same!

[79] K. Bell, *op. cit.* (above, n. 47); Genn and Genn (1989), p. 68 (S.S.A.T.s); this is not a surprising finding. Attendance at least allows the tribunal the possibility of questioning the claimant.

[80] This does not mean that a high proportion of the recipients of adverse D.S.S. decisions appeal: see Genn and Genn (1989), pp. 130–134.

[81] Genn and Genn (1989), pp. 138–147.

This may seem quite a late stage to be arriving at the representative's job of representing. At the hearing, the function of the representative is to put forward the applicant's case without coming completely between the applicant and the tribunal. The representative should not forget that the tribunal will be interested to hear from the applicant directly.[82] The need to marshal the arguments for the benefit of the tribunal will be dictated partly by the complexity of the subject matter and partly by the procedure adopted.[83] The skills required are not necessarily those of the advocate—but it helps the tribunal if the representative can present a logical, orderly, relevant analysis of the issues and the evidence. Statistics show that the represented claimant is better off at a tribunal.[84] This point is confirmed by the study by Genn and Genn,[84a] which also indicates that specialist representatives have the greatest effect on the probability of success.[85]

Finally, the expertise gained by the representative and his or her familiarity with the system may be used for the benefit of others in the exchange of information and pressure for reform. In the informal world of tribunals the shared experience is invaluable. This sharing may be formal, through publications,[86] or informal, through word of mouth but it is undoubtedly a factor in the increasing success of lay representatives.

Much of this section has been directed towards the less formal tribunals and the experience of the Industrial Tribunal is somewhat different. There, the actual representation at the hearing takes on the major significance and the other functions are consequently diminished.[87] It is not surprising that with considerable lawyer representation the emphasis has been placed upon advocacy.

Overall it was the clear conclusion of the study by Genn and Genn that representation of appellants and applicants increases the accuracy of tribunal decision-making and improves the fairness of the process by which decisions are reached.[88] Arguments that tribunals proceedings are informal and simple, and that representation is accordingly unnecessary and undesirable, are ill-founded.[89] The view of tribunals, representatives and presenting officers in the four areas studied

> "was that much of the law with which they were concerned was complex and the adjudicative function of tribunals was often a highly technical forensic process."[90]

---

[82] The Social Security Commissioner has, on occasion, criticised a representative who appears to have dominated the hearing to the exclusion of the applicant. (See R.(I) 36/61).

[83] In the Industrial Tribunal, for example, the representative has his or her job defined by the adoption of a fairly standard, adversarial procedure. See pp. 721–722 above.

[84] Although there are some reservations about the interpretation of the evidence: R. Lawrence, *Tribunal Representation* (1980), pp. 19–20.

[84a] Genn and Genn (1989), Chap. 3. Other factors independently associated with success were the type of case, number of witnesses, geographical location (S.S.A.T.s) and the identity of the chair or the adjudicator (S.S.A.T.s, I.T.s, Immigration hearings).

[85] Welfare rights centres, tribunal units and law centres for social security appeals, U.K.I.A.S. and lawyers for immigration hearings.

[86] For example, information is disseminated through NACAB and CPAG literature (*e.g.*, respectively, through *The Adviser* and the *Welfare Rights Bulletin*), and other periodicals.

[87] The negotiation function is, to some extent, undertaken by the conciliation officers of A.C.A.S., see above, p. 576.

[88] Genn and Genn (1989), pp. 247–248.

[89] *Ibid.*

[90] *Ibid.*, p. 244; and generally Chap. 4.

Moreover,

"the experience of unrepresented appellants and applicants indicates that, even in the most informal hearings, they have difficulty in expressing themselves; they do not understand the relevance of the rules and regulations that are quoted to them; and when they lose, frequently leave in a state of disappointment and frustration."[91]

It was the unanimous belief of representatives interviewed that "no matter how well-intentioned tribunals might be, it was impossible to compensate for lack of representation;" on the other hand, the majority of chairs of S.S.A.T.s and industrial tribunals believed that they could compensate for lack of representation. The observation of hearings for the purpose of the study tended to confirm the former view.[92]

Finally, some fears have been expressed about the extent to which an involvement with representation will inevitably result in a commitment to reform of the system, an over-identification with the position of the applicants, or an engagement in political activity.[93] How objective/disinterested can a representative remain? This anxiety has been examined and answered effectively by David Bull, whose analysis of the range of advocacy and its implications for the representatives is very convincing.[94]

4. SHOULD LAWYERS BE INVOLVED MORE? LESS? AT ALL?

The answer to this particular question depends upon the skills which lawyers bring to tribunal representation and the effect that the deployment of those skills is likely to have on the style and procedure of tribunals. It further depends upon the objectives which a system of tribunals seeks to achieve, and upon the complexity of the law which is being administered, the nature of the particular tribunal under consideration and upon the nature of the particular case under consideration, for there may be especial circumstances which warrant the attention of a lawyer.

Given all these variables it is difficult to formulate a single answer. Perhaps the convenient starting-point is to ask whether lawyers have a place in tribunal representation at all. Against the proposition that a citizen should have a right to legal representation in all forms of judicial or quasi-judicial proceedings[95] may be put the assertion that lawyers "spoil" tribunal adjudication by detracting from those qualities which tribunals are alleged to display, namely speed, informality, cheapness and expertise.[96] In particular, it has been argued that, in respect of areas in which discretion is an important element, the introduction of "legalism" is likely to hinder the operation of discretion to the disadvantage of the claimant.[97] These arguments have not

[91] *Ibid.*, pp. 246–247; and generally Chap. 7.
[92] *Ibid.*, pp. 215–216.
[93] This has been a particular fear of NACAB who are very sensitive about allegations of political involvement and campaigning.
[94] D. Bull, "The Anti-Discretion Movement in Britain: Fact or Phantom?" [1980] J.S.W.L. 65.
[95] See above, pp. 736–737.
[96] For the virtues (alleged) of tribunal adjudication, see above, pp. 39–40. It is interesting to note that in the county court small claims procedure (see above, p. 532) legal representation is not prohibited but it is discouraged because of the no-costs rule. Some commentators would have argued for a complete ban on lawyers.
[97] R. M. Titmuss, "Welfare 'Rights', Law and Discretion," (1971) 42 *Political Quarterly*, pp. 113–132. The subject is discussed fully in J. Fulbrook, *Administrative Justice and the Unemployed* (1978), pp. 276–293.

prevailed[98] and there is, apparently, only one example of a tribunal which positively prohibits legal representation.[99] It would certainly be difficult now to make a case for a blanket prohibition on legal representation, and it is generally accepted that lawyers have *some* part to play.

The more difficult question is the *extent* to which lawyer-representation is desirable. In practice, this question is closely linked with the possibility of providing public funds for such representation, for without funding the likelihood that an applicant will be able to pay for the services of a lawyer is slim.[1] However, until a positive case has been made for legal representation, funds will not be made available. What is the strength of the case?

There has been comparatively little evidence of the extent to which lawyers are involved in tribunal work or, incidentally, of their likely response if money were to be made available to allow them to undertake more.[2] Statistics from the research studies that have been done demonstrate the very low proportion of cases in social security tribunals which have lawyer representatives[3] and although the proportion is much higher in Industrial Tribunals[4] there is little to indicate whether a few firms provide representation as a specialist service or whether most firms will undertake this type of work.[5] If the Industrial Tribunal is any guide the presence of lawyer-representatives is likely to formalise procedure and reinforce the adversarial style of the proceedings. This fear has been expressed also in respect of social security tribunals, not least because the criticisms levelled at such tribunals by lawyers tend to focus on the failure to follow a consistent and clear judicial process in adjudication.[6] The lawyers' response to such a failure is normally to formulate procedural rules and safeguards to be operated by lawyers.

The research conducted by Professor Bell indicated that there was no great enthusiasm amongst appellants for professional advocates; rather they were anxious to see the tribunal play a more *enabling* role thereby improving the opportunity for appellants to put their own case.[7] Few among the tribunals and representatives interviewed for the study by Genn and Genn believed that lawyers were necessarily best equipped to conduct tribunal representations; the most common view was that specialisation and experience were the most important qualifications.[8]

Despite fears that lawyerly skills may frustrate some of the objectives of tribunal adjudication, the prevailing view is that legal representation is desirable in particular circumstances. This view is based mainly upon the

---

[98] Indeed, in the social security field benefits (first supplementary benefit, now income support) have become rule—rather than discretion-based and there is no longer a right of appeal to a tribunal in respect of the main remaining discretion-based benefit (social fund payments).
[99] The service committees of the Family Practitioner Committee, see p. 736 and n. 51, above.
[1] This is especially the case in social security tribunals where there is likely to be only a relatively small amount of money at stake. Costs are not normally awarded by tribunals, see pp. 478–479, above.
[2] R. Lawrence, "Solicitors and Tribunals" [1980] J.S.W.L. 13; N. Harris, "Solicitors and Supplementary Benefit Cases" (1983) 34 N.I.L.Q. 144.
[3] K. Bell, *op. cit.* below, n. 6; R.C.L.S. Vol. 2, Section 4; Genn and Genn (1989), p. 20..
[4] R.C.L.S. Vol. 2, Section 4, Tables 4.7, 4.8; Genn and Genn (1989), pp. 44–45, 50.
[5] R. Lawrence, *op. cit.* n. 47 above, inclines to the former view.
[6] K. Bell, *Research Study on Supplementary Benefit Appeal Tribunals. Review of Main Findings: Conclusions: Recommendations.* (DHSS, 1975), at pp. 19–20.
[7] *Ibid.*, p. 18.
[8] Genn and Genn (1989), p. 245; generally pp. 171–178, 193–198, 210–215.

combined arguments of legal complexity in certain fields and the importance of the issues to the individual claimant. The Royal Commission on Legal Services was content merely to state, ".... there are cases when a denial of legal aid for representation by a lawyer will put the applicant at a disadvantage. We have in mind, for example, cases before Supplementary Benefit Appeal Tribunals which involve allegations of cohabitation or dishonesty, and some of the claims before Industrial Tribunals which involve difficult problems of law and fact."[9] The study by Genn and Genn concluded that while the main development should be in the direction of increased funding to lay agencies, this would not provide the complete answer. There might be a need for skilled legal representation before the explicitly adversarial Industrial Tribunals, and to fill gaps left by the uneven geographical coverage of lay advice and representation agencies.[10]

The Benson Commission had considered much evidence on the provision of legal representation in tribunals and concluded that there are *some* cases before *all* tribunals in which it was necessary. The identification of those cases is problematic, but some indication of the factors which might necessitate legal representation is given by the tests formulated to govern the granting of legal aid. The assumption seems to have been made that legal representation will only really be available when legal aid is available[11] and we discuss in the next section the criteria which might be adopted in determining eligibility.

5. When Should Legal Aid be Available for Tribunals?

There is no serious dispute that it would be inadvisable for legal aid to be made immediately available for all cases in all tribunals. Different reasons would be given by different people. The expense; the inappropriateness; the difficulty of applying the "merits" test[12]; the availability of skilled lay representation; the possible lack of interest amongst the solicitors' profession[13] would all be reasons used to reject the extension of legal aid to all cases. There is an equal measure of agreement about the need to extend legal aid to *some* tribunal cases, but two difficulties arise. First, it is difficult to agree the criteria which would establish eligibility; second, the advocates of the development of lay representation would not wish the extension of legal aid to be viewed as an alternative to funding better organised and more comprehensive schemes of lay representation.

The Council on Tribunals has consistently advocated the extension of legal aid,[14] and its view has been supported by the Lord Chancellor's

---

[9] R.C.L.S. Vol. 1 para. 15.24.

[10] Genn and Genn (1989), pp. 249–250.

[11] This is why the two issues of whether lawyers should be involved, and whether they should be paid out of the Legal Aid Fund are extremely difficult to disentangle. When they are needed, they should be paid for ... See the evidence of The Law Society in *R.C.L.S. Memorandum No. 3* (1978). Evidence to the same effect was received from the Council on Tribunals, the President of Industrial Tribunals and other individuals. This view was supported by the Lord Chancellor's Advisory Committee on Legal Aid.

[12] This is the standard test for legal aid—"Would a solicitor advise a private client to pursue or defend the action?"—see above, p. 510. The test is almost unworkable in relation to many tribunals because of the lack of correlation between the amount at stake and the cost of legal representation.

[13] See R. Lawrence, "Solicitors and Tribunals" [1980] J.S.W.L. 13, at pp. 19–25.

[14] *e.g. Annual Reports*, 1976–77, p. 6; 1987–88, pp. 17–21. The Franks Committee had made such a recommendation in 1958: *Report*, para. 89.

Advisory Committee,[15] by the President of Industrial Tribunals[16] and by other groups and individuals. It was the formulation of the test of eligibility submitted by the Council on Tribunals which won the approval of the Benson Commission, subject to some additions. The Council proposed in their evidence to the Commission that an applicant for legal aid should show "... that in the particular circumstances of his case he reasonably requires the services of a lawyer, and the certifying committee shall in this respect have regard to the suitability and availability of any other forms of assistance." The Council instanced several situations where representation by a lawyer might be regarded as appropriate—

"(i) where a significant point of law arises,
(ii) where evidence is likely to be so complex or specialised that the average layman could reasonably wish for expert help in assembling and evaluating the evidence and in its testing or interpretation,
(iii) where a test case arises,
(iv) where deprivation of liberty or the ability of an individual to follow his occupation is at stake."[17]

To these situations the Commission added three others: where the amount at stake is significant *to the claimant*; where suitable lay representation is unavailable; where the special circumstances of the individual make legal representation desirable.[18]

These criteria, it is suggested, would be applied by the appropriate legal aid committee[19] and used to determine whether the "merits" tests for legal aid had been satisfied. An alternative view, that legal aid should be granted or recommended by the chairman of the appropriate tribunal,[20] was not supported by the Benson Commission.

It is evident that these criteria were formulated upon the assumption that there would be an adequate lay representation service available, and the supporters of such a service feared that these might be regarded as alternative, rather than complementary, developments. This dilemma confronts the reformer who wishes to advance the cause of tribunal representation but takes the view that the more important use of public funds is in the training and organisation of lay representatives. To oppose the extension of legal aid may appear to be siding with the forces of darkness; to support it, with limited funds available, may be reducing the possibility of more general improvement.

The Government's response to the Benson Commission was not encouraging;[21] it noted that all those involved in tribunal proceedings were already

---

[15] This subject was first considered at length in the *24th Report of the Law Society on Legal Aid and Advice*, 1973/74, pp. 47–55. Thereafter it recurs in the *33rd Legal Aid Annual Reports* [1982–83], pp. 194–209; the *35th Reports* [1984–85], pp. 232–243; *38th Reports* (1987–88), pp. 103–105; *39th Reports* (1988–89), pp. 112–114.

[16] In his evidence to the Royal Commission on Legal Services, referred to in R.C.L.S. Vol. 1, at para. 15.28.

[17] *Ibid.*, para. 15.28; endorsed by the Lord Chancellor's Advisory Committee on Legal Aid: *33rd Legal Aid Annual Reports* [1982–83], at p. 205.

[18] *Ibid.*, The Commission's additions were criticised and rejected by the Lord Chancellor's Advisory Committee: *33rd Annual Reports* [1982–83], at p. 205.

[19] Now the Area Director, see p. 508, above.

[20] See, for example, R. Micklethwait, *The National Insurance Commissioners* (1976), at p. 56.

[21] *The Government Response to the Report of The Royal Commission on Legal Services*, (Cmnd. 9077, 1983).

eligible, subject to means, for legal advice and assistance[22] and that assistance by way of representation was available for proceedings in mental health
review tribunals.[23] "Extensions of assistance by way of representation and
legal aid are made where it is shown to be necessary and resources allow."[24]

The Lord Chancellor's Advisory Committee on Legal Aid and the Council on Tribunals have not given up. The former have recommended that legal
aid should be extended as a matter of priority to bail applications to the
immigration appellate authorities, and to the Immigration Appeal Tribunal,
the Social Security Commissioners, Industrial Tribunals and the Vaccine
Damage Tribunal.[25] The Government's position has been to reiterate its
response to the Benson Royal Commission. Indeed, it was stated that,
pending the outcome of the research project on the effectiveness of representation, "the Government does not intend that there should be any
general extension of publicly funded tribunal representation."[26] Given that
outcome, noted at a number of points in the chapter, it is likely that any
future development will be in the area of lay representation. This position
has been supported by the Legal Aid Efficiency Scrutiny[27] and the Legal Aid
Board,[28] but their respective suggestions that the extension of representation might be funded by restricting the scope of the green form scheme have
been widely criticised as unrealistic and undesirable.[29]

6. HOW SHOULD LAY REPRESENTATION BE DEVELOPED?

"If agencies which provide advice and representation before tribunals
are to give an adequate service, they should have enough money to
provide training for staff, an up-to-date information service and proper
administrative support . . . we recommend that public funds should be
made available to approved agencies to assist in the training of tribunal
representatives."[30]

"[The recommendation is] accepted in principle subject to further
consideration being given to timing and the availability of resources."[31]

If the Government were to make available resources to implement the
Benson Commission recommendation, then consideration would have to be
given to the most effective method of organising schemes of lay representation. There is a variety of schemes already in existence which might provide
a guide for national development.

[22] See above, pp. 443–446.
[23] Introduced in December 1982, see above, p. 447.
[24] *Response*, above n. 21, p. 18.
[25] *33rd Legal Aid Annual Reports* [1982–83], pp. 194–209; *35th Annual Reports* [1984–85], pp.
236–242 (adding the Vaccine Damage Tribunal to the list). The Council on Tribunals' list of
priorities is longer, and includes M.H.R.T.s, Medical Appeal Tribunals and Immigration
Adjudicators (see Annual Report for 1987–88 (1988–89 H.C. 102), p. 18).
[26] White Paper on *Legal Aid in England and Wales, A New Framework* (Cm. 118, 1987), para.
30.
[27] (L.C.D. 1986), Vol. 2, Part IV. See further above pp. 462–464.
[28] *Second Stage Consultation on the Future of the Green Form Scheme* (1989), para. 12.
[29] *e.g.* responses to the Legal Aid Board by the Lord Chancellor's Advisory Committee (*39th
Legal Aid Annual Reports* (1988–89), p. 96), the Law Society (Response, p. 28) and NACAB
(Response, p. 7).
[30] R.C.L.S. Vol. 1, paras. 15.20, 15.21.
[31] *Response*, above n. 21, at p. 18.

Lawrence[32] distinguished three types of scheme which could be observed amongst the 16 or so existing tribunal units. He characterised these types as *referral agencies*, *advice bureau based* and *support units*.[33]

The *referral agencies* accept tribunal cases at the hearing stage from another agency which has done all the preparatory work and got the case ready for the tribunal. The representatives attached to such agencies operate purely as advocates and will send the applicant back to the original agency if there is any follow-up work to be done after the hearing has taken place. Typical of this kind of organisation of specialist advocates is the Free Representation Unit which draws its members from amongst Bar students and young barristers.[33a] Such a unit relies heavily on the initial competence of some other agency[34] to prepare the case in such a way that it is ready for a hearing.

Advice bureau based units operate from or alongside established agencies, often C.A.Bx., with particular responsibility for taking on the tribunal representation work of that agency. This is, in some ways, the easiest unit to develop since it can emerge from the expertise of workers in the bureau in response to a perceived need for the work.[35] The Newcastle Tribunal Assistance Unit[36] exemplifies that process, and the Chapeltown unit in Leeds is similarly bureau-based.[37] These units have a wider role because of the close connection with a bureau and find themselves involved in formal and informal training of bureau workers as well as advice and representation. The value of having a unit attached in this way is the effect it has of raising the general level of advice-giving in the host agency. It is clear that the tendency at first is for the agency to push *all* problems in the subject area of the unit onto the unit, including perfectly routine enquiries. After an initial period, however, the general competence to handle such enquiries increases and the work of the agency is consequently strengthened.[38]

Support units are those which are not intended directly to offer representation, but rather to train, inform, advise and assist other representatives in the area which is served by the unit. The NACAB/EEC Tribunal Project in the West Midlands[39] operated in this way from the outset although the staff found the need to deal with some casework in order to retain their own expertise in representation. Of course, such units depend on their ability to stimulate interest in representation amongst agencies in the area and it can be difficult to break down reluctance on the part of volunteers.[40] The task is

[32] R. Lawrence, *Tribunal Representation* (1980).

[33] *Ibid.*, at p. 84.

[33a] Above, p. 571.

[34] This is an unsatisfactory feature of such a scheme. The particularly fruitful parts of the other two types of scheme depend on the contact between representative and adviser and the building up of the general level of advice-giving.

[35] The drawback of this type of unit is that it relies heavily on the skills of few people. Holidays, illness, pressure of work can then disrupt the representation service quite significantly.

[36] Established in 1974 with the support of the Newcastle CAB. It experienced a rapid rise in workload and subsequently attracted work from a wide area.

[37] See *Chapeltown CAB, Leeds, Tribunal Assistance Unit Progress Report—First Two Years Aug. 1976—Aug. 1978* (NACAB Occasional Paper No. 6, 1979); *Tribunal Assistance, The Chapeltown experience* (NACAB Occasional Paper No. 14, 1982).

[38] R. Lawrence, *op. cit.*, esp. Chap. 5; *Tribunal Assistance* (above, n. 37), pp. 56–58.

[39] *Combatting Poverty*: *CABx, Claimants and Tribunals* (NACAB Occasional Paper No. 11, 1980); above, p. 740, n. 74.

[40] *Ibid.*, pp. 47–56.

less easy for support units than for bureau-based services with their constant contact with both workers and clients.

This categorisation does not take account of all the units presently in operation[41] but it may offer some guidance for future development. The Citizens Advice Bureaux network would seem to provide a good basis for bureau-based units, but the bureaux are autonomous and might not welcome such a development. Geographical coverage is still incomplete and it might prove hopelessly expensive to provide bureau-based units in rural areas where there is relatively less work to do. Support units are not directly effective and seem to take longer to stimulate a reliable service. In the longer term, however, they have a much broader effect on the area they serve.

A further kind of service, commended by Genn and Genn,[42] is the single-purpose agency, exemplified by the United Kingdom Immigration Advisory Service. It is, however, doubtful that it would be practicable to extend this model generally to all tribunals in which there is a representation problem.[43]

The Lord Chancellor's Advisory Committee advocate the development of a strong voluntary lay representation service, possibly based on the CABx, utilising the skills of "resource lawyers." This scheme would complement legal representation funded by legal aid in difficult cases and would be closest to the *support units* of the models we have discussed.[44]

7. PROCEDURAL REFORM

The preceding sections have all made one important assumption: that the tribunal system will continue in much the same way, becoming, if anything, rather more legalistic. The need for improved representation is based on that assumption.

The Benson Commission recommended a review of the procedures of tribunals in order to ensure that applicants in person are able to conduct their own cases whenever possible.[45] Such a review might have an effect on the need for representation, but would raise again the fundamental principles of tribunal adjudication. In the end, the question, "What kind of representation do we need?" is linked inextricably with the question, "What kind of tribunals do we want?" As we have seen, the study by Genn and Genn strongly reinforces the view that the idea that procedures can be simplified, given the great complexity of much of the law dealt with by tribunals, is unduly optimistic.

---

[41] R. Lawrence, *op. cit.* at p. 85.
[42] Genn and Genn (1989), pp. 193–198, 250.
[43] See T. Mullen, (1990) 53 M.L.R. 230, 234–235.
[44] *33rd Annual Legal Aid Reports* [1982–83], pp. 201–203; 35th Reports [1984–85], pp. 235–236.
[45] R.C.L.S., Vol. 1., paras. 15.12, 15.13.

CHAPTER 16

THE CRIMINAL TRIAL

THIS chapter examines the criminal trial. It should be read taking a critical approach, bearing in mind Packer's two models of criminal justice.[1] The crime control model emphasises the importance of the repression of criminal behaviour in the most efficient manner. There is a requirement for high rates of arrest and conviction, and a major interest in speed and finality in the system. There is, therefore, a reliance on informal, routine procedures, relying heavily on the work of the police to determine guilt. Consequently, whatever procedures are used presume guilt. The due process model stresses the need to protect the accused against error. Whereas the crime control model looks like a conveyor-belt approach to criminal justice, the due process model looks more like an obstacle course. Every stage in the due process model assumes the innocence of the accused and requires formidable impediments to be overcome to establish guilt. Essential, therefore, to the due process model is the trial stage.

The rhetoric of the English criminal justice system reflects the due process model, as will be indicated by this chapter. Examples to consider are the presumption of innocence, reflected in the prosecution having the burden of proof in a criminal trial, the right to silence of the accused, and the rules relating to the admissibility of evidence. However, as White makes clear,[2] it is inappropriate quickly to dismiss the crime control model since, for example, many cases are diverted from trial, the police, it is alleged, have on occasion violated the rules governing their powers and many, perhaps too many, guilty pleas are entered.[3] The crime control model plays a greater role in the English criminal justice system than would at first appear.

It may also be of some value in reading this chapter to consider that there is a difference between methods of establishing the truth and the procedure

---

[1] See H. L. Packer, *The Limits of the Criminal Sanction* (1968). Packer's models are discussed more fully in relation to pre-trial criminal procedure at pp. 680–684 above, where also attention is drawn to the "fundamental balance" between the interests of the community and the rights and liberties of individual citizens considered by the Royal Commission on Criminal Procedure. For a summary of Packer's models, see R. C. A. White, *The Administration of Justice* (1985), Chap. 7, esp. pp. 113–114. For the enthusiastic student, M. King, *The Framework of Criminal Justice* (1981) provides a method of examining the criminal justice system by building more models on to those created by Packer. A summary of King's work is also to be found in White (1985), pp. 114–116.
[2] White (1985), p. 114.
[3] As to diversion from trial, see above pp. 630–636 and the fixed penalty notice scheme noted briefly below at p. 752; the Police and Criminal Evidence Act 1984 is now preventing what may have been regular violations, see above Chap. 13; as to the debate concerned with "plea bargaining" at pp. 767–769, 772–774, 777–778, 784–786 below.

in the criminal trial.[4] At the criminal trial, it is for the prosecution to establish its case against the accused to the satisfaction of the magistrates or jury beyond a reasonable doubt through an adversarial procedure. Considerable efforts are made to ensure "fairness" in the procedure, so the court cannot take account of all possible forms of evidence. Outside the criminal trial, judgments as to the truth of a matter are likely to be made, not by adversarial methods, but inquisitorial; not so as to be satisfied beyond reasonable doubt, but as more likely than not; not by evidence which passes the rules of legal admissibility, but on any reliable evidence. It is not the objective of the criminal trial to establish the truth of what happened, although it is presumably believed that the criminal trial will produce results which closely resemble the truth of the matter.

A. SUMMARY TRIAL[5]

Whilst the bulk of the work of magistrates' courts concerns minor offences, their powers of sentencing are limited and their decisions create no legal precedents, they do deal with the vast majority of criminal cases[6] and they constitute the tribunal most likely to be encountered by the "ordinary" person. Thus the manner in which they perform their function is of considerable significance.

We have already considered the ways in which the appearance of a person accused of a summary offence or an offence triable either way can be secured.[7] We have also explained the procedure adopted by the court in selecting the mode of trial of an offence triable either way.[8] If summary trial is the appropriate way of determining liability for the offence charged, the first formal step is for the magistrates' clerk to read the information to the

---

[4] See, further, Z. Bankowski, "The Jury and Reality" in M. Findlay and P. Duff (eds.), *The Jury Under Attack* (1988) and works referred to there.

[5] The body of literature on the summary trial is increasing. The practitioners' work is Stone's *Justices Manual*, published annually. The main books relied on in this chapter are A. E. Bottoms and J. D. McLean, *Defendants in the Criminal Process* (1976); E. Burney, *J.P., Magistrate, Court and Community* (1979); P. Carlen, *Magistrates' Justice* (1976); A. P. Carr, *Criminal Procedure in Magistrates' Court* (1983); P. Darbyshire, *The Magistrates' Clerk* (1984); J. Gregory, *Crown Court or Magistrates' Court?* Office of Population Censuses and Surveys (HMSO 1976); B. Harris, *The Criminal Jurisdiction of Magistrates* (11th ed., 1988); H. Parker, M. Sumner and J. Jarvis, *Unmasking the Magistrates* (1989); J. W. Raine, *Local Justice* (1989); P. J. Rowe and S. J. Knapp, *Evidence and Procedure in Magistrates' Courts* (3rd ed., 1989); R. Tarling, *Sentencing Practice in Magistrates' Courts*, Home Office Research Study No. 56 (1981), J. Vennard, *Contested Trials in Magistrates' Courts*, R.C.C.P. Research Study No. 6 (1980); J. Vennard, *Contested Trials in Magistrates' Courts*, Home Office Research Study No. 71 (1981); For a brief summary of the work of the Home Office Research and Planning Unit, see D. Moxon, "Current Research Bearing on the Work of Magistrates' Courts" (1984) 148 J.P.N. 634.

[6] In 1989, 1,864,000 defendants were proceeded against at magistrates' courts, of whom 55,000 were aged between 10 and 17; 24 per cent. of these proceedings were for indictable offences; 30 per cent. for summary, non-motoring offences; and 45 per cent. for summary motoring offences: *Criminal Statistics 1989* (Cm. 1322, 1990), Table 6.1. In the same year, 104,400 defendants were proceeded against in the Crown Court, of whom 1,700 were aged between 10 and 17. A further 7,200 appeared in the Crown Court for sentence after summary conviction (of whom 100 were aged between 10 and 17), because the magistrates' sentencing powers were not sufficient in the circumstances: *Ibid.* Table 6.5.

[7] See pp. 642–645, above.

[8] See pp. 639–641, above.

accused or the defendant (these terms are used inter-changeably), and secure a plea.

1. THE INFORMATION

The information is the formal document containing the allegation(s) against the accused.[9] Unlike an indictment it does not contain a separate statement of the alleged offence and then the particulars alleged to constitute the offence.[10] It merely contains a statement which combines the essential facts and the alleged offence. It is sufficient if the accused is given reasonable notice of the charge to be met and the way in which it is alleged the offence was committed.[11] The use of plain, non-technical language is intended to simplify matters for the accused. Specimen informations[12] relating to criminal damage, theft and carrying an offensive weapon follow:

(i) Henry Frederick Smailey on the 1st day of March 1991 did without lawful excuse damage a motor vehicle, namely a Ford Escort number ABC 123, belonging to John Smith intending to damage the property or being reckless as to whether that property would be damaged; contrary to section 1(1) of the Criminal Damage Act 1971.

(ii) Henry Frederick Smailey on the 1st day of March 1991 stole £15 belonging to John Smith; contrary to sections 1 and 7 of the Theft Act 1968.

(iii) Henry Frederick Smailey on the 1st day of March 1991 without lawful authority or reasonable excuse had with him in a public place, namely the Victoria Shopping Centre, Nottingham, an offensive weapon namely a bayonet; contrary to section 1(1) of the Prevention of Crime Act 1953.

2. PRESENCE OF THE ACCUSED

At a trial on indictment, the accused must be in court to enter a plea and is normally present through the whole trial.[13] Summary trial is different in that provision is made for guilty pleas to be made by post and also, where the accused fails to appear at the appointed time and place, for trial in the absence of the accused. Both these procedures are designed to spare the time and expense of the participants where there is no real intention to defend the charge, but they are hedged with certain safeguards to ensure that injustice does not result.

Written pleas of guilty made by post may be entered only if the offence is a summary offence punishable by not more than three months' imprisonment. The safeguards ensuring no injustices result are that the accused must be served with a statement of the facts alleged by the prosecution and an explanatory note, in addition to the usual summons; a wish not to be present

---

[9] For the full form of an information, see p. 643, above.

[10] Specimen indictments are set out at pp. 760–761, below.

[11] The rules relating to the drafting of an information are contained in the Magistrates' Courts Rules 1981 (S.I. 1981, No. 552). The most informal style permitted is to be found in rule 100.

[12] The prescribed full form of information is to be found in the Magistrates' Courts (Forms) Rules 1981 (S.I. 1981, No. 553), Form 1.

[13] See p. 767, below.

must be made clear by the accused; the statement of facts, the plea and anything which the accused has written in relation to mitigation or personal financial circumstances must be read out in court by the clerk; and no information is given to the court by the prosecution other than that contained in the documents.[14] This procedure is very strict and any deviation will result in the proceedings being a nullity.[15]

A magistrates' court has a discretion to proceed with a trial in the absence of the accused[16] where the right to be present has been voluntarily waived. The right is voluntarily waived by the accused, for example, abusing it as a consequence of indecent, outrageous or unseemly behaviour, or ceasing to claim it by deliberately jumping bail. In any case, the court must exercise its discretion with great reluctance, never for anyone's convenience, but solely in the interests of the administration of justice.[17]

Note should also be made of the fixed penalty notice system, used not only for parking offences, but also, for example, for speeding, not wearing a seat belt or crash helmet and violating a red light. The motorist is issued a ticket giving brief particulars of the offence and the name of the clerk to whom payment of a fixed sum must be made. This system produces an end result similar to that where the full court system were used, but there are significant time and costs savings for all involved.[18]

3. THE PLEA

A plea is usually only sought to the general issue, that is, the accused is asked to plead guilty or not guilty. However, special pleas may be entered and other preliminary points may be raised. For example, a point may be raised whether the court has jurisdiction to try the accused or whether the information charges more than one offence. If it is successfully raised, the trial cannot continue.[19]

In a summary trial where the accused is present, the information is read out by the magistrates' clerk. The accused is asked to plead guilty or not guilty. The accused's plea must be freely made and unambiguous, and should normally be made personally.[20] The accused's response determines the remainder of the procedure.

There is, however, no specific procedure to deal with the situation where the accused does not reply. The procedure available in the Crown Court to

---

[14] Magistrates' Courts Act 1980, s.12.

[15] See Harris (1988), p. 261.

[16] Under the Magistrates Courts Act 1980, s.11. A plea of not guilty is entered on behalf of the accused and the prosecution evidence is heard. Service of the summons must be proved and the accused is permitted to show, within 21 days after finding out about the proceedings, that he or she did not know of the summons or proceedings until after their commencement. See C. J. Emmins, *A Practical Approach to Criminal Procedure* (4th ed., 1988), pp. 176–177.

[17] Harris (1988), p. 242.

[18] See Emmins (1988), pp. 14–15.

[19] The special pleas are the same as those in response to an indictment: see pp. 762–764, below, although technically the pleas of autrefois acquit and autrefois convict only apply to indictments. The same effect is achieved in magistrates' courts by dealing with the matter on a plea of not guilty. See Harris (1988), pp. 243–254.

[20] *R. v. Wakefield JJ., ex p. Butterworth* [1970] 1 All E.R. 1181; *R. v. Gowerton JJ., ex p. Davies* [1974] Crim.L.R. 253; *R. v. Kingston upon Thames Magistrates' Court, ex p. Davey* (1985) 149 J.P. 744.

consider fitness to plead is not available to a magistrates' court.[21] The possibilities are either to discontinue the proceedings, and perhaps contact the social services department; or to commit the accused for trial in the Crown Court if the offence can be tried on indictment; or to enter a plea of not guilty, and then determine whether the accused did the act or made the omission charged and, if so, impose a hospital order without convicting the accused.[22]

4. THE GUILTY PLEA

If the accused enters a guilty plea, the court can proceed to hear the facts of the case from the prosecution, including any further offences which the accused wishes to have taken into consideration and any previous convictions. These facts are not usually elicited from witnesses unless there is some substantial disagreement,[23] but are presented by the prosecutor concerned.

The magistrates have a discretion whether to take other crimes into consideration[24] and may decline to do so where the offences are more serious than those with which the accused has actually been charged. If the offences are taken into consideration on sentence it is technically still possible for the accused to be prosecuted for them at a later date[25] but in practice this is not done and the procedure operates as a useful means of clearing up outstanding crimes.[26]

In certain circumstances social inquiry reports are required, for example, before a community service order can be imposed, and it is normal for a case to be adjourned if such a report is necessary or desirable.[27] The probation service is responsible for compiling a report and it will be available to the bench at the adjourned hearing, when the defence will have the opportunity of seeing and commenting upon it. With or without a report, the bench will listen to anything that may be said by the defence by way of mitigation of sentence.

5. THE NOT GUILTY PLEA

A plea of not guilty normally results in an immediate adjournment to an agreed date so that the prosecution and defence can assemble their witnesses and court time can be allocated. At the adjourned hearing the procedure will follow the normal adversarial lines. The prosecution is entitled to address the court through an opening speech and will then lead evidence through

---

[21] R. v. Metropolitan Stipendiary Magistrate Tower Bridge, ex p. Aniifowosi (1985) 149 J.P. 748. As to "fitness to plead" see below pp. 770–771.

[22] Mental Health Act 1983, s.37(3); see R. v. Lincoln (Kesteven) JJ., ex p. O'Connor [1983] 1 W.L.R. 335; and M. Wasik, "Hospital Orders without Trial" (1983) 147 J.P.N. 211.

[23] Magistrates' Courts Act 1980, s.9(3).

[24] R. v. Collins [1947] K.B. 560. Magistrates should not take into consideration any indictable offences.

[25] R. v. Nicholson [1947] W.N. 272.

[26] The benefit for the accused is that the admission of other offences wipes the slate clean so as to prevent future prosecution without very substantially increasing sentence in respect of the offence(s) charged.

[27] It is also recommended that a report should be obtained before certain other sentences are passed: see Carr (1983), p. 94. The defence is entitled to request a social inquiry report either to investigate the accused's personal circumstances, or suitability for a particular kind of sentence.

witnesses who will be subject to examination in chief, cross-examination and, perhaps, re-examination.[28] If the case is not especially difficult, the prosecution will often start with witnesses, since, with an experienced bench, there is no need to stress general points which might be necessary at a trial on indictment.[29]

At the close of the prosecution case, the defence may submit that there is no case to answer. The magistrates stop the hearing if they find that no reasonable tribunal could convict on the prosecution evidence, either because an essential element of the offence has not been proved or because the evidence has been discredited on cross-examination.[30] The magistrates must not say whether *they* would convict on the evidence so far presented, merely whether a reasonable bench *could* convict. If the submission is accepted, the accused is discharged. If it is rejected, the right of the defence to call witnesses and build a defence is not prejudiced.

At the close of the defence case, the defence is entitled to make a closing speech to the bench. Exceptionally, the prosecution may be permitted to speak again and, if so, the defence will be given a second opportunity[31]; the defence is entitled to the last word.

The rules of evidence are the same for summary trial as for trial on indictment. A particular problem in summary trial exists when there is a challenge to the admissibility of an item of evidence.[32] It is for the magistrates to decide, for example, whether a confession is admissible in accordance with the Police and Criminal Evidence Act 1984.[33] They must obviously be informed of the accused's confession. If they decide it is not admissible, they must attempt to determine the guilt of the accused without taking account of the confession. Such a task is extraordinarily difficult, but is nevertheless essential where the deciders of fact and law are one (or three) and the same.[34]

6. THE UNREPRESENTED DEFENDANT

It has so far been assumed that the accused who appears[35] at a magistrates' court is represented. The availability of legal aid[36] and the existence of duty

---

[28] Magistrates Court Rules 1981, r. 13, and see Harris (1988), pp. 257–261. The order of proceedings is similar to that in trial on indictment, see pp. 762–766, below.

[29] *e.g.* the burden and standard of proof, the need to listen carefully to the evidence, etc.

[30] The criteria are contained in a *Practice Note* [1962] 1 All E.R. 448 (criticised by E. C. J. McBride, (1990) 154 J.P.N. 99). Justices are warned against forming a view without hearing the whole of the evidence save in the two cases mentioned in the text.

[31] Magistrates' Courts Rules 1981, r. 13.

[32] See Rowe and Knapp (1989), pp. 76–79.

[33] In magistrates' courts the dual function of the justices as judges of both fact and law generally renders the "trial within a trial" an unnecessary sophistication, though one must be held where the admissibility of a confession is in issue: *R.* v. *Liverpool Juvenile Court, ex parte R.* [1988] Q.B. 1. See R. Pattenden, *Judicial Discretion and Criminal Litigation* (2nd ed., 1990), pp. 313–314. As to the admissibility of confessions, see pp. 787–788, below.

[34] See also p. 50, above, and for the situation in a trial on indictment, p. 788.

[35] For trial in the absence of the accused, see p. 751, above. Legal aid would not be granted for such work, but legal advice and assistance might.

[36] As to the granting of legal aid, see pp. 675–680, above. Emmins (1988), p. 447 points out that in 1983 (i) of the 425,000 people appearing in magistrates' courts charged with an indictable offence, 380,000 applications were made and 89 per cent. were granted; (ii) of the 1.7 million people appearing at a magistrates' court charged with summary offences, 60,000 legal aid applications were made and 62 per cent. were granted.

solicitor schemes at magistrates' courts[37] means that representation is more readily available than in the past. However, many defendants in magistrates' courts are unrepresented, and this is not likely to change for the foreseeable future.[38] At least when pleading not guilty, the lack of representation is a major disadvantage.[39] The difficulties for an unrepresented defendant include ignorance of procedure; the pressure imposed by a bewildering situation; an inability to understand, or even hear, what is going on; and the difficulty of putting forward one's own case sensibly, clearly and intelligibly.[40] The willingness of the clerk to assist an unrepresented defendant as far as pressure of business and the responsibility to the justices permit may ameliorate these difficulties.[41]

7. THE VERDICT

The magistrates normally retire to consider their decision. Where the trial is before a bench of lay magistrates, rather than a stipendiary magistrate, a majority[42] must be satisfied beyond reasonable doubt that the charge is proved before they can convict. The magistrates decide questions of both fact and law. On matters of practice and procedure, law and mixed law and fact relating to the charge they will have the benefit of advice from their clerk, which, in practice, they accept.[43] The clerk is also able to offer advice on sentencing. The clerk must not appear to be influencing the magistrates' decision on the facts when giving legal advice.

The appellate courts have been quick to establish that justice must be seen to be done in magistrates' courts. It is improper for a third party to be with the magistrates in the retiring room whilst they consider their verdict. Even the briefest of interventions may raise doubts about what has transpired between an outsider and the magistrates, and so is strictly forbidden.[44] A similar rule is imposed to preserve the inviolability of the deliberations of a jury.[45]

There is, however, a difference between a jury engaged in fact-finding and the position of magistrates. The jury have already received instruction on

---

[37] See above, pp. 452–455, and Emmins (1988), pp. 453–454.

[38] See H. Astor, "The Unrepresented Defendant: A Consideration of the Role of the Clerk in Magistrates' Courts" (1986) 13 J.L.S. 225, at 237.

[39] One study showed that of 111 defendants who pleaded not guilty at a magistrates' court, 30 per cent of those unrepresented were acquitted, whereas 64 per cent of those represented by lawyers were acquitted: M. Zander, "Unrepresented Defendants in Magistrates' Courts" (1972) 122 N.L.J. 1041. On the other hand, a study by the Lord Chancellor's Department suggested that acquittal rates did not vary on the basis of representation: Lord Chancellor's Department, *Report of a Survey of the Grant of Legal Aid in Magistrates' Courts* (1983), Table 17, quoted in M. Zander, *Cases and Materials on the English Legal System* (5th ed., 1988), p. 325 [hereafter Zander, *Cases and Materials* (1988)].

[40] See S. Dell, *Silent in Court* (1971) and Carlen (1976), both quoted in Zander, *Cases and Materials* (1988), pp. 327–329.

[41] Astor (1986), p. 238. See, further, Darbyshire (1984), pp. 170–181. An unrepresented defendant has no right to the assistance of a "friend"; *R. v. Leicester City JJ., ex p. Barrow* (1991) *The Times*, January 9.

[42] Which is the reason why magistrates normally sit in threes, see p. 50, above. The chairperson has no casting vote so that if a two person court is divided the case must be retried.

[43] The advice from the clerk is regulated by *Practice Direction* [1981] 1 All E.R. 1163. For a fuller consideration of the status and role of the clerk, see p. 194, above. As to the practice of accepting that advice, see *R. v. Jones-Nicks* [1977] R.T.R. 72 and see Emmins (1988), p. 187.

[44] *R. v. Stratford upon Avon JJ., ex p. Edmonds* [1973] R.T.R. 356.

[45] See pp. 810–811, below.

the law from the judge in a summing-up. The magistrates will receive advice if they ask for it from the clerk, which they may seek in the course of their deliberations. The influence a clerk has over the magistrates is a matter of conjecture. Speculation that the clerk may have played too substantial a role in the verdict can be fuelled by his or her presence in the retiring room for a substantial period. The courts will quash a conviction if the clerk visits the retiring room where there is no good reason for doing so.[46] The best approach is for legal advice, including not only advice on questions of law and practice and procedure but also refreshing the magistrates' memory as to matters of evidence and principles of sentencing, to be given in open court, when the advocates on both sides can contribute to the advice being proffered.[47] However, if it is thought that the magistrates have retired to consider their verdict having been misinformed as to the law, the clerk may inform them of the correct position.[48]

On returning to court the magistrates give their verdict of guilty or not guilty without giving any reason.[49] If the verdict is guilty the procedure will follow the same course as after a plea of guilty. If not guilty, the accused will be discharged.

8. SENTENCING

Not only is it the function of the magistrates to determine guilt, but they must also impose a sentence upon the offender. Sentences are laid down in respect of each offence, involving a maximum term of imprisonment and/or a maximum fine. Some offences can be punished by a fine, or lesser sentence, alone. Where the offence is one triable summarily only, magistrates may not at present impose a term of imprisonment greater than six months for any single offence. The maximum fine is laid down by reference to the standard scale of fines which was introduced in 1982. It has five levels. Currently level 1 imposes a maximum fine of £50, level 2 a maximum fine of £100, level 3 a maximum fine of £400, level 4 a maximum fine of £1,000 and level 5 (otherwise known as the statutory maximum) a maximum fine of £2,000. Where the offence is triable either way and is being tried summarily, magistrates still cannot impose a term of imprisonment more than six months, but the maximum fine they may impose is at least £2,000 and is greater if the statute so provides.[50]

Rarely would the maximum term of imprisonment or fine be imposed. In addition, it is not necessarily the case that imprisonment, for example, will be imposed when it is available as a sentencing option. Indeed a major

---

[46] In R. v. Guildford JJ., ex p. Harding (1981) 145 J.P. 174 the conviction was quashed because the clerk had retired with the magistrates to advise them when the case was absolutely straightforward.

[47] See, Practice Direction [1981] 1 W.L.R. 1163, para. 3; Carr (1983), pp. 9–10; Emmins (1988), p. 188.

[48] See Justices of the Peace Act 1979, s.28(3) and R. v. Uxbridge JJ., ex p. Smith [1985] Crim.L.R. 670 and commentary by D. J. Birch.

[49] Juries are similarly excused from explaining the basis of their decisions: see p. 809, below. However, magistrates may be required to record their findings of fact and the principles of law upon which they reach their decision, if required by the convicted defendant to state a case for consideration by the Divisional Court: see pp. 827–828, below.

[50] If the magistrates' court finds that their powers of sentence are not sufficient for an offence triable either way, they may commit the offender to Crown Court for sentence: Magistrates' Courts Act 1980, s.38, see Emmins (1988), pp. 200–206.

question for the magistrates is whether to impose a custodial sentence or not. The range of non-custodial sentences available includes, not only imposing a fine, but also placing someone on probation, ordering attendance at an attendance centre, suspending or partially suspending a sentence of imprisonment, ordering someone to do community service or granting an absolute or conditional discharge, as well as specific options available for young people.[51]

How any given bench of magistrates chooses a particular sentencing option is a matter of some speculation. Unlike sentencing at the Crown Court, the use of guidelines for magistrates is infrequent. The only official guidelines that are regularly observed are those in relation to motoring offences. Whilst there may be local policies, the most significant factors seem to be what has been called the "bench effect"[52] which is a more unconscious application of consistent principles by a particular bench of magistrates than the following of a policy would suggest, the role of the clerk in drawing the bench's attention to what the legislation permits and the higher courts have decided,[53] and what has been described as the gifts of "a sound judicial sense" and "sound judgment,"[54] which reflect that magistrates appear to think that sentencing is very much a matter of responding to each individual situation to which generalised approaches may be inapplicable or unhelpful.[55]

It is perhaps not surprising that there is considerable variation in the sentences imposed by different magistrates. Whilst benches of magistrates may not be too concerned about such inconsistency, it has excited the concern of researchers, the Magistrates Association and the Lord Chancellor.[56]

9. Do Magistrates Reach the Right Result?

The answer to this question, as with the question whether juries arrive at the right result,[57] depends upon what is meant by "right result" and may well be impressionistic. Care must be taken with assertions either that magistrates or that juries acquit too many people. The rate of acquittals in 1989 in both magistrates' courts and the Crown Court was similar.[58] Even so, there are many different, often inconsistent beliefs, or perhaps a better word would be myths, about summary trial, including that an accused has a greater chance

---

[51] As to sentencing in magistrates' courts, see Emmins (1988), pp. 185–187 (for offences triable summarily only) and pp. 201–202 (for offences triable either way).

[52] See Tarling (1981). See also Raine (1989), pp. 94–100. The "bench effect" is produced by magistrates working and training together and the influence of the senior magistrates who chair any given individual bench.

[53] See Parker, Sumner and Jarvis (1989), pp. 99–100 and Raine (1989), pp. 100–106. See also M. Wasik "Sentencing and the Divisional Court" [1984] Crim.L.R. 272.

[54] As appears in advice by a Metropolitan Stipendiary Magistrate: R. Bartle, *Crime and the New Magistrate* (1985), quoted in Parker, Sumner and Jarvis (1989).

[55] For a detailed consideration of the various factors involved see Parker, Sumner and Jarvis (1989), esp. Chaps. 4, 5 & 6.

[56] For the outcome of the numerous research studies see Raine (1989), pp. 86–94 and Parker, Sumner and Jarvis (1989). For the views of the Magistrates Association and the Lord Chancellor, see Raine (1989), pp. 97–98.

[57] See pp. 814–816, below.

[58] 16.7 per cent. of defendants were acquitted at magistrates' courts, compared with 17.9 per cent. at the Crown Court: *Criminal Statistics 1989* (Cm. 1322, 1990), Tables 8.6, 8.9.

of acquittal before a jury, that magistrates' impose lighter sentences in circumstances where the Crown Court and magistrates have the same sentencing powers, that judges impose lighter sentences in the same circumstances, and that magistrates' courts are biased in favour of the prosecution.[59] Further, there is some evidence that the criminal fraternity lack confidence in magisterial decision-making.[60] Is that because magistrates get decisions wrong, or because they get them right?

Vennard's study of contested trials in the magistrates' court[61] gives some support to the view that magistrates weigh evidence carefully and reach a verdict which is broadly in line with identifiable features of the evidence heard. The criticism that is most frequently made of magistrates is that they place too much credibility on the evidence of police officers and are generally too "prosecution-minded."[62] This criticism emanates not only from the accused who opt for trial by jury because it is "fairer," or because magistrates are amateurs who cannot be expected to get it right, or because they estimate that there is a better chance of acquittal,[63] but also from amongst those individuals and organisations who gave evidence to the James Committee.[64] The research study undertaken by Vennard had as its aims[65]:

(i) to appraise and itemise for contested cases the substance of the evidence presented by the prosecution and the defence, and attempt to quantify weaknesses and strengths in that evidence— such as whether or not the credibility of witnesses was impugned; and

(ii) to attempt to explain trial outcome in contested cases in relation to the type of evidence presented by both parties and to criteria pertaining to witness credibility.

On somewhat limited evidence Vennard concluded that her findings indicated that "... magistrates' decisions whether to convict or acquit are strongly associated with a few quantifiable indices of the evidence adduced by the parties and the credibility of witnesses."[66] Strong associations were detected between direct evidence implicating the accused given by the prosecution witnesses whose credibility was not impugned and conviction. Conversely there was a strong association between acquittal, the prosecution witnesses' lack of credibility, and the lack of direct evidence. These findings are not startling but they may reassure critics that magistrates are generally operating along rational lines.

For an alternative view, which relies partly upon different work by Vennard on acquittal rates, one may look at King's response[67] to proposals by

---

[59] Bottoms and McLean (1976), Chap. 4; Parker, Sumner and Jarvis (1989), p. 60; and D. Riley and J. Vennard, "Triable-either-way cases: Crown Court or magistrates' court?" (1988) 25 *Home Office Research Bulletin* 31, at p. 34.

[60] Riley and Vennard (1988), p. 34.

[61] Vennard (1980); Vennard (1981) and J. Vennard, "Acquittal Rates in Magistrates' Courts" (1981) 11 *Home Office Research Bulletin* 21.

[62] See, *e.g.*, evidence to the James Committee, *The Distribution of Criminal Business Between the Crown Court and the Magistrates Court* (Cmnd. 6323, 1975); B. Wootton, *Crime and Penal Policy* (1978).

[63] Gregory (1976).

[64] See n. 62, above.

[65] Vennard (1981), p. 4.

[66] *Ibid*. p. 20.

[67] M. King, "Against Summary Trial" *LAG Bulletin*, April 1982, p. 14.

the Justices' Clerks Society[68] that more trials should be diverted into the magistrates' court. King is dismissive of claims that magistrates offer a better quality of justice than juries and argues vigorously against proposals to reduce the right to jury trial.[69]

B. TRIAL ON INDICTMENT

If the prosecution has secured the committal of the accused for trial following committal proceedings[70] or has obtained a voluntary bill,[71] proceedings in the Crown Court are begun by the "preferment of a bill of indictment." This procedure simply involves sending the bill of indictment[72] to the appropriate officer of the Crown Court for signature.[73] Once it is signed, the accused may be brought before the court.[74] Then the accused must be asked to plead to the indictment, in a process known as arraignment.

The indictment is the formal statement of the charge(s) against the accused and should contain the statement of the offence, that is a description of the offence, and the particulars of the offence, that is a brief statement of the essential facts which constitute the offence. The statement of the offence should be precise, using the recognisable common law name,[75] the statutory name and derivation,[76] or sufficient details of a statutory offence.[77] The particulars must give "reasonable information as to the nature of the charge,"[78] so that the accused knows the details of the charge and the prosecution may not shift its ground during the trial.[79] Three specimen indictments follow: a common law offence, a precise statutory description

[68] "A Case for Summary Trial—Proposals for a Redistribution of Criminal Business" published by the Justices' Clerks Society.

[69] It was certainly the experience of the James Committee (1975) that their proposals to remove the right to trial by jury for minor thefts brought an outraged response, not least in the House of Commons. The proposal, originally incorporated in the Criminal Law Bill 1977, disappeared during the Bill's progress through Parliament. The opposition was, it is true, based more on a commitment to jury trial than on an antipathy to magisterial justice. See p. 637, above.

[70] See pp. 657–664, above.

[71] See pp. 664–665, above.

[72] In most cases it is now the responsibility of the Crown Prosecution Service to draft and determine the form of an indictment: Procedural Notice issued by the Crown Prosecution Service and the Lord Chancellor's Department: (1989) 139 N.L.J. 188.

[73] The appropriate officer retains for the time being the responsibility for signing indictments: *ibid.*

[74] Where the accused has been committed for trial, the bill of indictment must be preferred within 28 days of the date of committal, unless that period is extended: Indictment (Procedure) Rules 1971 (S.I. 1971 No. 2084), r. 5, as amended. The time limit is not mandatory: *R.* v. *Urbanowski* (1976) 62 Cr.App.R. 229, C.A.; *R.* v. *Soffe* (1982) 75 Cr.App.R. 133, C.A. Delay in bringing proceedings may be regarded as an abuse of process and thus cause criminal proceedings to be stopped, see Pattenden (1990), pp. 33–38. If it is a serious fraud case, the 28 day limit commences on the date of the notice of transfer, as provided for in the Criminal Justice Act 1987 and the Indictment (Procedure) Rules 1971, r. 5, as amended.

[75] *e.g.* murder; manslaughter; blasphemy; conspiracy to corrupt public morals.

[76] *e.g.* theft, contrary to s.1 of the Theft Act 1968; robbery, contrary to s.8(1) of the Theft Act 1968; arson, contrary to s.1(1) and (3) of the Criminal Damage Act 1971.

[77] *e.g.* removing an article from a place open to the public, contrary to s.11(1) of the Theft Act 1968; sexual intercourse with a girl under 13, contrary to s.5 of the Sexual Offences Act 1956.

[78] Indictment Rules 1971 (S.I. 1971 No. 1253), r. 5(1).

[79] The accused, if he or she requests, is entitled to a copy of the indictment free of charge: *ibid.* r. 10(1).

and a statutory offence for which there is no short description. They are taken from decided cases and reflect particular difficulties of those cases. Simpler cases will produce simpler indictments.

(i) *Shaw* v. *D.P.P.*[80]

STATEMENT OF OFFENCE

Conspiracy to corrupt public morals

PARTICULARS OF OFFENCE

Frederick Charles Shaw on divers days between the 1st day of October 1959 and the 23rd day of July 1960 within the jurisdiction of the Central Criminal Court, conspired with certain persons who inserted advertisements in issues of a magazine entitled "Ladies' Directory" numbered 7, 7 revised, 8, 9, 10 and a supplement thereto, and with certain other persons whose names are unknown, by means of the said magazine and the said advertisements to induce readers thereof to resort to the said advertisers for the purposes of fornication and of taking part in or witnessing other disgusting and immoral acts and exhibitions, with intent thereby to debauch and corrupt the morals as well of youth as of divers other liege subjects of Our Lady the Queen and to raise and create in their minds inordinate and lustful desires.

(ii) *R.* v. *Miller*[81]

STATEMENT OF OFFENCE

Arson, contrary to section 1(1) and (3) of Criminal Damage Act 1971

PARTICULARS OF OFFENCE

James Miller on a date unknown between August 13 and 16, 1980, without lawful excuse, damaged by fire a house known as No. 9, Grantham Road, Sparkbrook, intending to do damage to such property or reckless as to whether such property would be damaged.

---

[80] [1962] A.C. 220.
[81] [1983] 2 A.C. 161.

(iii) *R. v. Markus*[82]

STATEMENT OF OFFENCE

Conniving at a corporation fraudulently inducing the investment of money contrary to sections 13(1)(*b*) and 19 of the Prevention of Fraud (Investments) Act 1958

PARTICULARS OF OFFENCE

Edward Jules Markus between August 25, 1970, and January 15, 1971, within the jurisdiction of the Central Criminal Court being a director of Agricultural Investment Corporation S.A. of the First National Investment Corporation S.A. and of Agri-International S.A. and of Agri-International (U.K.) Ltd. connived at the fraudulent inducement of Agricultural Investment Corporation S.A., through its agents First National Investment Corporation S.A. and Agri-International S.A. and Agri-International (U.K.) Ltd. of Dr. Hermann Schlick and Mrs. Theodoline Schlick to take part in an arrangement to invest $1038.32 in Agri-Fund (the said investment being an arrangement with respect of property other than securities, the purpose or pretended purpose of which was to enable the said Dr. Hermann Schlick and the said Mrs. Theodoline Schlick to participate in the profits alleged to be likely to arise from the holding of Agri-Fund) by representations that Agricultural Investment Corporation S.A. was genuinely carrying on an honest business and that moneys invested in Agri-Fund were immediately redeemable at the option of the investor which representations both he and the said corporation knew to be misleading false and deceptive.

These examples satisfy the requirements that an indictment should include such information as to the time and place of the offence as to indicate to the accused the acts which are alleged to constitute the offence,[83] a reasonably clear description of any property involved,[84] the identity of any "victim" or a description reasonable so as to be identifiable,[85] any factual circumstances necessary to the offence,[86] and any special mental element

---

[82] [1976] A.C. 35.
[83] An allegation as to time may be made in ordinary language, and the dates between which the offence may be quite a long way apart, as in Shaw's indictment. It is only in a few cases that either time or place is of the essence of the offence, in which case greater particularity is required.
[84] In Miller's indictment, No. 9 Grantham Road, Sparkbrook. The name of the owner of the property is unnecessary in most cases.
[85] In Markus' indictment, Dr. Herman Schlick and Mrs. Theodoline Schlick.
[86] *e.g.* in an indictment for theft, the particulars must state that the property in question belonged to another, but does not have to state who that other was.

required by the offence which is not inherent in the statement of the offence.[87]

Indictments may contain more than one offence provided they are founded on the same facts or for part of a series of offences of the same or a similar character, but the charges must be separated and are then known as "counts."[88]

1. HEARING IN OPEN COURT

It is often regarded as essential to the administration of justice that hearings take place in open court.[89] In the recent past increasing concern has been expressed with regard to the number of trials taking place out of the public view.[90] In consequence, a right of appeal against orders restricting or preventing reports of or restricting public access to trials on indictment has been introduced by section 159 of the Criminal Justice Act 1988.[91]

2. THE ORDER OF PROCEEDINGS

We shall consider the proceedings at trial in some detail in this chapter and see them from the point of view of the various parties to the trial: the accused, counsel, witnesses, the judge and the jury. At the outset it is useful to set out the chronology of the trial from the first appearance of the accused until he or she leaves the court.[92]

(a) The arraignment

The accused is brought to the bar of the court and the indictment is read out and a plea in respect of each count is sought. The plea may be to the "general issue," that is a plea of "guilty" or "not guilty." Alternatively, a plea of a special nature may be entered. This is the point of the trial where

---

[87] *e.g.* the particulars on an indictment for an offence under s.18 of the Offences Against the Person Act 1861 should allege an intent to do grievous bodily harm to the victim or to resist or prevent lawful apprehension, as appropriate. The particulars of an indictment for arson under s.1(1) and (3) of the Criminal Damage Act 1971 must allege either an intent to destroy or damage another's property, or recklessness as to whether such property would be destroyed or damaged.

[88] See p. 764, below.

[89] *e.g.* Article 6(1) of the European Convention on Human Rights provides: "In the determination of . . . any criminal charge against him, everyone is entitled to a fair and public hearing within a reasonable time by an independent and impartial tribunal established by law. Judgment shall be pronounced publicly but the press and public may be excluded from all or part of the trial in the interests of morals, public order, or national security in a democratic society, where the interests of juveniles or the protection of the private life of the parties so require, or to the extent strictly necessary in the opinion of the court in special circumstances where publicity would prejudice the interests of justice." Articles 10 and 13 may also be relevant.

[90] Much of the credit for this provision must go to Tim Crook and the National Union of Journalists who were concerned about the prevention of reporting newsworthy cases and the lack of challenge to such decisions by trial judges, see, *e.g. R.* v. *Central Criminal Court, ex p. Crook, The Times,* November 8, 1984.

[91] As regards summary trial, the Magistrates' Courts Act 1980, s.121(4) requires courts to sit in open court, but there is an inherent jurisdiction to sit *in camera* if required by the administration of justice: see Archbold, *Criminal Pleading, Evidence and Practice* (43rd ed., 1988), para. 4–1.

[92] See also D. Barnard, *The Criminal Court in Action* (3rd ed., 1987).

issues such as double jeopardy, the jurisdiction of the court to try the accused and errors in the indictment may be raised.[93]

(i) Double jeopardy

A basic principle is that no person should be tried twice for the same offence. Consequently "the unwarranted harassment of the accused by multiple prosecutions" is avoided.[94] The principle is established in English law by the availability of the special pleas in bar: the pleas of autrefois acquit; of autrefois convict; and of pardon.[95] These pleas are rarely used in practice, because the accuracy of court records ensures that people are rarely prosecuted for the same offence twice.[96]

—*Autrefois acquit* and *autrefois convict*[97]

The appropriate plea, depending upon whether the accused has already been acquitted (*autrefois acquit*) or convicted (*autrefois convict*) of the same offence, or substantially the same offence, is normally made in writing before the beginning of the trial, although it may be made at any stage. After such a plea, it is for the judge without a jury to decide whether the plea is successful.[98]

The circumstances in which either plea will be available were explored in *Connelly* v. *D.P.P.*,[99] The House of Lords, mainly through the speech of Lord Morris, indicated that the pleas are not limited to circumstances where an accused has been charged with exactly the same offence arising out of the same set of circumstances. A person previously acquitted or convicted of an offence cannot be tried again for that same offence or a substantially similar offence or an offence which was a proper alternative.[1] A proper alternative offence is one of which the accused could have been found guilty at the earlier trial instead of that named in the indictment. So, for example, if Fred is acquitted of murdering Ann, he cannot later be charged with her murder, even if there is fresh evidence, nor can he be charged with her manslaughter or causing her death by reckless driving or causing her grievous bodily harm with intent. Further, if the accused has previously been acquitted of an offence which, as a matter of fact, is essential to establish guilt of the offence charged, he or she cannot be tried for that lesser offence later.[2] However, the plea of autrefois convict does not operate to prevent a person being tried

---

[93] As will be seen in the relevant passage, these issues can also be raised at other points in the sequence of the trial.

[94] See M. L. Friedland, *Double Jeopardy* (1969), pp. 3–4. See also below, p. 840.

[95] The possibility of similar questions arising through issue estoppel must be recognised, although such an argument is probably inapplicable to the criminal law: *D.P.P.* v. *Humphrys* [1977] A.C. 1. The more likely method of raising these questions is through the inherent power of the judges to prevent oppression of an accused where there is an abuse of process. Abuse of process is a claim being considered by the courts much more frequently in recent years, see Pattenden (1990), pp. 32–38.

[96] See Emmins (1988), p. 90.

[97] For a full treatment of the law, see Archbold (1988), paras. 4–67 to 4–106; Emmins (1988), pp. 90–93.

[98] Criminal Justice Act 1988, s.122.

[99] [1964] A.C. 1254.

[1] The power to enter an alternative verdict is provided by the Criminal Law Act 1967, s.6, which has been widely interpreted by the House of Lords in *R.* v. *Wilson*; *R.* v. *Jenkins and another* [1984] A.C. 242.

[2] Consequently, an earlier acquittal of theft precludes a trial for robbery on the same facts, because theft is an essential element in proving robbery, see Theft Act 1968, ss.1 and 8.

on a charge which is more serious than the one of which he or she has originally been convicted. So, for example, if Dorothy attacks and seriously injures Michael she may be convicted of causing grievous bodily harm with intent. If Michael dies after the trial from the injuries, Dorothy may be tried for murder, provided Michael's death takes place within a year and a day of the attack.[3]

—Pardon

The plea is that the accused has already been pardoned for the offence.

(ii) *Jurisdiction*

The plea is that the court has no jurisdiction to try the accused for the relevant offence.[4]

(iii) *Errors in the indictment*

There are many technical rules about the drafting of indictments, primarily concerned with the requirements that indictments must be (a) positive and (b) not duplicitous. The rules are discussed in the works on criminal procedure.[5] Such errors perceived by the accused may be raised for consideration through a number of avenues, but primarily by applying to the judge to quash the indictment[6] or by an abuse of process claim. These are not pleas as such. It is most unlikely that the almost obsolete demurrer will be used to object to the wording of the indictment.[7]

(b) The empanelling and swearing of the jury

If a plea of not guilty is entered, a jury of twelve people will be empanelled and, after an opportunity for challenges, sworn. The indictment will be read over to the jury which will be told of its obligation to listen to the evidence and to determine guilt or innocence.

(c) The opening speech

Counsel for the prosecution addresses the jury. The function of the opening is to explain to the jury the basic elements of the prosecution case, the evidence that is to be called and the burden and standard of proof. Even allowing for the fact that any mistakes may ultimately be corrected by the judge in the summing-up, it is vital that prosecution counsel does not claim

---

[3] See *R. v. Dyson* [1908] 2 K.B. 454 and J. C. Smith and B. Hogan, *Criminal Law* (6th ed., 1988), pp. 309–330, esp, p. 312.

[4] The issue of jurisdiction may be raised under the general issue during the course of the trial. The issue will arise where there is a point to be raised about the territorial jurisdiction of the court. The Crown Court can, as a general rule, only try crimes committed in England and Wales. There may well be debate about where the crime was committed, especially, for example, in relation to conspiracies (see Smith and Hogan (1988), pp. 268–269) and theft through the use of computers (see, *e.g.*, J. C. Smith, *The Law of Theft* (6th ed., 1989), para. 56); see also Law Commission Report No. 180, *Criminal Law: Jurisdiction over Offences of Fraud and Dishonesty with a Foreign Element* (1989).

[5] Archbold (1988); Emmins (1988); C. Hampton, *Criminal Procedure* (3rd ed., 1982).

[6] As to a motion to quash the indictment and the errors that may be raised, see, Archbold (1988), paras. 1–110 to 1–114; Emmins (1988), pp. 69–70.

[7] Archbold (1988), para. 4–65.

more than can be proved for it may eventually be difficult for the jury to remember whether allegations made in the speech were actually substantiated by the evidence.[8] Equally counsel must not refer to any evidence which is inadmissible,[9] or which defending counsel has indicated will be challenged as inadmissible.

(d) The prosecution case

Witnesses called by the prosecution give their evidence in turn (examination-in-chief) and may be subjected to questioning by the defence (cross-examination). Counsel for the prosecution may have the final word with each witness (re-examination) but must ask questions only on matters raised in the course of cross-examination. The way in which and the sort of questions counsel asks and whether evidence is admissible are both decided upon by the judge alone.[10]

(e) Defence submission of no case to answer

At the close of the prosecution case the defence may ask the trial judge to direct the jury to acquit the accused because there is no case to answer. If this submission is accepted, the trial ends and the accused is acquitted.

(f) Defence opening speech

Defence counsel is only entitled to make an opening speech to the jury if at least one witness (other than the accused) is to be called as to the *facts* of the case. Otherwise, counsel must simply start to call evidence.

(g) The defence case

Witnesses called by the defence are examined. They may be cross-examined by prosecution counsel and re-examined by defence counsel.

(h) Closing speeches

Both counsel may address the jury at the close of the evidence. The prosecution goes first and the defence has the last word. In the closing speech prosecution counsel may review the evidence and emphasise alleged strengths in the prosecution case and weaknesses in the defence. The jury is likely to be reminded once again of the burden and standard of proof.

(i) The summing-up

The trial judge must sum up the evidence to the jury, directing it as to the law and explaining its function.

---

[8] A particular example of the dangers is to be found in the trial of James Hanratty, where a vital piece of evidence was referred to in the opening speech but never proved in evidence, see L. Blom-Cooper, *The A6 Murder*. In any event, it may be tactically more sensible to pitch the opening on a relatively low key lest the jury should later be disappointed with the prosecution witnesses.

[9] The opening of such evidence will not automatically lead to the quashing of a subsequent conviction: *R.* v. *Jackson* [1953] 1 W.L.R. 591. The normal course would be for the judge to discharge the jury and recommence the trial if the defendant has been seriously prejudiced.

[10] See pp. 775, 786, below.

(j) The verdict

The jury retire to consider its verdict. Only very exceptionally is evidence admitted after the retirement of the jury. An unanimous verdict is the first objective, but a majority verdict may eventually be acceptable. The verdict of the jury is announced by the person known as the "foreman" in open court.

(k) Information for sentencing

Since not all the necessary information is provided during the trial to enable an appropriate sentence to be imposed, after conviction an information gathering exercise is often undertaken, which includes the possibility of a plea in mitigation being made by either defence counsel or the accused in person.

(l) Sentence

The judge passes sentence on the accused.

3. THE ACCUSED

Historically, the accused laboured under a considerable disadvantage in the criminal trial. The Criminal Law Revision Committee, considering the rules of evidence in criminal cases identified the following difficulties which had hindered the accused[11]:

i. The "indecent haste" with which trials were conducted, in a potentially unfair manner.[12] Representation, legal aid and judicial unwillingness to curtail trials now ensure that there are few complaints of brevity. If anything, now the complaint is that trials go on too long.

ii. Legal representation was severely restricted before 1836.[13] The arrival of legal aid has ensured representation in at least all serious cases, although the accused may occasionally still be unrepresented.[14]

iii. The accused was not permitted to give evidence on oath in all cases.[15] The Criminal Evidence Act 1898 provided the accused with this right in all cases.

iv. There was only rarely a right to appeal against conviction. A general right of appeal was provided by the Criminal Appeal Act 1907.[16]

Since all these obstacles to a fair trial have been removed, and, according to the C.L.R.C., because of the improved quality of juries and magistrates, it

---

[11] Criminal Law Revision Committee, *Eleventh Report, Evidence (General)* (Cmnd. 4991, 1972), pp. 10–12.

[12] Mr. Justice Hawkins described one 1840's Old Bailey Trial which lasted two minutes 53 seconds as "a high example of expedition," and stated that trials after dinner lasted on average four minutes: Hawkins, *Memoirs*, cited in the C.L.R.C. 11th Report (1972), p. 11.

[13] Prior to the Trials for Felony Act 1836, the defence counsel in felony trials was limited to arguments on points of law and giving advice to the defendant on how he or she should conduct his or her case.

[14] As to the availability of legal aid, see above, pp. 675–680.

[15] The accused could only make an unsworn statement from the dock, which would carry little credibility with the jury: see M. Cohen, "The Unsworn Statement from the Dock" [1981] Crim.L.R. 224.

[16] As to criminal appeals, see pp. 830–847, below.

has been suggested that the accused is in a very strong position in the criminal trial.[17] This view is not accepted by all commentators. McBarnet,[18] on completion of a critical examination of the criminal justice system, concluded that the "process of conviction is easier than the rhetoric of justice would have us expect—and easier still the lower the status of the defendant."[19] Whilst the law appears to provide considerable protection for the accused, there are many exceptions to that law, which reduce the protection in reality. Thus, for example, McBarnet points to the fact that the actual operation of the right to silence does not guarantee that the accused need not incriminate himself or herself; and whilst there is in many cases a formal right to jury trial, the vast majority of cases are tried without a jury.[20]

The first procedural question concerns the attendance of the accused at court. If in custody, the accused is brought to court from prison; if on bail, the accused is informed of the time and date of the trial and told to attend. The accused *must* attend court so as to answer in person when the indictment is put, because no-one else may enter a plea.[21] Whilst needing to be present at the arraignment, the accused may be absent for the trial, although that will happen only in exceptional cases, because the accused needs to be present in order to "hear the case against him and have the opportunity . . . of answering it."[22] Such cases include those where the accused is violent or disorderly,[23] is ill,[24] or absconds from the trial.[25] An accused who is likely to intimidate a witness may be removed from the presence of the witness, but not out of hearing.[26]

The second procedural question relates to the accused's response on arraignment after the indictment has been read. The accused is required to answer to every count on the indictment and each plea will be recorded. In the great majority of cases the plea will be "guilty" or "not guilty," although there are several other possibilities.[27]

(a) The plea of guilty

This acknowledgment of guilt must be unmistakeable. It must be made

---

[17] C.L.R.C. Eleventh Report (1972), pp. 10–12.

[18] D. J. McBarnet, *Conviction: Law, the State and the Construction of Justice* (1981).

[19] *Ibid.*, p. 155.

[20] *Ibid.*, pp. 154–155.

[21] *R.* v. *Heyes* [1951] 1 K.B. 29. In some circumstances, the failure of the accused to plead personally to the indictment results in a mistrial: *R.* v. *Boyle* [1954] 2 Q.B. 292; *R.* v. *Ellis* (1973) 57 Cr.App.R. 571. However, if the trial had proceeded as though a "not guilty" plea had been recorded no material irregularity had necessarily occurred: *R.* v. *Williams* [1978] Q.B. 373. As to the position in summary trials, see pp. 751–752, above.

[22] *R.* v. *Lee Kun* (1916) 11 Cr.App.R. 293, 300, *per* Lord Reading. See also *R.* v. *Howson* (1982) 74 Cr.App.R. 172. See generally, G. Zellick, "The Criminal Trial and the Disruptive Defendant" (1980) 43 M.L.R. 121, 284.

[23] It is possible to handcuff or restrain an accused, but only if there is a danger of escape or violence, and whether such restraint is justified should be investigated in court without the jury, see *R.* v. *Vratsides* [1988] Crim.L.R. 251. See also *R.* v. *Berry* (1897) 104 L.T.Journ. 110, where the accused performed an impromptu striptease on the clerk's table.

[24] *R.* v. *Orton* (1873), cited in Archbold (1988), para. 3–47; *R.* v. *Howson* (1981) 74 Cr.App.R. 172, where it was indicated that the discretion must not be exercised if the accused's defence could be prejudiced by his or her absence.

[25] *R.* v. *Jones (No. 2)* [1972] 1 W.L.R. 887.

[26] *R.* v. *Smellie* (1919) 14 Cr.App.R. 128. As to the statutory extension of this power in relation to the use of live television links, especially in child abuse cases, see p. 782 below.

[27] See pp. 762–764, above.

freely by the accused in person who must have knowledge of the elements of the offence.[28] The accused must not be under pressure from counsel or the court. It is quite proper for defence counsel to advise the accused, perhaps in very forceful terms, that a plea of guilty could be advantageous in securing a lesser sentence and/or that the evidence seems to point strongly to guilt. Counsel must also stress that a guilty plea should only be entered if the accused has actually committed the alleged offence.[29]

The importance attached to the accused's freedom to enter the plea desired is reflected in the "plea bargaining" cases where it was suspected that unfair pressure had been placed on the accused.[30] "Plea bargaining ... describes the practice whereby the accused enters a plea of guilty in return for which he will be given some consideration that results in a sentence concession."[31]

The first method by which the sentence concession is obtained is a plea of guilty to the offence charged. A guilty plea attracts a lighter sentence.[32] The amount of discount can be substantial.[33] In some cases the discount will operate not only to reduce the severity of a particular form of sentence but also to alter the type of sentence from, for example, custodial to non-custodial. The second method is by a plea arrangement made between prosecuting and defence counsel whereby a plea of guilty to a lesser charge on the indictment is accepted in return for the prosecution not proceeding with the more serious charges.[34]

The value of a guilty plea in the criminal process is that it reduces the time and money spent on achieving convictions, it obviates the need for a trial and the inherent difficulties of proof, it spares the witnesses an experience which can be both unpleasant and distressing,[35] and it is alleged to demonstrate an attitude of contrition and remorse on the part of the accused. The advantages to the prosecution of offering concessions or inducements to persuade

[28] *R.* v. *Golathan* (1915) 11 Cr.App.R. 79.
[29] See below, p. 777 on the obligations of defence counsel.
[30] The particular pressure that gives rise to concern is where it appears to the accused that the judge has indicated to counsel that an unsuccessful plea of not guilty will attract a heavier sentence: *R.* v. *Turner* [1970] 2 Q.B. 321, see pp. 784–786, below.
[31] J. Baldwin and M. McConville, *Negotiated Justice* (1977), p. 19. This research study is a prerequisite for any detailed study of the subject of plea bargaining. See also, P. Thomas, "Plea Bargaining and the Turner Case" [1970] Crim.L.R. 559; A. Davis, "Sentences for Sale: A New Look at Plea Bargaining in England and America" [1970] Crim.L.R. 150 and 218; R. Purves, "That Plea-Bargaining Business" [1971] Crim.L.R. 470; S. McCabe and R. Purves, *By-Passing the Jury* (1972); Bottoms and McLean (1976); J. Baldwin and M. McConville, "Plea Bargaining: legal carve-up or legal cover-up" (1978) 5 B.J.L.S. 228, "Plea Bargaining and the Court of Appeal" (1979) 6 B.J.L.S. 200, "The Influence of the Sentencing Discount in Inducing Guilty Pleas" in J. Baldwin and A. K. Bottomley (eds.), *Criminal Justice*: *Selected Readings*, "Preserving the Good Face of Justice: Some Recent Plea Bargain Cases" (1978) 128 N.L.J. 872 and *Court, Prosecution and Conviction* (1981); S. Moody and J. Tombs, "Plea Negotiations and Scotland" [1983] Crim.L.R. 297; S. Moody and J. Toombs, *Prosecution in the Public Interest* (1982).
[32] See D. A. Thomas, *Current Sentencing Practice*, para. A8.2(b) and see *R.* v. *Cain* [1976] Q.B. 496.
[33] *Current Sentencing Practice*, at para A8.2(c), suggests that the extent of the reduction is between one quarter and one third of what would otherwise have been the sentence. See also Baldwin and McConville (1977), pp. 213–214.
[34] See pp. 772–774, below.
[35] This may be a particularly significant factor where the charges include sexual offences: *R.* v. *Grice* (1977) 66 Cr.App.R. 167.

the accused to plead guilty are the certainty and economy thereby secured. These advantages must be balanced against the need to ensure that offenders are convicted of offences which properly represent the seriousness of their behaviour.[36]

For the truly guilty defendant and the prosecution, a plea bargain represents a mutually beneficial compromise. A guilty plea is obtained and so is a sentence concession. However, these concessions also operate (intentionally) as inducements and must create pressure on the accused. How severe are these pressures on the innocent accused, or on the accused against whom the prosecution have a less than cast-iron case? To what extent, if at all, is it legitimate to serve the interests of the prosecution and the guilty accused by establishing principles and procedures which will inevitably place some pressure to plead guilty on the accused who would, or might, be acquitted after trial?

If a guilty plea is made in error by the accused, it may be withdrawn, and the trial judge may permit a change of plea at any time before sentence.[37]

(b) The plea of not guilty

This plea occasions little difficulty. It constitutes a denial of the prosecution's allegations and requires them to prove all the elements of their case, except those facts admitted by the defence.[38] The plea must be entered by the accused personally.[39]

A plea of not guilty may be changed during the trial with the leave of the judge.[40] There are many reasons for a change of plea, including a realisation of the effect of sentence discount when there has been a guilty plea and the possibility of an unwelcome outcome of the trial if the plea of not guilty is maintained.[41]

(c) The accused not pleading

The expectation is that the accused will be able, with legal representation, to plead. However, the accused may "stand mute," that is make no reply or no intelligible reply, when the charge is put. A jury must be empanelled[42] to determine whether the accused is "mute of malice" or "mute by visitation of God." The issue is tried like any other jury matter by the bringing of evidence, examination of witnesses, summing-up and verdict. If the accused is found to be mute of malice (the prosecution having proved it beyond a reasonable doubt) a plea of not guilty is formally entered on behalf of the accused.[43] If found to be mute by visitation of God the question arises as to

---

[36] See below, p. 773 for the obligations of prosecuting counsel.

[37] *S.* v. *Manchester Recorder* [1971] A.C. 481. Late changes of plea may well be made when the accused indicates that his or her original plea was made as a result of threats, see *e.g. R.* v. *Dodd, Pack and others* (1982) 74 Cr.App.R. 50.

[38] Admissions may be made at various stages of criminal proceedings in accordance with the Criminal Justice Act 1967, s.10: see Emmins (1988), pp. 128–129.

[39] For instances where a plea of not guilty is entered on behalf of the accused, see below.

[40] As to the procedure to be adopted on change of plea, see *R.* v. *Ellis* (1973) 57 Cr.App.R. 571.

[41] In *R.* v. *Sullivan* [1984] A.C. 156 the accused changed his plea to guilty, because when he raised the claim that he assaulted someone when in an epileptic fit it was made clear that he was raising the defence of insanity which would result in his being sent to a mental hospital.

[42] In the normal way, see pp. 801–802, below.

[43] Criminal Law Act 1967, s.6(1)(c).

whether the accused is fit to plead to the charge at all. If found fit to plead, a not guilty plea is entered.

(d) Fitness to plead

The question of fitness to plead may arise not only where the accused has remained silent on arraignment and been found mute by visitation of God, but also where there is a defence submission of unfitness or the prosecution bring the matter to the judge's attention. The question is "whether the accused is under disability, that is to say under any disability such that . . . it would constitute a bar to his being tried. . . ."[44] This issue is determined by a jury[45] considering the evidence and reaching a verdict in the normal way. If there is a verdict of unfitness to plead, the court must direct that the accused be detained in a mental hospital without limitation of time, only being released with the consent of the Home Secretary or by a Mental Health Review Tribunal.[46]

If the matter goes to the jury, they must determine whether or not the accused can instruct a solicitor and counsel, plead to the indictment, that is understand the charge and the significance of a plea, challenge jurors, understand the evidence, and give evidence.[47]

Because it is desirable that a person charged with a criminal offence should stand trial if possible and should have the chance to show that the prosecution case is inadequate, the question of fitness to plead may be deferred until the opening of the defence case, at the discretion of the trial judge.[48] The onus of proving the question of fitness lies with the party raising it. If raised by the defence it must be proved on a balance of probabilities; if raised by the prosecution or the judge it must be proved beyond reasonable doubt.[49]

The mandatory consequence of a finding of unfitness to plead is that there are very few such submissions. First, if a person suffers mental ill-health, there are compulsory powers which may mean treatment can be provided so that the accused is able to plead when the trial commences.[50] Secondly, although the automatic consequence of a finding is admission to a mental hospital, lack of fitness to plead cannot be equated with mental ill-health or insanity.[51] There is no requirement in the conditions for fitness to plead that a person be suffering from a mental disorder, which is required for admis-

[44] Criminal Procedure (Insanity) Act 1964, s.4(1).
[45] If a jury has found the accused mute by visitation of God the same jury may be resworn to try the issue of fitness, or a new jury may be used.
[46] Criminal Procedure (Insanity) Act 1964, s.5(1)(c), Sched. 1; Mental Health Act 1983, ss.23, 70, 79(1)(b), Sched. 1, Part II, para. 7.
[47] R. v. Pritchard (1836) 7 C. & P. 303; R. v. Robertson [1968] 1 W.L.R. 1767. See, generally, Archbold (1988), paras. 4–114 to 4–120; Emmins (1988), pp. 89–90; and Smith and Hogan (1988), pp. 182–185.
[48] Criminal Procedure (Insanity) Act 1964, s.4(2).
[49] The question of the onus and standard of proof is considered in R. v. Podola [1960] 1 Q.B. 325, which is of general interest on the question of fitness to plead.
[50] In particular, it is possible to remand an accused to hospital for treatment, if he or she suffers from mental illness or severe mental impairment: Mental Health Act 1983, s.36. It may also be possible to persuade the Crown Prosecution Service to discontinue the proceedings, see p. 625, above.
[51] It is not the case that all people with mental disorder are unfit: Royal Commission on Capital Punishment, Report, (Cmnd. 8932, 1953), p. 78.

sion to hospital under the Mental Health Act 1983, nor is there even a need for a finding of insanity akin to that which provides a defence at criminal trials. The problems with the fitness to plead procedure are exemplified by the experience of Glenn Pearson. On a charge of theft he was found unfit to plead when as a deaf mute he was unable to communicate with the court. He was admitted to a mental hospital. There he had a right of appeal to a mental health review tribunal, which had to discharge him because he suffered from no form of mental disorder.[52] To prevent this happening continually either a form of communication with Glenn had to be found or the proceedings against him had to be dropped.

Fitness to plead was considered by the Butler Committee.[53] It recommended that there should always be a trial of the facts in the case at an appropriate time, that the issue of fitness should normally be decided by the trial judge, that two doctors should always give evidence on the question and that the phrase "under disability in relation to the trial" should be substituted for "fitness to plead."[54]

There are other procedural matters concerning the accused as well as his or her attendance and arraignment, particularly the extent to which character and antecedents can be referred to and the extent to which the credibility of prosecution witnesses can be attacked. These matters are dealt with in discussing the roles of other participants in the trial.

4. REPRESENTATION AND THE OBLIGATIONS OF COUNSEL

The availability of legal aid[55] ensures that it is very unusual to find an unrepresented accused in the Crown Court. Those who are unrepresented have normally chosen to conduct their own defence.[55a] Both prosecution and defence counsel are under obligations to behave in a particular manner in the course of the trial and we shall examine some examples. Counsel should always act in accordance with the rules and etiquette of the Bar.[56] "A practising barrister has an overriding duty to the Court to ensure in the public interest that the proper and efficient administration of justice is achieved: he must assist the court in the administration of justice and must not deceive or knowingly or recklessly mislead the court."[57] The latter

---

[52] See C. J. Emmins, "Unfitness to Plead: Some Thoughts Prompted by Glenn Pearson's Case" [1986] Crim.L.R. 604.

[53] *Report of the Committee on Mentally Abnormal Offenders*, Cmnd. 6244 (1975).

[54] *Ibid*. Chapter 10. See also N. Walker, "Butler v. C.L.R.C. and others" [1981] Crim.L.R. 596 and A. R. Poole, "Standing Mute and Fitness to Plead" [1968] Crim.L.R. 6. A Private Members' Bill, the Criminal Procedure (Insanity and Unfitness to Plead) Bill 1990 will, if enacted, make important changes. It is the first Bill sponsored by the Law Society.

[55] See pp. 675–680, above.

[55a] If the defendant is unrepresented, the judge is under an obligation to ensure the proper conduct of the trial: Archbold (1988), para. 4–392.

[56] *Code of Conduct for the Bar of England and Wales* (5th ed., 1990), as amended. "The general purpose of the Code is to provide the standards of conduct on the part of barristers which are appropriate in the interests of justice in England and Wales . . .": *ibid*. para. 102 and see above, Chap. 3.

[57] *Ibid*. para. 208. A barrister's other duties include the obligation to act honestly and with proper regard to the public confidence in the profession, to exercise independent, professional judgment and to promote fearlessly the client's best interests: *ibid*. paras. 201, 206, 207.

principle is of the utmost importance and impinges upon the task of counsel at several points in the trial.

(a) Prosecuting counsel

The Standards Applicable in Criminal Cases annexed to the Code of Conduct for the Bar of England and Wales state that:

"Prosecuting counsel should not attempt to obtain a conviction by all means at his command. He should not regard himself as appearing for a party. He should lay before the Court fairly and impartially the whole of the facts which comprise the case for the prosecution and should assist the Court on all matters of law applicable to the case."[58]

This view has found judicial expression at various times and prosecuting counsel have even been described as "ministers of justice assisting in the administration of justice."[59] A distinguished Old Bailey judge, who had been Senior Prosecuting Counsel at that court, warned a prosecutor against feeling pride or satisfaction in the mere fact of success, or boasting of the percentage of convictions secured over a period of time. It is, he said, ". . . no rebuff to his prestige if he fails to convince the tribunal of the prisoner's guilt."[60] It is highly undesirable for prosecuting counsel to use unnecessarily emotive language which can only excite sympathy for the victim or prejudice against the accused.[61]

What is required of prosecuting counsel is an element of objectivity in conducting the trial process. This will often be difficult to achieve.

Three broad areas may be identified which necessitate careful consideration and the exercise of judgment by counsel: the desirability and propriety of a plea arrangement; the nature and presentation of the prosecution case at trial; the amount of assistance which needs to be given to the defence or the judge.

(i) *The plea arrangement*[62]

Where there are a number of counts in the indictment or where one count contains alternative charges or where the jury might convict of a lesser charge, it is not uncommon for the defence to offer a plea of guilty to a lesser charge in return for an agreement from the prosecution to offer no evidence on the more serious charge. This is a form of plea bargaining. In a sense, there is a double advantage in these circumstances. Assume that the accused is charged on one indictment containing two separate counts of rape and one count of indecent assault. If, in return for an agreement to accept not guilty pleas to the counts of rape, the accused agrees to plead guilty to the other count he will render himself liable to a less severe sentence on the lesser

---

[58] *Ibid.* Annex H, *Standards Applicable in Criminal Cases*, para. 1.1 (hereinafter, *Standards in Criminal Cases*). See also the Report of Mr. Justice Farquharson's Committee on the Role of Prosecuting Counsel (1986), set out in Archbold (1988), para. 4–47a.

[59] *R.* v. *Puddick* (1865) 4 F. & F. 497; *R.* v. *Banks* [1916] 2 K.B. 621. See also the Farquharson Report (1986).

[60] C. Humphreys, "The Duties and Responsibilities of Prosecuting Counsel" [1955] Crim.L.R. 739.

[61] Archbold (1988), para. 4–177.

[62] As to the research on plea bargaining, see n. 31, above.

charge and also receive credit for a guilty plea. Clearly, the offer of a plea arrangement creates a certain amount of pressure on the accused.[63] In this context, however, we are more interested in the problems it may create for prosecuting counsel and what the approach should be in deciding when it is proper to accept a plea of guilty to less than the full charges in the indictment.

The advantages of a guilty plea for the prosecution are obvious: there is a saving of time and money; witnesses are spared the experience of testifying; the inevitable uncertainty of the trial is exchanged for the certainty of a plea. On the other hand, "administrative convenience in the form of a rapid guilty plea should not take precedence over the interests of justice."[64] Justice demands first that the offence in the indictment should be prosecuted where the evidence supports the charge,[65] unless there are exceptional factors suggesting otherwise, and secondly that the court should be able to pass a proper sentence consistent with the gravity of the accused's actions, and if a plea is accepted the case cannot be put by counsel on the basis that what the accused did was more serious than what appears in the charge upon which the accused is being tried.[66]

Defence counsel will merely be negotiating for an "offer" which can be put to the client, whilst reminding the client that a plea of guilty should be entered only if he or she is actually guilty. The vigour with which defence counsel commends the arrangement which has been negotiated may be related to factors other than the strength of the evidence and the story of the client.[67]

The arrangement of pleas is a common feature of the trial on indictment and it is alleged that it can be improperly facilitated by "overcharging" the accused at the outset. If more serious charges are included on the indictment when the evidence is, at best, equivocal, prosecuting counsel has more to bargain with. This touches both on the discretion of the police and the Crown Prosecution Service in selecting appropriate charges and the inadequacy of committal proceedings for eliminating dubious charges at an early stage.

There are two constraints on plea arrangement. First, prosecuting counsel exercise no significant influence over sentence.[68] No bargain is directly permissible about the length of sentence on particular charges, but is permissible about the charges to be proceeded with. In the United States, on the

---

[63] For a consideration of the pressures on the accused, see pp. 768–769, above.

[64] Code for Crown Prosecutors, para. 11. See also the Home Affairs Committee Fourth Report for Session 1989–90, *Crown Prosecution Service* H.C. 118–1, paras. 36–44. The Code is not binding upon counsel, but may be regarded as reflecting the appropriate balance to be borne in mind. As to the relationship between counsel and the instructing solicitor, see the Farquharson Report (1986) and see *Standards in Criminal Cases*, paras. 1.1–1.6.

[65] Whilst this is based upon *R. v. Soanes* (1948) 32 Cr.App.R. 136, which, in part, does not represent the present position, as will be seen from the following discussion in the text, it does represent a commonly held view.

[66] Code for Crown Prosecutors, para. 11.

[67] See further, pp. 777–778.

[68] Prosecuting counsel is limited, in effect, to rehearsing the facts about the previous record of the defendant. See G. Zellick, "The Role of Prosecuting Counsel in Sentencing" [1979] Crim.L.R. 493; M. King, "The Role of Prosecuting Counsel in Sentencing—What about Magistrates' Courts?" [1979] Crim.L.R. 775 and *Standard in Criminal Cases*, para. 1.8.

other hand, it is possible in many states for the prosecutor to make direct recommendations about sentence.[69]

Secondly, consideration must be given to the role of the judge. The respective roles of prosecuting counsel and judge have not been clearly defined, but it would seem that counsel has the right to offer no evidence on the indictment as a whole or to offer no evidence on a particular count. Consequently, it is the responsibility of the prosecution to decide whether to drop a particular charge. This seems to have been accepted by Lawton L.J. in *R.* v. *Coward*,[70] but is contrary to the statement of Lord Goddard C.J. in *R.* v. *Soanes*.[71] The solution propounded by the Farquharson Committee on the Role of Prosecuting Counsel[72] is to accept that the decision is for prosecuting counsel, but that such a decision is subject to three important qualifications:

(1) If counsel seeks the approval of the judge, in particular where it is desirable to reassure the public at large that the course proposed is a proper one, counsel must abide by the judge's decision.[73]

(2) Where the judge takes a view on the basis of the information available that counsel is taking the wrong decision, the judge may decline to proceed with the case until counsel has consulted with the Director of Public Prosecutions on whether to proceed in the light of the judge's comments. In the final analysis, the judge has no right to prevent counsel proceeding as decided.[74]

(3) Where a decision has to be made on whether to proceed during the course of the trial, that decision is to be made by counsel. The prosecution cannot discontinue proceedings after the end of its case without the leave of the judge.

None of this guidance relates to the power of the Attorney-General to enter a nolle prosequi to end the proceedings, which may be done at any stage.

---

[69] Sentencing structures also differ: see J. Baldwin and M. McConville (1977), pp. 18–24. The prosecutor's discretion in the United States is considered in B. Grossman, *The Prosecutor: An Inquiry into the Exercise of Discretion* (1969).

[70] (1979) 123 S.J. 785.

[71] 112 J.P. 193.

[72] A copy of the Report is to be found in Archbold (1988), para. 4–47a. On the basis of that Report, Sir Thomas Hetherington, the previous D.P.P., considers the relationship between the prosecution and the courts: *Prosecution and the Public Interest* (1989), pp. 169–171. See also Crown Prosecution Service, *The Crown Court: A Guide to Good Practice for the Courts* (1990).

[73] This proposition is supported by *R.* v. *Broad* (1978) 68 Cr.App.R. 281. In the Yorkshire Ripper case, the judge was asked whether he would accept the agreement between the prosecution and the defence to accept a plea by Peter Sutcliffe of guilty of manslaughter by diminished responsibility when charged with murder. The judge refused to accept the agreement, presumably because the public interest demanded a trial for murder.

[74] See also the Guidelines to Prosecution Counsel given by the Bar Committee of the Senate of the Four Inns of Court and the Bar (1984), as approved in *R* v. *Jenkins* (1986) 83 Cr.App.R. 152. In *R.* v. *Renshaw* [1989] Crim.L.R. 811, the Court of Appeal, referring to the Farquharson Report (1986), emphasised that it is important for the judge to listen to the reasons of counsel for offering no evidence, in particular since counsel may well have information not available to the judge, otherwise the judge is not in a position to decide whether to approve or disapprove counsel's proposed course of action.

(ii) *The presentation of the prosecution case*

Apart from planning the general strategy of the prosecution case, counsel has four specific tasks in its presentation. Opening and closing speeches are made, prosecution witnesses are examined and defence witnesses are cross-examined. In each of these tasks rules of conduct as well as rules of procedure and evidence must be observed.

The *opening speech* to the jury is of the utmost importance. The greatest level of concentration and understanding is likely to be exhibited at the beginning and end of a trial. Jurors, especially, are likely to be taking their duties very seriously at the outset of the trial and the opening speech is bound to have considerable impact. It is highly undesirable that prosecuting counsel should open the case with unnecessarily emotive language, and where the offences charged are likely to excite particular sympathy for the victim or prejudice against the accused counsel should warn the jury not to be influenced by such emotions in weighing the evidence.[75]

In *examination-in-chief* of prosecution witnesses, counsel must obey the golden rule of sticking to the facts in issue. Counsel should not use leading questions[76] (except on uncontentious matters and with the agreement of the defence[77]) and there are certain other constraints on the lines of questioning.[78] Whether a question is a leading one is a matter for the judge to decide.

In *cross-examination* of defence witnesses, prosecuting counsel is entitled to test their evidence fully and fairly subject to the normal constraints on the line of questioning.[79] Counsel may ask leading questions. If prosecuting counsel does choose to question the accused, there are statutory restrictions upon the putting of questions about the criminal past and bad character of the accused.[80]

(iii) *Assisting the other participants—the defence and the judge*

Prosecuting counsel has an obligation to assist the defence by the disclosure of certain evidence. The disclosure provisions are considered more fully elsewhere,[81] but in brief the prosecution must inform the defence of the name and address of any person who has made a statement related to the prosecution but is not to be called as a witness; of the existence of statements made previously by a prosecution witness which are inconsistent with evidence given at trial by the witness; and of the previous convictions, if any, of

---

[75] Archbold (1988), para. 4–177. See also the Farquharson Report (1986).

[76] *i.e.* a question which by its form suggests the desired answer. "You saw the defendant take the jewellery and put it in his pocket, didn't you?"

[77] There are other exceptions to the general rule, *e.g.*, when the witness called for the prosecution turns out to be hostile, *i.e.* deliberately obstructive, the Criminal Procedure Act 1865, s.3, permits the use of leading questions to cross-examine the witness to elicit the expected information; see J. A. Andrews and M. Hirst, *Criminal Evidence* (1987), paras. 7.06ff.

[78] *e.g.* questions about previous inconsistent statements may not generally be put (unless the witness is hostile), nor questions impugning the witness's credit. Counsel must not vilify, insult or annoy any witness: *Code of Conduct*, para. 610(e).

[79] That is it should be directed to an issue in the case or to the credit of a witness. Questions can be put about previous inconsistent statements, see the Criminal Procedure Act 1865, ss.4 and 5.

[80] See Criminal Evidence Act 1898, s.1(f).

[81] See p. 666, above.

prosecution witnesses which are known to the prosecution. These disclosures may materially assist the defence case and further assistance requested by the defence may be rendered by the prosecution at their discretion.[82]

The obligation to assist the judge is made clear in the Code of Conduct. Not only must counsel assist by arguments on point of law or procedure arising during the trial, but it is also "the duty of prosecuting counsel to assist the court at the conclusion of the summing-up by drawing attention to any apparent errors or omissions of fact or law."[83] Needless to say, this duty has to be discharged with considerable tact.

Influencing the court with regard to sentence is not part of the duties of prosecuting counsel, although the prosecution may now request that the Attorney-General seek a review by the Court of Appeal of a sentence believed to be unduly lenient.[84]

(b) Defence counsel

Counsel defending a client in a criminal case may face conflict between the duty to the court and the duty to the client. It may be asked how counsel can act as advocate for someone who is "obviously guilty," or put forward a defence or a mitigation which appears to be based on the slenderest of evidence. The answer given by the Bar is that, consistent with counsel's duty not knowingly to deceive or mislead the court,[85] every accused person has a right to have the prosecution case tested and their own case put.[86] In a statement following the case of *R. v. McFadden*,[87] in which the trial judge had criticised counsel for wasting time, the Chairman of the Bar said[88]:

> "It is the duty of counsel when defending an accused on a criminal charge to present to the court, fearlessly and without regard to his personal interests, the defence of that accused. It is not his function to determine the truth or falsity of that defence, nor should he permit his personal opinion of that defence to influence his conduct of it.... Counsel also has a duty to the court and to the public. This duty includes the clear presentation of the issues and the avoidance of waste of time, repetition and prolixity. In the conduct of every case counsel must be mindful of this public responsibility."[89]

---

[82] See *Standards in Criminal Cases*, para. 1.2. For examples of assistance, see Humphreys (1955).

[83] *Standards in Criminal Cases*, para. 1.7.

[84] *Ibid.* para. 1.8. As to the review of sentencing, see the Criminal Justice Act 1988, s.36, and pp. 839–841, below.

[85] *Code of Conduct*, para. 208.

[86] This is one of the fundamental principles of the Bar: see *Standards in Criminal Cases*, section 2: Responsibilities of Defence Counsel and pp. 157–159, above.

[87] (1976) 62 Cr.App.R. 187.

[88] Melford Stevenson J. had taken a very dim view of the length of the trial in which the evidence had occupied over 30 days, and the closing speeches for the defence six and a half days. There were seven defendants, but the judge thought that counsel had behaved improperly and took the unusual course of inviting the taxing master to look carefully at the fees allowed counsel on legal aid taxation.

[89] (1976) 62 Cr.App.R. 193. The complaints against defending counsel were investigated by the Professional Conduct Committee of the Bar, and rejected. See *Code of Conduct*, paras. 206–208 and 610 and *Standards in Criminal Cases*, paras. 2.1 and 2.2.

The "cab-rank" principle is intended to ensure that every accused can engage an advocate.[90] Counsel must ". . . endeavour to protect his client from conviction except by a competent tribunal and upon legally admissible evidence sufficient to support a conviction for the offence charged."[91] Counsel's opinion of the weight of evidence and the credibility of any defence being suggested by the client will obviously be factors in the advice which defence counsel gives.

(i) *Advising on plea and the accused's confession*

Counsel cannot leave a client unaware of the concessions to be gained from a sentence discount[92] or plea arrangement.[93] However, it must be made clear to the accused that there is complete freedom of choice of plea and that the accused has complete responsibility for it.[94] In practice the advice and attitude of defence counsel can be crucial, as the study of Baldwin and McConville[95] demonstrates. For example, 48 accused people gave as their reason for their changing plea the advice that they had received from counsel. It is difficult to offer advice which will inevitably carry great weight whilst leaving the accused free to make up his or her mind. In 21 out of 121 cases there was evidence that the advice given was not fair or proper.

Counsel may give an assessment of the strength of the prosecution case and the likelihood of acquittal, the details of any plea arrangement which has been or might be negotiated, the possible range of sentence and the discount for a guilty plea, the credibility of any defence which may be advanced, and the dangers of attempting to discredit prosecution witnesses, especially the police. Also important is counsel's attitude and demeanour. If the accused is given the impression that counsel has no hope or confidence of an acquittal or appears indifferent to the accused's protestations of innocence, the pressure on the accused will be further increased.

The Court of Appeal, considering defence counsel's obligations to advise a client, said that if need be the advice may be in strong terms, but that counsel must emphasise that the accused should only plead guilty if actually guilty.[96] If defence counsel deprives the accused of the freedom of plea, a guilty plea would be a nullity.[97] However, such cases are rare since the advice needs to be couched in extreme terms to contravene the guidelines.

If an innocent client decides to plead guilty, counsel must continue to represent the client, "but only after he has advised what the consequences will be and what can be submitted in mitigation can only be on the basis that the client is guilty."[98]

Counsel may discover that the client is guilty of the offence charged. This may emerge from the client in clear terms in the form of a confession or as a result of inconsistent statements or from supposition on the part of counsel. A conflict then arises between the duty to the client and the duty to the

[90] See pp. 158–159, above.
[91] *Standards in Criminal Cases*, para. 2.1.
[92] See pp. 768–769, above, and p. 797, below.
[93] See pp. 772–774, above.
[94] *Ibid.*
[95] *Negotiated Justice* (1977), Chap. 3.
[96] *R. v. Turner* [1970] 2 Q.B. 321, 326. See also *Standards in Criminal Cases*, para. 2.3.
[97] *R. v. Peace* [1976] Crim.L.R. 119; *R. v. Inns* (1975) 60 Cr.App.R. 231.
[98] *Standards in Criminal Cases*, para. 2.5.

court. If the discovery is based upon inconsistent statements or counsel's suspicions or speculations, no general guidance is provided by the Code of Conduct since it all depends on the actual circumstances of the particular case.[99] If the discovery is based upon a confession, it is made .clear that counsel is not prevented from appearing in the accused's defence, nor does it release counsel from "his imperative duty to do all that he honourably can for his client."[1] However, a confession limits what counsel may do. Counsel "must not assert as true that which he knows to be false. He may not connive at, much less attempt to substantiate, a fraud."[2] Counsel may not suggest that someone else committed the crime or call any evidence known to be false. Counsel may take objections to the competency of the court, to the form of the indictment, to the admissibility of evidence and to the evidence admitted. "In other words, a barrister must not . . . set up an affirmative case inconsistent with the confession made to him."[3] Further, since the issue in a criminal trial is whether or not the accused is guilty and the burden of proof lies on the prosecution, counsel may test the prosecution evidence and may argue that the case against the accused has not been established.[4]

(ii) *Correcting defects*

The conflict between the duty to the client and the duty to the court may also arise with regard to defence counsel's obligations in respect of procedural error, or factual or legal errors made by the court, not noticed by the prosecution.[5] One view, proceeding partly from the conception of the trial as a game in which the underdog (the accused) is entitled to the benefit of any errors, is that defence counsel is under no obligation to correct the judge. The Code of Conduct, however, requires counsel to bring all authorities, that is all relevant statutes and cases, and any procedural irregularity to the attention of the court before the summing up has begun.[6] Points of procedural irregularity must not be reserved so as to form the basis of an appeal.[7]

(iii) *The conduct of the defence*

If, at the end of the prosecution presentation, defence counsel believes that a case has not been established against the accused, a submission of no case to answer may be made which, if successful, results in the acquittal of the accused. The judge must decide whether or not the prosecution have adduced evidence on which a jury, properly directed, could convict in

---

[99] *Ibid.*, para. 3.6.
[1] *Ibid.* para. 3.2. It is also important to bear in mind: "(a) that every punishable crime is a breach of common or statute law committed by a person of sound mind and understanding; (b) that the issue in a criminal trial is always whether the defendant is guilty of the offence charged, never whether he is innocent; (c) that the burden of proof rests on the prosecution:" *ibid.* para. 3.1.
[2] *Ibid.* para. 3.3.
[3] *Ibid.* para. 3.4.
[4] *Ibid.* para. 3.5.
[5] If they are noticed by the prosecution, they should be raised with the judge: see p. 776, above.
[6] *Code of Conduct*, para. 610(c).
[7] *Ibid.*

accordance with the law.[8] If the Crown Prosecution Service carefully consider whether or not to prosecute, and the magistrates consider the case for the prosecution at committal proceedings, there should be relatively few successful submissions, unless, for example, the prosecution witnesses fail to appear or do not support the case for the prosecution.[9]

The formal procedure for the defence case, if the case proceeds, will be the same as for the prosecution, with an opening speech, witnesses and a closing speech, but it is the tactical conduct of the case which gives rise to greater difficulties. A major problem will often be the extent to which prosecution witnesses can be attacked without allowing the prosecution to place in evidence details of the (bad) character of the accused, including any previous convictions.

The normal rules of evidence prevent evidence being given by prosecution witnesses about the accused's character[10] and also forbid cross-examination of the accused on that subject.[11] Such cross-examination may, however, be permitted where the defence has sought to establish the accused's good character or cast imputations upon the character of the prosecutor or prosecution witnesses.[12] It is this latter rule which creates the problem, for the dividing line between an emphatic denial of guilt and an allegation of lies or misconduct by prosecution witnesses (particularly police officers) may be a very narrow one.[13] Counsel, if instructed by the accused to allege that the whole of the prosecution case is a "put-up job," will have to advise on the consequences of running that particular defence. To assist counsel, the trial judge will usually give a warning when a line of cross-examination is being used which may expose the accused to cross-examination as to character.[14]

(iv) *After the verdict*

Defence counsel, after a plea or verdict of guilty, will usually make a plea in mitigation of sentence on behalf of the client. As favourable a view as possible is put on the client's circumstances and suggestions may be made as to why particular sentences would or would not be appropriate. Care must be taken in referring to third parties during mitigation, for they will have no opportunity to contest any assertions. No allegation may be made which is ". . . merely scandalous, or intended or calculated to villify insult or annoy a . . . person."[15]

---

[8] *R.* v. *Galbraith* [1981] 1 W.L.R. 1039 and see Emmins (1988), pp. 129–131.
[9] See above, Chap. 13.
[10] See below n. 63.
[11] See generally, Sir Rupert Cross and C. Tapper, *Cross on Evidence* (7th ed., 1990), Chaps. 8, 9 and 10.
[12] Criminal Evidence Act 1898, s.1(f).
[13] See *R.* v. *Tanner* (1977) 76 Cr.App.R. 56 and the discussion in Archbold (1988), para. 4–360. The most helpful dictum is that of Lord Hewart C.J. in *R.* v. *Jones* (1924) 17 Cr.App.R. 117, 120: It is ". . . one thing to deny that he had made the confession, but it is another thing to say that the whole thing was a deliberate and elaborate concoction on the part of the inspector: that seems to be an attack on the character of the witness." General guidance is to be found in a decision of the House of Lords, *Selvey* v. *D.P.P.* [1970] A.C. 304.
[14] *Ibid.* at p. 342A; *R.* v. *Cook* [1959] 2 Q.B. 340, 348.
[15] *Code of Conduct*, para. 610(e).

Save in exceptional circumstances, it is defence counsel's duty to see the client after conviction and sentence.[16] Counsel may give initial advice on appeal or the existence of grounds of appeal.[17]

5. WITNESSES

In most contested trials witness evidence will be called by either or both the prosecution and the defence.[18] People who might be witnesses may be unwilling to appear or there may be some doubt about their capacity to give evidence. Whether a witness satisfies the legal requirements to give evidence is a matter of law for the judge. Prosecuting and defence counsel exercise considerable discretion in who they will call. They must bear in mind not only the legal requirements but also the practical consideration that there is no point in calling someone who will not "come up to proof," that is, someone who will not be able to provide a convincing and consistent story in court, particularly under cross-examination. In certain cases it may be necessary to call expert witnesses.

(i) *Competence of witnesses*

"Competence" in this respect is used in two different ways. First it raises the question of whether the accused and the accused's spouse are allowed to give evidence. The accused has been allowed to give evidence on his or her own behalf since the Criminal Evidence Act 1898, s.1. The accused's spouse has been competent for the defence since the 1898 Act,[19] but only became generally competent for the prosecution by virtue of the Police and Criminal Evidence Act 1984, s.80.[20]

Secondly, it raises the question of whether a person will be capable of giving evidence. A person must be competent both to take the oath and to give evidence. Competence in this sense may be questioned when the proposed witness is either a young child or someone suffering from a mental disorder affecting the ability to give evidence. The matter is one for the judge,[21] who must determine whether the particular proposed witness[22] has

---

[16] *Standards in Criminal Cases*, para. 6.2.

[17] As to appeals in criminal cases, see pp. 830–847, below esp. p. 831.

[18] Some cases, *e.g.* can be proved on scientific evidence alone.

[19] See now the Police and Criminal Evidence Act 1984, s.80(1)(*b*).

[20] Police and Criminal Evidence Act 1984, s.80(1)(*a*). He or she is not competent if jointly charged with the accused: *ibid.* s.80(4). As to both the competence and compellability of spouses, see P. Creighton, "Spouse Competence and Compellability" [1990] Crim.L.R. 34.

[21] *R.* v. *Khan* [1981] 73 Cr.App.R. 190; *R.* v. *Dunne* (1929) 143 L.T. 120; *R.* v. *Reynolds* [1950] 1 K.B. 606.

[22] Issues arise, in particular, with regard to children and people with a mental disorder. When the proposed witness is a child, the question is "whether the child is possessed of sufficient intelligence to justify the reception of the evidence, and understands the duty of speaking the truth. Those criteria will inevitably vary widely from child to child, and may indeed vary according to the circumstances of the case, the nature of the case, and the nature of the evidence which the child is called upon to give. Obviously the younger the child, the more care the judge must take before he allows the evidence to be received. But the statute [Children and Young Persons Act 1933] lays down no minimum age and the matter accordingly remains in the discretion of the judge in each case. It may be very rarely that a five year old will satisfy the requirements . . . But nevertheless the discretion remains to be exercised judicially by the judge. . . .": *R.* v. *Z.* [1990] 2 Q.B. 355, 359–360. When the proposed witness is a person with a mental disorder, *R.* v. *Hill* (1851) 2 Den. 254 made clear that such a person is not necessarily incapable of giving evidence. It is probable that a similar approach to that taken with regard to children will be taken.

the capacity to understand the solemnity of the proceedings and the special obligation to tell the truth.[23]

Particular problems arise in child sexual abuse cases, when the nature of the incidents may well be such that the victim is the only witness. It is possible for a child to give unsworn evidence[24] although such evidence may not carry the same weight as that given under oath.

(ii) *Compellability of witnesses*

Most people can be compelled to be witnesses, with the exception of the accused and the accused's spouse. However, the accused's spouse is compellable on behalf of the accused generally, and for the prosecution and co-accused in cases of assault or worse offences on the spouse witness or people under 16 and sexual offences committed against the spouse witness or someone under 16.[25]

(iv) *Giving evidence*

A witness gives evidence initially in response to questions from counsel by whom he or she was called.[26] "Leading" questions must be avoided.[27] The witness is then available to counsel for the other side for cross-examination, where the object will be to elicit evidence favourable to the cross-examiner's case and to discredit unfavourable evidence. Finally, counsel who called the witness is entitled to re-examine the witness, but must not raise any new issues.[28]

Giving evidence in court is a trying experience. Consequently, counsel has to be aware of the possibility of the witness not coming up to proof. What is meant here is the capacity of the witness not only to retell the story convincingly when responding to examination-in-chief, but also to be able to stick to that story when subject to cross examination.

For some witnesses, the trauma of a court appearance will be particularly severe. This has been made graphically apparent in child sexual abuse cases.

[23] R. v. *Hayes* [1977] 2 All E.R. 288; R. v. *Campbell* [1983] Crim.L.R. 174; R v. *Bellamy* [1986] Crim.L.R. 54.

[24] Children and Young Persons Act 1933, s 38, as amended by the Criminal Justice Act 1988, s.34.

[25] A spouse is not compellable where jointly charged with the accused. The offences when a spouse is compellable include those involving injury or the threat of injury, which may be caused to the spouse witness. The offences also include attempting to, conspiring to, aiding, abetting or counselling or procuring such offences, see the Police and Criminal Evidence Act 1984, s.80 and Creighton (1990).

[26] Usually, the witness will be giving evidence in conformity with the case which counsel is putting; however, as to the position if the witness turns out to be hostile, see p. 775, above. As to the usual rule of the inadmissibility of out-of-court statements which are to the same effect as the in-court evidence, see *Fox* v. *G.M.C.* [1960] 3 All E.R. 225; usually, a witness may not refresh memory in court but must speak from their own recollection of the events, but there is an exception in that a witness may refer to a contemporaneous note of the matters to which the testimony relates. Witnesses are encouraged to refresh their memories out of court by reference to their original witness statements, and in some cases may interrupt their testimony in order to do so, see R. v. *Da Silva* (1990) 90 Cr.App.R. 233. There are rules which provide that the prosecution must tell the defence if their witnesses have seen their statements prior to giving evidence, see Archbold (1988), para. 4–300.

[27] See p. 775, above.

[28] R. v. *Harman* [1985] Crim.L.R. 326.

Many of these cases have not been prosecutions of the alleged abuser, but child care cases where the rules of evidence are less stringent. However, if a prosecution is instituted, it will be necessary to consider whether the victim can give evidence. As has already been seen, the first hurdle is whether or not the child is competent to give evidence. If so, it has to be considered whether the child will be able to give evidence in the daunting atmosphere of the court under the gaze of the alleged abuser. The court has always had the power to screen the witness from the gaze of the accused, although the witness must be open to the view of the court.[29] The Criminal Justice Act 1988 added to this by providing for the possibility of children in certain cases to give their evidence through a live television link.[30] These provisions still mean that, consonant with the ethos of the criminal trial as an adversarial procedure, the witness must be available for cross-examination. The *Report of the Advisory Group on Video Evidence* makes a particularly important recommendation amongst a number of crucial recommendations, that in trials on indictment for serious child abuse cases, video-recorded interviews with children under 14 should be admissible as evidence.[31]

(v) *Expert witnesses*

The function of an expert witness in a criminal trial is to assist the jury in matters outside the jury's competence or normal knowledge.[32] For example an expert may prove, from scientific tests, that the accused has handled explosives[33] or, from DNA testing, that the accused had sexual intercourse with the victim[34] or, from examining a vehicle, that a road traffic accident was caused by brake failure. Expert evidence will not be admitted to resolve a question on which the jury can bring their own experience to bear, for example, on a defence of provocation, the effect on an ordinary man of discovering that his girlfriend was pregnant by another man[35] or, on a

---

[29] *R.* v. *Smellie* (1919) 14 Cr.App.R. 128 and *R.* v. *X.* (1990) 91 Cr.App.R. 36.

[30] Criminal Justice Act 1988, s.32, and see J. R. Spencer and R. Flin, *The Evidence of Children* (1990).

[31] The Group was chaired by Judge Pigot. See also J. McEwan, "In the Box or on the Box? The Pigot Report and Child Witnesses" [1990] Crim.L.R. 363. Some of the Pigot Report recommendations are to be introduced, see The Criminal Justice Bill 1991, Part III. Similar problems may apply with regard to adults with a mental handicap who have been abused, see M. J. Gunn, "How Can the Law Help?" in H. Brown and A. Craft (eds.), *Thinking the Unthinkable* (1989), but the live television links do not apply to such witnesses and the proposal to use videoed interviews does not actually extend to such witnesses, although the Pigot Report envisages future extensions of their recommendations.

[32] See *Cross on Evidence* (1990), pp. 440–443 & 446–448. As to the work of such experts, see I. R. Freckleton, *The Trial of the Expert* (1987) and D. J. Gee, "The Expert Witness in the Criminal Trial" [1987] Crim.L.R. 307.

[33] Care must, of course, be taken in what tests are used and what they establish and in presenting the evidence accurately, reliably, fairly and credibly. Failure in these respects was part of the reason for the interim report on the Maguire case concluding that their convictions for taking part in IRA explosions were unsafe, see Sir John May, *Interim Report on the Maguire Case* (1990). The case has been referred to the Court of Appeal, which is expected to quash the convictions.

[34] See K. F. Kelly, J. J. Rankin and R. C. Wink, "Method and Application of DNA Finger-printing: A Guide for the Non-Scientist" [1987] Crim.L.R. 105 and R. M. White and J. J. D. Greenwood, "DNA fingerprinting and the law" (1988) 51 M.L.R. 145. DNA fingerprinting, otherwise known as genetic fingerprinting, played a crucial role in the arrest and conviction of Colin Pitchfork for murder of two young girls, see J. Wambaugh, *The Blooding* (1989).

[35] See *R.* v. *Turner* [1975] Q.B. 834.

prosecution for publishing an obscene book, the effect it may have on an ordinary person likely to read it.[36]

6. THE ROLE OF THE JUDGE[37]

The characterisation of the judge as the umpire or referee in our adversarial system is not entirely appropriate in the context of the trial on indictment. It is true that the judge should apply the rules, allow counsel to present the case without undue hindrance, not intervene unduly and that ultimately the decision on matters of fact belongs to the jury. However, it is equally true that the judge exercises a very considerable discretion in respect of many aspects of the trial and it is reasonably clear that the way in which that discretion is exercised may have a significant bearing on the outcome. Indeed, in certain circumstances, the judge's ruling will determine the case. In considering the extent of the judge's discretion and the possible effects of its exercise we should bear in mind the relationship between judge and jury.

The separation of functions between the judge and the jury is that the judge is to deal with matters of law and the jury with matters of fact. Consequently, it is the judge's function to determine certain procedural matters; to consider any plea bargaining; to decide upon the admissibility of evidence; to sum up on the law and the evidence for the benefit of the jury; and to pass sentence. It will be seen that the distinction between matters of law and matters of fact is often blurred, and that the judge, in any case, has considerable influence in the determination of matters of fact.

(a) Procedural matters

From the outset, the judge has control over the progress of the trial and the administrative and procedural problems that may arise. The judge must decide questions relating to the form of the indictment and any necessary amendment to it[38]; the taking of the plea from the accused and its acceptability[39]; whether a special plea of autrefois acquit or autrefois convict has been successfully raised by the accused; the determination of preliminary points

---

[36] See *R.* v. *Anderson* [1972] 1 Q.B. 304. By contrast, if the question was the effect a publication would have on a child, expert evidence might be admissible, see *D.P.P.* v. *A & BC Chewing Gum Ltd.* [1968] 1 Q.B. 159.

[37] See *Jones* v. *National Coal Board* [1957] 2 Q.B. 55, discussed by Lord Denning in *The Due Process of Law* (1980), pp. 58–62, see p. 707, above. See P. Devlin, *The Judge* (1979) and, for an unique account by the judge of a criminal trial, P. Devlin, *Easing the Passing* (1985). See also Pattenden (1990); A. Samuels, "Judicial Misconduct and the Criminal Trial" [1982] Crim.L.R. 221.

[38] As to questions relating to the form of the indictment, for example, whether the indictment discloses any offence, see Archbold (1988), paras. 1–110 to 1–115. Under the Indictments Act 1915, s.5 the judge may allow amendment to the indictment at any stage of a trial provided there will be no injustice in all the circumstances. See Archbold (1988), para. 1–63 to 1–69 and *R.* v. *Nelson* (1977) 65 Cr.App.R. 119, which is also instructive on the obligations of defence counsel to draw irregularities to the notice of the court, *cf.* p. 778, above.

[39] For the role of the judge in relation to prosecuting counsel's obligations in plea arrangements, see p. 774, above. In *R.* v. *Winterflood* (1978) 68 Cr.App.R. 291, the trial judge appears to have taken the initiative in suggesting the addition of a charge to the indictment to which the accused might plead guilty.

raised by counsel; and the desirability of separate trials.[40] Whilst these may be classed as procedural questions, their importance should not be under-estimated. In some cases the determination of the procedural point may settle the whole issue.

The empanelling and swearing of the jury is subject to judicial control. The judge will settle any question over challenges.[41] Once sworn, with the case proceeding, the jury may be discharged by the judge for a variety of reasons.[42] The effect of discharging the jury is not to acquit the accused—he or she may be remanded for a second trial.[43]

It is also the judge's responsibility to maintain order in court. The judge has powers of punishment for contempt where there is misbehaviour.[44]

Although counsel for the prosecution and the defence must conduct their respective cases in accordance with the Code of Conduct, the judge has a significant role in controlling the questioning of witnesses by counsel[45] and in restraining counsel from improper practices. Control should be discreet and the judge must resist the temptation to take over the questioning or to criticise counsel's conduct to such an extent that the jury might thereby be prejudiced.[46]

(b) Plea bargaining[47]

The judge has to be very careful in playing any role in plea arrangements. The extent to which it is proper for the judge to indicate the nature of the sentence discount[48] appropriate in a particular case if the accused enters a guilty plea gives rise to difficulties. Whilst the benefit to the accused is tangible when the prosecution offers an arrangement, it is not precisely

---

[40] The practice is to join several charges together on one indictment where they are founded on the same facts or form part of a series of offences of the same or similar character and so have one trial: Indictment Rules 1971, r. 9. See C. Yates, "How Many Counts to an Indictment?" [1976] Crim.L.R. 428.

[41] See p. 806, below.

[42] See pp. 808–809, below.

[43] *R.* v. *Randall* [1960] Crim.L.R. 435. In this case the jury was discharged after returning verdicts of not guilty, which were then stated to be majority verdicts. (Majority verdicts were not at that time acceptable). The plea of autrefous acquit at the second trial was rejected.

[44] There is a summary power to punish contempts "in the face of the court" which exists to maintain the dignity and authority of the judge and to ensure a fair trial. See *Balogh* v. *Crown Court at St. Albans* [1975] 1 Q.B. 73, discussed in Lord Denning, *The Due Process of Law* (1980), pp. 12–18. The accused was apprehended before he livened up court proceedings by introducing "laughing gas" into the ventilating system at St. Albans Crown Court. See also, *Morris* v. *Crown Office* [1970] 2 Q.B. 114 (group of students breaking up a libel trial); *R.* v. *Aquarius* [1974] Crim.L.R. 373 (disruptive behaviour of defendant); *R.* v. *Logan* [1974] Crim.L.R. 609 (outburst by defendant after sentence); *Lecointe* v. *Courts Administrator of the Central Criminal Court* (1973, unreported) (distribution of leaflets at the Old Bailey inciting people to picket the court). Judge Pickles sentenced a witness to five days imprisonment for her failure to give evidence against her ex-boyfriend. The Court of Appeal in *R.* v. *Renshaw* [1989] Crim.L.R. 811 quashed the finding of contempt because the trial was not fair, but made clear that a person who refuses without adequate excuse to give evidence to the court may be punished, which will usually mean imprisonment.

[45] The line of questioning must be relevant and material and witnesses should be treated courteously.

[46] *R.* v. *McFadden* (1976) 62 Cr.App.R. 187, and see Samuels (1982), p. 223.

[47] As to the position of the accused, prosecuting and defence counsel, see pp. 767, 772, 777, above.

[48] As to the reduction in sentence in response to a guilty plea, see p. 777, above.

quantifiable. When the judge indicates a view about sentence, the induce-ment is precise and the pressure greatly increased.

The Court of Appeal considered the matters of principle involved in judicial intervention in the case of R. v. Turner.[49] Turner had pleaded not guilty on a charge of theft. During an adjournment he was advised by counsel to change his plea. Turner knew that counsel had seen the judge and thought that counsel was relaying the views of the judge when he said that a guilty plea was likely to result in a non-custodial sentence, whereas a finding of guilty would bring a custodial sentence. Turner was repeatedly told that the choice of plea was his. He changed his plea to guilty and later appealed on the ground that he did not have a free choice in retracting his original plea.

The appeal was allowed on the basis that the accused may have felt that the views expressed were those of the trial judge and might, therefore, have been deprived of his freedom of plea.[50] On the general issue Lord Parker C.J. made four observations[51]:

(i) Counsel must give the best advice he or she can, in strong terms if need be, including the advice that a plea of guilty is a mitigating factor which may allow the court to pass a lesser sentence. The accused must be told not to plead guilty unless he or she has committed the offence charged.[52]

(ii) The accused must have freedom of choice of plea.[53]

(iii) There must be freedom of access between counsel and judge in order that matters which cannot be mentioned in open court may be com-municated. Counsel for the defence and the prosecution should both be present as well as the defence solicitor, if he or she so wishes. Any such meetings should only take place when really necessary and the judge should only treat them as private where necessary.[54]

(iv) A judge should never indicate the sentence he or she is minded to impose, save that counsel may be told that whatever the plea, he or she is minded to impose a particular type of sentence, e.g. probation, or a fine, or a custodial sentence. A judge should never say that on a finding of guilt a more severe sentence would be passed, nor should it be indicated that on a guilty plea he or she would pass a particular sen-tence, lest it be thought that a more severe sentence would result after a finding of guilt. Any discussion on sentence should be communicated by counsel to the accused.

---

[49] [1970] 2 Q.B. 321.

[50] This is the basic question which the court will consider in all cases of this kind—"Has the plea been made freely and voluntarily?" cf. R. v. Inns (1975) 60 Cr.App.R. 251; R. v. Peace [1976] Crim.L.R. 119.

[51] [1970] 2 Q.B. 321, pp. 326–327.

[52] See, further, p. 777, above.

[53] See p. 768, above.

[54] The necessity to limit the discussions in the judge's room has been emphasised by the Court of Appeal in R. v. Smith [1990] 1 W.L.R. 1311, drawing attention to the words of Mustill L.J. in R. v. Harper-Taylor (1988) 138 N.L.J. 80 where the requirement that justice be done in public for all to see and hear was emphasised. Thus, whilst the jury may have to be required to withdraw, rarely should meetings take place outside the courtroom. If such meetings do take place, there must be a shorthand note-taker present, as stated in R. v. Smith, in part to avoid the sort of unseemly dialogue between judge and counsel which took place at the end of Smith's trial. See also R. v. Pitman, The Times, October 31, 1990.

Those observations appear to have limited the judicial role substantially and established a clear code of procedure, but they contain one major difficulty. The judge is told never to indicate that a sentence passed after a conviction would be more severe than a sentence passed after a guilty plea. Given the generally acknowledged rule that guilty pleas lead to sentence discounts, how can this principle be observed? The judge is not permitted to say what everyone knows. The Court of Appeal in *R.* v. *Cain*[55] subsequently acknowledged this difficulty, but the authority of *R.* v. *Turner* was strengthened by a subsequent *Practice Direction*[56] which reaffirmed the procedure set out by Lord Parker.

To sum up, the judicial role should be limited to the consideration of arrangements negotiated between counsel, although the ultimate decision on plea arrangements lies with counsel,[57] and to the indication of the particular type of sentence whether the sentence follows a guilty plea or conviction after a not guilty plea. Once the judge becomes involved in indicating alternative sentences any accused is likely to be under the same pressure as Turner and, ". . . once he felt that this was an intimation emanating from the judge, it is really idle in the opinion of this court to think that he really had a free choice in the matter."[58]

(b) Admissibility of evidence

One of the functions of the trial judge is to control the input of material upon which the jury will ultimately base its decision. This the judge does by applying the complex body of rules which make up the law of evidence.[59]

Relevance and admissibility

The evidence a jury hears must be both relevant and admissible. Evidence is relevant if it is logically probative or disprobative of some matter which requires proof, *i.e.* if it makes that matter more or less probable.[60] Thus when a person is accused of murder it is relevant to prove that he or she had a motive to kill the victim, that he or she was seen in possession of the murder weapon, and that he or she was unwilling to account for his or her movements at the time the murder was committed. None of these matters would, standing alone, be likely to establish beyond reasonable doubt that the accused committed the offence, but the proof of each tends to render guilt more probable, which is all that is required.

Not all evidence which is relevant is also admissible. Relevant evidence may have various deficiencies, the most common of which are that it may be unreliable or prejudicial to a fair trial. Rules of exclusion have therefore developed to prevent such evidence being given. Thus the hearsay rule operates to exclude statements not made in court as evidence of the truth of the facts stated, since statements which are not made while giving evidence

---

[55] [1976] Q.B. 496.
[56] [1976] Crim.L.R. 561.
[57] See p. 772, above.
[58] [1970] 2 Q.B. 321, 326B, *per* Lord Parker C.J.
[59] See generally *Cross on Evidence* (1990); Andrews and Hirst (1987).
[60] *Per* Lord Simon in *D.P.P.* v. *Kilbourne* [1973] A.C. 729, 756, H.L.

are considered insufficiently *reliable* to be acted upon by a jury.[61] Thus, for example, it would be inadmissible hearsay for a police officer to give evidence that a person interviewed during the investigation told the police officer that the accused had committed the crime. It would be a different matter if the person concerned came to court and made the same accusation on oath.[62] An example of a rule which operates to exclude *prejudicial* evidence is that which prohibits the giving of evidence of the accused's bad character, including previous convictions. If the jury heard such evidence, it is feared that it would be so incensed that it would give it undue weight in assessing the case against the accused.[63]

The rules of exclusion are seldom absolute and the judge must be familiar with the various exceptions which exist and under which evidence may be received. Exceptions are frequently made in respect of evidence which is not subject to the deficiency against which the rule of exclusion is designed to guard. Thus a confession made by an accused person, though hearsay, may be given in evidence, as it is a statement which goes against the interest of the person making it and so is unlikely to be unreliable.[64] Exceptions may also be made where the need to prevent the giving of certain evidence is outweighed by other factors. Thus evidence of the bad character of the accused may be received where it is of particular value in proving the case against him or her; for instance where a man is charged with drowning his wife in the bath and it is proved that his previous wives drowned in similar circumstances.[65]

Exceptions to the rules of exclusion are generally hedged about with conditions to prevent the admission of undesirable evidence. Thus, for example, where it is proposed to rely upon a confession made by an accused person, the prosecution must, by virtue of section 76 of the Police and Criminal Evidence Act 1984, be able to prove beyond reasonable doubt that it was not obtained either:

"(a) by oppression of the person who made it; or
(b) in consequence of anything said or done which was likely, in the circumstances existing at the time, to render unreliable any confession which might be made by him in consequence thereof."[66]

---

[61] "[Hearsay evidence] is not the best evidence and it is not delivered on oath. The truthfulness and accuracy of the person whose words are spoken to by another witness cannot be tested by cross-examination, and the light which his demeanour would throw on his testimony is lost": *Teper* v. *R.* [1952] A.C. 480, 486, *per* Lord Normand.

[62] When evidence is presented directly to the court in this way, not only is it subject to the sanction of the oath, but also the reliability of the evidence can be tested by cross-examination, and the witness's demeanour seen by the jury.

[63] Such evidence is not necessarily devoid of probative value: *D.P.P.* v. *Kilbourne* [1973] A.C. 729, 757, *per* Lord Simon. But a jury might think it proved more than it does: in other words, the probative value of the evidence is outweighed by its prejudicial effect, see *Boardman* v. *D.P.P.* [1975] A.C. 421, 456, *per* Lord Cross.

[64] Numerous other exceptions to the hearsay rule exist. Much documentary hearsay is admissible under Part II of the Criminal Justice Act 1988, for example, while oral statements made by participants in events in the heat of the moment and before they have had time to concoct anything to their advantage are admissible at common law, see *R.* v. *Andrews* [1987] A.C. 281. For a more complete statement of the exceptions see Andrews and Hirst (1987), Chaps. 18–20.

[65] *R.* v. *Smith* (1915) 11 Cr.App.R. 229.

[66] Police and Criminal Evidence Act 1984, s.76(2).

Determining admissibility

Where the admissibility of an item of evidence, such as a confession, is contested, it would obviously be inadvisable for argument to take place in front of the jury, which would then hear that a confession had been made, even if it were subsequently ruled to be inadmissible. There is therefore a special procedure whereby matters relating to the admissibility of evidence may be determined in the absence of the jury,[67] and this is known as the trial within a trial or *voir dire*. Witnesses may be called in the usual way,[68] and legal argument heard, after which the judge makes his or her ruling.[69]

Discretionary exclusion

Where the strict rules of evidence might operate unfairly, a trial judge has various discretionary powers to exclude from the jury's consideration evidence which is both relevant and admissible.[70] The best known and most frequently exercised power is to be found in section 78 of the Police and Criminal Evidence Act 1984, which provides that the judge:

> "may refuse to allow evidence on which the prosecution proposes to rely to be given if it appears to the court that, having regard to all the circumstances, including the circumstances in which the evidence was obtained, the admission of the evidence would have such an adverse effect on the fairness of the proceedings that the court ought not to admit it."

An example of the use of this power might be in respect of a confession which, though it was not obtained in circumstances rendering it inadmissible under section 76 of the 1984 Act,[71] was nevertheless procured in breach of the rules governing interrogation in such a way that it would be unfair to admit it.[72] In addition to the power conferred by section 78, the trial judge may exclude evidence by virtue of the discretion vested in him or her by the common law[73] and by various statutes.[74]

---

[67] This is something that the magistrates must attempt, see p. 754 above.

[68] Although a special oath is used, which is known as the *"voire dire,"* and from which the procedure takes its name. "I swear I will true answer make to all such questions as the court shall demand of me."

[69] The trial within a trial may form a significant, and sometimes lengthy, part of the proceedings. When the "Birmingham Six" came to trial, a "trial within a trial" was held to determine the admissibility of confessions made by the accused, which lasted eight days, at the end of which the statements were admitted by the judge, Bridge J, who gave a reasoned decision covering fifteen pages: *McIlkenny* v. *Chief Constable of West Midlands Police Force* [1980] Q.B. 283, 314, *per* Lord Denning M.R.

[70] See generally Pattenden (1990), Chap. 7.

[71] See above.

[72] See, *e.g. R.* v. *Samuel* [1988] Q.B. 615 in which the accused confessed to robbery after having been denied access to his solicitor in breach of s.58 of the Police and Criminal Evidence Act 1984. The court regarded this denial of "one of the most important and fundamental rights of a citizen" as sufficient justification for exclusion of the confession under s.78.

[73] The judge has power at common law to exclude evidence at his or her discretion where the prejudicial effect of prosecution evidence outweighs its probative value, and (in certain cases) where evidence has been improperly obtained, see *R.* v. *Sang* [1980] A.C. 402.

[74] See, *e.g.* Criminal Justice Act 1988, s.25: power to exclude admissible documentary evidence where not in the "interests of justice" to admit it.

(c) Summing up

The other major matters of law which are the responsibility of the judge are those which must be explained to the jury so that it can reach a proper decision. The judge will deal with these matters in the summing up, telling the jury that it must accept his or her direction on issues of law.

Lord Hailsham, at the time the Lord Chancellor, emphasised the judge's obligations in summing up:

"The purpose of a direction to a jury is not best achieved by a disquisition on jurisprudence or philosophy or a universally applicable circular tour round the area of law affected by the case. The search for universally applicable definitions is often productive of more obscurity than light. A direction is seldom improved and may be considerably damaged by copious recitations from the total content of a judge's notebook. A direction to a jury should be custom-built to make the jury understand their task in relation to a particular case. Of course, it must include references to the burden of proof and the respective role of jury and judge. But it should also include a succinct but accurate summary of the issues of fact as to which a decision is required, a correct but concise summary of the evidence and arguments on both sides and a correct statement of the inferences which the jury are entitled to draw from their particular conclusions about the primary facts."[75]

Achieving such a summing up may well be difficult, especially in the case of long and complex trials.[76] It would seem proper to suggest that many of the problems might be avoided if judges were careful to ensure that the language they use is that which a jury is likely to understand.[77]

A summing up usually consists of the following elements.[78]

(i) A direction as to the respective tasks of judge and jury

The jury is told that it is for the judge to decide upon matters of law and for it to decide upon matters of fact and that it should not be influenced by any judicial opinions expressed about the evidence; it is for the jury to decide what facts have been proved.[79] It would be naive to think, however, that the views of the judge, if expressed, have no bearing on the jury's decision.[80]

[75] R. v. Lawrence [1982] A.C. 510. See also R. v. McVey [1988] Crim.L.R. 127.
[76] See p. 817, below for consideration of whether the jury should be involved in long complex cases, especially fraud cases.
[77] The point is made, e.g. by R. Harding, "Jury Performance in Complex Cases" in Findlay and Duff (1988), Chap. 5; by M. Levi, "The Role of the Jury in Complex Cases" in Findlay and Duff (1988), Chap. 6; and by Edward Griew, "Summing Up the Law" [1989] Crim.L.R. 768, who supports his argument, at p. 773, with American research which suggests "that a good many vocabulary items freely used in jury instructions are incomprehensible to an alarming percentage of jurors. . . ."
[78] Always to include all these elements is likely to be unnecessary and, sometimes, very confusing, see Griew (1989) and Pattenden (1990), pp. 177–212.
[79] R. v. Bradbury (1920) 15 Cr.App.R. 76; R. v. Mason (1924) 18 Cr.App.R. 131. See Emmins (1988), p. 137. The jury may decide upon a verdict which may appear to be "perverse" despite this statement, provided it realises it has that opportunity: see p. 814, below. There are also some rare circumstances in which the judge may direct a conviction, see below, p. 793.
[80] At its lowest, the position of the summing-up at the end of the trial must give it significance. Add to that the respect accorded to a professional's view by lay people and their natural tendency to rely on the judge's analysis and the judge's influence is clear.

(ii) *A direction as to the burden and standard of proof*

The judge should tell the jury about the burden and standard of proof.[81] Prosecuting counsel may have done so in the opening speech and it may have been referred to during the trial. The judge tells the jury that the burden of proving the guilt of the accused lies on the prosecution save in the case of the common law defence of insanity,[82] and subject to any statutory exception.[83] The standard that must be satisfied is proof beyond a reasonable doubt.[84] So if, for example, Vera, a defendant, raises the issue by stating that an apparent attack was carried out in self-defence, it is for the prosecution to prove beyond reasonable doubt that she was not acting in self defence, rather than on Vera to prove on a balance of probabilities that she was so acting.

The judge directs that the jury must be satisfied of the accused's guilt. This has not been thought to create any problems. Recently, however, it has been observed to cause some difficulties in cases where the crime can be established on the basis of a number of different, mutually exclusive grounds. If, for example, six jurors are satisfied as to one ground for a conviction, and the other six as to a different, mutually exclusive ground, how can the jury be satisfied as to the guilt of the accused?[85]

(iii) *A direction as to the definition of the offence charged and the facts which have to be proved before there can be a conviction*

The judge must explain to the jury the legal requirements of the offence charged and the facts of which the jury must be convinced before it can convict. This often is not easy. In a case of theft, for example, the judge should say that the property stolen must have belonged to someone else and must have been appropriated by the accused, who must have been dishonest and intending to deprive the other person permanently of the property.[86] Yet there are already difficulties. What is an appropriation? What amounts

[81] If a case gets to the stage of a summing-up, it has been questioned whether talk of the burden of proof is appropriate, since the prosecution must have established a prima facie case, otherwise a submission of no case to answer would have succeeded and, in reality, the jury must rely on all the evidence, not just that provided by the prosecution, but also that provided by the defence: Griew (1989). If the jury ask for futher guidance, the judge should use similar words to that used in the original direction: *R.* v. *Milligan*, *The Times*, March 11, 1989.

[82] As established in *M'Naghten's Case* (1843) 10 Cl. & F. 200.

[83] Such exceptions may be express, see, *e.g.* the defence of diminished responsibility in the law of murder, Homicide Act 1957, s.3(2); or implied, see *R.* v. *Hunt* [1986] A.C. 352, H.L. The possibility that the burden may be imposed on the accused impliedly by statute and how it can be decided that the burden is so imposed have been vigorously criticised by P. Mirfield in "The Legacy of Hunt" [1988] Crim.L.R. 19. D.J. Birch in "Hunting the Snark: the Elusive Statutory Exception" [1988] Crim.L.R. 221, arguing against Mirfield, suggests that *R.* v. *Hunt* is in fact helpful in determining when the burden is impliedly imposed on the accused by statute.

[84] If the burden lies upon the defence, the standard is the lower one of the balance of probabilities: *R.* v. *Carr-Briant* (1943) 29 Cr.App.R. 76. As to the prosecution standard, the actual formulation of the direction to the jury has varied. "Satisfied so that you feel sure" has its supporters: *Walters* v. *The Queen* [1960] 2 A.C. 26; *R.* v. *Summers* (1952) 36 Cr.App.R. 14. So does, "satisfied beyond all/any/a reasonable doubt": *D.P.P.* v. *Woolmington* [1935] A.C. 462; *R.* v. *Lawrence* [1982] A.C. 510. For the judge who wishes to be doubly safe, the direction, "... satisfied beyond reasonable doubt so that you feel sure of the defendant's guilt" has also been approved: *Ferguson* v. *The Queen* [1979] 1 W.L.R. 94.

[85] See J. C. Smith, "Satisfying the Jury" [1988] Crim.L.R. 335.

[86] Theft Act 1968, s.1.

to dishonesty? What if the property has been "borrowed," to be returned at some (distant) future date?[87] Some difficulties may be resolved by judges relying on model directions created by the courts[88] and specimen directions produced by the Judicial Studies Board with the approval of the Lord Chief Justice.[89] On the other hand, it might be questioned whether use of such directions may not introduce excess rigidity[90] and, in particular, whether it might not confuse the jury both by using overly complex (lawyerly) language and by introducing superfluous law.[91]

The example of theft raises starkly the problem of the distinction between matters of law and matters of fact when considering what to say about words like "dishonesty." The judge must direct the jury on issues of law. The problem that arises is the tendency that the courts have had to regard at least some words appearing in criminal offences as words of the ordinary English language whose meaning is not, therefore, a question of law.[92] This was the approach taken with regard to "dishonesty" by the Court of Appeal in R. v. Feely,[93] which was trenchantly criticised largely on the ground that it was leaving to the jury a decision which was properly that of the judge.[94] However, it seems that, even if the courts ever really did follow this trend,[95] they generally no longer do so, but are providing juries with directions as to the legal meaning of words which the jury must then be satisfied have been proved on the facts of the case.[96] Of course, the greater the number of issues of law upon which the judge gives a direction, the fewer the opportunities for the exercise of discretion or common sense by the jury and the greater is the control of the judge.[97]

As to "dishonesty," the Court of Appeal in R. v. Ghosh[98] has decided not to leave the matter entirely to the jury, which would mean that the jury could in effect apply its own standards.[99] Neither has the court provided a detailed legal definition, which would perhaps be impossible to achieve. Instead it has indicated that, as a matter of law, the accused will be dishonest if the jury

---

[87] All these questions give rise to considerable difficulty in the law of theft as will immediately be apparent from a perusal of Smith (1989), paras. 18–53; 120–129; 138–141.

[88] See, e.g. the model direction as to the meaning of "recklessness" in the offences under the Criminal Damage Act 1971 established by Lord Diplock in Commissioner of Police for the Metropolis v. Caldwell [1982] A.C. 341, 354.

[89] Judicial Studies Report for 1983–1987 at para. 10.10.

[90] See Lord Hailsham's statement in R. v. Lawrence, above.

[91] Griew (1989), who points out that there may be a temptation amongst trial judges to provide too much legal information in order to make their directions unappealable.

[92] See Lord Reid in Brutus v. Cozens [1973] A.C. 854 (on the meaning of the word "insulting" in the Public Order Act 1936, s.5, since repealed); Lawton L.J. in W. v. L. [1974] Q.B. 711 (on the meaning of "mental illness" in the Mental Health Act 1959).

[93] [1973] Q.B. 530.

[94] See, e.g. D. W. Elliott, "Law and Fact in Theft Act Cases" [1976] Crim.L.R. 707; G. Williams, "Law and Facts" [1976] Crim.L.R. 472, 537; E. J. Griew, Dishonesty and the Jury (1974); A. Briggs, "Judges, Juries and the Meaning of Words" (1985) 5 L.S. 314.

[95] D. W. Elliott, "Brutus v. Cozens: Decline and Fall" [1989] Crim.L.R. 323, shows that there are very few instances where Brutus v. Cozens was actually utilised.

[96] See Elliott (1989).

[97] The jury will usually follow such a direction by the judge, and thus the exercise of discretion is limited. The jury is, of course, permitted to exercise discretion outside the judge's direction, which some might describe as not legitimate or perverse, see p. 814, below.

[98] [1982] 2 Q.B. 1053. See commentary at [1982] Crim.L.R. 608, and D. W. Elliott, "Dishonesty in Theft: A Dispensable Concept" [1982] Crim.L.R. 395.

[99] R. v. Feely [1973] Q.B. 530, C.A. See Smith (1989), para. 127.

decides: (i) that what was done was dishonest by the standards of ordinary, decent people; and (ii) that the accused must have realised that what was being done was by those standards dishonest.[1]

(iv) *A direction as to evidential points*

It may be necessary for the judge to give directions about the evidence which the jury has heard. The jury may have to be warned of the legal requirements in relation to certain evidence lest it rely upon that evidence too readily in deciding questions of fact. The judge again exercises control over the jury.

An example is where the defence is one of mistaken identity, since eye-witness evidence may be based on a fleeting glimpse. Rarely would, for example, a by-passer have more than a swift glimpse of the bank robber running out of a bank to the getaway car. In such circumstances it is possible for witnesses genuinely and honestly to be convinced that they are right. They may, in fact, be mistaken. The jury must be informed of the problems which can arise. Before the summing up, the judge may withdraw the evidence from the jury if it is "poor" and the prosecution should inform the defence of any material discrepancies between the description originally given and the accused's actual appearance. In the summing-up, the judge should warn the jury of the need for caution; the circumstances in which the identification took place should be drawn to the attention of the jury, in particular the length of time the observation could have lasted and the conditions; the judge should remind the jury of any weaknesses that have become apparent and point out to the jury that evidence of recognition of someone known can be relied upon more satisfactorily than identification of a stranger.[2]

(v) *A summary of the evidence in the case*

It is for the judge to put the case before the jury which, in particular in a complex case, will involve a substantial amount of the evidence being rehearsed for the jury's benefit.[3] Whether this is really an appropriate function, especially as it may be unnecessary, may provide the judge with too much influence over the jury, and may make it appear as though the prosecution is being supported by the judge, may be doubted.[4]

---

[1] *R.* v. *Ghosh* [1982] 2 Q.B. 1053, 1064.

[2] *R.* v. *Turnbull* [1977] 2 Q.B. 224.

[3] *R.* v. *Attfield* (1961) 45 Cr.App.R. 309. The judge keeps a note of the evidence—a process which has a significant effect on the speed of the criminal trial—and will remind the jury of it in the summing-up. However, merely reading out such notes, especially in complex cases, was criticised by the Court of Appeal in *R.* v. *Charles* (1979) 68 Cr.App.R. 334, see Emmins (1988), p. 139. The judge must also be careful to put the defence case fully and properly, see *R.* v. *Tillman* [1962] Crim.L.R. 261; *R.* v. *Hamilton* [1972] Crim.L.R. 266. For a particularly abbreviated summing-up consisting almost entirely of a low, prolonged whistle, see *Piepowder*, by a circuit tramp (1911), p. 70, cited in Samuels (1982). For an incisive consideration of the function of summing up, see Griew (1989).

[4] D. Wolchover, "Should Judges Sum Up on the Facts?" [1989] Crim.L.R. 781.

Whilst the determination of matters of fact is for the jury, the judge is entitled to comment on matters arising out of the evidence,[5] including the strength of the respective cases,[6] the demeanour and quality of witnesses,[7] the credibility of evidence and the quality of any argument. Comment may be in strong terms provided that, overall, it is not unfair[8] and the jury is reminded clearly and forcefully that they have the ultimate responsibility for deciding issues of fact.[9] Comments may be other than verbal: gesture, tone of voice and facial expression can all speak volumes in indicating the judge's view of the merits, and such matters do not appear in the transcript.[10] The Court of Appeal appears to be unwilling to interfere with a conviction on the ground that the judge has overstepped the permissible limits of comment unless the summing-up is very defective.[11] An informal constraint on the extent of judicial comment is the possibility that the jury will react against a very strong direction to convict and, out of perversity or sympathy for the accused or some other motivation, bring in a verdict of acquittal.

The judge may even possibly indicate the verdict considered appropriate.[12] However, it is only in exceptionally rare cases, if at all, that the judge would be able to direct a conviction.[13] The better view[14] is that even if the judge believes that the only possible result is a conviction, the ultimate issue of guilt or innocence must be left to the jury.[15]

There are two circumstances in which a judge must be particularly careful in addressing the jury, namely when the accused has made no answer to the police and/or has not disclosed a defence until trial, and when the accused has not exercised the right to give evidence at trial. Both are examples of the

[5] See *R.* v. *Evans* (1990) 91 Cr.App.R. 173. For an interesting account of the summing up in the *Oz* case, see T. Palmer, *The Trials of Oz* (1971). There was a great deal of comment contained in that summing-up which was later the subject of appeal: *R.* v. *Anderson* [1972] 1 Q.B. 304.

[6] "[I]n *R.* v. *O'Donnell* (1917) 12 Cr.App.R. 219 a conviction was upheld even though the judge described the accused's story as a 'remarkable' one and contrary to previous statements he had made, but in *R.* v. *Canny* (1945) 30 Cr.App.R. 143 repeatedly telling the jury that the defence was 'absurd' and that there was no foundation for defence allegations amounted to a direction to find the case against the accused proved. The conviction was therefore quashed.": Emmins (1988), p. 139.

[7] "I thought he was a jolly good witness. He wasn't prepared to whitewash all of *Oz* like some of the other so-called experts and I can't say fairer than that": *per* Judge Argyle, quoted in Palmer (1971), p. 252.

[8] *R.* v. *Middlesex Justices, ex p. D.P.P.* [1952] 2 Q.B. 758, *R.* v. *O'Donnell* (1917) 12 Cr.App.R. 219; *R.* v. *Canny* (1945) 30 Cr.App.R. 143.

[9] *R.* v. *West* (1910) 4 Cr.App.R. 179; *R.* v. *Beeby* (1911) 6 Cr.App.R. 138; *R.* v. *Frampton* (1917) 12 Cr.App.R. 202. The following is an example of such a direction: "... if I now express an opinion and you agree, well, that's alright. If not, you can disagree. You do not have to do what I tell you. What I think is irrelevant. *You* have to decide": *per* Judge Argyle: Palmer (1971), p. 239.

[10] See Wolchover (1989).

[11] *cf. R.* v. *Anderson* [1972] 1 Q.B. 304. Such defects will occur where the judge usurps the jury's function, as in *R.* v. *Canny* (1945) 30 Cr.App.R. 143, see, n. 6, above. This issue may also overlap with the question of whether a judge can direct a conviction, see text below.

[12] *D.P.P.* v. *Stonehouse* [1978] A.C. 55.

[13] See, *e.g. R.* v. *Ferguson* (1970) 54 Cr.App.R. 410 and Archbold (1988), para. 4–437.

[14] Both on the law and in theory. As to the latter, see below, pp. 798–799.

[15] *D.P.P.* v. *Stonehouse* [1978] A.C. 55; *R.* v. *Thompson* [1984] 3 All E.R. 565; *R.* v. *Challinor* (1985) 80 Cr.App.R. 253; *R.* v. *Gent* (1989) 89 Cr.App.R. 247. See Archbold (1988), para. 4–437; Emmins (1988), p. 139. In *R.* v. *Ponting* [1985] Crim.L.R. 318 the judge gave a direction which, on the law, clearly indicated that Ponting was guilty of an offence under the Official Secrets Act 1911, s.2. The jury found him not guilty.

so-called "right to silence" based upon the propositions that the accused should not be required to provide any evidence which might be incriminating and is entitled to make the prosecution prove its case without answering questions before or at the trial. To what extent is the jury able or obliged to draw prejudicial inferences from the silence of the accused?

It will be safest for the judge to make no comment on the accused's failure to disclose a defence until trial or to answer questions before trial.[16] The judge must certainly avoid inviting the jury to draw inferences adverse to the accused[17] and it will be difficult to find an appropriate comment which does not have that effect.

On the failure of the accused to testify, the accepted comment that the judge may make in most cases is that established by Lord Parker C.J. in R. v. Bathurst[18]:

> ". . . the accused is not bound to give evidence, that he can sit back and see if the prosecution have proved their case, and that, while the jury have been deprived of the opportunity of hearing his story tested in cross-examination, the one thing that they must not do is to assume that he is guilty because he has not gone into the witness box."

What the judge must never do is to suggest to the jury that guilt may be assumed from silence. The Criminal Law Revision Committee has recommended, with regard to out-of-court silence that inferences should be permissible when the accused has failed to reveal facts upon which reliance is subsequently placed. The C.L.R.C. also recommended, with regard to in-court silence, that it should be possible for inferences to be drawn from the accused's failure to counter a prima facie case by going into the witness box.[19] In 1988 the law was changed accordingly in Northern Ireland and it has been recommended that such changes be made in England. These reforms have been doubted as not providing sufficient protection to the concept of the fair trial.[20]

(d) Sentencing[21]

Once the jury have found the accused to be guilty of an offence or after the

---

[16] R. v. Tune (1944) 29 Cr.App.R. 162, ". . . observations of different sorts by judges have from time to time been made the subject of appeals to this court. If nothing is said by way of comment, no point can be raised."

[17] R. v. Sullivan (1967) 51 Cr.App.R. 102.

[18] [1968] 1 All E.R. 1175, 1178. In some cases stronger comment can be made, e.g. in R. v. Brigden [1973] Crim.L.R. 579, where what was permitted was to the effect that since Brigden had alleged that the police had planted evidence on him but he had not given evidence, the jury might consider that that failure would assist them in deciding whether there was any truth in the allegation.

[19] Eleventh Report: Evidence (General) (Cmnd. 4991, 1972). See also R.C.C.P. (Cmnd. 8092, 1981), pp. 80–91.

[20] A. A. S. Zuckerman, "Trial by Unfair Means—The Report of the Working Group on the Right of Silence" [1989] Crim.L.R. 855. He suggests that the balance between the need to control crime and the need to preserve the interests of the individual is not properly struck, thus arguing along lines similar to those of the Packer models; see above, pp. 687–688.

[21] For a brief description of the sentencing function of magistrates, see pp. 756–757 above. The leading writer in the field of sentencing is D. A. Thomas, see his Principles of Sentencing (2nd ed., 1979) and Current Sentencing Practice; he is also the Editor of Criminal Appeal Reports (Sentencing) and the Sentencing Case Commentator for the Criminal Law Review. Other

accused has pleaded guilty, it is for the judge to pass sentence on the offender. The judge must have the necessary information available about the offence and the offender. If this is available, sentencing may occur immediately; if not, there may be an adjournment.

Information for sentencing[22]

The judge must be provided with the facts of the offence. Where the accused has pleaded guilty, these facts will not as yet have been set out. They are now given by the prosecutor, unless disputed, in which case there may be a "Newton" hearing at which the prosecutor is obliged to prove them.[23]

A police officer will then provide evidence as to the offender's "antecedents," that is previous convictions, educational history, employment record, home circumstances and resources. The defence may challenge the evidence, in which case the prosecutor must prove it. Further information may be contained in a variety of reports, in particular a social inquiry report, prepared by either a probation officer or a social worker, considering the factors leading to the offence and a recommendation as to appropriate sentence. Other reports include medical and psychiatric reports and reports from places where a person has been held, such as a remand centre or prison when on remand in custody.

The defence may then make a plea in mitigation.[24]

Finally, an offender may have other cases taken into consideration. This clears up outstanding offences and the offender is likely to get a substantial sentencing reduction for those offences so as to reward honesty.

What sentence is imposed?[25]

A sentence is laid down for each offence.[26] For a very limited range of offences the penalty is fixed by law. Murder is the main example, since the judge is obliged to impose a sentence of life imprisonment. If the offence is a common law offence, the sentence is a maximum of life imprisonment or a fine. If the offence is a statutory offence, the statute will lay down the punishment.

Any sentence laid down is a maximum and that maximum is rarely imposed. The judge has a wide range of possible sentences from which to choose. Broadly speaking, for people over 21,[27] these fall into the non-

works of reference are: A. Ashworth, *Sentencing and Penal Policy* (1983); C. J. Emmins, *A Practical Approach to Sentencing* (1985); C. J. Emmins, *A Practical Approach to Criminal Procedure* (4th ed., 1988); C. Harding and L. Koffman, *Sentencing and the Penal System: Text and Materials* (1988); E. Stockdale and K. Devlin, *Sentencing* (1987); N. Walker, *Sentencing: Theory, Law and Practice* (1985); M. Wasik and D. Pease, *Sentencing Reform* (1987).

[22] See Emmins (1988), pp. 222–236, 476–477 and the works referred to a n. 21 above.

[23] So-called after the decision of the Court of Appeal in *R.* v. *Newton* (1983) 77 Cr.App.R. 13.

[24] See also p. 779, above.

[25] See Emmins (1988), Chap. 16 and the works referred to in n. 21, above. A number of additional options are open where an offender is under 21, see Emmins (1988), Chap. 17.

[26] If the offender has been committed by the magistrates to trial on indictment for an offence triable either way and also a related summary offence within s.41 of the Criminal Justice Act 1988, the Crown Court has the sentencing powers which the magistrates' court would have had on conviction at summary trial.

[27] The sentences available where the offender is under 21 are different, see Emmins (1988), Chap. 17 and the works referred to at n. 21 above.

custodial and the custodial options. The non-custodial option includes fines, probation, community service orders and an absolute or conditional discharge. Further, there are a variety of other orders, such as an order to pay costs to the prosecution or compensation to the victim, which, whilst not being sentences, have much the same effect as a fine as far as the offender is concerned. The custodial option is imprisonment, which may be suspended or partly suspended.

The judge chooses a particular sentence by initially considering the "tariff" for the offence. The tariff is established by decisions of the Court of Appeal. The best collated source is D. A. Thomas' *Current Sentencing Practice*. In recent years the Court of Appeal has been using particular cases to give clear and specific guidelines as to whether a custodial or non-custodial sentence is appropriate and, especially if the former, the range of sentences appropriate for an offence in specified circumstances. Not only is this now possible where the offender appeals against sentence, but also where the Attorney-General refers a case to the Court of Appeal when the sentence imposed is believed to have been too lenient.[28] The first exercise of this power provides an example of a guidelines case: *Attorney General's References (No. 1 of 1989)*, which concerned sentencing for incest.[29] As is usual, the guidelines assume that the offender pleads not guilty, since if there is a guilty plea a lesser sentence may be imposed. The guidelines consider the circumstances where the victim is a girl and are as follows:

(1) Where the girl is over 16, the range of sentence is from three years' imprisonment to a non-custodial penalty depending upon whether or not force was used, the degree of harm caused to the girl, the degree to which it is desirable to keep family disruption to a minimum and "the lower the degree of corruption, the lower the penalty";

(2) Where the girl is aged from 13 to 16, the range of sentence is from five to three years' imprisonment depending upon similar principles to those already mentioned although corruption of the girl is more likely because the girl is younger;

(3) Where the girl is under 13, then the widest range of sentence is to be found since there are many factors which may have to be taken into account;

   (a) if the girl has taken on "the wife's role," if she is near 13 and if there are no particularly adverse or favourable features, the sentence should be about six years;

   (b) the younger the girl, the more she was coerced and thus the sentence should be higher;

   (c) the presence of aggravating factors will increase the sentence, including physical or psychological suffering to the girl, frequent acts of incest over a long period of time, abhorrent perversions involved in the acts, and if the girl has become pregnant;

   (d) the presence of mitigating factors will decrease the sentence, including a guilty plea, genuine affection for the girl, if the girl seduced the offender, and if a shorter sentence is for the benefit of the victim.

---

[28] The latter power is provided by ss.35 & 36 of the Criminal Justice Act 1988.
[29] [1989] 3 All E.R. 571; [1989] Crim.L.R. 925.

As this case indicates, whilst the tariff provides a starting point, it is still for the judge to take account of factors, other than the nature of the offence, raised by the information provided. If it is a first time offence, a sentence of imprisonment should not be imposed unless no other method is appropriate for dealing with the offender[30]; a guilty plea will almost invariably lead to a lesser sentence, frequently one below the tariff; a person who co-operates with the police, especially the "supergrass" whose information leads to the conviction of numerous criminals, may get a much reduced sentence; the effect of a particular sentence option on other members of the offender's family may lead to a reduced sentence, frequently a non-custodial one; a person's good character may well be a reason for imposing a non-custodial sentence; and persistent offenders are more likely to receive a tariff sentence.

The judge will go outside the tariff where there are factors about the individual which suggest other options. Life imprisonment, which is the maximum for common law and a number of statutory offences, may be imposed where the offender is mentally unstable and dangerous and will remain so for a long or indeterminable time. Where the offender has a mental disorder and life imprisonment is not appropriate, a hospital order under the Mental Health Act 1983 may be imposed.[31]

Sentencing may undergo considerable change in the near future if the proposals contained in the government's White Paper, *Crime, Justice and Protecting the Public*[32] are enacted, since it proposes a statute to provide "a coherent framework for the use of financial, community and custodial punishments," basing its sentencing philosophy on "proportionality."[32a] Whether the proposals will satisfy those who have called for a Sentencing Commission or Council to bring greater coherence, rationality and consistency to sentencing remains to be seen.[33]

7. THE JURY[34]

(a) Historical background[35]

The decision of the Fourth Lateran Council in 1215 to withdraw the

---

[30] Powers of Criminal Courts Act 1973, s.20.

[31] See Emmins (1988), Chaps 16 & 18, esp. pp. 243–244, 250–252, 305–310 and the other works referred to at n. 21 above.

[32] Cm. 1965, 1990. See M. Wasik and A. von Hirsch "Statutory Sentencing Principles: the 1990 White Paper" (1990) 53 M.L.R. 508.

[32a] The Criminal Justice Bill 1991 will, if it is enacted, introduce a new framework for the sentencing of offenders. It will lay down the grounds on which a custodial sentence may be imposed and the criteria for determining the length of a custodial sentence.

[33] See, *e.g.* M. Wasik and K. Pease (eds.), *Sentencing Reform* (1987); A. Ashworth, "Crime and punishment: towards a national sentencing policy" (1988) 138 N.L.J. 726; R. Morgan, "Making sense of Sentencing" (1989) 139 N.L.J. 1521.

[34] Much material is available. That to which we shall particularly be referring in this section includes: W. R. Cornish, *The Jury* (1971); Lord Devlin, *Trial by Jury* (1956); N. Walker with A. Pearson (ed.), *The British Jury System* (1975); J. Baldwin and M. McConville, *Jury Trials* (1979); M. McConville and J. Baldwin, *Courts, Prosecution and Conviction* (1981); M. D. A. Freeman, "The Jury on Trial" (1981) 34 C.L.P. 65; M. Findlay and P. Duff (eds.), *The Jury Under Attack* (1988).

[35] Sir Frederick Pollock and F. W. Maitland, *History of English Law* (2nd ed., 1898), Vol. II, pp. 618–650; W. S. Holdsworth, *History of English Law* (3rd ed., 1922), Vol. 1, pp. 312–350; J. H. Baker, *An Introduction to English Legal History* (3rd ed., 1990), Chap. 5.

support of the Roman Catholic Church from the process of trial by ordeal is generally recognised as the factor which prompted the adoption of the jury system for the determination of criminal cases. That the jury was in existence before 1215 is undisputed, since it would have been almost the only means of collecting information in administrative as well as judicial matters.[36] In addition to determining issues which were relevant to the king, juries came to be used for determining issues of interest to private individuals and were available to replace trial by battle.[37] When trespass was alleged, including the allegation of a breach of the king's peace, a writ of *venire facias* went to the sheriff who summoned a group of twelve[38] men to meet and give a verdict on the allegation. On the demise of trial by ordeal the jury was used to determine the guilt of alleged criminals.[39]

In the beginning, the role of the jury was unclear.[40] Were the twelve individuals to deliberate and deliver a verdict to the judge, or was the judge to treat them as witnesses, examine them and then come to a decision? The resolution of this question shaped the future of the jury and the future of criminal procedure.[41] In the event, the collective deliberative role of the jury prevailed and the transition from knowledge to ignorance as the primary characteristic of a juror began. The landmarks are well known. By 1367 it had become established that the verdict had to be unanimous.[42] Witnesses began to give evidence and the jury were prevented from talking to any outsider until they reached a verdict.[43] In *Bushell's* case it was established that the jury had the right to give a verdict according to its conscience.[44] By the eighteenth century it was finally established that a juror should not take part in a case of which he had personal knowledge. Now a juror should be excused where he or she is personally concerned in the facts of the case or is closely connected with a party or prospective witness.[45]

(b) The role of the jury

The jury has been described as having three functions.[46] First, it is the jury that is to decide the facts and it is on those facts which it then determines guilt. The jury is to arrive at its verdict by considering whether it is satisfied that the prosecution has proved its case solely on the evidence presented at the trial and in accordance with the direction of the judge as to the law.[47]

---

[36] The practice of getting a group together and putting them under oath to tell the truth had been highly effective for the Normans.

[37] Under Henry II two assizes existed: the grand assize and the petty assize. It was the petty assize which evolved into the jury.

[38] Why twelve? The answer is unknown, although it is the same number as the Apostles of Christ and the ancient tribes of Israel.

[39] C. Wells, "Instructions given by Henry III to Itinerant Justices 1219" (1914) 30 L.Q.R. 97.

[40] Pollock and Maitland (1898), pp. 622 ff.

[41] Guiding procedure into the adversarial system and away from the inquisitorial system with its emphasis on judicial involvement.

[42] Baker (1990), p. 90.

[43] *Ibid.*, p. 89.

[44] *R. v. Sheriffs of London, ex p. Bushell* (1670) Vaughn 135.

[45] *Practice Direction* (1988) 87 Cr.App.R. 294.

[46] See P. Duff and M. Findlay, "The Jury in England: Practice and Ideology" (1982) 10 International Journal of the Sociology of Law 253. See also, M. Findlay, "The Role of the Jury in a Fair Trial" in Findlay and Duff (1988), Chap. 10.

[47] As to the respective roles of judge and jury, see pp. 783, 786–788, 789–794, above and as to the obligation upon the prosecution, see pp. 775–776, above.

Secondly, the jury adds certainty to the law, since it gives a general verdict. The jury merely states that the accused is either guilty or not guilty, and gives no reasons. Consequently, the decision is not open to dispute. Thirdly, the jury represents the "just face" of the criminal justice system, since it can arrive at its unchallengeable decision on any basis it chooses. In particular, it is proper for the jury to arrive at an acquittal according to its conscience,[48] even if a conviction is clearly required according to the relevant law.

Whilst the jury has these functions, it is not all that should be said about its role, particularly since they could be performed by other bodies. Jury service is described as an important public duty.[49] It has been suggested that the jury satisfies the constitutional role that no-one should be tried apart from judgment by one's peers. Whilst this claim is frequently made, however, it does not follow that the phrase "judgment by one's peers" has a consistent meaning. Marshall suggests that it can mean one, or more, of the following:

"1. A claim to the judgment of one's peers, or equals or neighbours
2. A claim to the judgment of a body of fair-minded persons
3. A claim to judgment by an independent or impartial body of persons
4. A claim to the judgment of a randomly chosen body of persons
5. A claim to the judgment of a representative body of persons."[50]

In fulfilling its functions and its constitutional role, there are a number of qualities which enable a jury to perform effectively. Thus a jury, it is said, should be independent, impartial and representative, and it should be randomly selected. It is not the case that these qualities are always consistent; for example, a representative jury may be partial.[51]

(c) Qualification for jury service and selection

To *qualify* for selection as a juror, a person must be aged between 18 and 70,[52] registered as a parliamentary or local government elector, and have been ordinarily resident in the United Kingdom for any period of at least five years since the age of 13.[53] In addition, a person must not fall into the categories of people disqualified or ineligible by Schedule 1 of the Juries Act 1974.

The people *disqualified* are those who (1) at any time have been sentenced in the United Kingdom to life imprisonment, custody for life, or a term of five years or more imprisonment or youth custody, or to be detained during Her Majesty's pleasure; or (2) at any time in the last ten years have in the United Kingdom served any part of a sentence of imprisonment, youth custody or detention, or been detained in a Borstal institution, or had

---

[48] As established in *Bushell's Case*, see n. 44, above. See also T. A. Green, *Verdict According to Conscience, 1200–1800* (1985) for a history of the jury in this role.

[49] *Practice Direction* (1988) 87 Cr.App.R. 294.

[50] G. Marshall, "The judgement of one's peers: some aims and ideal of jury trial" in Walker with Pearson (1975), p. 5.

[51] See M. Findlay with P. Byrne, "Introduction" in Findlay and Duff (1988).

[52] People who are aged more than 65 are entitled, if they wish, to be excused from jury service: Juries Act 1974, s.9, Sched. 1, Part III, as amended by the Criminal Justice Act 1988, s.119(2). As to excusal from jury service, see p. 804, below.

[53] Juries Act 1974, s.1, as amended by the Criminal Justice Act 1988, s.119(1).

imposed a suspended sentence of imprisonment or order for detention or a community service order; or (3) at any time in the last five years has been placed on probation in the United Kingdom.[54]

The people who are *ineligible* for jury service fall into four categories[55]: (1) the judiciary,[56] (2) others concerned with the administration of justice, including barristers, solicitors, the staff of the Crown Prosecution Service, court staff, prison officers, police officers and forensic scientists, (3) the clergy,[57] and (4) mentally disordered persons.[58]

The objectives of disqualification and ineligibility are first to exclude from participation people who are or have been intimately concerned with the administration of justice, presumably on the basis either that a jury with lawyers on it will not decide according to the judge's direction but might use its own knowledge of the law, or that current or previous involvement in the criminal justice system will deprive the jury of its impartiality. The second objective is to exclude from participation those who are demonstrably incompetent. There is at least an implicit assumption that a basic level of intellectual ability is necessary for a person to be able to be involved in the performance by the jury of its various functions.[59] Inevitably a number of people are excluded who might make very good jurors and such exclusions mean that the jury is not representative of the whole of society.

The qualifications for jury service were revised in 1972,[60] when the requirement that a juror should be an occupier of a house with a prescribed rateable value was abolished, and the electoral register adopted as the basis of qualification. There had been growing criticism of the composition of the jury, and its unrepresentative nature.[61] Since the adoption of the new qualification, research has demonstrated[62] that the composition of juries has changed profoundly. Juries are less middle class[63] and much younger than before,[64] but there is still an under-representation of women and members of

---

[54] Juries Act 1974, Sched. 1, Part II, as amended by the Juries (Disqualification) Act 1984. This amending legislation significantly increased the number of people who were consequently disqualified from jury service.

[55] Juries Act 1974, Sched. 1, Part I, as amended.

[56] The "judiciary" includes not only the holders of high judicial office, but also, amongst others, Circuit judges, recorders, masters of the Supreme Court.

[57] Including vowed members of a religious order living in a religious community.

[58] The definition of such people within the Juries Act 1974 has been amended by the Mental Health (Amendment) Act 1982 and the Mental Health Act 1983.

[59] Such reasoning does not explain the exclusion of the clergy, but may explain the exclusion of monks and nuns who choose to live in a religious community removed from everyday life. See further the Report of the Departmental Committee on Jury Service, Chair: Lord Morris (Cmnd. 2627, 1965); White (1985), p. 78. As to the discharge of people who cannot understand a case, see p. 808 below.

[60] By the Criminal Justice Act 1972, which implemented some of the recommendations of the Morris Committee (1965).

[61] In Lord Devlin's oft-quoted phrase, the property qualification produced a jury which was, "... predominantly male, middle-aged, middle-minded and middle-class": *Trial by Jury*, p. 20. It is reported that when Bernard Rothman and others were tried at Derby Assizes in 1932 on charges relating to a mass trespass on private land near Kinder Scout in the Peak District, the jury consisted of two brigadier-generals, three colonels, two majors, three captains and two aldermen: *The Guardian*, January 18, 1982.

[62] *Jury Trials*, pp. 94–99.

[63] *Ibid*. Table 10, p. 95.

[64] *Ibid*. Table 11, p. 96. 27 per cent. of jurors empanelled in Birmingham in 1975 and 1976 were under 30.

ethnic minorities. These latter deficiencies may be partly explicable by selection policy,[65] excusal of women jurors and language problems.[66] It appears that the totally representative jury has not yet been achieved.[67]

Trial judges have a discretion to discharge a juror to prevent scandal and perversion of justice, and this may permit the exclusion of someone who is, for example, completely deaf.[68] However, the discretion does not extend to securing the establishment of a representative jury. The Court of Appeal in *R. v. Ford*[69] decided that a trial judge has no power to interfere with the composition of the jury or the jury panel in order to produce a multiracial jury and that there is no principle that a jury should be racially balanced. The argument in favour of racially balancing the jury is to avoid partiality as, for example, in the trial of Rose, a black man accused of murder, where the judge had asked potential jurors to disqualify themselves if they had strong views against black people or supported the extreme Right or the extreme Left.[70] This would not, however, now be appropriate in the light of *R. v. Ford*.

Selection of jurors from the electoral register used to be a matter for individual summoning officers. Since February 1981, random selection by computer has been utilised.[71] A number is allotted to every person on the electoral register, and a random number programme is then run through the computer to produce the jury list. It is not possible to challenge the summoning officer on the basis that the jury panel is not representative, because no black person is on the panel, although if bias or other impropriety could be shown then a challenge could be founded.[72]

(d) Summons, empanelling and vetting

The people selected for jury service receive a summons requiring them to

---

[65] A policy of summoning twice the number of male jurors than females has now been abandoned in Birmingham but would have influenced the figures.

[66] The judge has the power to determine whether a person's insufficient understanding of English means that he or she cannot act as a juror: Juries Act 1974, s.10, see below p. 808.

[67] As to the debate on the requirement, if any, for a representative jury, see p. 807, below.

[68] R. Buxton, "Challenging and Discharging Jurors—1" [1990] Crim.L.R. 225. The judicial power to discharge jurors is considered further at p. 808 below.

[69] [1989] 3 All E.R. 445. The court's reasons for rejecting the power were that it would interfere with random selection, that the power would have to be granted by statute and thirdly it interferes with the responsibility of the Lord Chancellor's Department to summon jurors, *ibid.* pp. 448–449.

[70] This, and other examples, are to be found in M. Zander, *A Matter of Justice* (1988), at pp. 222–226. See also *R. v. Broderick* [1970] Crim.L.R. 155, where the Court of Appeal had said that the trial judge could go no further than ascertaining whether there was a coloured juror on the panel. This possibility is now questionable in the light of the decision in *R. v. Ford*; see also *R. v. Danvers* [1982] Crim.L.R. where the judge, Mr. Recorder Cowley Q.C. at Nottingham Crown Court, rejected a challenge to the array (*i.e.* the whole panel), on the ground that it was unrepresentative, holding that it was no requirement in law that there should be a coloured member of a jury or a jury panel, approved in *R. v. Ford*. See Baldwin and McConville (1979), pp. 97–98; A. Dashwood, "Juries in a Multi-racial Society" [1972] Crim.L.R. 85; the commentary to *R. v. Danvers* by G. W. Hoon at [1982] Crim.L.R. 681; and Buxton, [1990] Crim.L.R. 225, 234–235.

[71] See Zander, *A Matter of Justice* (1988), p. 217; see also, R. Tarling, "The Random Selection of Jurors," Home Office Research Bulletin No. 13 (1982) and Lord Chancellor's Department, *The Crown Court: A Guide to Good Practice for the Courts* (1990), paras. 9.1–9.2.

[72] *R. v. Ford* [1989] 3 All E.R. 445, 450. As to challenge, see below pp. 804–808.

attend at the Crown Court at a specified time.[73] Accompanying the summons are a form, which is intended to identify those ineligible or disqualified, and a set of notes, which explains something of the procedure of jury service and the functions of the juror.[74] A failure to attend the Crown Court can result in a fine, as can unfitness for service through drink or drugs after attendance.[75] Again, the implicit assumption is that a person must be competent in order to act as a juror. This principle, in the circumstances, permits derogation from the requirement that the jury be randomly selected.

Those summoned for service constitute the jury panel and from the panel the jury for an individual case will be selected.[76] The panel may be divided into parts relating to different days or sittings.[77] The jury list contains the names, addresses and dates for attendance of the panel. The parties to the case and their lawyers are entitled to inspect the list before or during the trial.[78] Such information may assist counsel in deciding whether to challenge any of the jurors but, since the occupation of jurors is no longer provided, there is very little on which defence counsel may rely for a challenge for cause.[79]

The subject of *jury vetting* has arisen for consideration in the last few years. It surfaced in 1978 as a result of the trial of a soldier and two journalists (Aubrey, Berry and Campbell) on charges under the Official Secrets Act 1911. It became apparent during the trial that the jury panel had been investigated[80] and, in the ensuing public debate, the Attorney-General published the guidelines under which the vetting had been carried out.[81]

---

[73] The power to summon is granted to the Lord Chancellor by the Juries Act 1974, s.2, who delegates it to such officers. In so summoning jurors, the officer is required to have regard to the convenience of the persons summoned and where they live, in particular to the desirability of selecting jurors within reasonable daily travelling distance of the place where they are to attend: *ibid*. s.2(2). See Lord Chancellor's Department (1990), paras. 9.3–9.5.

[74] The notes assist the juror in the task by dealing with the swearing-in and challenges, trial procedure, the verdict, secrecy, taking notes, etc.

[75] Juries Act 1974, s.20, as amended. The person summonsed must attend and not someone standing in for them. In response to claims of juror personation (see, S. Enright, "Britain's reluctant jurors" (1989) 138 N.L.J. 538), the Lord Chancellor's Department has emphasised that it is a criminal offence for any person to impersonate a juror, and as a matter of routine court staff will check on identity: (1989) 138 N.L.J. 758.

[76] See p. 804 below. The Lord Chancellor's Department has set targets and introduced management controls to monitor and review the number of jurors who are summoned to attend court each day against the number who actually sit on trials: Lord Chancellor's Department (1990), para. 9.6.

[77] Juries Act 1974, s.5.

[78] *Ibid*. s.5(2), (3).

[79] See below, pp. 804–806. In 1973 the occupation of jurors was removed from the list by the Lord Chancellor in the exercise of powers, under the Courts Act 1971, s.32, now the Juries Act 1974, s.5(1), to determine the information included on the list; see H. Harman and J. Griffith *Justice Deserted: The Subversion of the Jury* (1979). Such information would have been of considerable assistance to counsel in deciding whether to exercise the right of challenge, see p. 806, below.

[80] In the first trial, defence counsel made an application to have the jury discharged. One of the accused said so on television with the result that the first trial was stopped and the jury discharged. This gave the opportunity for the matter to be raised directly at the beginning of the second trial. The Attorney-General's Guidelines were first published during the course of the second trial on October 11, 1978.

[81] The current full text is to be found at (1989) 88 Cr.App.R. 124. These guidelines were amended in February 1986; see Hansard, Vol. 91, H.C. Debs., February 3, 1986, col. 39, written answer. For the original text, see (1981) 72 Cr.App.R. 14.

The guidelines make clear that vetting may involve the search of criminal records for the purpose of ascertaining whether or not a member of the panel is a disqualified person,[82] or the limited further investigation of members of the panel (a) in security or terrorist cases[83] with the object of revealing political beliefs which are so biased that they might interfere with the juror's fair assessment of the facts or lead a juror to exert improper pressure on fellow jurors, or (b) in security cases alone with the object of discovering whether a juror might be in danger of making improper use of evidence given *in camera*.[84] A further investigation is made, on the personal authority of the Attorney-General, using the records of Police Special Branches and, with regard to the cases in (b), the security services, and is known as an "authorised check." No checks other than with these sources and no general enquiries may be made except to the limited extent that they may be needed to confirm the identity of a juror. The information gleaned from an authorised check is sent to the Director of Public Prosecutions, who decides what information ought to be provided to prosecuting counsel. Consequently a juror may be asked to stand by for the Crown[85] provided it is appropriate to exercise that power in the circumstances.[86]

The legality of the original guidelines was contested in *R.* v. *Sheffield Crown Court, ex p. Brownlow*, where a majority of the Court of Appeal (Civil Division) said *obiter* that they were unconstitutional.[87] The point was not strictly in issue since the court decided, in any event, that it had no jurisdiction to review an order made by a Crown Court judge, but the condemnation of the practice was clear. However, in the Criminal Division of the Court of Appeal the point was argued in *R.* v. *Mason*[88] and the court had no hesitation in upholding the legality of vetting, although the judgment is specifically restricted to the use of vetting for the purpose of ascertaining convictions. The Court confirmed the propriety of vetting the panel for convictions, passing the information to the prosecution, using it to exercise the right to stand by and passing the information to defence counsel if it would be fair so to do. Whether jury vetting in security and terrorist cases is acceptable remains to be argued.

The practice of jury vetting is alleged to undermine the jury as a random selection of fellow citizens assembled for the purpose of determining guilt.[89]

---

[82] The Annex to the Guidelines contains the Recommendations of the Association of Chief Police Officers with regard to the carrying out of checks on the previous convictions of the jury panel to ensure that disqualified persons do not sit on a jury. For the full text, see (1989) 88 Cr.App.R. 125.

[83] These are cases described as being exceptional types of cases of public importance for which the provisions as to majority verdicts and the disqualification of jurors may not be sufficient to ensure the proper administration of justice. Jury vetting is thus a further safeguard in (a) security cases, defined as cases in which national security is involved and part of the evidence is likely to be heard *in camera*, and (b) terrorist cases, of which no definition is provided: Attorney-General's Guidelines (1989) 88 Cr.App.R. 124.

[84] *Ibid.*

[85] See below, p. 807.

[86] As to the guidance on the exercise of the power of stand by as a consequence of jury vetting, see the Attorney-General's Guidelines, paras. 9, 10, 11 and 12.

[87] [1980] Q.B. 530, Lord Denning M.R. and Shaw L.J. Brandon L.J. expressed serious doubts about the practice.

[88] [1981] Q.B. 881.

[89] See Harman and Griffith (1979); A. Nicol, "Official Secrets and Jury Vetting" [1979] Crim.L.R. 284; Zander, *Cases and Materials* (1988), pp. 399–402; Freeman (1981).

On the other hand, exclusion of people within the Attorney-General's Guidelines may prevent partiality on the part of the jury, and prevent the verdict of the jury being unduly swayed by the prejudices of one particular member, consequently maintaining public confidence in the general verdict.[90]

(e) Excusal and discretionary deferral

Any member of a jury panel may be excused service on the basis of previous service,[91] or on showing entitlement to be excused,[92] or at the discretion of the appropriate officer.[93]

The first two provisions are straightforward, but the discretion to excuse from service is not one which is widely known. The notes which accompany the jury summons make no mention of excusal. The discretion is exercised in accordance with a *Practice Direction*[94] which makes clear that the normal presumption where a person is not entitled to be excused as of right is in favour of requiring a person to serve when summoned, because "jury service is an important public duty which individual members of the public are chosen at random to undertake.... There will however be circumstances where a juror should be excused, for instance where he or she is personally concerned in the facts of the particular case or is closely connected with a party or prospective witness. He or she may also be excused on grounds of personal hardship or conscientious objection to jury service. Each application should be dealt with sensitively and sympathetically."[95]

A person's attendance may be deferred, if it is shown to the appropriate officer that there is good reason for it.[96]

(f) Ballot, challenges and swearing in

From the jury panel, the jury for a particular case is selected by ballot in open court.[97] The clerk of the court has the names of all members of the panel. The names are put on cards, the cards are shuffled and the clerk reads out the names from the pile of cards. Hence, a random selection should be achieved from a randomly-selected panel.

On entering the jury box to be sworn, each juror may be challenged by the prosecution or the defence.[98] The defence has only the right to challenge for

[90] See, further, A. Freiberg, "Jury Selection in Trials of Commonwealth Offences" in Findlay and Duff (1988), Chap. 7 and Zander, *A Matter of Justice* (Revised edn. 1989), pp. 227–228.
[91] Juries Act 1974, s.8. People summoned who have served or attended to serve on a jury in the preceeding two years or been excused jury service for a period which has not finished are entitled to be excused.
[92] *Ibid.* s.9(1) and Sched. 1, Part III, as amended by the Criminal Justice Act 1988, s.119(2). Those entitled to be excused include people aged more than 65, peers and peeresses entitled to attend the House of Lords, M.P.s, M.E.P.s, members of the armed forces and members of the medical and other similar professions.
[93] *Ibid.*, s.9(2). If the appropriate officer refuses to excuse a person from jury service an appeal to the court may be made: *ibid.* s.9(3). Any person who so appeals must be given an opportunity to make representations in support of the appeal: *Practice Direction* (1988) 87 Cr.App.R. 294.
[94] (1988) 87 Cr.App.R. 294.
[95] Concern has been expressed that the frequency of the grant of excusal adversely affects the representativeness of the jury, see *The Times*, October 25, 1988.
[96] Juries Act 1974, s.9A, inserted by the Criminal Justice Act 1988, s.120.
[97] Juries Act 1974, s.11.
[98] See R. Buxton, "Challenging and Discharging Jurors—1" [1990] Crim.L.R. 225.

cause. The prosecution has the right to challenge for cause or to require a juror to stand by.

Challenge for cause has been fairly unusual,[99] but the abolition of peremptory challenge and the imposition of restrictions on the prosecution's right to stand by[1] "have given new practical importance to what had been thought to be [this] largely obsolescent institution."[2] It is possible to challenge the panel,[3] but the most likely use of challenge is to individual jurors. Challenge can be on statutory grounds, that is on the basis of ineligibility or disqualification, or common law grounds.[4] There are four possible forms of common law challenge all still properly known by their Latin titles:

(i) *propter honoris respectum*, that is privilege of peerage;
(ii) *propter delictum*, that is past criminal conviction;
(iii) *propter defectum*, that is lack of requisite qualification;
(iv) *propter affectum*, that is presumed or actual bias in the juror.

Of these grounds of challenge, the first three are relatively straightforward, since they refer back to ineligibility and disqualification.[5] Bias requires further consideration. In this context it means "whether the individual juror will be able to, and will, be loyal to his oath to give a true verdict according to the evidence."[6] Buxton classifies bias into three headings:

(a) Connection with the case[7] or with the parties,[8] and if there is a connection, bias is in effect assumed;
(b) Knowledge of the accused's character,[9] and if there is knowledge, bias is also in effect assumed;
(c) General hostility,[10] in this case, bias is not assumed but must be established.

It follows from the meaning of bias that the fact that a juror is of a particular race or holds a particular religious belief cannot be the basis of a challenge for cause on the grounds of bias (or any other ground).[11]

---

[99] In a survey of 3,165 cases the defence challenged for cause in 39 cases, *i.e.* 1 per cent. and the prosecution challenged for cause in 25 cases, *i.e.* 1 per cent.: J. Vennard and D. Riley, "The Use of Peremptory Challenge and Stand by of Jurors and their Relationship to Trial Outcome" [1988] Crim.L.R. 731.

[1] See below.

[2] Buxton, *op. cit.*, p. 225.

[3] *Ibid.* pp. 225–226.

[4] As to ineligibility for and disqualification from jury service, see pp. 799–801 above. On statutory challenge, see Buxton *op. cit.*, p. 227 and on common law challenge, see *ibid.* pp. 227–234 and Archbold (1988), para. 4–155ff.

[5] See Buxton *op. cit.*, pp. 228–229. Buxton, at p. 228, points out that whilst not all criminal convictions can ground a challenge for cause as such, nevertheless a criminal conviction might ground a challenge on some other basis such as bias, as indicated by the Court of Appeal in *R.* v. *Mason* [1981] Q.B. 881.

[6] Buxton *op. cit.*, p. 229–230.

[7] *e.g.* that the juror is personally connected with the facts of the particular case, see *ibid.* p. 230.

[8] *e.g.* that the juror is related to one of the parties, see *ibid.*

[9] Personal knowledge is intended here, not that gained through the media, which may, though, in exceptional circumstances be sufficient, see *ibid.* pp. 231–232.

[10] *e.g.* the holding of political opinions, the Court in *R.* v. *Swain* (1838) 2 M. & Rob. 112 emphasised the need to establish more than mere general hostility. In that case two jurors' active opposition to the Poor Law Act 1834 founded such a challenge, see Buxton *op. cit.*, p. 232.

[11] *R.* v. *Ford* [1989] 3 All E.R. 445, 449.

Jurors cannot be questioned before being challenged to ascertain whether there is ground for it, consequently basing a challenge on heads (iii) and (iv) may be particularly difficult, especially since the defence only has information as to the juror's name and address and not as to occupation.[12] If a challenge is made, it is tried by the trial judge.[13] The burden of proof lies on the party challenging. Witnesses may be called to support or defeat the challenge, but a prima facie case must be made before the challenged juror may be cross-examined, upon which fairly stringent limits are placed.[14]

In 1988 the defence right of peremptory challenge was abolished. This right had meant that the defence could exclude, without reason, up to three[15] members of the jury. Abolition of the right was proposed by the Roskill Committee[16] in fraud trials. The call for complete abolition appears to have followed on from the acquittal of the accused in the "Cyprus Secrets" trial.[17]

The main objection to this form of challenge was that it interfered with the random selection of a jury and that the effect of this unacceptable possibility would be heightened where in a trial involving more than one accused they combine their challenges and consequently radically alter the composition of the jury. The other objections were that the use of a challenge would lead either to juries being more likely to acquit or to juries being more likely to convict, and that the form of challenge brought the criminal justice system into disrepute.

TABLE 3

Number of Peremptory Challenges Used Per Defendant					
Number of defendants	Peremptory challenges per defendant				Trials
	0	>0 to 1	>1 to <3	3(max)	
1	80%	8%	6%	6%	2611
2	71%	18%	10%	1%	411
3	62%	23%	14%	1%	93
4 or more	46%	46%	8%	0%	50
				TOTAL	3165[18]

However, the evidence suggested that the peremptory challenge was not excessively used. In a survey of 3,165 cases undertaken by Vennard and

[12] The restriction on questioning is imposed by *R.* v. *Dowling* (1845) 7 St.Tr.(N.S.) 381; *R.* v. *Stewart* (1845) 1 Cox C.C. 174; Buxton *op. cit.*, p. 226. Compare the very different position in the United States where potential jurors may be questioned to ascertain whether they might be prejudiced. In one case it took four months to question 1,035 people before a jury could be sworn. See Harman and Griffith (1979), pp. 26–27 and M. George, "Jury selection, Texas style" (1988) 138 N.L.J. 438. Buxton *op. cit.*, p. 227, n. 15 points out that the recommendation of the Roskill Committee on Fraud Trials to re-instate the provision of a juror's occupation has not been implemented.

[13] Juries Act 1974, s.12(1). The judge may order that the hearing of a challenge for cause be *in camera* or in chambers: Criminal Justice Act 1988, s.118(2).

[14] See Archbold (1988), para. 4–162.

[15] Until the Criminal Law Act 1977, s.43, it had been possible to challenge seven jurors.

[16] *Report of the Departmental Inquiry on Fraud Trials* (HMSO, 1986), para. 7.38.

[17] The accused pooled their peremptory challenges. Consequently they were able to alter the composition of the jury. For a survey of the recent history to the abolition of the peremptory challenge, see Zander (1989), pp. 217–222.

[18] Vennard and Riley (1988), pp. 735, 736, 738.

Riley the peremptory challenge was used in 704 cases, *i.e.* 22 per cent. More detailed figures show its use in relation to the number of accused people, which suggests that "there was no evidence of the widespread pooling of challenges which is often thought to alter the balance of the jury in multi-defendant cases."

The evidence also suggested that the peremptory challenge did not have a significant effect on the rate of acquittals. Indeed the number of convictions was higher where the right of challenge had been exercised! Further, the available evidence suggests that the composition of the jury has little effect upon verdict.[19]

This evidence, however, was only addressed to the question of the practical use and effect of the challenge and not to the question of principle whether such interference with random selection adversely affecting the impartiality of the jury should be permitted.

The case for retaining the challenge included the argument that the peremptory challenge assisted in the obtaining of a non-biased jury by excluding people having the characteristics believed by experienced defence lawyers to predispose them to fail to decide a case in accordance with the evidence.[20] On the other hand, peremptory challenge was one of the few, admittedly limited, ways in which the accused could attempt to achieve a representative jury in terms of race[21] and sex and thus a jury which would more likely be impartial.[22] It will be noted that both sides were able to argue that their proposal more satisfactorily provided for the impartiality of the jury.[23]

The prosecution still retains the right to stand by for the Crown, which is similar to the peremptory challenge.[24] The prosecution has the right to require someone not to sit on the jury (stand by) unless there are not enough members of the panel left from which to produce a jury.[25] Any challenges thereafter have to be for cause. Whilst this right of stand by still exists, its use has been limited through the issuing of guidelines by the Attorney-General which specifically state that the abolition of the peremptory challenge means that "the Crown should assert its right to stand by only on the basis of clearly defined and restrictive criteria."[26] These criteria do not include the right to

---

[19] See Vennard and Riley (1988), p. 738, referring to the review of research by Hastie and Penrod: R. Hastie and S. Penrod, *Inside the Jury* (1983). The same conclusion is arrived at by Baldwin and McConville (1979), pp. 104–5; by Zander (1989), p. 226 and by J. J. Gobert "The Peremptory Challenge—An Obituary" [1989] Crim.L.R. 528.

[20] Whether the views of the lawyers as to who will be biased and who will not are accurate is doubtful, but a challenge means that lawyers may give full vent to their sad experiences of jurors not deciding cases according to the evidence, see Gobert (1989).

[21] Since there is no power in the judge to achieve such a jury by exercise of the power of discharge, according to the Court of Appeal in *R.* v. *Ford* [1989] 3 All E.R. 445, the racial composition of a jury is a matter purely of chance.

[22] See N. Blake, "The Case for the Jury" in Findlay and Duff (1988), Chap. 9; Zander (1989), pp. 217–222 and Gobert (1989).

[23] As to the arguments for and against the peremptory challenge, see Blake in Findlay & Duff (1988) and Zander (1989), pp. 217–222.

[24] The prosecution had a right of peremptory challenge until 1305.

[25] Technically, the Crown is exercising a challenge for cause but the trial of the cause is postponed until the panel is exhausted: *R.* v. *Parry* (1837) 7 C. & P. 836; *R.* v. *Casement* [1917] 1 K.B. 98. See also, J. F. McEldowney, "Stand By for the Crown: an Historical Analysis" [1979] Crim.L.R. 272.

[26] (1989) 88 Cr.App.R. 123, para. 3.

influence the overall composition of the jury nor should the right be exercised with a view to tactical advantage,[27] but the right may be used in connection with jury vetting or where a juror is manifestly unsuitable and the defence agree with the exercise of the power.[28]

A juror, having entered the jury box and remained unchallenged, is then sworn[29] in. The juror's oath makes no reference to the possibility of deciding according to conscience:

> "I swear by Almighty God that I will faithfully try the defendant[s] and give a true verdict[s] according to the evidence."[30]

When 12 have been sworn the accused may be "given in charge" to the jury and the trial can begin.[31]

(g) Discharge[32]

The judicial power to discharge[32a] the jury or individual jurors once the trial has begun is closely related to the challenge for cause considered above. Consequently, there is no power to discharge a jury because it is not racially mixed.[33] A judge's decision to discharge a jury or juror is unchallengeable, whereas if the judge decides not to discharge, that decision may be challenged on appeal against conviction by the accused on the basis that the conviction is to be regarded as unsafe and unsatisfactory because there was no discharge.[34]

If doubt arises about the capacity to act as a juror because of physical disability or insufficient understanding of English, an individual juror may be discharged. It may also be appropriate to accommodate a juror by exercising the discharge power, for example, on the death of a spouse.[35]

The discharge power enables the judge to deal with irregularities and improprieties before and after the retirement of the jury to consider its verdict. Before retirement, the sort of matters which may lead the judge to discharge a juror are: drunkenness; inattention to the proceedings; frivolous behaviour; acquisition of information which ought not to be available to a juror, such as existing knowledge of the accused's bad character; or contact

---

[27] Ibid. para. 1.

[28] The power, therefore, can be used where it becomes apparent that a juror selected to try a complex case is illiterate: ibid. para. 5. The limitation on the right of stand by would not entirely satisfy Gobert, who argued that peremptory challenge did not need to be abolished, but that any perceived problems should have been resolved by less drastic methods. For example, in a multi-defendant trial do not permit the aggregation of challenges: Gobert (1989).

[29] Some jurors may wish to affirm, either because of having a faith which will not permit them to swear on the New or Old Testament, or having no faith.

[30] Oaths Act 1978, ss.1, 4; Practice Direction [1984] 3 All E.R. 528. An alternative form is provided for jurors who wish to affirm.

[31] This is not an essential part of trial procedure. At the end of the swearing-in, the clerk may read the indictment to the jury and tell them that it is their "charge" to say whether the accused is guilty or not.

[32] See R. Buxton, "Challenging and Discharging Jurors—2" [1990] Crim.L.R. 284, and Archbold (1988) at paras. 4–169 to 4–172.

[32a] Juries Act 1974, s.16. This power is exercisable in any trial except when it is for an offence punishable with death: ibid., s.16(1)(2) as amended by the Criminal Justice Act 1988, s.121.

[33] R. v. Ford [1989] 3 All E.R. 445, and see p. 801 above.

[34] Buxton, [1990] Crim.L.R. 284, 284–285.

[35] Ibid. p. 285. The power must be exercised by a High Court or Circuit judge or recorder.

with someone outside the jury which in the circumstances is an irregularity rather than acceptable conduct and which may interfere with the course of justice.[36] In view of the nexus between challenge and discharge, an important ground for discharge is bias in a juror becoming apparent later than the time for challenge. In some cases the bias of an individual juror may lead to the discharge of the jury as a whole, since the accused's right to a fair trial has been prejudiced.[37]

A long trial can place a considerable strain on the jury and there are provisions which allow the discharge of individual jurors in the course of a trial in the event of illness or other good reason.[38] So long as the jury does not fall below nine members, the trial can proceed.[39]

After retirement, the jury must not separate or speak to anyone.[40] If there is any such separation or communication the jury will normally be discharged.[41]

(h) The trial, the summing up and the deliberations

During the course of the trial the members of the jury sit together in the jury box and listen to the evidence and the speeches of counsel. Jurors are entitled to take notes if they wish.[42] Such notes taken are subject to the same restrictions of secrecy as the jurors' deliberations. At an early stage of the trial, probably at the first adjournment, the jurors will be warned not to discuss the case with anyone except amongst themselves, and then only in the jury room. This instruction is designed to prevent outside influences on jurors[43] and may be reinforced by a reminder not to come to a view about the case until all the evidence and arguments have been heard.[44]

The contents of the summing up have been noted in the preceding section, as well as the significant place it has in the sequence of the trial. The initial direction on verdict will be that unanimity should be achieved, and although the jurors will know from the notes provided that a majority verdict is possible, the object of the deliberations should be unanimity. At the end of the summing up the jury retires to the jury room to consider its verdict and

---

[36] *Ibid.* pp. 286–287.

[37] *Ibid.* pp. 287–288, commenting on *R. v. Spencer* [1987] A.C. 128 where the House of Lords decided that the failure to discharge the jury after three of them had been in discussion with a biased, discharged juror who may well have influenced them, meant that the conviction had to be quashed as being unsafe.

[38] Juries Act 1974, s.16, provides that a juror can be discharged when incapable of continuing to act through illness or for any other reason. The power to discharge should be exercised generously. Trial by jury depends upon the willing co-operation of the public and, in any event, an aggrieved and inconvenienced juror is not likely to be a good one: *R. v. Hambery* [1977] Q.B. 924.

[39] Juries Act 1974, s.16(1). The number required for a majority verdict is adjusted accordingly: see p. 811, below.

[40] As to other aspects of the secrecy of the jury room, see below pp. 810–811.

[41] Buxton, [1990] Crim.L.R. 284, 288–291.

[42] This is a dubious advantage unless the juror happens to be reasonably skilled at note-taking. See Cornish (1971), pp. 50–51.

[43] Not necessarily sinister influences: the juror must give a verdict according to the evidence adduced in court and not on any other basis.

[44] This instruction may not always be heeded. The anonymous juror in the Thorpe trial revealed that the jury had decided on acquittal on the first day of the trial: see "Thorpe's trial: how the jury saw it" *New Statesman*, July 27, 1979.

are kept together privately until a verdict is reached or it is discharged.[45] The jury bailiff must ensure that no one comes into contact with the jury except by leave of the court.[46] In particularly difficult cases it may be necessary to provide overnight hotel accommodation for the jurors under the close supervision of the court. If the jury requires further information from the judge to explain a point in the summing up, or if guidance is required, the normal practice is for counsel to be consulted and the jury, if necessary, brought back into court. The judge then tries to resolve the problem and may, if appropriate, remind the jury of the evidence.

The jurors will select a person known as a "foreman" to speak for the jury on all matters and, ultimately, to deliver the verdict. An important aspect of the role of the "foreman" is to chair the jury's deliberations. Consequently, he or she has the possibility of significantly influencing the decision.[47] The method of selection is a matter for the jury.[48]

The deliberations of the jury are kept secret. Jurors are told that what is said in the jury room should not be disclosed to anyone even after the trial is over.[49] There have been examples of this instruction being ignored and some of what is known about the jury and the way in which it approaches its task emanates from the published experiences of individual jurors.[50] Statute makes it contempt of court to obtain, disclose or solicit any particulars of statements made, opinions expressed, arguments advanced or votes cast by members of a jury in the course of their deliberations in any legal proceedings.[51]

The secrecy of the jury room is said to be the basis on which trial by jury continues to exist. The arguments in favour of secrecy have been stated by Mr. Justice McHugh[52]: (1) it is necessary to ensure freedom of discussion in the jury room; (2) it protects jurors from outside influences; (3) if the public knew how juries reached decisions, the jury would lose its place in the public esteem; (4) without it citizens would be reluctant to serve as jurors; (5) it is necessary to ensure the finality of the verdict; (6) it protects the community satisfaction which flows from a unanimous verdict; (7) it enables juries to bring in unpopular verdicts; (8) it prevents unreliable disclosures by jurors and prevents verdicts being misunderstood; (9) it protects the privacy of the individual juror and prevents harassment; (10) it protects jurors from pres-

---

[45] Circumstances are now somewhat less primitive than when juries were locked up without refreshment to encourage them to concentrate. Juries are now allowed refreshment at their own expense: Juries Act 1974, s.15.

[46] Juries Act 1974, s.13. This rule is enforced very strictly and any breach of it is likely to lead to the discharge of the jury or the later quashing of any conviction: *R.* v. *Prime* (1973) 57 Cr.App.R. 632; *R.* v. *Goodson* [1975] 1 W.L.R. 549; *R.* v. *Davis* (1960) 44 Cr.App.R. 235.

[47] J. Baldwin and M. McConville, "Juries, Foremen and Verdicts" (1980) 20 Brit.J.Criminol. 35.

[48] The question apparently often put is, "Has anybody been on a jury before?" A juror who admits to experience often becomes "foreman".

[49] As they are informed in the notes accompanying the jury summons.

[50] E. Devons, "Serving as a Juryman in Britain" (1965) 28 M.L.R. 561; D. Barber and G. Gordon (ed.), *Members of the Jury* (1976).

[51] Contempt of Court Act 1981, s.8(1). Such proceedings for contempt may only be brought by, or with the permission of, the Attorney-General, or on the motion of a competent court: s.8(3). A competent court for this purpose is one which has jurisdiction to deal with the alleged contempt.

[52] "Jurors' Deliberations, Jury Secrecy, Public Policy and the Law of Contempt" in Findlay and Duff (1988), pp. 62–65.

sure to explain their reasons for a verdict; (11) it prevents vendettas against jurors; (12) it prevents enormous public pressures being placed on jurors.

The arguments against secrecy and in favour of disclosure have been stated by the same author[53]: (1) it will make juries more accountable; (2) it will enable injustices to be cured; (3) it could lead to inquiries into the reliability of convictions; (4) it could lead to worthwhile reforms of the legal system; (5) it may have an educational effect on the public; (6) it is necessary to ensure that jury trial can be properly examined to see if it is working[54]; (7) it is required by each juror's freedom of expression.

(i) Majority verdicts[55]

The requirement that the verdict be unanimous, which had stood since the thirteenth century, was abandoned by the Criminal Justice Act 1967, which introduced the majority verdict. The governing provision is now the Juries Act 1974, s.17:

"(1) ... the verdict of a jury in proceedings in the Crown Court or the High Court need not be unanimous if—

    (*a*) in a case where there are not less then eleven jurors, ten of them agree on a verdict; and

    (*b*) in a case where there are ten jurors, nine of them agree on a verdict.

    ...

(3) The Crown Court shall not accept a verdict of guilty by virtue of subsection (1) above unless the foreman of the jury has stated in open court the number of jurors who respectively agreed to and dissented from the verdict.

(4) No court shall accept a verdict by virtue of subsection (*a*) ... unless it appears to the court that the jury have had such period of time for deliberation as the court thinks reasonable having regard to the nature and complexity of the case; and the Crown Court shall in any event not accept such a verdict unless it appears to the court that the jury have had at least two hours for deliberation."

At the outset the jury is directed to reach an unanimous verdict[56] and no mention should normally be made of the majority verdict procedure.[57] However, as has been mentioned, the jurors know of the procedure from the notes accompanying the jury summons.

A *Practice Direction*[58] sets out the procedure which ensures that the safeguards contained in the Act (a minimum period of deliberation and a

---

[53] *Ibid.* pp. 65–67.

[54] Jury research is not made impossible, but is made much harder, by the secrecy requirement; see S. McCabe, "Is Jury Research Dead"? in Findlay and Duff (1988), Chap. 2, and see pp. 815–816, below.

[55] See generally, Archbold (1988), paras. 4–444ff; Emmins (1988), pp. 155–157. At a summary trial, there is normally a bench of three magistrates and conviction is by majority, see p. 755, above.

[56] See p. 809, above.

[57] *R.* v. *Thomas* [1983] Crim.L.R. 745. The fact that the judge told the jury in the summing-up that he was entitled to take a majority verdict after at least two hours was held not to be such a significant irregularity that there was the risk of a miscarriage of justice. The fear is of "inviting" the jury to disagree from the start: see also *R.* v. *Modeste* [1983] Crim.L.R. 746.

[58] [1967] 1 W.L.R. 1198, as clarified by *Practice Direction* [1970] 1 W.L.R. 916.

statement in open court of the majority) are observed. The stages are as follows:

1. If the jury returns[59] within two hours,[60] only a unanimous verdict is acceptable. If there is no unanimity the jury is sent back for further deliberation.
2. If the jury returns after two hours ten minutes[61] have elapsed it is asked if a verdict has been reached. If it is not unanimous and the judge considers that the jury has had a reasonable time for deliberation and having regard to the nature and complexity of the case the judge will direct it that a majority verdict is acceptable, although they should still try to reach unanimity.
3. When the jury finally returns, a precise set of questions is asked:
   (i) Have at least ten (or nine as the case may be) of you agreed upon your verdict? If "Yes,"
   (ii) What is your verdict? Please answer only "Guilty" or "Not Guilty."
   (iii) (a) If "Not Guilty"—accept the verdict without more ado.
        (b) If "Guilty"—is that the verdict of you all or by a majority?
   (iv) If "Guilty" by a majority, how many of you agreed to the verdict and how many dissented?

The foreman must state in open court the number of jurors who agreed to and dissented from the verdict before the judge can properly accept a guilty verdict, but there is no requirement that the precise words of the *Practice Direction* be used so long as it is clear to the ordinary person how the jury divided.[62] The formulation of the questions in the *Practice Direction* is intended to prevent anyone (other than the jurors) knowing whether or not a guilty verdict was reached by a majority.[63]

Before the introduction of the majority verdict, it was the case that if a jury failed to reach a unanimous verdict it was discharged and the accused might or might not be retried at the discretion of the prosecution. The majority verdict was introduced because fears of jury "nobbling" had been expressed and it was argued that the unanimity rule made it too easy for professional criminals to threaten or intimidate one member of a jury into holding out for a not guilty verdict.[64] However, the evidence to support these arguments put forward by the government to support the majority verdict was at best scanty.[65] The government mentioned also the argument that the

---

[59] "Returns" in the context of the *Practice Direction* includes being sent for by the judge who may be wondering how the deliberations are progressing.

[60] The statutory requirement that not less than two hours should be allowed for the initial deliberation is mandatory: *R.* v. *Barry* [1975] 1 W.L.R. 1190. The initial period may be such longer time as the judge thinks reasonable. A complicated case is an instance where a longer period is to be expected: Juries Act 1974, s.17(4); *R.* v. *Bateson* (1969) 54 Cr.App.R. 11; *R.* v. *Thornton, R.* v. *Stead* (1989) 89 Cr.App.R. 54.

[61] *Practice Direction* [1970] 1 W.L.R. 916. The period that has elapsed since the last member of the jury left the jury box must be stated in open court before the jury is asked for its verdict. The extra ten minutes allows for the practical necessities of returning from the jury room to the court room: Emmins (1988), p. 155.

[62] *R.* v. *Pigg* [1983] 1 W.L.R. 6.

[63] Thus avoiding a sort of second-class acquittal. See *R.* v. *Adams* [1969] 1 W.L.R. 106.

[64] See P. Duff and M. Findlay, "The Politics of Jury Reform" in Findlay and Duff (1988), Chap. 13, at pp. 212–215 and N. Blake in *ibid.*, p. 143. See also, P. Byrne, "Jury Reform and the Future" in *ibid.*, Chap. 12, at p. 191.

[65] See, *e.g.* Blake, *op. cit.*

reform would save resources in avoiding the consumption of time for the police and others involved in a second trial, although little importance was attached to this argument.[66]

It has been suggested that there are very strong arguments against the use of majority verdicts since the unanimity principle rather than the majority verdict reduces the risk of convicting the innocent, unanimous verdicts command greater community acceptance and thus the public has greater confidence in the criminal justice system, and the evidence suggests that the rate of hung juries, that is where the jury is discharged after being unable to agree, has not been much affected by the introduction of the majority verdict.[67] Further, Freeman has argued that the introduction of the majority verdict weakens the effect of the requirement that the prosecution must prove its case beyond a reasonable doubt, since if one member of a jury of twelve people is not satisfied of the guilt of the accused that is a clear indication that there is a reasonable doubt as to the prosecution's case and so the accused should be acquitted.[68] Maher has pointed out that this argument rather assumes that proof beyond a reasonable doubt is a concept which can be described in terms of probability. However, "it can be said that insisting on an unanimity rule is not always necessary in order to show that the principle of proof of the guilt of the accused beyond reasonable doubt is being taken seriously. For if a jury is large in size and is also representative of the community or society in general, then some relaxation of the rule may not frustrate the purpose of the principle which is to give the accused a right not to be convicted of a charge unless the case against him has been made out at a level of practical certainty. The rule of unanimity may also be relaxed where this right receives adequate protection by other means. . . . But it can be said that if no such safeguards exist for an accused then jury verdicts must be unanimous, or be near to unanimity, if the accused's right to proof of his guilt at the level of practical certainty is to be upheld."[69]

The introduction of majority verdicts and the consequent debate is an example of an instance where the Packer models may be helpful. The government appears to have been aware that most of its arguments in favour of majority verdicts were crime control model arguments, which may be why emphasis was placed on the change to majority verdicts improving fairness to the accused by preventing jury nobbling. This approach emphasises a value of the due process model.[70] Further, Maher's argument for accepting the majority verdict is conditional upon true respect being granted to the principles of due process.

(j) Is the jury competent to make decisions?

Is the jury actually competent to perform its functions?[71] It has been

---

[66] See Duff and Findlay in Findlay & Duff (1988), p. 213.
[67] D. Brown and D. Neal, "Show Trials: The Media and the Gang of Twelve" in *ibid.*, Chap. 8, at p. 134.
[68] Freeman (1981). See also Brown and Neal in Findlay & Duff (1988), p. 134.
[69] G. Maher, "The Verdict of the Jury" in *ibid.*, Chap. 3 at pp. 45–49, esp. p. 49.
[70] Duff and Findlay in *ibid.*, pp. 212–215.
[71] As to the functions of the jury, see p. 799, above.

asserted that the jury acquits too many people accused of crime.[72] The
evidence to support such a claim is, at best, equivocal.[73]

The question, further, raises doubts, first, whether it is proper for juries to
decide cases on any grounds, regardless of the direction on the law by the
judge, and, secondly, whether the jury is capable of understanding the
evidence and making decisions in complex cases. These doubts may be
regarded as an attack on the independence of the jury since some would
argue that the very arbitrariness and prejudice of which complaint is made
proves that independence.[74]

(i) Do juries arrive at "perverse" verdicts?

There are two aspects of the question whether juries reach "perverse"
verdicts: first, whether a jury's decisions according to conscience should be
permitted, and, secondly, what the function of the jury is when matters of
conscience are not raised.

"Perverse" verdicts and the conscience of the jury
If the value of trial by jury lies in the involvement of the public in the criminal
process, thus permitting the exercise of "community conscience" and providing the "just face" of the law,[75] the jury, it can be argued, must be entitled
to arrive at decisions which appear to be contrary to the law. Thus the jury's
acquittal of Clive Ponting of charges under the section 2 of the Official
Secrets Act 1911 may be viewed as the jury exercising its constitutional role
to arrive at a decision according to its conscience.[76]

Ponting had passed to Tam Dalyell M.P. documents relating to the
sinking of the Argentinian battleship, the *General Belgrano*, by a British
submarine during the Falklands War in 1982. These documents were clearly
covered by section 2, and the judge directed the jury that, on his understanding of section 2, Ponting had no authorisation to pass them to someone such
as Dalyell and there was no other lawful justification for Ponting's act.
Nevertheless the jury acquitted him.

On the other hand, it can be argued that permitting juries to decide
according to their conscience is completely inappropriate in "enlightened
times."[77] Consequently, the acquittal of Ponting may be regarded as wholly
improper. If the law is wrong, the proper means of challenge and change is
through the democratic process.

"Perverse" verdicts and jury decision-making
Whatever view is taken as to the acceptability of the jury acting according to
its conscience, there may be an argument about "perverse" verdicts in a

---

[72] See, in particular, Sir R. Mark, "Minority Verdicts" (1973), extracted in M. Zander, *Cases and Materials on the English Legal System* (5th ed., 1988), pp. 430–434.
[73] See the statistics referred to at p. 757, n. 58 above, which do not distinguish between pleas of guilty and not guilty; S. Butler, "Acquittal Rates" and J. Vennard, "The Outcome of Contested Trials" in D. Moxon (ed.), *Managing Criminal Justice* (1985); M. Zander, *Cases and Materials on the English Legal System* (5th ed., 1988), pp. 435–436. Sir Robert Mark's other grounds of complaint such as the professional criminal being let off too frequently, and the activities of crooked lawyers are responded to by Zander at pp. 435–437.
[74] See, *e.g.* Brown and Neal in Findlay & Duff (1988); and Mr. Justice McHugh in *ibid*.
[75] As to this function of the jury, see p. 799, above.
[76] C. Ponting, *The Right to Know: The Inside Story of the Belgrano Affair* (1985). See also N. MacCormick, "The Interest of the State and the Rule of Law" in P. Wallington and R. M. Merkin, *Essays in Memory of Professor F. H. Lawson* (1986).
[77] The phrase is that of Jeremy Bentham in *Draught of a Code for the Organisation of the Judicial Establishment in France* (1790), quoted in G. Marshall, "The judgement of one's peers: some aims and ideal of jury trial" in Walker with Pearson (1975), p. 1.

different sense. Whether juries' verdicts may be described as "perverse" on a more general basis depends upon what the role of the jury in decision-making is perceived to be. If a narrow approach is taken, a verdict is right if it is reached by the jury after an honest, careful and reasonable attempt to apply the law (as explained by the judge in the summing up) to the facts as it finds them, taking no other circumstances into account.[78] What is then achieved is both greater certainty in the outcome of trials and greater consistency in juries' decisions.[79] A broad approach might perceive a verdict to be right where it is a verdict of acquittal, say, after a consideration of the evidence which indicated guilt or even without any consideration of the evidence at all, provided it nevertheless results from a reasonable exercise of discretion in favour of the accused reflecting the jury's sympathy, clemency or disapproval of the prosecution.

The narrow approach will view more acquittals as perverse verdicts and hence leads to the argument that reform of the jury is necessary. Jury research has been undertaken to attempt to consider whether juries do arrive at "perverse verdicts." Because of the limitations imposed upon researchers, the methods employed to analyse and explain the decision-making process and the verdicts reached in particular cases have necessarily been indirect.[80] One approach has been to compare the verdict of the jury in selected cases with the "verdict" of the professional participants in the trial; the other has been to arrange for a "mock" or "shadow" jury to listen to a case and then observe its deliberations when required to give a verdict. Both methods have their drawbacks but the results are illustrative of different features of jury decisions.

Two major English studies have been conducted which take account of the views of the professionals.[81] The first, by McCabe and Purves,[82] dealt with 475 accused tried on indictment over a two-year period, concentrating solely on the 115 who were acquitted by the jury. The second, by Baldwin and McConville,[83] dealt with 2,406 accused who appeared in the Birmingham Crown Court over an eighteen month period, concentrating on the 500 accused who contested their cases. The latter study is, therefore, of wider significance since it looks at all jury verdicts and not solely acquittals. There were some differences of methodology but both studies sought to explain the relevant verdicts by reference to the views of counsel,[84] solicitors, the judge and police officers.[85]

The first study attempted to categorise the 115 acquittals[86] according to the views of the professionals. It appeared that only 15 of the 115 acquittals

[78] The argument is not denying the jury's function to be the decider of the facts.
[79] See, e.g. on the general point about consistency, Lord Devlin, *The Judge* (1979), Chap. 5; also E. J. Griew, *Dishonesty and the Jury* (1974) and G. Williams, *The Proof of Guilt* (1963), Chap. 10.
[80] See McCabe in Findlay and Duff (1988). See also R. Eldin, "A Juror's Tale" (1988) 138 N.L.J. 37.
[81] Reference should also be made to M. Zander, "Are Too Many Professional Criminals Avoiding Conviction?—A Study of Britain's Two Busiest Courts" (1974) 37 M.L.R. 28.
[82] S. McCabe and R. Purves, *The Jury at Work* (1972).
[83] J. Baldwin and M. McConville, *Jury Trials* (1979).
[84] The Bar did not co-operate in the Birmingham survey.
[85] The police did not co-operate in the Oxford survey.
[86] In the Oxford study there were a further 58 cases in which the accused was acquitted on the direction of the judge.

were based on a deliberate decision to go against the evidence. All the others were explicable on the grounds of weakness in the prosecution case, the failure of prosecution witnesses or the credibility of the accused's explanation. Many of the acquittals were regarded as correct by the professionals and the proportion of perverse verdicts was established as low in relation to acquittals[87] and very low in relation to all contested cases.[88]

In the second study, Baldwin and McConville concluded that it was not possible to determine an overall pattern in the cases where the outcome was regarded as questionable. Those cases included convictions as well as acquittals and so doubts are raised about the conventional wisdom that the accused gets the benefit of the doubt from the jury. A similar proportion of wayward verdicts occurred in this study[89] and the authors agreed that it was a tiny fraction of all cases that pass through the criminal courts, yet they pointed out the serious nature of the cases tried by the jury and concluded that trial by jury is "... an arbitrary and unpredictable business."[90] The authors recognised that the significance of their research was limited to an assessment of the accuracy of verdicts and that the political and constitutional issues were also very important. They believed, however, that the political and constitutional debate should be informed by as much knowledge as possible about the veracity of jury verdicts.

In sum, the English evidence[91] demonstrates that there is an identifiable, if relatively small, number of cases in which juries reach perverse verdicts, although views differ on whether these deviations can be explained on any particular basis.

In the course of the Oxford study,[92] McCabe and Purves also utilised the "shadow" jury technique. In 30 cases, a second "jury" was installed in the court to listen to the proceedings and then to deliberate and reach a verdict. This method has the drawback that the degree of pressure which exists when a jury is dealing with the fate of an accused is lacking in mock deliberations, but the main conclusions pointed to the care and determination of the jurors to go about their task methodically, discount their prejudices and look for evidence on which to base their verdict.[93] This would suggest that in real cases the jury is likely to display the same, or an even greater, degree of conscientiousness and application. On the other hand, some evidence suggests that jury trial is a lottery when considering the competence of jurors to follow and remember evidence and think through the issues raised logically and carefully.[94]

(ii) *The jury in complex cases*

A similar debate is encountered when considering the role of the jury in

---

[87] One verdict in eight amongst the jury acquittals, and one verdict in eleven amongst all acquittals.
[88] One verdict in thirty-two amongst the accused dealt with in the period of the study.
[89] *Jury Trials*, Chaps. 4 and 5.
[90] *Ibid*. p. 132.
[91] There has been more extensive research in America, starting with H. Kalven and H. Zeisel, *The American Jury* (1966) (The Chicago Jury Project); see McCabe in Findlay and Duff (1988). In England, Zander's conclusions are broadly in line with the other studies.
[92] S. McCabe and R. Purves, *The Shadow Jury At Work* (1974). See also, A. P. Sealy, "What Can Be Learned from the Analysis of Simulated Juries?" in Walker with Pearson (1975).
[93] *Ibid*. p. 61.
[94] See *The Times*, October 24, 1988.

complex cases. The debate relies more upon the nature of the trials, such as fraud trials and trials involving scientific evidence, which, it is suggested, means that the jury cannot competently arrive at proper decisions. The inherent complexity of some cases was part of the argument that led to the abolition of the jury in most civil cases.[95] In the context of criminal cases, the Roskill Committee on Fraud Trials concluded that "we do not find trial by a random jury a satisfactory way of achieving justice in cases as long and complex as [many fraud trials]. We believe that many jurors are out of their depth."[96] Consequently, the Committee recommended that for complex fraud cases, the jury should be abolished and trial should take place before a Fraud Trials Tribunal.[97] This conclusion was reached even though the Committee stated that it was unable to obtain accurate evidence to suggest "that there has been a higher proportion of acquittals in complex fraud cases than in fraud cases or other criminal cases generally."[98] Indeed the Roskill Committee appears to have based its view, in so far as it was based on any evidence, at least in part on the conclusions of the study by Baldwin and McConville.[99] However, Baldwin and McConville had concluded that none of the questionable acquittals that they reported had been in a complex fraud case. In fact the jury had convicted in six of the eight cases which involved complex fraud issues and the two acquittals appeared to have been regarded as broadly justified.[1]

On that basis one author has suggested that the assertion of the Roskill Committee about the incompetence of the jury is really an article of faith.[2] Similar doubts about jury competence have been raised in cases involving scientific evidence.[3] The research on the decision-making of juries[4] suggests that juries are competent to make decisions, including decisions in complex cases. It has been suggested that the real fault in complex cases lies not with the jury, but rather with other participants in the criminal trial.[5]

Levi concluded that jury performance would be considerably improved if "greater care were devoted to the instruction of the jury on points of evidence and on the method to be followed when assessing it."[6] In particular there appears to be a tendency for judges to attempt to make their decisions

[95] See pp. 703–706, above.
[96] *Fraud Trials Committee: Report*; Chair: Lord Roskill (1986), para. 8.35.
[97] *Ibid.* para 8.51.
[98] *Ibid.* para 8.35.
[99] J. Baldwin and M. McConville, *Jury Trials* (1979), see above.
[1] *Ibid.* pp. 61–62.
[2] R. Harding, "Jury Performance in Complex Cases" in Findlay and Duff (1988), p. 77. Mr. Merricks, a member of the Roskill Committee, felt that the case for change was not made out, partly because of the evidence and partly because most people making submissions were in favour of the jury. See also, M. Zander, "The Report of the Roskill Committee on Fraud Trials" [1986] Crim.L.R. 423.
[3] See, *e.g.* Harding in Findlay and Duff (1988), pp. 82–90, concentrating on the Australian criticism of jury performance in such cases as the *Chamberlain* case. See also the criticisms of jury competence considered in M. Levi, "The Role of the Jury in Complex Cases" in Findlay and Duff, (1988), Chap. 6; and Lord McCluskey, *Law, Justice and Democracy* (1986) (Reith Lectures).
[4] See above.
[5] As pointed out by both Harding in Findlay & Duff and Levi in *ibid.*
[6] Levi *op. cit.*, p. 109. The Roskill Committee recognised this problem and, in fraud cases where there was still to be jury trial, made a number of recommendations to improve jury comprehension, including the use of visual aids and proper preparation of documentation: *Fraud Trials Committee* (1986), Chap. 9. The same point is made with regard to the judge's responsibility in summing up to the jury, see pp. 789–794, above.

to the jury "appeal proof" by full, undifferentiated reference to all the
relevant law and any guideline judgments that exist, without taking sufficient care to emphasise simply and only those matters necessary for the
decision of the jury on the facts of the particular case and in response to the
actual issues raised by counsel.[7]

(k) Replacing the jury?[8]

Questions have been raised about the role and efficacy of the jury.
Although not frequently suggested, replacement of the jury by some other
method of determining facts in criminal matters must be considered. There
would appear to be four options.[9]

(i) The single judge

Most civil trials are conducted by a judge alone[10] deciding both fact and
law. In criminal matters the stipendiary magistrate has the same function.
The role of the stipendiary is somewhat restricted because of the lesser
degree of seriousness of the offences tried and also because any appeal
against conviction is by way of rehearing, so that there would be significant
differences in merely translating a stipendiary to the Crown Court.

The advantages of this option include time-saving at trials through not
having to explain so many matters to the jury which it then decides, the
reduction in the likelihood of decision-making being affected by outside
influences,[11] and the reduction in the likelihood of verdicts not in accordance
with the law.

The disadvantages of this option include the lack of community participation, the loss of the independence and impartiality of the jury, and the
possibility that the judge would become case-hardened or prosecution-
minded. Further, there would be little protection against eccentricity, and
decisions on guilt being taken by one person might be too onerous a
burden.[12]

(ii) The bench of judges

Some of the disadvantages of the single judge option, such as the possibility of becoming prosecution-minded or making eccentric decisions, might be
avoided by a bench of three or five judges. The disadvantages of this option
include that it would be enormously expensive and recruitment might be
difficult and that the nature of the judiciary would be transformed because a

---

[7] *Ibid.* pp. 109–111. The same point is made by E. Griew, "Summing Up the Law" [1989]
Crim.L.R. 768. See also p. 791, above.
[8] See, W. R. Cornish, *The Jury* (1968), Chap. 10.
[9] Assuming that we are considering alternative types of tribunal rather than adjustment to the
jury, such as the reduction of the number of jurors to six.
[10] See p. 703, for the significance of the jury in civil trials.
[11] The judge may be more immune to threats. This line of reasoning lay behind the introduction
of single judge courts in certain trials in Northern Ireland in 1973 as a result of the Diplock
Report (Report of the Commission to Consider Legal Procedures to Deal with Terrorist
Activities in Northern Ireland, Cmnd. 5185, 1972), see now, the Northern Ireland (Emergency Provisions) Act 1978.
[12] See, *e.g.* S. Greer and A. White, "Restoring Jury Trial to Terrorist Offences in Northern
Ireland" in Findlay and Duff (1988), Chap. 11.

considerable increase in the number of judges would allegedly weaken the bench. There would be considerable implications for the legal profession if a career judiciary were necessitated.

Many of the disadvantages associated with decision-making by professionals remain, in particular the absence of community participation in trial. The dislike of such decision-making will not have been lessened by the willingness of benches of judges of the Court of Appeal to permit convictions to stand where new evidence has emerged after the trial which might cause a jury to entertain reasonable doubt.[13]

(iii) *The composite tribunal*

On certain appeals from the magistrates' court, a Crown Court judge sits with two lay magistrates.[14] Some European jurisdictions[15] rely heavily upon the composite tribunal of lay people and judge and one observer, at least, has professed himself to be impressed by the system.[16]

The advantages would include the probability that trials would be speedier because the judge would be involved in all discussions, and that the lay people involved would be able to outvote the judge thus maintaining the overriding influence of representatives of the community.

Possible disadvantages would include whether the judge would have too large a say in most cases and whether decision-making would still be independent and impartial so as to preserve a fair trial. The lay people might have to be trained which could mean that they would no longer be representatives of the community.

(iv) *The special jury*

The special jury is an option which seeks to satisfy the demand for community participation and independence, but to ensure competence through training. Thus a jury is still selected from non-lawyers, but the only people eligible to serve on such a jury are those who have been trained for jury service. Consequently, the objective of random selection may be defeated and trial would be in the hands of a select group of people, albeit not all lawyers.

C. EVALUATIONS

Critical analysis of the criminal trial is essential. It may be that the Packer's two model system[17] will help students to think through the many issues in relation to the criminal trial. For example, it might be suggested that the crime control model, emphasising the necessity to reduce criminal conduct and requiring that the system operate efficiently, helps to explain why it has

---

[13] A development initiated by the decision of the House of Lords in *Stafford* v. *D.P.P.* [1974] A.C. 878. It is heavily criticised in Lord Devlin, *The Judge* (1979) at pp. 148–176.

[14] See pp. 198–199, above. It used to be possible for lay magistrates to sit with a judge at a trial on indictment, but that was unusual and they did not take part in the decision: Supreme Court Act 1981, s.8(1).

[15] Described in Cornish (1968).

[16] Cornish was particularly complimentary about the Scandinavian system: *ibid*. Chap. 10.

[17] For a description of these models, see above, pp. 682–683 and p. 749.

been proposed that more offences be tried summarily where the accused does not need to be present, why plea bargaining is permitted, and why proposals for jury reform are made, especially in relation to the alternatives to the jury, and on particular aspects such as the majority verdict, jury vetting and jury composition.[18] On the other hand, it could be suggested that the due process model helps to explain certain developments with regard to the criminal trial, for example, the developments as to the exclusion of evidence under the Police and Criminal Evidence Act 1984.

However, Packer's models are intended to be extremes, recognising that systems actually adopt a balance,[19] as the Royal Commission on Criminal Procedure set out to achieve in its "fundamental balance."[20] It is also necessary, therefore, to consider whether that balance is actually being achieved, or whether too much emphasis is being placed on the desire to control crime or on the desire to ensure that the accused gets a fair trial.

An approach on the basis of these models or the fundamental balance can be undertaken on any of the topics in this chapter, but attention might, for example, be drawn to the following arguments:

(a) Magistrates' court or Crown Court trial?

Frequently suggestions are made to increase the number of offences triable in the magistrates' courts. The arguments in favour tend to be based upon efficiency since magistrates trials will be cheaper and will not last as long, there is the possibility of written pleas of guilty, and the trial may proceed in the absence of the accused. Sometimes, the additional argument that magistrates are less likely to acquit is also put forward, although the evidence does not clearly support such an argument.[21]

These appear to be arguments founded on the concept of crime control. However, that does not necessarily make them bad or wrong, if adequate protections for the accused are provided. It is this side of the balance which may be missing, in view of the poor levels of legal representation[22] and the need of the magistrates to decide matters of both law and fact.[23]

A move towards magistrates' court trial may, of course, be thought to be fundamentally inappropriate if, for example, there is a belief that jury trial is an essential element in a fair trial or that only jury trial represents the essential requirement of community participation.

(b) Plea bargaining

In the course of this chapter two forms of plea bargaining have been considered from the perspective of the various participants in the criminal trial, not least the accused. They are the plea arrangement between counsel for the accused to plead guilty to a lesser charge[24] and the sentencing discount available on a plea of guilty by the accused.[25]

[18] See P. Duff and M. Findlay, "The Politics of Jury Reform" in Findlay and Duff (1988), Chap. 13.
[19] See p. 749, above.
[20] See pp. 680–684, above.
[21] See p. 757, n. 58.
[22] See pp. 675–680, above.
[23] See pp. 755–756, above.
[24] See pp. 768, 772–774, 777, above.
[25] See pp. 768–769, 777–778, above.

If the crime control model is thought to be the proper model to adopt, plea bargaining has much to say for it in encouraging the guilty to plead guilty, and in saving considerable resources by having fewer contested trials.

However, it seems generally to be accepted that the inducements to plead guilty, if they are regarded as legitimate at all, should not be such that they create a substantial danger of the innocent pleading guilty. The pressures exerted by defence counsel giving advice to the accused "in strong terms" were identified by Baldwin and McConville in their research study which concentrated on 121 Crown Court defendants who made late changes of plea from not guilty to guilty.[26] The criticisms made of the attitude and performance of counsel caused the publication of the research to be surrounded with controversy, but the conclusions of the study were that the sentencing discount and the rules governing the interrogation of suspects by the police were primarily responsible for any deficiencies exposed, rather than the conduct of the participants in the criminal process.[27]

Although lip-service is paid to the notion that the discount is based on the expression of remorse, the primary justification for the inducements to plead guilty is administrative expediency. In a system which places so much emphasis upon the assumed innocence of the accused and the right to require the prosecution to prove their case, the existence of strong pressures to plead guilty may appear quite contradictory. The evidence currently available allows no complacency and suggests that more attention needs to be focused on those who plead guilty and, as a result, do not participate in the elaborate procedures described in the rest of this chapter.[28]

(c) Jury reform

If crime control were the dominant motive in jury reform, arguments for abolition of the jury would be anticipated, since juries are inefficient and may acquit too many people, their decisions are unpredictable, and there is no appeal against an acquittal. In fact, proposals for the abolition of the jury are very rarely put forward, perhaps because of the popular support the jury receives through an ingrained belief that it is a constitutional protection against improper action by the State or simply that it is every person's right to be tried by one's peers.

The arguments are actually concerned with what crimes should be tried by the jury.[29] Many advocates of the jury are firmly of the view that it is under attack, but that the attack is not direct or frontal against the institution of the jury itself.[30] Some advocates take the view that the attack is predicated on the basis of the crime control model. This model explains, it is argued, the

---

[26] *Negotiated Justice* (1977). The research technique involved detailed interviews with defendants accused of serious crimes. The interviews were conducted soon after the trial had finished and it is inevitable that the particular sample might be inclined to protest innocence and exaggerate the pressures involved. Nevertheless, it would appear that the number of people wrongly convicted after a guilty plea may be underestimated.

[27] *Ibid.* Chap. 6.

[28] See further, S. Dell, *Silent in Court* (1971); S. McCabe and R. Purves, *By-Passing the Jury* (1972); Bottoms and McClean (1976). See also McBarnet (1981).

[29] See above.

[30] See, *e.g.* P. Duff and M. Findlay, "The Politics of Jury Reform" in Findlay and Duff (1988), Chap. 13; Freeman (1981); Lord Devlin, *Trial by Jury* (1956); Lord Devlin, "Trial By Jury for Fraud" (1986) 6 O.J.L.S. 311.

move in favour of majority verdicts,[31] the change in disqualification conditions excluding a considerable number of potential jurors,[32] and the acceptance of jury vetting.[33] On the other hand, it might be suggested that the recent alterations are merely redressing the balance from a position where too many of the provisions were far too favourable to the accused.

[31] See pp. 812–813, above.
[32] See pp. 799–800, above.
[33] See pp. 802–804, above.

CHAPTER 17

APPEALS AND JUDICIAL REVIEW

A. INTRODUCTION

IN this chapter we consider the various mechanisms for correcting errors in, and otherwise reviewing, the decisions of courts and tribunals. There are two basic kinds of legal procedure that are available for these purposes. An *appeal* may be provided by statute: indeed it will only be available if a statute has so provided, as the common law does not recognise any rights of appeal as such. The common law has provided only for the *review* of decisions either on the ground that the body which made the decision had no jurisdiction in the matter, or on the ground that the formal record of proceedings revealed that there had been some error of law. Where the body was an inferior body of limited jurisdiction, the appropriate remedy was a writ of certiorari to remove the proceedings into the Court of King's Bench: if the decision was shown to be defective it would be quashed. If such a body was proposing to act outside the jurisdiction in the future, a writ of prohibition would lie to prevent it from so acting; if it failed to perform a duty, the appropriate remedy was a writ of mandamus. These "prerogative" remedies would be available to challenge, for example, the decisions of justices of the peace in summary criminal proceedings or in civil cases. Where, however, the decision was that of one of the superior courts, or followed a criminal trial on indictment at the assizes or quarter sessions, the remedy was a writ of error, closely analogous to certiorari.[1] There were also informal devices whereby matters could be adjourned so that the views of other judges could be obtained[2] and special procedures for the review of decisions in the Court of Chancery.[3]

In the nineteenth and early twentieth centuries, writs of error were replaced by statutory appeals. The prerogative writs continued to be available in respect of the courts of summary jurisdiction, but now in parallel to statutory appeals. They were also increasingly used to correct the decisions of local authorities, government departments and statutory tribunals. In 1938 they became prerogative "orders" rather than writs,[4] and in 1978 they came to be exclusively available on a new procedure termed an "application for judicial review."[5]

Apart from these basic options there are various other avenues for the redress of grievances, some of which are enshrined in statute (*e.g.* references

[1] See above, p. 33.
[2] *Ibid.*
[3] *Ibid.*
[4] Administration of Justice (Miscellaneous Provisions) Act 1938, s.7.
[5] See below, pp. 871–878.

by the Home Secretary to the Court of Appeal (Criminal Division)), some dependent on an exercise of the royal prerogative (*e.g.* the prerogative of mercy) and some informal.

There are two basic functions fulfilled by mechanisms for appeal or review. The first is that of the correction of errors of fact, substantive law or procedure made by the court or tribunal below. The second is that of the harmonious development of the law. Appellate courts commonly comprise a number of judges whereas trial courts and tribunals normally have a single judge or legally-qualified chairman, sitting alone or with a jury or lay members. Appellate judges tend to be of greater experience and seniority than trial judges and their case load tends to be smaller, giving greater time for consideration; these factors become more pronounced the higher one moves up the courts hierarchy. In limited circumstances fresh evidence may be admitted before the reviewing court. Appellate courts may also correct divergences of approach among different courts of first instance.[6]

B. VARIABLE FACTORS IN APPEAL AND REVIEW MECHANISMS

There are a number of factors which must be taken into account when considering any legal procedure for redressing a grievance:

(1) Who can institute an appeal?[7]
(2) Can the appeal be brought as of right or only by the leave of a court or other body?
(3) What are the permissible grounds for an appeal?
(4) What is the time limit within which an appeal must be brought?
(5) To which court or tribunal does the appeal lie?
(6) What material may the appellate body consider?
(7) Who may appear as parties on the appeal?
(8) What are the powers of the appellate court?

C. APPEALS

In this section we consider appeals from courts and tribunals.[8] We concentrate on appeals in basic civil and criminal cases: in addition a vast number of rights of appeal have been created in special cases which cannot be covered in detail.[9] The appeals are presented in four groups:

(1) Summary criminal proceedings and civil proceedings originating in magistrates' courts;
(2) Criminal proceedings on indictment;
(3) Civil cases originating in a county court or the High Court;
(4) Appeals in administrative law matters.

---

[6] *e.g.* the Court of Appeal in *Froom* v. *Butcher* [1976] Q.B. 286 settled the difference between judges who held that failure to wear a seat belt in a car would normally constitute contributory negligence and those who did not: the former approach was approved.
[7] For convenience this is to be taken here to include "seek review."
[8] As to the constitution and functions of appellate courts, see Chap. 2.
[9] A full list may be found in D. Price, *Appeals* (1982).

The basic principles governing rights of appeal from a court seem to be that: (1) there should be one chance to appeal on the facts or merits and a series of opportunities to take points of law up the hierarchy of the courts; (2) there should be one chance to appeal as of right, with further appeals being dependent upon obtaining leave; and (3) that an acquittal by a jury in a criminal case should be regarded as final. Appeals from tribunals or public authorities tend to be limited to points of law.

1. APPEALS FROM MAGISTRATES' COURTS

A person aggrieved by a decision of a magistrates' court in a criminal case, or in certain civil cases, has the option of (1) appealing on fact or law to the Crown Court or (2) appealing on a point of law alone direct to the High Court, by way of "case stated." If the first option is chosen, an appeal lies thereafter to the High Court as in (2). In domestic (family) cases, the appeal lies only to the High Court.

Once a case reaches the High Court, further appeals in criminal cases lie only to the House of Lords, and further appeals in civil cases lie on the same basis as in other civil cases determined by the High Court. In a criminal case, where the magistrates commit a convicted person to the Crown Court for sentence, the appeal thereafter lies to the Court of Appeal (Criminal Division).[10]

(a) Appeals from magistrates' courts to the Crown Court

The defendant in a criminal case may appeal to the Crown Court, as of right, (a) if he or she pleaded guilty,[11] against sentence; or (b) if he or she did not plead guilty, against the conviction or sentence.[12] "Sentence" includes any order made on conviction other than an order for costs and certain other orders.[13] Similarly, a person may appeal against an order for contempt of a magistrates' court[14] or an order binding him or her over to keep the peace or to be of good behaviour.[15] The prosecutor or complainant may not appeal against an acquittal or a refusal to make an order.[16]

---

[10] Criminal Appeal Act 1968, s.10: see below, p. 839.

[11] If the plea of guilty was "equivocal" the defendant may appeal to the Crown Court to set aside the conviction and remit the case to the magistrates with a direction to enter a plea of "not guilty" and try the case summarily: the magistrates' court is obliged to comply with the direction provided that there has been a proper inquiry by the Crown Court and sufficient evidence from which it could find that the plea had been equivocal: *R.* v. *Plymouth JJ.*, *ex p. Hart* [1986] Q.B. 950. A plea is equivocal where something emerges during the trial which throws doubt on it, *e.g.* "guilty, but I took it by mistake." See *R.* v. *Durham Quarter Sessions, ex p. Virgo* [1952] 2 Q.B. 1. The Crown Court should seek affidavit evidence from the chairman of the bench or the clerk before sending it back: *R.* v. *Rochdale JJ.*, *ex p. Allwork* [1981] 3 All E.R. 433. The Crown Court may also remit a case where it subsequently transpires that a plea of guilty was made under duress: *R.* v. *Huntingdon Crown Court, ex p. Jordan* [1981] Q.B. 857.

[12] Magistrates' Courts Act 1980, s.108(1).

[13] *Ibid.*, s.108(3). Probation orders and orders for conditional discharge were formerly excluded : see now the Criminal Justice Act 1982, s.66(2).

[14] Contempt of Court Act 1981, s.12(5).

[15] Magistrates' Courts (Appeals from Binding Over Orders) Act 1956, s.1.

[16] Such a right may be expressly conferred, *e.g.* the Customs and Excise Management Act 1979, s.147: offences under the Customs and Excise Acts.

Notice of appeal must be given within 21 days after the day on which the decision or sentence appealed against was given.[17] The notice must state the grounds for appeal. The Crown Court may extend the time for giving notice of appeal either before or after it expires.[18] If the defendant is legally aided, the clerk to the justices must supply a copy of his or her notes[19]; if the defendant is not, the clerk should view requests for notes sympathetically.[20]

The appeal is treated as a complete rehearing,[21] and the procedure is exactly the same as at a summary trial in the magistrates' court. The appeal can be heard notwithstanding the absence of the appellant,[22] even where he or she has not instructed counsel to appear on his or her behalf.[23] For example, the relevant witnesses will attend the court and give evidence as at the original trial. The parties are not, however, confined to the evidence placed before the magistrates. Where the appeal is against sentence only, it is usual for the prosecution merely to put forward facts which had been admitted or found by the magistrates, although there is no technical reason why sworn evidence should not be given.[24]

The powers of the Crown Court are as follows.[25] It may correct any error or mistake in the order or judgment against which the appeal is brought, and at the end of the hearing may:

(a) confirm, reverse or vary any part of the decision appealed against, including a determination not to impose a separate penalty in respect of an offence.[26]

(b) remit the matter with its opinion thereon to the authority whose decision is appealed against; or

[17] Crown Court Rules 1982 (S.I. 1982 No. 1109), r. 7.
[18] *Ibid.*
[19] Legal Aid in Criminal and Care Proceedings (General) Regulations 1989 (S.I. 1989 No. 344), reg. 42.
[20] *R.* v. *Clerk to Highbury Corner JJ, ex p. Hussein* [1986] 1 W.L.R. 1266, following *R.* v. *Clerk to Lancaster JJ, ex p. Hill* (1983) 148 J.P. 65, in preference to *dicta* in *Hill* v. *Wilson* (1984) 149 J.P. 252.
[21] See *Drover* v. *Rugman* [1951] 1 K.B. 380; *Northern Ireland Trailers* v. *Preston Corporation* [1972] 1 W.L.R. 203; *Hughes* v. *Holley* (1986) 86 Cr.App.R. 130: these cases show that the court must, however, consider the state of affairs existing at the time the order was appealed against. Appeals against binding-over orders are to be conducted as a rehearing: *Shaw* v. *Hamilton* [1982] 1 W.L.R. 1308.
[22] *R.* v. *Croydon Crown Court, ex p. Clair* [1986] 1 W.L.R. 746 (the Crown Court had refused to hear the appeal in the appellant's absence: mandamus was granted requiring them to do so).
[23] *R.* v. *Crown Court at Guildford, ex p. Brewer* (1987) 87 Cr.App.R. 265 (the appellant's counsel was present, but, following refusal of an application for an adjournment, took no further part in the proceedings as he had no instructions to do so). The Crown Court has power to set aside its own order dismissing an appeal, *e.g.* where the appellant is absent as the result of a misunderstanding: *R.* v. *Knightsbridge Crown Court, ex p. Johnson* [1986] Crim.L.R. 803.
[24] *Paprika Ltd.* v. *Board of Trade* [1944] K.B.327; *Shaw* v. *Hamilton* [1982] 1 W.L.R. 1308; *Williams* v. *R.* (1983) 77 Cr.App.R. 329; *R.* v. *Telford JJ., ex p. Darlington* (1987) 87 Cr.App.R. 194.
[25] Supreme Court Act 1981, s.48, as amended by the Criminal Justice Act 1988, s.156.
[26] Prior to the enactment of s.156 of the 1988 Act, the subsection merely referred to a power to vary "the decision appealed against;" the Divisional Court in *Dutta* v. *Westcott* [1987] Q.B. 291 gave the words a strained interpretation in holding that the Crown Court was empowered to vary the penalty imposed for another offence dealt with by the magistrates on the same occasion, but which was not appealed against: the amendment gave express authority for this.

(c) make any order in the matter as it thinks just and exercise any power which that authority might have exercised.

These powers are subject to any limit or restriction imposed by any other enactment. A punishment in a criminal case may be more or less severe than that awarded by the magistrates' court, provided that it could have been imposed by that court.[27]

In civil matters, appeals lie to the Crown Court in respect of the making or refusal of care orders[28] and a variety of licensing matters.[29]

(b) Appeals from magistrates' courts to the High Court by "case stated"

Any person who was party[30] to any proceedings before a magistrates' court or who is "aggrieved"[31] by its decision may question the decision on the ground that it is wrong in law or in excess of jurisdiction by applying to the justices for them to state a case for the opinion of the High Court.[32] An application may not be made following committal proceedings,[33] at an interlocutory stage in a summary hearing,[34] to challenge a decision by the magistrates declining jurisdiction,[35] where there is otherwise a right of appeal to the High Court or where the decision is said by an enactment to be "final."[36] The application must be made within 21 days, and any right to appeal to the Crown Court is lost when this is done.[37] The justices may refuse to state a case if they are of opinion that the application is "frivolous,"[38] but may not do so where the application is made by or under the direction of the Attorney-General. If they do exercise their power to refuse, the applicant may seek an order of mandamus from the High Court to compel them to state a case, and the High Court has a discretion whether to make an order.

[27] See *Arthur* v. *Stringer* (1986) 84 Cr.App.R. 361.
[28] See the Children and Young Persons Act 1969, ss.2(12), 3(8), 16(8), 21(4), as amended. To be replaced by an appeal to the High Court under the Children Act 1989, s.94.
[29] See, *e.g.* Licensing Act 1964, ss.21, 50, 81B, 146, 154.
[30] *e.g.* defendant *or prosecutor* in a criminal case: *R.* v. *Newport (Salop) JJ. ex p. Wright* [1929] 2 K.B. 416.
[31] This covers a person who is not a party but whose legal rights are affected by the decision: *Drapers Company* v. *Hodder* (1892) 57 J.P. 200, *e.g.* the owner of stolen goods who seeks a restitution order.
[32] Magistrates' Courts Act 1980, s.111(1).
[33] *Atkinson* v. *United States Government* [1971] A.C. 197; *Cragg* v. *Lewes District Council* [1986] Crim.L.R. 800.
[34] *Streames* v. *Copping* [1985] Q.B. 920 (to challenge a disputed ruling that the magistrates had jurisdiction). *Cf. Loade* v. *D.P.P.* [1990] 1 Q.B. 1052 (Divisional Court has no jurisdiction in a criminal case to entertain an appeal by case stated at an interlocutory stage of an appeal to the Crown Court); there is such a jurisdiction in civil cases, but justices should exercise their power only in exceptional circumstances (*R.* v. *Chesterfield JJ.*, *ex p. Kovacs* (1990) 154 J.P. 1023.
[35] *Pratt* v. *A. A. Sites Ltd.* [1938] 2 K.B. 459: the remedy here is to apply for judicial review: see *Streames* v. *Copping*, *supra*, at p. 928 (May L.J.).
[36] 1980 Act, s.111(1).
[37] *Ibid.*, s.111(4). See *P. & M. Supplies (Essex) Ltd.* v. *Hackney London Borough Council* (1990) 154 J.P. 814. An appeal by case stated against conviction will not debar an appeal to the Crown Court against sentence, and vice versa: an appeal by case stated on both matters debars the appeal to Crown Court completely: *R.* v. *Winchester Crown Court, ex p. Lewington* [1982] 1 W.L.R. 1277.
[38] This term includes cases where the argument on the point of law cannot succeed, *e.g.* where the law has been authoritatively stated in a superior court.

The procedure for stating a case is regulated by the Magistrates' Courts Rules 1981.[39] The application is made to the clerk to the justices. Unless the application is refused, a draft case must be sent to the parties, and it may be amended by the justices in the light of any representations received. The case must state the facts found and the questions of law or jurisdiction on which guidance is sought. It must specify any finding of fact which is claimed to be unsupported by evidence, but it may not otherwise contain a statement of evidence. In practice it is normally prepared by the clerk.

In criminal cases the appeal is heard by a Divisional Court of the Queen's Bench Division; otherwise, it is normally heard by a single judge. Where the appeal relates to care proceedings, or the enforcement of a maintenance order, the appeal lies to the Family Division.[40] The appellant must lodge the case in the Crown Office or the Principal Registry of the Family Division within 10 days of receiving it, and must serve a copy on the respondent within four days of so lodging it. The High Court may return the case for amendment.[41]

On an appeal, the High Court may reverse, affirm or amend the decision or remit it to the justices for their reconsideration in the light of the court's opinion, or make such other order as the court thinks fit.[42] Apart from the obvious power to correct errors of law, such as the misinterpretation of a statute, the court will treat any decision unsupported by the evidence, or otherwise one which no reasonable magistrates could reach, as erroneous in law.[43] The court may take the view that in the light of its ruling on the law in a criminal case the defendant is clearly guilty or clearly innocent, in which event it will direct the magistrates to convict or acquit as the case may be. Otherwise the matter will be left to the magistrates. However, the Divisional Court may only order the magistrates' court to make an appropriate order or otherwise to complete unfinished proceedings: it may not order a retrial.[44]

(c) Appeals from magistrates' courts to the High Court in family cases

In certain family matters an appeal lies to the Family Division of the High Court. These include the making or refusal of orders under the Domestic Proceedings and Magistrates' Courts Act 1978,[45] adoption orders and variations of maintenance orders. The appeal can raise matters of fact or law and is not by case stated. A notice of appeal must be served and the appeal entered within six weeks of the decision challenged.[46] The court may receive further evidence, draw its own inferences of fact and may make any order

---

[39] S.I. 1981 No. 552, as amended, rr. 76–81.
[40] R.S.C., Ord. 56, rr. 4A, 5. An appeal is normally heard by a single judge unless the court directs that it should be heard by a Divisional Court.
[41] Summary Jurisdiction Act 1857, s.7.
[42] *Ibid.*, s.6, as amended.
[43] *Bracegirdle* v. *Oxley* [1947] 1 K.B. 349. This is significantly narrower than the appeal on the merits to the Crown Court: see section (a) above.
[44] *Rigby* v. *Woodward* [1957] 1 W.L.R. 250; *Maydew* v. *Flint* (1984) 80 Cr.App.R. 49.
[45] Other than interim maintenance orders, against which no appeal lies. Appeals as to the *enforcement* of maintenance orders lie by case stated: see section (b), above. The position is the same in respect of decisions to remit, or refuse to remit, maintenance arrears: *Berry* v. *Berry* [1987] Fam. 1.
[46] R.S.C., Ord. 55, r. 4(2), applied by Ord. 90, r. 16(2), and Ord. 109.

that the magistrates might have made and any other order that the case might require, or may remit the matter with its opinion for rehearing by the magistrates.[47] When in force, appeals will also lie in respect of orders made under the Children Act 1989.[47a]

(d) Appeals from the Crown Court to the High Court

Where there has been an appeal from a magistrates' court to the Crown Court, any party to the proceedings[48] may appeal by case stated on a point of law or jurisdiction to the High Court.[49] The procedure is similar to that for such appeals from the magistrates' court direct to the High Court.[50] The same right of appeal is available in respect of any other decision of the Crown Court[51] except one relating to trial on indictment and in certain licensing matters.[52]

(e) Appeals from the High Court to the House of Lords

In civil cases which have reached the High Court on appeal, further appeals lie on the same bases as in other civil matters determined by the High Court.[53] Until 1960 there was, however, no further right of appeal in a criminal case, and the Divisional Court of the Queen's Bench Division was the final authority on many matters concerning summary offences.[54] Under the Administration of Justice Act 1960[55] either the prosecutor or the defendant may appeal to the House of Lords on a point of law of public general importance. Leave must be obtained from either the Divisional Court or the House of Lords: the Divisional Court must certify that a point of law of general public importance is involved,[56] and it must appear either to that court or to the House of Lords[57] that the point ought to be considered by the House. On the appeal, the House may exercise any of the powers of the Divisional Court or may remit the case to it.

---

[47] R.S.C., Ord. 55, r. 7.

[47a] See s.94.

[48] *i.e.* in a criminal case, either prosecutor or defendant.

[49] Supreme Court Act 1981, s.28.

[50] Crown Court Rules 1982, (S.I. 1982 No. 1109), r. 26, and *cf.* above pp. 827–828.

[51] *e.g.* matters such as firearms licensing where an appeal lies direct to the Crown Court: see P. J. Clarke and J. W. Ellis, *The Law Relating to Firearms* (1981), pp. 104–111; *Kavanagh* v. *Chief Constable of Devon and Cornwall* [1974] Q.B. 624.

[52] Supreme Court Act 1981, s.28(2) *cf.* s.29(3), below p. 878. As to appeals in relation to trials on indictment, see below, pp. 830–845, and on the relationship between appeals by case stated and applications for judicial review, see below, p. 878.

[53] See below, pp. 849–866.

[54] For example, there was no right to appeal against the unsatisfactory decisions in *Thomas* v. *Sawkins* [1935] 2 K.B. 249 and *Duncan* v. *Jones* [1936] K.B. 218: see S. H. Bailey, D. J. Harris and B. L. Jones, *Civil Liberties: Cases and Materials* (2nd ed., 1985), pp. 177–180, 184–188.

[55] ss.1–9.

[56] There is no right to appeal against the refusal of a certificate: *Gelberg* v. *Miller* [1961] 1 All E.R. 618n, H.L.

[57] The application for leave is made first to the Divisional Court and only if that court refuses to the House of Lords.

2. APPEALS FOLLOWING TRIAL ON INDICTMENT

(a) Appeals from the Crown Court to the Court of Appeal (Criminal Division)

An acquittal by a jury in a criminal case is regarded as sacrosanct: the prosecutor has no right of appeal however perverse the verdict of the jury.[58] However, persons convicted[59] of an offence on indictment may appeal to the Court of Appeal (Criminal Division).[60]

(i) Appeals against conviction

(1) Grounds and procedure. The person convicted may appeal as of right on any ground which involves a question of law alone.[61] Where a ground is one of fact alone or of mixed law and fact he or she may only appeal if either (a) a certificate from the trial judge that the case is fit for appeal[62] or (b) leave of the Court of Appeal (Criminal Division) is obtained. In addition, the Court of Appeal may grant leave "on any other ground which appears . . . to be a sufficient ground of appeal."[63]

Where a point of law alone is involved the appellant or his or her legal advisers must serve a notice of appeal on the appropriate officer of the Crown Court, at the centre where the proceedings took place, within 28 days of the conviction.[64] The time limit may be extended by the court.[65] The notice must contain the grounds of appeal.[66]

In other cases, the appellant must either serve the trial judge's certificate on the appropriate officer of the Crown Court with the notice of appeal, or serve notice of application for leave to appeal. The notice must be served within 28 days of conviction and the grounds of the appeal or application stated. The grounds of an appeal or application may be varied or amplified

---

[58] The Attorney-General may refer cases where there has been an acquittal to the Court of Appeal (Criminal Division), but not so as to affect the defendant: see below, pp. 843–844.

[59] This includes a person who pleaded guilty; R. v. Lee (Bruce) [1984] 1 W.L.R. 578; R. v. Swain [1986] Crim.L.R. 480; and where a verdict has been returned, but the judge has postponed sentence: R. v. Drew [1985] 1 W.L.R. 914.

[60] See above, pp. 88–89; Criminal Appeal Act 1968; Criminal Appeal Rules 1968 (S.I. 1968 No. 1262, as amended) (hereafter "C.A.R."); Guide to Proceedings in the Court of Appeal Criminal Division [1983] Crim.L.R. 415; (1983) 77 Cr.App.R. 138; P, O'Connor, [1990] Crim.L.R. 615.

[61] 1968 Act, s.1(2)(a). See A. W. Barsby, [1982] Crim.L.R. 642.

[62] Such a certificate may also be granted where the appeal is on a question of law alone (and where, accordingly, leave is not required): this enables the Crown Court to grant bail: Supreme Court Act 1981, s.1B, inserted by the Criminal Justice Act 1982, s.29(1). On bail, see below, n. 68.

[63] Ibid., s.1(2)(b).

[64] Ibid. s.18(1); C.A.R. 1968, r. 2(1). The Crown Court forwards the notice to the Criminal Appeal Office with the trial documents and any others which may be required: Practice Direction (Crime: Notices of Appeal) [1988] 1 W.L.R. 34. Prior to the amendment of r. 2 in 1987 (by S.I. 1987 No. 1977), notices were served directly on the Registrar of Criminal Appeals at the Criminal Appeal Office; the purpose of the change was to reduce delays: see ibid.; Practice Note, The Times, March 15, 1988.

[65] 1968 Act, s.18(2). Leave may be granted some years later. See e.g. R. v. Foster [1985] Q.B. 115, where F. was convicted of rape in 1977, following a plea of guilty. Another man confessed to and was convicted of the offence in 1981. F. was granted a free pardon in 1982 (see below, p. 888), and leave to appeal in 1984, when the conviction was quashed.

[66] C.A.R. 1968, r. 2(2)(a).

within such time as the court may allow.[67] The appellant may apply for bail,[68] and be present at the hearing.[69]

If it appears to the registrar that the notice of appeal or of application for leave to appeal does not show any substantial ground he or she may refer the appeal or application to the court for summary determination, and the court, if it considers the appeal to be frivolous[70] or vexatious may dismiss the appeal summarily.[71]

The defendant at the trial should be seen by his or her solicitor and counsel in the event of conviction or sentence and advised on whether there appear to be reasonable grounds for an appeal.[72] The defendant may only pursue an appeal under sections 1 and 2 of the 1968 Act once, even where he or she seeks to adduce fresh evidence on the second occasion.[73]

Applications for leave to appeal are normally dealt with by a single judge who examines the papers and may grant leave, refuse it, or refer the case to the court. If leave is refused an application may be renewed to the court within 14 days.[74] The court will hold a hearing, which may be combined with the hearing of the appeal on the merits. Legal aid may be granted for further advice and assistance and for representation before the single judge or the court.[75] The single judge and the court have power, when refusing an application for leave to appeal, to direct that part of the time during which a person has been in custody after lodging his application should not count

---

[67] C.A.R. 1968 r. 2(2)(c). This may be after the 28-day period.

[68] Bail may be granted by the Crown Court (Supreme Court Act 1981, s.81(1)(f) and (1A) to (1G), inserted by the Criminal Justice Act 1982, s.29(1)) or the Court of Appeal (Criminal Division) (Criminal Appeal Act 1968, s.19, as substituted by the 1982 Act, s.29(2)(b)). See *Practice Direction (Crown Court: Bail Pending Appeal)* [1983] 1 W.L.R. 1292.

[69] *Ibid.*, s.22. He or she is entitled to be present except in four cases where the leave of the court is necessary: (1) the appeal is on a point of law alone; (2) for an application for leave to appeal; (3) for an ancillary application; (4) where he or she is in custody after a verdict of not guilty by reason of insanity or of a finding of disability.

[70] *e.g.* the ground of appeal could not possibly succeed on argument: *R.* v. *Taylor* [1979] Crim.L.R. 649.

[71] Criminal Appeal Act 1968, s.20, as substituted by the Criminal Justice Act 1988, s.157. The original form of s.20 made this procedure available only in respect of appeals involving a question of law alone.

[72] *Guide to proceedings in the Court of Appeal Criminal Division* (1983) 77 Cr.App.R. 138. See also M. Zander, [1972] Crim.L.R. 132, [1975] Crim.L.R. 364 and *Practice Note* [1974] 2 All E.R. 805. This work should be covered by any trial legal aid order: see the Legal Aid Act 1988, s.2(4), which provides that a grant of representation in a criminal case includes "advice and assistance as to any appeal."

[73] *R.* v. *Pinfold* [1988] Q.B. 462: there are two apparent exceptions: where the decision on the original appeal is a nullity and where, owing to some defect in procedure, the appellant on the first appeal being dismissed suffered an injustice, (*e.g.* the appellant has not been notified of the hearing of the appeal, or counsel has been unable to attend (*ibid.*)). A case may also be referred back to the Court of Appeal by the Home Secretary, see below, pp. 841–843.

[74] An extension to the initial 28-day period will readily be granted if reasonable grounds are shown; however, the time limit of 14 days for a renewal application will be enforced strictly and only extended in exceptional circumstances: *R.* v. *Towers* (1984) 30 Cr.App.R. 231.

[75] Legal Aid Act 1988, ss.19(1)(c)(2), 20(1)(2). Where an application is made before the giving of notice of appeal or an application for leave to appeal, the grant of legal aid may be limited to advice on whether there appears to be reasonable grounds of appeal, and assistance in the preparation of the notice or application: *ibid.*, s.21(8). Legal aid may be granted by the Court of Appeal, a single judge, or the registrar, who may specify the stage at which it shall commence: see the Legal Aid in Criminal and Care Proceedings (General) Regulations 1989 (S.I. 1989 No. 344), reg. 22. An order granted by the court may be limited to representation by counsel only: *ibid.*, reg. 44(4).

towards sentence.[76] In both 1970 and 1980 the then Lord Chief Justice issued a reminder of the existence of this power in view of the delay caused to the hearing of meritorious appeals by the lodging of huge numbers of hopeless applications.[77] In the two years after 1970 the number of applications for leave to appeal was cut by a half, although the problem subsequently recurred. In the 1980 Direction, it was stated a direction for loss of time "will normally be made unless the grounds are not only settled and signed by counsel, but also supported by the written opinion of counsel." Counsel should only so act where he or she considers that the proposed appeal is properly arguable. Moreover, a direction will also normally be made where an application is renewed to the court after the single judge has refused it as wholly devoid of merit: here, whether or not the grounds have been settled and signed by counsel.[78]

The administrative tasks in relation to appeals are performed by the Criminal Appeal Office, headed by the Registrar of Criminal Appeals. The documents in the case, including, if appropriate, a transcript, are assembled by the office.[79] If leave is granted, a lawyer on the staff of the office then prepares a descriptive "summary" of the facts and grounds of appeal to assist the full court.

(2) *Evidence.*[80] The court, under section 23(1) and (3) of the Criminal Appeal Act 1968, *may* "if they think it necessary or expedient in the interests of justice": (a) order the production of any document, exhibit or other thing connected with the proceedings; (b) order the examination of any witness who would have been a compellable witness at the trial, whether or not he or she was called; and (c) hear evidence from a non-compellable witness.[81]

Without prejudice to these powers, the court by virtue of section 23(2) of the 1968 Act, *must* receive any evidence if:

"(a) it appears to them that the evidence is likely to be credible[82] and would have been admissible in the proceedings from which the appeal lies on an issue which is the subject of the appeal[83]; and

---

[76] Criminal Appeal Act 1968, s.29(1), as amended by the Criminal Justice Act 1988, Sched. 15, para. 27. Thus a direction may not be made if leave is granted, or where there is a certificate under ss.1 or 11(1A) of the 1968 Act, or s.81(1B) of the Supreme Court Act 1981.

[77] Lord Parker C.J.: (1970) 54 Cr.App.R. 280; Lord Widgery C.J.: (1980) 70 Cr.App.R. 186.

[78] R. v. *Gayle, The Times*, May 28, 1986.

[79] Criminal Appeal Act 1968, s.32; C.A.R., rr. 18–20. The Registrar may determine that only a "short transcript" is necessary, covering charges, pleas, summing-up and evidence after verdict. The appellant here may obtain a full transcript at his or her own expense. In practice, a transcript of evidence is rarely needed: R. v. *Campbell, The Times*, July 21, 1981.

[80] See R. Pattenden, *Judicial Discretion and Criminal Litigation* (2nd ed., 1990), pp. 355–358.

[81] The court may examine such material as it thinks fit in deciding whether to order production of documents or the attendance of witnesses at the hearing of the appeal: it is not confined to material relating to the trial and the documents placed before the court by the parties: R. v. *Callaghan* [1988] 1 W.L.R. 1, a pre-appeal review in the Birmingham pub bombers' case: the appellants sought to prevent the judges reading documents relating to other litigation and police inquiries arising out of the case, unless raised by the parties; the court held that its *jurisdiction* was not so confined, but acceded to the appellants' request in the exercise of its discretion.

[82] This has been interpreted to mean "evidence well capable of belief": *per* Edmund Davies L.J. in R. v. *Stafford and Luvaglio* (1968) 53 Cr.App.R. 1, 3.

[83] *i.e.* the issue must have been raised first at the trial: R. v. *Melville* [1976] 1 W.L.R. 181.

(b) they are satisfied that it was not adduced at the trial but there is a reasonable explanation of the failure to adduce it."[84]

The court can only refuse to receive such evidence if it is satisfied that it would not afford any ground for allowing the appeal. This *duty* to receive evidence in the circumstances stated was first introduced by the Criminal Appeal Act 1966: the conditions stated are similar to those on which the *discretion* to receive fresh evidence, which dates back to the Criminal Appeal Act 1907, was exercised in pre-1966 cases.[85] The discretion under section 23(1) must now logically be available in a wider range of circumstances than those specified in section 23(2). However in *Stafford and Luvaglio* Edmund Davies L.J. stated that notwithstanding this development:

"Public mischief would ensue and legal process could become indefinitely prolonged were it the case that evidence produced at any time will generally be admitted by this Court when verdicts are being reviewed. There must be some curbs, the section specifies them. . . ."[86]

Subsequently, the Court of Appeal (Criminal Division) emphasised in *R. v. Lattimore and others*[87] that this did not mean that the conditions limiting the duty of section 23(2) were to be read as limiting the discretion under section 23(1).[88] This case arose out of the killing of Maxwell Confait, which was shortly followed by a fire at the house where he lived. Two youths were convicted of killing him (one for murder, one manslaughter) and those two and another were convicted of arson, solely on the basis of their own confessions. Three years later the Home Secretary referred the cases to the Court of Appeal (Criminal Division).[89] The court, acting under section 23(1), received the evidence of three expert witnesses who had given evidence at the trial (two fire experts and a pathologist) and two further medical witnesses who gave evidence as to the time of death. However, they refused to admit evidence of persons who sought to throw light on the killer's identity, as they doubted its credibility and admissibility and in any event did not need to rely upon it. In addition, the Crown was permitted to call a fire expert and a forensic pathologist who had given evidence at the trial. The court held that this evidence showed that the lapse of time between the killing and the fire was much greater than had originally been thought and it threw sufficient doubt on the confessions for the homicide and arson convictions to be quashed. Scarman L.J. stated that the medical evidence was presented to the Court of Appeal "in a much sharper focus than it was at the

---

[84] *Ibid.*, s.23(2). Under (b) the test is whether evidence could with "reasonable diligence" have been obtained for use at the trial: *R. v. Beresford* (1971) 56 Cr.App.R. 143: B had failed to mention his presence at the "Poco a Poco Club" until he sought leave to introduce an alibi witness on the appeal. The court held that he had not used reasonable diligence and in any event disbelieved the witness.

[85] *R. v. Parks* [1961] 1 W.L.R. 1484. The pre–1964 position was narrower than s.23(2) in that evidence available at the date of trial but not introduced was not normally admitted on an appeal, even where there was a reasonable explanation. There was some relaxation between 1964 and 1966: see M. Knight, *Criminal Appeals* (1970), pp. 93–96, 115–118.

[86] (1968) 53 Cr.App.R. 1, 3. The court declined to hear evidence from any additional witnesses.

[87] (1975) 62 Cr.App.R. 53.

[88] *Ibid.*, p. 56.

[89] See below, pp. 841–843.

trial."[90] In other cases fresh evidence has been admitted where another person confesses to the crime for which the appellant was convicted,[91] where prosecution witnesses subsequently make statements inconsistent with their testimony[92] and where it is claimed that there was an irregularity at the trial.[93] Exceptionally, fresh evidence may be admitted following an unequivocal plea of guilty.[94]

(3) *Disposition*. There are a number of ways in which the Court of Appeal may dispose of an appeal. The key section is section 2 of the Criminal Appeal Act 1968:

"2(1) Except as provided by this Act, the Court of Appeal shall allow an appeal against conviction if they think—
> (*a*) that the verdict of the jury should be set aside on the ground that under the circumstances of the case it is unsafe or unsatisfactory; or
> (*b*) that the judgment of the court of trial should be set aside on the ground of a wrong decision of any question of law; or
> (*c*) that there was a material irregularity in the course of the trial,
and in any other case shall dismiss the appeal:

Provided that the Court may, notwithstanding that they are of the opinion that the point raised in the appeal might be decided in favour of the appellant, dismiss the appeal if they consider that no miscarriage of justice has actually occurred.

(2) In the case of an appeal against conviction the Court shall, if they allow the appeal, quash the conviction."

These grounds for intervention are somewhat wider than those that were open to the Court of Criminal Appeal under the Criminal Appeal Act 1907.[95]

Verdicts have been set aside as unsafe and unsatisfactory where, for example, there has been a misdirection as to the ingredients of the offence charged or the burden of proof, the judge has improperly withdrawn an issue from the jury or failed to put a line of defence to them, or evidence was wrongfully admitted or excluded. Decisions on some of these points may also amount to a wrong decision on a point of law under section 2(1)(*b*). The "material irregularity" ground in section 2(1)(*c*) was designed to cover

---

[90] *Ibid.* p. 60. The events were subsequently the subject of an Inquiry by Sir Henry Fisher: 1977–78 H.C. 90, which concluded that "on a balance of probabilities" all three were involved in the arson and that two (excluding one of the two originally convicted for it) were involved in the killing. The report made a number of recommendations concerning the interrogation process and other aspects of the case. See further above, pp. 660–661.

[91] *R.* v. *Ditch* (1969) 53 Cr.App.R. 627.

[92] *R.* v. *Conway* (1979) 70 Cr.App.R. 4.

[93] *R.* v. *Leggett and others* (1969) 53 Cr.App. 51: interruptions by the Chairman of Quarter Sessions (*e.g.* when it appeared that an address by counsel to the jury would be protracted "he observed in a loud voice, 'Oh, God,' and then laid his head across his arm and made groaning noises": p. 56). Appeal dismissed.

[94] *R.* v. *Lee (Bruce)* [1984] 1 W.L.R. 578; *R.* v. *Foster* [1985] Q.B. 115 (F. had received a free pardon for offences of which another had now been convicted); *R.* v. *Swain* [1986] Crim.L.R. 480 (evidence that there was a risk that D's mind was affected by L.S.D. when he changed his plea to guilty).

[95] The court could allow an appeal if they thought that the verdict was unreasonable, or could not be supported by the evidence or otherwise there was an error of law or a miscarriage of justice. The wider grounds were first enacted in the Criminal Appeal Act 1966.

procedural irregularities,[96] although other defects are sometimes so described. Under this head the Court of Appeal may interfere with an exercise of discretion[97] by the judge where he or she has "erred in principle or there is no material on which he could properly have arrived at his decision,"[98] or the court thinks that the judge's ruling may have resulted in injustice to the defendant.[98a]

The approach to section 2(1)(a) was described as follows by Widgery L.J. in *R. v. Cooper*[99]:

"[I]n cases of this kind the court must in the end ask itself a subjective question, whether we are content to let the matter stand as it is, or whether there is not some lurking doubt in our minds which makes us wonder whether an injustice has been done. This is a reaction which may not be based strictly on the evidence as such; it is a reaction which can be produced by the general feel of the case as the court experiences it."

Indeed, a conviction may be quashed as unsafe and unsatisfactory where the specific grounds of appeal are rejected.[1]

Where fresh evidence is admitted, the question for the court is still whether, in the light of the evidence overall, the verdict is unsafe and unsatisfactory.[2] This point was made by the House of Lords in *Stafford* v. *D.P.P.*[3] After referring to the concept of the "lurking doubt" mentioned in *R. v. Cooper*[4] Viscount Dilhorne continued, "That this is the effect of section 2(1)(a) is not to be doubted,"[5] although he also emphasised that the Court of Appeal should not place any fetter or restriction on its power under section 2. The court was not bound to ask in a case where new evidence was admitted whether that evidence "might . . . have led to the jury returning a verdict of not guilty?": if *it* was satisfied that there was no reasonable doubt about the guilt of the accused the conviction should not be quashed even though the jury might have come to a different view.

This approach to "fresh evidence" cases has been roundly criticised by Lord Devlin[6] on the basis that it is wrong in principle for judges rather than juries to determine whether the appellant is guilty: the proper course of

[96] *Per* Lord Salmon in *D.P.P.* v. *Shannon* [1975] A.C. 717, 773.
[97] *e.g.* to sever counts in an indictment, to permit cross-examination of a defendant on his or her previous convictions or to discharge a jury.
[98] Devlin J. in *R.* v. *Cook* (1959) 43 Cr.App.R. 138, 147.
[98a] *R.* v. *Cullen* (1990) 140 N.L.J. 629: the court held that the trial judge should have ordered a retrial of the three charged with conspiracy to murder Mr. Tom King following public statements made by Mr. King and Lord Denning concerning the proposal to change the law on the right to silence.
[99] [1969] 1 Q.B. 267, 271. The case was one of alleged mistaken identification and another man of similar appearance had admitted to a witness that he had committed the crime: even though all the evidence had been before the jury, the conviction was quashed. For other examples of "lurking doubts" see *R.* v. *Pattinson* (1973) 58 Cr.App.R. 417; *R.* v. *Spencer* [1987] A.C. 128.
[1] *R.* v. *Bracewell* (1978) 68 Cr.App.R. 44.
[2] The fresh evidence will not reveal an error of law or constitute a "material irregularity" under s.2(1)(b) and (c) of the Criminal Appeal Act 1968.
[3] [1974] A.C. 878. Followed in *R.* v. *Callaghan* (1988) 88 Cr.App.R. 40 (the first reference to the Court of Appeal in the Birmingham pub bombing case); *R.* v. *Byrne* (1988) 88 Cr.App.R. 33.
[4] Above.
[5] *Ibid.*, p. 892.
[6] *The Judge* (1979), pp. 133–135, 148–176.

action where the fresh evidence *could* have made a difference to the verdict[7] would be for the court to order a new trial.[8] The first verdict should be regarded as unsatisfactory simply on the ground that it was not given upon the whole of the evidence.[9] Given that the appeal in *Stafford* v. *D.P.P.* was dismissed, the appellants were thereafter imprisoned on the basis of the verdict of the judges.

Given that the matter is to be tested by reference to the views of the appeal court judges rather than the views of a hypothetical jury, a further question arises whether that is so in all fresh evidence cases. In particular, should the judges determine issues as to whether the oral testimony of a new or re-examined witness is credible?[10] In a number of cases the court has ordered a new trial,[11] but in *R.* v. *Cooper and McMahon*[12] the court determined such a question itself. The case is one of the most publicised examples of a miscarriage of justice, and came before the Court of Appeal on no less than five occasions. Three men, Cooper, McMahon and Murphy, were convicted of the murder of a Luton subpostmaster during an unsuccessful robbery. They were identified by a professional criminal, Mathews, who admitted taking part in the robbery but denied involvement in the murder. He turned Queen's evidence and the men were convicted solely on his testimony. They appealed without success to the Court of Appeal. Mathews subsequently received part of the reward offered by the Post Office. In 1973 Murphy's conviction was quashed by the Court of Appeal following the discovery of a fresh alibi witness. This naturally threw doubt on Mathews' identification of Cooper and McMahon and the Home Secretary referred the case to the Court of Appeal on three further occasions. On the first of these in 1975, the court refused to permit Mathews to be recalled for further cross-examination, indicated that the jury "could" have acquitted Murphy and convicted the others, and dismissed the appeal. The court refused leave to appeal to the House of Lords, reaffirming that in the light of *Stafford* v. *D.P.P.*[13] it was "not a necessary function of this Court, when considering fresh evidence, to evaluate the effect which it would have on the jury at the trial."[14] On the second, in 1976, Mathews was recalled and cross-examined: the judges concluded from their observations that he was telling the truth on the "vital part of his story" although other parts were discredited (a "cock and bull story"). This self-evidently surprising result does not inspire confidence in trial (or at least partial trial) by judges alone. The final reference by the Home Secretary (of the case of McMahon alone) was unsuccessful on the ground that the fresh alibi evidence sought to be tendered was not likely to be credible, and even if believed would be insufficient to afford a ground for allowing the appeal.[15] In 1980, following the publication of a book on the case edited by Ludovic Kennedy (*Wicked Beyond Belief*), the Home Secre-

---

[7] This is in effect the same test as that for applying the proviso: see below, p. 837.

[8] See below, p. 837. Indeed, until 1989 the court could *only* order a new trial in fresh evidence cases.

[9] See counsel's argument in *Stafford* v. *D.P.P.* [1974] A.C. 878, 884C.

[10] The test for admissibility is merely whether the fresh evidence is *capable* of belief: see above, p. 832.

[11] See Devlin (1979), pp. 165–166.

[12] See Devlin (1979), pp. 166–173; L. Kennedy (ed.), *Wicked Beyond Belief* (1980).

[13] [1974] A.C. 878.

[14] (1975) 61 Cr.App.R. 215.

[15] *R.* v. *McMahon* (1978) 68 Cr.App.R. 18: criticised in Kennedy (1980), pp. 132–135.

tary, William Whitelaw, ordered the release of Cooper and McMahon[16]: the case was "wholly exceptional" and there was a "widely felt sense of unease about it" which he shared. He was not to be taken as criticising his predecessors, who had "acted with scrupulous regard to the constitutional conventions in referring each piece of alleged new evidence to the Court of Appeal and in acting in accordance with the court's judgment. Any general departure from that rule would clearly be disastrous." His action was not to be taken as a precedent.

It is commonly the case that an appeal is dismissed under the proviso at the end of section 2(1). The test for applying the proviso was stated as follows by Viscount Simon L.C. in *Stirland* v. *D.P.P.*[17]:

> "When the transcript is examined, it is evident that no reasonable jury, after a proper summing-up, could have failed to convict the appellant on the rest of the evidence to which no objection could be taken. There was, therefore, no miscarriage of justice. . . . [The proviso] assumes a situation where a reasonable jury, after being properly directed, would, on the evidence properly admissible, without doubt convict."

Other possibilities that may be open to the Court of Appeal are the substitution of a conviction for an alternative offence, where the jury would have found the defendant guilty of that offence and it appears to the court that the jury must have been satisfied of facts which proved him or her guilty of it,[18] and the substitution of a finding of insanity or of unfitness to plead.[19]

(4) *New Trials.* Where the Court of Appeal allows an appeal against conviction, it may order that the appellant be retried where it appears that this is required by the interests of justice.[20] The appellant may only be retried for the offence in respect of which the appeal was allowed, an offence of which he or she could have been convicted at the original trial on an indictment for that offence or an offence charged in an alternative count of the indictment at the trial on which the jury were discharged from giving a verdict.[21]

Prior to the amendment made by section 43 of the Criminal Justice Act 1988, the Court of Appeal could only order a retrial where fresh evidence was received under section 23 of the Criminal Appeal Act 1968.[22] This limitation was cogently criticised, and the case for its removal powerful.[23] In particular, in a number of cases where (1) the appellant appeared to have a good argument in law but little or none on the merits, but (2) the case was not suitable for an application of the proviso,[24] the Court of Appeal or House of Lords succumbed to the temptation to "bend" the law to enable

---

[16] 988 H.C.Deb., July 18, 1980, written answers, cols. 719–720.

[17] (1944) 30 Cr.App.R. 40, 46–47. See Pattenden (1990), pp. 361–365.

[18] Criminal Appeal Act 1968, s.3. The sentence may not be higher than that originally passed.

[19] *Ibid.*, s.6, Sched. 1.

[20] 1968 Act, s.7(1), as amended by the Criminal Justice Act 1988, s.43(2). See Pattenden (1990), pp. 366–370. For the procedure on retrial see s.8 and Sched. 1. Any sentence passed after a retrial may not be longer than the original one.

[21] *Ibid.* s.7(2). For the analogous power to award a *venire de novo*, see below, p. 844. This can only be done where the original trial is a nullity.

[22] See above, pp. 832–833.

[23] See the previous edition of this book at pp. 712–714.

[24] See above.

the appeal to be dismissed. Justice appeared to be done in the case itself but at the expense of the development of the law in a consistent, coherent and principled way.[25] Unfortunately, the change can still be criticised as not going far enough,[26] in that the power does not extend to ordering a retrial for an offence which arises out of the same facts, but which is different from those charged in the original indictment. Such a power might well be necessary where there is a flaw in the indictment which is not so serious as to render the trial a nullity (in which case a *venire de novo* may be ordered). This could arise where the defendant is convicted of the wrong or a non-existent offence,[27] and the indictment contains no suitable alternative count. The omission was drawn to the government's attention, but the position was defended on the basis that

"It is one thing to legislate for the differing interpretations of the law by higher and lower courts, but quite another to build into the law the assumption that the prosecution will occasionally blunder. And in addition there might be difficulties in principle in conferring on the Court of Appeal what might appear to be prosecutorial function if it was to have a role in specifying the charges on which a retrial could be based."[28]

A wider retrial power exists in Scotland.[29]

Where a retrial is ordered, arrangements must normally take place within two months. Thereafter, if the prosecution wishes to proceed, it must apply to the Court of Appeal for leave; conversely, the defendant may apply to the Court of Appeal to set aside the retrial order and enter a verdict of acquittal of the offence for which he or she was ordered to be retried. On either application, the court may grant leave, but may only do so if it is satisfied that the prosecution has acted with due expedition, and that there is a good and sufficient cause for a retrial in spite of the lapse of time since the retrial order was made.

(ii) *Appeals against sentence and reviews of sentencing*

A person who has been convicted of an offence on indictment may appeal to the Court of Appeal (Criminal Division) against any sentence[30] passed on him or her for the offence, except where the sentence is fixed by law.[31] Leave

[25] J. R. Spencer, "Criminal law and criminal appeals" [1982] Crim.L.R. 260.
[26] J. R. Spencer, "Retrials and tribulations" (1988) 138 N.L.J. 315.
[27] *e.g.* "anal rape:" *R.* v. *Gaston* (1981) 73 Cr.App.R. 164.
[28] Home Office letter in response to Spencer: (1988) 138 N.L.J. 641.
[29] Criminal Procedure (Scotland) Act 1975, s.452B.
[30] This includes any order made by the court when dealing with an offender including a hospital order under the Mental Health Act 1983, a recommendation for deportation, a probation order or an absolute or conditional discharge: Criminal Appeal Act 1968, s.50, amended by the Criminal Justice Act 1982, s.66(1). Apart from the orders expressly mentioned in s.50, the section covers such matters as driving disqualifications, costs orders, compensation orders: see *R.* v. *Hayden* [1975] 1 W.L.R. 852. It also includes binding-over orders contingent on a conviction: *R.* v. *Williams (Carl)* [1982] 1 W.L.R. 1398, but not a recommendation as to the minimum period that a person convicted of murder should serve (Murder (Abolition of Death Penalty) Act 1965, s.1(2)): *R.* v. *Aitken* [1966] 1 W.L.R. 1076; *R.* v. *Bowden and Begley* (1983) 77 Cr.App.R. 66; or an order to contribute toward legal aid costs: *R.* v. *Hayden* [1975] 1 W.L.R. 852; *R.* v. *Raeburn* (1981) 74 Cr.App.R. 21.
[31] Criminal Appeal Act 1968, s.9(1). He or she may also appeal against any sentence passed for a summary offence dealt with by the Crown Court under s.41 of the Criminal Justice Act 1988 (above, p. 642); 1968 Act, s.9(2), inserted by the 1988 Act, Sched. 15, para. 21.

to appeal must be obtained from the Court of Appeal, or the judge who passed the sentence must certify that the case is fit for appeal,[32] and the procedure is essentially the same as in appeals against conviction. The court, if it considers that the appellant should be sentenced differently, may quash any sentence or order which is the subject of the appeal and substitute any other sentence or order that it thinks appropriate, provided that it would have been within the jurisdiction of the court below. The appellant may not, however, be dealt with more severely than by the court below,[33] except that the court may bring a suspended sentence into effect.[34]

The court will interfere with an exercise of discretion as to sentence where the sentence is not justified by law, where matters are improperly taken into account or improperly ignored, where fresh matters are to be taken into account, or where the sentence is manifestly excessive or wrong in principle. One of the accepted functions of the Court of Appeal is that of laying down guidelines for sentencing.[35]

The court has the same powers to deal with sentences imposed in cases where a person convicted after summary trial is committed to the Crown Court for sentence,[36] or where a person previously made the subject of a probation order, a community service order, conditional discharge, attendance centre order or suspended sentence is further dealt with by the Crown Court for the offence.[37] However, an appeal in such a case only lies if the sentence of imprisonment or youth custody is for six months or more,[38] or the sentence is outside the power of the court which convicted him or her, or the court recommends deportation, orders disqualification from driving, or activates a suspended sentence.[39]

Part 1V of the Criminal Justice Act 1988[40] introduced a new procedure whereby the Attorney-General may refer certain sentences[41] to the Court of Appeal (Criminal Division). It is available in respect of offences triable only on indictment, and triable either way offences specified by statutory instrument made by the Secretary of State.[42] The power may be exercised where

---

[32] 1968 Act, s.11 as amended by the Criminal Justice Acts 1982, s.29(2)(a), and 1988, Sched. 15, para. 23.

[33] *Ibid.* A hospital order with an indefinite restriction order was held not to be more severe than a sentence of three years' imprisonment in *R.* v. *Bennett* [1968] 1 W.L.R. 980. The court may add a recommendation for deportation.

[34] 1968 Act, s.11(4), substituted by the Criminal Justice Act 1988, Sched. 15, para. 24.

[35] See generally, *R.* v. *Newsome and Browne* [1970] 2 Q.B. 711, and above, pp. 796–797.

[36] Not in cases where the defendant *appeals* to the Crown Court.

[37] 1968 Act, s.10, as amended by the Criminal Justice Acts 1982, Sched. 14, para. 23, and 1988, Sched. 15, para. 22.

[38] Two sentences are treated as a single sentence if they are passed on the same day, or expressed by the court to be a single sentence, or are consecutive sentences.

[39] 1968 Act, s.10(3).

[40] ss.35, 36: in force from February 1, 1989. See also Sched. 3 and the Criminal Appeal (Reviews of Sentencing) Rules 1989 (S.I. 1989 No. 19). See the notes by I. Leigh in *Current Law Statutes Annotated 1988* and A. Green, (1990) 43 C.L.P.55.

[41] The term has the same meaning as in the Criminal Appeal Act 1968, except that it does not include an interim hospital order under Part III of the Mental Health Act 1983: 1988 Act, s.35(6).

[42] The Home Secretary stated that he would want to consider how the procedure operated in relation to indictable only offences before extending it: Standing Committee H, February 23, 1988, col. 219.

"it appears to the Attorney-General that the sentencing of a person in a proceeding in the Crown Court has been unduly lenient." Without prejudice to the generality of this, the condition may be satisfied if it appears that the judge erred in law as to his or her powers of sentencing.[43] The Attorney-General must apply for leave to refer a case within 28 days of the passing of the sentence. The Court of Appeal may quash any sentence passed on the defendant, and in place of it pass such sentence (including a heavier sentence) as it thinks appropriate and as the court below had power to pass when dealing with him or her. When the Court of Appeal has concluded its review, the Attorney-General or the defendant may refer a point of law to the House of Lords. The Court of Appeal must certify that it is a point of law of general public importance, and the leave of either the Court of Appeal or the House of Lords is necessary.

The Government had previously proposed a procedure analogous to the Attorney-General's reference procedure, in which the Court of Appeal would have had power to give guidance as to sentencing principles but no power to vary the sentence in question. This had been included in the Prosecution of Offences Bill 1985, but had been defeated in the House of Lords.[44] The present procedure gives the Court of Appeal power to increase or otherwise vary the sentence in question. The Home Secretary indicated that he did not expect the procedure to be employed frequently, suggesting a dozen cases a year as the probable number of such references.[45] The arguments in favour of the new procedure were marshalled by J. R. Spencer,[46] who wrote that under-sentencing: (i) blunts the deterrent effect of the criminal law; (ii) causes outrage to the victim; (iii) is demoralising to the police; (iv) causes injustice to those who were appropriately sentenced; (v) undermines public confidence in the administration of justice and the authority of the courts; (vi) may cause public danger; and (vii) hinders development of a rational sentencing policy by the Court of Appeal. The main[47] contrary argument is that the procedure offends the principle against double jeopardy, in particular the need "to prevent the state . . . abusing its power and control over the prosecution process in order to harass and oppress an individual or minority."[48] While it is "virtually unthinkable" that the government would seek to abuse its powers in this way, the risk should nevertheless be recognised.[49] One weakness in the new procedure is that no provision is made for the comprehensive review of sentences: the possible, undesirable, consequence is that it will be sentences that happen to attract adverse comment in the media that will be referred.[50]

---

[43] 1988 Act, ss.36(1)(a), (2).
[44] See J. R. Spencer, (1985) 149 J.P.N. 262.
[45] Standing Committee H, February 23, 1988, col. 219, cited by Leigh, op. cit. The decision is, however, the Attorney-General's and not the Home Secretary's.
[46] "Do we need a prosecution appeal against sentence?" [1987] Crim.L.R. 724.
[47] Others are summarised, and dismissed by Spencer, ibid., pp. 729–736.
[48] S. Seabrook, "Two-timing the double jeopardy principle" [1988] Crim.L.R. 103, 104. Spencer takes a narrower view of the double jeopardy principle: [1987] Crim.L.R. 724, 735, as meaning (1) that it is wrong to punish a person twice for the same offence; and (2) that a person must not be put in peril of conviction twice.
[49] Seabrooke, [1988] Crim.L.R, 103.
[50] Spencer, [1987] Crim.L.R. 724, 730; A. Heaton-Armstrong, (1988) 152 J.P. 278.

The Court of Appeal has stated that an application will not be granted unless there was some error of principle in the judge's sentence and that public confidence would be damaged if the sentence was not altered.[51]

(iii) *Appeals against findings of insanity*

A person in whose case a verdict of not guilty by reasons of insanity[52] is returned may appeal to the Court of Appeal on the same grounds as against a conviction.[53] The powers of the court are similar. However it may dismiss the appeal if none of the grounds for allowing it relates to the question of the appellant's insanity under the *M'Naghten* rules and, but for that insanity, the proper verdict would have been that he was guilty of some other offence.[54] In appropriate cases, the court may substitute a conviction for an offence, or a verdict of acquittal[55]: in the former case it has power to pass an appropriate sentence or make a hospital order, in the latter it may order that the appellant be admitted to hospital for assessment.[56]

Similar provisions govern appeals against a finding that a person is under a disability and is accordingly unfit to be tried[57]: if the appeal is successful other than by the entry of an acquittal the defendant is returned to the court below for trial. A hospital order may be continued.

(iv) *Appeals against conviction on special verdict*

If the Court of Appeal considers that the trial judge has drawn an incorrect conclusion from a special verdict entered by a jury, it may substitute the correct conclusion, and pass any sentence that may be authorised by law.[58]

(v) *References by the Home Secretary*

Where a person has been (1) convicted on indictment or (2) tried on indictment and found not guilty by reason of insanity or (3) found by a jury to be under a disability, the Home Secretary may refer the case to the Court of Appeal.[59] Two kinds of reference are possible. The first is a reference of the whole case, in which event the reference is treated as an appeal.[60] The

---

[51] *Attorney-General's Reference No. 5 of 1989 (R. v. Hill-Trevor)* [1990] Crim.L.R. 278 (custodial sentence substituted for a fine for causing death by reckless driving). The first was *Attorney-General's Reference No. 1 of 1989* (1989) 90 Cr.App.R. 141, which set guidelines for sentencing for incest: see above, p. 796.

[52] "Insanity" here means insanity under the *M'Naghten* rules, which do not cover all cases of mental disorder and do cover some situations where there is no mental disorder: see generally J. C. Smith and B. Hogan, *Criminal Law* (6th ed., 1988), pp. 185–200.

[53] 1968 Act, s.12: see above, p. 834.

[54] *Ibid.*, s.13(3).

[55] *Ibid.*, s.23(4).

[56] *Ibid.*, s.24 and Sched. 1, as amended by the Mental Health (Amendment) Act 1982, Sched. 3, Part I, para. 38.

[57] *Ibid.*, ss.15, 16; *cf.* above, pp. 770–771.

[58] 1968 Act, s.5.

[59] 1968 Act, s.17.

[60] *Ibid.*, s.17(1)(*a*). The powers of the court are the same whether a case comes before it as an appeal or a reference of this kind: *Stafford* v. *D.P.P.* [1974] A.C. 878, although the criteria for permitting fresh evidence to be adduced may be applied less strictly than on ordinary appeals so that the court can consider the matters mentioned in the letter of reference: *R.* v. *Swabey* [1972] 1 W.L.R. 925.

court is not limited to the grounds mentioned in the Home Secretary's letter of reference.[61] A further appeal may then lie to the House of Lords. The other possibility is that a particular point may be referred for the opinion of the court.[62] The court gives what is essentially only an advisory opinion, with any further action to be taken by the Home Secretary.[63] This form of reference is uncommon.[64]

The Home Secretary prefers to refer a case to the Court of Appeal rather than to recommend the exercise of the prerogative to grant a pardon or remit a sentence[65]: it is thought that persistent use of the power to recommend a pardon would undermine the distinction between the functions of the executive and of the judiciary.[66] Indeed it was, in part, dissatisfaction with the review by the Home Office of criminal convictions that led to the establishment of the Court of Criminal Appeal. The Home Secretary's approach was summarised in a memorandum to the Home Affairs Committee[67]:

"In considering convictions on indictment, the Home Secretary . . .
  (a) will not normally intervene where normal avenues of appeal to the Court of Appeal have not been exhausted;
  (b) will, where the normal avenues are not available and intervention seems justified, consider using his power of reference to enable the Court to hear the case;
  (c) will consider recommending the exercise of the Royal Prerogative where intervention seems justified but for some reason (e.g. lapse of time, inadmissibility as evidence of salient new facts) a resort to the judicial appeal process would not be appropriate."

However, the Home Secretary will not intervene on the basis of evidence already considered by the courts. A case will only be referred where there is fresh evidence that might lead to the view being taken that the conviction was unsafe and unsatisfactory.[68] Moreover, if a case is referred to the Court of Appeal and the conviction is upheld, the Home Secretary will only intervene thereafter if the case is wholly exceptional.[69]

A further point is that it is only the Court of Appeal that can quash a conviction: a pardon does not have that effect.[70] Thus, in a number of cases the reference procedure has been used to secure the formal quashing of a

[61] R. v. Chard [1984] A.C. 279; followed in R. v. Callaghan [1988] 1 W.L.R. 1.
[62] 1968 Act, s.17(1)(b).
[63] See Thomas (Arthur) v. The Queen [1980] A.C. 125, where the Privy Council held that advice given to the Governor-General under an identically worded provision was not binding on him, and could not be the subject of an appeal to the Privy Council.
[64] See, e.g. R. v. O'Neill (1948) 33 Cr.App.R. 19; R. v. McCartan (1958) 42 Cr.App.R. 262; R. v. McMahon (1978) 68 Cr.App.R. 18.
[65] See below, pp. 888–889.
[66] 1981–82 H.C. 421, 6th Report on Miscarriages of Justice, p. 2.
[67] Ibid.
[68] Ibid. It has been suggested this restrictive approach cannot be a proper exercise of the discretion: Bar Council response to the May Committee of Inquiry into the Guildford and Woolwich cases: (1990) 140 N.L.J. 430. See also R. v. Secretary of State for the Home Department, ex p. Pegg, The Times, July 16, 1990.
[69] e.g. R. v. Cooper and McMahon, above, p. 836. The previous Home Secretaries had firmly taken the view that they should not override the court's decision: see L. Kennedy, (ed.), Wicked Beyond Belief (1980), pp. 130, 159–160, 169.
[70] R. v. Foster [1985] Q.B. 115: see above, p. 830, n. 65; below, p. 888.

conviction[71] or a sentence[72] that fell outside the powers of the trial court, often for reasons of some technicality. Indeed, it is uncommon for the Court of Appeal to quash a conviction, following a reference, on the basis of its doubts about the merits of the conviction.[73] "Judicial distaste for the whole reference procedure has verged at times upon open hostility."[74] Doubts as to the effectiveness of the Court of Appeal in correcting miscarriages of justice have led to proposals for the establishment of a separate, independent review tribunal.[75]

A decision of the Home Secretary to refuse to refer a case to the Court of Appeal may be challenged on an application for judicial review: to date, such challenges have failed.[76]

(vi) *Attorney-General's References*[77]

Section 36 of the Criminal Justice Act 1972 introduced a procedure whereby the Attorney-General may refer a point of law to the Court of Appeal where the defendant in a trial on indictment has been acquitted. The point must actually have arisen in the case. The court gives its opinion and may thereafter refer the point to the House of Lords. The Attorney-General may appear in person or be represented by counsel: the acquitted person may be represented by counsel, or with leave may appear in person.[78]

The reference has no effect on the trial or the acquittal. No mention must be made in the reference of the proper name of any person or place which is likely to lead to the identification of the acquitted person.[79] His or her identity must not be disclosed during the proceedings except with consent.

The aim of this procedure is to ensure that an erroneous direction by a trial judge on the law is corrected at the earliest opportunity and without the need for legislation. Whereas the defendant may appeal where such a direction

---

[71] *R.* v. *Davies* (1981) 76 Cr.App.R. 120 (following D.'s extradition, a new count was added to the indictment with D.'s agreement, but contrary to the Extradition Act 1870, s.19).

[72] *e.g. R.* v. *Bardoe* [1969] 1 W.L.R. 398 (youth of 17 wrongly sentenced to life imprisonment); *R.* v. *McKenna* (1985) 7 Cr.App.R.(S) 348; *R.* v. *Seafield, The Times,* May 17, 1988 (suspended sentence supervision order wrongly attached to six month and three month sentences, neither being a sentence of "more than six months").

[73] Widely publicised rejections of appeals include the Cooper and McMahon case, above, p. 836; the Birmingham pub bombing case (*R.* v. *Callaghan* (1988) 88 Cr.App.R. 40; C. Mullin, *Error of Judgment* (Rev. ed., 1990); J. Yahuda, (1988) 152 J.P.N. 230; B. Hilliard, (1990) 140 N.L.J. 160); the Carl Bridgwater murder case (see P. Foot, *Murder at the Farm* (1988)). By contrast, the Court of Appeal allowed an appeal in case of the Guildford Four (*R.* v. *Richardson, The Times,* October 20, 1989) although here the prosecution felt itself unable to support the convictions (see G. McKee and R. Franey, *Time Bomb* (1988); S. Edwards, (1989) 139 N.L.J. 1449). It also ultimately allowed an appeal in the Birmingham case: *R.* v. *McIlkenny, The Independent,* March 28, 1991.

[74] P. O'Connor, [1990] Crim.L.R. 615, 617.

[75] *Ibid.*; below, pp. 890–891.

[76] *R.* v. *Secretary of State for the Home Department, ex p. Cleeland* (Unreported, October 8, 1987); *R.* v. *Same ex p. Ewing* (Unreported, July 28, 1988); *R.* v. *Same ex p. Garner* (Unreported, January 26, 1989): available on *Lexis*; *ex p. Pegg* (fn. 68, *supra*).

[77] See J. Jaconelli, [1981] Crim.L.R. 543.

[78] In practice, however, the defendant is normally not represented and counsel for the Attorney-General is opposed by counsel appearing as *amicus curiae,* instructed by the Treasury Solicitor. In *Attorney-General's References (Nos. 1 and 2 of 1979)* [1980] Q.B. 180, the Law Commission, who had instigated the references in order to secure clarification of the law concerning conditional intention to steal, submitted a memorandum for the assistance of the court.

[79] Criminal Appeal (Reference of Points of Law) Rules 1973 (S.I. 1973 No. 1114), r. 3.

leads to an erroneous conviction, the prosecution has no right to appeal against an erroneous acquittal in a trial on indictment. The sanctity of an acquittal by a jury is maintained by the provisions designed to secure that the reference procedure cannot operate to the detriment of the person acquitted.

In general, judges have resisted the introduction of procedures whereby matters may be referred to them for an advisory opinion.[80] One of the grounds for refusing in the exercise of their discretion to grant a declaration on a disputed matter of law is that the dispute is hypothetical rather than real.[81] However, the opinions under the reference procedure relate to a real case, and, moreover, one in which an opinion has already been expressed by the trial judge. The exact status of the opinions as precedent is, however, uncertain: as they have no actual effect on the outcome of the case as far as the defendant is concerned, it is arguable that they are not binding, either on trial judges or on the Court of Appeal itself; however, they are obviously of strong persuasive force.

The reference procedure has been characterised as "problematic"[82] in view of the doubts as to precedental status and the fact that the defendant often has little interest in contesting the case.[83] Nevertheless, the procedure has been of value in providing authoritative guidance in a number of areas of criminal law, most notably that of conditional intention to steal, where the Court of Appeal's decision on a reference put an end to a line of argument that had led to a large number of undeserved acquittals.[84]

(vii) *Venire de novo*

Where there has been a "mistrial," in the sense either that the trial has never been validly commenced or the jury has not validly returned a verdict, the Court of Appeal may order the issue of a writ of *venire de novo* for a "new" trial: the first "trial" is treated as a nullity.[85] This may be done, for example,[86] where proceedings have not been properly instituted,[87] where the court is not properly constituted,[88] where the defendants although

---

[80] There was weighty judicial opposition to clause 4 of the Rating and Valuation Bill 1928, which would have enabled the Minister of Health to seek advisory opinions from the High Court on questions of rating law: the clause was dropped: see Lord Hewart, *The New Despotism* (1929) Chap. 7; E. C. S. Wade, (1930) 46 L.Q.R. 169 and (1931) 47 L.Q.R. 58; C. K. Allen, (1931) 47 L.Q.R. 43, 60.

[81] *e.g. Blackburn* v. *Att.-Gen.* [1971] 1 W.L.R. 1037, where the court declined to make a declaration on the hypothetical question whether by signing the Treaty of Rome, Her Majesty's Government would irreversibly surrender in part the sovereignty of Parliament.

[82] J. Jaconelli, *op. cit.*

[83] The Supreme Court of the United States refuses to consider "moot" points even where they arise out of real and not hypothetical situations.

[84] *Attorney-General's References* (*Nos.* 1 *and* 2 *of* 1979) [1980] Q.B. 180. See *R.* v. *Bayley and Easterbrook* [1980] Crim.L.R. 503.

[85] This jurisdiction, formerly exercised by the Court for Crown Cases Reserved, was preserved for the Court of Criminal Appeal (*Crane* v. *D.P.P.* [1921] 2 A.C. 299) and is now exercised by the Court of Appeal under the Supreme Court Act 1981, s.53(2).

[86] See R. B. Cooke, (1955) 71 L.Q.R. 100; M. Knight, *Criminal Appeals* (1970), pp. 216–219.

[87] *R.* v. *Angel* (1968) 52 Cr.App.R. 280: the consent of the D.P.P. was necessary but had not been obtained; *R.* v. *Newland* [1988] Q.B. 402: the indictment was a nullity as it joined disparate offences (*cf. R.* v. *O'Reilly* (1989) 90 Cr.App.R. 40).

[88] *R.* v. *Cronin* (1940) 27 Cr.App.R. 179: trial presided over by a person unqualified to act as a deputy recorder.

separately indicted are tried together,[89] where there is an equivocal plea of guilty which should not have been accepted as such,[90] where the jury is not properly constituted,[91] where the jury is improperly discharged before giving a verdict,[92] or the verdict is ambiguous.[93] It is open to the Court of Appeal simply to quash a conviction without ordering a retrial.[94] Moreover, there may be a rule that the court may not order a *venire de novo* where the "mistrial" led to an acquittal.[95]

In *R. v. Rose*[96] the House of Lords emphasised that the power to order a *venire de novo* was not available where there was an irregularity in the course of the trial occurring between the time that it had been validly commenced and the discharge of the jury after returning a verdict. Here, the judge had applied improper pressure on the jury to reach a verdict by imposing a time limit: the House held that the Court of Appeal had no alternative but to quash the conviction under section 2 of the Criminal Appeal Act 1968, and had no jurisdiction to order a *venire de novo*.[97]

The court of trial may direct a *venire de novo* where the jury is discharged before giving a verdict, for example where they fail to agree or there is an irregularity in the conduct of proceedings.[98]

(b) Appeals from the Court of Appeal (Criminal Division) to the House of Lords)

An appeal lies from the Court of Appeal (Criminal Division) to the House of Lords at the instance of either the defendant or the prosecutor.[99] The Court of Appeal must certify that a point of law of general public importance is involved. In addition, leave must be obtained from either the Court of

---

[89] *Crane* v. *D.P.P.*, *supra*.

[90] See above, p 825, n. 11; see, *e.g. R.* v. *Baker* (1912) 7 Cr.App.R. 217, 252.

[91] *e.g.* where a juror was personated by his bailiff, who was neither on the jury panel nor qualified to be so: *R.* v. *Wakefield* (1918) 13 Cr.App.R. 56, or where the defendant is denied his right of challenge: *R.* v. *Williams* (1925) 19 Cr.App.R. 67; *R.* v. *Gash* (1967) 51 Cr.App.R. 37.

[92] *R.* v. *Hancock* (1931) 100 L.J.K.B. 419: the defendant changed his pleas from not guilty to guilty, but the jury did not formally return a guilty verdict.

[93] *R.* v. *Lewis* (1988) 87 Cr.App.R. 270: the way the verdicts were taken left it unclear whether they were unanimous or majority.

[94] See, *e.g. R.* v. *Golathan* (1915) 11 Cr.App.R. 79; *R.* v. *Lewis* (1988) 87 Cr App.R. 270. It is not clear whether it is open to the prosecution to recommence proceedings: if the court is simply regarded as holding the decision of the "first" trial to be a nullity, it seems that there could be such proceedings; if, however, the conviction is quashed under the Criminal Appeal Act 1968, s.2, the position is as if there had been a judgment and verdict of acquittal and fresh proceedings could be met by a plea of *autrefois acquit*.

[95] *R.* v. *Middlesex Quarter Sessions, ex p. D.P.P.* [1952] 2 Q.B. 758. An alternative ground for the decision was that the irregularity was not such as to cause a mistrial. There may be exceptions to the supposed rule where the defendant is party to the irregularity or is tried by a court with no jurisdiction over charges of the kind in question: R. B. Cooke, (1955) 71 L.Q.R. 100, 116.

[96] [1982] A.C. 822.

[97] The position is the same where the defendant changes his or her plea to guilty in reliance on the judge's ruling on a point of law that is subsequently shown to be erroneous: *R.* v. *Hunt* [1986] Q.B. 125, 132 (an appeal was allowed by the House of Lords, but this point was not dealt with: [1987] A.C. 352.)

[98] See R. B. Cooke, *op. cit.* pp. 120–125; Juries Act 1974, s.21(4).

[99] Criminal Appeal Act 1968, s.33(1). Where a point of law is referred to the Court of Appeal by the Attorney-General under the Criminal Justice Act 1972, s.36 (see above, p. 843) the court may thereafter refer the point to the House of Lords.

Appeal or the House of Lords and this can only be granted where it appears that the point is "one which ought to be considered by the House."[1] If leave is granted, the House may in its discretion allow a point to be argued that is not connected with the point certified.[2]

An application for leave to appeal is normally made immediately after the Court of Appeal's decision, but may be made in writing within 14 days.[3] The point is normally formulated by counsel for the applicant, sometimes with the assistance of counsel for the other side. If a certificate is refused the matter may not be taken any further: the refusal is not itself a decision that may be subject to appeal.[4] Reasons are not normally given for refusing a certificate.[5] Where a certificate is granted, the application for leave should be made first to the Court of Appeal, and only if leave then is refused by that court, to the House of Lords, within 14 days.[6] The Court of Appeal may grant bail[7] and legal aid.[8]

Where the prosecutor is granted leave to appeal or gives notice of intention to apply for leave, and but for the decision of the Court of Appeal the defendant would be liable to be detained, the Court of Appeal may make an order for his or her detention or direct that he or she is not to be released except on bail so long as the appeal is pending.[9] An order under the Mental Health Act 1983 may be continued.[10] A defendant who is detained may apply to the Court of Appeal or House of Lords to be present at the hearing of the appeal of preliminary or incidental matters.[11] If no order for continued detention is made, or the defendant is released or discharged before the appeal is disposed of, the defendant cannot be detained again as the result of the decision of the House of Lords on the appeal.[12]

The rules governing petitions to the House of Lords for leave to appeal and petitions of appeal are prescribed by the House of Lords Directions as to Procedure, 1988.[13] The former are heard by an Appeal Committee, the latter by the House itself or an Appellate Committee.[14] If leave is granted by

[1] 1968 Act, s.33(2).
[2] *Att.-Gen. for Northern Ireland* v. *Gallagher* [1963] A.C. 349. Where, however, the certificate relates to conviction only the House will not deal with matters of sentence: *Jones* v. *D.P.P.* [1962] A.C. 635. The House's judgment is the final judgment in the appeal; the case cannot subsequently be re-listed before the Court of Appeal for unargued points to be dealt with: *R.* v. *Berry* [1991] 1 W.L.R. 125.
[3] Criminal Appeal Act 1968, s.34. The time limit may be extended: *ibid.*
[4] *Cf.* in relation to appeals to the House of Lords from the Divisional Court, *Gelberg* v. *Miller* [1961] 1 W.L.R. 459, above, p. 829, n. 56.
[5] *R.* v. *Jones* (1975) 61 Cr.App.R. 120; *R.* v. *Cooper, R.* v. *McMahon* (1975) 61 Cr.App.R. 215.
[6] Criminal Appeal Act 1968, s.34. The time limit may be extended.
[7] *Ibid.*, s.36.
[8] Legal Aid Act 1988, s.19(1)(*d*), 20(3): legal aid may be granted by the Registrar or the single judge, but not the House of Lords. If the prosecutor appeals or applies for leave to appeal legal aid must be granted if the defendant's means warrant it: *ibid.*, s.20(3)(*b*).
[9] Criminal Appeal Act 1968, s.37(2). The order ceases to have effect if leave is refused, or the application for leave is not made within the due time, or the appeal is determined, or the liability for detention otherwise ceases, as the case may be: *ibid.*, ss.34(3), 37(3).
[10] *Ibid.*, s.37(4)(4A).
[11] *Ibid.*, s.38.
[12] *Ibid.*, s.37(5). See *D.P.P.* v. *Merriman* [1973] A.C. 584, 606; *U.S. Government* v. *McCaffery* [1984] 1 W.L.R. 867, 873; *R.* v. *Hollinshead* [1985] A.C. 975, 998–999, *per* Lord Roskill, who stated that an order should be made unless there were strong reasons for not so doing.
[13] See (1988) 88 Cr.App.R. 105.
[14] See above, pp. 91–94.

the Court of Appeal there is no statutory time limit for lodging the petition of appeal although it is recommended that this is done within three months: if leave is granted by an Appeal Committee, the committee may set a time limit.[15] The appellant must lodge 15 copies of a record of the proceedings, which now include printed cases on the same pattern as for civil appeals.[16] If any of the parties intend to invite the House to depart from one of its own previous decisions, this intention must be clearly stated.

The House in disposing of an appeal may exercise any of the powers of the Court of Appeal or remit the case to that court.[17] Any sentence substituted by the House of Lords runs from the time when the other sentence would have begun to run, unless the House otherwise directs.[18] Any time spent on bail pending hearing of the appeal does not count towards the sentence.[19]

Until 1960, an appeal could only be taken from the Court of Criminal Appeal to the House of Lords if the Attorney-General granted a *fiat* or certificate that a point of law of exceptional public importance was involved and that it was in the public interest that a further appeal be brought.[20] Between 1907 and 1960 there were 23 successful applications for a *fiat*. The exercise of the Attorney-General's discretion to grant or refuse a *fiat* was in certain instances highly controversial. The Administration of Justice Act 1960[21] introduced the present arrangements which, *inter alia*, brought an end to the involvement of the Attorney-General. The number of criminal appeals to the House of Lords has, accordingly, increased. However, it has been debated whether, on balance, the increased involvement of the House in criminal law matters has proved beneficial. In his commentary on *R.* v. *Caldwell*,[22] Professor J. C. Smith noted that the "House of Lords has a dismal record in criminal cases. All too often their Lordships' decisions have to be reversed by legislation."[23] His criticisms were echoed by Professor Glanville Williams,[24] who remarked that the average age of Law Lords is higher than that of members of the Court of Appeal, and that "old men" are "often fixed in their opinions" and "tend to ignore the opinions of others." He noted that a further drawback was the breadth of the House's jurisdiction: "It is particularly inapt that a Chancery judge should have the casting vote in the House of Lords in a criminal case, as Lord Cross did in *Hyam*."[25]

After a survey of the record of the House in criminal cases between 1960 and 1984, Professor A. T. H. Smith concluded that appeals by the Crown in such cases should be abolished, and replaced by the Attorney-General's Reference procedure. Decisions from the Divisional Court could go to the Court of Appeal (Criminal Division), but no further.[26]

---

[15] House of Lords Criminal Appeals Directions as to Procedure 1988, Dir. 17.
[16] See above, p. 93. The change was introduced in 1988.
[17] Criminal Appeal Act 1968, s.35(3).
[18] *Ibid.*, s.43(2).
[19] *Ibid.*, s.43(1).
[20] See "Appeals to the House of Lords" [1957] Crim.L.R. 566.
[21] See D. G. T. Williams, [1961] Crim.L.R.87.
[22] [1982] A.C. 341.
[23] [1981] Crim.L.R. 393.
[24] *Ibid.*, pp. 581–582.
[25] [1975] A.C. 55.
[26] "Criminal Appeals in the House of Lords" (1984) 47 M.L.R. 133.

3. APPEALS IN CIVIL CASES

In this section we consider appeals in civil cases originating in the county court or the High Court. Appeals in civil cases originating in the magistrates' court or Crown Court have already been discussed.[27]

(a) Appeals from the county court to the Court of Appeal (Civil Division)

In general, a person dissatisfied with a decision of a county court may appeal to the Court of Appeal.[28] In certain cases, however, the appeal is expressly excluded[29]:

—questions of fact arising in certain actions by a landlord for possession of the premises;
—an order extending the time for appealing;
—an order expressed by statute to be final[30];
—a decree absolute of divorce or nullity of marriage, by a party who, having had time and opportunity to appeal from the decree nisi, has not done so;
—where the parties have agreed in writing that the judge's decision shall be final.

An appeal only lies with the leave of the county court judge from any order made with the consent of the parties or relating only to costs which are by law left to the discretion of the court.[31]

In certain cases an appeal may only be brought with the leave of the county court judge or the Court of Appeal: the classes prescribed[32] include those where the claim (or counter-claim if larger) is for an amount not exceeding one-half of the relevant county court limit for contract and tort, equity, probate and miscellaneous matters,[33] and where the decision of the county court judge is made in an appellate capacity. However, no leave is required where the court's determination includes or preserves an injunction or is related to the custody of, or access to, a child.[34]

In other cases, an appeal lies as of right.

---

[27] See above, pp. 825–829.

[28] County Courts Act 1984, s.77(1). Until 1934 the appeal lay first to a Divisional Court and thereafter to the Court of Appeal. In bankruptcy cases the appeal lies to a Divisional Court of the Chancery Division; an appeal lies from that court to the Court of Appeal with the leave of either, and the decision of the Court of Appeal is final: Insolvency Act 1986, s.375(2).

[29] County Courts Act 1984, s.77(6); Supreme Court Act 1981, s.18(1)(b)(c)(d); 1984 Act, s.79(1).

[30] A final order may be set aside if procured by fraud: cf. *Lazarus Estates Ltd.* v. *Beasley* [1956] 1 Q.B. 702, and in matrimonial cases, a final order may be set aside if there is fraud, mistake or material non-disclosure: *Robinson* v. *Robinson* (*Practice Note*) [1982] 1 W.L.R. 786.

[31] Supreme Court Act 1981, s.18(1)(f). To be repealed by the Courts and Legal Services Act 1990, s.7.

[32] By the Lord Chancellor under the County Courts Act 1984, s.77(2)–(4): the County Court Appeals Order 1981 (S.I. 1981 No. 1749). See also the restrictions on appealing from interlocutory orders or judgments imposed by the Supreme Court Act 1981, s.18(1)(h): below, p. 850 (also to be repealed by the 1990 Act, s.7).

[33] See above, pp. 64–67.

[34] S.I. 1981, No. 1749, art. 3.

Appeals may be based on questions of fact, discretion or law.[35] The procedure for appealing and the powers of the Court of Appeal are discussed in the section on appeals from the High Court.[36]

Appeals lie from decisions of a district judge to the county court judge.[37] In interlocutory matters, the judge considers the issue *de novo*, and may substitute his or her view for that of the district judge. Where the appeal is from a judgment or final order, the role of the county court judge is analogous to that of the Court of Appeal on appeals from decisions of the judge.[38] Accordingly, he or she may only order a new trial in the same circumstances as the Court of Appeal,[39] and may only interfere with a discretionary decision if no reasonable registrar could have so decided.[40]

(b) Appeals from the High Court to the Court of Appeal (Civil Division)

(i) *When does an appeal lie?*

Appeals normally lie from any judgment or order of the High Court to the Court of Appeal (Civil Division).[41] In some circumstances, the appeal may be direct to the House of Lords.[42] Generally, there is a right to appeal. In respect of some matters, however, the appeal is expressly excluded by statute:

    —any criminal cause or matter[43];
    —any order allowing an extension of time for appealing[44];
    —any decision expressed by statute to be final[45];
    —a decree absolute of divorce or nullity of marriage, by a party who, having had time and opportunity to appeal from the decree nisi, has not done so[46];
    —any decision of the High Court on an appeal under section 1 of the Arbitration Act 1979 on a question of law arising out of an arbitration award, or under section 2 of the Act on a question of law arising in the course of a reference, other than as provided by the 1979 Act[47];
    —a judgment or order of the High Court sitting as a Prize Court[48];

---

[35] The circumstances in which the Court of Appeal will consider a point of law not raised in the county court are now the same as for appeals from the High Court to the Court of Appeal (below, pp. 856–857): *Pittalis* v. *Grant* [1989] Q.B. 605. Formerly, a more restrictive approach was adopted.

[36] See below, pp. 851–863.

[37] County Court Rules 1981, Ord. 13 r. 1(10) (interlocutory matters) and Ord. 37, r. 6 (final orders or judgments).

[38] See below, pp. 851–863.

[39] *Devenish* v. *P.D.I. Homes (Hythe) Ltd.* [1959] 1 W.L.R. 1188.

[40] *Woodspring District Council* v. *Taylor, The Times* May 15, 1982.

[41] Supreme Court Act 1981, s.16(1).

[42] See below, pp. 863–864.

[43] Supreme Court Act 1981, s.18(1)(*a*). Here, the appeal lies to the House of Lords under the Administration of Justice Act 1960: see above, p. 829.

[44] 1981 Act, s.18(1)(*b*). An appeal lies from a refusal to make such an order: *Rickards* v. *Rickards* [1990] Fam. 194.

[45] *Ibid.*, s.18(1)(*c*).

[46] *Ibid.*, s.18(1)(*d*).

[47] *Ibid.*, s.18(1)(*g*).

[48] *Ibid.*, s.16(2). An appeal lies to the Privy Council.

—an order refusing leave to a vexatious litigant to institute or continue legal proceedings.[49]

In other cases an appeal only lies if leave is obtained[50]:

(1) The leave of the High Court is necessary for appeals in relation to orders made with the consent of the parties or relating only to costs which are by law left to the discretion of the court.[51]

(2) The leave of the Divisional Court or the Court of Appeal is necessary for appeals from the determination by a Divisional Court of any appeal to the High Court.[52]

(3) The leave of the High Court or the Court of Appeal is necessary for appeals from an interlocutory order or judgment,[53] except:

—where the liberty of the subject or the custody, education[54] or welfare of a minor is concerned;
—where an applicant for access to a minor is refused all access to the minor;
—where an injunction or the appointment of a receiver is granted or refused;
—in the case of a decision determining the claim of any creditor, or the liability of any contributory or of any director or other officer, under company law;
—in the case of a decree nisi in a matrimonial cause, or a judgment or order in an admiralty action determining liability;
—in such other cases as may be prescribed.[55]

In situations (2) and (3) the application for leave must be made first to the court below,[56] unless there are special circumstances which make that impossible or inappropriate,[57] and if leave is refused, then to the Court of Appeal. In the latter event the application may be determined by a single judge of the Court of Appeal[58] initially on paper, but otherwise in open

---

[49] *Ibid.*, s.42(4).

[50] See generally N. Harris, "Leave to appeal in civil cases" (1985) VII (1) Liverpool L.R. 51.

[51] *Ibid.*, s.18(1)(f). Where leave is refused, the Court of Appeal can nevertheless entertain an appeal on costs where the judge has either not exercised his or her discretion as to costs at all or has not exercised it judicially: *Scherer* v. *Counting Instruments Ltd.* (1977) [1986] 1 W.L.R. 615; *Marshall* v. *Levine* [1985] 1 W.L.R. 814; *Smiths Ltd.* v. *Middleton (No. 2)* [1986] 1 W.L.R. 598; *Bankamerica Finance Ltd.* v. *Nock* [1988] A.C. 1002. An appeal is not entered unless the Court of Appeal is satisfied on an ex parte application that there is an arguable case (*ibid.*). An order that a solicitor is personally liable for costs does not fall within s.18(1)(f): *Thompson* v. *Fraser* [1986] 1 W.L.R. 17.

[52] *Ibid.*, s.18(1)(e), *i.e.* in civil cases: *cf.* above, p. 829.

[53] The distinction between final and interlocutory orders caused much uncertainty and gave rise to a large body of case law: see, *e.g. Salter Rex & Co.* v. *Ghosh* [1971] 2 Q.B. 597, 601; *White* v. *Brunton* [1984] Q.B. 570. A classification is now provided by R.S.C. Ord. 59 r. 1A, inserted by S.I. 1988 No. 1340, r. 7. An order refusing unconditional leave to defend an action is not to be treated as an interlocutory order: 1981 Act, s.18(2)(a).

[54] "Education" includes training and religious instruction: *ibid.* s.18(2)(b).

[55] *Ibid.*, s.18(1)(h). Subss. (1) (e), (f) and (h) and (2) are to be repealed by the Courts and Legal Servcies Act 1990, and the cases requiring leave will be specified in Rules of the Supreme Court.

[56] An application in situation (3) may be made to any judge of the High Court, not necessarily the judge who heard the case: *Warren* v. *T. Kilroe & Sons Ltd.* [1988] 1 W.L.R. 516.

[57] R.S.C. Ord. 59, r. 14(4).

[58] 1981 Act, s.54(6). See *Practice Direction (Court of Appeal: Single Judge)* [1985] 1 W.L.R. 739.

court[59]: he or she may, if he or she thinks fit, refer the application to a full court.[60]

Even where leave to appeal is not necessary, the Court of Appeal may decline to entertain an appeal where, for example, the issue is or has become hypothetical,[61] or the parties have agreed not to appeal.[62]

(ii) *Who may appeal?*

Where in principle an appeal lies, any party to proceedings in the court below and any person on whom notice of the order or judgment is served[63] may appeal. In addition, any person who *could* have been made a party to the action may appeal, provided he or she obtains leave from the Court of Appeal.[64]

(iii) *Procedure for appealing*

The appellant must serve a "notice of appeal" on all parties to the proceedings in the court below who are directly affected by the proceedings,[65] and any other person directed by the Court of Appeal, the single judge or the Registrar of Civil Appeals.[66] The notice may be given in respect of the whole or a specified part of the judgment or order of the court below. For example in a personal injuries case there might be an appeal against the quantum of damages only. The notice must specify the grounds of the appeal and the precise form of the order which the appellant proposes to ask the Court of Appeal to make: the appellant will need leave to rely on any ground or apply for any relief at the hearing not specified in the notice of appeal.[67]

The notice must normally be served within four weeks from the date on which the judgment or order of the court below was sealed or otherwise perfected.[68] The exceptions are (1) where a certificate is granted for an appeal direct to the House of Lords, but the House refuses leave, where the four week period runs from the date of refusal,[69] and (2) social security appeals, where there is a six week time limit.[70] The time limit may be extended or abridged by the court below, provided that the application for extension or abridgment is made within the specified period,[71] or by the Registrar of Civil Appeals, the single judge, or the Court of Appeal.[72]

---

[59] *Carter (R.G.) Ltd.* v. *Clarke* [1990] 1 W.L.R. 578; *The Iran Nabuvat* [1990] 1 W.L.R. 1115.
[60] R.S.C. Ord. 59, r. 14(10).
[61] *e.g. Sutch* v. *Burns* [1944] K.B. 406; *Sun Life Assurance Co. of Canada* v. *Jervis* [1944] A.C. 111.
[62] *Jones* v. *Victoria Graving Dock Co.* [1877] 2 Q.B.D. 314.
[63] R.S.C. Ord. 44, r. 3.
[64] *per* Jessel M.R. in *Crawcour* v. *Salter* (1882) 30 W.R. 329; *Re B (an infant)* [1958] 1 Q.B. 12.
[65] R.S.C. Ord. 59, r. 3(5).
[66] *Ibid.*, r. 8.
[67] *Ibid.*, r. 3(2)(3).
[68] R.S.C. Ord. 59, r. 4(1), as amended.
[69] R.S.C. Ord. 59, r. 4(2): see below, pp. 863–864.
[70] R.S.C. Ord. 59, r. 21.
[71] R.S.C. Ord. 59, r. 15.
[72] R.S.C. Ord. 3, r. 5. Where leave to appeal is required and granted by the Court of Appeal, time for serving notice of appeal is automatically extended by seven days from the grant of leave, provided the application for leave was made within the four week time limit: R.S.C. Ord. 59, r. 4(3).

Where, however, the time limit for appealing has expired, an extension will only be granted in exceptional cases[73]: a more liberal exercise of this discretion would be unfair to the other party or parties. The court has an inherent jurisdiction to strike out a notice of appeal if it is hopeless or an abuse of process.[74]

A respondent who is served with a notice of appeal may, within 21 days,[75] serve a "respondent's notice" on the appellant and all parties to the proceedings in the court below directly affected. This must be done where the respondent wishes to contend that the decision of the court below, in respect of the cause of action related to the notice of appeal,

(a) should be varied; or
(b) should be affirmed on grounds other than those relied upon by that court; or
(c) was wrong in whole or in part.

The notice must specify the grounds of the respondent's contention, and, in cases (a) and (c), the precise form of the order which he or she proposes to ask the court to make: the respondent will need leave to apply for any relief not specified in the notice or to rely upon any ground which is either not specified in the notice or relied upon by the court below.[76]

Where the respondent is dissatisfied with the decision of the court on a *separate* cause of action from that raised in the notice of appeal, the proper course is to serve a separate notice of appeal.[77]

The notice of appeal or respondent's notice may be amended without leave before the date on which the appeal appears in the List of Forthcoming Appeals, and, thereafter, with the leave of the Court of Appeal, the single judge or the Registrar.[78]

The purpose of the notice of appeal is to:

"define and confine the area of controversy on the hearing of the appeal, thus saving both time and expense to the parties. It is intended that wherever possible the members of the court will have read the notice of appeal and any respondent's notice and the reasons for the judgment under appeal before the appeal is called on, and a properly drawn notice of appeal will enable counsel to come at once to the central issues without any prolonged opening."[79]

---

[73] *Practice Note (Court of Appeal: New Procedure)* [1982] 1 W.L.R. 1312 (Sir John Donaldson, M.R.). See, *e.g. Palata Investments* v. *Burt & Sinfield* [1985] 1 W.L.R. 942 (extension granted where there was a very short delay and an acceptable excuse); *cf. Hollis* v. *R. B. Jenkins* (*a firm*), *The Times*, January 31, 1984 (seven-month delay inexcusable); *Nestle* v. *National Westminster Bank plc*, *The Times*, March 28, 1990 (three month delay excusable where most of the time had been occupied in attempts to get legal aid).
[74] *Burgess* v. *Stafford Hotel Ltd.* [1990] 1 W.L.R. 1215.
[75] The time can be extended: Ord. 59, r. 6(3): see *V.C.S.* v. *Magmasters* [1984] 1 W.L.R. 1208.
[76] R.S.C. Ord. 59, r. 6.
[77] *National Society for the Distribution of Electricity by Secondary Generators* v. *Gibbs* [1900] 2 Ch. 280.
[78] R.S.C. Ord. 59, r. 7. Applications for leave are made first to the Registrar, who will require good reasons why the amendment was not made earlier and to be satisfied that the application is made at the earliest possible moment: *Practice Note (Court of Appeal: New Procedure)* [1982] 1 W.L.R. 1312, 1313–14.
[79] *Ibid.*, p. 1312.

The same principles apply to a respondent's notice.[80] The grounds should be stated shortly and simply: these notices are not designed to be as elaborate as pleadings.[81]

Within seven days of the later of (i) service of the notice of appeal or (ii) the date on which the judgment or order of the court below was sealed or otherwise perfected, or within such further time as may be allowed by the Registrar of Civil Appeals,[82] the appellant must leave certain specified documents, including two copies of the notice of appeal, with the Registrar. The Registrar thereupon causes the appeal to be set down in the proper list of appeals[83]: there is a series of lists depending on the court or tribunal from which the appeal is taken.[84]

The next stage is the appearance of the appeal in the "List of Forthcoming Appeals." The appellant then has 14 days to lodge copies of a series of specified documents, including the notice of appeal, any respondent's notice, the judgment or order of the court below, the pleadings, a record of the judge's reasons, relevant parts of the transcript or judge's note of evidence and relevant affidavits and exhibits.[85]

At any time after an appeal has been set down in the appropriate list of appeals the Registrar may give:

". . . such directions in relation to the documents to be produced at the appeal, and the manner in which they are to be presented, and as to other matters incidental to the conduct of the appeal, as appear best adapted to secure the just, expeditious and economical disposal of the appeal."[86]

This was described as "perhaps the most important single change in the rules."[87] The hope was expressed that as experience of the new system built up, the rate of disposal of appeals could be increased without detriment to, and even with an improvement in, the quality of the justice which was administered.[88] Possible time-saving devices included "perfected grounds of appeal," which refer to the key authorities and the relevant portions of the summing-up and evidence or the provision of a skeleton outline of the argument annotated by reference to the documents and authorities.[89] Notice has also been given that time limits will be strictly enforced unless there are good grounds for granting an extension.[90] Doubts have, however, been expressed:

[80] *Ibid.*, pp. 1313–14.
[81] *Sansom* v. *Sansom (Practice Note)* [1956] 1 W.L.R. 945.
[82] See *C.M. Van Stillevoldt BV* v. *El Carriers Inc.* [1983] 1 W.L.R. 297; *Hollis* v. *R. B. Jenkins, The Times*, January 31, 1984.
[83] R.S.C. Ord. 59, r. 5, as amended by S.I. 1986 No. 1187.
[84] *Practice Note (Court of Appeal: New Procedure)* [1982] 1 W.L.R. 1312, 1313. The papers are vetted by a lawyer in the Civil Appeals Office: *Practice Statements (Civil Appeals: Setting down)* [1990] 1 W.L.R. 1436.
[85] R.S.C. Ord. 59, r. 9(1) (2) (2A); *Practice Direction (Appeals: Documentation)* [1986] 1 W.L.R. 1316.
[86] *Ibid.*, r. 9(3).
[87] *Practice Note (Court of Appeal: New Procedure)* [1982] 1 W.L.R. 1312, 1315.
[88] *Ibid.*
[89] See *Practice Note (Court of Appeal: Skeleton Arguments)* [1983] 1 W.L.R. 1055; *Practice Direction (Court of Appeal: Skeleton Argument Time Limits)* [1990] 1 W.L.R. 794.
[90] *Practice Direction (Appeals: Documentation)* [1986] 1 W.L.R. 1318.

"[T]here prevails at present an emphasis on efficiency, time saving and expedition, which tends to undermine the English system of appeal (which is predicated upon the advocate's right to conduct the appeal in the way most beneficial to his client's interests) and to assimilate it to American and continental procedure. For all practical purposes this has dispensed with oral presentation and leaves the conduct of a very short hearing to the court rather than Counsel, while in England tradition entitles Counsel to be to a large extent 'in possession of the court.' "[91]

Notwithstanding such doubts, the Court of Appeal has reinforced the emphasis in question, while denying that the effect has been deleterious in the way suggested.[92] From June 6, 1989, skeleton arguments have been compulsory in all cases, except where appeals are heard as a matter of great urgency and in any individual case where the court otherwise directs. They must normally be lodged not less than 14 days[93] before the expected date of the hearing. The appellant's skeleton argument must be accompanied by a chronology of events. Counsel must certify time estimates for the length of the appeal hearing[94] and check periodically that the estimate is correct.[95] At the oral hearing, counsel are normally expected to proceed direct to the grounds of and issues in the appeal without any preamble.[96]

(iv) Interlocutory applications

Interlocutory applications, for example for a stay of execution,[97] for leave to adduce fresh evidence,[98] or for security for the costs of appeal, are heard by a single judge or the Registrar: only the judge, however, may deal with matters concerning an injunction or a stay of execution.[99] The Court of Appeal has all the powers and duties as to amendment and otherwise of the High Court.[1]

An appeal lies respectively from the Registrar to the single judge and from the single judge to the Court of Appeal, by means of a fresh application brought within 10 days. However, an appeal does not lie to the Court of Appeal without leave of that court in respect of a determination of the Registrar which has been reviewed by the single judge.[2] No appeal lies from the determination by the judge of an application for leave to appeal.[3]

---

[91] F. A. Mann, (1983) 2 C.J.Q. 320, 322–325, at p. 325.
[92] *Practice Direction (Court of Appeal: Presentation of Argument)* [1989] 1 W.L.R. 281: Introduction (pp. 281–284). This followed a working party, chaired by Purchas L.J.
[93] Reduced from four weeks by *Practice Note* [1990] 2 All E.R. 318.
[94] *Practice Direction (List of Forthcoming Appeals)* [1987] 1 W.L.R. 1422.
[95] [1989] 1 W.L.R. 281, 286.
[96] *Ibid.*, pp. 286–287.
[97] R.S.C. Ord. 59, r. 13: an appeal does not operate as a stay of execution unless directed by the court below, a single judge of the Court of Appeal or the court itself.
[98] See below, p. 856.
[99] R.S.C. Ord. 59, r. 10(9).
[1] R.S.C. Ord. 59, r. 10(1).
[2] R.S.C. Ord. 59, r. 14(11) and (12). The judge must consider the matter afresh and use his own discretion: *C.M. Van Stillevoldt BV* v. *E.L. Carriers Ltd.* [1983] 1 W.L.R. 207; thereafter, the Court of Appeal will only interfere where the single judge has erred in principle: *Kloeckner & Co. SA* v. *Gatoil Overseas Inc.* [1990] 1 Lloyd's Rep. 177.
[3] *Ibid.*, r. 14(12).

(v) Evidence in the Court of Appeal (Civil Division)

An appeal to the Court of Appeal is expressed to be "by way of rehearing."[4] This is not a rehearing in the same sense as appeals from magistrates' courts to the Crown Court[5] but a rehearing "on the documents." The court has power:

—"to draw inferences of fact and to give any judgment and make any order which ought to have been given or made, and to make such further or other order as the case may require;"[6]

and

—"to make any order, on such terms as the Court thinks just, to ensure the determination on the merits of the real question in controversy between the parties."[7]

The court should take account of any new authorities and of any relevant, retrospective, legislation. For example, in *Attorney-General* v. *Vernazza*,[8] Mr. Vernazza was declared to be a vexatious litigant and prohibited by the High Court from *instituting* legal proceedings without leave. By the time his appeal was heard by the Court of Appeal, the High Court had been given a new statutory power to prohibit vexatious litigants from *continuing existing* proceedings without leave. The House of Lords held that the new legislation, as it affected procedural and not substantive rights, was retrospective, should have been applied to Mr. Vernazza by the Court of Appeal, and should be applied to him now. Where there are new authorities or legislative provisions which are relevant to a decision of the High Court, leave to appeal out of time will be granted if it is just to do so.[9]

Similarly, the court should take account of any material changes in the facts since the trial. For example, in *Murphy* v. *Stone-Wallwork (Charlton) Ltd.*[10] an action was brought by an employee against his employers for breach of statutory duty. The judge and the Court of Appeal assessed the damages on the assumption that the plaintiff would continue to be employed by the defendants on lighter work. A fortnight after the decision in the Court of Appeal, the plaintiff was dismissed because of his incapacity. The House of Lords[11] held that even though it did not appear that the employers had

---

[4] R.S.C. Ord. 59, r. 3(1).

[5] See above, pp. 825–827.

[6] R.S.C. Ord. 59, r. 10(3). This power may be exercised notwithstanding that the relevant point is not covered by a notice of appeal or respondent's notice: r. 10(4).

[7] R.S.C. Ord. 59, r. 10(4).

[8] [1960] A.C. 965.

[9] *In Re Earl of Berkeley, Borrer* v. *Berkeley* [1945] Ch. 1; *Anns* v. *Walcroft Property Co. Ltd.* [1976] Q.B. 882; *Property and Reversionary Investment Corporation Ltd.* v. *Templar* [1977] 1 W.L.R. 1223.

[10] [1969] 1 W.L.R. 1023. See also *Mulholland* v. *Mitchell* [1971] A.C. 666. Evidence concerning post-hearing developments is "readily admitted" in cases concerning the welfare of children: *G.* v. *G. (Minors: Custody Appeal)* [1985] 1 W.L.R. 647, 654, *per* Lord Fraser. See, *e.g. M.* v. *M. (Minor: Custody Appeal)* [1987] 1 W.L.R. 404; *A.* v. *A. (Custody Appeal: Role of Appellate Court)*) [1988] 1 F.L.R. 193; *Re A. (A. Minor) (Abduction)* [1989] 1 F.L.R. 365.

[11] The same principle would have applied by the Court of Appeal if the change had occurred after the trial.

acted in bad faith or oppressively, evidence of the change of circumstances was admissible, as the basis on which the case had been conducted on both sides had been suddenly and materially falsified. It should, however, be noted that the change occurred within the time limit for appealing: it is unlikely that a leave to appeal out of time would be granted in such circumstances, in view of the need for finality in litigation, unless, perhaps, there was bad faith or oppression.

Where a party to an appeal seeks to adduce fresh evidence concerning matters other than events that have occurred since the trial, a more restrictive approach is adopted. Where judgment has been given after trial or hearing of the cause or matter on the merits,[12] such fresh evidence is only admitted on "special grounds."[13] Three conditions were laid down by Denning L.J. in *Ladd* v. *Marshall*[14]:

(1) It must be shown that the evidence could not have been obtained with reasonable diligence for use at the trial.

(2) The evidence must be such that, if given, it would probably have an important influence on the result of the case, although it need not be decisive.

(3) The evidence must be such as is presumably to be believed, or, in other words, must be apparently credible, though it need not be incontrovertible.[15]

These conditions may be relaxed where the welfare of a child is at stake,[16] or on appeals concerning applications for judicial review.[17]

The Court of Appeal similarly adopts a restrictive approach to points not taken at the trial and presented for the first time in the Court of Appeal. The court will not decide in favour of an appellant on a new point unless it is satisfied beyond doubt (1) that it has before it all the facts bearing upon the new contention as completely as if it had been raised at the trial, and (2) that no evidence could have been adduced at the trial which by any possibility could prevent the point from succeeding.[18] Accordingly it may permit a new

---

[12] This includes summary judgment under R.S.C. Ords. 14 or 86: *Langdale* v. *Danby* [1982] 1 W.L.R. 1123.

[13] R.S.C. Ord. 59, r. 10(2).

[14] [1954] 1 W.L.R. 1489, 1491: approved by the House of Lords in *Skone* v. *Skone* [1971] 1 W.L.R. 812 and *Langdale* v. *Danby, supra.*

[15] See, *e.g. Roe* v. *Robert McGregor & Sons* [1968] 1 W.L.R. 925; *Williams* v. *Reason* (Note) [1988] 1 W.L.R. 96; *Mason* v. *Mason* [1986] 2 F.L.R. 212 and *Krywald* v. *Krywald* [1988] 2 F.L.R. 401 (financial provision); *Ferguson* v. *Welsh* [1987] 1 W.L.R. 1553; *Sutcliffe* v. *Pressdram Ltd.* [1990] 2 W.L.R. 271. The points that a large sum of money is at stake and that a foreign element is involved do not justify relaxing the requirements: *The Gudermes* [1984] 1 Lloyd's L.R. 5.

[16] *M.* v. *M.* (*Minor: Custody Appeal*) [1987] 1 W.L.R. 404, 409; *cf.* Sheldon J. in *Devon County Council* v. *C.* [1985] F.L.R. 619, and *Re G.* (*A Minor*) (*Wardship: Access*) [1988] 1 F.L.R. 305. It has, however, been suggested that such a relaxation could only be effected by the House of Lords or by legislation: Latey J. in *P.* v. *P.* (*Minors: Custody Appeal*) [1984] F.L.R. 99, 113.

[17] *R.* v. *Secretary of State for the Home Department, ex p. Momin Ali* [1984] 1 W.L.R. 663, 669–670 (Sir John Donaldson M.R.: the principles underlying *Ladd* v. *Marshall* were applicable "subject always to the discretion of the court to depart from them if the wider interests of justice so require"), and 673 (Fox L.J.) on the facts, the principles did apply, and fresh evidence which could have been placed before the judge was excluded.

[18] See Lord Herschell in *The Tasmania* (1890) 15 App.Cas. at p. 225 and Jessell M.R. in *Ex p. Firth, re Cowburn* (1882) 19 Ch.D. 419, 429; *Ashcroft* v. *Mersey Regional Health Authority* [1985] 2 All E.R. 96; *Transcontainer Express Ltd.* v. *Custodian Security Ltd.* [1988] 1 Lloyd's L.R. 128.

question to be raised on the construction and application of a regulation where the facts are not disputed.[19]

(vi) *Decision-making in the Court of Appeal*

The approach of the Court of Appeal varies according to whether the appeal concerns (1) questions of fact; (2) awards of damages; (3) exercises of judicial discretion; and (4) questions of law.

(1) *Questions of fact.* In the vast majority of cases, the trial will have been conducted by a judge sitting without a jury. The findings of fact will be set out in the judgment. On an appeal, a distinction will be drawn by the Court of Appeal between findings of "primary fact" and inferences of fact drawn from those primary facts (sometimes termed "secondary facts").[20] The Court of Appeal is most reluctant to disturb findings of primary fact where they are based on the testimony of witnesses who have been seen by the judge, and who, in accordance with the practice of the Court of Appeal, will not be seen in person on the appeal.[21] The judge's finding will normally have been based, at least in part, on his or her observations of manner and demeanour, and this advantage is denied to the Court of Appeal. In exceptional cases, the court may find that the trial judge has "failed to use or has palpably misused his advantage."[22] The judge's impression of the witnesses' demeanour "should be carefully checked by a critical examination of the whole of the evidence."[23] A judgment:

> ". . . may be demonstrated . . . to be affected by material inconsistencies and inaccuracies or [the trial judge] may be shown to have failed to appreciate the weight or bearing of circumstances admitted or proved or otherwise to have gone plainly wrong."[24]

The court is a little less reluctant to interfere with findings based upon expert evidence.[25]

On the other hand, the Court of Appeal is much more willing to draw inferences from the primary facts different from those drawn by the trial judge: it is generally in as good a position as the judge to draw such inferences.[26]

The role of the Court of Appeal in appeals on questions of fact was considered in *Whitehouse* v. *Jordan*.[27] The trial judge held a senior hospital registrar to have been negligent in the course of delivering a baby by pulling too hard and too long on obstetric forceps, causing brain damage. This

---

[19] *Donaghey* v. *P. O'Brien & Co.* [1966] 1 W.L.R. 1170, 1180; on appeal: *Donaghey* v. *Boulton & Paul Ltd.* [1968] A.C. 1, 14, 23, 31; *cf. Jones* v. *Department of Employment* [1989] Q.B. 1 (Court of Appeal willing to entertain a new argument on a point of law on an appeal against striking out, where the facts are assumed).

[20] See above, p. 11.

[21] *SS. Hontestroom (Owners)* v. *SS. Sagaporack (Owners)* [1927] A.C. 37; *Powell* v. *Streatham Manor Nursing Home* [1935] A.C. 243; *Watt or Thomas* v. *Thomas* [1947] A.C. 484.

[22] *Per* Lord Sumner in *SS. Hontestroom* v. *SS. Sagaporack, supra,* at p. 47.

[23] *Per* Lord Greene M.R. in *Yuill* v. *Yuill* [1945] P. 15, 22.

[24] *Per* Lord Macmillan in *Watt or Thomas* v. *Thomas* [1947] A.C. 484 at p. 491.

[25] *Joyce* v. *Yeomans* [1981] 1 W.L.R. 549 (medical witnesses).

[26] *Benmax* v. *Austin Motor Co. Ltd.* [1955] A.C. 370.

[27] [1981] 1 W.L.R. 246.

finding was based on a combination of expert evidence, a report by the consultant professor who was the registrar's head of department, and the testimony of the mother. This finding was reversed by the Court of Appeal (Lord Denning M.R. and Lawton L.J., Donaldson L.J. dissenting). The majority held that the expert evidence against the registrar was defective in certain respects, and could not stand up against the expert evidence in his favour; that the judge had acted incorrectly in interpreting a crucial word in the report in its dictionary sense rather than in that now stated by the professor to be the sense intended; and that as the judge had disbelieved most of the mother's evidence, he ought not to have relied upon any of it. The mother had testified that force had been applied to the extent that her hips had been lifted off the table. The judge accepted that this could not literally have been true, but held that it showed that she "could" have been pulled towards the bottom of the delivery bed. On this last point, Lawton L.J. said that this was one of the rare cases where the appeal court was entitled to disregard the trial judge's assessment of the reliability of a witness. He had "palpably misused his advantage" in seeing the witness by turning her account of what had happened, which physically could not have taken place, into one which could. The House of Lords unanimously endorsed the conclusion of the majority of the Court of Appeal. They stressed the point that apart from the mother's testimony, the issues concerned inferences from the primary facts in the sense of the evaluation of testimony accepted to have been honestly given.[28] As to the mother's testimony, the House agreed unanimously that the judge's "reconstruction" of it should be disregarded.

Where the trial is conducted with a jury, the powers of the Court of Appeal are more limited. A verdict will be set aside if the evidence was such that no jury properly directed could reasonably have returned it.[29]

(2) *Awards of damages.* The Court of Appeal will not vary an award of damages merely because the judges sitting on the appeal would have awarded a different figure. It will only do so:

"... if satisfied that the judge has acted on a wrong principle of law or has misapprehended the facts, or has, for those or other reasons, made a wholly erroneous estimate of the damage suffered."[30]

In practice, the Court of Appeal is much more likely to interfere with an award of damages than a finding of fact, especially where, as with large personal injuries awards, complex calculations are necessary.

Where damages were assessed by a jury, the Court of Appeal was only prepared to interfere with an award where it was "so excessive or so inadequate that no 12 reasonable jurors could reasonably have awarded it."[31] The consequence of this cautious approach was that awards of significantly different amounts in similar cases were permitted to stand. This was

---

[28] See Lord Wilberforce, *ibid.* pp. 249–250; Lord Fraser of Tullybelton, *ibid.*, p. 263.
[29] See below, pp. 861–862.
[30] *Per* Morris L.J. in *Scott* v. *Musial* [1959] 2 Q.B. 429, 437.
[31] *Ibid.*, pp. 437–8.

one of the factors in the move away from trial by jury in civil cases.[32] In *Ward v. James*,[33] Lord Denning M.R. said[34]:

> "In future this court will not feel the same hesitation as it formerly did in upsetting an award of damages by a jury. If it is 'out of all proportion to the circumstances of the case' (that is, if it is far too high or far too low), this court will set it aside."

This approach appears to bring the position closer to that applied to awards by judges. In *Sutcliffe v. Pressdram Ltd.*[35] the Court of Appeal set aside a libel award of £600,000 to the wife of the so-called "Yorkshire Ripper." The traditional approach was followed, and it was not regarded as having been changed by *Ward v. James*.[36]

The Court of Appeal may substitute an award of damages for that made by a judge. If the award was made by a jury the Court of Appeal may only vary an award with the consent of the parties[37]: otherwise it must order a new trial, which may be by judge alone. However, there is now power to make rules of court enabling the Court of Appeal in specified cases to substitute an award for that made by the jury.[38]

(3) *Exercises of discretion.* On many matters, a decision may be left to an exercise of the judge's discretion. This is commonly so in interlocutory matters such as pleading, discovery, venue and mode of trial. Here, the matter will normally have been considered first by a master or registrar, and then, by way of a fresh application to the judge. At this stage the judge will consider the matter afresh and may substitute his or her discretion for that of the master. However, if the matter is then taken to the Court of Appeal, that court will only interfere with the judge's exercise of discretion if he or she has erred in law, applied an incorrect principle, misapprehended the facts, taken irrelevant matters into consideration or ignored relevant considerations, or if the court is satisfied that the decision was wrong.[39] This is not regarded as enabling the Court of Appeal to interfere merely because the judges sitting on the appeal would have exercised the discretion differently.[40] An example is *Charles Osenton & Co. v. Johnston*,[41] where the House of Lords reversed an order for trial by an official referee on the ground that the judge had not given sufficient weight to the point that the professional reputation of surveyors was at stake.

[32] See above, pp. 703–706.
[33] [1966] 1 Q.B. 273.
[34] *Ibid.*, p. 301.
[35] [1990] 2 W.L.R. 271.
[36] *Supra.* A majority of the Court of Appeal regarded the jury in the *Sutcliffe* case as having wrongly included an award of exemplary damages. Mrs. Sutcliffe settled the case for £60,000.
[37] R.S.C. Ord. 59, r. 11(4). Where a head of damages has been erroneously included or excluded the only consent required is that of the person entitled to receive or the person liable to pay the damages, as the case may be: *ibid.*
[38] Courts and Legal Services Act 1990, s.8.
[39] *Evans v. Bartlam* [1937] A.C. 473. This is regarded as broader than the tests applied by the court in reviewing exercises of administrative discretion under the principles stated in the *Wednesbury* case (see below, p. 873, n. 59): *Tsai v. Woodworth, The Times*, November 30, 1983.
[40] *Per* Viscount Simon L.C. in *Charles Osenton & Co. v. Johnston* [1942] A.C. 130, 138.
[41] *Ibid.*

In addition, modern statutes commonly leave decisions on substantive as distinct from procedural matters to the discretion of judges. Examples include awards under the Inheritance (Provision for Family and Dependants) Act 1975, financial provision after divorce and decisions concerning custody of and access to children. The same principles have been applied to the role of the Court of Appeal here,[42] and it has been stressed that the court should be particularly unwilling to interfere where the exercise of discretion is based on the impression made by a person in the witness box.[43]

However, in custody cases there has been a difference between: (1) those who take the view that the appellate court should only interfere where the judge has erred in law, taken some irrelevant matter into account or failed to take some relevant matter into account, or where the decision is "plainly wrong" in the sense that no reasonable judge could have so decided[44]; and (2) those who take the view that, in addition, the appellate court may interfere on the ground that the judge's decision is "plainly wrong" as a consequence of erring in the course of balancing the relevant factors.[45] The House of Lords in G. v. G. (Minors: Custody Appeal)[46] clearly endorsed the second school of thought. It expressly rejected as too narrow the "no reasonable judge" formulation: this was based on the "Wednesbury unreasonableness" principle[47] applicable to judicial control over the decision of an administrative body, and was not the appropriate test here. The distinction between the tests was admittedly "a fine one." Furthermore, it was clear that even under the less restricted approach approved by the House of Lords, the Court of Appeal would only exceptionally interfere with a decision where it could not point to an error of law or to a particular factor that should (or should not) have been taken into account: i.e. only in a case where the judge had "exceeded the generous ambit within which a reasonable disagreement is possible."[48]

A further point made by the House of Lords in G. v. G. (Minors: Custody Appeal)[49] was that the principles set out are generally applicable to all judicial exercises of discretion: appeals concerning the welfare of children do not form a special category.[50] The principles have subsequently been cited in connection with financial provision after divorce,[51] the award of

---

[42] See, e.g. In re Thornley, Decd. [1969] 1 W.L.R. 1037; Preston v. Preston [1982] Fam. 17.

[43] B. v. W. (Wardship: Appeal) [1979] 1 W.L.R. 1041.

[44] Stamp L.J. dissenting, in Re F (A Minor) (Wardship: Appeal) [1976] Fam. 238, 249–255; Sir John Arnold P. in Clode v. Clode (1982) 3 F.L.R. 360, 363.

[45] Re O (Infants) (Wardship: Appeal) [1971] Ch. 748; Browne and Bridge L.JJ. in Re F (A Minor) (Wardship: Appeal) [1976] Fam. 238; B. v. W. (Wardship: Appeal) [1979] 1 W.L.R. 1041; D. v. M. (Minor: Custody Appeal) [1983] Fam. 33.

[46] [1985] 1 W.L.R. 647. See J. Eekelaar, (1985) 48 M.L.R. 704; C. Forder and R. Ward, "Child custody appeals: the search for principle" [1987] C.L.J. 489; S. P. de Cruz, (1986) 130 S.J. 563.

[47] Below, p. 873.

[48] Per Lord Bridge at [1985] 1 W.L.R. 647, 656.

[49] Per Lord Fraser at p. 652, based on Asquith L.J. in Bellenden (formerly Satterthwaite) v. Satterthwaite [1948] 1 All E.R. 343, 345. The point that this formulation should not apply where there is an error of law or principle is emphasised by Eekelaar, and by Forder and Ward, op. cit. Most of the post-G. v. G. cases in which an appeal has been allowed have been characterised as involving errors of principle, rather than errors in balancing the relevant factors.

[50] Ibid., p. 651, per Lord Fraser.

[51] Morris v. Morris [1985] 1 F.L.R. 1176; Mason v. Mason [1986] 2 F.L.R. 212; Allen v. Allen [1986] 2 F.L.R. 265; Whiting v. Whiting [1988] 1 W.L.R. 565.

costs[52] and the grant of injunctions.[53] The adherents of both schools were agreed that the Court of Appeal may not interfere merely because the members of that court would have exercised the discretion differently.[54]

If an appellate court wishes to vary a discretionary order, it may either substitute an appropriate order, remit the case to the judge (or to another judge) or, in exceptional cases, hear evidence in order to resolve any doubts.[55]

(4) *Questions of law.* Here, the Court of Appeal may simply substitute its opinion for that of the court below.

(vii) *Applications for a new trial*

Section 17 of the Supreme Court Act 1981 provides that applications for a new trial must normally be directed to the Court of Appeal. However, rules of court may prescribe cases or classes of cases where applications are to be made to the High Court: such cases can only be those where trial was by a judge alone and no error of the court at the trial is alleged.[56] The procedure for applications to the Court of Appeal for a new trial is virtually the same as for an appeal.[57]

Where a case is tried by judge alone, the proper course for a dissatisfied party is normally[58] to appeal. On an appeal, the Court of Appeal may, as we have noted, correct any error of fact or law and may vary the judgment. However, in some cases it may be appropriate for the Court of Appeal to order a new trial.[59] This may be so where, for example, the essence of the complaint is that there has not been a fair trial. For example, a party may be "taken by surprise" where a case is called on for hearing unexpectedly, or develops in a wholly unexpected manner. Similarly, a new trial may be ordered where fresh evidence is discovered,[60] or a witness confesses that his or her evidence was false,[61] or in cases of misconduct by the judge[62] or counsel.

Where a case is tried by a judge sitting with a jury, the proper course for a party dissatisfied is to apply for a new trial. The grounds for such applications mentioned above in relation to trial by judge alone will also be relevant here. In addition, there are a number of grounds related particularly to jury trial, including misdirection of the jury, the improper admission or rejection of evidence, and claims that there was no evidence to go to the jury, that the verdict was against the weight of evidence or that the damages are excessive or inadequate.[63] However, the court is not bound to grant a new trial on the

[52] *Hawkins* v. *Dhawan* [1987] 2 E.G.L.R. 157.
[53] *Att.-Gen.* v. *Guardian Newspapers Ltd.* [1987] 1 W.L.R. 1248.
[54] *Re F (A Minor), supra,* at pp. 250 (Stamp L.J.); 257–258 (Browne L.J.); *Clarke-Hunt* v. *Newcombe* (1983) 4 F.L.R. 482, 486–487 (Cumming-Bruce L.J.).
[55] *Per* Lord Scarman in *B.* v. *W., supra,* at p. 1055, in relation to custody orders.
[56] *e.g.* where judgment has been obtained in the absence of a party: Ord. 35, r. 2(1) (see *Re Edwards' Will Trusts, Edwards* v. *Edwards* [1982] Ch. 30).
[57] R.S.C. Ord. 59, r. 2.
[58] *i.e.* unless an application must be made to the High Court: n. 56, *supra.*
[59] Jurisdiction to do so is conferred by R.S.C. Ord. 59, r. 11(1).
[60] See above, p. 856: *Meek* v. *Fleming* [1961] 2 Q.B. 366 (court misled by concealment of material evidence).
[61] *Piotrowska* v. *Piotrowski* [1958] 1 W.L.R. 798.
[62] *Jones* v. *National Coal Board* [1957] 2 Q.B. 55, above, p. 707.
[63] See above, p. 858.

ground of misdirection, or the improper admission or rejection of evidence, or because the verdict of the jury was not taken upon a question which the judge at the trial was not asked to leave to them, unless the Court of Appeal is of the opinion that this caused some "substantial wrong or miscarriage."[64] In other words, there will be no new trial in these circumstances if the court is satisfied that the jury, if rightly directed, would still have returned the same verdict.[65]

A verdict supported by no evidence is regarded as erroneous in law: if it is claimed, however, that a verdict is against the weight of evidence, it will only be set aside if it was one that no reasonable jury could have found.[66]

A new trial may be ordered on one particular aspect of a case, without affecting the other aspects.[67] For example, there may be a new trial on a question of damages without prejudice to a finding of liability.

(viii) *Appeals from masters, district judges and referees*

Generally speaking, an appeal lies from the decision of a High Court master or a district judge of the High Court, to a judge of the appropriate division sitting in chambers.[68] The judge will rehear the matter and is not fettered by the decision of the master or district judge.[69] An appeal lies from a decision of a judge in chambers, whether or not the matter has previously been before a master or district judge, to the Court of Appeal, subject to the restrictions applicable generally to appeals to that court.[70]

In certain cases, an appeal lies direct from a master of the Queen's Bench or Chancery Divisions to the Court of Appeal.[71] These are cases where a matter has been tried by the master or referred to him or her for a final decision, and decisions on an assessment of damages.[72]

An appeal lies from a decision of an official referee[73] to the Court of Appeal:

(1) on a point of law; or, when section 18(1)(*f*) of the Supreme Court Act 1981[74] does not apply, on a question only of costs;

(2) with the leave of the official referee or the Court of Appeal, on a question of fact, or, when section 18(1)(*f*) does apply, on a question only of costs[75];

---

[64] R.S.C. Ord. 59, r. 11(5).
[65] *Rowell* v. *Pratt* [1938] A.C. 101, 116.
[66] *Metropolitan Ry. Co.* v. *Wright* (1886) 11 App.Cas. 152; *Mechanical Inventions Co. Ltd.* v. *Austin* [1935] A.C. 346. If it is obvious that no verdict for the plaintiff on all the available evidence could be supported, the court may save the waste of time in ordering a new trial by ordering judgment to be entered for the defendant: *Mechanical Inventions Co. Ltd.* v. *Austin, ibid.*
[67] R.S.C. Ord. 59, r. 11(3).
[68] R.S.C. Ord. 58, rr. 1(1), 3.
[69] *Evans* v. *Bartlam* [1937] A.C. 473, 478. All relevant evidence should be considered, including evidence that was not but could have been adduced before the registrar: *Wales Tourist Board* v. *Roberts, The Times,* January 10, 1987.
[70] See above, pp. 849–850; and see also R.S.C. Ord. 58, r. 6, as amended by S.I. 1988 No. 298, r. 4.
[71] R.S.C. Ord. 58, r. 2.
[72] Under, respectively, R.S.C. Ord. 36, r. 11 and Ord. 37.
[73] See above, pp. 83–84.
[74] See above, p. 850.
[75] R.S.C. Ord. 58, r. 4., substituted by S.I. 1988 No. 1340, r. 6. Formerly, an appeal on a question of fact lay only if it related to a charge of fraud or breach of professional duty.

(3) where he or she has made or refused to make an order of committal for contempt of court.[76]

(c) Appeals from the High Court to the House of Lords

In certain circumstances an appeal in a civil case may be taken directly from the High Court (whether a single judge or a Divisional Court) to the House of Lords, "leap-frogging" the Court of Appeal. The conditions are prescribed by Part II of the Administration of Justice Act 1969.[77]

Any of the parties to civil proceedings[78] in the High Court may apply to the trial judge[79] for a certificate to the effect that he is satisfied:

(1) that the "relevant conditions" are fulfilled in relation to his decision in the proceedings;
(2) that a sufficient case for a "leap-frog" appeal has been made out to justify an application for leave to appeal; and
(3) that all the parties consent to the grant of a certificate.[80]

Where apart from the provisions of Part II of the 1969 Act no appeal would lie to the Court of Appeal without the leave of the trial judge or the Court of Appeal, the judge is not to grant a certificate unless it appears to the judge that apart from those provisions "it would be a proper case for granting leave."[81]

The "relevant conditions" are:

(1) that a point of law of general public importance is involved in the decision; and
(2) that the point of law either—
   "(a) relates wholly or mainly to the construction of an enactment or of a statutory instrument, and has been fully argued in the proceedings and fully considered in the judgment of the judge in the proceedings, or
   (b) is one in respect of which the judge is bound by a decision of the Court of Appeal or of the House of Lords in previous proceedings, and was fully considered in the judgments given by the Court of Appeal or the House of Lords (as the case may be) in those previous proceedings."[82]

No certificate can be granted if by virtue of any enactment no appeal would lie from the High Court to the Court of Appeal or from the Court of

---

[76] Administration of Justice 1960, s.13(2)(b).
[77] This possibility was recommended by the Evershed Committee on Supreme Court Practice and Procedure, Final Report (Cmd. 8878, 1953), paras. 483–503. The Law Lords at the time were not in favour of the proposal, but attitudes had changed by the late 1960s. See L. Blom-Cooper and G. Drewry, Final Appeal (1972), pp. 149–151.
[78] i.e. "proceedings other than proceedings in a criminal cause or matter": Administration of Justice Act 1969, s.12(8).
[79] Or Divisional Court, as the case may be: ibid.
[80] 1969 Act, s.12(1).
[81] Ibid. s.15(3).
[82] Ibid. s.12(3).

Appeal to the House of Lords, or if the decision or order of the judge was made in the exercise of jurisdiction to punish for contempt of court.[83]

Otherwise, the judge has a discretion whether to grant a certificate,[84] and no appeal lies from a refusal.[85] The application for a certificate should normally be made at the hearing but may be made within 14 days.[86]

If a certificate is granted any party may apply within one month to the House of Lords for leave to appeal directly.[87] No hearing is held. The House may grant leave "if . . . it appears . . . to be expedient to do so," whereupon no appeal will lie to the Court of Appeal.[88] Moreover, no appeal will lie to the Court of Appeal once a certificate is granted until either the time for an application for leave has expired or, where an application is made, until it has been determined by the House.[89]

The "leap-frog" procedure is used in comparatively few cases,[90] although it does enable there to be a significant saving in time and expense if a case is destined for the House of Lords. One of the problems is that it may be difficult for a trial judge to perceive that a case is so destined: it may only become so in the light of the decision in the Court of Appeal.[91]

(d) Appeals from the Court of Appeal to the House of Lords

An appeal lies from any judgment or order of the Court of Appeal to the House of Lords, provided that leave is obtained from either court.[92] No appeal lies from a decision of the Court of Appeal to refuse leave for an appeal to itself; such a refusal does not constitute a "judgment or order."[93] An application for leave is made first to the Court of Appeal, normally immediately after judgment. It is only if leave is refused that a petition for leave may be made to the House.

Among grounds commonly given by the Court of Appeal for refusing leave to appeal are that the point concerns an interlocutory matter, the point is one of fact rather than law, the subject matter is trivial, the matter has become of academic interest only to one or both of the parties[94] and that the Court of Appeal was unanimous and not divided. On the other hand, leave is normally granted in revenue cases.[95]

Petitions to the House of Lords for leave are heard by an Appeal Committee of three Law Lords,[96] and must be lodged within one month from the

---

[83] Ibid. s.15(1)(2)(4).
[84] I.R.C. v. Church Commissioners for England [1975] 1 W.L.R. 1383.
[85] 1969 Act s.12(5).
[86] Ibid. s.12(4).
[87] The House may grant an extension of time: ibid. s.13(1).
[88] Ibid. s.13(2).
[89] Ibid. s.13(5).
[90] The early practice is reviewed by G. Drewry in "Leapfrogging—And a Lord Justices' Eye View of the Final Appeal" (1973) 89 L.Q.R. 260.
[91] e.g. as in Cassell & Co. Ltd. v. Broome [1972] A.C. 1027: see above, pp. 380–382. The Lord Chancellor suggested that in view of the doubts raised about the direction in Rookes v. Barnard [1964] A.C. 1129, the proper course would have been to wait for a case in which the point was directly raised and suggest that the parties take that case directly to the House of Lords: ibid., p. 1053.
[92] Appellate Jurisdiction Act 1876, s.3; Administration of Justice (Appeals) Act 1934, s.1.
[93] Lane v. Esdaile [1891] A.C. 210; Whitehouse v. The Board of Control [1960] 1 W.L.R. 1093.
[94] cf. Ainsbury v. Millington [1987] 1 W.L.R. 379, where the House refused to hear arguments on this ground in a case in which leave had been granted.
[95] See L. Blom-Cooper and G. Drewry, Final Appeal (1972), pp. 146–149.
[96] See above, p. 93 and L. Blom-Cooper and G. Drewry, Final Appeal (1972), Chap. VII.

date of the order of which complaint is made.[97] The committee considers the petition, and if all three members are unanimously of the opinion that it is incompetent and should not be allowed it is dismissed without a hearing. If all three are unanimously of the opinion that leave should be granted, the respondents are notified, and given 14 days to lodge written objections. If the committee's opinion remains the same, leave is granted without a further hearing. In any case in which the members are not unanimous, the petition is referred for an oral hearing by the committee.[98] The parties may appear in person or may be represented by solicitors (known as "agents" on appeals to the House) or counsel. In the case of "leapfrog" appeals from the High Court[99] the petition for leave must be lodged within one month from the date on which the necessary certificate was granted: the time can be extended. The petition is considered by the Appeal Committee without a hearing.[1] No reasons are normally given for refusing leave. Conditions may be attached to a grant of leave: this is commonly done on appeals by the Inland Revenue in tax cases, where leave is only granted if the Revenue undertake to pay the costs of the appeal for the respondent in any event. If a condition is imposed by the Court of Appeal, the applicant may treat this as a refusal and apply for leave to the House of Lords.

Where an application for leave to appeal has been refused, it is nevertheless possible, in exceptional cases, for a fresh application to be made and granted.[2]

An appeal must be lodged in the House of Lords within three months of the date of the order appealed from, unless the House otherwise orders,[3] or a different period is fixed by statute. Leave to appeal out of time may be obtained. Unless legal aid has been granted, or the respondent agrees to waive the requirement, the appellant must give security for costs in the sum of £4,000.[4]

The appeal is normally considered by an Appellate Committee of five Law Lords.[5] The parties may appear in person or be represented by counsel. The parties must each lodge a printed "Case," "being a succinct statement of their argument in the Appeal, settled by counsel" and stating "what are, in their view, the issues arising in the Appeal."[6] All members of the Appellate Committee will have read the Case and the judgments in the court below in advance of the hearing. The House has noted and deprecated a tendency to expand the written cases to incorporate and develop in them detailed written arguments, supported by lengthy citations and references to numerous authorities:

[97] House of Lords Civil Appeals, Directions as to Procedure, Dir. 2: *Supreme Court Practice 1991*, para. 4907.
[98] Directions as to Procedure, Dir. 9.
[99] See above, pp. 863–864.
[1] Directions as to Procedure, Dir. 13.
[2] See *Buttes Gas* v. *Hammer* [1982] A.C. 888 (leave to appeal from [1975] Q.B. 557 in the light of related proceedings: but note the criticisms of F. A. Mann, (1983) 2 C.J.Q. 320, 325–326); *R.* v. *Home Secretary, ex p. Khera* [1984] A.C. 74, (the House of Lords invited the appellant to re-apply for leave following their Lordships' decision to review *R.* v. *Home Secretary, ex p. Zamir* [1980] A.C. 930).
[3] Directions as to Procedure, Dir. 15.
[4] Directions as to Procedure, Dir. 23; [1981] 1 W.L.R. 1213.
[5] See above, p. 93.
[6] See above, p. 93. Directions as to Procedure, Dir. 25.

"... much on the same lines as the written "briefs" submitted by the parties in appeals to appellate courts in the United States, which have resulted in oral argument playing a relatively insignificant role in the decision-making process adopted by appellate courts in that country."[7]

The pre-reading was, it was emphasised, not intended to reduce the process played by oral argument in the decision-making process. Cases should include the *heads* of argument on each issue, and only *key* authorities should be mentioned. It has, however, been doubted whether all members of the Committee do always read all the papers in advance, and whether all the members always come to a hearing without at least a provisional conclusion in mind.[8] It would obviously be undesirable for preconceived opinions to be based on limited information. Indeed, it has been suggested that changes in the practice of both the Court of Appeal[9] and the House of Lords may inevitably transform the nature of oral argument:

"... which is bound to lose its force where it is no longer a dialogue in the traditional sense, but an attempt to dislodge or fortify an existing impression, however provisional it may be said to be....
[T]he introduction of radical changes under the heading of practice and procedure is outside the province of judges."[10]

The respective approaches of the House to question of fact, discretion and law are similar to that taken by the Court of Appeal.[11] The House "may determine what of right, and according to the law and custom of this realm, ought to be done" in relation to the appeal. Where the House reverses or varies an order of the court below, or orders anything to be done by the court below, the order of the House of Lords must be made an order of the High Court[12]: the House itself has no machinery for enforcement.

4. APPEALS IN ADMINISTRATIVE LAW MATTERS

(a) Introduction

No neat classification is possible of the vast range of functions performed by administrative authorities. Neither is it possible to discern any clear pattern in the availability of rights of appeal from administrative decisions.[13]
The Franks Committee[14] noted that:

"... over most of the field of public administration no formal procedure is provided for objecting or deciding on objections.... Of course the aggrieved individual can always complain to the appropriate administrative authority, to his Member of Parliament, to a representative organisation or to the press. But there is no formal procedure on which he can insist.... It may be thought that in these cases the individual is

---

[7] *M.V. Yorke Motors* v. *Edwards* [1982] 1 W.L.R. 444, 446–448; reaffirmed in *G.* v. *G.* (*Minors: Custody Appeal*) [1985] 1 W.L.R. 647.
[8] F. A. Mann, (1983) 2 C.J.Q. 320, 327–328, 334–335.
[9] See above, pp. 853–854.
[10] F. A. Mann, *supra*, pp. 334, 335.
[11] See above, pp. 857–861.
[12] See R.S.C. Ord. 32, r. 10.
[13] See S. A. de Smith and R. Brazier, *Constitutional and Administrative Law* (6th ed., 1989), pp. 542–544.
[14] See above, pp. 35–36.

less protected against unfair or wrong decisions [than where there is provision for a formal procedure involving a tribunal or inquiry]."[15]

Such decisions were outside the committee's terms of reference, although it did express "much sympathy" with the proposal by Professor W. A. Robson that there should be a general administrative appeal tribunal, with jurisdiction to hear not only appeals from tribunals and from ministers after a public inquiry, "but also appeals against harsh or unfair administrative decisions in that considerable field of administration in which no special tribunal or enquiry procedure is provided."[16] The committee, however, felt that it had to consider the proposal in relation to its limited terms of reference, and that, viewed from that standpoint, the proposal was to be rejected.

Since then, the problem noted by the Franks Committee has been partly met by the establishment of "Ombudsmen" of various kinds. The Parliamentary Commissioner for Administration and Local Commissioners have power to investigate complaints that there has been injustice consequent on "maladministration" in central and local government.[17] The concept of "maladministration" covers such matters as corruption, bias, unfair discrimination, giving misleading advice, failure to explain the reasons for a decision, losing correspondence and unreasonable delay. The relevant defects are mostly procedural, although where a decision is "thoroughly bad in quality" maladministration may be inferred, and in certain circumstances authorities may be required to reconsider a rule that has caused hardship. The commissioners may not, however, question the merits of a discretionary decision taken without maladministration,[18] and may not entertain a complaint in respect of which there is a right of appeal to a tribunal or a remedy by way of proceedings in a court of law, unless it is not reasonable to expect the complainant to utilise those possibilities.[19]

As to the availability of statutory appeals against administrative decisions, the late Professor de Smith noted[20] that there is in general no appeal against discretionary decisions of central government involving questions of national policy or the allocation of scarce resources, against decisions of public corporations or against most discretionary decisions of local authorities on the allocation of limited resources.

However, in certain other areas of public administration, particularly where no sensitive issue of policy is involved, where questions of law may loom large or where a decision has a significant impact on individual rights of liberty or property there may be provision for an appeal.

(b) Particular areas

(i) *Regulatory functions*

Many activities are subjected to state regulation for such purposes as the

[15] Cmnd. 218, pp. 2–3.
[16] Cmnd. 218, p. 28.
[17] See generally, de Smith and Brazier (1989), Chap 33; Sir William Wade, *Administrative Law* (6th ed., 1988), pp. 77–101, 135–140; P. P. Craig, *Administrative Law* (2nd ed., 1989), pp. 102–113. There is also an office of National Health Service Commissioner (held by the P.C.A.) and there are two Commissioners in Northern Ireland.
[18] Parliamentary Commissioner Act 1967, s.12(3); Local Government Act 1974, s.34(3).
[19] *Ibid.* ss.5(2) and 26(6) respectively.
[20] de Smith and Brazier (1989), p. 543.

protection of public health and welfare. Certain activities are prohibited by law. Others are permitted provided that those who participate in them register with a public authority.[21] Yet others require a specific permission or licence from a public authority: the ease with which a licence may be obtained, and the grounds upon which a licence may be refused are almost infinitely variable.

Control may also be exerted by procedures for inspection. For example, health and safety inspectors may inspect factory premises, offer advice on safety matters, issue notices requiring the cessation of dangerous activities, and, in the last resort, bring criminal proceedings for breaches of the law.

Decisions made in the course of regulatory procedures of this kind are commonly subject to a statutory right of appeal to a tribunal,[22] the Crown Court,[23] a county court[24] or, most commonly, a magistrates' court.[25]

In a small number of cases, such as decisions of the Director-General of Fair Trading concerning consumer credit licensing and the supervision of estate agency work, an appeal lies to a minister, in these examples the Secretary of State for Trade and Industry.

It is normal for it to be possible on such appeals to challenge a decision on the merits as well as on any point of law. This may be so even where it is expressly stated that the decision is "at the discretion" of the authority in question. For example, a grant of a permit for amusements with prizes[26] is "at the discretion of the local authority."[27] An appeal lies to the Crown Court. In *Sagnata Ltd.* v. *Norwich Corporation*,[28] the Court of Appeal held that the recorder at quarter sessions (now the Crown Court) had been correct to go into the merits of a refusal of a permit afresh on appeal, although this did not mean that he "ought not to pay great attention to the fact that the duly constituted and elected local authority have come to an opinion on the matter, and ought not lightly to reverse their opinion."[29]

(ii) *Welfare benefits*

Another important sphere of state activity is that of the provision of many

---

[21] Registration requirements may also be imposed to raise revenue.

[22] *e.g.* appeals to an Industrial Tribunal against an improvement or prohibition notice served by a health and safety inspector.

[23] *e.g.* decisions of a chief officer of police in relation to firearms certificates and the registration of firearms; refusal of a permit for the commercial provision of amusements with prizes and many decisions of justices of the peace in administrative matters: see D. Price, *Appeals* (1982), pp. 37–40.

[24] *e.g.* a person aggrieved by a notice requiring him or her to carry out works of repair, by a demand for the recovery of expenses where the authority has acted in default or by a demolition or closing order: Housing Act 1985, ss.191, 269, and Sched. 10, para. 6; Price (1982), pp. 46–49.

[25] *e.g.* revocation of a pilot's or slaughterman's licence; refusal of a pet shop or knacker's yard licence; refusal of registration of a nursery, child minder, or nursing home: Price (1982), pp. 53–60.

[26] *e.g.* fruit machines.

[27] Lotteries and Amusements Act 1976, Sched. 3. para. 7(1)(a).

[28] [1971] 2 Q.B. 614.

[29] *Per* Lord Goddard C.J. in *Stepney Borough Council* v. *Joffe* [1949] 1 K.B. 599, 603, endorsed by Edmund Davies L.J. in *Sagnata, supra*, at p. 637. See also *Darlington Borough Council* v. *Paul Wakefield* (1988) 153 J.P. 481.

kinds of welfare benefits. Here, it is common for rights of appeal to be granted to a tribunal[30] or, in a few cases,[31] a minister.

(iii) *Tribunals*

Where a decision-making function has been entrusted to a tribunal, it is normal for there to be a further appeal on points of law, either to a special appellate tribunal such as the Social Security Commissioners or the Employment Appeal Tribunal,[32] to the High Court or to the Court of Appeal.[33] For example, the Tribunals and Inquiries Act 1971 provides[34] for a right of appeal on a point of law to the High Court from the decisions of over 10 tribunals,[35] and there are several others for which similar provision is made by specific statutes. Appeals from tribunals to the High Court on points of law may be required to be made by means of a case stated procedure. Most lie to the Queen's Bench Division, but some, such as those against decisions of the Commons Commissioners and the Special and General Commissioners of Income Tax, lie to the Chancery Division. Appeals are generally heard by a single judge, unless the High Court's decision will be final, in which case the appeal will normally be heard by a Divisional Court.[36]

(iv) *Land use*

Given the traditional concern of the law for the protection of property rights it is perhaps not surprising that statutory rights to appeal figure prominently in respect of governmental decisions that infringe or affect property rights. Two kinds of procedure require special mention here. First, planning permission is generally necessary for "the carrying out of building, engineering, mining or other operations in, on, over or under land" or "the making of any material change in the use" of buildings or land.[37] Applications for permission are made to the local planning authority and an appeal on merits, fact or law lies against a refusal to the Secretary of State for the Environment. An appeal may involve a hearing by way of a public local inquiry conducted by an inspector appointed by the Secretary of State, unless the appellant wishes simply to make written representations. The inspector may make the decision personally, except in the thirty per cent. or so of larger scale applications, where the decision is taken by the Secretary of State. An appeal thereafter lies on a point of law to the Queen's Bench Division.

Secondly, there are many powers which authorise the compulsory acquisition of land. The typical procedure provides for a compulsory purchase order to be made by a local authority, subject to confirmation by a minister.

---

[30] See above, pp. 60–62.
[31] *e.g.* on questions whether contribution conditions for national insurance conditions have been satisfied: Social Security Act 1975, s.93(1)(*b*).
[32] See above, pp. 59–60, 62.
[33] *e.g.* from the Lands Tribunal and the Foreign Compensation Commission.
[34] s.13.
[35] *e.g.* Industrial Tribunals (for certain matters), Rent Assessment Committees and Pension Appeal Tribunals.
[36] The procedure on ordinary appeals is regulated by R.S.C. Ord. 55 and on appeals by case stated by Ord. 56. R.S.C. Ord. 57 makes further provision for appeals to Divisional Courts.
[37] Town and Country Planning Act 1990, s.55.

If there are objections, a hearing before an inspector must be held on behalf of the minister. If the minister confirms the order, the typical provision[38] governing further appeals enables a person aggrieved by the order to apply within six weeks to the High Court for the order to be quashed on the ground either:

(1) that it is "not within the powers of the Act"; or
(2) that the applicant has been substantially prejudiced by failure to comply with a requirement of the Act.

The order may not otherwise be challenged: thus the person aggrieved may not, for example, seek to challenge an order by applying for judicial review[39] whether within the six week period or not.[40]

The first limb of the grounds of challenge purports to approximate to judicial review under the *ultra vires* doctrine,[41] although it has been given a wider interpretation by the courts. The correct approach was stated as follows by Lord Denning M.R. in *Ashbridge Investments Ltd.* v. *Minister of Housing and Local Government*[42]:

> "The court can only interfere on the ground that the Minister has gone outside the powers of the Act or that any requirement of the Act has not been complied with. Under this section it seems to me that the court can interfere with the Minister's decision if he has acted on no evidence; or if he has come to a conclusion to which on the evidence he could not reasonably come; or if he has given a wrong interpretation to the words of the statute; or if he has taken into consideration matters which he ought not to have taken into account, or vice versa; or has otherwise gone wrong in law. It is identical with the position when the court has power to interfere with the decision of a lower tribunal which has erred in point of law."

This would appear to extend the grounds of challenge to include errors of law not of a kind to cause the authority to act *ultra vires*.

(v) *Appeals from ministers*

In a small number of situations where ministers have to determine questions which may have a significant legal content, there is a further right of appeal on a point of law (or analogous grounds) to the High Court. These include the procedures mentioned in the previous section, decisions of the Secretary of State for Trade and Industry on appeals from the Director-General of Fair Trading, decisions of the Secretary of State for Social Security on national insurance contribution conditions and deportation decisions.[43]

---

[38] *e.g.* Acquisition of Land Act 1981, ss.23–25; Housing Act 1985, Sched. 22, para. 7; Town and Country Planning Act 1990, ss.287, 288.
[39] See below, pp. 871–878.
[40] See *Smith* v. *East Elloe R.D.C.* [1956] A.C. 736; *R.* v. *Secretary of State for the Environment, ex p. Ostler* [1977] Q.B. 122.
[41] See below, pp. 871–874.
[42] [1965] 1 W.L.R. 1320, 1326. Applied by the Court of Appeal in *Coleen Properties Ltd.* v. *Minister of Housing and Local Government* [1971] 1 W.L.R. 433, and subsequent cases.
[43] See below.

(vi) *Immigration*

The impact on individual liberty of decisions to refuse entry to or to deport persons who have no legal right to enter or remain in the United Kingdom is such that a special appellate structure has been established.[44] The decisions of immigration officers or the Home Secretary, whether discretionary or not, may normally be the subject of an appeal to an Immigration Adjudicator, and then to the Immigration Appeal Tribunal.[45] The decision of the tribunal is final, but may be the subject of judicial review.[46] Where a deportation order is made on the ground that it is conducive to the public good "as being in the interests of national security or of the relations between the United Kingdom and any other country or for other reasons of a political nature," there is no appeal, but representations may be made to "three advisors," who may advise the Home Secretary but may not make a binding decision.[47]

D. APPLICATIONS FOR JUDICIAL REVIEW

An appeal will only lie if expressly provided by statute. Apart from, but parallel to, any appellate structure is the control exercised by the High Court over the decisions of any statutory authority[48] with a limited jurisdiction or area of power. This "judicial" control is exercised on the basis of two doctrines. By far the more significant is the *ultra vires* doctrine. The other is the power of the High Court to quash any decision within the reach of the prerogative order of certiorari if an error of law is apparent on the face of the decision-making body's record of proceedings; for this purpose it is immaterial whether the error of law is such as to cause the body to act *ultra vires*.[49] There is not the space here to give more than a very brief account of the *ultra vires* doctrine, and the procedures for seeking judicial review.[50]

1. THE ULTRA VIRES DOCTRINE

Public authorities are normally given a circumscribed area of authority by Parliament. The function of the courts is to ensure that such authorities, whether inferior courts, tribunals, ministers or local authorities, do not exceed any of the limits expressly set by Parliament, and that they perform

---

[44] Immigration Act 1971, Part II.
[45] In certain cases, the appeal lies directly to the I.A.T.
[46] See below.
[47] Immigration Act 1971, s.15(3). See *R. v. Secretary of State for the Home Department, ex p. Hosenball* [1977] 1 W.L.R. 766.
[48] Or bodies established under the royal prerogative: *R. v. Criminal Injuries Compensation Board, ex p. Lain* [1967] 2 Q.B. 864; or otherwise performing public functions: *R. v. Panel on Take-Overs and Mergers, ex p. Datafin plc.* [1987] Q.B. 815.
[49] *R. v. Northumberland Compensation Appeal Tribunal, ex p. Shaw* [1952] 1 K.B. 338.
[50] The leading works include J. M. Evans, *de Smith's Judicial Review of Administrative Action* (4th ed. 1980); Sir William Wade, *Administrative Law* (6th ed., 1988); P. P. Craig, *Administrative Law* (2nd ed., 1989). For a briefer account see S. A. de Smith and R. Brazier, *Constitutional and Administrative Law* (6th ed., 1989), Chaps. 29, 30. On the application for judicial review, see R. J. Gordon, *Judicial Review: Law and Procedure* (1985); G. Aldous and J. Alder, *Applications for Judicial Review* (1985); C. Emery and B. Smythe, *Judicial Review* (1986); R. J. Gordon, *Crown Office Proceedings* (1990).

any statutory duties. If that were all to be done, the *ultra vires* doctrine would simply be an exercise in statutory interpretation, and more or less straightforward as the case might be. However, the courts have in addition read certain implied limitations into governmental powers aimed at ensuring that those powers are not abused, and that decision-making processes are fair procedurally. It is assumed that these limitations are to be observed unless Parliament expressly provides otherwise.

If express or implied limits are exceeded, the body in question is said to have acted "*ultra vires*" *i.e.* beyond its powers: if they are not, the body has acted "*intra vires*." Where a decision is judicial rather than administrative[51] the term "jurisdiction" is used rather than "power," but the difference is one of terminology rather than substance. For convenience of exposition a number of different *ultra vires* situations are commonly distinguished.

(a) Straightforward situations

In some cases a question may arise whether a particular activity falls within the scope of existing statutory authority. For example, in *Attorney-General* v. *Fulham Corporation*[52] the establishment of a municipal laundry was held not to be within the corporation's statutory powers to provide wash-houses. The courts, however, accept that authority may be "reasonably implied" from the express provisions of a statute,[53] and, furthermore, that matters "reasonably incidental" to activities expressly or impliedly authorised will also be held to be *intra vires*.[54]

(b) Jurisdiction over fact and law

In many situations, a body may only act where it is first established that a given state of affairs exists. For example, a court or tribunal may only have jurisdiction over a certain geographical area; a rent tribunal may only have jurisdiction in respect of "leases" of "furnished" premises; there may be a monetary limit to jurisdiction. In these examples, the "preliminary," "collateral" or "threshold" question is clearly distinguishable from the "main" question the court or tribunal has to determine. Moreover, the former is determinable at the commencement of that body's hearing. The superior courts have taken the view that inferior courts and tribunals may not extend their jurisdiction by erroneous determinations of these "preliminary," "collateral" or "jurisdictional" issues, whether or not the error is one of fact or law.[55] If challenged, decisions on these points will be redetermined by the High Court on an application for judicial review.

In other cases, however, the distinction between "preliminary" and "main" questions is less easy to draw. This is particularly so where it is alleged that a tribunal with jurisdiction at the commencement of an inquiry has "wandered outside its designated territory" by misconstruing the statute which gives it power to act. This area of administrative law has been the subject of much sophisticated analysis: it has, however, been doubted

---

[51] These categories represent each end of a spectrum rather than two discrete categories.
[52] [1921] 1 Ch. 440.
[53] *Baroness Wenlock* v. *River Dee Co.* (1885) 10 App.Cas. 354, 362.
[54] *Att.-Gen.* v. *Great Eastern Railway Co.* (1880) 5 App.Cas. 473, 478.
[55] See, *e.g. R.* v. *City of London, etc. Rent Tribunal, ex p. Honig* [1951] 1 K.B. 641.

whether there is any clear cut or convincing test to distinguish "jurisdictional" questions from others. It may be that in the last resort the classification applied by a reviewing court turns more on whether that court wishes to intervene than on the application of any clear principle.

The decision of the House of Lords in *Anisminic Ltd.* v. *Foreign Compensation Commission*[56] was widely regarded as broadening significantly the range of errors of law that would be regarded as causing a tribunal to exceed its jurisdiction.

In *Pearlman* v. *Keepers and Governors of Harrow School*[57] Lord Denning M.R. said that the traditional distinction between jurisdictional and nonjurisdictional errors should be discarded and replaced by a rule that all errors of law, as distinct from errors of fact, should be regarded as jurisdictional. This view has been broadly endorsed by certain members of the House of Lords, but only in respect of tribunals other than courts of law.[58]

(c) Discretion

The courts under the *ultra vires* doctrine ensure that bodies entrusted with a discretion do not fetter it unlawfully by developing rigid rules which preclude a genuine consideration of each case on its merits or by entering contracts or other agreements incompatible with a proper exercise of discretion. Similarly, a body may not be estopped from exercising a statutory discretion and may not delegate the exercise of a discretion without express or implied statutory authority.

Furthermore, an administrative body may not "abuse" its discretion by exercising powers in bad faith or for an improper purpose, by taking account of irrelevant considerations or ignoring relevant considerations, or by making a decision that is so unreasonable, no reasonable authority could make it.[59]

(d) Natural Justice

There are two basic principles of natural justice. The first, the *nemo judex in sua causa* rule, provides that no person should be a judge in his or her own cause, and is applied to judicial or quasi-judicial decisions. The rule is breached where the adjudicator has a direct financial interest[60] or has acted both as prosecutor and judge, or where there is a reasonable suspicion or real likelihood of bias.[61]

The other, the *audi alteram partem* rule, applies to a wider range of decision-making functions and requires prior notice to be given of a decision

---

[56] [1969] 2 A.C. 147.

[57] [1979] Q.B. 56.

[58] *In Re Racal Communications Ltd.* [1981] A.C. 374 *per* Lord Diplock and Lord Keith. It was regarded as applicable to courts of law by the Divisional Court in *R.* v. *Greater Manchester Coroner, ex p. Tal* [1985] Q.B. 67.

[59] These principles were expounded by Lord Greene M.R. in *Associated Provincial Picture Houses Ltd.* v. *Wednesbury Corporation* [1948] 1 K.B. 223.

[60] *e.g. Dimes* v. *Grand Junction Canal Proprietors* (1852) 3 H.L.Cas. 759 (decision of Lord Cottenham L.C. set aside by the House of Lords on the ground that he held shares in the plaintiff company).

[61] The test currently favoured was expounded by Lord Denning M.R. in *Metropolitan Properties Co.* v. *Lannon* [1969] 1 Q.B. 577, 599: whether "right-minded persons would think that, in the circumstances, there was a real likelihood of bias."

adverse to individual interests together with an opportunity to make representations. The detailed content of this rule varies from the rigorous procedural standards expected of courts to the minimal standards of "fairness" required in respect of purely administrative decisions: the content in any given case will depend on the court's appraisal of what is appropriate in the circumstances.[62]

(e) Procedural Ultra Vires

The procedure to be adopted for a particular decision-making process may be expressly prescribed by statute or statutory instrument. However, the consequences of failure to observe a particular step are not commonly spelled out. The courts draw a distinction between *mandatory* and *directory* requirements: failure to observe a mandatory step renders the ultimate decision *ultra vires*; failure to observe a directory step does not have this effect, although in some cases "substantial compliance" may be necessary. Important safeguards such as an obligation to consult[63] or to inform a person of rights of appeal[64] are normally held to be mandatory: trivial typographical errors which do not mislead[65] are normally regarded as directory matters, although the distinction is not always easy to draw.[66]

2. THE METHODS OF OBTAINING JUDICIAL REVIEW

(a) Introduction

Judicial review of judicial and administrative decisions and delegated legislation may be sought "directly" or "collaterally." A direct challenge may be made either:

(1) by an "application for judicial review" in the Queen's Bench Division where the court may award one or more of a number of remedies: namely, certiorari, mandamus, prohibition, an injunction, a declaration and damages; or

(2) in an ordinary action in the Queen's Bench or Chancery Divisions for an injunction, a declaration, or damages.

A challenge is made collaterally where the argument that an act or decision, such as a bye-law, is *ultra vires* is raised as a defence to enforcement proceedings or prosecution.[67]

The new, unified, procedure for an application for judicial review was introduced in 1978. In 1982, the House of Lords held that as a general rule it will be contrary to public policy and an abuse of the process of the court for a plaintiff complaining of a public authority's infringement of his or her

---

[62] See, *e.g. Ridge* v. *Baldwin* [1964] A.C. 40 (dismissal of a chief constable without prior notice and a proper hearing held to be void); *R.* v. *Commission for Racial Equality, ex p. Cottrell & Rothon* [1980] 1 W.L.R. 1580, 1586–7 (emphasising the variable content of the *audi alteram partem* rule and the duty to act fairly).

[63] *Agricultural etc. Training Board* v. *Aylesbury Mushrooms Ltd.* [1972] 1 W.L.R. 190.

[64] *London & Clydeside Ltd.* v. *Aberdeen District Council* [1980] 1 W.L.R. 182.

[65] *e.g. R.* v. *Dacorum Gaming Licensing Committee* [1971] 3 All E.R. 666.

[66] Lord Hailsham in the *London & Clydeside* case, *supra,* suggested *obiter* that the courts should adopt a more flexible approach to this issue: this view is beginning to find favour: see, *e.g* the Court of Appeal in *R.* v. *Lambeth Borough Council, ex p. Sharp* [1987] J.P.L. 440.

[67] See, *e.g. Kruse* v. *Johnson* [1898] 2 Q.B. 91.

"public law rights" to seek redress by an ordinary action rather than an application for judicial review.[68] Private law claims against public authorities, such as actions for damages, may still be brought by ordinary proceedings.[69] The distinction between public law and private law matters is, however, a novel one, and may prove in some, if not many, cases difficult to draw. After some hesitation,[70] it has been held that the principle of *O'Reilly* v. *Mackman*[71] does not prevent a defendant in criminal proceedings for breach of a bye-law raising the validity of the bye-law collaterally by way of defence at the trial.[72] Similarly, in a civil case, matters of *vires* may be raised in defence of private law rights, where those rights are not dependent upon a public law decision.[73]

(b) Procedure on applications for judicial review

The procedure on applications for judicial review is prescribed by section 31 of the Supreme Court Act 1981 and R.S.C. Order 53. An application for mandamus, prohibition or certiorari, or for an injunction restraining a person from acting in an office in which he or she is not entitled to act, *must* be brought under Order 53. An application for a declaration or injunction (other than of the kind just mentioned) *may* be brought under Order 53,[74] and such a remedy may be granted where the court considers it just and convenient so to do, having regard to the nature of the matters in respect of which, and the persons and bodies against whom, mandamus, prohibition or certiorari may be granted, and all the circumstances of the case.

On an application for judicial review, the applicant may claim any one or more of the remedies listed above, and may be awarded damages if there is a good cause of action. The procedure is in two stages. The applicant must first obtain leave from a High Court judge of the Queen's Bench Division. Where the application for leave is refused, the applicant may renew it by applying, in a criminal case, to a Divisional Court, and in a civil case, to a judge sitting in open court. The applicant must specify the relief sought and the grounds for his claim and file an affidavit verifying the facts relied on. He or she may be allowed to amend his claim on such terms, if any, as the court thinks fit.

The court may not grant leave unless it considers that the applicant has a "sufficient interest" in the matter (*locus standi*): it is not necessary, however, for him or her to show that his or her legal rights are affected.[75]

Once leave is granted, the application is made to a judge sitting in open court, unless the court directs that it be made to a judge in chambers or a

---

[68] *O'Reilly* v. *Mackman* [1983] 2 A.C. 237.
[69] *Davy* v. *Spelthorne Borough Council* [1984] A.C. 262.
[70] *Quietlynn Ltd.* v. *Plymouth City Council* [1988] Q.B. 114, D.C. (pet.dis. [1987] 1 W.L.R. 1090, H.L.).
[71] *Supra.*
[72] *R.* v. *Reading Crown Court, ex p. Hutchinson* [1988] Q.B. 384, D.C. (pet.dis. [1988] 1 W.L.R. 308). The challenge was ultimately successful: *D.P.P.* v. *Hutchinson* [1990] 2 A.C. 783.
[73] *Wandsworth London Borough Council* v. *Winder* [1985] A.C. 461 (council tenant entitled to raise in defence to an action for arrears of rent that the council's decision to raise the rent was an *ultra vires* abuse of discretion under the *Wednesbury* principles: the argument ultimately failed: *Wandsworth London Borough Council* v. *Winder (No. 2)* (1988) 20 H.L.R. 400).
[74] Subject to the principle expressed in *O'Reilly* v. *Mackman, supra.*
[75] *Inland Revenue Commissioners* v. *National Federation of Small Businesses* [1982] A.C. 617.

Divisional Court: criminal cases are, however, always heard by a Divisional Court. The court may entertain interlocutory applications for orders such as those for discovery, interrogatories and cross-examination on affidavits. Evidence is given in affidavit form,[76] and leave to cross-examine is in practice rarely granted.

An application must be made promptly, and in any event within three months from the date when grounds for the application first arose, unless the court considers there are good grounds for extending the period.[77]

All the remedies are discretionary, and may be refused, for example, where the applicant is actuated by improper motives or on the ground of undue delay.[78]

(c) A comparison with ordinary actions

It should be noted that in ordinary actions for a declaration or injunction there is no requirement of leave, the limitation period is normally six years, although a remedy may still be refused on the ground of undue delay, and the applicant is not required to swear an affidavit in support of his or her factual allegations. Moreover, it is the more useful procedure where it is necessary for a witness to give evidence orally. However, a person will only have *locus standi* to be granted a declaration or injunction in an ordinary action if his or her legal rights are affected or he or she has suffered special damage.[79] Otherwise, that person must either apply for judicial review under Order 53, where the test for *locus standi* is less strict, or seek the consent of the Attorney-General for "relator proceedings." Here, the Attorney-General is the nominal plaintiff, although the proceedings are taken at the expense of the applicant (or "relator").[80] The Attorney-General's decision to grant or refuse consent may not be challenged.[81]

(d) The remedies

(i) *Mandamus*

The prerogative[82] order of mandamus[83] lies to compel performance of a public (not necessarily statutory) duty. For example, it may be granted where a tribunal wrongfully declines to hear a matter that does in fact lie

---

[76] As to the principles governing the admission of fresh evidence, see *R. v. Secretary of State for the Environment, ex p. Powis* [1982] 1 All E.R. 788, 797–798.

[77] Ord. 53, r. 4, as amended by S.I. 1980 No. 2000, and S.I. 1987 No. 1423, r. 63, Sched. See *R. v. Stratford-on-Avon District Council, ex p. Jackson* [1985] 1 W.L.R. 1319; *R. v. Dairy Produce Quota Tribunal for England and Wales, ex p. Caswell* [1990] 2 A.C. 738.

[78] The Supreme Court Act 1981, s.31(6) provides that where the court considers there has been undue delay, it may refuse to grant leave to apply, or any relief sought, "if it considers that the granting of the relief sought would be likely to cause substantial hardship to, or substantially prejudice the right of any person or would be detrimental to good administration." This is regarded as complementing Ord. 53, r. 4: *ex p. Jackson* and *ex p. Caswell, supra.*

[79] *Boyce* v. *Paddington Corporation* [1903] 1 Ch. 109; *Gouriet* v. *Union of Post Office Workers* [1978] A.C. 435.

[80] See, *e.g. Att.-Gen ex rel. McWhirter* v. *Independent Broadcasting Authority* [1973] Q.B. 629.

[81] *Gouriet* v. *Union of Post Office Workers, supra.*

[82] So called because the writ replaced by the modern order was thought to be especially associated with the Crown.

[83] Normally pronounced "mandaymus."

within its jurisdiction, or, where there has been an *ultra vires* abuse of discretion, to ensure that the matter is reconsidered according to law.[84]

(ii) *Prohibition and Certiorari*

The prerogative orders of prohibition and certiorari[85] are similar in scope. Prohibition lies to restrain a tribunal or other authority where it is about to act *ultra vires* or to complete an *ultra vires* act already begun. Certiorari lies to quash[86] a decision already made where:
(1) it is *ultra vires*; or
(2) it has been obtained by fraud[87]; or
(3) there is an error of law apparent on the face of the record of proceedings.

These orders were formerly confined to decisions in respect of which there was a duty to act judicially, but they may now be sought in respect of any judicial or administrative[88] (but not legislative) act.

(iii) *Declarations and Injunctions*

A person may obtain a declaration on a disputed matter of law, or an injunction, whereby a party to an action is required to do or refrain from doing a particular thing.[89] These were in origin private law remedies but are today frequently sought in respect of the decisions of public authorities.

(iv) *Habeas Corpus*[90]

The prerogative writ of *habeas corpus ad subjiciendum* lies to secure a person's release from wrongful imprisonment. An *ex parte* application for a writ must be made to a Divisional Court of the Queen's Bench Division or, if no such court is sitting, to a single judge of any Division of the High Court, and takes precedence over other business. In an emergency, an application may be made to a judge out of court, for example at home at night. If prima facie grounds are shown by an affidavit by or on behalf of the prisoner the matter is normally adjourned to a Divisional Court for a full hearing. In exceptional cases the writ may be issued forthwith to the custodian, requiring that the prisoner be produced to the court at the time specified for the full hearing. In either event, the burden of justifying the detention lies on the custodian: if he or she fails, the prisoner's release is ordered.

The grounds for granting a writ of habeas corpus are essentially the same as for an application for judicial review. An appeal lies in civil cases as of right to the Court of Appeal and then with leave to the House of Lords. In criminal cases, no appeal can lie from an order made by a single judge,[91] but

---

[84] *e.g. Padfield* v. *Minister of Agriculture* [1968] A.C. 997.
[85] Normally pronounced "sersheeorair'eye."
[86] Not "squash," "quosh" or "gnash" (*cf. R.* v. *Pressick* [1978] Crim.L.R. 377).
[87] See *R.* v. *Wolverhampton Crown Court, ex p. Crofts* [1983] 1 W.L.R. 204.
[88] *R.* v. *Hillingdon London Borough Council, ex p. Royco Homes Ltd.* [1974] Q.B. 720.
[89] See further above, p. 708.
[90] See R. J. Sharpe, *The Law of Habeas Corpus* (2nd ed., 1989); J. M. Evans, *de Smith's Judicial Review of Administrative Action* (4th ed., 1980), appendix 2; R.S.C. Order 54.
[91] Administration of Justice Act 1960, s.15(2): a single judge may only grant an application: the matter must otherwise be referred to a Divisional Court: *ibid.* s.14(1).

an appeal does lie from the Divisional Court to the House of Lords, with the leave of either.[92] An appeal may be taken from a refusal to discharge the prisoner or an order of release: in the latter event the person's right to remain at large cannot be affected by the outcome of the appeal.[93] After a refusal to grant habeas corpus no further application may be made on the same grounds and evidence.[94]

An application for habeas corpus is the standard method of challenging extradition decisions.

(e) Relationship between applications for judicial review and appeals

The remedies available on an application for judicial review are discretionary, and will not be awarded if there is some equally convenient and beneficial remedy such as a right of appeal. However, an appeal to a minister against a planning condition will not, for example, be regarded as convenient as certiorari where the issue is purely one of law.[95] Indeed, it has sometimes been stated that an application for judicial review must be made where a challenge is based on the *ultra vires* doctrine, rather than exercising a right to appeal on a point of law.[96]

Conversely, an application for judicial review will be less appropriate than an appeal by case stated where complicated findings of fact are involved,[97] and will not be entertained in respect of points arising in the course of trials or committal proceedings[98]: such proceedings must be concluded before any challenge can take place, whether by appeal or application for judicial review.

Statutory provisions may purport to exclude or restrict judicial review. For example, the Crown Court is made amenable to the supervisory jurisdiction of the High Court in respect of matters other than those relating to trial on indictment.[99]

An application for judicial review may be made to challenge a sentence or order on the ground that it is harsh or oppressive.[1]

---

[92] *Ibid.*, ss.1, 15(3).

[93] *Ibid.*, s.15(1)(4). In criminal cases an order may be made providing for the continued detention of the defendant or directing that he or she shall not be released except on bail: *ibid.* s.5.

[94] *Ibid.*, s.14(2).

[95] *R.* v. *Hillingdon London Borough Council, ex p. Royco Homes Ltd.* [1974] Q.B. 720.

[96] *Metropolitan Properties Co.* v. *Lannon* [1968] 1 W.L.R. 815; *Chapman* v. *Earl* [1968] 1 W.L.R. 1315; *Henry Moss Ltd.* v. *Customs and Excise Commissioners* [1981] 2 All E.R. 86, 90 (*per* Lord Denning M.R.), criticised by A. W. Bradley [1981] P.L. 476; *contra, Elliott* v. *Brighton Borough Council* (1980) 79 L.G.R. 506.

[97] *R.* v. *Crown Court at Ipswich, ex p. Baldwin* [1981] 1 All E.R. 596.

[98] *R.* v. *Wells Street Stipendiary Magistrate, ex p. Seillon* [1978] 1 W.L.R. 1002 (committal proceedings); *R.* v. *Rochford JJ. ex p. Buck* (1978) 68 Cr.App.R. 114. (summary trial).

[99] Supreme Court Act 1981, s.29(3); *R.* v. *Sheffield Crown Court, ex p. Brownlow* [1980] Q.B. 530: jury vetting order held to relate to trial on indictment; J. Kodwo Bentil, (1988) 152 J.P.N. 323. See also above, p. 803.

[1] *R.* v. *St. Albans Crown Court, ex p. Cinnamond* [1981] Q.B. 480; *R.* v. *Tottenham JJ., ex p. Joshi* [1982] 1 W.L.R. 631. It has been suggested that *Cinnamond* was wrongly decided (Watkins L.J. in *Arthur* v. *Stringer* (1986) 84 Cr.App.R. 361, 368), or should at least be confined to cases where the sentence is "truly astonishing" (Watkins L.J. in *R.* v. *Crown Court at Croydon, ex p. Miller* (1986) 85 Cr.App.R. 152 (decided before *Arthur* v. *Stringer*)). The court may, however, refuse in the exercise of its discretion to entertain an application for judicial review if a right to appeal against sentence has not been exercised: *R.* v. *Battle Magistrates' Court, ex p. Shepherd* (1983) 5 Cr.App.R. (S.) 124.

E. REFERENCES TO THE EUROPEAN COURT OF JUSTICE[2]

One of the major functions of the Court of Justice of the European Communities[3] is that of ensuring consistency in the decision making of national courts in community law matters. The governing provision in the EEC Treaty is Article 177[4]:

"(1) The Court of Justice shall have jurisdiction to give preliminary rulings concerning:
　(a)　the interpretation of this Treaty;
　(b)　the validity and interpretation of acts of the institutions of the Community;
　(c)　the interpretation of the statutes of bodies established by an act of the Council, where those statutes so provide.
(2) Where such a question is raised before any court or tribunal of a Member State, that court or tribunal may, if it considers that a decision on the question is necessary to enable it to give judgment, request the Court of Justice to give a ruling thereon.
(3) Where any such question is raised in a case pending before a court or tribunal of a Member State, against whose decisions there is no judicial remedy under national law, that court or tribunal shall bring the matter before the Court of Justice."

The equivalent provision in the European Coal and Steel Community Treaty (Art. 41) is more narrowly drawn:

"The Court shall have sole jurisdiction to give preliminary rulings on the validity of acts of the High Authority and of the Council where such validity is in issue in proceedings brought before a national court or tribunal."

Thus only questions of *validity* can be referred. It should be noted, however, that within these narrower limits the jurisdiction of the court is exclusive: the label "preliminary" ruling is in this context misleading.

It should be noted that the reference procedure is not strictly an appeal: the decision to refer is taken by the national court and not a party and the court will only rule on the point of Community law raised and remit the case to the national court to apply the law to the facts of the case. The remainder of this discussion will relate to the EEC and Euratom. We now examine the elements of Article 177 in more detail.

1. The Matters that may be Referred

The Court may give rulings concerning (1) the interpretation of Treaty

---

[2] F. G. Jacobs and A. Durand, *References to the European Court* (1975); L. Collins, *European Community Law in the United Kingdom* (4th ed., 1990) Chap. 3; T. C. Hartley, *The Foundations of European Community Law* (2nd ed., 1988), Chap. 9; L. N. Brown and F. G. Jacobs, *The Court of Justice of the European Communities* (3rd ed., 1989), Chap. 10; H. G. Shermers, *et al.* (eds.), *Article 177 EEC: Experiences and Problems* (1987); A. Arnull, "The Use and Abuse of Article 177 EEC" (1989) 52 M.L.R. 622 and "References to the European Court" (1990) 15 E.L.Rev. 375.

[3] See above, pp. 96–100.

[4] The equivalent provision in the Euratom Treaty (Art. 150) is virtually identical.

provisions[5]; and (2) the interpretation and validity of acts of the Community institutions (certainly the Council[6] and Commission and probably the Parliament and the Court itself[7]). Where, however, the act of the Council in question is the "statute" regulating the operation of an institution or body established by the Council, the court may only give a ruling if the statute so provides,[8] and the ruling may only concern interpretation, not validity.[9] The task of "interpretation" is taken to include that of determining whether a provision is directly effective.[10] A question of validity *must* be referred as the European Court has the exclusive jurisdiction to rule on such a question.[11]

2. "ANY COURT OR TRIBUNAL"

Article 177(2) of the EEC Treaty provides that "any court or tribunal" may refer a question if the conditions stated are applicable. In the United Kingdom, procedural rules have been made governing references from the High Court and the Court of Appeal (Civil Division),[12] the Court of Appeal (Criminal Division),[13] the Crown Court[14] and county courts.[15] However, it is clear that magistrates' courts[16] and statutory tribunals[17] have power to refer matters to the European Court even though no procedural rules have been made. The meaning of the expression "court or tribunal" will in the last resort be determined by the European Court, and the title of an institution

---

[5] Art. 177(1)(*a*)/EEC covers the EEC Treaty and all Treaties amending or supplementing it: subsidiary conventions are not covered: Case 44/84, *Hurd* v. *Jones (Inspector of Taxes)* [1986] E.C.R. 29 (agreement between the Member States setting up European Schools in Community countries not within Art. 177): see L. N. Brown, (1986) 23 C.M.L. Rev. 895; Case 152/83, *Demouche* v. *Fonds de Garantie Automobile* [1989] 1 C.M.L.R. 544 (agreement between national bureaux of motor vehicle insurers not within Art. 177, notwithstanding that it implemented a Council Directive).

[6] The Court has asserted jurisdiction under Art. 177 to interpret agreements between the Community and non-Member States, concluded on behalf of the Community by the Council: Case 181/73, *Haegeman* v. *Belgium* [1974] E.C.R. 449 (Association Agreement between the EEC and Greece); or even agreements involving Member States to which the Community is not formally a party: Cases 267–269/81, *SPI* [1983] E.C.R. 801 (General Agreement on Tariffs and Trade). See Hartley (1988), pp. 251–254.

[7] Although a preliminary ruling is not itself an act that can be questioned on an application for a further preliminary ruling: Case 69/85, *Wunsche Handelsgesellschaft* v. *Germany* [1986] E.C.R. 947: see G. Bebr, (1987) 24 C.M.L.Rev. 719; this does not prevent the national court making a subsequent reference in the same proceedings: *ibid.*; Case 14/86, *Pretore di Salo* v. *Persons Unknown* [1989] 1 C.M.L.R. 71.

[8] Under Art. 150/Euratom, rulings concerning "statutes" may be given "save where those statutes provide otherwise."

[9] Art. 177(1)(*c*)/EEC.

[10] See above, pp. 288–294.

[11] This is expressly provided by Art. 41/ECSC, and the same position has been reached as regards the EEC by the Court in Cases 314/85, *Firma Foto Frost* v. *Haupzollamt Lübeck-Ost* [1988] 3 C.M.L.R. 57, applied in *R.* v. *Ministry of Agriculture, Fisheries and Food, ex p. F.E.D.E.S.A.* [1988] 3 C.M.L.R. 661.

[12] R.S.C. Ord. 114.

[13] Criminal Appeal (References to the European Court) Rules 1972 (S.I. 1972 No. 1786).

[14] Crown Court Rules 1982 (S.I. 1982 No. 1109), r. 29.

[15] County Court Rules 1981, Ord. 19, r. 11.

[16] See, *e.g. R.* v. *Plymouth JJ., ex p. Rogers* [1982] Q.B. 863.

[17] By 1989 references had been made by the Employment Appeal Tribunal, a National Insurance Commissioner, Social Security Commissioners, Special Income Tax Commissioners, Value Added Tax Tribunals and a Northern Ireland industrial tribunal.

and its status in national law is not decisive.[18] It seems that any institution which exercises judicial or quasi-judicial functions and which has at least "a measure of official recognition"[19] will be included, and not, therefore, bodies whose functions are advisory,[20] investigatory, conciliatory, legislative or executive,[21] and not arbitrators[22] or (probably) domestic tribunals which exercise jurisdiction solely by virtue of a contractual arrangement between the parties.[23] Where a court or tribunal performs both judicial and non-judicial functions in respect of particular proceedings, (*e.g.* as examining magistrate and public prosecutor), the European Court will accept a reference from it in the first of those capacities.[24]

3. THE POWER TO REFER

Where any "question" within the scope of the preliminary rulings procedure is "raised before" any national court or tribunal that body may, "if it considers that a decision on the question is necessary to enable it to give judgment," refer the question to the European Court.

(a) "Question . . . raised before"

The question can be raised by a party or by the court itself.[25] Moreover, it is immaterial that the parties take the same position on the point of Community law.[26] The question for reference will be formulated by the national court, although the European Court will confine itself to ruling on matters of *interpretation* and *validity*: it will not rule on the *application* of Community law to the facts or the compatibility of national law with Community law even if requested to do so. The Court will reformulate questions put too widely, and may even formulate the question for itself if the national court fails to do so.[27]

---

[18] See W. Alexander and E. Grabandt, (1982) 19 C.M.L.Rev. 413; Case 61/65, *Vaassen* [1966] E.C.R. 261; Case 36/73, *Nederlandse Spoorwegen* [1973] E.C.R. 1299; Case 138/80, *Borker* [1980] E.C.R. 1975; Case 246/80, *Broekmeulen* [1981] E.C.R. 2311; Case 102/81, *Nordsee* v. *Reederei Mond* [1982] E.C.R. 1095.

[19] *e.g.* supervision or regulation by a minister: *Vaassen* and *Broekmeulen, supra.*

[20] The fact that functions are technically advisory will not prevent the institution from being regarded as a "court or tribunal" if in reality it operates as a judicial body; accordingly, the Dutch *Raad van State* (Council of State), in practice the supreme administrative court, has been held to be within Article 177: *Nederlandse Spoorwegen, supra.* By contrast, the *commissione consultiva per la infrazioni valutarie* (Consultative Commission for Currency Offences), which gives reasoned opinions to the Italian Treasury on sanctions to be imposed for foreign exchange violations, was held not to fall within Art. 177 in Case 318/85, *Criminal proceedings against Undterweger* [1986] E.C.R. 955: its opinions were not binding on the Treasury minister.

[21] *e.g.* the professional association of the Paris Bar: *Borker, supra.*

[22] *Nordsee, supra*: See G. Bebr, (1985) 22 C.M.L.Rev. 489; C. M. Schmitthoff, (1987) 24 C.M.L.Rev. 143.

[23] Hartley (1988), pp. 255–258.

[24] Case 14/86, *Pretore di Salo* v. *Persons Unknown* [1989] 1 C.M.L.R. 71.

[25] See, *e.g.* R.S.C. Ord. 114, r. 2(1).

[26] Advocate General Slynn in Case 244/80, *Foglia* v. *Novello (No 2)* [1981] E.C.R. 3045, 3071–3072.

[27] This was done in Case 6/64, *Costa* v. *E.N.E.L.* [1964] E.C.R. 585; however, the Court may be unable to do so: Case 14/86, *Pretore di Salo* v. *Persons Unknown* [1989] 1 C.M.L.R. 71, where the Court could not make anything of a very general question posed by the Italian court.

(b) "A decision on the question is necessary to enable it to give judgment"

This wording makes it clear that the material issue is whether a *decision* on the point of Community law is necessary and not whether a *reference* is necessary. The European Court will not normally review the decision of the national court that a reference is "necessary,"[28] although in exceptional circumstances it may decline to accept a reference on the ground that the matter has not arisen in real, genuine, litigation: it is not willing to render advisory opinions, of academic interest only, on "general or hypothetical questions."[29] Accordingly, the Court has now said that the national court should state in its order for reference the reasons for which it considers it necessary to obtain a preliminary ruling, unless these can be clearly deduced from the file on the case.[30]

Essentially, however, the decision to refer is for the national court or tribunal. However, in the *Rheinmuhlen* cases the European Court held that: (1) "a rule of national law whereby a court is bound on points of law by the rulings of a superior court cannot deprive the inferior courts of their power to refer . . . questions" to the Court,[31] but that (2) Article 177 does not preclude a decision of an inferior court to refer a question "from remaining subject to the remedies normally available under national law."[32] This suggests that any attempt to fetter the discretion of a court under Article 177(2) will be contrary to Community law. Nevertheless, in *Bulmer* v. *Bollinger*[33] Lord Denning M.R. laid down certain "guidelines," which have been relied upon in a number of cases since, but which have also, in some respects, been the subject of widespread criticism, not least on the basis that they may constitute "fetters" which are contrary to Community law.[34] His Lordship set out the guidelines in two groups: (1) guidelines as to whether a decision is "necessary"; and (2) guidelines as to the exercise of the "discretion" to refer. He regarded the question of "necessity" as a condition precedent to the exercise of the discretion and, presumably, as raising matters of law or jurisdiction rather than discretion.[35] However, it seems

---

[28] *Ibid.*; Cases 98, 162 and 258/85, *Bertini* v. *Regione Lazio* [1986] E.C.R. 1885.

[29] Case 104/79, *Foglia* v. *Novello (No. 1)* [1980] E.C.R. 745; Case 244/80, *Foglia* v. *Novello (No. 2)* [1981] E.C.R. 3045: see A. Barav, (1980) 5 E.L. Rev. 443, G. Bebr, (1980) 17 C.M.L.Rev. 525 (*Foglia No. 1*); D. Wyatt, (1981) 6 E.L. Rev. 449, G. Bebr, (1982) 19 C.M.L.Rev. 421 (*Foglia No. 2*). It should be noted that this litigation was between private parties in Italy but was in reality directed at the alleged incompatibility of a French law with Community law. *Cf.* Cases 98, 162 and 258/85, *Bertini*, *supra*.

[30] *Foglia* v. *Novello (No. 2)*, *supra*, at p. 3062.

[31] Case 166/73, *Rheinmühlen-Düsseldorf* v. *EVSt (No. 1)* [1974] E.C.R. 33: the lower court was, under German law, bound on points of law by decisions of a superior court; the European Court held that this could not take away the lower court's power to refer under Art. 177(2). See also Case 106/77, *Italian Minister for Finance* v. *Simmenthal (No. 2)* [1978] E.C.R. 629.

[32] Case 166/73, *Ibid.* (*No. 2*) [1974] E.C.R. 139. The court rejected the suggestion by A. G. Warner that the existence of a right to appeal against an order referring a question to the European Court was contrary to Community law: see [1974] E.C.R. 33, 43–44.

[33] [1974] Ch. 401, 422–425.

[34] See, *e.g.* F. G. Jacobs, (1974) 90 L.Q.R. 486; J. D. B. Mitchell, (1974) 11 C.M.L.Rev. 351; E. Freeman, [1975] C.L.P. 176; Collins (1990), pp. 176–183. In *Bulmer* v. *Bollinger*, Stephenson L.J. (with whom Stamp L.J. agreed) stated that judges should "bear in mind" the considerations set out by Lord Denning M.R. ([1974] Ch. 401, 430) but was also conscious of the requirement that the discretion must not be fettered (*ibid.*, p. 431).

[35] Collins (1990), p. 179.

that his Lordship erroneously thought that it was the *reference* that had to be "necessary," whereas Article 177(2) makes it clear that the significant point is whether a *decision* by the national court on the point is "necessary."[36] Accordingly, two of the matters mentioned by Lord Denning M.R. in relation to "necessity" should have been placed with the other group: the presentation here has been revised accordingly.

(i) *Jurisdiction to refer: is a decision "necessary?"*

(1) *"The point must be conclusive"* and (2) *"find the facts first."* According to Lord Denning M.R. the point must be conclusive in the sense that a decision one way must lead to judgment for one party and a decision the other way to judgment for the other. Where the point would only be conclusive if decided one way, and the trial would have to go its full course in respect of the contested issues of fact or of English law if decided the other, then, according to Lord Denning M.R., a reference might be "desirable" or "convenient" but could not be "necessary." Moreover, "[a]s a rule you cannot tell whether it is necessary to decide a point until all the facts are ascertained. So in general it is best to decide the facts first."[37]

It seems to be generally agreed that this is too narrow, and that the correct view is that it may be appropriate to refer a point where there are still matters outstanding which will have to be determined should the European Court's decision go one way rather than another.[38] This broader view has been adopted by Ormrod L.J. in the Court of Appeal,[39] by the Divisional Court[40] and by Bingham J. in the High Court.[41] These cases suggest, however, that while there is jurisdiction to refer at an early stage, the facts should normally be found first.[42] A difficulty here is that it may not be clear which facts are relevant for the purposes of Community law until after the reference has been made. On the other hand, it has also been stressed by English courts that it may be impossible to formulate the questions to be referred until after a case has been argued.[43]

A further point is that it is not necessary that the whole of a case be affected by Community law for a decision to be necessary: it is sufficient if a particular aspect, such as the measure of damages or the terms of a court order should be so affected.

---

[36] *Ibid.* p. 177.

[37] [1974] Ch. 401 at p. 422, 423.

[38] R.S.C. Ord. 114, r. 2(1) provides that an order for reference may be made at any stage.

[39] *Polydor Ltd.* v. *Harlequin Record Shops Ltd.* [1980] 2 C.M.L.R. 413, 428: "necessary" to mean "reasonably necessary" and not "unavoidable."

[40] *R.* v. *Plymouth JJ., ex p. Rogers* [1982] Q.B. 863, 867–870.

[41] *Customs and Excise Commissioners* v. *ApS Samex* [1983] 1 All E.R. 1042, 1054.

[42] Templeman L.J. in *Polydor, supra,* at p. 426; Lord Lane C.J. in *R.* v. *Plymouth JJ., supra,* at p. 182; Bingham J. in *Samex, supra,* at p. 1056c. See also Lord Diplock in *R.* v. *Henn and Darby* [1981] A.C. 850, 904. In *R.* v. *Plymouth JJ.* and *Samex* the matters outstanding were not significant in extent; a reference was, however, made at an early stage by Taylor J., with the agreement of both sides, in *R.* v. *Ministry of Agriculture, Fisheries and Food, ex p. Agegate Ltd.* [1987] 3 C.M.L.R. 939, and by Henry J. in *R.* v. *Ministry of Agriculture, Fisheries and Food, ex p. F.E.D.E.S.A.* [1988] 3 C.M.L.R. 661; a reference was made notwithstanding that there was an unresolved conflict on some factual matters, and over the objections of one party, by the Court of Appeal in *R.* v. *Pharmaceutical Society of Great Britain, ex p. Association of Pharmaceutical Importers* [1987] C.M.L.R. 951.

[43] *Church of Scientology* v. *Customs and Excise Commissioners* [1981] 1 All E.R. 1035, 1039 (Brightman L.J.); *Lord Bethell* v. *S.A.B.E.N.A.* [1983] 3 C.M.L.R. 1 (Parker J.).

The move away from Lord Denning M.R.'s attempt to formulate a narrow, clear-cut rule in this context means that the matter is so much one for the appreciation of the court itself that it would be artificial to seek to perpetuate the supposed distinction between "necessity" and "discretion": the approach of an appellate court is in practice likely to be similar in each case.

(ii) *Exercise of the discretion to refer*

(1) *Previous ruling.* In *Da Costa* v. *Nederlandse Belastringadministratie*[44] the European Court stated that where it has given a ruling on a particular question of interpretation, and the same question arises in a subsequent case before a national court of last resort, the earlier ruling may "deprive the obligation [under Art. 177(3)] of its purpose and thus empty it of its substance."[45] There would thus be no *obligation* to refer, although the Court also stressed that a national court still had a *discretion* to refer the question. In *Bulmer* v. *Bollinger*[46] Lord Denning M.R. noted that the European Court was not bound by its own previous decisions and said that an English court should only refer a case in such circumstances if it thinks the earlier ruling to be wrong or if there are new factors which ought to be brought to the notice of the European Court.

(2) *Acte clair.* It has been a matter of much controversy whether a national court, whether a court of last resort or not, may decline to refer a question to the European Court on the ground that, notwithstanding the absence of any prior ruling on the point by the European Court, the point is clear and so no "question" arises. Commentators, both academic and judicial, have argued against the *acte clair* doctrine on the basis that there is a real risk that the national courts of different countries may each regard a question as "clear" but in fact decide it differently.[47] Conversely, national courts in several member states have endorsed and relied upon the doctrine. In *Bulmer* v. *Bollinger*[48] Lord Denning M.R. stated that there was no need to refer a question if the point is considered to be "reasonably clear and free from doubt."[49] Rather to everyone's surprise, in *C.I.L.F.I.T.* v. *Ministry of Health*[50] the European Court approved the doctrine, although not in nearly so broad a formulation as Lord Denning's: thus, there is no *obligation* to refer if:

[44] Cases 28, 29 and 30/62, [1963] E.C.R. 31.
[45] *Ibid.* p. 38. The same effect may be produced where previous decisions of the court have already dealt with the point of law in question "irrespective of the nature of the proceedings which led to those decisions, even though the questions at issue are not strictly identical": Case 283/81, *C.I.L.F.I.T.* v. *Ministry of Health* [1982] E.C.R. 3415, 3429.
[46] [1974] Ch. 401, 422.
[47] See, *e.g.* Judge Pescatore in M. E. Bathhurst *et al.* (eds.), *Legal Problems of an Enlarged European Community* (1972), pp. 27–46 (but *cf.* M. Lagrange, (1971) 8 C.M.L.Rev. 313); A. G. Capotorti in Case 283/81, *C.I.L.F.I.T.* v. *Ministry of Health* [1982] E.C.R. 3415; G. Bebr, (1981) 18 C.M.L.Rev. 475, 484–489.
[48] [1974] Ch. 401. See also the decision of the Conseil d'Etat in *Cohn-Bendit* [1980] 1 C.M.L.R. 543; G. Bebr, (1983) 20 C.M.L.Rev. 439.
[49] *Ibid.*, p. 423.
[50] [1982] E.C.R. 3415. See D. Wyatt, (1983) 8 E.L. Rev. 179; N. P. Gravells, (1983) 99 L.Q.R. 518; H. Rasmussen, (1984) 9 E.L. Rev. 242.

". . . the correct application of Community law is so obvious as to leave no scope for possible doubt. The existence of such a possibility must be assessed in the light of the specific characteristics of Community law, the particular difficulties to which its interpretation gives rise and the risk of divergences in judicial decisions within the Community."

In practice in United Kingdom courts the *acte clair* issue has arisen in courts other than of last resort, which accordingly have a discretion to refer.[51] There appears to have been a variation in approach depending on the context. Thus, the unwillingess of judges to refer possible defences arising under European law to actions for breach of intellectual property rights has been contrasted with an apparent willingness to refer questions concerning equal pay and sex discrimination in employment law.[52] Points regarded by judges as clear turn out on closer examination by commentators to be at least arguable. The dangers of a reluctance to refer questions have been stressed by the House of Lords in *R.* v. *Henn and Darby,*[53] where Lord Diplock noted the different approaches to statutory interpretation adopted respectively by the European Court and English courts[54] and the point that each of the six texts of Community law is of equal authority. His Lordship said that English judges should not be "too ready to hold that because the meaning of the English text . . . seems plain to them no question of interpretation can be involved."[55] However, where the point was one "to which an established body of case law plainly applies" an English court might properly take the view that no real question of interpretation was involved.[56]

(3) *Other points.* Other factors identified by Lord Denning M.R. in *Bulmer* v. *Bollinger*[57] as relevant to the exercise of a court's discretion included: (1) the time to get a ruling; (2) the need not to overload the European Court; (3) the need to formulate the question clearly, which was another reason for finding the facts first; (4) "Unless the point is really difficult and important, it would seem better for the English judge to decide it himself;" (5) expense; and (6) the wishes of the parties:

[51] But *cf. S.A. Magnavision* v. *General Optical Council (No. 2)* [1987] 2 C.M.L.R. 262, below, p. 887.
[52] A. M. Arnull, "Article 177 and the Retreat from Van Duyn" (1983) 8 E.L. Rev. 365. See also A. Dashwood and A. Arnull, "English Courts and Article 177 of the EEC Treaty" (1984) 4 Y.E.L. 255; L. W. Gormley, "The Application of Community Law in the United Kingdom, 1976–1985" (1986) 23 C.M.L.Rev. 287, 288–303.
[53] [1981] A.C. 850.
[54] See above, pp. 367–368.
[55] [1981] A.C. 850 at p. 906. See also Lord Diplock's speech in *Garland* v. *British Rail Engineering Ltd.* [1983] 2 A.C. 751; *cf.* Bingham J. in *Customs and Excise Commissioners* v. *Ap S Samex* [1983] 1 All E.R. 1042: on three of four points the judge held clear views, but accepted that each was not so clear as to be *acte clair*; the Court of Appeal in *R.* v. *Pharmaceutical Society of Great Britain, ex p. Association of Pharmaceutical Importers* [1987] 3 C.M.L.R. 951, *per* Kerr L.J. at pp. 969–970; and McCullough J. in *R.* v. *Dairy Produce Quota Tribunal, ex p. Hall & Sons (Dairy Farmers) Ltd.* [1988] 1 C.M.L.R. 592 (discussed by Arnull, (1989) 52 M.L.R. 622, 628–631).
[56] [1981] A.C. 850, 906. Lord Diplock thought that the interpretation of Art. 30 was clear in this sense, but as the Court of Appeal had taken a different view, the point was referred to the European Court. See also *R.* v. *Secretary of State for Social Services, ex p. Bomore Medical Supplies Ltd.* [1986] 1 C.M.L.R. 228 (and other cases, discussed by Arnull, (1989) 52 M.L.R. 622, 631–636).
[57] [1974] Ch. 401, 423–425.

"If both parties want the point to be referred to the European Court, the English court should have regard to their wishes, but it should not give them undue weight. The English court should hesitate before making a reference against the wishes of one of the parties, seeing the expense and delay which it involves."

The tenor of Lord Denning's judgment was obviously restrictive: references should only be made in exceptional cases, and (possibly) only by the House of Lords. The possibility that the guidelines may, to an extent, conflict with Community law has already been noted.[58] However, the breadth of the discretion to refer has also been noted:

"The matters referred to by Lord Denning are specifically stated only to be guidelines and, as Lord Denning himself said, when referring to the guidelines laid down by the House of Lords in *The Nema*,[59] with reference to applications for leave to appeal in matters of arbitration, 'guidelines may be stepped over, and are flexible.' I take it that he would apply the same standard to his own guidelines. At all events, it is perfectly clear that, where a discretion is conferred upon the court, that discretion cannot be fettered."[60]

One point not stressed expressly in *Bulmer* v. *Bollinger*[61] is whether references should normally only be made by appellate courts. It has since been suggested that references should only exceptionally be made by trial judges in the Crown Court[62] and by magistrates' courts.[63] It is, however, often argued that an early reference may save time and expense.

4. The Obligation to Refer

Article 177(3) of the EEC Treaty provides that where a decision on a question of Community law is necessary to enable a court or tribunal to give judgment in a pending case, and that court or tribunal is one "against whose decisions there is no judicial remedy under national law," an *obligation* to refer arises. The points discussed above concerning "necessity," previous rulings and the *acte clair* doctrine are equally applicable here: indeed the decision in *C.I.L.F.I.T.* v. *Ministry of Health*[64] arose in respect of Article 177(3).

In addition, there is the question as to which courts are covered by Article 177(3). The wording of the paragraph suggests that it applies only to courts from which an appeal never lies.[65] The view more widely favoured, however, is that it applies to any court from which an appeal or other "judicial remedy" does not lie in the case in question.[66] One difficulty that has not

---

[58] See above, p. 882.
[59] [1980] 2 Lloyd's Rep. 83.
[60] *Per* Parker J. in *Lord Bethell* v. *S.A.B.E.N.A.* [1983] 3 C.M.L.R. 1, 4.
[61] [1974] Ch. 401.
[62] *R.* v. *Henn and Darby* [1981] A.C. 850, 906: Lord Diplock regarded this as equivalent to referring before the facts are found. The Crown Court is presumably not so inhibited when dealing with an appeal from the magistrates in a summary criminal case: *cf. Charles Robertson (Developments) Ltd.* v. *Caradon District Council* [1988] 1 C.M.L.R. 293.
[63] *R.* v. *Plymouth JJ., ex p. Rogers* [1982] Q.B. 863, 870–871.
[64] Above, pp. 884–885.
[65] This was stated to be the correct view by Lord Denning M.R. *obiter* in *Bulmer* v. *Bollinger* [1974] Ch. 401: the other members of the Court of Appeal expressed no view on the matter.
[66] See the European Court, *obiter*, in Case 6/64, *Costa* v. *E.N.E.L.* [1964] E.C.R. 585, 592.

been settled is whether the remedy has to be available as of right. In *Hagen v. Fratelli D. & G. Moretti S.N.C.*[67] Buckley L.J. stated that the "ultimate court of appeal" in this country "is either [the Court of Appeal] if leave to appeal to the House of Lords is not obtainable, or the House of Lords."[68] It is not clear whether "obtainable" means "obtainable ever" or "obtainable in the particular case" but the latter interpretation seems more likely. In *S.A. Magnavision NV v. General Optical Council (No. 2)*,[69] it was argued that once the Divisional Court, on an appeal by case stated from a magistrates' court in a criminal matter, had refused to certify a point of law of general public importance, it fell within Art. 177(3). The refusal of the certificate would block any further appeal (to the House of Lords) and could not itself be challenged on appeal.[70] The Divisional Court sidestepped the argument, holding (1) that as it had already dismissed the appeal, it was *functus officio*,[71] notwithstanding that the order had not yet been drawn up and (2) that in any event the point of Community law was clear and the *acte clair* doctrine applicable. It is also uncertain whether the availability of the remedy of certiorari, which may only be sought if leave to apply is obtained, counts as a "judicial remedy."[72]

The fact that an interlocutory order may not be the subject of an appeal does not render it final for the purposes of Article 177(3) provided that the decision is subject to review in the main or subsequent proceedings from which a reference may be made.[73]

5. PROCEDURE

As mentioned above, procedural rules have been made for county courts, the Crown Court, the High Court and the Court of Appeal.[74] All references from these courts must be channelled through the Senior Master of the Queen's Bench Division.

An appeal lies against a decision or refusal to refer in the ordinary way. An order for reference by the High Court is deemed to be a final order and so an appeal lies without leave. Notice of appeal must be served within 14 days and the order is not transmitted until this time limit has expired, and, if an appeal is lodged, until after it has been disposed of.[75] Leave is necessary to appeal against refusal of an order for reference.[76]

---

[67] [1980] 3 C.M.L.R. 253.
[68] *Ibid.* p. 255. *cf.* Kerr L.J. (for a unanimous Court of Appeal) in *R. v. Pharmaceutical Society of Great Britain, ex p. Association of Pharmaceutical Importers* [1987] 3 C.M.L.R. 951, 969: "A court or tribunal below the House of Lords can only fall within [Art. 177(3)] where there is no possibility of any further appeal from it."
[69] [1987] 2 C.M.L.R. 262.
[70] See above, p. 829.
[71] "having performed his function": *i.e.* the function of the judge is exhausted: D. M. Walker, *The Oxford Companion to Law* (1980), p. 508.
[72] It was so held by Mr. J. G. Monroe in *Re a Holiday in Italy* [1975] 1 C.M.L.R. 184 (decision of a National Insurance Commissioner) but see F. G. Jacobs, (1977) 2 E.L. Rev. 119.
[73] Case 107/76, *Hoffman-La Roche v. Centrafarm* [1977] E.C.R. 957: see F. G. Jacobs, (1977) 2 E.L. Rev. 354; Cases 35 and 36/82, *Morson v. Netherlands; Jhanjan v. Netherlands* [1982] E.C.R. 3723: see N. P. Gravells, (1983) 8 E.L. Rev. 250.
[74] See above, p. 880.
[75] R.S.C. Ord. 114, rr. 4, 5, 6.
[76] *Bulmer v. Bollinger* [1974] Ch. 401, 420–421, 430–431.

F. THE ROYAL PREROGATIVE OF MERCY

The Crown has retained certain of its prerogative powers as "fountain of justice" in the field of the administration of justice. One such area is the prerogative of mercy exercised by the Crown on the advice of the Home Secretary. This may take one of three forms[77]:

> "(i) A Free Pardon, the effect of which is that a conviction is to be disregarded, so that, so far as is possible, the person is relieved of all penalties and other consequences of the conviction; or
>
> (ii) A Conditional Pardon, which excuses or varies the consequences of the conviction subject to conditions—this power has been used primarily to commute a sentence of death to one of life imprisonment, a purpose which it still serves in respect of sentences in the Isle of Man and Jersey; or
>
> (iii) Remission of all or part of the penalty imposed by the Court."

The power to recommend special remission is normally used for reasons unconnected with the merits of the conviction, for example, to reward assistance to the prison authorities or to release a dying prisoner. Occasionally it may be used where new information casts doubt on the rightness of a conviction but the case is not suitable for reference to the Court of Appeal.[78] A free pardon[79] is "normally only recommended when there are not merely doubts about the defendant's guilt but convincing grounds for thinking that he was innocent"; and this means "morally as well as technically innocent. This 'clean hands' doctrine implies that the Home Secretary must be satisfied . . . that in the incident in question the defendant had no intention of committing an offence and did not in fact commit one."[80] In practice the prerogative is more freely used in respect of cases tried summarily than tried on indictment.

A person who is acquitted on a criminal charge or whose conviction is quashed on appeal normally has no legal right to compensation.[81] However, for many years it has been the normal practice of the Home Secretary to offer ex gratia compensation where a person is granted a free pardon, or,

---

[77] Sixth report from the Home Affairs Committee of the House of Commons (1981–82, H.C. 421), Home Office Memorandum, p. 1. The Home Secretary may refer cases to the Court of Appeal (Criminal Division): see above, pp. 841–843. The following summary is based on this Memorandum. See also the comprehensive survey by A. T. H. Smith, [1983] P.L. 398, and the works cited therein; C. H. Rolph, The Queen's Pardon (1978); C. H. W. Gane, 1980 J.R. 18.

[78] Home Office Memorandum, pp. 2–3.

[79] There is much confusion over the exact implications of a "free pardon": see A. T. H. Smith, op. cit., pp. 417–422. It seems to depend on the exact terms of the pardon in question. The terminology is clearly inappropriate where a person has been pronounced to be innocent. In New Zealand it has been held to be technically no more than an indication that the person concerned was wrongfully convicted: Re Royal Commission on Thomas [1980] 1 N.Z.L.R. 602, and in R. v. Foster [1985] Q.B. 115, the Court of Appeal (Criminal Division) held that the effect of a free pardon was to remove from the subject of the pardon all pain, penalties and punishments ensuing from the conviction but not to eliminate the conviction. (The court proceeded to quash the conviction: see A. Wolfgarten and A. N. Khan, (1986) 130 S.J. 157.) Compare the current Home Office view, above.

[80] Ibid. p. 3.

[81] It is difficult to establish a cause of action for malicious prosecution: it is necessary to prove, inter alia, that the prosecution lacked reasonable and probable cause and that the defendant acted maliciously: Winfield and Jolowicz on Tort, (13th ed., 1989), pp. 545–551.

following the emergence of new evidence, has had his or her conviction quashed on appeal out of time or after the Home Secretary has referred the case to the Court of Appeal. A payment may also be made where there has been misconduct or default by the police or some other agency of the criminal justice system and in other, exceptional, cases. Payments are not, however, made simply because there has been an acquittal or a quashed conviction. The amount of compensation is fixed on the recommendation of an independent assessor (in practice the chairman of the Criminal Injuries Compensation Board) whose advice is always accepted.[82] The assessor takes account of pecuniary losses, damage to character or reputation and physical hardship. The offer is made without admission of liability, and while the claimant is free to accept or refuse, if he or she accepts any legal claim must be waived.[83]

In 1985, the Home Secretary stated that he would pay compensation

(1) wherever that was required by the United Kingdom's international obligations; the provision in point was article 14.6 of the International Covenant on Civil and Political Rights, which provides:

"When a person has by a final decision been convicted of a criminal offence and when subsequently his conviction has been reversed or he has been pardoned on the ground that a new or newly discovered fact shows conclusively that there has been a miscarriage of justice, the person who has suffered punishment as a result of such conviction shall be compensated according to law, unless it is proved that the non-disclosure of the unknown fact in time is wholly or partly attributable to him."

He remained willing to pay compensation in two further situations:

(2) to people who did not fall within the terms of the preceding paragraph but who had spent time in custody following a wrongful conviction or charge, where he was satisfied that it had resulted from serious default on the part of a member of a police force or of some other public authority;

(3) in other, exceptional, circumstances; in particular where facts emerged at trial or on appeal within time that completely exonerated the accused person (and not merely where the prosecution had been unable to sustain the burden of proof beyond reasonable doubt). The Home Secretary also stated that he would regard any recommendation as to amount made by the assessor as binding upon him.[84]

A further step was taken by section 133 of the Criminal Justice Act 1988, which enacted a statutory right to compensation in situation (1) above. The right follows the terms of article 14.6, except that it must be shown "beyond

---

[82] The procedure was set out in H.C. Deb, 29 July 1976, written answers, cols. 328–330.

[83] Between 1972 and 1981 there were 47 *ex gratia* payments: 16 of £10,000 or more and 3 of £20,000 or more: *Home Office Memorandum*, Appendix A(4). In 1983, £77,000 was paid to a man convicted of murder in 1973 on the basis of evidence of a Home Office scientist subsequently discredited. In 1984 Patrick Meehan accepted an offer of £50,500 after 7 years in prison: he had previously rejected an offer of £7,500 and the amount was reassessed by an Edinburgh advocate: *Daily Telegraph*, February 2, 1984.

[84] 87 H.C. Deb, November 29, 1985, written answers, cols. 691–692: see P. Ashman, (1986) 136 N.L.J. 497.

reasonable doubt" (not "conclusively") that there has been a miscarriage of justice. The compensation is paid to the accused person or, if he or she is dead, to the personal representatives. Whether there is a right to compensation is determined by the Secretary of State; the amount by an assessor appointed under Schedule 12 to the 1988 Act.[85]

Cases for the exercise of the prerogative of mercy and requests for compensation are considered by the Home Office's Criminal Department.[86] The relevant papers are scrutinised, and, if it is thought to be necessary, further inquiries are commissioned.

The working of the system has been considered in recent reports by the Home Affairs Committee and JUSTICE.[87] The Home Affairs Committee thought that cases should continue to be processed by the Home Office, but noted that decisions were often presented in such a way as to seem arbitrary: delays should be explained and reasons given for a refusal to take action normally given. However, there should be an independent review body to advise the Home Secretary on the exercise of the prerogative of mercy. This body should be able to take into account a wider range of matters than those currently considered by the Home Office, including evidence which was known to counsel or the police but not put before the jury, for example for tactical reasons that turn out to have been misguided. It should also be able to advise the exercise of the royal prerogative where its investigation has shown the verdict to be unsafe and unsatisfactory: it should not be necessary for the convicted person to prove his or her innocence. The committee were impressed by Sir David Napley's statement that he was unable from his own experience to recall "a single case where the Home Office has, as a result of its own investigations, felt able to recommend a pardon or any other recognition that a conviction was necessarily wrongful." On the other hand, officials had expressed disquiet about certain cases where the courts had refused to interfere with a verdict.[88]

The government rejected most of the Committee's proposals, apart from those concerning matters of presentation.[89] The Home Secretary indicated that he would in future be prepared to exercise his power of reference more readily and the Lord Chief Justice that there was scope for the Court of Appeal to be more ready to exercise its powers to receive evidence or order a retrial. The Home Office would also examine the possibility of legislation to allow the Home Secretary to refer doubtful summary convictions back to the courts.

---

[85] An assessor must be a lawyer who possesses a 7 year general qualification under the Courts and Legal Services Act 1990, s.71, or an advocate or solicitor in Scotland or a Northern Ireland barrister or solicitor of 7 years' standing, a person who holds or has held judicial office in any part of the United Kingdom, or the chairman or a member of the Criminal Injuries Compensation Board: Criminal Justice Act 1988, Sched. 6, para. 2, as amended by the 1990 Act, Sched. 10, para. 72(1).

[86] See the Devlin Report on *Evidence of Identification in Criminal Cases*, 1975–76 H.C. 338, pp. 55–56, 142–145; *Home Office Memorandum*, pp. 4–5.

[87] 1981–82, H.C. 421; JUSTICE Report, *Compensation for Wrongful Imprisonment* (1982); JUSTICE Report, *Miscarriages of Justice* (1989). See also the JUSTICE Report, *Home Office Reviews of Criminal Convictions* (1968); B. Woffinden, *Miscarriages of Justice* (1987); and, on the compensation issue, G. H. L. Fridman, (1963) 26 M.L.R. 481; C. Shelbourn, [1978] Crim.L.R. 22.

[88] 1981–82 H.C. 421, p. x.

[89] *Government Reply to the Sixth Report from the Home Affairs Committee Session 1981–82 H.C. 421* (Cmnd. 8856, 1983).

The JUSTICE Committee considered the issue of compensation. It thought that persons given a free pardon and those whose convictions are quashed after a reference by the Home Secretary should have a *right* to compensation. Other persons whose convictions are quashed on appeal should be entitled to apply for compensation although that compensation could be refused or reduced in the light of the claimant's conduct or if the conviction was quashed on a technicality. In certain circumstances compensation should be paid to persons committed for trial in custody and acquitted or discharged, and persons who have had part of their sentence remitted. Claims should be dealt with by an Imprisonment Compensation Board established on the lines of the Criminal Injuries Compensation Board. The recent reforms constitute only a partial move in this direction.[90]

JUSTICE returned to these matters in its 1989 Report on *Miscarriages of Justice*. It summarised its own case work in connection with alleged miscarriages of justice, and examined the reasons why such miscarriages occur. Many of its recommendations concern the investigation, trial and appeal stages of the criminal process. As regards the post-appeal stage, it took the view that the government's response to the Home Affairs Committee's report had not met the criticisms, and that there had been no discernible change in the practice of the Home Office and the Court of Appeal since then. It recommended[91]

(i) that the Secretary of State should not exclude cases from investigation just because there is no fresh information;

(ii) that where an investigation without fresh information reveals serious doubts about the correctness of a conviction, the Secretary of State should remit the remainder of the sentence;

(iii) that the Home Affairs Committee's previous recommendation for an independent review body should be implemented. The body should be chaired by lawyers, but with a membership not so confined, and operate throughout the U.K. It would only deal with cases after trial on indictment and its case load would be small. Normally, only cases turning on points of law or procedure should be referred to the Court of Appeal.

---

[90] JUSTICE described the details of the scheme as "disappointing": 31st Annual Report of JUSTICE, pp. 27–28.
[91] Chap. 5. See B. Woffinden, (1989) 139 N.L.J. 1108.

INDEX